Turkish Dictionary

Turkish-English
English-Turkish

Hugo's Language Books Limited

Original edition published as:
English Learner's Dicitonary
by Fono (Istanbul)

Compiled by

Ali Bayram, Ş. Serdar Türet and **Gordon Jones**

Typeset, printed and bound in Turkey by
FONO
Gündoğdu Cad. 49 Merter 34016 Istanbul

PREFACE

Concise and accurate translations combined with clear type and layout make this fully up-to-date dictionary a most accessible reference for use in any situation - at home when learning the language via Hugo's *Turkish in Three Months* self-tuition course, in class if you are attending formal lessons, and when you travel to Turkey on holidays or business. Turkish students of English will find the dictionary equally useful.

Compiled by experts at Fono, one of Turkey's leading language publishers, it contains approximately 35,000 headwords and in excess of 70,000 definitions. There's a brief guide to the essentials of Turkish pronunciation, immediately following this preface; similar notes relating to English will be found just before the English-Turkish half of the dictionary.

ÖNSÖZ

Türkçe'nin çağdaş sözvarlığının dikkate alınarak hazırlandığı bu Türkçe-İngilizce bölümünde, gündelik dile ait binlerce sözcük ve deyimin yanı sıra çeşitli bilimlere ait binlerce terime de yer verilmiştir.

Karşılıkları verilen Türkçe sözcüklerin anlamları, kullanımlarındaki önem sırasına göre dizilmiş, İngilizce-Türkçe bölümünde olduğu gibi, eşanlamlı ve/veya yakın anlamlı karşılıklar virgül ile, ayrı anlamı yansıtan karşılık(lar) noktalı virgül ile ayrılmıştır.

Orta ve lise öğrencilerinin olduğu gibi İngilizce ile ilgili hemen herkesin orta boy bir Türkçe-İngilizce sözlüğe duyacakları gereksinimler göz önüne alınarak hazırlanan bu sözlüğün güvenilir ve yararlı bir kılavuz olacağı inancındayız.

PRONUNCIATION OF TURKISH

Vowels and Diphthongs

The vowels are usually short or of medium length, but there are numerous foreign words (mostly Arabic) with long vowels.

a	as in *but*, sometimes long as in *far*.
e	as in *bed*.
ı	something between the *i* in *big* and the *a* in *along*.
i	as in *hit*.
o	as in *doll* or *hot*.
ö	as French *œu* in *œuvre*.
u	as in *bull*.
ü	as French *u* in *plume*.

The diphthongs are as follows:

ay	as *uy* in *buy*.
ey	as *a* in *make*.
oy	as *oi* in *boil*.
uy	as French *oui* in *Louis*.

Consonants

The consonants sound as they do in English, except:

c	as *j* in *jam*.
ç	as *ch* in *chalk*.
g	as in English, but when followed by *â* or *û* it is palatalized: thus *gâ* is very nearly *gya*, *gû* like *gyoo*.
ğ	with soft vowels (*e, ö, ü*) is a consonantal *y*. With hard vowels (*a, ı, o, u*), it is a very guttural but hardly perceptible *g* and very little more than a lengthening of the preceding vowel.
h	is always pronounced.
j	as French *j* in *journal*.
k	with soft vowels is frontal like *k* in *kill*; with hard vowels it is backward like the *c* and *ck* in *cuckoo* or the two *c*'s in *cocoa*. When followed by *â* or *û* it is highly palatalized - thus *kâ* is almost like *kya*.

l	is much like the English *l*, but before soft vowels and *â* or *û* it is frontal and similar to the German *l*.
r	is much like a slightly rolled Scottish *r*, but at the end of word it is practically unvoiced.
ş	as *sh* in *she*.
v	as in *vile*; after a vowel it sometimes changes to the English *w* in *we* (e.g. *levha, lavta*). This happens especially in foreign words.

Circumflex and Apostrophe

The circumflex (^) denotes:

1. On *a* and *u* the frontal pronunciation of the preceding consonants *g*, *k* and *l* (*ikametgâh, kâtip, lûtfen*).
2. The lengthening of a vowel when two words are spelled in the same way (*alem, flag*; *âlem, world*).

The apostrophe (') denotes:

1. The separate pronunciation of two syllables; thus *kat'etmek* is pronounced "kat/etmek" and not "kat/tetmek".
2. The separation of suffixes from a proper name; thus, *İngiltere'de* (*in England*).

Stress

The stress is usually on the final syllable; important exceptions to this rule are:

1. The stress lies always on the final syllable <u>before</u> the interrogative and negative particles *mı, mi, mu, mü, ma, me*: *geldí mi?, yápma!*
2. The suffix *-le* (from *ile with*) is never stressed; thus, *bu surétle* (*in this way*).
3. The syllables denoting the tense of the verb (like *-yor-, -ir-,* etc) are usually stressed: *geliyórum, gidérsin*, etc.

ABBREVIATIONS

a.	– ad	(*noun*)
adl.	– adıl	(*pronoun*)
Aİ.	– Amerikan İngilizcesi	(*American English*)
anat.	– anatomi	(*anatomy*)
arg.	– argo	(*slang*)
ask.	– askerlik	(*military*)
ats.	– atasözü	(*proverb*)
bağ.	– bağlaç	(*conjunction*)
be.	– belirteç	(*adverb*)
bitk.	– bitkibilim	(*botany*)
biy.	– biyoloji	(*biology*)
bkz.	– bakınız	(*see*)
bş.	– bir şey	(*something*)
coğ.	– coğrafya	(*geography*)
ç.	– çoğul	(*plural*)
den.	– denizcilik	(*nautical*)
dilb.	– dilbilim	(*linguistics*)
e.	– eylem	(*verb*)
fel.	– felsefe	(*philosophy*)
fiz.	– fizik	(*physics*)
hayb.	– hayvanbilim	(*zoology*)
hek.	– hekimlik	(*medical*)
huk.	– hukuk	(*law*)
İİ.	– İngiliz İngilizcesi	(*British English*)
ilg.	– ilgeç	(*preposition*)
kim.	– kimya	(*chemistry*)
kon.	– konuşma dili	(*colloquial*)
mat.	– matematik	(*mathematics*)
müz.	– müzik	(*music*)
ruhb.	– ruhbilim	(*psychology*)
s.	– sıfat	(*adjective*)
sb	– birisi	(*somebody*)
sp.	– spor	(*sports*)
sth	– bir şey	(*something*)
tek.	– teknoloji	(*technology*)
tic.	– ticaret	(*commerce*)
topb.	– toplumbilim	(*sociology*)
ünl.	– ünlem	(*exclamation*)
yaz.	– yazın	(*literature*)

A

aba coarse woollen cloth **abayı yakmak** to fall in love (with sb)

abajur lampshade

abaküs abacus

abanmak to lean forward/against

abanoz ebony

abartı exaggeration

abartmak to exaggerate

abece alphabet

abecesel alphabetic(al)

abes unnecessary, useless; foolish; unreasonable

abi *bkz.* ağabey

abide monument, memorial

abla elder sister

ablak chubby, round

abluka blockade **abluka etmek** to blockade **ablukayı kaldırmak** to raise the blockade

abone subscriber; subscription **abone bedeli/ücreti** subscription fee **abone olmak** to subscribe (to)

abonman subscription; season ticket; *kon.* bus ticket

abstre abstract

abuk sabuk nonsensical, incoherent **abuk subuk konuşmak** to talk nonsense, to babble

abur cubur kickshaw

acaba I wonder (if/whether)

acar bold, plucky, hardy; clever, cunning

acayip strange, weird, peculiar, odd **acayibine gitmek** to seem strange (to sb)

acayiplik peculiarity, strangeness

acele hurry, haste; urgent; hurried, hasty **acele etmek** to make haste, to be in a hurry **Acele işe şeytan karışır.** Haste makes waste.

aceleci hasty, impatient

acemi untrained, inexperienced, callow; beginner, tyro

acemice clumsily

acemilik inexperience, callowness **acemilik çekmek** to suffer from inexperience

acente agent, representative; agency

acı bitter; biting, harsh; pain, ache; sorrow, grief **acı çekmek** to suffer, to feel pain **acısını çekmek** to pay the consequence (for) **acısını çıkarmak** be/get even (with sb)

acıbadem bitter almond **acıbadem kurabiyesi** almond cooky, macaroon

acıklı touching, pathetic, tragic, sad

acıkmak to feel hungry, to be hungry

acılaşmak to get bitter/sour

acılı spicy; sad, grieved, mourning

acılık bitterness, sourness

acıma pity, mercy

acımasız pitiless, merciless

acımasızlık pitilessness, mercilessness

acımak to hurt, to feel pain; to feel sorry for, to have/take pity on

acımsı, acımtırak somewhat bitter

acındırmak to arouse pity for sb; to ask for sympathy

acınmak to feel sorrow (for); to be regretted/pitied

acıtmak to hurt, to cause pain (to)

acil urgent, immediate, pressing **acil bakım** emergency maintenance **acil servis** casualty department, casualty ward **acil şifalar dilemek** to wish sb a quick recovery

acilen urgently, promptly

aciz inability, helplessness, weakness

âciz incapable, uncapable; weak, helpless **âciz kalmak** to be incapable (of)

acizane humbly, modestly

acuze hag

aç hungry; insatiable, greedy **aç açına** with an hungry stomach **aç kalmak** to be left hungry; to be poor **aç karnına** on an empty stomach **aç kurt gibi** hungry as a wolf **aç kurt gibi yemek** to wolf **aç susuz** without food and water **acından ölmek** to starve to death; to starve, to be famished

açacak opener

açalya azalea

açgözlü greedy, insatiable

açgözlülük greed, avarice açgözlülük etmek to act greedily

açı angle; point of view dar açı acute angle dik açı right angle geniş açı obtuse angle

açık open; uncovered; clear, distinct; naked, bare; clear, cloudless; weak (tea); light (colour); unoccupied, vacant; open air; open sea; vacant position; deficit; wing; openly, frankly açık açık frankly açık alan open space, opening açık artırma public auction açık çek blank cheque açık deniz open sea; high seas açık eksiltme purchase by Dutch auction açık elli generous açık fikirli broad minded açık hava open air açık hava tiyatrosu open-air theatre açık kalpli open-hearted açık konuşmak to talk frankly açık liman free port açık pazar open market açık saçık indecent, obscene açık seçik explicit, obvious açık yürekle open hearted

açıkça frankly, openly, clearly

açıkçası to tell the truth, frankly speaking

açıkgöz cunning, shrewd, sharp

açıkgöz(lü)lük cunning, slyness

açıklama explanation açıklama yapmak to make an explanation

açıklamak to explain; to clarify

açıklayıcı explanatory, illustrative

açıklık openness; clearness; opening; open space, blank space

açıkoturum panel discussion

açıköğretim the Open University

açıksözlü outspoken, straightforward, frank

açıksözlülük outspokenness, frankness

açıktan from a distance; without effort; extra açıktan açığa openly, frankly

açılır kapanır collapsible, folding

açılış opening, inauguration

açılmak to be opened, to open; (weather) to become clear; to put out (to sea); to become relaxed, to be at ease; to overspend

açımlamak to elucidate, to expound; to comment (on)

açındırmak to develop

açınmak to develop

açıortay bisector

açıölçer protractor

açlık hunger; famine açlık çekmek to go hungry; to be poor açlık grevi hunger strike açlıktan ölmek to starve

açmak to open; to draw aside, to lift; to unfold; to break through, to clear away; to reveal (a secret); to turn on (switch, light, radio, etc.); to begin, to open (a meeting/conversation); to clear up (weather); to sharpen (pencil); to make lighter (colour); (flower) to bloom

açmaz difficult position; impasse, dilemma

ad name; fame; dilb. noun ad durumu dilb. case ad koymak to give a name ad takmak to nickname, to call ad vermek to give a name adı çıkmak to be talked about, to get a bad reputation adı geçen above-mentioned adı karışmak to be involved in adına in the name of adını anmak to mention

ada island

adalı islander

adabımuaşeret manners, etiquette

adaçayı sage tea; garden sage

adak vow, oblation adak adamak to vow

adale muscle

adaleli muscular

adalet justice Adalet Bakanı Minister of Justice Adalet Bakanlığı Ministry of Justice Adalet Divanı International Court of Justice

adaletli just, fair

adaletsiz unjust, unfair

adaletsizlik injustice

adam man; human being; person, individual; employee, servant; agent adam almak to recruit adam başına a/per head, apiece adam beğenmemek to be overcritical adam etmek to lick sb/sth into shape adam gibi properly adam içine çıkmak to go out in public adam olmak to grow into manhood, to grow to be a man adam olmaz hopeless, incorrigible adam öldürme manslaughter, homicide a-

dam sarrafı a good judge of character **adam sen de** who cares?, never mind! **adam tutmak** *sp.* to mark a man **adam yerine koymak** not to disregard, to consider important **adamdan saymak** to treat with respect, to consider important **adamına çatmak** to meet one's match

adamak to vow (a pledge); to dedicate oneself to

adamakıllı thoroughly, fully

adamotu *bitk.* mandrake

adamsendecilik indifference, callousness

adamsızlık lack of employees/servants

adap customs; good manners **adaba aykırı** contrary to the rules of accepted ways **adap erkân** rules and conventions, customary practices

adaptasyon adaptation

adapte adapted **adapte etmek** to adapt **adapte olmak** to be adapted

adaş namesake

adatavşanı *hayb.* rabbit, cony

aday candidate; nominee; applicant **aday adayı** candidate for nomination **aday göstermek** to put sb in for

adçekme lot, drawing of lots

adçekmek to draw lots

addetmek to count, to esteem

Adem Adam

âdemelması *anat.* adam's apple

âdemoğlu mankind

adet number; piece

âdet habit; custom; *hek.* menstruation, periods **âdet bezi** sanitary towel/pad **âdet çıkarmak** to start a new custom **âdet edinmek/etmek** to get into the habit (of) **âdet görmek** to have one's periods, to menstruate **âdetten kesilmek** to reach menopause **âdet yerini bulsun diye** as a matter of form, for form's sake

âdeta nearly, almost; simply, merely

adıl *dilb.* pronoun

adım step; pace **adım adım** step by step **adım atmak** to walk, to step; to take the first step, to begin **adım atmamak** not to visit **adım başı(nda)** at every step **adımlarını açmak** to walk

faster **adımlamak** to pace

adi customary, usual; common, ordinary; base, low, mean; cheap, tacky; commonplace, banal **adi alacak** unsecured claim **adi iflas** non-fraudulent bankruptcy **adi mektup** ordinary letter **adi şirket/ortaklık** unincorporated association

adil just, fair

adilane justly

adilik vulgarity, baseness

adlandırmak to denominate, to name

adli juridical; judicial **adli hata** legal error **adli sicil** police record, record of previous convictions **adli takibat** judiciary proceedings **adli tebligat** summons **adli tıp** forensic medicine **adli yıl** legal year, court year

adliye (administration of) justice; law court **adliye mahkemeleri** ordinary tribunals **adliye sarayı** courthouse

adrenalin *hek.* adrenalin(e)

adres address **adres defteri** address book

Adriyatik Adriatic Sea

adsız nameless; anonymous

aerobik aerobics

aerodinamik aerodynamic; aerodynamics

af pardon, forgiveness; amnesty; exemption **af dilemek** to apologize (to sb), to beg pardon **affa uğramak** to be pardoned

afacan unruly, naughty (child)

afalla(ş)mak to be bewildered, to be taken aback

aferin Bravo! Well done! Good for you! **aferin almak** to receive a good mention; to be praised

afet disaster, calamity, catastrophe *kd.* femme fatale, siren

afetzede disaster stricken

affedilmek to be forgiven, to be pardoned

affetmek to pardon, to forgive; to excuse **Affedersiniz!** Excuse me! I'm sorry!

Afgan Afghan

Afganca Pushtu

Afganistan Afghanistan

Afganlı Afghan
afiş poster, placard, bill
afiyet good health, well-being **Afiyet (şeker) olsun!** Have a nice meal, Enjoy your meal!
aforoz excommunication **aforoz etmek** to excommunicate
Afrika Africa
Afrikalı African
afsun spell, charm
afsuncu sorcerer, witch
afsunlamak to bewitch
Afşar Turkoman tribe (in North Iran and South Anatolia)
afyon opium
afyonkeş opium addict
agrandisman (photo) enlargement
agrandisör enlarger
ağ net; network; (trousers) crotch; web **ağ atmak/bırakmak** to cast a net **ağına düşürmek** to trap **ağ tabaka** retina
ağa master, lord; landowner, agha
ağabey elder brother
ağaç tree; wood, timber; wooden **ağaç budamak** to prune trees **ağaç işleri** woodwork **ağaç kabuğu** bark **ağaç kaplama** wooden wainscotting **ağaç kovuğu** hollow of a tree **ağaç olmak** arg. to have been waiting for ages **Ağaç yaşken eğilir.** ats. Train the mind while it is young.
ağaççık bush, shrub
ağaççileği bitk. raspberry
ağaçkakan woodpecker
ağaçkavunu bitk. citron
ağaçkurdu woodworm
ağaçlandırmak, ağaçlamak to afforest
ağaçlıklı tree-lined, wooded
ağarmak to turn white; to become light; to bleach, to whiten
ağda semi-solid sweel, syrup; epilating wax **ağda yapmak** to remove hairs (with sticky boiled sugar)
ağdalı viscous; bombastic, pompous, overloaded (style)
ağı poison, venom **ağı gibi** very bitter; very strong
ağıl sheep-fold, fold
ağılamak to poison

ağılanmak to be poisoned
ağılı poisonous
ağılıböcek hayb. ground beetle
ağınmak to roll on the ground (animal)
ağıotu bitk. hemlock
ağır heavy; difficult, hard; slow; serious, severe, grave (illness); precious, valuable; offensive, hurtful; slow **ağır ağır** slowly **ağır aksak** very slowly **ağır basmak** to carry weight, to turn the scale **ağır ceza** severe punishment **ağır ceza mahkemesi** criminal court **ağır çekim** slow motion **ağır endüstri** heavy industry **ağır gelmek** to offend, to hurt; to find sth difficult **ağır hapis (cezası)** solitary confinement, heavy imprisonment **ağır işitmek** to be hard of hearing **ağır kayıp** heavy casualities, great losses **ağır para cezası** heavy fine **ağır sanayi** heavy industry **ağır sıklet** heavyweight **ağır söz** harsh word **ağır yaralı** seriously wounded **ağırdan almak** to take it easy, to play for time **ağırına gitmek** to offend, to hurt (the feelings of)
ağırbaşlı serious, dignified, sedate
ağırbaşlılık dignity, sedateness
ağırlamak to entertain, to put sb up, to show hospitality
ağırlaşmak to become heavier; to become more difficult; to become slower; to become more serious (illness)
ağırlık weight, heaviness; importance; severity; gravity; slowness; burden; oppressiveness; drowsiness, lethargy **ağırlık basmak/çökmek** to come upon sb (sleep); to oppress sb (nightmare) **ağırlık merkezi** the centre of gravity **ağırlık olmak** to be a burden to **ağırlık vermek** to attach importance (to) **ağırlığını koymak** to use one's influences
ağıt requiem, lament, elegy, dirge **ağıt yakmak** to wail for, to lament
ağız mouth; edge, blade; rim, brim; muzzle, snout; opening, entrance; crossroads; persuasive words; local language, accent **ağız açtırmamak** not to let sb speak **ağız alışkanlığı**

manner of speech **ağız dalaşı** quarrel **ağız kavgası** quarrel, battle of words **ağız şakası** joke **ağız tadı** enjoyment; peace, harmony **ağızdan ağza dolaşmak** to be rumoured **ağza alınmaz** unspeakable, vulgar **ağzı (bir karış) açık kalmak** to gape with astonishment **ağzı bozuk** coarse-mouthed **ağzı kokmak** to have bad breath **ağzı kulaklarına varmak** to grin from ear to ear **ağzı pis** foulmouthed **ağzı sıkı** secretive, reticent **ağzı sulanmak** to water (mouth); to be envious **ağzı süt kokmak** to be young/inexperienced **ağzı var dili yok** (he is) very silent **ağzı yanmak** to burn one's fingers **ağzına almamak** not to mention **ağzına bakmak** to obey sb blind **ağzına geleni söylemek** to say disagreeable things (without thinking); to scold severely **ağzında gevelemek** to beat around the bush **ağzından baklayı çıkarmak** to spill the beans **ağzından bal akmak** to talk pleasantly **ağzından çıkanı kulağı duymamak/işitmemek** not to realize what one is saying **ağzından düşürmemek** to talk about sb/sth constantly **ağzından kaçırmak** to let sth slip out **ağzını açıp gözünü yummak** to let oneself go, to say bitter words **ağzını açmak** to give vent to one's feelings **ağzını açmamak** not to open one's lips **ağzını aramak** to sound out **ağzını bozmak** to swear, to curse **ağzını burnunu dağıtmak** to beat sb up **Ağzını hayra aç!** Speak no evil! Heaven forbid! **ağzını sulandırmak** to make one's mouth water **Ağzını topla!** Mind your language! **ağzını yoklamak** to sound out **ağzının payını almak** to be snubbed **ağzının payını vermek** to snub sb **ağzının tadını kaçırmak** to spoil sb's pleasure **ağızbirliği** agreement on what to say/do **ağızbirliği etmek** to agree to tell the same story

ağızlık cigarette holder; mouthpiece
ağlamak to cry, to weep
ağlamaklı ready to cry, tearful **ağlamaklı olmak** to fee like crying

ağlaşmak to weep together
ağlatmak to make sb cry, to reduce sb to tears
ağlatı tragedy
ağrı pain, ache **ağrı vermek** to hurt
ağrıkesici painkiller, analgesic
Ağrıdağı Mount Ararat
ağrımak to ache, to hurt
ağtabaka retina
ağustos August
ağustosböceği cicada
ah! Ah! Oh! Alas! ah çekmek to sigh, to utter a sigh **ahı gitmiş vahı kalmış** *kon.* clapped out **ahı tutmak** (one's curse) to take effect
aha here, there
ahali inhabitants; people, population
ahbap friend, fellow, chap **ahbap çavuşlar** chums, cronies **ahbap olmak** to make friends with
ahbaplık friendship, acquaintance
ahçı cook
ahçıbaşı chef, head cook
ahçılık cooking, cookery, cuisine
ahdetmek to resolve, to take an oath
ahenk harmony
aheste slow, gentle
ahım şahım *kon.* beautiful, excellent, favourable **ahım şahım bir şey değil** It's not much of a thing
ahır stable, shed, barn
ahit oath; promise; agreement, pact, treaty
ahize (telephone) receiver
ahkâm judgements **ahkâm kesmek** to make judgements without hesitation
ahlak morals; ethics; manners, conduct **ahlaka aykırı** immoral **ahlakını bozmak** to debauch, to deprave, to pervert **ahlakı bozuk** depraved
ahlakbilim ethics
ahlakçı moralist
ahlakdışı amoral
ahlaki moral, ethical
ahlaklı well-behaved, decent
ahlaksız immoral, dissolute
ahlaksızca immorally
ahlaksızlık immorality, depravity
ahlamak to sigh
ahlat wild pear

ahmak stupid, foolish; fool, idiot
ahmaklık stupidity
ahret afterlife, the hereafter, the next world
ahşap wooden
ahtapot octopus
ahu gazelle
ahududu raspberry
ahval circumstances, conditions
aidat dues, revenues
aile family aile bireyleri/efradı members of a family aile hayatı family life, domesticity aile ocağı home aile planlaması family planning aile reisi head of the family, householder
ailesel, ailevi domestic, regarding the family
ait concerning; belonging (to) ait olmak to concern; to belong (to)
ajan agent; secret agent, spy ajan provokatör agent provocateur
ajanda date book, engagement calendar
ajans news-agency; agency ajans bülteni news-agency, bulletin
ak white; hoary (hair); clean; honest Ak akçe kara gün içindir ats. One must put by for a rainy day ak düşmek to begin to turn white akla karayı seçmek to meet a lot of difficulties; to be hard put to do sth
akabinde immediately, afterwards
akaç drain pipe
akaçlama drainage
akaçlamak to drain
akademi academy
akademik academic
akağaç (white) birch
akaju mahogany
akanyıldız shooting star
akar landed property, real estate
akarca hek. fistula
akaret property rented out
akarsu river, stream akarsu kavşağı confluence akarsu yatağı stream bed
akaryakıt liquid fuel akaryakıt tankeri fuel tanker
akasya acacia
akbaba vulture
akciğer lungs akciğer zarı pleura

akça whitish, quite white
akça (small silver) coin
akçaağaç maple
akçakavak white poplar
akçe coin, small silver coin
Akdeniz the Mediterranean Akdeniz iklimi Mediterranean climate
akdetmek to make, to contract, to draw up
akdiken hawthorn
akıbet end, consequence, outcome
akıcı fluid, liquid; fluent
akıcılık fluency
akıl intelligence, mind, brain; memory; opinion, idea; advice Akıl akıldan üstündür ats. It pays to ask advice. Two heads are better than one. akıl almak/danışmak to consult akıl almaz unimaginable, unbelievable akıl erdirememek not to make head or tail of sth, not to make of akıl hastalığı mental illness akıl hastanesi mental home, psychiatric hospital akıl hastası mental patient akıl hocası mentor, advisor akıl vermek to give sb advice Akıl yaşta değil, baştadır. ats. Intelligence doesn't go by age. akılda tutmak to keep in mind akıllara durgunluk vermek to astound akla gelmedik unthinkable aklı almak to conceive aklı başına gelmek to come to one's senses aklı gitmek to be taken (with); to be astonished; to be taken (with) aklı yatmak to be convinced aklıma gelmişken by the way, incidentally aklına esmek to feel like doing, to come into one's head aklına koymak to take it into one's head (to), to have a mind aklına takılmak to run in one's head aklında kalmak not to forget, to remember aklından çıkmak to slip one's mind aklından geçirmek to happen to think (of sth) aklından geçmek to occur to sb aklından zoru olmak to have sth wrong with one's mind aklını başına toplamak to gather/collect one's wits together aklını başından almak to make sb unable to think, to turn one's head aklını bozmak to be ob-

sessed by sth **aklını çelmek** to bias, to dissuade (from) **aklını kaçırmak** to be/go out of one's mind **aklını oynatmak** to be out of one's senses **aklını peynir ekmekle yemek** to lose one's senses
akılcı rationalist
akılcılık rationalism
akıldışı irrational
akıldişi wisdom tooth
akıllanmak to become wiser (by experience)
akıllı clever, intelligent
akıllıca cleverly, intelligently
akıllılık cleverness, intelligence
akılsız stupid, foolish
akılsızlık stupidity
akım current; movement, ırend
akın raid; run; rush **akın akın** in crowds **akın etmek** to rush (into); to raid, to attack
akıntı current, stream; flow **akıntıya kapılmak** to go adrift **akıntıya kürek çekmek** to beat the air
akış flow, course
akışkan fluid
akışkanlık fluidity
akıtmak to make/let sth flow; to shed
akide faith, creed
akide candy sugar
akik agate
akis reflection; echo; reaction
akkan lymph
akkor incandescent
aklama acquittal
aklamak to acquit
aklanmak to be acquitted
aklıselim common sense
akmadde white matter
akmak to flow; to leak; to run down
akordeon accordion
akort tune; accord **akort etmek** to tune **akordu bozuk** out of tune **akordu bozulmak** to go out of tune
akraba relative, kin, kindred
akrabalık relationship, kinship, affinity
akran equal, peer
akreditif letter of credit
akrep scorpion; hour-hand (watch) **Akrep burcu** Scorpio

akrobasi acrobatics
akrobat acrobat
akrobatik acrobatic
aks axle, journal
aksak lame, limping
aksam parts, portions, sections
aksaklık trouble, breakdown, hitch; limp
aksamak to limp, to hitch; to run wrong, not to work right
aksan accent, stress
aksetmek to hinder
aksesuar accessory; stage prop; spare part
aksırık sneeze
aksırmak to sneeze
aksi contrary, opposite; perverse, cross **aksi gibi** *kon.* unfortunately **aksi halde** otherwise, if not **aksi tesadüf** unfortunate coincidence; unluckily
aksilik misfortune; crossness, obstinacy **aksilik çıkmak** to have a difficulty come up **aksilik etmek** to make difficulties, to be obstinate
aksine on the contrary
aksiyom axiom
akşam evening; in the evening **akşam** this time of the night **akşam gazetesi** evening paper **akşam güneşi** yellowish pink; afternoon sun **akşam karanlığı** dusk **akşam namazı** evening worship **akşam sabah** all the time, constantly **akşam yemeği** dinner; supper **akşama** this evening, tonight **akşamları** in the evening **akşamdan akşama** every evening **akşamdan kalma** having a hangover
akşamcı night worker; habitual drinker
akşamlamak to stay until evening; to stay the night
akşamleyin in the evening
akşamlık for an evening, evening; evening clothes
akşamüstü, akşamüzeri at sunset, at dusk; towards evening
Akşamyıldızı evening star, Venus
akşın albino
akşınlık albinism
aktar seller of medicinal herbs, herbalist; haberdasher's, herbalist's

aktarıcı tiler; passer; transmitter
aktarma transfer; change; quotation **aktarma bileti** transfer ticket **aktarma yapmak** to change (trains, etc.)
aktarmak to transfer; to quote; to transmit; to empty; *hek.* transplant
aktarmalı connecting (train, etc.)
aktarmasız without change, through, direct
aktif active; assets
aktiflik activity
aktinik actinic
aktör actor
aktöre morals
aktörlük acting
aktris actress
aktüalite the news of the day; newsreel
aktüel actual, present
akuple coupled
akupleman coupling
akupunktur acupuncture
akustik acoustic; acoustics
akümülatör storage battery, car battery
akvaryum aquarium
akyuvar leucocyte
al vermilion, crimson, scarlet; chestnut, bay (horse); rouge; trick, intrigue **al al olmak** to become red **al basmak** to catch puerperal fever; to blush **al bayrak/sancak** The Turkish flag **al kanlara boyanmak** to die a bloody death; to be wounded **al yanaklar** rosy cheeks
ala variegated, pied; light brown
âlâ very good, excellent
alabalık trout
alabanda *den.* broadside **alabanda etmek** to put the helm hard over **alabanda iskele** hard to board
alabildiğine to the utmost; at full speed; extremely
alabora capsizing, overturn **alabora etmek** to overturn **alabora olmak** to capsize, to turn over
alaca speckled, pied, variegated **alaca bulaca** incongruously coloured
alacak money owed to sb, credit; *huk.* claim **alacak bakiyesi** credit balance, effect **alacak davası** action of debt **alacak senedi** note receivable, bill re-

ceivable **alacağı olsun!** I will make him pay for it, I'll show him!
alacaklı payee, creditor **alacaklı taraf** credit side
alacalanmak to become speckled
alafranga European, in the European style **alafranga müzik** European music **alafranga tuvalet** Western style toilet
alageyik fallow-deer
alaka interest, concern; connection, relationship; affection **alaka duymak** to be interested (in) **alaka göstermek** to take interest (in) **alakasını kesmek** to break off relations (with) **alaka uyandırmak** to arouse interest
alakadar concerned, interested **alakadar etmek** to concern, to interest **alakadar olmak** to be interested (in)
alakalanmak to be interested (in)
alakalı interested, concerned
alakarga jay
alakasız uninterested, indifferent; unconnected
alamet sign, mark **alameti farika** trademark
alan open space; area; field; clearing; (public) square **alan araştırması** fieldwork
alarm alarm
alaşağı etmek to overthrow, to depose
alaşım alloy
alaturka in the Ottoman/Turkish style **alaturka müzik** Turkish music **alaturka tuvalet** squat toilet
alavere passing (from hand to hand); gangway (for loading/unloading) **alavere dalavere çevirmek** to play a trick
alay procession, parade; *ask.* regiment; crowd, troop; mockery, ridicule **alay alay** in large crowds **alay etmek** to make fun (of), to gibe at **alay konusu** object of derision **alay konusu olmak** to become an object of derision **alaya almak** to make fun (of), to laugh (at), to guy **alayında olmak** not to take sth seriously
alaycı mocking; mocker, joker
alaylı joking, mocking
alaz flame, blaze

albastı puerperal fever
albay colonel; (navy) captain
albeni charm, appeal, attraction
albino albino
albüm album
albümin albumin
alçak low; mean, vile **alçak basınç** low pressure
alçakça rather low; viciously, shamefully
alçaklık lowness; meanness, baseness; cowardice
alçalmak to decline, to descend; to lose value; to abase oneself
alçakgönüllü humble, modest
alçakgönüllülük humility, modesty
alçaklık lowness; shamefulness, vileness
alçı plaster of Paris, plaster **alçıya almak/koymak** to encase in plaster
alçıtaşı gypsum, parget
aldanmak to be deceived, to be duped; to be mistaken; to bloom early
aldatıcı deceptive, misleading
aldatmaca trick, deception
aldatmak to deceive, to cheat; to be unfaithful (to)
aldehit aldehyde
aldırış attention, care **aldırış etmemek** not to care, not to pay attention
aldırmak to mind, to pay attention (to) **Aldırma!** Never mind! Don't worry!
aldırmazlık indifference **aldırmazlıktan gelmek** to pretend to be indifferent, not to care
alegori allegory
alelacele in a big hurry, hastily
alelade ordinary, common
âlem world, universe; state, condition; all the world, people; merrymaking, party, orgy; kingdom **âlem yapmak** to have a rave-up, to go on a spree
alemdar standard bearer; leader
alenen openly, publicly
alengirli arg. showy, flashy
aleni open, public
alerji allergy
alerjik allergic
alet tool, instrument; apparatus, appliance; tool, means, agent **alet edavat** tools **alet etmek** to make a tool of sb **alet olmak** to be a tool
alev flame **alev almak** to catch fire
Alevi partisan of the caliph Ali, shiite
Alevilik Shiism
alevlendirmek to set on fire, to cause to blaze; to incite, to inflame
alevlenmek to take fire, to blaze; to become excited
aleyh against **aleyhinde bulunmak/-söylemek** to run down, to backbite **aleyhinde olmak** to be against sb **aleyhine dönmek** to boomerang on, to backfire **aleyhine olmak** to be disadvantageous to sb
aleyhtar opponent; opposed to
aleyhtarlık opposition
aleykümselam Peace be to you! (in reply to the Muslim greeting selamünaleyküm)
alfa alpha **alfa ışınları** alpha-rays
alfabe alphabet
alfabetik alphabetic(al)
algı perception
algılamak to perceive, to sense
algılanmak to be perceived
algler bitk. seaweeds
alıcı buyer, customer, purchaser, client; receiver, addressee; movie camera **alıcı gözüyle bakmak** to look carefully **alıcı kuş** bird of prey **alıcı yönetmeni** cameraman
alık clumsy, silly
alıkoymak to keep; to hinder, to stop; to arrest, to detain; to put aside, to reserve
alım taking; buying; attraction, charm **alım satım** business, trade
alımlı attractive, charming
alımlılık attraction, charm
alın forehead, brow; front **alın teri** great effort **alın teri dökmek** to graft (away), to work like a black **alın teriyle kazanmak** to earn by hard work **alnı açık** blameless, innocent **alnına yazılmış olmak** to be one's destiny **Alnını karışlarım!** I'll show you! I dare you!
alındı receipt
alıngan touchy

alınganlık touchiness
alınmak to take offence, to be hurt
alınyazısı fate, destiny
alışık accustomed (to), used (to)
alışkanlık habit, custom
alışkı custom, practice, habit
alışkın accustomed (to)
alışmak to be used (to); to get used to; to become addicted (to); to be in the habit of; to catch fire
alıştırma exercise; training
alıştırmak to accustom, to familiarize; to domesticate, to tame; to addict; to set on fire
alışveriş trade, business, commerce; shopping; relation **alışveriş etmek** to shop, to do shopping; to trade; to do dealings (with) **alışverişi olmamak** not to have anything to do (with)
âli high, sublime
âlim learned, wise; scholar, scientist
alimallah by God!
alize trade wind
alkali alkali
alkış applause, clapping **alkış tutmak** to clap (for); to cheer
alkışlamak to clap (for), to applaud
alkol alcohol
alkolik alcoholic
alkolizm alcoholism
alkollü alcoholic, spirituous **alkollü içki** alcoholic drink, alcohol, liquor
alkolsüz non-alcoholic, soft
Allah Allah, God **Allah Allah!** Goodness gracious! How strange! **Allah aşkına** for heaven's sake **Allah bağışlasın.** May God bless sb. **Allah belanı versin!** God damn you! **Allah belasını versin!** Damn him! Curse him! **Allah bilir.** Only God knows. **Allah bir yastıkta kocatsın.** May you/they have a happy life together (to married couple) **Allah büyüktür.** God is great; God will put things right. **Allah cezanı versin!** God damn you! **Allah esirgesin/saklasın** unless something goes wrong **Allah kazadan beladan korusun/saklasın** May god protect you from all evil. **Allah korusun!** God forbid! **Allah ömürler versin!** May

god give you/him, etc. a long life! **Allah rahatlık versin!** Good night! **Allah rahmet eylesin!** God rest his soul! **Allah senden razı olsun!** Thank you, May God be pleased with you! **Allaha bin şükür** Thank God **Allahın cezası** damn, damned **Allahını seversen** for God's sake **Allahın kulu** person, anybody **Allahtan** luckily **Allahtan bulsun.** Let God punish him. **Allahtan kork!** Don't do it! You should be shamed! **Allahtan korkmaz** pitiless, cruel **Allahtan umut kesilmez** While there is life, there is hope.
allahaısmarladık good-bye
allahlık simpleton, nitwit
allahsız godless, atheistic; merciless, cruel, cold-hearted
allak bullak confused, messed-up, tangled; upside down **allak bullak etmek** to make a mess (of), to upset; to confuse **allak bullak olmak** to turn into a mess; to be confused
allamak pullamak to decorate, to deck out, to smarten up
allegretto müz. allegretto
allegro müz. allegro
allık redness; rouge
alma receiver
almak to take; to get, to obtain; to buy; to receive; to accept; to contain, to hold; to conquer; to clean, to dust, to sweep; to last, to take; to cover (a distance); to employ, to hire; to mark
Alman German **Alman usulü** a Dutch treat **Alman usulü yapmak** to go Dutch (with sb)
Almanca German
Almanya Germany
almanak almanac
almangümüşü nickel silver
almaş permutation; alternative
almaşık alternative
alo hallo! (on telephone)
alt bottom, underside, underneath; under, lower, inferior; base **alt alta üst üste** rough-and-tumble **alt etmek** to beat, to defeat, to overcome **alt kat** downstairs; ground floor **altına kaçırmak** to wet one's clothes/bed **altın-**

da kalmak to have no answer to altında kalmamak not to be outdone altından girip üstünden çıkmak to squander, to blow altından kalkamamak not to be successful enough to cope with altını çizmek to underline; to emphasize altını ıslatmak to wet one's clothes/bed altını üstüne getirmek to turn upside down alttan almak to answer gently enough; not to make sb angrier

altbölüm sub-section, sub-division

altcins sub-genus

altçene lower jaw, mandible

altderi derma, corium

alternatif alternative **alternatif akım** alternative current ·

altgeçit underpass; subway

altı six

altıgen hexagon

altın gold; gold coin; golden **altın bilezik** skill that will earn one's living **altın çağı** golden age **altın kaplama** gold-plating; gold-plated **altın sarısı** golden blond **altın sikke** gold coin **altın topu gibi** chubby (baby)

altınbaş muskmelon, cantaloupe

altıncı sixth

altınsuyu aqua regia

altıntop grapefruit

altıpatlar six-shooter, revolver

altışar six each, six apiece

altlık support, base; pad

altmış sixty

altmışıncı sixtieth

alto alto

altsınıf sub-class

alttakım sub-order

alttür sub-species

altüst upside down, topsy-turvy **altüst etmek** to mess up, to upset **altüst olmak** to be in a mess, to be upset

altyapı substructure; infrastructure

altyazı subtitles

alüminyum aluminium

alüvyon alluvium, alluvion

alyans wedding ring

alyuvar red blood cell, erythrocyte

ama but, yet, still **aması maması yok** There are no buts about it! But me no buts!

âmâ blind

amaç aim, goal **amacına erişememek** to miss one's aim **amacına ulaşmak** to achieve one's aim

amaçlamak to aim (at); to intend

amaçlı purposeful

amaçsız aimless, purposeless

amaçsızca aimlessly

amade ready, prepared

aman pardon, mercy; help! mercy! alas! **aman Allahım** oh dear!, my god!, good God! **aman dilemek** to ask for mercy **aman vermek** to give quarter

amanın ünl. oh my!, what now!

amansız merciless, pitiless; deadly, incurable

amatör amateur

ambalaj packing, wrapping; package **ambalaj kâğıdı** wrapping paper **ambalaj yapmak** to wrap up, to pack

ambalajlamak to wrap up, to pack

ambar barn, granary; warehouse, storehouse; *den.* hold

ambargo embargo **ambargo koymak** to embargo, to put an embargo **ambargoyu kaldırmak** to lift the embargo (from)

amber ambergris; scent, perfume

ambulans ambulance

amca (paternal) uncle **amca kızı** daughter of one's paternal uncle, cousin **amca oğlu** son of one's uncle, cousin

amcazade cousin

amel action, deed, work; diarrhoea **amel olmak** to have diarrhea

amele worker, workman, labourer

ameli practical, applied

ameliye process, procedure, operation

ameliyat *hek* operation **ameliyat olmak** to be operated, to have an operation

ameliyathane *hek.* operating theatre, theatre

Amerika America **Amerika Birleşik Devletleri, ABD** the United States of America, USA

Amerikalı American

Amerikan American **Amerikan İngilizcesi** American English

amerikanbezi nettle cloth, grey cotton cloth

ametal non-metalic

amfi amphitheatre; lecture room

amfibi amphibian **amfibi tank** amphibian tank

amfiteatr lecture hall, lecture theatre; amphitheatre

amigo cheerleader

amin amen

amip amoeba

amir superior, chief; boss

amiral admiral

amiyane vulgar, common **amiyene tabiriyle** in the colloquial

amme the public **amme hizmeti** public service

amonyak ammonia

amorti redemption of a bond issue; the smallest prize (in lottery)

amortisman amortization; redemption (of a bond)

amortisör shock-absorber; damper

amper ampere

amperölçer ampermetre

ampul bulb, lamp; *hek.* ampoule

amut perpendicular **amuda kalkmak** to do a hand-stand

amyant asbestos

an moment, instant; intelligence, mind

ana mother; main, principal, basic **ana avrat düz gitmek** to swear like a trooper **ana baba** parents **ana baba günü** doomsday, tumult **ana kuzusu** baby-in-arms **ana sütü** breast milk **ana tarafından** on the mother's side **ana yüreği** mother's love **anadan doğma** stark naked; from birth, congenital **Anan güzel mi?** I'm no fool **anasından doğduğuna pişman etmek** to make sb sorry he has been born **anasından emdiği süt burnundan gelmek** to have a hell of time **anasının gözü** very cunning

anadil primitive language

anadili native language, mother tongue

anaerki matriarchy

anaerkil matriarchal

anafor eddy; counterflow; *arg.* rake-off, unearned money, illicit profit

anaforcu parasite, sponger

anahtar key; spanner, wrench

anakara continent

analık motherhood; adoptive mother; motherly woman

analiz analysis **analiz etmek** to analyse

anamal capital

anamalcı capitalist

anamalcılık capitalism

ananas pineapple

anane tradition

ananevi traditional

anaokulu kindergarten, nursery school

anarşi anarchy

anarşist anarchist

anarşizm anarchism

anason *bitk.* anise; aniseed

anatomi anatomy

anatomik anatomical

anayasa constitution

anayasal constitutional

anayol main road

anayön cardinal point

anayurt mother country, homeland

ancak only, merely; hardly, barely; but, however; at the earliest

ançüez anchovy

andaç gift, souvenir

andırış resemblance, similarity

andırmak to resemble, to be reminiscent

anestezi anaesthesia

angarya drudgery, donkeywork

Anglikan Anglican

Anglikanlık Anglicanism

Anglosakson Anglo-Saxon

angut ruddy shelduck; *kon.* fool

anı memory

anılmak to be remembered; to be mentioned

anımsamak to remember, to recall

anında instantly; immediately

anırmak to bray, to hee-haw

anıt monument

anıtsal monumental

anıtkabir mausoleum

Anıtkabir Atatürk's tomb

ani sudden, unexpected; suddenly, all at once, short

aniden suddenly

animasyon animation
anjin angina
Anka phoenix
anket public survey, inquiry, questionnaire **anket yapmak** to take a poll, to make a survey
anlak intelligence
anlam meaning, sense **anlam çıkarmak** to make sth of sb/sth **anlamı olmak** to make sense **anlamına gelmek** to mean, to signify, to amount (to)
anlama understanding comprehension, apprehension
anlamak to understand, to comprehend, to conceive; to find out; to appreciate
anlamazlık lack of understanding **anlamazlıktan gelmek** to feign ignorance
anlambilim semantics
anlamdaş synonymous
anlamlandırmak to give meaning (to). to explain
anlamlı meaningful
anlamsız meaningless
anlaşılır clear, lucid, comprehensible
anlaşılmak to be understood; to be evident
anlaşılmaz incomprehensible, unintelligible
anlaşma agreement, contract **anlaşma yapmak** to make an agreement, to contract **anlaşmayı bozmak** to break an agreement
anlaşmak to understand one another; to reach an agreement
anlaşmazlık disagreement; misunderstanding
anlatı narration, narrative; short story
anlatmak to tell, to express; to explain, to expound; to describe
anlayış understanding, comprehension; perceptiveness, intelligence; mind, intellect
anlayışlı understanding; intelligent
anlayışsız inconsiderate, intolerant
anlık intellect, understanding
anma remembrance; commemoration, celebration **anma töreni** commemorative ceremony

anmak to call to mind, to remember; to mention; to commemorate
anne mother, ma, mummy **anneciğim** mummy, ma, mum **anneler günü** Mother's Day
anneanne grandmother
annelik motherhood
anofel anopheles
anonim anonymous **anonim şirket/ortaklık** incorporated company, joint stock company
anons announcement **anons etmek** to announce
anormal abnormal
anormalleşmek to become abnormal
anormallik abnormality
anot anode
ansızın suddenly, all of a sudden
ansiklopedi encyclopaedia
ansiklopedik encyclopaedic
ant oath, pledge **ant içmek** to take an oath **andını bozmak** to violate an oath
antarktik antarctic
Antarktika Antarctica
anten antenna, aerial; *hayb.* antenna, feeler
antepfıstığı pistachio
antibiyotik antibiotic
antidemokratik antidemocratic
antika antique; *kon.* odd, weird, funny **antika eşya** antique
antikacı antique dealer
antikalık antiqueness; eccentricity
antikor antibody
antilop antelope
antimuan antimony
antipati antipathy
antipatik disagreeable, unpleasant, cold
antitez antithesis
antitoksin antitoxin
antlaşma pact, treaty
antoloji anthology
antrakt (theatre, concert) interval, interlude; (cinema) interval, intermission
antrasit anthracite
antre entrance, entry
antrenman training, exercise **antrenman yapmak** to train, to work out, to

exercise
antrenör trainer, coach
antrenörlük being a trainer/coach
antrepo bonded warehouse
antropolog anthropologist
antropoloji anthropology
anüs anus
Anzak Anzac
aort aorta
apaçık very clear, evident
apak pure white, all white
apandis appendix
apandisit appendicitis
apansız(ın) unexpectedly, all of a sudden
apartman block of flats, apartment block *il.* **apartman katı** flat, apartment
apar topar pell-mell, helter-skelter, at a moments notice
apayrı quite separate, quite different
aperitif aperitif, (pre-dinner etc.) drink
apış fork (of the body), crotch
apışmak to collapse from tiredness; to be astonished **apışıp kalmak** to be nonplussed
apolet epaulet
apse abscess
aptal stupid, silly
aptallaşmak to become stupid; to be dazed, to be flabbergasted
aptallık stupidity, foolishness
aptes ritual ablution, faeces, bowel movement **aptes almak** *din.* to perform ritual ablution **aptes bozmak** to defecate, to urinate **aptesi kaçmak** *din.* to perform ritual ablution again because one has relieved oneself
apteshane toilet, water closet
ar are (100 m2)
ar shame **ar damarı çatlamak** to feel no sense of shame
ara distance, space; interval, pause; break; *sp.* half-time, time out; terms, relation, footing **ara bozmak** to destroy the friendship (between) **ara bulmak** to reconcile, to mediate **ara seçimi** by-election **ara sıra** now and then **ara vermek** to take a break, to pause **arada bir** at times, from time

to time **arası açık/bozuk olmak** to be on bad terms (with, ile) **arası iyi olmak** to be on good terms (with) **arasına, arasında** between; among **araya girmek** to meddle, to interfere
araba car, automobile; cart; wagon **araba gezisi** drive **araba kazası** smash, smash-up **araba kullanmak** to drive a car **araba vapuru** ferryboat, car ferry **araba yarışı** car racing
arabacı driver; coachman; cartwright
arabesk arabesque
arabozan mischief-maker
arabozanlık mischief-making
arabulucu mediator, peacemaker; go--between
arabuluculuk mediation peacemaking
aracı mediator, intermediary; agent, broker, middleman
aracılık mediation, intervention
araç means; tool, apparatus, implement, device; vehicle
arada in between; sometimes **arada bir** (every) now and then, occasionally **arada sırada** occasionally, now and then, now and again
arakesit intersection
araklamak to pilfer, to swipe, to walk of (with)
aralamak to half-open, to leave ajar
aralık space, gap, opening; time, interval, moment; corridor; *fiz.* range; (month) December; half-open, ajar **aralık bırakmak** to leave a space; to leave half-open **aralık vermek** to put off sth for a time
aralıklı spaced out; periodic, intermittent
aralıksız continuous, uninterrupted; continuously, uninterruptedly
arama search, searching **arama emri** search-warrant **arama tarama** (police) searching **arama yapmak** to carry out a search
aramak to look for, to seek; to search; to long for, to miss **arayıp taramak** to search carefully
aranağme instrumental passage
aranjman *müz.* arrangement
aranmak to be searched; to be in de-

mand; to be missed; to search oneself, to search one's pockets, etc.; to look for trouble

Arap Arab; Arabian; very dark, black

Arapça Arabic

arapsabunu soft soup

arapsaçı tangled affair, mess **arapsaçına çevirmek** to tangle **arapsaçına dönmek** to be too difficult to sort out

araştırma research, investigation, study

araştırmacı researcher

araştırmak to research, to investigate; to search

aratmamak to be a complete substitute (for)

arayış searching, seeking

arazi land **arazi olmak** arg. to sneak off **arazi sahibi** landowner **arazi vergisi** land tax

arazöz street sprinkler

ardıç bitk. juniper

ardıçkuşu hayb. fieldfare

ardıl consecutive; successor

ardınca behind, following

ardışık consecutive, successive

ardiye warehouse; storehouse **ardiye ücreti** storage

arena arena, bullring

argo slang, cant

argon argon

arı bee **arı gibi** hard working **arı kovanı** beehive **arı yuvası** hornet's nest **arıbeyi** queen-bee

arı clean; pure; innocent

arıcılık beekeeping, apiculture

arılık cleanliness; purity; innocence

arılaşmak to become pure

arınmak to become clean; to be purified

arıtımevi refinery

arıtmak to cleanse, to purify; to refine

arıza breakdown, defect, fault **arıza bulucu** fault-finder; trouble-shooter **arıza yapmak** to break down

arızalanmak to break down

arızalı broken-down, out of order, defective; uneven, rough, rugged, broken

arızi fortuitous

arif wise, knowing

arife eve

aristokrasi aristocracy

aristokrat aristocrat; aristocratic

aristokratlık aristocracy

aritmetik arithmetic; arithmetical **aritmetik dizi** arithmetical progression **aritmetik işlem** arithmetical operation

Arjantin Argentina

Arjantinli Argentinian

ark dike, ditch; canal

arka back; back part, rear; posterior; support, protection; supporter, backer; continuation, sequel **arka plan** background **arka arkaya** one after the other **arkadan** from behind; afterwards **arkadan vurmak** to stab sb in the back **arkası gelmek** to continue **arkası kesilmek** to come to an end, to run out **arkası yere gelmemek** not to be defeated, to have powerful supporters **arkasına, arkasında** behind **arkasına düşmek/takılmak** to follow up (a matter); to follow, to pursuit, to dog **arkasından** after **arkasından konuşmak** to backbite **arkasını bırakmamak** to follow up, to tag after **arkasını getirememek** to be unable to complete **arkasını vermek** to lean one's back (against); to rely (on)

arkadaş friend; companion **arkadaş canlısı** friendly, sociable, social **arkadaş olmak** to become friends

arkadaşlık friendship **arkadaşlık etmek** to be a friend (of), to rub shoulders (with)

arkalamak to hoist sth onto one's back, to shoulder; to support, to back

arkalık back (of a chair, etc.); porter's saddle

arkeolog archaeologist

arkeoloji archaeology

arkeolojik archeological

Arktik Arctic

arlanmak to be ashamed

arlanmaz shameless

arma coat of arms; den. rigging

armağan present, gift **armağan etmek** to present (to)

armatör shipowner

22

armatür armature
armoni *müz.* harmony
armonika harmonica; accordion
armut pear
Arnavut Albanian
Arnavutça Albanian
arpa barley
arpacık sty, stye; *ask.* front sight (of a gun)
arsa building plot
arsenik arsenic
arsız shameless, cheeky
arsızlık shamelessness, impudence
arsızlaşmak to become shameless, to act shamelessly
arslan *bkz.* aslan
arş the highest heaven
arşın Turkish yard (approximately 68 cm.)
arşidük archduke
arşiv archives arşiv filmi library film
art back, near, behind art arda one after another art niyet hidden intent ardı arkası gelmeyen never-ending, endless ardına düşmek to follow up, to pursue
artçı *ask.* rear guard
artezyen artesian well
artı *mat.* plus; positive
artık left, remaining; remainder, remnant; waste, rubbish
artık at last, finally; from now on; any more Artık bu kadarı fazla. That's more than enough. Artık canıma yetti. I've had enough of it.
artıkdeğer surplus value
artıkgün leap-year day, leap day (29 February)
artıkyıl leap-year
artırım economy, saving
artırma increase, economizing; auction
artırmak to increase, to raise, to expand; to save, to economize; to raise a bid (at auction)
artış increase, increment
artist actor, actress artist gibi beautiful; handsome
artistik artistic artistik patinaj artistic skating
artmak to increase, to rise; to remain

over
aruz prosody
arya aria
arz the earth
arz *tic.* supply; presentation, submission arz etmek to present (a gift, a petition, one's respects); to submit (a proposal); to offer (an opinion) arz ve talep supply and demand
arzu wish, desire arzu etmek to wish, to desire arzusunda olmak to have a wish (to) arzu üzerine on request
arzuhal petition
arzuhalci street letter-writer, petition writer
arzulamak to desire, to wish (for)
as ace
as ermine, stoat
asa scepter, stick
asabi nervous, irritable; neurotic
asabileşmek to get nervous, to become irritated
asabilik nervousness, irritability
asabiye nervous diseases; neurology
asabiyeci neurologist
asal basic, fundamental asal sayı prime number
asalak, parasite; *kon.* sponger
asalaklık parasitism; sponging
asalet nobility
asaleten *huk.* acting as principal
asansör *İi.* lift, *Aİ.* elevator
asap nerves asap bozukluğu nervous disorder asabı bozulmak to chafe, to get nervous
asayiş order, public order, public security asayişi bozmak to break the peace asayişi korumak to keep the peace
asbest asbestos
asetilen acetylene
aseton acetone
asfalt asphalt; motorway asfalt kaplamak to asphalt
asgari minimum; least asgari ücret minimum wage
asıl origin, source; reality, truth; real, true; main, principal; original asıl sayılar cardinal numbers aslı astarı olmamak not to be true aslı çıkmak to be

confirmed

asılı hanging, suspended; hanged, executed

asılmak to hang; to be hanged/hung; to try to pick sb up; to pester, to insist

asılsız baseless, groundless

asır century; age, time, period

asi rebel, insurgent; rebellious

asil noble, aristocratic; permanent, definitively appointed

asileşmek to rebel

asilik rebellion **asilik etmek** to rebel

asillik nobility

asistan assistant; assistant to a professor; *hek.* assistant doctor, intern

asistanlık assistantship; internship

asit acid

asker soldier; military service; troops **asker kaçağı** absent-without-leave, deserter **asker ocağı** place for military service **asker olmak** to join the army **asker tayını** soldier's rations **askere almak** to enlist, to conscript **askere gitmek** to join the army, to go into the army

askeri military **askeri bando** military band **askeri bölge/mıntıka** military zone **askeri hastane** military hospital **askeri inzibat** military police, military policeman **askeri lise** cadets school **askeri mahkeme** court-martial, military court **askeri öğrenci** cadet

askerileştirmek to militarize

askerlik military service **askerlik şubesi** local draft office **askerlik yoklaması** rollcall

askı hook; hanger, clothes-hanger; *İİ.* braces, *Aİ.* suspenders; the posting **askıda** in suspense **askıya çıkarmak** to publish the banns

asla never, in no way

aslan lion **aslan ağzında olmak** to be very hard to get **aslan gibi** well-built, healthy **aslan kesilmek** to become as brave as a lion **aslan payı** the lion's share **aslan sütü** *kon.* rakı **aslan yürekli** lion-hearted

Aslan (burcu) Leo

aslanağzı *bitk.* snapdragon

aslen originally, essentially

aslında actually, in fact

asli fundamental, essential

asma *bitk.* vine; grape-vine

asmak to hang; *arg.* to play truant, to cut

aspiratör aspirator

aspirin aspirin

asri modern

assubay noncommissioned officer

ast under, below; junior; subordinate

astar lining; undercoat, priming

astarlamak to line; to apply priming

asteğmen second lieutenant

astım *hek.* asthma

astigmat *hek.* astigmatic

astigmatizm astigmatism

astragan astrakhan

astroid astroid

astronom astronomer

astronomi astronomy

astronomik astronomical

astronot astronaut

Asya Asia

Asyalı Asiatic

aş cooked food

aşağı lower part, bottom; lower, inferior; common, mean; less; down; below **aşağı görmek** to look down on, to despise **aşağı kalmamak** not to fall short (of), to be second to none **aşağı yukarı** more or less, approximately

aşağıda below; downstairs

aşağıdan from below **aşağıdan almak** to sing another song, to sing small

aşağılamak to lower, to reduce, to snub, to debase

aşağılık vulgarity; lowness; base; common, inferior; coarse, vulgar **aşağılık duygusu/kompleksi** inferiority complex

aşağıya down, downwards; downstairs

aşama phase, stage; rank; grade

aşamalı gradual **aşamalı olarak** in echelon; by stages, gradually

aşçı cook

aşçıbaşı head-cook, chef

aşçılık cooking, cookery, cuisine

aşevi restaurant; soup kitchen

aşı inoculation; graft; vaccine **aşı olmak** to be inoculated **aşı yapmak** to inoculate, to vaccinate; to graft, to bud

aşıboyası red ocher; brick-red

aşık knuckle-bone

âşık lover, admirer; wandering minstrel, bard; in love (with)

aşılamak *hek.* to vaccinate, to inoculate; to graft, to bud; to infect; to instil (ideas)

aşındırmak to wear out, to abrade; to eat away, to corrode

aşınma abrasion; corrosion; erosion

aşınmak to be abraded, to be eroded

aşırı excessive, extreme; excessively, extremely; beyond, over

aşırıdoyma *fiz.* supersaturation

aşırıergime *fiz.* superfusion; supercooling

aşırılık excessiveness, excess

aşırmacılık stealing; plagiarism, piracy

aşırmak to pass over; to steal, to swipe; to plagiarize

aşikâr obvious, clear, apparent, evident

aşina acquaintance; acquainted, conversant, knowing

aşinalık acquaintance, intimacy

aşiret tribe

aşk love; passion **aşka gelmek** to get excited, to be enraptured

aşkın excessive; exceeding, over; transcendent(al)

aşmak to pass over, to go beyond, to exceed

aşure Noah's pudding, a dessert with wheat grains, nuts, dried fruit, etc.

at horse **at arabası** coach, cat, carriage **at oynatmak** to ride skilfully; to compete (with), to vie (with); to go on one's way **at yarışı** horse race **ata binmek** to ride a horse **attan düşmek** to fall off a horse

ata father; ancestor **atadan kalma** ancestral, traditional

ataerki patriarchy

ataerkil patriarchal

atak reckless, rash, bold; *sp.* attack

atama appointment

atamak to appoint (sb), (to)

atanmak to be appointed (to)

atardamar *anat.* artery

atasözü proverb

ataşe attache

Atatürkçü Kemalist

Atatürkçülük Kemalism

ateist atheist

ateizm atheism

atelye workshop; studio

ateş fire; *hek.* temperature, fever; vehemence, ardour **ateş açmak** to open fire (on), **ateş almak** to catch fire **ateş almamak** to hang fire, to miss fire **ateş altında** under fire **ateş basmak** to feel hot **ateş etmek** to fire (on) to shoot (at) **ateş gibi** very hot, fiery; agile, quick **ateş pahası(na)**, very expensive **ateş püskürmek** to be furious **ateş yakmak** to light a fire **(kendini) ateşe atmak** to go through fire and water (for, için) **ateşe vermek** to set fire to **ateşi başına vurmak** to become very excited, to blow one's cap **ateşi çıkmak** (one's temperature) to rise **ateşi düşmek** (one's temperature) to drop **ateşi yükselmek** (one's temperature) to rise **ateşle oynamak** to play with fire **ateşten gömlek** ordeal

ateşböceği *hayb.* firefly

ateşçi fireman, stoker

ateşkes cease-fire, armistice

ateşlemek to set fire (to), to ignite; to provoke

ateşlenmek to be lit, to be ignited; to have a temperature; to get excited

ateşli burning, fiery, passionate, fervent *hek.* feverish **ateşli silah** firearm

ateşperest fire-worshipper

atıcı marksman, good shot; braggart, boaster

atıf attribution, ascribing

atık waste; effluent **atık madde** effluent **atık su** waste water

atılgan dashing, reckless, bold

atılım leap, rush; development, progress

atılmak to be thrown; to be fired; to be dismissed; to attack; to burst into (a conversation), to cut in

atım range (of a gun)

atımlık charge

atış throwing; firing, shooting; (heart)

beating **atış alanı/yeri** rifle range, artillery range
atışmak to quarrel, to bicker
atıştırmak to gobble, to bolt, to gulp; to spit, to drizzle
atik alert, agile
atkestanesi *bitk.* horse chestnut
atkı scarf, shawl, wrap; hay-fork; shoe-buckle; weft
atkuyruğu pony-tail; *bitk.* marestail
atlama jumping, jump; skipping, omission **atlama beygiri** vaulting horse
atlamak to jump; to leap; to skip, to omit; to miss (an item of news)
atlas satin; *coğ.* atlas; *anat.* atlas
Atlas Okyanusu The Atlantic Ocean
atlasçiçeği *bitk.* cactus
atlatmak to cause to jump; to recover from (a disease); to weather, to overcome, to weather; to put off, to get rid of
atlet athlete; undershirt
atletik athletic
atletizm athletics
atlı horseman, rider
atlıkarınca merry-go-round, roundabout, carousel *Al.*
atmaca *hayb.* sparrow-hawk
atmak to throw; to throw away; to drop; to put into; to put out, to extend; to fire (a gun); to shoot (an arrow, etc.); to write (one's signature, the date); to expel, to dismiss; to cast, to impute; to carry to take (sth, to a place); to send, to post; to lie, to fib; to drink; to crack, to split; to pulsate, to beat; to land (a blow); (colour) to fade **atıp tutmak** to run down; to talk big, to boast
atmasyon *arg.* lie, story; false, made up
atmosfer atmosphere **atmosfer tabakası** atmospheric layer
atol coral island, atoll
atom atom **atom ağırlığı** atomic weight **atom bombası** atom bomb **atom çağı** atomic age **atom çekirdeği** atomic nucleus **atom enerjisi** atomic energy **atom reaktörü** nuclear reactor **atom sayısı** atomic number
atomal atomic

atölye workshop; studio, atelier
atsineği horsefly
aut *sp.* out (of play)
av hunting, shooting, fishing; game, prey **av hayvanı** game animal **av köpeği** hunting dog, hound **ava çıkmak** to go out hunting **Ava giden avlanır** *ats.* The biter is sometimes bit.
avadanlık set of tools
avam the public, the common people **Avam Kamarası** the House of Commons, the Commons
avanak gull, boob, mug; gullible
avans advance (of money) **avans almak** to get an advance **avans vermek** to advance money
avanta *arg.* rake-off, pickings, gravy
avantaj advantage
avantajlı advantageous
avare vagabond, good-for-nothing
avcı hunter, huntsman **avcı mangası** skirmishers **avcı uçağı** fighter plane, fighter
avcılık huntsmanship, hunting, shooting
avize chandelier
avlak hunting ground
avlamak to hunt, to shoot; to deceive, to entice
avlanmak to be hunted; to be caught; to go out hunting
avlu courtyard
avokado *bitk.* avocado
Avrasya Eurasia
avrat woman; wife
Avrupa Europe
Avrupai European (manner/style)
Avrupalı European
Avrupalılaşmak to become Europeanized
Avrupalılaştırmak to Europeanize
avuç the hallow of the hand; handful **avuç açmak** to beg **avuç dolusu** handful; plenty of **avucunun içi gibi bilmek** to know (a place) like the palm of one's hand **avucunu yalamak** to go away empty-handed
avukat lawyer, barrister, solicitor
avukatlık profession/work of a barrister; loquacity

avunmak to be consoled; to be distracted
avuntu consolation; distraction
avurt pouch, cheek pocket
Avustralya Australia
Avustralyalı Australian
Avusturya Austria
Avusturyalı Austrian
avutmak to soothe, to distract; to console, to comfort; to amuse, to divert
ay Ah! Oh! Ouch!
ay moon; month **ay başı** first days of a month **ay ışığı** moonlight **ay parçası** a beauty **ay takvimi** lunar calendar **ay tutulması** lunar eclipse **ay yıldız** star and crescent (on the Turkish flag) **ayda yılda bir** once in a blue moon **aydan aya** once a month, monthly **Ayın kaçı?** What is the date?
aya palm (of the hand); sole (of the foot)
ayak foot; leg; pedal (of a machine); treadle (of a sewing machine); rung (of a ladder); rhyme **ayak bağı** hindrance, impediment **ayak basmak** to set foot in, to arrive **ayak bileği** ankle **ayak diremek** to put one's foot down, to insist **ayak yapmak** to put on an act, to fake **ayağa kalkmak** to stand up; to get better, to recover **ayağı alışmak** to frequent (a place) **ayağına bağ olmak** to hinder **ayağına dolanmak/dolaşmak** to be in the way **ayağına getirmek** to have sth/sb brought to one **ayağına gitmek** to visit sb personally **ayağını çabuk tutmak** to hurry **ayağını giymek** to put on one's shoes **ayağını çıkarmak** to take off one's shoes **ayağını denk almak** to watch one's step **ayağını kaydırmak** to supplant, to oust **ayağının altına almak** to thrash, to beat; to violate, to ignore **ayakaltında dolaşmak** to get under foot, to be in the way **ayaklar altına almak** to disregard **ayakta** on foot, standing; excited, worried **ayakta kalmak** to be left without a seat; to remain standing **ayakta uyumak** to be excessively tired; not to know what is going on

ayakaltı much-frequented place **ayakaltında dolaşmak** to get in sb's way
ayakkabı footwear, shoe
ayakkabıcı shoe-maker; shoe-seller; cobbler
ayakkabıcılık shoemaking; shoe trade
ayaklandırmak to make revolt, to cause to revolt; to arouse, to provoke
ayaklanma rebel, rebellion, uprising, revolt, mutiny
ayaklanmak (child) to begin to walk; (patient) to be able to walk; to rebel, to revolt
ayaklı footed, legged
ayaktakımı rabble, mob
ayakucu foot, tiptoe **ayakucuna basarak yürümek** to walk on tiptoe
ayaküstü, ayaküzeri without sitting down, in haste
ayakyolu water-closet, lavatory
ayar adjustment, setting; standard (of fineness); carat; quality, character **ayar etmek** to regulate, to adjust **ayarı bozuk** out of order
ayarlamak to adjust, to regulate, to fix, to test, to gauge, to assay; to arrange
ayarlı adjusted, regulated; adjustable
ayarsız not regulated
ayartmak to tempt, to seduce, to pervert
ayaz dry cold (daytime); frost (at night)
aybaşı menstruation, periods
ayça new moon, crescent
ayçiçeği sunflower
aydın educated, enlightened; bright; intellectual
aydınger tracing paper
aydınlanmak to become bright, to brighten up; to become informed, to be enlightened
aydınlatıcı illuminating; informative, explanation
aydınlatmak to light up, to illuminate; to enlighten, to elucidate
aydınlık bright, sunlit; light, daylight
ayet verse of the Koran
aygın baygın languid; languishing; languidly
aygır *hayb.* stallion **aygır gibi** huge, bury

aygıt apparatus, instrument, tool; *biy.* system

ayı bear **ayı gibi** bearish; huge

ayıbalığı *hayb.* seal

ayık sober; wide-awake

ayıklamak to sort sth out; to clean, to pick, to shell (rice, vegetables); to shell (peas, beans, nuts) **Ayıkla şimdi pirincin taşını!** Here's a nice/pretty kettle of fish!

ayılmak to sober up, to recover; to come to, to come round (after fainting); to come to one's senses, to see the light

ayıltmak to sober up, to bring round

ayıp shame; defect, fault; shameful; shame on you! **ayıp etmek** to behave shamefully **ayıptır söylemesi** without wishing to boast

ayıplamak to find fault with, to censure, to blame

ayıraç *kim.* reagent

ayırmak to separate; to disconnect, to detach; to select, to pick, to choose; to divide; to save, to reserve; to distinguish

ayırt etmek to distinguish, to discriminate

ayırtman examiner

ayin rite; ceremony

ayıüzümü *bitk.* bearberry

aykırı against, contrary to; crosswise, across **aykırı düşmek** to contradict, to be incongruous (with)

aykırılaşmak to become contrary

ayla halo

aylak unemployed, idle **aylak aylak** idly

aylık monthly salary; monthly; ... months old; lasting ... months

aylıkçı salaried employee

aylıklı salaried

aymak to come to; to come to one's senses

ayna mirror, looking-glass

aynen without change, exactly

aynı the same, identical **aynı kapıya çıkmak** to reach the same conclusion **aynı şekilde** in the same way **aynı şey** it makes no difference **aynı zamanda** at the same time; meanwhile

ayol Say! Well! Hey! You! (mostly by women)

ayraç bracket, parenthesis

ayran drink made with yoghurt and water

ayrı separate, apart; different, distinct; exceptional **ayrı tutmak** to make a distinction

ayrıbasım offprint, reprint

ayrıca separately, specially; in addition, moreover, also

ayrıcalık privilege, concession

ayrıcalıklı privileged; preferential

ayrık separated, disjointed; exceptional

ayrıkotu *bitk.* couch grass

ayrıksı eccentric, different

ayrılık separation; difference; deviation

ayrılmak to separate from one another, to part; to leave, to depart from; to be distinguished; to be divorced

ayrım distinction; difference; disparity; part, chapter

ayrımlaşma differentiation

ayrımlaşmak to differentiate

ayrımlı different

ayrıntı detail

ayrıntılı detailed, comprehensive **ayrıntılı olarak** in detail

ayrışık decomposed; different, various

ayrışmak to be decomposed

ayrıştırmak to decompose

ayrıt *mat.* edge

aysberg iceberg

ayva quince **ayvayı yemek** to get into difficulties, to be in hot water *kon.*

ayvaz footman **Ayvaz kasap hep bir hesap.** It makes no difference.

ayyaş drunkard, alcoholic

ayyaşlık alcoholism, drunkenness

az little, few; insufficient, skimpy; seldom **az bir şey** only a little **az buçuk** a little, somewhat; slight **az bulmak** to consider insufficient **Az buz şey değil** It's no small matter. **az çok** more or less **az daha** almost, nearly **az gelmek** to be insufficient **az kaldı/kalsın** almost, nearly

aza member; limps, organs

azalmak to become less, to lessen, to diminish

azaltmak to lessen, to reduce, to lower, to decrease, to diminish

azamet greatness, grandeur; conceit, arrogance

azametli magnificent, grand; arrogant, conceited, ostentatious

azami maximum, greatest, utmost

azap pain, torture, torment

azar scolding,reproach **azar işitmek** to be scolded, to get a rocket

azar azar little by little, inch by inch, bit by bit

azarlamak to give sb a rocket, to tell off, to scold

azat liberation, emancipation; free **azat etmek** to set free; to emancipate

azdırmak to irritate, to make worse; to excite, to incite; to spoil (a child); to lead astray

azelya *bitk.* azalea

Azerbaycan Azerbaijan

Azerbaycanlı Azerbaijani

Azeri Azerbaijani

Azerice Azerbaijani, Azeri

azgelişmiş underdeveloped **azgelişmiş ülke** underdeveloped country

azgelişmişlik underdevelopment

azgın furious, mad, wild, fierce; tender, sensitive (skin); naughty, mischievous (child); oversexed, lustful; wild, strong (wind); very rough (sea)

azı molar tooth

azıcık very little, very few; little; for a moment

azıdişi molar tooth

azık food; provisions

azılı ferocious, savage

azımsamak to consider sth too little

azınlık minority **azınlıkla kalmak** to be in the minority

azılmak to get out of control, to get wild

azim resolution, determination

azimli resolute, determined

aziz dear, beloved; saint

azizlik preciousness; sainthood; trick, practical joke

azletmek to dismiss

azmak to go too far, to overstep the mark; to become depraved; to feel

horny, to rut; to get wild, to become furious; to get rough (sea); to fester, to get inflamed (wound); (river) to be in flood; to be a hybrid

azman monstrous, enormous

azmetmek to be determined (to), to resolve (upon)

azoik azoic

azot nitrogen, azote

Azrail Azrael **Azrailin elinden kurtulmak** to be saved from death

B

baba father; *den.* bollard; newel post **baba tarafı** the father's side **babadan kalma** inherited from one's father

babaanne (paternal) grandmother

babacan good-natured, fatherly

babalık fatherhood; stepfather; father-in-law

babayiğit brave, virile

babayiğitlik bravery, virility

baca chimney; *den.* funnel

bacak leg; jack, knave **bacak kadar** tiny, shorty

bacaksız without legs; short-legged, squat; *kon.* naughty, urchin

bacanak the husband of one's wife's sister

bacı (elder) sister

badana whitewash, limewash **badana etmek/vurmak** to whitewash

badanacı whitewasher

badanalamak to whitewash

badanalı whitewashed

badem almond **badem gibi** fresh and crisp **badem gözlü** almond-eyed **badem kurabiyesi** macaroon

bademcik *anat.* tonsil

bademezmesi almond paste

bademşekeri sugared almond

badi duck **badi badi yürümek** to waddle

badire (unexpected) calamity, difficult situation

bagaj luggage, baggage; boot, trunk

bağ tie, string, cord; bandage; bunch, bundle; relation, link; *anat.* ligament; vineyard; garden, orchard
bağbozumu vintage
bağcı grape grower
bağcık cord, strap; shoe lace
bağcılık viniculture
bağdaş sitting cross-legged **bağdaş kurmak** to sit cross-legged
bağdaşık harmonious
bağdaşmak to accord, to agree, to suit
bağdoku connectiive tissue
bağıl relative
bağım dependence
bağımlı dependent
bağımlılık dependence
bağımsız independent
bağımsızlık independence
bağıntı relation
bağıntılı relative
bağır breast, bosom; viscera **bağrı yanık** heartsick, distressed **bağrına basmak** to embrace; to protect, to shelter **bağrına taş basmak** to grin and bear it
bağırmak to shout, to yell **bağırıp çağırmak** to make a big fuss, to make a lot of noise
bağırsak intestine(s), bowel(s), gut(s)
bağırtı shout, outcry
bağış donation, grant
bağışık immune
bağışıklık immunity
bağışlamak to donate; to forgive, to pardon
bağlaç *dilb.* conjunction
bağlam context; bunch, bundle
bağlama a plucked string instrument; crossbar
bağlamak to tie, to fasten, to connect; to bandage; to form; to hinder, to obstruct, to appropriate, to assign
bağlantı tie, connection
bağlayıcı connecting; binding, obliging; conjunctive
bağlı bound, tied, fastened, connected; dependent; faithful
bağnaz fanatical
bağnazlık fanaticism
bağrışmak to cry out together

bahadır brave, valiant
bahane excuse, pretext **bahane aramak** to seek a pretext **bahane etmek** to plead; to allege
bahar spring
baharat, bahar spices
baharatçı spice-seller
bahçe garden
bahçıvan gardener
bahçıvanlık gardening
bahis subject, topic; wager, bet **bahse girişmek/girmek** to bet, to wager **bahsi kaybetmek** to lose the wager **bahsi kazanmak** to gain the wager
bahriye navy
bahriyeli sailor; naval officer
bahsetmek to mention, to speak of, to talk about
bahşiş tip **bahşiş vermek** to tip
baht fortune, luck **bahtı açık** lucky, fortunate **bahtı kara** unlucky, unfortunate
bahtiyar lucky, fortunate
bakakalmak to stand in astonishment, to gape
bakan minister
bakanlık ministry
bakarkör unobservant person
bakıcı attendant, guard; nurse
bakım care; attention, upkeep; point of view
bakımevi dispensary
bakımlı well-cared for, well-kept
bakımsız neglected, unkempt
bakınmak to look around
bakır copper
bakırcı coppersmith
bakış glance, look
bakışım symmetry
bakışımlı symmetric
bakışımsız asymmetric
bakışımsızlık asymmetry
bakışmak to look at one another
baki everlasting
bakir virgin, untouched
bakire virgin, maiden
bakiye remainder
bakkal grocer; grocery **bakkal dükkânı** grocery
bakkaliye groceries; grocery shop

bakla broad-bean(s), horsebean; chain link **baklayı ağzından çıkarmak** to spill the beans

baklagiller leguminous plants

baklava finely layered pastry filled with nuts and steeped in syrup

bakmak to look; to look for; to face; to look after; to see to; to treat; to be in charge (of); to depend (on); (waiter) to serve **bakarız** we'll see **bakar mısınız** excuse me

bakraç copper bucket

bakteri bacterium

bakteriyolog bacteriologist

bakteriyoloji bacteriology

bal honey **bal gibi** like honey; certainly

balarısı honeybee

balast ballast

balata brake lining

balayı honeymoon

balçık clay, mud

baldır *anat.* calf **baldır kemiği** tibia, shin-bone

baldıran *bitk.* poison; hemlock

baldız sister-in-law, wife's sister

bale ballet

balerin ballerina

balgam mucus, phlegm **balgam çıkarmak/sökmek** to expectorate

balık fish; Pisces **balık ağı** fishing net **balık avlamak/tutmak** to fish **balık etinde** attractively fleshy/plump **balık oltası** fishing line **balık pazarı** fish market **balık yumurtası** hard roe, spawn **balığa çıkmak** to go fishing

balıkadam skin diver

balıkçı fisherman; fishmonger **balıkçı teknesi** smack **balıkçı yaka** turtleneck, poloneck; turtlenecked

balıkçıl *hayb.* heron, egret, bittern

balıkçılık fishery, fishing

balıkgözü eyelet

balıklama headfirst, headlong; like a shot, unthinkingly

balıksırtı camber, ridge; hog-backed, ridge

balıkyağı fish oil; cod-liver oil

balina whale

balistik balistics; ballistic

balkabağı squash

Balkanlar the Balkans

balkon balcony

ballandırmak to praise extravagantly, to exaggerate **ballandıra ballandıra** praising extravagantly

ballı containing honey, honeyed *kon.* unusually lucky

ballıbaba *bitk.* dead-nettle

balmumu wax

balo ball, dance

balon baloon

balözü nectar

balta axe, hatchet **balta girmemiş orman** virgin forest

baltalama sabotage, blow

baltalamak to sabotage, to paralyze, to block; to hack (with an axe)

Baltık the Baltic

Baltık Denizi the Baltic Sea

balya bale

balyoz sledgehammer

bambaşka utterly different

bambu bamboo

bamya okra, gumbo

bana (to) me **Bana bak!** Look here! **Bana bakma** Don't count on me **Bana göre hava hoş** It doesn't make any difference (to me) **Bana kalırsa** as far as I'm concerned **bana mısın dememek** to show no reaction to; to have no effect

bandaj bandage

bandıra flag, colours

bandırmak to dip (into)

bando *müz.* band

bandrol monopoly tax label

bangır bangır too loudly **bangır bangır bağırmak** to shout loudly

bank bench

banka bank **banka cüzdanı** passbook, bank-book **banka çeki** bank cheque **banka hesabı** bank account **banka kartı** bank card **banka soygunu** bank robbery **banka şubesi** branch bank **bankaya yatırmak** to deposit (in a bank), to bank

bankacı banker; bank employee

bankacılık banking

banker banker; stockbroker

banket shoulder (of a road)

banknot banknote, bill
banko bench; counter
banliyö suburb **banliyö treni** suburban train
banmak to dip (into), to dunk
bant band; tape; hairband **banda almak** to record on tape
banyo bath; bathroom; (film) development **banyo yapmak** to have a bath, (film) to develop
bar bar; tarnish, dirt; a folk dance of Eastern Anatolia
baraj dam; (football) wall **barajı aşmak** to pass (the examination)
baraka hut, shed
barbar barbarian; barbarous
barbarlık barbarism
bar bar loudly and angrily **bar bar bağırmak** to shout at the top of one's voice
barbunya *hayb.* red mullet; *bitk.* kidney bean **barbunya fasulyesi** small reddish bean
bardak glass **bardağı taşıran son damla** the last straw **bardaktan boşanırcasına yağmur yağmak** to rain cats and dogs
bardakeriği greengage, egg-plum
barem a scale of official salaries
barfiks *sp.* horizontal bar
barınak shelter
barındırmak to give shelter, to shelter, to harbour
barınmak to take shelter (in)
barış peace
barışçı, barışçıl peace-loving, pacific
barışçılık pacifism
barışık at peace, reconciled
barışmak to make peace (with), to be reconciled, to bury the hatchet
barıştırmak to reconcile, to conciliate
bari at least, for once; if so, then; may/might as well
barikat barricade
bariton baritone
bariz clear, obvious
barmen barman, bartender
baro bar, the body of lawyers
barok baroque
barometre barometer

baron baron
baroskop baroscope
barut gunpowder **barut gibi** brusque, irritable; too sour/hot **barut kesilmek** to fly into a rage
baryum barium
bas *müz.* bass
basamak step, stair; *mat.* order, degree **basamak basamak** step by step
basamaklı having steps
basbayağı quite common, ordinary
basık low, squat; compressed
basıklık lowness
basılı printed; pressed
basım printing, impression
basımcı printer
basımevi printing house, press
basın press, newspapers **basın ataşesi** press attache **basın toplantısı** press conference
basınç pressure
basınçölçer barometer
basil bacillus
basiret prudence, insight, foresight **basireti bağlanmak** to become blind (to a danger)
basiretli prudent, cautious
basiretsiz imprudent
basit simple, plain, easy; common, ordinary
basitlik simplicity
basket *kon.* basketball **basket atmak** to make/shoot a basket
basketbol basketball
baskı press; constraint, oppression; edition; (newspaper) circulation **baskı altında tutmak** to oppress, to suppress **baskı yapmak** to bring pressure on, to put pressure on
baskın sudden attack, raid; *kon.* unexpected visit; overpowering, superior **baskın çıkmak** to get the upper hand, to surpass **baskın yapmak** to swoop down on **baskına uğramak** to be raided; to be caught red-handed; to be flooded
baskıncı raider
baskül weigh-bridge, scales
basma printed cotton
basmak to press, to weigh down; (age)

to enter; to print; to step (on)

bastıbacak shortlegged, squat

bastırmak to push down, to press; to suppress, to quench; to surpass; to satisfy, to appease (hunger); to set in, to close in

baston walking-stick, cane

basur hemorrhoids, piles

baş head; leader, chief; beginning; *den.* bow; main, chief, principal **baş ağrısı** headache; trouble **baş aşağı** upside down **baş başa** face to face **baş başa kalmak** to stay alone (with) **baş başa vermek** to put their heads together, to collaborate **baş belası** trouble, nuisance **baş döndürücü** astounding; stupefying **baş dönmesi** dizziness, vertigo **baş edememek** to be unable to cope with **baş göstermek** to break out, to arise **baş göz etmek** to give in marriage, to marry **baş göz olmak** to marry **baş koymak** to risk one's life **Baş üstüne!** With pleasure! **baş kaldırmak** to rebel **baş sayfa** title page **baş tacı** crown; a greatly respected and loved person **başa çıkmak** to handle, to cope with **Başa gelen çekilir** One has to take what comes **başı bağlı** fastened by the head; married **başı dönmek** to feel dizzy **başı sıkıya gelmek** to be in trouble **başı üstünde yeri olmak** to be highly respected, to be welcome **başına bela olmak** to worry, to cause trouble to **başına bir hal gelmek** to get into hot water, to have a misfortune **başına buyruk** independent **başına dert açmak** to borrow trouble; to cause trouble to **başına devlet kuşu konmak** to have a stroke of luck **başına dikilmek** to stand over sb, to breathe down sb's neck **başına ekşimek** to be a burden (to) **başına geçmek** to become the chief of **başına gelmek** to happen (to) **başına iş açmak** to cause trouble (to) **başına iş çıkarmak** to cause sb to see to a burden **başına kakmak** to hurt by reminding him of a favour done to him **başına patlamak** (undesirable thing) to fall to one's lot, to be-

fall **başına yıkmak** to throw a burden on sb **başında beklemek/durmak** to watch over, to watch by **başından aşağı kaynar sular dökülmek** to have a nasty shock, to be shocked **başından aşkın** (work) too much for sb **başından atmak** to get rid **başından büyük işlere girişmek** to bite off more than one can chew **başından geçmek** to happen (to), to experience **başından savmak** to get rid (of) **başını ağrıtmak** to bother, to annoy **başını belaya sokmak** to bring trouble (to); to get into trouble **başını boş bırakmak** to leave alone; to leave without control **başını derde sokmak** to get oneself into trouble; to get sb into trouble **başını dinlemek** to rest **başını kaldır(a)mamak** to be engrossed in **başını ütülemek** to nag, to badger **başını yakmak** to get sb into trouble **başının altından çıkmak** to be hatched out in sb's head **başının çaresine bakmak** to save oneself, to fend for oneself, to look after oneself **başının derdine düşmek** to be too involved in his own affairs not to be interested in anything else **başının etini yemek** to nag **başta gelmek** to be first **baştan aşağı** from head to foot, throughout **baştan başa** from end to end **baştan çıkarmak** to lead astray, to seduce **baştan çıkmak** to go astray, to be corrupted **baştan savma** carelessly, improperly

başak ear, spike **Başak (burcu)** Virgo

başaltı (wrestling) second class; *den.* steerage, forward crew-quarters

başarı success **başarı göstermek** to show success

başarılı successful

başarısız unsuccessful **başarısız olmak** to fail

başarısızlık failure

başarmak to succeed, to achieve

başbakan prime minister, premier

başbakanlık prime ministry, premiership

başbuğ (formerly) commander, chief, leader

başçavuş sergeant major

başhekim head doctor
başhemşire head nurse
başıboş untied, free, loose; untamed; neglected, unattended **başıboş bırakmak** to leave uncontrolled, to leave to oneself **başıboş kalmak** to run wild
başıbozuk irregular, undisciplined
başından from the beginning, again
başka other, another, different (-den) **başka** apart from, except **başka başka** separately, one by one; different
başkaca besides, furthermore, further, otherwise
başkaları others
başkaldırı rebellion, revolt
başkaldırmak to rebel, to revolt
başkalık difference; alteration, change
başkan president, chief, chairman
başkanlık presidency, chairmanship
başkası another, someone else
başkâtip head clerk
başkent capital
başkomutan commander-in-chief
başkomutanlık supreme military command
başkonsolos consul general
başkonsolosluk consulate general
başlamak to begin, to start, to come on, to commence
başlangıç beginning, start; foreword **başlangıç noktası** starting point
başlatmak to make (let) begin, to start; to cause sb to swear
başlı başına independently, by oneself, on one's own
başlıca main, principal
başlık cowl, cap, headgear; headline, title; caption; money paid by the bride-groom to the bride's family
başmakale leading article, editorial
başmüfettiş chief inspector
başoyuncu leading player, featured actor/actress
başöğretmen (school) principal
başörtüsü head-scarf
başparmak thumb; big toe
başpehlivan wrestling champion
başpiskopos archbishop
başrol leading part, lead
başsağlığı condolence **başsağlığı dilemek** to give one's condolences
başsavcı attorney-general
başsız headless
başşehir capital
baştanbaşa entirely
başucu head end; zenith
başvurmak to apply (to); to resort to
başvuru application **başvuru formu** application form **başvuruda bulunmak** to make an application
başvurucu applicant
başyapıt masterpiece
başyazar editorial writer, editor
başyazı leading article, editorial
batak marsh, swamp; marshy, swampy
batakhane den, den of thieves
bataklık marsh, swamp
batarya battery
bateri *müz.* drums
batı west; the West; western
batık sunken, hallow
batıl superstitious, false; unreasoning **batıl itikat** superstition
batılı western; Westerner
batılılaşma westernization
batılılaşmak to become westernized
batırmak to sink, to submerge; to dip, to plunge; to stick; to dirty, to ruin; to run down, to disparage
batmak to sink; to set (sun, etc); to hurt, to prick; to go bankrupt; to be lost, to perish; to irk, to hurt
battal useless, void; oversize
battaniye blanket
bavul suitcase, case
bay gentleman; Mr
bayağı ordinary, common; mean, vulgar, coarse; quite
bayağıkesir common fraction
bayağılaşmak to become vulgar
bayan lady, madam; Mrs, Miss, Ms
bayat stale; trite, insipid
bayatlamak to get stale
baygın faint; unconscious, fainted **baygın düşmek** to be exhausted
baygınlık faintness **baygınlık geçirmek** to feel faint, to have a blackout
bayılmak to faint, to swoon; to be fond of; *arg.* to shell out, to pay
bayındır prosperous, developed

bayındırlık prosperity; public works
bayır slope, ascent
bayi vendor, seller, dealer
baykuş owl
bayrak flag bayrak çekmek to hoist the flag bayrak dikmek to plant the flag bayrak direği flag-pole
bayram religious festival, Bairam bayram etmek/yapmak to be overjoyed bayramdan bayrama very seldom, once in a blue moon, rarely
bayramlaşmak to exchange Bairam greetings
bayramlık fit for a festival; Bairam present; one's best dress, Sunday best
baytar veterinary surgeon
baz *kim.* base
bazal basic
bazen sometimes
bazı some, certain
bazilika basilica
be Hi! Hey! I say!
bebe baby
bebek baby; doll bebek beklemek to be pregnant bebek gibi (woman) beautiful; babyish, babylike
bebeklik babyhood
beceri skill
becerikli skillful, capable
beceriklilik skill, dexterity
beceriksiz unskillful, incapable
beceriksizlik clumsiness, incapability
becermek to pull off, fo manage; *kon.* to ruin, to spoil
bedava free, for nothing
bedavacı freeloader, sponger
bedbin pessimistic
beddua curse, malediction beddua etmek to curse bedduasını almak to be cursed (by sb)
bedel equivalent; worth, value; price; substitute
beden body beden eğitimi physical education, gym
bedenen physically
bedensel bodily, physical
begonya begonia
beğeni taste, liking, gusto
beğenilmek to win approval
beğenmek to like, to admire, to enjoy;

to choose, to prefer
beğenmemek to disapprove (of)
beğenmezlik disapproval
behemehal in any case, for sure
beher to each, for each, per
behey Hey!
bej beige
bek (football) back; gas burner
bekâr unmarried, single, bachelor
bekâret virginity
bekârlık bachelorhood, celibacy
bekçi (night) watchman; guard, sentry
bekleme waiting bekleme salonu/odası waiting room
beklemek to wait (for); to expect; to watch, to attend
beklenmedik unexpected
beklenmek to be expected
beklenti expectation
bekletmek to make sb wait, to keep sb waiting; to delay, to postpone
bekri drunkard
Bektaşi dervish of the Bektashi order
Bektaşilik the Bektashi order
bel waist, loins; mountain pass, notch; *den.* midship body; sperm, come; spade bel ağrısı lumbago bel bağlamak to rely on belini doğrultmak to recover
bela trouble, misfortune, calamity bela aramak to ask for trouble bela çıkarmak to stir up trouble bela okumak to curse belasını bulmak to get one's desert belaya girmek/çatmak to run into trouble belaya sokmak to get sb into trouble
belalı tiresome, troublesome; toughy, quarrelsome
belde city
belediye municipality belediye başkanı mayor belediye binası town hall belediye meclisi town council
belediyeci municipal employee
beleş free, buckshee beleşe konmak to get on the gravy train
beleşten for nothing, buckshee
beleşçi free-loader, sponger
belge document, certificate belge almak to be expelled from school
belgelemek to document, to confirm

belgeli dismissed from school

belgesel documentary **belgesel film** documentary film

belgin clear

belgisiz *dilb.* indefinite **belgisiz adıl** indefinite pronoun **belgisiz sıfat** non-restrictive adjective **belgisiz tanımlık** indefinite article

belirgin clear, manifest

belirginleşmek to become clear

belirginlik clarity

belirlemek to determine, to fix

belirli determined, definite **belirli belirsiz** dim, indistinct

belirmek to appear, to come into sight

belirsiz undetermined, indefinite, uncertain; imperceptible

belirsizlik uncertainty, indefiniteness

belirteç *dilb.* adverb

belirti sign, mark, indication; symptom

belirtili defined, qualified

belirtisiz undefined, unqualified

belirtmek to state, to specify; to determine

belkemiği backbone, spine

belki perhaps, maybe

bellek memory; (computer) memory, storage **belleğini yitirmek** to lose one's memory

bellemek to memorize, to learn by heart; to suppose, to think; to spade

belleten bulletin, notice

belli clear, evident; certain, definite **belli başlı** main, chief; definite, proper **belli belirsiz** hardly visible **belli etmek** to show, to reveal **Belli olmaz** One never knows; It all depends

belsoğukluğu gonorrhea

bembeyaz snow-white, pure white

bemol *müz.* flat

ben I, me; ego; mole; beauty-spot

bence in my opinion, as for me, as far as I'm concerned, I think ...

bencil selfish

bencileyin like me

bencilleşmek to be selfish

bencillik egotism; solipsism

benek spot freckle

benekli speckled, spotted

benimsemek to adopt, to appropriate

to oneself, to identify oneself with

beniz colour of the face, complexion **benzi atmak** to grow pale **benzi soluk** pale

benlik personality, ego; egotism; conceit

bent dam, dyke, weir, barrage; paragraph; stanza (in a poem)

benzemek to look like, to resemble

benzer similar, like

benzerlik similarity, resemblance

benzersiz unique

benzeşmek to resemble each other

benzetme imitation; *yaz.* simile

benzetmek to liken (sth to sth) to compare (sth with sth); to mistake for; to ruin, to smash; to beat

benzeyiş resemblance, similarity

benzin petrol, gasoline **benzin istasyonu** petrol station, filling station

benzol benzol

beraat acquittal **beraat etmek** to be acquitted **beraat ettirmek** to acquit

beraber together **berabere bitmek** *sp.* to finish in a dead heat **berabere kalmak** *sp.* to draw, to tie **bununla beraber** nevertheless, however **olmakla beraber** although, though

beraberlik draw, tie; unity, cooperation

berat patent, warrant

berbat very bad, terrible, awful, horrid; ruined, spoilt; filthy, dirty **berbat etmek** to ruin

berber barber; hairdresser **berber dükkânı** barbershop

berduş vagabond, tramp

bere bruise; beret

bereket abundance, fruitfulness, fertility; blessing; rain; luckily, fortunately **Bereket versin!** God bless you! Thank you!; fortunately, thank God

bereketli abundant, fruitful

bereketsiz unfruitful, scanty

bergamot *bitk.* bergamot

beri the near side, this side, here; since

beriki the nearest, the nearer one; this one

berilyum beryllium

berk hard, strong

berkelyum berkelium

berrak clear
berraklaşmak to become clear
berraklık clearness
besbelli very clear, evident
besbeter altogether bad
besi nutrition, nourishing; fattening
besici breeder, stockbreeder
besili (animal) well-fed, fleshy, fat
besin nourishment, food
besleme feeding, nourishing, nutrition; girl servant brought up in the household
beslemek to feed, to nourish; to breed, to rear; to support, to keep
beslenmek to be nourished
besleyici nutritious, nutritive, nourishing
besmele the formula (Bismillahirrahim)
   besmele çekmek to pronounce the formula (Bismillahirrahmanirrahim)
beste *müz.* composition, tune
besteci, bestekâr composer
bestelemek to compose
beş five beş para etmez worthless beş parasız penniless
beşer mankind, man, human
beşeriyet mankind, humanity
beşgen pentagon
beşik cradlev
beşinci fifth
beter worse beterin beteri the worst
betimleme description
betimlemek to describe
beton concrete
betonarme reinforced concrete
betonyer cement mixer
bevliye urology
bevliyeci urologist
bey gentleman, sir; Mr; ruler, head; *kon.* husband, hubby; ace
beyan declaration, announcement
beyanat statement, declaration
beyanname written statement, declaration
beyaz white; white person Beyaz Saray the White House
beyazımsı, beyazımtırak whitish
beyazlaşmak to get white
beyazlatmak to whiten
beyazlık whiteness
beyazperde movie screen; the cinema,

the movies
beyazpeynir white cheese, Turkish cottage cheese
beyefendi sir; Mr
beygir horse, packhorse, carthorse
beygirgücü horsepower
beyin brain beyin göçü brain drain beyin kanaması cerebral hemorrhage beyin yıkama brain washing beyin yıkamak to brainwash beyninden vurulmuşa dönmek to be shocked
beyincik cerebellum
beyinsiz brainless, stupid
beyit *yaz.* couplet, distich
beylik rank of a ruler; principality; commonplace, trite; stateowned
beysbol baseball
beyzi oval, elliptical
bez cloth, dustcloth; *ana.* gland
bezdirmek to sicken, to disgust, to annoy
beze *ana.* gland; lump of dough
bezek ornament
bezelye pea(s)
bezemek to adorn, to deck
bezgin disgusted, wearied, depressed
bezginlik weariness, lethargy
bezik bezique
bezir linseed oil; flaxseed
beziryağı linseed oil
bezmek to get tired of, to be fed up with
bıçak knife bıçak altına yatmak to have an operation bıçak kemiğe dayanmak to become unbearable
bıçaklamak to stab, to knife
bıçkı two-handed saw, bucksaw
bıçkın rascal, rowdy, bully
bıkkın bored, tired
bıkkınlık boredom, disgust
bıkmak to get tired (with), to get tired (of)
bıktırıcı tiresome, boring
bıktırmak to bore, to annoy
bıldırcın quail
bıngıldak *anat.* fontanella
bırakmak to leave; to give up, to quit; to release, to allow, to let; to put off, to postpone; to set free, to let go
bıyık moustache; *hayb.* whiskers bıyık

altından gülmek to laugh up one's sleeve **bıyık bırakmak** to grow a moustache **bıyık burmak** to twist the moustache; to show off, to swagger
bıyıklı moustached
bıyıksız without a moustache
bızdık child, nipper, kiddie
bızır clitoris
biber pepper **biber gibi** very sharp/hot
biberli peppered, peppery
biberlik *İİ.* pepper pot *Aİ.* pepperbox
biberiye rosemary
biberon feeding bottle
bibliyografi bibliography
biblo knicknack trinket
biçare poor, helpless
biçerbağlar reaper
biçerdöver combine (-harvester)
biçim form, shape; manner, way; cut **biçim vermek, biçime sokmak** to give a shape (to)
biçimli well-shaped, shapely
biçimsiz ill-shaped, ugly; improper, awkward
biçki cutting out (clothes) **biçki dikiş yurdu** tailoring school
biçme cutting; mowing; *mat.* prism
biçmek to cut; to mow, to reap
bidon can, drum, barrel
biftek beefsteak, steak
bigudi hair curler
bihaber unaware (of)
bikini bikini
bilakis on the contrary
bilanço balance (sheet)
bilardo billiards
bildik known; acquaintance
bildirge written statement, declaration
bildirim announcement, declaration, notice
bildirme announcing, informing **bildirme kipi** *dilb.* indicative mood
bildirmek to tell, to notify, to inform
bile even; already
bileği sharpening instrument
bileğitaşı whetstone
bilek wrist **bileğine güvenmek** to trust to one's fists **bileğinin hakkı ile** purely by one's own hard working
bileklik wrist supporter

bilemek to sharpen, to whet
bileşen component
bileşik compound **bileşik faiz** *tic.* compound interest **bileşik kesir** *mat.* compound fraction **bileşik sözcük** *dilb.* compound word
bileşim composition
bileşke resultant
bileşmek to combine
bileştirmek to compound, to combine
bilet ticket **bilet gişesi** box office, ticket window
biletçi ticket seller; ticket collector, conductor
bileyici knife-grinder
bilezik bracelet; metal ring
bilfiil effectively, actually
bilge learned, wise
bilgelik sagacity, wisdom
bilgi knowledge; information **bilgi almak** to get information **bilgi edinmek** to obtain information **bilgi kuramı** epistemology
bilgiç pedant; pedantic
bilgiçlik pedantry **bilgiçlik taslamak** to pretend to know a lot
bilgiişlem data processing
bilgili learned, well-informed
bilgin scholar; scientist
bilgisayar computer
bilgisiz ignorant
bilgisizlik ignorance
bilhassa especially
bilim science **bilim adamı** scientist
bilimkurgu science fiction
bilimsel scientific
bilinç the conscious **bilincinde olmak** to be conscious of
bilinçaltı the subconscious
bilinçdışı the unconscious
bilinçlenmek to become conscious
bilinçli conscious
bilinçsizce unconsciously
bilinen known
bilinmedik unknown
bilinmek to be known
bilinmeyen unknown
bilinmez unknown; unidentified
bilirkişi expert **bilirkişi raporu** expertise
bilişim data processing

billur

billur crystal **billur gibi** very clear
billurlaşmak to crystallize
bilmece riddle, puzzle
bilmek to know; to understand; to think, to guess; to learn, to hear; to experience **bildiğini okumak/yapmak** to go/ take one's own way **bile bile, bilerek** on purpose, intentionally, purposely **bilemedin** at most **bilmeden** unintentionally
bilmezlik ignorance **bilmezlikten gelmek** to pretend not to know, to ignore
bilmukabele in exchange; and the same to you
bilumum in general, all
bilya, bilye marble; ball
bilyalı having a ball
bilyon a thousand million
bin thousand **bin bir** great many, all kinds of **bin dereden su getirmek** to beat about the bush **bin pişman olmak** to regret greatly **bin tarakta bezi olmak** to have too many irons in the fire **binde bir** very rarely, scarcely
binlerce thousands of
bina building; construction **bina etmek** to build, to construct **bina vergisi** building tax
binaenaleyh therefore
binbaşı major; commander; squadron leader
bindallı purple velvet with silver thread
bindirmek to cause to mount; to add on; to run into, to collide; to overlap
binek mount **binek atı** saddle horse
binici rider, horseman
binicilik horse-riding
bininci thousandth
binmek to get on, to get into, to board, to mount; to ride; to overlap
bir one; a, an; the same, equal; unique **bir ağızdan** with one voice **bir an önce** as soon as possible **bir ara** for a moment **bir araya gelmek** to come together **bir avuç** a handful **bir bakıma** in a sense, in a way **bir baltaya sap olmak** to find a job, to be employed **bir başına** all alone **bir bir** one by one **bir çırpıda** at once **Bir çiçekle yaz ol-**

maz *ats.* One swallow does not make a summer **bir çift sözü olmak** to have a word or two to say **bir daha** once more; never again **bir de** in addition, also **bir dediği bir dediğini tutmamak** to contradict oneself **bir dediğini iki etmemek** to dance attendance on sb **bir defa** once **Bir elin nesi var, iki elin sesi var.** *ats.* United we stand, divided we fall. **bir hoş olmak** to have a strange feeling, to feel sad **bir içim su** very beautiful (woman) **bir kapıya çıkmak** to come to the same thing **bir kere** once; for once **bir kerecik** just once **bir kulağından girip (öbür) kulağından çıkmak** to go in at one ear and out at the other **bir miktar** a little some **bir nebze** a modicum of **bir olmak** to collaborate, to unite **bir parça** a little, one piece **bir sürü** lots of **bir şey** something **bir şey değil** you are welcome, don't mention it, not at all **bir şeyler olmak** to behave strangely, to give oneself airs **bir taşla iki kuş vurmak** to kill two birds with one stone **bir türlü** somehow, in a way or another **bir varmış bir yokmuş** once upon a time **bir yana** apart from **bir yastığa baş koymak** to be husband and wife **bir zamanlar** at one time **bire bin katmak** to exaggerate
bira beer
birader brother; fellow, buddy
birahane pub, beer-house
biraz a little, some **biraz sonra** a little later, soon
birazcık a little bit
birazdan a little later
birbiri, biribiri each other, one another **birbiri ardınca** one after the other **birbirine düşmek** to start quarrelling **birbirine düşürmek** to set sb against sb, to set at loggerheads **birbirine girmek** to start quarrelling **birbirini yemek** to be constantly quarreling
birçenekliler monocotyledoneae
birçoğu most (of them)
birçok a lot of, lots of, many
birden suddenly; at a time, in one lot
birdenbire all of a sudden, suddenly

birdirbir leapfrog **birdirbir oynamak** to play leapfrog

birebir the most effective (remedy)

birer one each, one apiece **birer birer** one by one

bireşim synthesis

birey individual

bireyci individualist

bireycilik individualism

bireysel individual

birgözeli unicellular, one-celled

biri, birisi someone, somebody; one of them

biricik unique, sole, only

birikim accumulation, buildup

birikinti accumulation, heap

birikmek to come together, to accumulate, to collect

biriktirmek to gather, to assemble; to save up; to collect

birileri some people

birim unit

birinci first; first-class **birinci elden** at first hand **birinci gelmek** to be first **birinci mevki** first class (in a train, bus), cabin class (on a ship) **birinci olmak** to be first **birinci sınıf** first class; first rate, excellent; first grade (at school)

birincilik first rank, championship

birincil primary

birkaç some, a few, several

birleşik united, joint; compound, composite

birleşim session, sitting; union

birleşmek to unite; to meet; to agree

birleşmiş united **Birleşmiş Milletler** the United Nations

birleştirici uniting, unifying

birleştirmek to unite, to connect, to bind, to joint

birli ace

birlik unity; union, association, corporation; sameness; *ask.* unit

birlikte together

birtakım some, a certain number of

birterimli *mat.* monomial

bisiklet bicycle, cycle *kon.* bike

bisküvi biscuit

bisturi lancet

bit louse **bit kadar** tiny, very small

bitap exhausted, feeble **bitap düşmek** to become exhausted

bitaraf impartial

biteviye continuously, monotonously

bitik exhausted, worn out

bitim ending, end

bitirim *arg.* smart, appealing

bitirmek to finish, to end, to complete; to exhaust, to destroy

bitiş ending, end; finish

bitişik contiguous, adjacent, touching, joining, neighbouring; next door

bitişmek to be contiguous, to adhere, to join

bitiştirmek to join, to attach

bitki plant **bitki örtüsü** plant cover

bitkibilim botany

bitkibilimci botanist

bitkin exhausted, worn out **bitkin düşmek** to collapse from exhaustion

bitkinlik exhaustion

bitkisel vegetal, vegetable **bitkisel hayat** cabbage/vegetable existence

bitlenmek to become lousy; to clear oneself of lice

bitmek to finish, to end, to be over; to be exhausted; to be fond of, to fall for; to grow, to sprout **bitmez tükenmez** never ending

bitpazarı flea market

bityeniği something fishy, catch

biyofizik biophysics

biyografi biography

biyokimya biochemistry

biyolog biologist

biyoloji biology

biyolojik biological

biyonik bionic

biyopsi biopsy

biyosfer biosphere

biz awl, bradawl

biz we **biz bize** by ourselves, without outsiders

bizce in our opinion, according to us

bize to us, us

bizden from us

bizi us

bizim our; ours

bizimki ours; my wife, my husband

bizon bison

blok block; writing pad
blokaj blockage; covering
bloke blocked **bloke etmek** to close, to stop
bloknot writing pad
blöf bluff **blöf yapmak** to bluff
blucin (blue) jeans
bluz blouse
boa *hayb.* boa
bobin reel, spool; coil
boca *den.* lee (side) **boca etmek** *den.* to bear away to leeward; to turn over, to dump out
bocalamak to falter, to reel; *den.* to veer
bocurgat *den.* capstan, crab
bodrum cellar, dungeon **bodrum katı** basement
bodur dumpy, squat
boğa bull **boğa güreşi** bullfight **boğa güreşçisi** bullfighter, toreador, matador
Boğa (burcu) Taurus
boğaz throat; (bottle) neck; defile, pass; strait **boğaz ağrısı** sore throat **boğaz boğaza gelmek** to be at daggers drawn, to quarrel fiercely **boğaz tokluğuna çalışmak** to work for one's food only **boğazı ağrımak** to have a sore throat **boğazına düşkün** gourmet, glutton **boğazına kadar borç içinde olmak** to be in debt up to one's neck **boğazına sarılmak** to clasp sb by the throat, to choke **boğazında kalmak** to stick in one's throat
Boğaziçi the Bosphorus
boğazlamak to strangle, to slaughter
boğazlı gluttonous
boğmaca whooping-cough
boğmak to choke, to strangle, to suffocate; to drown; to overwhelm, to heap
boğucu suffocating, sultry
boğuk hoarse, raucous
boğulmak to be suffocated, to be strangled; to be drowned; (engine) to be flooded
boğum joint, knot, node; internode
boğuntu cheating, duping; suffocation **boğuntuya getirmek** to prevaricate; to gull (sb)
boğuşmak to fight, to scuffle; to struggle, to tussle

bohça bundle, package
bohem bohemian
bok *arg.* excrement, shit, dung, feces **bok atmak** to defame, to throw mud on **boku bokuna** for nothing, in vain **bok etmek** to spoil **boktan** worthless
boks box **boks yapmak** to box
boksör boxer
bol loose, wide; abundant, plentiful **bol bol** abundantly, generously **bol keseden atmak** to be free with, to scatter promises around
bolca amply, abundantly; quite loose, quite wide
bollanmak, bollaşmak to loosen, to get wide, to widen; to become abundant
bolluk looseness, wideness; plenty, abundance
bomba bomb
bombalamak to bomb
bombardıman bombardment **bombardıman etmek** to bombard **bombardıman uçağı** bomber
bombok *arg.* terrible, awful, foul **bombok etmek** to make a mess of
bomboş quite empty
bonbon candy
boncuk bead
bone bonnet; bathing cap
bonfile sirloin (steak), sirloin steak
bono bond bill **açık bono** blank cheque **bono vermek** to give a promissory note
bonservis certificate of good service, testimonial
bora squall,tempest
boraks borax
borazan trumpet
borç debt, loan; duty **borca girmek** to go into debt **borcunu kapatmak** to pay one's debt **borç almak** to borrow (money) **borç etmek/yapmak** to get into debt **borç harç** on loan **borç para** loan **borç vermek** to lend (money) **borçtan kurtulmak** to get out of debt
borçlanmak to get into debt
borçlu debtor; obliged, grateful
borda *den.* broadside
bordo claret red

bordro payroll; docket, list

bornoz, bornuz bathrobe

borsa stock-exchange, exchange, market **borsa tellalı** stockbroker, broker

boru tube, pipe; trumpet,horn **borusu ötmek** *kon.* to be in authority, to be domineering

bostan vegetable garden, kitchen garden **bostan korkuluğu** scarecrow; figure-head, puppet

boş empty; vacant; unemployed; free; vain, futile **boş bulunmak** to be taken unawares **boş durmak** to do nothing, not to be working **boş gezenin boş kalfası** loafer, idler **boş oturmak** to be unemployed, to do nothing **boş söz** empty words, vain promises **boş vakit** spare time, leisure **boş vermek** not to worry, not to give a damn **boş yere** in vain, uselessly **boşa gitmek** to come to nothing, to be in vain **boşta** unemployed **boşta gezmek** to be unemployed **boşu boşuna** in vain, uselessly

boşalmak to be emptied; to become vacant

boşaltım excretion

boşaltmak to empty, to pour out; to unload, to unship, to discharge

boşamak to divorce

boşanma divorce **boşanma davası** divorce case

boşanmak to be divorced; to get loose

boşluk empty space; blank; emptiness; cavity; vacuum

Boşnak Bosnian

boşuna in vain

bot boat, dinghy; boot

botanik botany

bovling bowling

boy length; size; height; tribe **boy atmak** to grow tall **boy aynası** full--length mirror **boy bos** stature, figure **boy boy** of different sizes **boy göstermek** to show oneself **boy ölçüşmek** to compete with **boy vermek** to show how deep the water is **boya çekmek** (child) to shoot up **boydan boya** from end to end **boyu bosu yerinde** tall, well-proportioned **boyu kısa** short **bo-**

yunun ölçüsünü almak to get one's deserts, to learn one's lesson

boya paint, dye

boya vurmak/çekmek to paint

boyacı dyer; housepainter; shoeblack, bootblack

boyamak to paint, to dye, to colour; (shoes) to polish, to black

boykot boycott **boykot etmek** to boycott

boylam longitude

boylamak to end up in, to land in

boylu tall **boylu boyunca** at full length; from end to end

boynuz horn; antler

boynuzlamak to gore; *arg.* to cuckold

boynuzlanmak to sprout horns; to be gored; *arg.* to be cuckolded

boynuzlu horned; *arg.* cuckold

boysuz short, not tall

boyun neck **boynu bükük** unhappy, sad, disappointed **boynu tutulmak** to have a stiff neck **boynuna sarılmak** to embrace **boynunu bükmek** to become very sad/disappointed **boyun atkısı** scarf **boyun borcu** incumbent duty **boyun eğmek** to submit, to yield

boyuna lengthwise; continually

boyunbağı necktie

boyunca along; throughout; during; lengthwise

boyunduruk yoke; bondage; *sp.* headlock **boyunduruk altına almak** to put under the yoke, to enslave

boyut dimension

boz grey, gray

boza thick fermented grain drink

bozayı brown bear

bozarmak to turn pale; to become grey

bozdurmak to cause to spoil/ruin; to change, to cash

bozgun rout, defeat **bozguna uğramak** to be routed, to be defeated **bozguna uğratmak** to rout

bozguncu defeatist

bozkır steppe

bozmak to spoil, to ruin, to destroy; to change, to cash; to upset, to foil, to baffle; to cancel, to annul; to be crazy

about; to violate, to infringe; (weather) to become worse **ağzını bozmak** to swear, to abuse **kafasını bozmak** to rub sb the wrong way
bozuk spoilt, destroyed ruined; broken; out of order, on the bum; corrupt, depraved; (weather) bad **bozuk para** small money
bozukluk defect, trouble, breakdown; corruption, disorder; small change
bozulmak to be spoilt; to degenerate; to break down; to be humiliated, to resent
bozum embarrassment, humiliation **bozum etmek** to embarrass, to discomfort **bozum olmak** to be mortified, to be discomfited
bozuntu embarrassment, discomfiture **bozuntuya vermemek** to hide one's displeasure
bozuşmak to fall out with, to break with
böbrek kidney
böbürlenmek to boast, to crow
böcek insect; bug, beetle; louse
böğür side, flank
böğürmek to bellow, to low
böğürtlen blackberry, bramble
bölen mat. divisor **ortak bölen** common divisor **en büyük ortak bölen** greatest common divisor
bölge region, district, zone, section
bölgecilik regionalism
bölgesel regional
bölme division; compartment; den. bulkhead
bölmek to divide (into); to separate
bölü mat. divided by
bölücü separationist, intriguer
bölücülük divisive behaviour
bölük ask. company; squadron; mat. order; division, part **bölük bölük** in groups **bölük pörçük** in bits
bölüm part, chapter; portion, division; mat. quotient; department
bölümlemek to classify
bölünen mat. dividend
bölüşmek to share out
bölüştürmek to distribute, to share out
bön naive, silly, simple **bön bön bakmak** to gawp (at), to gape (at)

börek pastry, pie
börülce kidney-bean
böyle so, such, thus, like this, in this way **bundan böyle** from this time on, henceforth **böyle olunca** in that case, then **Böyle gelmiş böyle gider** That's life; It's inevitable
böylece then, so
böylelikle in this way, thus
böylesi such a, this kind of
böylesine as ... as this, such
branda sailor's hammock **branda bezi** canvas
branş branch, department
bravo! Bravo! Well done!
Brezilya Brazil
Brezilyalı Brazilian
briç bridge
brifing briefing
briket briquette, briquet
Britanya Britain, Great Britain
Britanyalı Briton, Englishman
briyantin brilliantine
brokar brocade
brom bromine
bromür bromide
bronş bronchus
bronşit bronchitis
bronz bronze
bronzlaşmak to bronze, to get brown
broş brooch
broşür brochure, booklet
bröve certificate, diploma
brüksellahanası Brussels sprout
brülör burner
brüt gross
bu this **bu arada** meanwhile **bu bakımdan** from this point of view **bu defa** this time **bu gibi** of this kind, such **bu yana** since
bucak subdistrict; corner, nook **uçsuz bucaksız** immense, vast **bucak bucak aramak** to search in every nook and cranny
buçuk half
budak knot
budaklı knotty
budala silly, foolish, imbecile; crazy about
budalalık stupidity, foolishness **budala-**

lık etmek to behave foolishly, to be silly
budamak to prune, to lop, to trim
Budist Buddhist
Budizm Buddhism
budun tribe, people, nation
budunbetim ethnography
budunbilim ethnology
bugün today **bugün yarın** soon **bugünden tezi yok** right now **bugüne bugün** unquestionably, sure enough **bugünlerde** in these days, nowadays, recently
bugünkü of today, today's, present
bugünlük for today
buğday wheat
buğu vapour, steam, fog
buğulanmak to be steamed up, to mist over
buğulu steamy, misty, fogged
buhar steam, vapour
buharlaşmak to vaporize, to evaporate
buhran crisis
buhur incensev
buhurdan censer, thurible
buji spark plug
bukağı fetter, hobble
bukalemun chameleon
buket bunch of flowers, bouquet
bukle haircurl, lock
bukleli curly
bulandırmak to muddy, to roil, to render turbid; (stomach) to turn, to nauseate
bulanık turbid, muddy; cloudy, overcast **bulanık suda balık avlamak** to fish in troubled waters
bulanmak to become turbid, to get muddy; to be smeared; (stomach) to be upset
bulantı nausea
bulaşıcı infectious, contagious
bulaşık dirty dishes, dishes; smeared, bedaubed; infected, contagious **bulaşık bezi** dishcloth **bulaşık makinesi** dishwasher **bulaşık suyu** dishwater **bulaşık yıkamak** to wash the dishes
bulaşıkçı dishwasher (person)
bulaşkan sticky; troublesome
bulaşmak to be smeared, to become

dirty; *hek.* to spread, to be infected; to pester, to annoy, to molest; to be involved
bulaştırmak to smear, to daub; *hek.* to infect; to involve in
buldok bulldog
buldozer bulldozer
Bulgar Bulgarian
Bulgarca Bulgarian
Bulgaristan Bulgaria
bulgu discovery; invention, finding
bulgur boiled and pounded wheat **bulgur pilavı** cracked wheat cooked with tomatoes
bulmaca crossword puzzle
bulmak to find; to discover; to invent; to amount to
buluğ puberty **buluğa ermek** to reach puberty
bulundurmak to have present, to have in stock, to provide
bulunmak to be found; to be, to exist; to be located; to participate, to attend **(bir) ricada bulunmak** to make a request
buluş invention; discovery; original thought, idea
buluşma meeting
buluşmak to meet, to come together
bulut cloud **bulut gibi (sarhoş)** dead drunk **buluttan nem kapmak** to be very touchy/suspicious
bulutlanmak to get cloudy
bulutlu cloudy
bulutsuz cloudless
bulvar boulevard, avenue
bumburuşuk very creased, wrinkled all over
bunak senile, dotard
bunaklık senility, dotage
bunalım crisis; depression
bunalmak to feel suffocated; to get bored, to be depressed
bunaltmak to suffocate; to oppress, to weary, to bore
bunamak to become senile, to dote
bunca this much, so much **bunca zaman** for such a long time
buncağız this poor little thing
bundan from this, about this **bundan**

başka besides, furthermore **bundan böyle** from now on, henceforth; after this **bundan dolayı** for this reason, therefore

bunun of this **bunun üzerine** thereupon **bununla birlikte** nevertheless, however

bura this place, this spot

burada here

buradan from here, hence

buraları these places

buralı native of this place

burası here

buraya here **buraya kadar** thus far

burç tower; zodiacal constellation, sign of the zodiac

burçak vetch

burgaç vortex, whirlwind

burgu corkscrew; auger, gimlet

burjuva bourgeois

burjuvazi bourgeoisie

burkmak to twist, to sprain, to wrench

burkulmak to be sprained

burmak to twist, to wring, to castrate

burs scholarship, bursary

buruk acrid, astringent, puckery

burulmak to be twisted

burun nose; beak, bill; *coğ.* cape, headland **burun buruna** very close **burun buruna gelmek** almost to collide with; to come face to face **burun deliği** nostril **burun kanaması** nosebleed **burnu büyük** conceited, arrogant **burnu büyümek** to have a swollen head, to become conceited **burnu havada** conceited **burnu kanamak** to bleed at the nose **burnunda tütmek** to long for **burnundan gelmek** to suffer so much after having sth good **burnunu kıvırmak** to turn one's nose up **burnunu sokmak** to poke one's nose into, to nose into **burnunun dibinde** under sb's very nose **burnunun doğrusuna gitmek** to follow one's nose **burnunun ucunu görememek** to be dead drunk

buruş buruş very wrinkled **buruş buruş olmak** te be badly wrinkled

buruşmak to be wrinkled, to crease, to crumple

buruşturmak to wrinkle, to crumple, to pucker

buruşuk wrinkled, crumpled, puckered

but thigh; rump

butik boutique

buyruk order, command **kendi başına buyruk olmak** to be one's own master

buyurmak to order, to decree; to command

Buyurun! Come in! Help yourself!

buz ice **buz gibi** very cold, icy **buz kesilmek** to freeze; to be stunned **buz kesmek** to freeze, to feel very cold **buz tutmak** to ice up/over, to freeze (over)

buzağı calf

buzağılamak to calve

buzdağı iceberg

buzdolabı refrigerator, fridge

buzhane icehouse; cold storage plant

buzlanmak to get icy; to ice up/over

buzlu icy, iced; (glass) frosted, translucent

buzlucam frosted glass

buzluk icebox

buzul glacier **buzul çağı** ice age

bücür squat, shorty, dwarf

büfe sideboard; refreshment stall, buffet; kiosk

büklüm twist, curl; fold **büklüm büklüm** in curls, curly

bükmek to twist, to wrench; to bend, to flex; to spin

bükülgen flexible

bülbül nightingale **bülbül gibi** fluently

bülten bulletin

bünye structure, constitution

büro office, bureau

bürokrasi bureaucracy, red tape

bürokrat bureaucrat

bürümek to wrap, to enfold; (smoke) to cover up, to fill

bürünmek to wrap oneself up (in)

büsbütün completely, entirely, wholly

büst bust

bütan butane

bütçe budget

bütün whole, entire, complete; all, the whole

bütün bütün entirely
bütünleme completion
bütünlemek to complete, to integrate
bütünleşmek to become integrated
bütünlük wholeness, completeness, integrity
bütünüyle completely, entirely, fully
büyü magic, spell büyü yapmak to cast a spell on
büyücü witch; magician, sorcerer
büyücülük sorcery, witchcraft
büyük big, large; great, grand; older, elder; important, serious büyük aptes yapmak to defecate büyük bir olasılıkla most likely büyük defter ledger büyük harf capital letter büyük ikramiye first prize Büyük Millet Meclisi the Grand National Assembly (of Turkey) büyük ölçüde on a large scale büyük (söz) söylemek to talk big
büyükanne grandmother
Büyükayı Big Dipper, the Great Bear
büyükbaba grandfather
büyükbaş cattle
büyükçe somewhat large
büyükelçi ambassador
büyükelçilik embassy
büyüklük largeness, bigness; greatness; size
büyülemek to bewitch; to fascinate, to charm
büyüleyici fascinating, charming
büyültmek to make bigger to enlarge; to exaggerate
büyülü bewitched, charmed, magic
büyümek to grow; to become large; to expand; to develop büyümüş de küçülmüş (child) precocious
büyüteç magnifying glass
büyütmek to make bigger; to enlarge; to bring up, to rear; to exaggerate; (business) to extend
büz cement pipe
büzgü smocking, shirr
büzmek to constrict, to pucker, to contract
büzük constricted, puckered
büzülmek to contract, to be puckered; to crouch, to cower
büzüşük puckered, wrinkled

C

caba gratis, free
cabadan for nothing, free
cacık a dish made of chopped cucumber and garlic flavoured yoghurt
cadaloz shrew, hag, vixen
cadde street, main road
cadı witch, hag, shrew
cafcaf showiness, pomp
cafcaflı showy, pompous
cahil ignorant, uneducated, illiterate; inexperienced, greenhorn
cahillik ignorance, inexperience cahillik etmek to act foolishly
caiz admissible, allowable, permitted
caka show-off, swagger, ostentation caka satmak to show off, to swagger
cakalı showy, swaggering
cam glass, paneş
camcı glazier
cambaz rope dancer, acrobat, swindler, juggler
cambazlık acrobatism; cunning, trick
camgöbeği glass-green
camgöz hayb. tope
camız water buffalo
cami mosque
camia community
can soul, spirit; life; person, soul; darling, love; energy, zeal, vigour can alıcı (nokta) crucial (point) can atmak to starve for, to crave, to desire can çekişmek to be at one's last gasp can damarı vital point can damarına basmak to touch sb on the raw can düşmanı mortal enemy can evi the vital spot can havliyle desperately can korkusu fear of death can kulağı ile dinlemek to be all ears, to breathe in can sıkıcı boring, annoying, dull can sıkıntısı boredom, annoyance can sıkıntısından patlamak to get bored to death can vermek to die, to pass away cana can katmak to enliven, to refresh cana yakın friendly canı acımak to feel pain Canı cehenneme! To hell with him! canı çekmek to long

canan

46

for **canı çıkmak** to die; to get very tired **canı istemek** to feel like (doing sth) **canı sıkılmak** to be bored; to be annoyed **canı tez** impatient **canı yanmak** to feel pain **canım** dear, my darling **canımın içi** my darling **canın isterse** as you like, I don't care **Canın sağ olsun!** Never mind, It doesn't matter **canına değmek** to hit/touch the spot **canına kıymak** to kill oneself; to kill **canına okumak** to destroy; to kill; to harass **canına susamak** to want to die **canına tak demek** to get to be intolerable **canından bezmek (bıkmak) usanmak** to be tired of living **canını almak** to take one's life **canını acıtmak** to hurt, to inflict pain **canını bağışlamak** to spare sb's life **canını çıkarmak** to wear out, to tire out **canını kurtarmak** to save one's/sb's life **canını sıkmak** to annoy, to bother **canını vermek** to sacrifice oneself **canını yakmak** to cause pain (to) **canla başla** with heart and soul

canan sweetheart, beloved

canavar monster, brute **canavar düdüğü** siren

canciğer intimate

candan sincere, hearty

caneriği green plum

canhıraş heart-rending, bitter; horrible

cani criminal, murderer

cankurtaran ambulance; life-saver **cankurtaran simidi** life buoy **cankurtaran yeleği** life jacket

canlandırmak to animate, to revive; to impersonate, to perform

canlanmak to come to life, to revive; (business) to boom

canlı alive, living; active, lively **canlı yayın** live broadcast

canlılar the living

cansız lifeless, dead; weak, feeble; slack, still; dull

cari current; valid, effective **cari hesap** current account

cascavlak bald-headed; stark naked

casus spy, agent

casusluk espionage

cavlak naked, bare; hairless, featherless

caydırmak to dissuade, to disincline, to deter

cayırtı creak, rattle, crash

caymak to back out of, to give up, to go back on, to renounce

caz jazz

cazcı jazz musician

cazgır (wrestling) announcer

cazırdamak to crackle

cazibe attraction, charm

cazibeli attractive, charming

cazip attractive, charming

cebir algebra

cebren by force

Cebrail the Archangel Gabriel

cefa suffering, pain; ill-treatment, cruelty **cefa çekmek** to suffer

cefakâr who has suffered much

cehalet ignorance

cehennem hell, inferno **cehennem azabı** hellish torture **cehennem gibi** like hell, hellish **cehennem ol!** Go to hell! **cehennem zebanisi** demon, devil **cehenneme kadar yolu olmak** to go to hell **cehennemin dibine gitmek** to get the hell out, to go away

cehennemi infernal

cehennemlik deserving of hell

ceket jacket, coat

celep cattle-dealer, drover

cellat executioner

celp attraction; *huk.* summons; *ask.* call

celse session; hearing, sitting

cemaat congregation, community

cemiyet society; assembly, union

cemre increase of warmth in February

cenabet impure, unclean

cenah wing

cenap majesty, excellency

Cenabı Hak God, Lord

cenaze corpse; funeral **cenaze alayı** funeral procession

cendere press, mangle

cengâver warlike

cenin foetus, embryo

cenk combat, battle, war, fight

cennet paradise, heaven

cennetkuşu bird of paradise

cennetlik deserving of heaven

centilmen gentleman

centilmence in a gentlemanlike way
centilmenlik gentlemanliness
cep pocket cep feneri torch cep harçlığı pocket money cep saati pocket watch cep sözlüğü pocket dictionary cebi delik penniless broke cebine indirmek to pocket cebinden çıkarmak to outdo (sb), to excel cebini doldurmak to fill one's pockets cepten vermek to pay (money) out of one's own pocket
cephane ammunition, munitions
cephanelik ammunition store, arsenal
cephe front cephe almak to take sides (against)
cepken short embroidered jacket
cerahat matter, pus cerahat bağlamak/toplamak to suppurate
cerahatli suppurating
cereme penalty, fine ceremesini çekmek to pay the penalty of
cereyan current; draught cereyan etmek to take place, to happen, to occur
cerrah surgeon
cerrahi surgical
cerrahlık surgery
cesaret courage, bravery cesaret almak/bulmak to take courage (from) cesaret etmek to dare, to venture cesaret göstermek to show courage cesaretini kırmak to discourage cesaret vermek to encourage
cesaretlendirmek to encourage
cesaretlenmek to gather one's courage
cesaretli courageous, brave
cesaretsiz cowardly, timid
ceset corpse, dead body
cesur courageous, brave
cesurluk courage, bravery
cet ancestor, forefather; grandfather
cetvel ruler; list, schedule, table
cevaben in reply (to)
cevahir jewellery
cevap answer, reply cevap almak to get an answer, to receive an answer cevap vermek to answer, to reply
cevaplandırmak to answer, to reply
cevapsız unanswered
cevher jewel, gem; ore; ability, capacity; substance, essence
ceviz walnut
ceylan gazelle, antelope ceylan bakışlı having alluring eyes ceylan gibi shapely and agile
ceza punishment, penalty; fine ceza almak to be punished ceza çekmek to serve a sentence ceza hukuku criminal law ceza kesmek/yazmak to fine ceza mahkemesi criminal court ceza sahası sp. penalty area ceza vermek to punish; to fine; to pay a fine ceza vuruşu sp. penalty kick ceza yemek to be punished; to be fined cezasını bulmak to get one's deserts cezasını çekmek to serve a sentence; to suffer for cezaya çarptırılmak to be fined; to be punished cezaya çarptırmak to punish; to fine
cezaevi prison
cezalandırmak to punish; to fine
cezalı punished; fined
cezbetmek to attract, to draw
cezir ebb tide
cezve coffee-pot
cıgara cigarette
cılız puny, thin, undersized
cılk (egg) rotten; (wound) inflamed, festered cılk çıkmak to be spoilt
cımbız tweezers
cırcır babbler; hayb. cricket
cırcırböceği cricket
cırıldamak to chirr
cırlak strident, shrill; cricket
cırnak claw
cıva mercury, quicksilver cıva gibi mercurial, restless
cıvata bolt
cıvık sticky, greasy, wet, viscid; saucy, impertinent
cıvıl cıvıl twittering
cıvıldamak to twitter, to chirp
cıvıldaşmak to chirp together
cıvımak to become soft and sticky; to become impertinent
cıvıtmak to make soft and sticky; to become impertinent
cıyak cıyak with a shrill voice
cız sizzling sound; fire
cızbız grilled meat cızbız köfte grilled

meatball(s)
cızırdamak to sizzle; to creak
cızırtı sizzling or creaking sound
cibilliyet character, nature
cibinlik mosquito net
cici good, pretty, nice cici bici trinket, gimcrack
cicili bicili gaudy, glaring, fussy
cicianne granma
cidden seriously, really
ciddi serious, earnest; real, true; important ciddiye almak to take seriously
ciddiyet seriousness; importance
ciğer liver, lungs; heart ciğeri beş para etmez despicable ciğerine işlemek to hurt deeply ciğeri sızlamak to feel greet compassion
ciğerci seller of liver and lungs
cihan world; universe
cihat holy war
cihaz apparatus, device, equipment; anat. system
cihet direction, side; point of view
cila polish, varnish, glaze cila vurmak to polish, to varnish
cilalamak to polish, to varnish
cilalı polished, varnished
cilasız unpolished, unvarnished
cilt skin, complexion; binding, volume
ciltçi bookbinder
ciltçilik bookbindery
ciltlemek (book) to bind
ciltli bound
ciltsiz unbound
cilve coquetry, grace; manifestation
cilveli coquettish, flirtatious, coy
cimnastik gymnastics, gym
cimri mean, stingy, miserly; niggard, miser
cimrilik stinginess, meanness
cin genie, demon, sprite cin fikirli shrewd, crafty cin gibi very clever, cunning cinleri başına çıkmak to get furious
cin (drink) gin
cinai criminal
cinas play on words, pun
cinayet crime, murder cinayet işlemek to commit murder
cingöz cunning, clever

cinnet insanity, madness cinnet getirmek to go mad
cins kind, sort, type, variety; species, genus; breed, race; dilb. gender; arg. queer, weird
cinsel sexual cinsel birleşme (sexual) intercourse cinsel cazibe/çekicilik sex appeal cinsel ilişki sexual intercourse cinsel ilişkide bulunmak to have sex with
cinsellik sexuality
cinsiyet sex; sexuality
cip jeep
cirit javelin cirit atma the javelin throw cirit atmak to run wild
ciro tic. endorsement ciro etmek to endorse
cisim substance, body, matter
cisimsiz insubstantial
cisimlenmek to take a material form
cisimcik corpuscle
civar neighbourhood, environments, vicinity; neighbouring
civarında near; about, approximately
civciv chick
civelek lively, playful, brisk
coğrafi geographical
coğrafya geography
coğrafyacı geographer
cokey jockey
conta gasket
cop truncheon, cosh
coplamak to truncheon
coşku enthusiasm, vigour
coşkun enthusiastic, vigorous, exuberant, ebullient
coşkunluk enthusiasm, ebullience, exuberance
coşmak to become enthusiastic, to get carried away, to effervesce
coşturmak to exite, to carry away, to incite
cömert generous, liberal
cömertlik generosity, liberality
cuma Friday
cumartesi Saturday
cumburlop plop! splash!
cumhurbaşkanı president (of a republic)
cumhuriyet republic

cumhuriyetçi republican
cumhuriyetçilik republicanism
cunta junta
cup! plop!
cura three-stringed lute
curcuna uproar, carousal, hullabaloo, hubbub **curcunaya çevirmek** to raise an uproar (in a place)
cüce dwarf
cücük bud, shoot; heart of an onion
cülüs accession to the throne
cümbür cemaat the whole caboodle, the whole lot
cümbüş carousal, merrymaking, binge **cümbüş etmek/yapmak** to carouse, to revel
cümle sentence; whole, all **cümle alem** all the world, everybody **cümlemiz** all of us, we all
cümlecik dilb. clause
cümleten all together **cümleten Allahaısmarladık** goodbye everybody!
cüppe robe
cüret boldness, impudence, audacity **cüret etmek** to dare, to venture
cüretkâr, cüretli courageous, brave; bold, impudent
cüruf slag, scoria
cürüm crime, felony, offence **cürüm işlemek** to commit a crime
cüsse body, bulk
cüsseli big-bodied, huge
cüzam leprosy
cüzamlı leprous
cüzdan wallet, purse; account-book; portfolio
cüzi small, slight, trifling; partial

Ç

çaba effort, exertion **çaba göstermek** to make an effort to, to strive
çabalamak to strive, to endeavour, to struggle, to strain
çabuk quick, fast, swift; quickly, soon **çabuk çabuk** quickly **Çabuk ol!** Be quick! Hurry up! **çabuk olmak** to

hurry
çabuklaşmak to gain speed, to quicken
çabuklaştırmak to accelerate, to speed
çabukluk quickness, rapidness
çadır tent **çadır bezi** tent canvas **çadır direği** tent pole **çadır kurmak** to pitch a tent
çağ time; age; period; era, epoch **çağ açmak** to open a period
çağanoz hayb. crab
çağcıl modern
çağdaş contemporary; modern, up-to-date
çağdaşlaş(tır)mak to modernize
çağdışı outdated, old-fashioned, antiquated
çağıldamak to burble, to bubble, to purr
çağırmak to call; to invite; to send for, to call in
çağla green almond
çağlamak to burble, to murmur, to babble
çağlayan waterfall, cascade
çağrı call, invitation
çağrılı invited person
çağrışım association
çağrıştırmak to associate
çakal jackal
çakaleriği wild plum, sloe
çakı pocket-knife
çakıl pebble, gravel
çakıllı pebbly, gravelled
çakıltaşı rounded pebble
çakılmak to be nailed; to be fixed; arg. to be noticed
çakır greyish-blue
çakırkeyf slightly drunk, tipsy, happy
çakışmak to coincide; to fit into one another; mat. to be congruent
çakmak lighter
çakmak to nail; to pound; to light; to strike; to notice, to twig, to cotton on; (exam) to fail, to pip, to muff
çakmaktaşı flint
çakozlamak arg. to understand, to latch on, to twig
çaktırmak arg. to let be noticed; to fail (a student), to pluck
çaktırmadan on the sly, stealthily

çalakalem writing hastily and carelessly

çalar saat alarm clock

çalçene chatterbox, chatterer

çaldırmak to make sb play (a musical instrument, song, etc.); to get sth stolen

çalgı musical instrument

çalgıcı musician

çalı bush, shrub çalı çırpı brushwood

çalıbülbülü orphean warbler

çalıfasulyesi string bean

çalık crooked, awry, slanting

çalıkuşu goldcrest

çalılık thicket, bushes, brushwood

çalım swagger, swank, dash, strut; sp. dribble çalımından geçilmemek to swagger unbearably çalım satmak to swagger, to show off, to swank

çalımlamak sp. to dribble

çalıntı stolen; stolen goods

çalışkan hard-working, studious, diligent

çalışkanlık diligence, industriousness

çalışma work, study Çalışma Bakanlığı Ministry of Labour çalışma koşulları working conditions çalışma saatleri working hours

çalışmak to work; to study; to strive, to try; to work, to run

çalıştırmak to employ, to run, to work, to operate

çalka(la)mak to shake, to agitate; (egg) to beat, to whip

çalka(la)nmak to be shaken; (sea) to be rough; to be talked everywhere

çalkantı fluctuation; agitation; nausea

çalmak to steal; to lift; to play; to ring; to knock; to strike

çam pine çam devirmek to drop a brick/clanger çam yarması gibi (person) gigantic, huge

çamaşır underwear; laundry çamaşır asmak to hang out the laundry çamaşır değiştirmek to change one's underwear çamaşır ipi clothes line çamaşır makinesi washing machine çamaşır mandalı clothes-peg çamaşır sepeti clothes basket, linen basket çamaşır yıkamak to wash the clothes, to do the washing

çamaşırcı washerwoman, laundryman

çamaşırhane laundry

çamfıstığı pine nut

çamlık pine grove

çamsakızı pine resin çamsakızı çoban armağanı small present

çamur mud; aggressive, obtrusive, importunate çamur atmak to throw mud at, to slander çamur sıçratmak to splash with mud, to spatter çamurdan çekip çıkarmak to raise sb from the dunghill

çamurlu muddy, miry

çamurluk wing, mudguard, fender; muddy place

çan bell; gong

çanak pot; bitk. calyx çanak çömlek pots and pats çanak tutmak to ask for (trouble) çanak yalamak to bootlick

Çanakkale Boğazı the Dardanelles

çançiçeği bellflower

çanta bag; handbag; purse; suitcase, case; rucksack, knapsack çantada keklik in the bag, in hand

çap diameter ask. calibre; size, scale çaptan düşmek to go downhill, to decline

çapa hoe, mattock; den. anchor

çapak viscous crust round the eyes; burr

çapaklanmak (eye) to become gummy

çapar spotted, mottled; albino

çapari trawl, trotline

çapkın womanizer, casanova, wolf; coquettish, sensual

çapkınlık debauchery, profligacy çapkınlık etmek/yapmak to have one's fling, to go on the loose

çapraşık complicated, entangled

çapraz crosswise, transversal, diagonal; crosswise, diagonally, transversely

çaprazlama diagonally, transversely, crosswise

çapul booty, loot, plunder

çapulcu plunderer, looter

çaput rag; cloth

çar czar, tzar

çarçabuk very quickly

çarçur extravagance **çarçur etmek** to squander, to waste **çarçur olmak** to be squandered

çardak arbour, bower

çare remedy, cure; way, means **çare bulmak** to find a way, to remedy **çaresine bakmak** to see to, to settle

çaresiz uncurable; helpless; inevitably **çaresiz kalmak** to be helpless

çaresizlik incurability; helplessness, despair; poverty

çarık rawhide, sandal

çariçe czarina, tsarina

çark wheel **çark etmek** to turn, to wheel

çarkçı engineer, mechanic; knifegrinder

çarkıfelek *bitk.* passion flower; destiny, fate

çarlık czardom, tsardom

çarliston charleston

çarmıh cross, crucifix **çarmıha germek** to crucify

çarpan *mat.* multiplier **çarpanlara ayırmak** to factor

çarpı *mat.* multiplication sign; times, multiplied by

çarpıcı striking, impressive, dramatic

çarpık crooked, distorted, awry **çarpık bacaklı** bandylegged, crooked **çarpık çurpuk** crooked

çarpılan *mat.* multiplicand

çarpım *mat.* product **çarpım tablosu** multiplication table

çarpıntı palpitation, throbbing

çarpışma collision, smash; fight, clash, conflict

çarpışmak to collide; to fight, to clash

çarpıtmak to make crooked, to contort; to distort

çarpmak to strike; to hit; to run into, to dash, to bump; (heart) to beat; (evil spirit) to distort, to paralyze, to strike; *mat.* to multiply; (drink) to go to one's head

çarşaf sheet **çarşaf gibi** (sea) very calm

çarşamba Wednesday

çarşı market, bazaar, shopping centre, downtown **çarşı pazar** shopping district **çarşıya çıkmak** to go shopping

çatal fork; forked, bifurcated **çatal bıçak** knives and forks, silver

çatallaşmak to become forked, to bifurcate

çatalağız *coğ.* delta

çatı roof; framework, skeleton; fabric; *dilb.* voice **çatı arası** attic **çatı katı** penthouse, attic

çatık frowning, sulky; (rifles) stacked **çatık kaşlı** beetle-browed, frowning

çatırdamak to creak, to crackle; to chatter

çatırtı crack, crash, snap, crunch

çatışık contradictory

çatışma *ask.* skirmish, short fight; clash, conflict

çatışmak to collide, to clash; to contradict; to have a quarrel

çatkı headband

çatlak cracked; off one's head, crazy; mad; crack, fissure

çatlaklık crack; *kon* stupidity

çatlamak to crack, to split; (hand) to chap; to die (from overeating/exhaustion)

çatmak (arms) to stack, to pile; to tack, to baste together; to attack, to tilt at, to pick a quarrel with; to come up, to meet; to wrinkle, to knit

çat pat a little, somewhat

çavdar rye **çavdar ekmeği** rye bread

çavlan waterfall

çavuş sergeant

çavuşkuşu hoopoe

çavuşüzümü sweet-water

çay tea; stream, brook **çay bahçesi** tea-garden **çay demlemek** to steep tea **çay demliği** teapot **çay fincanı** teacup **çay kaşığı** teaspoon

çaycı keeper of a tea-shop; seller of tea

çaydanlık teapot

çayevi, çayhane tea-shop, tea-room

çayır meadow, pasture

çaylak *hayb.* kite; inexperienced person

çehre face, countenance; appearance, aspect

çek cheque *İİ*, check *Aİ.* **çek bozdurmak** to cash a cheque **çek defteri** chequebook

Çek Czech

çekap check-up

çekecek shoehorn

çekememek to be unable to stand; to be jealous of

çekememezlik jealousy, envy

çeker weighing capacity

çeki a measure of weight (250 kilos)

çekici attractive, charming

çekicilik attractiveness, charm

çekiç hammer

çekidüzen tidiness, orderliness çekidüzen vermek to tidy up

çekik slanting

çekiliş draw (for a lottery)

çekilme *ask.* withdrawal; resignation

çekilmek to be pulled; to draw back, to withdraw; to resign; to shrink, to contract

çekilmez unbearable, intolerable

çekim attraction; shooting; filming; *dilb.* conjugation, inflection, declination çekim eki ending, termination

çekimser abstainer

çekimserlik abstention

çekince drawback; risk, danger

çekingen timid, shy, hesitant

çekingenlik timidity, shyness

çekinmeden without hesitation

çekinmek to avoid, to abstain, to shun; to beware of, to shrink

çekirdek seed, stone; nucleus çekirdek kahve coffee beans çekirdekten yetişme trained from the cradle

çekirdekli having seeds

çekirdeksiz seedless çekirdeksiz kuru üzüm sultana

çekirge grasshopper,locust

çekişme argument, quarrel, strife; competition

çekişmek to argue, to quarrel; to pull in opposite directions; to compete, to contest

çekişmeli contentious

çekiştirmek to pull at both ends; to run down, to backbite

çekmece drawer; till

çekmek to pull, to draw; to withdraw; to attract, to draw; to pull out, to extract; to bear, to suffer; to take, to last; to contract, to shrink; to take after, to resemble; to copy; *dilb.* to inflect, to conjugate, to decline Çek arabanı!

Off with you! Clear out! çekip çevirmek to manage, to run çekip çıkarmak to pull out çekip gitmek to go away

çekmekat penthouse

çekmez unshrinkable

Çekoslovak Czechoslovakian

Çekoslovakya Czechoslovakia

çektirmek to cause to pull; to cause to suffer

çekül plumb-line

çelebi gentleman, educated person; well-mannered

çelenk wreathe, garland

çelik steel; cutting, slip

çelim stature

çelimsiz puny, frail

çelişik contradictory

çelişki contradiction

çelişkili contradictory

çelişmek to be in contradiction (with)

çello *müz.* violoncello, cello

çelme trip çelme takmak to trip up

çelmelemek to trip

çeltik rice in the husk

çember *mat.* circle; ring, belt; hoop çember sakal round trimmed beard

çemen cummin

çene chin, jaw; talkativeness, gab çene çalmak to chatter çene yarıştırmak to talk incessantly çene yormak to talk in vain çenesi düşük chatterbox, garrulous çenesi kuvvetli olmak to have the gift of the gab çenesini bıçak açmamak to be silent because of sorrow çenesini tutmak to hold one's tongue

çenebaz talkative, garrulous

çeneli talkative chatty

çengel hook

çengelli hooked

çengelliiğne safety pin

çengi dancing girl

çentik notch; notched

çentiklemek to notch, to nick

çentikli notched

çep(e)çevre all around

çeper membrane

çerçeve frame; window frame; limitation

çerçevelemek to frame

çerçeveli framed

çerçi peddler, hawker

çerçöp twigs; sweepings çerden çöpten jerry-built, flimsy

çerez hors d'oeuvres, appetizers; snack, nuts

Çerkez Circassian

çeşit kind, sort, variety; sample çeşit çeşit assorted, various

çeşitleme *müz.* variation

çeşitli different, various

çeşitlilik variety, variation

çeşme fountain

çeşni flavour, taste

çeşnici taster

çete band, gang; guerilla

çetele tally-stick

çetin hard, difficult çetin ceviz a hard nut to crack

çetrefil complicated, confusing

çevik agile, swift

çeviklik agility

çevirgeç commutator

çeviri translation

çevirim shooting, filming

çevirmek to turn; to rotate, to spin; to translate; to convert, to change; to surround, to encircle; to hold up, to stop

çevirmen translator

çevre surroundings; environment; circumference, periphery çevre kirlenmesi environmental pollution

çevrebilim ecology

çevrelemek to surround, to encircle

çevrili surrounded

çevrim cycle

çevrimsel cyclic

çevriyazı transcription

çeyiz trousseau, dowry

çeyrek quarter çeyrek final quarter final

çıban abscess, boil çıban başı head of a boil; delicate matter

çığ avalanche çığ gibi büyümek to snowball

çığır path, way; epoch çığır açmak to break new ground, to mark a new epoch çığırından çıkmak to go off the rails

çığırtkan tout, crier

çığlık scream, cry, shriek çığlık atmak to scream, to shriek çığlık çığlığa with shrieks and cries

çıkagelmek to come up, to blow in

çıkar self-interest; benefit, advantage, interest, profit çıkar sağlamak to profit by çıkar yol way out

çıkarcı self-seeking, selfish

çıkarcılık opportunism, avarice

çıkarım deduction

çıkarma *mat.* subtraction; ask landing

çıkarmak to take out, to get out, to pull out; to remove; (garment) to take off; to produce, to bring out; to publish; to strike out, to omit; to throw out, to oust; to subtract; (food) to vomit; to make out, to figure out; (telephone) to get through

çıkartma decal, transfer, sticker

çıkık prominent, projecting; dislocated; dislocation

çıkıkçı bone-setter

çıkın knotted bundle

çıkıntı projecting part; marginal note; promontory

çıkıntılı projecting, protruding

çıkış exit; *ask.* sortie; *sp.* start

çıkışma scolding, rebuke

çıkışmak to scold, to rebuke; to be enough, to suffice

çıkma going out; projection, promontory; bow-window, bay window; marginal note

çıkmak to go out to come out; to depart, to leave; to go up, to climb up; to move out (of a house); to graduate; to set off, to start on; to come up, to appear; to break out; to arise, to spring; (sun, moon) to come up, to come out, to rise; to turn out to be, to prove; to lead (to); (rumour) to get about, to be issued; (winter, month) to be over

çıkmaz blind alley, cul-de-sac; dead end, impasse, deadlock çıkmaz ayın son çarşambası at Greek Kalends çıkmaz sokak blind alley çıkmaza girmek to come to an impasse

çıkrık spinning wheel

çıktı output

çılbır dish of poached eggs with yo-ghurt

çıldırmak to go mad, to lose one's mind

çıldırtmak to drive mad, to make wild

çılgın mad, crazy, insane, frenzied

çılgınca madly

çılgınlık madness

çıma *den.* hawser

çınar plane tree

çın çın ringing sound çın çın ötmek to make a ringing sound, to resound with

çıngar quarrel row çıngar çıkarmak to kick up a row, to make a scene

çıngırak small bell; rattle

çıngıraklıyılan rattlesnake

çıngırdamak to tinkle

çıngırtı tinkle

çınlamak to tinkle, to ring; to echo

çıplak naked, nude; bare çıplaklar kam-pı nudist camp

çıplaklık nakedness, nudity

çıra resinous wood

çırak apprentice; pupil, novice

çıraklık apprenticeship

çır(ıl)çıplak naked, nude; in the nude

çırçır cotton gin; cricket

çırılçıplak stark naked, in the buff

çırpı dry twigs, chip

çırpınmak to flutter, to struggle, to flop about; to be all in a fluster, to bustle about

çırpıntı flurry; slight agitation

çırpıştırmak to scribble, to scrawl

çırpmak to beat, to flutter; (hands) to clap; (laundry) to rinse

çıt cracking sound, crack çıt çıkarma-mak to keep silent çıt çıkmamak to be dead silent Çıt yok. There is a dead silence.

çıta lath, narrow strip of wood

çıtçıt snap fastener, press-button

çıtı pıtı small and lovely, dainty

çıtır çıtır with a crackling sound çıtır çı-tır etmek to crackle çıtır çıtır yemek to crunch

çıtırdamak to crackle

çıtırtı crackle

çıtkırıldım overdelicate, fragile; dandy, effeminate

çıtlatmak to crack; to hint, to break

çıyan centipede

çızıktırmak to scribble, to scrawl

çiçek flower; bloom, blossom; *hek.* small-pox çiçek açmak to bloom, to blossom çiçek gibi very clean çiçek çı-karmak to have smallpox çiçeği bur-nunda quite fresh, brand new

çiçekçi florist

çiçeklenmek to blossom, to flower, to bloom

çiçekli in flower, in bloom; ornamented with flowers

çiçeklik flower garden; vase

çiçektozu pollen

çift pair, couple; double; *mat.* even çift çift in pairs, two by two çift koşmak to harness to the plough çift sürmek to plough

çiftçi farmer

çiftçilik farming, agriculture

çifte paired, double; kick; shotgun çifte atmak (horse, etc) to kick

çifter çifter in pairs

çiftleşme copulation

çiftleşmek to mate, to copulate; to pair, to couple

çiftleştirmek to mate, to breed; to make a pair

çiftlik farm, ranch

çiftsayı even number

çiğ raw; crude; immature, rough; dew çiğ köfte a dish made of minced meat, pounded wheat and chilli pep-per

çiğdem crocus, meadow saffron

çiğnemek to chew; to run over; to tread, to crush; to disobey, to violate

çiklet chewing-gum çiklet çiğnemek to chew (a gum)

çikolata chocolate

çil freckle speckle

çillenmek to freckle

çile ordeal, sufferance; hank, skein çile çekmek to suffer greatly çileden çıkar-mak to infuriate, to exasperate çile-den çıkmak to be in a rage, to lose one's temper

çilek strawberry

çilekeş sufferer; suffering
çileli suffering; enduring
çilingir locksmith
çilli freckled, speckled
çim grass, lawn
çimdik pinch **çimdik atmak** to pinch
çimdiklemek to pinch
çimen grass, meadow, lawn
çimenlik meadow, lawn; grassy
çimento cement
çimentolamak to cement
çimlendirmek to grass over
çimlenmek to germinate, to sprout; to become grassy
çimmek to duck under water, to swim
Çin China
Çince, Çinli Chinese
çini tile; porcelain, china **çini mürekkebi** India ink
çinicilik the art of tile-making
çinko zinc
çiriş paste, glue
çirkef filthy water, slop; loathsome, disgusting
çirkin ugly; unbecoming, unseemly, disgusting
çirkinleşmek to become ugly
çirkinleştirmek to make ugly
çirkinlik ugliness
çiroz salted and dried mackerel; *kon.* skinny person
çiselemek to drizzle
çisenti drizzle
çiş urine, piss **çiş etmek** *kon.* to wee, to piddle, to piss
çit fence, hedge
çitilemek to rub (clothes) together while washing
çitlembik terebinth berry, nettle tree berry
çivi nail; peg, pin **çivi çakmak** to drive a nail **çivi gibi** healthy, strong; very cold **çivi kesmek** to freeze, to feel very cold
çivileme feet-first jump; *sp.* smash
çivilemek to nail
çivit indigo, blue dye **çivit mavisi** indigo
çivitlemek to dye with indigo
çiviyazısı cuneiform
çiy dew

çizelge list, table
çizge graph, diagram
çizgi line; stripe, band; dash; scratch, mark **çizgi çizmek** to draw a line **çizgi film** (animated) cartoon **çizgi roman** comics
çizgili lined, ruled; striped, banded
çizgisel linear
çizik line; scratch
çiziktirmek to scribble, to scrawl
çizim drawing
çizinti scratch
çizme (top) boot **çizmeden yukarı çıkmak** to meddle with things one should not to
çizmek to draw; to cross out, to cancel; to scratch
çoban shepherd, herdsman **çoban köpeği** sheepdog
Çobanyıldızı Venus
çocuk child, infant; boy kid **çocuk aldırmak** to have one's child aborted **çocuk arabası** baby carriage, pram, pushchair **çocuk bahçesi** children's ark, playground **çocuk bakımı** child care **çocuk bezi** diaper, nappy **çocuk büyütmek** to bring up children **çocuk doğurmak** to give birth to a child **çocuk doktoru** pediatrician **çocuk düşürmek** to have an abortion, to abort **çocuk gibi** childlike **çocuk işi** child's play, pushover **çocuk mahkemesi** juvenile court **çocuk maması** baby food **çocuk oyuncağı** toy; child's play, gift **çocuk yuvası** nursery school **çocuk zammı** child allowance **çocuğu olmak** to have a child
çocukbilim pedagogy
çocukça childish; childishly
çocukcağız poor little child
çocuklaşmak to become childish, to act childishly
çocukluk childhood; childishness
çocuksu childish
çoğalmak to increase, to multiply
çoğaltmak to increase, to augment; to reproduce
çoğu most (of); mostly **çoğu zaman** usually
çoğul plural

çoğun often
çoğunluk majority
çoğunlukla with a majority of votes; usually
çok very; a lot of, many, much; too; too much, too many çok çok at (the) most çok fazla too much çok geçmeden before long, soon çok görmek to begrudge, to grudge çok olmak to go too far çok şükür! Thank God! çok yaşa! long live! God bless you! çoktan already çoktan beri for a long time
çokanlamlı dilb. polysemous
çokanlamlılık polysemy
çokayaklılar myriapoda
çokdüzlemli mat. polyhedral
çokeşli polygamous
çokeşlilik polygamy
çokgen polygon
çokgözeli multicellular
çokkarılı polygynous
çokkarılılık polygyny
çokkocalı polyandrous
çokkocalılık polyandry
çokluk abundance; majority; often
çoksesli müz. polyphonic
çokseslilik polyphony
çoktanrıcılık polytheism
çoktanrılı polytheist
çokterimli mat. polynomial
çokuluslu multinational
çokyüzlü mat. polyhedron
çolak one-handed, one-armed
Çolpan Venus
çoluk çocuk wife and children, household, family
çomak stick, cudgel, club
çomar watchdog, mastiff
çopur pockmark; pockmarked
çorak barren, arid; brackish, bitter
çoraklaşmak to become arid
çoraklık aridity; brackishness
çorap stocking, sock, hose çorap kaçığı ladder, run çorap kaçmak to ladder, Aİ. to run çorap söküğü gibi in rapid succession, easily and quickly
çorapçı hosier
çorba soup; mess çorba gibi in a mess, confused çorba kaşığı tablespoon çorbaya döndürmek to make a mess of

çorbaya dönmek to become a mess
çökelek skim-milk cheese, curds; kim. precipitate
çökelmek to precipitate
çökelti precipitate
çökertmek to make kneel; to cause to collapse, to break in, to stave in
çökkün collapsed; depressed
çökkünlük collapse; depression
çökmek to collapse, to fall in; to fall down, to sink; to kneel down; (darkness) to fall; (health) to break down; to precipitate, to subside; (sorrow) to descend upon one
çökük collapsed; sunken; prostrated
çöküntü wreckage, debris; sinking, collapse; depression
çöküş collapse; decline
çöl desert
çömelmek to squat (down)
çömez disciple
çömlek earthenware pot
çömlekçi potter
çöp garbage, rubbish, litter; small stick, chip; (fruit) stalk çöp arabası garbage truck çöp gibi very thin, skinny çöp kebabı pieces of grilled meat on a stick çöp tenekesi garbage can, dustbin, trashcan çöpe dönmek to get very thin
çöpçatan matchmaker
çöpçatanlık matchmaking çöpçatanlık etmek to arrange a marriage
çöpçü dustman, garbage collector Aİ.
çöplenmek to get pickings
çöplük dump
çörek bun
çöreklenmek to coil oneself up
çöreotu black cumin
çörkü abacus
çözelti (liquid) solution
çözgü warp
çözmek to unfasten, to untie; to solve; to unravel, to crack
çözücü solvent
çözülmek to become unfastened; to be solved; to ravel; to break up; (ice) to thaw
çözüm solution
çözümleme analysis

çözümlemeli analytic

çözümlemek to analyze

çözünme *kim.* dissolving

çözünmek to dissolve

çözünürlük solubility

çözüşmek to dissociate

çubuk rod, stick, bar; shoot, twig; pipe, stripe **çubuk aşısı** grafting **çubuk kraker** pretzel

çuha broadcloth

çuhaçiçeği polyanthus

çukur hole, hollow, pit; dimple; hollow, sunk **çukur kazmak** to dig a hole

çul haircloth; horsecloth

çulha weaver

çullanmak to swoop on; to fall upon

çulluk woodcock

çulsuz poor, penniless

çuval sack **çuval gibi** loose, untidy **bir çuval inciri berbat etmek** to upset the applecart

çuvaldız packing needle

çuvallamak *arg.* to fail, to flunk

çünkü because, for

çürük rotten, decayed, spoilt; unsound, sandy, flimsy; untenable, worthless; *ask.* disabled; bruise black-and-blue spot **çürük çıkmak** to turn out rotten; to prove to be untrue **çürük tahtaya basmak** to fall into a trap **çürüğe çıkarmak** *ask.* to invalid out

çürüklük rottenness; unsoundness

çürümek to rot, to decay, to go bad; to be bruised; to be refuted

çürütmek to make decay; to bruise, to contuse; to refute, to explode

D

da, de also, too; and; so

-da,-de at, on, in

dadanmak to frequent, to haunt; to acquire a taste for, to want to have

dadı nurse, nanny

dağ brand, mark

dağ mountain **dağ başı** mountain top, summit; wild and remote place **dağ**
eteği lower slopes of a mountain **dağ gibi** mountainous **dağ(lar) kadar** enormous **dağ sırtı** mountain ridge **dağ silsilesi** mountain range **dağdan gelip bağdakini kovmak** to be an upstart who does not like the old times

dağarcık knowledge; repertoire

dağcı mountain climber, mountaineer

dağcılık mountaineering, mountain climbing

dağılım dispersion; distribution

dağılmak to scatter, to disperse; to diffuse; to disintegrate, to break up; to fall to pieces

dağınık scattered, dispersed; untidy

dağınıklık untidiness, disorder

dağıtıcı distributor

dağıtım distribution

dağıtmak to scatter, to disperse; to distribute, to deliver; to disorder, to mess up; to dissolve; to break up

dağkeçisi chamois

dağlamak to brand; to cauterize

dağlıç a kind of fat-tailed sheep

dağlık mountainous

daha more, further; yet, still; plus **daha çok** more **daha iyi** better **Daha iyisi can sağlığı** Nothing could be better **daha kötü** worse **Daha neler!** What next!, How absurd! **daha sonra** later, afterwards **Dahası var** That's not all

dahi also, too, even

dâhi genius

dahil including, included; the interior, inside **dahil etmek** to include, to insert **dahil olmak** to be included (in), to be inserted

dahili internal, interior, inner

dahiliye internal diseases

dahiliyeci internist, doctor of internal medicine

daima always

daimi constant, permanent

dair about, concerning

daire circle; department, office; flat, apartment *AI.*; limit, range

dakik punctual, exact; minute, precise, accurate

dakika minute **dakikası dakikasına** punctually, on time

daktilo typewriter; typist **daktilo etmek** to type **daktilo makinesi** typewriter

daktilograf typist

daktilografi typewriting

dal branch, bough, offshoot; branch, subdivision **dal budak salmak** to shoot out branches, to spread **daldan dala konmak** to jump from one thing to the other

dal back, shoulder **dalına basmak** to tread on sb's corns, to annoy

dalak spleen

dalamak to bite; to sting to prick

dalaş dogfight, fight

dalaşmak to bite One another; to brawl, to wrangle

dalavere trick, intrigue, plot **dalavere çevirmek** to intrigue, to plot

dalavereci trickster, intriguer

daldırma dipping, immersion

daldırmak to plunge, to dip; (shoot) to layer

dalga wave; ripple; undulation; *arg.* trick, intrigue; *arg.* gadget, jigger; *arg.* affair, sweetie **dalga dalga** wavy; in waves **dalga geçmek** to make fun of, to kid; not to pay attention, to be woolgathering **dalgaya getirmek** to pull the wool over sb's eyes

dalgacı *arg.* daydreamer, woolgatherer; shirker, slacker

dalgakıran breakwater

dalgalandırmak to wave, to agitate

dalgalanmak to wave, to undulate; to fluctuate

dalgalı (sea) rough, wavy; (silk) watery; (metal) corrugated

dalgıç diver **dalgıç oksijen tüpü** aqualung

dalgıçlık diving

dalgın absent-minded, abstracted

dalgınlık absent-mindedness, absence of mind, abstractedness

dalkavuk flatterer, bootlicker, toady

dalkavukluk flattery, toadyism **dalkavukluk etmek** to flatter, to blandish

dallanmak to branch out, to ramify; to become complicated

dallı branched, ramified **dallı budaklı** ramified; complicated

dalmak to dive, to plunge; to drop off, to doze off; to be lost in thought, to be absorbed in

dalyan fishpond, fishgarth **dalyan gibi** well-built, strapping

dam roof; stable; lady partner; (cards) queen **damdan düşer gibi** out of the blue, bluntly

dama draughts, *Aİ.* checkers **damalı** chequered, checked

damacana demijohn

damak palate

damaksıl palatal

damar blood vessel, vein; bad temper **damarına basmak** to tread on one's corns, to exasperate **damar sertliği** arteriosclerosis **damar tıkanıklığı** embolism

damarlı veined

damat bridegroom; son-in-law

damga stamp; mark, brand **damga basmak** to stamp **damga pulu** revenue stamp

damgalamak to stamp; to brand, to stigmatize

damıtık distilled

damıtmak to distil

damızlık animal kept for breeding, stallion; yeast

damla drop, bead; medicine dropper; *hek.* gout **damla damla** drop by drop

damlalık *hek.* dropper; dripstone

damlamak to drop, to drip; to turn up, to pop in

damper dumper (truck)

damping dumping

-dan, -den from; out of; than; because of; through, via

dana calf **dana eti** veal

dangalak *arg.* blockhead, dumb, boor

danışıklı sham, feigned **danışıklı dövüş** sham fight; put-up job

danışma information; inquiry

danışmak to consult, to confer

danışman adviser, counsellor

danışmanlık counseling

Danıştay Council of State

daniska the best, the finest **daniskası** the best of

dank etmek (kafasına) to dawn upon

dans dance **dans etmek** to dance
dansçı dancer
dansör dancer (man)
dansöz dancer (woman)
dantel lace, lacework
dapdaracık very narrow/tight
dar narrow, tight; scanty, scant; difficulty, straits; narrowly, barely **dar açı** acute angle **dar boğaz** bottleneck **dar darına** narrowly, hardly, barely **dar gelirli** of small income **dar görüşlü** narrow-minded **dar kafalı** petty, old-fashioned **dara düşmek** to be in a difficulty **darda kalmak** to be short of money; to feel the pinch
dara tare **darasını almak/düşmek** to deduct the tare of
daracık quite narrow
darağacı gallows, scaffold
daralmak to narrow; to shrink, to contract; to become scanty
daraltmak to narrow; to take in
darbe blow, stroke
darbuka earthenware kettle-drum
darbukacı, darbukatör earthenware kettle-drum player
dargın cross, offended, angry
dargınlık irritability, anger, falling-out
darı millet **Darısı başınıza!** May your turn come next!
darılmak to take offence;to get angry, to fall out with **Darılmaca yok!** No offence
darıltmak to give offence, to offend
darlık narrowness; shortage, scarcity; need, poverty
darmadağın(ık) in a mess in a clutter **darmadağınık etmek** to clutter up, to mess up
darphane mint
darülaceze poorhouse, alms-house
dava lawsuit, suit, case, action; claim, assertion; thesis, problem, cause **dava açmak/etmek** to bring a suit, to sue **dava vekili** lawyer, barrister **davadan vazgeçmek** to give up a claim **davanın düşmesi** discontinuance of action **davaya bakmak** to hear a case
davacı plaintiff, litigant
davalı defendant; contested, in dispute; pretentious
davar sheep, goat(s)
davavekili lawyer, barrister
davet invitation; party, reception **davet etmek** to invite
davetiye invitation card
davetkâr inviting
davetli (person) invited, guest
davetsiz uninvited **davetsiz misafir** intruder
davlumbaz chimney hood
davranış behaviour, attitude
davranmak to behave, to act, to treat; to make (for), to reach (for) **Davranma!** Don't stir!
davul drum **davul çalmak** to drum, to beat the drum **davul gibi** bloated
davulcu drummer
dayak beating, hiding, thrashing; support, prop, stay **dayak atmak** to give a thrashing, to beat **dayak yemek** to get a thrashing **dayağı hak etmek** to deserve a whacking
dayalı leaning against; based on **dayalı döşeli** completely furnished
dayamak to lean against, to rest
dayanak support, prop
dayandırmak to base on, to ground on
dayanıklı strong, lasting, enduring; resistant, tough
dayanıklılık endurance, resistance
dayanıksız not lasting, weak, flimsy
dayanılmaz irresistible; unbearable
dayanışma solidarity
dayanmak to lean against; to be based on; to endure, to last; to tolerate, to bear; to rely on, to be backed (by) **dayanacak gücü kalmamak** to be at the end of one's tether
dayatmak to insist on
dayı mother's brother, maternal uncle; protector, backer
dayıoğlu cousin
dayılık being an uncle; nepotism, protection; *arg.* bullying
dazlak bald
dazlaklık baldness
de too, also
debdebe pomp, splendour
debdebeli magnificent, splendid,

showy

debelenmek to thrash about, to welter; to struggle desperately

debriyaj clutch **debriyaj pedalı** clutch pedal

dede grandfather

dedektif detective

dedektör detector

dedikodu gossip **dedikodu yapmak** to gossip

dedikoducu gossip, gossiper

defa time, turn **bir defa** once **bir defa daha** once again, once more **bir iki defa** once or twice **birkaç defa** several times **bu defa** this time **çok defa** often **iki defa** twice **üç defa** three times

defalarca again and again, repeatedly

defetmek to drive away, to repel; to expel, to eject

defile fashion show

defin burial

define treasure

deflasyon deflation

defne laurel, bay-tree **defne yaprağı** bay leaf

defnetmek to bury, to inter

defo flaw

defolu having a flaw, faulty

defolmak to go away, to clear out **Defol!** Off with you! Piss off!

deforme deformed

defter notebook, copybook, exercise book; (account) book; register **defter tutma** bookkeeping **defter tutmak** to keep the books **defterden silmek** to finish with sb **deftere geçirmek** to enter in the book **defteri kapamak** to close a subject, to give up **defteri kebir** ledger **defterini dürmek** to finish off, to kill

defterdar head of the financial department (of a province)

defterdarlık financial office

değdirmek to touch

değer value, worth; price **değer biçmek** to evaluate, to value **değerden düşmek** to lose its value **değeri düşmek** to go down in value **değer vermek** to esteem, to appreciate

değerbilir appreciative

değerbilmez unappreciative

değerlendirmek to put to good use, to turn to account, to utilize; to evaluate, to appraise

değerlenmek to increase in value, to gain value

değerli valuable, precious; estimable, worthy **değerli taş** gem, jewel

değersiz worthless

değgin concerning, about

değil not

değin until, till

değinmek to touch on, to mention

değirmen mill; grinder

değirmenci miller

değirmentaşı millstone

değirmi round

değiş exchange **değiş etmek** to exchange **değiş tokuş** exchange, barter **değiş tokuş etmek** to exchange, to barter

değişik different; various, varied; novel, original **değişik olmak** to vary, to differ

değişiklik change, variation

değişim change

değişke biy. variation

değişken changeable, variable

değişme change; exchange

değişmek to change; to alter; to vary; to exchange, to barter

değişmez unchangeable

değiştirme change, alternation

değiştirmek to change, to alter, to convert; to exchange

değme contact, touch; every, any

değmek to touch; to reach, to attain; to be worth

değnek stick, rod, cane

deha genius

dehliz entrance-hall, vestibule, corridor

dehşet horror, terror, dread; marvellous **dehşet saçmak** to spread terror **dehşete kapılmak** to be horrified

dehşetli terrible, dreadful

dejenere degenerate **dejenere olmak** to degenerate

dek until, till

dekalitre decalitre

dekametre decametre
dekan dean (of a faculty)
dekanlık dean's office
dekar decare
deklanşör shutter release
dekolte low-cut
dekont statement of account, deduction
dekor scenery; set, setting; decoration
dekorasyon decoration
dekoratif decorative
dekoratör set-designer; internal decorator
dekore decorated **dekore etmek** to decorate
delâlet indication, denotation **delâlet etmek** to indicate, to denote
delegasyon delegation
delege delegate
delgeç punch
delgi drill, gimlet
deli mad, insane, crazy, lunatic, loony; crazy about, fond of; madman, madwoman **deli divane olmak** to be wild about **deli etmek** to drive sb mad **deli gibi** madly; recklessly **deli olmak** to go mad; to be crazy about **Deli olmak işten değil.** It drives one crazy. **deliye dönmek** to go crazy
delice madly, crazily
delicesine madly
delidolu thoughtless, reckless, rash
deliduman foolhardy, daredevil
delifişek unbalanced, flippant
delilik madness; foolishness **delilik etmek** to act foolishly **deliliğe vurmak** to pretend to be mad
delirmek to go mad, to flip
delirtmek to drive mad, to craze
delişmen unbalanced, madcap
delik hole, opening, orifice; *arg.* prison, clink; pierced, bored **delik açmak** to make a hole, to drill, to bore **delik deşik etmek** to riddle **delik deşik olmak** to be riddled **deliğe tıkmak** *arg.* to put into jail
delikanlı young man, youth
delikanlılık adolescence, youth
delikli having a hole, perforated
deliksiz without a hole; (sleep) sound

delil proof, evidence **delil göstermek** to adduce proofs
delinmek to be pierced, to burst
delmek to pierce, to drill, to bore
delta *coğ.* delta
dem blood **dem gelmek** to have a menstrual hemorrhage
dem breath; moment, time; (tea) being steeped **dem vurmak** to talk about
demli (tea) well-steeped, strong
demagog demagogue
demagoji demagogy
demeç speech, statement **demeç vermek** to make a statement
demek to say; to call, to name; to mean **Deme!** You don't say so! **demeğe gelmek** to come to mean, to add up to **demek istemek** to mean **demeye getirmek** to imply **demeye kalmadan** no sooner than **deyip geçmek** to underrate
demet bunch, bouquet; bundle
demin(cek) a second ago, just now
demir iron; anchor; bar **demir almak** to weigh anchor **demir atmak** to cast anchor **demir gibi** strong, tough **demir leblebi** a hard nut to crack **Demir tavında dövülür** Strike while the iron's hot
demirbaş inventory, furnishings
demirci blacksmith, smith
demirlemek to cast anchor, to anchor
Demir Perde the Iron Curtain
demiryolu railway, railroad
demlemek to steep, to brew
demlenmek to be steeped, to brew; to drink, to booze
demlik tea-pot
demode old-fashioned
demokrasi democracy
demokrat democrat; democratic
demokratik democratic
demokratlaş(tır)mak to democratize
denden ditto mark
denek subject
denektaşı touchstone
deneme test, trial; attempt, try; essay
denemeci essayist
denemek to try, to test; to attempt, to essay

denet control, supervision
denetçi supervisor, controller
denetici controlling device
denetim control, supervision, check; censure
denetimli controlled
denetimsiz uncontrolled
denetleme control, inspection **denetleme kurulu** censor board
denetlemek to control, to inspect, to check
denetleyici controlling, supervisory; controller, inspector
deney experiment
deneyim experience
deneyimli experienced
deneyimsiz inexperienced
deneysel experimental
denge balance, equilibrium
dengelemek to balance
dengeli balanced
dengesiz unbalanced
deniz sea, ocean; maritime, marine, naval, nautical **deniz kazası** shipwreck **deniz kuvvetleri** naval forces **deniz mili** nautical mile **deniz nakliyat şirketi** shipping company **deniz suyu** sea water **deniz tutmak** to get seasick **deniz tutması** seasickness **deniz üssü** naval base **deniz yolları** maritime lines **deniz yoluyla** by sea **deniz yosunu** seaweed **denizden çıkmış balığa dönmek** to feel like a fish out of water **denize açılmak** to put out to sea **denize düşen yılana sarılır** ats. a drowning man will clutch at a straw **denize girmek** to go swimming, to have a swim **denize indirmek** to launch
denizaltı submarine
denizanası jellyfish, medusa
denizaşırı overseas
denizatı seahorse
denizayısı sea cow, manatee
denizbilim oceanography
denizci seaman, sailor
denizcilik seamanship; sailing, navigation
denizdibi submarine
denizgergedanı narwhal

denizkestanesi sea urchin
denizkızı mermaid
denk bale; equal, balanced; suitable, match **denk gelmek** to be suitable, to be timely, to suit **denk getirmek** to choose the right time, to act in the right **denk olmak** to be equal
denkleştirmek to balance
denklem equation **cebirsel denklem** algebraic equation
denli so, so that; tactful
densiz tactless
depar sp. start
deplasman sp. playing away **deplasman maçı** away match, away game
depo depot; warehouse **depo etmek** to store
deprem earthquake
depremyazar seismograph
depresyon depression
depreşmek to recur, to relapse
derbeder untidy, slovenly
dere brook, stream, rivulet; eaves trough **dere tepe düz gitmek** to go up hill and down dale **dereden tepeden konuşmak** to have a small talk **dereyi görmeden paçaları sıvamak** to count one's chickens before they are hatched
derebeyi feudal lord
derebeylik feudalism
derece degree; grade, rank; extent, point; thermometer **bir dereceye kadar** to a certain degree **derece almak** to place (in a competition) **son derece** utterly, extremely
dereceli graded; graduated
dereotu dill
dergâh dervish convent
dergi magazine, review, periodical
derhal at once, immediately
deri skin; leather; peel **derisini yüzmek** to skin, to flay; to strip, to rob; to torture to dead
derialtı subcutaneous
derici leather dealer
dericilik leather trade
derin deep **derin derin** deeply **derin derin düşünmek** to think deeply **derin dondurucu** deep freeze **derinlere**

dalmak to be plunged in thought
derinlemesine in depth, deeply
derinleşmek to become deep
derinlik depth
derişik concentrated
derken while trying to, when intending to; just at that moment
derleme collecting, compilation; selected, collected
derlemek to collect, to compile **derleyip toplamak** to tidy up
derleyici compiler
derli toplu tidy, in order
derman remedy, cure; strength, energy **derman aramak** to seek a remedy **derman olmak** to be a remedy (for)
dermansız incurable; exhausted
derme collection; collected **derme çatma** jerry-built, rambling
dermek to collect, to pick, to gather
dernek association, club, society
ders lesson, lecture, class; warning, example, lesson **ders almak** to take lessons from **ders çalışmak** to study **ders vermek** to give a lesson **dersi asmak** to play truant, to cut a class **dersini yapmak** to prepare one's lesson, to do one's homework
dershane classroom; private schools offering specialized courses
derslik classroom
dert trouble, worry, sorrow; suffering, pain; nuisance, bother; disease **derde girmek** to get into trouble **derdine düşmek** to be deeply occupied with **dert çekmek** to suffer **dert dökmek** to unbosom oneself **dert olmak** to become a worry to **dert ortağı** fellow sufferer **dert yanmak** to complain
dertlenmek to be troubled, to get worried
dertleşmek to talk about each other's troubles, to have a heart-to-heart talk (with)
dertli pained, sorrowful
dertsiz untroubled, carefree
derviş dervish; humble, tolerant
derya sea, ocean
desen design; drawing
desenli figured

desilitre decilitre
desimetre decimetre
desise trick, intrigue
despot despot
destan epic, legend **destan gibi** very long **dillere destan olmak** to become very famous
deste bunch, packet
destek support, prop, shore **destek olmak** to support **destek vurmak** to put a prop to
destekleme support **destekleme alımı** support buying
desteklemek to support
destroyer destroyer
deşik pierced
deşmek (boil) to lance; (subject) to open up, to recall
detay detail
detaylı detailed
dev giant; gigantic **dev gibi** enormous, huge
deva cure, remedy
devalüasyon devaluation
devam continuation; attendance **devam etmek** to continue, to go on; to attend **devamı var** to be continued
devamlı continuous, lasting; assiduous, regular
devamsız without continuity; irregular
devamsızlık lack of continuity; irregular attendance, absenteeism
deve camel **deve gibi** huge and awkward **devede kulak** a drop in the ocean **Devenin başı!** Stuff and nonsense!, Incredible!
deveboynu tube with "S" or "U" shape
devedikeni thistle
devekuşu ostrich
deveran circulation
devetabanı bitk. philodendron
devetüyü camelhair
devim movement, motion
devimbilim dynamics
devimsel kinetic
devingen dynamic
devinim motion
devinmek to move
devir period, epoch; rotation, turn, tour; transfer

devirli periodic

devirmek to knock down, to turn over; to overthrow, to subvert; to drink down, to toss off; to capsize

devlet state; government **devlet adamı** statesman **devlet baba** the state **devlet bakanı** state minister **devlet başkanı** head of the state, president **devlet hazinesi** state treasury **devlet hizmeti** government service, public service **devlet kuşu** wind-fall, godsend **devlet tahvilleri** state bonds

devletçe on the part of the government

devletlerarası international

devletleştirmek to nationalize

devralmak to take over

devre period, term; circuit; *sp.* half-time

devren by cession, by transfer

devretmek to turn over, to transfer; to sublet

devrik folded over; overthrown; *dilb.* inverted

devrim revolution; reform

devrimci revolutionist; revolutionary

devriye patrol **devriye gezmek** to patrol **devriye polisi** *Aİ.* patrolman

devşirmek to gather, to collect; to roll up, to fold

deyim idiom

deyiş style of speech; folk poem, song

dezavantaj disadvantage

dezenfekte disinfected **dezenfekte etmek** to disinfect

dırdır nagging **dırdır etmek** to nag, to grumble

dırıltı grumbling; squabble **dırıltı çıkarmak** to cause a squabble

dış outside, exterior; outer, external; foreign **dış gebelik** ectopic pregnancy **dış görünüş** exterior, façade **dış hat** external line; international line **dış pazar** foreign market **dış ticaret** foreign trade

dışadönük extroverted

dışalım importation; import(s)

dışalımcı importer

dışarı out; outside, exterior; outdoor; abroad **dışarı gitmek** to go out; to go abroad **dışarı vurmak** to manifest, to show

dışavurumcu expressionist

dışavurumculuk expressionism

dışbükey convex

dışında outside; except, exclusive of, with the exception of

dışişleri foreign affairs **Dışişleri Bakanı** Minister of Foreign Affairs **Dışişleri Bakanlığı** Ministry of Foreign Affairs

dışkı feces, excrement

dışlamak to exclude

dışmerkezli eccentric

dışsatım exportation; export

dışsatımcı exporter

Dicle the Tigris

didaktik didactic; didactics

didiklemek to pull to shreds

didinmek to toil, to slog, to drudge

didişmek to scuffle, to quarrel

diferansiyel differential gear

difteri diphtheria

diftong diphthong

diğer other; different; another

dik perpendicular, vertical; erect, upright; *mat.* right; steep **dik açı** right angle **dik başlı/kafalı** pig-headed, obstinate **dik dik bakmak** to stare (angrily) **dik durmak** to stand upright **dik üçgen** right triangle

dikdörtgen rectangle

dikelmek to become steep; to stand; to be defiant

diken thorn; spine **diken üstünde oturmak** to be on tenterhooks

dikenli thorny, prickly

dikensiz without thorns

dikey vertical, perpendicular

dikilitaş obelisk

dikilmek to be planted; to be erected; to be sewn; to stand; (eyes) to be fixed on

dikim sewing; planting

dikimevi sewing workshop

dikine vertically

dikiş sewing, stitching; planting; seam; *hek.* suture **dikiş dikmek** to sew **dikiş iğnesi** sewing needle **dikiş makinesi** sewing machine

dikit stalagmite

dikiz peep, peek **dikiz aynası** rear view mirror **dikiz etmek** to peep

dikizci *arg.* peeper
dikizlemek to peep, to peek
dikkat attention, caution; care, heed
Dikkat! Look out!, Watch out!
dikkat çekmek to attract attention **dikkat etmek** to pay attention (to); to be careful **dikkate almak** to consider, to take into consideration **dikkatini çekmek** to call sb's attention (to)
dikkatle carefully
dikkatli careful
dikkatsiz careless
dikkatsizlik carelessness
diklenmek to become steep; to get stubborn
dikleşmek to become steep; to get stubborn
dikme sewing; planting; seedling; *mat.* perpendicular
dikmek to sew, to stitch; to plant; to erect; (eyes) to stare; (ears) to prick up; to drink off, to drain
diksiyon diction
diktatör dictator
diktatörlük dictatorship
dikte dictation **dikte etmek** to dictate
dil language; tongue; *coğ.* promontory, spit **dil çıkarmak** to put out the tongue **dil dökmek** to flatter, to talk sb round/over **dil uzatmak** to talk against to defame **dile gelmek** to start to talk **dile getirmek** to express, to depict **dile kolay** easier said than done, easy to say **dili çözülmek** to start to talk **dili dolaşmak** to splutter, to mumble **Dili kurusun!** Curse his tongue! **dili tutuk** tongue-tied **dili tutulmak** to be tongue-tied **dili varmamak** not to be willing to say **dilinde tüy bitmek** to be tired of repeating **dilinden düşürmemek** to keep on saying, to harp on **dilini tutmak** to hold one's tongue **dilini yutmak** to have lost one's tongue **dilinin altında bir şey olmak** to seem to be hiding sth **dilinin ucunda olmak** to be on the tip of one's tongue **dillerde dolaşmak** to be in the limelight **dillere destan olmak** to be on everybody's tongue **dillere düşmek** to become a subject of gossip
dilbalığı sole
dilbasan *hek.* spatula
dilbaz eloquent, glib, talkative
dilber beautiful, attractive
dilbilgisi grammar
dilbilgisel grammatical
dilbilim linguistics
dilbilimci linguist
dilbilimsel linguistic
dilci linguist
dilcik *bitk.* ligule
dilek wish, desire, request **dilek dilemek** to make a wish **dilek kipi** *dilb.* optative mood **dilekte bulunmak** to make a wish
dilekçe petition, application **dilekçe vermek** to make a petition, to petition
dilemek to wish (for), to desire; to ask (for), to beg
dilenci beggar
dilencilik mendicancy, begging
dilenmek to beg
dilim slice **dilim dilim** in slices
dilimlemek to slice
dillenmek to begin to talk; to find one's tongue
dilli talkative, glib
dilmek to slice
dilsel linguistic
dilsiz dumb
dimağ brain
dimdik bolt upright, erect **dimdik ayakta durmak** not to collapse
din religion **dinden imandan çıkarmak** to be enough to make a saint swear **dini bütün** pious, religious **Dini imanı para** All he/she thinks of is money
dindar pious, religious
dini, dinsel religious
dinsiz irreligious, atheistic
dinsizlik irreligion, atheism
dinamik dynamic; dynamics
dinamit dynamite
dinamizm dynamism
dinamo dynamo
dinar dinar
dinç robust, vigorous
dinçleşmek to become robust
dinçlik robustness

dindar

dindar religious, pious, faithful
dindarlık devotion, piety
dindirmek to stop; to slake, to satisfy
dingil axle
dingildemek to rattle, to wobble
dingin calm, tranquil
dini religious
dinlemek to listen (to); to obey, to follow; *hek.* auscultate
dinlence holiday, vacation
dinlendirici relaxing
dinlendirmek (to allow) to rest
dinlenmek to be listened (to); to rest, to relax
dinleti concert
dinleyici listener
dinleyiciler the audience
dinmek to stop, to cease, to calm down
dinozor dinosaur
dinsiz irreligious, godless; atheist, pagan
dip bottom dibine darı ekmek to use up
dipçik butt (of a rifle)
diploma diploma, degree
diplomasi diplomacy
diplomat diplomat
diplomatik diplomatic
dipnot footnote
dirayet ability; intelligence
direk pole, post
direksiyon steering-wheel
direkt direct; directly
direktif directive, instructions
direktör director
direnç resistance
direniş resistance, opposition
direnmek to insist (on); to hold out, to resist
diretmek to put one's foot down, to insist
direy fauna
dirhem drachma
diri alive, living; fresh; energetic, lively
dirilmek to be resuscitated/revived
diriltmek to bring to life, to resuscitate
dirim life
dirimbilim biology
dirlik peace; affluence dirlik düzenlik

peace and harmony
dirsek elbow dirsek çevirmek to turn one's back on, to drop dirsek çürütmek to study long and hard
disiplin discipline
disiplinli disciplined
disiplinsiz undisciplined
disk discus disk atma throwing the discus
diskalifiye disqualified diskalifiye olmak to be disqualified
disket disk, diskette
disko(tek) disco(theque)
dispanser dispensary
distribütör distributor
diş tooth; clove; cog; thread diş ağrısı toothache diş bilemek to nurse a grudge diş çekmek to pull out a tooth diş çıkarmak to cut one's tooth diş fırçası toothbrush diş geçirmek to be able to influence diş gıcırdatmak to gnash one's teeth diş göstermek to show one's teeth diş hekimi dentist diş hekimliği dentistry diş macunu toothpaste dişini sıkmak to set one's teeth, to endure dişinden tırnağından artırmak to pinch and save dişini tırnağına takmak to work tooth and nail
dişbudak ash tree
dişçi dentist
dişçilik dentistry
dişeti gum
dişi female, she
dişil *dilb.* feminine
dişlek bucktoothed, toothy
dişlemek to bite, to nibble
dişli toothed, serrated, notched; influential, formidable; cogwheel, gear
dişözü dental pulp
ditmek to card, to tease
divane crazy, insane
divanıharp court martial, military court
diyabet diabetes
diyafram diaphragm
diyalekt dialect
diyalektik dialectic; dialectics
diyaliz dialysis diyaliz cihazı dialyzer
diyalog dialogue
diyanet piety; religion

diyapazon diapason, tuning fork
diyar country, land
diyare *hek.* diarrhea
diye so that; in case; because; thinking that, by mistake; called, named
diyecek something say **diyeceği olmamak** to have no objection; to have nothing to say
diyet diet
diyez *müz.* flat, diesis
diz knee **diz boyu** knee-deep **diz çökmek** to kneel (down) **dize gelmek** to give up, to surrender **dize getirmek** to bring sb to his knees, to bring to heel **dizini dövmek** to repent bitterly **dizlerine kapanmak** to fall at sb's feet **dizlerinin bağı çözülmek** to give way at the knees
dizanteri dysentery
dizbağı garter
dizayn design
dize *ed.* line
dizel diesel
dizge system
dizgeli systematic
dizgi composition, typesetting
dizgici typesetter, compositor
dizgin rein, bridle **dizginleri ele almak** to take control
dizginlemek to bridle; to restrain, to curb
dizginsiz uncontrolled, unbridled
dizi line, row; series; string; serial; *mat.* progression
dizici typesetter, compositor
dizin index
dizkapağı kneecap
dizlik knee pad
dizmek to arrange in a row, to line up, to array; to string; to set up, to compose
do *müz.* do
dobra blunt, frank **dobra dobra** bluntly, frankly
doçent assistant professor, lecturer
dogma dogma
dogmatik dogmatic
doğa nature **doğa bilgisi** natural history **doğa bilimleri** natural sciences
doğal natural **doğal gaz** natural gas **do-ğal kaynaklar** natural resources **doğal olarak** naturally
doğan falcon
doğmak to be born; (sun) to rise; to happen, to arise, to spring
doğrama woodwork, joinery
doğramacı carpenter, joiner
doğru straight; true, right; honest; truth; *mat.* line **doğru bulmak** to approve **doğru çıkmak** to come true **doğrudan doğruya** directly **doğru durmak** to behave oneself, to sit still **doğru dürüst** proper; properly **doğru söylemek** to speak the truth
doğruca, doğrudan directly
doğrucu truthful
doğrulamak to confirm, to verify
doğrulmak to straighten out; to become erect; to direct one's steps to, to head (for)
doğrultmak to straighten; to correct; to point (at), to aim
doğrultu direction
doğruluk straightness; rightness; truth; honesty
doğrusu the truth of the matter; to speak honestly **daha doğrusu** to be more exact **doğrusunu isterseniz** to tell the truth
doğu east; eastern
doğum birth **doğum günü** birthday **doğum kontrolü** birth control **doğum sancısı** labour pain
doğumevi maternity hospital
doğurgan prolific
doğurmak to give birth to, to bear; to bring about, to produce
doğuştan by birth; inborn
doksan ninety
doksanıncı ninetieth
doksanlık nonagenarian
doktor doctor, physician
doktora doctorate; doctoral examination
doktorluk medical profession
doktrin doctrine
doku tissue; texture
dokuma weaving; woven
dokumacı weaver
dokumacılık textile industry

dokumak to weave
dokunaklı touching pathetic
dokunmak to be woven; to touch; to upset, to harm; to concern
dokunulmazlık immunity
dokuz nine dokuz doğurmak to be on pins and needles
dokuzuncu ninth
doküman document
dolamak to twist, to wind
dolambaç curve, bend; labyrinth
dolambaçlı sinuous, winding, devious; complicated
dolandırıcı swindler, crook, cheat
dolandırmak to swindle, to cheat, to nick
dolanmak to be wrapped (around); to go round, to circulate; to rove, to hang about, to stroll
dolap cupboard, wardrobe; plot, trick dolap çevirmek to pull a trick, to plot
dolaşık sinuous, roundabout; tangled, confused
dolaşım circulation
dolaşmak to walk about, to stroll; to get tangled; (rumour) to go around; to circulate
dolay surroundings, environment
dolayı because of, owing to
dolayısıyla consequently; on account of, because of
dolaylı indirect; indirectly
dolaysız direct; directly
doldurmak to fill; to load; (battery) to charge
dolgu filling dolgu yaptırmak to have a tooth filled
dolgun plump, buxom; full, filled; (wages) high
dolma stuffed vegetables; stuffed
dolmak to become full; to be packed; (period) to expire
dolmakalem fountain-pen
dolmuş shared-taxi, shared cab, jitney
dolu full; loaded; charged
dolu hail dolu yağmak to hail
dolunay full moon
domalmak to squat down in a humped position
domates tomato

domino dominoes
domuz pig, swine domuz gibi sturdy; obstinate
don frost; underpants
donakalmak to stand aghast, to freeze
donanım den. rigging
donanma fleet, navy; illumination
donanmak to be equipped; to dress up
donatım equipment
donatmak to deck out, to ornament; to equip; to illuminate
dondurma ice-cream
dondurmak to freeze
donmak to freeze; (cement) to set, to harden; to curdle
donuk frozen; dull
doping doping doping yapmak to dope
doru bay
doruk summit, peak
dosdoğru straight (ahead)
dost friend; lover, mistress, steady dost edinmek to make (one's) friends dost olmak to become friends
dostça friendly; in a friendly way
dostluk friendship
dosya file, dossier
dosyalamak to file
doygun satiated
doymak to be full up, to be satiated
doyum satisfaction, satiety doyum olmamak not to have enough of, not to get tired of
doyurmak to fill up, to satisfy, to satiate; to saturate
doyurucu satisfying
doz dose
dozaj dosage
dökme poured; (metal) cast
dökmek to pour, to empty, to spill; to cast; to shed
dökülmek to be poured, to be spilled; to fall into ruin, to moulder; (hair, etc.) to fall out, to lose; to spill over
döküm casting; enumeration; fall
dökümcü founder
dökümevi foundry
döküntü remains, remnants, remainder; debris; rubbish, trash
döl semen, sperm; offspring, young;

race, stock

döllemek to inseminate, to fertilize

dölüt foetus

dölyatağı womb, uterus

dölyolu vagina

döndürmek to turn round, to rotate, to spin

dönek fickle, untrustworthy

dönem period; term

dönemeç bend, curve

dönence tropic

döner turning, revolving, rotary **döner kapı** revolving door, swing door **döner kebap** meat roasted on a revolving spit **döner sermaye** circulating capital

döngel medlar

dönmek to turn, to revolve, to rotate; to return; to swim, to whirl; to break one's promise; to be converted, to apostatize

dönüm a land measure ot about 920 m2; turning, **dönüm noktası** turning point

dönüşlü *dilb.* reflexive

dönüşmek to be transformed into, to change

dönüştürmek to transform, to change

dönüşüm transformation

döpiyes two-piece

dördül square

dördüncü fourth

dört four **dört ayak üstüne düşmek** to fall on all fours, to land on one's feet **dört dönmek** to search everywhere **dört elle sarılmak** to stick hard and soul, to work wholeheartedly **dört gözle beklemek** to look forward to **dört köşeli** four-cornered, foursided

dörtgen quadrangle

dörtlü (cards) four; quartet

dörtlük *yaz.* quatrain; *müz.* quarter note

dörtnal gallop **dörtnala gitmek** to go at a gallop

dörtyol crossroads

döş breast, bosom

döşek mattress, bed

döşeli furnished

döşem installation

döşeme floor; upholstery; furniture

döşemeci upholsterer

döşemek to furnish; to spread, to lay down; to pave, to floor

döviz foreign exchange, foreign currency; motto, slogan

dövme beating; tattoo; forging

dövmek to beat, to thrash; to hammer, to forge; to bombard

dövünmek to beat one's breast, to lament

döviş fight

dövüşçü fighter

dövüşken combative, bellicose

dövüşmek to fight; to box

drahmi drachma

draje sugar-coated pill; dragée

dram drama; tragedy

dramatik dramatic; tragic

dramatize etmek to dramatize

drenaj drainage

dua prayer **dua etmek** to pray

duba pontoon, barge

dublaj dubbing **dublaj yapmak** to dub

duble double

dubleks duplex

dublör stunt-man

dudak lip **dudak boyası** lipstick **dudak bükmek** to curl one's lip **dudak ısırmak** to bite one's lip

duhuliye entrance fee

duka duke

dul widow; widower; widowed

duman smoke; mist, fog

dumanlanmak to get smoky

dumanlı smoky; misty, fogy

dumansız smokeless

durağan stable, fixed

durak stop; break, pause

duraklama pause; hesitation

duraklamak to stop, to pause; to hesitate

duraksamak to hesitate

durgun calm, quiet; stationary, stagnant

durgunlaşmak to get calm

durgunluk calmness; stagnation

durmak to stop, to cease; to remain, to stay; to stand; to wait

duru clear, limpid

durulamak to rinse

durulmak to become clear; to calm down

durum condition, situation, state, case; position; *dilb.* case

duruş position, pose, posture

duruşma trial, hearing

duş shower **duş yapmak/almak** to have a shower

dut mullberry **dut yemiş bülbüle dönmek** to be tongue-tied

duvak bridal veil

duvar wall **duvar ilanı** poster **duvar kâğıdı** wallpaper **duvar saati** clock

duvarcı bricklayer, mason

duy socket

duyarga antenna

duyarlı sensible, sensitive

duyarlık sensibility, sensitivity

duyarsız insensitive

duygu feeling; sensation, sense

duygulandırmak to affect, to move

duygulanmak to be affected, to be moved

duygulu sensitive, emotional

duygusal emotional, sentimental

duygusuz insensitive, hardhearted, unfeeling

duymak to hear; to feel, to sense **duymazlıktan gelmek** to pretend not to have heard

duyu sense

duyum sensation

duyuru announcement

düdük whistle, pipe

düello duel

düet *müz.* duet

düğme button; switch

düğmelemek to button up

düğüm knot; difficulty, rub **düğüm açmak** to untie a knot **düğüm atmak** to tie a knot **düğüm noktası** crucial point, nodal point **düğüm olmak** to get knotted

düğümlemek to knot

düğümlenmek to become knotted

düğün wedding (feast) **düğün alayı** wedding procession **düğün etmek** to rejoice, to exult **düğün yapmak** to hold a wedding

düğünçiçeği buttercup

dük duke

dükkân shop **dükkân açmak** to set up business, to open a shop

dükkâncı shopkeeper

dülger carpenter; builder

dülgerlik carpentry

dümbelek tabor, timbal

dümdüz perfectly smooth; straight ahead

dümen rudder, helm; *arg.* trick **dümen kırmak** to change course, to veer, to swerve **dümen çevirmek** to play tricks, to trick **dümen kullanmak** to steer

dümenci helmsman, steersman

dün yesterday **dün akşam** yesterday evening **dün değil evvelsi gün** the day before yesterday **dün gece** last night **dünden hazır/razı** very eager

dünkü of yesterday, yesterday's

dünür the father-in-law or mother-in-law of one's child

dünya world, earth; everybody **dünya âlem** all the world, everybody **dünya durdukça** for ever and ever **dünya evine girmek** to get married **dünya gözüyle görmek** to see (sb/sth) before one dies **dünya kadar** a world of, lots of **Dünya varmış!** How wonderful! What a relief! **Dünya yıkılsa umurunda değil!** He doesn't give a damn **dünya zindan olmak** to be in great distress, to lead a dog's life **dünyadan elini eteğini çekmek** to give up all worldly things **dünyadan haberi olmamak** to be unaware of what is going on around one **dünyanın kaç bucak olduğunu göstermek** to teach sb a lesson **dünyanın öbür ucu** the far end of the world **dünyanın parası** a lot of money **dünyaya gelmek** to be born **dünyaya getirmek** to bring into the world, to bear **dünyaya gözlerini kapamak** to pass away **dünyayı tozpembe görmek** to see things through rosecoloured glasses **dünyayı zindan etmek** to lead sb a dog's life

dünyevi worldly

düpedüz openly, sheer

dürbün binoculars, field glasses

dürmek to roll up

dürtmek to prod, to goad; to stimulate, to incite

dürtü drive, motive

dürtüklemek to nudge

dürüm roll, fold

dürüst honest, upright, straight

dürüstlük honesty, uprightness

düstur principle, rule

düş dream, daydream **düş görmek** to have a dream **düş kırıklığı** disappointment **düş kurmak** to daydream

düşes duchess

düşeş bargain, windfall; double six

düşey vertical

düşkün down-and-out, poor; addicted to, devoted to, fond of; devotee, addict, buff, bug

düşman enemy, foe

düşmanlık hostility, enmity

düşmek to fall; to drop; (child) to be born dead; to subtract, to deduct; to fall on hard times; to end up, to wind up, to land up

düşük fallen; drooping; (price) low; (sentence) misconstructed; *hek.* miscarriage, abortion

düşün thought

düşünce thought, idea; anxiety, worry **düşünceye dalmak** to be lost in thought

düşünceli thoughtful; considerate

düşüncesiz thoughtless, inconsiderate

düşüncesizlik thoughtlessness, inconsiderateness

düşündürmek to make (sb) think, to worry

düşünmek to think of; to think (about), to consider **düşünüp taşınmak** to think over

düşünür thinker

düşürmek to let fall to drop; to reduce; (government) to overthrow; (child) to miscarry, to abort

düşüş fall, falling

düz smooth, even, flat; straight

düzelmek to improve, to get better; to be put in order; to be straightened

düzeltme proofreading

düzeltmek to correct, to improve; to put in order, to straighten

düzeltmen proofreader

düzen order, regularity; regime; *müz.* tuning; trick, ruse **düzene koymak/sokmak** to put in order

düzenbaz, düzenci trickster, cheat; tricky

düzenleme arrangement

düzenlemek to arrange, to organize; to put in order

düzenli tidy, in order; systematic; regular

düzensiz untidy, out of order; unsystematic, irregular

düzensizlik disorder

düzey level

düzgün smooth, level; correct; tidy, in order

düzine dozen

düzlem *mat.* plane

düzlemek to smooth, to level

düzlük smoothness, levelness; straightness; level place, plain

düzme(ce) made up, false, forged, sham

düzmek to arrange, to compose; to invent, to make up **düzüp koşmak** to arrange, to compose

düztaban flat-footed; ill-omened, Jonah

düztabanlık flat-footedness

düzyazı prose

E

ebat dimensions

ebe midwife; (game) it

ebedi eternal

ebediyen eternally, forever

ebediyet eternity

ebegümeci mallow

ebelik midwifery

ebe(m)kuşağı rainbow

ebeveyn parents

ebleh stupid, idiot

ebonit ebonite

ebru marbling, watering
ecdat ancestors
ece queen
ecel time of death, death ecel teri dökmek to be in mortal fear eceli gelmek (the term of one's life) to expire ecelne susamak to run into the jaws of death, to be daredevil eceliyle ölmek to die a natural death
ecnebi foreign; foreigner
ecza drugs, chemicals
eczacı chemist, druggist
eczane chemist's (shop), drugstore
eda manner, air, tone
edalı charming, gracious
edat *dilb.* preposition
edebi literary
edebiyat literature
edebiyatçı man of letters
edep breeding, manners, politeness, modesty
edepli well-behaved, polite
edepsiz ill-mannered, rude
edepsizlik bad manners, rudeness edepsizlik etmek to misbehave
eder price, cost
edilgen passive edilgen çatı *dilb.* passive voice
edinmek to acquire, to obtain, to get
edip man of letters
editör editor, publisher
efe swashbuckler
efekt (theatrical) effect(s)
efektif ready money, cash
efendi gentleman; master, Mr; gentlemanly, polite
efkâr thoughts; worry, anxiety efkâr basmak to have the blues efkâr dağıtmak to drown one's sorrows
efkârlanmak to become worried
efkârlı worried, anxious
eflatun lilac-coloured, lilac
efsane myth, legend
efsaneleşmek to become legendary
efsanevi legendary, mythical
efsun spell, charm
Ege Aegean Ege Denizi the Aegean Sea
egemen sovereign, dominant
egemenlik sovereignty, domination
egoist egoism; egotist

egzama eczema
egzersiz exercise
egzoz exhaust
egzotik exotic
eğe file
eğelemek to file
eğer if
eğik oblique; bent, inclined
eğilim tendency; inclination
eğilmek to bend; to incline; to lean
eğim slope, declivity
eğirmek to spin
eğitbilim pedagogy
eğitici pedagogue; instructive
eğitim education, training
eğitimci educator, pedagogue
eğitimli educated
eğitimsiz untrained; uneducated
eğitmek to educate, to train
eğitsel educational
eğlemek to delay, to stop
eğlence amusement, entertainment
eğlenceli amusing, entertaining
eğlencelik kicksaw, titbits
eğlendirmek to amuse, to entertain
eğlenmek to have a good time, to enjoy oneself; to make fun of; to delay, to dawdle
eğlenti party, feast, jollity
eğmek to bend, to bow
eğreltiotu fern, bracken
eğreti borrowed; temporary; artificial, false eğreti almak to borrow eğreti vermek to lend
eğri crooked, bent; aw eğri büğrü contorted, twisted
eğrilik crookedness
eğrilmek to become bent
eğriltmek to bend, to twist
eh well, all right, well enough
ehemmiyet importance
ehil efficient, capable
ehli tame, domestic
ehlileştirmek to tame, to domesticate
ehliyet efficiency, capacity; driving licence
ehliyetli capable, qualified
ehliyetsiz incapable, unqualified
ehram pyramid
ejderha dragon

ek addition; appendix; joint, patch; dilb.
   affix; additional, supplementary
ekâbir great persons, bigwigs
ekili sown, planted
ekim sowing, planting; October
ekin crop; culture ekin biçmek to harvest,to reap
ekinsel cultural
ekip team, group
eklem joint, articulation
eklemek to add; to join together
eklenmek to be added; to be joined
eklenti addition
ekmek to sow, to plant; to spread, to
   sprinkle; arg. to give sb the slip, to
   drop, to ditch
ekmek bread; food; living, job ekmek
   elden su gölden living on others ekmek kapısı a place where one earns
   his livelihood ekmek parası living,
   modest livelihood ekmeğine yağ sürmek to play into sb's hands ekmeği-
   ni çıkarmak to make a living ekmeği-
   ni eline almak to have a job ekmeği-
   ni taştan çıkartmak to make a living
   under difficult conditions ekmeğiyle
   oynamak to threaten (one's) job
ekoloji ecology
ekonomi economy; economics
ekonomik economic; economical
ekose checkered, plaided
ekran screen
ekselans Excellency
eksen axis; axle
ekseriya usually
ekseriyet majority
eksi minus; negative
eksik lacking, missing, absent, short;
   defective, incomplete; less (than); deficiency, lack, defect eksik çıkmak to
   be lacking eksik doldurmak to fill the
   gap eksik etmemek to have always
   in stock eksik gedik small necessities
   Eksik olma! Thank you! eksik olmamak always to turn up
eksiklik lack, absence, deficiency
eksiksiz complete, perfect; completely,
   perfectly
eksilmek to decrease, to lessen
eksiltme reduction; putting up to ten-

der
eksiltmek to reduce, to decrease
ekskavatör excavator
ekspres express (train)
ekstra extra
ekşi sour, acid ekşi yüzlü/suratlı sour--
   faced
ekşilik sourness, acidity
ekşimek to sour; to ferment; (stomach)
   to be upset
ekşimsi sourish
ekşitmek to make sour
ekvator equator
el hand; forefoot; handle; discharge,
   shot; times; possession; (cards) deal
   el altında handy, on hand, ready el
   altından underhandedly, secretly el
   arabası wheelbarrow el atmak to lay
   hands upon, to seize; to attempt el
   ayak çekilmek to be deserted el bebek gül bebek spoiled, coy el bezi
   hand towel el bombası hand grenade
   el çekmek to give up, to relinquish el
   değiştirmek to change hands el ele
   hand in hand el ele tutuşmak to take
   each other by the hand el ele vermek
   to cooperate el etmek to wave (to sb)
   el feneri flashlight el freni hand brake
   el ilanı handbill el işi handwork; hand-
   made el kaldırmak to raise one's
   hand to el kapısı another's house el
   koymak to seize, to confiscate el öpmek to kiss sb's hand (in respect) el
   sürmemek not to touch; not to begin
   el şakası practical joke played on sb
   using the hand el üstünde tutmak to
   treat with honour, to cherish el yazısı
   handwriting elde etmek to get, to obtain elden çıkarmak to sell off, to dispose of elden düşme second-hand
   elden ele from hand to hand elden
   geçirmek to overhaul, to go over ele
   alınır in good condition ele almak to
   take up, to deal with ele avuca sığmaz out of hand, mischievous ele
   geçmek to be caught ele vermek to
   inform, to betray eli açık generous eli
   ağır slow-working eli alışmak to get
   used to; to become skilful eli ayağı
   buz kesilmek to be very cold eli aya-

ğı düzgün lacking in bodily defects **eli boş** empty-handed **eli boş dönmek** to return empty-handed **eli ekmek tutmak** to earn one's bread **eli kulağında** about to happen, impending **eli sıkı** close-fisted, stingy **eli uzun** thievish **eli yüzü düzgün** presentable **elinde kalmak** to remain unsold **elinde olmak** to be in one's power **elinde tutmak** to monopolize; not to sell **elinden bir şey gelmemek** not to be in a position to do sth **elinden geleni yapmak** to do one's best **elinden gelmek** to be able to **elinden kaçırmak** to slip through one's fingers **elinden kurtulmak** to manage to escape from (sb) **elinden tutmak** to help **eline bakmak** to depend on (sb for a living) **eline düşmek** to be caught; to need sb; to meet, to come across **eline geçmek** to earn; to find; to catch **elini ayağını kesmek** to stop going (to) **elini eteğini çekmek** to withdraw **elini çabuk tutmak** to hurry up **elini sıcak sudan soğuk suya sokmamak** not to do any housework, to lead a comfortable life **eliyle koymuş gibi bulmak** to find very easily **Eller yukarı!** Hands up!

el stranger; people; country **ele güne karşı** in the eyes of everybody **el oğlu** stranger, outsider

elâ (eyes) hazel

elâlem all the world, everybody

elastiki elastic, flexible

elastikiyet elasticity

elbet, elbette of course, certainly

elbirliği cooperation

elbise clothes, garments, dress

elçi ambassador; envoy

elçilik embassy

eldiven glove

elebaşı ringleader, chief

elek sieve

elektrik electricity **elektrik akımı** electric current **elektrik düğmesi** switch

elektrikçi electrician; electrician's

elektrikli electric; (wire) live

elektrokardiyografi electrocardiography

elektrolit electrolyte

elektroliz electrolysis

elektromanyetik electromagnetic

elektron electron

elektronik electronic; electronics

elem pain, sorrow

eleman staff member, worker; element

eleme elimination; selected, sifted **eleme sınavı** preliminary examination

elemek to sieve; to eliminate, to select

element element

eleştiri criticism

eleştirici, eleştirmen critic

eleştirmek to criticize

elhamdülillah thank God, thank Allah

elim painful, sorrowful

elişi handwork; hand-made

elkitabı handbook, manual

ellemek to touch with the hand, to handle

elli fifty

ellinci fiftieth

elma apple

elmas diamond

elti sister-in-law

elveda farewell, goodbye

elverişli convenient, suitable

elvermek to be convenient; to suffice, to be enough

elyaf fibres

elzem indispensable

emanet trust, deposit; left luggage office, cloakroom **emanet etmek** to commend, to entrust **emanete vermek** to check

emanetçi depository

emaneten on deposit

emare sign, indication

emaye enamel; enamelled

embriyon *anat.* embryo

emek labour, work; pains, effort **emek vermek** to take pains with, to labour **emeği geçmek** to contribute efforts

emekçi proletarian, labourer

emeksiz effortless, easy

emeklemek to creep, to crawl

emekli retired; pensioner **emekli aylığı** pension, retirement pay **emekli olmak** to retire

emeklilik retirement

emektar old and faithful

emel ambition, desire, wish, ideal, goal
emici absorbent
emin confident, sure; safe, secure; trustworthy **emin olmak** to be sure (of); to make certain
emir order, command; decree **emir almak** to receive orders **emir eri** *ask.* orderly **emir subayı** *ask.* adjutant **emir vermek** to order, to command **emre amade** at one's service, ready **emre yazılı senet** promissory note
emir emeer
emirlik emirate
emisyon emission
emlak real estate, property **emlak komisyoncusu** estate agent
emmek to suck; to absorb, to take in
emniyet safety, security; the police **emniyet altına almak** to make safe, to secure **emniyet amiri** chief of police **emniyet etmek** to trust; to entrust **emniyet kemeri** safety belt **emniyet mandalı** split pin **emniyet somunu** lock nut **emniyet supabı** safety valve **emniyet tedbiri** security measure
emniyetli safe, secure
emniyetsiz unsafe, insecure
emperyalist imperialist; imperialistic
emperyalizm imperialism
empresyonist impressionist
empresyonizm impressionism
emprime printed cloth
emretmek to order, to command
emrivaki accomplished fact, fait accompli
emsal similars, equals; peer, compeer
emsalsiz peerless, matchless
emtia goods, merchandise
emzik nipple; (baby's) feeding bottle
emzirmek to breast-feed, to suckle
en width, breadth
en most **en aşağı** at least **en az** minimum least; at least **en başından** from the very beginning **en önce** first of all **en sonra** last of all
enayi fool, gull, suckle, goof
enayilik foolishness
encik pub, cub
encümen council, committee
endam shape, figure, stature

endamlı well-proportioned, shapely
endeks index
ender rare; rarely
endirekt indirect
endişe anxiety, worry, care **endişe etmek** to be anxious
endişeli anxious, thoughtful
endişesiz unworried, carefree
Endonezya Indonesia
Endonezyalı Indonesian
endüstri industry
endüstrileşmek to be industrialized
endüstriyel industrial
enerji energy
enerjik energic
enfarktüs infarction
enfeksiyon infection
enfes delicious, excellent
enfiye snuff
enflasyon inflation
enfraruj infrared
engebe rough ground, unevenness
engebeli uneven, rough, broken
engel obstacle, hindrance, barrier **engel olmak** to prevent, to obstruct, to stop **engelli koşu** hurdle race
engerek adder, viper
engin vast, wide, boundless
enginar artichoke
enik puppy, cup
enikonu thoroughly, fully
eninde sonunda in the end
enine broadways, breadthways **enine boyuna** in length and breadth; fully, completely
enişte sister's or aunt's husband
enjeksiyon injection
enkaz ruins; wreckage
enlem latitude
ense back of the neck, nape
enselemek *arg.* to nab, to nick
ensiz narrow
enstantane snapshot
enstitü institute
enstrüman instrument
entari loose robe, dress
ensülin insulin
entrika intrigue **entrika çevirmek** to intrigue, to plot
envanter inventory

epey, epeyce pretty, fairly
epidemi epidemic
epik epic
er man, male; private (soldier); manly man
erat *ask.* privates, recruits
erbap expert, master
erbaş non-com
erdem virtue
erdemli virtuous
erek aim, goal
ergen adolescent; unmarried
ergenlik adolescence; youthful acne
ergime melting, fusion
ergimek to melt, to fuse
ergin ripe, mature; adult, major
erginleşmek to mature, to ripen
erginlik maturity; *huk.* majority
erguvan judas-tree
erguvani purple
erik plum
eril masculine
erim reach, range
erimek to melt, to fuse, to dissolve, to thaw
erinç peace, rest
erişmek to arrive, to reach; to mature, to ripen
erişte vermicelli
eritmek to melt, to dissolve
eriyik solution
erk power
erkân high officials, great men
erke energy
erkek man, male; manly, virile, honest erkek gibi mannish
erkekçe manly; manfully
erkeklik masculinity; manliness, courage; male sexual potency, virility
erken early
erkenci early riser
ermek to reach, to attain; to ripen, to mature
ermiş saint
eroin heroin
erotik erotic
erotizm erotism
erozyon erosion
ertelemek to postpone, to delay, to put off

ertesi next, following ertesi gün the next/following day
erzak provisions
es *müz.* rest es geçmek to pass over, to skip
esans perfume
esaret slavery
esas foundation, basis, base; fundamental, essential, basic
esasen fundamentally, essentially
esaslı based, founded; principal, basic, main; true, solid
esassız baseless, unfounded
esef regret
esefle regretfully
esen healthy, sound
esenlik health, soundness
eser work (of art); sign, mark, trace
esin inspiration
esinlemek to inspire
esinlenmek to be inspired
esinti breeze
esir slave; prisoner of war, captive esir düşmek to be taken prisoner esir ticareti slave trade
esirgemek to spare, to protect; to grudge
esirlik slavery, captivity
eski old; ancient; secondhand; former, ex; old-fashioned eski çamlar bardak oldu a lot of water has flowed under the bridge eski defterleri kapamak to let bygones be bygones eski eserler antiques, antiquities eski kafalı (person) old-fashioned eski püskü shabby, tattered, ragged eski zaman antiquity; old days eskisi gibi the way it used to be, as before
eskici ragman, ragpicker; cobbler
eskiçağ prehistoric period
eskiden in the past, formerly eskiden kalma handed down, passed down
eskilik oldness; seniority
eskimek to wear out, to become old; to get old in the service
eskitmek to wear sth out, to age
Eskimo Eskimo
eskiz sketch
eskrim fencing eskrim yapmak to fence
eskrimci fencer

77 **etraf**

esmek (wind) to blow; to come to one's mind
esmer dark, brown, brunette
esmerleşmek to get brown, to tan
esmerlik darkness, brownness
esna moment, instant
esnasında during, while
esnaf tradesman, artisan
esnek elastic, flexible
esneklik elasticity
esnemek to yawn; to stretch, to bend
espri wit, joke, crack, quip espri yapmak to make a wisecrack; to crack a joke
esrar hashish
esrarkeş hashish addict
esrar mystery
esrarengiz mysterious
estağfurullah Don't mention it, Not at all
estetik aesthetic; aesthetics estetik cerrahi plastic surgery
estetikçi aesthetician
eş match, counterpart; partner; mate; spouse, consort eş dost friends and acquaintances
eşsiz matchless, peerless
eşanlamlı synonymous
eşantiyon sample, model
eşarp scarf
eşcinsel homosexual
eşdeğer equivalence
eşdeğerli equivalent
eşek donkey, ass; stupid, ass Eşek hoşaftan ne anlar It's like casting pearls before swine eşek sudan gelinceye kadar dövmek to give sb a good thrashing eşek şakası coarse practical joke eşekten düşmüş karpuza dönmek to be shocked
eşekarısı wasp, hornet
eşeklik assinity, stupidity
eşelemek to scratch, to paw
eşey sex
eşeysel sexual
eşgüdüm coordination
eşik threshold
eşinmek to scratch the soil
eşit equal
eşitlik equality

eşkâl forms, figures
eşkenar equilateral
eşkıya bandit, brigand
eşkin canter; cantering
eşlemek to pair, to match; (film) to synchronize
eşlik accompaniment eşlik etmek to accompany, to escort
eşmek to dig up, to scratch
eşofman tracksuit
eşraf notables
eşsesli homophone
eşya things, objects; furniture; luggage, belongings
eşzamanlı synchronic
et meat; flesh; pulp et suyu broth etine dolgun plump
etajer whatnot
etap stage, lap
etçil carnivorous
etek skirt; bottom; fool etekleri tutuşmak to be exceedingly alarmed etekleri zil çalmak to walk on air
eteklik skirt
eter ether
Eti Hittite
etiket label, tag, sticker
etiketlemek to label
etilen ethylene
etimoloji etymology
etimolojik etymological
etken factor; dilb. active
etki effect, influence; impression
etkilemek to effect, to influence, to impress
etkileyici impressive
etkili effective, effectual; influential; impressive, touching
etkisiz ineffective, ineffectual
etkileşim interaction
etkin effective, active
etkinlik activity
etli fleshy, plump; meaty
etmek to make, to do; to cost, to be worth
etnik ethnic
etnografya ethnography
etoburlar carnivores
etol stole
etraf surroundings, environment; sides

etrafına, etrafında around, round etrafına bakınmak to look around
etraflı detailed, exhaustive
etraflıca in detail, fully
etraftan from all around from all directions
ettirgen *dilb.* causative
etüt study, research etüt etmek to
study, to investigate
ev house; home; household, family ev
bark household ev bark sahibi family
man ev halkı household family ev
hayvanı domestic animal ev idaresi
housekeeping ev kadını housewife ev
kirası (house) rent ev sahibesi hostess ev sahibi host; landlord ev tutmak to rent a house evde kalmak
(girl) not to be able to get married; to
have been left on the shelf
evcek with the whole family
evci weekly boarder
evcil domestic, tame
evcilleştirmek to domesticate
evermek to marry off
evet yes
evham apprehensions, suspicions
evhamlı hypochondriac, suspicious
evirmek to change, to alter evirip çevirmek to turn over and over
evlat son, daughter, child evlat edinmek to adopt a child
evlatlık adopted child evlatlıktan reddetmek to disown
evlendirmek to give in marriage, to
marry (off)
evlenmek to get married, to marry
evli married, hitched
evlilik marriage
evliya saint
evrak documents, papers
evre phase
evren universe; cosmos
evrensel universal
evrim evolution
evrimci evolutionist
evrimsel evolutionary
evsaf qualities
evvel ago, before, earlier; the first part,
beginning evvel Allah with God's
help evvel zaman içinde once upon a

time
evvela in the first place, first of all
evvelce previously, formerly
evvelden previously, formerly
evveliyat first stages, beginnings
evvelki, evvelsi the previous evvelki gün
the day before yesterday
eyalet province
eyer saddle
eyerlemek to saddle
eylem action; *dilb.* verb eylem çekimi
dilb. conjugation
eylemek to make, to do
eylül September
eyvah alas! alack!
eyvallah thanks!, ta!; goodbye!, ta-ra!
eza torment
ezan call to prayer, the azan ezan okumak to recite the azan
ezber learning by heart, memorizing
ezbere by heart; without knowing ezbere konuşmak to talk without knowing
it
ezberci (a student) who learns parrot
fashion
ezbercilik learning parrot fashion
ezberlemek to learn by heart, to memorize
ezcümle among other things; for
example
ezel past eternity
ezeli eternal ezeli ve ebedi without beginning or end, etarnal
ezeliyet past eternity
ezgi tune, melody, song
ezgin crushed, squashed
ezici crushing, overwhelming
ezik crushed, squashed
eziklik worry, depression
ezilmek to be crushed; to be run over
eziyet torment, torture eziyet çekmek
to suffer pain eziyet etmek to torment, to torture
eziyetli painful, fatiguing, hard
ezme crushing; purée, paste; crushed,
mashed
ezmek to crush, to squash, to mash; to
run over; to tread, to trample; to
overwhelm, to suppress; to trounce
Ezrail Azrail

F

fa *müz.* fa
faal active
faaliyet activity
fabl fable
fabrika factory, plant
fabrikasyon fabrication
fabrikatör factory owner
facia disaster, calamity
fagot *müz.* bassoon
fahiş excessive, exorbitant
fahişe prostitute
fahrenhayt Fahrenheit
fahri honorary
faik superior
fail author, agent; *dilb.* subject
faiz interest **faiz oranı** the rate of interest **faize vermek** to lend (money) at interest **faize yatırmak** to put out at interest
faizci usurer, moneylender
faizcilik usury
faizli interest-bearing, at interest
faizsiz free of interest
fakat but
fakir poor **fakir fukara** the poor
fakirleşmek to become poor
fakirlik poverty
faktör factor
fakülte faculty
faks fax, facsimile
fal fortune **fal bakmak** to tell fortunes **falına baktırmak** to have one's fortune told
falaka bastinado
falan such and such, so and so **falan filan** and so on
falanca so-and-so
falcı fortune-teller
falso blundel, error; *müz.* false note
falsolu faulty
familya *biy.* family
fanatik fanatic
fani mortal, transient
fanila flannel, vest

fantezi fancy; fantasy
fanus lantern; lamp glass
far headlight; eye shadow
faraş dustpan
faraza supposing (that)
fare mouse
fark difference **fark etmek** to notice, to realize; to differ **fark etmez** It doesn't make any difference **fark gözetmek** to treat differently **farkına varmak** to realize, to notice **farkında olmak** to be aware of
farklı different
farklılık difference
farksız same, identical
farmakoloji pharmacology
fars farce
Farsça Persian
farz religious precept; obligation; supposition
Fas Morocco
fasa fiso fiddle-faddle, nonsense
fasarya empty talk, nonsense
fasıl chapter, section
fasıla interval
fasikül fascicle
fasulye bean
faşing fasching
faşist fascist
faşizm fascism
fatih conqueror
fatura invoice, bill
faul foul **faul yapmak** *sp.* to foul
favori whiskers; favourite
fay *coğ.* fault
fayans faience
fayda use, profit, advantage, benefit **faydalı olmak** to help **fayda etmemek** to cut no ice
faydalanmak to make use of
faydalı useful
faydasız useless
fayton phaeton
faz phase
fazilet virtue
faziletli virtuous
fazla excess, spare; excessive, extra; too much **fazla gelmek** to be too much **Fazla mal göz çıkarmaz** Store is no sore **fazla mesai** overtime **fazla**

mesai yapmak to work overtime
fazlasıyla abundantly
fazlalaşmak to increase
fazlalık excess, superfluity
fecaat calamity
feci tragic, terrible
feda sacrifice **feda etmek** to sacrifice
fedakâr self-sacrificing
fedakârlık sacrifice
fedai bodyguard, bouncer
federal federal
federasyon federation
federatif federative
federe federate, federated
felaket disaster, calamity, misfortune **felakete uğramak** to meet with a disaster
felaketzede victim
felç paralysis, apoplexy, palsy **felce uğramak** to be paralysed **felce uğratmak** to paralyse
felçli paralytic, paralysed
felek fate, destiny **feleğin çemberinden geçmek** to go through the mill **felekten bir gün çalmak** to go on a spree, to go to town
felsefe philosophy
felsefi philosophical
feminist feminist
feminizm feminism
fen science
fena bad **fena halde** badly **fena olmak** to feel bad
fenalaşmak to grow worse; to feel taint
fenalık evil, mischief; harm; fainting **fenalık geçirmek** to feel faint
fener lantern; lighthouse
feodal feudal
feodalite feudalism
feragat abnegation, self-sacrifice; renunciation, cession
ferağ cession, renunciation
ferah roomy, spacious; relieved
ferahlamak to feel relieved
ferahlatmak to relieve
ferahlık spaciousness, roominess; relief
ferdi individual
feribot ferryboat
ferman decree, command
fermantasyon fermentation

fermuar zipper
fersah league, five kilometres
fersiz lustreless, dull
fersizlik lack of lustre
fert individual
feryat cry, scream **feryat etmek** to cry out, to scream
fes fez
fesat conspiracy, intrigue, malice
fesatçı mischief-maker
feshetmek to abolish, to cancel
fesih abolition
fesleğen (sweet) basil
festival festival
fethetmek to conquer
fetih conquest
fetiş fetish
fetişizm fetishism
fettan seducing, cunning
feveran effervescence, ebullition
fevk upper part, top
fevkinde above
fevkalade extraordinary
fıçı barrel, cask **fıçı birası** draught beer
fıkırdak coquettish
fıkırdamak to bubble; to giggle, to flirt
fıkırtı bubbling noise
fıkra anecdote, joke; column; paragraph
fındık hazel-nut
fındıkkıran nutcrackers
Fırat the Euphrates
fırça brush **fırça atmak** to chew out, to give sb a rocket **fırça çekmek** to scold, to rebuke
fırçalamak to brush
fırdöndü swivel
fırfır furbelow
fırıldak weather-cock; windmill; trick, intrigue **fırıldak çevirmek** to intrigue
fırın oven; furnace; bakery
fırınlamak to bake
fırıncı baker
fırlak protruding
fırlama bastard
fırlamak to rush out to fly off; to stick out, to protrude
fırlatmak to fling, to launch
fırsat opportunity, chance, occasion **fırsat aramak** to seek an opportunity **fır-**

sat beklemek to wait for an opportunity **fırsat bulmak** to find an opportunity **fırsat düşkünü** opportunist **fırsat kollamak** to watch for an opportunity **fırsat vermek** to give an opportunity **fırsatı kaçırmak** to miss an opportunity **fırsattan yararlanmak** to take advantage of an opportunity

fırtına storm, tempest **fırtınaya yakalanmak** to be caught in a storm

fırtınalı stormy, tempestuous

fısıldamak to whisper

fısıldaşmak to whisper to each other

fısıltı whisper

fıskıye jet, fountain

fıstık peanut, pistachio nut; (girl) *arg.* bundle

fışırdamak to rustle; to fizz

fışırtı a rustling noise

fışkı dung, manure

fışkın shoot, sucker

fışkırmak to gush out, to squirt

fışkırtmak to spout, to spurt

fıtık hernia

fıttırmak to go off one's head, to flip

fıttırtmak to drive sb mad, to go to sb's head

fiberglas fibreglass

fidan sapling, shoot

fidanlık nursery

fide seedling

fidye ransom

figan wail, lamentation

figür figure

figüran walk-on, extra

fihrist index; catalogue, list

fiil act, action; *dilb.* verb, predicate

fikir idea, thought, opinion **fikir edinmek** to form an opinion about **fikir yürütmek** to put forward an idea **fikrinde olmak** to be of the opinion **fikrini almak** to ask sb's opinion **fikrini söylemek** to state one's opinion

fikstür fixture

fil elephant

filaman filament

filarmonik philharmonic

filatelist philatelist

fildişi ivory

file net, nettng

fileto fillet

filika ship's boat

filinta carbine

Filipin Philippine **Filipin Adaları** Philippine Islands

Filipinli Filipino

Filistin Palestine

Filistinli Palestinian

filiz ore; young shoot; bud, sprout

filizlenmek to sprout

film film **film yıldızı** film star **filme almak/çekmek** to film **filmini çekmek** to film; to x-ray

filmci film maker

filmcilik film industry

filo fleet

filotilla flotilla

filoloji philology

filozof philosopher

filtre filter

Fin Finn; Finnish

final *sp.* final **finale kalmak** to be left in the final **finale katılmak** to take part in the finals

finalist finalist

finans finance

finanse etmek to finance

finansman financing

fincan cup

fingirdek coquettish, frivolous

fingirdemek to coquet, to flirt

Finlandiya Finland

Finli Finn

Firavun Pharaoh

fire loss, diminution **fire vermek** to suffer wastage, to diminish

firkete hairpin

firma firm

firuze turquoise

fiske flick, flip **fiske vurmak** to flick

fiskos whispering; gossip **fiskos etmek** to whisper; to gossip

fistan dress

fistül *hek.* fistula

fiş card, slip; plug; counter, token

fişek cartridge

fit instigation, provocation **fit vermek** to instigate, to incite

fit quits **fit olmak** to be quits

fitçi provoker

fitil wick; *ask.* fuse; *hek.* suppository **fitil gibi sarhoş** blind drunk
fitlemek to incite, to instigate
fitne instigation, mischiefmaking **fitne fücur** mischiefmaker, intriguer
fitneci mischiefmaker, instigator
fitnelemek to denounce, to inform
fitre alms
fiyaka showing-off, ostentation **fiyaka yapmak** to swank, to show off
fiyakacı swaggerer
fiyakalı showy, ostentatious
fiyasko fiasco, failure
fiyat price
fiyonk bow-tie
fiyort *coğ.* fiord
fizibilite feasibility
fizik physics; physique
fizikçi physicist
fiziki, fiziksel physical
fizyoloji physiology
fizyolojik physiological
fizyonomi physiognomy
fizyoterapi physiotherapy
flama signal flag, pennant
flamankuşu flamenco
flaş flash
floresan fluorescent, fluorescence
flurya *hayb.* greenfinch
floş floss silk; flush
flört flirt **flört etmek** to flirt
flu blurred
flüt flute
flütçü flutist
fobi phobia
fodul vain
fodulluk vanity
fok seal
fokurdamak to bubble noisily
fokurtu bubbling noise
fol nest egg
folluk egg nest
folklor folklore
folklorcu folklorist
folyo folio
fon fund; background
fondöten liquid make-up, foundation cream
fonetik phonetics; phonetic
fonksiyon function

fora Open!; Unfurl!
form form
forma uniform; colours; sheet of 16 pages
formalite formality
formasyon formation
formika formica
formül formula
fors influence, power
forsa galley-slave, convict
forslu influential
forum forum
forvet *sp.* forward
fos false **fos çıkmak** to fizzle out
fosfat phosphate
fosfor phosphorus
fosforlu phosphorous, phosphoric
fosil fosil
fosilleşmek to fossilize
fosseptik septic tank
fosurdatmak to puff
foto photo
fotoğraf photograph **fotoğraf çekmek** to take a photograph **fotoğraf çektirmek** to have one's photo taken **fotoğraf makinesi** camera
fotoğrafçı photographer
fotoğrafçılık photography
fotojenik photogenic
fotokopi photocopy, xerox **fotokopi çekmek** to photocopy, to xerox **fotokopi makinesi** photo-copier
fotomontaj photomontage
fotoroman photo-story
fotosentez *bitk.* photosynthesis
foya foil; fraud, eyewash **foyası meydana çıkmak** to give oneself away **foyasını meydana çıkarmak** to debunk
fötr felt **fötr şapka** felt hat
frak swallow-tailed coat
francala fine white bread
frank franc
Fransa France
Fransız Frenchman; French
Fransızca French
frekans frequency
fren brake **fren yapmak** to brake
frenlemek to brake; to restrain, to hold back
frengi syphilis

frengili syphilitic
frenkinciri prickly pear
frenküzümü redcurrant
fresk fresco
freze milling cutter
frigorifik frigorific
frikik free kick
fuar fair
fuaye (theatre) foyer
fueloyl fuel-oil
fuhuş prostitution
fukara poor
fukaralık poverty
fular foulard
fulya jonquil
funda heath
fundalık shrubbery
furgon freight-car
furya glut, rush
futbol football, soccer **futbol sahası** football field **futbol sezonu** football seoson **futbol takımı** football team
futbolcu football player, footballer
fuzuli unnecessary
fücceten suddenly
fünye *ask.* primer
füsun charm, enchantment
füze missile, rocket

G

gabardin gabardine
gacırdamak to creak
gacır gucur creakily
gacırtı creak
gaddar cruel, pitiless
gaddarlık cruelty
gaf gaffe, blunder **gaf yapmak** to blunder
gafil inattentive, unwary **gafil avlamak** to catch unawares **gafil avlanmak** to be caught unawares
gaflet inattention, headlessness **gaflete düşmek** to be unaware, to be careless
gaga beak, bill
gaile worry, anxiety

gaileli worried
gailesiz carefree
gaip absent, invisible; the invisible world **gaipten haber vermek** to foretell the future
gaklamak to croak
gala gala, festivity
galaksi galaxy
galebe victory; supremacy **galebe çalmak** to overcome
galeri gallery
galeta hard biscuit, cracker; rusk, dried bread
galeyan excitement, rage, agitation **galeyana gelmek** to get worked up
galiba probably, I think (so); apparently, seemingly
galibiyet victory
galip winner, victor; victorious **galip gelmek** to win, to be victorious
galon gallon
galoş galosh
galvanizlemek to galvanize
galvanizli galvanized
gam *müz.* scale
gam care, worry, sadness
gama gamma **gama ışınları** gamma rays
gamet gamete
gamlı sad, gloomy
gammaz talebearer, informer
gammazlamak to inform, to tell on
gamsız untroubled, light hearted
gamze dimple
gangren gangrene **gangren olmak** to gangrene
gangster gangster
gangsterlik gangsterism
gani abundant, plentiful
ganimet booty, loot
ganyan (horse) winner; winning ticket
gar railway station
garaj garage
garanti guarantee, guaranty **garanti etmek** to guarantee
garantilemek to guarantee; to make sure, to cinch
garantili guaranteed
garantör guarantor
garaz, garez rancour, grudge **garaz**

bağlamak to bear a grudge
gardırop wardrobe
gardiyan prison guard
gargara gargle **gargara yapmak** to gargle
gariban miserable
garip odd, queer, strange; needy, poor **garibine gitmek** to seem odd
gariplik strangeness; poverty
garipsemek to feel out of place; to find strange
gark drowning **gark etmek** to drown, to submerge; to overwhelm, to load with -e **gark olmak** to be submerged; to be overwhelmed (with)
garnitür garnish, trimmings
garnizon garrison
garp west
garson waiter
garsoniyer bachelor's flat
gasp usurpation **gasp etmek** to usurp, to extort
gastrit *hek.* gastritis
gâvur unbeliever, atheist
gayda bagpipe
gaye aim, goal, purpose
gayet extremely, quite
gayret effort, endeavour **gayret etmek** to exert oneself, to strive
gayretli persevering, zealous
gayrı henceforth, henceforward; any more, no more
gayri other than, besides **gayri ihtiyari** involuntary; involuntarily **gayri menkul** real estate **gayri meşru** illegal **gayri resmi** unofficial, informal **gayri safi** gross **gayri tabii** unnatural
gayzer geyser
gaz kerosene; *fiz.* gas **gaz bombası** gas bomb **gaz lambası** oil lamp **gaz maskesi** gas mask **gaz pedalı** accelerator pedal **gaz sobası** gas stove **gaza basmak** (car) to step on the gas
gaza holy war
gazal *hayb.* gazelle
gazap wrath, fury
gazel *yaz.* lyric poem
gazete newspaper, paper
gazeteci journalist
gazetecilik journalism

gazi ghazi, war veteran
gazino musichall
gazlamak to gas; (car) to speed up; *arg.* to run away
gazlı gaseous
gazoz fizzy lemonade, pop
gazyağı kerosene
gebe pregnant **gebe kalmak** to fall pregnant
gebelik pregnancy **gebelik önleyici** contraceptive
gebermek to die, to peg out
gebertmek to kill, to croak
gece night **gece bekçisi** night watchman **gece gündüz** day and night **gece yarısı** midnight **gece yatısına kalmak** to stay the night
gececi night worker
gecekondu shanty, squatter's house
gecelemek to spend the night **geceleyin** at night
gecelik nightdress, nightie
gecikme delay
gecikmek to be late, to delay
geciktirmek to delay, to hold up
geç late **geç kalmak** to be late
geçen last **geçen gün** the other day
geçenlerde recently, lately
geçer current; valid; passing
geçerli current, valid
geçersiz invalid
geçici temporary; infectious
geçim living, livelihood, subsistence
geçimsiz difficult to get on with
geçimsizlik inability to get on with others, incompatibility
geçindirmek to support, to maintain
geçinmek to live on, to subsist; to get along/on well with others; to pretend to be **geçinip gitmek** to scrape along, to keep the pot boiling
geçirgen permeable
geçirmek to pass; (time) to spend; to undergo, to experience; (disease) to get over; (disease) to pass on, to infect; to cure; to see off (a person)
geçiş passing; transition **geçiş üstünlüğü** right of way
geçişli *dilb.* transitive
geçişsiz *dilb.* intransitie

geçiştirmek to avoid, to weather, to escape; to evade, to parry
geçit passage; mountain pass; parade **geçit resmi** parade
geçkin elderly; overripe
geçmek to pass; to expire, to lapse; to surpass, to exceed; to be valid; to blow over; to happen, to take place; to skip, to omit; (disease) to be transmitted; to transfer **geçip gitmek** to go by **geçmek bilmemek** to drag on
geçmiş past
geçmişte in the past
gedik breach, gap
geğirmek to belch
geğirti belch
gelecek future; coming **gelecek zaman** *dilb.* future tense **gelecekte** in the future
gelenek tradition
gelenekçi traditionalist
gelenekçilik traditionalism
geleneksel traditional
gelgelelim however, but
gelgit tides
gelin bride; daughter-in-law **gelin alayı** bridal procession
gelinlik wedding-dress; marriageable
gelincik *bitk.* poppy; *hayb.* weasel
gelir income, revenue, receits **gelir vergisi** income tax
gelişigüzel casual; casually
gelişim development, progress
gelişmek to develop, to progress
gelişmiş developed
geliştirmek to develop, to improve
gelmek to come; to seem, to appear; to cost **gelip geçici** passing, transient
gem bit **gemi azıya almak** to get out of, control -e **gem vurmak** to restrain, to bridle
gemi ship, boat **gemiye binmek** to go on board **gemi mürettebatı** crew
gemici sailor
gemicilik navigation; seaman-ship
gencecik very young
genç young; young man
gençleşmek to become youthful
gençleştirmek to rejuvenate
gençlik youth **gençliğine doyamamak**
to die young
gene again; still, yet, even so **gene de** all the same, yet
genel general **genel grev** general strike **genel kurul** general meeting **genel müdür** general director **genel olarak** in general, by and large **genel sekreter** secretary general
genelev brothel
genelge circular, notice
genelkurmay General Staff
genelleme generalization
genellemek to generalize
genellikle generally
general general
generallik generalship
genetik genetics; genetic
geniş broad, wide; spacious, vast **geniş fikirli** broad-minded **geniş ölçüde** on a large scale
genişlemek to broaden, to widen; to expand
genişletmek to widen, to enlarge; to expand
genişlik breadth, width
geniz nasal fossae **genizden konuşmak** to speak through the nose
genleşmek to expand
genlik amplitude
gensoru interpellation
geometri geometry
geometrik geometrical
gerçek true, real; truth, reality **gerçeği söylemek** to tell the truth
gerçekçi realist; realistic
gerçekçilik realism
gerçekdışı unreal
gerçekleşmek to come true; to become fact, to materialize
gerçekleştirmek to realize
gerçeklik reality
gerçekte in reality
gerçekten in fact, indeed
gerçeküstü surrealist
gerçeküstücülük surrealism
gerçi although, though
gerdan neck, throat
gerdanlık necklace
gerdek nuptial chamber **gerdeğe girmek** to enter the nuptial chamber

gereç material equipment
gerek necessary, requisite; necessity
gereğince according to
gerekirse if necessary
gerekli necessary
gereklik necessity
gerekmek to be necessary; to need; to have to, must, should
gereksinim, gereksinme need, necessity
gereksiz unnecessary gereksiz yere unnecessarily
gerektirmek to necessitate, to require, to involve
gerek whether ... or
gergedan rhinoceros
gergef embroidery frame
gergin stretched, tight, tense
gerginleşmek to become tense
gerginlik tension, tightness
gerekçe reason, justification
geri back; backward; (watch) slow geri almak to take back; to put back geri çekmek to draw back, to withdraw geri çekilmek to withdraw geri çevirmek to send back geri dönmek to return geri gelmek to come back geri gitmek to go back geri göndermek to send back geri tepmek to kick back, to recoil geri vermek to give back geri zekâlı mentally retarded
gerici reactionary
gericilik reaction
geride behind
gerilemek to draw back, to recede; to retrograde
gerilim tension, stress; voltage
gerilimli tense
gerilla guerilla
gerilmek to be stretched
gerinmek to stretch oneself
germek to stretch, to tense
getirmek to bring
gevelemek to chew; to mumble
geveze talkative, chatty; chatterbox, chatterer
gevezelik babbling, chattering gevezelik etmek to babble, to chatter
geviş chewing the cud geviş getirmek to chew the cud

gevrek crisp, brittle
gevremek to become brittle
gevşek loose, slack
gevşeklik looseness, slackness
gevşemek to become slack, to loosen; to relax, to slacken
gevşetmek to loosen, to slacken
geyik deer
geyşa geisha
gez back-sight
gezdirmek to take sb for a walk, to walk, to show around
gezegen planet
gezgin traveller
gezi excursion, trip
gezici itinerant, peripatetic
gezinmek to go for a walk, to stroll
gezinti walk, stroll
gezmek to go about, to walk about; to visit, to tour (round) gezmeğe gitmek to go for a walk
gıcık tickling sensation in the throat, tickle; arg. pain, nuisance
gıcırdamak to creak, to squeak
gıcırdatmak to make creak
gıcır gıcır very clean; brand-new
gıcırtı creak
gıda food, nourishment
gıdalı nutritious
gıdasız undernourished
gıdaklamak to cackle
gıdıklamak to tickle
gıdıklanmak to feel ticklish
gık dememek not to object
gına satiety, disgust gına gelmek to be sick (of), to be fed up (with)
gıpta envy gıpta etmek to envy
gırgır distraction, fun, teasing; carpet sweeper gırgır geçmek to make fun (of)
gırtlak windpipe, larynx, throat gırtlağına kadar borç içinde olmak to be in debt up to one's neck
gırtlaklamak to strangle
gıyaben in the absence of; by name
gıyabında in his absence
gıyap absence
gibi like; as; as if gibi gelmek to seem, to appear
gider expense, expenditure

giderayak just before leaving
giderek gradually
gidermek to remove; to quench, to satisfy
gidiş going, departure gidiş dönüş bileti return ticket, Al. round-trip ticket
gidişat course of events, goings-on
girdap whirlpool, vortex
girdi input girdisini çıktısını bilmek to have sth at one's fingertips, to know what's what
girgin go-ahead, pushing, bold
girift complicated
girinti recess, indentation girintili çıkıntılı serrated, indented
giriş entering; entrance; introduction; müz. prelude
girişim enterprise
girişken enterprising, pushful
girişmek to attempt, to undertake
Girit coğ. Crete
girmek to go in, to enter Girilmez! No entrance!
gişe box office, ticket-office gişe rekoru kırmak to be a box-office success
gitar guitar
gitarist guitarist
gitgide gradually
gitmek to go; to suffice, to last
gittikçe gradually
giydirmek to dress, to clothe
giyecek clothing, dress, garment, gear, clothes
giyim clothing, dress, attire giyim kuşam clothes, attire
giyinmek to dress oneself, to put on one's clothes giyinip kuşanmak to dress oneself up, to prink oneself up
giymek to put on, to wear
giysi clothes, garments, dress
giyotin guillotine
giz secret; mystery
gizem mystery
gizemli mysterious
gizlemek to hide, to secrete, to veil
gizlenmek to hide oneself, to lurk; to be kept secret
gizli secret, hidden gizli ajan secret agent gizli kapaklı very secret, suspicious gizli oturum secret session gizli oy secret vote gizli tutmak to keep secret
gizlice secretly
gizlilik secrecy
gladyatör gladiator
glikoz glucose
gliserin glycerine
gocuk sheepskin cloak
gocunmak to take offence
gofret chocolate water biscuit
gol goal gol atmak to score a goal
golf golf
Golfstrim coğ. Gulf Stream
gonca bud
gondol gondola
gonk gong
goril gorilla
gotik Gothic
göbek navel; belly; centre. heart göbek atmak to dance a belly-dance göbek bağı umbilical cord göbek bağlamak to become paunchy göbek dansı belly-dance
göbeklenmek to become paunchy
göbekli paunchy, pot-bellied
göç emigration, immigration göç etmek to migrate, to emigrate, to immigrate
göçebe nomad; nomadic
göçebelik nomadism
göçer nomadic, migratory
göçmek to migrate; to fall down; to die
göçmen emigrant, immigrant; migratory
göçmenlik migration
göçük landslide, landslip
göğüs chest, breast, bosom göğüs germek to face, to stand up to göğsü kabarmak to swell with pride
göğüslük bib, apron, pinafore
gök sky gök gürlemek to thunder gök gürültüsü thunder gök mavisi sky blue göklere çıkarmak to exalt, to extol
gökada galaxy
gökbilim astronomy
gökbilimci astronomer
gökcismi celestial body
gökdelen skyscraper
gökkuşağı rainbow
gökkubbesi celestial vault

gökküresi 88

gökküresi celestial sphere
göktaşı meteor
gökyakut sapphire
gökyüzü sky, firmament
göl lake
gölcük pond
gölge shadow, shade gölge etmek to cast a shadow (upon)
gölgelemek to overshadow
gölgeli shadowy, shady
gölgelik shady spot
gömlek shirt
gömlekçi shirt-maker or seller
gömme burial; let-in, recessed, inset
gömü treasure
gömüt grave, tomb
gön leather
gönder flag-staff, pole
gönderen sender
gönderme sending; reference
göndermek to send; to transmit; to refer
gönül heart, feelings; inclination, desire gönül almak to placate, to please gönül bağlamak to set one's heart on gönül eğlencesi toy of love gönül eğlendirmek to amuse oneself, to dally gönül kırmak to hurt the feelings gönül vermek to lose one's heart to, to fall for gönlü olmak to be willing; to be in love with gönlünü almak to placate, to make up to gönlünü etmek to prevail on, to coax gönlünü kırmak to hurt the feelings of
gönlünce after one's heart
gönüllü volunteer; willing
gönülsüz unwilling
gönye square, setsquare
göre according to, as to
görecilik relativism
göreli relative
görelilik relativity
görenek custom, usage
göreneksel customary
görev duty, task; mission
görevlendirmek to charge, to entrust
görevli in charge (of)
görgü good manners, etiquette görgü kuralları rules of good manners görgü tanığı eyewitness

görgülü having good manners
görgüsüz unmannerly, ill-bred
görgüsüzlük unmannerliness
görkem splendour, magnificence
görkemli splendid, magnificent
görmek to see; to notice, to recognize göresi gelmek to miss görüp geçirmek to go through, to experience
görmemezlik connivance görmemezlikten gelmek to pretend not to see, to cut, to ignore
görsel visual
görücü female go-between
görülmemiş unseen, unprecedented
görümce wife's sister-in-law, husband's sister
görünmek to be seen; to show oneself, to be visible; to appear, to seem
görünmez invisible
görünürde apparently
görüntü image, picture
görünüm appearance; aspect
görünüş appearance; aspect
görünüşte apparently
görüş sight, view; viewpoint, opinion
görüşme talk, conversation, discussion; interview
görüşmek to talk; to have an interview, to confer with
gösterge indicator; sign
gösteri show; demonstration gösteri yapmak to demonstrate
gösterici demonstrator
gösterim (film) projection
gösteriş showing-off, ostentation gösteriş yapmak to splurge, to show off
gösterişçi ostentatious
gösterişsiz modest, simple
göstermek to show
göstermelik specimen, sample; for show only, not real
göt a, arg. arse; bottom; courage, guts götü yemek arg. to have the guts (to do sth)
götürmek to take with, to take (to); to take away, to carry off; to lead (to); to accompany
götürü in the lump, by the piece götürü çalışmak to do piece-work götürü iş job work, piecework

gövde body, trunk **gövde gösterisi** show of strength
göz eye; drawer; cell; spring, source **göz açıp kapayıncaya kadar** in the twinkling of an eye **göz alıcı** striking, eye-catching **göz almak** to dazzle, to blind **göz aşinalığı** bowing acquaintance, knowing sb by sight **göz atmak** to glance at **göz aydına gitmek** to pay a visit of congratulation **göz banyosu** free show **göz boyamak** to hoodwink **göz dikmek** to long to possess, to covet **göz etmek** to wink at **göz göre göre** openly, publicly **göz kamaştırmak** to dazzle, to blind **göz kırpmadan** without batting an eyelid, pitilessly **göz kırpmak** to wink, to blink **göz koymak** to covet, to lust after **göz kulak olmak** to look after, to watch over **göz nuru** eye-straining work **göz önünde tutmak** to take into consideration **göz ucuyla bakmak** to look out of the corner of one's eye **göz yummak** to close one's eyes (to) **gözden çıkarmak** to sacrifice **gözden düşmek** to fail from favour **gözden geçirmek** to look over, to review **gözden kaçmak** to escape notice **gözden kaybolmak** to risk **göze batmak** to be very inappropriate **göze çarpmak** to strike the eye **göze gelmek** to be coveted **gözleri fal taşı gibi açılmak** to be moon-eyed **gözleri yollarda kalmak** to have been waiting for a long time **gözü açık** shrewd **gözü doymak** to be quite satisfied **gözü gönlü açılmak** to be cheered up **gözü ısırmak** to seem to know sb. **gözü ilişmek** to catch one's eye **gözü kalmak** to hanker after **gözü olmak** to have one's eyes on sth **gözü korkmak** to show the white feather **gözü pek** plucky, bold **gözü tutmak** to take a fancy to **gözünde tütmek** to long for **gözünden uyku akmak** to feel very sleepy **gözüne girmek** to find favour in sb's eyes, to win sb's favour **gözüne kestirmek** to feel oneself capable of **gözünü boyamak** to throw dust in sb's eyes **gözünü dikmek** to stare, to

fix one's eyes on **gözünü dört açmak** to keep one's eyes skinned **gözünü kan bürümek** to see red **gözünü korkutmak** to intimidate, to daunt **gözünün içine bakmak** to fuss over sb, to cherish dearly **gözünün yaşına bakmamak** to have no pity (on) **gözüyle bakmak** to regard as, to consider
gözaltı custody, surveillance **gözaltına almak** to take into custody
gözbağı magic, spell
gözbebeği pupil; the apple of one's eye
gözcü watchman
gözdağı intimidation, threat **gözdağı vermek** to intimidate, to threaten
gözde in favour, favourite **göze** cell
gözenek pore
gözetim custody, care
gözetleme observation
gözetlemek to observe secretly, to watch
gözetmek to take care, to protect
gözkapağı eyelid
gözlem observation
gözlemci observer
gözlemevi observatory
gözlemek to watch (for), to wait (for)
gözlük spectacles, glasses **gözlük takmak** to wear glasses
gözlükçü optician
göztaşı copper sulfate, bluestone
gözükmek to show oneself, to become visible
gözyaşı tear **gözyaşı dökmek** to shed tears, to weep
grafik graph; graphics
grafit graphite
gram gram
gramer grammar
gramofon gramophone
granit granite
granül granule
gravür engraving
gravyer Gruyere cheese
Grek Greek
Grekçe Greek
grekoromen Greco-Roman **grekoromen güreş** Greco-Roman wrestling
gres lubricating grease
grev strike **grev yapmak** to go on strike,

to be on strike
grevci striker
greyder grader
grey(p)frut grapefruit
gri grey
grip influenza, flu grip olmak to have influenza
grizu firedamp
gros gross
grosa tic. gross, 12 dozen
grotesk grotesque
grup group
gruplaşmak to group
guatr goitre
gudde gland
gudubet ugly, hideous
guguk cuckoo
gulden gulden
gurbet absence from home; foreign land, abroad
gurbette away from home
gurbetçi one living away from home; guestworker
guruldamak to rumble
gurultu rumbling noise
gurup sunset, sundown
gurur pride; honour gurur duymak to feel proud of
gururlanmak to be proud of
gururlu proud
gusül ritual ablution
gut hek. gout
guvaş gouache
gübre dung, manure
gübrelemek to manure, to dung
gücendirmek to offend, to hurt
gücenmek to be offended, to be hurt
güç difficult, hard
güç strength, force; power gücüne gitmek to offend sb's feelings gücü yetmek to afford
güçlendirmek to strengthen, to fortify
güçlenmek to be strengthened, to grow stronger
güçlü strong, powerful
güçlük difficulty, trouble güçlük çekmek to have difficulty in güçlük çıkarmak to make difficulties
güçlükle with great difficulty, hardly
güçsüz weak, feeble

güderi chamois (leather)
güdü ruhb. motive, drive
güdük tailless; incomplete, deficient güdük kalmak to be stunted
güdüm driving, management
güdümlü controlled, guided güdümlü mermi guided missile
güfte words, lyrics
güğüm copper jug with a handle
gül rose gül gibi swimmingly gül gibi geçinmek to get along quite well
güldürmek to make laugh
güldürü comedy
güleç smiling, merry
güle güle goodbye! bye-bye!
güler yüzlü cheerful, friendly
gülle ask. cannon ball, shell; sp. shot, weight gülle atmak sp. to put the shot
gülmece humour
gülmek to laugh gülmekten katılmak/kırılmak to split one's sides, to be doubled up with laughter gülmekten kırmak to make sb split his sides
gülsuyu rose water
gülücük smile, chuckle
gülümseme smile
gülümsemek to smile
gülünç funny, ridiculous
gülüşmek to laugh together
güm bang!, boom! güm güm atmak (heart) to throb, to beat violently güme gitmek to perish in a confusion; to die in vain
gümbürdemek to boom, to roar
gümbürtü booming, roar
gümeç honeycomb
gümlemek to bang, to boom; (examination) to tail
gümrük customs; tariff, duty gümrük beyannamesi customs declaration gümrük dairesi customs house gümrük kontrolü customs control gümrük komisyoncusu customs broker gümrük vergisi customs duty gümrüğe tâbi dutiable gümrükçü customs officer
gümrüksüz duty-free
gümüş silver gümüş kaplama silver plating; silver-plated

gümüşbalığı silver atherine
gün day; time, period; lady's at-home day **gün ağarmak** (day) to dawn **gün aşırı** every other day **gün batışı** sunset **gün doğmak** (sun, morning) to dawn, to rise **gün gibi açık** obvious, evident **gün görmek** to live happily **gün ışığı** daylight **gün ışığına çıkarmak** to bring to light **günlerce** day after day, for days **günlerden bir gün** once upon a time **günden güne** from day to day, gradually **günü geçmiş** (bill) overdue **günü gelmek** (bill) to fall due **günü gününe** punctually **günün birinde** one day, some day **gününü gün etmek** to enjoy oneself
günah sin **günah çıkartmak** to confess **günah işlemek** to commit a sin **günaha girmek** to sin **günaha sokmak** to tempt **günahına girmek** to accuse wrongly
günahkâr sinner; sinful
günahsız sinless, innocent
Günaydın! Good morning!
günbegün from day to day
günberi perihelion
güncel actual, current
güncellik actuality
günçiçeği sunflower
gündelik daily; daily wages **gündelikle çalışmak** to work by the day
gündelikçi day-labourer
gündem agenda
gündöndü sunflower
gündönümü solstice
gündüz daytime
gündüzleri, gündüzün in the daytime
gündüzlü day student
gündüzsefası convolvulus, bindweed
günebakan sunflower
güneş sun, sunshine **güneş banyosu** sun bath **güneş çarpmak** to get/have sunstroke **güneş çarpması** sunstroke **güneş görmek** (a place) to be light and sunny **güneş gözlüğü** shades, sunglasses **güneş ışığı** sunlight, sunshine **güneş ışını** sunbeam, sun ray **güneş sistemi** solar system **güneş tutulması** solar eclipse **güneş yanığı** sunburn, tan **güneşte** in the sun **gü-**

neşte yanmak to be sunburnt
güneşlenmek to sunbathe, to bask, to sun oneself
güneşli sunny
güneşlik sunshade; sunny place; sun--hat
güney south; southern **güney kutbu** South Pole
güneybatı southwest; southwestern
güneydoğu southeast; southeastern
güneyli Southerner
günlük daily; diary **günlük güneşlik** sunny
günöte aphelion
günübirlik a day visit **günübirliğine gitmek** to make a day visit
güpegündüz in broad daylight
gür abundant, dense, thick
gürlük abundance, luxuriance
gürbüz robust, sturdy
gürbüzlük sturdiness
Gürcü Georgian
güreş wrestling
güreşçi wrestler
güreşmek to wrestle
gürgen hornbeam
gürlemek to thunder, to roar
güruh gang, mob
gürüldemek to burble; to thunder
gürül gürül with a gurgling sound **gürül gürül akmak** to flow with a gurgling sound
gürültü noise **gürültü çıkarmak** to kick up a row **gürültü yapmak** to make a noise
gürültücü noisy
gürültülü noisy
gürültüsüz noiseless, quiet
gürültüsüzce noiselessly
gürz iron club, mace
gütmek to drive, to pursue; to nourish, to nurse
güve moth
güveç casserole
güven confidence, trust **güveni olmak** to have confidence in
güvence guarantee
güvenç trust
güvenilir reliable
güvenli safe

güvenlik security
güvenmek to rely on, to trust in
güvenoyu vote of confidence
güvensiz distrustful
güvensizlik distrust
güvercin pigeon
güverte deck
güvey, güveyi bridegroom; son-in-law
güya as if, as though
güz autumn, fall
güzün in autumn
güzel pretty, beautiful, nice; good, fine
güzel güzel calmly, meekly güzel sanatlar fine arts
güzelavratotu belladonna
güzelleşmek to become beautiful, to grow handsomer
güzelleştirmek to beautify
güzellik beauty; goodness güzellik enstitüsü beauty parlour
güzellikle gently, softly
güzergâh route
güzide distinguished, select

H

ha I see! Oh yes!; What!; either... or ha babam all the time, continuously ha bire continuously ha bugün ha yarın soon, in a short time Ha şöyle. That's better.
habbe grain, seed, kernel
haber news, information, message haber ajansı news agency haber alma intelligence haber almak to receive information haber göndermek to send a message haber toplamak to gather news haber vermek to inform, to report, to tell haberi olmak to have heard (of/about) haberini almak to hear, to learn
haberci messenger, forerunner
haberdar informed haberdar etmek to inform sb. of sth
haberleşme communication
haberleşmek to communicate
haberli informed, knowing, having

knowledge about
habersiz uninformed, unaware; without warning
habis wicked, evil; malignant
hac pilgrimage (to Mecca) hacca gitmek to go on a pilgrimage to Mecca
hacet need, necessity hacet yok there is no need
hacı pilgrim, hadji
hacıyatmaz tumbler
hacim volume
haciz sequestration, seizure
hacizli distrained
haczetmek to distrain
haç cross haça germek to crucify
Haçlılar the Crusaders
had limit, boundary haddi zatında in itself, essentially haddinden fazla excessive; excessively haddini aşmak to go too far haddini bildirmek to put sb. in his place haddini bilmek to know one's place haddini bilmez presumptuous
hadde rolling mill
hademe servant, janitor
hadım eunuch hadım etmek to castrate
hadise event, incident hadise çıkarmak to provoke an incident
haf sp. half-back
hafıza memory
hafif light, slight; easy hafife almak to make light of
hafifçe lightly
hafifleşmek to become lightly
hafifletmek to lighten
hafifletici extenuating
hafiflik lightness, slightness
hafifsemek to make light of
hafifsıklet light-weight
hafifmeşrep frivolous, loose
hafiye detective
hafriyat excavation(s)
hafta week hafta sonu weekend haftalarca for weeks haftaya next week
haftalık weekly; weekly wages haftalık almak to be paid by the week
haftaym half-time
hain traitor; ungrateful
hainlik treachery

haiz possessing, containing
Hak God **Hakkın rahmetine kavuşmak** to die
hak right **hak etmek** to deserve **hak sahibi** holder of a right **hak vermek** to acknowledge to be right **hak yemek** to be unjust **hakkından gelmek** to get the better of; to defeat **hakkını vermek** to give sb his due
hak engraving
hakan khan, sultan
hakaret insult **hakaret etmek** to insult **hakarete uğramak** to be insulted
hakça justly, rightly
hakem referee, (tennis) umpire
haki khaki
hakikat truth, reality
hakikaten really, actually
hakikatli faithful
hakiki true, real; genuine
hâkim judge
hâkim dominating, ruling; overlooking **hâkim olmak** to rule, to dominate; to overlook
hâkimiyet sovereignty
hakir despicable, mean **hakir görmek** to despise
hakkaniyet justice, equity
hakkaniyetli just, equitable
hakkaniyetsiz unjust
hakketmek to engrave
hakkında about, on
hakkıyla properly, duly
haklamak to beat, to defeat; to kill
haklı right **haklı çıkarmak** to justify **haklı çıkmak** to be justified
haksever just, fair
haksız unjust, unfair **haksız çıkarmak** to put sb. in the wrong **haksız çıkmak** to turn out to be in the wrong
haksızlık injustice, unfairness **haksızlık etmek** to act unjustly
haktanır just, equitable
hal condition, circumstance, situation, state; strength, energy **hal hatır sormak** to inquire after sb's health **halden anlamak** to be understanding **hali kalmamak** to have no strength left **hali vakti yerinde** well off
hal market-place

hâlâ still, yet
hala aunt
halat rope
halayık female servant
halazade cousin
halbuki whereas
hale halo; *anat.* areola
halel injury, harm **halel gelmek** to be injured
halen at present
halet successor
halhal bangle, anklet
halı carpet, rug
haliç estuary, bay
Haliç the Golden Horn
halife caliph
halifelik caliphate
halihazır the present time
halihazırda at present
halim gentle, mild
halis pure, genuine
haliyle naturally, consequently
halk people, nation **halk edebiyatı** folk literature **halk kütüphanesi** public library **halk müziği** folk dance **halk ozanı** folk poet **halk türküsü** folk song
halka ring, hoop; circle
halkbilim folklore
halkbilimci folklorist
halkçı populist, democrat
halkoylaması referendum
halkoyu people's vote
hallaç (wool or cotton) carder **hallaç pamuğu gibi atmak** to scatter about
halletmek to solve, to settle
halsiz exhausted, weary
halsizlik weakness
halt improper act, blunder **halt karıştırmak/yemek** to make a great blunder
halter *sp.* weight lifting; dumbbell, barbell
halterci weight lifter
ham crude, raw; unripe, green; *sp.* out of training **ham madde** raw material **ham petrol** crude oil
hamak hammock
hamal porter, carrier
hamaliye porterage
hamam (Turkish) bath; bathroom **ha-**

mam gibi very hot

hamamböceği cockroach

hamarat hardworking, diligent

hamburger hamburger

ham hum etmek to hum and haw

hami protector

hamil bearer hamiline yazılı (pay) to bearer

hamile pregnant hamile kalmak to become pregnant

hamilelik pregnancy

haminne granny

hamiyet public spirit, patriotism

hamiyetli public-spirited

hamlaç blowpipe

hamla(ş)mak to get out of condition

hamlık crudeness; unripeness, greenness

hamle attack, rush; (chess) move, turn hamle yapmak to make an attack, to dash

hamsi anchovy

hamt giving praise to God hamt etmek to praise God hamt olsun thank God!; thank Allah

hamule cargo

hamur dough, paste; half-baked hamur açmak to roll out dough hamur işi pastry hamur yoğurmak to knead dough

han khan

han inn; large commercial building

hançer dagger

hançere larynx

handikap handicap

hane house, building; mat. column

hanedan dynasty

hanedanlık nobility

hangar hangar

hangi which, what

hangisi which one

hanım woman, lady; wife hanım evladı milksop, mollycoddle

hanımefendi lady, madam

hanımeli honeysuckle

hani where?

hantal clumsy, awkward

hap pill hapı yutmak to be in the soup

hapis imprisonment; prison hapse atmak to put in jail

hapishane prison hapishaneyi boylamak to end up in jail

hapsetmek to put in prison

hapşırmak to sneeze

Hapşu! Atishoo! Atchoo!

harabe ruin

haraç tribute haraç yemek to sponge on sb haraca bağlamak to lay sb under tribute

haraççı extortionist, racketeer

harakiri harakiri

haram forbidden by religion; unlawful haram etmek to forbid the use/enjoyment of

harap ruined harap etmek to ruin, to destroy harap olmak to fall into ruin

hararet heat, warmth; thirst hararet basmak to feel thirsty

hararetli ardent, fervent; vehement, intense

harbi ramrod; straight, trustworthy, outspoken

harcama expenditure

harcamak to spend; to expend, to use; to sacrifice

harcırah travelling allowance

harç expenditure; charge, cost; mortar, plaster

harçlık pocket-money

hardal mustard

harekât operation(s)

hareket movement; action, behaviour; departure hareket etmek to move; to act, to behave; to depart, to leave harekete geçmek to start action

hareketlendirmek to get into motion

hareketli active, lively

hareketsiz motionless, inactive

harem harem

harf letter

harfiyen word for word

harıl harıl continuously, assiduously harıl harıl çalışmak to work hard

haricen externally

harici external

hariciye external diseases

hariciyeci diplomat; specialist in external diseases

hariç except; exterior, outside

harika marvellous, wonderful; wonder,

miracle
harikulade marvellous, wonderful
haris ambitious, greedy
harita map
harlamak to flare up
harman harvest; blend, mixture **harman dövmek** to thresh **harman makinesi** threshing machine
harmanlamak to blend
harp war; *müz.* harp
has peculiar to; pure
hasar damage **hasara uğramak** to suffer damage
hasat harvest **hasat etmek** to reap
hasbıhal chitchat, friendly chat **hasbıhal etmek** to have a friendly chat, to chat
haset jealousy, envy **haset etmek** to envy **hasetten çatlamak** to be green with envy
hasıl resulting, produced **hasıl olmak** to result; to be obtained
hasılat returns, revenue; products
hasım opponent; enemy
hasımlık antagonism; enmity
hasır rush mat, matting
hasis stingy, mean
hasislik stinginess, meanness
haslet virtue, merit
hasret longing, homesickness **hasret çekmek** to long for, to yearn for
hasretlik separation, nostalgia
hasretmek to devote, to dedicate
hassa property quality
hassas sensitive
hassasiyet sensitivity
hasta sick, ill; patient **hasta etmek** to make ill **hasta olmak** to become ill, to get sick **-ın hastası olmak** to be a fan of sth
hastabakıcı nurse
hastabakıcılık nursing
hastalanmak to become ill
hastalık disease; sickness; passion, addiction
hastalıklı diseased, morbid
hastane hospital **hastaneye kaldırmak** to take to hospital **hastaneye yatırmak** to hospitalize
haşa God forbid!

haşarat insects
haşarı naughty, mischievous
haşat *arg.* very bad, worn out
haşere insect
haşhaş poppy
haşin harsh, rude
haşinlik harshness
haşiye footnote
haşlama boiled
haşlamak to boil; to scold, to reprimand
haşmet majesty
haşmetli majestic
hat line; handwriting, calligraphy
hata fault, error, mistake **hata etmek** to make a mistake
hatalı erroneous, faulty, wrong
hatır memory, mind; consideration, influence; one's feelings, heart **hatır senedi** accommodation bill **hatıra gelmek** to come to mind **hatırda kalmak** to be remembered **hatırda tutmak** to bear in mind **hatırı için** for the sake of **hatırı sayılır** considerable, remarkable; respected **hatırı sayılmak** to have influence **hatırım için** for my sake **hatırına gelmek** to occur to one **hatırına getirmek** to remind sb of sth **hatırından çıkmak** to pass out of one's mind **hatırını kırmak** to hurt the feelings of **hatırını sormak** to inquire after sb's health
hatıra memory, reminiscence; souvenir **hatıra defteri** diary
hatır hutur yemek to crunch, to munch
hatırlamak to remember, to recollect, to recall
hatırlatmak to remind
hatırşinas obliging, considerate
hatim reading the Koran from beginning to end **hatim indirmek** to finish the reading of the whole Koran
hatip orator
hatmetmek to read from beginning to end
hatta even, in fact
hattat calligrapher
hattatlık calligraphy
hatun woman
hav nap, pile

hava weather; air, atmosphere; climate; tune, air **hava akımı** draught **hava akını** air raid **hava almak** to go for a walk in the fresh air; *arg.* to get nothing, to draw a blank **hava atmak** to show off, to cut a dash **hava basıncı** atmospheric pressure **hava boşluğu** atmospheric vacuum **hava geçmez** airtight **hava kabarcığı** air bubble **hava kirlenmesi** air pollution **hava koridoru** air corridor **hava kuvvetleri** air forces **hava otobüsü** airbus **hava raporu** weather report **hava üssü** air base **hava yolları** airlines **havaya uçurmak** to blow up

havaalanı airfield

havacı aviator

havacılık aviation

havacıva trivial useless

havadan for nothing, out of the blue

havadar airy

havadis news

havagazı coal gas

havai aerial; flighty, frivolous

havalandırmak to air

havalanmak to take off, to lift off; to be aired

havale transfer; assignment; money order; hek. eclampsia **havale etmek** to transfer; to assign; to refer **havale göndermek** to send a money order

havaleli bulky, top-heavy, cumbersome

havalı airy, breezy; eye-catching, attractive; pneumatic

havali neighbourhood

havalimanı airport

havan mortar **havan topu** howitzer

havari apostle

havasız airless, stuffy

havlamak to hark

havlu towel

havra synagogue

havsala comprehension; pelvis **havsalası almamak** to be unable to comprehend

havuç carrot

havuz pond, pool

Havva Eve

havyar caviar

havza *coğ.* river-basin

haya testicle

haya shame, modesty

hayasız shameless

hayal image; fancy, imagination; phantom, spectre **hayal kurmak** to dream **hayal kırıklığı** disappointment, letdown **hayal kırıklığına uğramak** to be disappointed **hayal kırıklığına uğratmak** to disappoint **hayale dalmak** to fall into a reverie **hayal meyal** faint, indistinct

hayalet ghost

hayalci daydreamer

hayali imaginary

hayalperest dreamer

hayat life **hayat kadını** prostitute **hayat memat meselesi** a matter of life and death **hayata atılmak** to begin to work **hayatını kazanmak** to earn one's living

hayati vital

haydi, hadi come on! **Haydi bakalım!** Come on then! **Haydi ordan!** Be off!, Clear out!

haydut bandit, robber, highwayman

hayhay All right! Certainly! Sure! With pleasure!

hayıflanmak to bemoan, to lament

hayır no

hayır goodness; benefaction, charity **hayır işlemek** to do good **hayır sahibi** benefactor, donor **hayra alamet değil** it augurs no good **hayra yormak** to interpret favourably **hayrını görmek** to enjoy the advantage of

Hayrola! What's the matter?

hayırdua blessing

hayırlı auspicious, blessed **hayırlısı olsun** let's hope for the best **Hayırlı yolculuklar!** Bon voyage! Have a good trip!

hayırsever benevolent, charitable

hayırsız useless, good-for-nothing; unfaithful

haykırış shouting, cry

haykırmak to cry out, to shout

haylaz lazy, idle

haylazlık idleness

hayli a good deal (of); fairly, pretty

hayran admirer, lover, fan **hayran bırak-**

mak to strike with admiration **hayran olmak** to admire
hayranlık admiration
hayranlıkla with admiration
hayrat pious foundations
hayret astonishment, amazement **hayret etmek** to be astonished
haysiyet dignity, honour
haysiyetli dignified, honourable
haysiyetsiz undignified, dishonourable
haysiyetsizlik dishonour
hayvan animal **hayvanat bahçesi** zoo
hayvansal animal
hayvanbilim zoology
haz pleasure, delight, gusto **haz duymak** to feel pleasure
hazan autumn
Hazar Denizi Caspian Sea
hazım digestion
hazımsızlık indigestion
hazır ready; present **hazır bulunmak** to be present, to attend **hazır etmek** to prepare, to get ready **Hazır ol!** Attention! **hazır olmak** to prepare oneself; to be prepared; to be present (at) **hazır para** ready money, cash
hazırcevap quick-witted, witty
hazırlamak to prepare
hazırlanmak to prepare, to get ready; to be prepared
hazırlık preparation **hazırlık yapmak** to make preparations
hazırlıklı prepared
hazırlıksız unprepared
hazırlop hard-boiled
hazin sad pathetic
hazine treasure; treasury
haziran June
hazmetmek to digest
hazne storehouse; (gun) chamber
heba waste, loss **heba etmek** to waste, to spoil **heba olmak** to be wasted
hece syllable
hecelemek to syllable
hedef target
hediye present, gift; price **hediye etmek** to give as a gift
hekim physician, doctor
hekimlik medical science, medicine
hektar hectare

hektolitre hectolitre
hektometre hectometre
hela water-closet, toilet
helak destruction **helak etmek** to kill, to destroy **helak olmak** to perish
helal lawful, legitimate **helal etmek** to give up sth to sb
hele especially, above all
helezon spiral
helezoni spiral
helikopter helicopter
helva halvah, halva
helyum *kim.* helium
hem and also; both ... and
hemen at once, immediately **hemen hemen** nearly, almost
hemencecik right away
hemfikir like-minded
hemoglobin hemoglobin
hemoroit hemorrhoid, piles
hemşeri fellow countryman, townsman
hemşerilik citizenship
hemşire nurse
hemzemin geçit level crossing
hendek ditch, trench
hengame uproar, confusion
hentbol handball
henüz yet, still, just
hep all whole; always **hep beraber** all together
hepsi all ot it; all of them
hepten entirely, completely
her even, each **her an** (at) any moment **her bakımdan** in every respect **her daim** every time, always **her günkü** everyday **her halde** in any case **her kim** whoever **her nasılsa** somehow, someway *Aİ.* **her ne** whatever **her ne kadar** although **her ne pahasına olursa olsun** at all costs **her ne zaman** whenever **her nedense** for some reason or other **her nerede** wherever **her nereye** wherever **her neyse** anyway, anyhow **her şey** everything **her şeyden önce** above all **her şeye rağmen** after all **her tarafta** on all sides, everywhere **her taraftan** from everywhere **her yerde/yere** everywhere **her yerinde** all over **her zaman** always

hercai fickle, capricious
hercaimenekşe pansy
hergele scoundrel, rake
herhalde probably
herhangi whoever, whatever, whichever
herif fellow, guy, bloke
herifçioğlu fellow, guy
herkes everybody, everyone
hesap calculation; bill; account hesabı kapamak to close the account hesabına gelmek to suit hesap açmak to open an account hesap cetveli slide rule hesap cüzdanı bank book, passbook hesap defteri account book hesap etmek to calculate, to work out hesap görmek to settle accounts, to pay the bill hesap pusulası bill hesap sormak to call to account hesap vermek to account for
hesaplamak to calculate
hesaplaşmak to settle accounts mutually
hesaplı economical
hesapsız countless, innumerable; unplanned
heterojen heterogeneous
heves desire, inclination heves etmek to have a fancy for
hevesli desirous, keen
hey! Look here!
heybe saddle-bag
heybet majesty, grandeur
heybetli majestic, grand
heyecan excitement
heyecanlandırmak to excite
heyecanlanmak to get excited
heyecanlı exciting; excited
heyecansız unexciting; unexcited
heyelan landslide
heyet commission, committee; board
heykel statue
heykeltıraş sculptor
heykeltıraşlık sculpture
hezimet rout hezimete uğramak to be completely defeated hezimete uğratmak to rout
hıçkırık hiccup, hiccough hıçkırık tutmak to have the hiccups
hıçkırmak to hiccup; to sob

hıfzısıhha hygiene
hık mık etmek to hum and haw
hımbıl slothful, slack, bone-lazy
hınç rancour, hatred hıncını almak to revenge
hınzır swine
hınzırlık dirty trick
hır row, quarrel hır çıkarmak to kick up a row, to start a quarrel
hırçın ill-tempered, peevish, cross
hırçınlaşmak to become cross
hırçınlık bad temper, peevishness
hırdavat hardware
hırgür squabble
hırıldamak to snarl
hırıltı growl, snarling
hırızma nose-ring
Hıristiyan Christian
Hıristiyanlık Christianity
hırka cardigan
hırlamak to snarl, to growl
hırpalamak to maltreat, to maul, to manhandle
hırpani ragged, tattered
hırs ambition, greed; anger, rage hırsını alamamak to be unable to vent one's anger hırsından çatlamak to be ready to burst with anger hırsını -dan almak to wreak one's wrath on sb
hırsız thief, burglar, robber
hırsızlık theft, burglary hırsızlık etmek to steal, to burgle
hırslanmak to get angry
hırslı ambitious, avaricious; furious, angry
hısım relative, kin hısım akraba kith and kin
hısımlık relationship, kinship
hışım anger, fury
hışırdamak to rustle
hışırtı rustling
hıyanet treacher, treason
hıyar cucumber; duffer, dolt, blockhead
hız speed hız göstergesi speedometer hızını alamamak to be unable to slow down
hızar large saw
hızlandırmak to accelerate
hızlı quick, fast, rapid; fast, quickly

hibe donation **hibe etmek** to donate
hiciv satire
hicvetmek to satirize
hicviye satirical poem
hiç no, none; never; not at all; ever; any; nothing **hiç değilse** at least **hiçe saymak** to disregard **hiç kimse** nobody, no one **hiç olmazsa** at least **hiç yoktan** for no reason
hiçbir no **hiçbiri** none **hiçbir şekilde** in no way **hiçbir şey** nothing **hiçbir yerde/yere** nowhere **hiçbir zaman** never
hiççilik nihilism
hiddet anger, rage
hiddetlenmek to become angry
hiddetli angry
hidrat hydrate
hidrodinamik hydrodynamics; hydrodynamics
hidroelektrik hydroelectric
hidrofil hydrophilic; absorbent
hidrofor air pressure tank
hidrograf hydrographer
hidrografi hydrography
hidrojen hydrogen **hidrojen bombası** hydrogen bomb
hidrokarbon hydrocarbon
hidroklorik asit hydrochloric acid
hidroksil hydroxyl
hidrolik hydraulic; hydraulics
hidroloji hydrology
hidrosfer hydrosphere
hidrostat hydrostat
hidroterapi *hek.* hydrotherapy
hikâye story, tale
hikâyeci short story writer
hikmet wisdom; hidden cause, reason
hilafet Caliphate
hilal crescent
hile trick, ruse, shift **hile yapmak** to swindle **-e hile karıştırmak** to rig
hileci deceitful, tricky, false
hilesiz genuine, pure
hilkat creation **hilkat garibesi** freak
himaye protection, defence **himaye etmek** to protect **himayesine almak** to patronize
himayesiz unprotected
hindi turkey
hindiba chicory

Hindistan India
hindistancevizi coconut
Hindistanlı Indian
hintfıstığı physic nut
Hint Okyanusu Indian Ocean
hinthurması palmyra
hintkamışı bamboo
hintkeneviri (Indian) hemp
hintyağı castor oil
hipermetrop far-sighted, longsighted
hipertansiyon hypertension
hipnotizma hypnotism
hipodrom hippodrome
hipofiz *anat.* hypophysis
hipotenüs hypotenuse
hipotez hypothesis
hippi hippie, hippy
his feeling, sensation; sense **hislerine kapılmak** to be carried away by one's feelings
hisar castle, fort
hisli sensitive
hisse share **hisse senedi** share, stock share
hissetmek to feel
hissi sentimental
hissiz insensitive, unfeeling
hissedar shareholder
hisseli divided into shares
histoloji histology
hişt! Psst! Look here!
hitabe address, speech
hitaben addressing
hitap addressing, address **hitap etmek** to address
Hitit Hittite
hiyerarşi hierarchy
hiyerarşik hierarchical
hiyeroglif hieroglyph
hiza level, line, alignment **hizaya gelmek** to get into line
hizip clique
hizipçilik cliquishness
hizmetçi servant
hizmetkâr servant
hoca hodja; teacher
hodbin selfish
hodbinlik selfishness
hohlamak to breathe (upon)
hokey hockey

hokka inkpot
hokkabaz juggler, conjurer
hokkabazlık jugglery, trickery
hol hall, vestibule
holding *tic.* holding company
Hollanda Holland, the Netherlands
Hollandaca Dutch
Hollandalı Dutchman, Hollander
homojen homogeneous
homolog homologous
homoseksüel homosexual
homoseksüellik homosexuality
homurdanmak to grumble, to grouch
homurtu grumbling, muttering
hoparlör loudspeaker
hoplamak to leap, to hop
hoppa flighty, frivolous
hoppalık flightiness, frivolity
hor contemptible, despicable **hor gör-mek** to look down upon, to despise **hor kullanmak** to misuse
horlamak to snore
horlamak to ill-treat, to despise
hormon hormone
horoz cock, rooster **horoz döğüşü** cock-fight
horozlanmak to strut about, to bluster
hortlak ghost
hortlamak to rise from the grave/dead; to arise again
hortum hose; whirlwind; trunk
horuldamak to snore
horultu snore, snoring
hostes stewardess, air hostess
hoş pleasant, nice, pretty **Hoş geldiniz! Welcome! hoş görmek** to tolerate, to allow **hoş görmemek** to disapprove **hoş karşılamak** to approve, to con-nive **hoşa gitmek** to be liked **hoşça kalın!** goodbye! **hoşuna gitmek** to ap-peal (to sb), to relish, to please
hoşaf stewed fruit, compote **hoşaf gibi** exhausted
hoşbeş chat
hoşgörü tolerance
hoşgörülü tolerant
hoşgörülülük tolerance
hoşgörüsüz intolerant
hoşgörüsüzlük intolerance
hoşlanmak to enjoy, to like

hoşlanmamak to dislike
hoşnut contented, pleased
hoşnutluk contentment
hoşnutsuz discontented
hoşnutsuzluk discontent
hoşsohbet conversationalist, good com-pany
hovarda gadabout, debauchee; prodi-gal, spendthrift
hovardalık debauchery, profligacy **ho-vardalık etmek** to go to town
hoyrat rough, coarse
hödük boor, bumpkin, hick
höpürdetmek to slurp
hörgüç hump
hörgüçlü humped
höyük mound, tumulus
hububat grain, cereals
hudut border, boundary; limit
hudutsuz boundless, unlimited
hukuk law; rights **Hukuk Fakültesi** the Law Faculty **hukuk müşaviri** legal ad-viser
hukukçu jurist
hukuki legal
hulasa summary; extract; in short
hulya daydream, fancy
humma fever
hummalı feverish
humus humus
hunhar bloodthirsty
huni funnel
hurafe superstition
hurda scrap, junk **hurda demir** scrap iron **hurda fiyatına** for its scrap value **hurdaya çıkarmak** to scrap, to junk
hurdacı scrap dealer, junkman
huri houri
hurma date
hurufat type
husul occuring, taking place **husule gelmek** to come into existence, to oc-cur **husule getirmek** to bring about, to produce
husumet hostility
husus matter, subject; point, respect
hususi special, private, personal
hususiyet particularity, peculiarity
husye testicle
huşu deep reverence, awe

huy temper, temperament; habit huy edinmek to form the habit of

huylanmak to feel suspicious; to be restless, to become touchy

huysuz bad tempered, cross, peevish

huysuzluk bad temper, snappishness

huysuzlanmak to fret, to become bad--tempered

huzur peace, comfort

huzurevi old age asylum

huzurlu at ease, in peace

huzursuz uneasy, unquiet

huzursuzluk unease, unrest

hücre cell

hücum attack, assault hücum etmek to attack, to assail

hücumbot assault boat

hükmen legally; sp. by the decision of the referee hükmen mağlup sayılmak to default

hükmetmek to rule, to command; to sentence, to judge

hüküm rule, authority; command; sentence, judgement; importance, effect hüküm giymek to be condemned hüküm sürmek to reign, to rule

hükümdar monarch, ruler

hükümdarlık sovereignty; kingdom

hükümet government, administration hükümet darbesi coup d'etat hükümet etmek to govern hükümet konağı government office

hükümlü sentenced, condemned

hükümran ruling, sovereign

hükümranlık sovereignty

hükümsüz null, invalid

hümanist humanist

hümanizm humanism

hüner skill

hünerli skilful

hünersiz unskilled

hüngürdemek to sob hüngür hüngür ağlamak to weep bitterly

hür free, independent

hürriyet freedom, liberty

hürmet respect, regard hürmet etmek to respect

hürmeten out ot respect

hürmetsizlik disrespect

hüsnükuruntu fond imagination, wishful thinking

hüsnüniyet goodwill

hüsran disappointment hüsrana uğramak to be disappointed

hüviyet identity hüviyet cüzdanı identity card

hüzün sadness, sorrow, grief

hüzünlenmek to feel sad

hüzünlü sad, sorrowful, gloomy

I

ıhlamur lime tree, linden tree; lime tea

ıkınmak to strain while defecating ıkına sıkına with great effort ıkınıp sıkınmak to grunt and strain

ılgıt ılgıt gently

ılıca hot spring, spa

ılık lukewarm

ılıklaşmak to become lukewarm

ılıklık lukewarmness

ılım moderation

ılıman mild, temperate

ılımlı moderate, equable, temperate

ılımlılık moderation

ılıştırmak to make tepid

ıpıslak very wet, soaked

ıra character

ırak distant, far

Irak Iraq

Iraklı Iraqi, Iraki

ıraksak divergent

ırgalamak to shake; arg. to concern, to interest

ırgat day labourer, workman; capstan

ırk race

ırkçı racialist

ırkçılık racialism

ırmak river

ırz chastity ırz düşmanı rapist ırza tecavüz rape, violation ırzına geçmek to violate, to rape

ısı heat

ısıl thermal, thermic

ısın calorie

ısındırmak to break in, to cause to like

ısınma heating, warming up

ısınmak to warm; to warm oneself; *sp.* to warm up

ısıölçer calorimeter

ısırgan nettle

ısırık bite, sting

ısırmak to bite

ısıtıcı heater

ısıtmak to heat, to warm

ıska miss ıska geçmek to miss; *arg.* to disregard, to ignore

ıskalamak to miss

ıskarmoz *den.* oarlock, rowlock, thole pin; *hayb.* barracuda

ıskarta discard, scrap; discarded ıskartaya çıkarmak to discard, to scrap, to junk

ıskonto discount ıskonto etmek to discount

ıskuna schooner

ıslah improvement, reform ıslah etmek to improve, to better ıslah olmak to improve one's conduct ıslah olmaz incorrigible

ıslahat reforms, improvements ıslahat yapmak to make reforms

ıslahatçı reformer

ıslahevi reformatory

ıslak wet

ıslaklık wetness

ıslatmak to wet

ıslık whistle ıslık çalmak to whistle

ısmarlama order; ordered, made to order

ısmarlamak to order

ıspanak spinach

ıspatula spatula

ıspazmoz spasm

ısrar insistence ısrar etmek to insist

ısrarla insistently

ısrarlı insistent

ıssız lonely, deserted

ıssızlık loneliness

ıstakoz lobster

ıstampa inkpad

ıstırap suffering, pain ıstırap çekmek to suffer

ışık light; lamp ışık tutmak to shed light (on); to light the way (for)

ışıklandırmak to illuminate

ışıklı illuminated, lighted ışıklı reklam neon sign

ışıldak searchlight, projector

ışıldamak to sparkle, to twinkle

ışıl ışıl sparklingly, glitteringly

ışıltı glitter, twinkle

ışıltılı glittering

ışımak to glow, to radiate

ışın ray

ışınım radiation

ışınlamak to radiate

ıtır perfume, aroma ıtır çiçeği geranium

ıtırlı aromatic, perfumed

ıtriyat perfumes

ıvır zıvır trifles, baubles, bunkum

ızbandut hulk, colossus ızbandut gibi giantlike

ızgara grill, grilled, gridiron ızgara köfte grilled meatballs ızgara yapmak to grill

i

iade giving back iade etmek to give back, to return iadeli taahhütlü registered and reply paid

iane donation, aid

iaşe subsistence, feeding

ibadet worship ibadet etmek to worship

ibadethane house of God, temple

ibare sentence, paragraph, clause

ibaret consisting of, composed of

ibibik hoopoe

ibik *hayb.* comb, crest *anat.* crista

iblis Satan, the Devil

ibra acquittal ibra etmek to acquit

İbrani Hebrew

İbranice Hebrew

ibraz presentation ibraz etmek to present, to show

ibre needle, pointer

ibret lesson, example ibret almak to draw a lesson (from) ibret olmak to be a lesson to

ibrik ewer

ibrişim silk thread

icabet acceptance icabet etmek (invitation) to accept

icap requirement, necessity **icap etmek** to be necessary **icabına bakmak** to see to **icabında** if needed, if need be, if necessary

icar rent, hire **icara vermek** to let out

icat invention **icat etmek** to invent

icra execution; performance **icra etmek** to execute, to perform **icra memuru** bailiff, executive officer **icraya vermek** to refer to the court bailiff

icraat activities, performances

icracı performer

iç inside, interior; heart, mind; stomach, intestines; kernel; interior, internal, inner **iç açıcı** cheering, pleasant **iç çamaşırı** underclothing, underwear **iç çekmek** to sigh **iç etmek** to appropriate, to pocket **iç hastalıkları** internal diseases **iç içe** one within the other **iç lastik** inner tube **iç savaş** civil war **iç sıkıcı** boring **iç sıkıntısı** boredom **iç ticaret** home trade **iç tüketim** home consumption **iç tüzük** house regulations **içi açılmak** to be cheered up **içi cız etmek** to be deeply moved **içi dışı bir** sincere **içi geçmek** to doze off **içi gitmek** to desire strongly **içi içine sığmamak** to be unable to contain oneself **içi içini yemek** to fret about **içi kan ağlamak** to be in deep sorrow **içi parçalanmak** to be cut to the heart **içinden geçirmek** to think **içinden gelmek** to feel like **içinden okumak** to read to oneself **içine almak** to contain **içine dert olmak** to be a thorn in one's flesh **içine doğmak** to have a hunch **içine etmek** to spoil **içine kurt düşmek** to feel suspicious **içini açmak/dökmek** to unburden one's heart

içbükey concave

içderi endoderm

içecek drink, beverage

içedönük introvert

içegöç immigration

içekapanık autistic

içerde inside

içeri inside, interior; in **içeri girmek** to go in, to enter

içerik content

içerlek set back, standing back

içerlemek to resent, to be grieved

içermek to contain, to include, to comprise

içevlilik endogamy

içgöç internal migration

içgüdü instinct

içgüdüsel instinctive

içgüvey(si) bridegroom who lives in his wife's house

içilir drinkable

içilmez undrinkable

içim draught, sip

için for

içinde in; inside

içindekiler contents

içinden from the inside

içişleri internal affairs **İçişleri Bakanlığı** Ministry of the Interior **İçişleri Bakanı** Interior Minister

içki drink, booze **içki âlemi** drinking bout, binge **içkiye düşkün** addicted to drink **içkiyi fazla kaçırmak** to have taken a drop too much

içkici drinker

içkili drunk

içkulak inner ear

içli sensitive; sad, touching

içlidışlı familiar, intimate

içme drinking; mineral spring **içme suyu** drinking water

içmek to drink

içmimar interior decorator

içmimarlık interior decoration

içten sincere; from within

içtenlik sincerity

içtenlikle sincerely

içtima meeting

içtimai social

içyağı suet

içyüz inside story, real truth

idam capital punishment, execution **idam etmek** to execute

idame continuance

idare management, direction; administration, government; economy, thrift **idare etmek** to administer, to govern; to manage; to economize **idare etmez** it doesn't pay **idare heyeti** board of directors

idareci
104

idareci manager, administrator

idarecilik administration

idareli economical, thrifty idareli kullanmak to use economically

idareten temporarily

idari administrative

iddia claim; bet, wager iddia etmek to claim; to pretend, to purport iddiaya girmek/tutuşmak to bet

iddiacı assertive, persistent

iddialı pretentious

iddianame indictment

iddiasız unpretentious

ideal ideal

idealist idealist; idealistic

idealize etmek to idealize

idealizm idealism

ideoloji ideology

ideolojik ideological

idman workout, training

idrak perception; reaching idrak etmek to perceive; to reach

idrar urine idrar torbası urinary bladder

idraryolu urethra

ifa performance, execution ifa etmek to perform, to execute

ifade expression; deposition, statement ifadesini almak to question, to interrogate ifade vermek to give evidence, to testify

iffet chastity

iffetli chaste

iffetsiz unchaste

iflah salvation iflah olmaz incorrigible iflahı kesilmek to be exhausted iflahını kesmek to exhaust

iflas bankruptcy iflas etmek to go bankrupt iflas ettirmek to bankrupt

ifrat excess, overdoing ifrata kaçmak to overdo ifrata vardırmak to carry to excess

ifraz separation; biy. secretion

ifşa divulgation, disclosure ifşa etmek to divulge, to disclose

ifşaat revelations

iftar the breaking of the Ramadan fast; the evening meal during Ramadan iftar etmek to break one's fast

iftihar pride iftihar etmek to be proud ot

iftira slander iftira etmek to slander

iftiracı slanderer

iğ spindle

iğde oleaster, elaeagnus

iğdiş castrated iğdiş etmek to castrate

iğfal rape iğfal etmek to rape

iğne needle, pin; fish hook; syringe; biting word, pinprick iğne deliği the eye of a needle iğne ipliğe dönmek to become skin and bones iğne olmak to have an injection iğne yapmak to give an injection iğneye iplik geçirmek to thread a needle

iğnelemek to pin, to prick; to hurt with words

iğneleyici picking; biting

iğneli having a pin; biting

iğrenç disgusting, loathsome, abhorrent

iğrençlik repulsiveness

iğrendirmek to disgust

iğrenmek to loathe, to abhor

iğreti borrowed

ihale adjudication, awarding ihale etmek to adjudicate, to award ihaleye çıkarmak to put out to tender

ihanet treachery, betrayal ihanet etmek to betray

ihbar denunciation ihbar etmek to denounce

ihbarname notice, warning

ihlal disobeying, violation ihlal etmek to break, to violate

ihmal negligence, inattention ihmal etmek to neglect

ihmalci neglectful

ihracat exports

ihracatçı exporter

ihraç exportation, expulsion ihraç etmek to export; to expel

ihsan gift, grant ihsan etmek to grant, to bestow

ihtar warning ihtar etmek to warn

ihtisas specialization ihtisas yapmak to specialize in

ihtilaf dispute, conflict

ihtilaflı controversial

ihtilal revolution

ihtilalci revolutionary

ihtimal probability; probably ihtimal

vermek to deem likely
ihtimam care, painstaking **ihtimam göstermek** to take pains
ihtimamlı painstaking, careful
ihtimamsız careless, slipshod
ihtiras passion
ihtiraslı passionate
ihtişam magnificence, splendour
ihtiva containing, inclusion **ihtiva etmek** to contain, to include
ihtiyaç necessity, need **ihtiyacı olmak** to need
ihtiyar old, aged
ihtiyarlamak to grow old
ihtiyarlık oldness, old age
ihtiyar choice, option
ihtiyari optional
ihtiyat precaution; *ask.* reserves **ihtiyat akçesi** *tic.* reserve fund **ihtiyat kuvvetleri** *ask.* reserve forces
ihtiyatla cautiously
ihtiyatlı cautious
ihtiyatsız imprudent, incautious
ihtiyatsızlık imprudence, rashness **ihtiyatsızlık etmek** to act imprudently
ihya vivification, revitalization **ihya etmek** to vivify, to revitalize
ikamet dwelling, residing **ikamet etmek** to dwell, to reside
ikametgâh residence
ikaz warning **ikaz etmek** to warn
iken while, when
iki two **iki ayağını bir pabuca sokmak** to run sb (clean) off his feet **iki dirhem bir çekirdek** dressed up to kill **iki eli kanda olsa** no matter how busy he is **iki yakası bir araya gelmemek** to be unable to make two ends meet **ikide bir** now and then
ikidilli bilingual
ikilem dilemma
ikili bilateral; (cards) two
ikilik disunion, disagreement; duality
ikinci second
ikincil secondary
ikindi afternoon
ikindiüstü in the afternoon
ikircik hesitancy
ikirciklenmek to hesitate
ikircikli hesitant

ikişer two each, two at a time **ikişer ikişer** two by two, in twos
ikiyaşayışlı amphibious
ikiyüzlü hypocritical, twofaced, insincere; hypocrite
ikiyüzlülük hypocrisy
ikiz twin **İkizler (burcu)** Gemini
ikizkenar *mat.* isosceles **ikizkenar üçgen** isosceles triangle
iklim climate
ikmal completing, finishing; *ask.* supply, reinforcement; (exam) condition, make-up **ikmal etmek** to complete, to finish
ikna persuasion, inducement **ikna etmek** to persuade, to convince
ikram honouring; discount **ikram etmek** to show honour to; to offer, to treat to; to discount
ikramiye bonus; prize **ikramiye kazanmak** to win a prize
ikrar confession **ikrar etmek** to confess, to acknowledge
iksir elixir
iktibas quotation, citation **iktibas etmek** to quote
iktidar power; sexual potency **iktidar partisi** the party in power **iktidara gelmek** to come to power **iktidarda olmak** to be in power
iktidarsız impotent
iktidarsızlık impotence
iktisaden economically
iktisadi economic
iktisat economy; economics **İktisat Fakültesi** the School of Economics
iktisatçı economist
iktisap acquisition **iktisap etmek** to acquire
ila to, up to; until
ilaç medicine
ilaçlamak to medicate
ilaçlı medicated
ilah god
ilahe goddess
ilahi divine, heavenly
ilahiyat theology **İlahiyat Fakültesi** the School of Theology
ilahiyatçı theologian
ilam judicial decree, engrossment

ilan announcement, declaration; advertisement **ilan etmek** to declare, to announce; to advertise

ilave addition; additional **ilave etmek** to add

ilçe county, district

ile with; by; and

ilelebet for ever

ileri forward part, front; future; advanced; forward, ahead **ileri atılmak** to spring forward, to rush forward **ileri gelenler** notables **ileri gitmek** to go forward; to go too far **ileri sürmek** to put forward, to bring forward **ileriyi görmek** to foresee

ilerici progressive

ileride, ilerde in the future; ahead

ilerisi the farther part; the future

ileriye forward

ilerlemek to go forward, to proceed; to progress, to advance; (time) to pass away

iletim transmission; *fiz.* conduction

iletişim communication

iletken conductor

iletkenlik conductivity

iletki protractor

iletmek to transmit, to carry; to conduct, to convey

ilga abolition **ilga etmek** to abolish

ilgi interest; relation, connection **ilgi göstermek** to show interest **ilgi uyandırmak** to arouse sb's interest

ilgilendirmek to interest, to concern

ilgilenmek to be interested (in, ile)

ilgili interested; relevant

ilginç interesting

ilgisiz indifferent, unconcerned

ilgisizlik indifference, unconcern

ilham inspiration

ilik buttonhole

ilik marrow **iliklerine kadar ıslanmak** to be soaked to the skin

iliklemek to button up

ilim science

ilinti connection

ilişik attached; connection, relation **ilişiğini kesmek** to sever one's connection with; to discharge

ilişki relation, connection; affinity, bond

ilişki kurmak to get in touch with; to have an affair (with)

ilişkili connected, relevant

ilişmek to touch

iliştirmek to attach, to fasten

ilk first; initial **ilk defa** for the first time **ilk fırsatta** at the first opportunity **ilk göz ağrısı** first child; first love

ilkçağ antiquity

ilkin at first, to begin with

ilkbahar spring

ilke principle, basis

ilkel primitive

ilkellik primitiveness

ilkin first, in the first place; at first, at the beginning

ilkokul primary school

ilköğretim primary education

ilkönce first of all

ilkyardım first aid

illa, illaki whatever happens, come what may

illallah I'm sick of it!

ille by all means; especially

illet disease

illüstrasyon illustration

ilmek, ilmik loop; noose

ilmi scientific

ilmiklemek to loop

ilmühaber certificate

iltica taking refuge **iltica etmek** to take refuge in

iltifat compliment **iltifat etmek** to pay a compliment

iltihap inflammation

iltihaplanmak to become inflamed

iltimas favouritism, protection **iltimas etmek** to favour, to protect

iltimasçı protector, patron

ima allusion, hint **ima etmek** to hint at, to allude to

imal manufacture **imal etmek** to manufacture, to produce

imalat products

imalatçı manufacturer

imalathane workshop, small factory

imalı allusive

imam imam

imambayıldı a dish of eggplants with olive oil

iman faith, belief **iman etmek** to have faith in Allah (God) **imana gelmek** to be converted to Islam; to see reason **imanı gevremek** to suffer a lot; to be exhausted

imanlı believing, religious

imansız unbelieving; cruel; unbeliever

imar public improvement, public works **imar etmek** to improve, to render prosperous

imbat daytime summer sea breeze

imbik retort, still **imbikten geçirmek** to distil

imdat help

imece doing a work together for one of the members of the community

imge image

imgelem imagination

imgelemek to imagine

imha destruction, annihilation **imha etmek** to destroy, to annihilate

imkân possibility, means

imkânsız impossible

imla spelling, orthography

imparator emperor

imparatoriçe empress

imparatorluk empire

imrenmek to envy, to covet

imtihan examination

imtiyaz privilege, distinction

imtiyazlı privileged

imza signature **imza etmek** to sign **imza sahibi** signer, signatory

imzalamak to sign

imzalı signed

imzasız unsigned

in den, lair

inak *fel.* dogma

inan belief

inanç belief; confidence

inançlı believer; believing

inandırıcı persuasive

inanılmaz unbelievable, incredible

inanış belief, faith

inanmak to believe; to trust

inat obstinacy, stubbornness **inat etmek** to be obstinate **inadı tutmak** to have a fit of obstinacy

inatçı stubborn, obstinate

inatçılık obstinacy

inayet favour, grace

ince thin; subtle; slim **inceden inceye** minutely **ince eleyip sık dokumak** to split hairs

incebağırsak *anat.* small intestine

incehastalık *kon.* tuberculosis

inceleme research, study

incelemek to examine, to study

incelik thinness; subtlety; slimness

incelmek to become thin

inceltmek to thin spect

inceyağ thin oil

inci pearl

incik shin **incik kemiği** shinbone

İncil the New Testament; the Gospel

incinmek to be hurt; to be injured; to be bruised; to be sprained

incir fig **incir çekirdeğini doldurmaz** trivial, trifling

incitici hurting

incitmek to hurt

inç inch

indeks index

indirgeme reduction

indirgemek to reduce

indirim reduction, discount

indirimli reduced in price **indirimli satış** sale

indirmek to take down, to lower; to bring down, to reduce

inek cow; *arg.* swot, grind

ineklemek *arg.* to swot, to grind

infaz execution **infaz etmek** to execute

infilak explosion, burst **infilak etmek** to explode, to burst

infraruj infrared

İngiliz English; Englishman **İngiliz anahtarı** monkey wrench

İngilizce English

İngiltere England

inhisar monopoly

inildemek to moan

inilti moan, groan

inisiyatif initiative

iniş downward slope, descent, downhill **iniş aşağı** downhill, downwards **iniş çıkış** descent and ascent

inkâr denial, refusal **inkâr etmek** to deny, to gainsay

inkılap revolution

inkıta interruption inkıtaa uğramak to be interrupted, to cease
inkişaf development inkişaf etmek to develop
inlemek to moan, to groan
inme stroke, apoplexy, paralysis inme inmek to have a stroke
inmek to descend; to alight, to dismount; (plane) to land; (prices) to fall
inmeli paralysed
inorganik inorganic
insaf justice, fairness; Have a heart! insaf etmek to take pity (on) insafa gelmek to show mercy
insaflı just, fair
insafsız unjust, unfairly
insafsızlık injustice, unfairness
insan human being, human insan hakları human rights insan içine çıkmak to go out in public
insanbilim anthropology
insanbilimci anthropologist
insanca properly, decently
insancıl humanitarian
insani human, humanely
insaniyet humanity, mankind; humaneness, kindness
insaniyetli humane, kind
insaniyetsiz inhuman
insanlık humanity, mankind; humaneness
insanoğlu man, mankind
insanüstü superhuman
inşa building inşa etmek to build
inşaat constructions, buildings inşaat mühendisi civil engineer
inşaatçı builder, constructor
inşallah God willing! I hope so! I hope that...
integrasyon mat. integration
intiba impression
intibak adaptation intibak etmek to adjust oneself to
intifa benefit
intihar suicide intihar etmek to commit suicide
intikal transition; perception intikal etmek to be inherited
intikam revenge intikam almak to revenge, to avenge

intizam order, tidiness
intizamlı tidy, neat
intizamsız untidy, irregular
inzibat discipline; military policeman
inziva seclusion inzivaya çekilmek to seclude oneself
ip rope, string ip atlamak to skip rope ipe çekmek to hang ipe sapa gelmez irrelevant, nonsensical ipin ucunu kaçırmak to lose control of iple çekmek to look forward to
ipsiz vagabond
ipek silk ipek gibi silken, silky
ipekböceği silkworm
ipince very thin
iplemek to mind, to respect, to heed
iplememek not to give a damn, not to care
iplik thread
ipnotize hypnotized ipnotize etmek to hypnotize
ipnotizma hypnotism
ipnotizmacı hypnotizer
ipnoz hypnosis
ipotek mortgage ipotek etmek to mortgage
ipotekli mortgaged
iptal cancellation, annulment iptal etmek to cancel, to annual
iptidai primitive
ipucu clue ipucu vermek to give a clue
irade will, volition; command, decree
iradedışı involuntary
iradeli strongwilled
iradesiz irresolute, weak
iradi voluntary
İran Iran, Persia
İranlı Iranian, Persian
irat income
irdeleme examination
irdelemek to examine, to scrutinize, to discuss
irfan knowledge
iri large huge
iribaş hayb. tadpole
irice largish
irikıyım huge; large chopped
irileşmek to become large
irili ufaklı large and small
irilik largeness

irin pus
irinlenmek to suppurate
iris *anat.* iris
iriyarı huge, burly
irkilmek to be startled
İrlanda Ireland
İrlandalı Irish
irmik semolina irmik helvası semolina
  halva
irs inheritance
irsi hereditary
irsiyet heredity
irtibat connection; communication irtibat subayı liaison officer
irtical improvisation
irticalen extemporaneously, impromptu
irtifa altitude
is soot
İsa Jesus Christ
isabet hitting (the mark); saying/doing
  exactly the right thing; falling (by
  chance) to isabet etmek to hit the
  mark; to say/do just the right thing;
  (prize, etc.) to fall to, to win
isabetli right, exact
isabetsiz inexact, improper
ise if ise de even if, although
ishal diarrhoea ishal olmak to have diarrhoea
isilik heat spots isilik olmak to have
  heat spots
isim name; noun; title; reputation isim
  takmak to nickname isim vermek to
  give a name, to name
isimsiz anonymous, innominate
iskambil playing card iskambil kâğıdı
  playing cards iskambil oynamak to
  play cards
iskân settling iskân etmek to house; to
  settle
İskandinavya Scandinavia
İskandinavyalı Scandinavian
iskarpin shoe
iskele landing-place, wharf, quay, pier;
  scaffolding; seaport iskele kurmak to
  erect scaffolding
iskelet skeleton; framework
iskemle chair
iskete finch

İskoç Scotch
İskoçya Scotland
İskoçyalı Scotsman, Scot; Scottish
iskonto discount iskonto etmek to discount
iskorbüt scurvy
İslam Islam
İslami Islamic
İslamiyet Islamism
İslamlaştırmak to Islamize
İslav Slav; Slavic
islemek to soot
isli sooty
ismen by name
isnat ascribing, attributing isnat etmek
  to ascribe, to attribute
İspanya Spain
İspanyol Spaniard; Spanish
İspanyolca Spanish
ispat proof ispat etmek to prove
ispatlamak to prove
ispati (cards) clubs
ispinoz chaffinch
ispirto alcohol
ispiyon informer, snitcher
ispiyonlamak to inform on, to sneak, to
  snitch
israf squandering, waste israf etmek to
  squander, to waste
İsrail Israel; Israeli
istasyon station
istatistik statistics; statistic
istavrit horse mackerel
istavroz cross; crucifix
istek desire, wish; request istek duymak to want, to feel a desire for
isteka billiard cue
istekli desirous, willing
isteksiz unwilling, reluctant
isteksizlik reluctance, unwillingness
istem request, demand; *ruhb.* volition
istemek to want, to desire, to wish; to
  ask for; to need, to want istemeyerek
  unwillingly, reluctantly istemiye istemiye unwillingly ister istemez willy--
  nilly isteyerek freely, willingly, readily
istemli voluntary
istemsiz involuntary
isteri hysteria
isterik hysterical

istiap capacity istiap haddi maximum capacity

istibdat despotism

istida petition

istidat aptitude, talent

istidatlı talented

istif storage, stacking istif etmek to stow istifini bozmamak to keep up appearances

istifçi packer, stevedore

istifçilik packing, stowage

istiflemek to stow, to pack

istifa resignation istifa etmek to resign

istifade profit, advantage istifade etmek to benefit by, to take advantage of

istifadeli profitable

istifrağ vomiting istifrağ etmek to vomit

istihbarat information, intelligence istihbarat bürosu information office istihbarat dairesi intelligence department

istihdam employment istihdam etmek to employ

istihkak merit, deserts; ration

istihkâm fortification; ask. military engineering istihkâm subayı engineer officer

istihsal production istihsal etmek to produce

istiklal independence İstiklal Marşı the Turkish National Anthem İstiklal Savaşı the War of Independence

istikrar stabilization

istikrarlı stabilized, settled

istikrarsızlık instability

istikraz loan

istila invasion istila etmek to invade

istilacı invader

istimlak expropriation istimlak etmek to expropriate

istinaden based on, relying on

istinat support istinat etmek to lean upon, to be based istinat ettirmek to base, to ground

istirahat rest, repose istirahat etmek to rest, to repose

istirham imploring, requesting istirham etmek to implore, to plead

istiridye oyster

istismar exploiting istismar etmek to exploit

istismarcı exploiter

istisna exception

istisnai exceptional

istisnasız without exception

istişare consultation istişare etmek to consult

istişari consultative

İsveç Sweden

İsveçli Swedish

İsviçre Switzerland

İsviçreli Swiss

isyan rebellion, revolt, mutiny isyan etmek to rebel, to revolt

isyancı rebel, mutineer

isyankâr rebellious, mutinous

iş work; job, occupation; business; affair, matter; service iş başında at work iş bitirmek to finish a job iş bölümü division of labour iş çıkarmak to raise difficulties iş görmek to do a job, to work, to be of use iş güç occupation, business iş günü working day, workday iş güvenliği security of work iş hukuku labour legislation iş kazası industrial accident iş işten geçti! It's too late! iş olacağına varır what will be will be iş sözleşmesi labour contract iş olsun diye just for the sake of doing sth. iş ve işçi bulma kurumu employment exchange işe yaramak to be of use, to work işi azıtmak to go too far işi başından aşkın olmak to be up to one's ears in work işi oluruna bırakmak to let things take their own course işi sağlama bağlamak to make sure of işi yüzüne gözüne bulaştırmak to make a mess of things işinden olmak to lose one's job işine gelmek to suit one's book işin içinde iş var there are wheels within wheels işin içinden çıkamamak to be unable to settle sth işin içinden çıkmak to get out of a difficulty işin içyüzü the inside story, the real truth işini bitirmek to finish one's work; to finish sb off işten çıkarmak to dismiss, to sack

işadamı businessman

işaret sign, mark; signal işaret etmek to point, to point out, to indicate; to

make a mark **işaret koymak** to mark
işaret sıfatı demonstrative adjective
işaret zamiri demonstrative pronoun
işaretlemek to mark
işaretparmağı forefinger, index finger
işbaşı hour at which work begins **işbaşı yapmak** to start work, to clock in
işbirliği collaboration
işbirlikçi collaborator
işçi worker, labourer **işçi sınıfı** working class
işemek to urinate, to piss
işgal occupation, possession **işgal altında** under military occupation **işgal etmek** to occupy
işgücü working power, laborer-power
işgüzar officious
işgüzarlık officiousness
işitmek to hear **işitmemezlikten gelmek** to pretend not to hear
işitsel auditory
işkembe paunch; tripe **işkembe çorbası** tripe soup
işkembeci tripe restaurant
işkence torture **işkence etmek/yapmak** to torture
işkil suspicion
işkillenmek to be suspicious
işkilli suspicious
işlek busy
işlem procedure; *mat.* operation
işleme handwork, embroidery
işlemek to work, to run, to operate; (a subject) to treat of, to deal with; to embroider; to carve
işlemeli embroidered
işlenmemiş raw, unprocessed
işlenmiş processed
işletme enterprise; running, working; exploitation **İşletme Fakültesi** School of Business Administration **işletme müdürü** managing director
işletmeci administrator, manager
işletmecilik business administration, management
işletmek to operate, to run; to exploit, to work; to have sb on, to hoax
işlev function
işlevsel functional
işlik workshop

işporta pedlar's pushcart **işporta malı** shoddy goods
işportacı pedlar, peddler
işportacılık peddling
işret carousal
işsiz unemployed
işsizlik unemployment **işsizlik sigortası** unemployment insurance
iştah appetite **iştah açıcı** appetizing **iştah açmak** to whet the appetite
iştahlı having an appetite
iştahsız having no appetite
işte Here! Here it is!; Look! See! **işte böyle** Such is the matter
iştigal occupation
iştirak participation **iştirak etmek** to participate (in)
işve coquetry
işveli coquettish
işveren employer
işyeri office, workplace
it dog **itoğlu it** son of a bitch
itaat obedience **itaat etmek** to obey
itaatli obedient
itaatsiz disobedient
itaatsizlik disobedience
italik italic
İtalya Italy
İtalyan Italian
İtalyanca Italian
itelemek to nudge
itfaiye fire brigade
itfaiyeci fireman
ithaf dedication **ithaf etmek** to dedicate
ithal import, importation **ithal etmek** to import **ithal malı** imported goods
ithalat imports
ithalatçı importer
itham accusation, charge **itham etmek** to accuse, to charge
itibar esteem, prestige, regard **itibar etmek** to esteem, to consider **itibar görmek** to be respected
itibari nominal, fictitious
itibarlı esteemed; influential
itikat creed, belief, faith **itikat etmek** to believe in
itikatlı believing
itilaf entente, agreement

itimat confidence, trust **itimat etmek** to have confidence in, to trust

itimatname credentials

itina care **itina göstermek** to give close attention to **itina ile** carefully

itinalı careful, attentive

itinasız careless, inattentive

itiraf confession, admission

itiraz objection **itiraz etmek** to object

itirazcı objector

itirazsız without any objection

itişmek to push one another **itişip kakışmak** to push and shove one another

itiyat habit **itiyat edinmek** to form the habit of

itmek to push **itip kakmak** to push and shove

ittifak alliance, agreement

ittifakla unanimously

ittihat union

ivedi haste, hurry; urgent

ivedilik urgency

ivedilikle urgently, hurriedly

ivme acceleration

iye possessor

iyelik possession **iyelik adılı/zamiri** possessive pronoun

iyi good; well **iyi etmek** to cure; to do well **iyi gelmek** to do good, to benefit **iyi gitmek** to go well; to suit **iyi gün dostu** fair weather friend **iyi hal kâğıdı** certificate of good conduct **iyi huylu** good-natured, mild **iyi kalpli** kind-hearted **iyi ki** fortunately, luckily **iyi kötü** somehow, more or less **iyi olmak** to recover, to get better **iyisi mi** the best thing to do is ...

iyice pretty well, rather good, thoroughly, completely

iyileşmek to get better, to improve; to recover

iyileştirmek to make better, to improve, to cure

iyilik goodness; favour **iyilik etmek** to do good

iyilikbilir grateful

iyilikbilmez ungrateful

iyiliksever benevolent

iyimser optimist; optimistic

iyimserlik optimism

iyon *kim.* ion

iyot *kim.* iodine

iyotlu iodic

iz trace, track; print, mark **iz sürmek** to trace, to trail

izafi relative

izafiyet relativity

izah explanation **izah etmek** to explain

izahat explanations

izale removing **izale etmek** to remove

izan understanding, intelligence

izci scout, boy scout

izdüşüm *mat.* projection

izdiham crowd

izin permission; licence **izin almak** to get permission **izin vermek** to permit, to give permission

izinli on leave; on vacation

izinsiz without permission

İzlanda Iceland

İzlandalı Icelander

izlemek to follow, to trace; to watch

izleyici spectator

izlenim impression

izmarit sea bream; cigarette butt, stub

izolasyon isolation

izolatör isolator

izole insulated; isolated **izole bant** insulating tape **izole etmek** to isolate, to insulate

izoterm isotherm

izotop isotope

izzet might, honour

izzetinefis self-respect

J

jaguar jaguar

jale dew

jaluzi Venetian blind

jambon ham

jandarma police soldier, gendarme; gendarmerie

jant rim

Japon Japanese

Japonca Japanese

japongülü camellia
Japonya Japan
jarse jersey
jartiyer garter
jelatin gelatine
jelatinli gelatinous
jeneratör generator
jenerik (film) credits
jeodezi geodesy
jeofizik geophysics
jeolog geologist
jeoloji geology
jeolojik geologic
jeopolitik geopolitics; geopolitical
jeotermal geothermal
jeotermik geothermic
jest gesture
jet jet (plane)
jeton token
jigolo gigolo
jikle choke
jilet safety-razor
jimnastik gymnastic
jimnastikçi gymnast
jinekolog gynecologist
jinekoloji gynecology
jiujitsu jiujitsu
joker joker
jokey jockey
jöle jelly
jön juvenile; handsome/young man
judo judo
judocu judoist
jul joule
jumbo jet jumbo jet
jurnal denunciation, report **jurnal et-mek** to denounce, to report
jurnalci denouncer, informer
jübile jübile
Jüpiter Jupiter
jüpon underskirt
jüri jury **jüri üyesi** juror

K

kaba rough **kaba et** buttocks **kaba sa-ba** common, coarse **kaba söz** vulgar
expression
kabaca roughly; biggish
kabadayı bully, tough guy, roughneck
kabadayılık bravado **kabadayılık tasla-mak** to play the tough, to bluster
kabahat fault, offence **kabahat bulmak** to find fault with **kabahati birinin üze-rine atmak** to lay the blame on sb
kabahatli faulty, guilty
kabahatsiz innocent, faultless
kabak squash, pumpkin, gourd; bald, bare; (watermelon) unripe **kabak çe-kirdeği** pumpkin seed **kabak kafalı** baldheaded **kabak başına patlamak** to carry the can **kabak çıkmak** to turn out to be tasteless **kabak tadı ver-mek** to pall, to cloy **kabak tatlısı** pumpkin with syrup and walnuts
kabakulak hek. mumps **kabakulak ol-mak** to have the mumps
kabalaşmak to become impolite
kabalık roughness, coarseness **kabalık etmek** to behave rudely
kaban hooded overcoat
kabarcık bubble; blister
kabare cabaret
kabarık swollen, puffy
kabarıklık swelling, puffiness
kabarmak to swell, to bloat; to puff out; to increase; (sea) to become rough
kabartı swelling, bulge
kabartma relief; in relief
kabataslak roughly drawn; in outline
Kabe the Kaaba
kabız constipation; constipated **kabız olmak** to be constipated
kabızlık constipation
kabile tribe, clan
kabiliyet ability, talent
kabiliyetli talented, capable
kabiliyetsiz incapable, untalented
kabin cabin
kabine cabinet; small room
kabir grave, tomb
kablo cable **kablo döşemek** to lay a cable
kabotaj cabotage
kabristan cemetery, graveyard
kabuk (fruit, vegetable) peel, skin, shell, jacket; (animal, nut, egg) shell;

(bean, pea) pod; (tree) bark; (wound) scab **kabuk bağlamak** to form a crust; to form a scab **kabuğuna çekilmek** to withdraw into one's shell **kabuğunu soymak** to peel, to skin, to husk
kabuklu having a shell, barky **kabuklu deniz hayvanı** shellfish
kabuklular *hayb.* crustaceae
kabuksuz without bark; shelled, peeled
kabul acceptance; reception **kabul etmek** to accept; to receive **kabul salonu** reception-room
kabullenmek to accept; to appropriate
kaburga rib
kabus nightmare
kabza handle, butt
kabzımal middlemen
kaç how many, how much?
kaça What is the price? How much is it?
kaçak fugitive, escapee; (liquid gas) escape, leakage; smuggled, contraband
kaçakçı smuggler
kaçakçılık smuggling
kaçamak subterfuge, evasion, shift; evasive
kaçamaklı evasive, elusive
kaçar How many each? How much each?
kaçık crazy; cracked, nuts
kaçıklık craziness
kaçılmak to get out of the way
kaçıncı which (in order), how manyth
kaçınmak to avoid, to shun, to evade, to abstain, to refrain
kaçınılmaz inevitable
kaçırmak to kidnap, to abduct; to miss; to hijack, to skyjack; to drive away, to frighten away
kaçış escape, flight
kaçkın fugitive, runaway
kaçmak to run away, to flee, to escape; (stocking) to ladder, to run; (dust, insect etc.) to get into, to slip into; to avoid, to spare; to verge on
kadar until, till, up to; as ... as; about
kadastro land survey; cadastral
kadavra corpse, cadaver, carcass

kadeh glass, cup, wineglass **kadeh kaldırmak** to propose a toast **kadeh tokuşturmak** to clink glasses
kademe grade, degree; *ask.* echelon
kademeli graded, in steps
kader destiny, fate, fortune **kaderi ilahi** divine providence **kaderin cilvesi** irony of fate
kaderci fatalist
kadercilik fatalism
kadı cadi, Muslim judge
kadın woman; lady; servant; female **kadın berberi** hairdresser **kadın doktoru** gynaecologist **kadın hastalıkları** gynaecological diseases **kadın peşinde koşmak** to run after women, to phelander **kadın terzisi** dressmaker
kadınlık womanhood
kadınsı womanish, effeminate
kadırga galley
kadife velvet **kadife gibi** soft and bright, velvety
kadir value, worth **Kadir Gecesi** the Night of Power **Kadir Gecesi doğmak** to be born under a lucky star **kadrini bilmek** to appreciate, to know the value of
kadir powerful, capable
kadirbilir appreciative, grateful
kadirşinas appreciative, grateful
kadran dial, face
kadro staff, personnel
kadrolu on the permanent staff
kafa head; mind, brain, intelligence **kafa dengi** like-minded **kafa kâğıdı** *kon.* official identity card **kafa patlatmak** to rack one's brains to cudgel one's brains **kafa şişirmek** to bore **kafa tutmak** to oppose, to resist **kafa vurmak** to head **kafadan** ad lib, off the cuff **kafadan atmak** to talk through one's hat **kafası almamak** to be unable to take in **kafası işlemek** to have a quick mind **kafası kızmak** to fly into a temper **kafasına dank etmek** to dawn on sb **kafasına koymak** to make up one's mind **kafasına sokmak** to drum sth into sb **kafayı çekmek** to have a booze-up, to booze
kafadar intimate friend, buddy, chum

kafalı intelligent
kafasız stupid, thickheaded
kafasızlık stupidity
kafatası skull, cranium
kafein caffeine
kafes cage
kafeterya cafeteria
kâfi enough **kâfi derecede** sufficiently **kâfi gelmek** to be enough
kafile convoy, procession
kâfir unbeliever
kâfirlik unbelief, irreligion
kafiye rhyme
kafiyeli rhyming
kafiyesiz rhymeless
Kafkasya Caucasia
Kafkasyalı Caucasian
kaftan robe, caftan
kâgir built of stone or brick
kağan khan, ruler
kâğıt paper; playing card; of paper **kâğıt dağıtmak** to deal (out) cards **kâğıt helvası** pastry wafers **kâğıt kaplamak** to paper **kâğıt mendil** tissue, paper hanky **kâğıt oynamak** to play cards **kâğıt para** paper money, note, bill **kâğıt sepeti** wastepaper basket
kağnı ox-cart
kâh sometimes **kâh ... kâh** now ... now
kahır distress, sorrow, anxiety **kahrını çekmek** to have to put up with sb.
kâhin soothsayer
kahkaha loud laughter **kahkaha atmak** to laugh loudly **kahkahayı basmak** to burst into laughter
kahpe prostitute; perfidious, fickle
kahpelik prostitution; treachery, dirty trick
kahraman hero
kahramanca heroically
kahramanlık heroic deed, feat; heroism, bravery
kahretmek to overpower, to overwhelm
kahrolmak to be depressed
kahrolası damned, blasted
kahrolsun! kahretsin Damn it! Down with!
kahvaltı breakfast **kahvaltı etmek** to have breakfast
kahve coffee; cafe, coffee house **kahve**

cezvesi coffeepot **kahve değirmeni** coffee mill **kahve fincanı** coffee cup **kahve kaşığı** coffee spoon **kahve telvesi** coffee grounds **kahve yapmak** to make coffee
kahveci keeper of a coffee-house
kahvehane coffee house, coffee shop
kahverengi brown
kâhya steward, majordomo
kaide rule; base
kâinat universe
kaka faeces, big one; poop **kaka yapmak** to poo-poo, to defecate
kakao cocoa
kakırdamak to crackle, to rattle
kakma relief work, repoussé work
kakmak to push, to prod; to drive in, to nail
kaktüs cactus
kâkül forelock, fringe
kala to; before
kalabalık crowd; crowded
kalan remaining; remainder
kalantor well-to-do man
kalas beam, plank
kalay tin
kalaycı tinner, tinsmith
kalaylamak to tin
kalaylı tinned
kalaysız untinned
kalben cordially, heartily
kalbur sieve, riddle **kalbur gibi** riddled **kalbura çevirmek** to riddle **kalbura dönmek** to be riddled
kalburüstü select, elite
kalça hip, haunch **kalça kemiği** haunch bone, hipbone
kaldıraç crank, lever
kaldırım pavement **kaldırım kenarı** curb **kaldırım mühendisi** loafer
kaldırmak to lift, to raise; to erect; to put away; to wake, to rouse; to bear, to tolerate; to abolish, to repeal
kale fortress, castle; *sp.* goal post
kaleci *sp.* goalkeeper, goalie
kalem pencil, pen; item, entry **kalem açmak** to sharpen a pencil **kalem aşısı** graft **kalem kutusu** pencil box **kaleme almak** to draw up
kalemtıraş pencil sharpener

kalender carefree, easygoing, unconventional

kalfa assistant master, qualified workman

kalıcı lasting, permanent

kalın thick; coarse **kalın kafalı** thick headed, dull

kalınlaşmak to thicken

kalınlık thickness

kalınbağırsak large intestine

kalıntı remnant; ruin, ruins; residue; mark, trace

kalıp mould; cake, bar; shape, form; pattern **kalıba dökmek** to mould, to cast **kalıbını basmak** *kon.* to be dead certain about

kalıplaşmış stereotyped

kalıtım *biy.* heritage, heredity

kalıtımsal, kalıtsal hereditary

kalibre calibre

kalifiye qualified

kaligrafi calligraphy

kalipso calypso

kalite quality

kaliteli of good quality, high-quality

kalitesiz of poor quality, shoddy

kalkan shield, buckler; *hayb.* turbot

kalker limestone

kalkık raised, risen; erect; lifted

kalkındırmak to develop

kalkınma development, progress

kalkınmak to develop, to progress, to make progress

kalkış departure

kalkışmak to attempt, to try, to dare

kalkmak to get up; to leave, to depart; to become erect; to disappear, to lift; to try, to attempt; (custom) to fall into disuse; to be abolished **kalk borusu** *ask.* reveille **kalk borusu çalmak** to sound the reveille

kalleş untrustworthy, unreliable, deceitful

kalleşlik deceit, treachery **kalleşlik etmek** to play a dirty trick on

kalmak to remain; to be left; to stay, to dwell; to fail (a class); to be inherited, to pass **kala kala** there only remains **kaldı ki** moreover, besides

kalori calorie, calory

kalorifer central heating

kalp heart; centre **kalp ağrısı** heartache **kalp atışı** heartbeat **kalp krizi** heart attack **kalp para** counterfeit money **kalbi atmak** to beat, to pulsate **kalbi çarpmak** to palpitate, to throb **kalbini kırmak** to break sb's heart

kalp false, forged

kalpak fur cap

kalpazanlık counterfeiting

kalpazan counterfeiter

kalpsiz heartless, cruel

kalsiyum *kim.* calcium

kaltak saddletree; whore, floozy

kalyon galleon

kama dagger

kamara (ship) cabin

kamarot steward, cabin boy

kamaşmak to be dazzled

kamaştırmak to dazzle

kambiyo foreign exchange **kambiyo kuru** rate of exchange, exchange rate

kambur hump, hunch; humpbacked, hunchbacked **kamburu çıkmak** to become hunchbacked **kamburunu çıkarmak** to arch, to stoop

kamçı whip, scourge

kamçılamak to whip, to lash; to whip up, to stimulate

kamelya *bitk.* camellia

kamera camera

kameraman cameraman

kameriye arbour, bower

kamış reed, cane; penis

kamp camp **kamp kurmak** to pitch camp **kamp yeri** camp ground, campsite **kampa çıkmak** to go camping **kampa girmek** *sp.* to go into camp

kampçı camper

kampana bell

kampanya campaign

kampus campus

kamu the public, the people **kamu düzeni** public order, public safety **kamu giderleri** public expenditure **kamu hakları** public rights **kamu hizmeti** public service **kamu hukuku** public law, civil law **kamu kesimi** public sector **kamu personeli** civil servant **kamu sağlığı** public health **kamu yararı**

public interest
kamuflaj camouflage
kamufle camouflaged **kamufle etmek** to camouflage
kamulaştırma nationalization
kamulaştırmak to nationalize
kamuoyu public opinion
kamyon lorry *İİ*, truck *Aİ.*
kamyoncu lorry driver, truck driver
kamyonet pickup (truck)
kan blood **kan ağlamak** to shed tears of blood **kan akıtmak** to shed blood **kan almak** to take blood **kan bağışlamak** to donate blood **kan bankası** blood bank **kan basıncı** blood pressure **kan çanağı gibi** (eyes) bloodshot **kan çıbanı** furuncle, boil **kan damarı** blood vessel **kan damlası** drop of blood **kan davası** blood feud, vendetta **kan dolaşımı** blood circulation **kan grubu** blood group, blood type **kan kardeşi** blood brother **kan nakli** blood transfusion **kan sayımı** blood count **kan tahlili** blood test, blood analysis **kan vermek** to donate blood **kana kana** to one's heart's content **kana susamış** bloodthirsty **kanı dindirmek** to stanch blood **kanı kaynamak** to take to sb
Kanada Canada
Kanadalı Canadian
kanaat conviction, opinion; contentment, satisfaction **kanaat etmek** to be satisfied **kanaat getirmek** to be convinced, to satisfy oneself
kanaatkâr contented
kanal canal, waterway; channel
kanalizasyon sewerage, drainage
kanama bleeding
kanamak to bleed
kanarya canary **Kanarya Adaları** Canary Islands
kanat wing
kanatçık winglet
kanatlanmak to take wing, to fly away
kanatlı winged
kanatsız wingless
kanaviçe canvas
kanca hook **kancayı takmak** to get one's knife into, to set one's cap at

kancalı hooked **kancalı iğne** safety pin
kancık bitch; mean
kandırmak to convince, to persuade; to seduce, to cheat
kandil oil lamp
kanepe sofa, couch
kangal coil, skein
kangren gangrene
kanguru *hayb.* kangaroo
kanı conviction, opinion **kanımca** in my opinion **kanısında olmak** be of the opinion that
kanıksamak to be satiated, to get used (to), to be inured (to)
kanır(t)mak to force back, to bend, to twist
kanıt proof
kanıtlamak to prove
kaniş poodle
kanlanmak to be stained with blood
kanlı bloody
kanmak to be persuaded, to believe; to be seduced, to be duped; to be satisfied
kano canoe
kanser cancer
kanserli cancerous
kansız bloodless
kansızlık anaemia
kantar steelyard; weighing-machine
kantin canteen
kanun *müz.* zither
kanun law **kanun hükmünde olmak** to have the force of law **kanun koymak** to make a law, to legislate **kanun koyucu** legislator **kanun namına** in the name of the law **kanun tasarısı** bill, draft of a law **kanun tasarısını kabul etmek** to pass a bill **kanun tasarısını reddetmek** to throw out a bill **kanuna aykırı** unlawful, illegal
kanunen by law, according to the law
kanuni legal, lawful
kanunlaşmak to become a law
kanunsuz lawless, illegal
kanyak cognac, brandy
kanyon canyon
kaos chaos
kap vessel, container **kap kacak** pots and pans

kapak lid, cover
kapaklanmak to fall flat on one's face
kapalı shut, closed; covered; overcast **kapalı çarşı** covered market **kapalı devre** closed circuit **kapalı gişe oynamak** to play to a full house **kapalı kutu** closed book **kapalı spor salonu** arena **kapalı tribün** covered grandstand **kapalı zarf usulüyle** by sealed tender
kapamak to shut, to close; to turn off
kapan trap **kapan kurmak** to set a trap **kapana kısılmak** to be caught in a trap
kapanık confined, shut in; cloudy, dark
kapanış closure; (radio, TV) close down
kapanmak to shut, to close; to confine oneself in, to shut oneself up; to be blocked off; (weather) to become overcast
kaparo earnest money, key money
kapasite capacity
kapatma kept woman, mistress
kapatmak to close, to shut; to turn off
kapı door; gate **kapı aralığı** doorway **kapı dışarı etmek** to throw out, to dismiss **kapı gibi** large **kapı kapı dolaşmak** to go from door to door **kapı tokmağı** knocker
kapıcı doorkeeper, caretaker, janitor, porter
kapılanmak to secure a job
kapılmak to be carried away, to yield to, to abandon oneself to
kapış snatch **kapış kapış** grabbingly, greedily **kapış kapış gitmek** to sell like hot cakes
kapışmak to snatch (at), to scramble (for); to get to grips with sb
kapışılmak to be sold like hot cakes
kapital capital, funds
kapitalist capitalist; capitalistic
kapitalizm capitalism
kapitülasyon capitulation
kaplam extension
kaplama coat, plate; coating, plating; coated, plated
kaplamak to cover; to overlay, to plate, to coat
kaplan tiger

kaplıca thermal spring, hot spring
kaplumbağa tortoise, turtle
kapmak to snatch, to seize, to grasp; to learn quickly, to pick up
kaporta bonnet *Al.* hood
kapris caprice, fancy, whim
kaprisli capricious, whimsical
kapsam scope, coverage, range
kapsamak to comprise, to include, to involve
kapsamlı comprehensive, overall
kapsül capsule
kaptan captain
kapuska cabbage stew
kaput military cloak, greatcoat; condom, rubber; bonnet, hood
kar snow **kar düşmek** (snow) to fall **kar gibi** snow-white **kar fırtınası** snowstorm **kar tanesi** snow flake **kar temizleme makinesi** snow plough **kar tutmak** (snow) to stick, to lie **kar yağıyor** It is snowing. **kar yağmak** (snow) to fall, to snow **kardan adam** snowman
kâr profit, gain **kâr bırakmak** to yield a profit **kâr etmek** to make a profit **kâr getirmek** to bring profit **kâr haddi** profit limit **kâr kalmak** to remain as profit **kâr oranı** rate of profit **kâr ve zarar** profit and loss
kara land, shore; territorial **kara kuvvetleri** land forces **karaya ayak basmak** to land, to disembark **karaya oturmak** (ship) to run aground
kara black; dark; bad, unlucky **kara cahil** crassly ignorant **kara cehalet** crass ignorance **kara çalmak** to calumniate, to slander **kara gün dostu** a friend in need **kara kara düşünmek** to brood (on/over sth) **kara kutu** flight recorder **kara listeye almak** to blacklist **kara mizah** black humour
karaağaç elm
karabasan nightmare
karabatak cormorant
karabiber black pepper
karaborsa black market **karaborsadan almak** to buy on the black market
karaborsacı black marketeer
karabulut nimbus

karaca roe (deer)
karacı officer or soldier in land office
karaciğer liver
Karadeniz the Black Sea
karafatma cockroach
karagöz Turkish shadow show; *hayb.* sargo, sea bream
karahumma *hek.* typhus
karakabarcık *hek.* anthrax
karakalem charcoal pencil
karakış severe winter, midwinter
karakol police station; patrol
karakter character **karakter oyuncusu** character actor **karakter sahibi** person of firm character
karakteristik characteristic
karaktersiz characterless
karalamak to blacken; to scribble, to draft; to backbite
karalık blackness
karaltı blur, silhouette
karambol collision, smashup
karamela caramel
karamsar pessimistic
karamsarlık pessimism
karanfil carnation
karanlık dark, darkness; dark, obscure **karanlık basmak** (night) to fall **karanlık oda** darkroom
karanlıkta in the dark
karantina quarantine **karantinaya almak** to put in quarantine
karar decision, resolution; judgement, sentence; constancy, stability **karar almak** to take a decision **karar vermek** to decide, to make a decision **karara varmak** to come to a decision, to reach a decision
karargâh headquarters
kararlama estimated by guess
kararlamadan at a guess
kararlaştırmak to decide, to arrange, to fix
kararlı decided, determined; stable, fixed
kararlılık determination
kararmak to grow dark, to darken
kararname decree, legal decision
kararsız irresolute, undecided; unstable
kararsızlık indecision, hesitation

karartma blackout
karasaban primitive plough
karasevda melancholy
karasevdalı melancholic
karasinek common housefly
karasu glaucoma
karasuları territorial water
karatavuk blackbird
karate karate
karateci katateist
karavan caravan
karavana mess-tin; mess
karayel northwest wind
karayolu highway, main road
karbon carbon **karbon kâğıdı** carbon paper
karbonat carbonate
karbondioksit carbon-dioxide
karbonhidrat carbohydrate
karbüratör carburettor
kardeş brother, sister
kardeşlik brotherhood, sisterhood
kardinal cardinal
kardiyograf cardiograph
kardiyografi cardiography
kardiyolog cardiologist
kardiyoloji cardiology
kare square **karesini almak** to square
karekök square root **karekökünü almak** *mat.* to extract the square root of
kareli chequered, squared
karga crow, raven
kargaburnu round pliers
kargacık burgacık yazmak to scrawl, to scribble
kargaşa confusion, disorder, tumult
kargo cargo
karı wife; woman **karı koca** husband and wife
karın belly, abdomen; stomach **karın ağrısı** stomachache; pain in the neck, pain **karnı acıkmak** to be hungry **karnı ağrımak** to have stomachache **karnı zil çalmak** to feel peckish **Karnım tok.** I am full. **karnını doyurmak** to eat one's fill
karınca ant
karıncalanmak to prickle, to have pins and nedles
karıncık *anat.* ventricle

karış span, hand span **karış karış** inch by inch, every inch of **karış karış bilmek** to know every inch of (a place)

karışık mixed; complicated, complex; miscellaneous, assorted

karışıklık disorder, confusion **karışıklık çıkarmak** to stir up trouble, to kick up a row

karışlamak to measure by the span

karışım mixture

karışmak to mix, to mingle; to interfere, to meddle; to be involved in

karıştırıcı mixer

karıştırmak to mix, to blend; to mix up, to confuse; to fumble about in, to rummage about

karides shrimp

karikatür cartoon; caricature

karikatürcü caricaturist

karlı snowy

kârlı profitable, fruitful

karma mixing; mixed **karma öğretim** coeducation

karmak to mix, to blend; (playing cards) to shuffle

karmakarışık in a mess, in utter disorder

karmaşa disorder; complex

karmaşık complex

karnabahar cauliflower

karnaval carnival

karne report card, school report; ration card

karnıyarık dish of eggplants stuffed with mincemeat

karo (playing cards) diamond

karoser (car) body

karpuz watermelon; globe

kârsız profitless

karşı opposite; against; toward, towards **karşı karşıya gelmek** to come face to face with **(karşıdan) karşıya geçmek** to cross over **karşı çıkmak** to oppose; to object **karşı gelmek** to oppose, to buck **karşı koymak** to resist, to withstand, to oppose **karşı olmak** to be against; to face **karşı casusluk** counterespionage

karşılamak (to go) to meet, to welcome; to receive, to greet; to meet, to cover

karşılaşmak to meet, to confront

karşılaştırma comparison

karşılaştırmak to compare, to contrast

karşılaştırmalı comparative

karşılık answer, reply; equivalent; return, recompense **karşılık vermek** to answer back

karşılıklı mutual, reciprocal **karşılıklı olarak** mutually, reciprocally

karşılıksız unreturned, unanswered **karşılıksız çıkmak** (cheque) to bounce

karşın in spite of, despite

karşıt opposite, contrary **karşıt anlamlı** antonymous

karşıtlık contrast

karşısında opposite, facing; in the face of

kart card; postcard

kart tough, hard; old

kartal eagle

kartel cartel

kartlaşmak to become tough (old)

kartlık toughness; oldness

karton cardboard, pasteboard

kartonpiyer papier-mâché

kartopu snowball **kartopu oynamak** to play snowball

kartotek card catalogue, card index

kartpostal postcard

kartuş cartridge

kartvizit visiting card, card

karyola bed, bedstead

kas muscle

kasa safe, strongbox; till; cash; case, box; (car) body **kasa açığı** cash deficit **kasa defteri** cash book **kasa hesabı** cash account

kasaba small town **kasaba halkı** townsfolk, townspeople

kasabalı townsman, townswoman

kasadar cashier

kasap butcher; butcher's shop

kasatura bayonet

kasavet gloom, depression

kasavetli gloomy, depressed, desolate

kasdoku muscular tissue

kâse bowl

kaset cassette

kasık groin

kasılmak to contract; to give oneself airs, to swank, to swagger

kasım November

kasımpatı chrysanthemum

kasıntı swagger, swank

kasırga whirlwind, cyclone

kasıt intention, purpose

kasıtlı intentional, deliberate

kaside eulogy

kasiyer cashier

kaskatı very hard, rigid

kasket cap

kasko automobile insurance

kaslı muscular

kasmak to stretch tight; (garment) to take in **kasıp kavurmak** to terrorize, to tyrannize

kasnak rim, hoop

kasten on purpose, intentionally

kastetmek to mean

kasti deliberate, intentional

kasvet depression, gloom **kasvet basmak** to become depressed **kasvet vermek** to depress

kasvetli sad, depressing, gloomy

kaş eyebrow **kaş(larını) çatmak** to knit one's brows, to frown **kaş göz etmek** to wink at **kaşla göz arasında** in the twinkling of an eye **kaş yapayım derken göz çıkarmak** to make matters worse (while trying to be helpful)

kaşağı currycomb, back-scratcher

kaşağılamak to curry, to groom

kaşar a kind of yellow cheese made of sheep's milk

kaşarlanmış callous, hard-boiled

kaşe cachet

kaşık spoon

kaşıkçıkuşu pelican

kaşıklamak to spoon up

kaşımak to scratch

kaşındırmak to irritate

kaşınmak to itch; to scratch oneself; to ask for a beating

kaşıntı itching, irritation

kâşif explorer, discoverer

kaşkol scarf, neckerchief

kat storey, floor; layer, stratum; coat, coating; times **kat çıkmak** to add a storey **kat kat** in layers; much more,

by far **kat mülkiyeti** ownership of a flat, condominium

katafalk catafalque

katakulli cheat, ruse

kataliz catalysis

katalizör catalyst

katalog catalogue

katar file; train

katarakt *hek.* cataract

katedral cathedral

kategori category

katetmek to travel, to cover

katı hard, rigid, stiff; (egg) hard-boiled **katı yürekli** hard hearted

katılaşmak to harden

katılık hardness, rigidness, stiffness

katık anything eaten with bread, relish

katıksız pure, unmixed

katılım participation, joining in

katılmak to be added, to be mixed; to participate, to join (in); to agree with; to get out of breath (from laughing)

katır mule

katır kutur with a crunching sound

katışık mixed

katışıksız pure

katıyağ grease

kati decisive, definite, final

kâtibe woman secretary

katiyen definitely, absolutely

katiyet definiteness

katil murderer, killer

kâtip clerk, secretary

katkı contribution, addition **katkıda bulunmak** to contribute to

katkısız pure, unadulterated

katlamak to fold, to pleat

katlanmak to put up with, to bear, to stand

katlanır folding, collapsible

katletmek to kill, to murder

katliam massacre, slaughter

katma added, additional **katma bütçe** supplementary budget **katma değer vergisi, KDV** value added tax, VAT

katmak to add, to join

katman layer, stratum

katmer layer

katmerli in layers, manifold, multiplied

Katolik Catholic

Katoliklik Catholicism
katot cathode katot ışınları cathode rays
katran tar
katranlamak to tar
katranlı tarred
katsayı *mat.* coefficient
katyon cation
kauçuk rubber
kavaf dealer in ready-made shoes
kavak poplar
kaval pipe, flageolet
kavalkemiği fibula
kavalye escort, partner
kavanoz jar, pot
kavga quarrel, brawl, fight kavga çıkarmak to kick up a row kavga etmek to quarrel, to fight
kavgacı quarrelsome
kavgalı quarrelled, angry
kavim ethny, tribe
kavis bend, curve
kavram concept, notion
kavrama comprehension; coupling, clutch kavrama pedalı clutch pedal
kavramak to grab, to seize, to clutch; to comprehend, to grasp, to understand
kavrayış comprehension, conception
kavrayışlı quick-witted
kavrayışsız thick-witted
kavşak junction, crossroads
kavuk quilted turban
kavun melon
kavuniçi light yellow colour
kavurma fried meat; fried
kavurmak to fry, to roast
kavuşmak to meet; to reach, to attain
kavuşturmak to bring together, to unite
kaya rock kaya gibi rocky kayalara bindirmek to run on the rocks
kayalık rocky
kayabalığı goby
kayağan slippery
kayak ski kayak yapmak to ski
kayakçı skier
kayakçılık skiing
kaybetmek to lose
kaybolmak to be lost; to disappear
kaydetmek to enrol, to register; to note down

kaydırak hopscotch; slide; flat round stone
kaygan slippery
kayganlık slipperiness
kaygı worry, anxiety
kaygılandırmak to make anxious, to worry
kaygılanmak to worry, to feel anxious
kaygılı worried, anxious
kaygısız carefree, jaunty
kayık boat, rowboat
kayıkçı boatman
kayıkhane boathouse
kayın beech
kayın brother-in-law
kayınbaba father-in-law
kayınbirader brother-in-law
kayınpeder father-in-law
kayınvalide mother-in-law
kayıp loss; casualties; lost kayıp eşya lost property kayıplara karışmak to disappear, to vanish
kayırmak to protect, to favour, to back
kayısı apricot
kayış strap, belt
kayıt enrolment, registration kayıt defteri register kayda değer noteworthy kayda geçirmek to register kaydını silmek to delete the record of
kayıtlı registered, recorded
kayıtsız unregistered; indifferent, unconcerned kayıtsız kalmak to be indifferent (to) kayıtsız şartsız unconditionally
kayıtsızlık indifference, unconcern
kaykılmak to lean (back)
kaymak to slip, to slide, to skate
kaymak cream
kaymaklı creamy
kaymakam head official of a district
kaynaç geyser
kaynak spring, fountain; source kaynak suyu spring water
kaynak weld, welding kaynak çubuğu welding bar kaynak yapmak to weld
kaynakça bibliography
kaynakçı welder
kaynaklanmak to arise from, to result from
kaynama boiling, ebullition kaynama

noktası boiling point
kaynamak to boil; to swarm, to crawl with
kaynana mother-in-law
kaynanadili cactus
kaynanazırıltısı rattle, clacker
kaynarca spring; hot spring
kaynaşmak to unite, to coalesce; to be welded; to swarm, to mill around
kaynata father-in-law
kaynatmak to boil
kaypak slippery, shifty
kaytan braid, cord
kaytarmak to shirk, to dodge, to goldbrick
kaz goose **kaz adımı** goosestep **kaz kafalı** stupid, thickheaded
kaza accident, mishap, crash **kaza sigortası** accident insurance **kaza yapmak** to have an accident **kazaen, kaza ile** by accident, by chance **kazaya uğramak** to have an accident
kaza (administrative) district
kazak pullover, jersey; (husband) despotic, dominating
kazan boiler, cauldron **kazan kaldırmak** to rebel against
kazanç profit, earnings; benefit, gain
kazançlı gainful, lucrative, profitable; advantageous
kazanmak to win; to acquire, to obtain
kazara by chance, by accident
kazazede wrecked, ruined, victim
kazı excavation
kazıbilim arch(a)eology
kazıbilimci archeologist
kazık stake, pale; trick, overcharge, cheat; exorbitant **kazık atmak** to overcharge, to stick, to soak
kazıkçı extortioner, extortionist, trickster
kazıklanmak to be overcharged, to pay through the nose
kazıklıhumma tetanus
kazımak to scrape
kazıntı scrapings
kazma pickaxe, mattock
kazmak ta dig, to excavate
kebap roasted meat, roast meat, kebap
keççap ketchup, catchup

keçe felt; mat
keçi goat; obstinate **keçileri kaçırmak** to go out of one's mind
keçiboynuzu carob (bean)
keçisakal goatee
keçiyolu path
keder grief, sorrow
kederlenmek to become sorrowful
kederli grieved, sorrowful
kedi cat
kedigözü rear reflector
kefal grey mullet
kefalet bail **kefalet senedi** surety bond
kefaletle on bail **kefaletle salıvermek** to release on bail
kefaletname surety bond, bail bond
kefaret atonement, expiation **kefaretini ödemek** to atone, to expiate
kefe (balance) scale
kefen shroud **kefeni yırtmak** to cheat death
kefil guarantor, sponsor **kefil olmak** to stand as surety
kefillik guarantee, security
kehanet soothsaying, prediction **kehanette bulunmak** to prophesy, to predict
kehribar amber
kek cake
keke stuttering, stammering
kekelemek to stutter, to stammer
kekeme stutterer, stammerer
kekemelik stuttering, stammer
kekik thyme
keklik partridge
kekre acrid, pungent
kekrelik acridity
kel bald **kel başa şimşir tarak** unnecessary luxury **kel olmak** to become baldheaded
kelaynak ibis, kahlibis
kelebek butterfly; throttle
kelek unripe melon; *arg.* stupid, silly
kelepçe handcuffs; pipe clip **kelepçe takmak** to put handcuffs on sb
kelepçelemek to handcuff
kelepir bargain, buy **kelepire konmak** to get a bargain
kelepirci bargain hunter
keleş brave; beautiful, handsome; hair-

less
kelime word **kelimesi kelimesine** word for word
kelle head, bean **kellesini uçurmak** to decapitate, to behead
kellifelli well-dressed, dignified
kellik baldness
kem bad, evil
Kemalist Kemalist
Kemalizm Kemalism
keman violin
kemancı violinist
kemençe *müz.* small violin with three strings
kement lasso **kement atmak** to throw a lasso at
kemer belt, girdle; arch **kemerini sıkmak** to tighten one's belt
kemik bone **kemik çıkmak** (bone) to be dislocated **kemik gibi** as hard as a bone; bone-dry **kemik veremi** tuberculosis of the bones
kemikli having bones, bony
kemiksiz boneless, without bones
kemirmek to gnaw, to nibble
kemiyet quantity
kem küm etmek to hum and haw
kenar edge, border, brink **kenar mahalle** slums, outskirts **kenara çekilmek** to get out of the way, to step aside **kenara kaldırmak** to put aside
kenarortay median
kendi self; own **kendi aleminde yaşamak** to live in one's own world **kendi başına** on one's own, by himself **kendi bildiğini okumak** to get one's own way **kendi derdine düşmek** to be preoccupied with one's own troubles **kendi düşen ağlamaz** as you make your bed, so you must lie in it **kendi halinde** harmless, quiet **kendi kazdığı kuyuya kendi düşmek** to be hoist with one's own petard **kendi kendime** by myself, to myself **kendi kendine gelin güvey olmak** to reckon without one's host **kendi kendisine** by himself to himself **kendi yağıyla kavrulmak** to stand on one's own feet **kendileri** themselves **kendiliğinden** by oneself, automatically **kendim** my-

self **kendimiz** ourselves **kendinden geçmek** to lose one's self-control; to lose consciousness **kendinde olmamak** to be unconscious **kendinden pay biçmek** to live and let live **Kendine gel!** Pull yourself together! **kendine gelmek** to come round, to come to oneself again **kendine ... süsü vermek** to pretend to be **kendine yediremek** to be unable to bring oneself to **kendini beğenmek** to be full of oneself **kendini beğenmiş** conceited, self-satisfied **kendini beğenmişlik** conceitedness **kendini bilmez** presumptuous, impertinent **kendini birşey sanmak** to think oneself important **kendini fasulye gibi nimetten saymak** to think no small beer of oneself **kendini toparlamak** to pull oneself together **kendini -ye vermek** to devote oneself to, to give oneself over to **kendiniz** yourself; yourselves
kendir hemp
kene tick
kenef water-closed
kenet clamp
kenetlemek to clamp (together)
kenetli clamped together
kenevir hemp
kent city, town
kentleşme urbanization
kentleşmek to be urbanized
kentsoylu bourgeois
kepaze vile, contemptible, ridiculous **kepaze etmek** to disgrace, to dishonour **kepaze olmak** to disgrace oneself, to be humiliated
kepazelik vileness, ignominy
kepçe ladle, scoop
kepek bran; dandruff (in the hair), scurf
kepeklenmek to become scurfy
kepekli containing bran; scurfy
kepenk pull-down shutter
keramet miracle
kerata shoehorn; son of a gun, dog; cuckold
kere time(s)
kereste timber, lumber; *arg.* lout, boor
kereviz celery
kerhane brothel, whorehouse

kerhen unwillingly
keriz *arg.* sucker, dupe
kerkenez kestrel
kermes fair, kermis, flea market
kerpeten pincers
kerpiç sun-dried brick, adobe
kerrat cetveli multiplication table
kerte degree, point
kertenkele lizard
kerteriz bearing
kertik notch, tally
kertikli notched
kertmek to notch, to gash
kervan caravan
kesat slackness; stagnant, slack
kese purse; pouch; coarse bath glove; cyst **kesenin ağzını açmak** to loosen one's purse strings
kese shortcut
kesecik small purse; *anat.* saccule
kesekâğıdı paper bag
keselemek to rub the body with a bath glove
keseliler *hayb.* marsupials
kesen secant
keser adze
kesici cutting, incisive; cutter
kesicidiş incisor
kesif dense, thick
kesik cut, broken **kesik kesik** brokenly
kesikli discontinued
kesiksiz continuous
kesilmek to be cut; to be interrupted; to cease, to stop; to pretend to be
kesim cutting, slaughter; section, sector
kesimevi slaughterhouse
kesin definite, certain **kesin olarak** for certain, certainly
kesinkes decisive, definite; decisively, definitely
kesinleşmek to become definite
kesinlik decisiveness, certainty
kesinlikle definitely, definitively
kesinti deduction; interruption
kesintili interrupted, discontinuous
kesintisiz uninterrupted, continuous; without deduction, net
kesir traction
kesirli fractional

kesişmek to intersect, to cross
kesit section, cross-section
keskin sharp; bitter, tart **keskin nişancı** sharp shooter, marksman **keskin viraj** hairpin bend, sharp bend **keskin zekâlı** sharp-witted
keskinleştirmek to sharpen
keskinlik sharpness
kesme cutting; *mat.* sector **kesme almak** to pinch one's cheek
kesmece (watermelon) on condition that it is cut for examination
kesmek to cut; to interrupt; to stop, to kill; *arg.* to shut up, to cut the cackle; *arg.* to ogle at (a girl) **kesip atmak** to settle once and for all
kesmeşeker lump sugar
kestane chestnut **kestane kebabı** roasted chestnuts
kestanerengi red dishbrown, auburn
kestaneşekeri candied chestnuts
kestirme direct, decisive **kestirme yol** short cut **kestirmeden gitmek** to take a short cut
kestirmek to cause to cut; to estimate, to guess; to have a snap, to doze
keşfetmek to discover, to explore
keşif discovery, exploration; *ask.* reconnaissance
keşiş monk
keşişleme southeast wind
keşke I wish, if only
keşkül milk pudding with coconut
keşmekeş great confusion, disorder
ket obstacle **ket vurmak** to hinder
ketçap ketchup, catchup, catsup
keten flax; linen **keten bezi** linen cloth
kevgir colander, skimmer
keyfi arbitrary
keyfiyet quality; state of affairs, circumstance
keyif pleasure, enjoyment, joy; humour, disposition, inclination **keyif çatmak** to enjoy oneself **keyif için** for fun for pleasure **keyif sürmek** to lead a life of pleasure **keyif vermek** to intoxicate **keyfi gelmek** to feel in a good mood **keyfi kaçmak** to be out ot spirits, to be annoyed **keyfi olmamak** to be out of sorts **keyfi yerinde olmak** to be in

high spirits **keyfine bakmak** to take one's ease **keyfini çıkarmak** to get a kick out to, to enjoy **keyfini kaçırmak** to dispirit

keyiflenmek to become merry

keyifli in high spirits, merry

keyifsiz out of sorts, unwell

keyifsizlik indisposition, ailment

kez time

keza also, too; likewise

kezzap nitric acid, aqua fortis

kıble direction of Mecca

Kıbrıs Cyprus

Kıbrıslı Cypriot

kıç buttock, behind, bottom

kıdem seniority, priority

kıdemli senior

kıdemsiz junior

kıkırdak cartilage

kıkırdakdoku cartilaginous tissue

kıkırdamak to giggle, to chuckle

kıl hair; bristle; *arg.* nerk, nerd **kıl payı** by a neck **kıl payı kaybetmek** to lose by a hair's breadth **kıl payı kurtulmak** to escape by a hair's breadth **kıl testere** fret saw **kılı kırk yarmak** to split hairs **kılına dokunmamak** not to lay a finger on sb **kılını bile kıpırdatmamak** not to turn a hair

kılavuz guide; leader

kılcal capillary **kılcal damar** capillary vessel

kılçık fishbone

kılçıklı bony

kılçıksız without bones

kılıbık henpecked

kılıç sword **kılıç çekmek** to draw the sword **kılıçtan geçirmek** to put to the sword

kılıçbalığı swordfish

kılıf case, cover

kılık appearance, shape **kılık değiştirmek** to disguise oneself **kılık kıyafet** attire, dress **kılığında** in the guise of

kılıksız shabby, frumpish

kıllanmak to become hairy

kıllı hairy

kılmak to make, to render

kılsız hairless

kımıldamak to move, to stir

kımıldatmak to move, to budge

kın sheath, scabbard **kınına koymak** to sheathe **kınından çıkarmak** to unsheathe

kına henna **kına sürmek** to dye with henna

kınaçiçeği balsam

kınakına cinchona tree

kınamak to condemn, to blame

kınkanatlılar beetles

kınnap twine, string

kıpırdamak to move, to budge, to quiver

kıpırdatmak to move, to budge

kıpırtı stirring, quiver

kıpkırmızı crimson, very red **kıpkırmızı olmak** (face) to glow

kır country, countryside **kır çiçeği** wildflower **kır koşusu** cross-country run

kır grey, gray **kır düşmek** to turn grey **kır saçlı** grey haired

kıraathane coffee house

kıracak nutcrackers

kıraç barren, arid

kırağı hoarfrost, frost **kırağı çalmak** to become frostbitten

kırat carat

kırbaç whip

kırbaçlamak to whip

kırçıl grizzled

kırgın offended, hurt, resentful

kırgınlık offence, resentment

kırıcı offensive

kırık broken; break fracture; (school) bad mark **kırık dökük** in pieces

kırıkçı bone-setter

kırıklık fatigue, indisposition

kırılgan brittle, fragile

kırılmak to be broken; to take offence

kırım slaughter, massacre

Kırım Crimea

kırıntı fragment; crumb

kırışık wrinkle; wrinkled

kırışmak to become wrinkled; to divide among/between themselves

kırıştırmak to wrinkle; to carry on with, to flirt with

kırıtkan coquettish, mincing

kırıtmak to mince, to coquet

kırk forty **kırk yılda bir** once in a blue

moon
kırkayak centipede
kırkıncı fortieth
kırkmak to shear
kırlangıç swallow
kırlangıçbalığı gurnard
kırmak to break, to fracture; to fold, to pleat; to offend, to hurt; to destroy, to kill; (price) to lower **kırıp dökmek** to destroy **kırıp geçirmek** to tyrannize, to rage
kırmızı red **kırmızı balık** goldfish
kırmızıbiber red pepper, cayenne pepper
kırmızılaşmak to redden
kırmızılık redness
kırmızımsı reddish
kırpıntı clippings
kırpıştırmak to blink
kırpmak to clip, to shear; (eye) to wink
kırsal rural
kırtasiye stationery
kırtasiyeci stationer; bureaucrat
kırtasiyecilik bureaucracy, red tape; the stationery business
kısa short **kısa dalga** short wave **kısa devre** short circuit **kısa kesmek** to cut short, to curtail **kısa sürmek** to take a short time
kısaca shortly
kısacık very short
kısalık shortness
kısalmak to become short, to shorten; to shrink
kısaltma abbreviation
kısaltmak to shorten; to abbreviate
kısas retaliation, reprisal **kısasa kısas** an eye for an eye
kısık turned down; hoarse, choked **kısık sesli** hoarse voiced
kısım part, portion; section
kısıntı restriction, curtailment
kısır sterile, barren
kısırlaşmak to become sterile
kısırlaştırmak to make sterile
kısırlık sterility, barrenness
kısırdöngü vicious circle
kısırganmak to grudge, to skimp
kısıtlama restriction
kısıtlamak to restrict

kısıtlayıcı restrictive
kısıtlı restricted
kıskaç pincers, pliers; *tek.* grips
kıskanç jealous
kıskançlık jealousy
kıskanmak to be jealous of, to envy
kıskandırmak to make jealous
kıskıvrak tightly
kısmak to reduce, to cut down; (radio, lamp) to turn down; (eyes) to narrow
kısmen partly, partially
kısmet destiny, lot, fortune, chance **kısmet olmamak** not to be possible **kısmeti açık** fortunate, lucky **kısmeti açılmak** to be in luck; (girl) to receive a marriage proposal
kısmetli lucky
kısmetsiz unlucky
kısmi partial
kısrak mare
kıssa story, tale, anecdote **kıssadan hisse** the moral of the story; the lesson learned from an experience
kıstak *coğ.* isthmus
kıstas criterion
kıstırmak to pinch, to corner
kış winter **kış kıyamet** severe winter cold **kış uykusu** *hayb.* hibernation **kışı çıkarmak** to spend the whole winter **kışı geçirmek** to spend the winter **kışta kıyamette** in the depth of winter
kışın in (the) winter
kışır crust, bark, peel
kışkırtıcı provocative, inciting; instigator, provoker
kışkırtıcılık provocation
kışkırtmak to incite, to provoke
kışla barracks
kışlamak (winter) to set in; to winter
kışlık wintery, hibernal
kıt scarce, scanty **kıt kanaat geçinmek** to live from hand to mouth, to make both ends meet
kıta continent; stanza; *ask.* detachment **kıta sahanlığı** continental shelf
kıtalararası intercontinental
kıtır kıtır brittle, crisp; with a cracking sound **kıtır kıtır yemek** to munch
kıtlaşmak to become scarce
kıtlık scarcity; famine

kıvam thickness, density; the right moment/stage

kıvanç pleasure, joy; pride **kıvanç duymak** to feel proud of

kıvançlı joyful; proud

kıvılcım spark

kıvırcık curly, frizzy **kıvırcık salata** cabbage lettuce; head lettuce

kıvırmak (hair) to curl, to frizz; to twist, to bend; to pull off, to bring off; to invent, to make up

kıvrak brisk, agile, lithe

kıvraklık briskness, agility

kıvrandırmak to convulse, to torment

kıvranmak to writhe, to squirm

kıvrık curled; bent, crooked

kıvrım curl, twist

kıyafet dress, costume, attire, clothes **kıyafet balosu** fancy dress ball

kıyak fine, smart, swell, great

kıyamamak not to have the heart to

kıyamet doomsday; tumult, uproar **kıyamet gibi** heaps of **kıyamet günü** day of judgement **kıyameti koparmak** to make a row, to raise hell/the roof

kıyas comparison **kıyasla** in comparison (with)

kıyasıya mercilessly

kıyaslamak to compare

kıyı edge, border; shore, coast

kıyıcı cruel

kıyım mincing, cutting; wrongdoing

kıyma minced meat

kıymak to mince, to chop up fine; not to spare, to sacrifice

kıymet value, worth **kıymet biçmek** to evaluate, to value **kıymet vermek** to esteem, to appreciate **kıymet takdir etmek** to value **kıymetini bilmek** to appreciate, to value **kıymetten düşmek** to depreciate

kıymetlendirmek to increase the value of

kıymetlenmek to rise in value, to gain value

kıymetli valuable

kıymetsiz valueless

kıymık splinter

kız girl; maiden, virgin; (cards) queen **kız evlat** daughter **kız gibi** new; girlish **kız kaçırmak** to kidnap a girl **kız kardeş** sister **kız kurusu** spinster, old maid **kız tarafı** the bride's relatives **kız oğlan kız** virgin

kızak sledge, sled **kızak kaymak** to sledge **kızağa çekmek** to lay on the stocks **kızaktan indirmek** (ship) to launch

kızamık measles **kızamık çıkarmak** to have the measles

kızarmak to turn red; to blush **kızarıp bozarmak** to change colour

kızartma fried, roasted **kızartma tavası** frying pan

kızartmak to make red; to fry, to grill, to roast, to toast

kızdırmak to make angry, to annoy

kızgın hot; angry, furious

kızgınlık hotness; anger, fury

kızıl red, scarlet; scarlet fever; red, communist **Kızıl Deniz** the Red Sea **kızıl saçlı** red haired

kızılağaç alder

Kızılay Red Crescent

Kızılderili American Indian

Kızılhaç Red Cross

kızıllık redness

kızılötesi infrared

kızışmak to become heated, to get hot

kızıştırmak to excite, to incite

kızlık virginity, madinhood; girlhood **kızlık zarı** hymen

kızmak to get angry; to get hot

ki who, which, that

kibar polite, refined

kibarca politely

kibarlaşmak to become polite

kibarlık politeness, refinement **kibarlık taslamak** to play the fine gentleman

kibir pride, conceit

kibirlenmek to become haughty

kibirli haughty, conceited

kibrit match **kibrit çakmak** to strike a match **kibrit çöpü** match stick **kibrit kutusu** match box

kifayet sufficiency

kil clay, argil

kile bushel

kiler larder, pantry

kilim rug, kilim

kilise church
kilit lock, padlock **kilit açmak** to unlock **kilit noktası** key position **kilit vurmak** to lock
kilitlemek to lock
kilitli locked
kilo kilo **kilo almak** to put on weight **kilo vermek** to lose weight
kilogram kilogramme
kilohertz kilohertz
kilometre kilometre **kilometre kare** square kilometre
kilovat kilowatt
kim who **Kim bilir?** Who knows? **Kim o?** Who is it?
kime to whom, for whom, whom, who
kimi whom, who
kimi some **kimi zaman** sometimes
kimin whose
kimlik identity (card) **kimlik belgesi/-kartı** identity card
kimono kimono
kimse somebody, someone; anyone; nobody, no one **Kimsecikler yok.** There is not a soul here.
kimsesiz without relations/friends; empty, forlorn
kimsesizlik destitution
kimya chemistry **kimya mühendisi** chemical engineer **kimya mühendisliği** chemical engineering
kimyacı chemist; teacher of chemistry
kimyager chemist
kimyasal chemical **kimyasal maddeler** chemicals
kimyon cumin
kin grudge, hatred, spite **kin beslemek** to bear a grudge
kinaye allusion, innuendo
kinci vindictive
kinetik kinetics; kinetic
kinin quinine
kip mood
kir dirt, filth
kira hire, rent **kira getirmek** to rent **kira ile tutmak** to hire, to rent, to tenant **kira müddeti** lease, tenancy **kira sözleşmesi** lease, rental contract **kiraya vermek** to let, to rent, to lease, to rent out

kiracı tenant, leaseholder **kiracıyı çıkartmak** to evict
kiralamak to hire, to rent, to tenant
kiralayan lessee
kiralık for hire, to let **kiralık ev** house to let **kiralık katil** hired killer
kiraz cherry
kireç lime, chalk **kireç gibi** very white **kireç kuyusu** lime pit **kireç ocağı** limestone quarry
kireçlenmek to be limed; to calcity
kireçli calcareous, limy
kiremit tile **kiremit kaplamak** to tile
kiriş joist, rafter; string; *mat.* chord; *anat.* tendon **kirişi kırmak** to take to one's heels
kirlenmek to become dirty/filthy
kirletmek to make dirty, to dirty, to pollute
kirli dirty, filthy, foul, nasty **kirli çamaşır** dirty linen **kirli çamaşırlarını ortaya çıkarmak** to wash one's dirty linen in public
kirlilik dirtiness, filthiness
kirpi hedgehog
kirpik eyelash
kist cyst
kişi person, individual
kişileştirmek to personify
kişisel personal
kişilik personality
kişilikli having a strong personality
kişiliksiz characterless
kişnemek to neigh, to whinny
kitabe inscription, epitaph
kitabevi bookshop, bookstore
kitap book **kitaba el basmak** to swear on the Koran
kitapçı bookseller; publisher
kitaplık library; bookcase
kitapsever bibliophile
kitle mass **kitle iletişim araçları** mass media
klakson horn
klan clan
klarnet clarinet
klasik classic; classical
klasman classification
klasör file
klavye keyboard

klik clique
klima air-conditioner
klinik clinic; clinical
klişe cliché; trile
klişeleşmek to become hackneyed
klor chlorine
klorlamak to chlorinate
klorofil chlorophyll
kloroform chloroform
kloş bell-shaped, flared
koalisyon coalition
kobalt *kim.* cobalt
kobay guinea pig
kobra cobra
koca husband **koca bulmak** to find a hubby **kocaya kaçmak** to elope **kocaya vermek** to marry off
koca large, huge
kocakarı old woman, crone
kocalı having a husband
kocalık husbandhood
kocasız unmarried; widow
kocamak to grow old, to age
kocaman huge, large, enormous
koç ram
Koç (burcu) Aries
koçan corn cob; stump
kod code
kodaman magnate, big pot, big shot
kodeks codex
kodes jail, clink, jug
kodlamak to codify
kof hollow
kofana large bluefish
kofluk hollowness
kofra conduit box
koğuş ward; dormitory
kok coke
kokain cocaine
kokarca polecat, skunk
koklamak to smell, to sniff
koklatmak to cause to smell, to let smell; to give a very tiny bit of
kokmak to smell; to go bad
kokmuş rotten, spoiled, putrid
kokoreç roasted sheep's intestines
kokteyl cocktail
koku smell, scent; perfume
kokulu fragrant, perfumed, odorous
kokusuz scentless

kokuşmak to go bad, to putrefy
kokutmak to stink out, to smell up
kol arm; sleeve; handle, bar, lever; patrol; column **kol düğmesi** cuff-link **kol gezmek** to go the rounds, to patrol **kol kola** arm in arm **kol saati** wrist watch **koluna girmek** to take sb by the arm
kola starch
kolalamak to starch
kolalı starched
kola cola
kolaçan rummage, prowl **kolaçan etmek** to rummage about, to prowl
kolay easy **Kolay gelsin!** May it be easy! **kolay iş** easy job, cushy **kolayını bulmak** to find an easy way
kolayca easily
kolaylamak to break the back of
kolaylaşmak to become easier
kolaylaştırmak to facilitate, to make easy
kolaylık easiness; facility, means
kolaylıkla easily
kolcu guard, watchman
kolej private high school
kolejli student at a private high school
koleksiyon collection
koleksiyoncu collector
kolektif collective, joint **kolektif ortaklık** general partnership
kolektör collector
kolera cholera
kolestrol cholesterol
koli parcel, packet
kolit colitis
kollamak to watch for; to look after, to protect
kolluk cuff; armband
Kolombiya Colombia
kolon column
koloni colony
kolonya cologne
kolordu army corps
koltuk armchair; armpit; protection **koltuk altı** armpit **koltuk değneği** crutch **koltukları kabarmak** to swell with pride
koltuklamak to take sth under the arm; to flatter

kolye necklace, chain
koma coma **koma halinde** comatose **komaya girmek** to go into a coma
komandit limited partnership
komando commando
kombina combine
kombine combined
kombinezon slip
komedi comedy
komedyen comedian
komi bellboy
komiser superintendent of police
komisyon commission
komisyoncu commission agent
komite committee
komodin commode, bedside table
kompartıman compartment
kompas caliper rule
kompetan expert
komple full, complete
kompleks complex
komplikasyon complication
komplike complicated
kompliman compliment **kompliman yapmak** to pay compliments to
komplo plot, conspiracy **komplo kurmak** to conspire
komposto compote
kompozisyon composition
kompozitör composer
komprador comprador
kompresör compressor
komprime *hek.* tablet
komşu neighbour; neighbouring **komşu açı** adjacent angle
komşuluk neighbourhood
komut order, command
komuta command
komutan commander
komutanlık commandership
komünist communist
komünistlik, komünizm communism
komütatör commutator
konak mansion
konaklamak to stay for the night
konca bud
konç leg (of a boot/a stocking)
konçerto *müz.* concerto
kondansatör condenser
kondisyon condition, form

kondurmak to put on
kondüktör conductor
konfederasyon confederation
konfedere confederate
konfeksiyon ready-made clothes
konfeksiyoncu ready-made seller
konferans lecture **konferans vermek** to give a lecture
konferansçı lecturer
kongre congress
koni cone
konik conic, conical
konjonktür conjuncture
konkordato concordat
konmak to settle on, to alight
konsantrasyon concentration
konsantre concentrated **konsantre olmak** to concentrate (on)
konser concert **konser vermek** to give a concert
konservatuvar conservatoire, conservatory
konserve tinned food, canned food; preserved, tinned
konsey council
konsol chest of drawers
konsolos consul
konsolosluk consulate
konsomatris hostess (in a bar)
konsorsiyum consortium
konsültasyon medical consultation
konşimento bill of lading
kont count, earl
kontak short circuit; ignition **kontak açmak** to turn on the engine **kontak anahtarı** car key **kontak kapamak** to turn off the engine
kontenjan quota; contingent
kontes countess
kontluk county
kontralto contralto
kontrat contract
kontratak counterattack
kontrbas contrabass
kontrbasçı contra bassist
kontrol control **kontrol etmek** to control
kontrolör controller
kontrplak plywood
konu subject, topic

konuk guest, visitor
konukevi guest house
konuksever hospitable
konukseverlik hospitality
konu komşu the neighbours
konum position, location
konuşkan talkative
konuşkanlık talkativeness
konuşma talk, conversation; speech
konuşmacı speaker
konuşmak to talk, to speak
konut house, residence
konvansiyonel conventional
konveks convex
konvertibilite convertibility
konvertisör convertor
konvoy convoy
konyak brandy, cognac
kooperatif cooperative
koordinasyon coordination
koordinat *mat.* coordinate
koparmak to pluck, to pick; to break off; to extort, to wangle
kopça hook and eye
kopçalamak to hook
kopmak to break, to snap; to break out, to burst
kopuk broken; *kon.* hobo, bum
kopya copy; cheating **kopya çekmek** to cheat, to crib from **kopya kâğıdı** carbon paper
kopyacı copyist; cribber, cheater
kor ember
koramiral vice-admiral
kordiplomatik diplomatic corps
kordon cordon
Kore Korea
Koreli Korean
koreografi choreography
korgeneral lieutenant-general
koridor corridor
korkak cowardly; coward
korkaklık cowardice
korkmak to be afraid (of), to be scared
korku fear, dread, scare **korku salmak** to spread terror **korkuya kapılmak** to be seized with tear
korkulu frightening, dreadful
korkuluk scarecrow; banister, parapet, balustrade

korkunç terrible, dreadful, awful
korkusuz fearless, undaunted
korkusuzca fearlessly
korkusuzluk fearlessness
korkutmak to frighten, to scare, to cow, to daunt
korna horn **korna çalmak** to honk the horn
kornea *anat.* cornea
korner corner **korner atışı** corner kick
kornet cornet
korniş cornice
koro chorus **koro halinde** in chorus
korsan pirate, hijacker
korsanlık piracy, hijacking **korsanlık etmek** to pirate, to hijack
kortej cortege
koru grove copse
korucu forest watchman
korugan blockhouse
korumak to protect, to defend
korunma defence
korunmak to defend oneself
koruyucu protective, preventive; protector
kosinüs cosine
koskoca enormous, huge
koskocaman colossal, huge
kostüm costume
koşmak to run
koşturmak to cause to run; to rush, to buzz about, to scurry
koşu run, running **koşu alanı** hippodrome **koşu atı** racehorse
koşucu runner
koşul condition
koşullandırmak to condition
koşullu conditional, conditioned
koşulmak to run about
koşulsuz unconditional, unconditioned
koşuluyla on condition that
koşum harness
kot jeans
kota quota
kotarmak to dish up; to complete, to fulfil
kotra cutter
kova bucket **Kova burcu** Aquarius
kovalamak to run after, to chase
kovan hive; cartridge case

kovboy cowboy
kovmak to drive away, to expel, to discharge
kovuk hollow, cavity
kovuşturma prosecution kovuşturma açmak to start a prosecution
kovuşturmak to prosecute
koy bay, inlet
koymak to put, to place; *arg.* to upset, to move, to affect
koyu thick, dense; (colour) dark, deep; extreme, fanatic
koyulaştırmak to become dense; to become dark
koyuluk density; (colour) depth
koyulmak (work) to set to; to become dense/dark
koyultmak to darken; to thicken
koyun sheep koyun eti mutton
koyun bosom, breast koynuna girmek to go to bed with sb.
koy(u)vermek to let go, to release
koz (cards) trump; walnut kozunu oynamak to play one's trump card kozunu paylaşmak to settle accounts (with)
koza cocoon
kozalak cone
kozmetik cosmetic
kozmopolit cosmopolitan
köfte meatball
köfteci seller of meat balls
köftehor rascal, son of a gun
köhne old, ramshackle, dilapidated
kök root; origin kök işareti radical sign kök salmak to take root kökünden sökmek to uproot kökünü kurutmak to extirpate, to eradicate
kökboyası madder, alizarin
köken origin, source
kökenbilim etymology
köklemek to uproot
köklenmek to take root
kökleşmek to take root
köklü rooted
köknar fir
köksüz rootless
kökten radical
köktenci radical
köktencilik radicalism

köle slave
kölelik slavery
kömür charcoal; coal kömür gibi as black as coal, coal-black kömür kovası coal scuttle kömür ocağı coal mine
kömürcü coal dealer
kömürlük coalhole
kömürleşmek to become carbonized
köpek dog
köpekbalığı shark, dogfish
köpekdişi canine tooth
köprü bridge köprü kurmak to build a bridge; (wrestling) to bridge
köprücük collar bone, clavicle
köpük foam, froth
köpüklü frothy, foamy
köpürmek to froth, to foam; (soap) to lather
köpürtmek to froth up
kör blind; (knife, etc.) blunt kör dövüşü muddle kör kütük blind drunk kör olası(ca) cursed, damned; bloody kör şeytan evil destiny kör talih bad luck kör topal after a fashion, perfunctorily körü körüne blindly körler alfabesi Braille alphabet
körbağırsak cecum, blind gut
kördüğüm Gordian knot
körebe blind man's buff
körelme *biy.* atrophy
körelmek to become blunt; to atrophy; to become extinct
körfez gulf, bay
körkaya submerged rock
körkuyu dry well
körleşmek to become blunt; to become blind
körletmek to blunt; to deaden to damp
körlük blindness; bluntness
körpe fresh, tender
körpecik very fresh
körük bellows
körüklemek to fan with bellows; to fan, to incite
körüklü having bellows
köse beardless
kösele stout leather
kösnü lust
kösnül lustful, erotic
köstebek mole

kösteklemek to fetter; to hobble; to foil, to hinder

köşe corner **köşe atışı** corner-kick **köşe başı** street-corner **köşe bucak** even nook and cranny **köşe kapmaca** puss-in-the-corner **köşeyi dönmek** to strike it rich

köşebent angle iron

köşegen diagonal

köşeli cornered, angled

köşk villa, summer-house

kötek beating, thrashing **kötek atmak** to give a beating **kötek yemek** to get a beating

kötü bad, evil, nasty **kötü kadın** prostitute **kötüye kullanmak** to abuse, to misuse **kötü yola düşmek** to be on the streets **kötü niyetli** evil-minded, malicious

kötücül malicious; malignant

kötülemek to speak ill of, to run down

kötüleşmek to grow worse, to worsen

kötülük wickedness badness; harm, wrong **kötülük etmek** to do sb harm

kötümsemek to think ill of, to belittle

kötümser pessimist; pessimistic

kötümserlik pessimism

kötürüm crippled; cripple **kötürüm olmak** to be paralysed

köy village **köy muhtarı** village headman

köylü villager, peasant

köz embers, cinders

közlemek to barbecue

kral king; tycoon **kral gibi** king like **kral naibi** regent

kralcı royalist

kralcılık royalism

kraliçe queen

kraliyet kingdom, royally

kramp cramp **kramp girmek** to have cramp

krampon crampon, cleat

krank crankshaft

krater crater

kravat necktie, tie

kredi credit **kredi açmak** to give credit **kredi ile almak** to buy sth on credit **kredi kartı** credit card **kredi mektubu** letter of credit **kredili satış** sale on credit

krem cream **krem rengi** cream **krem şantiyi** whipped cream

krema cream

kremşantiye whipped cream

krepon crepon

kreş nursery

kreşendo crescendo

kriket cricket

kriko jack

kriminoloji criminology

kristal crystal

kriter criterion

kritik critical

kriz crisis; heart attack

krizantem chrysanthemum

kroki sketch

krom chromium

kromozom chromosome

kronik chronic

kronoloji chronology

kronolojik chronologic

kronometre chronometer

kros cross-country race

kroşe (boxing) hook

krupiye croupier

kruvaze double-breasted

kruvazör cruiser

kuaför hairdresser, coiffeur

kuartet *müz.* quartet

kubbe dome, cupola

kubbeli domed

kucak lap, embrace **kucak açmak** to receive with open arms **kucağına almak** to take on one's lap **kucağına oturmak** to sit on sb's lap

kucaklamak to embrace, to hug

kucaklaşmak to embrace one another

kudret power, strength **kudret helvası** manna

kudretli powerful

kudretsiz powerless

kudurgan furious, raging

kudurmak to go mad; to be enraged, to fume

kudurmuş mad; rabid, furious

kudurtmak to enrage, to infuriate

kuduruk rabid; enraged, furious

kuduz rabies; mad, rabid

Kudüs Jerusalem

kuğu swan
kukla puppet
kukuleta hood, cowl
kukumav little owl **kukumav gibi** all alone
kul slave; human being, man **kul köle olmak** to be at sb's back and call
kulaç fathom; *sp.* stroke
kulak ear **kulak ağrısı** earache **kulak ardı etmek** to turn a deaf ear **kulak asmak** to pay attention **kulak dolgunluğu** knowledge picked up here and there **kulak iltihabı** otitis **kulak kabartmak** to prick up one's ears **kulak kesilmek** to be all ears **kulak misafiri olmak** to overhear **kulak vermek** to give ear, to listen **kulağı ağır işitmek** to be herd of hearing **kulağı ağrımak** to have an earache **kulağına çalınmak** to come to one's ears **kulağına söylemek** to whisper in sb's ear **kulağını açmak** to open one's ears **kulağını çekmek** to pull sb's ears **Kulakları çınlasın!** I hope his ears are burning! **Kulaklarıma inanamadım!** I couldn't believe my ears! **kulaktan kapmak** to pick up a language **kulaktan kulağa** on the grapevine
kulakçık auricle
kulakkepçesi earlap
kulaklık headphone, earphone; hearing aid
kulakmemesi earlobe
kulakzarı eardrum
kulampara pederast, bugger
kule tower
kulis back stage, wing
kullanılmış used, second hand
kullanım use, usage
kullanış use, usage
kullanışlı handy, practical
kullanışsız unhandy
kullanmak to use, to employ
kulluk slavery; worship
kulp handle **kulp takmak** to invent a pretext
kuluçka broody hen **kuluçka dönemi** incubation period **kuluçka makinesi** incubator **kuluçkaya yatmak** to brood
kulunç shoulder pain, pain

kulübe hut, shed
kulüp club
kulvar track, course
kum sand **kum fırtınası** sandstorm **kum saati** hourglass
kumlu sandy
kumluk sandy place
kuma second wife, fellow wife
kumanda command **kumanda etmek** to command
kumandan commander
kumandanlık commandership
kumanya portable rations
kumar gambling, gamble **kumar oynamak** to gamble
kumarbaz, kumarcı gambler
kumarbazlık gambling
kumarhane casino, gambling house
kumaş cloth, fabric
kumbara moneybox
kumpanya company; troupe
kumpas plot, conspiracy **kumpas kurmak** to conspire
kumral light brown
kumru turtledove **kumrular gibi sevişmek** to bill and coo
kumsal beach, sands
kundak swaddling clothes
kundakçı incendiary, arsonist
kundakçılık arson
kundaklamak to swaddle; to set fire (to)
kundura shoe
kunduracı shoemaker
kunduz beaver
kupa cup; (cards) hearts
kupkuru bone-dry
kupon coupon
kupür cutting
kur rate of exchange; course
kur courtship, flirtation **kur yapmak** to pay court to
kurabiye cookie, cooky
kurak arid, dry
kuraklık drought
kural rule
kuraldışı exceptional
kurallı regular
kuralsız irregular
kuram theory

kuramsal theoretical
Kuran the Koran
kurbağa frog, toad
kurbağalama breaststroke, frog-style
kurban sacrifice, offering; victim **Kurban Bayramı** the Moslem Festival of Sacrifices **kurban kesmek** to kill as a sacrifice **kurban olmak** to be a victim **kurban vermek** to lose as casualties
kurbanlık sacrificial
kurcalamak to monkey with, to meddle with
kurdele ribbon
kurdeşen rash, urticaria
kurgu montage, editing
kuriye courier
kurmak to set up, to found, to establish, to found; to make up, to form; to set, to lay; to wind (up)
kurmay staff **kurmay subay** staff officer
kurnaz sly, cunning, foxy
kurnazlık slyness, cunning, foxiness
kurs course **kurs görmek** to take a course
kurs disc, disk
kursak crop, craw
kurşun lead; bullet **kurşun geçirmez** bullet-proof **kurşuna gibi** very heavy **kurşun yarası** bullet wound **kurşuna dizmek** to execute by shooting
kurşuni grey, leaden
kurşunkalem pencil
kurşunlamak to shoot
kurşunlu leaden
kurt wolf; worm **kurt dökmek** to pass a worm **kurt gibi aç** ravenous **kurt köpeği** wolf dog, wolfhound **kurtlarını dökmek** to have one's fling
kurtağzı dovetail
kurtarıcı liberator
kurtarma saving, rescue **kurtarma ekibi** rescue party
kurtarmak to save, to rescue
kurtçuk larva
kurtlanmak to get wormy; to fidget, to become impatient
kurtlu maggoty, wormy; fidgety
kurtulmak to escape; to be saved; to get rid of
kurtuluş escape, liberation, independence **Kurtuluş Savaşı** Turkish War of Independence
kuru dry; dried; arid **kuru fasulye** haricot bean(s) **kuru gürültü** much ado about nothing **kuru hava** dry weather **kuru iftira** sheer calumny **kuru incir** dried fig **kuru kalabalık** useless crowd **kuru pil** dry cell **kuru temizleme** dry cleaning **kuru temizleyici** dry cleaner's **kuru üzüm** raisin
kurucu founder; founding **kurucu meclis** constituent assembly
kurukafa skull
kurukahve (roasted and ground) coffee
kurul committee, council
kurulamak to dry
kurulmak to be set up; to nestle down; to swagger, to pose
kurultay congress, assembly
kuruluk dryness
kuruluş organization, foundation, establishment; *dilb.* construction
kurum institution, association, society, foundation; swagger, swank; soot **kurum kurum kurulmak** to be stuck-up **kurum satmak** to put on airs, to swagger
kurumak to get dry, to dry
kurumlu sooty; conceited
kuruntu delusion, fancy, illusion
kuruntulu suspicious, hypochondriac
kurusıkı blank (shot); bluff
kuruş Turkish piastre, kurush
kurutma drying **kurutma kâğıdı** blotting paper
kurutmak to dry
kurye courier
kuskus couscous
kusmak to vomit; to throw up
kusmuk vomit, puke
kusturmak to cause to vomit
kusur defect, fault, flaw **kusur bulmak** to find fault with **kusur etmek** to be at fault **Kusura bakma!** I beg your pardon!, Excuse me! **kusura bakmamak** to overlook, to excuse **kusuruna bakmamak** to excuse
kusurlu defective, faulty
kusursuz perfect, faultless
kusursuzluk perfection, faultlessness

kuş bird kuş beyinli bird-brained kuş kafesi bird cage kuş uçmaz kervan geçmez out-of-the-way, desolate kuş uçurtmamak to keep a sharp lookout kuşa benzetmek to mess up, to spoil
kuşak sash, girdle; generation; zone
kuşanmak to gird on, to carry; to dress
kuşatma *ask*. siege
kuşatmak to surround, to besiege
kuşbakışı bird's-eye view
kuşbaşı in small chunks; in big flakes
kuşekâğıdı glazed paper
kuşet couchette, bert
kuşku suspicion, doubt kuşku duymak to feel suspicious
kuşkucu suspicious
kuşkulanmak to suspect
kuşkulu suspicious, doubtful
kuşkusuz of course, certainly
kuşluk midmorning
kuşpalazı diphtheria
kuşsütü any nonexistent thing kuşsütüyle beslemek to cherish, to pamper
kuştüyü down kuştüyü yatak feather bed
kuşüzümü currant
kutlama celebration; congratulation
kutlamak to celebrate; to congratulate
kutlu blessed, lucky, happy
kutsal sacred, holy
kutsallık sacredness, holiness
kutsama sanctification
kutsamak to sanctify
kutu box, case
kutulamak to box
kutup pole
Kutupyıldızı the North Star, Polaris
kuvars quartz
kuvvet strength, power kuvvetten düşmek to lose strength
kuvvetle strongly
kuvvetlendirmek to strengthen, to fortify, to reinforce
kuvvetlenmek to become strong, to strengthen
kuvvetli strong, powerful
kuvvetsiz weak
kuyruk tail; queue kuyruğu kapana kısılmak to have one's back against the wall kuyruk olmak to queue up

kuyruk sallamak to wag the tail; to play up to, to cringe
kuyruklu tailed kuyruklu piyano grand piano kuyruklu yalan whopper, big lie
kuyruksuz tailless
kuyrukluyıldız comet
kuyruksokumu sacrum
kuytu snug; out-of-the-way, cosy
kuyu well kuyu açmak to dig a well kuyusunu kazmak to dig a pit for sb
kuyumcu jeweller, goldsmith kuyumcu dükkânı jeweller's shop
kuzen cousin
kuzey north; northern kuzey kutbu northpole
kuzeybatı northwest
kuzeydoğu northeast
kuzeyli northern
kuzgun raven
kuzu lamb kuzu gibi as meek as a lamb
kuzudişi milk tooth
kuzugöbeği *bitk.* button mushroom
kuzukulağı sheep's sorrel
kuzulamak to lamb
kuzumantarı morel
Küba Cuba
kübik cubic
kübizm cubism
küçücük tiny, wee
küçük small, little; child küçük aptes urination küçük dilini yutmak to fall off one's chair küçük düşmek to lose face küçük düşürmek to humiliate, to abase, to degrade küçük düşürücü humiliating küçük harf minuscule, lower case küçük su dökmek to urinate, to make water, to piss
Küçükayı Little Bear, Asia Minor
küçükbaş sheep and goats
küçükdil uvula
küçüklük smallness, littleness; childhood
küçülmek to become small, to dwindle; to be humiliated
küçültmek to make smaller, to diminish; to belittle, to humiliate
küçültücü humiliating
küçümsemek to belittle, to look down

küf   138

on, to scorn
küf mould **küf bağlamak** to become
mouldy
küfe pannier
küfelik basketful; dead drunk **küfelik olmak** to be blind drunk
küflenmek to mould, to mildew
küflü mouldy, musty
küfretmek to curse, to swear
küfür oath, bad language, cursing;
blasphemy **küfürü basmak** to swear,
to cuss
küfürbaz foul-mouthed
küfürlü foul-mouthed
küheylan purebred Arab horse
kükremek to roar
kükürt sulphur
kükürtlü sulphurous
kül ash **kül etmek** to ruin **kül olmak** to
be reduced to ashes **kül tablası** ashtray **kül yutmak** to be sucked, to be
duped
külah conical hat; cone, cornet **külah
giydirmek** to play a trick on sb **Külahı-
ma anlat!** Tell me another! **külahları
değişmek** to fall out with
külbastı grilled cutlet
külçe ingot
külfet trouble, burden, inconvenience
külfetli troublesome
külfetsiz easy, painless
külhanbeyi rowdy, roughneck, tough
külliyat complete works
küllü ashy
küllük ashtray
külot (men's) underpants, undershorts,
briefs; (women's) panties
külrengi ashy, grey
kültür culture
kültürel cultural
kültürfizik gymnastics
kültürlü cultured
kültürsüz uncultured
külüstür ramshackle, shabby, dilapidated; beat-up **külüstür otomobil** ja-
lopy, rattletrap
kümbet cupola, dome
küme heap, pile; group; sp. league
kümelemek to heap
kümelenmek to form a group

kümebulut cumulus
kümes coop **kümes hayvanları** poultry
kümülüs cumulus
künk water pipe
künye personal data; identification tag,
identification bracelet
küp large earthenware jar **küplere binmek** to fly into a rage **küpünü doldurmak** to feather one's nest
küp cube **küp kök** cube root
küpe earring **küpe takmak** to wear earrings
küpeçiçeği fuchsia
küpeşte gunwale, bulwark
kür health cure
kürdan toothpick
küre globe, sphere
küresel spherical
kürek shovel; oar **kürek çekmek** to row
kürekçi oarsman, rower
kürekkemiği shoulder blade
küremek to shovel up
kürk fur
kürkçü furrier **kürkçü dükkânı** furrier's
shop
kürkçülük furriery, furring
kürsü podium, pulpit, rostrum; professorship, chair **kürsü başkanı** chairman
kürtaj curetting, curettage
küs offended, peeved
küskü crowbar
küskün offended, sore, sulky
küskünlük sulk, vexation
küsmek to be offended, to sulk, to miff
küspe bagasse, residue
küstah insolent, impertinent
küstahça insolently
küstahlaşmak to start behaving insolently
küstahlık insolence, impertinence **küstahlık etmek** to act insolently
küstümotu mimosa
küsur remainder, odd
küsurat fractions, remainder
küsüşmek not to be on speaking terms
küt blunt, obtuse **küt küt etmek** (heart)
to pound
kütle mass
kütleşmek to become blunt

139   **lastik**

küttedek with a thud
kütük trunk; stum, stub; ledger, register **kütük gibi** greatly swollen; dead
  drunk **kütüğe kaydetmek** to enrol in
  the register
kütüklük cartridge-pouch
kütüphane library; bookcase
kütüphaneci librarian
kütürdemek to crack, to make a crash-
  ing sound
kütürdetmek to snap to crunch
kütür kütür (fruit) crisp, fresh; with a
  crunching sound, crunchingly
kütürtü crunching sound, crunch
küvet bath-tub; washbasin, sink

L

labada *bitk.* patience dock
labirent labyrinth
laborant laboratory assistant
laboratuvar laboratory, lab
lacivert navy blue, dark blue
laçka slack **laçka olmak** to get slack
lades a bet with a wishbone **lades kemiği** wishbone **lades tutuşmak** to make
  a bet by pulling a wishbone
ladin spruce
laf word; talk, chat; empty words **laf altında kalmamak** to be quick to retord
  laf anlamaz thickheaded, obstinate
  laf aramızda between us **laf atmak** to
  make passes at (a girl), to molest **laf
  dinlemek** to listen to advice **laf ebesi**
  chatterbox **laf etmek** to talk (with); to
  gossip **laf işitmek** to be told off **Laf
  ola beri gele!** Stuff and nonsense! **laf
  olsun diye** just for the sake of conversation **laf taşımak** to be a talebearer
  lafa dalmak to be lost in conversation
  lafa karışmak to interrupt, to chime in
  lafa tutmak to buttonhole **lafı ağzına
  tıkamak** to shut (sb) up **lafı ağzında
  gevelemek** to beat about the bush **lafı ağzından almak** to take the words
  out of sb's mouth **lafı çevirmek** to
  change the subject **lafı ağzında geve-**

lemek to beat about the bush **Lafı mı
  olur?** It is not worth mentioning **lafını
  bilmek** to weigh one's words **lafını
  esirgememek** not to mince one's
  words **lafını etmek** to talk about, to
  mention **lafını kesmek** to interrupt sb
  lafla peynir gemisi yürümez fine
  words butter no parsnips
lafazan talkative, windy
laflamak to chat away
lağım sewer, drain
lağımcı sewerman
lağvetmek to cancel
lağvolmak to be cancelled
lahana cabbage **lahana turşusu** pickled cabbage
lahit tomb, sarcophagus
lahza instant
laik secular
laikleştirmek to secularize
laiklik secularism, laicism
lakap nickname **lakap takmak** to give a
  nickname (to)
lakayt indifferent, unconcerned **lakayt
  kalmak** to be indifferent (to)
lakaytlık indifference, unconcern
lake lacquer; lacquered
lakırdı word, talk **lakırdı etmek** to talk
lakin but, however
laklak chatter, clatter
laktoz lactose
lale tulip
lalettayin whatsoever, any; at random,
  indiscriminately
lam microscope slide
lama *hayb.* lama; Lama, the Buddhist
  monk
lamba lamp
lan bud, buddy, man
lanet curse, imprecation; bloody, cursed, damned **lanet etmek** to curse, to
  damn **Lanet olsun!** Damn it!
lanetli cursed
lapa porridge, mushy **lapa gibi** soft,
  mushy **lapa lapa** in large flakes
lappadak with a plop
larenjit *hek.* laryngitis
largetto larghetto
larva larva
lastik rubber; tyre, tire

laterna *müz.* barrel organ
latife joke, leg-pull latife etmek to joke
latifeci joker
latilokum Turkish delight
Latin Latin Latin harfleri Latin characters
Latince Latin language, Latin
laubali saucy, pert, free and easy
laubalileşmek to become saucy
laubalilik sauciness, pertness
lav lava
lavabo washbasin
lavaj washing
lavanta lavender water
lavantaçiçeği lavender
layık worthy of, deserving layık olmak to deserve layığını bulmak to get one's deserts
layıkıyla properly, duly
layiha proposal, memorandum
Laz Laz
lazer laser
lazım necessary, required lazım olmak to be necessary
lazımlı necessary
lazımlık chamber pot
leblebi roasted chickpeas
legorn *hayb.* leghorn
leğen basin; *anat.* pelvis
leh benefit lehimde in my favour lehinde in favour of him (her) lehinde karar vermek to decide in favour of lehine in one's favour
Leh Pole; Polish
lehçe dialect
lehim solder
lehimlemek to solder
lehimli soldered
lejyon legion
leke stain, blot, smear leke çıkarmak to remove stain leke etmek to stain leke olmak to become stained leke sürmek to besmirch, to taint leke yapmak to stain
lekelemek to stain, to soil; to blemish, to taint
lekeli stained, spotted
lekesiz spotless, stainless
lenf lymph
lens lens

leopar leopard
lepiska flaxen, fair
leş carcass leş gibi kokmak to stink, to reek
leşkargası hooded crow
levazım supplies, provisions levazım albayı commissary officer
levha sign, signboard
levrek sea bass
levye lever; crank
leylak lilac
leylek stork
leziz delicious
lezzet taste, flavour lezzet almak to find pleasure in
lezzetlenmek to become tasty
lezzetli tasty, savoury
lezzetsiz tasteless
lıkırdamak to gurgle
lıkırtı gurgle
liberal liberal
liberalizm liberalism
libretto libretto
Libya Libya
Libyalı Libyan
lider leader
liderlik leadership
lif fibre; loofah
lifli fibrous
lig league
likör liqueur
liman harbour, seaport
limanlamak to anchor in a harbour
lime strip
lime lime in strips
limit *mat.* limit
limitet şirket limited company
limon lemon limon gibi olmak to turn pale
limoni pale yellow; touchy; bad, sour
limonlu lemon-flavoured
limonluk greenhouse; lemon squeezer
limonata lemonade
limontuzu citric acid
linç lynching linç etmek to lynch
linear *mat.* linear
linotip linotype
linyit lignite
lir lyre
lira lira, pound

liret Italian lira
lirik lyrical
lirizm lyricism
lisan language
lisansüstü postgraduate
lise high school, lycée
liseli high school student
liste list
literatür literature
litografya lithography
litre litre, liter
liyakat merit, capacity
liyakatli capable, efficient
liyakatsiz incapable, inefficient
lobi lobby
loca (theatre) box; masonic lodge
lodos southwest wind
logaritma logarithm
logaritmik logarithmic
loğusa woman in child-bed
loğusalık lying-in, confinement
lojistik logistic; logistics
lojman flat/house (provided to employees/workers)
lokal club; local
lokanta restaurant
lokantacı restaurateur
lokavt lockout
lokma morsel
lokmanruhu ether
lokomotif locomotive
lokum Turkish delight
lombar *den.* port
lomboz port-hole
lonca guild
Londra London
Londralı Londoner
lop round and soft; (egg) hard-boiled **lop et** boneless meat **lop yumurta** hard-boiled egg
lort lord
lostra shoe polish **lostra salonu** shoe-shine shop
losyon lotion
loş dim, murky, dark
lotus lotus
lökosit leucocyte
lösemi leukemia
lumbago lumbago
lunapark amusement park

Lübnan Lebanon
Lübnanlı Lebanese
lüfer bluefish
lügat dictionary **lügat paralamak** to use a pompous language
lüks luxury; luxurious, de luxe **lüks mevki** deluxe class
lüle curl, ringlet, fold; spout
lületaşı meerschaum
lüp windfall **lüp diye yutmak** to gulp down
lüpçü sponger, moocher
lütfen please
lütfetmek to be so kind as to, to deign, to condescend
lütuf favour kindness
lütufkâr gracious, kind
lüzum necessity, need **lüzum görmek** to deem necessary
lüzumlu necessary

M

maada besides
maalesef unfortunately
maarif education, instruction
maaş salary **maaş günü** payday
maaşlı salaried
mabet temple
Macar Hungarian
Macarca Hungarian language
Macaristan Hungary
macera adventure **macera aramak** to seek adventure **macera romanı** adventure novel
maceracı adventurer
maceralı adventurous
macun paste; putty
maç match, game, bout
maça spade **maça beyi** jack of spades **maça kızı** queen of spades
maçuna *den.* crane, winch, derrick
madam madam
madde matter, substance; stuff; article, clause, paragraph
maddeci materialist
maddecilik materialism

maddesel material
maddeten materially
maddi material, physical, corporal
maddiyat material things
madem, mademki since, as, now that
maden mine, mineral; metal maden işçisi miner maden cevheri mineral ore maden mühendisi mining engineer maden ocağı mine maden yatağı ore-bed
madeni mineral, inorganic; metallic
madenkömürü coal
madensel mineral; metallic
madensuyu mineral water
madenyünü mineral wool
madik trick madik atmak to cheat
madrabaz middleman; cheat, crook
madrabazlık cheating, trickery
maestro *müz.* maestro
mafiş finished
mafsal articulation, joint
mafya Mafia, Maffia
magazin magazine
magma magma
magnezyum magnesium
mağara cave mağara adamı caveman
mağaza large store
mağdur wronged; victim, dupe
mağduriyet unjust treatment
mağfiret forgiveness
mağlubiyet defeat
mağlup defeated, overcome mağlup etmek to defeat, to overcome mağlup olmak to be defeated
mağrur proud, conceited
mağrurluk conceit
mahal place, spot mahal vermemek not to give occasion for mahallinde on the spot
mahalle quarter, district
mahalli local
maharet skill, dexterity
maharetli skilful, dexterous
maharetsiz unskilful
mahcubiyet shyness
mahcup shy, ashamed mahcup etmek to shame, to mortify mahcup olmak to be ashamed, to be embarrassed
mahdum son
mahdut limited

mahfaza case, box
mahıv destruction
mahiyet nature, character
mahkeme court mahkeme kararı sentence, verdict
mahkûm sentenced, condemned; convict mahkûm etmek to condemn, to sentence mahkûm olmak to be sentenced, to be condemned
mahkûmiyet sentence, condemnation
mahlep *bitk.* mahaleb
mahluk creature
mahmur sleepy, drowsy
mahmurluk sleepiness, drowsiness
mahmuz spur
mahmuzlamak to spur
mahpus prisoner; imprisoned
mahpushane prison
mahrem secret, private, intimate
mahremiyet privacy, intimacy
mahrum deprived mahrum etmek to deprive of
mahrumiyet deprivation mahrumiyet bölgesi hardship area mahrumiyet içinde yaşamak to lead a life of privation, to rough it
mahsuben to the account of
mahsul crop, produce; product
mahsur confined, cut off; stuck mahsur kalmak to be stuck (in)
mahsus special, peculiar to; reserved for; on purpose, deliberately
mahşer the last judgement; great crowd, great confusion
mahşeri (crowd) tremendous
mahvetmek to destroy
mahvolmak to be destroyed
mahzen cellar, granary
mahzun sad, gloomy
mahzur drawback, objection
mahzurlu disadvantageous, objectionable
maiyet suite, retinue, attendants
majeste majesty
majör *müz.* major
majüskül capital letter
makale article
makam position, office; tune
makara bobbin, reel, spool makaraya almak to make fun (of)

makarna macaroni

makas scissors, shears **makas almak** to pinch sb's cheek

makaslamak to scissor; to pinch sb's cheek; to censor (films)

makat anus

makber grave

makbul acceptable, welcome **makbule geçmek** to be welcome

makbuz receipt

Makedonya Macedonia

Makedonyalı Macedonian

maket model

maki bush, scrub

makine machine; engine **makine dairesi** engine room **makine mühendisi** mechanical engineer

makineci mechanic

makineleştirmek to mechanize

makineli having a machine **makineli tüfek** machine-gun

makineyağı lubricating oil, machine oil

makinist engine-driver; mechanic

makrama macrame

makro macro

maksadıyla with the intention of

maksat purpose, intention

maksatlı purposeful

maksatsız purposeless

maksi maxi

maksimum maximum

maktul killed, murdered

makul reasonable, sensible

makyaj make-up **makyaj yapmak** to make up

mal goods, commodity, merchandise; property; wealth; cattle, livestock; hash, heroin; loose woman **mal bildirimi** declaration of property **mal canlısı** avaricious **mal etmek** to appropriate for oneself; to produce at **mal müdürü** head of the finance office **mal mülk** property, goods **mal olmak** to cost **mal sahibi** owner **malın gözü** tricky, sly; (woman) loose

mala trowel

malak buffalo calf

malarya malaria

Malezya Malaysia

mali financial, fiscal **mali yıl** fiscal year

malik owning, possessing; owner, possessor **malik olmak** to have, to own

malikâne large estate, stately home

maliye finance **Maliye Bakanı** Minister of Finance **Maliye Bakanlığı** Ministry of Finance

maliyeci financier

maliyet cost **maliyet fiyatı** cost price

malmüdür head of the finance office

malt malt

Malta Malta

maltaeriği loquat

malul invalid, disabled

maluliyet disablement

malum known **malum olmak** to sense, to surmise

malumat information **malumat vermek** to inform **malumatı olmak** to know about

malzeme material, necessaries

mama baby's food

mamafih however, yet

mamul manufactured

mamulat manufactures

mamur prosperous

mamut *hayb.* mammoth

mana meaning **mana vermek** to interpret

manalı meaningful

manasız meaningless

manastır monastery

manav greengrocer, fruiteror; greengrocer's

mancınık catapult

manda water buffalo

manda mandate

mandal clothes-peg *Aİ.* clothespin; latch, tumbler

mandallamak to peg up *Aİ.* to pin up; to latch

mandalina mandarin, tangerine

mandıra dairy farm

mandolin mandolin

manen morally, spiritually

manevi moral, spiritual **menevi evlat** adopted child

maneviyat morale **maneviyatı bozulmak** to lose morale

manevra manoeuvres **manevra fişeği** *ask.* blank cartridge **manevra yap-**

mak to manoeuvre
manga *ask.* squad
mangal brazier mangal kömürü charcoal
manganez *kim.* manganese
mangır money dough
mangırsız penniless, broke
mangiz *arg.* money, dough, brass
mâni hindrance, impediment, obstacle mâni olmak to prevent, to hinder, to obstruct
mânia obstacle, barrier
manifatura drapery, textiles
manifaturacı draper
manifesto manifest
manikür manicure manikür yapmak to manicure
manikürcü manicurist
manita girlfriend, bird, *Aİ.* chick
manivela lever, crank
mankafa blockheaded, thick-headed
mankafalık thick-headness
manken model
mankenlik modelling
manolya magnolia
manometre manometer
mansiyon honourable mention
Manş Denizi the English Channel
manşet head-line; cuff
manşon muff
mantar mushroom; fungus; cork mantar gibi yerden bitmek to mushroom
mantık logic mantığa aykırı against logic
mantıkçı logician
mantıki logical, reasonable
mantıkdışı alogical
mantıklı logical, reasonable
mantıksal logical, reasonable
mantıksız illogical, unreasonable
mantıksızlık illogicality, unreasonableness
manto coat
manyak maniac
manyakça maniacal; maniacally
manyetik magnetic manyetik alan magnetic field manyetik bant magnetic tape manyetik kutup magnetic pole
manyetizma megnetism

manyeto magneto
manyezi magnesia
manzara view, landscape, panorama
manzaralı having a fine view, scenic
manzum in verse
manzume poem
marangoz joiner, carpenter
marangozluk joinery, carpentry
maraton marathon
maraz disease, illness
marazi pathological, morbid
mareşal marshal
mareşallik marshalship
margarin margarine
marifet skill
marifetli skilled
mariz *arg.* beating, thrashing
marizlemek to beat, to thrash
marj margin
marka make, mark, brand; ticket; counter
markaj (football) marking
markalamak to mark
markalı marked
marke etmek (football) to mark
marki marquis, marquess
markiz marchioness
marley vinyl floor covering
marmelat marmalade
maroken morocco (leather)
marpuç tube of a water-pipe
mars gammon mars etmek to gammon, to skunk *Aİ.*
Mars Mars
marş starter; march; Forward march! marşa basmak to press the starter Marş marş! *ask.* Run!; *kon.* Get going!
marşandiz goods train
mart March Mart kapıdan baktırır, kazma kürek yaktırır *ats.* Cast ne'er a clout till May is out.
martaval bunkum, hot air, humbug, baloney martaval atmak/okumak to spin a yarn
martavalcı liar, bullshitter
martı sea-gull
martini martini
maruf known, notorious
marul cos lettuce, cos

maruz exposed to **maruz kalmak** to experience, to be exposed to
maruzat representations, petitions
masa table; desk **masa örtüsü** table cloth
masaj massage **masaj yapmak** to massage
masal tale, story; lie, yarn **masal okumak** to spin a yarn **masal anlatmak** to tell a tale
masalcı story teller
masatenisi table tennis, ping pong
masatopu table tennis, ping pong
masif massive
mask mask
maskara buffoon, clown; mascara; frisky, playful **maskara etmek** to make a laughing-stock **maskaraya çevirmek** to make a fool of
maskaralık drollery, buffoonery **maskaralık etmek** to play the fool
maske mask **maskesi düşmek** to show one's true colours
maskelemek to mask
maskeli masked **maskeli balo** masked ball
maskot mascot
maslahat affair, business
maslahatgüzar charge d'affaires
masmavi very blue
mason freemason, mason
masonluk freemason
masör masseur
masraf expense, expenditure, cost **masrafa girmek** to put oneself to expense **masrafa sokmak** to put sb to expense **masraf etmek** to go to expense **masrafı çekmek** to bear the expense **masrafı karşılamak** to cover expenses **masrafını çıkarmak** to pay for itself **masraftan kaçmak** to avoid expense **masraftan kaçmamak** to spare no expense
masraflı expensive
masrafsız without expense
mastar infinitive
mastika mastic
mastürbasyon masturbation
masum innocent
masumiyet innocence

masura bobbin
maşa tongs; cat's-paw, tool **maşa gibi kullanmak** to use sb as a tool **maşası olmak** to be sb's pawn
maşallah May God preserve him from evil!; Wonderful!, Magnificent!
maşrapa mug
mat dull, mat
mat checkmate **mat etmek** to checkmate **mat olmak** to be checkmated
matador matador, bullfighter
matah thing, object
matara canteen, waterbottle
matbaa printing-press, press
matbaacı printer
matbaacılık printing
matbu printed
matbua printed matter
matbuat the Press
matem mourning **matem tutmak** to mourn
matemli mournful
matematik mathematics
matematikçi mathematician; mathematics teacher
materyal material
materyalist materialist
materyalizm materialism
matine matinee
matkap drill, gimlet; auger
matmazel mademoiselle, Miss
matrah tax assessment
matrak joke, fun; droll, funny **matrağa almak** to make fun of **matrak geçmek** to rib, to tease
matris matrix
maun mahogany
maval story, yarn, lie **maval okumak** to tell lies
mavi blue
mavilik blueness
mavimsi bluish
mavna barge, lighter
mavzer Mauser rifle
maya ferment, yeast, leaven
mayalamak to ferment, to leaven
mayalanma fermentation
mayalanmak to ferment
mayalı fermented
mayasıl hemorrhoids, piles

maydanoz parsley

mayhoş sourish, tart

mayhoşluk tartness

mayın *ask.* mine **mayın detektörü** mine detector **mayın gemisi** mine-layer **mayın taramak** to sweep mines **mayın tarama gemisi** mine-sweeper **mayın tarlası** mine-field

mayınlamak to mine

mayıs May

mayısböceği cockchafer, maybeetle

mayi liquid, fluid

maymun monkey, ape **maymun iştahlı** capricious,inconstant

mayna down sails **mayna etmek** to down sails, to haul down

mayo bathing suit, trunks

mayonez mayonnaise

mayonezli dressed with mayonnaise

maytap fireworks

mazeret excuse, apology **mazeret beyan etmek** to make excuses

mazeretli excused

mazeretsiz unexcused

mazgal embrasure

mazgallı embrasured

mazı arborvitae

mazi past bygone **maziye karışmak** to belong to past days

mazlum wronged, oppressed

mazoşist masochist; masochistic

mazoşizm masochism

mazot diesel oil, fuel oil

mazur excused, excusable **mazur görmek** to excuse, to pardon

mebus deputy, member of Parliament

mecal strength, power **mecali kalmamak** to have no strength left

mecaz figure of speech, trope'

mecazi figurative, metaphorical

mecbur compelled, forced, bound **mecbur etmek** to compel, to force **mecbur olmak** to be compelled

mecburen compulsorily

mecburi compulsory, obligatory **mecburi iniş** forced landing **mecburi istikamet** one way

mecburiyet compulsion, obligation **mecburiyetinde kalmak** to have to, to be obliged to

meclis assembly, council

mecmua magazine

mecnun madly in love, love-crazed

mecra watercourse, conduit

Mecusi Zorastrian, Mazdean

Mecusilik Zoroastiianism

meç rapier, foil

meç (hair) streak, hair-piece

meçhul unknown

meddücezir ebb and flow

medeni civilized, civil **medeni cesaret** moral courage **medeni haklar** civil rights **medeni kanun** civil code, civil law

medenileşmek to become civilized

medenileştirmek to civilize

medeniyet civilization

medeniyetsiz uncivilized

medet help, aid **medet ummak** to hope for help

medrese Moslem theological school, medresseh, madrasa

medya media, mass-media, mass communications

medyum fortune teller; medium

mefhum concept

mefkure ideal

mefruşat furnishings; fabrics

meftun infatuated, fascinated

megafon megaphone

megalomani *ruhb.* megalomania

megaton megaton

megavat *fiz.* megawatt

meğer but, however

Mehmetçik the Turkish Tommy

mehtap moonlight

mehter band of musicians performing military music

mekân place; residence, abode; space

mekanik mechanics; mechanical

mekanize mechanized

mekanizm *fel.* mechanism

mekanizma mechanism

mekik shuttle **mekik dokumak** to shuttle

Mekke Mecca

mektep school

mektup letter

mektuplaşma correspondence

mektuplaşmak to correspond

melamin melamine
melankoli melancholy
melankolik melancholic
melek angel **melek gibi** angelic
meleke faculty, aptitude, bent, knack
melekotu angelica
meleme bleat
melemek to bleat
melez cross-bred, hybrid
melezlemek to cross
melezleşmek to become crossed
melhem ointment
melodi melody
melodram melodrama
melodramatik melodramatic
melon bowler-hat
meltem breeze
melun cursed, damned
memba spring, fountain **memba suyu** spring water
meme breast, nipple, boobs **memeden kesmek** to wean **meme emmek** to suckle **meme vermek** to suckle
memeli mammiferous **memeli hayvanlar** mammals
memleket country
memnun glad, happy, pleased **memnun etmek** to please, to satisfy **memnun olmak** to be pleased
memnunluk gladness, pleasure
memorandum memorandum
memur official, employee **memur etmek** to appoint, to commission
memuriyet government job, official post, charge
memurluk official post, charge
menajer manager
mendebur disgusting, slovenly
menderes meander
mendil handkerchief **mendil açmak** to beg
mendirek breakwater, mole
menecer manager
menekşe violet
menekşegülü China rose, Bengel rose
menenjit meningitis
menetmek to forbid
menfaat interest, advantage
menfaatçi, menfaatperest self-seeking
menfi negative

mengene vice; press; clamp
meni sperm, semen
menkıbe legend
menkul movable, transferable **menkul değerler** stocks and bonds **menkul mallar** movable goods
menopoz menopause
mensubiyet relationship
mensucat textiles
mensup belonging to; member
menşe origin
menteşe hinge
menteşeli hinged
mentol menthol
mentollü mentholated
menzil range
mera pasture
merak curiosity; worry, anxiety; hobby, whim, bug **Merak etme!** Don't worry!
merak etmek to worry, to be curious about sth **merak içinde** anxios **merak sarmak** to develop a passion for **merakta bırakmak** to keep sb in suspense
meraklanmak to worry, to be anxious
meraklı curious, inquisitive; fond of, bug, devotee, hound
meraksız indifferent, uninterested
meram intention, aim **meramını anlatmak** to explain oneself
merasim ceremony, celebration **merasim kıtası** guard of honour, honour guard
mercan coral
mercanada atoll
mercanbalığı red seabream
mercanköşk marjoram
mercanotu pearlweed
mercek lens
merci reference, recourse
mercimek lentil **mercimeği fırına vermek** to fall in love with
merdane cylinder, roller
merdiven stairs; steps; ladder **merdiven basamağı** step, stair **merdiven parmaklığı** balustrade **merdiven sahanlığı** landing
meret damn
merhaba Hello! Hi! **merhabayı kesmek** to break off with sb

merhabalaşmak to greet one another
merhale stage, phase
merhamet pity, mercy **merhamete gelmek** to become merciful **merhamet etmek** to pity
merhametli pitiful, merciful
merhametsiz merciless, pitiless
merhametsizlik mercilessness, cruelty
merhem ointment, salve
merhum deceased, the late
meridyen meridian
Merih Mars
merinos merino
merkep donkey, ass
merkez centre, center; headquarters; police station **Merkez Bankası** Central Bank
merkezci centralist
merkezcilik centralism
merkezi central **merkezi ısıtma** central heating
merkezileşmek to centralize
merkeziyet centralization
merkeziyetçi centralist
merkeziyetçilik centralism
merkezkaç centrifugal
Merkür Mercury
mermer marble
mermi bullet, projectile
merserize mercerized
mersi thank you
mersin myrtle
mersinbalığı sturgeon
mersiye elegy
mert brave, manly
mertçe bravely
mertlik bravery
mertebe rank, grade
Meryem Ana the Virgin Mary
mesafe distance
mesai efforts, work **mesai arkadaşı** fellow worker **mesai saatleri** working hours, office hours **mesaiye kalmak** to work overtime
mesaj message
mesane bladder
mescit small mosque
mesel proverb, parable
mesela for example, for instance
mesele problem; matter **mesele çıkar-**
mak to make a fuss **mesele yapmak** to make a to-do about sth
meshetmek to wipe with the palm of the hand
Mesih Messiah
mesire promenade
mesken dwelling, house
meskûn inhabited
meslek profession, career
meslektaş colleague
mesleki professional
mesnet support, prop
mest drunk; enchanted **mest etmek** to intoxicate; to enrapture **mest olmak** to be intoxicated; to be enraptured
mest light soleless boot
mesul responsible
mesuliyet responsibility
mesuliyetli responsible
mesut happy
meşakkat trouble, hardship
meşakkatli troublesome, difficult
meşale torch
meşe oak
meşgale occupation, activity
meşgul busy **meşgul etmek** to keep busy **meşgul olmak** to be busy (with)
meşguliyet occupation, activity
meşhur famous, well-known **meşhur olmak** to become famous
meşin leather
meşru legitimate, lawful **meşru müdafaa** self-defence
meşrubat beverage, drinks
meşrutiyet constitutional government
meşum inauspicious, portentous
met high tide
meta merchandise
metabolizma biy. metabolism
metafaz biy. metaphase
metafizik metaphysics; metaphysical
metal metal
metalbilim metallurgy
metalurji metallurgy
metamorfoz metamorphosis
metan kim. methane
metanet firmness, fortitude **metanet göstermek** to show firmness
metanetli firm, steady
metanetsiz spineless, yielding, weak

metapsişik metapsychical
metastaz metastasis
metazori by force
metelik red cent, bean **meteliğe kurşun atmak** to be stony broke **metelik vermemek** not to care a fig
meteliksiz stony broke, penniless
meteor meteor
meteoroloji meteorology
meteorolojik meteorological
methetmek to praise, to extol
methiye eulogy, panegyric
metil methyl **metil alkol** methyl alcohol
metilen methylene
metin text
metin firm, solid
metodoloji methodology
metodolojik methodological
metot method
metotlu methodic
metotsuz unmethodical
metraj measurement in metres
metre metre, meter **metre kare** square metre **metre küp** cubic metre
metres mistress, keptie **metres tutmak** to keep a mistress
metrik metric **metrik sistem** metric system
metris *ask.* entrenchment, breastwork
metro underground, tube *Aİ.* subway
metronom *müz.* metronome
metropol metropolis
metropolit metropolitan
metruk abandoned, deserted
mevcudiyet existence; presence
mevcut existent, existing **mevcut olmak** to exist, to be present
mevduat deposits **mevduat hesabı** deposit account
mevki place; site; position, post; seat, class
Mevla God
mevlit poem depicting the birth and life of Mohammed
mevsim season
mevsimlik seasonal
mevsimsiz unseasonable, untimely
mevzi place, position **mevzi almak** *ask.* to take up a position
mevzu subject, topic

mevzuat the laws, the regulations
mevzubahis in question
meyankökü liquorice root
meydan square, open space **meydana atılmak** to come forward, to offer oneself **meydana atmak** to put forward, to suggest **meydana çıkarmak** to bring out, to bring to light; to reveal, to disclose **meydana çıkmak** to come into view, to appear; to come out, to be revealed **meydana gelmek** to happen, to occur; to come into existence **meydana getirmek** to bring into being, to produce **meydanda** clear, obvious **meydanı boş bulmak** to do what ever he wants in the absence of rivals **meydan muharebesi** pitched battle **meydan okumak** to challenge **meydan vermek** to give an opportunity **meydan vermemek** to avoid, to prevent
meyhane bar, saloon, pub, joint
meyhaneci barkeep, barkeeper
meyil slope, slant; inclination, tendency **meyil vermek** to fall in love with
meyilli sloping, slanting; inclined
meyletmek to incline
meymenetsiz inauspicious, unlucky, sulky, disagreeable
meyve fruit **meyve bahçesi** orchard **meyve suyu** fruit juice **meyve vermek** to fruit
meyveli fruitful, fruited
meyvesiz fruitless
mezar grave, tomb **mezarlık** cemetery, graveyard
mezat auction **mezata çıkarmak** to put up for auction **mezat malı** cheap, ordinary merchandise
mezatçı auctioneer
mezbaha slaughterhouse
meze appetizer, snack, hors d'oeuvre
mezgit whiting
mezhep creed, denomination
meziyet virtue, merit
meziyetli virtuous, meritorious
mezoderm mesoderm
mezon *fiz.* meson
mezosfer mesosphere
mezozoik *coğ.* mesozoic

mezun graduated from; graduate
mezuniyet graduation
mezura tape-measure
mezzosoprano *müz.* mezzo-soprano
mıh nail, stud
mıhlamak to nail
mıhlanmak to be nailed; to be nailed to the spot
mıknatıs magnet
mıknatısiyet magnetism
mıknatıslamak to magnetize
mıknatıslı magnetic
mıncıklamak to squeeze and squash, to knead
mıntıka district, zone
mırıldanmak to murmur, to mutter
mırıltı murmur, mutter mırın kırın etmek to show reluctance, to grumble
mırnav miaow
mısır maize *Aİ.* corn mısır koçanı corncob mısır patlatmak to pop corn mısır tarlası cornfield
Mısır Egypt
Mısırlı Egyptian
mısıryağı corn oil
mısra line (of poetry)
mışıl mışıl soundly mışıl mışıl uyumak to sleep soundly
mıymıntı sluggish, slack
mızıka military band
mızıkçılık spoilsport, killjoy mızıkçılık etmek not to play the game
mızmız fussy, persnickety, whiny
mızmızlanmak to make a fuss about trifles
mızrak lance, spear
mızrap plectrum
mi *müz.* mi
miço cabin boy
mide stomach, tummy mide bozukluğu stomach upset mide bulandırmak to turn one's stomach mide bulantısı nausea mide iltihabı gastritis mide kanaması gastric bleeding mideye indirmek to put sth away mideye oturmak to lie heavy on the stomach
midesiz having bad taste; eating anything
midi midi

midilli pony
midye mussel
migren migraine
miğfer helmet
mihenk touchstone, test
mihmandar host, hostess
mihnet trouble, worry mihnet çekmek to suffer
mihrace maharaja, maharajah
mihrap niche in a mosque, mihrab
mihver axis
mika mica
mikado mikado
mikro- micro
mikrobik mikrobic
mikrobiyoloji microbiology
mikrofilm microfilm
mikrofon microphone
mikrofonik microphonic
mikrometre micrometer
mikron micron
mikroorganizma microorganism
mikrop microbe, germ
mikroplu microbic
mikropsuz sterilized
mikroskop microscope
mikroskopik microscopic
mikser mixer
miktar quantity amount
mikyas scale
mil pivot, axle, axis
mil mile
miladi of the Christian era miladi takvim the Gregorian calender
milat birth of Christ milattan önce, MÖ. before Christ, B.C. milattan sonra, MS. after Christ, A.D.
mili- milli
milibar millibar
miligram milligramme
milim millimetre milimi milimine exactly
milimetre milimetre
milis militia
militan militant
millet nation, people Millet Meclisi the National Assembly
milletlerarası international
milletvekili deputy milletvekili dokunulmazlığı parliamentary immunity

milli national milli bayram national holiday Milli Eğitim Bakanlığı the Ministry of Education milli gelir national income milli marş national anthem Milli Savunma Bakanlığı the Ministry of Defence milli takım national team

millileştirmek to nationalize

milliyet nationality

milliyetçi nationalist

milliyetçilik nationalism

milyar milliard *Aİ.* billion

milyarder billionaire

milyon million

milyoner millionaire

mimar architect

mimari architectural; architecture

mimarlık architecture

mimlemek to mark down, to blacklist

mimoza *bitk.* mimosa

minare minaret

minber pulpit (in a mosque)

minder mattress, cushion; wrestling mat

mine enamel

mineçiçeği vervain, verbena

mineral mineral

mineraloji mineralogy

mini mini mini etek miniskirt

minibüs minibus

minicik tiny, wee

minik small and nice

minimal minimal

minimini teensy-weensy, tiny

minimum minimum

mink *hayb.* mink

minnacık teeny-weeny, wee

minnet gratitude, indebtedness minnet altında kalmak to be under obligation minnet altında kalmamak to repay a favour minnet etmek to ask a favour, to plead

minnettar grateful, indebted

minnettarlık gratitude, indebtedness

minnoş little darling

minör *müz.* minor

minüskül minuscule

minyatür miniature

minyon petite, slender, small

miraç the Prophet Mohammed's ascent to heaven

miras inheritance, heritage mirasa konmak to inherit

mirasçı heir, inheritor

mirasyedi (one) who has inherited a fortune; spendthrift, prodigal

mis musk mis gibi fragrant; excellent, proper

misafir guest, visitor misafir ağırlamak to entertain a guest misafir etmek to put sb up misafir odası guestroom misafireten as a guest

misafirlik visit misafirliğe gitmek to pay a visit to; to go on a visit to

misafirhane guesthouse

misafirperver hospitable

misafirperverlik hospitality

misal example

misil a similar one misliyle mukabele retaliation

misilleme retaliation misillemede bulunmak to retaliate misilleme olarak as a reprisal

misina fishline

misket marble

miskin indolent, bone-lazy, supine

miskinleşmek to become indolent

miskinlik indolence, sluggishness

mistik mystic, mystical

misyon mission

misyoner missionary

mit myth

miting meeting, demonstration miting yapmak to hold a public demonstration

mitoloji mythology

mitolojik mythological

mitoz *biy.* mitosis

mitral *anat.* mitral

mitralyöz machine gun

miyar standard; *kim.* reagent

miyav miaow, meow

miyavlamak to miaow, to meow

miyop nearsighted, shortsighted

miyopluk shortsightedness, myopia

mizaç temperament, nature

mizah humour mizah dergisi humour magazine

mizahçı humorist

mizahi humorous

mizanpaj page-setting, layout

mizanpli (hair) set
mizansen mise-en-scéne
mobilya furniture
mobilyacı maker/seller of furniture; furniture shop
mobilyalı furnished
moda fashion **moda(da)** in fashion **moda olmak** to be in fashion **modası geçmek** to be out of fashion **modası geçmiş** old-fashioned, out of date, **modaya uygun** fashionable **modayı izlemek** to follow the fashion
modacı fashion designer, modiste
model model
modellik modelling
moderato *müz.* moderato
modern modern
modernize modernized
modernleşmek to become modern
modernleştirmek to modernize
modernlik modernity
modül module
modülasyon modulation
Moğol Mongol; Mongolian
Moğolistan Mongolia
mokasen moccasin
mola pause, break **mola vermek** to halt, to take a break
molekül molecule
moleküler molecular
molla mullah, mollah
molotof kokteyli Molotov cocktail
moloz rubble, debris; *arg.* worthless person/thing
moment momentum
monarşi monarchy
monarşik monarchic
monarşist monarchist
monarşizm monarchism
monitör monitor
monogami *topb.* monogamy
monografi monograph
monolog monologue
monopol monopoly
monoteist monotheist; monotheistic
monoteizm monotheism
monotip monotype
monoton monotonous
monotonluk monotony
montaj mounting, assembly

montajcı assembler
monte etmek to put together, to assemble, to put together
mor violet, purple
moral morale **moral vermek** to cheer sb up, to reassure **morali bozulmak** to become low-spirited **morali düzelmek** to recover one's morale **moralini bozmak** to get sb down, to demoralize
morarmak to turn purple, to be black and blue
morartı bruise
morartmak to make purple; to make black and blue
moratoryum moratorium
morfem *dilb.* morpheme
morfin morphine
morfinman morphine addict
morfoloji morphology
morfolojik morphologic
morg morgue
morina cod, codfish
morötesi ultraviolet
Mors Morse **Mors alfabesi** Morse Alphabet
morto dead **mortoyu çekmek** to kick the bucket, to die
moruk *arg.* old man
mosmor deep purple; black and blue all over **mosmor kesilmek** to turn red in the face
mostra sample, pattern
mostralık figurehead; sample, model
motel motel
motif motif
motivasyon motivation
motor engine, motor; motorboat, boat; motorcycle
motorlu motorized
motorsuz motorless
motorbot motorboat
motorize motorized
motosiklet motorcycle
mozaik mosaic
möble furniture
möbleli furnished
möblesiz unfurnished
mönü menu
mösyö Monsieur

muadil equivalent

muaf exempt, freed **muaf tutmak** to exempt (from)

muafiyet exemption

muallak suspended **muallakta** in suspense, in abeyance **muallakta kalmak** to remain in suspense

muamele treatment, conduct; transaction, procedure **muamele etmek** to treat

muamma enigma, mystery

muaşeret social intercourse **muaşeret adabı** etiquette

muavin helper, assistant

muayene examination **muayene etmek** to examine

muayenehane consulting room, surgery

muayyen certain, definite

muazzam enormous, tremendous

mubah permissible, tolerated

mucibince in accordance with

mucip cause, reason

mucit inventor

mucize miracle **mucizeler yaratmak** to work miracles

mucizevi miraculous

muço cabin-boy

mudi depositor

muğlak abstruse, recondite, obscure

muhabbet affection, love **muhabbet etmek** to have a friendly chat **muhabbet tellalı** procurer, pimp

muhabbetçiçeği mignonette

muhabbetkuşu lovebird, budgerigar

muhabere correspondence, communication **muhabere sınıfı** *ask.* signal corps

muhabir correspondent

muhafaza protection **muhafaza altına almak** to guard, to protect **muhafaza etmek** to keep, to preserve, to protect

muhafazakâr conservative

muhafazakârlık conservatism

muhafız guard, defender **muhafız alayı** troop of guardsmen

muhakeme trial; judgement; reasoning **muhakeme etmek** to hear a case, to judge; to reason

muhakkak certain, sure; certainly

muhalefet opposition **muhalefet etmek** to oppose **muhalefet partisi** the opposition party

muhalif opponent

muhallebi milk pudding **muhallebi çocuğu** milksop, namby-pamby

muharebe battle, war **muharebe meydanı** battlefield

muharip combatant, belligerent

muharrik motive, moving; agitator, instigator

muhasara siege

muhasebe accountancy, bookkeeping

muhasebeci accountant

muhatap one spoken to; *tic.* drawee

muhayyel imaginary

muhayyer on approval

muhayyile imagination

muhbir informer

muhit surroundings, environment

muhkem strong, firm

muhtaç needy, dependent, destitute **muhtaç olmak** to be in need of

muhtar autonomous; headman, chief

muhtelif various

muhtemel probable, likely

muhtemelen probably

muhterem respected

muhteşem magnificent, splendid

muhteva contents

muhteviyat contents

muhtıra memorandum

mukabele retaliation, retort, response **mukabelede bulunmak** to return, to repay **mukabele etmek** to retaliate, to reciprocate

mukabil counter; equivalent, counterpart; in response to; in return for

mukadderat destiny, fate

mukaddes holy, sacred

mukavele agreement, contract **mukavele yapmak** to make a contract

mukavemet resistance **mukavemet etmek** to resist **mukavemet göstermek** to show resistance **mukavemet koşusu** long distance race

mukavemetli resisting, strong

mukavemetsiz resistless

mukavva cardboard

mukayese comparison **mukayese etmek** to compare
mukoza mucosa
muktedir capable **muktedir olmak** to be able to
mum candle; wax **mumla aramak** to crave for, to hanker for
mumlu waxed **mumlu kâğıt** stencil
mumçiçeği waxflower
mumya mummy
mumyalamak to mummify
mundar unclean, filthy
munis sociable
muntazam regular; regularly
muntazaman regularly
murakabe inspection, supervision
murakıp inspector, supervisor
murat desire, wish **muradına ermek** to attain one's desire
murdar dirty, filthy
Musa Moses
musahhih proof reader
musallat worrying, pestering **musallat olmak** to worry, to pester
Musevi Jew; Jewish
Mushaf the Koran
musibet calamity, disaster
musiki music
muska amulet, charm
muslin muslin
musluk tap, faucet
muson monsoon
mustarip suffering **mustarip olmak** to suffer
muşamba oilcloth, oilskin
muşmula medlar
muşta brass knuckles
muştu good news
mut happiness
mutaassıp fanatical
mutabakat agreement, conformity
mutabık conforming, agreeing **mutabık kalmak** to agree upon
mutasyon mutation
mutat habitual, usual
muteber esteemed, respected; trustworthy; valid
mutedil moderate; *coğ.* temperate
mutemet fiduciary, paymaster, trustee
mutena select, choice, elaborate

mutfak kitchen **mutfak takımı** set of kitchen utensils
mutlak absolute; absolutely
mutlaka absolutely, certainly
mutlakıyet absolutism; autocracy
mutlu happy, lucky
mutluluk happiness
mutsuz unhappy
mutsuzluk unhappiness
muvafakat consent **muvafakat etmek** to agree, to consent
muvaffak successful
muvaffakiyet success
muvakkat temporary
muvakkaten temporarily
muvazene equilibrium, balance
muvazeneli balanced
muvezenesiz unbalanced
muvazzaf *ask.* regular **muvazzaf hizmet** *ask.* active service **muvazzaf subay** active officer
muz banana
muzaffer victorious
muzır harmful, detrimental; mischievous
muzırlık harmfulness; mischievousness
muzip teasing, tormenting; mischievous
muziplik teasing, practical joke
mübadele exchange
mübalağa exaggeration **mübalağa etmek** to exaggerate
mübalağacı exaggerator
mübalağalı exaggerated
mübarek holy, sacred; fertile, bountiful; auspicious
mübaşir usher
mücadele struggle, fight, combat **mücadele etmek** to struggle, to fight
mücadeleci combative
mücahit combatant, fighter
mücbir compelling **mücbir sebep** force majeure
mücehhez equipped **mücehhez olmak** to be equipped
mücellit bookbinder
mücerret abstract
mücevher jewel
mücevherat jewellery

mücevherci jeweller

müdafaa defence müdafaa etmek to defend

müdafaasız defenceless

müdafi defender

müdahale interference, intervention müdahale etmek to interfere, to intervene

müdavim habitué, frequenter

müddet period, duration

müdire directress, manageress

müdür director, manager; headmaster, principal

müdürlük, müdüriyet directorate; directorship

müebbet perpetual, eternal; lifelong müebbet hapis life imprisonment müebbeten forever

müessese establishment, institution, foundation

müessif regrettable, sad

müessir effective, effectual

müeyyide sanction

müezzin muezzin

müfettiş inspector

müfettişlik inspectorship

müflis bankrupt

müfredat details müfredat programı curriculum

müfreze *ask.* detachment

müfrit excessive

müftü mufti

mühendis engineer

mühendislik engineering

mühim important

mühimmat *ask.* munitions

mühlet delay, respite, term

mühür seal mühür basmak to seal

mühürlemek to seal

mühürlü sealed

mühürsüz unsealed

müjde good news

müjdeci herald, harbinger

müjdelemek to give a piece of good news

mükâfat reward

mükâfatlandırmak to give a reward

mükellef charged, obliged; taxpayer

mükellefiyet obligation, liability

mükemmel perfect, excellent

mükemmelen perfectly

mükemmeliyet perfection

mükerrer repeated, reiterated

mülakat interview mülakat yapmak to have an interview (with)

mülayim mild, gentle

mülk property, real estate mülk sahibi property owner, landowner

mülkiyet possession, ownership

mülteci refugee

mümbit fertile

mümessil representative, agent

mümessillik agency

mümeyyiz examiner

mümin believer

mümkün possible

mümtaz distinguished

münafık hypocrite, double-dealer

münakaşa argument, dispute münakaşa etmek to argue, to dispute

münasebet relation, connection

münasebetiyle on the occasion of

münasebetsiz improper, unseemly; inconsiderate, tactless, impertinent

münasebetsizlik impertinence

münasip suitable, proper münasip görmek to see fit, to approve

münavebe alternation münavebe ile alternately

münazara debate, discussion

müneccim astrologer

münevver enlightened, intellectual

münferit separate

münhal vacant, empty

münzevi reclusive, hermitic

müphem vague, uncertain

müptela addicted to

müracaat application; information desk müracaat etmek to apply (to), to consult

müracaatçı applicant

mürdümeriği damson

mürebbiye governess

müreffeh prosperous

mürekkep ink

mürekkepbalığı cuttlefish

mürekkepli inky, having ink mürekkepli kalem fountain pen

mürettebat crew

mürettip typesetter, compositor

mürit disciple

mürüruzaman *huk.* prescription, limitation

mürüvvet joy felt by parents when they see their child get married, be circumcised etc. mürüvvetini görmek to live to see one's children grow up and get married

müsaade permission müsaade etmek to permit, to allow

müsabaka competition, contest

müsademe *ask.* clash, skirmish

müsadere confiscation, seizure müsadere etmek to confiscate, to seize

müsait suitable, convenient

müsamaha indulgence, tolerance müsamaha etmek to indulge, to tolerate

müsamahakâr indulgent, tolerant

müsamahalı indulgent, tolerant

müsamahasız intolerant

müsamere (school) show

müsavi equal

müseccel officially registered müseccel marka registered trademark

müsekkin sedative, tranquilizer

müshil purgative, laxative

Müslüman Moslem, Muslim; pious, religious

Müslümanlık Islam

müspet positive

müsrif spendthrift, prodigal

müstahak deserving, worthy müstahakını bulmak to get one's deserts

müstahdem employee, servant

müstahkem fortified

müstahzar preparation

müstakbel future, prospective

müstakil independent

müstebit despotic, tyrannical

müstehcen obscene, pornographic, smutty

müstehcenlik obscenity

müsterih at ease müsterih olmak to be at ease

müstesna exceptional, extraordinary; except, excluding

müsteşar undersecretary

müsteşarlık undersecretaryship

müsvedde rough copy, draft müsvedde defteri notebook, exercise book

müşahede observation müşahede altına almak to place under observation müşahede etmek to observe

müşavere consultation

müşavir adviser, consultant

müşerref honoured müşerref olmak to be honoured

müşfik kind, tender, compassionate

müşkül difficult, hard

müşkülat difficulties müşkülat çıkarmak to raise difficulties

müşkülpesent particular, fastidious, fussy

müştemilat annexes, outhouses

müşterek common, collective, joint müşterek bahis pari-mutuel

müşteri customer, buyer, purchaser, client

mütalaa observation, opinion, comment mütalaa etmek to examine, to scrutinize

mütareke armistice, truce

müteaddit numerous, many

müteahhit (building) contractor

müteakiben subsequently

müteakip following, subsequent

mütecaviz aggressor

müteessir grieved, sorry müteessir olmak to be grieved, to be sorry

mütehakkim domineering, bossy

müteharrik moving, movable; driven by, powered by

mütehassıs specialist

mütehassis moved, touched mütehassis olmak to be moved

mütemadi continual, continuous

mütemadiyen continually, continuously

mütemayil inclined

mütercim translator

mütereddit undecided, hesitant

müteselsil uninterrupted; *huk.* joint müteselsil alacaklılar joint creditors müteselsil borçlular joint debtors müteselsil mesuliyet joint liability

müteşebbis enterprising

müteşekkil composed (of)

müteşekkir thankful, grateful

mütevazı humble, modest

müteveccih aimed, directed

müteveffa the deceased
mütevekkil resigned
mütevelli trustee **mütevelli heyeti** board of trustees
mütevellit caused, resulting
müthiş extraordinary, terrible, fearful, awful, amazing, super, terrific
münafık allied; ally
müvekkil client
müvezzi distributor
müzakere discussion, deliberation, consultation; oral exam **müzakere etmek** to discuss, to debate, to talk over
müzayede auction
müze museum
müzeci museum curator
müzecilik museology
müzelik worth putting in a museum; kon. ramshackle, ancient
müzevir sneak, talebearer, telltale
müzevirlemek to sneak, to tell on
müziç troublesome
müzik music
müzikal musical
müzikbilim musicology
müzikbilimci musicologist
müzikçi musician; teacher of music
müzikhol music hall
müzikli musical
müzikolog musicologist
müzikoloji musicology
müziksever music lover
müzisyen musician
müzmin chronic **müzmin bekâr** confirmed bachelor
müzminleşmek to become chronic

N

na, nah There it is
naaş corpse
nabız pulse **nabzına bakmak** to feel sb's pulse **nabzına göre şerbet vermek** to handle sb with tact **nabzı atmak** to pulsate **nabzını yoklamak** to put out a feeler, to sound sb out

nacak hatchet
naçar helpless
naçiz worthless, insignificant
naçizane humbly
nadas fallowing **nadasa bırakmak** to fallow
nadide rare, curious
nadir rare, scarce; rarely
nadiren rarely, seldom
nafaka huk. alimony; subsistence, livelihood
nafile useless, in vain **nafile yere** uselessly, in vain
naftalin naphthalene
nağme tune, melody
nahiye sub-district
nahoş unpleasant
nail who attains/gains/obtains **nail olmak** to attain, to gain
naip regent
nakarat refrain
nakavt knock-out
nakden in cash
nakış embroidery **nakış işlemek** to embroider
nakil transport, transfer; transplanting; narration **nakil vasıtaları** means of transport
nakit ready money, cash
naklen live **naklen yayın** live broadcast
nakletmek to transport, to convey, to transfer; to narrate, to relate
nakliyat transport, freighting, forwarding
nakliyatçı freighter, shipper
nakliye transport, shipping; transport expenses, freight
nakliyeci freighter, shipper
nakşetmek to imprint, to engrave
nal horseshoe **nalları dikmek** to croak, to peg out
nalbant horseshoer, farrier
nalbantlık horseshoeing, farriery
nalbur hardware dealer, ironmonger; hardware store
nalça iron tip (on a boot)
nalın clogs, pattens
nallamak to shoe; arg. to kill, to croak
nam name; fame, reputation **nam kazanmak** to become famous

namına on behalf of, in sb's name

namında called, named

namıyla under the name of

namağlup undefeated

namaz ritual worship, prayer, namaz namaz kılmak to perform the namaz namaz vakti prayer time

name (love) letter

namert cowardly, despicable

namertlik cowardice, vileness

namlu (gun) barrel

namus honour, chastity; honesty

namuslu honourable, chaste; honest

namussuz dishonourable, unchaste; dishonest

namussuzca dishonestly

namussuzluk dishonesty, deceit, unchasteness

namüsait unfavourable

namzet candidate namzet göstermek to nominate

nanay arg. there isn't

nane mint, peppermint nane yemek to make a blunder

naneruhu oil of peppermint

naneşekeri peppermint

naneli (pepper) minty

nanemolla weakling

nanik yapmak to cock a snook at, to make a long nose

nankör ungrateful, unthankful

nankörlük ungratefulness, ingratitude nankörlük etmek to show ingratitude

napalm napalm

nar pomegranate nar gibi well toasted, well roasted

nara cry, shout nara atmak to shout out, to yell

narenciye citrus fruits

nargile water-pipe, hubble bubble, narghile

narh officially fixed price narh koymak to set a fixed price

narin slender, slim; delicate, fragile

narinlik slimness, slenderness; delicacy

narkotik narcotic

narkoz narcosis narkoz vermek to narcotize

narsisizm narcissism

nasıl how

nasılsa in any case, somehow or other

nasır corn, callus nasır bağlamak to become calloused

nasırlaşmak to form a corn

nasırlı calloused, warty

nasihat advice, counsel nasihat etmek/vermek to advise nasihat tutmak to follow sb's advice

nasip portion, share; destiny, luck nasip etmek to vouchsafe nasip olmak to be vouchsafed nasibini almak to enjoy

natüralist naturalist; naturalistic

natüralizm naturalism

natürel natural

natürist naturist

natürizm naturism

natürmort still life

navlun freight charge for cargo

naylon nylon

naz coquetry, whims; disdain, coyness naz etmek/yapmak to show coyness, to feign reluctance nazı geçmek to have influence (over) nazını çekmek to put up with sb's whims

nazar look, glance; the evil eye; consideration, opinion nazara almak to take into account nazar boncuğu blue bead (worn to avert the evil eye) nazar değmek to be affected by the evil eye Nazar değmesin! Touch wood! nazarı dikkatini çekmek to attract sb's attention consideration nazarıyla bakmak to consider, to regard as

nazarımda in my opinion

nazaran in comparison to; according to

nazari theoretical

nazariye theory

nazarlık amulet, charm

nazım verse

nazır overlooking, facing

nazik kind, polite; delicate, ticklish

nazikane politely

naziklik politeness; delicacy

nazikleşmek to become delicate

nazlanmak to behave coquettishly; to feign reluctance

nazlı spoilt, petted; coquettish, coy

ne what **ne âlâ!** How nice! **ne alemde?** How? **ne biçim?** what kind of? **ne çare!** It can't be helped! **ne çıkar?** so what? **ne de olsa** after all **ne demek** what does it mean?; Not at all! **ne demeye?** why (on earth)? **ne denli** how **ne diye?** why (on earth)? **Ne ekersen onu biçersin.** *ats.* As you sow, so shall you reap. **ne gibi?** what sort? **ne güzel!** How nice! **ne haber?** what's the news? **ne haddine?** how would he dare? **Ne hali varsa görsün!** Let him stew in his own juice! **ne hikmetse** heaven knows why **ne için?** what for? why? **ne kadar?** how much?; how **Ne münasebet!** Not by a long chalk! Of course not! **ne oldum delisi** parvenu **Ne olur!** Please **ne olur ne olmaz** just in case **ne pahasına olursa olsun** at any cost, at all costs **ne var?** what's the matter? **ne var ki** but **ne var ne yok?** what's the news? **ne vakit?** when? **ne zaman?** when? **ne ... ne** neither ... nor

nebat plant

nebati vegetable, botanical **nebati yağ** vegetable oil

nebi prophet

nebülöz nebula

nebze particle, bit, trace

nece what language

neceftaşı rock-crystal

neci of what trade?

nedamet regret, repentance, reason, cause

neden cause, reason; why? what for? **neden olmak** to cause **nedenini açıklamak** to account for sth

nedeniyle because of, due to

nedenli having a reason

nedense for some reason or other

nedensiz without a reason, causeless

nedime lady-in-waiting

nefaset excellence, exquisiteness

nefer *ask.* private

nefes breath **nefes aldırmamak** to give no rest **nefes almak** to breathe; to catch one's breath **nefes borusu** *anat.* trachea **nefes darlığı** asthma **nefesi daralmak** to be short of breath

nefesi kesilmek to be out of breath **nefesini kesmek** to take sb's breath away **nefes nefese** out of breath **nefes nefese kalmak** to get out of breath **nefes vermek** to breathe out

nefesli çalgılar wind instruments

nefis exquisite, delicious

nefis self, essence; one's desires, concupiscence **nefsine düşkün** self indulgent **nefsine uymak** to yield to the flesh, to sin **nefsine yedirememek** to be unable to bring oneself to do sth **nefsini köreltmek** to take the edge off one's desire

nefret hatred, abhorrence, hate **nefret etmek** to hate, to abhor, to loathe **nefret uyandırmak** to arouse hatred

nefretle with hatred

nefrit *hek.* nephritis

nefsi sensual

neft naphtha

negatif negative

nehir river **nehir ağzı** mouth of a river **nehir kenarı** riverside **nehir kıyısı** bank **nehir yatağı** riverbed, channel

nekahet convalescence

nekes stingy, mean

nektar nectar

nem moisture, damp

nemelazımcı indifferent, unconcerned

nemelazımcılık indifference, unconcern

nemlendirici moisturizing, humidifying; moisturizer

nemlenmek to become damp

nemli moist, damp, humid

nemrut cruel, grim, obstinate

nene granny

neolitik neolithic

neon *kim.* neon

neozoik Neozoic

Neptün Neptune

nere what place, what part, whatsoever place?

nerde, nerede where **nerede ise, neredeyse** before long, soon

nereden from where, whence

nereli where from **nerelisiniz?** where are you from? where do you come from?

neresi what place, what part
nereye to what place **nereye olursa olsun** anywhere
nergis narcissus
nesep ancestry, pedigree
nesil generation
nesir prose
neskafe instant coffee
nesne thing, object
nesnel objective
nesnellik objectivity
neşe gaiety, joy **neşesi yerinde olmak** to be in high spirits
neşelendirmek to cheer up, to make cheerful
neşelenmek to grow merry, to cheer up
neşeli cheerful, merry, joyful
neşesiz in low spirits, joyless
neşeyle joyfully, gaily
neşir broadcasting; publication
neşretmek to spread; to publish
neşriyat publications
neşter lancet
net clear; net **net ağırlık** net weight **net gelir** net income **net kazanç** net income
netameli sinister; accident-prone
netice result, outcome
neticelendirmek to bring to an end
neticelenmek to result in, to come to a conclusion
neticesiz fruitless, useless
nevale food, chow
nevi kind, sort **nevi şahsına münhasır** the only one of its kind
nevir complexion **nevri dönmek** to become angry
nevralji neuralgia
nevrasteni neurasthenia
nevresim sheet of a quilt
nevroloji neurology
nevropot neuropathic
nevroz neurosis
ney reed flute
neyse anyway **neyse ki** luckily, fortunately
neyzen flute player
nezaket politeness
nezaketli polite
nezaketsiz impolite

nezaketsizlik impoliteness
nezaret surveillance, custody; inspection **nezaret altına almak** to take under surveillance **nezaret etmek** to inspect, to superintend
nezarethane custodial prison
nezih pure, clean
nezle cold, common cold, catarrh **nezle olmak** to catch (a) cold
nışadır ammonia, salammoniac
nice how many, many a; how **nice nice** a great many
nicel quantitative
nicelik quantity
niçin why, what for
nifak discord, strife **nifak sokmak** to bring discord into
nihai final, ultimate
nihayet end; at last, finally
nihayetsiz endless, infinite
nihilist nihilist; nihilistic
nihilizm nihilism
nikâh marriage **nikâh dairesi** marriage office **nikâh düşmek** (marriage) to be legally possible **nikâh kıymak** to perform a marriage ceremony
nikâhlı married
nikâhsız unmarried, out of wedlock **nikâhsız yaşamak** to cohabit
nikel nickel
nikotin nicotine
Nil *coğ.* the Nile
nilüfer water lily
nimbus nimbus
nimet blessing; food, bread
nine granny, grannie
ninni lullaby **ninni söylemek** to sing a lullaby
nirengi triangulation
nisaiye gyn(a)ecology
nisaiyeci gyn(a)ecologist
nisan April
nispet proportion, ratio **nispet vermek/yapmak** to say sth out of spite
nispeten comparatively, relatively
nispetle in comparison (with)
nispetli proportional
nispetsiz disproportional
nispi proportional; relative **nispi temsil** proportional representation

nişan mark, sign; aim, target; engagement, betrothal; decoration, order **nişan almak** to take aim at **nişan koymak** to make a mark **nişan yamak** to arrange an engagement **nişan yüzüğü** engagement ring **nişanı bozmak** to break off an engagement

nişanlamak to engage, to betroth; to take aim at

nişanlanmak to get engaged (to)

nişanlı engaged; fiancé, fiancée

nişasta starch

nitekim just as, besides

nitel qualitative

niteleme qualification **niteleme sıfatı** descriptive adjective

nitelemek to qualify

nitelendirmek to qualify

nitelik quality

nitelikli qualified

niteliksiz unqualified

nitrat nitrate

nitrik nitric **nitrik asit** nitric acid

nitrogliserin nitroglycerin(e)

nitrojen nitrogen

niyaz entreaty **niyaz etmek** to entreat for

niye why?

niyet intention, intent, purpose **niyet etmek** to intend **niyeti bozuk** having an evil intention

niyetiyle with the intention of

niyetli who has an intention; fasting

nizam order, regularity; law, regulation

nizami regular; legal

nizamlı regular; legal

nizamsız irregular; illegal

nizamname regulation

nizamiye the regular army **nizamiye kapısı** the main entrance (to a barracks or garrison)

Noel Christmas **Noel ağacı** Christmas tree **Noel arifesi** Christmas Eve **Noel Baba** Father Christmas

nohut chickpea

noksan deficiency, defect, want; deficient, defective, wanting, lacking

noksanlık deficiency, lack

noksansız complete, perfect

nokta dot, point; speck, spot; full stop,

period *Al.*

noktalama punctuation **noktalama işareti** punctuation mark

noktalamak to punctuate; to finish

noktalı punctuated; dotted **noktalı virgül** semicolon

noktasız undotted

nonoş little darling

norm norm

normal normal

normalleşmek to normalize

normallik normality, *Al.* normalcy

Norveç Norway

Norveççe Norwegian

Norveçli Norwegian

not note; (school) mark, grade **not etmek** to note down **not tutmak** to take notes **not vermek** to give marks to; to size up

nota *müz.* note; (diplomatic) note

noter notary (public)

nöbet turn; guard, watch; fit, attack **nöbet beklemek/tutmak** stand guard

nöbetleşe in turns

nöbetleşmek to take turns

nöbetçi sentry, watchman; on duty, on guard **nöbetçi subayı** duty officer

nörolog neurologist

nöroloji neurology

nöron *biy.* neuron

nötr neutral

nötrleşmek to be neutralized

nötrlük neutrality

nötron neutron

Nuh Noah **Nuh'un gemisi** Noah's Ark

numara number; size, number; trick, blind, stall **numara yapmak** to act, to pretend

numaracı faker, phony

numaralamak to number

numaralı numbered

numarasız unnumbered

numune sample, model

numunelik sample

nur light, brilliance **Nur içinde yatsın!** May he rest in peace! **Nur ol!** Bravo! **nur topu gibi** cherubic, healthy and beautiful

nurlu shining, bright

nutuk speech, oration **nutuk atmak/-**

çekmek to sermonize **nutuk vermek** to make a speech

nüfus population, inhabitants **nüfus kâ-ğıdı** identity card, identity certificate **nüfus kütüğü** state register of persons **nüfus memurluğu** Registry of Births **nüfus patlaması** population explosion **nüfus planlaması** family planning **nüfus sayımı** census **nüfus yoğunluğu** population density

nüfusbilim demography

nüfuz influence hold; penetration **nüfuz etmek** to penetrate; to influence **nüfuz sahibi** influential

nüfuzlu influential

nükleer nuclear **nükleer enerji** nuclear energy **nükleer reaktör** nuclear reactor, atomic reactor **nükleer santral** nuclear power station **nükleer savaş** nuclear war **nükleer silahlar** nuclear arms, nuclear weapons

nükleon nucleon

nüksetmek to relapse, to recur

nükte witticism **nükte yapmak** to make witty remarks

nükteci witty

nükteli witty

nüsha copy; (newspaper, etc.) issue, number

nüve nucleus

nüzul epoplexy, stroke

O

o he; she; it **o anda** at that moment **o gün bugün(dür)** since that day **o halde** then, in that case **o kadar** so ..., so much; such; that's all **o taktirde** in that case **o taraflı olmamak** to take no notice of

oba large nomad tent; nomad group

obelisk obelisk

obje object, thing

objektif objective

obua *müz.* oboe

obuacı oboist

obur gluttonous, greedy

oburca greedily

oburlaşmak to become gluttonous

oburluk gluttony, greediness

obüs howitzer

ocak January

ocak cooker, range, oven; furnace, kiln; fireplace, hearth; quarry, mine **ocağına düşmek** to be at the mercy of **ocağına incir dikmek** to ruin sb's family, to destroy the family of

ocakçı chimney sweep; stoker

oda room; chamber **oda hizmetçisi** chamber maid **oda müziği** chamber music **oda orkestrası** chamber orchestra

odacı janitor, servant

odak focus, focal point

odaklamak to focus

odaklanmak to be focused

odun firewood, log

oduncu woodcutter, seller of firewood

odunkömürü charcoal

odunluk woodshed

ofis office

oflamak to breathe a sigh

ofsayt *sp.* offside

ofset ofset (printing) **ofset baskı** ofset printing

oğalamak to rub

oğlak kid **Oğlak burcu** Capricorn **Oğlak dönencesi** tropic of Capricorn

oğlan boy; (cards) Jack, knave; queen, catemite

oğmak to rub

oğul son; swarm of bees

oğulcuk little son; *biy.* embryo

oğulluk sonship; adopted son

oğulotu balm

oğuşturmak to rub

oh *ünl.* ah! good! **oh çekmek** to gloat over another's misfortunes **oh demek** to have a breather

oha stop! whoa!

ohm ohm **Ohm yasası** Ohm's Law

oje nail polish

ok arrow **ok atmak** to shoot arrows

okaliptüs eucalyptus

okçu archer

okluk quiver

okka oke (a weight of 2.8 pounds) **okka-**

nın altına gitmek to bear the brunt

okkalı heavy; large, big

oklava rolling-pin

oksijen oxygen **oksijen çadırı** oxygen tent **oksijen maskesi** oxygen mask

oksijenli oxygenic, oxygenous

oksit oxide

oksitlemek to oxidize

okşamak to caress, to pat, to pet; to tan, to beat, to trash

oktan octane

oktav octave

okul school **okul arkadaşı** schoolmate, schoolfellow **okul harcı/ücreti** tuition **okul kaçağı** truant, hooky **okul müdürü** headmaster, principal **okuldan kaçmak** to play truant **okulu asmak** to cut classes **okulu bırakmak** to drop out **okulu kırmak** *arg.* to cut classes

okulöncesi preschool time; preschool

okulsonrası post-school time; post-school

okuma reading **okuma yazma** reading and writing

okumak to read; to sing

okumamış uneducated

okumuş educated, well-read, learned

okunaklı legible

okunaksız illegible

okunuş way of reading; pronunciation

okur reader

okuryazar literate

okuryazarlık literacy

okutmak to teach, to instruct; *arg.* to dispose of, to sell, to fob off on

okutman lecturer

okutmanlık lectureship

okuyucu reader

okyanus ocean

olabilir possible

olabilirlik possibility

olacak suitable; reasonable; something inevitable **Olacak gibi değil** It's impossible **Olacak iş (şey) değil** It's incredible

olagelmek to go on, to continue

olağan usual, ordinary, common

olağandışı unusual, abnormal

olağanüstü extraordinary; unusual

olamaz impossible

olanak possibility, chance **olanak vermek** to enable

olanaklı possible

olanaksız impossible

olanaksızlık impossibility

olanca utmost, all of

olarak as

olası probable, likely, possible

olasılık probability

olay event, incident, case **olay çıkarmak** to kick up a fuss/row **olay yeri** scene

olaylı eventful

olaysız eventless

oldu all right, okay!

oldubitti fait accompli **oldubittiye getirmek** to confront sb with a fait accompli

oldukça rather, fairly

olgu tact, event

olgucu positivist; positivistic

olguculuk *fel.* positivism

olgun ripe; mature

olgunlaşmak to become ripe, to ripen; to become mature, to mature

olgunlaştırmak to ripen; to mature

olgunluk ripeness; maturity

oligarşi oligarchy

olimpiyat Olympiad **olimpiyat oyunları** (the) Olympic games

olmadık unusual; impossible, unreasonable

olmak to be; to become, to get, to grow; to happen, to take place **olan oldu** what's done is done, it's too late now **olanlar** happenings **olup bitenler** events, happenings

olmamış unripe

olmaz no, impossible

olmuş ripe, mature

olsa olsa at most

olsun let it be; never mind! **olsun olsun** at most

olta fishing line **olta iğnesi** fish hook **olta yemi** bait

oluk gutter, pipe; groove

oluklu grooved

olumlu positive, affirmative

olumsuz negative

olur possible; all right, okay, OK **olur**

şey değil It's incredible **olur olmaz** whatever, any; whoever, anybody **oluruna bırakmak** *kon.* to let sth ride
oluş state of being or becoming
oluşma formation
oluşmak to come into existence/being; to be formed; to take shape
oluşturmak to form, to constitute
oluşum formation
om ohm
omlet omelette
omur *anat.* vertebra
omurga spine, backbone
omurgalılar *hayb.* vertebrates
omurgasızlar *hayb.* invertebrates
omurilik *anat.* spinal cord
omuz shoulder **omuz omuza** shoulder to shoulder **omuz silkmek** to shrug one's shoulders **omuza vurmak** to shoulder **omuzuna almak** to shoulder
omuzlamak to shoulder
omuzluk epaulette
on ten **on altı** sixteen **on altıncı** sixteenth **on beş** fifteen **on beşinci** fifteenth **on bir** eleven **on birinci** eleventh **on dokuz** nineteen **on dokuzuncu** nineteenth **on dört** fourteen **on dördüncü** fourteenth **on sekiz** eighteen **on sekizinci** eighteenth **on üç** thirteen **on üçüncü** thirteenth **on yedi** seventeen **on yedinci** seventeenth **on para etmez** worthless
ona (to) him; (to) her; (to) it
onamak to approve
onar ten each **onar onar** ten by ten
onarım repair
onarımcı repairman
onarmak to repair, to mend
onay approval, consent, okay, OK
onaylı approved **onaylı suret** certified copy
onaylamak to approve, to certify
onbaşı corporal
onca in his/her opinion, according to him/her; so much, so many
ondalık a tenth; decimal **ondalık hanesi** decimal place **ondalık kesir** decimal fraction **ondalık sayı** decimal number **ondalık sistem** decimal sys-

tem **ondalık virgülü** decimal point
ondan for that reason; from him/her/it **ondan sonra** then, thereafter
ondülasyon permanent wave
ondüle curle, curly
ongun productive; prosperous; happy; totem
onikiparmakbağırsağı duodenum
onlar they
onlara (to) them
onları them
onlu (cards) the ten
onmak to heal, to recover; to be happy
onmaz, onulmaz incurable
ons ounce
onsuz without him/her/it
onu him, her, it
onun his, her, its **onun için** for that reason, that's why
onunki his, hers
onur honour; self respect, pride
onuruna in honour of **onuruna dokunmak** to hurt sb's pride **onuruna yedirememek** not to be able to stomach
onurlandırmak, onur vermek to honour
onurlanmak to be honoured
onurlu self respecting, dignified, proud
onursal honorary
onursuz dishonourable, undignified
onursuzluk dishonour
opera opera
operasyon operation
operatör surgeon; operator
operet operetta
optimum optimum
ora that place
oracıkta just over there
orada there, in that place **orada burada** here and there
oraları those places
orası that place
oraya there
orak sickle
oralı of that place **oralı olmamak** to pay no attention
oramiral vice-admiral
oran proportion, ratio, rate
orangutan orangutan, orangoutang
oranla in proportion (to)
oranlamak to measure, to calculate; to

estimate; to compare
oranlı proportioned
oransız badly proportioned
orantı proportion
orantılı proportional
oratoryo oratorio
ordino delivery order
ordonat *ask.* ordnance
ordövr hors d'oeuvre, appetizer
ordu army; crowd
ordubozan spoil-sport, marplot
orduevi officer's club
ordugâh military camp
organ organ, member **organ nakli** transplantation
organik organic
organizasyon organization
organizatör organizer
organizma *biy.* organism
orgazm orgasm, climax
orgeneral full general
orijinal original
orijinallik originality
orkestra orchestra **orkestra şefi** conductor, maestro
orkide *bitk.* orchid
orkinos tuna fish
orlon orlon
orman forest **orman bekçisi** ranger **Orman Fakültesi** School of Forestry
ormancı forester
ormancılık forestry
ormanlık wooded, covered with trees **ormanlık arazi** timberland
ornitoloji ornithology
orospu prostitute, whore, hustler
orospuluk prostitution
orsa *den.* windward side **Orsa alabanda!** Down with the helm!
orsalamak to hug the wind
orta middle, centre; average, medium; intermediate **orta boy** middle size **orta boylu** medium-sized **orta dalga** mediumwave **orta direk** mainmast; *kon.* middleclass **orta halli** of moderate means **orta karar** moderate **orta malı** common to all; prostitute **orta sınıf** middle class **orta yaşlı** middle aged **ortada bırakmak** to leave sb in the lurch **ortada** in the middle; clear,

obvious, apparent **ortada kalmak** to be in a fix **ortadan kaldırmak** to destroy, to remove **ortadan kaybolmak** to disappear **ortaya atılmak** to come forward, to offer oneself; to be put forward **ortaya atmak** to put forward, to bring up, to throw up, to suggest **ortaya çıkarmak** to bring to light; to find out, to discover **ortaya çıkmak** to show oneself, to appear; to come out, to be revealed **ortaya koymak** to put forward, to expose
ortaç *dilb.* participle
ortaçağ the Middle Ages; medieval
ortadamar median vein
ortaderi mesoderm
Ortadoğu the Middle East
ortaelçi minister plenipotentiary, minister
ortak partner, associate; common, joint **ortak çarpan** *mat.* ratio of a geometrical progression **ortak olmak** to share; to become a partner (with)
ortakkat *mat.* common multiple
ortaklaşa in common, collectively
ortaklık partnership; company, firm **ortaklık sözleşmesi** deed of partnership
ortakulak middle ear, tympanum
ortakyapım joint production, co-production
ortakyaşama symbiosis
ortakyönetim coalition
ortalama average **ortalama olarak** on an average
ortalamak to centre
ortalık surroundings, the world around **ortalığı birbirine katmak** to turn the place upside down **ortalığı toplamak** to tidy up **ortalık ağarmak** (dawn) to break **ortalık kararmak** (night) to get dark, to close in **ortalık karışmak** to be upside down
ortalıkta in sight, around
ortam environment, surroundings; atmosphere
ortanca middle, middling; middle child of three
ortanca *bitk.* hydrangea
ortaokul secondary school, middle school, junior high school

ortaöğretim secondary education
ortasıklet middleweight
Ortodoks Orthodox
Ortodoksluk Orthodoxy
ortopedi orthopedics
ortopedik orthopedic
oruç fast, fasting oruç bozmak to break the fast oruç tutmak to fast oruç yemek not to observe the fast
Osmanlı Ottoman Osmanlı İmparatorluğu the Ottoman Empire
Osmanlıca the Ottoman Turkish language
osurmak to fart, to break wind
osuruk fart
ot grass, herb
otağ, otak pavilion
otel hotel
otelci hotel-keeper
otlak pasture, grassland
otlakçı sponger, parasite
otlakçılık sponging, freeloading otlakçılık etmek to sponge on
otlamak to graze, to pasture; to sponge
otluk haystack
oto- auto
oto car, auto
otoban motorway *İi.*, freeway *İi.*, expressway *Ai*
otobiyografi autobiography
otobur *hayb.* herbivorous
otobüs bus; coach otobüs durağı bus stop
otogar coach station, bus terminal
otokrasi autocracy
otokritik self-criticism
otomasyon automation
otomat automaton
otomatik automatic otomatik olarak automatically
otomatikleştirmek to automatize
otomatikman automatically
otomobil car, motorcar, automobile, auto otomobil tamircisi car mechanic
otomotiv automotive
otonom autonomous
otonomi autonomy
otopark İi. car park *Ai.* parking lot
otopsi autopsy
otorite authority

otoriter authoritarian
otostop hitchhiking otostop yapmak to hitchhike
otostopçu hitchhiker
otoyol motorway, expressway
otsu, otsul herbaceous
oturacak seat
oturak seat; chamber pot
oturaklı well settled, foursquare; sober, dignified; well-chosen, timely
oturma sitting oturma grevi sit-down strike oturma odası living room, sitting room
oturmak to sit; to live, to stay; to settle
oturtmak to seat, to place
oturum session, sitting
otuz thirty
otuzar thirty each
otuzuncu thirtieth
ova plain
ovalık grass land
oval oval
ovmak to rub with the hand, to massage
ovuşturmak to massage, to knead, to rub
oy vote oy çokluğuyla by a large majority oy pusulası ballot-paper oy sandığı ballot box oy vermek to vote oya koymak to put sth to the vote
oylama voting
oylamak to put sth to the vote
oya pinking, embroidery
oyalamak to put sb off, to detain, to stall; to amuse, to divert
oyalanmak to dally, to linger, to loiter
oyalı pinked
oybirliği unanimity
oybirliğiyle by a unanimous vote
oyluk thigh
oylum volume, size
oyma carving, engraving; engraved, cut in
oymacı carver, engraver
oymalı caned engraved
oymak to carve, to engrave; to bore; *arg.* to punish, to beat, to tell off
oymak tribe, clan; troop of boy-scouts
oynak playful, frisky; fickle, flirtatious; loose, shifting

oynamak to play; to dance; to fiddle with, to trifle; to move; to be loose; (film play) to be on

oynaş lover, lovemate

oynaşmak to play with one another; to carry on a love affair

oynatmak (to cause) to play; (to cause) to dance; to move, to stir; to lose one's mind

oysa, oysaki yet, but, however, whereas

oyuk hollowed out; cavity, hollow

oyun play, game; performance; trick; gamble oyun oynamak to play a trick on, to deceive oyun yazarı playwright oyuna gelmek to be deceived

oyunbaz playful, frisky

oyunbozan spoilsport, killjoy

oyunbozanlık being a killjoy oyunbozanlık etmek to be a killjoy

oyuncak toy, plaything; laughingstock, plaything; child's play, cinch

oyuncu player; actor, actress; dancer

oyunlaştırmak to dramatize

ozan poet

ozon kim. ozone

Ö

öbek heap, group öbek öbek in groups

öbür the other öbür dünya the other world öbür gün the day after tomorrow

öbürkü, öbürü the other one

öbürleri the other ones

öcü ogre, bogyman

öç revenge öç almak to take revenge on öcünü almak to revenge

öd gall, bile ödü kopmak/patlatmak to be frightened to death ödünü koparmak/patlatmak to frighten sb out of his wits

ödeme payment ödeme emri order of payment ödeme gücü solvency ödemeli (teslim) cash on delivery (C.O.D.)

ödemek to pay

ödenek appropriation, allowance öde-

nek ayırmak to appropriate funds (for)

ödenti subscription, fee

ödeşmek to settle accounts (with one another)

ödev duty; homework

ödkesesi gallbladder

ödlek cowardly, timid

ödleklik cowardice

ödül prize, award, reward ödül kazanmak to win a prize

ödüllendirmek to reward

ödün concession, compensation ödün vermek to make concessions

ödünç loan; borrowed ödünç almak to borrow ödünç alan borrower ödünç veren lender ödünç vermek to lend, to loan

ödünleme compensation

ödünlemek to compensate

öfke anger, fury, rage

öfkelendirmek to anger, to make angry

öfkelenmek to get angry

öfkeli choleric, hot tempered; angry, furious

öge element

öğle noon, midday öğle üstü around noon öğle yemeği lunch öğleden önce in the forenoon öğleden sonra in the afternoon

öğleyin at noon

öğrenci student, pupil öğrenci yurdu students' hostel

öğrenim education, study öğrenim görmek to receive education

öğrenmek to learn

öğreti doctrine

öğretici instructive, didactic

öğretim instruction, education öğretim görevlisi lecturer öğretim üyesi professor, assistant professor, lecturer öğretim yılı academic year, school year

öğretmek to teach, to instruct

öğretmen teacher, instructor, tutor öğretmen okulu teacher's training school

öğretmenlik teaching, being a teacher

öğün meal

öğünmek to boast, to brag

öğür of the same age, peer; used to, ac-

customed **öğür olmak** to get used to
öğürmek to retch; to bellow
öğürtü retching
öğüt advice **öğüt vermek** to give advice
öğütlemek to advise, to recommend
öğütmek to grind, to mill
öğütücü diş molar
ökçe heel
ökçeli heeled
ökçesiz heelless
ökse birdlime
ökseotu mistletoe
öksü firebrand, half-burnt piece of
wood
öksürmek to cough
öksürük cough
öksüz orphan, motherless **öksüz kalmak** to be orphaned
öksüzlük orphanage
öküz ox; lout, oat, stupid person **öküz gibi bakmak** to stare like a fool
ölçek measure, scale
ölçme measuring
ölçmek to measure **ölçüp biçmek** to consider carefully
ölçü measure; measurement; moderation; (poetry) metre **ölçüsünü almak** to take the measurements of **ölçüyü kaçırmak** to pass the limit, to overdo
ölçülü measured; moderate
ölçüsüz unmeasured; immoderate
ölçüm measure; measurement
ölçüt criterion
öldüresiye to death, ruthlessly
öldürmek to kill, to murder
öldürücü mortal, deadly
ölesiye excessively
ölgün faded, withered
ölmek to die
ölmez immortal, eternal
ölmüş dead, lifeless
ölü dead; dead body, corpse
ölüm death **ölüm cezası** capital punishment, death-penalty **ölüm döşeğinde olmak** to be on one's deathbed **ölüm ilanı** obituary notice **ölüm kalım meselesi** a matter of life or death **ölümü göze almak** to risk one's life **ölümüne susamak** to run into the jaws of death

ölümcül deadly, mortal
ölümlü mortal, transitory
ölümsüz immortal
ölümsüzleştirmek to immortalize
ölümsüzlük immortality
ömür life, existence **ömür boyu maaş** pension for life **ömür boyu hapis** life imprisonment, life sentence **ömür çürütmek** to waste one's life **ömrü vefa etmemek** not to live long enough to
ömürsüz short-lived
ön front; preparatory, preliminary **ön ayak** foreleg; mitt, paw **ön ayak olmak** to pioneer, to lead **önde** ahead **önde gelmek** to be in the most important place **önden** from the front **önden çekişli** (car) front-wheel drive **öne** to the front **öne geçmek** to go to the fore **öne sürmek** to put forward, to bring forward **önü alınmak** to be prevented **önümüzdeki** next **önünde** in front of **önüne düşmek** to show sb the way **önüne gelen** anyone, everybody **önünü kesmek** to waylay
önalım preemption **önalım hakkı** right of preemption
önce before, ago; first, at first
önceden beforehand, in advance
önceki the former
öncel predecessor
önceleri previously, formerly
öncelik priority
öncü avant-garda; *ask.* vanguard
öncül premise, premiss
öncülük pioneering **öncülük etmek** to pioneer
önder leader, chief
önderlik leadership
öndeyiş *yaz.* prologue
önek prefix
önem importance **önem vermek** to attach importance to
önemsiz unimportant
önerge motion, proposal **önerge vermek** to make a motion
öneri proposal, suggestion **öneride bulunmak** to propose, to suggest
önerme proposition
önermek to propose, to suggest, to offer

önerti antecedent
öngörmek to anticipate, to foresee
öngörü foresight, prudence
öngörülü farseeing, prudent
önkol forearm
önlem measure, precaution önlem almak to take measures
önlemek to prevent
önleyici preventive
önlük apron
önseçim primary election
önsel a priori
önsezi presentiment, intuition
önsöz preface, foreword
önsözleşme preliminary agreement
önyargı prejudice
önyargılı prejudiced
önyargısız unprejudiced
önyüzbaşı lieutenant commander, senior captain
öpmek to kiss, to smooch
öpücük kiss, smooch öpücük göndermek to kiss one's hand to sb
öpüşmek to kiss(each other)
ördek duck
ördekbalığı striped wrasse
ördekbaşı greenish blue
ören ruin
örf custom, convention örf ve âdet usage and custom
örfi customary, conventional örfi idare martial law, state of siege
örgen organ
örgü knitting; plait, braid
örgülü plaited, braided
örgüt organization
örgütlemek to organize
örgütlenmek to be organized
örgütlü organized
örgütsel organizational
örme knitting; knitted
örmek to knit, to plait
örneğin for example, for instance
örnek sample, pattern, model; example; exemplary örnek almak to take sb/sth as one's model örnek olmak to be a model, to set an example
örnekle(ndir)mek to give an example of, to illustrate
örs anvil

örselemek to spoil, to batter, to rumple
örtbas hushing up örtbas etmek to hush up, to suppress, to conceal
örtmece euphemism
örtmek to cover
örtü cover, wrap
örtülü covered; shut, closed
örtünmek to cover oneself
örümcek spider örümcek ağı spider's web, cobweb örümcek bağlamak to be covered with cobwebs örümcek kafalı old-fashioned, square
örümcekkuşu shrike
östaki borusu anat. eustachian tube
öte the farther side; farther, further öte yandan on the other hand
ötede over there ötede beride here and there
öteden from the other side öteden beri for a long time
öteberi this and that, various things
öteki the other öteki beriki anybody and everybody
ötleğen hayb. warbler
ötmek to sing, to warble
öttürmek to sound, to blow
ötücü singing ötücü kuş singing bird, songbird
ötürü because of
övendire ox-goad
övgü praise, panegyric övgüye değer praiseworthy
övmek to praise, to extol övülmeye değer praiseworthy
övülmek to be praised övülmeye değer praiseworthy
övünç pride, self-respect
övüngen boastful, bragging; boaster, braggart
övünmek to boast, to brag, to blow Övünmek gibi olmasın I don't mean to boast, but ...
öykü story
öykücü (short) story writer
öykülemek to narrate
öykünmek to imitate
öyle such; so öyle mi? Is that so? öyle olsun! So be it! öyle ya Of course! öyle yağma yok Not on your life!
öyleyse if so, then

öz self; essence, kernel; essential, real; own **öz anne** one's own mother **öz kardeş** full brother/sister **öz Türkçe** pure Turkish
Özbek Uzbek
Özbekistan Uzbekistan
özbeöz real, true, german
özdek matter
özdekçilik *fel.* materialism
özden genuine, true
özdenetim *ruhb.* selfcontrol
özdeş identical
özdeşleşme identification
özdeşleşmek to identify oneself with
özdeşleştirmek to identify
özdeşlik identity
özdevim automation
özdevinim automatism
özdeyiş aphorism, saying
özdirenç resistivity
özek centre
özel private; personal; special **özel ad** *dilb.* proper noun **özel ders** private lesson **özel dedektif** private detective **özel hastane** private hospital **özel hayat** private life **özel mülkiyet** private property **özel okul** private school **özel sekreter** private secretary **özel uçak** private plane **özel ulak** express delivery
özeleştiri self-criticism
özellik peculiarity, property, characteristic
özellikle especially, particularly
özen care, attention, pains **özen göstermek** to take pains **özene bezene** painstakingly
özendirmek to encourage, to tempt
özenli painstaking, careful
özenmek to take pains; to imitate, to ape **özenip bezenmek** to take great pains
özensiz careless
özensizlik carelessness
özenti affectation, emulation
özentili affected
özentisiz genuine
özerk autonomous
özerklik autonomy
özet summary, outline, synopsis

özetle in brief, briefly
özetlemek to summarize
özezerlik *ruhb.* masochism
özge other (than)
özgeci altruist
özgecilik altruism
özgeçmiş biography **özgeçmiş (belgesi)** CV, curriculum vitae, résumé *Aİ.*, biodata *Aİ.*
özgü peculiar to, proper to
özgül specific **özgül ağırlık** specific gravity **özgül ısı** specific heat
özgülemek to devote
özgün original; authentic, genuine
özgünlük originality
özgür free **özgür bırakmak** to set free
özgürce freely
özgürlük freedom, liberty
özgürlükçü liberalist; liberalistic
özgüven self-confidence
özgüvenli self-reliant
özlem longing, yearning; aspiration, desire
özlemek to long for, to miss, to yearn for
özleştirmek to purify
özlü sappy, juicy; pithy, concise, terse
özlük essence, nature; individual, person **özlük işleri** personnel affairs
özne subject
öznel subjective
öznellik subjectivity
özöğrenim self-education
özöğrenimli selfeducated
özsaygı self-respect
özseverlik narcissism
özsu juice, sap
özümleme assimilation
özümlemek to assimilate
özümsemek to assimilate
özür excuse, apology, put-off; defect **özür dilemek** to apologize (to) **özürü kabahatinden büyük** his excuse is worse than his fault
özürlü having an excuse; defective
özüt extract
özveren self-sacrificing
özveri self-denial, self-sacrifice
özverili self-denying, self-sacrificing
özyaşamöyküsü autobiography

P

pabuç shoe **pabuç bırakmamak** not to be discouraged by **pabucu dama atılmak** to fall into discredit

paça lower part of the trouser leg; trotters **paçaları sıvamak** to gird up one's loins **paçaları tutuşmak** to be in a stew **paçasını kurtarmak** to evade, to elude

paçavra rag; worthless thing **paçavraya çevirmek** to make a mess of, to botch

padavra shingle

padişah (Ottoman) ruler, sultan

padişahlık sultanate; reign

pafta section of a large map

pagan pagan

paganizm paganism

paha price, value **paha biçilmez** priceless **paha biçmek** to estimate a price **pahadan düşmek** to fall in price

pahalanmak to become (more) expensive

pahalı expensive, dear

pahalılaşmak to become (more) expensive

pahalılık expensiveness

pak clean, pure

paket package, parcel **paket etmek** to parcel up, to pack up

paketlemek to parcel up, to pack up

Pakistan Pakistan

Pakistanlı Pakistani

paklamak to clean

pakt pact

pala scimitar

palabıyık long thick and curved moustache

palamar *den.* hawser

palamut *hayb.* bonito; *bitk.* valonia oak

palanga tackle, pulley-block

palas sumptuous building, palace **palas pandıras** helter-skelter

palaska cartridge belt, bandolier

palavra bunk, baloney, humbug **palavra atmak** to shoot the bull, to swagger

palavracı braggart, boaster, blowhard

palaz duckling, squab, gosling

palazlanmak to grow fat; (child) to grow up

paldır küldür headlong, pell-mell

paleontoloji paleontology

paleozoik paleozoic

palet palette; *den.* flippers; caterpiller tread

palmiye palm-tree, palm

palto overcoat

palyaço clown, buffoon

pamuk cotton **pamuk gibi** very soft

pamukçuk *hek.* aphtha, thrush

pamuklu of cotton; cotton cloth

pamuktaş travertine

Panama Panama

Panamalı Panamanian

panayır fair, market **panayır yeri** fairground

pancar beet, beetroot **pancar gibi olmak, pancar kesilmek** to turn as red as a beetroot **pancar şekeri** beet sugar

pancur shutter

panda *hayb.* panda

pandantif pendant

pandispanya sponge cake

pandomima pantomime

panel panel discussion

panik panic **paniğe kapılmak** to panic, to be seized with panic **panik yaratmak** to cause a panic

Panislamizm Panislamism

Panislavizm Panslavizm

panjur shutter

pankart banner

pankreas *anat.* pancreas

pankreas *sp.* pancratium

pano panel, notice board

panorama panorama

pansiyon boarding-house, pension

pansiyoncu boarding-house keeper

pansiyoner boarder, lodger

pansuman dressing **pansuman yapmak** to dress (a wound)

panteizm *fel.* pantheism

panter panther, leopard

pantolon trousers

panzehir antidote

panzer panzer
papa Pope
papalık papacy
papağan parrot
papara dish of dry bread and broth; scolding papara yemek to get a rocket
papatya daisy
papaz priest, monk; (cards) king papaza dönmek (one's hair) to be too long (and untidy) papaza kızıp oruç (perhiz) bozmak to cut off one's nose to spite one's face
papazlık priesthood
papirüs papyrus
papyon bow-tie
para money para babası moneybags para basmak to mint, to coin para biriktirmek to save money para birimi monetary unit para bozdurmak to change money para cezası fine, penalty para cüzdanı wallet, purse para çekmek to draw money para çıkarmak to issue money para çıkışmamak (money) not to suffice para darlığı deflation para dökmek to spend a lot of money para etmek to be worth; to tell, to work para getirmek to bring in money para harcamak to spend money para ile değil very cheap para kazanmak to earn money para kesmek to mint; to rake in money para kırmak to make a lot of money para parayı çeker money begets money para saymak to pay para sızdırmak to squeeze money out of sb para tutmak to save money para yapmak to earn money para yedirmek to bribe para yemek to play ducks and drakes with money; to accept a bribe paranın üstü change parasını sokağa atmak to throw one's money away parasını yemek to live at sb's expense paraya çevirmek to cash in paraya kıymak to spare no expense parayı bayılmak/sökülmek to shell out parayı denize atmak to waste money Parayı veren düdüğü çalar. ats. He who pays the piper calls the tune.
parabol parabola

parabolik parabolic
paradoks paradox
parafe initialled parafe etmek to initial
parafin paraffin
paragöz money-grubber
paragraf paragraph
paraka groundline, setline
parakete multi-hooked fishing line, setline Ai.; den. logline
paralamak to tear to pieces
paralanmak to be broken to pieces; to strain every nerve; to become rich
paralel parallel
paralellik parallelism
paralelkenar parallelogram
paralı moneyed, rich; requiring payment
parametre parameter
paramparça all in pieces paramparça etmek to break to pieces paramparça olmak to be broken to pieces
paranoya paranoia
paranoyak paranoiac
parantez parenthesis
parasal monetary
parasız penniless, broke; free, gratis
parasızlık pennilessness
paraşüt parachute
paraşütçü parachutist, paratrooper
paratoner lightning conductor
paravan paravana, (folding) screen
parazit parasite; atmospherics, interference
parça piece parça başına per piece parça mal piece goods parça parça in pieces, in bits parça parça etmek to break to pieces parça parça olmak to be broken to pieces
parçalamak to break into pieces, to shatter
parçalı in parts, pieced
pardon pardon me, excuse me
pardösü light overcoat
parfüm perfume
parfümeri perfumery
parıldamak to gleam, to glitter, to sparkle
parıl parıl brilliantly, glitteringly parıl parıl parlamak to shine brightly
parıltı gleam, glitter, sparkle

parıltılı gleaming, glittering, sparkling
park park; car park, *Aİ.* parking lot **park etmek** to park
parka parka
parke parquet, parquetry
parkur course, track
parlak bright, shining, brilliant
parlaklık brightness, brilliance
parlamak to shine, to beam; to flare up; to gain distinction, to shine
parlamenter member of parliament, parliamentary
parlamento parliament
parmak finger **parmak atmak** *arg.* to goose sb **parmak basmak** to draw attention (to) **parmak hesabı** counting on the fingers **parmak ısırmak** to be astonished **parmak ısırtmak** to cause sb to marvel **parmak izi** fingerprint **parmak izini almak** to fingerprint sb **parmak kaldırmak** to raise the hand **parmağı olmak** to have a finger in **parmağında oynatmak** to twist sb round one's little finger **parmağını bile kıpırdatmamak** not to move a finger **parmakla göstermek** to point at **parmakla gösterilmek** to be pointed at
parmaklamak to finger
parmaklık railing, balustrade
parodi parody
parola password, watchword
pars leopard
parsa money (collected from listeners/-onlookers) **parsa toplamak** to pass the hat round **parsayı başkası toplamak** sb else to get the benefit
parsel plot, parcel
parsellemek to divide into parcels
parşömen parchment
partal worn out, shabby
parti party; (goods) consignment **parti vermek** to give a party **partiyi kaybetmek** to lose the game
partici partisan
particilik partisanship
partisyon *müz.* score
partizan partisan
partizanlık partisanship
parttaym part-time

pas rust, tarnish **pas tutmak** to rust
pas *sp.* pass **pas vermek** *sp.* to pass; (woman) to give (sb) the glad eye
pasaj arcade; passage
pasak dirt, filth
pasaklı slovenly, dowdy, slipshod
pasaport passport
pasif passive; *tic.* liabilities
paskalya Easter
paslanmak to rust
paslanmaz rustless
paslaşmak *sp.* to pass the ball to each other; *arg.* to give each other the glad eye
paslı rusty
paso pass
paspal slovenly, untidy
paspas doormat
pasta cake, pastry, tart
pastane pastry shop
pastırma pastrami, preserve of dried meat **pastırmasını çıkarmak** to give a good beating (to) **pastırma yazı** Indian Summer
pastil lozenge, pastille
pastoral pastoral
pastörize pasteurized
paşa pasha general
pat thud! whop! **pat diye** with a thud
patak beating, hiding
pataklamak to beat to thrash
patates potato **patates tava** fried potatoes
patavatsız indiscreet, tactless
paten skate
patent patent, licence
patentli patented
patırdamak to make a knocking noise, to patter
patırtı noise, clatter, patter; tumult, row **patırtı çıkarmak** to kick up a row **patırtıya vermek** to put into confusion
patırtılı noisy, tumultuous
patik bootee
patika path, track
patinaj ice skating; skidding **patinaj yapmak** to skid, to slip **patinaj zinciri** antiskid chain
patiska cambric
patlak burst; puncture **patlak gözlü**

goggle-eyed, pop eyed **patlak vermek** to break out

patlama explosion

patlamak to burst, to explode

patlangaç pop-gun

patlatmak to blow up, to blast, to burst; (blow) to land, to slap

patlayıcı explosive

patlıcan egg-plant, aubergine

patoloji pathology

patolojik pathological

patrik patriarch

patrikhane patriarchate

patron boss, employer

patladak, pattadan all of a sudden, suddenly

pavyon night club; pavilion

pay share, lot, portion **pay bırakmak** to leave a margin **pay biçmek** to take as an example **pay etmek** to share out **payını almak** to get one's share

payanda prop, support

payda denominator

paydaş partner, shareholder

paydos break, rest **paydos etmek** to stop working, to knock off

paye rank, grade

paylamak to scold

paylaşmak to share

payreks Pyrex

paytak bandy-legged

payton phaeton

pazar Sunday

pazar market, marketplace **pazara çıkarmak** to put on sale **pazar kurmak** to set up an open market

pazarcı seller in a market

pazarlama marketing

pazarlamacı marketing expert

pazarlamak to market

pazartesi Monday

pazaryeri market-place

pazen cotton flannel

pazı *bitk.* chard

pazı biceps, muscle

pazıbent armlet

peçe veil

peçeli veiled

peçete napkin

pedagog pedagogue

pedagoji pedagogy

pedal pedal

peder father

pederşahi *topb.* patriarchal

pediatri pediatrics

pedikür pedicure

pehlivan wrestler

pejmürde shabby, ragged

pek very; hard, firm **pek çok** very much

pekâlâ very good; all right! okay!

pekdoku collenchyma

peki all right! okay!

pekişmek to harden

pekiştirmek to harden, to stiffen

peklik constipation **peklik çekmek** to suffer from constipation

pekmez grape-molasses

peksimet hardtack, ship biscuit

pelerin cape, cloak

pelesenk balsam, balm

pelesenkağacı balsam tree

pelikan *hayb.* pelican

pelin wormwood

pelit acorn, valonia

pelte jelly

peltek lisping **peltek konuşmak** to lisp

pelteklik lisp

pelteleşmek to jelly

pelür onion skin **pelür kâğıdı** onion skin paper

pelüş plush

pembe pink

pembeleşmek to turn pink

pembelik rosiness

pembemsi pinkish

penaltı *sp.* penalty

pencere window

pencüdü a five and a two

pencüse a five and a three

pencüyek a five and a one

pençe paw, claw; (shoe) sole **pençe atmak** to paw, to claw **pençe vurmak, pençelemek** to claw, to paw; to sole (a shoe)

pençeleşmek to grapple (with), to struggle

penguen penguin

peni penny, pence

penis penis

penisilin penicillin

pens pense, pliers, pincers; (dress) dart, pleat

pentatlon *sp.* pentathlon

pepe stammering

pepelemek to stammer, to stutter

pepsin *biy.* pepsin

perakende retail **perakende fiyatı** retail price **perakende satın almak** to buy sth retail **perakende satmak** to retail

perakendeci retailer

perçem tuft of hair

perçin clinch bolt, rivet

perçinlemek to rivet, to clench

perçinli riveted, clenched

perdah sheen, finish

perdahlı polished

perdahsız unpolished

perde curtain; screen; (play) act **perde inmek** (eye) to have cataract **perdeyi kapamak** to draw the curtain

perdelemek to curtain, to veil; to veil, to conceal

perdeli curtained, veiled

perende somersault **perende atmak** to turn a somersault

performans performance

pergel pair of compasses **pergelleri açmak** to take long steps

perhiz diet **perhiz yapmak** to diet

perhizli on a diet

peri fairy **peri gibi** fairylike

peribacası fairy chimney, earth pyramid, earth pillar

perihastalığı epilepsy; hysteria

perikart pericardium

perili haunted

periskop periscope

perişan perturbed, miserable, ruined; scattered, disordered **perişan etmek** to perturb, to ruin; to scatter **perişan olmak** to become miserable, to be wretched; to be scattered

periyodik periodic periodical

perma(nant) permanent

permanganat permanganate

permi permit

peroksit peroxide

peron platform

personel personnel, staff

perspektif perspective

perşembe Thursday

peruk, peruka wig

perukalı wigged

pervasız fearless

pervasızca fearlessly

pervane propeller, screw

pervaz cornice, fringe

pes (voice) low, soft **pes demek** to give in, to say uncle *Al.* **pes doğrusu** that beats all! **pes etmek** to cry small, to give in

pesek (tooth) tartar

peseta peseta

pespaye vulgar, common

pespembe very pink

pestil dried fruit pulp **pestile çevirmek** to tire out **pestili çıkmak** to be tired out **pestilini çıkarmak** to beat sb to a jelly

peş back **peş peşe** one after the other **peşi sıra** behind him, following him **peşinde dolaşmak** to go around with sb **peşinde koşmak** to run after **peşinden gitmek** to go after **peşine düşmek** to pursue **peşine takılmak** to tail after **peşini bırakmak** to stop following

peşin paid in advance, cash, ready; in advance, beforehand **peşin almak** to buy for cash **peşin fiyat** cash price **peşin hüküm** prejudice, preconception **peşin para** ready money, cash **peşin satış** cash sale **peşin söylemek** to tell in advance **peşin yargı** prejudice

peşinat advance payment

peşinen in advance, beforehand

peşkir napkin; towel

peşrev overture, prelude

peştemal cloth worn around the waist

petek honeycomb

petrol petroleum, oil **petrol boru hattı** pipeline **petrol bulmak** to strike oil **petrol kuyusu** oil well **petrol rafinerisi** oil refinery

pey earnest money, deposit **pey akçesi** earnest money, deposit **pey sürmek** to make a bid

peyda manifest, visible **peyda etmek** to beget, to create **peyda olmak** to appear, to spring up

peydahlamak to procure
peyderpey step by step, little by little
peygamber prophet
peygamberlik prophethood, prophecy
peygamberağacı guaiacum, lignum vitae
peygamberçiçeği cornflower
peyk satellite
peylemek to book, to engage
peynir cheese
peynirli containing cheese
peyzaj landscape
pezevenk pimp, procurer
pezevenklik procuration **pezevenklik etmek** to pimp, to procure
pezo Peso
pıhtı clot, coagulum
pıhtılaşmak to clot, to coagulate
pılı pırtı junk, traps; belongings
pır whirring, whizzling **pır pır etmek** to whirr, to whizz
pırasa leek
pırıldamak to glitter, to gleam
pırıl pırıl glittering, sparkling; brand-new; very clean
pırıltı glitter, gleam, sparkle
pırlamak (bird) to flutter; to take to one's heels
pırtlak bulging
pısırık diffident, pusillanimous
pısırıklık diffidence
pıtırdamak to crackle, to patter
pıtırtı tapping, patter
pıtrak burr
piç bastard **piç kurusu** brat
pide fat bread
pigment pigment
pik cast iron **pik boru** cast iron pipe
pikap record player; pick-up
pike piqué
pike nosedive **pike yapmak** to dive
piknik picnic **piknik yapmak** to picnic, to have a picnic
pil battery
pilav pilaf, rice
piliç chicken
pilot pilot
pilotluk pilotage
pin pin

pineklemek to doze, to slumber
pingpong ping-pong
pinti miserly, stingy
pintileşmek to become stingy
pintilik miserliness, stinginess
pipo pipe **pipo içmek** to smoke a pipe
piramit pyramid
pire flea **pire gibi** very agile **pire için yorgan yakmak** to cut off one's nose to spite one's face **pireyi deve yapmak** to make a mountain out of a molehill
pirelendirmek to make suspicious
pirelenmek to become flea-ridden; to smell a rat
pirinç rice
pirinç brass
pirzola cutlet, chop
pis dirty, filthy **pisi pisine** for nothing, in vain **pis pis bakmak** to leer (at) **pis pis gülmek** to grin, to chuckle
pisboğaz greedy
pisi pussy-cat
pisibalığı plaice
piskopos bishop
pislemek to dirty, to soil
pisletmek to dirty, to soil
pislik dirt, filth; dirtiness, filthiness
pissu sewage
pist running track; dance floor; runway
piston piston
pişik prickly heat, heat rash
pişirim amount to be cooked at one time
pişirmek to cook, to bake
pişkin well-cooked, well-done; experienced, hardened
pişkinlik being well-cooked; experience, maturity
pişman regretful, penitent, sorry **pişman etmek** to make sb feel sorry **pişman olmak** to feel sorry, to repent
pişmanlık regret, penitence
pişmek to be cooked, to cook; to become experienced, to toughen **pişmiş kelle gibi sırıtmak** to grin like a Cheshire cat
pişti a card game
piton *hayb.* phyton
pitoresk picturesque

piyade infantry, infantryman
piyango lottery; raffle piyango bileti lottery ticket piyango çıkmak to win a lottery
piyanist pianist
piyano piano
piyasa market piyasada on the market piyasaya çıkarmak to put on the market piyasaya çıkmak to come on the market; to show oneself, to appear piyasaya sürmek to throw on the market
piyaz bean salad
piyes play
piyon pawn
plaj beach
plak record
plaka number platev
plaket plate, plaque
plan plan plan yapmak to make a plan plan kurmak to plan
planet planet
plankton plankton
planlamak to plan
planlı planned
planör glider
plantasyon plantation
planya carpenter's plane
plasenta placenta
plasman investment
plaster plaster
plastik plastic plastik ameliyat plastic surgery plastik sanatlar the plastic arts
platform platform
platin platinum
plato plateau
platonik platonic
plazma plasma
plevra pleura
pleybek playback
pli pleat, fold
pliyosen pliocene
podyum podium, dais
pofurdamak to snort, to puff pofur pofur in great puffs
poğaça flaky pastry
pohpoh flattery
pohpohçu flatterer
pohpohlamak to flatter

poker poker
polarma polarization
polarmak to polarize
polemik polemic
poli- poly
poliandri topb. polyandry
poliçe bill of exchange, draft; insurance policy
polietilen polyethylene
poligami polygamy
poligon gunnery range, artillery range; polygon
polijini topb. polygyny
poliklinik polyclinic
polimer kim. polymer
polip polyp
polis police; policeman
polisiye detective polisiye film detective film polisiye roman detective novel
politeknik polytechnic
politeizm topb. polytheism
politik political
politika politics; policy politikaya atılmak to go into politics
politikacı politician
poliüretan polyurethane
poliyester polyester
Polonya Poland
Polonyalı Polish, Pole
pomat pomade
pompa pump
pompalamak to pump
ponpon pompom; powder puff
pop pop pop müzik pop music
poplin poplin
popo buttocks, butt, bum
popüler popular
pornografi pornography
pornografik pornographic
porselen porcelain
porsiyon portion, helping
porsuk badger
porsumak to shrivel up, to wizen
portakal orange
portakalrengi orange
portatif portable, movable
porte müz. stave
Portekiz Portugal; Portuguese
Portekizce Portuguese
Portekizli Portuguese

portföy wallet, purse
portmanto coat-stand, hallstand
portre portrait
posa sediment, dregs posasını çıkarmak to squeeze almost to death
posbıyık having a bushy moustache
post skin, hide postu deldirmek to be shot, to be killed postu kurtarmak to save one's skin postu sermek to outstay one's welcome
posta post, mail; postal service posta havalesi postal order, money order posta kartı postcard posta koymak to cow, to intimidate posta kutusu post box posta pulu postage stamp postaya atmak to post postayla göndermek to post
postacı postman
postal combat boot, half boot
postalamak to post
postane post office
postrestant poste restante
poşet small bag
pot crease, pucker; blunder, boner, howler pot kırmak to drop a brick, to put one's foot in it
pota crucible, cupel
potansiyel potential
potasyum potassium
potin boot
potpuri müz. potpourri
pound pound
poyra (wheel) hub
poyraz northeast wind
poz pose; exposure poz vermek to pose for
pozisyon position
pozitif positive
pöf ugh!
pörsük shrivelled up, wizened
pörsümek to shrivel up, to wizen
pörtlek (eye) bulging
pösteki sheepskin pösteki saydırmak to make sb do a tiresome job pöstekisini sermek to beat sb all to pieces
pranga shackles, fetters prangaya vurmak to shackle, to fetter
pratik practical; practice
pratisyen general practitioner
prehistorya prehistory

prehistorik prehistoric
prelüd prelude
prens prince
prenses princess
prensip principle
prenslik principality; princedom
pres press
presbit long-sighted
presbitlik presbyopia
prevantoryum sanatorium for the early stages of tuberculosis
prezervatif condom, rubber
prim premium; bonus
primadonna müz. prima donna
primatlar hayb. primates
priz socket, wall-plug
prizma prism
problem problem
prodüksiyon production
prodüktivite productivity
prodüktör producer
profesör professor
profesörlük professorship
profesyonel professional
profesyonellik professionalism
profil profile
program programme, program
programcı programmer
programlamak to program
programlı systematical, programmed
proje project
projeksiyon projection
projektör projector
proletarya proletariat
proleter proletarian
propaganda propaganda propaganda yapmak to propagandize
propagandacı propagandist
prosedür procedure
prospektüs prospectus
prostat anat. prostate
protein protein
proteinli proteinaceous
Protestan Protestant
Protestanlık Protestantism
protesto protest protesto çekmek to make a formal protest protesto etmek to protest
protez prosthesis
protokol protocol

proton proton
protoplazma protoplasm
prova fitting; rehearsal; proof **prova et-mek** (dress) to try on
provizyon provision
provokasyon provocation
provokatör provocateur
pruva *den.* bow, head
psikanaliz psychoanalysis
psikanalizci psychoanalyst
psikiyatr psychiatrist
psikiyatri psychiatry
psikolog psychologist
psikoloji psychology
psikolojik psychological
psikopat psychopath
psikoterapi psychotherapy
psikoz psychosis
psişik psychic, psychical
puan point **puan almak** to score
puanlamak to grade (a test)
puding pudding
pudra powder
pudralı powdered
pudralık, pudriyer compact, powder-box
pudraşeker castor sugar
puf pouf, poufle, pouff
pufla eider, eider duck
puflamak to puff, to blow
puhu eagle owl
pul stamp; (fish) scale; washer, nut
pulcu seller of stamps; philatelist
pulculuk philately
pullamak to stamp; to ornament with spangles
pullu stamped; scaly
pulluk plough
Pulman Pullman
pulsuz unstamped
puma puma
punç punch
punt appropriate time **punduna getir-mek** to find a suitable opportunity
punto size (of type)
pupa stern **pupa yelken gitmek** to go in full sail
puro cigar
pus haze, mist; (on fruit) bloom
pusarmak to get misty

puset pram
puslu hazy, misty
pusmak to crouch down
pusu ambush **pusu kurmak** to lay an ambush **pusuya düşürmek** to trap **pusuya yatmak** to lie in wait
pusula compass **pusulayı şaşırmak** to lose one's bearings
pusula note, memorandum
puşt catamite, fairy; son of a bitch, bastard
put idol, fetish; cross **put gibi** as still as a statue **put kesilmek** to be petrified
putperest idolater
putperestlik idolatry
putrel iron beam
püf puff **püf noktası** the weak spot (of sth)
püflemek to blow out, to blow on
püfür püfür gently and coolingly **püfür püfür esmek** to blow gently
pünez drawing pin, thumbtack
püre purée, puree
pürtük knob, protuberance **pürtük pürtük** full of knobs
pürtüklü knobby, rough
pürüz roughness, unevenness; difficulty, hitch
pürüzlü rough, uneven; difficult, knotty
pürüzsüz smooth, even; without a hitch
püskül tassel
püsküllü tasseled **püsküllü belâ** a great nuisance
püskürme eruption
püskürmek to spray from one's mouth; (volcano) to erupt
püskürteç atomizer, spray
pütür small protuberance, knob **pütür pütür** full of small protuberances, rough; chapped, cracked
pütürlü chapped, cracked; rough, shaggy

R

Rab God
Rabbim my God

rabıta relation, connection, tie
rabıtalı coherent; regular
rabıtasız incoherent;irregular
raca rajah, raja
racon way, method, procedure; showing off, swagger **racon kesmek** to show off, to swagger
radar radar
radde degree, point
radikal radical
radikalizm radicalism
radyan radian
radyasyon radiation
radyatör radiator
radyo radio
radyoaktif radioactive
radyoaktivite radioactivity
radyoevi broadcasting studio/house
radyografi radiography
radyolog radiologist
radyoloji radiology
radyoskopi radioscopy
radyoskopik radioscopic
radyoterapi radiotherapy
radyum radium
raf shelf **rafa koymak/kaldırmak** to put on a shelf, to shelve; to postpone
rafadan (egg) soft-boiled
rafine refined, purified
rafineri refinery
rağbet demand; popularity **rağbet etmek** to demand, to like **rağbet görmek** to be in demand **rağbetten düşmek** to be no longer in demand
rağmen in spite of, despite
rahat comfort, peace; comfortable; at ease! **rahat durmak** to behave oneself **rahat etmek** to be at ease **rahat vermemek** to bother, to pester **rahat yüzü görmemek** to have no peace **rahatına bakmak** to mind one's own comfort, to see to one's pleasures
rahatça comfortably
rahatlamak to feel relieved
rahatlatmak to relieve, to reassure, to relax
rahatlık comfort, quiet
rahatlıkla easily
rahatsız uncomfortable; ill, unwell; uneasy, anxious **rahatsız etmek** to dis-

turb, to bother, to annoy **rahatsız olmayın!** Don't trouble yourself!
rahatsızlanmak to become ill, to fall ill
rahatsızlık discomfort, illness **rahatsızlık vermek** to disturb, to bother
rahibe nun
rahim uterus, womb
rahip monk; priest
rahle low reading-desk
rahmet God's compassion, clemency; rain
rahmetli the deceased, the late
rahvan ambling; amble
rakam figure, number
raket (in tennis) racket; (in table tennis) bat
rakı (Turkish) raki, arrack
rakım altitude
rakip rival
rakipsiz unrivalled
rakkas pendulum
rali rally
ramak kalmak almost to happen
ramazan Ramadan, Ramazan
rampa incline, slope, grade
randevu appointment, date **randevu almak** to get an appointment (from/-with) **randevu vermek** to make an appointment (with) **randevusu olmak** to have an appointment (with, ile)
rendevuevi unlicensed brothel
randıman output, yield
randımanlı productive
ranza bunk, berth
rapor report **rapor vermek** to make a report **rapor yazmak** to draw up a report
raportör reporter
rapsodi müz. rhapsody
raptetmek to attach, to fasten
raptiye drawing pin, thumbtack
raptiyelemek to thumbtack
rasat observation
rasathane observatory
rasgele at random, casually, haphazardly **Rasgele!** Good luck!
raspa scraper
raspalamak to scrape
rast gitmek to come across, to run into, to encounter

rast getirmek to choose the right time, to watch for the best time; (God) to allow to succeed

rastık kohl

rastlamak to meet by chance, to come across, to run into, to encounter; to coincide with, to fall on

rastlantı chance, coincidence, encounter

rastlaşmak to chance upon each other

rasyonalist rationalist; rationalistic

rasyonalizm rationalism

rasyonel rational

raşitizm rachitism, rickets

raunt sp. round

ray rail, track **raydan çıkmak** to go off the rails **rayına oturmak** to set to rights **rayına girmek** to begin to go smoothly

rayiç market price, current value

razı contented, willing **razı etmek** to persuade, to satisfy **razı olmak** to consent, to agree to

re müz. re

reaksiyon reaction

reaktör reactor

realist realist

realizm realism

reçel jam

reçete prescription; recipe

reçine resin

reçineli resinous

redaksiyon redaction

redaktör redactor, redacteur

reddetmek to refuse, to reject, to turn down

redingot frock coat

redoks redox

refah prosperity, comfort

refakat accompaniment; companionship **refakat etmek** to accompany

refakatçi accompanier

referandum referendum

referans reference

refleks reflex

reflektör reflector.

reform reform

reformcu reformer, reformist

regülatör regulator

rehabilitasyon rehabilitation

rehavet slackness, languor **rehavet çökmek** to feel sluggish

rehber guide; guide book

rehberlik guidance **rehberlik etmek** to guide

rehin pledge, pawn **rehine koymak** to pawn, to pledge

rehinci pawnbroker

rehine hostage **rehine olarak tutmak** to hold as a hostage

reis chief, head

rejim regime; diet **rejim yapmak** to diet

rejisör director

rekabet rivalry **rekabet etmek** to rival, to compete

reklam advertisement **reklamını yapmak** to advertise, to boom

reklamcı advertiser

reklamcılık advertising **reklam acentası** advertising agency

rekolte harvest, crop

rekor record **rekor kırmak** to break a record

rekortmen record-holder

rektör rector, president

rektörlük presidency, rectorship

rektum rectum

rencide hurt, injured **rencide etmek** to hurt

rençber farm-hand; farmer

rende (carpenter's) plane; grater

rendelemek to plane; to grate

rengârenk multicoloured

rengeyiği reindeer

renk colour **renk atmak** to lose colour, to fade **rengi atmak** to turn pale **renk körlüğü** colour blindness **renkten renge girmek** to go all shades of red, to change colour **renk vermemek** not to show one's colours

renklendirmek to add colour; to liven up, to enliven

renklenmek to become colourful; to become more amusing/interesting

renkli coloured; colourful

renksiz colourless; nondescript, dull

renksemez achromatic

renkser chromatic

reorganizasyon reorganization

repertuar repertoire, repertory

replik (theatre) cue
re'sen on one's own account
resepsiyon reception
reseptör receiver
resif reef
resim picture; photograph, photo; illustration; drawing; painting; due, duty **resim çekmek** to take a photograph **resim yapmak** to draw,to paint **resmini çekmek** to take a photograph of
resimlemek to illustrate
resimli illustrated, pictorial **resimli roman** comic (strip)
resital *müz.* recital
resmen officially, formally; *kon.* openly, publicly
resmetmek to draw, to picture; to describe, to depict
resmi official; formal **resmi elbise** uniform **resmi gazete** official gazette
resmiyet formality, ceremony; official character, offcialism **resmiyete dökmek** to officialize; to become official in one's tone
ressam artist, painter
restoran restaurant
restorasyon restoration
restore etmek to restore
resul prophet
reşit adult, major
ret refusal, denial
retina retina
retorik rhetoric
reva suitable, proper **reva görmek** to deem proper
revaç demand, request
revaçta in demand **revaçta olmak** to be in demand
revak porch, colonnade
reverans courtesy
revir infirmary; *den.* sickbay
revizyon revision **revizyondan geçirmek** to overhaul
revizyonist revisionist
revü revue
rey vote
reyhan sweet basil
reyon department
rezalet scandal, disgrace **rezelet çıkarmak** to cause a scandal

reze hinge
rezene *bitk.* fennel
rezerv reserve
rezervasyon reservation
rezil vile, scandalous, disgraceful **rezil etmek** to disgrace **rezil olmak** to be disgraced
rezillik disgrace, scandal
rezistans resistance
rezonans resonance
rıhtım quay, wharf
rıza consent, approval **rıza göstermek** to consent
rızk one's daily bread, food **rızkını çıkarmak** to earn daily bread
riayet respect, esteem; obedience **riayet etmek** to respect, to obey
rica request **rica etmek** to request, to ask
ricat retreat **ricat etmek** to retreat
rimel mascara
ring ring
ringa herring
risk risk
riskli risky
ritim rhythm
ritmik rhythmic
rivayet rumour, hearsay **rivayet olunmak** to be rumoured **rivayete göre** rumour has it that
riya hypocrisy
riyakâr hypocritical
riyakârlık hypocrisy
riyal riyal
riziko risk
rizikolu risky
robdöşambr dressing-gown
robot robot
rodeo rodeo
Rodos Rhodes
roket rocket **roket atmak** to launch a rocket
rokoko rococo
rol role, part **rol almak** to have a part (in) **rol oynamak, rolü olmak** to play a part in **rolünü oynamak** to act to play the part of **rol yapmak** to act
rom rum
Roma Rome
Romalı Roman

roman novel
romancı novelist
romans romance
romantik romantic
romantizm romanticism
Romanya Romania
romatizma rheumatism
romatizmalı rheumatic
Romen Roman Romen rakamları Roman numerals
rosto roast meat
rot rod
rota ship's course
rotasyon rotation
rozet badge, rosette
rölanti (engine) idling rölantide çalışmak to idle rölantiye almak to idle
rölativite relativity
röle relay
rölyef relief
römork trailer
römorkör tugboat
Rönesans Renaissance
röntgen X-ray; arg. peeping röntgenini çekmek to X-ray
röntgenci X-ray specialist; arg. peeper
röportaj interview, reporting röportaj yapmak to interview
röportajcı interviewer, reporter
röprodüksiyon reproduction
rötar delay
rötarlı delayed
rötuş retouch rötuş etmek to retouch
ruble rouble, ruble
rugbi sp. rugby
ruh soul, spirit; essence; energy ruh çağırma necromancy ruh haleti the psychological condition, mood ruh hastası psychopath ruh hekimi psychiatrist ruh hekimliği psychiatry ruhu şad olsun May his soul be happy
ruhani spiritual
ruhban clergy
ruhbilim psychology
ruhbilimci psychologist
ruhbilimsel psychological
ruhi psychological
ruhsal psychological
ruhsat licence, permission ruhsat vermek to license

ruhsatlı licensed
ruhsatname permit, licence
ruhsatsız unlicensed
ruhsuz inanimate, lifeless, spiritless
ruj lipstick
rulet roulette
rulman bearing
rulo roll, rouleau
Rum Greek (of Turkish nationality)
Rumca modern Greek
Rumeli European Turkey, Roumelia, Rumelia
Rumen Romanian, Roumanian, Rumanian
Rumence Romanian
rumuz symbol
Rus Russian
Rusça Russian
Rusya Russia
rutubet humidity, dampness
rutubetlenmek to become damp
rutubetli damp, humid
rüçhan priority, preference rüçhan hakkı precedence, priority
rüküş comically dressed
rüsum dues, taxes
rüşt majority
rüşvet bribe, pay-off rüşvet almak to accept a bribe rüşvet vermek to bribe
rüşvetçilik bribery
rütbe rank rütbe almak to rise in rank
rüya dream rüya gibi dreamlike rüya görmek to dream, to have a dream rüya tabiri interpretation of dreams
rüzgâr wind, breeze rüzgâr altı den. lee side rüzgâr üstü den windward side Rüzgâr eken fırtına biçer. ats. Sow the wind and reap the whirlwind.
rüzgârgülü compass rose
rüzgârlı windy, breezy

S

saadet happiness
saat hour; watch, clock; meter saat gibi işlemek to run smoothly saat kaç? what's the time? what time is it? saat

kaçta? at what time? saat kulesi clock tower saat tutmak (a race) to time saati kurmak to wind a watch saati saatine punctually
saatçi maker/seller of watches/clocks, watchmaker, watchseller
saatli bomba time bomb
sabah morning; in the morning sabah akşam all the time sabah sabah early in the morning sabahın köründe early in the morning
sabahçı early riser
sabahki morning's
sabahlamak to sit up all night
sabahları in the morning; every morning
sabahleyin in the morning
sabahlık dressing gown
saban plough saban sürmek to plough
sabanbalığı fox shark
sabankemiği anat. vomer
sabık former, previous, ex
sabıka previous conviction
sabıkalı previously convicted
sabır patience sabrını taşırmak to put sb out of patience
sabırla patiently
sabırlı patient
sabırsız impatient
sabırsızlanmak to grow impatient, to champ
sabırsızlık impatience
sabırsızlıkla impatiently
sabit fixed stationary sabit fikir fixed idea sabit olmak to be fixed; to be confirmed
sabitleştirmek to fix
sabitlik fixity
sabotaj sabotage sabotaj yapmak to sabotage
sabotajcı saboteur
sabote etmek to sabotage
sabretmek to show patience, to be patient Sabreden derviş muradına ermiş. ats. Everything comes to him who waits.
sabuklama delirium
sabun soap
sabunlamak to soap
sabunlanmak to soap oneself

sabunlu soapy
sabunotu soapwort
sabuntaşı soapstone, steatite
sac sheet iron
sacayağı, sacayak trivet
saç hair saç bağı hair-band saç boyası hair dye saç filesi hair-net saç kurutma makinesi hair drier saç örgüsü plait saç saça baş başa gelmek to come to blows saçı başı ağarmak to grow old saçına ak düşmek (hair) to turn grey saçını başını yolmak to tear out one's hair saçını kestirmek to have one's hair cut saçını süpürge etmek (woman) to exert oneself saçları dökülmek to lose one's hair
saçak eaves (of a house); fringe
saçakbulut cirrus
saçaklı eaved; fringed
saçkıran alopecia, ringworm
saçma scattering, strewing; nonsense, bilge, piffle; buckshot, pellet; nonsensical saçma sapan konuşmak to talk nonsense
saçmak to scatter, to strew saçıp savurmak to play ducks and drakes with (money), to squander
saçmalamak to talk nonsense, to piffle
saçmalık nonsense
sadaka alms
sadakat faithfulness, loyalty sadakat göstermek to show loyalty
sadakatli faithful, loyal
sadakatsiz unfaithful, disloyal
sade simple, plain
sadece only, simply
sadeleşmek to become simple
sadeleştirmek to simplify
sadelik simplicity, plainness
sadet point, subject sadede gelmek to come to the point
sadeyağ clarified butter, run butter
sadık loyal, faithful; true, accurate
sadist sadist; sadistic
sadizm sadism
sadrazam Grand Vizier
saf row, line saf saf in rows
saf pure unmixed; ingenuous, gullible, naive
safa bkz. sefa

safari safari
safha phase
safi pure; net; merely, purely
safir sapphire
safkan purebred, thoroughbred
saflık purity; ingenuousness
safran *bitk.* saffron
safsata sophistry, casuistry
safsatacı sophist, casuist
safra bile, gall
sağ right sağ yapmak (auto) to pull over to the right sağa to the right sağa dönmek to turn right sağda on the right sağda solda everywhere, right and left sağdan from the right sağdan gidiniz! Keep to the right! sağına soluna bakmak to look about one sağı solu olmamak to chop and change sağlı sollu right and left, on both sides sağ alive sağ kalanlar the survivors sağ kalmak to remain alive, to survive sağ kurtulmak to save one's skin sağ ol Thank you! sağ olmak to be alive sağ salim sate and sound
sağalmak to become well, to recover
sağaltıcı curative, healing
sağaltım medical treatment
sağaltmak to cure, to heal
sağanak downpour
sağbeğeni good taste
sağcı rightist
sağcılık rightism
sağdıç (bridegroom's) best man
sağduyu common sense
sağgörü foresight
sağgörülü farsighted
sağı bird excrement
sağım milking; milk-giving animal
sağımlı milch
sağır deaf sağır etmek to deafen
sağırlaşmak to grow deaf
sağırlık deafness
sağıryılan adder, viper
sağlam strong, solid, firm; safe, secure, sound; healthy sağlama bağlamak to make sure
sağlama *mat.* check, proof
sağlamak to supply, to obtain, to get
sağlamlaşmak to become sound
sağlamlaştırmak to strengthen, to con-

solidate
sağlamlık solidity, firmness; safety
sağlık health sağlık görevlisi government health official sağlık merkezi health centre sağlık ocağı village clinic Sağlık olsun! Never mind! sağlık sigortası health insurance sağlığında while he was alive Sağlığınıza To your health!, Cheers!
sağlıklı healthy
sağlıksız unhealthy
sağlıkbilgisi hygiene
sağmak to milk
sağmal milk-giving, milch
sağrı rump
saha area, field
sahaf dealer in old books
sahan shallow cooking pan
sahanlık lending; platform
sahi really, truly
sahibe female owner
sahici genuine, real
sahiden really, truly
sahil coast, shore
sahip owner; master sahip çıkmak to claim
sahiplik ownership
sahipsiz ownerless; unprotected
sahne stage; scene sahneye çıkmak to appear sahneye koymak to stage
sahra desert, wilderness sahra topu *ask.* field-gun
sahte false, counterfeit, forged, sham, phoney
sahtekâr forger, counterfeiter
sahtekârlık forgery, counterfeiting
sahur meal before dawn
sair other
saka water-carrier
saka, sakakuşu goldfinch
sakağı glanders
sakal beard sakal bırakmak to grow a beard sakalı ele vermek to allow oneself to be led by the nose
sakallı bearded
sakalsız beardless
sakar butterfingered, clumsy, awkward
sakarin saccharine
sakaroz saccharose
sakat disabled, invalid, crippled; un-

sound, defective
sakatat offals, giblets
sakatlamak to damage, to main, to cripple
sakatlık impairment, disability, handicap
sakın Mind! Beware! Don't do it!
sakınca drawback, objection
sakıncalı objectionable
sakıngan cautious, prudent
sakınmak to avoid, to abstain (from), to beware (of)
sakız mastic, chewing gum sakız çiğnemek to chew gum
sakızkabağı vegetable marrow
sakin calm quiet; inhabitant
sakinleşmek to calm down
sakinleştirmek to calm down, to soothe
saklamak to hide, to conceal; to mask, to disguise
saklambaç hide-and-seek
saklanmak to hide
saklı hidden; secret
saksağan magpie
saksı flowerpot, vase
saksofon *müz.* saxophone
saksofoncu saxophonist
sal raft
salahiyet authority
salak silly, foolish
salaklık silliness
salam salami
salamandra *hayb.* salamander
salamanje dining room
salamura brine, pickle; pickled
salapurya *den.* small lighter
salata salad
salatalık cucumber
salça tomato sauce
saldırgan aggressive; attacker, aggressor
saldırganlık aggressiveness
saldırı aggression, attack
saldırmak to attack
saldırmazlık nonaggression saldırmazlık antlaşması nonaggression agreement
salep salep
salgı secretion
salgılamak to secrete

salgın epidemic
salhane slaughterhouse
salı Tuesday
salık advice salık vermek to recommend, to advise
salıncak swing
salınım oscillation
salınmak to sway; to oscillate
salıvermek to let go, to release
salimen safe and sound, safely
salkım bunch, cluster; wistaria salkım saçak hanging down in rags
salkımsöğüt weeping-willow
sallamak to swing, to rock; to shake, to wag, to whisk
sallanmak to swing, to sway, to bob; to linger over, to loiter
sallantı swinging, rocking sallantıda bırakmak to leave up in the air
sallapati tactless; tactlessly, carelessly
sallasırt etmek to shoulder
salmak to let go, to loose, to release
salmastra gasket
salon parlour, hall; sitting room
saloz *arg.* stupid
salt mere; merely, solely salt çoğunluk absolute majority
saltanat sovereignty, reign saltanat sürmek to reign; to live in luxury
saltık absolute
salvo salvo
salya saliva
salyangoz snail
sam samiel, simoom, simoon
saman straw saman altından su yürütmek to act on the sly, to do sth secretly saman gibi insipid saman nezlesi hay fever
samanlık hayloft, barn
samankâğıdı tracing paper
samankapan amber
samanrengi straw yellow
Samanyolu the Milky Way
samba samba
Sami Semitic
samimi sincere
samimiyet sincerity
samimiyetle sincerely
samimiyetsiz insincere
samimiyetsizlik insincerity

samur sable **samur kürk** sable skin coat, sable
samyeli samiel, simoom
san reputation
sana to you, for you **sana ne?** What's that to you?
sanat art; trade, craft **sanat eseri** work of art
sanatçı artist
sanatkâr artist; artisan, craftsman
sanatsal artistic
sanatoryum sanatorium
sanayi industry **sanayi devrimi** industrial revolution
sanayileşme industrialization
sanayileşmek to industrialize
sancak flag, standard; starboard side
sancı pain, grips, stitch
sancılanmak to have a pain
sancımak to ache
sandal rowboat
sandalcı boatman
sandalet sandal
sandalye chair
sandık chest, box, coffer
sandıklamak to crate, to box
sandviç sandwich
sanı supposition
sanık accused
saniye second
sanki as if, as though
sanlı famous
sanmak to think, to suppose
sanrı hallucination
sansar marten
sansasyon sensation **sansasyon yaratmak** to cause a sensation
sansasyonel sensational
Sanskrit Sanskrit; Sanskritic
sansür censorship
sansürcü censor
sansürlemek to censor
santigram centigramme
santigrat centigrade
santilitre centilitre
santim centimetre
santimetre centimetre **santimetre kare** square centimetre **santimetre küp** cubic centimetre
santra (football) centre spot

santral telephone exchange, switchboard
santrfor (football) centreforward
santrifüj centrifugal
santur *müz.* dulcimer
sap handle; stem, stalk **sapına kadar** to the core, utterly
sapa out-of-the-way, secluded
sapak turnoff, turning
sapan sling; catapult
saparta broadside
sapasağlam in the pink; quite healthy
sapık perverted; pervert
sapıklık perversion
sapınç deviation; aberration
sapır sapır dökülmek to fall abundantly and continuously
sapıtmak to go off one's head, to go nuts; to drivel, to rave
sapkın perverse, astray
saplama thrusting; stud
saplamak to thrust into, to plunge into
saplanmak to sink into, to be stuck in, to lodge
saplantı fixed idea
sapma deviation
sapmak to turn off into, to swing into; to deviate, to digress
saprofit saprophyte
sapsarı yellow; very pale **sapsarı kesilmek** to turn pale
saptamak to fix to determine
sara epilepsy **sarası tutmak** to have an epileptic fit
saraç saddler
saralı epileptic
sararmak to turn yellow, to turn pale
saray palace; government house
sardalye sardine, pilchard
sardunya geranium
sarf expenditure **sarf etmek** to spend, to expend; to use, to exert
sarfınazar apart from **sarfınazar etmek** to disregard, to overlook
sarfiyat expenses, expenditure
sargı bandage, dressing **sargı sarmak** to bandage
sarhoş drunk; boozer **sarhoş etmek** to make drunk, to intoxicate **sarhoş olmak** to get drunk

sarı yellow

sarıağız *hayb.* meagre, shadefish

sarıasma golden oriole

sarıçalı barberry

sarıgöz *hayb.* sargo

sarıhumma yellow fever

sarık turban

sarıkanat medium-sized bluefish

sarılgan *bitk.* climbing

sarılık yellowness; *hek.* jaundice

sarılmak to embrace, to hug; to be surrounded; to be bandaged

sarımsı, sarımtırak yellowish

sarınmak to wrap oneself in

sarısabır *bitk.* aloe

sarısalkım laburnum

sarışın blond, blonde

sarih clear, evident

sarkaç pendulum

sarkık hanging, pendulous, flabby

sarkıntılık molestation sarkıntılık etmek to molest

sarkıt stalactite

sarkmak to hang down, to dangle, to droop

sarmak to wrap up, to muffle up, to lap; to wind ... round, to wrap ... around; to appeal to, to interest

sarmal spiral

sarman enormous; yellow cat

sarmaşan winding

sarmaş dolaş in a close embrace sarmaş dolaş olmak to be locked in a close embrace

sarmaşık ivy

sarmısak garlic

sarnıç cistern

sarp arduous, precipitous sarpa sarmak to become complicated

sarpa sea-bream

sarplaşmak to become steep

sarraf money-changer

sarsak shaky, tottery

sarsılmak to be shaken; to be shocked; to be enfeebled

sarsıntı shake, jolt; earthquake; *hek.* concussion; *ruhb.* shock

sarsıntılı shaky, jolty

sarsıntısız smooth

sarsmak to shake, to jolt; to shock, to

shake

sataşmak to tease, to annoy, to taunt; to ask for trouble; to molest

saten satin

sathi superficial, shallow

satı sale satıya çıkarmak to put up for sale

satıcı seller, salesman

satıcılık salesmanship

satıh surface

satılık for sale, on sale satılığa çıkarmak to put up for sale

satım sale

satın almak to buy

satır line; meat cleaver

satırbaşı paragraph indentation

satış safe satışa çıkarmak to put up for sale

satlıcan *hek.* pleurisy

satmak to sell satıp savmak to sell all one has

satranç chess satranç tahtası chessboard satranç taşı piece

Satürn Saturn

sauna sauna

sav assertion, thesis

savaş war, battle

savaşçı combatant, fighter

savaşkan bellicose, warlike

savaşmak to fight, to struggle, to combat

savaşım struggle savaşım vermek to struggle

savcı public prosecutor

savcılık attorney generalship

savmak to drive away, to dismiss; to escape from, to avoid

savruk untidy, slapdash, messy

savsaklamak to neglect

savrulmak to stand aside, to get out of the way

savulmak to stand aside Savulun! Get out ot the way!

savunma defence, defense

savunmasız defenceless

savunmak to defend; to advocate, to champion, to maintain

savurgan prodigal, extravagant

savurganlık prodigality, extravagance

savurmak to throw, to scatter, to hurl,

to fling
savuşmak to slip away, to sneak off
savuşturmak to fend off; to avoid, to escape, to evade
saya vamp, shoe-upper
sayaç counter, meter
saydam transparent
saydamlık transparency
saye protection, assistance **sayesinde** thanks to, owing to
sayfa page
sayfiye summer house
saygı respect, esteem, regard **saygı duymak** to respect **saygı göstermek** to show respect **saygılarımla** yours respectfully
saygıdeğer estimable, respected
saygılı respectful
saygısız disrespectful
saygısızca disrespectfully
saygısızlık disrespect, disregard
saygın respected, esteemed
saygınlık esteem, prestige, credit
sayı number; issue, number **sayı saymak** to count
sayılı counted; numbered; limited; top-notch
sayıboncuğu abacus
sayıklamak to talk in one's sleep, to rave
sayım enumeration census
sayın esteemed, honourable; dear
sayısal numerical
sayısız innumerable, countless
sayışmak to settle accounts with one another
Sayıştay the Government Accounting Bureau
saymaca nominal, arbitrary
saymak to count; to include; to respect; to consider, to regard **sayıp dökmek** to enumerate
sayman accountant
saymanlık accountancy
sayrı sick,ill
sayrılık sickness, disease
sayvan awning, tent
saz rush, reed
saz Turkish guitar; musical instrument **saz şairi** minstrel

sazan carp
seans sitting, session
sebat perseverance **sebat etmek** to persevere
sebatkâr persevering
sebatsız inconstant, fickle
sebebiyet vermek to cause
sebebiyle because of, owing to
sebep cause, reason **sebep olmak** to cause
sebeplenmek to get a share of the pie
sebepsiz without any reason
sebil public fountain; free distribution of water
sebze vegetable
sebzeci greengrocer
seccade prayer rug
secde prostrating oneself (while performing the namaz)
seçenek alternative
seçici selector
seçim election; choice, preference **seçimini yapmak** to make one's choice
seçimle by election
seçkin distinguished, select, choice
seçme choice; select, choice
seçmece by choice, for choice
seçmek to choose, to select, to elect; to distinguish, to discern, to spot
seçmeli elective, optional
seçmen elector, voter **seçmen kütüğü** electoral roll, register of electors
seda sound, voice
sedef mother-of-pearl, nacre **sedef hastalığı** psoriasis
sedefotu rue
sedir divan, sofa
sedir *bitk.* cedar
sedye stretcher
sefa enjoyment, pleasure **sefa bulduk** Thank you! (said in reply to 'welcome!') **sefa geldin(iz)** Welcome! **sefa geldine gitmek** to visit sb in order to welcome him **sefa sürmek** to enjoy oneself, to have a good time **sefasını sürmek** to enjoy sth to the utmost
sefahat dissipation, debauch
sefalet misery, poverty **sefalet çekmek** to suffer privation
sefaret embassy

sefer expedition, journey; time
seferber mobilized for war seferber etmek to mobilize
seferberlik mobilization
sefertası travelling food box
sefil miserable, poor
sefir ambassador
sefire ambassadoress
seğirdim (gun) recoil; footrace
seğirmek to flicker, to twitch
seğirtmek to run, to rush
seher daybreak, dawn
sehpa coffee table, end table; easel
seki tenace, bench, shelf
sekiz eight
sekizer eight each
sekizinci eighth
sekmek to hop; to ricochet, to skim
sekreter secretary
sekreterlik secretariat, secretaryship
seks sex
seksapel sex appeal
seksek hopscotch
seksen eighty
seksener eighty each
sekseninci eightieth
seksi sexy
seksolojl sexology
seksüel sexual
sekte stoppage, interruption sekte vurmak to interrupt, to impede
sektör sector
sel flood sel basmak to flood
selam greeting, salutation Selam dur! Present arms! selam göndermek to send one's compliments selamı sabahı kesmek to break with selam söylemek to give one's kind regards to selam vermek to greet, to salute
selamet safety, security; healthiness, soundness selamete çıkmak to reach safety
selamlamak to greet, to salute
selamlaşmak to greet each other
Selanik Salonica
Selçuklu Seljuk, Seljukian
sele flattish basket; saddle
selef predecessor
selektör selector
selenterler coelentera

selfservis self-service
selim hek. benign
seloteyp sellotape
selüloit celluloid
selüloz cellulose
selvi cypress
sema sky
semafor semaphore
semaver samovar
semavi celestial
sembol symbol
sembolik symbolic, symbolical
semender hayb. salamander
semer packsaddle; pad, stout semer vurmak to put a packsaddle (on)
semere fruit, result semeresini vermek to prove fruitful
seminer seminar
semirgin fat and lazy
semirmek to grow fat
semirtmek to fatten
semiyoloji hek. semiology
semiz fat sleek
semizotu purslane
sempati attraction, liking sempati duymak to take to, to like
sempatik likable, congenial; anat. sympathetic sempatik sinir sistemi sympathetic nervous system
sempatizan sympathizer
sempozyum symposium
semptom hek. symptom
semt neighbourhood, quarter semtine uğramamak to stop going
sen you
senarist scenarist
senaryo scenario, script
senato senate
senatör senator
sence in your opinion
sendelemek to totter, to stagger, to stumble
senden from you
sendika trade union, labour union
sendikacı trade unionist
sendikacılık trade unionism
sendrom hek. syndrome
sene year
senelik yearly, annual
senet voucher, security, receipt; promis-

sory note **senet vermek** to give sb
written certification; to guarantee
senetleşmek to give one another written certifications
senetli certified
senetsiz uncertified
senfoni *müz.* symphony **senfoni orkestrası** symphony orchestra
senfonik symphonic
sen you
senin your
seninki yours
senkronizasyon synchronization
senlibenli free-and-easy, familiar **senlibenli olmak** to hobnob with
sentaks syntax
sentetik synthetic
sentez synthesis
sepet basket; sidecar **sepet havası çalmak** to give sb the boot
sepetlemek to get rid of, to fire, to sack
sepettopu basketball
sepi tanning
sepici tenner
sepilemek to tan
sera greenhouse
seramik ceramic; ceramics
serap mirage
serbest free **serbest bırakmak** to set
free **serbest bölge** free zone **serbest
güreş** catch-as-catch-can (wrestling)
serbest meslek sahibi self-employed
person **serbest nazım** free verse **serbest stil** freestyle **serbest vuruş** (football) free kick
serbestçe freely
serbesti freedom
serbestlik freedom
serçe sparrow
serçeparmak little finger
serdümen quartermaster
seren *den.* yard
serenat serenade
sere serpe yatmak to sprawl oüt
sergi exhibition
sergilemek to exhibit
seri series **seri halinde** in series **seri
imalat** mass production **seri numarası** serial number
seri swift, rapid

serifgrafi serigraphy, silk screen
serin cool
serinkanlı cool-headed
serinlemek to become cool
serinletmek to cool
serinlik coolness
serkeş rebellious
serkeşlik rebelliousness
sermaye capital; riches, wealth; prostitute **sermaye koymak** to invest capital
sermayeci, sermayedar capitalist
sermayeli having a capital
sermayesiz without capital
sermek to spread, to lay; to beat down
to the ground; to neglect
serpelemek to sprinkle down, to drizzle
serpilmek to be sprinkled; to grow
serpinti drizzle, sprinkle
serpiştirmek (rain) to drizzle, to mizzle;
(snow) to spit down; sprinkle, to scatter
serpmek to sprinkle, to scatter, to strew
sersem stupid, silly; stunned, dazed
sersemlemek to be stunned
sersemletmek to daze,,to stun
serseri tramp, vagabond, vagrant; stray
serserilik vagabondage, vagrancy
sert hard, tough; severe, harsh
sertleşmek to become hard
sertleştirmek to harden
sertlik hardness, toughness; severity,
harshness
sertifika certificate
serum serum
serüven adventure
serüvenci adventurous; adventurer
serüvenli adventurous
servet riches, wealth
servi cypress
servis service; department **servis yapmak** to serve food (to); *sp.* to serve
the ball
serzeniş reproach **serzenişte bulunmak** to reproach
ses sound, voice; noise **ses çıkarmamak** to say nothing **ses dalgası** sonic
wave **ses geçirmez** soundproof **sesini
çıkarmamak** to say nothing **sesini
kesmek** to shut up **sesini kısmak** to
turn down

sesbilgisi phonetics
sesbilim phonology
seselim resonance
seslenmek to call out
sesli voiced; aloud sesli harf vowel sesli okumak to read aloud
sessiz soundless, voiceless; silent, quiet, meek sessiz harf consonant
sessizce silently
sessizlik silence
sesteş *dilb.* homophone
set barrier, dam; *sp.* set set çekmek to dike; to hinder, to barricade
sevap good deed sevaba girmek to acquire merit in God's sight sevap işlemek to acquire merit
sevda love, passion sevda çekmek to be passionately in love
sevdalanmak to fall in love (with), to lose one's heart (to)
sevdalı in love
sevecen compassionate, kind
sevgi love
sevgili darling, lover, sweetie
sevi love
sevici lesbian
sevicilik lesbianism
sevimli lovable, congenial, charming
sevimsiz unlikeable, unattractive, charmless
sevinç joy, delight sevincinden uçmak to exult, to walk on air
sevinçli joyful, glad
sevindirmek to gladden, to delight, to please
sevinmek to be pleased, to rejoice
sevişmek to love one another; to make love
seviye level
sevk sending, consignment, dispatch; inciting, urging sevk etmek to send, to consign, to dispatch; to incite, to urge
sevkıyat consignments; *ask.* dispatch of troops
sevmek to love seve seve with pleasure, willingly
seyahat travel, journey, voyage seyahat acentesi travel agency seyahat çeki traveller's cheque seyahat etmek to travel
seyahatname book of travels
seyir course, progress; wotching, looking at; cruising seyir defteri logbook
seyirci spectator, onlooker seyirci kalmak not to be involved in, to be a mere spectator seyirciler audience
seyis groom
seyrek wide apart; rare; rarely
seyretmek to watch, to see; to move, to sail, to cruise
seyyah traveller
seyyar travelling, itinerant; movable seyyar satıcı street hawker, pedlar
sezaryen caesarean operation sezaryenle doğmak to be born by caesarean section
sezgi intuition
sezgili intuitive
sezi intuition
sezinlemek to sense, to feel
sezmek to perceive, to sense, to discern
sezon season
sıcacık cosy, cozy
sıcak hot, warm; heat sıcak renkler warm colours sıcak tutmak to keep warm sıcağı sıcağına while the iron is hot
sıcakkanlı warm blooded; friendly, warm-hearted
sıcaklık heat, warmth
sıçan rat, mouse
sıçankuyruğu rat-tailed file
sıçanotu arsenic
sıçmak to defecate, to shit
sıçrama jumping sıçrama tahtası springboard
sıçramak to jump, to spring, to leap
sıçratmak to splash, to spatter
sıfat capacity, position; *dilb.* adjective
sıfatıyla in the capacity of
sıfır zero, naught, nil sıfırdan başlamak to start from zero
sığ shallow
sığa capacity
sığdırmak to cram in, to jam in, to thrust in
sığınak shelter
sığınık refugee

sığınmak to take shelter, to shelter

sığıntı person whose presence is unwanted, intruder, sponger

sığır cattle sığır eti beef

sığırcık starling

sığırtmaç herdsman, drover

sığışmak to squeeze into

sığmak to go into, to fit into

sıhhat health Sıhhatinize! Cheers!, To your health! Sıhhatler olsun! Good health to you!

sıhhatli healthy

sıhhi hygienic

sıhhiye sanitary matters

sık close, dense, thick sık sık often, frequently

sıkacak squeezer

sıkboğaz etmek to keep on at, to rush sb, to importune sb

sıkı tight, firm; strict, rigorous; stingy; trouble, straits sıkı çalışmak to work hard sıkı durmak to hold fast sıkı tutmak to hold tight; to control firmly

sıkıca firmly, tightly

sıkıcı boring, dull

sıkıdenetim cencorship

sıkıdüzen discipline

sıkı fıkı intimate sıkı fıkı olmak to be on intimate terms (with)

sıkılık tightness, firmness

sıkılgan shy, bashful

sıkılganlık shyness

sıkılmak to be pressed; to be ashamed; to be bored; to be in straits

sıkılmaz shameless

sıkınmak to constrain oneself

sıkıntı boredom; bother, hardship, distress, trouble sıkıntı çekmek to have troubles sıkıntı vermek to annoy, to bother sıkıntıda olmak to be in straits sıkıntıya düşmek to be hard up sıkıntıya gelememek to be unable to stand the gaff

sıkıntılı troublesome, trying, uneasy

sıkışık tight; close, serried; crowded; cramped sıkışık durumda olmak to be hardpressed

sıkışmak to be jammed in, to squeeze into; to be in straits; to be taken short; to stick

sıkıştırmak to press, to squeeze

sıkıyönetim martial law

sıkkın annoyed

sıklaşmak to become frequent

sıklet weight

sıklık density; frequency

sıkmak to press, to squeeze; to tighten; to annoy, to bother; to put pressure on

sıla (one's) home, homeplace; reunion sılaya gitmek to go home

sımsıkı very tight; tightly

sınai industrial

sınamak to try, to test

sınav examination, exam sınav olmak to have an exam sınav vermek to pass an exam sınava girmek to take an exam sınavda kalmak to fail in an exam, to flunk

sınıf class; category; classroom sınıfta çakmak to flunk sınıfta kalmak to fail

sınıflandırma classification

sınıflandırmak to classify

sınır frontier, border sınır dışı etmek to deport sınır koymak to limit sınırı geçmek to cross the frontier

sınırdaş bordering

sınırlama limitation

sınırlamak to border, to limit

sınırlı limited

sınırsız limitless

sıpa donkey foal

sır secret, mystery sır saklamak/tutmak to keep (a) secret sır vermek to betray a secret sırra kadem basmak to vanish into thin air

sır glaze

sıra desk, bench; row; line; turn sıra beklemek to await one's turn sıra olmak to be lined up sıra sıra in rows sırası gelmişken by the way sırasını savmak to have done one's turn sıraya girmek to line up sıraya koymak to put in order

sıraca *hek* scrofula

sıradağ mountain range

sıradan ordinary

sıralamak to set up in order

sıralı in due order

sırasında when necessary

sırasız untimely, inconvenient, inopportune

sırça glass

sırdaş confidant

sırf pure, mere, sheer

sırık pole sırıkla atlama *sp.* pole vault

sırılsıklam *bkz.* sırsıklam

sırım leather thong sırım gibi wiry

sırıtkan given to grinning

sırıtmak to grin; (a defect) to show up

sırlamak to glaze; to silver

sırlı glazed

sırma silver thread sırma saçlı golden haired

sırnaşık pestering, importunate, saucy

sırnaşmak to pester, to importune

Sırp Serb; Serbian

Sırpça Serbian

Sırbistan Serbia

sırsıklam soaked to the skin sırsıklam âşık head over heels in love

sırt back sırt çevirmek to turn one's back on sırtından geçinmek to live at sb's expense sırtını yere getirmek to overcome sırtı yere gelmek to be overcome sırt sırta back to back

sırtlan hyena

sırtüstü on one's back sırtüstü gelmek to lie on one's back

sıska puny, skinny

sıtma malaria sıtmaya tutulmak to get malaria

sıtmalı malarial

sıva plaster sıva vurmak to plaster

sıvacı plasterer

sıvalı plastered

sıvamak to plaster; to roll up, to tuck up

sıvazlamak to stroke, to caress

sıvı liquid, fluid

sıvışmak to slip away, to sneak away

sıyırmak to skin, to graze, to scrape

sıyrık scrape, graze; scraped, grazed

sıyrılmak to be skinned; to get out of, to squeak through, to wriggle out ot

sıyrıntı scrapings; scratch

sızdırmak to leak, to ooze out; to leak; to squeeze (money) out of

sızı ache, pain

sızıltı complaint

sızıntı leakage, oozings

sızlamak to smart, to ache

sızlanmak to complain, to lament; to groan

sızmak to leak, to ooze; to drop into a drunken slumber

si *müz.* ti, te

sicil register sicile kaydetmek to enter into the register

sicilli registered

Sicilya Sicily

Sicilyalı Sicilian

sicim string

sidik urine

sidikborusu *anat.* ureter

sidiktorbası *anat.* bladder

sidikyolu urethra

sidikzoru *hek.* dysuria

sif *tic.* c.i.f.

sifilis syphilis

sifon siphon; flush tank

siftah first sale of the day, handsel siftah etmek to make the first sale of the day

sigara cigarette, cigaret *Aİ.* sigara içmek to smoke (a cigarette) Sigara içilmez! No smoking! sigara sarmak to roll a cigarette

sigorta insurance, assurance; fuse sigorta atmak (fuse) to blow sigorta etmek to insure, to assure sigorta poliçesi insurance policy sigorta primi insurance premium sigortayı attırmak to blow the fuses

sigortacı insurer

sigortalamak to insure

sigortalı insured

sigortasız uninsured

siğil wart

sihir magic, sorcery

sihirbaz magician, sorcerer

sihirbazlık magic, sorcery

sihirli bewitched, enchanted; bewitching, enchanting

silah weapon, arm silah altına almak to call to arms Silah başına! To arms! silah çatmak to pile arms

silahlanma armament silahlanma yarışı arms race

silahlanmak to arm oneself

silahlı armed silahlı kuvvetler armed

195   sirayet

forces
silahsız unarmed
silahsızlandırma disarmament
silahsızlandırmak to disarm
silahşor musketeer, warrior
silecek bath towel; windscreen wiper
silgi duster; eraser, rubber
silik rubbed out; indistinct, insignificant
silikon silicone
silindir cylinder; roller **silindir şapka** top hat
silindirik cylindrical
silinmek to wipe oneself dry; to wear away
silinmez indelible
silinti erasure
silis silica
silisyum silicon
silkelemek to shake off
silkinmek to shake oneself
silkmek to shake (out)
sille slap, box
silme wiping; full to the brim, brimful
silmek to rub off, to erase, to expunge; to wipe
silo silo
silsile chain, series
siluet silhouette
sima face; personage, figure
simetri symmetry
simetrik symmetric, symmetrical
simge symbol
simgelemek to symbolize
simgesel symbolic, symbolical
simit ring-shaped roll of bread covered with sesame seeds; life buoy
simpozyum symposium
simsar broker; middleman
simsarlık brokerage
simsiyah jet-black
simya alchemy
simyacı alchemist
sin grave, tomb
sinegog synagogue
sincap squirrel
sindirim digestion
sindirmek to digest; to cow, to daunt
sine breast, bosom **sineye çekmek** to take sth lying down
sinek fly; (cards) clubs **sinek avlamak**

(shopkeeper) to sit idly (because of no customers)
sinekkapan flycatcher
sinekkaydı (shave) very close
sinekkuşu hummingbird
sineklik fly-whisk
sineksıklet (boxing) feather weight
sinema cinema, movies
sinemaskop cinemascope
sini round metal or wooden tray
sinik cynical; cynic
sinir nerve; sinew **sinir argınlığı** neurasthenia, nervous breakdown **sinir etmek** to rub sb up the wrong way **sinir harbi** war of nerves **sinir hastalığı** neuropathy **sinir hücresi** nerve cell **sinir kesilmek** to become all nerves **sinir sistemi** nervous system **siniri tutmak** to have a fit of nerves **sinirine dokunmak** to get on sb's nerves **sinirleri altüst olmak** to be very upset **sinirleri bozmak** to get on sb's nerves
sinirbilim neurology
sinirce neurosis
sinirdoku neural tissue
sinirkanatlılar neuroptera, ant lions
sinirlendirmek to make nervous, to annoy, to rub sb the wrong way
sinirlenmek to get nervous, to become irritated
sinirli nervous, edgy; quick-tempered
sinirotu *bitk.* ribwort plantain
sinirsel neural, nervous
sinizm cynicism
sinmek to crouch down, to cower; to sink into, to penetrate
sinsi stealthy, sneaky
sinsice stealthily
sinsilik stealthiness
sinüs *anat.* sinus; *mat.* sine
sinüzit sinusitis
sinyal signal
sipahi cavalry soldier
sipariş order **sipariş etmek** to receive an order **sipariş etmek/vermek** to order
siper shelter, shield; *ask.* trench
sipsivri very sharp
sirayet contagion **sirayet etmek** (disease) to spread

siren siren
sirk circus
sirke vinegar
sirkülasyon circulation
sirküler circular
sis fog, mist
sisli foggy, misty
sismograf seismograph
sistem system
sistematik systematic
sistemleştirmek to systematize
sistemli systematical
sistemsiz unsystematic
sistit *hek.* cystitis
site housing estate; city-state
sitem reproach, rebuke sitem etmek to reproach
sitil style
sitoplazma *biy.* cytoplasm
sivil civilian, civil
sivilce pimple
sivilceli pimpled, pimply
sivri pointed, sharp sivri akıllı eccentric
sivribiber long green pepper
sivrilmek to become pointed; to come into prominence, to distinguish oneself
sivriltmek to make pointed, to sharpen
sivrisinek mosquito
siya *den.* rowing backwards
siyah black
siyahımsı blackish
siyahlık blackness
siyahi black, negro
siyanür cyanide
siyasa diplomacy, politics
siyasal political
siyasi political, diplomatic
siyatik *hek.* sciatica
siyek *anat.* urethra
Siyonizm Zionism
siz you siz bilirsiniz it's up to you, as you like
size to you, for you
sizi you
sizin your
sizinki yours
skandal scandal
skeç sketch
skleroz *hek.* sclerosis

skolastik scholastic
Slav Slav; Slavic
slayt slide
slogan slogan
smokin dinner jacket, tuxedo
soba stove
soda soda water
sodyum sodium
sofa hall, anteroom
sofizm sophism
sofra (dining) table sofra başında at the table sofra örtüsü tablecloth sofra takımı table service sofraya oturmak to sit down to a meal sofrayı kaldırmak to clear away sofrayı kurmak to lay the table
soğan onion; bulb
soğancık *anat.* medulla oblongata
soğuk cold soğuk almak to catch cold soğuk algınlığı cold soğuk damga embossed stamp soğuk davranmak to give sb the cold shoulder soğuk espri joke in bad taste soğuk savaş cold war soğuktan donmak to be frozen to death
soğukkanlı cool-headed, calm
soğukluk coldness; *ruhb.* frigidity; cold sweet compote
soğumak to get cold, to cool; to take a dislike to, to go off
soğutmak to cool, to chill; to alienate, to put off
soğutucu frigorific; fridge
soğurmak to absorb
sohbet chat, conversation sohbet etmek to have a chat
sokak street sokak çocuğu street Arab, (street) urchin sokak kadını street walker
sokmak to introduce, to insert, to put in; to let in, to admit; to sting, to bite
sokulgan sociable, friendly, folksy
sokulmak to be inserted in; to insinuate oneself (into), to snuggle up
sokuşturmak to squeeze (into)
sol left sol yapmak to steer to the left sola dön turn left solda on the left solda sıfır a mere cypher
sol *müz.* sol
solak left-handed

solaryum solarium
solcu leftist
solculuk leftism
soldurmak to fade, to discolour
solfej *müz.* solfége, solfeggio
solgun pale, faded
solist soloist
sollamak to overtake
solmak to fade, to wither
solmaz (colour) fast, fadeless
solo *müz.* solo **solo yapmak** to solo
solucan worm
soluk pale; faded
soluk breath **soluk aldırmamak** to give no respite **soluk almak** to breathe; to have a rest **soluk borusu** trachea, windpipe **soluk kesici** breathtaking **soluğu kesilmek** to be out of breath **soluk soluğa** out of breath
soluklanmak to take a breather
solumak to pant, to snort
solungaç gill
solunum respiration **solunum aygıtı/-sistemi** respiratory system
som solid
som *hayb.* salmon
somun loaf (of bread)
somun nut
somurtkan sulky, sullen
somurtmak to pout, to sulk
somut concrete
somutlaştırmak to concretize
somya spring mattress
son end; last, final **sona ermek** to end, to be over **sondan bir önceki** next to the last **son defa** (for) the last time **son derece** extremely **sone kalan donakalır** the early bird catches the worm **son kozunu oynamak** to play one's last card **son nefes** one's last breath **sonunu düşünmek** to think of the consequences
sonat *müz.* sonata
sonbahar autumn *Aİ.* fall
sonda probe, sound; drill
sondaj test bore; sounding **sondaj yapmak** to bore; to sound
sondalamak to sound; to bore
sone *yaz.* sonnet
sonek *dilb.* suffix

sonra after; then, later, afterwards
sonradan later, afterwards **sonradan görme** parvenu, upstart
sonraki following, subsequent
sonrasız eternal
sonsuz endless, infinite
sonsuzluk infinity, eternity
sonsuzlaştırmak to eternize
sonuç result, outcome, consequence **sonuç çıkarmak** to draw a conclusion
sonuçsuz fruitless, vain
sonuçlandırmak to conclude, to bring to a conclusion
sonuçlanmak to come to a conclusion, to conclude; to result (in, ile)
sonuncu last, final
sonunda in the end, finally
sopa stick, cudget; beating **sopa atmak** to give a beating (to) **sopa yemek** to get a beating
soprano soprano
sorgu interrogation **sorguya çekmek** to interrogate
sorguç crest
sorgulamak to interrogate
sorma to ask
soru question **soru işareti** question mark
sorumak to suck
sorumlu responsible (for, -den)
sorumluluk responsibility
sorumsuz irresponsible
sorumsuzluk irresponsibility
sorun problem, question, matter
soruşturma investigation
soruşturmak to investigate
sos sauce
sosis sausage
sosyal social **sosyal bilimler** social sciences
sosyalist socialist
sosyalizm socialism
sosyalleşme socialization
sosyete the upper classes, society
sosyoekonomik socioeconomic
sosyokültürel sociocultural
sosyolog sociologist
sosyoloji sociology
sosyolojik sociological
sote saute

Sovyet Soviet

soy lineage, descent, family; ancestors **soy sop** family, relations **soya çekmek** to take after one's family

soya soybean

soyaçekim heredity

soyadı family name, surname

soyağacı family tree, genealogical tree

soydaş of the same race

soykırımı genocide

soylu noble

soyluluk nobility

soygun robbery

soyguncu robber

soygunculuk robbery

soymak to undress; to rob; to shell, to peel, to shuck **soyup soğana çevirmek** to clean out, to rifle

soysuz of bad race; ignoble

soysuzlaşmak to degenerate

soytarı clown, buffoon

soyunmak to undress oneself

soyut abstract

soyutlamak to abstract

söğüş boiled meat

söğüt willow

sökmek to pull up, to uproot; to take to pieces, to tear ... down; to unsew, to unravel; *arg.* to work, to tell

sökük unravelled, unstitched; rent, tear

sökülmek to come unslitched; to be uprooted; *arg.* to pay up, to shell out

sömestr semester

sömürge colony

sömürgeci colonist

sömürgecilik colonialism

sömürgeleştirmek to colonize

sömürmek to exploit

sömürü exploitation

söndürmek to put out, to extinguish; to turn off, to switch off; to deflate

sönmek to go out

sönük extinguished; dull, lifeless; flat, deflated

sövgü swearword

sövmek to swear, to curse **sövüp saymak** to curse and swear

söylem discourse

söylemek to say, to tell; to pronounce

söylence myth

söyleniş pronunciation

söylenmek to be said; to be told; to be pronounced; to grumble, to mutter

söylenti rumour

söyleşi conversation, chat

söyleşmek to chat, to converse

söylev speech **söylev vermek** to give a speech

söz remark, word; speech, talk; rumour, gossip; promise **söz almak** to begin to speak; to obtain a promise **söz altında kalmamak** to give as good as one gets, to be quick to retort **söz anlamak** to be reasonable **söz aramızda** between you and me **söz dinlemek** to listen to advice, to obey **söz etmek** to talk about, to mention **söz geçirmek** to make oneself listened to **söz götürmez** indisputable, beyond doubt **söz işitmek** to be told off **söz kesmek** to agree to give in marriage **söz konusu** in question **söz olmak** to be the subject of gossip **söz vermek** to promise **söze karışmak** to interrupt by speaking **sözü ağzına tıkamak** to shut sb up **sözü ağzında gevelemek** to mince one's words **sözü çevirmek** to change the subject **sözü geçmek** to be talked about; to be influential **sözü uzatmak** to be wordy **sözünde durmamak** to break one's word **sözünden dönmek** to go back on one's word **sözünü esirgememek** not to mince one's words **sözünü geri almak** to retract **sözünü kesmek** to interrupt **sözünü tutmak** to keep one's word **sözünün eri** a man of his word

sözbirliği unanimity **sözbirliği etmek** to agree to say/do the same thing, to be unanimous in

sözbölükleri *dilb.* parts of speech

sözcü spokesman

sözcük word

sözcükbilim lexicology

sözde so-called, alleged, would-be

sözdizimi *dilb.* syntax

sözdizimsel syntactic

sözgelimi for example

sözgelişi for example

sözlendirici (film) dubber

sözlendirmek (film) to dub
sözleşme agreement, contract
sözleşmek to agree mutually; to make an appointment
sözlü oral, verbal; engaged; fiancé, fiancée sözlü sınav oral exam
sözlük dictionary
sözlükçü lexicographer
sözlükçülük lexicography
sözümona so-called, alleged
spazm spasm
spektroskop spectroscope
spekülasyon speculation
spekülatif speculative
spekülatör speculator
sperm(a) sperm
spiker announcer
spiral spiral; *hek.* loop
spontane spontaneous; spontaneously
spor *biy.* spore
spor sport; sports spor araba sports car spor yapmak to play sports
sporcu sportsman
sporsever sports fan
sportif sports, sportmen; sportsman; sportmanlike
sportoto football pools, pools
sprey spray; sprayer
stadyum stadium
staj apprenticeship, training staj görmek to be under training
stajyer trainee, probationer, intern
standart standard
statik static
statü status; statute
statüko status quo
steno shorthand, stenography; stenographer
stenograf stenographer
stenografi stenography
step steppe
stepne spare tyre
stereo stereo
stereofoni stereophony
stereofonik stereophonic
stereoskop stereoscope
steril sterile
sterilizasyon sterilization
sterilize, sterile sterilized sterilize etmek to sterilize

sterlin sterling
stetoskop stethoscope
steyşın station wagon
stil style
stoacılık *fel.* stoicism
stok stock stok etmek to stock
stokçu hoarder, stockist
stop stop stop etmek to stop
stopaj stoppage at source
stoplazma *biy.* cytoplasm
strateji strategy
stratejik strategical
stratosfer stratosphere
stres *hek.* stress
striptiz striptease
stüdyo studio
su water; broth; juice su almak (boat) to make water, to leak su bardağı water glass su baskını flood su basmak to flood su cenderesi hydraulic press su çekmek to draw water su değirmeni water mill su dökmek to make water, to urinate su geçirmez waterproof su gibi bilmek to know perfectly su gibi para harcamak to spend money like water su götürmez incontestable, indisputable su götürür disputable su koyuvermek to overstep the mark, to back on one's word su perisi nymph su sayacı water meter su toplamak to blister su vermek to water; (steel) to temper su yüzüne çıkmak to come to light sudan çıkmış balığa dönmek to be like a fish out of water sudan ucuz very cheap sularında about, around suya düşmek to fall to the ground, to fizzle out, to miscarry suya sabuna dokunmamak to avoid meddling suyunca gitmek to rub sb the right way suyunu çekmek to run out
sucu water seller
sucul hydrophile
sual question
sualtı underwater
suare evening performance
suaygırı hippopotamus
subay officer
sucuk sausage sucuğunu çıkarmak to give a good beating; to tire out sucuk

gibi ıslanmak to be wet through
suç offence, crime suç işlemek to commit an offence suçu bağışlamak to forgive an offence, to pardon
suçiçeği *hek.* chicken pox
suçlamak to accuse
suçlu guilty; criminal suçlu bulunmak to be found guilty
suçluluk guilt
suçortağı accomplice
suçsuz innocent
suçsuzluk innocence
suçüstü in flagrante delicto, in the act, red-handed
suçulluğu common sandpiper
sudan flimsy, trivial, lame
Sudan the Sudan
Sudalı Sudanese
suflör prompter
suiistimal abuse, misuse suiistimal etmek to abuse, to misuse
suikast conspiracy
suikastçı conspirator
sukabağı white gourd
sukamışı *bitk.* reedmace
sukeleri newt
sukemeri aqueduct
sukut fall
sulak watery
sulama watering; irrigation
sulamak to water; to irrigate
sulandırmak to dilute with water
sulanmak to be irrigated; to become watery; to water; *arg.* to get fresh with
sulh peace sulh hâkimi/yargıcı judge of the peace sulh mahkemesi court of first instance, minor court
sultan sultan, sultana
sulu watery; juicy; importunate, saucy
suluboya water colour
sulusepken sleet
sumen writing-pad
suna drake
sunak altar
sundurma shed, penthouse
sungur white falcon
suni artificial
sunmak to present, to offer; to perform, to play, to sing
sunturlu severe, awful

sunu offer sunu ve istem *tic.* offer and demand
sunucu compere, emcee
supap valve
sur city wall, rampart
surat face surat asmak to make a sour face suratından düşen bin parça olmak to pull a long face suratını buruşturmak to grimace surat mahkeme duvarı brazen-faced, sulky
suratsız sulky; ugly
sure section of the Koran, sura
suret copy; form, shape; manner, way suret çıkarmak to make a copy
Suriye Syria
Suriyeli Syrian
susak thirsty
susam sesame
susamak to be thirsty; to thirst for
susamış thirsty
susamuru common otter
suskun taciturn, quiet
susmak to hold one's tongue, to hush, to be quiet suspus olmak to keep silent, to be silenced
susta safety catch
sustalı clasp knife, flick knife sustalı çakı flick knife, switchblade
susturmak to silence, to hush, to shut up; to gag, to muzzle
susturucu silencer *Aİ.* muffler
susuz thirsty; waterless, arid, dry
susuzluk thirst; waterlessness
sutopu water polo
sutyen brassiere, bra
suvarmak to water (animals)
suyılanı grass-snake
suyolu waterline; watermark
suyosunu seaweed
suyuk body fluid, fluid
sübjektif subjective
sübvansiyon subvention
süet suede
süklüm püklüm sheepishly, with one's tail between one's legs
sükse success, hit, showy feat sükse yapmak to make a splash
sükûn, sükûnet calm, quiet
sükût silence, hush sükût ikrardan gelir silence gives consent

sülale family line, lineage
sülfat sulphate
sülfürik sulphuric **sülfürik asit** sulphuric acid
sülük leech **sülük gibi yapışmak** to cling like a leech
sülün pheasant
sümbül hyacinth
Sümer Sumerian
sümkürmek to blow one's nose
sümsük sluggish, slothful, uncouth
sümük mucus, snot
sümüklü mucous, snotty; snivelling
sümüksü mucous
sümüklüböcek slug
sünepe sluggish, slovenly
sünger sponge **(üzerine) sünger çekmek** to pass the sponge over sth **sünger gibi** spongy
süngerdoku spongy parenchyma
süngertaşı pumice-stone
süngü bayonet
süngülemek to bayonet
sünnet circumcision **sünnet etmek** to circumcise **sünnet olmak** to be circumcised
sünnetli circumcised
sünnetsiz uncircumcised
Sünnilik Sunnism
süper super **süper benzin** high-octane gasoline
süpermarket supermarket
süprüntü sweepings
süpürge broom
süpürgelik baseboard, mopboard
sürahi jug, decanter, pitcher
sürat speed
süratle quickly
süratli quick, rapid
sürç stumble **sürçü lisan** slip of the tongue
sürçmek to stumble, to slip; to make a mistake
sürdürmek to keep up, to continue
süre time, period **süresi sona ermek** to expire
süreaşımı prescription, limitation
süreç process
süredurum *fiz.* inertia
süregelen lasting, continual

süregelmek to continue
süreğen chronic
sürek duration; drove **sürek avı** drive
sürekli continuous, permanent
süreksiz transitory, transient
süreli periodical
süresince throughout
süresiz for an indefinite period of time, indefinitely
süreyazar chronograph
sürgü bolt; bedpan; harrow
sürgülemek to bolt; to harrow
sürgülü bolted; sliding **sürgülü cetvel** slide rule
sürgün exile; *hek.* diarrhoea; *bitk.* shoot **sürgün etmek** to banish, to exile **sürgüne göndermek** to send into exile
sürme kohl **sürme çekmek** to tinge with kohl
sürmek to continue, to last; to drive; to exile; to lay on, to spread, to smear; to plough; (life) to lead
sürmelemek to bolt (a door); to tinge with kohl
sürmenaj exhaustion (from overwork)
sürpriz surprise **sürpriz yapmak** to surprise (sb)
sürrealizm surrealism
sürtmek to rub (against); to loiter
sürtük (woman) gadabout; streetgirl, streetwalker
sürtünmek to rub oneself (against); to seek a quarrel
sürtüşme conflict, disagreement
sürtüşmek to rub against each other; to disagree, to dispute
sürü herd, flock
sürücü driver; drover
sürüklemek to drag, to trail; to carry with one, to absorb
sürükleyici absorbing, engrossing
sürüm demand, sale
sürümlü in great demand
sürümek to drag along
sürünceme delay **sürüncemede bırakmak** to drag out **sürüncemede kalmak** to be left hanging in the air, to drag on
süründürmek to make crawl; to lead sb a dog's life

sürüngen reptile

sürünmek to creep, to crawl; to rub against; to rub on, to rub in; to rough it, to vegetate, to lead a dog's life

süs ornament, decoration süsü vermek to pose as, to pretend to, to pass oneself off as

süsen iris

süslemek to adorn, to decorate, to ornament süsleyip püslemek to smarten up

süslenmek to be decorated; to deck oneself out süslenip püslenmek to smarten oneself up, to primp, to prink

süslü ornamented, decorated

süssüz unadorned, plain

süsmek to butt, to toss

süspansiyon suspension

süt milk süt çocuğu suckling süt dökmüş kedi gibi with his tail between his legs süt gibi white and clean süt kuzusu suckling lamb, suckling süt sağmak to milk Sütten ağzı yanan yoğurdu üfleyerek yer *ats.* Once bitten, twice shy sütü bozuk base, ignoble süt vermek to suckle, to nurse; (cow) to milk

sütana, sütanne wet nurse

sütbaba fosterfather

sütbaşı cream

sütbeyaz milk-white

sütçü milkman

sütdişi milk tooth, baby tooth

sütkardeş foster brother, foster sister

sütkız foster daughter

sütlaç rice pudding

sütleğen *bitk.* spurge

sütliman dead calm

sütlü milky sütlü kahve coffee with milk; white coffee

sütnine wet nurse

sütoğul foster son

sütsüz without milk; (coffee) black; untrustworthy, base

süttozu milkpowder

sütun column

süvari rider; cavalryman

süveter sweater

Süveyş Suez Süveyş Kanalı the Suez Canal

süzek sprayhead, rose

süzgeç strainer, filter

süzgün languid, languorous

süzmek to strain, to filter; to eye from head to foot, to look attentively

süzülmek to be filtered; to flow, to run; to get thin; to slip into, to creep in

Ş

şablon pattern

şadırvan water tank with a fountain

şafak dawn, daybreak şafak atmak to dawn on sb şafak sökmek (dawn) to break

şaft shaft

şah shah, king; (chess) king

şah (horse) rearing şaha kalkmak to rear

şahadet witnessing; martyrdom

şahadetname diploma, certificate

şahadetparmağı index finger

şahane magnificent, wonderful

şahdamarı aorta

şaheser masterpiece, masterwork

şahıs person, individual; *yaz.* character

şahin *hayb.* falcon

şahit witness şahit olmak to witness

şahitlik witnessing, testifying

şahlanmak (horse) to rear; to fly into a passion

şahmerdan battering-ram

şahsen in person; personally; by sight

şahsi personal, private

şahsiyet personality; individually

şahsiyetli having a strong personality

şahsiyetsiz characterless

şair poet

şairane poetic, poetical

şaka joke, jest, fun şaka bir yana joking apart şaka değil it's no joke şaka etmek to joke şaka götürmemek not to be a joking matter şaka kaldırmak to be able to take a joke şaka olarak söylemek to say sth in jest şaka söylemek to joke şaka yapmak to play a joke on sb **şakaya bozmak/dökmek** to turn sth into a joke **şakaya vurmak** to laugh sth off

şakacı joker, person given to joking

şakacıktan as a joke

şakak *anat.* temple

şakalaşmak to joke with one another

şakayık peony

şakımak to warble

şakırdamak to clank, to jingle, to rattle

şakırdatmak to clank, to rattle, to jingle

şakırtı clatter, rattle

şakkadak unexpectedly, all of a sudden

şaklaban buffoon, jester

şaklamak to crack, to snap

şaklatmak to crack, to snap

şakrak jovial, lively, mirthful

şakrakkuşu bullfinch

şakşak slap-stick; applause

şakşakçı toady

şal shawl

şalgam turnip

şalter power switch; circuit breaker

şalvar baggy trousers

şamandıra buoy, float

Şamanizm Shamanism

şamar slap, box on the ear **şamar atmak** to slap **şamar oğlanı** scapegoat

şamata commotion, hubbub, uproar

şamatacı noisy, boisterous

şamatalı noisy

şamdan candlestick

şamfıstığı pistachio nut

şampanya champagne

şampiyon champion

şampiyona championship

şampuan shampoo

şampuanlamak to shampoo

şan glory, fame, reputation **şanına yakışmak** to befit one's dignity

şangırdamak to clink, to crash **şangır şungur** with a crash

şangırtı crash

şanlı glorious, great

şans chance **şans eseri** by chance **şansı olmak** to have a chance **şansı ters gitmek** to have a run of bad luck **şansı yaver gitmek** to be lucky **şansını denemek** to take one's chance

şanslı lucky

şanssız unlucky

şanssızlık misfortune, badluck

şantaj blackmail, racket, shakedown **şantaj yapmak** to blackmail

şantajcı blackmailer, racketeer

şantiye shipyard; building-site

şanzıman gearbox, shift

şantör male singer

şantöz female singer

şap alum

şapırdamak to smack

şapırdatmak to smack

şapırtı smack

şapka hat

şaplak smack, slap **şaplak atmak** to give a smack

şaplamak to make a smacking noise, to smack

şappadak all of a sudden

şapşal silly, stupid; slovenly, untidy

şarampol shoulder (of a road)

şarap wine

şarapnel shrapnel

şarbon anthrax

şarıldamak to flow with a splashing noise

şarıltı splash, splashing sound

şarj charge **şarj etmek** to charge

şarjör clip

şarkı song **şarkı söylemek** to sing (a song)

şarkıcı singer

şarküteri delicatessen

şarlatan charlatan, quack

şarlatanlık charlatanism, quackery

şart condition, stipulation **şart koşmak** to stipulate **şart olmak** to become inevitable **şartıyla** on condition that

şartlandırmak to condition

şartlı conditional, conditioned

şartsız unconditional, unconditioned

şaryo carriage

şasi chasis

şaşakalmak to be taken aback

şaşalamak to be bewildered

şaşı cross-eyed, squinting

şaşılık crosseye, squint

şaşılası surprising, weird

şaşırmak to be surprised, to be con-

fused **şaşırıp kalmak** to be at a loss
şaşırtıcı amazing, surprising
şaşırtmak to amaze, to astonish, to surprise; to confuse, to baffle, to floor
şaşkın bewildered, confused, blank; stupid **şaşkına dönmek** to be stupefied **şaşkına çevirmek** to stupefy
şaşmak to be surprised; to deviate
şatafat ostentation, pomp
şatafatlı ostentatious, pompous
şato castle, chateau
şayan worthy, deserving
şayet if
şayia rumour
şebboy wallflower
şebek baboon
şebeke network; (student's) pass
şebnem dew
şecere genealogical tree
şef chief, leader **şef garson** headwaiter
şefaat intercession **şefaat etmek** to intercede
şeffaf transparent
şefkat compassion, affection
şefkatli compassionate, affectionate
şefkatsiz without affection
şeftali peach
şehir city, town
şehirlerarası interurban; long-distance (telephone call)
şehirli city dweller, townsman
şehit martyr
şehriye vermicelli
şehvani sensual
şehvet sexual desire, lust
şehvetli lustful, sensual
şehzade sultan's son, prince
şeker sugar; sweet, candy; *hek.* diabetes **Şeker Bayramı** the Ramadan holiday, the Lesser Bairam **şeker gibi** sweet **şeker hastalığı** diabetes
şekerci confectioner; candyseller; candymaker
şekerkamışı *bitk.* sugar cane
şekerleme candy, goody; nap, doze **şekerleme yapmak** to have a nap
şekerlemek to sugar
şekerleşmek to sugar
şekerli sugared; diabetic
şekerlik sugar bowl

şekersiz unsugared, unsweetened
şekerpancarı sugar beet
şekil form, shape; diagram, illustration **şekil almak** to take shape **şekil vermek** to give a form
şekilci formalist
şekilcilik formalism
şekillendirmek to shape, to form
şekillenmek to take shape
şekilsiz shapeless
şeklen in form
şelale waterfall
şelf shelf
şema diagram, plan
şematik diagramatic
şempanze chimpanzee
şemsiye umbrella, parasol
şen cheerful, joyful, merry
şenlendirmek to cheer, to enliven
şenlenmek to cheer up, to become cheerful; to be populated
şenlik cheerfulness, merriment; festival
şer evil, wickedness
şerbet sweet drink, sherbet
şerbetçiotu hop
şeref honour **şeref vermek** to honour, to grace
şerefe Cheerio! Cheers!
şerefine in honour of
şereflendirmek to honour, to grace
şerefli honoured, esteemed
şerefsiz dishonest, honourless
şerefsizlik dishonour
şerh explanation
şeriat Islamic law, canonical law
şerif sheriff
şerit ribbon, tape
şeş six **şeşi beş görmek** to get confused
şevk enthusiasm, eagerness **şevke gelmek** to become eager **şevki kırılmak** to be dispirited
şevkle eager
şey thing
şeyh sheik(h)
şeytan Satan, devil **şeytan aldatmak** to have nocturnal emissions **şeytan diyor ki** I have a good/half a mind to ... **şeytan gibi** as cunning as a fox **Şeytan kulağına kurşun!** Touch wood!

şeytan tüyü olmak to have an attractive personality şeytana uymak to yield to temptation şeytanın bacağını kırmak to get the show on the road at last

şeytanca devilish; devilishly

şeytani devilish, diabolical

şeytanlık devilment; mischief, trick

şezlong deck chair, chaise longue

şık smart, elegant, chic, high-hat

şık alternative

şıkırdamak to clink, to jingle

şıkırdatmak to clink, to jingle

şıkır şıkır with a clinking noise

şıkırtı clink, jingle

şıllık gaudily dressed woman

şımarık spoiled, saucy

şımarıklık sauciness, impertinence

şımarmak to get spoilt

şımartmak to spoil, to pamper

şıngırdamak to clink, to rattle

şıngırtı clink, rattle

şıp diye quickly, unexpectedly

şıpıdık heelless slipper

şıpırtı splash

şıpsevdi susceptible

şıra grape juice, must

şırak crack!, crash!

şırakkadak all of a sudden

şırfıntı tramp, slut

şırıldamak to splash, to babble

şırıltı splashing, babble

şırınga syringe

şiddet violence; intensity, strength şiddete başvurmak to resort to violence şiddet kullanmak to use violence

şiddetlendirmek to intensify

şiddetlenmek to become violent; to become intensified

şiddetli violent, impetuous, severe; hard, strong

şifa recovery, healing şifa bulmak to recover health şifa vermek to restore to health şifayı kapmak to fall ill

şifalı healing, curative

şifahen orally

şifon chiffon

şifoniyer chiffonier, chest of drawers

şifre code, cipher

şifrelemek to cipher şifreyi çözmek to decipher, to decode

şifreli in cipher

Şii Shiite

Şiilik Shiism

şikâyet complaint, grouch şikâyet etmek to complain, to grouch

şikâyetçi complainant

şike sp. rigging (a game/match/race)

şikeli sp. rigged

şilem slam

şilep cargo vessel, freighter

Şili Chile

Şilili Chilean

şilin Shilling

şilt shield

şilte mattress

şimdi now, at present şimdiye kadar until now, up to now

şimdiden from now on

şimdiki the present

şimdilik for the present, for the time being

şimşek lightning şimşek çakmak (lightning) to flash şimşek gibi like lightning

şimşir boxwood

şipşak quickly, in a flash

şiraze headband

şirin charming, pretty, lovely

şirket company, firm

şirpençe carbuncle

şirret bad-tempered, quarrelsome, malicious, fractious

şist schist

şiş swelling; swollen

şiş spit, skewer; knitting-needle şiş kebap shish kebab; roasted meat on skewers

şişe bottle

şişelemek to bottle

şişinmek to puff oneself up, to swell with importance

şişirmek to swell, to bloat, to inflate; to exaggerate; to knock off, to scamp, to skimp

şişkin swollen, puffy

şişkinlik swelling, puffiness

şişko fat, fatty

şişlemek to skewer, to spit; arg. to stab

şişlik swelling, bulge

şişman fat, obese
şişmanlamak to grow fat, to fatten
şişmanlık fatness, obesity
şişmek to swell, to be inflated, to be distended
şive accent
şizofren schizophrenic
şizofreni schizophrenia
şofben gas heater, geyser
şoför driver; chauffeur şoför ehliyetnamesi driving licence
şok shock
şoke shocked
şom ominous, sinister şom ağızlı who always predicts misfortune
şort shorts
şose paved road
şoson galoshes
şov show
şoven chauvinist; chauvinistic
şovenizm chauvinism
şöhret fame, reputation, renown
şöhretli famous, renowned
şölen feast, banquet
şömine fireplace
şövale easel
şövalye knight
şövalyelik chivalry
şöyle in this way, like this, like that, thus; this kind of, that kind of, such şöyle böyle so so şöyle dursun let alone şöyle ki in such a way that; as follows şöylece in this way, thus
şu that, this şu günlerde in these days şu halde in that case, then şu var ki however, only şundan bundan konuşmak to talk of this and that şunu bunu bilmem I'm not accepting any excuses! But me no buts! şunun şurasında just, only
şua ray
şubat February
şube branch; department, section
şuh coquettish, pert
şuhluk coquettishness, pertness
şunlar those
şura that place, this place
şurada there şurada burada here and there
şuralarda in these parts

şuraları these places
şuram this part of me
şura council
şurup syrup
şut (football) shoot, kick şut çekmek to shoot
şuur the conscious, consciousness
şuuraltı subconscious
şuurlu conscious
şuursuz unconscious
şükran gratitude, thanks
şükretmek to thank God; to give thanks (to)
şükür gratitude
şüphe doubt, suspicion; uncertainty şüphe etmek to doubt, to suspect şüphe uyandırmak to cause suspicion
şüphelendirmek to make ... suspicious
şüphelenmek to doubt, to suspect
şüpheli suspicious; doubtful; uncertain
şüphesiz doubtless, certain; of course! no doubt! certainly!
şüpheci sceptic, suspicious

T

ta even until, even as far as ta ki so that, even
taahhüt undertaking, commitment taahhüt etmek to undertake
taahhütlü (letter, etc.) registered
taahhütname written contract
taammüden huk. with premeditation, intentionally
taammüt huk. premeditation
taarruz attack, assault taarruz etmek to attack, to assault
taassup fanaticism
tab printing
taba tobacco-coloured
tabak plate, dish
tabak tanner
tabakhane tannery
tabaklamak to tan, to curry
tabaka layer, stratum; (of paper) sheet;

class, group

taban sole; base; floor **taban fiyat** the lowest price, minimum price **taban tabana zıt** diametrically opposite, antipodal **taban tepmek** to walk a long way **tabanları yağlamak** to take to one's heels

tabanca pistol, gun **tabanca çekmek** to draw one's gun

tabansız soleless; cowardly

tabanvayla on foot **tabanvayla gitmek** to go on foot, to walk

tabela sign, signboard; list of food; car of treatment

tabelacı sign-painter

tabetmek to print

tabi subject, dependent **tabi olmak** to be dependent on **tabi tutulmak** to be subjected to

tabiat nature; character, temperament **tabiat bilgisi** nature study **tabiat kanunu** law of nature **tabiatıyla** naturally

tabiatüstü supernatural

tabii natural; naturally, of course

tabiiyet nationality

tabip doctor, physician

tabir expression, idiom, phrase; (of a dream) interpretation **tabir caizse** if I may put in this way **tabir etmek** to express; to interpret (a dream)

tabla ashtray; circular tray

tabldot table d'hôte

tablet tablet

tablo painting, picture

tabu taboo

tabur *ask.* battalion; line, row, file

taburcu discharged from a hospital **taburcu etmek** to discharge **taburcu olmak** to be discharged

tabure stool, footstool

tabut coffin

tabya *ask.* bastion, redoubt

tacir merchant

taciz annoyance, disturbing, harassment **taciz etmek** to annoy, to bother, to harass

taç crown; corolla; *sp* touchdown **taç giymek** to be crowned

taçlandırmak to crown

taçlı crowned

taçsız uncrowned

taçyaprağı petal

tadım taste, small amount tasted; the sense of taste

tadımlık just enough to taste

tadil modification, alteration **tadil etmek** to modify, to amend

tadilat modifications

taflan cherry laurel

tafra conceit, pride

tafsilat details

tafsilatlı detailed

tafta taffeta

tahakkuk realization; verification **tahakkuk etmek** to be realized, to come true

tahakküm domination, oppression **tahakküm etmek** to dominate, to oppress, to tyrannize

tahammül endurance, patience **tahammül etmek** to put up with, to endure, to stand

taharet cleanliness; canonical purification

tahayyül imagination, fancy **tahayyül etmek** to imagine, to fancy

tahdit limitation **tahdit etmek** to limit

tahıl grain; cereal

tahin sesame oil

tahinhelvası halvah, halavah

tahkik investigation **tahkik etmek** to investigate

tahkikat investigations, inquiries

tahkim strengthening, fortification **tahkim etmek** to strengthen, to fortify

tahkir insult, affront **tahkir etmek** to insult, to affront

tahlil analysis **tahlil etmek** to analyse

tahliye evacuation, vacating; release; (cargo) discharge, unloading **tahliye etmek** to evacuate, to empty; to discharge, to release; (cargo) to unload, to discharge

tahmin estimate, guess **tahmin etmek** to estimate, to guess

tahminen approximately

tahmini approximate

tahribat destruction, devastation

tahrif falsification, distortion **tahrif et-**

tahrifat

mek to falsify, to distort

tahrifat falsification, alterations

tahrik provocation, incitement, excitation; excitement, stimulation **tahrik etmek** to provoke, to incite, to excite **tahrik edici** provocative

tahrip destruction, devastation, ruining **tahrip etmek** to destroy, to ruin, to devastate

tahriş irritation **tahriş etmek** to irritate

tahsil education, study; (money) collection **tahsil etmek** (money, taxes) to collect; to study **tahsil görmek** to receive an education

tahsilat collection of revenues

tahsildar tax-collector

tahsis assignment, allocation, allotment **tahsis etmek** to assign, to allot, to allocate

tahsisat allowance, fund

taht throne **tahta çıkmak** to ascend the throne **tahta geçirmek** to enthrone **tahttan indirmek** to dethrone

tahta board, plank, wood; wooden **tahtadan** wooden **tahtası eksik** having a screw loose, screwy **tahtaya kaldırmak** to call (a student) to the blackboard

tahtakurdu woodworm

tahtakurusu bug, bedbug

tahtalı boarded, planked **tahtalı köy** arg. cemetery **tahtalı köyü boylamak** arg. to kick the bucket, to die

tak knock **tak tak vurmak** to knock repeatedly

tak arch

taka small sailing-boat

takaddüm precedence **takaddüm etmek** to precede

takas clearing; exchange, barter **takas etmek** to clear; to exchange, to barter

takat strength **takati kalmamak** to be exhausted

takatsız exhausted, weak

takdim presentation; introduction **takdim etmek** to present, to offer; to introduce

takdir appreciation; predestination, fate **takdir etmek** to appreciate **takdirini**

kazanmak to win sb's approval

takdirde in the event of, if

takdirname letter of appreciation

takdis sanctification **takdis etmek** to sanctify

takı wedding present; jewellery, ornament; dilb. case ending

takılgan plaguing, teasing

takılmak to kid, to josh; to be afixed; to get stuck on, to get snagged on; arg. to frequent, to visit

takım team; gang, band, crew; set, service; suit; ask platoon **takım taklavat** sag and baggage, the whole push

takımada archipelago

takımyıldız constellation

takınmak to put on, to wear; to assume, to affect

takıntı relation, affair; small debt; subject which a student has flunked; condition

takırdamak to clatter, to rattle

takırtı clatter, rattle

takışmak to quarrel with each other, to squabble

takibat huk. prosecution

takip following, pursuit **takip etmek** to follow, to pursuit

takipçi follower, pursuer

takke skullcap

takla somersault **takla atmak** to turn a somersault

taklit imitation; counterfeit; imitated, counterfeit, sham **taklit etmek** to imitate; to counterfeit

taklitçi imitator; mimic

takma attaching; attached; false **takma ad** nickname **takma diş** false teeth **takma saç** false hair, wig

takmak to affix, to attach, to fix; to put on, to wear; arg. to fail, to flunk **takıp takıştırmak** to put on one's best bib and tucker

takmamak arg. to have no regard for, not to give a damn

takoz wooden wedge, chock **takoz koymak** to put a wedge

takriben approximately, about

takribi approximate

takrir huk. motion, proposal

taksi taxi *Al.* cab **taksi tutmak** to take a taxi

taksim division **taksim etmek** to divide

taksimetre taximeter

taksirat sins, faults

taksit instalment

taksitle by instalments **taksitle satış** instalment sale

taktik tactics

takunya clog, patten

takvim calendar

takviye reinforcement **takviye etmek** to reinforce

talan pillage, plunder **talan etmek** to pillage, to plunder

talaş wood shavings; sawdust

talebe student, pupil

talep demand **talep etmek** to demand, to request

tali secondary, subordinate

talih luck, good fortune, chance **talih kuşu** good luck **talihi yaver gitmek** to be lucky **talihine küsmek** to curse one's fate

talihli lucky, fortunate

talihsiz luckless, unlucky

talihsizlik bad luck

talim teaching; practice, exercise **talim etmek** to have to eat (the same food)

talimat instructions **talimat vermek** to give instructions

talimatname regulations

talimname field manual

talip desirous, seeking **talip olmak** to put oneself in for, to desire, to seek

talk talc **talk pudrası** talcum powder

taltif gratifying; rewarding **taltif etmek** to gratify; to reward

tam complete, entire, whole; exact, precise, perfect **tam adamına düşmek** to find the very man **tam gelmek** to fit well **tamı tamına** just, exactly **tam üstüne basmak** to hit the nail on the head **tam vaktinde** just in time **tam yetki** full authority **tam yol** full speed

tamah avarice, greed **tamah etmek** to covet, to desire

tamahkâr avaricious,greedy

tamam complete, ready; finished, over; correct, right; all right! OK! **tamam ol-**mak to end, to be over

tamamen completely, entirely, fully

tamamıyla completely, entirely, fully

tamamlamak to complete, to finish

tamamlayıcı supplementary, complementary

tambur a stringed instrument similar to the mandolin

tamim circular **tamim etmek** to circulate

tamir repair **tamir etmek** to repair, to mend

tamirat repairs

tamirci repairman

tamirhane repair shop

tamlama noun phrase, prepositional phrase

tamlanan *dilb.* noun modified by an adjective or a noun

tamlayan *dilb.* noun modifier **tamlayan durumu** *dilb.* genitive case

tampon bumper, buffer; *hek.* wad, plug **tampon devlet** buffer state

tamsayı *mat.* whole number, integer

tamtakır completely empty

tamtam tom-tom

tan dawn **tan ağarmak** (day) to break, to dawn

tane grain, seed, pip; piece **tane tane** piece by piece **tane tane konuşmak** to speak distinctly, to articulate

tanecik granule

tanelemek to granulate

tangırdamak to clang

tangırtı clang, discharge, to unload

tango tango

tanıdık acquaintance

tanık witness **tanık olmak** to witness

tanıklık testimony, witness **tanıklık etmek** to give evidence

tanım definition

tanımak to know; to recognize, to acknowledge **tanımazlıktan gelmek** to pretend not to know

tanımlama definition

tanımlamak to define

tanınmak to be known; to be recognized

tanınmış well-known, famous

tanış acquaintance

tanışık 210

tanışık acquaintance
tanışmak to get acquainted (with), to know one another, to meet
tanıtıcı introductory, promotional
tanıtım, tanıtma introduction, presentation; *tic.* promotion
tanıtma to introduce, to represent; to advertise, to promote
tanjant tangent
tank tank
tanker tanker
tanksavar antitank
Tanrı God Tanrı misafiri unexpected guest Tanrı vergisi gift, talent Tanrı'nın günü even blessed day
Tanrıbilim theology
Tanrıbilimci theologian
tanrıça goddess
tanrılaşmak to be deified
tanrılaştırmak to deify
tanrısal divine
tanrıtanımaz atheistic; atheist
tanrıtanımazlık atheism
tansiyon blood pressure tansiyon düşüklüğü hypotension tansiyon yüksekliği hypertension
tantal *kim.* tantalum
tantana pomp, display
tantanalı pompous
tanyeli zephyr, dawn breeze
tanyeri daybreak, dawn
tanzim putting in order, arrangement; organizing tanzim etmek to put in order; to arrange; to organize tanzim satışı sale of foodstuffs by a municipality so as to regulate the prices
tanzimat reforms
Tanzimat the political reforms made in the Ottoman State in 1839
tapa stopper, plug; fuse
tapınak temple
tapıncak fetish
tapınmak to worship, to adore
tapmak to worship, to adore
tapon trashy, shoddy
taptaze very fresh
tapu title-deed
tapulamak to register with a title-deed
taraça terrace
taraf side; place, site tarafa çıkmak to

take the part (of) to support taraf tutmak to take sides
taraflı having sides; supporter
tarafsız impartial
tarafsızlık impartiality
taraftar partisan, supporter taraftar olmak to be in favour of
taraftarlık partisanship, partiality
tarak comb; harrow, rake
taraklamak to comb; to harrow, to rake
tarakotu teasel
taramak to comb; to harrow, to rake; to search thoroughly, to comb; to scan, to rake
taranmak to be combed; to be raked; to comb oneself
tarçın cinnamon
taret *ask.* turret
tarh flower-bed; imposition (of a tax)
tarım agriculture
tarımcı agriculturist
tarımsal agricultural
tarif definition; description; recipe tarif etmek to describe; to define
tarife tariff; time-table; recipe
tarih history; date tarih atmak to date tarihe geçmek to make history tarihe karışmak to be a thing of the past, to vanish
tarihçi historian
tarihli dated
tarihsel tarihi, historic; historical
tarihsiz undated
tarihçe short history
tarihöncesi prehistory
tarikat religious order
tarla field
tarlafaresi vole
tarlakuşu skylark
tartaklamak to manhandle, to harass
tartı weight; weighing; scale, balance tartıya vurmak to weigh
tartılı weighed; balanced
tartılmak to be weighed; to weigh oneself
tartışılmaz indisputable
tartışma discussion; argument, dispute
tartışmacı debater
tartışmak to discuss, to debate; to argue, to dispute

211

tat

tartışmalı argumentative, controversial
tartmak to weigh; to balance
tarumar scattered, topsy-turvy tarumar
  etmek to rout, to disarray
tarz manner, way, style
tas bowl, cup tası tarağı toplamak to
  pack bag and baggage
tasa worry, anxiety tasa çekmek/etmek
  to worry Tasası sana mı düştü? It's
  none of your business! Mind your
  own business!
tasalı anxious
tasar plan
tasarçizim design
tasarçizimci designer
tasarı project; draft taw, bill
tasarım imagination, envisagement; design
tasarlamak to plan, to project, do design, to contrive
tasarruf saving, thrift, economy tasarruf etmek to save, to economize
tasarruflu economical, thrifty
tasasız carefree, lighthearted
tasavvuf Islamic mysticism, Sufism
tasavvufi mystical, Sufic
tasavvur imagination; idea tasavvur etmek to imagine
tasdik affirmation, confirmation; ratifica-
  tion, approval tasdik etmek to affirm,
  to confirm; to ratify
tasdikli certified
tasdiksiz uncertified
tasdikname certificate
tasfiye purification, cleaning; discharge
  (of the employees); tic. liquidation
  tasfiye etmek to purify, to refine; to
  discharge; to liquidate
tashih correction
taslak draft, sketch taslak halinde in
  draft
taslamak to pretend to, to feign, to fake
tasma collar
tasnif classification tasnif etmek to classify
tastamam absolutely, complete
tasvip approval, assent tasvip etmek to
  approve, to assent tasvip etmemek
  to disapprove
tasvir description, depiction tasvir et-

mek to describe, to depict
taş stone; rock taş atmak to make an allusion at sb taş çıkartmak to make
  rings round sb, to surpass taş devri
  stone age taş gibi very hard, stony
  taş kesilmek to be petrified taş taş üstünde bırakmamak to level with the
  ground taşa tutmak to stone taşı gediğine koymak to hit the nail on the
  head
taşak arg. testicle, ball
taşbaskı, taşbasması lithography
taşbebek doll
taşıl fossil
taşıllaşmak to fossilize
taşımacı transporter
taşımacılık transport
taşımak to carry; to transport, to convey
taşınır movable
taşınmaz immovable
taşırmak (to cause) to overflow
taşıt vehicle, conveyance
taşıyıcı carrier; porter
taşkın overflowing; exuberant, rowdy;
  flood
taşkınlık exuberance, rowdiness
taşkömürü coal
taşküre lithosphere
taşlama stoning; grinding; yaz. satire
taşlaşmak to be petrified
taşlı stony
taşmak to overflow, to flood; to boil
  over, to run over
taşocağı stone quarry
taşpamuğu asbestos
taşra the provinces
taşralı provincial
taşyuvarı lithosphere
taşyürekli stony-hearted, hard-hearted
tat taste tat almak to taste; to enjoy tat
  vermek to flavour tadı damağında
  kalmak to be unable to forget the delicious flavour of tadı kaçmak to lose
  its taste, to pall tadı tuzu yok tasteless tadına bakmak to taste tadında
  bırakmak not to overdo tadını almak
  to taste, to enjoy tadını çıkarmak to
  enjoy fully tadını kaçırmak to mar, to
  spoil, to go too far

Tatar Tartar, Tatar
tatarcık sandfly
tatbik application tatbik etmek to apply tatbik sahasına koymak to put into practice
tatbikat applications; ask. manoeuvres
tatbikatta in practice
tatbiki applied
tatil holiday, vacation; rest tatil etmek to close temporarily tatil olmak to be closed (for a holiday) tatil yapmak to take a holiday tatile çıkmak to go on a holiday
tatlandırmak to sweeten; to flavour
tatlanmak to sweeten
tatlı sweet tatlı bela sweet curse tatlı dil soft words tatlı dilli soft-spoken tatlı su fresh water tatlıya bağlamak to settle amicably
tatlılık sweetness; pleasantness
tatlılıkla kindly, gently
tatmak to taste; to experience
tatmin satisfaction tatmin etmek to satisfy tatmin olmak to be satisfied
tatminkâr satisfactory
tatsız tasteless
tatsızlık tastelessness, insipidity; disagreeableness, unpleasantness
tav proper heat; right moment tav vermek to dampen tavına getirmek to bring to the right condition
tava frying pan
tavan ceiling tavan arası attic tavan fiyatı maximum price, ceiling price
taverna tavern
tavır manner, attitude tavır takınmak to assume an attitude
taviz concession; compensation taviz vermek to compensate
tavla backgammon; stable
tavlamak to anneal; to cheat, to hoodwink; to pick up, to seduce
tavsiye recommendation tavsiye etmek to recommend, to advise tavsiye mektubu letter of recommendation
tavşan hare, rabbit
tavşandudağı harelip
tavşankanı bright carmine colour; (tea) dark and strong
tavşankulağı bitk. cyclamen

tavuk hen
tavukkarası night blindness
tavus peacock
tay colt, foal
tay counterpoise; equal, peer tay durmak (baby) to stand up
tayf spectrum
tayfa crew
tayfun typhoon
tayın ration
tayin appointment; designation tayin etmek to appoint; to designate
tayyör tailor-made costume
taze fresh; new, recent taze fasulye green beans taze kan fresh blood
tazelemek to freshen, to renew
tazelik freshness
tazı greyhound
taziye condolence
tazmin indemnification tazmin etmek to indemnify
tazminat indemnity, compensation tazminat davası action for damages
tazyik pressure
teamül custom, practice
teati exchange
tebaa subject
tebdil change
tebdilihava change of air
teberru donation teberru etmek to donate
tebessüm smile tebessüm etmek to smile
tebeşir chalk
tebligat notification
tebliğ notification, communique tebliğ etmek to notify, to communicate
tebrik congratulation tebrik etmek to congratulate
tecavüz attack, aggression; violation, transgression tecavüz etmek to attack; to transgress
tecelli manifestation; destiny tecelli etmek to be manifested, to appear
tecil delay, postponement tecil etmek to postpone
tecim commerce, trade
tecrit separation, isolation tecrit etmek to separate, to isolate
tecrübe trial, test; experience tecrübe

etmek to try, to test
tecrübeli experienced
tecrübesiz inexperienced
teçhiz equipping, equipment **teçhiz etmek** to equip
teçhizat equipment
tedarik procurement, preparation **tedarik etmek** to procure, to provide, to prepare
tedarikli prepared
tedariksiz unprepared
tedavi (medical) treatment **tedavi etmek** to treat
tedavül circulation; currency **tedavülde olmak** to circulate **tedavülden kalkmak** to be taken out of circulation **tedavüle çıkarmak** to put into circulation
tedbir measure, step, precaution **tedbir almak** to take measures
tedbirli prudent, cautious
tedbirsiz improvident, incautious
tedhiş terror
tedirgin uneasy, restless **tedirgin etmek** to discompose, to disquiet
tedirginlik uneasiness
tediye payment
tedricen gradually
teessüf regret **teessüf etmek** to regret
teessür sadness, sorrow
tef tambourine
tefeci usurer
tefecilik usury
tefekkür reflection, contemplation
teferruat details
teferruatlı detailed, exhaustive
tefsir commentary **tefsir etmek** to comment
teftiş inspection **teftiş etmek** to inspect
teğet tangent
teğmen lieutenant
teğmenlik lieutenancy
tehdit threat, menace **tehdit etmek** to threaten, to menace
tehir delay, postponement **tehir etmek** to delay, to postpone, to put off
tehlike danger **tehlikede** in danger **tehlikeye atılmak** to court danger **tehlikeye atmak** to risk **tehlikeye sokmak** to endanger

tehlikeli dangerous
tehlikesiz without danger
tehlikesizce safely
tek single; alone; only; unique; (number) odd **tek başına** alone **tek mi çift mi?** odd or even? **tek taraflı/yanlı** unilateral, one-sided **tek tek, teker teker** one by one **tek tük** only a few
tekdir scolding, reprimand
tekdüze monotonous
tekdüzelik monotony
teke male goat, he-goat
tekel monopoly **tekeli altına almak** to monopolize
tekelci monopolist
tekelcilik monopolism
teker wheel
tekerkçi monarchist
tekerkçilik monarchism
tekerklik monarchy
tekerlek wheel
tekerleme rigmarole
tekerlemek to roll
tekerlenmek to roll round; to topple over
tekeşlilik monogamy
tekhücreli unicellular
tekil *dilb.* singular
tekin deserted, empty; auspicious
tekir (cat) tabby; (fish) red mullet
tekke dervish lodge
teklemek to thin out; (piston of the engine) to work singly; *arg.* to stammer, to stutter
teklif proposal, offer **teklif etmek** to propose, to offer
teklifsiz unceremonious, familiar
teklik oneness
tekme kick **tekme atmak** to give a kick **tekme yemek** to get a kick
tekmelemek to kick
tekmil the whole, all
tekne trough; vessel, craft
teknik technique; technical
teknikçi technician
tekniker technician
teknikokul technical school
tekniköğretim technical training
teknisyen technician
teknokrasi technocracy

teknoloji technology
teknolojik technological
tekrar repetition; again **tekrar etmek** to repeat **tekrar tekrar** again and again
tekrarlamak to repeat
tekrarlanmak to be repeated
teksesli *müz.* monophonic
teksif concentration, condensation **teksif etmek** to concentrate, to condense
teksir multiplication; duplication **teksir etmek** to multiply; to duplicate **teksir makinesi** duplicator, mimeograph
tekstil textile
tektanrıcı monotheist; monotheistic
tektanrıcılık monotheism
tektonik tectonics; tectonic
tekzip contradiction, denial **tekzip etmek** to contradict, to deny
tel wire; string; fibre; string, cord; telegram, cable **tel çekmek** to enclose with wire; to send a wire, to cable **tel örgü** wire fence **tel şehriye** vermicelli
telaffuz pronunciation **telaffuz etmek** to pronounce
telafi compensation **telafi etmek** to compensate
telakki consideration; viewpoint **telakki etmek** to consider, to regard as
telaş hurry, flurry **telaş etmek** to bustle, to be flustered **telaşa düşmek** to get flurried, to take alarm
telaşçı restless, nervous
telaşlanmak to get flurried
telaşlı flurried, agitated
telaşsız unagitated, calm
telef destruction; waste **telef olmak** to be destroyed, to perish
teleferik cable railway
telefon telephone, phone; (telephone) call **telefon etmek** to telephone, to phone, to call (up), to ring (up) **telefon kulübesi** telephone booth **telefon rehberi** telephone directory **telefonu kapatmak** to hang up
telekız call girl
telekomünikasyon telecommunication
teleks telex
telem teletype, teleprinter
telemetre telemeter

teleobjektif teleobjective, telelens
telepati telepathy
teleskop telescope
televizyon television **televizyonda göstermek** to show on television, to televise
telgraf telegram, telegraph **telgraf çekmek** to send a telegram, to telegraph
telif compilation **telif hakkı** copyright **telif hakkı ücreti** royalty
telkin inspiration, suggestion **telkin etmek** to inspire, to inculcate
tellak bath attendant
tellemek to send a telegram, to wire
tellendirmek to smoke
telli wired **telli çalgılar** *müz.* stringed musical instruments
tellıturna demoiselle crane
telsiz wireless **telsiz telgraf** wireless telegraph
telsizci wireless operator
telve coffee-grounds
telyazı telegram, telegraph
temas contact **temas etmek** to touch **temasa geçmek** to get in touch (with, ile)
temaşa show, spectacle
temayül inclination, tendency
tembel lazy
tembelleşmek to grow lazy
tembellik laziness
tembih warning **tembih etmek** to warn
temel foundation, base; main, chief; basic, fundamental **temel atmak** to lay a foundation **temel taşı** foundation stone, cornerstone
temelli having a foundation; permanent; well-founded; permanently, for good
temelsiz without foundation; groundless, unfounded
temenni wish, desire **temenni etmek** to wish, to desire
temin assurance; obtaining, procurement **temin etmek** to assure, to ensure; to procure, to provide
teminat guarantee; security **teminat akçesi** guarantee fund
teminatlı guaranteed, secured
teminatsız insecure, unsecured

temiz clean; virtuous; clear, net **temiz bir dayak atmak** to give a good thrashing **temiz raporu** certificate of good health **temize çekmek** to make a fair copy **temize çıkarmak** to clear, to acquit
temizlik cleanliness
temizlemek to clean; to cleanse; to eat up, to polish off, to finish off; *arg.* to kill, to bump off, to rub out
temkin self-possession, poise
temkinli self-possessed, poised
temmuz July
tempo time, tempo **tempo tutmak** to keep time
temsil representation; performance **temsil etmek** to represent; (play) to present; to symbolize
temsilci representative, agent
temyiz discernment; *huk.* appeal **temyiz etmek** to discern; to appeal **temyiz mahkemesi** court of appeal
ten complexion; flesh, skin
tencere saucepan, pot **Tencere yuvarlanmış kapağını bulmuş** *ats.* Birds of a feather flock together
teneffüs respiration; recess, break **teneffüs etmek** to breathe
teneke tin
teneşir the bench on which the corpse is washed
tenezzül deigning, condescension **tenezzül etmek** to deign, to condescend
tenha uncrowded, lonely, solitary
tenis tennis **tenis kortu** tennis court
tenkıye *hek.* enema, clyster
tenkit criticism **tenkit etmek** to criticize
tenor tenor
tente awning
tentene lace
tentür *kim.* tincture
tentürdiyot tincture of iodine
tenya tapeworm, taenia
tenzilat reduction of prices
tenzilatlı reduced in price **tenzilatlı satış** sale
teokrasi theocracy
teoloji theology
teorem theorem

teori theory
teorik theoretical
tepe hill; peak, top **tepeden bakmak** to look down on **tepeden tırnağa** from top to toe **tepesi atmak** to fly into a rage **tepesinin tası atmak** to fly into a rage **tepe(si) üstü** head first, headlong
tepecam skylight
tepecik little hill; *bit.* stigma
tepelemek to tread; to defeat; to give a severe thrashing
tepelidalgıç great crested grebe
tepelitavuk hoatzin
tepetaklak headlong, headfirst
tepi *ruhb.* impulse
tepinmek to kick and stamp
tepişmek to kick one another; to push and shove one another
tepke reflex
tepki reaction
tepkime reaction
tepkimek to react
tepmek to kick; (illness) to relapse; to spurn, to scorn
tepsi tray
ter sweat, perspiration **ter basmak** to break out into a sweat **ter boşanmak** to perspire suddenly **ter dökmek** to sweat
terapi therapy
teras terrace
terazi balance, scales **Terazi (burcu)** libra, Balance
terazilemek to balance
terbiye education; training; good manners; seasoning **terbiye etmek** to bring up, to educate, to train; to season **terbiye görmek** to be trained **terbiyesini bozmak** to be rude
terbiyeli good-mannered, polite; flavoured (with a sauce etc.)
terbiyesiz ill-mannered, rude
terbiyesizce rudely, impolitely
terbiyesizlik rudeness **terbiyesizlik etmek** to behave rudely
tercih preference **tercih etmek** to prefer
tercihen preferably
tercihli preferential

tercüman translator, interpreter
tercümanlık work of interpreter **tercümanlık etmek** to act as translator/interpreter
tercüme translation **tercüme etmek** to translate (into)
tere cress
tereci seller of cress **tereciye tere satmak** to teach one's grandmother to suck eggs
terebentin turpentine
tereddüt hesitation **tereddüt etmek** to hesitate
terek shelf
terementi turpentine
teres *arg.* pimp, procurer
tereyağı butter **tereyağından kıl çeker gibi** very easily
terfi promotion, advancement **terfi etmek** to be promoted **terfi ettirmek** to promote
terhis *ask.* discharge, demobilization **terhis etmek** to discharge, to demobilize **terhis olmak** to be discharged **terhis tezkeresi** discharge papers
terilen terylene
terim term
terk abandonment **terk etmek** to abandon, to leave
terki back of a saddle
terkip composition, compound **terkip etmek** to compose, to compound
terlemek to sweat, to perspire
terli sweaty, perspiry
terlik slippers
termal thermal
termik thermic
terminal terminal
terminoloji terminology
termodinamik thermodynamics; thermodynamic
termoelektrik thermoelectric; thermoelectricity
termometre thermometer
termonükleer thermonuclear
termos thermos bottle, flask
termosifon hot-water heater; thermosiphon
termostat thermostat
terör terror

terörist terrorist
terörizm terrorism
ters reverse; opposite; awkward; inverted; upside down; backwards; sharp, curt; sharply, curtly; excrement, feces **ters anlamak** to misunderstand **ters gitmek** to go wrong **ters tarafından kalkmak** to get out of the wrong side **ters ters bakmak** to look daggers at
tersane dockyard
tersim drawing
tersine on the contrary **tersine çevirmek** to turn inside out
tersinir reversible
tersinirlik reversibility
terslemek to bite sb's head off, to snap at, to snub
terslik contrariness, setback; peevishness, awkwardness
tersyüz turning inside out **tersyüz etmek** to turn inside out **tersyüz geri dönmek** to return empty-handed **tersyüzüne çevirmek** to send back **tersyüzüne dönmek** to turn back
tertemiz absolutely clean
tertibat arrangement; mechanism, apparatus
tertip arrangement, setup; composition; plot, trick; *hek.* prescription **tertip etmek** to arrange; to organize
tertipçi organizer; planner; conspirator
tertiplemek to organize, to arrange
tertipli well-organized; tidy, neat
tertipsiz disarranged, disorderly, untidy
terzi tailor, dressmaker; tailor's shop
tesadüf chance, coincidence, encounter **tesadüf etmek** to come across, to meet by chance; to coincide with
tesadüfen by chance, by accident
tesadüfi fortuitous, casual, accidental
tescil registration
tescilli registered
tescilsiz unregistered
teselli consolation, comfort **teselli bulmak** to console oneself **teselli etmek** to console, to comfort **teselli mükâfatı** consolation prize
tesir effect, influence **tesir etmek** to act, to affect; to influence, to impress
tesirli effective; impressive

217   tezkere

tesirsiz ineffective
tesis establishment, foundation tesis etmek to found, to establish
tesisat installation
tesisatçı installer
teskin soothing, tranquilization teskin
  etmek to soothe, to calm, to pacify
teslim delivery; surrender, submission
  teslim etmek to take delivery of, to
  collect; to admit, to concede teslim
  bayrağı çekmek to strike one's flag,
  to yield teslim etmek to deliver; to admit, to concede teslim olmak to surrender, to submit
teslimiyet submission
teslis Trinity
tespih prayer beads, rosary tespih çekmek to tell one's beads
tespit fixing tespit etmek to fix
test test
testere saw
testerebalığı sawfish
testi pitcher, jug
tesviye levelling, smoothing tesviye etmek to level, to smooth
tesviyeci fitter
tesviyecilik fitting
teşbih simile teşbihte hata olmaz let it
  not be misunderstood
teşebbüs attempt; enterprise teşebbüs
  etmek to attempt
teşekkül formation; organization teşekkül etmek to be formed; to consist
  (of, -den)
teşekkür (giving) thanks teşekkür etmek to thank teşekkür ederim!
  Thank you!
teşhir exhibition, display teşhir etmek
  to exhibit, to display teşhir salonu
  showroom
teşhirci ruhb. exhibitionist
teşhircilik exhibitionism
teşhis identification, recognition; hek.
  diagnosis teşhis etmek to identify, to
  recognize; hek. to diagnose
teşkil formation teşkil etmek to form,
  to constitute
teşkilat organization
teşkilatçı organizer
teşkilatlandırmak to organize

teşkilatlanmak to be organized
teşkilatlı organized
teşkilatsız unorganized
teşrif honouring; visit, arrival teşrif etmek to honour
teşrifat protocol
teşrifatçı master of the ceremonies
teşriki mesai cooperation
teşvik encouragement teşvik etmek to
  encourage teşvik edici encouraging
tetanos hek. tetanus
tetik trigger; alert, vigilant tetikte beklemek to be on the alert
tetkik study, examination tetkik etmek
  to study, to examine
tevazu humility, modesty
tevcih turning towards; conferring tevcih etmek to turn towards; to confer
tevdi entrusting tevdi etmek to entrust
teveccüh turning towards; favour, kindness teveccüh göstermek to show favour, to be kind (to)
tevekkeli for no reason, for nothing
tevkif arrest tevkif etmek to arrest
Tevrat Pentateuch Torah
tevzi distribution tevzi etmek to distribute
teyel tacking, basting
teyellemek to tack, to baste
teyp tape recorder, casette-player tey-
  be almak to tape-record, to tape
tez thesis
tez quick, prompt; quickly, promptly
  tez canlı hustling, impetuous, impatient tez elden without delay
tezahür appearing tezahür etmek to
  appear
tezat contrast, contradiction tezata düşmek to contradict oneself
tezek dried dung
tezgâh counter, workbench; loom
tezgâhtar shop assistant, salesman,
  saleswoman; Aİ. sales clerk, salesgirl
tezgâhtarlık salesmanship
tezgâhlamak to concoct, to hatch
tezkere note, memorandum; ask. discharge papers tezkere almak ask. to
  receive one's discharge papers tezke-
  resini eline vermek to give sb his
  marching orders, to fire

tıbben medically
tıbbi medical
tıbbiye medical school
tıbbiyeli medical student
tıfıl child, kiddie, nipper
tığ crochet-needle **tığ gibi** wiry
tıka basa crammed full **tıka basa doldurmak** to cram full, to stuff **tıka basa yemek** to make a pig of oneself
tıkaç plug, stopper
tıkaçlamak to plug
tıkalı stopped up
tıkamak to stop up, to plug, to stuff; to obstruct, to block
tıkanık stopped up
tıkanıklık stoppage; (traffic) bottleneck, jam
tıkanmak to be stopped up; to lose one's breath
tıkır rattle **tıkırında gitmek** to go like clockwork
tıkırdamak to rattle
tıkırtı rattle, clatter
tıkız plump, dumpy
tıklatmak to tap
tıklım tıklım chock-a-block
tıkmak to cram, to jam
tıknaz plumpish, dumpy
tıknefes short-winded, pursy
tıksırık sneeze (with the mouth shut)
tıksırmak to sneeze
tılsım talisman, charm
tılsımlı enchanted
tımar grooming **tımar etmek** to groom
tımarhane insane asylum, mental hospital **tımarhane kaçkını** nutty, crazy
tınaz haystack
tıngır clinking noise
tıngırdamak to clink
tıngırtı clang, rattle
tınlamak to ring, to resound
tınmak to make a sound
tınmamak to take no notice
tıp medicine
tıpa plug, stopper
tıpatıp exactly
tıpırdamak to patter
tıpırtı patter
tıpış tıpış patteringly **tıpış tıpış gitmek** to patter, to toddle; to go willy-nilly

tıpkı exactly like, just like
tırabzan handrail, banister
tıraş shaving; haircut *arg.* boring talk, bragging **tıraş bıçağı** razor blade **tıraş etmek** to shave; to cut **tıraş fırçası** shaving-brush **tıraş macunu** shaving cream **tıraş makinesi** safety razor; electric shaver **tıraş olmak** to shave (oneself); to have a haircut
tıraşlı shaved
tıraşsız unshaved
tırıs trot **tırıs gitmek** to trot
tırmalamak to scratch
tırmanmak to climb
tırmık scratch; harrow, rake
tırmıklamak to scratch; to rake, to harrow
tırnak fingernail, toenail; claw, hoof **tırnak boyası** nail varnish, nail polish **tırnak işareti** inverted commas, quotation marks **tırnaklarını yemek** to bite one's nails
tırmıklamak to scratch; to claw
tırpan scythe
tırtık nick, notch
tırtıl *hayb.* caterpillar; caterpillar tread
tıs hiss
tıslamak to hiss
ticaret trade, commerce **ticaret filosu** merchant marine **ticaret gemisi** trader, merchantman **ticaret mahkemesi** commercial court **ticareti yapmak** to deal in **ticaret merkezi** commercial centre **Ticaret Odası** Chamber of Commerce **ticaret yasası** commercial law
ticarethane business, firm
ticari commercial
tifo typhoid fever
tiftik mohair
tifüs typhus
tik tic
tiksindirici loathsome, disgusting
tiksindirmek to sicken, to disgust
tiksinmek to loathe, to abhor
tiksinti disgust, loathing
tilki fox
tim team
timsah crocodile, alligator
timsal symbol

tin soul, spirit
tiner thinner
tinsel spiritual
tip type
tipi blizzard, snowstorm
tipik typical
tipografya typography
tiraj (of a newspaper) circulation
tirbuşon corkscrew
tire sewing cotton
tire ñyphen, dash
tirildemek to quiver, to shiver
tiroit *anat.* thyroid
tirsi *hayb.* shad
tir tir titremek to shake like a leaf
tiryaki addict **tiryakisi olmak** to be addicted to
tişört T-shirt
titiz fussy, fastidious, particular
titizlik fussiness, fastidiousness
titizlikle fastidiously
titrek shaky, tremulous
titremek to tremble, to shiver, to quiver
titreşim vibration
titreşmek to tremble, to quake; to vibrate
tiyatro theatre
tiz high-pitched, sharp
tohum seed
tok full, satiated; (cloth) thick, close; (voice) deep **tok karnına** on a full stomach **tok olmak** to be full
toka buckle
toka shaking hands **toka etmek** to shake hands
tokalaşmak to shake hands
tokat blow, slap, cuff **tokat atmak** to slap, to cuff, to box sb's ears **tokat yemek** to be slapped
tokatlamak to slap, to cuff
tokgözlü contented, satiated
tokmak mallet, beetle; door-knocker
tokmakçı *arg.* gigolo
toksin toxin
toksözlü outspoken
tokurdamak to bubble
tokurtu bubble
tokuşmak to collide
tokuşturmak to clink glasses
tolerans tolerance

toleranslı tolerant
toleranssız intolerant
tolga helmet
tomar roll
tombala lotto
tombalak plump, rounded
tombul plump
tomruk heavy log
tomurcuk bud
ton ton; tone
tonaj tonnage
tonbalığı tunny
tonga *arg.* trick **tongaya basmak** to be trapped, to be taken in **tongaya bastırmak** to trap, to take in
tonik tonic
tonilato tonnage
tonoz vault
tonton darling, dear
top ball **top oynamak** to play football **top sürmek** to dribble **topa tutmak** to bombard **topu atmak** to go bankrupt **topu topu** in all, altogether
topaç top, teetotum **topaç çevirmek** to spin a top
topak lump
topal lame, crippled
topallamak to limp
topallık lameness
toparlak round
toparlamak to collect (together); to tidy; to summarize
toparlanmak to be collected (together); to recover oneself; to pull oneself together
topçu artilleryman
topçuluk gunnery
toplaç collector
toplam total
toplama addition **toplama kampı** concentration camp
toplamak to collect, to gather; to pick, to pluck; to convene, to convoke; to sum up; to tidy up
toplanmak to be collected; to gather, to assemble
toplantı meeting
toplardamar vein
toplaşmak to gather together
toplu collected; plump; tidy; collective

toplu konut housing estate
topluiğne pin
topluluk community; group
toplum society
toplumbilim sociology
toplumbilimci sociologist
toplumsal social **toplumsal ayırım** social discrimination **toplumsal baskı** social repression **toplumsal ilerleme** social progress
toplusözleşme collective agreement
toplutaşıma mass transport
topografya topography
toprak earth, soil; land; country **toprağa vermek** to bury
toptan wholesale; collectively **toptan satış** wholesale trade
toptancı wholesaler
topuk heel
topuz (hair) knob, bun
topyekûn total; totally
toraman robust, sturdy
torba bag **torbada keklik** It's in the bag
torik large bonito
torna lathe
tornacı turner
tornavida screwdriver
tornistan den. stern-way **tornistan etmek** den. to go astern
torpido torpedo boat
torpil torpedo arg.pull, influence arg. backer, supporter **torpil yaptırmak** to pull strings
torpilli having a backer
tortu sediment, dregs, residue
torun grandchild
tos butt **tos vurmak** to butt
tosbağa tortoise
toslamak to butt; to bump, to ram; arg. to pay, to shell out
tost toast
tostoparlak quite round
tosun young bull, bullock
totaliter totalitarian
totem totem
toto sp. pools
toy inexperienced, raw
toy hayb. bustard
toynak hoof
toz dust; powder **toz bezi** dustcloth **toz bulutu** cloud of dust **toz kondurmamak** not to allow anything to be said against **toz koparmak** to raise the dust **toz olmak** arg. to run away **tozu dumana kalmak** to rise clouds of dust; to kick up a dust **tozunu silkmek** to beat out the dust **tozlanmak** to become dusty
tozlu dusty
tozluk gaiter
tozşeker granulated sugar
tozutmak to raise a dust
töhmet imputation
tökezlemek to stumble
töre custom, usage
törebilim ethics
törel moral, ethic
tören ceremony
törensel ceremonial
törpü file, rasp
törpülemek to tile, to rasp
tövbe penitence, repentance **tövbe etmek** forswear, to repent
tövbekâr, tövbeli penitent, repentant
trafik traffic **trafik ışığı** traffic light **trafik işaretleri** traffic signs **trafik polisi** traffic policeman **trafik sıkışıklığı** bottleneck, jam
trafo transformer
trahom trachoma
trajedi tragedy
trajik tragic
traktör tractor
Trakya Thrace
trampa barter, exchange **trampa etmek** to barter, to exchange
trampet side drum, snare drum
trampetçi drummer
tramplen springboard
tramvay streetcar, tram, trolley
transatlantik transatlantic
transfer transfer
transformasyon transformation
transformatör transformer
transfüzyon transfusion
transistor transistor
transit transit
transplantasyon transplantation
trapez trapeze
travers railway sleeper

travma *hek.* trauma

tren train **trene binmek** to get on the train **trenden inmek** to get off the train

trençkot trench coat

treyler trailer

tribün grandstand

trigonometri trigonometry

trigonometrik trigonometric

triko knitted fabric, tricot

trikotaj knitting

trilyon trillion

triptik pass sheet, triptyque

triyo *müz.* trio

trol trawl

troleybüs trolleybus

trombon *müz.* trombone

tromboncu trombonist

trompet trumpet

trompetçi trumpeter

tropik tropic

tropikal tropical

trotuar pavement

tröst trust

tufan flood

tugay *ask.* brigade

tuğ horse-tail

tuğamiral rear admiral

tuğgeneral brigadier general

tuhaf strange, odd, queer, weird

tuhafiye millinery, drapery

tuhafiyeci draper, milliner

tuluat improvisations **tuluat yapmak** to improvise

tulum overalls; bagpipes

tulumba pump

tulumcuk *biy.* utricle

tulumpeyniri cheese encased in a skin

tumturak bombast

tumturaklı bombastic, pompous

Tuna the Danube

tunç bronze

tungsten tungsten

Tunus Tunisia

tur tour; round **tur atmak** to take a stroll

turfanda early (vegetables, fruit)

turist tourist **turist rehberi** tourist guide

turistik touristic(al)

turizm tourism **turizm acentesi** tourist agency

turkuaz turquoise

turna crane **turnayı gözünden vurmak** to hit the jackpot

turnabalığı pike

turne tour **turneye çıkmak** to go on tour

turnike turnstile

turnusol litmus

turnuva tournament,tourney

turp radish **turp gibi** hale and hearty, robust

turşu pickle **turşu gibi** worn-out, dead beat **turşu kurmak** to pickle **turşusu çıkmak** to be exhausted, to be worn-out, to be exhausted

turuncu orange (colour)

turunç Seville orange

tuş key (of a piano, etc.)

tutacak pot holder

tutam pinch

tutamak handle, grip

tutanak minutes, record

tutar sum, total

tutarlı coherent, consistent

tutarlık coherence, consistency

tutarsız incoherent, inconsistent

tutarsızlık incoherence, inconsistency

tutkal glue, size

tutkallamak to glue, to size

tutku passion

tutkulu passionate

tutkun in love, smitten with, nuts over

tutmak to hold; to restrain, to bridle; to keep, to retain; to engage, to hire; to back up, to support; to amount; to tally, to agree with

tutsak prisoner, captive

tutsaklık captivity

tutturmak to cause to hold; to insist

tutucu conservative

tutuculuk conservatism

tutuk tongue-tied, stuttering; shy, timid

tutuklamak to arrest

tutuklu arrested; prisoner

tutukluluk detention, imprisonment

tutulmak to be held; to be eclipsed; to fall in love with, to fall for; to catch on, to succeed, to click with

tutum conduct, attitude; economy,

thrift

tutumlu thrifty, economical

tutumsuz thriftless, spendthrift

tutunmak to take a hold, to cling; to resist, to hold out

tutuşmak to catch fire, to ignite

tutuşturmak to set on fire, to ignite

tuval canvas

tuvalet water closet, lavatory, toilet; evening dress, toilet **tuvalet kâğıdı** toilet paper **tuvalet masası** dressing table

tuz salt **tuz ekmek/koymak** to salt **tuzla buz etmek** to smash to smithereens **tuzla buz olmak** to be smashed to smithereens **tuzu kuru olmak** to have nothing to worry about, to sit pretty

tuzak trap **tuzağa düşürmek** to entrap **tuzağa düşmek** to fall into a trap **tuzak kurmak** to lay a trap

tuzlamak to salt

tuzlu salted, salty; expensive

tuzluk saltcellars, saltshaker

tuzsuz unsalted

tuzla saltpan

tuzruhu *kim.* hydrochloric acid

tüberküloz tuberculosis

tüccar merchant

tüfek rifle, gun **tüfek atmak** to fire a rifle **tüfek çatmak** to stack arms

tükenmek to be used up, to run out; to become exhausted

tükenmez inexhaustible

tükenmezkalem ball-point pen

tüketici consumer

tüketim consumption

tüketmek to use up, to consume; to exhaust, to tire out

tükürmek to spit

tükürük spit, spittle, saliva **tükürük bezleri** salivary glands

tül tulle

tülbent gauze, muslin

tüm whole

tümamiral vice-admiral

tümce sentence

tümdengelim *fel* deduction

tümel universal

tümen *ask.* division

tümgeneral major-general

tümleç *dilb.* complement

tümlemek to complete

tümler *mat.* complementary **tümler açılar** complementary angles

tümör tumour

tümsek small mound; protuberance

tümtanrıcılık pantheism

tünek perch

tüneklemek to perch

tünel tunnel

tünemek to perch

tüp tube

tür kind, sort; species

türban turban

türbe shrine, tomb

türdeş homogeneous

türedi parvenu, mushroom

türemek to spring up, to appear

türetmek to originate, to produce; to derive

türev derivative

Türk Turk; Turkish

Türkçe Turkish

Türkçesi in plain Turkish

Türkçülük Turkism

Türkistan Turkistan

Türkiye Turkey **Türkiye Cumhuriyeti** the Turkish Republic

Türkmen Turkoman

Türkoloji Turcology

türkü folk song **türkü çağırmak/söylemek** to sing a song

türlü various, diverse, assorted; meat and vegetable stew **türlü türlü** all sorts of

tütmek to smoke, to fume

tütsü incense; smoke

tütsülemek to cense; to smoke

tüttürmek to smoke

tütün tobacco **tütün içmek** to smoke (tobacco)

tüvit tweed

tüy feather, down; hair **tüy gibi** as light as a feather, feathery **tüyler ürpertici** hair-raising, horrifying **tüyleri diken diken olmak** (hair) to stand on end, to get goose bumps

tüylenmek to glow feathers; to become rich

tüylü feathered

tüymek *arg.* to scram, to flee, to slip away

tüysıklet featherweight

tüysüz unfeathered; beardless, young

tüze jurisprudence, law

tüzel legal, judirral

tüzelkişi corporate body, juristic person

tüzük regulations, statutes

tvist twist

U

ucube freak, monstrosity

ucuz cheap, inexpensive **ucuz atlatmak/kurtulmak** to get off cheap **ucuza** on the cheap **ucuza almak** to get sth on the cheap

ucuzlamak to become cheap

ucuzlatmak to lower the price of

ucuzluk cheapness

uç point, tip; end **uç uca** end to end **uç uca gelmek** to be just enough **ucu bucağı olmamak** to be endless **ucunu kaçırmak** to lose the thread of

uçak aeroplane, airplane, plane **uçak kaçırmak** to skyjack **uçak korsanı** sky-jacker

uçaksavar antiaircraft weapon

uçandaire flying saucer

uçantop volleyball

uçarı unruly, incorrigible

uçkur waistband, waiststring **uçkuruna gevşek** promiscuous

uçlanmak *arg.* to give, to pay, to shell out

uçmak to fly; to evaporate; (colour) to fade; to vanish, to disappear

uçsuz pointless **uçsuz bucaksız** vast, immense

uçucu flying; volatile

uçuçböceği ladybird

uçuk pale, faded; *hek.* blain, bleb; herpes

uçurmak to fly; (wind) to blow; to blow up

uçurtma kite **uçurtma uçurmak** to fly a kite

uçurum precipice, abyss

uçuş flight, flying

uçuşmak to fly about

udi lute player

ufacık tiny, minute **ufacık tefecik** tiny

ufak small **ufak çapta** on a small scale **ufak para** small change **ufak tefek** (person) small and short; unimportant **ufak ufak** in small pieces *arg.* slowly

ufaklık smallness; small change; kid, boy

ufalamak to break up, to crumble

ufalmak to become smaller; to shorten, to shrink

ufarak somewhat small, smallish

uflamak to say "oof" **uflayıp puflamak** to keep saying "oof"

ufuk horizon

uğrak much frequented place, resort

uğramak to drop in, to stop by, to stop off; to call, to call at, to call in; to experience, to undergo

uğraş occupation, job; struggle

uğraşı occupation, occupation

uğraşmak to strive, to struggle

uğraştırmak to make sb struggle (with), to raise difficulties

uğuldamak to hum, to buzz

uğultu hum, buzz

uğur good luck, talisman **uğur getirmek** to bring good luck **uğurlar olsun!** Have a good trip!

uğur purpose, aim **uğruna** for the sake of

uğurböceği ladybird

uğurlamak to see sb off

uğurlu lucky, auspicious

uğursuz inauspicious, ill-omened

uğursuzluk bad luck, ill-omen

ukala wiseacre, know-it-all

ulak courier, messenger

ulam category

ulamak to join, to add

ulan hey! hi! man alive!

ulaşım communication, transport

ulaşmak to reach

ulaştırma communication **Ulaştırma Bakanlığı** Ministry of Communications

ulaştırmak to communicate, to transport

ulema theological scholars

ulu great

ululamak to extol, to exalt

ulumak to howl

uluorta rashly, recklessly

ulus nation, people

ulusal national

ulusallaştırmak to nationalize

ulusçu nationalist

ulusçuluk nationalism

uluslararası international

umacı ogre, bugaboo

ummadık unexpected

ummak to hope; to expect, to count on

umuduyla in the hope of

umulmadık unexpected

umum the public; general, universal

umumi general, public

umumiyet generality

umumiyetle in general

umur concern, minding **umurumda değil!** I don't care! I don't give a damn!

umursamak to care, to heed

umursamamak not to care, to be indifferent to

umursamaz indifferent

umursamazlık indifference

umut hope, expectation **umut etmek** to hope **umut vermek** to give hope to **umudunu kesmek** to give up hope of **umudunu kırmak** to destroy a person's hopes, to disappoint

umutlandırmak to give hope (to)

umutlanmak to be hopeful

umutlu hopeful

umutsuz hopeless

umutsuzluk hopelessness, despair **umutsuzluğa düşmek** to sink into despair **umutsuzluğa düşürmek** to drive to despair **umutsuzluğa kapılmak** to abandon oneself to despair

un flour **un ufak olmak** to be broken into pieces

unlamak to flour

unlu floury

unsur element

unutkan forgetful

unutkanlık forgetfulness

unutmabeni *bitk.* forget-me-not

unutmak to forget

unutulmaz unforgettable

unvan title

upuzun very long, very tall

ur tumour

urağan hurricane

Uranüs Uranus

uranyum uranium

urgan rope

us reason, intelligence **usa vurmak** to reason

usanç boredom **usanç getirmek** to be bored **usanç vermek** to bore, to disgust

usandırmak to bore, to sicken

usanmak to become bored, to be fed up (with)

usare sap, juice

usçu rationalist; rationalistic

usdışı irrational

uskumru mackerel

uskur propeller, screw

uslanmak to become sensible, to listen to reason

uslu well-behaved, docile, sensible **uslu durmak** to keep quiet **uslu oturmak** to sit still

ussal rational

usta master workman; foreman; clever, skilful

ustaca skilfully, cunningly

ustabaşı foreman

ustalık mastery, skill

ustura razor

usturmaça fender, padding

usul method, system; procedure **usul usul** slowly, gently

usulsüz unmethodical; irregular

usulsüzlük irregularity

uşak male servant; boy, child

utanacak shameful

utanç shame **utancından yerin dibine geçmek** to feel cheap, to feel like 30 cents

utandırmak to make ashamed, to embarrass, to wither

utangaç shy, timid

utangaçlık shyness

utanmak to feel ashamed, to be embar-

rassed; to blush
utanmaz shameless, impudent
utanmazlık impudence, shamelessness
utku victory, triumph
uvertür *müz.* overture
uyak rhyme
uyandırmak to awake, to wake (up); to arouse, to excite
uyanık awake; wide awake, sharp
uyanmak to wake up; to be aroused
uyaran stimulant
uyarı warning
uyarıcı stimulus
uyarınca in accordance with
uyarlama adaptation
uyarlamak to adapt
uyarmak to warn; to stimulate; to excite
uydu satellite
uydurma making up, fabrication; invented, made-up
uydurmak to invent, to fabricate
uydurmasyon invention, fable, fabrication; made-up, invented
uyduruk made-up,invented
uygar civilized
uygarlaşmak to be civilized
uygarlık civilization
uygulama application; practice **uygulamaya koymak** to put into practice
uygulamak to apply
uygulamalı applied, practical
uygulayım technics
uygun appropriate, fit, suitable, proper (price) reasonable, moderate **uygun bulmak/görmek** to see fit (to) **uygun gelmek** to suit
uygunluk suitability, fitness
uygunsuz inappropriate, unsuitable; improper, indecorous
uygunsuzluk unsuitability, unfitness; improperiety
Uygur Uighur
uyku sleep **uyku basmak** to feel very sleepy **uyku gözünden akmak** to be very sleepy **uyku hapı** sleeping pill **uyku sersemliği** drowsiness **uyku tutmamak** to be unable to get to sleep **uykusu açılmak** (one's sleepiness) to pass off **uykusu ağır** heavy sleeper

uykusu gelmek to feel sleepy **uykusu hafif** light sleeper **uykusu kaçmak** to lose one's sleep **uykusunu almak** to sleep the night through **uykuya dalmak** to fall asleep
uykucu late riser, sleepyhead
uykulu sleepy, drowsy
uykusuz sleepless
uykusuzluk sleeplessness, insomnia
uyluk thigh
uymak to fit, to suit; to agree with, to hew, to harmonize; to adapt oneself, to suit oneself; to follow, to listen to
uyruk subject, citizen
uyrukluk citizenship, nationality
uysal docile, easygoing, compliant, mild, flexible
uysallık docility, compliance
uyuklamak to doze, to drowse, to slumber
uyum harmony; accord
uyumlu harmonious
uyumsuz inharmonious
uyumak to sleep, to kip
uyuntu indolent, lazy
uyurgezer sleepwalker, somnambulist
uyurgezerlik somnambulism
uyuşmak to become numb; to reach an agreement, to come to terms
uyuşmazlık disagreement
uyuşturmak to benumb; to deaden, to dull
uyuşturmak to reconcile; to anesthetize, to narcotize; to benumb
uyuşturucu narcotic **uyuşturucu madde** narcotic drug
uyuşuk numb, insensible; indolent, bovine
uyuşukluk numbness; indolence
uyutmak to send to sleep; to deceive, to fool
uyuz scabies, itch; mangy, scabby; sluggish, indolent **uyuz etmek** to irritate **uyuz olmak** to have the itch; to become irritated
uyuzböceği itch mite
uyuzotu scabious
uz good, fine; skilful, clever; appropriate, fitting
uzaduyum telepathy

uzak far, distant, remote, off; distant place **uzağı görmek** to have foresight **uzak akraba** distant relative **uzak durmak** to keep away from **Uzaktan davulun sesi hoş gelir.** *ats.* Distance lends enchantment to the view.

uzaklaşmak to go away

uzaklaştırmak to take away, to send away

uzaklık distance; remoteness

Uzakdoğu Far East

uzamak to grow longer, to lengthen

uzanmak to stretch oneself out; to extend, to stretch

uzantı extension, prolongation

uzatma extension, prolongation; protraction, lengthening

uzatmak to extend, to stretch, to prolong; to lengthen, to elongate, to protract **uzatmıyalım** in short

uzatmalı prolonged

uzay space **uzay elbisesi** space suit **uzay geometri** solid geometry **uzay kapsülü** space capsule **uzay mekiği** space shuttle

uzayadamı spaceman, astronaut

uzaygemisi spaceship, spacecraft

uzgörür farseeing, farsighted

uziletişim telecommunication

uzlaşma agreement, understanding

uzlaşmak to come to an agreement, to come to terms

uzlaşmaz intransigent

uzlaşmazlık intransigence, disagreement

uzlaştırma conciliation **uzlaştırma kurulu** conciliation commission

uzlaştırmak to reconcile, to conciliate

uzluk skill, ability

uzman specialist, expert

uzmanlaşmak to specialize (in)

uzmanlık speciality, expertness

uzun long **uzun araç** long vehicle **uzun atlama** long jump **uzun boylu** tall **uzun çizgi** dash (-) **uzun dalga** long wave **uzun hikâye** long story **uzun sözün kısası** in short **uzun uzadıya** in great detail **uzun uzun** at length

uzunluk length

uzunçalar long play

uzuneşek leapfrog

uzuv organ, limb

Ü

ücra out-of-the-way, remote

ücret pay, wage; fee, charge; price, cost

ücretli paid, salaried

ücretsiz unpaid; free

üç three **üç aşağı beş yukarı** roughly, approximately **üç buçuk atmak** to shake in one's shoes

üçboyutlu three dimensional

üçdüzlemli trihedral

üçgen triangle

üçkâğıt swindling, trick **üçkâğıda getirmek** to decieve, to dupe

üçkâğıtçı crook, swindler

üçlü (playing card) the three *müz.* trio; ternary

üçteker three-wheeler; tricycle

üçüncü third **Üçüncü Dünya Ülkeleri** Third World

üçüncül tertiary

üçüz triplet

üfleç nozzle, blowpipe

üflemek to blow; to blow out

üfürmek to blow, to puff

üfürük exhaled breath

üfürükçü quack who claims to cure by breathing

üğrüm nutation

üleşmek to go shares, to divide

üleştirmek to share out, to distribute

ülke country; kingdom

Ülker the Pleiades

ülkü ideal

ülkücü idealist

ülkücülük idealism

ülküleştirmek to idealize

ülser ulcer

ültimatom ultimatum

ültraviyole ultraviolet

ümit hope **ümit etmek** to hope **ümit vermek** to give hope **ümidini kesmek**

to give up hope of
ümitlendirmek to fill with hope
ümitlenmek to be hopeful
ümitli hopeful
ümitsiz hopeless
ümitsizlik hopelessness, despair **ümitsizliğe kapılmak** to give way to despair
ümmet community, people **ümmeti Muhammed** the Moslems
ümük throat
ün fame, reputation, renown **ün kazanmak/salmak** to become famous; to acquire fame
ünlü famous; *dilb.* vowel
ünsüz unknown; *dilb.* consonant
üniforma uniform
ünite unit
üniversite university
ünlem interjection
ünlemek to cry out
Ürdün Jordan
Ürdünlü Jordanian
üre urea
üreme reproduction **üreme organları** genitals
üremek to reproduce; to multiply, to increase
üremi uremia
üreteç generator
üretici producer; productive
üretim production **üretim araçları** means of production
üretken productive
üretkenlik productiveness
üremek to produce; to breed, to raise
ürkek timid,fearful **ürkek ürkek** timidly
ürkmek to be scared, to start, to flinch, to wince
ürküntü sudden fright, panic
ürkütmek to frighten
ürolog urologist
üroloji urology
ürpermek to shudder, to shiver
ürperti shudder, shiver
ürtiker hek. urticaria
ürümek to howl, to yowl, to bay
ürün product
üs base; *mat.* exponent
üslup style, manner

üst upper part, top; outside surface; clothing, dress; body; remainder, change; upper, uppermost **üst baş** clothes **üste** in addition **üste vermek** to give in addition **üstesinden gelmek** to overcome, to cope with **üstü kalsın!** Keep the change! **üstü kapalı** covert, veiled **üstü kapalı söylemek** to hint **üstünde** on, over **üstüme iyilik sağlık!** Good heavens! **üstünden atmak** not to take over the **üstüne** about, on; onto, on, over **üstüne almak** to lay the blame on **üstüne basmak** to emphasize, to hit the nail on the head **üstüne bir bardak soğuk su iç!** You can whistle for it! **üstüne düşmek** to be very interested in **üstüne gitmek** to force, to press (sb to do sth) **üstüne kalmak** to be saddled with **üstüne oturmak** to pocket, to appropriate **üstüne titremek** to fuss over **üstüne toz kondurmamak** to consider above blame **üstüne tuz biber ekmek** to rub salt in the wound, to be the last straw **üst üste** one on the top of the other; one after the other, successively **üstüne varmak** to keep on at sb; to attack **üstüne yatmak** not to give back, to appropriate
üstat master, expert
üstbitken epiphyte
üstçavuş *ask.* staff sergeant
üstçene upper jaw
üstderi epidermis
üstdil metalanguage
üstdudak upper lip *hayb.* labrum
üsteğmen first lieutenant
üstelemek to dwell on, to insist; to recur, to relapse
üstelik furthermore, moreover, besides, in addition
üstenci contractor
üstgeçit flyover *Aİ.* overpass
üstsubay senior officer
üstübeç white lead
üstün superior **üstün gelmek** to surpass, to exceed **üstün olmak** to be superior to **üstün tutmak** to preter
üstünlük superiority **üstünlük derecesi** *dilb.* the superlative (degree) **üstün-**

lük duygusu/kompleksi superiority complex

üstünkörü superficial; superficially

üstüpü oakum, tow

üstyapı superstructure

üşengeç lazy, slothful

üşengeçlik laziness, sloth

üşenmek to be too lazy to

üşümek to be cold

üşüşmek to flock together, to crowd

üşütmek to catch cold; to go off one's head

üşütük nutty, crazy

ütopya utopia

ütü iron; crease

ütülemek to iron, to press

ütülü ironed

üvendire ox-goad

üvey step **üvey ana** stepmother **üvey baba** stepfather **üvey evlat** stepchild **üvey kardeş** stepbrother, stepsister **üvey kız** stepdaughter **üvey oğul** step-son **üvey evlat muamelesi yapmak** to ill-treat, to treat unfairly

üvez rowan, rowanberry

üye member

üyelik membership

üzengi stirrup

üzengikemiği stirrup bone, stapes

üzere just about to; (in order) to; on condition of

üzeri top; outer surface; clothing, attire; body; (money) remainder, change

üzgün unhappy, sad

üzmek to upset, to distress

üzücü upsetting, distressing

üzülmek to be upset, to be sorry

üzüm grape **üzüm asması** grapevine **üzüm salkımı** bunch of grapes

üzüntü sorrow, sadness

üzüntülü unhappy, sad

üzüntüsüz trouble-free, carefree

V

vaat promise **vaat etmek** to promise **vaatte bulunmak** to make a promise;

to promise

vaaz sermon **vaaz etmek** to preach

vacip necessary

vade due date, fixed term **vadesi geçmek** to be overdue **vadesi gelmek/-dolmak** to fall due **vadesini uzatmak** to prolong a term **vadeli hesap/mevduat** time deposit **vadeli satış** forward sale **vadesiz** having no fixed term **vadesiz hesap/mevduat** current account **A/** checking account

vadi valley

vaftiz baptism **vaftiz etmek** to baptise

vagina, vajina vagina

vagon railway car, railway wagon **vagon restoran** wagon restaurant, dining car

vah vah What a pity!

vaha oasis

vahdet unity

vahim grave, serious

vahşet atrocity, savage

vahşi savage, wild; brutal

vahşice wild, brutal; barbarously, brutally

vahşileşmek to become wild

vahşilik savageness; brutality

vaiz preacher

vaka event

vakar dignity, gravity

vakfetmek to devote, to dedicate

vakıf (pious) foundation

vâkıf aware, knowing

vaki happening, taking place **vaki olmak** to happen, to take place

vakit time **vakit bulmak** to get round to **vakit geçirmek** to pass the time **vakit kaybetmek** to lose time **vakit kazanmak** to play for time **Vakit nakittir. ats.** Time is money **vakit öldürmek** to kill time **vaktini almak** to take sb's time

vakitli timely **vakitli vakitsiz** at all sorts of times

vakitsiz premature, untimely, unseasonable

vaktinde on time

vakur dignified, grave

vakvak duck

vale (cards) knave, jack

valf valve
vali governor
valide mother
valilik governorship
valiz suitcase
vallahi by God! I swear it's so!
vals waltz **vals yapmak** to waltz
vampir vampire
vana valve
vanilya vanilla
vantilatör fan
vapur steamer, steamship; ship
var existent, available; there is, there are **var etmek** to create **varı yoğu** all that he has **var ol!** May you live long! **var olmak** to exist, to be
varagele den. pass-rope
varda Keep clear! Make way!
vardiya shift, relay; watch **vardiyalı çalışmak** to work in relays
vargel shaper
varış arrival
varil barrel, cask
vâris heir, inheritor
varis varicose vein, varix
varlık existence, presence; entity; life; riches, wealth **varlık göstermek** to make one's presence felt **varlık içinde yaşamak** to live in easy circumstances
varlıklı wealthy
varlıksız needy
varmak to arrive (at), to get to, to reach
varolmak to exist, to be
varoluş existence, being
varoluşçuluk existentialism
varoş suburb
varsayım hypothesis
varsayımlı hypothetical
varsaymak to suppose
varyant variant
varyasyon variation
varyete variety show
vasat average
vasıf quality
vasıflandırmak to qualify
vasıflı qualified, skilled
vasıfsız unqualified, unskilled
vasıta means; vehicle
vasıtasıyla by means of

vasi guardian; executor
vasiyet will, testament **vasiyet etmek** to bequeath
vasiyetname written will
vaşak lynx
vat watt
vatan motherland, fatherland, native country
vatandaş fellow countryman, citizen, compatriot
vatandaşlık citizenship
vatansever patriot; patriotic
vatanseverlik patriotism
vatansız stateless
vatka pad
vay Oh! Woe! **vay canına** by heaven! **vay vay ey**, Well, well!
vazelin vaseline
vazetmek to preach
vazgeçirmek to dissuade,to deter
vazgeçmek to give up, to quit, to abandon
vazife duty, task
vazifeli in charge; on duty
vazifeşinas dutiful
vaziyet position, situation
vazo vase
ve and
veba plague, pestilence
vebal sin
vecibe obligation
vecit ecstasy, rapture
veciz terse, laconic
vecize saying, maxim
veda farewell **veda etmek** to say farewell (to)
vedalaşmak to say good-bye to each other
vefa loyalty, faithfulness
vefakâr/vefalı faithful, loyal
vefasız disloyal, faithless
vefat death, decease **vefat etmek** to die, to decease
vahim groundless fear
vekâlet attorneyship, procuration **vekâlet etmek** to represent, to deputize, to substitute **vekâlet vermek** to give the procuration
vekâleten by proxy
vekâletname power of attorney, proxy

vekil representative, agent
vektör *mat.* vector
velet child, brat veledi zina bastard
velhasıl in short
veli guardian, protector; saint
veliaht heir to the throne
velinimet benefactor
Venüs Venus
veraset inheritance
verecek debt
verecekli debtor
verem tuberculosis
veremli tuberculous
veresiye on credit, on the cuff
vergi tax, duty; gift, talent vergi beyannamesi tax return vergi mükellefi tax-payer vergi tahsildarı tax collector vergiye tabi taxable
vergilendirmek to tax
veri datum
verici transmitter
verim output, yield, production
verimli productive
verimlilik productivity
verimsiz fruitless
verimsizlik fruitlessness
veriştirmek to swear at, to vituperate
verkaç *sp.* pass and run, one-two
vermek to give, to hand
vermut vermouth
vernik varnish
verniklemek to varnish
veronika veronica
vesaire etcetera
vesait means, ways
vesayet guardianship, executorship
vesika document
vesile means, cause; opportunity, occasion
vestiyer cloakroom
vesvese anxiety, misgiving
vesveseli scrupulous, apprehensive
veteriner veterinarian
veto veto veto etmek to veto
veya, veyahut or
vezin metre, meter
vezir vizier, vizir; (chess) queen
vezne cashier's desk, treasury
veznedar treasurer, cashier
vıcık sticky, gooey

vınlamak to buzz
vırlamak to nag
vırvır tiresome talk vırvır etmek to nag
vız buzz vız gelmek to be a matter of indifference vız gelir tırıs gider I don't give a damn
vızıldamak to buzz, to hum
vızıltı whiz, buzz
vızır vızır continuously
vızlamak to buzz, to hum
vicdan conscience vicdan azabı the pangs of conscience, remorse
vicdanlı conscientious
vicdansız remorseless, unscrupulous
vida screw
vidalamak to screw
video video; video player; video recorder
videoteyp videotape
Vietnam Vietnam
Vietnamlı Vietnamese
vikont viscount
vilayet province, vilayet
villa villa
vinç crane, winch
viraj curve, bend
viran devastated, ruined
virane ruin
virgül comma
virtüöz virtuoso
virüs virus
viski whisky
vişne morello cherry
vitamin vitamin
vites gear vites değiştirmek to shift gears vites kolu gear lever, gear shift *Aİ.* vites kutusu gearbox viteste in gear
vitray stained-glass
vitrin shop window; display cabinet
viyak squawk viyak viyak squawking
viyaklamak to squawk
viyola *müz.* viola
viyolin violin
viyolonist violonist
vize visa
vizite doctor's fee; medical visit
vizon mink
vodvil vaudeville
volan flywheel

vole volley **vole vurmak** to volley
voleybol volleyball
volkan volcano
volkanik volcanic
volt volt
volta *den.* fouling of a cable; *arg.* pacing back and forth **volta atmak** to pace back and forth
voltametre voltameter
voltaj voltage
votka vodka
vuku occurrence, event **vuku bulmak** to happen, to occur
vukuat events, incidents; police case, crime
vurdumduymaz thick-skinned
vurgu stress, accent
vurgulamak to stress, to emphasize
vurgulu stressed, accented
vurgusuz unstressed
vurgun struck on, sweet on, smitten; booty, scoop, killing **vurgun vurmak** to make a killing, to pull a deal
vurguncu profiteer, speculator
vurgunculuk profiteering
vurmak to hit; to strike, to dash; to knock; to shoot; (shoe) to pinch
vurucu striking, hitting; hitter **vurucu güç** striking power
vuruntu knock, detonation
vuruş blow, hit, stroke
vuruşkan combative
vuruşmak to strike one another, to have a fight
vücut body **vücut bulmak** to come into existence **vücuda getirmek** to bring into being, to create

Y

ya yes, of course; but what if
ya ... ya ... either ... or ...
yaban wilderness; stranger **yabana atmak** to sniff at, to sneeze at
yabanarısı wasp
yabancı foreigner; stranger; foreign **yabancı dil** foreign language **yabancı**

düşmanlığı xenophobia **yabancı gelmemek** to ring a bell **yabancısı olmak** to be a stranger to
yabancıl exotic
yabancılaşma estrangement, alienation
yabancılaşmak to estrange oneself
yabandomuzu wild boar
yabangülü shrub rose, dog rose
yabanıl primitive; wild
yabani wild, untamed
yabankazı wild goose, greylag
yabankedisi wildcat
yabanördeği wild duck, mallard
yabansı strange, weird
yabansımak to find strange
yabanturpu horseradish
yad strange **yad elde** in a foreign land, away from home
yad remembrance **yad etmek** to remember
yadırgamak to find strange
yadigâr souvenir
yadsımak to deny, to gainsay
Yafa Jaffa **Yafa portakalı** navel orange
yafta label
yağ oil, fat, butter; grease **yağ bağlamak** to put on fat **yağ çekmek** to butter sb up, to flatter, to toady **yağdan kıl çeker gibi** as easy as falling off a log **yağ sürmek** to butter (bread) **yağ tulumu** fatty
yağcı seller of oil/butter; softsoaper, toady, apple-polisher
yağdanlık oil-can
yağış rain
yağışlı rainy
yağışsız dry, arid
yağız swarthy, dark
yağlamak to oil, to grease, to lubricate
yağlı oily, fatty, greasy; profitable, lucrative
yağlıboya oil paint
yağma booty, loot **yağma etmek** to plunder; to loot, to pillage **yağma yok** Sold again! Nothing doing!
yağmacı plunderer, pillager
yağmak to rain
yağmalamak to pillage, to plunder
yağmur rain **yağmur yağmak** to rain **yağmurdan kaçarken doluya tutulmak**

to jump out of the frying pan into the fire

yağmurkuşu golden plover
yağmurlu rainy, wet
yağmurluk raincoat, mackintosh
yağmursuz without rain, dry
yağsız oilless; butterless; greaseless
yağyakıt fuel oil
yahni ragout, fricassee
yahu See here! Look here!; on earth
Yahudi Jew; Jewish
Yahudilik Jewishness; Judaism
yahut or
yak yak
yaka collar; shore, side **yaka paça** by the head and ears, by force **yaka silkmek** to be fed up (with) **yakası açılmadık** unheard-of **yakasına yapışmak** to collar, to badger **yakayı ele vermek** to be caught **yakayı kurtarmak** to get rid of, to escape, to evade
yakacak fuel
yakalamak to catch, to seize
yakamoz phosphorescence
yakarış entreaty
yakarmak to entreat
yakasız collarless
yakı plaster, cautery
yakıcı burning; caustic
yakın near **yakın akraba** close relative, near relation
yakında, yakınlarda near; soon, recently
yakından closely
Yakındoğu Near East
yakınlık closeness **yakınlık göstermek** to behave warmly, to be friendly
yakınmak to complain
yakınsak *mat* convergent
yakışık suitability **yakışık almak** to be suitable
yakışıklı handsome, comely
yakışıksız unsuitable, unbecoming
yakışmak to suit, to become
yakıştırmak to regard sth as suitable; to ascribe, to impute
yakıt fuel
yaklaşık approximate **yaklaşık olarak** approximately
yaklaşım approach

yaklaşmak to come near, to approach
yakmak to burn, to light; (light) to turn on
yakut ruby
yalabık sparkling
yalak trough
yalama worn **yalama olmak** to be worn
yalamak to lick
yalan lie; false, untrue **yalan söylemek** to lie, to tell lies **yalanını çıkarmak** to show up sb's lies
yalancı liar; false, counterfeit **yalancı çıkarmak** to belie, to contradict
yalancıktan in pretence
yalandan in pretence **yalandan yapmak** to pretend
yalanlamak to deny, to contradict
yalapşap superficially, perfunctorily
yalaz flame
yalçın steep, precipitous
yaldız gilding
yaldızlamak to gild
yaldızlı gilt
yalı waterside residence
yalım flame; blade
yalın simple; plain, modest **yalın durum** *dilb.* nominative case
yalınayak barefooted
yalınkat flimsy, weak; superficial
yalınkılıç drawn sword
yalıtıcı insulating; insulator
yalıtım insulating
yalıtmak to isolate, to insulate
yalnız alone, lonely; only, solely
yalnızlık loneliness
yalpa rolling lurching **yalpa vurmak** to roll, to lurch
yalpalamak to roll, to lurch
yalpak friendly
yaltak, yaltakçı fawning, cringing
yaltakçılık flattery, fawning
yaltaklanmak to fawn (on), to toady (to)
yalvarmak to beg, to implore
yama patch **yama vurmak** to put a patch (on)
yamaç slope, side
yamak assistant, apprentice
yamalamak to patch
yamalı patched

yamamak to patch; to pin on, to palm off (on)
yaman excellent, smart, crack
yamanmak to be patched on; to foist oneself on
yampiri crabwise
yamuk bent, crooked; *mat* trapezium
yamulmak to become crooked
yamyam cannibal
yamyamlık cannibalism
yamyassı very flat
yan side **yan bakmak** to look askance **yan çizmek** to shirk, to evade **yan gözle bakmak** to look askance; to look at hostilely **yan hakemi** linesman, lineman *A/.* **yan ödeme** fringe benefits **yan ürün** by-product **yan yana** side by side **yanına almak** to take into one's service **yanına bırakmamak** not to leave unpunished, to get even
yanak cheek
yanardağ volcano
yanardöner shot, chatoyant
yanaşık adjacent
yanaşma approaching; hireling
yanaşmak to draw near, to approach; to draw up alongside; (ship) to dock; to be willing (to), to incline
yanaştırmak to bring sth near to; to draw up alongside
yandaş partisan, supporter
yandaşlık partisanship, support
yangı inflammation
yangılanmak to become inflamed
yangın fire **yangın bombası** incendiary bomb **yangın çıkarmak** to start a fire **yangına körükle gitmek** to add fuel to the flames **yangını söndürmek** to put out the fire
yanık burnt; burn **yanık kokmak** to smell of burning
yanılgı mistake, error
yanılmak to make a mistake, to be mistaken
yanılmaz infallible
yanıltmak to lead into error
yanıltıcı misleading
yanıltmaca fallacy
yanıt answer

yanıtlamak to answer
yani that is, namely
yankesici pickpocket
yankı echo
yankıla(n)mak to echo
yanlamasına sideways
yanlış mistake; incorrect, wrong **yanlış kapı çalmak** to bark up the wrong tree
yanlışlık mistake
yanlışlıkla by mistake
yanmak to burn, to be on fire; (plant) to be blighted; to be ruined; (bulb) to blow
yansımak to be reflected
yansıtmak to reflect
yansıtıcı reflector
yansız impartial, neutral
yansızlık impartiality, neutrality
yampiri crabwise
yantümce subordinate clause, dependent clause
yapağı wool
yapay artificial
yapayalnız all alone
yapı building, construction; structure
yapısal structural
yapıbilim morphology
yapıcı maker; builder; constructive
yapılabilirlik feasibility
yapım making, building, manufacture; production
yapımcı maker, producer
yapımevi factory, workshop
yapışıcı sticky
yapışık stuck on, joined together
yapışkan sticky, adhesive; pertinacious, importunate
yapışkanlık stickiness; pertinacity
yapışmak to stick, to adhere; to stick to, to hang on
yapıştırmak to stick on, to fasten, to attach
yapıt work (of art/literature etc)
yapıtaşı building stone
yapma doing, making; artificial, false; sham, feigned
yapmacık artificial, affected, put on; affectation
yapmacıksız sincere, cordial

yapmak   234

yapmak to do, to make; to build, to
  construct
yaprak leaf; sheet (of paper) yaprak dol-
  ması stuffed vine-leaves
yaptırım sanction
yapyalnız all alone
yar precipice
yâr lover yâr olmak to assist
yara wound, injury yarası olan gocun-
  sun if the cap fits wear it
Yaradan Creator
yaradılış creation; nature, temperament
yaralamak to wound, to injure
yaralanmak to be wounded
yaralı wounded, injured
yaramak to be of use; to benefit, to do
  good
yaramaz useless; naughty, mischievous
yaramazlık uselessness; naughtiness;
  misbehaviour yaramazlık etmek to
  misbehave
yaranmak to curry favour (with), to
  cozy up (to)
yarar advantage, profit, use
yararlanmak to make use of, to profit,
  to benefit, to utilize
yararlı useful yararlı olmak to help, to
  benefit
yararsız useless
yarasa bat
yaraşmak to be fit, to suit, to become
yaratıcı creative; creator
yaratıcılık creativeness
yaratık creature
yaratmak to create; to cause, to occasion
yarbay lieutenant-colonel
yarda yard
yardakçı accomplice
yardakçılık complicity
yardım help, assistance, aid yardım etmek to help, to assist, to aid
yardımcı helper, assistant yardımcı fiil
  auxiliary verb
yardımlaşmak to help one another
yardımsever benevolent, charitable
yaren friend
yarenlik chat yarenlik etmek to have a
  chat

yargı judgement
yargılamak to try, to judge
yargıç judge
Yargıtay Supreme Court ot Appeal
yarı half; sp. half time yarı yarıya fifty--
  fifty yarı yolda half-way yarı yolda bırakmak to leave in the lurch yarıda bırakmak to interrupt, to discontinue yarıda kalmak to be left half-finished
yarıcı share-cropper
yarıçap radius
yarık split; crack, fissure, split
yarıküre hemisphere
yarılamak to be half-way through; to
  half finish
yarılmak to split
yarım half yarım ağızla half-hearted yarım saat half an hour yarım yamalak
  perfunctory, slipshod; incompletely,
  inadequately
yarımada peninsula
yarımay half-moon, crescent
yarımgün part-time
yarımküre hemisphere
yarın tomorrow yarın akşam tomorrow
  night yarın sabah tomorrow morning
yarınki of tomorrow
yarısaydam semitransparent
yarış race yarış etmek to race
yarışma competition, contest
yarışmacı competitor, contestant
yarışmak to race, to compete, to contest
yarıyıl semester
yarma splitting, cleaving; cleft, fissure;
  ask. breakthrough yarma şeftali free-
  stone peach
yarmak to split, to cleave, to chop; ask.
  to break through
yas mourning yas tutmak to lament, to
  be in mourning
yasa law
yasadışı illegal
yasak prohibition, ban; prohibited, forbidden yasak etmek to forbid, to prohibit
yasaklamak to forbid, to prohibit
yasal legal, lawful
yasallaştırmak to legalize
yasama legislation yasama dokunul-

mazlığı legislative immunity **yasama gücü** legislative power
yasamak to make laws
yasemin jasmine
yaslamak to prop, to lean
yaslanmak to lean against
yaslı in mourning
yassı flat
yastık pillow, cushion; pad **yastık yüzü** pillowcase, pillow slip
yaş damp, moist, wet; tear **yaş dökmek** to shed tears **yaş tahtaya basmak** to be cheated
yaş age **yaşına başına bakmadan** regardless of his age **yaşını başını almak** to be old **yaş günü** birthday **yaşını göstermek** to look one's age **kaç yaşındasın?** How old are you?
yaşadık We are in luck!
yaşam life
yaşamak to live; to experience
yaşamöyküsü biography
yaşantı experience
yaşarmak to moisten, to water
yaşatmak to cause to live, to revive; to keep alive, to keep up
yaşdönümü (women) menopause; (men) andropause
yaşıt of the same age
yaşlanmak to age, to grow old
yaşlı aged, old
yaşlık wetness
yaşlılık old age
yaşmak veil
yat yacht
yatak bed; den, lair; bearing **yatağa düşmek** to take to one's bed **yatak odası** bedroom **yatak örtüsü** counterpane, coverlet **yatak takımı** set of bedding
yatakhane dormitory
yataklı with a bed, having ... beds **yataklı vagon** sleeping car
yatalak bedridden
yatay horizontal
yatık leaning to one side
yatılı boarding; boarder, boarding student **yatılı okul** boarding school **yatılı öğrenci** boarder
yatır saint

yatırım investment **yatırım yapmak** to invest in
yatırımcı investor
yatırmak to put to bed; to lay down
yatışmak to calm down, to cool down
yatıştırmak to calm, to smooth, to ease, to soothe
yatıştırıcı calming, soothing
yatkın apt, inclined, predisposed
yatkınlık aptness, predisposition, inclination
yatmak to go to bed, to kip down, to flop; to be in bed; to lie (down), to lie flat
yatsı time about two hours after sunset
yavan (food) plain, dry; insipid, tasteless
yavaş slow; (voice) low, soft; slowly **yavaş yavaş** slowly
yavaşça slowly, gently
yavaşlamak to slow down
yaver aide-de-camp
yavru young
yavuklu betrothed, engaged; darling
yavuz good, excellent
yay bow; spring; arc **Yay (burcu)** Sagittarius
yaya pedestrian, walker **yaya geçidi** zebra crossing **yaya kaldırımı** pavement, sidewalk
yayan on foot **yayan gitmek** to go on foot
yaygara clamour, uproar, outcry **yaygarayı basmak** to make a great to do about nothing
yaygaracı noisy, clamorous, brawling
yaygı ground cloth
yaygın widespread, common
yaygınlaşmak to spread, to become common
yayık churn
yayılımcı imperialist; imperialistic
yayılımcılık imperialism
yayılmak to spread; to diffuse; to graze, to browse
yayım publication
yayımcı publisher
yayımlamak to publish; to broadcast
yayın publication
yayınbalığı sheatfish

yayınevi publishing house
yayınım, yayınma diffusion
yayla plateau, tableland
yaylanmak to spring, to bounce; *arg.* to
go away, to take a powder
yaylı having springs, springy
yaylım spreading yaylım ateşi volley
yaymak to spread
yayvan broad and shallow
yaz summer yaz kış in summer and winter yaz saati summer time
yazar writer, author
yazarlık authorship
yazgı destiny
yazı writing; article; destiny yazı dili literary language yazı kâğıdı writing paper yazı makinesi typewriter yazı mı
tura mı? Heads or tails? yazı tura
toss-up yazı tura atmak to toss up yazı tahtası blackboard
yazıcı scribe, secretary
yazıhane office
yazık pity, shame; what a pity! yazıklar
olsun sana! Shame on you!
yazılı written; destined; written examination
yazılım software
yazım spelling, orthography
yazın literature; in summer
yazışma correspondence
yazışmak to correspond
yazıt inscription
yazlık summer resort
yazma writing; manuscript; handwritten
yazmak to write
yazman secretary, clerk
yedek spare, extra yedek parça spare
part yedekte *sp.* on the bench ye-
dek(te) çekmek to tow
yedeksubay reserve officer
yedi seven
yedinci seventh
yedişer seven each
yedirmek to cause to eat, to feed
yegâne unique
yeğ better, preferable yeğ tutmak to
prefer
yeğen nephew, niece
yeğlemek to prefer
yeis despair

yek one
yeknesak monotonous
yekpare in one piece
yekûn sum, total
yel wind yel değirmeni windmill yel gibi
fast, quickly yel yeperek in a great
hurry
yele mane
yelek waistcoat, vest
yelken sail yelken açmak to hoist sails
yelkenleri indirmek to lower sails yelkenleri suya indirmek to knuckle under, to sing small
yelkenli sailboat
yelkovan minute-hand (of a clock/-
watch)
yellemek to tan
yellenmek to break wind, to fart
yelpaze fan
yeltenmek to try, to attempt
yem fodder, feed; bait
yemek food; meal; dish, course yemek
borusu esophagus; bugle-call for
food yemek listesi menu yemek seçmek to be choosy in eating yemek yemek to eat
yemek to eat; to spend; to consume yi-
yecekmiş gibi bakmak to glower at yiyip içmek to eat and drink
yemekhane dining hall
yemekli with food
yemeni hand-printed scarf
yemin oath yemin billah etmek to
swear to God yemin etmek to swear,
to take an oath yeminini bozmak to
break one's oath
yeminli under oath
yemiş fruit yemiş vermek to bear fruit
yemişçi fruiterer
yemlemek to feed; to bait
yemlik manger, trough; nose bag, feed
bag; bribe
yemyeşil very green
yen sleeve; cuff
yenge sister-in-law, brother's wife;
aunt-in-law; friend's wife
yengeç crab Yengeç (burcu) Cancer
Yengeç dönencesi Tropic of Cancer
yeni new; recent; newly, recently, just
yeni baştan over again

yeniay new moon, crescent
Yeniçeri Janissary
Yenidünya the New World, America
yenidünya Japanese medlar, loquat
yenik defeated **yenik düşmek** to be defeated
yenilemek to renew
yenileşmek to become new; to be modernized
yenileştirmek to renovate, to renew; to modernize
yenilgi defeat **yenilgiye uğramak** to suffer defeat, to get a beating
yenilik newness, novelty
yenilikçi reformist
yenilmek to be eaten; to lose
yenilmez invincible
yenir edible
yenişmek to beat one another
yeniyetme teenager
yenmek to defeat; to be eaten; to conquer; to beat; to master, to subdue
yepyeni brand-new, crisp
yer place, space; ground, floor; earth; seat; situation; position **yer açmak** to make room for **yer almak** to take part **yer etmek** to leave a mark; to make an impression **yer tutmak** to reserve a place; to occupy a place **yer vermek** to give place to **yerden göğe kadar** very much **yere inmek** to land **yerin dibine geçmek** to feel like 30 cents **yerinde** in its place; appropriate, timely **yerin kulağı var** walls have ears **yerinde saymak** to mark time; to make no progress **yerine** instead of, in place of **yerine geçmek** to replace, to substitute **yerine getirmek** to carry out, to fulfil, to perform **yerine koymak** to replace to substitute; to take sb for **yerini tutmak** to substitute for **yerle bir etmek** to level
yeraltı underground; subsurface **yeraltı geçidi** underground passage
yerbilim geology
yerçekimi gravitation, gravity
yerel local
yerelması Jerusalem artichoke
yerfıstığı peanut
yergi satire

yerinmek to feel sad; to be sorry for, to repent
yerkabuğu crust of the earth
yerleşik established, settled
yerleşme, yerleşim settlement
yerleşmek to settle in; to settle oneself in
yerleştirmek to settle; to place
yerli native; local **yerli malı** domestic good, home product **yerli yerinde** in its proper place **yerli yersiz** in season and out of season
yermek to run down, to disparage, to decry; to satirize
yermeli pejorative
yermerkezli geocentric
yermeşesi wall germander
yersakızı bitumen
yersarsıntısı earthquake
yersel terrestrial
yersiz homeless; out of place, irrelevant, untimely
yersolucanı earthworm
yeryuvarlağı terrestrial globe
yeryüzü the earth's surface, world
yeşermek to green
yeşil green **yeşil biber** green pepper **yeşil ışık** green light
Yeşilay the Green Crescent
yeşilbaş wild duck, mallard
yeşilimsi greenish
yeşillenmek to become green; to get fresh with, to molest
yeşillik greenness; greens; meadow
yeşim jade
yetenek aptitude, ability, gift, capacity
yetenekli talented, gifted, capable
yeteneksiz inefficient, incapable
yeter sufficient, enough
yeterince sufficiently
yeterli adequate, sufficient
yeterlik adequecy, efficiency, proficiency
yetersiz insufficient, inadequate, inefficient
yetersizlik insufficiency, inadequacy, inefficiency
yeti faculty, power
yetim orphan
yetimhane orphanage

yetimlik orphanage
yetinmek to be contented with
yetişkin grown-up, adult
yetişmek to reach, to attain; to catch; to be enough; to be brought up; to grow Yetişin! Help!
yetişmiş grown-up, mature
yetiştirici producer, breeder
yetiştirmek to grow, to raise; to breed; to bring up
yetke authority
yetki authority, power yetki vermek to give power, to authorize
yetkili authorized; competent; authority
yetkin perfect
yetkinlik perfection
yetmek to be enough, to suffice
yetmiş seventy
yetmişinci seventieth
yevmiye daily pay, day's wages
yezit scamp, devil
yığılmak to be heaped up, to bank up, to accumulate; to crowd together; to fall in a faint
yığın heap, pile, mass; lot, set
yığınak ask concentration
yığınla in heaps
yığıntı accumulation, heap
yığışmak to crowd together
yığmak to pile (up), to heap (up)
yıkamak to wash
yıkanmak to be washed; to wash oneself, to have a bath, to bathe
yıkıcı destructive
yıkık fallen down, broken, ruined
yıkılış ruin, fall
yıkılmak to be destroyed; to fall down, to collapse
yıkım ruin; disaster
yıkıntı ruins, debris
yıkmak to destroy, to ruin, to demolish; to overthrow, to subvert
yıl year
yılan snake
yılanbalığı eel
yılancık hek. erysipelas
yılankavi spiral, winding
yılbaşı the New Year
yıldırım thunderbolt, lightning yıldırım çarpmış struck by lightning yıldırım

telgrafı urgent telegram yıldırımla vurulmuşa dönmek to be thunderstruck
yıldırımlık, yıldırımkıran, yıldırımsavar lightning rod
yıldırmak to daunt, to cow
yıldız star; asterisk; ace yıldız falı horoscope yıldızı parlamak to be lucky, boom yıldızları barışmak to get along well with each other
yıldızlı stary; starred
yıldızçiçeği dahlia
yıldızkarayel north-north-west wind
yıldızpoyraz north-north-east wind
yıldızyağmuru meteoric shower
yıldönümü anniversary
yılgı phobia, terror
yılgın daunted, cowed
yılışık obtrusive, saucy, sticky
yılışmak to grin unpleasantly, to behave smarmily
yıllanmak to grow old, to age
yıllarca for years
yıllık annual, yearly; ... years old; yearly salary; yearbook, annual
yılmak to be daunted, to dread
yılmaz undaunted
yıpranmak to wear out; to frazzle, to fray
yıpratıcı exhausting, wearing
yıpratmak to wear out
yırtıcı rapacious, ferocious yırtıcı hayvan beast of prey
yırtık torn, rent; shameless, forward yırtık pırtık in rags
yırtınmak to shout at the top of one's voice; to strain even nerve, to wear oneself out
yırtmaç slit
yırtmak to tear, to rend
yiğit brave, courageous
yiğitçe bravely
yiğitlik bravery, courage yiğitliğe leke sürmemek to save one's face
yine (once) again; nevertheless, still
yineleme repetition
yinelemek to repeat
yirmi twenty yirmi yaş dişi wisdom tooth
yirminci twentieth

yirmişer twenty each
yitik lost
yitirmek to lose
yiv groove; chamfer
yivli grooved;chamfered
yiyecek food
yiyici corrupt, sharp
yobaz fanatic, bigot
yobazlık fanaticism, bigotry
Yoga yoga
yoğun thick, dense; intensive
yoğunlaşmak to become dense
yoğunlaştırmak to condense
yoğunluk density, thickness
yoğurmak to knead
yoğurt yoghurt, yogurt
yok there is/are not; non-existent, absent, lacking **Yok canım!** You don't say! **Yok devenin başı!** Impossible!, Incredible! **yok pahasına** dirt cheap **yok yere** without reason **yok etmek** to annihilate, to destroy, to exterminate, to remove **yok olmak** to disappear, to vanish, to be annihilated
yoklama quiz; roll-call
yoklamak to finger, to grope, to search, to grabble; to try, to test; to examine, to inspect
yokluk absence, non-existence; poverty
yoksa otherwise, if not, or
yoksul poor, needy
yoksullaşmak to grow poor
yoksulluk poverty,neediness
yoksun deprived of, devoid of **yoksun bırakmak** to deprive of
yokuş ascent, slope **yokuş aşağı** downhill **yokuş yukarı** uphill **yokuşa sürmek** to make difficulties
yol road, way, street; method, manner; means, medium; stripe **yol açmak** to open a road; to make way for; to bring about, to give rise to, to cause **yol almak** to advance, to proceed; to get up speed **yol göstermek** to show the way, to guide **yol kesmek** to waylay **yol vermek** to make way for; to dismiss, to discharge **yola çıkmak** to set out, to set off, to start (out) **yola gelmek** to come to reason; to come round **yola getirmek** to chasten, to

bring to reason **yoluna** for the sake of, for **yoluna girmek** to come right **yoluna koymak** to put right **yolunda** all right, well **yolunda gitmek** to go like clockwork **yolunu bulmak** to find a way (out); to make an illicit profit **yolunu kaybetmek** to lose one's way **yolunu şaşırmak** to go astray
yolcu passenger, traveller; goner
yolculuk travel, journey, voyage
yoldaş fellow traveller; companion, friend; comrade
yollamak to send, to dispatch, to forward
yollanmak to be sent; to set off, to advance, to head
yollu having roads; (cloth) striped, stripy; (woman) loose
yolluk travelling expenses; provisions for a journey
yolmak to pluck, to pull out; to tear out, to uproot
yolsuz roadless; unlawful, irregular; flat broke, penniless
yolsuzluk irregularity,malpractice
yoluyla by way of, via; by means of, through; properly, duly
yonca clover, trefoil
yonga chip
yontma chipping, cutting; chipped, cut **yontma taş** dressed stone **yontma taş çağı** paleolithic age
yontmak to chip, to cut
yontulmak to be chipped; to learn manners
yontulmamış uncut; unrefined, rough
yordam agility; method, way
yorga jogtrot
yorgan quilt **yorgan iğnesi** quilting needle
yorgun tired, weary **yorgun argın** dead tired
yorgunluk tiredness, fatigue **yorgunluktan canı çıkmak** to be worn out with fatigue
yormak to tire, to weary
yormak to interpret
yortu Christian feast
yorulmak to get tired, to be tired
yorum comment, commentary; interpre-

tation **yorum yok** No comment!
yorumcu commentator
yorumlamak to comment; to interpret
yosma coquette, vamp
yosun moss
yosunlu mossy
yozlaşmak to degenerate
yön direction; aspect, side **yön vermek** to direct
yönelim inclination; tropism
yönelmek to tend, to incline; to go towards
yöneltmek to direct towards; to aim, to point (at)
yönerge instructions, directive
yönetici administrator, manager; executive, managing
yöneticilik administration
yönetim direction, administration management **yönetim kurulu** board of directors
yönetmek to direct, to administer; to manage, to run
yönetmelik regulations, statutes
yönetmen director
yönlendirmek to direct, to orient
yöntem method
yöntemli methodic, methodical
yöntembilim methodology
yöre environs, vicinity, neighbourhood
yöresel local
yörük nomad
yörünge orbit
yudum sip, gulp, sup
yudumlamak to sip, to sup
yufka thin layer of dough **yufka yürekli** softhearted,tender-hearted
Yugoslav Yugoslav
Yugoslavya Yugoslavia
Yugoslavyalı Yugoslavian
yuha boo, hoot **yuha çekmek** to boo, to hoot
yuhalamak to boo, to hoot
yukarda above; upstairs
yukardaki above; above-mentioned
yukardan from above
yukarı upper part, top; up, upwards, above **yukarı çekmek** to hike up, to hitch up
yulaf oats

yular halter
yumak ball
yummak (eyes) to close; (fist) to clench
yumru lump, bump
yumruk fist; blow
yumruklamak to hit with the fist
yumulmak (eye) to shut, to close; to attack, to fall on, to wade into
yumurcak brat, urchin, kid
yumurta egg **yumurta akı** the white of an egg **yumurta sarısı** yolk
yumurtalık egg-cup; ovary
yumurtlamak to lay eggs; to invent, to blurt out
yumuşacık very soft
yumuşak soft, mild, tender **yumuşak başlı** docile, tractable
yumuşakçalar mollusks
yumuşamak to become soft, to soften; to relent, to mellow
Yunan Greek
Yunanca Greek
Yunanistan Greece
Yunanlı Greek
yunmak to wash oneself
yunusbalığı dolphin, porpoise
yurt native land, country, home; student dormitory, hostel
yurtsever patriotic; patriot
yurtseverlik patriotism
yurtsuz homeless
yurttaş fellow countryman, compatriot citizen
yurttaşlık citizenship **yurttaşlık bilgisi** civics
yusufçuk turtledove; dragonfly
yusyuvarlak very round
yutkunmak to swallow, to gulp
yutmak to swallow
yutturmak to cause to swallow; to sell, to make believe; to fob off on
yuva nest; home; den, lair; day nursery, kindergarten; socket **yuva bozmak** to break up a home **yuva kurmak** to build a nest; to set up a home **yuvasını yapmak** to teach sb a lesson **yuvasını yıkmak** to break up sb's marriage
yuvar corpuscle
yuvarlak round, spherical, globular, cir-

cular; globe, sphere; ball **yuvarlak hesap** even account **yuvarlak sayı** round number

yuvarlaklık roundness

yuvarlamak to roll; to roll up; to gulp down

yuvarlanmak to roll; to roll over, to tumble **yuvarlanıp gitmek** to rub along

yüce high, lofty, exalted

yücelik height, loftiness

yücelmek to become high

yüceltmek to exalt

yük burden, load, cargo, freight **yük hayvanı** pack animal **yükünü tutmak** to feather one's nest **yükünü boşaltmak** to unload, to unship

yüklem predicate

yüklemek to load, to burden; to impute, to attribute

yüklenmek to be loaded; to take upon oneself, to assume

yüklü loaded; pregnant

yüksek high; superior; (voice) loud **yüksek atlama** high jump **yüksek basınç** high pressure **yüksek sesle okumak** to read aloud **yüksekten atmak** to talk big, to boast, to bluster **yüksekten bakmak** to look down upon

yükseklik height, altitude

yüksekokul institution of higher education, college

yükseköğrenim higher education

yükseköğretim higher instruction

yükseliş ascent, rise

yükselmek to go up, to rise, to ascent

yükselteç amplifier

yükseltgen oxidizing; oxidizing agent

yükseltmek to raise, to hoist; to boost, to increase; to elevate, to uplift; to promote, to advance

yüksük thimble

yüküm obligation

yükümlü bound, liable

yükümlülük liability, obligation

yün wool; woollen

yünlü woollen, woolly

yürek heart; courage, guts **yürek istemek** to take a lot of nerve **yüreği ağzına gelmek** to have one's heart in

one's mouth **yüreği kabarmak** to feel nauseated **yüreğine inmek** to be struck with great fear **yürekler acısı** heartbreaking

yüreklendirmek to hearten, to encourage

yürekli plucky, brave

yüreksiz faint-hearted, cowardly

yürekten sincerely, hearty

yürümek to walk; to succeed, to work **yürüyen merdiven** moving stairs, escalator *Al.*

yürürlük validity **yürürlüğe girmek** to come into force **yürürlükte olmak** to be in force **yürürlüğe konulmak** to be put into effect **yürürlüğe koymak** to bring into force

yürütme carrying out, execution **yürütme gücü** executive power **yürütme kurulu** executive council

yürütmek to cause to walk; to carry out, to execute; *argo.* to walk off with, to pilfer, to filch

yürüyüş march, walk

yüz face; surface; impudence, cheek **yüz bulmak** to be spoilt by **yüz bulunca astar ister** if you give him an inch, he will take a mile **yüz çevirmek** to turn away from **yüz göz olmak** to be too familiar with **yüz kızartıcı** dishonourable, shameful **yüz suyu hürmetine** out of respect to, for the sake of **yüz tutmak** to tend, to begin **yüz vermek** to countenance, to spoil, to indulge **yüz vermemek** to keep sb at arm's length, to give sb the cold shoulder **yüz yüze gelmek** to come face to face with, to meet **yüze çıkmak** to come to the surface; to show up, to manifest itself **yüze gülmek** to feign friendship **yüzü gülmek** to be happy **yüzü kızarmak** to blush, to flush **yüzü olmamak** not to dare, not to have the face to **yüzünden düşen bin parça olmak** to pull a long face **yüzüne gözüne bulaştırmak** to make a bungle of, to bollix up **Yüzünü gören cennetlik** You're a sight for sore eyes **yüzüne gülmek** to feign friendship **yüzüne karşı** to sb's face **yüzü-**

nü buruşturmak to make a sour face
yüzünü güldürmek to make happy
yüz hundred
yüzbaşı captain
yüzde percentage yüzde on ten per cent yüzde yüz a hundred per cent; definitely
yüzdelik percentage, commission
yüzdürmek to sail, to float
yüzer floating yüzer havuz floating dock
yüzer hundred each
yüzergezer amphibious
yüzey surface
yüzeysel superficial, shallow
yüzgeç fin
yüzkarası disgrace, black sheep
yüzlemek to rub sb's nose in it, to rub in it
yüzlerce hundreds of
yüzleşmek to be confronted with one another
yüzleştirmek to confront
yüzme swim, swimming yüzme havuzu swimming pool yüzmeye gitmek to go for swimming
yüzmek to skin, to flay
yüzmek to swim; to float
yüznumara lavatory, toilet
yüzölçümü mat. area
yüzsüz cheeky, brassy, impudent
yüzsüzce cheekily
yüzsüzlük impudence yüzsüzlüğe vurmak to brazen it out
yüzücü swimmer
yüzük ring yüzüğü geri çevirmek to break off an engagement
yüzükoyun prone, face downwards yüzükoyun yatmak to lie face downwards
yüzükparmağı ring finger
yüzüncü hundredth yüzüncü yıldönümü centenary
yüzünden because of, due to
yüzüstü face downwards yüzüstü bırakmak to leave sb in the lurch, to desert; to leave sth unfinished yüzüstü kalmak to be left unfinished
yüzyıl century
yüzyıllık one hundred years old, centen-

nial

Z

zaaf weakness
zaafiyet weakness
zabıt minutes, record zabıt tutmak to take minutes, to write down a report
zabıta police
zaçyağı sulfuric acid
zafer victory zafer kazanmak to win a victory
zafiyet weakness
zağanos large owl
zağar hound, hunting dog
zahire stock of grain, cereals zahire ambarı granary
zahmet trouble pains, bother zahmet çekmek to suffer trouble zahmet etmek to take pains, to trouble zahmet vermek to trouble, to inconvenience zahmete sokmak to put sb to trouble
zahmetli troublesome, painful
zahmetsiz easy
zahmetsizce easily
zakkum oleander
zalim cruel; tyrant
zalimlik cruelty
zam addition, rise, Aİ. raise
zaman time; period, epoch; dilb. tense zaman kazanmak to gain time, to buy time zaman öldürmek to kill time zaman zaman from time to time, occasionally zamana uymak to keep up with the times zamanında at the right time
zamanaşımı huk. prescription
zamanla in the course of time
zamanlama timing
zamanlamak to time
zamanlı timely
zamansız untimely
zamazingo gadget, thingumabob; arg. mistress, kept woman
zambak lily
zamir pronoun

zamk gum, glue
zamklamak to gum
zampara woman chaser, womanizer, lecher
zamparalık running after women **zamparalık etmek** to run after women, to womanize
zan supposition, surmise; suspicion
zanaat craft, trade
zanaatçı craftsman
zangırdamak to rattle, to clatter
zangırtı rattle
zangır zangır rattlingly **zangır zangır titremek** to tremble like an aspen leaf
zangoç verger
zannetmek to think, to suppose
zapt restraining; seizure; conquest **zapt etmek** to hold back, to restrain; to seize; to conquer
zar membrane, film
zar dice **zar atmak** to throw dice
zarafet elegance, grace
zarar damage, harm, injury **zarar etmek** to lose money; to make a loss **zarar görmek** to be damaged **zarar vermek** to damage, to harm, to injure **zararı yok!** Never mind! **zararına satmak** to sell at loss
zararlı harmful **zararlı çıkmak** to end up a loser
zararsız harmless
zarf envelope; *dilb.jjjjvö* adverb
zarflamak to put into an envelope
zarfında during, within
zargana garfish, garpike
zarif elegant, graceful
zariflik elegance
zarkanatlılar hymenoptera
zart zurt bluster **zart zurt etmek** to bluster
zaruret necessity; poverty **zaruret halinde** in case of necessity
zaruri necessary
zar zor hardly, barely
zat person individual **zatı âlileri** your exalted person
zaten, zati as a matter of fact; besides, already
zatürree *hek* pneumonia
zavallı poor, miserable

zayıf weak, feeble; thin
zayıflamak to grow weak; to become thin
zayıflık weakness, thinness
zayi lost **zayi etmek** to lose **zayi olmak** to be lost
zayiat losses, casualties **zayiat vermek** to suffer casualties
zebani demon (of hell)
zebella huge man, strapper
zebra zebra
Zebur the Psalms of David
zedelemek to bruise, to contuse
zefir zephyr
zehir poison
zehirlemek to poison
zehirli poisonous
zehirsiz non-poisonous
zekâ intelligence
zekât alms
zeki intelligent, clever, shrewd
zelzele earthquake
zemberek spring
zemheri coldest time in winter
zemin ground; background **zemin katı** ground floor
zencefil ginger
zenci negro
zengin rich, wealthy; productive, rich, fertile
zenginleşmek to become rich
zenginlik riches, wealth; richness
zeplin zeppelin
zerdali wild apricot
Zerdüşt Zoroaster
zerk injection **zerk etmek** to inject
zerre atom, particle, bit **zerre kadar** in the slightest degree
zerrin jonquil
zerzevat vegetables
zerzevatçı vegetable seller
zevk pleasure, delight, fun **zevk almak** to enjoy, to find pleasure in **zevk için** for fun **zevk vermek** to give pleasure **zevkini çıkarmak** to enjoy sth to the full **zevkten dört köşe olmak** to be as happy as lark, to be as happy as Larry
zevklenmek to take pleasure; to make fun of

zevkli enjoyable, tasteful
zevksiz tasteless; unpleasant, boring, dull
zevzek silly, talkative
zevzeklik boring chatter, silly behaviour
zeytin olive
zeytinlik olive grove
zeytinyağı olive oil
zıbarmak to die; to sleep
zıbın wadded jacket for a baby
zıkkım poison
zıkkımlanmak to stuff oneself with, to eat
zılgıt dressing down, scolding zılgıt yemek to be told off, to be dressed down
zımba punch
zımbalamak to punch
zımbırdatmak to swang, to strum
zımbırtı twang; thingamabob, thingy, doohickey
zımnen indirectly, implicitly
zımpara emery zımpara kâğıdı emery paper, sandpaper
zımparalamak to sandpaper, to emery
zındık atheist
zıngırdamak to rattle, to clatter
zıngırtı rattling noise, rattle
zınk diye suddenly, with a jolt zınk diye durmak to come to an abrupt stop
zıpçıktı parvenu, upstart
zıpır cracked, loony, wild
zıpkın harpoon
zıpkınlamak to harpoon
zıplamak to jump, to bounce, to hop
zıpzıp marble
zırdeli raving mad
zırh armour
zırhlı armoured
zırıldamak to clatter continuously, to grumble; to weep continuously, to blubber
zırıltı continuous clatter; squabble, wrangle
zırlamak to bawl, to weep, to blubber
zırnık yellow arsenic, arpiment; the smallest bit zırnık (bile) koklatmamak not to give (even) a smallest bit
zırt pırt at any time whatsoever
zırva foolish talk, nonsense, bunkum, bullshit
zırvalamak to talk nonsense
zıt contrary, opposite zıttına gitmek to rile
zıtlık contrariness
zıvana tenon zıvanadan çıkmak to fly into a rage zıvanadan çıkarmak to infuriate
zibidi oddly dressed; crazy, screwy
zifaf entering the nuptial chamber zifaf gecesi wedding night zifaf odası nuptial chamber
zifir deposit in a pipe stem; dark
zifiri pitch-black zifiri karanlık pitch-dark
zifos splash of mud zifos atmak to slander, to spatter
zift pitch
ziftlemek to pitch
ziftli coated with pitch
zihin mind, intelligence; memory zihni karışmak to be confused zihnini bulandırmak to make one suspicious zihnini karıştırmak to confuse zihnini kurcalamak to strain one's mind, to worry zihnini bir şeyle bozmak to be obsessed by zihinde tutmak to bear in mind zihin yormak to rack one's brains zihin yorgunluğu mental fatigue
zihinsel mental
zihnen mentally
zihniyet mentality
zikzak zigzag zikzak yapmak to zigzag
zikzaklı zigzagging
zil bell
zilzurna blind drunk
zimmet debt zimmetine geçirmek to embezzle, to peculate
zina adultery
zincir chain zincire vurmak to chain
zincirleme successive zincirleme kaza pileup
zindan dungeon
zinde active, alive, energetic
zira because, for
ziraat agriculture
zirai agricultural
zirkon zircon
zirve summit, top, peak

zirzop crazy, loony, screwy
ziyade more, much; excessive **ziyade olsun** Thank you!
ziyadesiyle largely, excessively
ziyafet feast banquet **ziyafet vermek** to give a feast
ziyan loss, damage, harm **ziyan etmek** to waste **ziyanı yok** Never mind!
ziyaret visit **ziyaret etmek** to visit
ziyaretçi visitor
ziynet ornament
Zodyak zodiac
zom dead drunk, blotto
zonklamak to throb
zoolog zoologist
zooloji zoology
zor difficult, hard; difficulty; obligation, compulsion; force, strength; barely, hardly **zor gelmek** to be difficult for **zor kullanmak** to use force **zora gelememek** to be unable to withstand hardship **zora koşmak** to raise difficulties **zoru zoruna** with great difficulty **zorun ne?** What's the matter with you? What do you want? **zorunda kalmak** to have to, to be obliged to
zoraki forced
zoralım confiscation
zorba violent, despotic; extortioner, bully, bruiser
zorbalık bullying, bruising **zorbalık etmek** to bully

zorbalıkla high-handedly
zorbela with great difficulty
zorla by force **zorla almak** to usurp **zorla girmek** to break in **Zorla güzellik olmaz** No good can be achieved by force
zorlamak to force; to compel, to coerce, to oblige
zorlaşmak to grow difficult
zorlayıcı coercive, compelling
zorlu powerful, forceful; difficult, hard
zorluk difficulty
zorlukla with difficulty
zorunlu necessary, obligatory
zorunluk necessity, obligation
zulmetmek to oppress, to tyrannize
zulüm persecution, cruelty, tyranny
zücaciye glassware
züğürt penniless, broke **züğürt tesellisi** cold comfort
züğürtleşmek to become penniless
züğürtlük pennilessness
zührevi venereal **zührevi hastalıklar** venereal diseases
zülüf sidelock, earlock
zümre group, party, class
Zümrüdüanka phoenix
zümrüt emerald
züppe fop, dandy
züppelik foppishness, snobbery
zürafa giraffe
zürriyet progeny, offspring

English - Turkish
İngilizce - Türkçe

SÖZLÜĞÜN KULLANIMI

Girişler:

Madde başı sözcükler *temel giriş* olarak adlandırılır. Bu girişlerin altında yer alan türevler, deyimler ve deyişler *yan giriş*i oluşturur.

forest /'forist/ a. orman
  forester ormancı
  forestry ormancılık

guard /ga:d/ e. korumak; beklemek ...
  on guard nöbette, tetikte
  keep guard nöbet beklemek

Okunuşlar:

Bütün temel girişlerin sesletimi (telaffuz) verilmiş, yerden kazanmak amacıyla yan girişlerinki verilmemiştir.

forest /'forist/ a. orman
  forester ormancı
  forestry ormancılık

Aşağıda abecesel sırayla bir liste halinde verilen sonekler yardımıyla türev niteliğindeki bu yan girişlerin okunuşları kolayca öğrenilebilir. Buna göre, sözgelimi, **-er** soneki /ı/, **-ry** soneki /ri/ olarak okunduğuna göre, yukarıdaki yan girişlerin sesletimi şöyle olur:

forest /'forist/ a. orman
  forester /'foristı/ ormancı
  forestry /'foristri/ ormancılık

Bir türevin sesletimi temel girişin sesletiminden ayrı ise, bu ayrılık belirtilmiştir:

microscope /'maykrıskoup/ a. mikroskop
  microscopic /-'skopik/ mikroskobik

mortal /'mo:tl/ s. ölümlü
  mortality /-'telıti/ ölümlülük

Bu sözlükte okura kolaylık olması düşüncesiyle, uluslararası sesçil abece ya da başka bir yöntem yerine, söz konusu sese en yakın sesi gösteren bir Türk harfi kullanılmıştır. Aşağıda, koyu bir tonla verilen bu harflerin sağında yerini tuttuğu uluslararası sesçil abecenin harfi, altında ise bu sesin tanımı verilmiştir.

/ı/ - /ə/

Ağız Türkçe'deki /ı/ sesini çıkarmak için açıldığından biraz daha fazla açılarak /ı/ denirse bu ses çıkartılmış olur.

Örn: **about** /ı'baut/, **banana** /bı'na:nı/, **butter** /'batı/

/e/ - /ae/

Ağız /a/ demek için açılmışken /e/ sesi çıkarılırsa bu ses elde edilmiş olur.

Örn: **bad** /bed/, **cat** /ket/, **sat** /set/

/ö:/ - /ə:/

Yukarıdaki /ı/ sesinin uzun biçimi olan bu ses Türkçe'deki uzun /ö/ sesine çok yakındır.

Örn: **urge** /ö:c/, **bird** /bö:d/, **fur** /fö:/

/o/ - /ɔ/

Ağız /a/ demek için açılmışken /o/ sesi çıkarılırsa bu ses elde edilmiş olur.

Örn: **on** /on/, **dog** /dog/, **want** /wont/

/t/ - /θ/

Dilin ucu, üst dişlerin uç kısmına hafifçe dokunur durumdan ayrılırken /t/ denecek olursa bu ses çıkarılmış olur.

Örn: **thing** /ting/, **method** /'metıd/, **tooth** /tu:t/

/d/ - /δ/

Dilin ucu üst dişlerin uç kısmına hafifçe dokunur durumdan ayrılırken /d/ denecek olursa bu ses çıkarılmış olur.

Örn: **this** /dis/, **father** /'fa:dı/, **smooth** /smu:d/

Bunlara ekleyeceğimiz Türkçe'de olmayan bir ses de /w/ sesidir. Uluslararası sesçil abecede de aynı biçimde gösterilen bu ses, /duvak/ ve /duvar/'daki gibi dudakları yuvarlayarak söylenen /v/ sesine benzer.

:

Ünlüleri izleyen üst üste iki nokta (:), o sesin uzun okunacağını gösterir.

Örneğin: **car** /ka:/'daki /a:/ sesi, "ağlamak" ve "talim" sözcüklerindeki /a/ gibi biraz uzun okunur.

Sözcük Türleri :

Bütün temel girişlerin, dilbilgisel açıdan hangi sözcük türüne ait olduğu sözcüğün sesletiminden hemen sonra kullanılan kısaltmalarla belirtilmiştir. Türev niteliğindeki yan girişlerin sözcük türleri verilmemiş olmasına rağmen bunları Türkçe karşılıklarından ya da kullanılan soneklerinden kolayca anlamak olanaklıdır.

BAŞLICA SONEKLER

-able	/-ıbıl/	-er	/-ı/
-age	/-ic/	-ery	/-(ı)ri/
-al	/-(ı)l/	-ese	/-i:z/
-an	/-(ı)n/	-esque	/-esk/
-ance	/-(ı)ns/	-ess	/-ıs,-is,-es/
-ant	/-(ı)nt/	-ette	/-et/
-arian	/-eırıin/	-fic	/-fik/
-ary	/-(ı)ri/	-fold	/-fould/
-ate	/-ıt, it/	-form	/-fo:m/
-ation	/-eyşın/	-ful	/-fıl/
-ative	/-ıtiv/	-gamy	/-gımi/
-ator	/-eytı/	-gon	/-gın,-gon/
-cide	/-sayd/	-gram	/-grem/
-cracy	/-krısi/	-graph	/-gra:f/
-crat	/-kret/	-hood	/-hud/
-cy	/-(ı)si/	-ial	/-iıl,-l/
-d	/-d,-t,-id/	-ially	/-iıli,-li/
-dom	/-dım/	-ian	/-iın,-n/
-ed	/-d,-t,-id/	-(i)ana	/-(i)anı/
-ee	/-i:/	-ible	/-ıbıl/
-eer	/-iı/	-ic	/-ik/
-en	/-(ı)n/	-ical	/-ikıl/
-ence	/-(ı)ns/	-ically	/-ikli/
-ics	/-iks/	-ly	/-li/
-(i)fy	/-(i)fay/	-man	/-mın,-men/
-ing	/-ing/	-mania	/-meyniı/
-ise	/-ayz/	-maniac	/-meyniek/
-ish	/-iş/	-ment	/-mınt/
-ism	/-izm/	-most	/-moust/
-ist	/-ist/	-ness	/-nıs/
-ite	/-ayt/	-oid	/-oyd/
-ition	/-işın/	-or	/-ı/
-itis	/-aytis/	-ory	/-ıri/
-ity	/-ıti/	-ous	/-ıs/
-ive	/-iv/	-ry	/-ri/
-ize	/-ayz/	-ship	/-şip/
-less	/-lıs/	-sion	/-şın/
-lessly	/-lısli/	-some	/-sım/
-lessness	/-lısnıs/	-tion	/-şın/
-let	/-lıt/	-tude	/-tyu:d/
-like	/-layk/	-ure	/-yuı/
-ling	/-ling/	-ward	/-wıd/
-logue	/-log/	-wise	/-wayz/
-logy	/-lıci/	-y	/-i/

A

a /ı, ey/ (ünlü seslerden önce an /ın, en/ olur.) (herhangi) bir, bir; her
abacus /'ebıkıs/a. hesap cetveli, sayı boncuğu
abandon /ı'bendın/ e. terk etmek, bırakmak
abase /ı'beys/ e. küçük düşürmek, aşağılamak
abashed /ı'beşt/ s. şaşırmış; utanmış
abate /ı'beyt/ e. (rüzgâr, fırtına, ağrı) azalmak, hafiflemek
abbey /'ebi/a. manastır
abbreviate /ı'bri:vieyt/ e. kısaltmak **abbreviation** kısaltma
abdicate /'ebdikeyt/ e. vazgeçmek, çekilmek
abdomen /'ebdımın/a. karın
abduct /eb'dakt/ e. (birini) zorla kaçırmak
aberration /ebı'reyşın/a. doğru yoldan ayrılma, sapkınlık
abet /ı'bet/ e. (suça) katılmak
abhor /ıbho:/ e. nefret etmek, tiksinmek **abhorrence** nefret **abhorrent** nefret verici
abide /ı'bayd/ e. katlanmak, çekmek, tahammül etmek **abiding** sonsuz, ebedi
ability /ı'biliti/a. yetenek, beceri
ablative /'eblıtiv/a, dilb. ismin -den hali, çıkma durumu
ablaze /ı'bleyz/ s. tutuşmuş, yanan
able /eybıl/ s. yetenekli, becerikli **be able to** -ebilmek, **able-bodied** sağlıklı, sağlam
ablution /ı'blu:şın/a. aptes
abnormal /eb'no:mıl/ s. anormal, olağandışı **abnormality** anormallik
aboard /ı'bo:d/ ilg, be. gemide, gemiye; uçakta, uçağa, trende, trene
abolish /ı'boliş/ e. yürürlükten kaldır-

mak, durdurmak
abolition /ebı'lişın/ a. yürürlükten kaldırma
A-bomb /'eybom/a. atom bombası
abominable /ı'bominıbıl/ s. iğrenç, tiksindirici; kon. berbat, rezil
abort /ı'bo:t/ e. çocuk düşürmek **abortion** çocuk düşürme; düşük **abortive** başarısız
about /ı'baut/ ilg. hakkında; aşağı yukarı, yaklaşık; şurada burada, şuraya buraya; çevresinde, çevresine; yakın(-lar)da **be about to** -mek üzere olmak **What/how about ...** -e ne dersin?, ya ...?, -den ne haber?
above /ı'bav/ be. yukarıda, yukarı; ☆ ilg. üstünde, üstünden; -den yüksek, -den üstün; -den çok ☆ s. sözü edilen, yukarıdaki **above all** her şeyden önce **above mentioned** yukarıda sözü geçen **over and above** -den başka, -nin yanı sıra
abrasion /ı'breyjın/ a. aşınma, aşındırma
abrasive /ı'breysiv/ s. aşındırıcı, törpüleyici
abreast /ı'brest/ be. bir hizada, yan yana
abridge /ı'bric/ e. kısaltmak, özetlemek **abridgement** kısaltma, özet
abroad /ı'bro:d/ be. yurtdışında, yurtdışına
abrupt /ı'brapt/ s. ani, beklenmedik; (davranış, söz) kaba
abscess /'ebses/a. çıban, apse, irinşiş
abscond /ıb'skond/ e. gizlice kaçıp gitmek, sıvışmak
absence /'ebsıns/ a. yokluk, bulunmayış
absent /'ebsınt/ s. yok, bulunmayan **absent-minded** dalgın
absentee /ebsınti:/a. (işe) gelmeyen kişi
absolute /'ebsılu:t/ s. tam, eksiksiz; kesin, mutlak, salt **absolutely** tümüyle; kesinlikle
absolve /ıb'zolv/ e. bağışlamak, kurtarmak
absorb /ıb'so:b/ e. emmek, içine çekmek, soğurmak **absorbent** emici, so-

ğurucu **absorbing** sürükleyici **absorption** emme, içine çekme, soğurma

abstain /ıb'steyn/ e. uzak durmak, kaçınmak

abstinence /'ebstinıns/ a. uzak durma, kaçınma

abstract /'ebstrekt/ s. soyut, kuramsal ☆ a. özet ☆ e. çıkarmak, ayırmak, çekmek

absurd /ıb'sö:d, ıb'zö:d/ s. saçma, anlamsız

abundance /ı'bandıns/ a. bolluk **abundant** bol, çok

abuse /ı'byu:z/ e. kötüye kullanmak

abusive /ı'byu:siv/ s. küfürbaz, ağzı bozuk

abysmal /ı'bizmıl/ s. berbat, çok kötü

abyss /ı'bis/ a. cehennem çukuru

acacia /ı'keyşı/ a. akasya

academic /eki'demik/ s. akademik

academy /ı'kedımi/ a. akademi

accelerate /ık'selıreyt/ e. hızlandırmak; hızlanmak **acceleration** hızlandırma; fiz. ivme **accelerator** gaz pedalı

accent /'eksınt/ a. vurgu; şive, ağız

accept /ık'sept/ e. kabul etmek, almak; razı olmak **acceptable** kabul edilebilir; uygun, makul **acceptance** kabul, onama

access /'ekses/ a. giriş, yol; hek. nöbet **accessible** elde edilebilir, ulaşılabilir

accessory /ık'sesıri/ a. aksesuar; eklenti; yardımcı, suçortağı

accident /'eksidınt/ a. kaza; rastlantı **by accident** kazara, tesadüfen **accidental** tesadüfi **accidentally** tesadüfen, rasgele

acclaim /ı'kleym/ e. alkışlamak

acclimatize /ı'klaymıtayz/ e. yeni bir iklime/ortama alışmak/alıştırmak

accommodate /ı'komıdeyt/ e. barındırmak, yerleştirmek **accommodation** kalacak yer, yatacak yer

accompany /ı'kampıni/ e. eşlik etmek **accompaniment** eşlik

accomplice /ı'kamplis/ a. suçortağı, yardakçı

accomplish /ı'kampliş/ e. başarmak, becermek, üstesinden gelmek **accomplished** becerikli, hünerli **accom**-

plishment yerine getirme, yapma; başarı

according /ı'ko:ding/ **according to** -e göre **accordingly** bu nedenle

accordion /ı'ko:diın/ müz. akordeon

account /ı'kaunt/ a. hesap; rapor, açıklama; neden **on account of** yüzünden **on no account** hiçbir surette, asla **accountant** muhasebeci, sayman

accumulate /ı'kyu:myuleyt/ e. toplamak, biriktirmek; çoğalmak, yığılmak **accumulation** birikim; birikinti, yığın

accurate /'ekyırıt/ s. kesin, doğru, yanlışsız, tam

accuse /ı'kyu:z/ e. suçlamak **the accused** sanık(lar) **accusation** /ekyu'zeyşın/ suçlama

accustom /ı'kastım/ e. alıştırmak **accustomed** her zamanki **be accustomed to** -e alışmak

ace /eys/ a. as, birli, bey; as, yıldız

ache /eyk/ a. ağrı ☆ e. ağrımak

achieve /ı'çi:v/ e. başarmak; ulaşmak, elde etmek **achievement** başarma, yapma; başarı

acid /'esid/ s. ekşi; dokunaklı, acı ☆ a. asit, ekşi

acknowledge /ık'nolic/ e. kabul etmek, onaylamak; varlığını kabul etmek, tanımak; aldığını bildirmek; teşekkür etmek **acknowledgement** onaylama, kabul; aldığını bildirme

acne /'ekni/ a. sivilce

acorn /'eyko:n/ a, bitk. meşe palamudu

acoustic /ı'ku:stik/ s. akustik **acoustics** akustik, yankıbilim; akustik, yankılanım

acquaint /ı'kweynt/ e. bilgi vermek, bildirmek; göstermek, öğretmek **be acquainted (with)** (-den) haberi olmak, bilmek; (ile) tanışmak **acquaintance** tanıdık, tanış, haber; bilgi

acquire /ı'kwayı/ e. edinmek, kazanmak

acquisition /ekwi'zişın/ a. kazanma, edinme; kazanç, edinti

acquit /ı'kwit/ e. temize çıkarmak, aklamak **acquittal** beraat, aklanma

acre /'eykı/ a. İngiliz dönümü (0.404 hektar)

acrid /'ekrid/ s. acı, keskin, sert
acrobat /'ekrıbet/ a. akrobat, cambaz
acrobatic akrobatik acrobatics cambazlık, akrobasi
acronym /'ekrınim/ a. sözcüklerin baş harflerinden oluşan sözcük
across /ı'kros/ be, ilg. bir yanından öteki yanına; öbür yanında, karşısında; çaprazlama(sına)
act /ekt/ e. hareket etmek, davranmak; (rol) oynamak; etki yapmak, etkilemek ☆ a. hareket, iş; (oyun) perde; gösteri, numara acting oyunculuk; vekil, yerine bakan
action /'ekşın/ a. hareket, iş, eylem; etkinlik, işleme, etki; dava out of action bozuk, işlemez
activate /'ektiveyt/ e. harekete geçirmek, etkili hale getirmek
active /'ektiv/ s. çalışan, işleyen; faal, çalışkan; etkin, canlı; dilb. etken
activity /'ektiviti/ a. faaliyet, etkinlik
actor /'ektı/ a. erkek oyuncu, aktör
actress /'ektris/ a. kadın oyuncu, aktris
actual /'ekçuıl/ s. gerçek; şimdiki, bugünkü, güncel in actual fact aslında, gerçekte actually gerçekten, hakikaten; aslında
acumen /'ekyumın/ a. çabuk kavrayış
acupuncture /'ekyupankçı/ a. akupunktur
acute /'ıkyu:t/ s. zeki; şiddetli, ağır; (hastalık) ağır, ivegen
ad /ed/ a, kon. ilan, reklam
Adam's apple /edımz'epıl/ a, anat. gırtlak çıkıntısı
adapt /ı'dept/ e. uyarlamak adaptable kolayca uyum sağlayan adaptation /edep'teyşın/ adaptasyon, uyarlama adapter, adaptor adaptör
add /ed/ e. eklemek, katmak; toplamak
adder /'edı/ a, hayb. engerek
addict /'ıdikt/ be addicted to alışmak, bağımlı olmak
addict /'edikt/ a. uyuşturucu tutkunu; kon. bir şeye çok düşkün kimse
addition /ı'dişın/ a. ekleme, katma; zam mat. toplama in addition (to) bundan başka, ayrıca additional kat-

ma, ek
address /ı'dres/ a. adres; söylev ☆ e. hitap etmek, söz yöneltmek; adres yazmak
adequate /'edikwit/ s. elverişli, yeterli
adhere /ıd'hiı/ e. yapışmak; bağlı kalmak adherence (to) bağlılık, sadakat adherent taraftar, üye
adhesive /ıd'hi:siv/ s. yapışkan ☆ a. yapıştırıcı
adjacent /ı'ceysınt/ s. bitişik, komşu
adjective /'eciktiv/ a, dilb. sıfat, niteleç
adjourn /ı'cö:n/ e. ertelemek
adjust /ı'cast/ e. ayarlamak; uyum göstermek adjustment ayarlama; uyum
administer /ıd'ministı/ e. idare etmek, yönetmek; vermek, sağlamak; uygulamak administration idare, yönetim; hükümet administrative yönetimsel, idari administrator idareci, yönetici
admirable /'edmırıbıl/ s. çok güzel, beğenilen
admiral /'edmırıl/ a. amiral
admiration /edmi'reyşın/ a. takdir, hayranlık
admire /ıd'mayı/ e. hayran olmak, bayılmak admirer hayran
admission /ıd'mişın/ a. giriş; giriş ücreti; kabul
admit /ıd'mit/ e. kabul etmek, itiraf etmek admittance giriş; kabul
adolescence /edı'lesıns/ a. ergenlik adolescent ergen
adopt /ı'dopt/ e. kabul etmek, benimsemek; evlat edinmek
adore /ı'do:/ e. taparcasına sevmek; kon. bayılmak, bitmek adorable çok güzel adoration /edı'reyşın/ tapma
adorn /ı'do:n/ e. süslemek
adult /'edalt/ a, s. yetişkin, ergin
adultery /ı'daltıri/ a. eşini aldatma, zina
advance /ıd'va:ns/ e. ilerlemek; ilerletmek; yükselmek; yükseltmek ☆ a. ilerleme, yükselme; avans, öndelik in advance önceden advanced ileri advancement ilerleme
advantage /ıd'va:ntic/ a. yarar, çıkar; üstünlük advantageous avantajlı
advent /'edvent/ a. geliş; baş gösterme

adventure /ɪd'vençı/ a. serüven; tehlike, riziko adventurer maceracı serüven düşkünü

adverb /'edvö:b/ a, dilb. zarf, belirteç

adversary /'edvısıri/ a. düşman, hasım

adverse /'edvö:s/ s. ters, karşı, karşıt, zıt

advertise /'edvıtayz/ e. ilan etmek; ilan vermek

advertisement /ɪd'vö:tismınt/ a. reklam, ilan

advice /ɪd'vays/ a. öğüt, tavsiye; bilgi

advise /ɪd'vayz/ e. tavsiye etmek, öğüt vermek, haberdar etmek, uyarmak adviser danışman advisable makul, mantıklı

advocate /'edvıkit/ a. savunucu, yanlı; avukat ☆ e. desteklemek, savunmak

aerial /'eıriıl/ a. anten

aerodrome /'eırıdroum/ a. havaalanı

aerodynamics /eırouday'nemiks/ a. aerodinamik (bilimi)

aeroplane /'eırıpleyn/ a. uçak

aerosol /'eırısol/ a. aerosol

aesthetic(al) /i:s'tetik(ıl)/ s. estetik aesthetics estetik

afar /ı'fa:/ be. uzak, uzakta from afar uzaktan

affair /ı'feı/ a. mesele, iş; cinsel ilişki

affect /ı'fekt/ e. etkilemek; gibi görünmek, taslamak affectation yapmacık, gösteriş, özenti

affection /ı'fekşın/ a. sevgi; düşkünlük, eğilim affectioned sevecen

affiliate /ı'filieyt/ e. (with/to) birleştirmek, üye etmek; birleşmek, üye olmak

affinity /ı'finiti/ a. hoşlanma, eğilim; benzerlik

affirm /ı'fö:m/ e. doğrulamak; bildirmek, söylemek affirmation /efı'meyşın/ doğrulama affirmative (yanıt) olumlu

affix /ı'fiks/ a. önek, sonek

afford /ı'fo:d/ e. (parası, zamanı, olanağı) olmak, gücü yetmek

afraid /ı'freyd/ s. korkmuş be afraid of -den korkmak I'm afraid ... maalesef, üzgünüm ki

after /'a:ftı/ be, bağ, ilg. -den sonra; peşinden, ardından; -e karşın; -e göre, uyan; -dığı için, yüzünden; tarzında, biçeminde after all her şeye rağmen, yine de after you! Önce siz buyurun!

aftermath /'a:ftımet/ a. sonuç

afternoon /a:ftı'nu:n/ a. öğleden sonra in the afternoon öğleden sonra this afternoon bugün öğleden sonra

afterwards /'a:ftıwıdz/ be. sonradan, sonra

again /ı'gen/ be. tekrar, yine; bundan başka, ayrıca again and again sık sık, ikide bir, habire now and again arada sırada, bazen once/yet again bir kez daha

against /ı'genst/ ilg. -e karşı; -ye, -ya

age /eyc/ a. yaş; devir, dönem; kon. çok uzun süre ☆ e. yaşlanmak, kocalmak old age yaşlılık the Middle Ages Ortaçağ under age reşit olmayan, küçük aged ... yaşında; yaşlı middle aged orta yaşlı

agency /'eycınsi/ a. acenta, büro

agenda /ı'cendı/ a. gündem

agent /'eycınt/ a. acenta, temsilci

aggravate /'egrıveyt/ e. ağırlaştırmak; kon. kızdırmak, sinir etmek

aggregate /'egrigit/ s. toplam, toplu, bütün

aggression /ı'greşın/ a. saldırı

aggressive /ı'gresiv/ a. saldırgan

agility /ı'ciliti/ a. çeviklik, atiklik

agitate /'eciteyt/ e. çalkalamak, sallamak agitation heyecan, acı, üzüntü; kışkırtma, tahrik agitator tahrikçi; karıştırıcı

ago /ı'gou/ be. önce

agony /'egıni/ a. şiddetli acı

agree /ı'gri:/ e. aynı fikirde olmak, katılmak; kabul etmek, razı olmak; uyuşmak agreeable hoş, tatlı agreement anlaşma, uyuşma; ittifak

agriculture /'egrikalçı/ a. tarım agricultural tarımsal

aground /ı'graund/ be. karaya oturmuş, batık

ahead /ı'hed/ s, be. önde, ileride; ileri, ileriye straight ahead dosdoğru

aid /eyd/ a. yardım ☆ e. yardım et-

mek **first aid** ilkyardım
aim /eym/ e. nişan almak, yöneltmek; niyetinde olmak; amaçlamak ☆ a. amaç; nişan, hedef **aimless** amaçsız, başıboş **aimlessly** amaçsızca
air /eı/ a. hava ☆ e. havalandırmak **air base** hava üssü **air brake** havalı fren **air conditioning** havalandırma **aircraft** uçak **airfield** havaalanı, iniş pisti **airfoil** uçak kanadı **air force** hava kuvvetleri **air hostess** hostes **airless** havasız, boğucu **airline** havayolu **airmail** uçak postası; havayolu taşımacılığı **airplane** AI. uçak **airport** havalimanı **air raid** askeri hava saldırısı **airways** hava yolları **by air** uçakla **in the open air** açık havada, açıkta **on the air** radyoda, dinlenebilir
airs /eız/ a. hava, gösteriş **give oneself airs** havalara girmek **put on airs** havalara girmek, hava atmak
aisle /ayl/ a. (sinema, uçak, vb.'de) ara yol, geçit
ajar /ı'ca:/ s. (kapı) yarı açık, aralık
akin /ı'kin/ s. benzer
alarm /ı'la:m/ a. alarm, korku **alarm clock** çalar saat
alas /ı'les/ ünl. vah! yazık! tüh!
albino /el'bi:nou/ a. akşın, çapar
album /'elbım/ a. albüm; uzunçalar
alcohol /'elkıhol/ a. alkol; alkollü içki **alcoholic** alkollü; ayyaş **alcoholism** alkolizm
ale /eyl/ a. (açık renkli) bir tür bira
alert /ı'lö:t/ s. tetik, uyanık ☆ a. alarm
algebra /'elcibrı/ a, mat. cebir
alias /'eyliıs/ a. takma ad ☆ be. diğer adıyla
alibi /'elibay/ a. suçun işlenmesi sırasında başka yerde olduğunu kanıtlama
alien /'eyliın/ a. yabancı
align /ı'layn/ e. sıraya dizmek, aynı hizaya getirmek
alignment /ı'laynmınt/ a. sıraya dizme, düzenleme
alike /ı'layk/ s. aynı, benzer
alimentary /eli'mentırı/ s. beslenmeyle ilgili, besleyici **alimentary canal** sindi-

rim borusu
alimony /'elimını/ a. nafaka
alive /ı'layv/ s. canlı, hareketli
alkali /'elkılay/ a, kim. alkali
all /o:l/ s. bütün, tüm; her ☆ a. her şey ☆ adl. hep, hepsi; herkes; her şey ☆ be. bütün bütün, tümüyle **above all** her şeyden önce, hepsinden çok **after all** her şeye karşın, yine de **at all** hiç, hiç de **for all** -e karşın **in all** topu topu, hepsi **not at all** bir şey değil, estağfurullah **all alone** yapayalnız, tek başına, yardımsız **all night** bütün gece süren/açık **all of a sudden** birdenbire, ansızın **all over** he tarafına, her tarafında; her tarafı(nı); her tarafta **all right** peki, tamam; fena değil, idare eder; (sağlığına) bir şey olmamış, iyi
Allah /'elı/ a. Allah
allegiance /ı'li:cıns/ a. bağlılık, sadakat
allegory /'eligırı/ a. kinaye
allergy /'elıcı/ a. alerji; kon. hoşlanmama, sevmeme **allergic** alerjik; kon. nefret eden
alley /'eli/ a. dar yol
alliance /ı'layıns/ a. müttefik, bağlaşık
allied /'elayd/ s. müttefik, bağlaşık
alligator /'eligeytı/ a, hayb. timsah
alliteration /ılitı'reyşın/ a, yaz. aliterasyon
allocate /'elıkeyt/ e. paylaştırmak, dağıtmak **allocation** tahsisat, ödenek
allow /ı'lau/ e. izin vermek, bırakmak; kabul etmek; ayırmak, tahsis etmek; olanak vermek **allowable** izin verilebilir **allowance** izin; gelir, aylık, haftalık; indirim
alloy /'eloy/ a. metal alaşımı
allude /ı'lu:d/ e. dolaylı olarak anlatmak **allusion** dokundurma, ima, kinaye
ally /'ı'lay/ a. müttefik ülke; dost, arkadaş ☆ e. birleşmek; birleştirmek
almanac /'o:lmınek/ a. almanak, yıllık
almighty /o:l'mayti/ s. her şeye kadir **the Almighty** Allah
almond /'a:mınd/ a. badem
almost /'o:lmoust/ be. hemen hemen, neredeyse

alms /a:mz/ *a.* sadaka
alone /ı'loun/ *s, be.* tek başına, yalnız **let/leave sb/sth alone** kendi haline bırakmak, ilişmemek
along /ı'long/ *be.* ileri, ileriye, yanına, yanında, birlikte ☆ *ilg.* boyunca; süresince **all along** öteden beri **along with** ile birlikte **be along** gelmek, varmak **get along (with)** geçinmek, anlaşmak; gitmek
alongside /ılong'sayd/ *be.* yan yana ☆ *ilg.* yanına, yanında
aloof /ı'lu:f/ *be.* ayrı, uzakta
aloud /ı'laud/ *be.* yüksek sesle
alphabet /'elfıbet/ *a.* alfabe, abece **alphabetical** alfabetik, abecesel
already /o:l'redi/ *be.* daha şimdiden, çoktan, bile, zaten
alright /o:l'rayt/ *be, bkz.* **all right**
also /'o:lsou/ *be.* de, da, dahi; hem de, üstelik
altar /'o:ltı/ *a.* sunak, kurban taşı
alter /'o:ltı/ *e.* değişmek; değiştirmek **alteration** değiştirme; değişiklik
alternate /o:l'tö:nit/ *s.* (iki şey için) değişimli, bir o, bir öteki ☆ *e.* birbirini ardından gelmek, birbirini izlemek; sıra ile yapmak **on alternate days** günaşırı **alternate angles** ters açılar **alternating current** dalgalı akım
alternative /o:l'tö:nıtiv/ *s.* yerine geçebilen, başka ☆ *a.* ikisinden birisini seçme; seçenek
although /o:l'dou/ *bağ.* her ne kadar, ise de, -e karşın
altitude /'eltityu:d/ *a.* (denizden) yükseklik; *coğ.* yükselti, rakım
alto /'eltou/ *a, müz.* alto
altogether /o:ltı'gedı/ *be.* tamamen, tümüyle, bütün bütün
aluminium /elyu'minıım/ *a, kim.* alüminyum
always /'o:lwiz, 'o:lweyz/ *be.* her zaman, daima, hep
am /ım, em/ **'to be'** fiilinin **'I'** ile kullanılan biçimi: -im, -ım, -um
amateur /'emıtı/ *a.* amatör; deneyimsiz
amaze /ı'meyz/ *e.* şaşırtmak, hayrete düşürmek **be amazed** şaşırmak, hay-

rete düşmek **amazing** şaşırtıcı **amazement** şaşkınlık
ambassador /em'besıdı/ *a.* büyükelçi
amber /'embı/ *a.* kehribar; kehribar rengi
ambience /'embiıns/ *a.* bir yerin havası, ambiyans
ambiguity /embi'gyu:iti/ *a.* anlam belirsizliği; çokanlamlı söz **ambiguous** belirsiz, muğlak; çok anlamlı
ambition /em'bişın/ *a.* hırs, tutku **ambitious** hırslı, tutkulu; çok istekli
ambulance /'embyulıns/ *a.* cankurtaran
ambush /'embuş/ *e.* pusuya düşürmek, tuzak kurmak ☆ *a.* pusu, tuzak
amen /a:'men/ *ünl.* amin
amenable /ı'mi:nıbıl/ *s.* uysal; uyumlu
amendment /ı'mendmınt/ *a.* değişiklik, düzeltme
amends /ı'mendz/ *a:* **make amends** tazmin etmek, telafi etmek
amenity /ı'mi:niti/ *a.* rahatlık, konfor
amiable /'eymiıbıl/ *s.* sevimli, samimi
amicable /'emikıbıl/ *s.* dostça
amid /ı'mid/ *ilg.* ortasında, arasında
ammonia /ı'mouniı/ *a.* amonyak
ammunition /emyu'nişın/ *a.* cephane, mühimmat
amnesia /em'ni:ziı/ *a, hek.* bellek yitimi
amnesty /'emnısti/ *a.* genel af
amoeba /ı'mi:bı/ *a, biy.* amip
amount /ı'maunt/ *a.* miktar; tutar, toplam **amount to** olmak, etmek, varmak
ampere /'empiı/ *a, fiz.* amper
amphibian /em'fibiın/ *a, hayb.* ikiyaşayışlı, amfibi; *ask.* yüzergezer, amfibi **amphibious** ikiyaşayışlı; yüzergezer, yüzergezer
amphitheatre /'emfitiıtı/ *a.* amfiteatr
ample /'empıl/ *s.* bol, yeterli; geniş, büyük
amplify /'emplifay/ *e.* ayrıntılarını anlatmak, genişletmek; yükseltmek, güçlendirmek **amplification** büyütme, genişletme; geniş açıklama; yükseltme, güçlendirme **amplifier** *tek.* amplifikatör, yükselteç
amplitude /'emplityu:d/ *a, fiz.* genlik

ampoule /'empu:l/ *a, hek.* ampul
amulet /'emyulit/ *a.* muska, nazarlık
amuse /ı'myu:z/ *e.* eğlendirmek; güldürmek **amusement** eğlence; gülünçlük **amusing** eğlenceli, güldürücü
an /ın, en/ *bkz.* a
anaemia /ı'ni:mıı/ *a, hek.* kansızlık
anaesthesia /enis'ti:zıı/ *a.* anestezi, uyuşturum, duyum yitimi **anaesthetic** /enis'tetik/ uyuşturucu **anaesthetist** /ı'ni:stitist/ narkozcu **anaesthetize** /ı'ni:stitayz/ anestezi yapmak, narkoz vermek
anagram /'enıgrem/ *a.* **(name-mean** gibi) çevrik sözcük, evirmece
analogue /'enılog/ *a.* bir şeyin benzeri olan şey
analogy /ı'nelıci/ *a.* benzerlik; örnekseme **analogous** /ı'nelıgıs/ **(to/with)** benzer; yakın, paralel
analyse /'enılayz/ *e.* analiz etmek, çözümlemek
analysis /ı'nelisis/ *a.* çözümleme, analiz etme, analiz, tahlil **analyst** /'enılist/ analiz yapan kimse, analist *AI.* psikanalist, ruhçözümcü **analytical** /enı'litikıl/ çözümsel, analitik
anarchy /'enıki/ *a.* anarşi, kargaşa **anarchic** anarşik **anarchism** anarşizm, başsızlık, kargaşacılık
anatomy /ı'netimi/ *a.* anatomi, yapıbilim **anatomical** anatomik, yapısal
ancestor /'ensıstı/ *a.* ata, ced **ancestral** atalara ilişkin, atadan kalma **ancestry** soy; atalar
anchor /'enkı/ *a.* gemi demiri, çapa; güven veren şey/kimse, güven kaynağı ☆ *e.* demir atmak
anchovy /'ençvi/ *a, hayb.* hamsi
ancient /'eynşınt/ *s.* çok eski; Romalılar ve Yunanlılar zamanına ait
ancillary /en'silıri/ *s, tek.* yardımcı, yan
and /ınd, ın, end/ *bağ.* ve; ile **and so on** vesaire
anecdote /'enikdout/ *a.* eğlendirici kısa öykü, fıkra, anekdot
angel /'eyncıl/ *a.* melek; melek gibi kimse
angelica /en'celikı/ *a, bitk.* melekotu
anger /'engı/ *a.* öfke, kızgınlık, hiddet ☆ *e.* kızdırmak
angle /'engıl/ *a.* açı; köşe; bakım; görüş, açı; olta ☆ *e.* oltayla balık tutmak **acute angle** dar açı **right angle** dik açı **obtuse angle** geniş açı
Anglican /'englikın/ *a, s* Anglikan
angry /'engri/ *s.* kızgın, öfkeli; dargın
anguish /'engwiş/ *a.* şiddetli acı
angular /'engyulı/ *s.* köşeli, açılı, sivri; bir deri bir kemik, sıska
animal /'enimıl/ *a.* hayvan ☆ *s.* hayvani
animate /'enimeyt/ *e.* canlandırmak, diriltmek **animated cartoon** çizgi film **animation** animasyon, çizgi film; canlılık
animosity /enı'mositi/ *a.* kin, düşmanlık
ankle /'enkıl/ *a.* ayak bileği, topuk
annex /ı'neks/ *e.* kendi topraklarına katmak; eklemek, katmak, ilave etmek **annexation** müsadere, ilhak
annexe /'eneks/ *a.* ek yapı, müştemilat, ek
annihilate /ı'nayıleyt/ *e.* yok etmek **annihilation** yok etme
anniversary /eni'vö:sırı/ *a.* yıldönümü
annotate /'enıteyt/ *e.* notlar koymak, çıkmalar yapmak
announce /ı'nauns/ *e.* bildirmek, duyurmak **announcement** bildiri, duyuru **announcer** spiker
annoy /ı'noy/ *e.* rahatsız etmek, canını sıkmak, bıktırmak; kızdırmak, sinirlendirmek **annoyance** rahatsızlık, sıkıntı; baş belası, dert **annoying** can sıkıcı
annual /'enyuıl/ *s.* yıllık, yılda bir kez
annuity /ı'nyu:iti/ *a.* yıllık maaş, yıllık emekli maaşı
annul /ı'nal/ *e.* yürürlükten kaldırmak, bozmak **annulment** yürürlükten kaldırma
anode /'enoud/ *a.* anot, artıuç
anomalous /ı'nomılıs/ *s.* normal olmayan, anormal
anonymous /ı'nonimıs/ *s.* anonim, adsız, yazarı bilinmeyen
anorak /'enırek/ *a.* anorak, parka
another /ı'nadı/ *s.* başka bir; başka, diğer, öbür ☆ *adl.* bir başkası; başka-

answer

260

sı; diğeri, öbürü **one after another** birbiri arkasından **one another** birbirini
answer /'a:nsı/ *a.* yanıt, cevap, karşılık; (problem) cevap, sonuç ☆ *e.* yanıtlamak, karşılık vermek; (çağrılınca) gitmek, gelmek; (kapıya/telefona) bakmak **answer back** terbiyesizce cevap vermek **answerable (to, for)** sorumlu
ant /ent/ *a, hayb.* karınca
antagonism /en'tegınizım/ *a.* düşmanlık, kin **antagonist** hasım, rakip
antagonize /en'tegınayz/ *e.* düşman etmek
antarctic /en'ta:ktik/ *s.* Güney Kutbuyla ilgili **the Antarctic** Güney Kutbu ve çevresi, Antarktika
antecedent /enti'si:dınt/ *s.* önceki ☆ *a.* bir olaydan önce olan olay; *dilb.* adılın yerini tutan ad, öncül
antelope /'entiloup/ *a, hayb.* antilop
antenatal /enti'neytıl/ *s.* doğum öncesi
antenna /en'tenı/ *a.* anten; *hayb.* duyarga, anten
anthem /'entım/ *a.* şükran ve sevinç duası **national anthem** ulusal marş
anther /'entı/ *a, bitk.* başçık
anthology /en'tolıci/ *a.* antoloji, seçki
anthracite /'entrısayt/ *a.* antrasit, parlak kömür
anthrax /'entreks/ *a, hek.* şarbon, karakabarcık
anthropoid /'entrıpoyd/ *s.* insan benzeri, insansı, maymunsu
anthropology /entrı'polıci/ *a.* antropoloji, insanbilim
anthropologist /entrı'polıcist/ *a.* antropolog, insanbilimci
antiaircraft /'entieıkra:ft/ *a, s.* uçaksavar
antibiotic /entibay'otik/ *a.* antibiyotik
antibody /'entibodi/ *a.* antikor
anticipate /en'tisipeyt/ *e.* ummak, beklemek; olacağını sezmek **anticipation** umma, bekleme
anticlockwise /enti'klokwayz/ *be, s.* saat yelkovanının döndüğü yönün tersine
antics /'entiks/ *a.* maskaralık, soytarılık
antidote /'entidout/ *a.* panzehir, karşıtağı

antifreeze /'entifri:z/ *a.* antifriz, donmaönler
antigen /'enticın/ *a, biy.* antijen, bağıştıran
antipathy /en'tipıti/ *a.* hoşlanmama, beğenmeme, antipati, sevmezlik
antipathetic /entipı'tetik/ *s.* hoşlanılmayan, sevilmeyen, antipatik, sevimsiz
antiquarian /enti'kweıriın/ *a.* antika meraklısı, antikacı
antiquated /'entikweytid/ *s.* eski, modası geçmiş; yaşı ilerlemiş
antique /en'ti:k/ *s.* antik; eski moda; antika ☆ *a.* Eski Yunan ya da Roma sanatı; antika eşya **antiquity** /en'tikwiti/ eski çağlar, eski yapıtlar
antiseptic /enti'septik/ *a, s.* antiseptik, arıtkan
antitank /'entitenk/ *a, s, ask.* tanksavar
antithesis /en'titisis/ *a.* tezat, karşıtlık; antitez, karşısav
antonym /'entınim/ *a, dilb.* zıt/karşıt anlamlı sözcük
anus /'enıs/ *a, anat.* anüs, makat
anvil /'envil/ *a.* örs kemiği
anxiety /eng'zayıti/ *a.* tasa, kaygı, korku; şiddetli istek
anxious /'enkşıs/ *s.* kaygılı, üzüntülü; çok istekli
any /'eni/ *s.* herhangi bir, bir; hiç; bazı **any longer** artık, daha fazla **any more** daha çok, biraz daha **in any case** ne olursa olsun
anybody /'enibodi/ *adl.* (bir) kimse, birisi; herkes; hiç kimse **anybody else** başka birisi
anyhow /'enihau/ *adl.* hiçbir şekilde, ne olursa olsun; her şeye karşın, yine de; nasıl olsa, nasılsa
anyone /'eniwan/ *adl, bkz.* **anybody**
anything /'eniting/ *adl.* (herhangi) bir şey; hiçbir şey; her şey **anything else** başka bir şey **like anything** *kon.* deli gibi, çılgınca
anyway /'eniwey/ *be, kon.* ne olursa olsun, yine de; neyse, her neyse
anywhere /'eniweı/ *be.* her/hiç bir yerde/yere; neresi/nereye/nerede olursa olsun

aorta /ey'o:tı/ a. aort, ana atardamar

apart /ı'pa:t/ be. ayrı; bir yana, bir yanda **apart from** -den başka **joking apart** şaka bir yana

apartheid /ı'pa:theyt/ ırk ayrımı

apartment /ı'pa:tmınt/ a, Aİ. daire; İİ. lüks daire, apartman dairesi **apartment house** Aİ. apartman

apathy /'epıti/ a. duygusuzluk, duyarsızlık; ilgisizlik

apathetic duygusuz, duyarsız; ilgisiz

ape /eyp/ a. (kuyruksuz) maymun

aperitif /ıperi'ti:f/ a. aperitif, açar

aperture /'epıçı/ a. açık, delik, boşluk

apex /'eypeks/ a. (ç. **apexes, apices** /'eypisi:z/) zirve, doruk; uç, tepe

aphrodisiac /efrı'diziek/ a, s. afrodizyak

apiculture /'eypikalçı/ a. arıcılık

apiece /ı'pi:s/ be. her biri(ne); adam başı; tanesi

apish /'eypiş/ s. maymun gibi; salak

apocalypse /ı'pokılips/ a. kıyamet, dünyanın sonu

apologetic /ıpolı'cetik/ s. özür dileyen; savunan, savunmalı

apologize /ı'polıcayz/ e. özür dilemek

apology /ı'polıci/ a. özür; mazeret

apoplexy /'epıpleksi/ a, hek. felç, inme; beyin kanaması

apostle /ı'posıl/ a. 12 havariden biri

apostrophe /ı'postrıfi/ a, dilb. kesme işareti, apostrof

appal /ı'po:l/ e. şoka uğratmak, sarsmak **appalling** korkunç; kon. berbat, rezil

apparatus /epı'reytıs/ a. alet, cihaz

apparent /ı'perınt/ s. açık, ortada; görünüşte olan **apparently** görünüşe göre, anlaşılan

appeal /ı'pi:l/ e. yalvarmak, daha yüksek bir mahkemeye başvurmak; hoşuna gitmek, sarmak ☆ a. yalvarış, yakarış; cazibe, çekicilik, alımlılık; daha yüksek bir mahkemeye başvurma **appealing** çekici, hoş, tatlı; duygulandırıcı, dokunaklı

appear /ı'piı/ e. görünmek, ortaya çıkmak; varmak, gelmek; gibi görünmek **appearance** ortaya çıkma, göze gö-

rünme; görünüş, görünüm

appease /ı'pi:z/ e. gidermek, dindirmek, yatıştırmak; tatmin etmek

append /ı'pend/ e. eklemek

appendicitis /ıpendi'saytis/ a, hek. apandisit, ekbağırsak yangısı

appendix /ı'pendiks/ a. (ç. -es, -dices /disi:z/) ek, ek bölüm; apandis, körbağırsak

appetite /'epitayt/ a. iştah, arzu; şehvet

appetizer /'epitayzı/ a. iştah açıcı yiyecek, meze, çerez **appetizing** iştah açıcı

applaud /ı'plo:d/ e. alkışlamak; beğenmek, onaylamak, benimsemek

applause /ı'plo:z/ a. alkış

apple /'epıl/ a. elma

appliance /ı'playıns/ a. alet, araç

applicable /ı'plikıbıl/ s. uygulanabilir

applicant /'eplikınt/ a. başvuran kişi, aday, istekli

application /epli'keyşın/ a. başvuru; uygulama, uygulamaya koyma; merhem, sürme; ilaç **application form** başvuru formu

apply /ı'play/ e. başvurmak; uygulamak; sürmek, koymak **applied** uygulamalı

appoint /ı'poynt/ e. atamak, tayin etmek; kararlaştırmak, saptamak, belirlemek **appointment** randevu, iş, görev

appraise /ı'preyz/ e. değer biçmek

appreciable /ı'pri:şıbıl/ s. fark edilir, kayda değer

appreciate /ı'pri:şieyt/ e. takdir etmek, değerini bilmek; farkında olmak; değerini arttırmak **appreciation** minnettarlık, teşekkür; takdir, değerlendirme

appreciative /ı'pri:şıtiv/ s. değer bilen; anlayan, beğenen

apprehend /epri'hend/ e. anlamak, kavramak; huk. tutuklamak

apprehension /epri'henşın/ a. anlayış, kavrayış; korku; huk. tutuklama **apprehensive (of)** korkan, endişeli; kuruntulu

apprentice /ı'prentis/ a. çırak ☆ e. çırak olarak vermek **apprenticeship** çıraklık; çıraklık süresi

approach /ı'prouç/ *e.* yaklaşmak; ele almak, ile konuşmak; başvurmak ☆ *a.* yaklaşma, yanaşma; yol, geçit; ele alış biçimi, yaklaşım **approachable** yaklaşabilir, cana yakın, dostça

appropriate /ı'prouprieyt/ *e.* (for) ayırmak, tahsis etmek; kendine mal etmek, kendine ayırmak; çalmak

appropriate /ı'proupriıt/ *s.* uygun

approval /ı'pru:vıl/ *a.* onama, onaylama; uygun bulma, tasvip; resmi izin, onay **on approval** beğenilmediğinde geri verilmek koşuluyla

approve /ı'pru:v/ *e.* onaylamak, onamak, uygun bulmak, tasvip etmek **approvingly** onaylayarak

approximate /ı'proksimit/ *s.* yaklaşık **approximately** yaklaşık olarak

apricot /'eyprikot/ *a.* kayısı; zerdali

April /'eypril/ *a.* nisan **April fool** 1 nisanda aldatılan kimse **April Fools' Day** 1 nisan

apron /'eyprın/ *a.* önlük

apt /ept/ *s.* eğilimli, yatkın; uygun, yerinde; çabuk kavrayan **aptly** uygun bir biçimde, yerinde

aptitude /'eptityu:d/ *a.* yetenek

aqualung /'ekwılang/ *a.* dalgıç oksijen tüpü

aquarium /ı'kweıriım/ *a.* akvaryum

Aquarius /ı'kweıriıs/ *a.* Kova (burcu)

aquatic /ı'kwotik/ *s.* suda yaşayan; suyla ilgili **aquatic sports** su sporları

aqueduct /'ekwidakt/ *a.* sukemeri

arable /'erıbıl/ *s.* tarıma uygun, ekilebilir

arbitrary /'a:bitrıri/ *s.* isteğe bağlı, keyfi

arbitrate /a:bi'treyt/ *e.* (hakem sıfatıyla) karar vermek **arbitration** sorun ya da anlaşmazlığın hakem kararıyla çözümü **arbitrator** yansız aracı, hakem

arbour /'a:bı/ *a.* çardak, gölgelik

arc /a:k/ *a.* kavis, yay

arcade /a:'keyd/ *a.* pasaj, kemeraltı

arch /a:ç/ *a.* kemer altı, pasaj

archaeology /a:ki'olıci/ *a.* arkeoloji, kazıbilim **archaeological** /a:kiı'locikıl/ arkeolojik, kazıbilimsel **archaeologist** arkeolog, kazıbilimci

archaic /a:'keyik/ *s.* modası geçmiş, eski

archbishop /a:ç'bişıp/ *a.* başpiskopos

archer /'a:çı/ *a.* okçu **archery** okçuluk

archipelago /a:ki'pelıgou/ *a.* takımadalar

architect /'a:kitekt/ *a.* mimar ☆ *e.* tasarlamak, planlamak, yapmak

architectural /a:ki'tekçırıl/ *s.* mimari

architecture /'a:kitekçı/ *a.* mimarlık, mimari

archives /'a:kayvz/ *a.* resmi evrak, arşiv

archway /'a:çwey/ *a.* üst kemerli geçit

arctic /'a:ktik/ *s.* Kuzey Kutbuyla ilgili **the Arctic** Kuzey Kutbu

ardent /'a:dınt/ *s.* ateşli, coşkun

ardour /'a:dı/ *a.* gayret, istek; heyecan, heves, azim **arduous** güç, yorucu, çetin

are /ı, a:/ *e.* -sin, -iz, -siniz; -dirler

area /'eırıı/ *a.* alan, bölge, yüzölçümü

arena /ı'ri:nı/ *a.* arena, oyun alanı

argue /'a:gyu:/ *e.* tartışmak, atışmak; kanıtlamaya çalışmak; neden olarak göstermek **argue against** karşı çıkmak **argue for** -i savunmak

argument /'a:gyumınt/ *a.* tartışma, münakaşa, anlaşmazlık; tez, kanıt, sav, düşünce **argumentative** /a:gyu'mentıtiv/ tartışmayı seven

aria /'a:rıı/ *a, müz.* arya

arid /'erid/ *s.* kurak, kıraç

Aries /'eıri:z/ *a.* Koç burcu; Koç Takımyıldızı

arise /ı'rayz/ *e.* **arose** /ı'rouz/, **arisen** /ı'rizın/ ortaya çıkmak, ileri gelmek, kaynaklanmak; ayağa kalkmak, doğrulmak

arisen /ı'rizn/ *bkz.* arise

aristocracy /eri'stokrısi/ *a.* soylular sınıfı; aristokrasi

aristocrat /'eristıkret/ *a.* soylu, aristokrat

arithmetic /ı'ritmıtik/ *a, s.* aritmetik; ölçme, sayma, hesap; aritmetiksel

ark /a:k/ *a.* Nuh'un gemisi

arm /a:m/ *a.* kol; giysi/koltuk kolu; güç; otorite; dal, şube **arm in arm** kol kola **at arm's length** kol boyu uzaklıkta **keep sb at arm's length** soğuk davranmak, yüz vermemek

arm /a:m/ e. silahlandırmak, savaşa hazırlamak

armada /a:'madı/ a. donanma, deniz kuvvetleri

armament /'a:mımınt/ a. silahlanma; silahlandırma, donatım, teçhizat; ç. silahlar; ç. silahlı kuvvetler

armchair /'a:mçeı/ a. koltuk

armed /a:md/ s. silahlı **armed forces** silahlı kuvvetler

armistice /'a:mistis/ a. ateşkes

armour /'a:mı/ a. zırh; zırhlı güçler

armoured /'a:mıd/ s. zırhlı **armoured car** zırhlı araba **armoured division** zırhlı tümen

armpit /'a:mpit/ a. koltuk altı

arms /a:mz/ a. silahlar; cephane **arms race** silahlanma yarışı **under arms** silah altında, silahlanmış

army /'a:mi/ a. ordu, kara ordusu; kalabalık, sürü **army corps** kolordu **enter/join the army** askere gitmek, asker olmak

aroma /ı'roumı/ a. güzel koku **aromatic** /erı'metik/ güzel kokulu

arose /ı'rouz/ bkz. **arise**

around /ı'raund/ ilg. çevresine, çevresinde; dolayında, yakınında; sağında solunda, sağına soluna; sıralarında, sularında ☆ be. çevrede, ortalıkta; her yanına, çevresine; ötede beride, öteye beriye; aşağı yukarı, yaklaşık; arkaya, geriye **all around** çepçevre, dört yandan **have been around** çok deneyimli olmak, görmüş geçirmiş olmak **up and around** hastalıktan kalkmış, iyileşmiş

arouse /ı'rauz/ e. uyandırmak; canlandırmak, harekete geçirmek

arrange /ı'reync/ e. dizmek, düzeltmek; düzenlemek, ayarlamak; kararlaştırmak, saptamak; halletmek, çözümlemek **arrangement** düzenleme; anlaşma; müz. uyarlama, düzenleme; ç. hazırlık

array /ı'rey/ a. sıra, düzen; sergi ☆ e. sıraya koymak, dizmek

arrears /ı'riız/ s. gecikmiş borç; gecikmiş ve yapılmayı bekleyen iş

arrest /ı'rest/ e. tutuklamak; yakala-

mak; durdurmak, önlemek ☆ a. tutuklama

arrival /ı'rayvıl/ a. geliş, varış; gelen

arrive /ı'rayv/ e. varmak, gelmek; dönmek; (zaman) gelmek, gelip çatmak

arrogant /'erıgınt/ s. kendini beğenmiş, küstah **arrogance** kibir, kendini beğenme

arrow /'erou/ a. ok; ok işareti

arsenal /'a:sınıl/ a. cephanelik

arsenic /'a:sınik/ a, kim. arsenik

arson /'a:sın/ a. kundakçılık, yangın çıkarma **arsonist** kundakçı

art /a:t/ a. sanat; sanat ürünü; deneyim; ustalık; ç. güzel sanatlar **Bachelor of Arts** Edebiyat Fakültesi mezunu **fine arts** güzel sanatlar **liberal arts** toplumsal bilimler **Master of Arts** lisansüstü öğretim görmüş Edebiyat Fakültesi mezunu **work of art** sanat yapıtı

artery /'a:tıri/ a, hek. atardamar, arter; merkez yol **arterial** atardamarla ilgili

artesian well /a:ti:ziın'wel/ a. artezyen kuyusu

artful /'a:tfıl/ s. aldatıcı, hileci; akıllıca düşünülmüş, beceriyle yapılmış

arthritis /a:'traytis/ a, hek. kireçlenme, eklem yangısı

artichoke /'a:tiçouk/ a. enginar **Jerusalem artichoke** yerelması

article /'a:tikıl/ a. eşya, parça; makale, yazı; madde, fıkra; dilb. artikel, tanımlık **leading article** başyazı

articulate /a:'tikyulit/ s. açık seçik, anlaşılır; düşünce ve duygularını rahatça dile getirebilen; eklemli, boğumlu ☆ e. açık seçik konuşmak, tane tane söylemek; eklemlerle birleştirmek **articulation** dilb. boğumlanma; eklem

artificial /a:ti'fişıl/ s. yapay, suni; yapmacık, yalancı **artificial insemination** suni döllenme **artificial respiration** suni solunum

artillery /a:'tilıri/ a, ask. topçu sınıfı, toplar

artisan /a:ti'zen/ a. zanaatçı, esnaf

artist /'a:tist/ a. sanatçı, artist; ressam **artistic** sanatsal, artistik

artless /'a:tlis/ s. doğal; içten, yalın

as /ız, ez/ *be.* aynı derecede, o kadar; örneğin, sözgelimi ☆ *bağ.* -dığı sıra, -ken; -den dolayı; -dığı halde; -e karşın; -dığı gibi; gibi ☆ *ilg.* olarak; gibi **as a rule** genellikle **as ... as ... ...** kadar **as follows** aşağıdaki gibi **as for** -e gelince **as if/though** -miş gibi, sanki **as is** olduğu gibi **as it is** gerçekte, hakikatte **as it were** bir yerde, bir bakıma **as long as** sürece, -dikçe, -mek koşuluyla, yeterki **as regards** ... konusunda; ... ile ilgili olarak; -e göre **as to** konusunda, -le ilgili olarak; -e göre **as usual** her zamanki gibi **as well** de, da **as yet** şu ana kadar, şimdiye dek **so as** için, amacıyla, -cek biçimde **such as** gibi

asbestos /es'bestıs/ *a, kim.* asbest, amyant

ascend /ı'send/ *e.* yükselmek; tırmanmak, çıkmak

ascendancy /ı'sendınsi/ *a.* üstünlük, nüfuz, güç

ascent /ı'sent/ *a.* yükselme, tırmanma; yol, yokuş, yamaç

ascertain /esı'teyn/ *e.* doğrusunu bulmak, araştırmak

ascetic /ı'setik/ *s.* kendini her türlü dünyevi zevkten/işten soyutlamış

ascribe /ı'skrayb/ *e.* (to) atfetmek, yüklemek, -e yormak

ash /eş/ *a.* kül; dişbudak ağacı

ashes /'eşiz/ *a.* yakılmış cesedin külleri

ashamed /ı'şeymd/ *s.* utanmış, mahcup

ashen /'eşın/ *s.* kül renginde; küllü

ashore /ı'şo:/ *be.* kıyıda, kıyıya, karada, karaya

ashtray /'eştrey/ *a.* kül tablası

Asia /ey'şı/ *a* Asya **Asian, Asiatic** Asya ile ilgili, Asyalı

aside /ı'sayd/ *be.* bir yana; kenara, yana

asinine /'esinayn/ *s.* aptalca, saçma

ask /a:sk/ *e.* sormak; rica etmek, istemek; çağırmak, davet etmek **ask for** istemek, aramak

askew /ı'skyu:/ *be.* yanlamasına

asleep /ı'sli:p/ *s.* uykuda; uyumakta

asparagus /ı'sperıgıs/ *a, bitk.* kuşkonmaz

aspect /'espekt/ *a.* görünüş; bakım, yön

asperity /e'speriti/ *a.* sertlik, haşinlik; kötü söz, davranış

aspersion /ı'spö:şın/ *a.* iftira, kara çalma

asphalt /'esfelt/ *a.* asfalt ☆ *e.* asfaltlamak

aspiration /espi'reyşın/ *a.* tutku, istek

aspire /ı'spayı/ *e.* çabalarını bir amaca yöneltmek, çok istemek

ass /es/ *a.* eşek; *kon.* aptal, salak

assail /ı'seyl/ *e.* saldırmak **assailant** saldırgan

assassinate /ı'sesineyt/ *e.* suikast yapmak **assassin** suikastçı **assassination** suikast, cinayet

assault /ı'so:lt/ *e.* vahşice saldırmak ☆ *a.* ani saldırı, tecavüz

assemble /ı'sembıl/ *e.* toplamak; toplanmak; kurmak, takmak

assembly /ı'sembli/ *a.* toplantı, montaj **assembly line** montaj hattı

assert /ı'sö:t/ *e.* ileri sürmek, savunmak **assertion** iddia, açıklama, bildiri **assertive** iddialı, hakkını savunan

assess /ı'ses/ *e.* değer biçmek; vergi koymak

asset /'eset/ *a.* servet, varlık, mal; *ç.* aktif, alacak **assets and liabilities** alacak verecek **real assets** taşınmaz mallar

assiduous /ı'sidyuıs/ *s.* çalışkan

assign /ı'sayn/ *e.* ayırmak, vermek, atamak, seçmek **assignment** görev; ayırma

assimilate /ı'simileyt/ *e.* özümlemek, sindirmek **assimilation** özümseme, sindirim

assist /ı'sist/ *e.* yardım etmek; desteklemek **assistance** yardım, destek **assistant** yardımcı, asistan

assize /ı'sayz/ *a.* yargılama, muhakeme

associate /ı'souşieyt/ *e.* birleştirmek; birleşmek; arkadaşlık etmek *a.* ortak çalışma arkadaşı

association /ısousi'eyşın/ *a.* dernek, kurum, birlik; çağrışım **association foot-**

ball futbol

assort /ı'so:t/ e. sınıflandırmak, ayırmak **assorted** çeşitli **assortment** tasnif, sınıflandırma; cins, çeşit

assume /ı'syu:m/ e. varsaymak, farz etmek; (iş, görev) üzerine almak, üstlenmek; almak, takınmak **assumption** /ı'sampşın/ üzerine alma; farz, zan; azamet, kibir

assurance /ı'şuırıns/ a. güven, özgüveni; teminat, güvence; sigorta

assure /ı'şuı/ e. inandırmaya çalışmak; güven vermek, garanti etmek; inandırmak; sigortalamak **assured** kendine güvenen, kendinden emin

asterisk /'estırisk/ yıldız imi

asteroid /'estıroyd/ a. Mars ve Jüpiter arasındaki çok küçük gezegenlerden biri

asthma /'esmı/ a, hek. astım **asthmatic** astımlı

astigmatism /ı'stigmıtizım/ a, hek. astigmatizm, astigmatlık

astonish /ı'stoniş/ e. çok şaşırtmak, hayrete düşürmek **be astonished** hayret etmek, çok şaşırmak **astonishing** hayret verici, şaşırtıcı **astonishment** hayret, şaşkınlık

astound /ı'staund/ e. hayretler içinde bırakmak

astray /ı'strey/ s, be. doğru yoldan çıkmış, sapıtmış

astride /ı'strayd/ be. bacakları iki yana açık olarak

astrology /ı'strolıci/ a. astroloji, yıldızbilim **astrologer** yıldızbilimci

astronaut /'estrıno:t/ a. astronot

astronomy /ı'stronımi/ a. astronomi, gökbilim **astronomer** gökbilimci

astronomical /estrı'nomikıl/ s. astronomik, gökbilimsel; çok fazla, aşırı

astute /ı'styu:t/ s. akıllı, cin gibi

asylum /ı'saylım/ a. sığınak, barınak; himaye, koruma **political asylum** siyasi iltica, sığınma

at /ıt; et/ ilg. -de, -da, -e, -a, -ye, -ya

ate /et, eyt/ bkz. eat

atheism /'eytiizım/ a. ateizm, tanrıtanımazlık **atheist** ateist, tanrıtanımaz

athlete /'etli:t/ a. atlet, sporcu

athletic /'et'letik/ s. atletik, atletizmle ilgili; bedence güçlü, atletik

athletics atletizm

atlas /'etlıs/ a. atlas

atmosphere /'etmısfiı/ a. atmosfer, havaküre, gazyuvar; çevre, hava

atmospheric(al) /etmıs'ferik(ıl)/ s. atmosferle ilgili, atmosferik

atom /'etım/ a. atom, öğecik; zerre **atom bomb** atom bombası **atomic** /ı'tomik/ atomik, atomal **atomic energy** atom enerjisi **atomic number** atom sayısı **atomic pile/reactor** nükleer reaktör **atomic weight** atom ağırlığı

atone /ı'toun/ e. gönlünü almak, -i telafi etmek

atrocious /ı'trouşıs/ s. zalim; berbat

attach /ı'teç/ e. bağlamak, iliştirmek, bitiştirmek, takmak; yapıştırmak **attachment** bağ; bağlılık, sevgi

attache /ı'teşey/ a. ataşe

attack /ı'tek/ e. saldırmak, basmak; eleştirmek; çatmak; (işe) girişmek ☆ a. saldırı; nöbet, kriz

attain /ı'teyn/ e. elde etmek, erişmek

attempt /ı'tempt/ e. kalkışmak, girişmek, yeltenmek, çalışmak, denemek ☆ a. girişim, kalkışma; çaba, deneme

attend /ı'tend/ e. bakmak, ilgilenmek; hazır bulunmak, katılmak, gitmek; eşlik etmek **attendance** hazır bulunma, katılma, gitme; eşlik **attendant** yardımcı, hizmetçi; görevli

attention /ı'tenşın/ a. dikkat, özen; bakım, ilgi; ç. iltifat, kur **pay attention** dikkatini vermek, kulak vermek, dinlemek

attentive /ı'tentiv/ s. dikkatli; nazik, kibar

attest /ı'test/ e. ispat etmek, kanıtlamak; tasdik etmek, doğrulamak

attic /'etik/ a. çatı odası, tavan arası

attire /ı'tayı/ e. giydirmek, süslemek, donatmak ☆ a. elbise, üst baş, kıyafet

attitude /'etityu:d/ a. davranış, tutum; duruş, durum; fikir, düşünce

attorney /ı'tö:ni/ a. vekil, yetkili; dava vekili, avukat **attorney general** başsavcı

attract /ı'trekt/ e. cezbetmek, çekmek **attraction** cazibe, çekim; alımlılık, çekicilik, cazibe **attractive** çekici, cazip

attribute /ı'tribyu:t/ e. (to) atfetmek, bağlamak, vermek

attribute /'etribyu:t/ a. özellik, nitelik

aubergine /'oubıji:n/ a, İİ. patlıcan

auburn /'o:bın/ a, s. kestane rengi; (saç) kumral

auction /'o:kşın/ a. mezat, açık artırma ile satış **by auction** açık artırma ile **auctioneer** mezat tellalı

audacious /o:'deyşıs/ s. gözü pek, atılgan; arsız, yüzsüz

audible /'o:dibıl/ s. duyulabilir, işitilir

audience /'o:diıns/ a. dinleyiciler, izleyiciler, seyirciler; resmi görüşme; duruşma

audio /'o:diou/ önek işitme ile ilgili, işitsel **audio-visual** işitsel-görsel

audit /'o:dit/ a. (yıllık) hesap denetimi **auditor** murakıp, denetçi

auditorium /o:di'to:rıım/ a. konferans salonu, konser salonu

augment /o:g'ment/ e. artırmak

August /'o:gıst/ a. ağustos

aunt /a:nt/ a. teyze, hala, yenge **auntie** kon. teyze, hala, yenge

au pair /ou'peı/ a. yaptığı ev işlerine karşılık bir aile yanında kalan kız

aura /'o:rı/ a. hava, gizemli ortam; izlenim **aural** işitsel

auspices /'o:spisiz/ a. yardım, destek

austere /o'stiı/ s. hoşgörüsüz, sert; çetin, zor; yalın, süssüz **austerity** sertlik, güçlük; ciddiyet, katılık; idareli geçinme

authentic /o:'tentik/ s. esas, asıl, doğru, otantik **authenticate** gerçekliğini/doğruluğunu kanıtlamak; belgelemek **authenticity** gerçek olma özelliği, doğruluk

author /'o:tı/ a. yazar; yaratıcı, yapan **authorship** yazarlık

authoritative /o:'toritıtiv/ s. otoriter, sözünü geçirir; yetkili; güvenilir, inanılır

authority /o:'toriti/ a. otorite, yetkili; bilirkişi, uzman

authorize /'o:tırayz/ e. izin vermek; yet-

ki vermek; onaylamak

autobiography /o:tıbay'ogrıfi/ a. özyaşamöyküsü, özgeçmiş

autocracy /o:'tokrısi/ a. otokrasi, saltıkçı yönetim **autocrat** /'o:tıkret/ otokrat, saltıkçı **autocratic** /o:tı'kretik/ zorba

autograph /'o:tıgra:f/ a. (ünlü) birinin imzası ☆ e. (kitap, vb.) imzalamak

automate /'o:tımeyt/ e. otomatikleştirmek, makineleştirmek

automatic /o:tı'metik/ s. otomatik, farkında olmadan yapılan; istenç dışı **automatically** otomatik olarak, kendiliğinden

automation /o:tı'meyşın/ a, tek. otomasyon

automobile /'o:tımıbi:l/ a, Aİ. otomobil, araba

autonomous /o:'tonımıs/s. özerk

autonomy /o:'tonımi/ a. özerklik

autopsy /o:'topsi/ a. otopsi

autumn /'o:tım/ a. sonbahar, güz

auxiliary /o:g'zilyıri/ s, a. yardımcı, yedek **auxiliary verb** dilb. yardımcı fiil

available /ı'veylıbıl/ s. mevcut, elde; işe yarar, kullanılabilir, elde edilebilir **availability** hazır bulunma; işe yararlık; elde edilebilirlik

avalanche /'evıla:nş/ a. çığ

avenge /ı'venc/ e. öcünü almak

avenue /'evinyu:/ a. bulvar, geniş cadde

average /'evıric/ a, s. ortalama, orta ☆ e. ortalamasını almak

averse /ı'vö:s/ s. karşı, muhalif, isteksiz

aversion /ı'vö:şın/ a. nefret, tiksinti

avert /ı'vö:t/ e. başka yöne çevirmek; önlemek

aviary /'eyviiri/ a. kuşhane

aviation /eyvi'eyşın/ a. havacılık

avocado /evı'ka:dou/ a, bitk. avokado, amerikaarmudu

avoid /ı'voyd/ e. uzak durmak, kaçınmak, sakınmak; önüne geçmek, kurtarmak **avoidable** uzak durulabilir, kaçınılabilir

await /ı'weyt/ e. beklemek

awake /ı'weyk/ e. **awoke** /ı'wouk/ uyandırmak, uyanmak ☆ s. uyanık

awaken /ı'weykın/ e. **awoke** /ı'wouk/

uyandırmak, uyanmak
award /ı'wo:d/ e. ödül; hüküm, karar
☆ e. (ödül, vb.) vermek; hükmetmek, verilmesini istemek
aware /ı'weı/ s. farkında, haberdar, bilir **awareness** farkında olma
away /ı'wey/ be. uzağa, uzakta; -den, -dan; deplasmanda ☆ s. uzak, deplasmanda oynanan; başka yerde, yok **far away** çok uzakta **right away** hemen **play away** deplasmanda oynamak **take away** alıp götürmek, kaldırmak
awe /o:/ a. (saygıdan ileri gelen) korku
awesome /'o:sım/ s. korku veren
awful /'o:fıl/ s. korkunç; kon. berbat, rezil **awfully** çok, oldukça
awhile /ı'wayl/ be. kısa bir süre, biraz
awkward /'o:kwıd/ s. kullanımı zor, kullanışsız; uygunsuz; sakar; beceriksiz
awoke /ı'wouk/ bkz. awake
awl /o:l/ a. biz, tığ
axe /eks/ a. balta ☆ e. baltayla budamak; (gider, vb.) azaltmak, kısmak
axiom /'eksiım/ a. aksiyom, belit
axis /'eksis/ a. eksen
axle /'eksıl/ a. dingil, mil
azure /'ejı/ a, s. gök mavisi

B

babble /'bebıl/ e. gevezelik etmek, saçmalamak; mırıldanmak ☆ a. gevezelik, boşboğazlık; mırıltı
babe /beyb/ a. bebek
baboon /bı'bu:n/ a. köpek maymunu
baby /'beybi/ a. bebek; hayvan yavrusu **babyish** çocuksu **baby-sit** çocuk bakıcılığı yapmak **baby-sitter** çocuk bakıcısı
bachelor /'beçılı/ a. bekâr erkek; üniversite mezunu
bacillus /'bı'silıs/ a. basil, çomak bakteri; kon. bakteri
back /bek/ a. arka, sırt; belkemiği; ☆ be. arkaya, geriye; geçmişte, geçmi-

şe; eski yerine, yine; önce ☆ e. desteklemek, arka çıkmak; üzerine para koymak, üzerine oynamak **be back** geri dönmek **behind one's back** arkasından, yokken **get/put sb's back up** gıcık etmek **go back** dönmek **go back on** sözcünden caymak **back down** hatalı olduğunu kabul etmek, boyun eğmek **back out** vazgeçmek, caymak **back up** desteklemek **turn one's back on** sırtını çevirmek **backache** sırt ağrısı, bel ağrısı
backbone /'bekboun/ a. belkemiği, omurga; en büyük destek
backdate /bek'deyt/ e. eski bir tarih atmak
backer /'bekı/ a. destekçi, destek olan kimse
backfire /bek'fayı/ e. (plan, vb.) geri tepmek, olumsuz sonuç vermek
backgammon /'bekgemın/ a. tavla
background /'bekgraund/ a. arka plan; fon, zemin
backing /'beking/ a. destek, yardım
backlash /'bekleş/ a. geri tepme
backlog /'beklog/ a. geciktirilmiş, ihmal edilmiş işler
backmost /'bekmoust/ s. en geri, en arka
backside /'beksayd/ a. arka, kıç
backstage /bek'steyc/ a. perde arkasında ☆ s. perde gerisinde olan
backstroke /'bekstrouk/ a. sırtüstü yüzme
backward /'bekwıd/ s. geriye doğru yapılan; geç öğrenen, kafasız
backwards /'bekwıdz/ be. geriye doğru, arkaya; arka tarafa
backwater /'bekwo:tı/ a. durgun yer
backyard /bek'ya:d/ a. avlu
bacon /'beykın/ a. domuz pastırması
bacteria /bek'tiırıi/ a. bakteriler
bad /bed/ s. kötü; bozuk, çürük; geçersiz; yaramaz; şiddetli, sert; ahlaksız; zararlı; sağlıksız ☆ a. kötü şey, kötülük **bad fortune** şanssızlık, talihsizlik **not (so) bad** fena değil **not too bad** şöyle böyle **be bad of sth** pek iyi bilmemek **badly** kötü; kon. çok
badge /bec/ a. rozet

badger /'becı/ *a, hayb.* porsuk

badminton /'bedmintın/ *a, sp.* tenis benzeri bir oyun, badminton

baffle /'befıl/ *e.* şaşırtmak

bag /beg/ *a.* çanta; torba; ☆ *e.* çantaya/torbaya koymak

baggage /'begic/ *a.* bagaj

bail /beyl/ *a.* kefalet, kefalet ücreti

bailiff /'beylif/ *a.* mübaşir; çiftlik kâhyası; şerif yardımcısı

bait /beyt/ *a.* yem ☆ *e.* (oltaya/tuzağa) yem koymak; kasten kızdırmak

baize /beyz/ *a.* yeşil masa çuhası

bake /beyk/ *e.* fırında pişirmek/pişmek **baker** fırıncı **bakery** fırın

balance /'belıns/ *a.* denge; terazi; bakiye, kalıntı ☆ *e.* dengelemek; karşılaştırmak **balance of payments** ödemeler dengesi **balance sheet** bilanço **balanced** dengeli, aklı başında

balcony /'belkıni/ *a.* balkon

bald /bo:ld/ *s.* kel, dazlak

bale /beyl/ *a.* balya, denk **bale out** paraşütle uçaktan atlamak

baleful /'beylfıl/ *s.* şeytani

balk /bo:k/ *a.* kütük ☆ *e.* engel olmak; anlaşmaya yanaşmamak, duraksamak

ball /bo:l/ *a.* top; küre; yumak; misket; balo **keep the ball rolling** devam etmek, sürdürmek **play ball** *kon.* birlikte çalışmak, imece yapmak

ballad /'belıd/ *a.* türkü; şiirsel öykü

ballast /'belıst/ *a.* safra, ağırlık; balast, kırmataş

ballcock /'bo:lkok/ *a.* (sifon, su deposu, vb.) şamandıra

ballerina /belı'ri:nı/ *a.* balerin

ballet /'beley/ *a.* bale

ballistics /bı'listiks/ *a.* balistik, atış bilimi

balloon /bı'lu:n/ *a.* balon

ballot /'belıt/ *a.* oy pusulası; gizli oylama **ballot box** oy sandığı

ballpoint /'bo:lpoynt/ *a.* tükenmezkalem

ballroom /'bo:lrum/ *a.* dans salonu

balm /ba:m/ *a.* melisa, oğulotu

balsam /'bolsım/ *a.* belesan yağı

bamboo /bem'bu:/ *a, bitk.* bambu

ban /ben/ *e.* yasaklamak ☆ *a.* yasak, yasaklama

banal /bı'na:l/ *s.* adi, bayağı, banal, sıradan

banana /bı'na:nı/ *a.* muz

band /bend/ *a.* bağ, şerit, kayış, bant; *müz.* grup, topluluk

bandage /'bendic/ *a.* sargı ☆ *e.* sarmak, bağlamak

bandit /'bendit/ *a.* haydut

bandy /'bendi/ *s.* çarpık bacaklı ☆ *e.* lafa laf koymak; verip veriştirmek

bane /beyn/ *a.* felaket, kötülük, zarar, ziyan

bang /beng/ *a.* büyük patlama; şiddetli vuruş ☆ *e.* hızla çarpmak, vurmak

banger /'bengı/ *a.* sosis; külüstür araba

bangle /'bengıl/ *a.* bilezik, halka

banish /'beniş/ *e.* sürgün etmek; aklından çıkarmak

banister /'benistı/ *a.* tırabzan

banjo /'bencou/ *a, müz.* banço

bank /benk/ *a.* banka; nehir/göl kıyısı, kenar; yığın, küme; bayır; (oyun) banko **bank account** banka hesabı **bank holiday** resmi tatil **banknote** kâğıt para **bank rate** banka faiz oranı

banker /'benkı/ *a.* bankacı; çeşitli kumar oyunlarında kasa olan kişi, kasa

bankrupt /'benkrapt/ *s, a.* müflis, batkın, iflas etmiş **go bankrupt** iflas etmek **bankruptcy** iflas

banner /'benı/ *a.* bayrak; sancak, pankart

banquet /'benkwit/ *a.* ziyafet, şölen

baptize /'beptayz/ *e.* vaftiz etmek

baptism /'beptizım/ *a.* vaftiz

bar /ba:/ *a.* demir çubuk; engel, bariyer; sırık, çubuk; kalıp; bar ☆ *e.* parmaklıklarla örtmek, kapatmak; hapsetmek; kısıtlamak

barbarian /ba:'beıriın/ *a, s.* barbar, uygarlaşmamış kimse **barbaric** barbar, vahşi **barbarism** barbarlık **barbarity** acımasızlık, vahşilik **barbarous** uygarlaşmamış, kaba, barbar

barbecue /'ba:bikyu:/ *a.* açık hava ızgarası, ızgara; açıkta ızgara yemekleri yendiği toplantı

barbed wire /ba:bd'wayı/ *a.* dikenli tel
barber /'ba:bı/ *a.* berber
bard /ba:d/ *a.* ozan, şair
bare /beı/ *s.* çıplak; yalın; tamtakır; kılsız **bareback** eyersiz **barefaced** arsız **barefoot** yalınayak
barely /'beıli/ *be.* ancak, zar zor
bargain /'ba:gin/ *a.* pazarlık, anlaşma; kelepir; ucuz şey ☆ *e.* pazarlık etmek **bargain for** hesaba katmak, beklemek **drive a hard bargain** sıkı pazarlık etmek **into the bargain** üstelik, ayrıca
barge /ba:c/ *a.* mavna, salapurya ☆ *e.* çarpmak, toslamak **barge into** (konuşmayı) kesmek, bölmek, müdahale etmek **barge in** hızla içeri dalmak
baritone /'beritoun/ *a, müz.* bariton
bark /ba:k/ *e.* havlamak ☆ *a.* havlama, ağaç kabuğu
barley /'ba:li/ *a.* arpa
barmaid /'ba:meyd/ *a.* kadın barmen
barman /'ba:mın/ *a.* barmen
barn /ba:n/ *a.* ambar; ağıl, ahır
barnacle /'ba:nıkıl/ *a.* (kayalara, gemi diplerine yapışan) bir tür midye
barnyard /'ba:nya:d/ *a.* çiftlik avlusu
barometer /bı'romıtı/ *a.* barometre, basınçölçer
baron /'berın/ *a.* baron **baroness** baronun karısı; kadın baron
baroque /bı'rok/ *s, a.* barok
barrack /'berık/ *e, İİ, kon.* bağırarak sözünü kesmek
barracks /'berıks/ *a.* kışla
barrel /'berıl/ *a.* fıçı, varil; namlu
barren /'berın/ *s.* kıraç, çorak, verimsiz; kısır, sıkıcı, yavan
barricade /'berikeyd/ *a.* barikat, engel
barrier /'beriı/ *a.* engel; duvar, çit, korkuluk
barrister /'beristı/ *a.* avukat, dava vekili
barrow /'berou/ *a.* el arabası
barter /'ba:tı/ *a.* takas, değiş tokuş ☆ *e.* değiş tokuş etmek
base /beys/ *a.* temel; taban; esas; *ask.* üs; *mat.* doğru, düzlem; *kim.* baz; *dilb.* kök, gövde ☆ *s.* aşağılık, alçak; değersiz ☆ *e.* (**on**) dayandırmak; tesis etmek, kurmak

baseball /'beysbo:l/ *a, sp.* beysbol
basement /'beysmınt/ *a.* bodrum katı
bash /beş/ *e.* şiddetle vurmak ☆ *a.* şiddetli darbe **have a bash (at)** bir denemek
bashful /'beşfıl/ *s.* utangaç, sıkılgan
basic /'beysik/ *s.* temel, ana, esas
basics /'beysiks/ *a.* bir şeyin en basit ama en önemli kısımları
basin /'beysın/ *a.* leğen; çanak, tas; havuz; lavabo; *coğ.* havza
basis /'beysis/ *a.* (ç. **bases** /-si:z/) temel, esas; temel ilke
bask /ba:sk/ *e.* tadını çıkarmak; güneşlenmek
basket /'ba:skit/ *a.* sepet; *sp.* basket, sayı
basketball /'ba:skitbo:l/ *a, sp.* basketbol
bass /beys/ *a, müz.* bas
bass /bes/ *a, hayb.* (ç. **bass**) levrek
bassoon /bı'su:n/ *a, müz.* fagot
bastard /'ba:stıd/ *a.* piç
bat /bet/ *a.* yarasa; *sp.* kriket/beysbol sopası; *sp.* pinpon raketi ☆ *e.* topa sopayla vurmak **off one's own bat** kendi başına; kendisine söylenmeden
batch /beç/ *a.* dizi, grup, küme
bath /ba:t/ *a.* küvet; banyo yapma, yıkanma; banyo odası, banyo; ç. hamam; kaplıca; havuz ☆ *e.* banyo yapmak yıkanmak **bathroom** banyo odası; *Aİ.* tuvalet **bathrobe** bornoz
bathe /beyd/ *e.* yüzmek; suya/ilaca sokmak, yıkamak; yıkanmak
bathing yıkanma; yüzme **bathing suit** kadın mayosu
batman /'betmın/ *a, İİ.* emir eri
baton /'beton/ *a, müz.* baton; cop; sopa
batsman /'betsmın/ *a.* (kriket) vurucu
battalion /bı'teliın/ *a, ask.* tabur
batter /'betı/ *e.* dövmek; yumruklamak; ☆ *a.* pasta hamuru
battery /'betıri/ *a.* akü, pil; *ask.* batarya; takım, seri, dizi; *huk.* müessir fiil, dövme
battle /'betıl/ *a.* savaş, muharebe; çarpışma, vuruşma; mücadele ☆ *e.* sa-

bauble 270

vaşmak, çarpışmak; mücadele etmek
battlefield savaş alanı **battleship** savaş gemisi
bauble /'bo:bıl/ *a.* ucuz mücevher, incik boncuk
bauxite /'bo:ksayt/ *a.* boksit, alüminyumtaşı
bawl /bo:l/ *e.* bas bas bağırmak
bay /bey/ *a.* körfez, koy; *bitk.* defne; bölme, bölüm, kısım; çıkma, cumba; havlama, uluma; doru at ☆ *e.* havlamak, ulumak **at bay** köşeye sıkıştırılmış, çıkmazda
bayonet /'beyınit/ *a.* süngü, kasatura
bazaar /bı'za:/ *a.* çarşı
be /bi, bi:/ (**I** öznesiyle **am**; tekil öznelerle **is**; çoğul öznelerle **are** biçiminde çekimlenir. **Am** ve **is**'in geçmiş zaman biçimi **was, are**'ınki ise **were**'dür. Miş'li geçmiş zaman biçimi: **been**) olmak, var olmak, bulunmak
beach /bi:ç/ *a.* kıyı, sahil; plaj, kumsal
beacon /'bi:kın/ *a.* işaret ateşi; deniz feneri
bead /bi:d/ *a.* boncuk; *ç.* tespih, kolye
beak /bi:k/ *a.* gaga
beaker /'bi:kı/ *a.* büyük bardak; deney şişesi
beam /bi:m/ *a.* ışık, ışın, ışık demeti; sinyal, dalga; kiriş, direk; kalas ☆ *e.* (ışık vb.) saçmak, yaymak
bean /bi:n/ *a.* fasulye; tane, çekirdek **full of beans** hayat dolu, yerinde duramayan **spill the beans** baklayı ağzından kaçırmak
bear /beı/ *e.* **bore** /bo:/, **borne** /bo:n/ taşımak, götürmek; kabul etmek, üstlenmek, katlanmak, çekmek; sahip olmak, taşımak; (meyve, ürün) vermek **bearable** katlanılır, çekilir, dayanılır **bear down** yenmek, güç kullanmak **bear on** ile ilgili olmak; üstüne basmak, ezmek **bear out** doğrulamak, desteklemek **bear up** cesaretini elden bırakmamak **bear with** sabır göstermek, katlanmak
bear /beı/ *a.* ayı; spekülatör, vurguncu
beard /bıid/ *a.* sakal **bearded** sakallı
bearer /'beıtı/ *a, tic.* taşıyan, hamil
bearing /'beıring/ *a.* bedenin duruşu,

duruş biçimi; ilgi, ilişki; taşıma, dayanma; bağıntı; yön; mil yatağı
beast /bi:st/ *a.* (dört ayaklı) hayvan; kaba kimse, hayvan
beat /bi:t/ *e.* **beat, beaten** /bi:tın/ dövmek, vurmak; yenmek; (kalp, nabız) atmak; çırpmak; (davul, vb.) çalmak ☆ *a.* vurma, vuruş; yürek atışı; *müz.* ritm, tempo; devriye bölgesi **beat about/around the bush** lafı ağzında gevelemek **beat time** tempo tutmak **beat about** endişeyle aramak; rota değiştirmek **beat down** indirmek, azaltmak **beat into** kafasına sokmak, öğretmek **beat off** defetmek, püskürtmek **beat out** (ateş) vurarak söndürmek **beat up** pataklamak, döverek yaralamak **beat the air** akıntıya kürek çekmek **beaten** (metal) vurularak biçimlendirilmiş, dövme; (yol) ayak izleriyle belirginleşmiş; yenik, mağlup **off the beaten track** herkesce pek bilinmeyen
beater mikser **beating** dayak; (kalp, vb) atış, çarpma
beautician /byu:'tişın/ *a.* güzellik uzmanı
beautiful /'byu:tifıl/ *s.* güzel; *kon.* çok iyi, harika
beautify /'byu:tifay/ *e.* güzelleştirmek
beauty /'byu:ti/ *a.* güzellik; güzel şey/-kişi **beauty parlour/shop** güzellik salonu **beauty sleep** güzellik uykusu **beauty spot** güzelliğiyle bilinen yer
beaver /'bi:vı/ *a.* kunduz
became /bi'keym/ *bkz.* **become**
because /bi'koz/ *bağ.* çünkü, -dığı için **because of** ... yüzünden, -den dolayı
beckon /'bekın/ *e.* el etmek, çağırmak
become /bi'kam/ *e.* **became** /bi'keym/, **become** olmak; uymak, yakışmak; gitmek **becoming** uygun, üzerine yakışan; yerinde, doğru
bed /bed/ *a.* yatak, karyola; (ırmak, vb.) yatak; tarh; çiçeklik; taban, temel ☆ *e.* yerleştirmek, oturtmak; üzerinde ekim yapmak **bed and board** kalacak yer ve yiyecek **bed ridden** yatalak **go to bed** yatmak **bedclothes** yatak takımı **bedroom** yatak odası **bed-**

sitter bekâr odası **bedspread** yatak örtüsü **bedstead** karyola

bedbug /'bedbag/ a. tahtakurusu

bedding /'beding/ a. yatak takımı

bedevil /bi'devıl/ e. bozmak; şaşırtmak

bedlam /'bedlım/ a, kon. gürültülü patırtılı yer, çıfıt çarşısı

bedraggled /bi'dregıld/ s. üstü başı darmadağınık, pejmürde,

bee /bi:/ a. arı **beehive** arı kovanı **a bee in one's bonnet** fikri sabit, saplantı

beech /bi:ç/ a, bitk. kayın ağacı

beef /bi:f/ a. sığır; sığır eti **beefsteak** biftek

been /bi:n, bin/ e, bkz. be

beer /biı/ a. bira

beeswax /'bi:zweks/ a. bulmumu

beet /bi:t/ a, kon. pancar; şekerpancarı

beetle /'bi:tıl/ a. kanatlılardan herhangi bir böcek; iri kara böcek

beetroot /'bi:tru:t/ a, bitk. pancar

befall /bi'fo:l/ e. **befell** /bi'fel/, **befallen** /-'folın/ (kötü bir şey) olmak; başına gelmek

before /bi'fo:/ ilg. önünde; -den önce ☆ be. önde, önden; daha önce, önce ☆ bağ. -meden önce **before long** çok geçmeden

beforehand /bi'fo:hend/ be. önceden

befriend /'bi'frend/ e. arkadaşça davranmak, yardım etmek

beg /beg/ e. rica etmek, istemek, yalvarmak; dilenmek **I beg your pardon** affedersiniz; efendim!

began /bi'gen/ bkz. begin

beggar /'begı/ a. dilenci

begin /bi'gin/ e. **began** /bi'gen/ **begun** /bi'gan/ başlamak; başlatmak **to begin with** evvela, bir kere **beginner** yeni başlayan, acemi **beginning** başlangıç

begrudge /bi'grac/ e. istemeyerek vermek; çok görmek, içine oturmak

beguile /bi'gayl/ e. (into) aldatmak, kandırmak; büyülemek, çekmek, cezbetmek

begun /bi'gan/ bkz. begin

behalf /bi'ha:f/ a. taraf, leh **on behalf of** -in adına/yararına

behave /bi'heyv/ e. hareket etmek, davranmak; (makine) çalışmak, işlemek **behave oneself** terbiyesini takınmak, uslu oturmak **well-behaved** terbiyeli, uslu

behaviour /bi'heyvıı/ a. davranış, hareket, tavır **behaviourism** davranışçılık

behead /bi'hed/ e. başını kesmek, kellesini uçurmak

behind /bi'haynd/ ilg. arkasında, gerisinde ☆ be. arkada, arkaya, arkadan ☆ a. kıç **behindhand** gecikmiş, geç

behold /bi'hould/ e. farkına varmak, görmek

beige /beyj/ a, s. bej

being /'bi:ing/ a. varoluş, varlık; yaratık

belch /belç/ e. geğirmek; püskürtmek

belfry /'belfri/ a. çan kulesi

belie /'bi'lay/ e. yanıltmak; gizlemek, maskelemek

belief /bi'li:f/ a. inanç; güven; kanı

believe /bi'li:v/ e. inanmak, güvenmek; sanmak **believable** inanılır **believe in** varlığına inanmak; -e inancı olmak, inanmak **believer** inanan, inançlı

belittle /bi'litıl/ e. küçümsemek, küçük görmek

bell /bel/ a. çan, zil **bell-bottoms** İspanyol paça pantolon **bell boy** otel garsonu

belligerent /bi'licırınt/ s. (ülke) savaş halinde; (insan) kavgacı

bellow /'belou/ e. böğürmek

bellows /'belouz/ a. körük

belly /'beli/ a. karın, mide; göbek; kon. göbek deliği **bellyache** karın ağrısı **belly dance** göbek dansı **bellyful** çok fazla

belong /bi'long/ e. (to) ait olmak; (in) uygun olmak **belongings** birinin kişisel eşyaları

beloved /bi'lavd/ s, a. sevgili

below /bi'lou/ be. aşağı, aşağıda, altta ☆ ilg. -in altında; -den aşağı ☆ s. aşağıdaki, alttaki; kon. çok

belt /belt/ a. kemer, kuşak; kayış; bölge, yöre, kuşak ☆ e. kemerle bağlamak; kemerle dövmek **tighten one's belt** kon. kemerleri sıkmak

bemoan /bi'moun/ e. kederlenmek,

üzülmek; sızlanmak

bemused /bi'myu:zd/ *s.* aklı karışık, şaşkın

bench /benç/ *a.* sıra, bank; tezgâh; yargıç kürsüsü

bend /bend/ *e.* eğmek, bükmek; eğilmek, bükülmek; yöneltmek, çevirmek ☆ *a.* eğme, bükme; dönemeç, viraj **round the bend** *kon.* deli, çılgın

beneath /bi'ni:t/ *be.* altta, alta ☆ *ilg.* altında, altına

benediction /beni'dikşın/ *a.* kutsama

benefaction /beni'fekşın/ *a.* iyilik, hayır **benefactor** hayırsever

beneficent /bi'nefisınt/ *s.* hayır sahibi, hayırsever

beneficial /beni'fişıl/ *s.* yararlı, hayırlı

beneficiary /beni'fişıri/ *a.* yararlanan kimse

benefit /'benifit/ *a.* yarar, çıkar, kâr; kazanç; avantaj ☆ *e.* yaramak, yararı olmak **benefit from/by** -den yararlanmak

benevolence /bi'nevılıns/ *a.* hayırseverlik **benevolent** iyilikçi, hayırsever

benign /bi'nayn/ *s.* iyi huylu, tatlı, sevecen; (ur) tehlikesiz

bent /bent/ *a.* eğilim; yetenek

bent /bent/ *bkz.* **bend**

bequeath /bi'kwi:d/ *e.* miras olarak bırakmak

bequest /bi'kwest/ *a.* miras, kalıt

bereave /bi'ri:v/ *e.* **bereaved** ya da **bereft** /bi'reft/ elinden almak, yoksun bırakmak

bereavement /bi'ri:vmınt/ *a.* büyük kayıp, matem

bereft /bi'reft/ *bkz.* **bereave**

beret /'berey/ *a.* bere

berry /'beri/ *a.* (çilek, kiraz, vb. gibi) küçük, yumuşak meyve

berserk /bö:'sö:k/ *s.* çılgın gibi, delice

berth /bö:t/ *a.* (trende/gemide) ranza, yatak; (rıhtımda) palamar yeri ☆ *e.* (tekne) (bağlanmak için) limana girmek; limana sokmak

beseech /bi'si:ç/ *e.* yalvarmak, rica etmek; istemek

beseem /bi'si:m/ *e.* uygun düşmek

beset /bi'set/ *e.* **beset** kuşatmak, sarmak

beside /bi'sayd/ *ilg.* yanında, yanına **beside oneself** çılgın gibi **beside the point** konunun dışında

besides /bi'saydz/ *be.* bunun yanı sıra, ayrıca, bununla birlikte, üstelik, bir de ☆ *ilg.* -den başka, -e ilaveten

besiege /bi'si:c/ *e, ask.* kuşatmak; sıkıştırmak, rahat vermemek

best /best/ *s.* en iyi ☆ *be.* en iyi biçimde; en çok, en fazla; ☆ *a.* en iyi taraf/yan/kısım; en iyi **best man** sağdıç **best seller** en çok satılan kitap **at (the) best** en iyimser ihtimalle

bestial /'bestiıl/ *s.* hayvan gibi; kaba, hayvani **bestiality** kabalık, hayvanlık; acımasızlık

bestow /bi'stou/ *e.* bağışlamak

bet /bet/ *e.* **bet** ya da **betted** bahse girmek ☆ *a.* bahis, iddia **betting shop** müşterek bahis oynanan dükkân; ganyan bayii **I bet** *kon.* Bahse girerim ki

betray /bi'trey/ *e.* ihanet etmek; ele vermek; ağzından kaçırmak; baştan çıkarmak **betrayal** ihanet; ele verme **betrayer** hain

better /'betı/ *s, be.* daha iyi, daha çok ☆ *e.* gelişmek, daha iyi hale gelmek **better half** *kon.* eş, karı **better off** daha zengin **get better** iyileşmek **get the better off** -i yenmek **had better** iyi olur

between /bi'twi:n/ *be, ilg.* (iki şeyin) arasına, arasında **between you and me** laf aramızda

bevel /'bevıl/ *e.* eğmek

beverage /'bevıric/ *a.* içecek, meşrubat

bewail /bi'weyl/ *e.* ağlamak, dövünmek

beware /bi'weı/ *e.* **(of)** sakınmak, kaçınmak

bewilder /bi'wildı/ *e.* şaşırtmak **bewilderment** şaşkınlık

bewitch /bi'wiç/ *e.* büyülemek

beyond /bi'yond/ *be.* ötede, öteye, iler ☆ *ilg.* ötesinde, ötesine; -den başka

bi- /bay/ *önek* iki, çift

bias /'bayıs/ *a.* önyargı; eğilim **biase** önyargılı

bib /bib/ *a.* bebek önlüğü
Bible /'baybıl/ *a.* İncil, Kutsal Kitap
bibliography /bibli'ogrıfi/ *a.* kaynakça, bibliyografi
bicarbonate /bay'ka:bınit/ *a.* bikarbonat
bicentenary /baysen'ti:nıri/ *a.* iki yüzüncü yıldönümü
biceps /'bayseps/ *a.* pazı, iki başlı kol kası
bicker /'bıkı/ *e.* tartışmak, atışmak
bicycle /'baysikıl/ *a.* bisiklet ☆ *e.* bisiklete binmek, bisikletle gezmek
bid /bid/ *e.* bid fiyat teklif etmek; deklare etmek ☆ *a.* fiyat teklifi, teklif **bidding** buyruk, emir; deklarasyon
bide /bayd/ *e.* (uygun zamanı) sabırla beklemek
biennial /bay'eniıl/ *s.* iki yılda bir olan
bier /biı/ *a.* cenaze teskeresi
bifocals /bay'foukılz/ *a.* çift odaklı gözlük
big /big/ *s.* büyük, iri; önemli; *kon.* popüler, ünlü
bigamy /'bigımi/ *a.* ikieşlilik, bigami
bigot /'bigıt/ *a.* dar kafalı kimse, bağnaz **bigoted** dar kafalı, yobaz
bigwig /'bigwig/ *a, kon.* önemli kimse, kodaman
bike /bayk/ *a.* bisiklet; motosiklet
bikini /bi'ki:ni/ *a.* bikini
bilateral /bay'letırıl/ *s.* iki yönlü
bile /bayl/ *a.* safra, öd
bilingual /bay'lingwıl/ *s.* ikidilli
bill /bil/ *a.* hesap, fatura; yasa tasarısı; afiş, ilan; *Aİ.* kâğıt para; tahvil, poliçe; gaga **billboard** ilan tahtası
billet /'bilit/ *a.* kışla, baraka
billiards /'bilyıdz/ *a.* bilardo
billion /'bilyın/ *a. Aİ.* milyar; *İİ.* trilyon
billow /'bilou/ *a.* büyük dalga
billy goat /'bili gout/ *a.* erkek keçi, teke
bin /bin/ *a.* kutu, sandık, teneke
binary /'baynıri/ *s.* çift, ikili
bind /baynd/ *e.* **bound** /baund/ bağlamak; yarayı sarmak; ciltlemek; yasal olarak bağlamak **binder** bağlayan şey; sicim, tutkal; ciltçi **bindery** ciltevi **binding** ciltçilik; kitap kapağı; kenar süsü; bağlayıcı, zorunlu

bingo /'bingou/ *a.* bingo oyunu
binoculars /bi'nokyulız/ *a.* dürbün
biochemistry /bayou'kemistri/ *a.* biyokimya
biography /bay'ogrıfi/ *a.* yaşamöyküsü, biyografi
biology /bay'olıci/ *a.* biyoloji, yaşambilim **biologist** biyolog **biological** biyolojik
bionic /bay'onik/ *s.* insanüstü güçleri olan
biped /'bayped/ *a.* iki ayaklı yaratık
birch /bö:ç/ *a, bitk.* huş ağacı
bird /bö:d/ *a.* kuş **bird-brained** kuş beyinli, aptal **birdcage** kuş kafesi **bird's eye view** kuşbakışı görünüm **bird's nest** kuş yuvası **early bird** erken kalkan/gelen kimse **kill two birds with one stone** bir taşla iki kuş vurmak
biro /'bayırou/ *a.* tükenmezkalem
birth /bö:t/ *a.* doğum; doğurma; kaynak, köken **buy birth** doğuştan **birth control** doğum kontrolü **birthday** doğum günü **birthmark** doğum lekesi **birthplace** doğum yeri **birthrate** doğum oranı **birthright** doğuştan kazanılan ulusal hak, vatandaşlık hakkı
biscuit /'biskit/ *a.* bisküvi; *Aİ.* çörek, pasta
bisect /bay'sekt/ *e.* iki eşit parçaya bölmek
bisexual /bay'sekşuıl/ *s.* çift cinsiyetli, ikieşeyli, erselik
bishop /'bişıp/ *a.* piskopos
bison /'baysın/ *a, hayb.* bizon
bistro /'bi:strou/ *a.* küçük bar/lokanta
bit /bit/ *a.* miktar, parça; lokma, kırıntı; kısa süre; gem; matkap, delgi **a bit biraz bits and pieces** ıvır zıvır, ufak şeyler **bit by bit** azar azar, yavaş yavaş **not a bit** hiç değil, zerre kadar
bit /bit/ *bkz.* bite
bitch /biç/ *a.* dişi köpek, kancık; *kon.* orospu
bite /bayt/ *e.* bit /bit/, **bitten** /'bitın/ ısırmak; (böcek, yılan, vb.) sokmak; acıtmak; yakmak; aşındırmak; yemek ☆ *a.* ısırık; ısırma; sokma; lokma; parça; keskinlik; acılık
biting /'bayting/ *s.* kaskin, acı

bitten /'bitin/ *bkz.* **bite**

bitter /'bitı/ *a.* acı, keskin, yakıcı; üzücü, acı ☆ *a.* acılık, keskinlik; acı bira **bitterish** acımsı **bitterly** acı acı **bitterness** acılık, keskinlik

bizarre /bi'za:/ *s.* acayip, garip, tuhaf

black /'blek/ *s.* siyah, kara; karanlık; kirli, pis; çok kızgın; koyu tenli; (kahve) sütsüz, sade; uğursuz ☆ *a.* siyah renk; siyah giysi; zenci ☆ *e.* karartmak; (göz) morartmak **black belt** *sp.* siyah kuşak **black box** *hav.* kara kutu **black eye** morarmış göz **black letter** gotik matbaa harfi **black magic** kara büyü **black market** karaborsa **black out** karartma yapmak; bayılmak **black pepper** karabiber **Black Sea** Karadeniz **black sheep** yüz karası, kara koyun

blackberry /'blekbıri/ *a, bitk.* böğürtlen

blackbird /'blekbö:d/ *a, hayb.* karatavuk

blackboard /'blekbo:d/ *a.* karatahta, tahta

blackcurrant /'blekkarınt/ *a, bitk.* kuşüzümü

blacken /'blekın/ *e.* karartmak; kara çalmak, kötülemek

blackjack /'blekcek/ *a, isk.* yirmi bir oyunu

blacklist /'bleklist/ *a.* kara liste

blackmail /'blekmeyl/ *a.* şantaj ☆ *e.* şantaj yapmak

blackout /'blekaut/ *a.* karartma; bayılma, baygınlık

blacksmith /'bleksmit/ *a.* nalbant, demirci

bladder /'bledı/ *a.* sidiktorbası, mesane

blade /bleyd/ *a.* (bıçak, jilet, vb.) ağız

blame /bleym/ *e.* suçlamak, kınamak; sorumlu tutmak ☆ *a.* suç; kınama; sorumluluk **blameless** suçsuz **blameworthy** kusurlu, ayıp

blanch /bla:nç/ *e.* beyazlatmak, ağartmak; (with/at) (yüzünün rengi) solmak

bland /blend/ *s.* uysal, yumuşak başlı; (besin) hafif

blank /blenk/ *s.* yazısız, boş; (çek) açık; anlamsız, boş ☆ *a.* boş yer; boşluk **blank cartridge** kurusıkı kurşun **blank cheque** açık çek **blank signature** açığa atılan imza **blank verse** serbest nazım, uyaksız şiir

blanket /'blenkit/ *a.* battaniye

blare /bleı/ *a.* boru sesi

blarny /'bla:ni/ *e.* yaltaklanmak

blast /bla:st/ *a.* şiddetli rüzgâr; patlama ☆ *e.* havaya uçurmak; yok etmek; yakmak, kavurmak **blasted** kahrolası; yok olmuş **blast off** (uzay aracı) havalanma, fırlatılma

blatant /'bleytınt/ *s.* terbiyesiz, utanmaz

blaze /bleyz/ *a.* alev, ateş; parlak ışık ☆ *e.* alev alev yanmak, tutuşmak **blazing** /'bleyzing/ cayır cayır yanan; *kon.* aşikâr, gün gibi ortada

blazer /'bleyzı/ *a.* spor ceket, blazer

bleach /bli:ç/ *e.* beyazlatmak, ağartmak; beyazlamak, ağarmak ☆ *a.* beyazlatıcı madde

bleak /bli:k/ *s.* soğuk, tatsız, nahoş

bleary /'bliiri/ *s.* (göz) kızarmış, sulanmış

bleat /bli:t/ *e.* melemek ☆ *a.* meleme

bleed /bli:d/ **bled** /bled/ *e.* kanamak; (for) yüreği kan ağlamak, içi sızlamak

blemish /'blemiş/ *e.* güzelliğini bozmak, lekelemek ☆ *a.* leke, kusur

blench /blenç/ *e.* (korkudan) irkilmek

blend /blend/ *e.* harmanlamak; karıştırmak ☆ *a.* harman; karışım **blender** karıştırıcı, mikser

bless /bles/ *e.* kutsamak, takdis etmek; hayırdua etmek **blessed** /'blesid/ kutsal; mutlu, huzurlu

blessing /'blesing/ *a.* kutsama, takdis; lütuf, iyilik; şükran duası

blight /blayt/ *a.* bitki hastalığı; kötü etki ☆ *e.* bozmak, kötü etkilemek

blind /blaynd/ *s.* kör; düşüncesiz, akılsızca; görünmez; gizli ☆ *a.* perde, güneşlik ☆ *e.* kör etmek, körleştirmek **blind alley** çıkmaz sokak **blindfold** gözbağı **blind man's buff** körebe **blindly** gözü kapalı, körü körüne

blink /blink/ *e.* (göz) kırpmak/kırpıştır-

mak; (ışık) yanıp sönmek
blinkers /'blinkız/ a. at gözlüğü
blip /blip/ a. bip sesi
bliss /blis/ a. çok büyük mutluluk
blister /'blistı/ a. kabarcık, kabartı ☆ a. su toplamak, kabarmak
blithe /blayd/ s. mutlu, neşeli, kaygısız
blitz /blits/ a. ani saldırı
blizzard /'blizıd/ a. kar fırtınası, tipi
bloated /'bloutid/ s. davul gibi şişmiş; normalden fazla
blob /blob/ a. damla; leke
block /blok/ a. blok, birlik; kütük/kaya/taş parçası; blok; binalar dizisi, tıkanma, engel ☆ e. tıkamak, önünü kesmek, engellemek
blockade /blo'keyd/ a. abluka, kuşatma
blockage /'blokic/ a. tıkanma; tıkanıklık
blockhead /'blokhed/ s, kon. dangalak; mankafa, aptal
bloke /blouk/ a, İİ, kon. herif, adam
blond /blond/ a, s. (erkek) sarışın; (saç) sarı
blonde /blond/ a, s. (bayan) sarışın; (saç) sarı
blood /blad/ a. kan; akrabalık, kan bağı; mizaç, huy **blood bank** kan bankası **blood brother** kan kardeşi **blood feud** kan davası **blood group/type** kan grubu **blood poisoning** kan zehirlenmesi **blood pressure** kan basıncı, tansiyon **blood sport** kanlı spor, zevk için hayvan öldürme **blood test** kan tahlili **blood vessel** kan damarı **fresh/new blood** taze kan, yeni eleman **in cold blood** soğukkanlılıkla **make sb's blood boil** tepesini attırmak, kudurtmak **make sb's blood run cold** ödünü koparmak **bloodbath** kıyım, katliam **bloodless** kansız; öldürücü olmayan **bloodshed** kan dökme, katliam **bloodshot** (gözü) kanlanmış **bloodstain** kan lekesi **bloodstone** kantaşı **bloodstream** kan dolaşımı **bloodthirsty** kana susamış **bloody** kanlı; kanayan; kana susamış; acımasız; arg. lanet olası **bloody well** kesinlikle, pekâlâ, gayet iyi
bloom /blu:m/ a. çiçek; en güzel çağ/-

dönem, gençlik ☆ e. çiçek açmak, çiçeklenmek
blot /blot/ a. mürekkep lekesi; kusur, ayıp ☆ e. lekelemek, kirletmek **blotting paper** kurutma kâğıdı
blotch /bloç/ a. büyük leke
blouse /blauz/ a. bluz
blow /blou/ e. **blew** /blu:/ **blown** /bloun/ (rüzgâr) esmek; üflemek; çalmak; öttürmek; (sigorta, ampul) atmak, yanmak; açığa vurmak, söylemek ☆ a. darbe, vuruş; talihsizlik, darbe, şok **blow in** çıkagelmek **blow out** üfleyerek söndürmek **blow over** geçmek, dinmek **blow up** havaya uçurmak; (fotoğraf) büyültmek; kızmak
blown /bloun/ bkz. blow
blowout /'blouaut/ a. (lastik) patlama
blow-up /'blouap/ a. patlama
blubber /'blabı/ a. balina yağı
blue /blu:/ s. mavi; kon. üzgün, hüzünlü; morarmış ☆ a. mavi renk; çivit; ç. hüzün, keder ç. Amerikalılara özgü bir tür ezgi, blues ☆ e. maviye boyamak; çivitlemek **blue blood** doğuştan soyluluk **blue film** seks filmi **blue jacket** denizci, bahriyeli **once in a blue moon** kon. kırk yılda bir
bluebell /'blu:bel/ a, bitk. çançiçeği
blue-collar /blu:'kolı/ s. ağır işçi sınıfına ilişkin
blueprint /'blu:print/ a. mavi kopya, ozalit; ayrıntılı tasarı
bluff /blaf/ a. blöf; uçurum; kurusıkı ☆ s. dik, sarp ☆ e. blöf yapmak
blunder /'blandı/ e. gaf yapmak, pot kırmak ☆ a. gaf, pot
blunt /blant/ s. keskin olmayan, kör; patavatsız **bluntly** dobra dobra, açıkça
blur /blö:/ a. net görülmeyen şey, karaltı ☆ e. bulandırmak; bulanmak
blurt /'blö:t/ e. (out) ağzından kaçırmak, yumurtlamak
blush /blaş/ e. yüzü kızarmak, utanmak ☆ a. utanma, utanıp kızarma
bluster /'blastı/ e. kabadayılık taslamak; (rüzgâr) sert esmek **blustery** (hava) rüzgârlı

boa /bouı/ *a, hayb.* boa yılanı
boar /bo:/ *a, hayb.* (damızlık) erkek domuz; yaban domuzu
board /bo:d/ *a.* tahta, kereste; (satranç, dama, vb.) oyun tahtası; ilan tahtası; sofra, masa; yönetim kurulu; ç. sahne ☆ *e.* tahta döşemek; (gemi, tren, vb.) binmek; pansiyoner olarak almak **on board** gemide, gemiye; trende, trene; uçakta; uçağa **boarder** pansiyoner; yatılı öğrenci **boarding** tahta kaplama **boarding house** pansiyon **boarding school** yatılı okul
boast /boust/ *e.* övünmek; iftihar etmek; kıvanç duymak ☆ *a.* övünç; kıvanç **boastful** övüngen
boat /bout/ *a.* tekne; gemi; kayık; sandal ☆ *e.* sandalla/kayıkla gezmek **boathouse** kayıkhane
bob /bob/ *e.* aşağı yukarı hareket etmek; sallamak ☆ *a.* reverans; *kon.* şilin
bobbin /'bobin/ *a.* bobin, makara
bobsleigh /'bobsley/ *a.* kar kızağı
bodily /'bodili/ *be.* bütün olarak; tümüyle ☆ *s.* bedensel
body /bodi/ *a.* beden, vücut; gövde; ceset; kitle; heyet, kurul **bodyguard** koruyucu, muhafız **bodywork** (taşıt) karoser
bog /bog/ *a.* bataklık **boggy** batak
boggle /'bogıl/ *e.* çekinmek, ürkmek
bogus /'bougıs/ *s.* yapmacık, sahte
bohemian /bou'hi:miın/ *a, s.* bohem
boil /boyl/ *e.* kaynatmak; haşlamak; kaynamak; haşlanmak ☆ *a.* kaynama; kaynatma; kaynama noktası; çıban **boil away** kaynayıp gitmek **boil over** kaynayıp taşmak **boil up** tehlikeli bir boyuta ulaşmak, kızışmak
boisterous /'boystırıs/ *s.* gürültülü; (hava) kötü, sert
bold /bould/ *s.* cesur, yürekli, gözü pek, atılgan; küstah, arsız; (görünüş) keskin hatlı
bollard /'bolıd/ *a.* iskele babası; kısa kalın direk
boloney /bı'louni/ *a, arg.* zırva, palavra, boş laf
bolster /'boulstı/ *a.* uzun yastık ☆ *e.*

(up) desteklemek
bolt /boult/ *a.* cıvata; kapı sürgüsü, mandal; yıldırım; (kumaş, vb.) top
bomb /bom/ *a.* bomba ☆ *e.* bombalamak
bombard /bom'ba:d/ *a.* bombardıman etmek; (soru, vb.) yağmuruna tutmak **bombardment** bombardıman
bomber /'bomı/ *a.* bombardıman uçağı
bonanza /bı'nenzı/ *a.* çok kârlı iş/şey
bond /bond/ *a.* bono, senet; sözleşme; zincir; bağ ☆ *e.* yapıştırmak, birleştirmek; yapışmak, birleşmek
bondage /'bondic/ *a.* kölelik
bone /boun/ *a.* kemik; kılçık ☆ *e.* kemiklerini ayıklamak **bonedry** kupkuru **bone to pick** paylaşılacak koz **bonesetter** çıkıkçı **bony** kemikli, kılçıklı
bonfire /'bonfayı/ *a.* şenlik ateşi
bonnet /'bonit/ *a.* başlık, bone; motor kapağı
bonny /'boni/ *s.* sağlıklı, gürbüz, güzel; yeterli, iyi
bonus /'bounıs/ *a.* ikramiye; prim
boo /bu:/ *a, ünl.* yuh ☆ *e.* yuhalamak
book /buk/ *a.* kitap; defter; deste, paket; kayıt; *kon.* telefon rehberi **bookbinder** ciltçi **bookbinding** ciltçilik **bookcase** kitaplık **bookkeeper** muhasebeci, sayman **bookmaker** müşterek bahisleri düzenleyen kimse **bookseller** kitapçı **bookshop/bookstore** kitapevi **bookstall** kitap, dergi vb. satıldığı yer
book /buk/ *e.* (yer) ayırtmak; deftere geçirmek, kaydetmek **booking** rezervasyon, yer ayırtma **booking clerk** *İİ.* gişe memuru **booking office** *İİ.* gişe
booklet /'buklit/ *a.* kitapçık, broşür
boom /bu:m/ *a, den.* seren; gümbürtü; hızlı büyüme, artış, yükseliş ☆ *e.* gümbürdemek; birden artmak
boomerang /'bu:mıreng/ *a.* bumerang
boost /bu:st/ *e.* arttırmak, yükseltmek ☆ *a.* artış, yükselme; teşvik, yardım, destek **booster** etkiyi artırıcı
boot /bu:t/ *a.* çizme, bot; *oto, İİ.* baga ☆ *e, kon.* tekmelemek; sepetlemek kovmak

booth /bu:d/ *a.* kulübe, baraka
border /'bo:dı/ *a.* kenar; sınır, hudut ☆ *e.* sınır koymak; sınırdaş olmak, bitişik olmak **borderline** sınır çizgisi, sınır
bore /bo:/ *e.* canını sıkmak, başını ağrıtmak; delmek, oymak ☆ *a.* can sıkcı şey/kimse, baş belası; delik, oyuk; kalibre, çap **be bored** canı sıkılmak **boredom** can sıkıntısı **boring** can sıkıcı
bore /bo:/ *bkz.* **bear**
born /bo:n/ *bkz.* **bear; be born** doğmak
borne /bo:n/ *bkz.* **bear**
borough /'barı/ *a.* İngiltere'de Parlamentoya üye gönderen kent
borrow /'borou/ *e.* ödünç almak, borç almak **borrower** borç alan kimse **borrowing** ödünç alma, borç alma; alıntı
bosom /'buzım/ *a.* sine, koyun, göğüs
boss /bos/ *a.* patron; işveren ☆ *e.* yönetmek **bossy** emretmeyi seven
botany /'botıni/ *a.* bitkibilim, botanik **botanical** /bı'tenikıl/ bitkibilimsel **botanist** bitkibilimci
botch /boç/ *e.* beceriksizce onarmak ☆ *a.* baştan savma yapılmış şey
both /bout/ *adl.* her ikisi, her ikisi de ☆ *bağ.* (**both ... and ...**) sadece ... değil, aynı zamanda ☆ *s.* her iki, iki
bother /'bodı/ *e.* canını sıkmak, üzmek; (**with/about**) zahmet etmek ☆ *a.* sıkıntı, zahmet; *kon.* kavga, kargaşa, huzursuzluk
bottle /'botıl/ *a.* şişe; biberon **bottle--fed** biberonla beslenen **bottle-green** koyu yeşil **bottleneck** dar geçit; darboğaz
bottom /'botım/ *a.* alt; dip; kıç; etek **bottomless** dipsiz, çok derin
bough /bau/ *a.* ağaç (dal)
bought /bo:t/ *bkz.* **buy**
boulder /'bouldı/ *a.* büyük taş/kaya
boulevard /'bu:lva:d/ *a.* bulvar
bounce /bauns/ *e.* zıplamak; zıplatmak; hoplamak; *kon.* (çek) karşılıksız olduğu için geri çevrilmek ☆ *a.* zıplama, hoplama, sıçrama
bouncing /'baunsing/ *s.* (bebek) sağlıklı

bound /baund/ *s.* (**for**) gitmeye hazır; giden, gitmek üzere olan ☆ *e.* sınırlamak, sınır koymak ☆ *s.* bağlı, bağlanmış; kesin; yükümlü, mecbur; ciltli; kesin niyetli
bound /baund/ *a.* sıçrama, hoplama; sınır ☆ *e.* hoplamak, zıplamak, sıçramak; sekmek
boundary /'baundıri/ *a.* sınır
boundless /'baundlis/ *s.* sınırsız, sonsuz
bounty /'baunti/ *a.* cömertlik; cömertçe verilmiş şey; bağış
bouquet /bou'key/ *a.* buket; (şarap) koku
bourgeois /'buıjwa:/ *a, s.* kentsoylu, burjuva
bout /baut/ *a.* kısa dönem, devre; kriz, nöbet; boks maçı
boutique /bu:'ti:k/ *a.* butik
bow /bau/ *e.* başıyla selamlamak; reverans yapmak; eğmek; boyun eğmek ☆ *a.* reverans, başla selamlama
bow /bou/ *a.* (ok atmakta kullanılan) yay; *müz.* yay; kavis; fiyonk; gökkuşağı **bow legged** çarpık bacaklı **bow tie** papyon
bowels /'bauılz/ *a.* bağırsak; iç kısımlar
bowl /boul/ *a.* kâse, tas, çanak; bovling topu ☆ *e.* (kriket/bovling) topu atmak; bovling oynamak; yuvarlamak
bowling /'bouling/ *a.* bovling oyunu
box /boks/ *a.* kutu, sandık; (mahkeme) kürsü; *tiy.* loca; kulübe; ☆ *e.* kutuya/sandığa koymak **box office** bilet gişesi
box /boks/ *e.* yumruklaşmak; boks yapmak **boxer** boksör **boxing** boks
boy /boy/ *a.* erkek çocuk, oğlan; oğul **boy friend** erkek arkadaş
boycott /'boykot/ *a.* boykot ☆ *e.* boykot etmek
boyhood /'boyhud/ *a.* (erkek) çocukluk çağı
bra /bra:/ *a.* sutyen
brace /breys/ *a.* destek, bağ; dişlere takılan tel; *ç.* pantolon askısı ☆ *e.* sağlamlaştırmak, desteklemek
bracelet /'breyslit/ *a.* bilezik

bracket /'brekit/ *a.* destek, dirsek; ayraç, parantez; grup ☆ *e.* parantez içine almak
brackish /'brekiş/ *s.* (su) hafif tuzlu
brag /breg/ *e.* böbürlenmek
brad /bred/ *a.* tel çivi
braid /breyd/ *a.* saç örgüsü; şerit, kordon ☆ *e.* örmek
braille /breyl/ *a.* körler için kabartma yazı
brain /breyn/ *a.* beyin; zekâ, akıl; *kon.* zeki kimse **brain drain** beyin göçü **brainless** beyinsiz, kafasız **brainwash** beyin yıkamak **brainwashing** beyin yıkama **brainwave** (aniden akla gelen) parlak fikir **brainy** akıllı, kafalı
braise /breyz/ *e.* kapalı kapta ve ağır ateşte pişirmek
brake /breyk/ *a.* fren ☆ *e.* fren yapmak
bramble /'brembıl/ *a, bitk.* böğürtlen çalısı
bran /bren/ *a.* kepek
branch /bra:nç/ *a.* dal; (akarsu, yol) kol; şube, bölüm
brand /brend/ *e.* dağlamak, damgalamak; derinden etkilemek ☆ *a.* marka; damga, dağ **brand-new** yepyeni, gıcır gıcır
brandy /'brendi/ *a.* brendi
brash /breş/ *s.* küstah; toy, acemi
brass /bra:s/ *e.* pirinç; pirinçten yapılmış eşya **brassy** pirinç renkli
brave /breyv/ *s.* cesur, yiğit ☆ *e.* cesaretle karşılamak **bravery** cesaret, yiğitlik
bravo /'bra:vou/ *ünl.* Bravo! Aferin!
brawl /bro:l/ *e.* kavga, dalaş, dövüş ☆ *e.* dalaşmak, sesli sesli tartışmak
brawn /bro:n/ *a.* kas; kas gücü
brawny /'bro:ni/ *s.* kaslı
bray /brey/ *e.* anırmak ☆ *a.* anırma, anırtı
brazen /'breyzın/ *s.* arsız, yüzsüz, şımarık
brazier /'breyzyı/ *a.* mangal
breach /bri:ç/ *a.* (yasa) uymama, çiğneme; yerine getirmeme; gedik, yarık, oyuk ☆ *e.* gedik açmak, yarmak
bread /bred/ *a.* ekmek; rızk; geçim, ka-

zanç; *kon.* para **breadcrumb** ekmek kırıntısı
breadth /bredt, brett/ *a.* genişlik, en
break /breyk/ *e.* **broke** /brouk/, **broken** /'broukın/ kırmak, parçalamak; kırılmak; parçalanmak, kopmak; patlamak; bozmak; bozulmak; patlak vermek; çıkmak; uymamak; çiğnemek ☆ *a.* ara, mola; teneffüs, dinlenme; açıklık; kırık; ani değişim, değişiklik; tan, şafak vakti **break away** birinden kaçmak **break down** bozulmak, parçalamak **break even** ne kâr ne zarar **break in** zorla girmek **break off** kesmek; son vermek **break out** patlak vermek, çıkmak **break up** sona ermek, dağılmak **break with** ile bağını koparmak
breakage /'breykic/ *a.* kırma, kırılma kırık, çatlak
breakdown /'breykdaun/ *a.* arıza, bozulma; (sinirsel) bozukluk, çöküntü
breakfast /'brekfıst/ *a.* kahvaltı
breakthrough /'breyktru:/ *a.* atılım, ilerleme; ani saldırı, hücum
breakup /'breykap/ *a.* (arkadaşlık, birlik, vb.) sona erme, son bölüm, parsel
breakwater /'breykwo:tı/ *a.* dalgakıran
breast /brest/ *a.* meme, göğüs; gönül, sine **breaststroke** kurbağalama yüzüş
breath /bret/ *a.* soluk, nefes **breathless** soluk soluğa kalmış; soluk kesici **breathtaking** soluk kesici; heyecanlı **hold one's breath** nefesini tutmak; heyecanla beklemek **out of breath** nefes nefese **take one's breath away** birinin nefesini kesmek
breathe /bri:d/ *e.* solumak; nefes almak; fısıldamak; (koku, duygu, vb.) vermek **breather** *kon.* mola, ara
breeches /'briçiz/ *a.* golf pantolon
breed /bri:d/ *e.* (hayvan) doğurmak, yavrulamak; yetiştirmek, büyütmek ☆ *a.* cins, soy çeşit, tür
breeze /bri:z/ *a.* meltem, esinti
brew /bru:/ *e.* (bira) yapmak; (çay ya da kahve) yapmak **brewery** bira fabrikası

bribe /brayb/ e. rüşvet vermek ☆ a. rüşvet **bribery** rüşvetçilik, rüşvet
brick /brik/ a. tuğla **bricklayer** duvarcı **brickwork** tuğla işi
bridal /'braydıl/ s. gelin/düğün ile ilgili
bride /brayd/ a. gelin
bridegroom /'braydgru:m/ a. damat, güvey
bridesmaid /'braydzmeyd/ a. gelinin nedimesi
bridge /bric/ a. köprü; den. kaptan köprüsü burun kemiği; briç ☆ e. köprü kurmak
bridle /'braydıl/ a. at başlığı, yular ☆ e. (at) dizginlemek; yular takmak; tutmak, dizginlemek
brief /bri:f/ s. kısa ☆ a. özet; dava özeti; talimat, bilgi; ç. külot, don ☆ e. gerekli bilgiyi vermek; son talimatı vermek **in brief** kısaca, özetle, kısacası **briefcase** evrak çantası
briefing brifing
brier /'brayı/ a. yabangülü
brigade /bri'geyd/ a, ask. tugay; ekip, takım **fire brigade** itfaiye
brigadier /brigı'dıı/ a. tugay komutanı, tümgeneral
brigandage /'brigındic/ a. haydutluk, eşkıyalık, kanunsuzluk
bright /brayt/ s. parlak; aydınlık; akıllı, zeki, parlak; umut verici
brighten /'braytın/ e. parlamak, canlanmak; parlatmak; canlandırmak
brilliant /'brilıınt/ s. ışıl ışıl, pırıl pırıl, parlak; görkemli; akıllı
brim /brim/ a. (bardak, kap) ağız, kenar
brine /brayn/ a. tuzlu su, salamura
bring /bring/ e. **brought** /bro:t/ getirmek; neden olmak; ikna etmek, kandırmak **bring about** neden olmak **bring down** (vurup) düşürmek; fiyat indirmek; sürdürmek **bring forward** ileri sürmek, ortaya atmak **bring in** kâr getirmek; öne almak; tanıtmak **bring into** başlatmak **bring off** üstesinden gelmek **bring out** üretmek, ortaya çıkarmak **bring round** ayıltmak **bring through** -den kurtarmak **bring up** (çocuk) büyütmek, yetiştirmek; or-

taya atmak; kusmak
brink /brink/ a. kenar, kıyı
brisk /brisk/ s. çevik, canlı
bristle /'brisıl/ a. sert kıl ☆ e. (tüy, kıl, saç, vb.) diken diken olmak
British /'britiş/ s. Britanya ile ilgili, Britanyalı, İngiliz
brittle /'britıl/ s. kırılgan, gevrek
broad /'bro:d/ s. geniş, enli; ... genişliğinde; enlemesine; genel; serbest; hoşgörülü; açık, belli **broad bean** bakla **broad jump** sp, AI. uzun atlama **broad-minded** serbest fikirli, hoşgörülü
broadcast /'bro:dka:st/ a. radyo/televizyon yayını ☆ e. (radyo/televizyon) yayın yapmak; yayınlamak; yaymak, bildirmek **broadcasting** radyo veya televizyon ile yayın yapma, yayın
broaden /'bro:dın/ e. genişlemek; genişletmek
brocade /brı'keyd/ a. işlemeli, simli kumaş
broccoli /'brokıli/ a. karnabahara benzer bir bitki
brochure /'brouşı/ a. broşür, kitapçık
brogue /broug/ a. kalın ve dayanıklı ayakkabı; İrlanda aksanı
broil /broyl/ e. ızgara yapmak; kızartmak
broke /brouk/ bkz. **break**; s, kon. züğürt, meteliksiz
broken /'broukın/ bkz. **break**; s. kırık; kırılmış; bozuk
broker /'broukı/ a. komisyoncu, simsar
brolly /'broli/ a, İİ, kon. şemsiye
bronchitis /brong'kaytis/ a, hek. bronşit
bronze /bronz/ a. bronz, tunç; bronz rengi
brooch /brouç/ a. broş, süs iğnesi
brood /bru:d/ a. (kuş) yavruları ☆ e. kuluçkaya yatmak
brook /bruk/ a. dere, çay
broom /bru:m/ a. süpürge
broth /brot/ a. et suyu, çorba
brothel /'brotıl/ a. genelev
brother /'bradı/ a. erkek kardeş, birader **brotherhood** kardeşlik; birlik, camia, topluluk **brother-in-law** kayınbi-

rader; enişte; bacanak
brought /bro:t/ *bkz.* **bring**
brow /brau/ *a.* kaş; alın; tepe, yamaç
brown /braun/ *a, s.* kahverengi ☆ esmerleşmek; esmerleştirmek, kızartmak
browse /brauz/ *e.* otlamak; (kitap) gözden geçirmek, karıştırmak
bruise /bru:z/ *a.* çürük, bere, ezik ☆ *e.* çürütmek, berelemek; çürümek
brunch /branç/ *a, kon.* geç kahvaltı/erken öğle yemeği
brunette /bru:'net/ *a.* esmer kadın
brush /braş/ *a.* fırça; fırçalama; çalı ☆ *e.* fırçalamak; hafifçe değmek, sürtünmek
brusque /bru:sk/ *s.* kaba saba, ters
brussels sprout /brasılz'spraut/ *a, bitk.* brüksellahanası
brutal /'bru:tıl/ *s.* acımasız, vahşice, hayvanca
brute /bru:t/ *a.* hayvan; hayvan gibi kişi
brutish /'bru:tiş/ *s, hkr.* hayvani, hayvanlara yakışır, kaba
bubble /'babıl/ *a.* kabarcık; fokurtu
bubble gum balonlu çiklet
buck /bak/ *a.* erkek geyik/tavşan; antilop; *Aİ, kon.* bir dolar ☆ *e.* (at) sıçramak; (binicisini) üzerinden atmak
bucket /'bakit/ *a.* kova
buckle /'bakıl/ *a.* toka, kopça ☆ *e.* toka ile tutturmak; eğilmek, bükülmek
bud /bad/ *a.* gonca, tomurcuk ☆ *e.* tomurcuklanmak; gonca vermek
Buddhism /'budizım/ *a.* Budizm
Buddhist Budist
buddy /'badi/ *a, kon.* arkadaş, kafadar, ahbap
budge /bac/ *e.* kıpırdatmak; kıpırdamak
budgerigar /'bacıriga:/ *a.* muhabbetkuşu
budget /'bacit/ *a.* bütçe
buff /baf/ *a, s.* soluk sarı, kösele rengi ☆ *e.* yumuşak bir şeyle parlatmak
buffalo /'bafılou/ *a, hayb.* bufalo
buffer /'bafı/ *a.* tampon
buffet /'bufey/ *a.* büfe
buffoon /bı'fu:n/ *a.* soytarı, maskara

bug /bag/ *a, Aİ.* böcek; *kon.* mikrop, virüs; *kon.* gizli mikrofon; tahtakurusu
bugle /'byu:gıl/ *a.* borazan
build /bild/ *e.* kurmak, yapmak, inşa etmek ☆ *a.* beden yapısı, yapı **building** yapı, inşaat; inşaatçılık, inşa etme **building society** yapı kooperatifi **build up** gelişmek; büyümek; güçlenmek; geliştirmek; büyütmek
bulb /balb/ *a.* çiçek soğanı; ampul
bulge /balc/ *a.* şişkinlik, şiş ☆ *e.* şişmek, kabarmak
bulk /balk/ *a.* oylum, hacim; hantal gövde **in bulk** büyük miktarda, toptan **bulky** iri cüsseli, hantal; hacimli
bull /bul/ *a, hayb.* boğa **bulldog** buldok
bulldozer /'buldouzı/ *a.* buldozer
bullet /'bulit/ *a.* kurşun, mermi **bulletproof** kurşun geçirmez
bulletin /'bulıtin/ *a.* ilan, bildiri; bülten
bullfight /'bulfayt/ *a.* boğa güreşi
bullion /'bulyın/ *a.* külçe altın
bullock /'bulık/ *a.* iğdiş edilmiş boğa
bullring /'bulring/ *a.* arena
bullshit /'bulşit/ *a, arg.* bok
bully /'buli/ *a.* kabadayı, zorba ☆ *e.* kabadayılık etmek, zorbalık etmek
bulrush /'bulraş/ *a.* saz, hasırotu
bulwark /'bulwık/ *a.* siper, istihkâm
bum /bam/ *a, kon.* kıç, popo
bumblebee /'bambılbi:/ *a.* yabanarısı
bump /bamp/ *e.* çarpmak, vurmak, toslamak; çarpışmak; ☆ *a.* vurma, çarpma, gümbürtü; şişlik, yumru ☆ *be.* güm diye; aniden **bump into** rastlamak
bumper /'bampı/ *a.* tampon
bumpy /'bampi/ *s.* yamru yumru, çıkıntılı, tümsekli
bun /ban/ *a.* kurabiye, çörek; (saç) topuz
bunch /banç/ *a.* demet, deste, salkım; *kon.* grup ☆ *e.* demet yapmak, bir araya toplamak
bundle /'bandıl/ *a.* bohça, çıkın; deste, tomar ☆ *e.* paldır küldür gitmek; tıkıştırmak
bung /bang/ *a.* tapa, tıkaç
bungalow /'bangılou/ *a.* tek katlı ev,

bungalov
bungle /'bangıl/ *e.* yüzüne gözüne bulaştırmak **bungler** üstünkörü iş gören adam **bungling** üstünkörü iş; beceriksiz, hantal
bunk /bank/ *a.* ranza; kuşet, yatak
bunker /'bankı/ *a.* kömür ambarı, kömürlük; *ask.* yeraltı sığınağı
bunkum /'bankım/ *a.* saçma, zırva, palavra
bunny /'banki/ *a.* tavşan, tavşancık
buoy /boy/ *a.* şamandıra; cankurtaran simidi ☆ *e.* **(up)** su yüzünde tutmak, yüzdürmek; desteklemek **life buoy** cankurtaran simidi
buoyant /'boyınt/ *s.* batmaz, yüzen; neşeli, kaygısız
bur /'bö:/ *a.* dulavratotu, pıtrak
burden /'bö:dın/ *a.* ağır yük ☆ *e.* yüklemek; sıkıntı vermek
burdock /'bö:dok/ *a.* dulavratotu
bureau /'byuırou/ *a.* büro, yazıhane
bureaucracy /byuı'rokrısi/ *a.* bürokrasi
bureaucrat /'byuırıkret/ *a.* bürokrat
burglar /'bö:glı/ *a.* (ev, dükkân, vb. soyan) hırsız **burglary** ev soyma, hırsızlık
burial /'beriıl/ *a.* defin, gömme
burlesque /'bö:lesk/ *a.* alaya alma, taşlama, yerme
burly /'bö:li/ *s.* iriyarı, yapılı
burn /bö:n/ *e.* **burned** veya **burnt** /bö:nt/ yakmak; yanmak ☆ *a.* yanık **burn away** yakıp kül etmek **burning** yanan, yakıcı
burnish /'bö:niş/ *e.* cilalamak, parlatmak
burrow /'barou/ *a.* oyuk, yuva, in
bursar /'bö:sı/ *a.* veznedarlık
burst /bö:st/ *a.* patlamak; patlatmak; dolup taşmak; ☆ *a.* patlama **burst into** aceleyle girmek **burst out** aniden söylemek, patlamak
bury /'beri/ *e.* gömmek, defnetmek; gizlemek, saklamak
bus /bas/ *a.* otobüs **bus stop** otobüs durağı
bush /buş/ *a.* çalı, çalılık **bushy** (saç, vb.) gür; çalılı, çalılık
business /'biznis/ *a.* iş; ticaret; işyeri

Mind your own business. Sen kendi işine bak **none of your business** seni ilgilendirmez **businessman** işadamı **businesswoman** işkadını
bust /bast/ *a.* büst; (kadın) göğüsler; (kadın) göğüs çevresi ölçüsü
bustle /'basıl/ *e.* acele etmek ☆ *a.* telaş
busy /'bizi/ *s.* meşgul; hareketli; işlek
but /bıt, bat/ *bağ.* ama, ancak; ne var ki; oysa ☆ *ilg.* -den başka
butane /'byu:teyn/ *a.* bütan gazı
butcher /'buçı/ *a.* kasap; katil, cani ☆ *e.* (hayvan) kesmek; öldürmek, doğramak
butler /'batlı/ *a.* baş kâhya
butt /bat/ *e.* toslamak ☆ *a.* fıçı; sigara izmariti; dipçik
butter /'batı/ *a.* tereyağı **butter up** *kon.* yağlamak, yağ çekmek
butterfly /'batıflay/ *a.* kelebek
buttery /'batıri/ *s.* tereyağlı
buttock /'batık/ *a.* but, kaba et
button /'batın/ *a.* düğme; elektrik düğmesi, buton ☆ *e.* **(up)** düğmelemek **buttonhole** ilik, düğme iliği; yakaya takılan çiçek
buttress /'batris/ *a.* payanda, destek
buxom /'baksım/ *s.* (kadın) etli butlu, dolgun
buy /bay/ **bought** /bo:t/ *e.* satın almak **buyer** alıcı, müşteri
buzz /baz/ *e.* vızıldamak; **(for)** sinyalle çağırmak ☆ *a.* vızıltı; sinyal
buzzard /'bazıd/ *a, İİ.* bir tür şahin; *Aİ.* akbaba
by /bay/ *ilg.* yanında, yakınında; yanından; yoluyla, dan; -e kadar; ile, vasıtasıyla; tarafından; -e göre; -e bakarak; hakkı için, aşkına; (ölçü ve sayılarda) -le, -la; boyunca; -den, -dan ☆ *be.* geçerek, geçip; yakında; bir kenara **by the way** aklıma gelmişken, bu arada
bye, byebye /bay, bay'bay/ *ünl.* güle güle; allahaısmarladık, hoşça kal
byproduct /'bayprodakt/ *a.* yan ürün; yan etki
bystander /'baystendı/ *a.* görgü tanığı, seyirci

C

cab /keb/ a. taksi; fayton
cabaret /'kebırey/ a. kabare
cabbage /'kebic/ a, bitk. lahana
cabin /'kebin/ a, kon. kamara; kulübe
cabinet /'kebinit/ a. dolap; bakanlar kurulu
cable /'keybıl/ a. kablo; telgraf, telyazı
cacao /kı'ka:ou/ a. kakao
cachet /'keşey/ a. kaşe, mühür, damga
cackle /'kekıl/ e. (tavuk) gıdaklamak ☆ a. gıdaklama; kıkırtı
cactus /'kektıs/ a, bitk. kaktüs
cadaver /'kı'deyvı/ a. kadavra
cadet /kı'det/ a. harp okulu öğrencisi
caesarean /si'zeırıın/ a, hek. sezaryen
café /'kefey/ a. kafe
cafeteria /kefi'tiırıı/ a. (selfservis) kafeterya
caffeine /'kefi:n/ a. kafein
caftan /'keften/ a. kaftan
cage /keyc/ a. kafes
cagey /'keyci/ s, kon. ağzı sıkı, ketum
cake /keyk/ a. pasta, kek; kalıp, topak
calamity /kı'lemiti/ a. felaket, afet
calcify /'kelsifay/ e. kireçlenmek; kireçlendirmek
calcium /'kelsıım/ a. kalsiyum
calculate /'kelkyuleyt/ e. hesaplamak calculation hesap calculator hesap makinesi
calculus /'kelkyulıs/ a, mat. hesap
calendar /'kelindı/ a. takvim
calf /ka:f/ a. buzağı, dana; baldır
calibre /'kelibı/ a. kalite; kalibre, çap
calico /'kelikou/ a. patiska
caliph /'keylif/ a. halife caliphate halifelik
call /ko:l/ e. seslenmek, bağırmak; telefon etmek; adlandırmak, demek ☆ a. bağırış, sesleniş; çığlık; çağrı call for istemek; ihtiyaç duymak call in yardıma çağırmak call on uğramak call up telefon etmek call box İİ. telefon kulübesi caller telefonla arayan kimse, arayan

calligraphy /kı'ligrıfi/ a. güzel el yazısı (sanatı); hattatlık
calling /'ko:ling/ a. istek, heves; meslek, ticari unvan
callipers /'kelipız/ a. çap pergeli; kumpas
callus /'kelıs/ a. nasır
calm /ka:m/ a. (hava) sakinlik; (deniz) durgunluk; rahat, huzur ☆ s. (hava) rüzgârsız; (deniz) durgun, dalgasız; sakin, huzurlu ☆ e. sakinleştirmek calm down sakinleşmek; sakinleştirmek
calorie /'kelıri/ a. kalori
calypso /kı'lipsou/ a, müz. kalipso
camel /'kemıl/ a. deve
camellia /kı'mi:lıı/ a, bitk. kamelya
camera /'kemırı/ a. fotoğraf makinesi
camomile /'kemımayl/ a, bitk. papatya; papatya çayı
camouflage /'kemıfla:j/ a. kamuflaj ☆ e. kamufle etmek
camp /kemp/ a. kamp ☆ e. kamp yapmak
campaign /kem'peyn/ a. kampanya ☆ e. kampanya yapmak
camphor /'kemfı/ a. kâfur
camping /'kemping/ a. kamping
campus /'kempıs/ a. kampüs
can /kın, ken/ e. -ebilmek, -abilmek (olumsuzu cannot /'kenıt, -not/, can't /ka:nt/ geçmiş biçimi could /kud/, olumsuzu couldn't /'kudınt/)
can /ken/ a. teneke kutu ☆ e. konserve yapmak, konservelemek
canal /kı'nel/ a. kanal
canary /kı'neırı/ a. kanarya
cancel /'kensıl/ e. iptal etmek, feshetmek, bozmak cancellation iptal, fesih
cancer /'kensı/ a. Yengeç burcu; hek. kanser
candid /'kendid/ s. içten, samimi, dürüst; (kamera) gizli
candidate /'kendidit/ a. aday
candle /'kendıl/ a. mum candlestick şamdan
candy /'kendi/ a. şeker, şekerleme
cane /keyn/ a. kamış; sopa, değnek
canine /'keynayn/ s. köpeklerle ilgili
canister /'kenistı/ a. teneke kutu

283 **carpenter**

canker /'kenkı/ a, hek. pamukçuk
cannibal /'kenibıl/ a. yamyam
cannon /'kenın/ a, ask. büyük top
cannot /'kenıt, 'kenot/ e, bkz. can
canny /'keni/ a. kurnaz, akıllı, uyanık
canoe /kı'nu:/ a. kano
canon /'kenın/ a. genel kural, ilke
canopy /'kenıpi/ a. gölgelik, tente örtü
can't /ka:nt/ bkz. can
cantankerous /ken'tenkırıs/ s. huysuz, aksi, geçimsiz
canteen /ken'ti:n/ a. kantin; matara
canvas /'kenvıs/ a. çadır bezi; çadır; tuval
canyon /'kenyın/ a, coğ. kanyon, kapız
cap /kep/ a. kasket, başlık, kep; kapak ☆ e. kaplamak, örtmek
capability /keypı'biliti/ a. yetenek
capable /'keypıbıl/ s. yetenekli, elinden gelir
capacity /kı'pesiti/ a. kapasite; yetenek; sıfat, mevki
cape /keyp/ a, coğ. burun; pelerin
capillary /kı'pilıri/ a. kılcal damar
capital /'kepitıl/ a. başkent; büyük harf; sermaye, anamal capital letter büyük harf
capitalism /'kepitılizım/ a. kapitalizm capitalist kapitalist
capitulate /kı'piçuleyt/ e. (düşmana şartlı) teslim olmak, silahları bırakmak capitulation şartlı teslim olma, kapitülasyon
caprice /kı'pri:s/ a. kapris, şımarıklık
capricious /kı'prişıs/ s. kaprisli; dönek, değişken
Capricorn /'kepriko:n/ a. Oğlak burcu
capsicum /'kepsikım/ a, bitk. (dolmalık/uzun) biber
capsize /kep'sayz/ e. alabora olmak; ters dönmek
capsule /'kepsyu:l/ a. kapsül
captain /'keptın/ a, den. kaptan; takım başı; ask. yüzbaşı; den. kaptan
caption /'kepşın/ a. manşet, başlık
captive /'keptiv/ a, s. tutsak captivity tutsaklık, esaret
captor /'keptı/ a. esir alan kişi
capture /'kepçı/ a. esir alma; ganimet ☆ e. zapt etmek, ele geçirmek; tut-

sak etmek
car /ka:/ a. araba, oto, otomobil; vagon car park otopark dining car yemekli vagon sleeping car yataklı vagon
caramel /'kerımıl/ a. karamela
carat /'kerıt/ a. kırat, ayar
caravan /'kerıven/ a. kervan; karavan
caravanserai /kerı'vensıray/ a. kervansaray
carbohydrate /ka:bou'haydreyt/ a. karbonhidrat
carbon /'ka:bın/ a, kim. karbon; karbon kâğıdı
carbuncle /'ka:bankıl/ a. şirpençe, çıban
carburettor /ka:byu'retı/ a. karbüratör
carcass, carcase /'ka:kıs/ a. leş, ceset
card /ka:d/ a. oyun kâğıdı; kart; kartvizit; kartpostal
cardboard /'ka:dbo:d/ a. mukavva, karton
cardiac /'ka:diek/ s, hek. kalple ilgili
cardigan /'ka:digın/ a. hırka
cardinal /'ka:dinıl/ s. önemli, ana ☆ a. kardinal cardinal number asal sayı
care /keı/ a. kaygı, dikkat, özen; ilgi, bakım ☆ e. aldırmak, umursamak; ilgi duymak; kaygılanmak medical care tıbbi bakım take care of -e bakmak care for istemek; bakmak, ilgilenmek carefree kaygısız, tasasız careful dikkatli; özenli carefully dikkatle; özenle careless dikkatsiz; aldırışsız, ilgisiz; düşüncesizce yapılan carelessly dikkatsizce caretaker hademe, odacı; ev bekçisi
career /kı'riı/ a. meslek yaşamı, kariyer
caress /kı'res/ a. okşama; öpme ☆ e. okşamak; öpmek
cargo /'ka:gou/ a. yük, kargo
caricature /'kerikıçuı/ a. karikatür
carnage /'ka:nic/ a. katliam, kırım
carnation /ka:'neyşın/ a, bitk. karanfil
carnival /'ka:nivıl/ a. karnaval, şenlik
carnivore /'ka:nivo:/ a. etobur hayvan carnivorous etobur, etçil
carol /'kerıl/ a. Noel şarkısı, neşeli şarkı
carp /ka:p/ a. sazanbalığı ☆ e, kon. mızmızlanmak, dırdır etmek
carpenter /'ka:pıntı/ a. marangoz, doğ-

ramacı, dülger **carpentry** marangozluk, doğramacılık
carpet /'ka:pit/ a. halı; kilim ☆ e. halı
döşemek
carriage /'keric/ a. araba, at arabası;
nakliye, taşıma
carrier /'kerıı/ a. taşıyıcı; ask. kariyer
carrier bag saplı naylon çanta
carrot /'kerıt/ a. havuç
carry /keri/ e. taşımak, götürmek; ağırlığını çekmek; -e erişmek, -e varmak;
kazanmak **carry off** alıp götürmek; kazanmak **carry on** sürdürmek, yapmak; yönetmek **carry out/through** uygulamak, gerçekleştirmek
cart /ka:t/ a. at arabası
cartilage /'ka:tilic/ a. kıkırdak
carton /'ka:tın/ a. karton kutu
cartoon /ka:'tu:n/ a. karikatür; çizgi film
cartridge /'ka:tric/ a. fişek; kartuş
carve /ka:v/ e. oymak; kesmek, dilimlemek **carving** oyma; oymacılık
cascade /ke'skeyd/ a. çağlayan
case /keys/ a. hal, durum; olay; sorun;
huk. dava; kutu, sandık; çanta; kasa;
dilb. ad durumu **in any case** ne olursa
olsun **in case of** -dığı takdirde, ... du-
rumunda **(just) in case** ne olur ne olmaz
casement /'keysmınt/ a. pencere kanadı
cash /keş/ a. nakit para ☆ e. paraya
çevirmek, bozdurmak **cash register**
yazar kasa
cashew /'keşu:/ a, bitk. maun
cashier /ke'şıı/ a. kasiyer
cashmere /'keşmıı/ a. kaşmir
casino /kı'si:nou/ a. gazino
cask /ka:sk/ a. fıçı, varil
casket /'ka:skit/ a. küçük kutu; Aİ. tabut
casserole /'kesıroul/ a. güveç
cassette /kı'set/ a. kaset
cast /ka:st/ e. fırlatmak, atmak; dökmek; rol vermek ☆ a. atma, atış; kalıp, döküm; oynayanlar, oyuncular; çeşit, tür **cast iron** dökme demir
castaway /'ka:stıwey/ a. deniz kazaze-
desi
caste /ka:st/ a. sınıf, kast
castigate /'kestigeyt/ e. cezalandırmak

casting /'ka:sting/ a. döküm; oyuncu
seçme
castle /'ka:sıl/ a. şato, kale
castrate /ke'streyt/ e. hadım etmek
casual /'kejuıl/ s. tesadüfi; geçici; (giysi) günlük; gelişigüzel **casually** dikkatsizce, gelişigüzel
casualty /'kejuılti/ a. kaza, felaket; kazazede, yaralı; ask. zayiat, kayıp **Casualty Ward/Department** ilkyardım ko-
ğuşu
cat /ket/ a. kedi **rain cats and dogs**
kon. şakır şakır yağmur yağmak
catalogue /'ketılog/ a. katalog, liste
catapult /'ketıpalt/ a. sapan; mancınık
cataract /'ketırekt/ a. büyük çağlayan;
hek. katarakt, aksu
catarrh /kı'ta:/ a, hek. nezle, soğuk algınlığı
catastrophe /kı'testrıfi/ a. yıkım, felaket, facia
catch /keç/ e. **caught** /ko:t/ tutmak, yakalamak; yetişmek; anlamak; sıkıştırmak ☆ a. yakalama, tutma; tutulan
şey, av; bityeniği **catch on** sevilmek;
anlamak **catch up with** -e yetişmek
catchword slogan
catching /'keçing/ s, kon. bulaşıcı
catchy /'keçi/ s. kolayca akılda kalan
categorical /keti'gorikıl/ s. kesin, koşulsuz
categorize /'ketigırayz/ e. sınıflandırmak
category /'ketigıri/ a. sınıf, kategori
cater /'keytı/ e. yiyecek ve içecek sağlamak
caterpillar /'ketıpilı/ a, hayb. tırtıl
catfish /'ketfiş/ a, hayb. yayınbalığı
cathedral /kı'ti:drıl/ a. katedral, başkili-
se
cathode /'ketoud/ a. katot, eksiuç
catholic /'ketılik/ s. (beğeni, ilgi, vb.)
genel, yaygın, geniş **Catholic** Katolik
catsup /'ketsıp/ a. ketçap, domates sosu
cattle /'ketıl/ a. büyükbaş hayvan, sığır
caught /ko:t/ bkz. catch
cauliflower /'koliflauı/ a, bitk. karnabahar
causative /'ko:zıtiv/ s. neden olan; dilb.

285 **challenge**

ettirgen
cause /ko:z/ a. neden, sebep; huk. dava; amaç, hedef ☆ e. -e neden olmak
causeway /'ko:zwey/ a. geçici yol, geçit
caution /'ko:şın/a. dikkat, sakınma, ihtiyat **cautious** dikkatli, tedbirli, sakıngan
cavalry /'kevılri/ a, ask. süvari
cave /keyv/ a. mağara **caveman** mağara adamı
caviar /'kevia:/ a. havyar
cavity /'keviti/ a. çukur, oyuk, boşluk
cavy /'keyvi/ a. kobay
cayenne pepper /keyen'pepı/ a, bitk. arnavutbiberi
cease /si:s/ e. durdurmak, kesmek; durmak **without cease** sürekli, durmaksızın **cease-fire** ateşkes **ceaseless** sürekli, aralıksız
cedar /'si:dı/ a, bitk. sedir, dağservisi
ceiling /'si:ling/ a. tavan
celebrate /'selibreyt/ e. kutlamak; övmek **celebrated** ünlü, bilinen, meşhur **celebration** kutlama; tören
celebrity /si'lebriti/ a. ünlü kişi; ün, şöhret
celery /'selıri/ a, bitk. kereviz
cell /sel/ a. hücre; biy. hücre, göze; pil
cellar /'selı/ a. mahzen, kiler
cellist /'çelist/ a, müz. viyolonselist
cello /'çelou/ a, müz. viyolonsel
cellular /'selyulı/ s. hücresel, gözesel; hücreli, gözeli
celluloid /'selyuloyd/ a. selüloit
cellulose /'selyulous/ a. selüloz
Celsius /'selsiıs/ a, s. santigrat
cement /si'ment/ a. çimento; tutkal, macun, dolgu, çiriş
cemetery /'semitri/ a. gömütlük, mezarlık
censor /'sensı/ a. sansürcü ☆ e. sansürden geçirmek **censorship** sansür
censure /'senşı/ e. kınamak ☆ a. kınama
census /'sensıs/ a. nüfus sayımı, sayım
cent /sent/ a. doların yüzde biri değerindeki para, sent
centennial /sen'teniıl/ s. yüz yılda bir olan

center /'sentı/ a, e, Aİ, bkz. **centre**
centenary /sen'ti:nıri/ a. yüzüncü yıldönümü
Centigrade /sen'tigreyd/ a. santigrat
centimetre /'sentimi:tı/ a. santimetre
centipede /'sentipi:d/ a, hayb. kırkayak
central /'sentrıl/ s. merkezi; ana, temel; uygun **central heating** merkezi ısıtma sistemi
centralize /'sentrılayz/ e. merkezileştirmek
centre /'sentı/ a. merkez; orta ☆ e. bir merkezde toplamak; ortaya koymak
centrifugal /sentri'fyu:gıl/ s. merkezkaç
century /'sençıri/ a. yüzyıl, asır
ceramic /si'remik/ s. seramikle ilgili, seramik **ceramics** seramik, çömlek; seramikçilik
cereal /'siıriıl/ a. tahıl
cerebral /'seribrıl/ s, hek. beyinle ilgili
ceremony /'serimıni/ a. tören, merasim; resmiyet
certain /'sö:tın/ s. kesin, kati, muhakkak; emin, kuşkusuz; belirli, kesin **certainly** kesinlikle; tabii, elbette
certainty /'sö:tınti/a. kesinlik, kuşkusuzluk; kesin olan şey
certificate /sı'tifikıt/ a. sertifika, belge
certify /'sö:tifay/ e. doğrulamak, onaylamak
cesarean /si'zeıriın/ a, kon. sezaryen
cesspool /'sespu:l/ a. lağım çukuru
chafe /çeyf/ e. sürterek yaralamak, ovarak acıtmak; kızmak, sinirlenmek
chaff /ça:f/ a. tahıl kabuğu; saman; çöp
chain /çeyn/ a. zincir; sıra, dizi ☆ e. zincirle bağlamak **chain reaction** zincirleme reaksiyon **chain store** bir firmaya bağlı mağazalardan biri
chair /çeı/ a. iskemle, sandalye; makam, koltuk; profesörlük kürsüsü ☆ e. (toplantı) başkan olmak, yönetmek, başkanlık yapmak
chairman /'çeımın/ a. başkan, yönetici; toplantı başkanı
chalet /'şeley/ a. dağ evi, ahşap yazlık
chalice /'çelis/ a. kadeh
chalk /ço:k/ a. tebeşir
challenge /'çelinc/ e. meydan okumak; (düelloya, kavgaya, vb.) davet etmek;

chamber 286

karşı çıkmak ☆ *a.* meydan okuma; (düelloya/kavgaya) davet; karşı çıkma **challenger** meydan okuyan kimse

chamber /'çeymbı/ *a.* oda; meclis, kamara; toplantı salonu; yasama meclisi; (tüfek) hazne **chambermaid** oda hizmetçisi **chamber orchestra** oda orkestrası

champagne /şem'peyn/ *a.* şampanya

champion /'çempiın/ *a.* şampiyon; savunucu, destekleyici

championship /'çempiınşip/ *a.* şampiyona; şampiyonluk

chance /ça:ns/ *a.* şans, talih; ihtimal, olasılık; fırsat, olanak ☆ *e.* tesadüfen olmak, şans eseri olmak; riske girmek, göze almak **by chance** tesadüfen, şans eseri

chancellor /'ça:nsılı/ *a.* bakan; şansölye, başbakan; rektör

chandelier /şendı'liı/ *a.* avize

change /çeync/ *e.* değiştirmek; değişmek, değiş tokuş etmek; üstünü değiştirmek ☆ *a.* değiştirme, değişme, değişiklik; bozuk para **change one's mind** fikrini değiştirmek **changeable** değişebilir

channel /'çenıl/ *a.* kanal; oluk ☆ *e.* yönlendirmek; kanal açmak

chant /ça:nt/ *a.* (dinsel) şarkı

chaos /'keyos/ *a.* karışıklık, kargaşa, kaos

chap /çep/ *a.* (ciltte) çatlak; adam, arkadaş ☆ *e.* (cilt) çatlamak; çatlatmak

chapel /'çepıl/ *a.* küçük kilise; ibadet yeri

chaplain /'çeplin/ *a.* (okul, ordu, vb.'de) papaz, vaiz

chapter /'çeptı/ *a.* (kitap, yazı, vb.) bölüm

character /'kerıktı/ *a.* karakter, kişilik; nitelik, özellik

characteristic /kerıktı'ristik/ *s.* tipik, karakteristik

characterize /'kerıktırayz/ *e.* nitelendirmek, tanımlamak; -in ayırıcı özelliği olmak

charades /şı'ra:dz/ *a.* sessiz sinema oyunu

charcoal /'ça:koul/ *a.* mangalkömürü; odunkömürü

charge /ça:c/ *e.* fiyat istemek; suçlamak; yüklemek; doldurmak; saldırmak ☆ *a.* yük; yükleme; doldurma; saldırı **in charge of** görevli, sorumlu

chariot /'çerirt/ *a.* savaş arabası

charitable /'çeritıbıl/ *s.* cömert; hayırsever

charity /'çerıti/ *a.* hayırseverlik; sadaka; hayır kurumu

charlatan /'şa:lıtın/ *a, hkr.* şarlatan

charm /ça:m/ *a.* çekicilik, alım; muska, nazarlık ☆ *e.* hayran bırakmak, büyülemek **charming** çekici, büyüleyici, hoş

chart /ça:t/ *a.* harita; grafik, çizim

charter /'ça:tı/ *a.* kiralama, tutma; patent ☆ *e.* patent vermek; kiralamak **charter flight** çarter seferi

chase /çeys/ *e.* peşine düşmek, kovalamak; koşuşturmak ☆ *a.* takip, kovalama; av

chassis /'şesi/ *a.* şasi

chat /çet/ *e.* sohbet etmek ☆ *a.* sohbet, muhabbet, hoşbeş

chateau /'şetou/ *a.* şato

chatter /'çetı/ *e.* çene çalmak, sohbet etmek

chatterbox /'çetıboks/ *a, kon.* geveze

chatty /'çeti/ *s, kon.* geveze, çenebaz

chauffeur /'şoufı/ *a.* özel şoför

cheap /çi:p/ *s.* ucuz; kalitesiz, değersiz **cheapen** ucuzlamak; ucuzlatmak, itibarını düşürmek **cheaply** ucuz olarak

cheat /çi:t/ *a.* hile, aldatma, dolap; dolandırıcı ☆ *e.* aldatmak, dolandırmak

check /çek/ *e.* kontrol etmek, denetlemek; engel olmak, tutmak ☆ *a.* kontrol, denetim; zapt, tutma; emanet makbuzu, fiş; (satranç) şah; ekose desen **check in** (otel defteri vb.'ne) kaydolmak, bagaj kontrolü yaptırmak **check out** otelden ayrılmak **check-up** sağlık muayenesi

checkmate /'çekmeyt/ *e.* mat etmek; yenilgiye uğratmak ☆ *a.* (satranç) mat

cheddar /'çedı/ a. çedar peyniri
cheek /çi:k/ a. yanak; kon. yüzsüzlük, arsızlık, küstahlık cheekbone elmacık-kemiği cheeky kon. küstah, arsız, yüz-süz
cheer /'çiı/ a. alkış, bağırış; neşe, keyif ☆ e. neşelendirmek; alkışlamak, "ya-şa" diye bağırmak cheerful neşeli, şen, keyifli cheerfully neşeyle cheer-less keyifsiz, neşesiz
cheerio /çiiri'ou/ ünl, İİ, kon. hoşça kal!; gülegüle!
cheerleader /'çiili:dı/ a. amigo
cheese /çi:z/ a. peynir
cheetah /'çi:tı/ a, hayb. çita
chef /şef/ a. şef, aşçıbaşı
chemical /'kemikıl/ s. kimyasal ☆ a. kimyasal madde
chemist /'kemist/ a. kimyager, kimyacı chemistry kimya
cheque /çek/ a. çek cheque book çek defteri
cherish /'çeriş/ e. sevmek; hatırasında yaşatmak
cherry /'çeri/ a. kiraz
chess /çes/ a. satranç
chest /çest/ a. sandık, kutu; anat. gö-ğüs, bağır chest of drawers konsol
chestnut /'çesnat/ a. kestane
chew /çu:/ e. çiğnemek ☆ a. çiğne-me; lokma chewing gum çiklet, sakız
chick /çik/ a. civciv
chicken /'çikin/ a. piliç, tavuk; piliç eti chicken pox hek. suçiçeği
chickpea /'çikpi:/ a. nohut
chief /çi:f/ a. başkan, baş, amir, şef; re-is ☆ s. baş; en önemli, ana
child /çayld/ a. (ç. children /'çildrın/) çocuk; evlat, çocuk childhood çocuk-luk childish çocuksu, çocuk gibi
chill /çil/ e. soğumak; soğutmak; ür-pertmek ☆ s. soğuk ☆ a. titreme, ürperti; soğuk algınlığı chilly soğuk, serin
chilli /'çili/ a, bitk. kırmızıbiber
chime /çaym/ a. zil/çan sesi ☆ e. (sa-at, zil, vb.) çalmak
chimney /'çimni/ a. baca; yanardağ ağ-zı chimneysweep(er) baca temizleyi-cisi

chimp /çimp/ a, hayb. şempanze
chimpanzee /çimpen'zi:/ a, hayb. şem-panze
chin /çin/ a. çene
china /'çaynı/ a. çini, porselen
chinaware /'çaynıweı/ a. çin işi, çini/-porselen eşya
chink /çink/ a. yarık, çatlak ☆ e. şın-gırdamak, şıngırdatmak
chip /çip/ a. kırıntı, yonga; ç, İİ. patates kızartması; Aİ. cips ☆ e. yontmak; çentmek, dilimlemek
chipping /'çiping/ a. çakıltaşı
chiropody /ki'ropıdi/ a. ayak bakımı
chirp /çö:p/ a. cıvıltı ☆ e. cıvıldamak chirpy neşeli, cıvıl cıvıl
chisel /'çizıl/ a. keski ☆ e. oymak, yontmak
chivalry /'şivılri/ a. şövalyelik; yiğitlik, kahramanlık; incelik, kibarlık
chive /çayv/ a, bitk. frenksoğanı
chlorinate /'klo:rineyt/ e. klorlamak
chlorine /'klo:ri:n/ a. klor
chloroform /'klorıfo:m/ a. kloroform
chlorophyll /'klo:rıfil/ a. klorofil
chocolate /'çoklit/ a. çikolata
choice /çoys/ a. seçme; seçim; seçilen kişi/şey; seçenek ☆ s. seçkin
choir /'kwayı/ a. koro; koro üyelerinin yeri
choke /çouk/ e. boğmak; boğulmak; tı-kamak; tıkanmak ☆ a. jikle, hava kelebeği
choose /çu:z/ e. chose /çouz/, chosen /'çouzin/ seçmek; karar vermek; iste-mek choosy güç beğenen, titiz
chop /çop/ e. (balta, vb. ile) kesmek; kıymak, doğramak ☆ a. balta, vb. vuruşu; vuruş, darbe; (deniz) çırpıntı; pirzola, külbastı first chop birinci sı-nıf, kaliteli chopper balta; satır choppy (deniz) çırpıntılı, dalgalı; (rüz-gâr) değişken chopstick Çinlilerin kul-landığı yemek çubuğu
choral /'ko:rıl/ s. koro ile ilgili
chord /ko:d/ a. tel; müz. tel; müz. akor mat. kiriş
chore /ço:/ a. sıkıcı iş; günlük ev işi
choreography /kori'ogrıfi/ a. koreografi
chorus /'ko:rıs/ a. koro; nakarat; uğultu

chose /çouz/ *bkz.* choose
chosen /'çouzın/ *bkz.* choose
Christ /krayst/ *a.* İsa
christen /'krisın/ *e.* vaftiz etmek; ad koymak
Christendom /'krisındım/ *a.* Hıristiyan âlemi
Christian /'krişçın/ *a, s.* Hıristiyan Christian name ön ad, vaftiz adı
Christianity /kristi'eniti/ *a.* Hıristiyanlık
Christmas /'krismıs/ *a.* Noel Christmas Eve Noel arifesi
chrome /kroum/ *a.* krom
chromium /'kroumiım/ *a.* krom
chromosome /'kroumısoum/ *a, biy.* kromozom
chronic /'kronik/ *s.* müzmin, süregen
chronicle /'kronikıl/ *a.* kronik, vakayiname
chronological /'kronı'locikıl/ *s.* kronolojik, zamandizinsel
chronology /krı'nolıci/ *a.* kronoloji, zamandizin
chronometer /krı'nomıtı/ *a.* kronometre, süreölçer
chrysanthemum /kri'sentimım/ *a, bitk.* kasımpatı, krizantem
chuck /çak/ *e.* atmak, fırlatmak
chuckle /'çakıl/ *e.* kıkır kıkır gülmek ☆ *a.* kıkırdama
chug /çag/ *e.* (motor) pat pat etmek, teklemek
chum /çam/ *a, kon.* iyi arkadaş, ahbap chummy samimi, arkadaş canlısı
chump /çamp/ *a.* kütük, takoz
chunk /çank/ *a.* iri parça chunky bodur ve tıknaz
church /çö:ç/ *a.* kilise churchyard kilise mezarlığı
churlish /'çö:liş/ *s, hkr.* kaba, ters, aksi
churn /çö:n/ *a.* yayık ☆ *e.* yayıkta tereyağı yapmak; çalkalamak
chute /şu:t/ *a.* küçük çağlayan; oluk
chutney /'çatni/ *a.* bir tür acı sos
cider /'saydı/ *a, İİ.* elma şarabı, elma şırası
cigar /si'ga:/ *a.* puro
cigarette /sigı'ret/ *a.* sigara
cinder /'sindı/ *a.* kor, köz
cinema /'sinimı/ *a.* sinema

cinnamon /'sinımın/ *a.* tarçın
cipher, cypher /'sayfı/ *a.* sıfır; şifre
circa /'sö:kı/ *ilg.* tahminen; yaklaşık
circle /'sö:kıl/ *a.* çember, daire; halka; çevre; (tiyatro, vb.) balkon ☆ *e.* çember içine almak; çevresini dolaşmak
circuit /'sö:kit/ *a.* dolaşma, devir, tur; çevre; ring seferi; *fiz.* devre, çevrim circuit breaker şalter
circuitous /sö:'kyu:itıs/ *s.* dolambaçlı, kıvrımlı, dönemeçli
circular /'sö:kyulı/ *s.* dairesel; dolambaçlı ☆ *a.* genelge
circulate /'sö:kyuleyt/ *e.* dolaşmak; dolaştırmak; yaymak; yayılmak circulation dolaşım; tiraj
circumcise /'sö:kımsayz/ *e.* sünnet etmek circumcision sünnet
circumference /sı'kamfırıns/ *a, mat.* çember, çevre
circumflex /'sö:kımfleks/ *a.* düzeltme/uzatma işareti
circumstance /'sö:kımstens/ *a.* durum, koşul, hal; olay in/under no circumstances asla, hiçbir şekilde in/under the circumstances şartlar gerektirdiğinden
circumvent /sö:kım'vent/ *e.* -den kaçmak, kaçınmak; atlatmak
circus /'sö:kıs/ *a.* sirk; *İİ.* alan, meydan
cirrus /'sirıs/ *a.* sirrus, saçakbulut
cistern /'sistın/ *a.* sarnıç
citadel /'sitıdıl/ *a.* kale
citation /say'teyşın/ *huk.* celpname; alıntı
cite /sayt/ *e, huk.* mahkemeye çağırmak; celpname göndermek; bahsetmek; örnek olarak vermek/göstermek
citizen /'sitizın/ *a.* vatandaş, yurttaş citizenship vatandaşlık, yurttaşlık
citric acid /sitrik'esid/ *a.* sitrik asit
citrus /'sitrıs/ *s.* turunçgillerle ilgili
city /'siti/ *a.* kent, şehir
civic /'sivik/ *a.* şehirle ilgili, kentsel; yurttaşlıkla ilgili civics yurttaşlık bilgisi
civil /'sivıl/ *s.* devlete ait, milli, resmi; sivil; uygar; kibar, nazik; *huk.* medeni hukukla ilgili civil defence sivil savunma civil law medeni hukuk civil rights vatandaşlık hakları civil servant dev-

let memuru civil service devlet memurluğu, devlet hizmeti; devlet memurları civil war iç savaş

civilian /si'viliın/ a, s. sivil

civility /si'viliti/ a. incelik, nezaket, kibarlık

civilization /sivılay'zeyşın/ a. uygarlık, medeniyet; uygarlaştırma; uygarlaşma

civilize /'sivılayz/ e. uygarlaştırmak; adam etmek, kibarlaştırmak

claim /kleym/ e. hak talep etmek; almak, sahip çıkmak; iddia etmek ☆ e. istek, talep; hak; iddia

clam /klem/ a, hayb. deniztarağı

clamour /klemı/ a. gürültü, patırtı

clamp /klemp/ a. mengene, kenet, kıskaç ☆ e. mengeneyle sıkıştırmak

clan /klen/ a. kabile, oymak

clandestine /klen'destin/ s. gizli kapaklı, el altından yapılan

clang /kleng/ e. çınlamak ☆ a. çınlama

clap /klep/ e. (el) çırpmak; alkışlamak; dostça vurmak ☆ a. alkış; gürleme

clarify /'klerifay/ e. açıklamak, açıklık getirmek; açıklanmak; arıtmak

clarinet /kleri'net/ a, müz. klarnet

clarity /'kleriti/ a. açık seçiklik

clash /kleş/ e. çarpışmak, çatışmak; (renk) uymamak ☆ a. gürültü, patırtı; çatışma

clasp /kla:sp/ a. toka, kopça; sıkı tutma; kavrama ☆ e. sıkıca tutmak; kavramak; kopça/toka ile tutturmak

class /kla:s/ a. sınıf, zümre; (okul) sınıf; ders; çeşit, tür ☆ e. sınıflandırmak first class birinci mevki middle class orta sınıf classmate sınıf arkadaşı classroom derslik

classic /'klesik/ s. klasik; bilinen, tipik ☆ a. klasik yapıt, klasik

classical /'klesikıl/ s. klasik

classify /'klesifay/ e. sınıflandırmak, bölümlemek classification /klesifi'keyşın/ sınıflama; bölümleme, tasnif, sınıflandırma classified /'klesifayd/ sınıflandırılmış, tasnif edilmiş; (askeri bilgi, vb.) gizli classified ad küçük gazete ilanı

clatter /'kletı/ e. tangırdamak; tangırdatmak ☆ a. tangırtı

clause /klo:z/ a, dilb. cümlecik, yantümce; huk. madde, fıkra

claustrophobia /klo:strı'foubiı/ a. kapalı yer korkusu, klostrofobi

claw /klo:/ a. pençe; kıskaç ☆ e. pençelemek, tırmalamak

clay /kley/ a. kil

clean /kli:n/ s. temiz; masum; düzgün, adil, kurallara uygun; net ☆ be, kon. tam anlamıyla, bütünüyle ☆ e. temizlemek; temizlenmek, engeli aşmak clean-cut biçimli, düzgün; belirgin, açık seçik clean out temizlemek; kon. soyup soğana çevirmek clean up temizlemek, tertemiz yapmak; yoluna koymak, düzeltmek; kon. çok kâr etmek, vurgun vurmak cleaner temizlikçi; temizleyici cleaner's temizleyici dükkânı

cleanliness /'klenlinis/ a. temizlik

cleanly /'kli:nli/ be. temiz bir biçimde

cleanse /klenz/ e. (yara, vb.) temizlemek

clear /kliı/ s. açık, parlak; emin; açık, engelsiz; masum, temiz; belirgin, ortada, aşikâr ☆ be. açıkça; tamamen; uzağa, uzakta; dışarı ☆ e. temizlemek, açmak; temizlemek; temize çıkarmak, aklamak clear away kaldırıp götürmek clear off çekip gitmek clear out boşaltıp temizlemek, çekilip gitmek clear up (hava) açılmak; çözümlemek clearly kesinlikle

clearance /'kliırıns/ a. (gemi, vb.) geçiş izni

cleave /kli:v/ e. yarmak, ayırmak, bölmek cleaver kasap satırı

clef /klef/ a, müz. anahtar

clemency /'klemınsi/ a. acıma, merhamet; (hava) yumuşaklık

clench /klenç/ e. (diş, el, vb.) sıkmak, sımsıkı kapamak; sıkıca kavramak

clergy /'klö:ci/ a. ruhban sınıfı clergyman papaz, rahip

clerical /'klerikıl/ s. rahiplerle ilgili; daire/büro işleriyle ilgili

clerk /kla:k/ a. yazman, kâtip; tezgâhtar, satıcı

clever /'klevı/ s. akıllı, becerikli; usta
cliché /'kli:şey/ a. basmakalıp söz
click /klik/ a. tıkırtı ☆ e. tıkırdamak; tıkırdatmak
client /'klayınt/ a. müşteri, alıcı; huk. müvekkil clientele /kli:ın'tel/ müşteriler, müşteri
cliff /klif/ a. uçurum
climate /'klaymit/ a. iklim
climatic /'klaymetik/ s. iklimsel
climatology /klaymı'tolıci/ a. klimatoloji, iklimbilim
climax /'klaymeks/ a. zirve, doruk
climb /klaym/ e. tırmanmak; yükselmek ☆ a. tırmanış climber tırmanıcı; dağcı; bitk. sarmaşık
clinch /klinç/ e. çözümlemek; kucaklamak, sarılmak
cling /kling/ s. clung /klang/ tutunmak, yapışmak
clinic /'klinik/ a. klinik clinical klinik; soğuk, ilgisiz, umursamaz
clink /klink/ e. şangırdamak ☆ a. şangırtı
clip /klip/ a. ataş; toka; klips; şarjör; klip; kesme, kırılma ☆ e. (ataş, vb. ile) tutturmak; kırkmak; vurmak
clippers /'klipız/ a. kırpma makası, saç kesme makinesi nail clippers tırnak makası
clipping /'kliping/ a. kupür, kesik
clique /kli:k/ a. klik, hizip
clitoris /'klitıris/ a. klitoris, bızır
cloak /klouk/ a. pelerin ☆ e. gizlemek cloakroom vestiyer
clock /klok/ a. masa/duvar saati ☆ e. saat tutmak clockwise saat yelkovanı yönünde
clod /klod/ e. tıkamak; tıkanmak
cloister /'kloystı/ a. manastır
clop /klop/ a. nal sesi
close /klouz/ e. kapatmak; kapanmak; bitirmek, son vermek ☆ a. son, sonuç, nihayet ☆ s. yakın; samimi; sık, az aralıklı; dikkatli, titiz; az farklı, hemen hemen eşit ☆ be. yakın, yakından, yakına close by yakında, yanında close call/shave/thing kon. kıl payı kurtuluş close fitting dar, sıkı close-up yakından çekilen fotoğraf

closed circuit kapalı devre televizyon sistemi closely yakından; dikkatle
closet /'klozit/ a, AI. gömme dolap; tuvalet; küçük oda
clot /klot/ e. pıhtılaşmak ☆ a. pıhtı
cloth /klot/ a. kumaş; bez
clothe /kloud/ e. giydirmek
clothes /kloudz/ a. giysi, elbise
clothing /'klouding/ a. giyecek, giyim, kıyafet
cloud /klaud/ a. bulut ☆ e. bulutlanmak; karartmak; kararmak cloudy bulutlu; bulanık
clove /klouv/ a. karanfil; sarmısak dişi
clover /'klouvı/ a. yonca
clown /klaun/ a. palyaço; soytarı
club /klab/ a. kulüp, dernek; sopa; golf sopası; sinek, ispati
cluck /klak/ a. gıdaklama ☆ e. gıdaklamak
clue /klu:/ a. ipucu
clump /klamp/ a. küme, yığın ☆ e. ağır ve gürültülü adımlarla yürümek
clumsy /'klamzi/ s. beceriksiz, sakar; biçimsiz
cluster /'klastı/ a. salkım, demet, küme
clutch /klaç/ e. kavramak, yakalamak ☆ a. kavrama, tutma; debriyaj; pençe
clutter /'klatı/ a. karışıklık, darmadağınıklık e. karmakarışık etmek
coach /kouç/ a. at arabası, fayton; İl. yolcu otobüsü; yolcu vagonu; sp. antrenör, koç, çalıştırıcı ☆ e. çalıştırmak, yetiştirmek
coagulate /kou'egyuleyt/ e. koyulaşmak, pıhtılaşmak; koyulaştırmak, pıhtılaştırmak coagulant pıhtılaştırıc madde coagulation pıhtılaşma
coal /koul/ a. kömür coalgas havagaz coalminer maden kömürü işçisi
coalesce /kouı'les/ e. birleşmek
coalescence /kouı'lesıns/ a. birleşme bütünleşme
coalition /kouı'lişın/ a. koalisyon, birleş me
coarse /ko:s/ s. kaba, terbiyesiz; bayağı; adi; işlenmemiş
coast /koust/ a. kıyı, sahil ☆ e. kıyı bo yunca gitmek; yokuş aşağı inmel

coastguard sahil koruma görevlisi; sahil koruma **coastline** kıyı, sahil şeridi
coat /kout/ a. palto; ceket; mont; post; tabaka, kat ☆ e. kaplamak
coating /'kouting/ a. tabaka, kat, astar
coax /kouks/ e. tatlılıkla ikna etmek; tatlılıkla elde etmek
cob /kob/ a. mısır koçanı
cobalt /'koubo:lt/ a. kobalt
cobble /'kobıl/ a. arnavut kaldırım taşı ☆ e. kaldırım taşı döşemek
cobbler /'koblı/ a. ayakkabı tamircisi
cobra /'kobrı/ a, hayb. kobra
cobweb /'kobweb/ a. örümcek ağı
cocaine /kou'keyn/ a. kokain
cock /kok/ a. horoz; tetik; musluk ☆ e. (silah) kurmak, tetiğe almak; (kulak, vb.) dikilmek, kalkmak
cockcrow /'kokkrou/ a. şafak, sabahın ilk saatleri
cockerel /'kokırıl/ a. yavru horoz
cockle /'kokıl/ a. bir tür midye
Cockney /'kokni/ a, s. (Doğu) Londralı
cockpit /'kokpit/ a. horoz dövüşü yapılan küçük alan; pilot kabini; yarış arabasında sürücü yeri
cockroach /'kokrouç/ a, hayb. hamamböceği
cocktail /'kokteyl/ a. kokteyl
coco /'koukou/ a. hindistancevizi ağacı
cocoa /'koukou/ a, bitk. kakao
coconut /'koukınat/ a, bitk. hindistancevizi
cocoon /kı'ku:n/ a. koza
cod /kod/ a. morina balığı
coda /'koudı/ a, müz. koda, final
coddle /'kodıl/ e. ağır ateşte kaynatmak; üzerine titremek, şımartmak
code /koud/ a. şifre; kod; kural ☆ e. şifrelemek, şifreyle yazmak; kodlamak
codein /'koudi:n/ a. kodein
codify /'koudifay/ e. düzenlemek, kodlamak
coed /kou'ed/ s. (okul) karma eğitim yapan, karma
coeducation /kouecu'keyşın/ a. karma eğitim
coefficient /koui'fişınt/ a. katsayı
coerce /kou'ö:s/ e. zorlamak; baskı yapmak

coercion /kou'ö:şın/ a. zorlama, baskı
coexist /kouig'zist/ e. barış içinde birlikte yaşamak **coexistence** bir arada varoluş
coffee /'kofi/ a. kahve **coffeepot** cezve
coffer /'kofı/ a. sandık, kutu, çekmece
coffin /'kofin/ a. tabut
cog /kog/ a. çark dişi, diş
cogent /'koucınt/ s. ikna edici, inandırıcı, telkin edici
cogitate /'kociteyt/ e. (bir şey üzerinde) enine boyuna iyice düşünmek **cogitation** iyice düşünme
cognac /'konyek/ a. konyak
cognate /'kogneyt/ s. aynı kökenli, aynı soydan gelen, akraba
cognition /kog'nişın/ a. bilme, kavrama, idrak
cognitive /'kognitiv/ s. bilmeye, kavramaya ya da idrak etmeye ilişkin
cohabit /kou'hebit/ e. (nikâhsızca) birlikte yaşamak **cohabitation** birlikte yaşama
cohere /kou'hiı/ e. yapışmak; birbirini tutmak **coherent** uygun, tutarlı; yapışık
cohesion /kou'hi:jın/ a. yapışma
coiffeur /kwo'fö:/ a. kuaför
coil /koyl/ a. bobin, kangal ☆ e. sarmak
coin /koyn/ a. madeni para ☆ e. para basmak; (sözcük, vb.) uydurmak
coinage /'koynic/ a. madeni para basma; para sistemi; (yeni sözcük, vb.) uydurma
coincide /kouin'sayd/ e. aynı zamana rastlamak, çatışmak; (düşünce, vb.) uymak
coincidence /kou'insidıns/ a. rastlantı, tesadüf; uygunluk **coincidental** rastlantısal, tesadüfi
coke /kouk/ a. kok kömürü; *kon.* koka kola
cola /'koulı/ a. kolalı içecekler
colander /'kalındı/ a. süzgeç, kevgir
cold /kould/ s. soğuk; üşümüş ☆ a. soğuk; nezle **cold-blooded** soğukkanlı **cold-hearted** soğuk, duygusuz **cold war** soğuk savaş **catch a cold** nezle ol-

mak; üşütmek

collaborate /kı'lebıreyt/ *e.* işbirliği yapmak **collaboration** işbirliği

collage /'kola:j/ *a.* kolaj, kolaj resim

collapse /kı'leps/ *e.* çökmek; yıkılmak; açılır kapanır olmak ☆ *a.* çöküş, yıkılış, çökme; ani düşüş, yıkım; başarısızlık **collapsible** açılır kapanır

collar /'kolı/ *a.* yaka; tasma **collarbone** *anat.* köprücükkemiği

collateral /kı'letırıl/ *s.* yan yana, paralel; yardımcı, ek; aynı soydan gelen

colleague /'koli:g/ *a.* meslektaş

collect /kı'lekt/ *e.* toplamak, biriktirmek; uğrayıp almak **collection** toplama; toplanma; koleksiyon, biriktiri; yığın **collector** toplayan

collective /kı'lektiv/ *s.* ortaklaşa, ortak, toplu **collective agreement** toplusözleşme **collective bargaining** toplu pazarlık **collective noun** *dilb.* topluluk adı

college /'kolic/ *a.* yüksekokul, fakülte

collide /kı'layd/ *e.* çarpışmak; çatışmak, zıt olmak

collier /'kolıı/ *a.* kömür işçisi; kömür gemisi **colliery** /'kolyıri/ kömür ocağı, kömür madeni

collision /kı'lijın/ *a.* çarpışma; çatışma, düşünce ayrılığı

colloquial /kı'loukwiıl/ *s.* konuşma diline özgü

collude /kı'lu:d/ *e.* dolap çevirmek, tezgâh hazırlamak **collusion** gizli anlaşma, dolap, tezgâh

cologne /kı'loun/ *a.* kolonya

colon /'koulın/ *a.* iki nokta üst üste (:) ☆ *anat.* kolon

colonel /'kö:nıl/ *a.* albay

colonial /kı'louniıl/ *s.* sömürgeci

colonialism /kı'louniılizım/ *a.* sömürgecilik

colonize /'kolınayz/ *a.* kolonileştirmek, sömürgeleştirmek

colony /'kolıni/ *a.* sömürge; koloni

color /'kalı/ *a, Aİ, bkz.* **colour**

colossal /kı'losıl/ *s.* dev gibi, kocaman

colossus /kı'losıs/ *a.* dev

colour /'kalı/ *a.* renk; boya; ç. bayrak ☆ *e.* boyamak **colour bar** ırk ayrımı **oil**

colours yağlıboya **water colours** suluboya **colour-blind** renk körü **coloured** renkli **colourfast** boyası çıkmaz, solmaz **colourful** renkli, rengârenk; canlı, parlak **colouring** boya, gıda boyası; boyama, renklendirme **colourless** renksiz; solgun; sıkıcı, itici; donuk

colt /koult/ *a.* tay; sıpa

column /'kolım/ *a.* sütun **columnist** köşe yazarı

coma /'koumı/ *a, hek.* koma

comb /koum/ *a.* tarak ☆ *e.* taramak

combat /'kombet/ *a.* mücadele, savaşım; çarpışma, savaş ☆ *e.* mücadele etmek; savaşmak **combatant** savaşçı

combination /kombi'neyşın/ *a.* birleştirme; birleşme; *kim.* bileşim, terkip

combine /kım'bayn/ *e.* birleşmek; birleştirmek **combine harvester** biçerdöver

combustible /kım'bastibıl/ *s.* yanabilir, kolayca tutuşabilir, yanıcı

combustion /kım'basçın/ *a.* yanma, tutuşma

come /kam/ *e.* **came** /keym/ **come** /kam/ gelmek; varmak; ulaşmak; olmak **come about** olmak **come across** karşılaşmak, rastlamak **come along** ilerlemek, gelişmek; (sağlık) iyiye gitmek; olmak, ortaya çıkmak; takip etmek **come apart** kopuvermek, dağılıvermek **come back** yeniden gözde olmak **come by** elde etmek, sahip olmak; karşılaşmak; tesadüfen edinmek **come down** aşağıya inmek; (fiyat) düşmek **come in** (içeri) girmek **come into** girmek; mirasa konmak **come off** çıkmak, kopmak **come on** gelişmek, ilerlemek; elini çabuk tutmak **come out** çıkmak **come round** uğramak, ziyaret etmek; kendine gelmek **come through** kurtulmak; atlatmak **come to** ayılmak; tutmak, varmak **come true** gerçekleşmek **come up** çıkmak, yükselmek **comeback** eski güncüne kavuşma, yeniden başarma **comedown** düş kırıklığı, düşüş

comedian /kı'mi:dıın/ *a.* komedyen

comedy /'komidi/ *a.* komedi, güldürü

293 **communicate**

comet /'komit/ *a.* kuyrukluyıldız, komet

comfort /'kamfıt/ *a.* rahatlık; refah, konfor; teselli ☆ *e.* rahatlatmak, teselli etmek

comfortable /'kamfıtıbıl/ *s.* rahat; konforlu; huzurlu

comic /'komik/ *s.* komik, gülünç comic strips karikatür şeklinde öykü dizisi comics resimli mizah dergileri; karikatür öyküsü

coming /'kaming/ *a.* gelme, geliş, varış ☆ *s.* gelen, gelmekte olan

comma /'komı/ *a.* virgül

command /kı'ma:nd/ *e.* emretmek, buyurmak; komuta etmek, yönetmek; hâkim olmak ☆ *a.* buyruk, emir, komut; kontrol, komuta, kumanda yönetim; yetki; hâkimiyet

commandant /komın'dent/ *a.* komutan

commandeer /komın'diı/ *e, ask.* el koymak

commander /kı'ma:ndı/ *a.* komutan; deniz yarbayı commander-in-chief başkomutan

commando /kı'ma:ndou/ *a, ask.* komando

commemorate /kı'memıreyt/ *e.* anmak, anısını kutlamak; anısı olmak

commence /kı'mens/ *e.* başlamak commencement başlangıç, başlama; diploma töreni

commend /kı'mend/ *e.* övmek, takdir etmek; emanet etmek commendable övgüye layık commendation övgü; takdir; resmi takdirname, onurlandırma

commensurate /kı'menşırit/ *s.* uygun, oranlı, eşit

comment /'koment/ *a.* yorum ☆ *e.* yorum yapmak; yorumlamak

commentary /'komıntıri/ *a.* açıklama, yorum; (maç, vb.) anlatma, nakil

commentate /'komınteyt/ *e.* (maç, vb.) anlatmak

commentator /'komınteytı/ *a.* (maç, vb.) anlatıcı

commerce /'komö:s/ *a.* ticaret, tecim chamber of commerce ticaret odası

commercial /kı'mö:şıl/ *s.* ticari ☆ *a.* televizyon/radyo reklamı

commercialize /kı'mö:şılayz/ *e.* ticarete dökmek

commiserate /kı'mizıreyt/ *e.* (with) acısını paylaşmak commiseration acısını paylaşma, derdine ortak olma

commission /kı'mişın/ *a.* iş, görev; yetki; kurul, heyet, komisyon; komisyon, yüzde ☆ *e.* görevlendirmek

commissionaire /kımişı'neı/ *a.* (sinema, otel, vb.'de) kapıcı

commissioner /kı'mişını/ *a.* komisyon üyesi; hükümet temsilcisi; (devlet dairesinde) yetkili memur, şube müdürü

commit /kı'mit/ *e.* yapmak, işlemek; teslim etmek; üstlenmek commitment taahhüt, üstlenme; sorumluluk; söz; bağlantı committed kendini adamış

committee /kı'miti/ *a.* komisyon, heyet, komite

commodity /kı'moditi/ *a.* eşya, mal

commodore /'komıdo:/ *a.* tuğamiral

common /'komın/ *s.* ortak, genel; sıradan; toplumsal, kamusal; yaygın, bilinen ☆ *a.* halka açık yeşil alan, park; ortak, müşterek Common Market Ortak Pazar common noun *dilb.* cins ismi common sense sağduyu commonly genellikle, çoğunlukla, ekseriya

commoner /'komını/ *a.* halk tabakasından olan kimse

commonplace /'komınpleys/ *s.* alelade, sıradan, basit

Commons /'komınz/ *a.* Avam Kamarası

commonwealth /'komınwelt/ *a.* ulus; cumhuriyet The Commonwealth İngiliz Uluslar Topluluğu

commotion /kı'mouşın/ *a.* kargaşa

communal /'komyunıl/ *s.* halka ait, toplumsal; ortaklaşa kullanılan

communicate /kı'myu:nikeyt/ *e.* (haber, düşünce, vb.) geçirmek, nakletmek, iletmek, bildirmek, açıklamak; (with) görüş alışverişi yapmak, iletişim kurmak; birleşmek communication iletişim, haberleşme, komünikasyon; haber, mesaj; *ç.* komünikasyon sistemi communicative /kı'myu:nikıtiv/ konuşkan, geveze, boşboğaz

communion /kı'myu:niın/ a. görüş alışverişi; duygu, düşünce, vb. paylaşma
communiqué /kı'myu:nikey/ a. bildiri
communism /'komyunizım/ a. komünizm **communist** komünist
community /kı'myu:niti/ a. halk, toplum; topluluk; ortak iyelik, ortaklaşalık
commute /kı'myu:t/ e. (cezayı) hafifletmek; ev ile iş arasında gidip gelmek; değiş tokuş etmek
compact /kım'pekt/ s. yoğun, sıkı, sık
companion /kım'peniın/ a. arkadaş, yoldaş **companionship** arkadaşlık; dostluk
company /'kampıni/ a. şirket; arkadaşlık, eşlik; dost; birlik, grup; den. tayfa; ask. bölük
comparable /'kompırıbıl/ s. karşılaştırılabilir
comparative /kım'perıtiv/ s. karşılaştırmalı, mukayeseli; göreceli, nispi; dilb. üstünlük derecesi
compare /kım'peı/ e. karşılaştırmak, mukayese etmek; benzetmek
comparison /kım'perisın/ a. karşılaştırma, mukayese; benzerlik
compartment /kım'pa:tmınt/ a. bölme, daire; (tren) kompartıman; oto. torpido gözü, torpido
compass /'kampıs/ a. pusula; pergel; sınır, alan
compassion /kım'peşın/ a. acıma, şefkat **compassionate** merhametli, sevecen
compatible /kım'petıbıl/ s. bir arada olabilir, bağdaşabilir
compatriot /kım'petriıt/ a. yurttaş, hemşeri
compel /kım'pel/ e. zorlamak
compensate /'kompınseyt/ e. tazminat ödemek; bedelini vermek, zararı ödemek, telafi etmek **compensation** bedel, tazminat; yerini doldurma, telafi
compére /'kompeı/ a, İİ. (eğlence programında) sunucu ☆ e, İİ sunuculuk yapmak
compete /kım'pi:t/ e. yarışmak; yarışmaya katılmak
competence /'kompitıns/ a. yetenek, beceri, ustalık; yetki **competent** yete-

nekli, usta; doyurucu; yetkili
competition /kompi'tişın/ a. yarışma, müsabaka; rekabet, çekişme
competitive /kım'petitiv/ s. rekabete dayanan; rekabetçi
competitor /kım'petitı/ a. yarışmacı; rakip
compilation /kompi'leyşın/ a. derleme
compile /kım'payl/ e. derlemek, toplamak **compiler** derleyen
complacent /kım'pleysınt/ s. halinden memnun, keyfi yerinde
complain /kım'pleyn/ e. şikâyet etmek, yakınmak **complaint** yakınma, şikâyet; hastalık; dert
complement /'komplimınt/ a. tamamlayıcı şey; tam; bütün ☆ e. tamamlamak **complementary** /-'mentıri/ tamamlayıcı
complete /kım'pli:t/ s. tam, eksiksiz, bütün; tamam, bitmiş; yetkin ☆ e. tamamlamak, bitirmek; bütünlemek **completely** tamamen, bütünüyle
complex /'kompleks/ s. çok parçalı; karmaşık, karışık ☆ a. kompleks
complexion /kım'plekşın/ a. ten; ten rengi
compliance /kım'playıns/ a. rıza, uyum
compliant /kım'playınt/ s. yumuşakbaşlı, uysal, itaatkâr
complicate /'komplikeyt/ e. karıştırmak, güçleştirmek **complicated** karışık, zor **complication** karışıklık
complicity /kım'plisiti/ a. suçortaklığı
compliment /'komplimınt/ a. övgü, iltifat, kompliman; ç. selamlar, saygılar, iyi dilekler ☆ e. övmek, tebrik etmek **complimentary** övgü niteliğinde; parasız
comply /kım'play/ e. (with) uymak; razı olmak
component /kım'pounınt/ a. (makine, vb.) parça; bileşen
compose /kım'pouz/ e. birleştirmek, oluşturmak; yazmak; bestelemek; yatıştırmak, sakinleştirmek **composer** besteci **composing** yatıştırıcı, rahatlatıcı; dizgi, tertip
composite /'kompızit/ s. birçok parçalardan oluşan, karma, bileşik

composition /kompı'zişın/ a. bileşim; beste; kompozisyon; nitelik, yapı
compositor /kım'pozıtı/ a. dizgici
compost /'kompost/ a. çürümüş organik maddeli gübre
composure /kım'poujı/ a. soğukkanlılık, kendine hâkimiyet
compound /kım'paund/ s. bileşik ☆ e. katmak, eklemek, artırmak; birleştirmek ☆ a. bileşim **compound interest** bileşik faiz
comprehend /kompri'hend/ e. anlamak, kavramak; kapsamak **comprehensible** anlaşılabilir **comprehension** anlama, kavrama; (okulda) kavrama testi **comprehensive** geniş, ayrıntılı; **comprehensive (school)** sanat okulu, çok amaçlı okul
compress /kım'pres/ e. basmak, sıkıştırmak, bastırmak; birkaç sözcükle anlatmak, özetlemek **compression** sıkıştırma; özetleme
comprise /kım'prayz/ e. -den oluşmak; içermek, kapsamak
compromise /'komprımayz/ a. uzlaşma ☆ e. uzlaşmak; şerefine gölge düşürmek
compulsion /kım'palşın/ a. zorlama, baskı **compulsiv** zorunlu, mecburi
compulsory /kım'palsıri/ s. zorunlu
compunction /kım'pankşın/ a. vicdan azabı, pişmanlık; utanma
computation /kompyu'teyşın/ a. ölçüm, hesap, hesaplama
compute /kım'pyu:t/ e. hesap yapmak, hesaplamak **computer** bilgisayar
computerize /kım'pyu:tırayz/e. bilgisayarlaştırmak; bilgisayara yüklemek
comrade /'komrid/ a. arkadaş, yoldaş
con /kon/ a. aleyhte nokta/kimse; kon. kazık, üçkâğıt ☆ e, kon. kazıklamak, dolandırmak
concave /kon'keyv/ s. çukur, içbükey
conceal /kın'si:l/ e. gizlemek, saklamak
concede /kın'si:d/ e. teslim etmek; kabul etmek; vermek, bağışlamak
conceit /kın'si:t/ a. kendini beğenmişlik **conceited** kendini beğenmiş
conceive /kın'si:v/ e. tasarlamak, kurmak; gebe kalmak **conceivable** akla yatkın, olası

concentrate /'konsıntreyt/ e. toplanmak, derişmek; toplamak, deriştirmek; konsantre olmak
concentration /konsın'treyşın/ a. toplama; toplanma; konsantrasyon **concentration camp** toplama kampı
concentric /kın'sentrik/ s. eşmerkezli
concept /'konsept/ a. genel kavram, genel düşünce
conception /kın'sepşın/ a. anlayış, kavrayış, kavrama; düşünce, görüş, kavram, fikir; gebe kalma
concern /kın'sö:n/ e. ilgilendirmek, ilişiği olmak; kaygılandırmak, üzmek **concerned** ilgili, ilişkili; endişeli, kaygılı **as far as I'm concerned** bence, bana kalırsa **concerning** hakkında; -e dair, ile ilgili
concert /'konsıt/ a. konser **in concert** birlikte, işbirliği içinde
concerto /kın'çö:tou/ a, müz. konçerto
concession /kın'seşın/ a. ödün, taviz; ayrıcalık, imtiyaz
conciliate /kın'silieyt/ e. gönlünü almak, gönlünü yapmak **conciliation** gönül alma **conciliatory** gönül alıcı
concise /kın'says/ s. kısa, özlü
conclude /kın'klu:d/ e. bitirmek; bitmek; sonucuna varmak; karara varmak
conclusion /kın'klu:jın/ a. son; sonuç; yargı; anlaşma **in conclusion** neticede, sonuç olarak
conclusive /kın'klu:siv/ s. kesin, son
concord /'konko:d/ a. uyum, anlaşma; dostluk
concourse /'konko:s/ a. bir araya gelme, toplanma
concrete /'konkri:t/ s. somut; açık, kesin, belli ☆ a. beton ☆ e. beton dökmek
concur /kın'kö:/ e. anlaşmak, uyuşmak; aynı zamanda oluşmak **concurrent** aynı zamanda oluşan, rastlantısal
concussion /kın'kaşın/ a. beyin sarsıntısı
condemn /kın'dem/ e. kınamak, ayıplamak; mahkûm etmek
condensation /kondın'seyşın/ a. yoğun-

laşma, sıvılaşma; buğu
condense /kın'dens/ *e.* (gaz) yoğunlaşmak; özetlemek
condenser /kın'densı/ *a.* kondansatör;
kondansör
condescend /kondi'send/ *e.* tenezzül
etmek; lütfetmek
condiment /'kondimınt/ *a.* baharat,
sos, çeşni
condition /kın'dişın/*a.* durum, hal, vaziyet; koşul, şart; genel sağlık durumu,
kondisyon, form ☆ *e.* şart koşmak;
şartlandırmak; koşullandırmak; alıştırmak **on condition that** eğer, şartıyla
on no condition asla, hiçbir surette
conditional /kın'dişınıl/*s.* şartlı, koşulla-
ra bağlı **conditional clause** *dilb.* koşul
yantümcesi
condolence /kın'doulıns/ *a.* başsağlığı;
acısını paylaşma, avutma
condom /'kondım/ *a.* kaput, prezervatif
condone /kın'doun/ *e.* bağışlamak,
göz yummak
conduce /kın'dyu:s/ *e.* (**to/towards**)
yardım etmek, katkıda bulunmak
conducive /kındyu:siv/ *s.* yardım eden,
olanak sağlayan
conduct /'kondakt/ *a.* davranış; yönetme, idare
conduct /'kın'dakt/*e.* davranmak, hareket etmek; yönetmek, yürütmek; götürmek, kılavuzluk etmek, taşımak,
nakletmek; (elektrik, ısı, vb.) iletmek,
geçirmek; *müz.* orkestra yönetmek
conduction taşıma, götürme; iletme
conductive iletken **conductor** orkestra şefi; biletçi, kondüktör; iletken
cone /koun/ *a.* koni; kozalak; külah
confection /kın'fekşın/ *a.* şekerleme
confectioner şekerci **confectionery** şekerleme; şekerci dükkânı
confederacy /kın'fedırısi/*a.* konfederasyon, birlik
confederate /kın'fedırıt/ *s.* konfedere,
birleşik ☆ *a.* müttefik; suçortağı **confederation** konfederasyon, birlik
confer /kın'fö:/ *e.* (**on/upon**) (unvan,
vb.) vermek; (**with**) danışmak, görüşmek
conference /'konfırıns/ *a.* (fikir alışverişi

için düzenlenen) toplantı, görüşme,
müzakere
confess /kın'fes/ *e.* itiraf etmek; kabul
etmek; günah çıkarmak
confession /kın'feşın/ *a.* itiraf; günah çıkarma
confetti /kın'feti/ *a.* konfeti
confidant /'konfident/ *a.* sırdaş, dert ortağı
confide /kın'fayd/ *e.* (sır, vb.) vermek,
açmak; (**in**) güvenmek, açılmak **confidence** /'konfidıns/ güven; sır, gizli
şey **in confidence** gizlilikle **confident**
kendinden emin **confidential** gizli; güvenilir
configuration /konfigyu'reyşın/ *a.* biçim, şekil
confine /kın'fayn/ *e.* kapatmak, hapsetmek; sınırlandırmak **confinement**
hapsedilme, kapatılma; hapis; loğusalık
confines /'konfaynz/ *a.* sınırlar
confirm /kın'fö:m/ *e.* doğrulamak; pekiştirmek; onaylamak **confirmation**
/konfı'meyşın/ doğrulama, onaylama
confirmed /kın'fö:md/ alışkanlıklarını
değiştirmez
confiscate /'konfiskeyt/ *e.* el koymak
confiscation el koyma
conflict /'konflikt/*a.* çatışma, çarpışma;
uyuşmazlık, zıtlık, anlaşmazlık ☆ *e.*
bağdaşmamak, çatışmak
conform /kın'fo:m/*e.* uymak
conformity /kın'fo:miti/ *a.* uymacılık;
uyum
confound /kın'faund/ karıştırmak, allak
bullak etmek, şaşırtmak
confront /kın'frant/*e.* karşı koymak, göğüs germek; (**with**) yüzleştirmek
confuse /kın'fyu:z/ *e.* şaşırtmak, kafasını karıştırmak **confusion** kargaşa; karışıklık
congeal /kın'ci:l/ *e.* dondurmak, donmak
congenial /kın'ci:niıl/ *s.* hoş, kafa dengi, kafasına uygun
congenital /kın'cenitıl/ *s.* (hastalık) doğuştan
congestion /kın'cesçın/ *a, hek.* kan bi-
rikmesi; tıkanıklık

conglomerate /kın'glomırit/ *a.* küme, yı-ğın; büyük işletme/şirket; *tek.* çakıl ka-yaç

congratulate /kın'greçuleyt/ *e.* kutla-mak, tebrik etmek **congratulation** kut-lama, tebrik **Congratulations!** Tebrik-ler!

congregate /'kongrigeyt/ *e.* bir araya gelmek, toplanmak **congregation** ce-maat, topluluk

congress /'kongres/ *a.* kongre, kurul-tay, toplantı **Congress** (ABD'de) Millet Meclisi **congressman** ABD Millet Mec-lisi üyesi

congruous /'kongruıs/ *s.* uygun, yakışır

conical /'konikıl/ *s.* koni biçiminde, ko-nik

conifer /'kounifı/ *a, bitk.* kozalaklı ağaç

conjecture /kın'cekçı/ *a.* varsayım; tah-min

conjugal /'koncugıl/ *s.* evlilikle ilgili

conjugate /'koncugeyt/ *e, dilb.* (eylem) çekmek; (eylem) çekilmek **conjuga-tion** *dilb.* eylem çekimi

conjunction /kın'cankşın/ *a, dilb.* bağ-laç; birleşme, birleşim **in conjunction with** ile birlikte

conjure /'kancı/ *e.* hokkabazlık yap-mak; el çabukluğu ile çıkarmak; büyü-lemek **conjurer** hokkabaz, sihirbaz

connect /kı'nekt/ *e.* bağlamak, birleştir-mek **connected** bağlı, ilgili

connection /kı'nekşın/ *a.* bağlantı; iliş-ki, bağ; aktarma **in connection with** ile ilgili olarak

connive /kı'nayv/ *e.* gizlice işbirliği yap-mak; (**at**) görmezlikten gelmek

connoisseur /konı'sö:/ *a.* uzman, ehil

connotation /konı'teyşın/ *a.* yan anlam

conquer /'konkı/ *e.* fethetmek, zapt et-mek; yenmek **conqueror** fatih

conquest /'konkwest/ *a.* fetih, fethet-me; alt etme

conscience /'konşıns/ *a.* vicdan

conscientious /konşi'enşıs/ *s.* vicdanlı, dürüst; özenli

conscious /'konşıs/ *s.* bilinçli; farkında, bilincinde; kasıtlı, kasti **consciousness** bilinç

conscript /kın'skript/ *e.* askere almak

consecrate /'konsikreyt/ *e.* kutsamak; adamak

consecutive /kın'sekyutiv/ *s.* art arda gelen, ardışık

consensus /kın'sensıs/ *a.* ortak karar, oybirliği, anlaşma

consent /kın'sent/ *e.* izin vermek, razı olmak ☆ *a.* izin, rıza **age of consent** rüşt, erginlik

consequence /'konsikwıns/ *a.* sonuç; önem **consequently** sonuç olarak, bu nedenle

conservation /konsı'veyşın/ *a.* koruma **conservatism** tutuculuk

conservative /kın'sö:vıtiv/ *s.* muhafaza-kâr

conservatoire /kın'sö:vıtwa:/ *a.* konser-vatuvar

conservatory /kın'sö:vıtıri/ *a.* konserva-tuvar; limonluk, ser

conserve /kın'sö:v/ *e.* korumak

consider /kın'sidı/ *e.* düşünüp taşın-mak; olduğunu düşünmek, saymak; göz önünde tutmak

considerable /kın'sidırıbıl/ *s.* büyük, önemli, hatırı sayılır **considerably** çok

considerate /kın'sidırit/ *s.* düşünceli, saygılı

consideration /kınsidı'reyşın/ *a.* göz önüne alma; saygı; husus, etmen; önem

considering /kın'sidıring/ *ilg.* -e göre, -e karşın

consign /kın'sayn/ *e.* mal göndermek; vermek, teslim etmek; tahsis etmek **consignment** mal gönderme; gönderi-len mal

consist /kın'sist/ *e.* (**of**) oluşmak; (**in**) bağlı olmak, dayanmak

consistency /kın'sistınsi/ *a.* koyuluk, yo-ğunluk; tutarlılık, uyum

consistent /kın'sistınt/ *s.* istikrarlı, tutar-lı; devamlı, sürekli **consistent with** -e uygun olarak **consistently** sürekli ola-rak

console /kın'soul/ *e.* avutmak, teselli et-mek **consolation** /konsı'leyşın/ tesel-li; avuntu

console /'konsoul/ *a.* konsol; dirsek

consolidate /kın'solideyt/ *e.* sağlamlaş-

tırmak; birleştirmek; birleşmek **conso-
lidation** sağlamlaştırma; birleşim, ünite; birleştirme, birleşme
consommé /kın'somey, 'konsımey/ *a.*
et suyu
consonant /'konsınınt/ *a, dilb.* ünsüz
harf, ünsüz
consort /'konso:t/ *a.* karı, koca, eş
consortium /kın'so:tıım/ *a.* konsorsiyum, birlik
conspicuous /kın'spikyuıs/ *s.* göze çarpan, çarpıcı, dikkat çekici
conspiracy /kın'spirısi/ *a.* komplo, suikast **conspirator** komplocu
conspire /kın'spayı/ *e.* plan yapmak,
komplo kurmak; suikast hazırlamak
constable /'kanstıbıl/ *a, İİ.* polis memuru
constancy /'konstınsi/ *a.* karar, metanet, sebat; tutarlılık
constant /'konstınt/ *s.* değişmeyen; sadık; bağlı **constantly** sürekli olarak
constellation /konsti'leyşın/ *a.* takımyıldız
consternation /konstı'neyşın/ *a.* şaşkınlık, dehşet, korku
constipation /konsti'peyşın/ *a.* kabızlık,
peklik
constituency /kın'stiçuınsi/ *a.* seçmenler; seçim bölgesi
constituent /kın'stiçuınt/ *a.* seçmen; bileşen, öğe ☆ *s.* kurucu
constitute /'konstityu:t/ *e.* oluşturmak;
kurmak
constitution /konsti'tyu:şın/ *a.* oluşum,
bileşim; yapı, bünye; anayasa **constitutional** yapısal; bünyesel; anayasal
constrain /kın'streyn/ *e.* zorlamak, zorla yaptırmak **constraint** zorlama; baskı, tehdit
constrict /kın'strikt/ *e.* daraltmak; sıkmak; kısmak
construct /kın'strakt/ *e.* inşa etmek,
yapmak; kurmak **construction** yapı-
lış, yapım, inşa **constructive** yapıcı,
yardımcı, yararlı
construe /kın'stru:/ *e.* yorumlamak, anlam vermek; *dilb.* (cümle) analiz etmek
consul /'konsıl/ *a.* konsolos

consulate /'konsyulit/ *a.* konsolosluk
consult /kın'salt/ *e.* danışmak, başvurmak, sormak **consultant** danışman
consultation danışma, başvurma
consume /kın'syu:m/ *e.* tüketmek; yok
etmek, yakmak
consumer /kın'syu:mı/ *a.* tüketici
consummate /'konsımeyt/ *e.* tamamlamak, mükemmelleştirmek
consumption /kın'sampşın/ *a.* tüketim;
verem
contact /'kontekt/ *a.* dokunma, temas;
bağlantı, irtibat; kontak ☆ *e.* görüşmek, bağlantı kurmak **contact lens**
kontaklens
contagious /kın'teycıs/ *s.* bulaşıcı
contain /kın'teyn/ *e.* içermek, kapsamak; tutmak, bastırmak
container /kın'teynı/ *a.* (kutu, şişe, vb.)
kap
contaminate /kın'temineyt/ *e.* bulaştırmak, kirletmek; zehirlemek, bozmak
contemplate /'kontımpleyt/ *e.* bakmak;
niyetinde olmak, tasarlamak; üzerinde düşünmek **contemplation** düşünceye dalma **contemplative** /kın'-
templıtiv/ düşünceli, dalgın
contemporary /kın'tempırıri/ *s.* çağdaş
☆ *a.* çağdaş; yaşıt
contempt /kın'tempt/ *a.* küçümseme;
saygısızlık **contemptible** alçak, aşağılık **contemptuous** /-çuıs/ hor gören,
aşağılayıcı
contend /kın'tend/ *e.* yarışmak; iddia
etmek
content /kın'tent/ *s.* memnun, hoşnut
☆ *e.* doyurmak, tatmin etmek ☆ *a.*
içerik **contented** memnun, hoşnut
contents /'kontents/ *a.* içindekiler
contest /'kontest/ *a.* mücadele; yarışma ☆ *e.* yarışmak, çekişmek; doğru-
luğu hakkında tartışmak **contestant**
yarışmacı
context /'kontekst/ *a.* bağlam
continent /'kontinınt/ *a, coğ.* kıta, anakara **the Continent** *İİ.* Britanya dışın-
daki Avrupa ülkeleri **continental** /kon-
ti'nentıl/ kıtasal
contingency /kın'tincınsi/ *a.* olasılık
contingent /kın'tincınt/ *s.* -e bağlı;

şans eseri olan, umulmadık ☆ *a,
ask.* birlik, grup; bölüm

continual /kın'tinyuıl/ *s.* sürekli, devamlı

continue /kın'tinyu:/ *e.* devam etmek, sürmek; devam ettirmek, sürdürmek

continuity /konti'nyu:iti/ *a.* süreklilik

continuous /kın'tinyuıs/ *s.* sürekli, devamlı

contour /'kontuı/ *a.* dış hatlar; (haritada) yükseklik çizgisi, kontur

contraband /'kontrıbend/ *a.* kaçak eşya; kaçakçılık

contraception /kontrı'sepşın/ *a.* doğum kontrolü **contraceptive** gebelik önleyici

contract /'kontrekt/ *a.* sözleşme, kontrat

contract /kın'trekt/ *e.* sözleşme yapmak; (hastalık, vb.) kapmak; küçülmek, büzülmek

contraction /kın'trekşın/ *a.* küçülme, büzülme; küçültme; hastalık kapma; (kas) kasılma

contractor /kın'trektı/ *a.* müteahhit

contradict /kontrı'dikt/ *e.* inkâr etmek; yalanlamak; birbirini tutmamak, çelişmek **contradiction** tersini söyleme, inkâr; yalanlama; zıtlık, çelişki **contradictory** çelişkili, tutarsız

contrary /'kontrıri/ *s.* karşıt, aksi; ters **on the contrary** aksine, tersine

contrast /'kontra:st/ *a.* karşıtlık, tezat

contravene /kontrı'vi:n/ *e.* karşı gelmek; ihlal etmek

contribute /kın'tribyu:t/ *e.* katkıda bulunmak, katılmak; -de payı olmak; yazı hazırlamak **contribution** katılım; katkı, yardım **contributory** payı olan, neden olan

contrite /'kontrayt/ *s.* pişman

contrition /kın'trişın/ *a.* pişmanlık

contrive /kın'trayv/ *e.* bulmak, icat etmek; planlamak; bir yolunu bulup becermek

control /kın'troul/ *e.* kontrol etmek; dizginlemek; denetlemek ☆ *a.* denetim, kontrol; idare, hâkimiyet; ç. (uçak, vb.) kumanda donanımı **out of control** kontrolden çıkmış **under con-**trol kontrollu, disiplinli

controversial /kontrı'vö:şıl/ *s.* tartışmaya yol açan

controversy /'kontrıvö:si/ *a.* tartışma; anlaşmazlık, uyuşmazlık

convalesce /konvı'les/ *e.* iyileşmek **convalescence** nekahet, iyileşme dönemi **convalescent** iyileşen

convection /kın'vekşın/ *a, fiz.* konveksiyon, ısıyayım

convene /kın'vi:n/ *e.* toplantıya çağırmak; buluşmak, toplanmak

convenience /kın'vi:niıns/ *a.* uygunluk, elverişlilik; rahat, çıkar; uygun zaman **convenient** uygun, elverişli

convent /'konvınt/ *a.* rahibe manastırı

conventional /kın'venşınıl/ *s.* törel, geleneksel; (silah) konvansiyonel

converge /kın'vö:c/ *e.* bir noktada birleşmek

conversant /kın'vö:sınt/ *s.* (**with**) bilgisi olan, bilen

conversation /konvı'seyşın/ *a.* konuşma; sohbet, muhabbet

converse /kın'vö:s/ *e.* konuşmak

converse /'konvö:s/ *a, s.* zıt, ters, karşıt

conversion /kın'vö:şın/ *a.* değişme, dönüşme; din değiştirme

convert /kın'vö:t/ *e.* değiştirmek, dönüştürmek **convertible** (para) konvertibl; üstü açılır araba

convex /kon'veks/ *s.* dışbükey

convey /kın'vey/ *e.* taşımak, götürmek; ifade etmek **conveyance** taşıma, nakil; taşıt, vasıta **conveyor** taşıyıcı

convict /'konvikt/ *e.* suçluluğunu kanıtlamak ☆ *a.* mahkûm

conviction /kın'vikşın/ *a.* mahkûmiyet; inanç, kanı, kanaat

convince /kın'vins/ *e.* inandırmak, ikna etmek **convincing** inandırıcı

convoke /kın'vouk/ *e.* toplantıya çağırmak

convoy /'konvoy/ *e.* (korumak amacıyla) eşlik etmek

convulse /kın'vals/ *e.* şiddetle sarsmak **convulsion** çırpınma

coo /ku:/ *e.* (kumru gibi) ötmek

cook /kuk/ *a.* aşçı ☆ *e.* (yemek) pişirmek; pişmek **cook up** uydurmak, kafadan atmak

cooker /'kukı/ a. ocak **cookery** aşçılık

cookie /'kuki/ a. kurabiye, bisküvi

cooky /'kuki/ a, bkz. **cookie**

cool /ku:l/ s. serin; sakin, soğukkanlı, serinkanlı; (davranış) soğuk, uzak ☆ e. soğumak, serinlemek; soğutmak, serinletmek

coop /ku:p/ a. kümes

co-op /'kouop/ a, kon. kooperatif

cooperate /kou'opıreyt/ e. işbirliği yapmak **cooperation** birlikte çalışma, işbirliği, elbirliği; destek **cooperative** yardımcı; kooperatif

coordinate /kou'o:dineyt/ e. düzenlemek, ayarlamak **coordination** koordinasyon, eşgüdüm

cop /kop/ a, kon. polis, aynasız

cope /koup/ e. (with) başa çıkmak, üstesinden gelmek

copious /'koupiıs/ s. bol, çok

copper /'kopı/ a. bakır; ii, kon. polis, aynasız

copse /kops/ a. çalılık; koru

copulate /'kopyuleyt/ e. (hayvan) çiftleşmek

copy /'kopi/ a. kopya, suret; gazete vb.'nin bir tek sayısı, nüsha ☆ e. kopyasını çıkarmak; örnek almak, taklit etmek; hkr. kopya çekmek

copyright /'kopirayt/ a. telif hakkı

coral /'korıl/ a. mercan

cord /ko:d/ a. ip, sicim; tel, şerit; (ses) tel **spinal cord** omurilik **vocal cords** ses telleri

cordial /'ko:diıl/ s. candan, yürekten, içten ☆ a. meyve suyu; likör

cordially /'ko:diıli/ be. içtenlikle, yürekten

cordon /'ko:dın/ a. kordon

corduroy /'ko:dıroy/ a. fitilli kadife

core /ko:/ a. (meyve) göbek, koçan; öz, çekirdek

cork /ko:k/ a. şişe mantarı **corkscrew** tirbuşon; burgu, spiral

cormorant /'ko:mırınt/ a, hayb. karabatak

corn /ko:n/ a.ii tahıl; buğday; Aİ. mısır; tahıl; ekin, tane; nasır **corn flour** mısır unu

cornea /'ko:niı/ a, anat. kornea

corner /'ko:nı/ a. köşe ☆ e. kıstırmak, köşeye sıkıştırmak

cornet /'ko:nit/ a, müz. kornet; dondurma külahı, kornet

cornflakes /'ko:nfleyks/ a. mısır gevreği

cornice /'ko:nis/ a. pervaz, korniş; saçak silmesi

coronary /'korınıri/ s, anat. kalple ilgili

coronation /korı'neyşın/ a. taç giyme töreni

coroner /'korını/ a. sorgu yargıcı

coronet /'korınit/ a. küçük taç

corporal /'ko:pırıl/ s. bedensel ☆ a, ask. onbaşı

corporate /'ko:pırit/ s. birleşmiş; huk. tüzel

corporation /ko:pı'reyşın/ a. dernek, kurum; lonca; tüzel kişi; kuruluş, şirket

corps /ko:ps/ a. kurul, heyet; ask. kolordu

corpse /ko:ps/ a. ceset, ölü

corpulent /'kopyulınt/ s. çok şişman, şişko

corpuscle /'ko:pısıl/ a, anat. yuvar

corral /ko'ra:l/ a. ağıl

correct /kı'rekt/ e. düzeltmek ☆ s. doğru; kurala uygun **correction** düzeltme; ceza, cezalandırma **corrective** düzeltici

correlation /kori'leyşın/ a. karşılıklı bağıntı, ilişki

correspond /kori'spond/ e. uymak, uyuşmak; -in karşılığı olmak; (düzenli olarak) yazışmak, mektuplaşmak **corresponding** uyan, benzeyen

correspondence /kori'spondıns/ a. uygunluk, birbirini tutma; mektuplaşma, yazışma **correspondence course** mektupla öğretim **correspondent** mektup arkadaşı; muhabir

corridor /'korido:/ a. koridor, aralık

corroborate /kı'robıreyt/ e. desteklemek; güçlendirmek

corrode /kı'roud/ e. aşındırmak, çürütmek; paslanmak

corrosion /kı'roujin/ a. aşınma, aşındırma; korozyon **corrosive** aşındırıcı

corrugated /'korıgeytid/ s. dalgalı, kıvrımlı

corrupt /kı'rapt/ e. baştan çıkarmak; ayartmak, bozmak ☆ s. namussuz; bozuk; laçka

corset /'ko:sit/ a. korsa

cortege /ko:'teyj/ a. kortej, tören alayı

cosmetic /koz'metik/ s, a. kozmetik, güzelleştirici

cosmic /'kozmik/ s. evrensel; engin, geniş, sınırsız

cosmonaut /'kozmıno:t/ a. uzayadamı

cosmopolitan /kozmı'politın/ s. kozmopolit; evrendeş

cosmos /'kozmos/ a. evren

cost /kost/ a. fiyat; değer, paha; masraf, maliyet ☆ e. değerinde olmak; mal olmak **at all costs** ne pahasına olursa olsun **cost of living** geçim gideri

co-star /'kousta:/ a. başrol oyuncularından biri

costume /'kostyum/ a. giysi, kostüm

cosy /'kouzi/ s. rahat, sıcacık ☆ a. örtü, kılıf

cot /kot/ a. beşik; baraka, kulübe

cotangent /kou'tencınt/ a, mat. kotanjant

cottage /'kotic/ a. küçük ev, kulübe

cotton /'kotın/ a. pamuk **cotton wool** ham pamuk

couch /kauç/ a. sedir, kanape

couchette /ku:'şet/ a. (trende) kuşet

cougar /'ku:gı/ a, hayb. puma

cough /kof/ e. öksürmek ☆ a. öksürük; öksürme

could /kıd, kud/ e, bkz. **can**

council /'kaunsıl/ a. konsey, danışma kurulu, meclis

counsel /'kaunsıl/ a. öneri, tavsiye; avukat ☆ e. önermek **counsellor** danışman

count /kaunt/ e. (sayı) saymak; içermek, kapsamak; göz önünde tutmak, saymak ☆ a. sayma, sayım; hesap; toplam; huk. şikâyet maddesi **count out** hesaba katmamak, saymamak

countable /'kauntıbıl/ s. sayılabilen, sayılabilir

countdown /'kauntdaun/ a. gerisayım

countenance /'kauntinıns/ a. yüz ifadesi; uygun bulma, destek ☆ e. destek-

lemek, onaylamak

counter /'kauntı/ a. tezgâh; il. marka, fiş; sayaç ☆ e. karşı çıkmak; karşılık vermek ☆ s, be. karşı

counterattack /'kauntırıtek/ a. karşı saldırı

counterbalance /'kauntıbelıns/ a. eş ağırlık, karşılık ☆ e. denkleştirmek

counterclockwise /kauntı'klokwayz/ s, be. saat yönünün tersine

counterfeit /'kauntıfit/ s. sahte, taklit ☆ e. (para, vb.) sahtesini yapmak

counterfoil /'kauntıfoyl/ a. makbuz dip koçanı

counterpane /'kauntıpeyn/ a. yatak örtüsü

counterpart /'kauntıpa:t/ a. tam benzeri, kopyası

countersign /'kauntısayn/ a, ask. parola; onay imzası ☆ e. (onay için) ayrıca imzalamak

countess /'kauntis/ a. kontes

countless /'kauntlis/ s. çok fazla, sayısız

country /'kantri/ a. ülke, yurt; kır, taşra, kırsal kesim; ulus, halk; bölge, yöre

countryside /'kantrisayd/ a. kırsal bölge

county /'kaunti/ a, Aİ. ilçe; kontluk; il idare bölgesi

coup /ku:/ a. darbe **coup d'état** /ku:-dey'ta:/ hükümet darbesi

coupé /'ku:pey/ a. iki kapılı spor araba

coupe /ku:p/ a, bkz. **coupé**

couple /'kapıl/ a. çift; karı koca, çift; (of) kon. birkaç ☆ e. bağlamak, birleştirmek; cinsel ilişkide bulunmak, çiftleşmek

couplet /'kaplit/ a. beyit

coupon /'ku:pon/ a. kupon

courage /'karic/ a. yüreklilik, cesaret, mertlik **courageous** /kı'reycıs/ cesur, yiğit, mert

courier /'kuriı/ a. haberci, kurye

course /ko:s/ a. yön, rota; pist; akış; alan, pist; kurs; dizi, seri; kap, tabak; yemek **in due course** zamanında, vaktinde **of course** elbette, tabii

court /ko:t/ a. mahkeme; oturum; avlu; saray, saray halkı; sp. kort, saha; konak ☆ *e.* gözüne girmeye çalışmak; kur yapmak **courthouse** mahkeme; adliye sarayı **courtyard** avlu, iç bahçe

courteous /'kö:tiıs/ *s.* nazik, kibar

courtesy /'kö:tisi/ *a.* nezaket, kibarlık

courtier /'ko:tiı/ *a.* saraylı

court-martial /ko:t'ma:şıl/ *a.* askeri mahkeme, divanıharp

cousin /'kazın/ *a.* kuzen

cove /kouv/ *a.* koy, körfezcik

cover /'kavı/ *e.* örtmek, kaplamak; katetmek, yol almak; içine almak, kapsamak; korumak ☆ *a.* kapak, örtü; kılıf; sığınak; (kitap) kap **covering** kat, örtü

covert /'kavıt/ *s.* gizli, saklı, örtülü

covet /'kavit/ *e.* göz dikmek

cow /kau/ *a.* inek ☆ *e.* gözünü korkutmak, yıldırmak **cowboy** kovboy, sığırtmaç **cowhand** sığırtmaç **cowhide** sığır derisi

coward /'kauıd/ *a.* korkak **cowardice** korkaklık **cowardly** korkak

cower /'kauı/ *e.* sinmek, büzülmek

cowslip /'kauslip/ *a, bitk.* çuhaçiçeği

cox /koks/ *a, kon.* dümenci

coy /koy/ *s.* çekingen, utangaç; nazlı, cilveli

crab /kreb/ *a, hayb.* yengeç

crack /krek/ *e.* çatlamak; çatlatmak; şaklamak; şaklatmak ☆ *a.* çatlak; çatırtı; vuruş, darbe; *kon.* girişim

crackle /'krekıl/ *e.* çatırdamak; çıtırdatmak

cradle /'kreydıl/ *a.* beşik

craft /kra:ft/ *a.* beceri, hüner, ustalık, maharet; kurnazlık, hile; gemi, uçak; teknik eleman **craftsman** usta, zanaatçı **crafty** kurnaz

crag /kreg/ *a.* yalçın kayalık **craggy** dik ve pütürlü

cram /krem/ *e.* tıkmak, sıkıştırmak; tıka basa doldurmak; acele ile sınava hazırlanmak

cramp /kremp/ *a.* kramp, kasınç; mengene; engel ☆ *e.* engel olmak

cranberry /'krenbırı/ *a, bitk.* yabanmersini

crane /kreyn/ *a.* vinç; *hayb.* turna

cranium /'kreynıım/ *a, anat.* kafatası

crank /krenk/ *a, tek.* dirsek, kol; *kon.* saplantılı kimse; deli, kaçık

crash /kreş/ *e.* (araba, vb.) gürültüyle çarpmak; çarptırmak; düşmek; düşürmek ☆ *a.* çatırtı, gürültü; (uçak, otomobil, vb.) kaza; iflas

crate /kreyt/ *a.* kafesli sandık, kasa

crater /'kreytı/ *a.* krater, yanardağ ağzı

cravat /krı'vet/ *a, İİ.* boyunbağı, kravat

crawl /kro:l/ *e.* emeklemek, sürünmek; (böcek, vb. ile) dolu olmak; ürpermek ☆ *a.* krol yüzme; çok yavaş hareket; ağır gidiş

crayfish /'kreyfiş/ *a, hayb.* kerevit, kerevides

crayon /'kreyın/ *a.* renkli kalem, boyalı kalem

craze /kreyz/ *e.* çılgına çevirmek, çıldırtmak, deli etmek ☆ *a.* geçici akım, moda

crazy /'kreyzi/ *s.* deli, çılgın; (**about**) *kon.* hayran, tutkun

creak /kri:k/ *a.* gıcırtı **creaky** gıcırtılı

cream /kri:m/ *a.* kaymak, krema; krem; merhem ☆ *a, s.* krem rengi ☆ *e.* (sütün) kaymağını almak (**off**) (en iyileri) seçmek, ayıklamak

crease /kri:s/ *a.* buruşukluk, kırışıklık; kat, pli ☆ *e.* buruşmak, kırışmak

create /kri'eyt/ *e.* yaratmak; -e yol açmak, neden olmak **creation** yaratma; yaradılış; evren; kreasyon

creator /kri'eytı/ *a.* yaratıcı **the Creator** Tanrı, Yaradan

creature /'kri:çı/ *a.* yaratık

crèche /kreş/ *a.* kreş, bebekevi, yuva

credentials /kri'denşılz/ *a.* güven belgesi, itimatname

credible /'kredıbıl/ *s.* inanılır, güvenilir

credit /'kredit/ *a.* inanç, güven, sadakat; övgü, onur; kredi; saygınlık ☆ *e.* inanmak, güvenmek, itimat etmek; para yatırmak **creditable** şerefli, övgüye değer **creditor** alacaklı **credit card** kredi kartı

creed /kri:d/ *a.* inanç, iman, itikat

creek /kri:k/ *a. İİ.* çay, ırmak kolu

creep /kri:p/ *e.* **crept** /krept/ sürünmek; sessizce sokulmak; (sarmaşık, vb.) sarılmak

crumple

creepy /'kri:pi/ s. tüyler ürpertici

cremate /kri'meyt/ e. (ölüyü) yakmak

crepe /kreyp/ a. krep; crepe paper krepon kâğıdı

crescendo /kri'şendou/ a, müz. kreşendo

crescent /'kresınt/ a. hilal, ayça, yeniay

cress /kres/ a, bitk. tere

crest /krest/ a. ibik, taç; tepe, doruk

crew /kru:/ a. tayfa, mürettebat; ekip

crick /krik/ a. boyun tutulması, kasılma

cricket /'krikit/ a, hayb. cırcırböceği; sp. kriket

crime /kraym/ a. suç

criminal /'kriminıl/ s. suçla ilgili; cezai ☆ a. suçlu

crimson /'krimzın/ s, a. koyu kırmızı

cripple /'kripıl/ a. sakat, topal, kötürüm ☆ e. sakatlamak

crisis /'kraysis/ a. bunalım, kriz

crisp /krisp/ s. gevrek; körpe, taze; (hava) soğuk ☆ a, İİ. cips

crispy /'krispi/ s. gevrek, körpe, taze

criterion /kray'tiiriın/ a. ölçüt, kriter

critic /'kritik/ a. eleştirmen

critical /'kritikıl/ s. kritik, çok önemli; her şeye kusur bulan, eleştiren; eleştirel

criticism /'kritisizım/ a. eleştiri

criticize /'kritisayz/ e. eleştirmek

croak /krouk/ e. kurbağa gibi bağırmak ☆ a. kurbağa sesi, vırak

crock /krok/ a. çanak, çömlek, toprak kap crockery çanak, çömlek

crocodile /'krokıdayl/ a. hayb. timsah

crocus /'kroukıs/ a, bitk. çiğdem

croissant /'krwa:song/ a. ayçöreği

crook /kruk/ a. kanca; sopa, değnek; kon. hırsız, dolandırıcı ☆ e. kıvırmak, bükmek

crooked /'krukid/ s. eğri, yamuk; kon. namussuz

crop /krop/ a. ekin, ürün, mahsul ☆ e. (hayvan) otlamak, yemek; (saç/kuyruk) kesmek

cross /kros/ a. çarpı/artı işareti; çarmıh; haç; üzüntü, gam, elem; çapraz ☆ e. karşıdan karşıya geçmek; (kol, bacak) kavuşturmak, üst üste atmak; karşı koymak; engellemek ☆ s. kız-

gın, sinirli, aksi

crossbred /'krosbred/ s. melez

cross-country /kros'kantri/ s, be. kırlar boyunca, kırlarda

cross-examine /krosig'zemin/e. çaprazlama sorguya çekmek

cross-eyed /'krosayd/ s. şaşı

crossfire /'krosfayı/ a, ask. çapraz ateş

crossing /'krosing/ a. deniz yolculuğu; geçiş yeri, geçiş

crossroads /'krosroudz/ a. birkaç yolun kesiştiği yer; dönüm noktası

cross-section /'krossekşın/ a. yatay kesit

crossword (puzzle) /'kroswö:d (pazıl)/ a. çapraz bulmaca

crotch /kroç/ a. kasık; pantalon ağı, apışlık

crouch /krauç/ e. çömelmek, sinmek

croupier /'kru:piı/ a. krupiye

crow /krou/ a. karga ☆ e. (horoz) ötmek

crowd /kraud/ e. toplanmak, doluşmak, kalabalık oluşturmak ☆ a. kalabalık; yığın crowded kalabalık, tıkış tıkış, dopdolu

crown /kraun/ a. taç giydirmek ☆ a. taç; 25 penny değerinde madeni para; şampiyonluk

crucial /'kru:şıl/ s. çok önemli, kesin, son

crucifix /'kru:sifiks/ a. İsa'lı haç crucifixion çarmıha germe

crucify /'kru:sifay/ e. çarmıha germek

crude /kru:d/ s. ham, işlenmemiş; kaba

cruel /'kru:ıl/ s. acımasız, zalim, gaddar cruelty acımasızlık, gaddarlık, zulüm

cruise /kru:z/ e. gemiyle gezmek, deniz gezisi yapmak ☆ a. deniz gezisi, tekne gezisi

cruiser /'kru:zı/ a. kotra; kruvazör

crumb /kram/ a. ekmek kırıntısı, kırıntı

crumble /'krambıl/ e. ufalamak; ufalanmak

crumpet /'krampit/ a. hamburger ekmeği

crumple /'krampıl/ e. buruşturmak, kırıştırmak

crunch /kranç/ e. çatır çutur yemek; çatırdamak; çatırdatmak ☆ a. çatırtı, çuturtu

crusade /kru:'seyd/ a. Haçlı Seferi; mücadele, savaşım

crush /kraş/ e. ezmek; izdiham oluşturmak ☆ a. izdiham, kalabalık; sıkma meyve suyu

crust /krast/ a. kabuk, ekmek kabuğu; tabaka

crusty /'krasti/ s. kabuklu, gevrek; ters, huysuz

crutch /kraç/ a. koltuk değneği; kasık; pantolon ağı

cry /kray/ e. ağlamak; bağırmak ☆ a. çığlık, feryat; haykırma, bağırma

crypt /kript/ a. yeraltı türbesi

cryptic /'kriptik/ s. gizli, kapalı, örtük

crystal /'kristıl/ a. kristal; kırılca; billur

cub /kab/ a. yavru ayı/aslan/kaplan/tilki; yavrukurt, izci; acemi

cube /kyu:b/ a. küp ☆ e. (bir şeyi) küp biçiminde kesmek, doğramak; mat. küpünü almak

cubic /'kyu:bik/ s. küp biçiminde, kübik

cubicle /'kyu:bikıl/ a. küçük oda, kabin, odacık

cuckoo /'kuku:/ a. guguk kuşu

cucumber /'kyu:kambı/ a, bitk. salatalık, hıyar

cuddle /'kadıl/ e. sarılmak, kucaklamak

cudgel /'kacıl/ a. kısa kalın sopa

cue /kyu:/ a. işaret; ipucu; bilardo sopası, isteka

cuff /kaf/ a. kolluk, manşet, yen; tokat

cuisine /kwi'zi:n/ a. yemek pişirme yöntemi, aşçılık

cul-de-sac /'kaldısek/ a. çıkmaz sokak

culminate /'kalmineyt/ e. (in) doruğuna yükselmek; sonuçlanmak culmination sonuç, son; doruk

culprit /'kalprit/ a. sanık, suçlu

cult /kalt/ a. mezhep; tapınma; rağbet, moda

cultivate /'kaltiveyt/ e. toprağı işlemek, ekip biçmek; yetiştirmek cultivated kültürlü, terbiyeli cultivation toprağı işleme

culture /'kalçı/ a. kültür cultural kültürel cultured kültürlü

cumbersome /'kambısım/ s. biçimsiz, kullanışsız, taşıması zor

cumin /'kamin/ a. kimyon

cumulative /'kyu:myulıtiv/ s. gittikçe artan

cunning /'kaning/ s. kurnaz

cup /kap/ a. fincan; kupa

cupboard /'kabıd/ a. dolap

curative /'kyuırıtiv/ s. iyileştirici

curb /kö:b/ a. fren, engel, zapt, kontrol; ☆ e. tutmak, engellemek, dizginlemek

curd /kö:d/ a. kesmik, lor

curdle /'kö:dıl/ e. (süt) kesilmek

cure /kyuı/ e. (hastayı) iyileştirmek, tedavi etmek; tuzlamak; tütsülemek ☆ a. tedavi; ilaç, çare; iyileşme

curfew /'kö:fyu:/ a. sokağa çıkma yasağı

curio /'kyuıriou/ a. nadir ve değerli eşya, antika

curiosity /kyuıri'ositi/ a. merak; antika

curious /'kyuırııs/ s. meraklı; garip, acaip

curl /kö:l/ a. büklüm, kıvrım; bukle ☆ e. (saç) kıvırmak; kıvrılmak, bükülmek curler bigudi curly kıvırcık

curlew /'kö:lyu:/ a. çulluk

currant /'karınt/ a. kuşüzümü; frenküzümü

currency /'karınsi/ a. geçerlilik, revaç; para

current /'karınt/ s. şimdiki, bugünkü, güncel; yaygın, geçerli, genel, cari; ☆ a. akıntı; akım, cereyan current account cari hesap current exchange günlük kur

curriculum /kı'rikyulım/ a. müfredat programı curriculum vitae özgeçmiş belgesi

curry /'kari/ a. köri, acılı bir Hint yemeği

curse /kö:s/ a. lanet; lanetleme; küfür ☆ e. lanetlemek, beddua etmek; küfür etmek

curtail /kö:'teyl/ e. kısa kesmek; kısmak, azaltmak

curtain /'kö:tın/ a. perde; tiyatro perdesi

curtsy /'kö:tsi/ a. (kadınların yaptığı) reverans

curve /kö:v/ a. eğri, kavis, dönemeç ☆ e. eğmek; eğilmek

cushion /'kuşın/ a. minder, yastık; (bilardo) bant, kenar

custard /'kastıd/ a, İİ. muhallebi; krema

custodian /ka'stoudiın/ a. (kütüphane, müze, vb.) sorumlu, yönetici kimse

custody /'kastıdi/ a. gözetim, bakım; nezaret, gözaltı

custom /'kastım/ a. gelenek, görenek, töre; alışkanlık, âdet; müşteri **customary** geleneksel, alışılmış

customer /'kastımı/ a. alıcı, müşteri

customs /'kastımz/ a. gümrük vergisi; gümrük

cut /kat/ e. cut /kat/ kesmek; biçmek; dilimlemek; (ders) asmak; kesilmek ☆ a. kesik, yarık, yara; dilim, parça; kısıntı, kesinti; indirim **cut across** kestirmeden gitmek **cut back (on)** azaltmak **cut down** kesip düşürmek, devirmek; azaltmak, kısmak **cut in** sözünü kesmek; (arabayla) araya girmek, araya dalmak **cut off** kesmek **cut out** kesip çıkarmak; (içki, sigara, vb.) bırakmak **cut up** parçalamak **cutback** indirim **cut-out** elektrik akımını kesen aygıt

cute /kyu:t/ s. şirin, hoş, sevimli

cuticle /'kyu:tikıl/ a. tırnakların çevresindeki ölü deri, üst deri

cutlery /'katlıri/ a. çatal-bıçak-kaşık, sofra takımı

cutlet /'katlit/ a. pirzola, külbastı

cyanide /'sayınayd/ a. siyanür

cybernetics /saybı'netiks/ a. sibernetik, güdümbilim

cyclamen /'siklımın/ a, bitk. siklamen, tavşankulağı

cycle /'saykıl/ a. devir, tur, dönüş; bisiklet; motosiklet ☆ e. bisiklet sürmek **cyclist** bisikletçi

cyclone /'saykloun/ a. kasırga, siklon

cylinder /'silindı/ a. silindir **cylindrical** silindirik

cymbal /'simbıl/ a, müz. büyük zil

cynical /'sinikıl/ s. iyiliğe inanmayan

cypher /'sayfı/ a, bkz. cipher

cypress /'saypris/ a, bitk. servi

cyst /sist/ a, hek. kist

czar /za:/ a. çar

D

dab /deb/ a. dokunma, hafif vuruş ☆ e. hafifçe dokunmak, hafifçe vurmak

dabble /'debıl/ e. (at/in) bir işle amatörce uğraşmak, takılmak

dad /ded/ a, kon. baba

daddy /'dedi/ a, kon. baba, babacığım

daffodil /'defıdil/ a, bitk. zerrin, fulya, nergis

daft /da:ft/ s, kon. aptal, salak, budala

dagger /'degı/ a. hançer, kama

daily /'deyli/ s. günlük ☆ be. her gün ☆ a. günlük gazete

dainty /'deynti/ s. narin, sevimli; zarif

dairy /'deıri/ a. mandıra; süthane

dais /'deyis, deys/ a. konuşmacı kürsüsü

daisy /'deyzi/ a. papatya

dale /deyl/ a, yaz. vadi

dally /'deli/ e. (about/over) oyalanmak, sallanmak

dam /dem/ a. baraj, set ☆ e. baraj yapmak; set çekmek

damage /'demic/ a. zarar, hasar ☆ e. zarar vermek

damask /'demısk/ a. Şam kumaşı

dame /deym/ a, Aİ, kon. kadın

damn /dem/ e. lanetlemek, sövmek, mahkûm etmek **damn it** arg. Allah kahretsin! **damnation** lanet, bela **damned** melun; çok

damp /demp/ a. ıslaklık, nem ☆ s. nemli, rutubetli ☆ e. ıslatmak; söndürmek, azaltmak

dampen /'dempın/ e. ıslatmak, ıslanmak

damson /'demzın/ a, bitk. mürdümeriği

dance /da:ns/ e. dans etmek ☆ a. dans **dancer** dansör; dansöz

dandelion /'dendilayın/ a, bitk. karahindiba

dandy /'dendi/ a. züppe, çıtkırıldım
danger /'deyncı/ a. tehlike
dangerous /'deyncırıs/ s. tehlikeli
dangle /'dengıl/ e. sarkıtmak; sarkmak
dank /denk/ s. nemli, soğuk, yaş
dappled /'depıld/ s. benekli, puanlı
dare /deı/ e. cüret etmek; kalkışmak;
cesaret etmek I daresay galiba, sanı-
rım daredevil gözüpek, yiğit
daring /'deıring/ s. cüretkâr, cesur
dark /da:k/ s. karanlık; koyu; esmer ☆
a. karanlık darkness karanlık
darling /'da:ling/ a. sevgili
darn /da:n/ e. örerek onarmak, yamamak ☆ a. örülen yer
dart /da:t/ a. küçük ok; ani hareket; (dikiş) pens ☆ e. (across/out/to-
wards) fırlamak, atılmak; fırlatmak
darts dart oyunu
dash /deş/ e. çarpmak, vurmak; fırlamak, hızla koşmak; (ümit, vb.) yıkmak ☆ a. saldırma; fırlama; atılma;
darbe; vuruş; az miktar; eser; çizgi; tire (-) işareti; kısa mesafe koşusu
dashboard gösterge tablosu dashing
canlı, atılgan, enerjik
data /'deytı/ a. veri data processing veri işlem, bilgi işlem
date /deyt/ a. tarih; randevu; flört edilen (kimse); kurma ☆ e. tarih atmak;
tarihli olmak; birisiyle çıkmak out of
date modası geçmiş dated tarihli;
modası geçmiş
dative /'deytiv/ a, dilb. ismin -e hali, yö-
nelme durumu
daub /do:b/ e. (with/on) sıvamak, (yumuşak bir şeyle) kaplamak, sürmek
☆ a. harç, sıva; acemice yapılmış resim
daughter /'do:tı/ a. kız evlat, kız çocuk
daughter-in-law gelin
daunt /do:nt/ e. yıldırmak, korkutmak
dauntless gözü pek, korkusuz
dawdle /'do:dıl/ e, kon. salınmak, zaman harcamak
dawn /do:n/ a. şafak, tan ☆ e. (gün)
ağarmak
day /dey/ a. gün; gündüz; zaman, çağ,
ömür day by day günden güne from

day to day/day by day günden güne
günbegün one day bir gün, günün birinde some day (gelecekte) bir gün
make sb's day birini çok mutlu etmek, birini sevindirmek the other day
geçen gün, geçenlerde daybreak tan
şafak, seher daydream hayal, düş
daylight gün ışığı, gündüz daytime
gündüz
daze /deyz/ e. sersemletmek, afallatmak
dazzle /'dezıl/ e. (gözlerini) kamaştırmak
dead /ded/ s. ölü; uyuşmuş, uyuşuk
durgun; solgun; sıkıcı dead asleep
derin uykuda dead drunk zilzurna
sarhoş dead end açmaz, çıkmaz; çıkmaz sokak the dead ölüler deadly öldürücü; çok
deaden /'dedın/ e. hafifletmek, azaltmak
deadline /'dedlayn/ a. son teslim/bitir-
me tarihi
deadlock /'dedlok/ a. çözümleneme-
yen anlaşmazlık, çıkmaz
deaf /def/ s. sağır deafen sağırlaştır-
mak deafmute sağırdilsiz
deal /di:l/ e. pay etmek; dağıtmak; vermek; alışveriş etmek; ele almak, işlemek ☆ a. oyun kâğıtlarını dağıtma
alışveriş; iş a great deal of pek çok
dealer satıcı; oyunda kâğıtları dağı-
tan kişi dealings ilişkiler; alışveriş, iş
dealt /delt/ bkz. deal
dean /di:n/ a. dekan; baş papaz
dear /dıı/ s. sevgili; değerli; pahalı
(mektup başında) sevgili, sayın Oh
dear! Aman Allahım!, Hay Allah!, Deme! dearly pek çok
dearth /dö:t/ a. yokluk, kıtlık
death /det/ a. ölüm put to death öldürmek deathless ölümsüz
debar /di'ba:/ e. (from) mahrum bırakmak; engel olmak
debase /di'beys/ e. itibarını düşürmek
debatable /di'beytıbıl/ s. şüpheli, kuşku uyandıran
debate /di'beyt/ a. tartışma, müzakere
☆ e. tartışmak, görüşmek
debauch /di'bo:ç/ a. sefahat; ahlaksız-

lık ☆ e. ayartmak, baştan çıkartmak
debauchery sefahat, uçarılık; alemcilik
debilitate /di'biliteyt/ e. güçsüzleştirmek, takatten düşürmek
debility /di'biliti/ a. güçsüzlük, takatsızlık
debit /'debit/ a. deftere kaydedilen borç ☆ e. zimmetine geçirmek
debris /'debri, 'deybri/ a. enkaz, yıkıntı, çöküntü
debt /det/ a. borç **debtor** borçlu
debut /'deybyu:/ a. sosyal bir alanda ilk beliriş, sahneye ilk kez çıkış
decade /'dekeyd/ a. on yıl
decadent /'dekıdınt/ s. gözden düşen, itibarını yitiren
decanter /di'kentı/ a. şarap sürahisi
decathlon /di'ketlon/ a, sp. dekatlon, onlu yarış
decay /di'key/ e. çökmek, çürütmek ☆ a. çürüme, bozulma; çöküş
decease /di'si:s/ e. ölmek, vefat etmek **deceased** merhum, ölü
deceit /di'si:t/ a. aldatma, hile, yalan **deceitful** hilekâr, yalancı; aldatıcı
deceive /di'si:v/ e. aldatmak
December /di'sembı/ a. aralık (ayı)
decent /'di:sınt/ s. terbiyeli; saygılı; uygun, makul; hoş; kon. nazik, ince, kibar
decentralize /di:'sentrılayz/ e. merkezden birkaç yere yetki dağıtmak
deception /di'sepşın/ a. aldatma; aldanma; hile
deceptive /di'septiv/ s. aldatıcı, yanıltıcı
decibel /'desibel/ a, tek. desibel
decide /di'sayd/ e. karar vermek, kararlaştırmak **decided** açık, kesin; kararlı **decidedly** kuşkusuz
deciduous /di'sidyuıs/ s. (ağaç) her yıl yaprakları dökülen
decimal /'desimıl/ s, a. ondalık, onlu **decimal fraction** ondalık kesir **decimalize** ondalık sisteme çevirmek
decimate /'desimeyt/ e. büyük kısmını yok etmek
decipher /di'sayfı/ e. şifresini çözmek
decision /di'sijın/ a. karar

decisive /di'saysiv/ s. kararlı; kesin, sonuca götüren; şüphesiz
deck /dek/ a. güverte; Aİ. (iskambil) deste; kat ☆ e. süslemek, donatmak **deckchair** şezlong
declaim /di'kleym/ e. yüksek sesle ve el kol hareketleriyle konuşmak/söylemek
declaration /deklı'reyşın/ a. bildiri; demeç
declare /di'kleı/ e. ilan etmek; bildirmek; iddia etmek; huk. deklare etmek
decline /di'klayn/ e. geri çevirmek; çökmek; gerilemek ☆ a. iniş, gerileme, çöküş
decode /di:'koud/ e. şifresini çözmek
decompose /di:kım'pouz/ e. çürümek, bozulmak; çürütmek; ayrışmak; ayrıştırmak
décor /'deyko:/ a. dekor
decorate /'dekıreyt/ e. süslemek, donatmak, dekore etmek; badanalamak, boyamak; nişan vermek **decoration** süsleme, dekorasyon; süs; nişan, madalya **decorative** süsleyici, dekoratif **decorator** dekoratör
decoy /'di:koy/ a. tuzak; yem; hile
decrease /di'kri:s/ e. azalmak; azaltmak
decree /di'kri:/ a. emir, kararname; huk. karar, hüküm ☆ e. emretmek, buyurmak
decry /di'kray/ e. kötülemek, yermek
dedicate /'dedikeyt/ e. adamak; ithaf etmek **dedicated** (işine) kendini adamış **dedication** adama; ithaf
deduce /di'dyu:s/ e. sonuç çıkarmak
deduct /di'dakt/ e. çıkarmak, azaltmak
deduction /di'dakşın/ a. kesinti, indirme, azaltma; tümdengelim, türetim; sonuç
deed /di:d/ a. iş, hareket, eylem; huk. senet, tapu senedi
deem /di:m/ e. saymak, sanmak, zannetmek
deep /di:p/ s. derin; (renk) koyu; (ses) boğuk, alçak; (duygu) derin, içten; yoğun, ciddi ☆ be. derine, dibe, derinden **deep freeze** dipfriz, derin dondurucu **deep seated** köklü

deepen /'di:pın/ e. derinleşmek; derinleştirmek

deer /dıı/ a, hayb. geyik, karaca

deface /di'feys/ e. görünüşünü bozmak, çirkinleştirmek

defame /di'feym/ e. kara çalmak, ününe leke sürmek

default /di'fo:lt/ e. yapmama, savsama, gelmeme, hazır bulunmayış

defeat /di'fi:t/ e. yenmek, bozguna uğratmak ☆ a. yenilgi, bozgun

defect /'di:fekt/ a. kusur, eksiklik

defect /di'fekt/ e. kendi ülke/parti, vb.'ni terk etmek; iltica etmek

defective /di'fektiv/ s. hatalı, kusurlu, eksik

defence /di'fens/ a. savunma

defend /di'fend/ e. savunmak, korumak, müdafaa etmek **defendant** sanık, davalı **defender** savunucu; koruyucu

defensive /di'fensiv/ s. savunan, savunmalı, koruyucu

defer /di'fö:/ e. ertelemek, sonraya bırakmak **defer to** saygı göstermek, kabul etmek **deference** /'defırıns/ uyma, saygı gösterme, riayet etme

defiant /di'fayınt/ s. meydan okuyan, küstah

deficiency /di'fişınsi/ a. eksiklik, kusur; yetersizlik

deficient /di'fişınt/ s. yetersiz; eksik

deficit /'defisit/ a. (bütçe, hesap) açık

defile /di'fayl/ e. kirletmek

define /di'fayn/ e. tanımlamak; açıklamak

definite /'definit/ s. belirli, açık, kesin **definitely** kesinlikle

definition /defi'nişın/ a. tanım; (foto vb.) netlik

definitive /di'finitiv/ s. nihai, kesin

deflate /di:'fleyt, di'fleyt/ e. havasını boşaltmak, söndürmek; piyasadaki para miktarını azaltmak **deflation** deflasyon, paradarlığı

deflect /di'flekt/ e. saptırmak, çevirmek, sapmak

deform /di'fo:m/ e. biçimini bozmak, deforme etmek **deformed** biçimi bozulmuş **deformity** biçimsizlik, sakatlık

defraud /di'fro:d/ e. dolandırmak, aldatmak

defrost /di:'frost/ e. buzlarını çözmek/ temizlemek

deft /deft/ s. becerikli, usta

defunct /di'fankt/ s. ölü, ölmüş

defy /di'fay/ e. karşı gelmek, başkaldırmak; kafa tutmak; meydan okumak

degenerate /di'cenıreyt/ e. yozlaşmak **degeneration** yozlaşma

degrade /di'greyd/ e. küçük düşürmek, alçaltmak

degree /di'gri:/ a, tek. derece; düzey, derece, kademe; öğrenim derecesi

deify /'di:ifay, 'deyfay/ e. tanrılaştırmak, yüceltmek

deign /deyn/ e, hkr. tenezzül etmek

deity /'di:iti, 'deyti/ a. tanrı, tanrıça

dejected /di'cektid/ s. üzgün, hüzünlü

delay /di'ley/ e. gecikmek; geciktirmek; ertelemek ☆ a. gecikme

delectable /di'lektıbıl/ s. nefis

delegate /'deligit/ a. temsilci, delege ☆ e. temsilci olarak görevlendirmek/atamak; delege olarak göndermek

delegation /deli'geyşın/ a. delegasyon; yetki verme, görevlendirme

delete /di'li:t/ e. silmek, çıkarmak **deletion** silme, çıkarma

deliberate /di'libırıt/ s. kasıtlı; temkinli, dikkatli **deliberately** kasten, bile bile

delicacy /'delikısi/ a. duyarlılık, narinlik; az bulunur/pahalı/leziz yiyecek

delicate /'delikıt/ s. narin, zarif, ince; nazik; (yemek) leziz ve hafif

delicatessen /delikı'tesın/ a. mezeci dükkânı, şarküteri

delicious /di'lişıs/ s. nefis, leziz

delight /di'layt/ e. zevk vermek, memnun etmek, sevindirmek; (in) zevk almak; ☆ a. zevk, haz; sevinç **Turkish delight** lokum **delightful** zevkli, hoş

delinquency /di'linkwınsi/ a. görevin ihmali; kusur, kabahat; suçluluk **delinquent** suçlu

delirious /di'liıriıs/ s. sayıklayan; çılgın gibi, azgın

delirium /di'liırıım/ a. sayıklama; coşma

deliver /di'livı/ e. teslim etmek, götürmek; dağıtmak; serbest bırakmak; doğurtmak

delivery /di'livıri/ a. teslim, dağıtım, servis; doğum

delta /'deltı/ a, coğ. delta, çatalağız

delude /di'lu:d/ e. kandırmak, aldatmak

deluge /'delyu:c/ a. büyük sel, su baskını; şiddetli yağmur ☆ e. ... yağmuruna tutmak

delusion /di'lu:jın/ a. aldatma; aldanma; saplantı; yanlış inanç, kuruntu

de luxe /di'laks/ s. lüks, kaliteli

demagogic /demı'gogik/ s. demagojik

demagogue /'demıgog/ a. demagog, halkavcısı

demand /di'ma:nd/ a. istek, talep; rağbet e. istemek, talep etmek; gerektirmek **in demand** rağbette

demarcation /dima:'keyşın/ a. ayırma, sınırlarını belirtme

demean /di'mi:n/ e. küçük düşürmek, alçaltmak

demeanour /di'mi:nı/ a. davranış biçimi, tavır, tutum

demented /di'mentid/ s. deli, çılgın

demo /'demou/ a, kon. gösteri

demobilize /di:'moubilayz/ e. terhis etmek

demobilization /dimoubilay'zeyşın/ a, ask. terhis; seferberliğin bitmesi

democracy /di'mokrısi/ a. demokrasi

democrat /'demıkret/ a. demokrat, halkçı **democratic** demokratik

demography /di'mogrıfi/ a. demografi, nüfusbilim

demolish /di'moliş/ e. yıkmak, yok etmek

demolition /demı'lişın/ a. yıkma, yok etme; yıkılma, yıkım

demon /'di:mın/ a. şeytan

demonstrate /'demınstreyt/ e. göstermek; kanıtlamak; gösteri yapmak/düzenlemek **demonstration** gösteri; kanıt **demonstrative** duygularını gizlemeyen; dilb. işaret zamiri, gösterme adılı

demoralize /di'morılayz/ e. cesaretini kırmak, moralini bozmak

demote /di'mout/ e. rütbesini indirmek

demure /di'myuı/ s. ağırbaşlı, uslu

den /den/ a. in, mağara; yatak, uğrak; kon. çalışma odası

denial /di'nayıl/ a. inkâr; yalanlama

denim /'denim/ a. blucin kumaşı, kot; ç, kon. blucin, kot

denomination /dinomi'neyşın/ a. mezhep; birim; ad

denote /di'nout/ e. belirtmek, göstermek, anlamına gelmek

denounce /di'nauns/ e. alenen suçlamak, kınamak

dense /dens/ s. yoğun; koyu; kon. aptal, kalın kafalı

density /'densiti/ a. yoğunluk; sıklık

dent /dent/ a. ezik, çukur; kon. incinme ☆ e. göçürmek, yamultmak

dental /'dentıl/ s. dişlerle ilgili, diş ...

dentist /'dentist/ a. dişçi, diş hekimi **dentistry** dişçilik

denture /'dençı/ a. takma diş

denude /di'nyu:d/ e. soymak, çıplak hale getirmek

denunciation /dinansi'eyşın/ a. alenen suçlama, kınama; kınanma

deny /di'nay/ e. inkâr etmek; yalanlamak, tanımamak

deodorant /di:'oudırınt/ a. deodoran, kokugideren

depart /di'pa:t/ e. ayrılmak, hareket etmek, kalkmak

department /di'pa:tmınt/ a. kısım, bölüm, reyon; şube, daire, kol **department store** (çeşitli reyonlardan oluşan) büyük mağaza

departure /di'pa:çı/ a. hareket, gidiş, kalkış

depend /di'pend/ e. bağlı olmak; (on) güvenmek; göre değişmek **dependable** güvenilir

dependant /di'pendınt/ a. başkasının eline bakan, muhtaç

dependence /di'pendıns/ a. bağımlılık; güven, güvenme

dependent /di'pendınt/ s. başkasının eline bakan; muhtaç **(on)** bağlı

depict /di'pikt/ e. göstermek; dile getirmek

deplete /di'pli:t/ e. tüketmek; boşaltmak

deplore /di'plo:/ *e.* teessüf etmek, üzülmek

deploy /di'ploy/ *e, ask.* mevzilenmek, konuşlanmak; mevzilendirmek, konuşlandırmak

deployment /di'ploymınt/ *a, ask.* yayılma

deport /di'po:t/ *e.* sınırdışı etmek

depose /di'pouz/ *e.* tahttan indirmek; azletmek, görevden çıkarmak

deposit /di'pozit/ *e.* koymak, bırakmak; (bankaya) yatırmak; (kaparo) vermek; (tortu) bırakmak ☆ *a.* yatırılan para, mevduat; kaparo, depozit; tortu **deposit account** mevduat hesabı

depositor /di'pozitı/ *a.* mudi, yatıran

depot /'depou/ *a.* depo, ambar; *ask.* cephanelik; küçük istasyon

deprave /di'preyv/ *e.* ahlaksızlaştırmak

depraved /di'preyvd/ *s.* ahlaksız

depreciate /di'pri:şieyt/ *e.* (para, vb.) değer kaybetmek; küçümsemek, hor görmek

depress /di'pres/ *e.* üzmek, keyfini kaçırmak, içini karartmak; durgunlaştırmak

depression /di'preşın/ *a, hek.* depresyon, çökkünlük, çöküntü, bunalım; alçak basınç alanı

deprive /di'prayv/ *e.* (of) yoksun bırakmak, mahrum etmek

depth /dept/ *a.* derinlik

deputation /depyu'teyşın/ *a.* temsilciler heyeti

depute /di'pyu:t/ *e.* vekil tayin etmek, yetki vermek

deputy /'depyuti/ *a.* vekil; milletvekili

derby /'da:bi, 'dö:bi/ *a, Aİ.* melon şapka **the Derby** İngiltere'de Epsom'da her yıl yapılan geleneksel at yarışı

derelict /'derilikt/ *s.* terk edilmiş, sahipsiz

deride /di'rayd/ *e.* ile alay etmek

derision /di'rijın/ *a.* alay, hor görme **object of derision** alay konusu

derive /di'rayv/ *e.* (from) elde etmek, çıkarmak; türemek **derivation** türetme **derivative** türev

derogatory /di'rogıtıri/ *s.* küçültücü, onur kırıcı, aşağılayıcı

derrick /'derik/ *a.* vinç; petrol sondaj kulesi

descend /di'send/ *e.* (aşağı) inmek, alçalmak **descendant** torun

descent /di'sent/ *a.* iniş, inme; soy, nesil; baskın

describe /di'skrayb/ *e.* tanımlamak; (as) görmek, saymak, gözüyle bakmak; çizmek

description /di'skripşın/ *a.* tanımlama; tanım, tarif; *kon.* çeşit, tür **descriptive** tanımlayıcı

desecrate /'desikreyt/ *e.* kutsallığını bozmak

desert /'dezıt/ *a.* çöl

desert /di'zö:t/ *e.* terk etmek; firar etmek, kaçmak **deserter** asker kaçağı

deserve /di'zö:v/ *e.* hak etmek, layık olmak

design /di'zayn/ *e.* çizmek; plan çizmek; tasarlamak **designer** tasarımcı, tasarçizimci, dizayncı ☆ *a.* plan, proje; tasarım, çizim, dizayn; desen, taslak

designate /'dezigneyt/ *e.* göstermek, işaret etmek; görevlendirmek; (as) unvanlandırmak

desirable /di'zayırıbıl/ *s.* istenilir, hoş

desire /di'zayı/ *e.* arzu etmek, istemek; ☆ *a.* arzu, emel; istek, dilek

desist /di'zist/ *e.* vazgeçmek

desk /desk/ *a.* okul sırası; yazı masası; kürsü; resepsiyon

desolate /'desılıt/ *s.* ıssız, boş; yalnız

despair /di'speı/ *e.* (of) umudunu kesmek ☆ *a.* umutsuzluk

despatch /di'speç/ *a, e, bkz.* **dispatch**

desperate /'despırıt/ *a.* umutsuz, çaresiz; gözü dönmüş; çok ciddi

desperation /despı'reyşın/ *a.* gözü dönmüşlük, çaresizlik

despicable /di'spikıbıl/ *s.* aşağılık, adi

despise /di'spayz/ *e.* küçümsemek, hor görmek, aşağılamak

despite /di'spayt/ *ilg.* -e rağmen, -e karşın

despot /'despot/ *a,* despot, zorba

dessert /di'zö:t/ *a.* (yemeğin sonunda yenen) tatlı

destination /desti'neyşın/ *a.* gidile-

cek/gönderilen yer
destine /'destin/ e. kaderini/geleceğini
önceden belirlemek
destiny /'destini/ a. alınyazısı, yazgı, kader
destitute /'destityu:t/ s. yoksul; -den
yoksun
destroy /di'stroy/ e. yok etmek, mahvetmek; yıkmak **destroyer** destroyer,
muhrip
destruction /di'strakşın/ a. yıkma, yok
etme; yıkım
destructive /di'straktiv/ s. yıkıcı
detach /di'teç/ e. ayırmak, sökmek, çıkarmak **detached** ayrı; yansız; (ev)
müstakil **detachment** ayırma, çıkarma; ayrılma; ask. müfreze
detail /'di:teyl/ a. ayrıntı, detay
detailed /'di:teyld/ s. ayrıntılı, detaylı
detain /di'teyn/ e. alıkoymak, tutmak
detect /di'tekt/ e. bulmak, ortaya çıkarmak **detection** bulma, ortaya çıkarma **detector** dedektör, bulucu
detective /di'tektiv/ a. dedektif, hafiye
detention /di'tenşın/ a. alıkoyma, engelleme; alıkonma
deter /di'tö:/ e. vazgeçirmek, caydırmak
detergent /di'tö:cınt/ a. deterjan, arıtıcı
deteriorate /di'tiiriireyt/ e. kötüleşmek;
kötüleştirmek
determination /ditö:mi'neyşın/ a.
azim, kararlılık; belirleme, saptama
determine /di'tö:min/ e. karar vermek;
kararlaştırmak; belirlemek, saptamak
determined kararlı, azimli **determiner** dilb. belirtici, bir adın anlamını sınırlayan ve bu adı tanımlayan sözcük
determinism /di'tö:minizim/ a, fel. determinizm, gerekircilik
detest /di'test/ e. nefret etmek
detonate /'detıneyt/ e. patlamak; patlatmak
detour /'di:tuı/ a. dolambaçlı yol
detract /di'trekt/ e. (from) düşürmek,
eksiltmek, azaltmak
detriment /'detrimınt/ a. zarar, hasar
detrimental zararlı
deuce /dyu:s/ a. (tenis) düs, beraberlik; (zar) dü

devaluation /di:velyu'eyşın/ a. devalüasyon, değer düşürümü
devalue /di:'velyu:/ e. paranın değerini
düşürmek; değerini düşürmek
devastate /'devısteyt/ e. harap etmek
devastation harap etme/olma
develop /di'velıp/ e. gelişmek, büyümek, geliştirmek, büyütmek; harekete geçirmek; (filmi) banyo etmek **development** gelişme; geliştirme; kalkınma; (film) banyo
deviate /'di:vieyt/ e. sapmak, ayrılmak
deviation sapma
device /di'vays/ a. aygıt, alet; hile,
oyun
devil /'devıl/ a. (the) şeytan; kötü ruh
devious /'di:viis/ s. dolambaçlı
devise /di'vayz/ e. planlamak, bulmak
devoid /di'voyd/ s. (of) yoksun
devote /di'vout/ e. (to) -e adamak, vermek **devoted** sadık, bağlı **devotee**
hayran, düşkün **devotion** adama; bağlılık, düşkünlük; dindarlık
devour /di'vauı/ e. yiyip yutmak; bitirmek, yok etmek
devout /di'vaut/ s. dindar; içten, samimi
dew /dyu:/ a. çiy, şebnem **dewdrop** çiy
damlası
dexterity /dek'steriti/ a. yetenek, el becerisi **dexterous** becerikli, usta
diabetes /dayı'bi:ti:z/ a, hek. şeker hastalığı, diyabet **diabetic** /-'betik/ diyabetik; şeker hastası
diagnose /'dayıgnouz/ e. teşhis etmek,
tanılamak **diagnosis** /-'nousis/ teşhis, diyagnoz
diagonal /day'egınıl/ a. köşegen ☆ s.
çapraz
diagram /'dayıgrem/ a. diyagram, çizenek
dial /'dayıl/ a. (saat/telefon, vb.) kadran ☆ e. (telefon) numaraları çevirmek
dialect /'dayılekt/ a. lehçe, diyalekt
dialectic /dayı'lektik/ a. diyalektik, eytişim
dialogue /'dayılog/ a. diyalog, söyleşme
diameter /day'emitı/ a. çap

diamond /'dayımınd/ a. elmas; baklava biçimi; (iskambil) karo

diaper /'dayıpı/ a, Aİ. çocuk bezi

diaphragm /'dayıfrem/ a, anat. diyafram; fiz. diyafram, ışık bebeği, zar

diarrhea /dayı'rii/ a, bkz. **diarrhoea**

diarrhoea /dayı'rii/ a. ishal, amel

diary /'dayıri/ a. günlük; anı defteri; not defteri

dice /days/ a. zar, oyun zarları

dictate /dik'teyt/ e. (söyleyerek) yazdırmak

dictation /dik'teyşın/ a. dikte, yazdırma

dictator /dik'teytı/ a. diktatör

diction /'dikşın/ a. telaffuz, diksiyon

dictionary /'dikşınıri/ a. sözlük

didactic /day'dektik/ s. (konuşma ya da yazı) didaktik, öğretici

die /day/ e. ölmek; sona ermek ☆ a. metal kalıp; oyun zarı **die away** (ses, ışık, rüzgâr, vb.) azalmak **die out** tamamen yok olmak **be dying for** -i çok istemek

diesel /'di:zıl/ a. dizel motoru, dizel motorlu araç **diesel oil** mazot

diet /'dayıt/ a. perhiz, rejim; günlük besin **go on a diet** rejim yapmak ☆ e. perhiz yapmak, rejim yapmak

differ /'difı/ e. (**from**) farklı olmak; (**with**) farklı görüşte olmak

difference /'difrıns/ a. fark, ayrım, ayrılık **different** farklı; başka, değişik; ayrı; çeşitli

differential /difı'renşıl/ a. ücret farkı; diferansiyel

differentiate /difı'renşieyt/ e. ayırmak; fark gözetmek

difficult /'difikılt/ s. zor, güç; güç beğenir; huysuz **difficulty** zorluk, güçlük

diffident /'difidınt/ s. çekingen

diffuse /di'fyu:s/ s. yayılmış, dağınık; ☆ e. yaymak, dağıtmak; yayılmak **diffusion** yayma; yayılma

dig /dig/ e. **dug** /dag/ kazmak; kazı yapmak; arg. hoşlanmak ☆ a. kazı yeri; iğneli söz **dig out** kazıp ortaya çıkarmak

digest /day'cest/ e. sindirmek; anlamak, kavramak; sindirilmek ☆ a. özet

digestion /day'cesçın, di'cesçın/ a. sindirim

digit /'dicit/ a. rakam; parmak **digital** sayısal

dignified /'dignifayd/ s. ağırbaşlı

dignitary /'dignitıri/ a. yüksek mevki sahibi, ileri gelen

dignity /'digniti/ a. değer; saygınlık; ciddiyet; ağırbaşlılık

digress /day'gres/ e. konu dışına çıkmak

digs /digz/ a, İİ, kon. pansiyon

dike /dayk/ a. set, bent; hendek

dilate /day'leyt/ e. genişlemek; büyümek; genişletmek

dilemma /di'lemı/ a. ikilem

diligent /'dilicınt/ s. dikkatli, çalışkan, gayretli **diligence** dikkat, çalışkanlık

dilute /day'lu:t/ e. seyreltmek, sulandırmak

dim /dim/ s. loş, sönük, bulanık; kon. ahmak, budala

dime /daym/ a, Aİ. (ABD ve Kanada'da) 10 sent değerindeki madeni para

dimension /day'menşın, di'menşın/ a. boyut **dimensional** ... boyutlu

diminish /di'miniş/ e. azalmak; azaltmak

diminutive /di'minyutiv/ s. çok küçük, minik

dimple /'dimpıl/ a. gamze

din /din/ a. gürültü

dine /dayn/ e. akşam yemeği yemek **diner** yemek yiyen kimse; Aİ. vagon restoran **dine out** akşam yemeğini dışarıda yemek

dingdong /ding'dong/ a. çan/zil ses

dinghy /'dingi/ a. küçük sandal; lastik bot **rubber dinghy** lastik bot

dingy /'dinci/ s. kirli; soluk

dining room /'dayning ru:m/ a. yemek odası

dinner /'dinı/ a. akşam yemeği; (bazen) öğle yemeği; yemek, iş yemeği **dinner jacket** smokin

dinosaur /'daynıso:/ a, hayb. dinozor

dip /dip/ e. daldırmak, batırmak; (güneş, vb.) batmak; azalmak, azaltmak ☆ a. dalma, batma; kon. kısa yüzüş

diphtheria /dif'tiırıı/ a, hek. difteri
diphthong /'diftong/ a, dilb. diftong, ikili ünlü
diploma /di'ploumı/ a. diploma
diplomacy /di'ploumısi/ a. diplomasi,
diplomatlık diplomat diplomat diplomatic diplomatik
dire /'dayı/ s. korkunç; müthiş
direct /di'rekt, day'rekt/ s. doğru, düz;
dolaysız ☆ be. dosdoğru, durakla-
madan ☆ e. yolu tarif etmek; emretmek; yöneltmek; çevirmek; yönetmek
direct current doğru akım direct object dolaysız tümleç direct speech dolaysız anlatım directly doğrudan doğruya; derhal; hemen
direction /di'rekşın, day'rekşın/ a. yön;
idare, yönetim; talimat, yönerge
directive /di'rektiv/ a. direktif, yönerge
director /di'rektı/ a. müdür, yönetici; yönetmen
directory /di'rektıri/ a. adres rehberi; telefon rehberi
dirge /dö:c/ a. ağıt
dirt /dö:t/ a. kir, pislik; toz, toprak, çamur dirty pis, kirli; iğrenç; çirkin; kon.
(hava) bozuk, fırtınalı; kon. adi, alçakça
disable /dis'eybıl/ e. sakatlamak; mahrum etmek the disabled sakatlar
disadvantage /disıd'va:ntic/ a. dezavantaj; zarar, kayıp
disagree /dısı'gri:/ e. (with) aynı düşüncede olmamak; yaramamak, dokun-
mak disagreeable ters, huysuz; nahoş; tatsız disagreement anlaşmazlık, uyuşmazlık
disappear /dısı'piı/ e. gözden kaybolmak, ortadan kalkmak; unutulup gitmek disappearance kayboluş, kaybol-
ma, gözden kayboluş
disappoint /dısı'poynt/ e. hayal kırıklığına uğratmak disappointed düş kırıklığına uğramış, üzgün disappointing
düş kırıklığına uğratıcı disappointment düş kırıklığı; düş kırıklığına uğra-
tan şey/kimse
disapprove /dısı'pru:v/ e. (of) uygun
görmemek disapproval uygun görme-
me, onaylamama

disarm /dis'a:m/ e. silahsızlandırmak;
silahsızlanmak; yatıştırmak, yumuşatmak disarmament silahsızlanma
disaster /di'za:stı/ a. felaket, facia, yıkım disastrous felaket getiren, feci
disbelief /disbi'li:f/ a. inançsızlık, güvensizlik, inanmazlık
disc /disk/ a. yuvarlak yüzey; yuvarlak
şey; disk, plak disc jockey diskcokey,
plak sunucu
discard /dis'ka:d/ e. atmak, ıskartaya çıkarmak, başından atmak
discern /di'sö:n/ e. (güçlükle) görmek,
fark etmek, ayırt etmek discerning zeki, anlayışlı
discharge /dis'ça:c/ e. (yük) yerine getirmek, yapmak; boşaltmak; tahliye etmek; (borç) ödemek; (silah, ok, vb.)
ateşlemek, atmak; (gaz, sıvı, vb.) akıtmak ☆ a. boşaltma; ateş etme; tahliye; terhis; akma
disciple /di'saypıl/ a. mürit, havari
discipline /'disiplin/ a. disiplin; bilgi da-
lı ☆ e. kontrol altında tutmak, eğitmek
disclaim /dis'kleym/ e. -e ile ilişkisi ol-
madığını söylemek; vazgeçmek
disclose /dis'klouz/ e. açığa vurmak
disco /'diskou/ a, kon. disko
discolour /dis'kalı/ e. rengini değiştirmek; rengi değişmek, bozulmak
discomfort /dis'kamfıt/ a. rahatsızlık; sıkıntı
disconnect /dis'kınekt/ e. bağlantısını
kesmek; ayırmak
discontent /diskın'tent/ a. hoşnutsuzluk
discontinue /diskın'tinyu:/ e. devam etmemek, bırakmak, kesmek; durmak
discord /'disko:d/ a. düşünce ayrılığı,
uyuşmazlık; ihtilaf; müz. ahenksizlik
discotheque /'diskıtek/ a. diskotek, disko
discount /'diskaunt/ a. indirim ☆ e.
(senet, bono) kırmak
discourage /dis'karic/ e. cesaretini kırmak; vazgeçirmek, engellemek
discourse /'disko:s/ a. söylev
discourteous /dis'kö:tiıs/ s. kaba, saygısız discourtesy kabalık, saygısızlık

discover /dis'kavı/ e. keşfetmek, bulmak; farkına varmak discoverer kâşif discovery keşif, buluş

discredit /dis'kredit/ e. gözden düşürmek; kuşkuyla bakmak ☆ a. gözden düşme; yüzkarası, leke; inanmama, şüphe

discreet /di'skri:t/ s. sağduyulu, saygılı

discretion /di'skreşın/ a. sağduyu; denlilik

discriminate /di'skrimineyt/ e. ayırmak; farkı görmek; fark gözetmek, ayrım yapmak discrimination ayrım, fark gözetme; ince farkları görebilme yeteneği racial discrimination ırk ayrımı

discus /'diskıs/ a, sp. disk

discuss /di'skas/ e. ele almak, tartışmak, görüşmek discussion tartışma, görüşme

disdain /dis'deyn/ e. hor görmek, tepeden bakmak; tenezzül etmemek

disease /di'zi:z/ a. hastalık diseased hastalıklı

disembark /disim'ba:k/ e. karaya çıkmak

disembody /disim'bodi/ e. gövdeden ayırmak

disgrace /dis'greys/ e. küçük düşürmek, itibarını zedelemek; gözden düşürmek, rezil etmek ☆ a. yüzkarası; gözden düşme

disgruntled /dis'grantıld/ s. (at/with) üzgün, canı sıkılmış

disguise /dis'gayz/ e. görünüşünü/kılığını değiştirmek; saklamak, gizlemek ☆ a. sahte kılık; maske, numara

disgust /dis'gast/ a. iğrenme, tiksinme, tiksinti ☆ e. tiksindirmek, iğrendirmek disgusting iğrenç

dish /diş/ a. tabak; yemek dishes tabak çanak; bulaşık dishwasher bulaşık makinesi dishwater bulaşık suyu wash the dishes bulaşıkları yıkamak

dishonest /dis'onist/ s. namussuz

dishonour /dis'onı/ e. namusuna leke sürmek ☆ a. onursuzluk, şerefsizlik; leke

disillusion /disi'lu:jın/ e. gözünü açmak, yanlış bir düşünceden kurtarmak

disillusioned /disi'lu:jınd/ s. üzgün, kırgın, hayal kırıklığına uğramış

disinfect /disin'fekt/ e. dezenfekte etmek

disinfectant /disin'fektınt/ a. dezenfektan

disintegrate /dis'intigreyt/ e. parçalamak, dağıtmak, ufalamak; parçalanmak, dağılmak

disinterested /dis'intristid/ s. kişisel duygularla etkilenmeyen, yansız, önyargısız; kon. ilgisiz, umursamaz

disjoint /dis'coynt/ e. parçalarına ayırmak

disjointed /dis'coyntid/ s. (konuşma, yazı, vb.) bağlantısız, kopuk

disk /disk/ a, Aİ, bkz. disc

dislike /dis'layk/ e. sevmemek, hoşlanmamak ☆ a. sevmeme, hoşlanmama

dislocate /'dislıkeyt/ e. (kemik) yerinden çıkarmak; altüst etmek

disloyal /dis'loyıl/ s. vefasız disloyalty vefasızlık

dismal /'dizmıl/ s. kasvetli, iç karartıcı

dismantle /dis'mentıl/ e. sökmek

dismay /dis'mey/ e. dehşete düşürmek, korkutmak ☆ a. korku, dehşet

dismiss /dis'mis/ e. (işten) çıkarmak, yol vermek; gitmesine izin vermek dismissal çıkarma, kovma; izin, bırakma, gönderme

dismount /dis'maunt/ e. (at, bisiklet, vb.'den) inmek

disobedience /disı'bi:diıns/ a. söz dinlemezlik, itaatsizlik disobedient itaatsiz, söz dinlemez

disobey /disı'bey/ e. söz dinlememek, itaat etmemek; (kural, yasa, vb.) çiğnemek, uymamak

disorder /dis'o:dı/ a. karışıklık, düzensizlik; kargaşa, patırtı; hastalık, rahatsızlık ☆ e. karıştırmak, bozmak

disorganized /dis'o:gınayzd/ s. düzensiz

dispatch, despatch /di'speç/ e. göndermek; bitirivermek ☆ a. yollama, gönderme; mesaj; telyazı, telgraf

dispel /di'spel/ e. dağıtmak, def etmek; yok etmek, gidermek

dispense di'spens/ *e.* dağıtmak, vermek; (ilaç reçetesini) hazırlamak

dispensable /di'spensıbıl/ *s.* gereksiz; vazgeçilebilir

dispensary /di'spensıri/ *a.* dispanser, bakımevi

dispense /di'spens/ *e.* dağıtmak, vermek; (ilaç/reçete, vb.) hazırlamak

disperse /di'spö:s/ *e.* dağılmak, yayılmak; yaymak, dağıtmak

displace /dis'pleys/ *e.* yerinden çıkarmak; -in yerine geçmek; ülkesinden çıkarmak

display /di'spley/ *e.* göstermek; sergilemek ☆ *a.* gösterme; gösteri; sergi

displease /dis'pli:z/ *e.* canını sıkmak; gücendirmek **displeasure** hoşnutsuzluk, gücenme

dispose /di'spouz/ *e.* (of) kurtulmak, başından atmak; alt etmek; düzenlemek, yerleştirmek **disposable** kullandıktan sonra atılan **disposal** elden çıkarma; düzenleme; idare, yönetim; kurtulma

disposition /dispı'zişın/ *a.* yaradılış, huy; düzenleme; eğilim, istek

disproportionate /disprı'po:şınit/ *s.* oransız, çok fazla ya da çok az

disprove /dis'pru:v/ *e.* yanlış olduğunu kanıtlamak

dispute /di'spyu:t/ *e.* tartışmak; çekişmek; karşı çıkmak, itiraz etmek, kabul etmemek ☆ *a.* tartışma; çekişme, kavga; anlaşmazlık, uyuşmazlık **disputable** tartışılabilir, kuşkulu, su götürür

disqualify /dis'kwolifay/ *e.* diskalifiye etmek

disregard /disri'ga:d/ *e.* aldırmamak, önemsememek ☆ *a.* aldırmazlık, önemsememe; ihmal

disrepute /disri'pyu:t/ *a.* kötü şöhret **disreputable** adı çıkmış, kötü ünlü

disrespect /disri'spekt/ *a.* saygısızlık, kabalık

disrupt /dis'rapt/ *e.* dağıtmak, bozmak, bölmek

dissatisfy /dis'setisfay/ *e.* doyuramamak, memnun edememek **dissatis-**

faction doyumsuzluk, hoşnutsuzluk

dissect /di'sekt/ *e.* incelemek üzere kesip ayırmak; dikkatle incelemek

disseminate /di'semineyt/ *e.* (düşünce, haber, vb.) yaymak, saçmak

dissension /di'senşın/ *a.* anlaşmazlık, kavga

dissent /di'sent/ *e.* aynı görüşte olmamak ☆ *a.* görüş ayrılığı, uyuşmazlık, anlaşmazlık **dissenter** muhalif

dissidence /'disidıns/ *a.* görüş ayrılığı, muhalefet; anlaşmazlık

dissident /'disidınt/ *a, s.* muhalif

dissimilar /di'similı/ *s.* benzemez, ayrı

dissipate /'disipeyt/ *e.* dağıtmak, yok etmek; çarçur etmek, aptalca harcamak

dissociate /di'souşieyt/ *e.* ayırmak, ayrı tutmak

dissolve /di'zolv/ *e.* erimek; eritmek; feshetmek, dağıtmak; sona erdirmek, bozmak **dissolution** erime, eritme; sona erme; bozma, bozulma

dissuade /di'sweyd/ *e.* caydırmak, vazgeçirmek **dissuasion** caydırma, vazgeçirme

distance /'distıns/ *a.* mesafe, uzaklık; ara; süre **in the distance** uzakta

distant /'distınt/ *s.* uzak, uzakta; (akraba) uzaktan, uzak; soğuk, ilgisiz, mesafeli

distaste /dis'teyst/ *e.* sevmeme, hoşlanmama, nefret **distasteful** tatsız, nahoş

distend /di'stend/ *e.* şişmek; şişirmek

distil /di'stil/ *e.* imbikten çekmek, damıtmak; (konu, vb.) özünü çıkarmak, özünü almak **distillation** damıtma; damıtık madde **distillery** içki yapan fabrika

distinct /di'stinkt/ *s.* farklı, ayrı; açık, belirgin

distinction /di'stinkşın/ *a.* fark, ayırım; üstünlük; ün, şan; şeref; ödül

distinctive /di'stinktiv/ *s.* diğerlerinden ayrı, ayıran, özel

distinguish /di'stingwiş/ *e.* ayırt etmek, seçmek; kendini göstermek; sivrilmek; görmek, seçmek **distinguishable** ayırt edilebilir; görülebilir **distin-**

guished seçkin, ünlü

distort /di'sto:t/ e. biçimini bozmak; bükmek; çarpıtmak, saptırmak; değiştirmek

distract /di'strekt/ e. (dikkatini) başka yöne çekmek **distraction** dikkat dağıtıcı şey; dikkatini dağıtma; eğlence

distraught /di'stro:t/ s. aklı başından gitmiş, çılgına dönmüş

distress /di'stres/ a. acı, ıstırap, üzüntü ☆ e. sıkıntı vermek **distressing** acı veren, üzücü

distribute /di'stribyu:t/ e. dağıtmak, vermek; pay etmek, bölüştürmek; yaymak, saçmak **distribution** dağıtma, dağıtım **distributor** dağıtıcı, dağıtımcı; tek. distribütör

district /'distrikt/ a. bölge

distrust /dis'trast/ e. güvenmemek, itimat etmemek ☆ a. güvenmeme, itimatsızlık

disturb /di'stö:b/ e. rahatsız etmek; üzmek; bozmak; karıştırmak; allak bullak etmek **disturbance** rahatsızlık; karışıklık **disturbed** rahatsız, huzursuz

disuse /dis'yu:s/ a. kullanılmayış, geçersizlik

ditch /diç/ a. hendek ☆ e, kon. başından atmak, bırakmak

dither /'didı/ e, kon. telaşa kapılmak

ditto /'ditou/ a. aynı şey; denden (") işareti

ditty /'diti/ a. kısa ve basit şarkı

divan /di'ven/ a. divan, sedir

dive /dayv/ e. (suya) balıklama atlamak; dalmak **diver** dalgıç

diverge /day'vö:c/ e. (yol, görüş, vb.'-den) ayrılmak, uzaklaşmak; sapmak **divergence** ayrılma, uzaklaşma **divergent** birbirinden ayrılan

diverse /day'vö:s/ s. çeşitli; farklı, değişik **diversity** farklılık; çeşitlilik

diversify /day'vö:sifay/ e. çeşitlendirmek

diversion /day'vö:şın/ a. yönünü değiştirme, saptırma; eğlence; oyun

divert /day'vö:t/ e. başka yöne çevirmek; oyalamak, eğlendirmek

divide /di'vayd/ e. bölmek; ayrmak

dividend /di'vidınd/ a. kâr hissesi; mat. bölünen

dividers /di'vaydız/ a. pergel

divine /di'vayn/ s. kutsal, tanrısal; ilahi; kon. süper, çok iyi

divinity /di'viniti/ a. ilahiyat

divisible /di'vizıbıl/ s. bölünebilir

division /di'vijın/ a. bölme; bölünme; parça; fikir ayrılığı; ask. tümen

divisor /di'vayzı/ a, mat. bölen

divorce /di'vo:s/ a. boşanma ☆ e. boşanmak; boşamak

divorcé /di'vo:si:, di'vo:sey/ a. dul erkek

divorcee /divo:'si:/ a. boşanmış kimse, dul kimse

divorcée /di'vo:si:/ a. dul kadın

divulge /day'valc/ e. açığa vurmak

dizzy /'dizi/ s. başı dönen; baş döndürücü; kon. aptal **feel dizzy** başı dönmek

do /du:/ e. **did** /did/ **done** /dan/ yapmak, etmek **do away with** ortadan kaldırmak; yok etmek, öldürmek **do with** -e ihtiyacı olmak **do without** idare etmek, olmadan yapmak **have to do with** ile bir ilgisi olmak

dock /dok/ a. rıhtım; gemi havuzu, dok; (mahkemede) sanık yeri ☆ e. (kuyruğunu) kesmek; (ücret, vb.) kısmak, azaltmak; (gemi) limana girmek **be in the dock** sanık olmak **put in the dock** suçlamak

dockage /'dokic/ a. kesinti

dockyard /'dokya:d/ a. tersane

doctor /'doktı/ a. doktor, hekim; doktora yapmış kişi; Aİ. diş doktoru ☆ e, kon. tedavi etmek; onarmak; değiştirmek

doctorate /'doktırıt/ a. doktora

doctrinaire /doktri'neı/ s. kuramcı

doctrine /'doktrin/ a. öğreti, doktrin

document /'dokyumınt/ a. belge ☆ e. belgelemek **documentation** /dokyumen'teyşın/ belgelerle kanıtlama, belgeleme

documentary /dokyu'mentıri/ s. belgesel; belgeli ☆ a. belgesel (film)

dodge /doc/ e. hızla yana çekilmek; hile ile kurtulmak, atlatmak ☆ a. yana kaçış; kon. üçkâğıt, oyun; kon. plan, yol

dodgy /'doci/ s, İİ, kon. riskli, tehlikeli; üçkâğıtçı, namussuz

doe /dou/ a. dişi geyik ya da tavşan

dog /dog/ a. köpek; it ☆ e. izlemek, peşini bırakmamak **dog-cheap** sudan ucuz, çok ucuz **dog days** yılın en sıcak günleri **dogtooth** köpekdişi

dogma /'dogmı/ a. dogma **dogmatic** /-metik/ s. dogmatik **dogmatism** dogmatizm

doh /dou/ a, müz. do notası

doing /'du:ing/ a. (birisinin yaptığı) iş; sıkı çalışma

dole /doul/ a: **go/be on the dole** İİ, kon. hükümetten işsizlik maaşı almak ☆ e. (out) yoksulllara (para, yiyecek, vb.) dağıtmak **doleful** üzgün, kederli, mahzun

doll /dol/ a. oyuncak bebek; kon. (aptal) güzel kadın, bebek

dollar /'dolı/ a. dolar

dolly /'doli/ a, kon, bkz. **doll**

dolphin /'dolfin/ a, hayb. yunusbalığı

domain /dı'meyn/ a. beylik arazi; alan

dome /doum/ a. kubbe

domestic /dı'mestik/ s. ev/aile ile ilgili; evcil; yerli; evine bağlı, evcimen ☆ a. hizmetçi **domesticate** (hayvan) evcilleştirmek; ev işlerine alıştırmak

dominant /'dominınt/ s. egemen; üstün; bíy. başat, dominant

dominate /'domineyt/ e. egemen olmak, hâkim olmak; en önemli yeri tutmak **domination** egemenlik, hâkimiyet

domineering /domi'niıring/ s. despotça davranan, zorba

dominion /dı'miniın/ a. egemenlik; yönetme hakkı; dominyon; yönetilen bölge/ülke

domino /'dominou/ a. domino taşı; ç. domino oyunu

don /don/ a. (İngiltere'de) üniversitede öğretim görevlisi

donate /dou'neyt/ e. (para, vb.) bağışlamak, bağışta bulunmak **donation** /dou'neyşın/ bağış

done /dan/ s. bitmiş, sona ermiş; çok yorgun; pişmiş **Done!** Tamam! Kabul!

donkey /'donki/ a. eşek

donor /'dounı/ a. bağışta bulunan kimse

doom /du:m/ a. kötü kader, yazgı; ölüm **doomsday** kıyamet günü

door /do:/ a. kapı; giriş **next door** kapı komşu, yakın **out of doors** açık havada, dışarıda **doorbell** kapı zili **doorkeeper** kapıcı **doorknob** kapı tokmağı, kapı kolu **door-mat** paspas **doorstep** eşik **doorway** kapı yeri, giriş

dope /doup/ a. uyuşturucu madde; budala, salak; arg. bilgi

dormant /'do:mınt/ s. hareketsiz, etkin olmayan; uykuda

dormitory /'do:mitıri/ a. yatakhane, koğuş; Al. öğrenci yurdu

dormouse /'do:maus/ a, hayb. fındıkfaresi

dorsal /'do:sıl/ s, anat. sırtla ilgili, sırt ..., arka ...

dosage /'dousic/ a. dozaj, düzem

dose /dous/ a. doz; miktar

dot /dot/ a. nokta; benek ☆ e. noktasını koymak

dotage /'doutic/ a. bunaklık

double /'dabıl/ s. çift, iki; iki kişilik; iki misli, iki kat; ikili, çifte ☆ a. benzer, eş; (içki) duble ☆ be. iki misli, iki katı ☆ e. iki katına çıkartmak; iki misli olmak **doublebreasted** (giysi) kruvaze **doublecross** aldatmak, ihanet etmek **doubledealer** ikiyüzlü **doubledecker** iki katlı otobüs; iki katlı ev **doubleglazing** çift cam

doubles /'dabılz/ a. (tenis) çiftler maçı

doubly /'dabli/ be. iki misli, iki kat

doubt /daut/ e. -den kuşkulanmak; emin olmamak, kuşkusu olmak **no doubt** kuşkusuz **doubtful** kuşkulu, güvenilmez; kesin olmayan, şüpheli **doubtless** kuşkusuz, şüphesiz, kesin; muhtemelen

dough /dou/ a. hamur; kon. para

doughnut /'dounat/ a. lokma benzeri bir tür tatlı

douse /daus/ e. ıslatmak, sulamak; kon. söndürmek

dove /dav/ a. güvercin, kumru

down /daun/ be. aşağı, aşağıya; aşağıda ☆ *ilg.* aşağısına; aşağısında **down with ...!** kahrolsun ...! **down to earth** gerçekçi

downcast /'daunka:st/ *s.* üzgün, mahzun; (gözler) yere doğru bakan

downfall /'daunfo:l/ *a.* düşüş, çöküş, mahvolma; ani yağış, sağanak

downgrade /'daungreyd/ *e.* (rütbe, derece, vb.) indirmek, alçaltmak

downhearted /daun'ha:tid/ *s.* üzgün, mutsuz

downhill /'daunhil/ *be.* yokuş aşağı **go downhill** kötüye gitmek

downpour /'daunpo:/ *a.* sağanak

downstairs /daun'steız/ *be.* alt katta, aşağıda; alt kata, aşağıya

downstairs /daun'steız/ *a, s.* alt kat

downward /'daunwıd/ *s.* aşağı inen, düşen; *Aİ, bkz.* **downwards**

downwards /'daunwıdz/ *be.* aşağıya doğru

downwind /'daunwind/ *s, be.* rüzgâr yönünde

dowry /'dauıri/ *a.* çeyiz

doze /douz/ *a.* şekerleme, kestirme, kısa uyku ☆ *e.* şekerleme yapmak, kestirmek, uyuklamak

dozen /'dazın/ *a.* düzine

draft /dra:ft/ *e.* taslak; karalama, müsvedde; poliçe; *Aİ.* askere alma ☆ *e.* taslağını çizmek; *Aİ.* askere almak

drag /dreg/ *a.* çekme, sürükleme; sürüklenen şey; tırmık, tarak ☆ *e.* sürüklemek, sürümek, çekmek; (ağ, kanca, vb.) dibini yoklamak, taramak **drag on** gereksiz yere uzamak

dragon /'dregın/ *a.* ejder, ejderha; cadaloz kadın **dragonfly** yusufçuk, kızböceği

drain /dreyn/ *e.* akmak; akıtmak; kurumak; kurutmak; güçsüzleşmek ☆ *a.* pissu borusu; kanal, lağım; akaç; masraf **drainage** suları akıtma; kanalizasyon **drainpipe** pissu akıtma borusu

drake /dreyk/ *a.* erkek ördek

dram /drem/ *a.* dirhem

drama /'dra:mı/ *a.* (radyo, televizyon ya da tiyatroda oynanan) oyun; drama, tiyatro sanatı; heyecanlı olaylar

dizisi **dramatic** tiyatroyla ilgili, dramatik; heyecanlandırıcı **dramatics** oyun yazma (sanatı) **dramatist** oyun yazarı

dramatize /'dremıtayz/ *e.* oyunlaştırmak, sahneye uyarlamak; (olayı) heyecanlı bir biçimde anlatmak; abartmak

drape /dreyp/ *e.* (kumaş, vb. ile) üstünü örtmek, kaplamak; süslemek; katlamak, kıvırmak **draper** *İİ.* kumaşçı **drapery** *İİ.* kumaşçılık; kumaş

drastic /'drestik/ *s.* güçlü, şiddetli, etkili

draught /dra:ft/ *a.* cereyan, hava akımı; yudum; geminin yüzebileceği derinlik; *İİ.* dama taşı **draught beer** fıçı birası

draughts /'dra:fts/ *a, İİ.* dama oyunu **draughtsman** teknik ressam; dama taşı

draw /dro:/ *e.* **drew** /dru:/, **drawn** /dro:n/ (resim) çizmek; çekmek; ilgisini çekmek, cezbetmek; (oyun, savaş, vb.) berabere bitirmek/bitmek; ☆ *a.* kura, çekiliş; (maç, vb.) beraberlik; ilgi toplayan şey/kimse **draw away** hızla çekmek, uzaklaştırmak **draw back** gerilemek; düşünmekten/yapmaktan çekinmek **draw on/upon** kullanmak, yararlanmak **draw out** (zaman içinde) uzatmak, yaymak; hesabndan para çekmek; konuşturmak **draw up** oluşturmak; (taşıt) belli bir noktaya ulaşıp durmak; düzenlemek, yazmak; sıralamak, dizmek

drawback /'dro:bek/ *a.* dezavantaj; engel; sorun, güçlük

drawer /'dro:/ *a.* çekmece, göz

drawing /'dro:ing/ *a.* çizim; eskiz; resim, plan, tasar **drawing pin** raptiye; **drawing room** salon, misafir odası

drawn /dro:n/ *bkz.* **draw**

dread /dred/ *e.* çok korkmak ☆ *a.* korku, dehşet; korku nedeni **dreadful** korkutucu, ürkütücü, korkunç **dreadfully** çok; çok fena, korkunç bir şekilde

dream /dri:m/ *e.* **dreamed, dreamt** /dremt/, rüya görmek; rüyasında görmek; düşlemek, düş kurmak ☆ *a.* düş, rüya; hayal; *kon.* çok güzel şey

dream away (zaman) çarçur etmek
dreamer rüya gören kimse; hayalperest kimse **dreamy** hayalci; *kon.* harika, nefis
dreamt /dremt/ *bkz.* **dream**
dreary /'drııri/ *s.* can sıkıcı, kasvetli
dredge /drec/ *e.* (ırmak ya da denizin) dibini taramak ☆ *a.* dip tarama aracı, tarak
dregs /dregz/ *a.* tortu, çökelti
drench /drenç/ *e.* ıslatmak, sırılsıklam etmek
dress /dres/ *e.* giydirmek; giyinmek; yaraya pansuman yapmak, sarmak; saç yapmak; (yemeği) hazırlamak, süslemek ☆ *a.* giysi, elbise; kılık kıyafet, giyim ☆ *s.* elbiselik; (giysi) uygun, düzgün
dresser /'dresı/ *a.* mutfak rafı, tabaklık; *Aİ.* şifoniyer
dressing /'dresing/ *a.* giydirme; giyinme, kuşanma; pansuman, sargı; salça, mayonez, sos, vb. yemek malzemesi **dressing gown** sabahlık
dressing table tuvalet masası
drew /dru:/ *bkz.* **draw**
dribble /'dribıl/ *e.* (salya, vb.) damlamak; damlatmak; salya akıtmak; *sp.* top sürmek
drift /drift/ *a.* sürükleme, sürüklenme; sürüklenen şey; genel anlam ☆ *e.* sürüklemek; sürüklenmek; biriktirmek, yığmak; birikmek **drifter** avare, başıboş
drill /dril/ *e.* (matkapla delik) açmak, delmek; alıştırmak, eğitmek, talim yaptırmak ☆ *a.* delgi, matkap; alıştırma; talim
drink /drink/ *e.* **drank** /drenk/ **drunk** /drank/ içmek; içki içmek; emmek; yutmak ☆ *a.* içilecek şey, içecek; (alkollü) içki **drinkable** içilebilir, içilir **drinker** içkici
drip /drip/ *e.* damlamak; damlatmak ☆ *a.* damlama; damla; *arg.* sevimsiz, renksiz kimse
drip-dry /'dripdray/ *s.* (giysi) asılarak kurutulan, ütü istemeyen
dripping /'driping/ *a.* pişirilen etten damlayan yağ

drive /drayv/ *e.* **drove** /drouv/ **driven** /'drivın/ sürmek; (taşıt) kullanmak; (araba, vb. ile) götürmek; -e zorlamak; sıkıştırmak; ☆ *a.* taşıtta yolculuk; (park yerine) giriş yolu; girişim; dürtü; (araba, vb.) çekiş **drive-in** otomobille girilen (sinema, lokanta, vb. yer) **driver** sürücü, şoför **driver's licence** (*Aİ.* **license**) sürücü belgesi, ehliyet
driven /'drivın/ *bkz.* **drive**
drizzle /'drizıl/ *e.* (yağmur) ince ince yağmak, çiselemek ☆ *a.* ince yağmur, çisenti
drone /droun/ *a.* erkek arı; asalak, parazit
droop /dru:p/ *e.* sarkmak, eğilmek ☆ *a.* düşüş uzaklığı, düşüş
drop /drop/ *e.* (yere) düşürmek; düşmek; *kon.* (arabadan) indirmek; bırakmak; son vermek, kesmek; (artık) görüşmemek ☆ *a.* damla, azıcık şey; düşüş, iniş **drop by/in/on** şöyle bir uğramak **drop off** uyuyakalmak; azalmak **drop out** ayrılmak, bırakmak
dropper /'dropı/ damlalık
droppings /'dropingz/ *a.* ters, hayvan dışkısı
dross /dros/ *a.* cüruf, süprüntü, artık
drought /draut/ *a.* kuraklık, susuzluk
drove /drouv/ *bkz.* **drive;** *a.* sürü
drover davar çobanı, celep
drown /draun/ *e.* (suda) boğulmak; suda boğmak; (ses) bastırmak, boğmak
drowse /drauz/ *e.* kestirmek, uyuklamak **drowsy** uykulu; uyutan, uyutucu
drudge /drac/ *e.* ağır, zor ve tatsız iş yapmak **drudgery** ağır, tatsız iş
drug /drag/ *a.* ilaç; uyuşturucu madde ☆ *e.* ilaç vermek; uyuşturucu vermek, ilaçla uyutmak **druggist** *Aİ.* eczacı **drugstore** *Aİ.* eczane
drum /dram/ *a.* davul, bateri, dümbelek ☆ *e.* davul çalmak; davul sesi çıkartmak **drummer** davulcu, baterist **drumstick** davul sopası, baget
drunk /drank/ *a, s.* sarhoş, içkili
drunkard /'drankıd/ *a,* ayyaş, sarhoş
drunken /'drankın/ *s.* sarhoş
dry /dray/ *s.* kuru; kurumuş, kupkuru,

dryer

susuz; susamış; yavan, sevimsiz; basit, sade; (içki) sek ☆ *e.* kurumak; kurutmak **dry-clean** kuru temizleme yapmak **dry cleaner's** kuru temizleme dükkânı

dryer /'drayı/ *a.* kurutma makinesi

dual /'dyu:ıl/ *s.* ikili, iki eş parçalı, dual, çift

dub /dab/ *e.* (film, vb.) seslendirmek, dublaj yapmak

dubious /'dyu:biıs/ *s.* kuşkulu, belirsiz

duchess /'daçis/ *a.* düşes

duck /dak/ *a.* ördek ☆ *e.* (görülmemek, vurulmamak için) başını eğmek; (başını) suya daldırmak; *kon.* kaçmak, kaytarmak

duckling /'dakling/ *a.* yavru ördek

duct /dakt/ *a.* guddelerden salgıları akıtan kanal; boru

dud /dad/ *s, kon.* işe yaramaz; bozuk

due /dyu:/ *s.* hak edilen, gerekli; tam, uygun, yeterli; (para) ödeme zamanı gelmiş; beklenen ☆ *a.* hak, kişinin hakkı ☆ *be.* direkt olarak, tam olarak, doğruca **due to** ... yüzünden

duel /'dyu:ıl/ *a.* düello ☆ *e.* düello yapmak

dues /dyu:z/ *a.* resmi vergiler, aidat

duet /dyu:'et/ *a, müz.* düet

dugout /'dagaut/ *a.* kütükten oyularak yapılmış kayık; *ask.* yeraltı sığınağı

duke /dyu:k/ *a.* dük

dulcet /'dalsit/ *s.* (ses, vb.) tatlı, hoş, huzur veren

dull /dal/ *s.* sönük, donuk; boğuk; yavaş düşünen; sıkıcı; tekdüze ☆ *e.* sönükleştirmek, donuklaştırmak, köreltmek; körelmek

duly /'dyu:li/ *be.* zamanında; tam olarak, layıkıyla, hakkıyla

dumb /dam/ *s.* dilsiz; dilini yutmuş, sessiz, suskun; *kon.* aptal

dumbfound /dam'faund/ *e.* hayretten konuşamaz hale getirmek

dummy /'dami/ *a.* (cansız) manken; emzik; yapma şey, taklit; *arg.* aptal, salak

dump /damp/ *e.* yere dökmek, düşürmek; indirim yapmak, fiyatta damping yapmak ☆ *a.* çöplük/artık yığma yeri; *arg.* çöplük, batakhane

dumpling /'dampling/ *a.* meyveli bir tatlı; etli hamur

dumpy /'dampi/ *s.* tıknaz, bodur

dunce /dans/ *a.* kolay öğrenemeyen kimse; aptal

dune /dyu:n/ *a.* kum tepesi, kumul

dung /dang/ *a.* hayvan gübresi

dungarees /dangı'ri:z/ *a.* kalın işçi tulumu

dungeon /'dancın/ *a.* zindan

dunk /dank/ *e.* (çaya, kahveye, vb.) batırmak, banmak

duo /'dyu:ou/ *a,·müz.* düo, ikili

dupe /dyu:p/ *a.* kandırılan, aldatılan, kazıklanan ☆ *e.* kandırmak, aldatmak, kazıklamak

duplicate /'dyu:plikit/ *a, s.* diğerinin aynısı, kopyası, eşi; iki kısımlı, ikili, çift ☆ *e.* kopya etmek, aynısını yapmak **duplicator** teksir makinesi

duplicity /dyu:'plisiti/ *a.* ikiyüzlülük, düzenbazlık, hile

durable /'dyuırıbıl/ *s.* dayanıklı, uzun ömürlü **durability** dayanıklılık

duration /dyu'reyşın/ *a.* süre

duress /dyu'res/ *a.* zorlama, baskı

during /'dyuıring/ *be.* sırasında, esnasında, süresince

dusk /dask/ *a.* akşam karanlığı

dust /dast/ *a.* toz; pudra; toz toprak, çöp; toz bulutu ☆ *e.* toz almak **dustbin** çöp kutusu, çöp tenekesi **dustcart** *İl.* çöp kamyonu **duster** toz bezi; silgi **dustman** çöpçü **dustpan** faraş **dusty** tozlu; sıkıcı

Dutch /daç/ *s.* Hollandaya/Hollanda diline ilişkin; Hollanda'lı **Dutch treat** Alman usulü **go Dutch** masrafları paylaşmak

dutiful /'dyu:tifıl/ *s.* sorumluluk taşıyan, görevine bağlı

duty /'dyu:ti/ *a.* görev, sorumluluk; hizmet, iş; vergi **on duty** nöbetçi, işbaşında, nöbette **duty-free** gümrüksüz, gümrükten muaf

dwarf /dwo:f/ *a.* cüce ☆ küçük göstermek, gölgede bırakmak

dwell /dwel/ *e.* **dwelt** /dwelt/ oturmak, yaşamak, ikamet etmek **dweller** sa-

kin, oturan kimse **dwelling** ikametgâh
dwelt /dwelt/ *bkz.* **dwell**
dwindle /'dwindıl/ *e.* azalmak, küçülmek
dye /day/ *a.* kumaş boyası, boya maddesi ☆ *e.* boyamak
dynamic /day'nemik/ *s.* enerjik, hareketli **dynamics** devimbilim, dinamik
dynamism /'daynımizım/ *a.* devingen-
lik, canlılık, hareketlilik
dynamite /'daynımayt/ *a.* dinamit
dynamo /'daynımou/ *a.* dinamo
dynasty /'dinısti/ *a.* hanedan
dysentery /'disıntıri/ *a, hek.* dizanteri

E

each /i:ç/ *s.* her, her biri ☆ *be.* her biri, tanesi ☆ *adl.* her biri; herkes **each
other** birbiri(ni)
eager /'i:gı/ *s.* istekli, hevesli; sabırsız
eagerly büyük bir istekle **eagerness**
şevk, istek
eagle /'i:gıl/ *a.* kartal
ear /iı/ *a.* kulak; başak **eardrum** kulakzarı **earlobe** kulakmemesi **earmark**
bir kenara koymak, ayırmak, tahsis etmek **earphone** kulaklık **earrings** küpe
earshot işitme mesafesi
earl /ö:l/ *a.* İngiliz lordu
early /'ö:li/ *s, be.* erken; önceki, ilk; eski
earn /ö:n/ *e.* kazanmak
earnest /'ö:nist/ *s.* ciddi, ağırbaşlı; çalışkan, istekli **in good earnest** ciddiyetle
earnestly ciddiyetle, istekle **earnest-
ness** ciddiyet, içtenlik; istek
earnings /'ö:ningz/ *a.* kazanç
earth /ö:t/ *a.* yerküre, dünya; toprak,
yer; doğa; *elek.* toprak hattı; hayvan
ini **earthly** dünyevi; maddi; olanaklı
earthenware /'ö:tınweı/ *a.* çanak, çömlek
earthquake /'ö:tkweyk/ *a.* deprem
earthworm /'ö:twö:m/ *a.* solucan
ease /i:z/ *a.* rahatlık, kolaylık, rahat, huzur ☆ *e.* hafifletmek, dindirmek, ya-

tıştırmak; azalmak, dinmek; yavaşlatmak
easel /'i:zıl/ *a.* ressam sehpası
easily /'i:zili/ *be.* kolayca; kuşkusuz
east /i:st/ *a.* doğu **the Far East** Uzakdoğu **the Middle East** Ortadoğu **eastern**
doğu ... **easterly** doğudan, doğuda
eastward(s) doğuya (doğru)
Easter /'i:stı/ *a.* Paskalya yortusu
easy /'i:zi/ *s.* kolay; rahat **easy chair** koltuk **easy-going** kaygısız, yüreği geniş
eat /i:t/ *e.* ate /et/ eaten /'i:tın/ yemek,
yemek yemek; **(away/into)** çürüt-
mek, aşındırmak, kemirmek, yemek
eatable yenebilir
eaten /'i:tın/ *bkz.* **eat**
eau de cologne /ou dı kı'loun/ *a.* kolonya
eaves /i:vz/ *a.* dam saçağı
ebb /eb/ *a.* suların alçalması, çekilme
☆ *e.* (deniz) çekilmek; azalmak
ebony /'ebıni/ *a, s.* abanoz
eccentric /ik'sentrik/ *s.* tuhaf; *mat.* dışmerkezli
ecclesiastical /ikli:zi'estikıl/ *s.* Hıristiyan
kilisesine ilişkin
echo /'ekou/ *a.* yankı ☆ *e.* yankı yapmak; yankılanmak
eclipse /i'klips/ *a.* güneş/ay tutulması;
düşüş, çöküş; ☆ *e.* (güneş/ay) tutmak; gölgede bırakmak, geçmek
ecology /i'kolıci/ *a.* çevrebilim, ekoloji
economic /ekı'nomik/ *s.* ekonomik, iktisadi **economical** az masraflı, ekonomik
economics /ekı'nomiks/ *a.* ekonomi, iktisat bilimi **economist** /i'konımist/
ekonomist, iktisatçı
economize /i'konımayz/ *e.* idareli harcamak, masrafları kısmak
economy /i'konımi/ *a.* ekonomi, iktisat
ecstasy /'ekstısi/ *a.* kendinden geçme,
aşırı mutluluk, coşku
eczema /'eksimı/ *a, hek.* egzama, mayasıl
eddy /'edi/ *a.* burgaç, anafor, girdap
edge /ec/ *a.* kenar, uç; ağız, keskin kenar ☆ *e.* kenar yapmak **be on the
edge** sinirli olmak **have the edge on**
-den üstün olmak

edging /'ecing/ a. kenar, şerit

edible /'edıbıl/ s. yenilebilir

edit /'edit/ e. (kitap, film, vb.) yayına hazırlamak; (bilgisayar) edit etmek; biçimlemek

edition /i'dişın/ a. baskı, yayın

editor /'editı/ a. yayıncı, editör **editorial** (gazetede) başyazı

educate /'edyukeyt, 'ecıkeyt/ e. eğitmek, öğretmek, okutmak

education /ecu'keyşın/ a. eğitim; tahsil; öğretim **educational** eğitimsel, eğitsel

eel /i:l/ a, hayb. yılanbalığı

efface /i'feys/ e. silmek; silerek yüzeyini bozmak

effect /i'fekt/ a. sonuç; etki; anlam; ☆ e. gerçekleştirmek; sonuçlandırmak; başarmak **in effect** yürürlükte, geçerli; etki itibariyle **into effect** yürürlüğe, uygulamaya **take effect** yürürlüğe girmek; sonuç vermeye başlamak

effective /i'fektiv/ s. etkili; yürürlükte, geçerli **effectiveness** etki; geçerlilik

effectual /i'fekçuıl/ s. etkili, istenen sonucu veren

effervesce /efı'ves/ e. köpürmek, kabarmak, köpüklenmek

efficiency /i'fişınsi/ a. işbilirlik, yeterlik; etki; verim

efficient /i'fişınt/ s. iyi çalışan, hızlı ve verimli, becerikli

effluent /'efluınt/ a. fabrika artığı sıvı

effort /'efıt/ a. çaba, emek; uğraş; çaba harcama **effortless** zahmetsiz; çaba göstermeyen

effrontery /i'frantıri/ a. arsızlık, yüzsüzlük

effusive /i'fyu:siv/ s. taşkın, azgın

egg /eg/ a. yumurta **boiled egg** rafadan yumurta **fried egg** sahanda yumurta **egg-cup** yumurta kabı

eggplant /'egpla:nt/ a, bitk. patlıcan

ego /'i:gou/ a. ben, benlik, ego

egocentric /i:gou'sentrik/ s, hkr. bencil

egoism /'i:gouizım/ a. bencillik, egoizm **egoist** bencil, egoist

egotism /'i:goutizım/ a. hep kendinden söz etme **egotist** benlikçi

eiderdown /'aydıdaun/ a. kuştüyü yorgan

eight /eyt/ a, s. sekiz **eighth** /eitt/ sekizinci

eighteen /ey'ti:n/ a, s. on sekiz **eighteenth** /-tint/ on sekizinci

eightieth /'eytiıt/ a, s. sekseninci

eighty /'eyti/ a, s. seksen

either /'aydı/ s, adl. ikisinden biri; iki; her iki be. (olumsuz cümlelerde) de, da, de (değil) bağ. **either ... or** ya ... ya da

ejaculate /i'cekyuleyt/ e. fışkırtmak, atmak **ejaculation** fışkırtma, atma; haykırma

eject /i'cekt/ e. kovmak, dışarı atmak

eke /i:k/ e. (out) idareli kullanmak **eke out a living** güçlükle geçinmek

elaborate /i'lebırıt/ s. ayrıntılı, detaylı; özenle hazırlanmış

elapse /i'leps/ e. (zaman) geçmek

elastic /i'lestik/ s. esnek **elasticity** esneklik

elated /i'leytid/ s. mutlu, sevinçli

elbow /'elbou/ a. dirsek ☆ e. dirsek atmak, dirsekle dürtmek

elder /'eldı/ s. (yaşça) büyük **elderly** yaşlıca, geçkin **eldest** yaşça en büyük

elect /i'lekt/ e. oylayarak seçmek; (önemli bir) karar vermek **elector** seçmen **electoral** seçimle ilgili **electorate** seçmenler

election /i'lekşın/ a. seçim **by-election** ara seçim **general election** genel seçim **local election** yerel seçim

electric /i'lektrik/ s. elektrikle ilgili; elektrikli **electrical** elektrikle ilgili, elektrik ... **electrical engineer** elektrik mühendisi

electrician /ilek'trişın/ a. elektrikçi

electricity /ilek'trisiti/ a. elektrik

electrify /ilek'trifay/ e. elektriklendirmek; heyecanlandırmak

electrode /i'lektroud/ a. elektrot

electron /i'lektron/ a. elektron

electronic /ilek'tronik/ s. elektronik **electronics** elektronik, elektronik bilimi

elegant /'eligınt/ s. zarif, ince, güzel, şık **elegance** incelik, güzellik, zarafet

elegy /'elici/ a. ağıt

element /'elimınt/ a. öğe, unsur, eleman; element **the element** hava the **four elements** dört temel öğe: toprak, su, ateş, hava

elementary /eli'mentıri/ s. basit; ilk, temel

elephant /'elifınt/ a, hayb. fil

elevate /'eliveyt/ e. yükseltmek, kaldırmak; (aklı) geliştirmek

elevation /eli'veyşın/ a. yükseltme; yüksek yer

elevator /'eliveytı/ a, Aİ. asansör

eleven /i'levın/ a, s. on bir **eleventh** /i'-levınt / on birinci

elf /elf/ a. cin, peri

elicit /i'lisit/ e. çıkartmak, ortaya çıkarmak

eligible /'elicıbıl/ s. hak sahibi, haklı; uygun, seçilebilir

eliminate /i'limineyt/ e. elemek, atmak; -den kurtarmak, çıkarmak **elimination** eleme, çıkarma, atma

elite /ey'li:t/ a. seçkinler, elit

ellipse /i'lips/ a. elips

elm /elm/ a. karaağaç

elocution /elı'ku:şın/ a. hitabet

elope /i'loup/ e. sevgilisi ile kaçmak

else /els/ başka **or else** yoksa, aksi takdirde **elsewhere** başka yerde, başka yere

elucidate /i'lu:sideyt/ e. açıklamak

elude /i'lu:d/ e. -den kurtulmak, atlatmak

elusive /i'lu:siv/ s. yakalanması/bulunması zor; bir türlü akla gelmeyen

emaciated /i'meyşieytid/ s. sıska, bir deri bir kemik

emanate /'emıneyt/ e. (from) çıkmak, meydana gelmek

emancipate /i'mensipeyt/e. özgürlüğüne kavuşturmak, bağlarından kurtarmak, serbest bırakmak

embalm /im'ba:m/ e. (ölüyü) mumyalamak

embankment /im'benkmınt/ a. toprak set, set, bent

embargo /im'ba:gou/ a. ambargo ☆ e. ambargo koymak

embark /im'ba:k/ e. gemiye binmek; gemiye bindirmek

embarrass /im'berıs/ e. utandırmak, bozmak **embarrassed** sıkılgan, çekingen **embarrassing** can sıkıcı; utandırıcı **embarrasment** utanma, sıkılma, bozuntu

embassy /'embısi/ a. elçilik

embed /im'bed/ e. iyice yerleştirmek, oturtmak, sokmak, gömmek

embellish /im'beliş/ e. süsleyerek güzelleştirmek

ember /'embı/ a. kor, köz

embezzle /im'bezıl/ e. (para) zimmetine geçirmek, çalmak

embitter /im'bitı/ e. üzmek, canından bezdirmek

emblem /'emblım/ a. simge, amblem

embody /im'bodi/ e. somutlaştırmak; katmak, eklemek, dahil etmek

emboss /im'bos/ e. üzerine kabartma yapmak

embrace /im'breys/ a. kucaklama, bağrına basma, sarılma ☆ e. kucaklamak, sarılmak; içine almak, kapsamak; benimsemek, kabul etmek

embroider /im'broydı/ e. nakış işlemek **embroidery** nakış

embryo /'embriou/ a. embriyon, oğulcuk

emerald /'emırıld/ a, s. zümrüt; zümrüt yeşili

emerge /i'mö:c/ e. ortaya çıkmak **emergence** ortaya çıkma, belirme

emergency /i'mö:cınsi/ a. acil vaka, olağanüstü durum

emery /'emıri/ a. zımpara

emetic /i'metik/ a. kusturucu ilaç

emigrant /'emigrınt/ a. göçmen

emigrate /'emigreyt/ e. (başka bir ülkeye) göç etmek **emigration** göç, dışgöç

eminence /'emınıns/ a. şöhret, saygınlık, ün

eminent /'emınınt/ s. seçkin, ünlü, saygın **eminently** çok; son derece; müthiş

emirate /'emirıt/ a. emirlik

emissary /'emisıri/ a. kurye, gizli ajan

emit /i'mit/ e. göndermek, yollamak, vermek, yaymak, salmak

emolument /i'molyumınt/ a. ücret
emotion /i'mouşın/ a. heyecan, duygu
emotional duygusal, duygulu
emotive /i'moutiv/ s. duygulandırıcı
emperor /'empırı/ a. imparator
emphasis /'emfısis/ a. vurgu; bir şeye verilen önem, üzerinde durma
emphasize /'emfısayz/ e. üzerinde durmak, belirtmek, vurgulamak
emphatic /im'fetik/ s. vurgulu, önemli
empire /'empayı/ a. imparatorluk
employ /im'ploy/ e. iş vermek, çalıştırmak; kullanmak **employee** /im'ployi:/ işçi, hizmetli, çalışan **employer** /im'p-loyı/ işveren **employment** /im'ploymınt/ çalıştırma, iş verme
empower /im'pauı/ e. yetki vermek
empress /'empris/ a. imparatoriçe
empty /'empti/ s. boş ☆ e. boşaltmak; içmek, kafaya dikmek **empty--handed** eli boş **empty-headed** boş kafalı, ahmak **emptiness** boşluk
emulate /'emyuleyt/ e. bir diğer kişiden daha iyisini yapmaya çalışmak
emulsion /i'malşın/ a. merhem; sübye, emülsiyon
enable /i'neybıl/ e. imkân tanımak
enact /i'nekt/ e. (yasa) çıkarmak
enamel /i'nemıl/ a. emay; (diş) mine
enamoured /i'nemıd/ s. (of/with) düşkün, hayran
encampment /in'kempmınt/ a. kamp yeri
encase /in'keys/ e. kılıfa sokmak, kutulamak, örtmek
enchant /in'ça:nt/ e. büyülemek **enchanting** büyüleyici **enchantment** büyülenme; büyüleyici şey
encircle /in'sö:kıl/ e. kuşatmak, çevrelemek
enclose /in'klouz/ e. çevresini sarmak, kuşatmak; içine koymak, iliştirmek
enclosure /in'kloujı/ a. çevirme, kuşatma; çit, duvar; ilişkte gönderilen şey
encompass /in'kampıs/ e. kuşatmak, çevrelemek
encounter /in'kauntı/ e. (tehlike, sorun, vb. ile) karşılaşmak; (biriyle) tesadüfen karşılaşmak ☆ a. karşılaşma, rast gelme

encourage /in'karic/ e. yüreklendirmek, cesaretlendirmek
encroach /in'krouç/ e. ileri gitmek, haddini aşmak; (birinin hakkına) tecavüz etmek
encrusted /in'krastid/ s. (mücevher, vb.) kaplı, kaplanmış
encyclopedia /insayklı'pi:dıı/ a. ansiklopedi, bilgilik
end /end/ a. son; uç; amaç ☆ e. sona erdirmek, bitirmek **in the end** sonunda **endless** sonsuz **endlessly** sürekli olarak, durmadan
endanger /in'deyncı/ e. tehlike yaratmak
endear /in'dıı/ e. (to) sevdirmek
endeavour /in'deyvı/ e. çalışmak, çabalamak ☆ a. emek, çaba
endemic /en'demik/ s. (hastalık, vb.) belli bir yere özgü
endorse /in'do:s/ e. desteklemek; ciro etmek; (ceza, isim, vb.) yazmak
endow /in'dau/ e. (okul, hastane, vb.'ne) bağışta bulunmak
endurance /in'dyuırıns/ a. dayanma; tahammül, sabır
endure /in'dyuı/ e. dayanmak, katlanmak, sürmek **enduring** dayanıklı; sürekli
enemy /'enımi/ a. düşman
energetic /enı'cetik/ s. çalışkan, enerjik
energy /'enıci/ a. enerji, güç
enforce /in'fo:s/ e. zorlamak, zorla yaptırmak; uygulamak, yürütmek **enforcement** zorlama; uygulama
enfranchise /in'frençayz/ e. oy hakkı vermek
engage /in'geyc/ e. çalıştırmak; birbirine geçirmek, tutturmak; saldırmak **engaged** nişanlı; (telefon hattı) meşgul **engagement** nişan, nişanlanma; söz, randevu
engine /'encin/ a. motor; makine
engineer /enci'nıı/ a. mühendis **engineering** mühendislik
English /ingliş/ s, a. İngiliz; İngilizce **the English** İngilizler
engrave /in'greyv/ e. oymak, hakketmek
engrossing /in'grousing/ s. çok ilginç,

sürükleyici
engulf /in'galf/ e. içine çekmek, yutmak
enhance /in'ha:ns/ e. (değer, güç, güzellik, vb.) artırmak, çoğaltmak
enigma /i'nigmı/ a. muamma, anlaşılmaz şey **enigmatic** /enig'metik/ bilmece gibi; anlaşılmaz
enjoy /in'coy/ e. zevk almak, hoşlanmak, beğenmek **enjoy oneself** mutlu olmak, eğlenmek **enjoyable** zevkli, eğlenceli **enjoyment** zevk, haz
enlarge /in'la:c/ e. büyütmek, genişletmek; büyümek, genişlemek; (on) uzatmak **enlargement** büyütme, genişletme
enlighten /in'laytın/ e. aydınlatmak, bilgi vermek, açıklamak
enlist /in'list/ e. askere almak; asker olmak; (yardım, sempati, vb.) kazanmak
enliven /in'layvın/ e. canlandırmak, hareketlendirmek
enmity /'enmiti/ a. düşmanlık, husumet
enormity /i'no:miti/ a. büyük kötülük, alçaklık; büyüklük
enormous /i'no:mıs/ s. çok geniş, çok büyük, kocaman **enormously** pek çok
enough /i'naf/ s, be. yeterli; yeteri kadar ☆ a. yeter miktar
enquire /in'kwayı/ e. soruşturmak **enquiry** soruşturma
enrage /in'reyc/ e. çileden çıkarmak
enrich /in'riç/ e. zenginleştirmek
enrol, enroll /in'roul/ e. üye olmak; üye etmek, kaydetmek
en route /on'ru:t/ be. yolda, ... yolunda
ensemble /on'sombıl/ a. birlik, grup, takım; küçük müzik topluluğu
ensign /'ensayn, 'ensın/ a. (donanma, vb.) bayrak; Al. deniz teğmeni
ensue /in'syu:/ e. (sonuç olarak ya da sonra) ortaya çıkmak, ardından gelmek
ensure /in'şuı/ e. (olmasını) kesinleştirmek; sağlama almak, garantiye almak
entail /in'teyl/ e. gerektirmek, zorunlu kılmak, istemek

entangle /in'tengıl/ e. (ip, saç, vb.) dolaştırmak, karıştırmak
enter /'entı/ e. girmek; yazmak, kaydetmek; üyesi olmak **enter into** başlamak, girişmek; yer almak, katılmak
enterprise /'entıprayz/ a. girişim, yatırım; girişkenlik, cesaret **enterprising** girişken
entertain /entı'teyn/ e. eğlendirmek, hoşça vakit geçirtmek; (konuk) ağırlamak **entertaining** eğlendirici, eğlenceli **entertainment** eğlence
enthral, enthrall /in'tro:l/ e. (bir şey anlatarak) büyülemek
enthrone /in'troun/ e. tahta çıkarmak, taç giydirmek
enthusiasm /in'tyu:ziezım/ a. heves, büyük ilgi, isteklilik **enthusiastic** şevkli, ateşli
entice /in'tays/ e. ayartmak, kandırmak
entire /in'tayı/ s. bütün, tüm, tam, tamam **entirely** bütünüyle, tümüyle
entirety /in'tayırıti/ a. bütünlük, tamlık
entitle /in'taytıl/ e. ad vermek; yetki vermek
entity /'entiti/ a. varlık, mevcudiyet
entrails /'entreylz/ a. sakatat
entrance /'entrıns/ a. giriş
entrance /in'tra:ns/ e. kendinden geçirmek, büyülemek
entreat /in'tri:t/ e. yalvarmak, yakarmak
entrenched /in'trençt/ s. yerleşik, köklü
entrepreneur /ontrıprı'nö:/ a. müteşebbis, girişimci; müteahhit
entrust /in'trast/ e. emanet etmek
entry /'entri/ a. giriş; yarışmacı(lar)
entwine /in'twayn/ e. sarmak, dolaştırmak
enumerate /i'nyu:mıreyt/ e. sıralamak, belirtmek
enunciate /i'nansieyt/ e. telaffuz etmek; düşünceleri açıkça belirtmek
envelop /in'velıp/ e. sarmak, örtmek
envelope /'envıloup/ a. zarf
enviable /'enviıbıl/ s. imrenilecek; başarılı
envious /'enviıs/ s. kıskanç
environment /in'vayırınmınt/ a. çevre,

ortam **environmental** çevresel
envisage /in'vizic/ e. gözünün önüne getirmek
envoy /'envoy/ a. delege; elçi
envy /'envi/ e. gıpta etmek, kıskanmak, imrenmek ☆ a. kıskançlık, çekememezlik
enzyme /'enzaym/ a. enzim
epaulet, epaulette /epı'let/ a. apolet
ephemeral /i'femırıl/ s. kısa ömürlü, geçici
epic /'epik/ a. epik, destan
epidemic /epi'demik/ a, hek. salgın
epigram /'epigrem/ a. nükteli şiir/söz
epilepsy /'epilepsi/ a, hek. sara
epilogue /'epilog/ a. son deyiş; son bölüm, kapanış
episode /'episoud/ a. olay, serüven; (roman, vb.) bölüm
epitaph /'epita:f/ a. mezar taşı kitabesi
epitome /i'pitımi/ a. somut örnek, ideal
epitomize /i'pitımayz/ e. somut örneği olmak
epoch /'i:pok/ a. dönem, çağ
equable /'ekwıbıl/ s. değişmez, dengeli, sakin
equal /'i:kwıl/ s. eşit, eş, denk ☆ e. -e eşit olmak ☆ a. eş, akran **equality** /i'kwoliti/ eşitlik **equalize** /'i:kwılayz/ eşitlemek **equally** /'i:kwıli/ eşit olarak, aynı derecede
equanimity /i:kwı'nimiti/ a. soğukkanlılık, temkin, sakinlik
equate /i'kweyt/ e. eşit yapmak, eşit saymak, eşitlemek
equation /i'kweyjın/ a, mat. denklem
equator /i'kweytı/ a. ekvator
equestrian /i'kwestriın/ s, a. binicilikle ilgili; atlı, binici
equilateral /i:kwi'letırıl/s. (üçgen) eşkenar
equilibrium /i:kwi'libriım/ a. denge
equip /i'kwip/ e. donatmak, teçhiz etmek **equipment** /i'kwipmınt/ donatım, teçhizat, gereç
equity /'ekwiti/ a. adalet, dürüstlük
equivalent /i'kwivılınt/ a, s. eşdeğer, denk, eşit ☆ a. karşılık
equivocal /i'kwivıkıl/ s. (sözcük) iki anlamlı, iki anlama gelebilen

era /'iırı/ a. devir, çağ, dönem
eradicate /i'redike,t/ e. yok etmek, kökünü kurutmak
erase /i'reyz/ e. (yazı, vb.) silmek; kazımak **eraser** silgi
erect /i'rekt/ e. dikmek; yapmak, inşa etmek **erection** inşa; yapma, kurma, dikme, yapı, bina
ermine /'ö:min/ a, hayb. ermin, as
erode /i'roud/ e. yemek, aşındırmak, yıpratmak; aşınmak
erosion /i'roujın/ a. aşınma, aşındırma
erotic /i'rotik/ s. erotik
err /ö:/ e. yanılmak, hata etmek
errand /'erınd/ a. ayak işi; olmayacak iş
erratic /i'retik/ s. değişen, kararsız, düzensiz
erroneous /i'rouniıs/ s. hatalı, yanlış
error /'erı/ a. yanlışlık, hata
erudite /'erudayt/ s. bilgili, engin bilgili
erupt /i'rapt/ e. (yanardağ) patlamak, püskürmek; patlak vermek **eruption** patlama, püskürme
escalate /'eskıleyt/ e. (savaşı) kışkırtmak; (fiyat, ücret) yükselmek
escalator /'eskıleytı/ a. yürüyen merdiven
escapade /'eskıpeyd/ a. çılgınlık, aptalca hareket
escape /i'skeyp/ e. kaçmak; atlatmak, kurtulmak; hatırından çıkmak ☆ a. kaçış, firar; kurtuluş; (gaz, sıvı, vb.) sızıntı, kaçak
escort /'esko:t/ a. muhafız, maiyet; kavalye, refakatçi
escort /i'sko:t/ e. eşlik etmek
esoteric /esı'terik/ s. belirli bir kesime hitap eden
especial /i'speşıl/ s. özel, ayrı, müstesna **especially** özellikle
espionage /'espiına:j/ a. casusluk
esquire /i'skwayı/ a. bay, efendi
essay /'esey/ a. deneme **essayist** deneme yazarı
essence /'esıns/ a. öz, esas; esans
essential /i'senşıl/ s. gerekli; başlıca, esaslı, öz **essentially** esasen, aslında
establish /i'stebliş/ e. kurmak, tesis etmek; yerleştirmek; kanıtlamak **estab-**

lishment kuruluş, kurum, tesis
estate /i'steyt/ *a.* arazi, mülk, emlak; arsa **estate agent** emlak komisyoncusu **estate car** pikap **personal estate** taşınabilir mallar **real estate** taşınamaz mallar
esteem /i'sti:m/ *a.* saygı, itibar ☆ *e.* saygı göstermek; gözüyle bakmak
estimate /'estimeyt/ *e.* değer biçmek, tahmin etmek **estimation** tahmin, takdir
estimate /'estimit/ *a.* tahmin, hesap
estuary /'esçuıri/ *a, coğ.* haliç
et cetera /et'setırı/ *be.* vesaire, ve benzeri
etch /eç/ *e.* asitle maden üzerine resim oymak
eternal /i'tö:nıl/ *s.* sonsuz, öncesiz sonrasız, ebedi **eternally** ebediyen
eternity /i'tö:niti/ *a.* sonsuzluk
ether /'i:tı/ *a, kim.* eter
ethic /'etik/ *a.* ahlak sistemi
ethical /'etikıl/ *s.* ahlaki, törel; (davranış, vb.) ahlaklı **ethics** törebilim, ahlak bilimi; ahlak, ahlak kuralları
ethnic /'etnik/ *s.* budunsal, etnik
ethnology /et'nolıci/ *a.* budunbilim, etnoloji
etiquette /'etiket/ *a.* görgü kuralları
etymology /eti'molıci/ *a.* kökenbilim, etimoloji
eucalyptus /yu:kı'liptıs/ *a, bitk.* okaliptüs, sıtmaağacı
eulogize /'yu:lıcayz/ *e.* övmek, methetmek
eulogy /'yu:lıci/ *a.* övgü, methiye
eunuch /'yu:nık/ *a.* hadım, haremağası
Europe /yuırı'p/ *a.* Avrupa
European /yuırı'piın/ *s.* Avrupa ile ilgili ☆ *a.* Avrupalı **European Community** Avrupa Topluluğu, AT
euthanasia /yu:tı'neyziı/ *a.* acısız ölüm
evacuate /i'vekyueyt/ *e.* tahliye etmek; tehlikeden uzaklaştırmak
evade /i'veyd/ *e, hkr.* -den kaçmak, kaytarmak; sıvışmak
evaluate /i'velyueyt/ *e.* değer biçmek
evangelical /i:ven'celikıl/ *s.* İncil ya da İsa'nın öğretisi ile ilgili
evaporate /i'vepıreyt/ *e.* buharlaşmak;

buharlaştırmak; uçup gitmek, yok olmak
evasion /i'veyjın/ *a, hkr.* kaçma, atlatma
eve /i:v/ *a.* arife, öngün
even /'i:vın/ *s.* düz; yatay, pürüzsüz; eşit, aynı; (sayı) çift ☆ *be.* bile; hatta **even if/though** -se bile, -e rağmen, öyle olsa da **even now/so/then** ona rağmen, yine de **even out** denklemek, eşitlemek **get even with sb** birisinden öcünü almak, acısını çıkarmak
evening /'i:vning/ *a.* akşam
event /i'vent/ *a.* olay; sonuç; *sp.* karşılaşma **eventful** olaylı
eventual /i'vençuıl/ *s.* sonuç olarak **eventually** sonunda, neticede
ever /'evı/ *be.* hiç; her zaman; hep **ever so/such** *ii, kon.* çok
evergreen /'evıgri:n/ *s, a.* yaprak dökmeyen
everlasting /evı'la:sting/ *s.* ölümsüz, sonsuz
evermore /evı'mo:/ *be.* her zaman, sonsuza kadar
every /'evri/ *s.* her, her bir **everybody** herkes **everyday** her günkü, günlük **everything** her şey **everywhere** her yerde, her yere
evict /i'vikt/ *e, huk.* tahliye ettirmek
evidence /'evidıns/ *a.* kanıt, delil
evident /'evidınt/ *s.* besbelli, açık
evil /'i:vıl/ *s.* kötü, kem; uğursuz, aksi ☆ *a.* fenalık, kötülük
evoke /i'vouk/ *a.* uyandırmak; anımsatmak
evolution /i:vı'luşın, evı'lu:şın/ *a.* değişim, gelişim; evrim
evolve /i'volv/ *e.* gelişmek, evrim geçirmek
ewe /yu:/ *a.* dişi koyun
ewer /'yu:ı/ *a.* ibrik
exacerbate /ig'zesıbeyt/ *e.* kötüleştirmek, ağırlaştırmak
exact /ig'zekt/ *s.* tam, kesin, doğru, kati ☆ *e.* tehditle elde etmek, zorla almak; ısrarla istemek **exactly** tam, tamamen, tam olarak
exaggerate /ig'zecıreyt/ *e.* abartmak **exaggeration** abartma, şişirme

exalt

exalt /ig'zo:lt/ e. övmek, göklere çıkarmak; (rütbe) yükseltmek, paye vermek; yüceltmek

exam /ig'zem/a. sınav

examination /igzemi'neyşın/ a. sınav; yoklama, muayene

examine /ig'zemin/ e. incelemek; muayene etmek; sınamak, sınavdan geçirmek

example /ig'za:mpıl/ a. örnek for example örneğin, mesela

exasperate /ig'za:spıreyt/ e. kızdırmak, sinirlendirmek

excavate /'ekskıveyt/ e. kazmak, (çukur) açmak excavation kazı

excavator /ekskı'veytı/ a. kazı makinesi

exceed /ik'si:d/ e. aşmak, geçmek; üstün çıkmak exceedingly çok, son derece,

excel /ik'sel/ e. üstün olmak, geçmek

excellence /'eksılıns/ a. üstünlük, mükemmellik

Excellency /'eksılınsi/ a. ekselans

excellent /'eksılınt/ s. mükemmel, çok iyi, üstün, kusursuz

except /ik'sept/ ilg. hariç, -den başka ☆ e. hariç tutmak, dışlamak except for -den başka

exception /ik'sepşın/ a. istisna with the exception of -in dışında, -hariç exceptional olağanüstü, istisnai

excerpt /'eksö:pt/ a. alıntı

excess /'ekses/ s. aşırı, fazla ☆ a. aşırılık, fazlalık excessive aşırı, çok fazla

exchange /iks'çeync/ e. değiş tokuş etmek; değiştirmek ☆ a. değiştirme, değiş tokuş, takas; (borsa) kambiyo exchange rate döviz kuru

exchequer /iks'çekı/ a. finans kaynağı, mali kaynak; İİ. devlet hazinesi, maliye

excise /'eksayz/ a. bir ülkede üretilen ve kullanılan kimi mallardan alınan vergi

excite /ik'sayt/ e. heyecanlandırmak; yol açmak, uyandırmak, tahrik etmek excitable kolay heyecanlanır excited heyecanlı, heyecanlanmış excitement heyecan exciting heyecanlı, heyecan verici

exclaim /ik'skleym/ e. bağırmak, haykırmak exclamation bağırış, haykırış; ünlem exclamation mark ünlem işareti

exclude /ik'sklu:d/ e. kabul etmemek, içeri sokmamak; dışlamak, hesaba katmamak; dışarı atmak, kovmak

excluding /iks'klu:ding/ ilg. hariç, -den başka, -in dışında

exclusion /iks'klu:jın/ a. çıkarma, çıkarılma; hariç tutma

exclusive /ik'sklu:siv/ s. herkese açık olmayan; lüks; pahalı exclusive of ... hariç, -in dışında exclusively sadece, yalnız

excommunicate /ekskı'myu:nikeyt/ e. aforoz etmek

excrement /'ekskrimınt/ a. dışkı

excreta /ik'skri:tı/ a. dışkı, sidik, ter

excrete /ik'skri:t/ e. (dışkı, sidik, ter) vücuttan çıkarmak

excursion /ik'skö:şın/ a. kısa gezi, gezinti

excusable /ik'skyu:zıbıl/ s. bağışlanabilir, affedilebilir

excuse /ik'skyu:z/ e. bağışlamak, mazur görmek Excuse me Affedersiniz

excuse /ik'skyu:s/ a. özür, mazeret; bahane

execute /'eksikyu:t/ e. yürütmek, uygulamak; idam etmek; müz. çalmak, icra etmek execution yapma, yürütme; idam; infaz executioner cellat

executive /ig'zekyutiv/ a. yönetici, idareci ☆ s. yürütücü, yürütmeye ilişkin

executor /ig'zekyutı/ a, huk. vasiyet hükümlerini yerine getiren kimse

exemplary /ig'zemplıri/ s. örnek niteliğinde, örnek

exemplify /ig'zemplifay/ e. örneklerle açıklamak

exempt /ig'zempt/ s. bağışık, muaf ☆ e. muaf tutmak

exercise /'eksısayz/ a. antrenman, idman; ask. talim, tatbikat ☆ e. egzersiz/alıştırma yapmak; egzersiz yaptırmak; uygulamak

exert /ig'zö:t/ e. (çaba, gayret, vb.) sarf etmek exertion çaba, gayret, güç harcama

exhale /eks'heyl/ e. (soluk) dışarı ver

mek; (koku, gaz, vb.) çıkarmak, yaymak

exhaust /ig'zo:st/ *e.* yormak, halsiz bırakmak; tüketmek, bitirmek; ☆ *a.* egzoz **exhausted** çok yorgun, bitkin **exhaustion** yorgunluk, bitkinlik

exhaustive /ig'zo:stiv/ *s.* ayrıntılı, etraflı, eksiksiz

exhibit /ig'zibit/ *e.* sergilemek; göstermek ☆ *a.* sergilenen şey .

exhibition /eksi'bişın/ *a.* sergi **exhibitionist** teşhirci

exhilarate /ig'zilıreyt/ *e.* keyif vermek, neşelendirmek

exhort /ig'zo:t/ *e.* hararetle öğütlemek, teşvik etmek

exile /'eksayl, 'egzayl/ *e.* sürgüne göndermek ☆ *a.* sürgün

exist /ig'zist/ *e.* var olmak, mevcut olmak, olmak, bulunmak; yaşamak **existence** varlık, var oluş; yaşam

exit /'egzit, 'eksit/ *a.* çıkış; çıkış yeri

exonerate /ig'zonıreyt/ *e.* suçsuz çıkarmak; beraat ettirmek

exorbitant /ig'zo:bitınt/ *s.* fahiş, aşırı

exorcist /'ekso:sist/ *a.* kötü ruhları kovan kimse

exorcize /'ekso:sayz/ *e.* dua ya da büyü ile şeytan kovmak

exotic /ig'zotik/ *s.* egzotik, yabancıl; çekici

expand /ik'spend/ *e.* genişlemek, büyümek; genişletmek; büyütmek

expanse /ik'spens/ *a.* geniş alan

expansion /ik'spenşın/ *a.* genişleme, genleşme, büyüme

expect /ik'spekt/ *e.* (olmasını) beklemek; ummak; *kon.* sanmak **expectancy** ümit, beklenti **expectant** bekleyen, uman, umutlu **expectation** umut, beklenti

expedient /ik'spi:diınt/ *s.* uygun; yararlı

expedite /'ekspidayt/ *e.* çabuklaştırmak, kolaylaştırmak

expedition /ekspi'dişın/ *a.* yolculuk, sefer

expel /ik'spel/ *e.* çıkarmak, dışarı atmak

expend /ik'spend/ *e.* tüketmek, harcamak

expenditure /ik'spendiçı/ *a.* masraf, gider, harcama

expense /ik'spens/ *a.* masraf, gider, harcama **at the expense of** -i yitirerek **at sb's expense of** -in hesabından/parasıyla

expensive /ik'spensiv/ *s.* pahalı, masraflı

experience /ik'spiıriıns/ *a.* tecrübe, deneyim ☆ *e.* görmek, görüp geçirmek

experienced /ik'spiıriınst/ *s.* deneyimli, tecrübeli

experiment /ik'sperimınt/ *a.* deney ☆ *e.* deney yapmak **experimental** deneysel

expert /'ekspö:t/ *a.* uzman, bilirkişi

expertise /ekspö:'ti:z/ *a.* uzmanlık; bilirkişi raporu

expire /ik'spayı/ *e.* süresi dolmak, sona ermek ☆ *a.* süresi dolma

explain /ik'spleyn/ *e.* açıklamak **explanation** /ekspli'neyşın/ açıklama

explanatory /ik'splenıtıri/ *s.* açıklayıcı

explicit /ik'splisit/ *s.* açık, belirgin

explode /ik'sploud/ *e.* patlamak; patlatmak

exploit /'eksployt/ *a.* olağanüstü başarı, yiğitlik

exploit /ik'sployt/ *e.* işletmek, sömürmek

exploration /ekspli'reyşın/ *a.* araştırma, keşif

explore /ik'splo:/ *e.* keşfe çıkmak, inceleme gezisi yapmak; araştırmak

explorer /ik'splorı/ *a.* kâşif

explosion /ik'sploujın/ *a.* patlama

explosive /ik'splousiv/ *a, s.* patlayıcı

exponent /ik'spounınt/ *a.* (görüş, inanç) taraftar; *mat.* üs

export /ik'spo:t/ *e.* ihraç etmek ☆ /'ekspo:t/ dışsatım, ihracat **exporter** ihracatçı

expose /ik'spouz/ *e.* maruz bırakmak, karşı karşıya getirmek, ortaya çıkarmak

exposition /ekspı'zişın/ *a.* açıklama

exposure /ik'spoujı/ *a.* maruz kalma, açık olma; açığa vurma; poz

expound /ik'spaund/ e. açıklamak

express /ik'spres/ e. dile getirmek, anlatmak, göstermek ☆ s. açık, kesin; ekspres, hızlı ☆ a. ekspres tren

expression /ik'spreşın/ a. anlatım, ifade

expressionism /ik'spreşınizım/ a. dışavurumculuk

expressive /ik'spresiv/ s. anlamlı

expressway /ik'spreswey/ a, Aİ. otoyol, otoban

expropriate /ik'sprouprieyt/ e. kamulaştırmak, istimlak etmek

expulsion /ik'spalşın/ a. kovma, çıkarma

exquisite /ik'skwizit/ s. mükemmel, enfes, harika, ince

extend /ik'stend/ e. uzatmak; genişletmek; büyütmek; uzanmak; yayılmak

extension /ik'stenşın/ a. uzatma; genişletme; büyütme; ek; (telefon) dahili hat

extensive /ik'stensiv/ s. geniş, yaygın

extent /ik'stent/ a. uzunluk, genişlik, büyüklük, alan; derece; ölçü

exterior /ik'stiiriı/ s. dış, harici

exterminate /ik'stö:mineyt/ e. yok etmek, kökünü kazımak

external /ik'stö:nıl/ s. dış, harici

extinct /ik'stinkt/ s. (hayvan, vb.) nesli tükenmiş; sönmüş

extinguish /ik'stingwiş/ e. (ışık, ateş) söndürmek extinguisher yangın söndürücü

extort /ik'sto:t/ e. (from) tehditle almak, gasp etmek

extra /'ekstrı/ a. ek, ilave, ekstra ☆ s. gereğinden çok, ek; üstün ☆ a. ek; (gazete) özel baskı; ek ücret; figüran

extract /ik'strekt/ e. çekmek, çekip çıkarmak; elde etmek, çıkarmak; parça, vb. seçmek; aktarmak ☆ a. öz, ruh, esans; özet extraction çekme, çıkarma; soy, köken

extracurricular /ekstrıkı'rikyulı/ s. ders programının dışında, müfredat dışı

extraordinary /ik'stro:dınıri/ s. olağanüstü, görülmemiş

extraterrestrial /ekstrıtı'restriıl/ s. dünya dışından gelen, dünya dışı

extravagance /ik'strevıgıns/ a. savurganlık, israf

extravagant /ik'strevıgınt/ s. savurgan, müsrif; aşırı

extreme /ik'stri:m/ s. en uçtaki, son, aşırı; çok büyük, son derece, çok ☆ a. en uzak nokta, sınır, uç; son derece extremely son derece, çok

extremity /ik'stremiti/ a. (acı, üzüntü, vb.) en yüksek derece; ç. eller ve ayaklar

extrovert /'ekstrıvö:t/ a. dışadönük kişi

exuberant /ig'zyu:bırınt/ a. coşkun, taşkın; (bitki) bol, verimli

exude /ig'zyu:d/ e. sızmak; sızdırmak, akıtmak

exult /ig'zalt/ e. çok sevinmek, bayram etmek

eye /ay/ a. göz; görme gücü, görüş; iğne deliği; dişi kopça; bakış, nazar ☆ e. gözden geçirmek; dikkatle bakmak eyeball göz küresi, göz yuvarlağı eyebrow kaş eye-catching dikkat çekici, göze çarpan eyelash kirpik eyelid gözkapağı eyesight görme gücü, görme yeteneği eyesore gözü rahatsız eden eyestrain göz yorgunluğu eyewitness görgü tanığı, şahit in the eyes of -in gözünde keep an eye on kon. göz kulak olmak keep an eye out for anımsamaya çalışmak under/before one's very eyes -in gözü önünde with one's eyes open göz göre göre, bile bile

F

fable /'feybıl/ a. masal, hayvan masalı, fabl

fabric /'febrik/ a. dokuma, kumaş, bez; yapı, iskelet, bünye

fabricate /'febrikeyt/ e. uydurmak, yalan söylemek, biraraya getirmek, yapmak

fabrication /'febrikeyşın/ a. yapım; imalat; uydurma, yalan

fabulous /'febyulıs/ s. inanılmaz, şaşılacak; kon. mükemmel, harika, müthiş

facade /fı'sa:d/ *a.* binanın ön yüzü, bina cephesi
face /feys/ *a.* yüz, surat, çehre; görünüş, şekil ☆ *e.* cesaretle karşılamak, karşı koymak; yüzüne -e ye doğru çevirmek; -in karşısında olmak **face to face** yüz yüze **have the face** yüzü tutmak, cüret etmek **in the face of** -e karşın, -e rağmen **to sb's face** yüzüne karşı **facecloth** el-yüz havlusu **face-lift** yüz gerdirme ameliyatı
facial /'feyşıl/ *s.* yüze ilişkin, yüzle ilgili
facile /'fesayl/ *s.* kolay yapılmış
facilitate /fı'siliteyt/ *e.* kolaylaştırmak
facility /fı'siliti/ *a.* kolaylık ç. vasıta, bina, tesis, olanak
facsimile /fek'simili/ *a.* kopya, suret, tıpkısı, tıpkıbasım
fact /fekt/ *a.* gerçek, olgu, olmuş şey; durum **as a matter of fact, in (actual) fact, in point of fact** gerçekten, hakikatte, işin doğrusu, hatta
faction /'fekşın/ *a.* hizip, grup
factor /'fektı/ *a.* etmen, faktör; *mat.* çarpan
factory /'fektıri/ *a.* fabrika, üretimlik
factual /'fekçuıl/ *s.* gerçeklere, olgulara dayanan
faculty /'fekılti/ *a.* fakülte; yetenek, beceri
fad /fed/ *a.* geçici heves/merak
fade /feyd/ *e.* solmak; soldurmak **fade away** ortadan kaybolmak, yok olmak **fade out** (ses, vb.) yavaş yavaş kısmak; kısılmak
fag /feg/ *a, kon.* angarya; *İİ.* sigara
faggot /'fegıt/ *a.* çalı çırpı demeti, çıra demeti
fail /feyl/ *e.* başaramamak, becerememek, başarısız olmak; (sınavda) kalmak; (sınıfta) bırakmak; yetersiz kalmak ☆ *a.* başarısızlık
failure /'feylyı/ *a.* başarısızlık; yetersizlik, eksiklik; yetmezlik
faint /feynt/ *s.* zayıf, güçsüz; soluk, donuk, sönük, zayıf, silik ☆ *e.* bayılmak güçsüzleşmek ☆ *a.* baygınlık, bayılma
fair /feı/ *s.* adil, dürüst, doğru; sarışın, kumral; (hava) açık; orta, şöyle böyle

☆ *a.* fuar, panayır, pazar, sergi ☆ *be.* adilane, hakça, dürüstçe, kurallara uygun **fair and square** dürüst bir şekilde; doğrudan, direkt **fair play** dürüst davranış, yansızlık **fairly** dürüst bir biçimde, hakça; oldukça
fairy /'feırı/ *a.* peri **fairy tale** peri masalı; palavra, uydurma, yalan
faith /feyt/ *a.* güven, güçlü inanç, itikat **faithful** sadık, bağlı; aslına uygun, doğru **faithfully** içtenlikle; tam olarak **yours faithfully** (mektup sonlarında) saygılarımla **faithless** vefasız
fake /feyk/ *a.* sahte, taklit; sahtekâr ☆ *s.* sahte ☆ *e.* taklidini/sahtesini yapmak
falcon /'fo:lkın/ *a, hayb.* şahin, doğan
fall /fo:l/ **fell** /fel/, **fallen** /'fo:lın/ *e.* düşmek; azalmak; düşüş göstermek; inmek; yıkılmak, çökmek; rastlamak, denk gelmek ☆ *a.* düşüş, düşme; azalma; çöküş, yıkılma; *Aİ.* sonbahar, güz **fall back** geri çekilmek **fall back on** (başka bir yola/şeye) başvurmak **fall behind** zamanında bitirememek **fall for** kazıklanmak, aldatılmak; *kon.* -e âşık olmak **fall off** (kalite, miktar, vb.) düşmek
fallen /'fo:lın/ *bkz.* **fall**
false /fo:ls/ *s.* yanlış; takma; yapma, taklit **false teeth** takma dişler **falsehood** yalan; yalancılık
falsify /'fo:lsifay/ *e.* değiştirmek, tahrif etmek, saptırmak ☆ *a.* yanlışlık, yanlış olma; yalan
falter /'fo:ltı/ *e.* sendelemek; duraksamak, bocalamak, tereddüt etmek
fame /feym/ *a.* ün, şöhret
familiar /fı'milıı/ *s.* bildik, tanıdık; bilen, anlayan; alışık **familiarity** aşinalık; yakınlık, içtenlik; samimilik; laubalilik
family /'femılı/ *a.* aile; soy; çoluk çocuk; *biy.* familya **family planning** aile planlaması **family tree** soyağacı, şecere
famine /'femin/ *a.* kıtlık
famish /'femiş/ *e.* çok acıkmak *kon.* açlıktan ölmek
famous /'feymıs/ *s.* ünlü, meşhur
fan /fen/ *a.* yelpaze; pervane, vantilatör

fan /fen/ *a.* hayran

fanatic /fı'netik/ *s.* bağnaz, fanatik

fanciful /'fensifıl/ *s.* hayal ürünü

fancy /'fensi/ *e.* imgelemek, aklında canlandırmak, düşünmek; sanmak; hoşlanmak, beğenmek ☆ *a.* hayal gücü; kuruntu; istek, arzu ☆ *s.* süslü **fancy-dress party** maskeli balo

fantastic /fen'testik/ *s.* düşsel, inanılmaz, hayal ürünü; acayip; *kon.* harika, süper

fantasy /'fentısi/ *a.* düş, fantezi

far /fa:/ *s.* uzak ☆ *be.* uzakta; uzağa; epeyce; çok; bir hayli **far from** -den ziyade; -in yerine **how far** ne kadar so **far** şimdiye dek; bir yere kadar **far better** çok daha iyi **as far as I know** bildiğim kadarıyla **far sighted** ileriyi görür; öngörülü; uzağı gören

farce /fa:s/ *a.* sulu komedi, kaba güldürü

fare /feı/ *a.* yol parası; yiyecek

farewell /feı'wel/ *a.* veda ☆ *ünl.* elveda!

farm /fa:m/ *a.* çiftlik; çiftlik evi ☆ *e.* çiftçilik yapmak **farmer** çiftçi **farmhouse** çiftlik evi **farming** çiftçilik **farmyard** çiftlik avlusu

farther /'fa:dı/ *s.* uzak, daha uzaktaki, ötedeki ☆ *be.* daha ileri, daha uzağa, daha uzakta

farthest /'fa:dist/ *s, be.* en uzak, en ileri, en uzağa, en uzakta

fascinate /'fesineyt/ *e.* etkilemek, büyülemek **fascinating** etkileyici, büyüleyici

fascism /'feşizım/ *a.* faşizm **fascist** faşist

fashion /'feşın/ *a.* moda; biçim, tarz, üslup **fashion parade** defile **fashion plate** elbise modeli **fashionable** modaya uygun, moda **out of fashion** demode, modası geçmiş

fast /fa:st/ *s.* hızlı, süratli, çabuk; sıkı, sağlam; (renk) sabit, solmaz; (saat) ileri ☆ *be.* hızla, süratle; sıkıca, sağlamca **fast asleep** derin uykuda

fast /fa:st/ *e.* oruç tutmak ☆ *a.* oruç

fasten /'fa:sın/ *e.* bağlamak; iliştirmek, tutturmak; (giysi) iliklemek **fastener** tutturucu, bağlayıcı şey; bağ, toka

fastidious /fe'stidiıs/ *s.* müşkülpesent, zor beğenir

fat /fet/ *s.* şişman, tombul; (et) yağlı ☆ *a.* yağ, içyağı ☆ **fatty** (yiyecek) yağlı

fatal /'feytıl/ *s.* ölümcül, öldürücü, yok edici **fatalism** kadercilik

fatality /fı'teliti/ *a.* ölümle sonuçlanan kaza, ölüm, felaket

fate /feyt/ *a.* alınyazısı, yazgı, kader, kısmet **fateful** alında yazılı olan; kaçınılmaz; çok önemli

father /'fa:dı/ *a.* baba; papaz **Father Christmas** Noel Baba **The father** Tanrı **fatherhood** babalık **father-in-law** kayınpeder **fatherly** babacan, baba gibi

fathom /'fedım/ *a.* kulaç ☆ *e.* anlamak

fatigue /fı'ti:g/ *a.* aşırı yorgunluk, bitkinlik; *tek.* malzeme yorgunluğu ☆ *e.* yormak, yorgunluk vermek

fatten /'fetın/ *e.* şişmanlatmak, semirtmek

fatuous /'feçuıs/ *s.* saçma, akılsız

faucet /'fo:sit/ *a, Aİ.* musluk

fault /fo:lt/ *a.* hata, yanlışlık; suç; kusur, arıza, bozukluk; *coğ.* fay, çatlak ☆ *e.* hata bulmak, kusur bulmak **faultless** hatasız, kusursuz **faulty** hatalı; arızalı

favour /'feyvı/ *a.* dostça davranış, güler yüz, yakınlık; iyilik; yardım; destek ☆ *e.* lütfetmek, vermek; uygun görmek, desteklemek **in favour of** -in yanında, tarafında, lehinde **do sb a favour** birisine bir iyilikte bulunmak **favourable** olumlu, lehte; uygun

favourite /'feyvırit/ *a.* en çok sevilen, gözde ☆ *a.* favori

fear /fiı/ *a.* korku ☆ *e.* korkmak, ürkmek, çekinmek; (for) endişe etmek, telaşlanmak **I fear** korkarım, korkarım ki **fearful** korkunç, müthiş; endişeli, kaygılı **fearless** korkusuz, yürekli

feasible /'fi:zıbıl/ *s.* yapılabilir, makul, mantıklı

feast /fi:st/ *a.* şölen, ziyafet; bayram ☆ ziyafet vermek; bol bol yiyip içmek

feat /fi:t/ *a.* ustalık isteyen hareket, marifet

feather /'fedı/ a. kuştüyü, tüy **birds of a feather** aynı yolun yolcuları **featherweight** (boks) tüysıklet

feature /'fi:çı/ a. özellik, yüzün herhangi bir kısmı; uzun film; makale ☆ e. -in belirleyici/göze çarpan özelliği olmak; yer/rol vermek; yer/rol almak

February /'februiri/ a. şubat

feckless /'feklıs/ s. dikkatsiz, düşüncesiz, sorumsuz

fed /fed/ bkz. **feed**; **be fed up with** -den bıkıp usanmak

federal /'fedırıl/ s. federal, birleşik

federate /'fedıreyt/ e. federasyon halinde birleştirmek; birleşmek **federation** federasyon, birlik

fee /fi:/ a. ücret, vizite; giriş ücreti

feeble /'fi:bıl/ s. zayıf, güçsüz **feebleminded** geri zekâlı

feed /fi:d/ e. **fed** /fed/ beslemek, yiyecek vermek; beslenmek ☆ a. yiyecek, besin; yem, ot; mama

feedback /'fi:dbek/ a. geribesleme, besleni

feel /fi:l/ e. **felt** /felt/ hissetmek, duymak; dokunmak, ellemek; kanısında olmak; anlamak, sezmek **feel cold** üşümek **feel like** canı istemek

feeling /'fi:ling/ a. duygu, his; dokunma; hassasiyet; sezgi; izlenim

feign /feyn/ e. ... numarası yapmak, gibi yapmak; bahane uydurmak

feint /feynt/ a. savaş hilesi, sahte saldırı

feline /'fi:layn/ s, a, hayb. kedigil

fell /fel/ bkz. **fall**

fell /fel/ e. (ağaç) kesmek; düşürmek

fellow /'felou/ a, kon. adam, herif, ahbap; arkadaş; akademi üyesi

fellowship dernek, grup; üniversite bursu

felony /'felıni/ a. ağır suç

felt /felt/ bkz. **feel**; a. keçe, fötr **felttip pen** keçeli kalem

female /'fi:meyl/ a. dişi; kadın

feminine /'feminin/ s. kadınla ilgili; kadınsı **femininity** kadınsılık **feminism** feminizm

fen /fen/ a. bataklık arazi, bataklık

fence /fens/ a. çit, tahta perde, parmak-

lık ☆ e. çitle çevirmek; eskrim sporu yapmak

fencing /'fensing/ a, sp. eskrim; çit; duvar

fender /'fendı/ a. şömine paravanası; Ai, oto. çamurluk

ferment /fı'ment/ mayalanmak; mayalamak; heyecanlanmak, telaşlanmak **fermentation** mayalanma

fern /fö:n/ a, bitk. eğreltiotu

ferocious /fı'rouşıs/ s. vahşi, yırtıcı

ferret /'ferit/ a, hayb. yaban gelinciği

ferrous /'ferıs/ s. demirle ilgili

ferry /'feri/ a. feribot, araba vapuru **ferryboat** feribot, araba vapuru

fertile /'fö:tayl/ s. verimli, bereketli, doğurgan

fertility /'fö:tiliti/ a. verimlilik, bereketlilik, doğurganlık

fertilize /'fö:tilayz/ e. döllemek, aşılamak, gübrelemek **fertilizer** kimyasal gübre

fervent /'fö:vınt/ s. ateşli, coşkun

fester /'festı/ e. (yara) mikrop kapmak, irinlenmek

festival /'festivıl/ a. şenlik, festival

festive /'festiv/ s. festival/şenlik ile ilgili **festivity** şenlik, eğlence

festoon /fe'stu:n/ a. çiçek ya da yaprak zinciri

fetch /feç/ e. gidip getirmek, gidip almak; para getirmek, para kazandırmak

fête /feyt/ a. eğlence, şenlik, şölen

fetish /'fetiş/ a. fetiş, tapıncak

fetter /'fetı/ a. pranga, zincir ☆ e. pranga vurmak; engellemek

fetus /'fi:tıs/ a, bkz. **foetus**

feud /fyu:d/ a. kan davası, düşmanlık

feudal /'fyu:dıl/ s. derebeyliğe ilişkin, feodal **feudalism** derebeylik, feodalizm

fever /'fi:vı/ a, hek. ateş, hararet; heyecan, telaş **feverish** ateşli, hararetli; heyecanlı, telaşlı

few /fyu:/ s, adl, a. az **a few** birkaç **no fewer than** en azından, hiç yoksa **quite a few** birçok

fez /fez/ a. fes

fiancé /fi'onsey/ a. (erkek) nişanlı

fiancée /fi'onsey/ a. (kız) nişanlı
fiasco /fi'eskou/ a. başarısızlık, fiyasko
fib /fib/ e. küçük yalan söylemek
fiberglass /'faybıgla:s/ a, Aİ, bkz. fibreglass
fibre /'faybı/ a. lif; tel, elyaf; iplik
fibreglass /'faybıgla:s/ a. fiberglas, camyünü
fickle /'fikıl/ s. vefasız, dönek
fiction /'fikşın/ a. hayal ürünü; uyduruk; roman, öykü türü
fictitious /fik'tişıs/ s. gerçek olmayan, uydurma, kurmaca
fiddle /'fidıl/ a. keman; dolandırıcılık, üçkâğıt ☆ e. keman çalmak; (with/about/around) oyalanmak; zaman öldürmek fiddler kemancı; arg. düzenbaz, üçkâğıtçı
fidelity /fi'deliti/ a. bağlılık, sadakat; aslına uygunluk
fidget /'ficit/ e. kıpırdanmak, yerinde duramamak
field /fi:ld/ a. tarla; alan, saha; açık arazi; kırlık; iş, etkinlik alanı field day manevra günü field events atlama ve atma karşılaşmaları field glasses arazi dürbünü field marshal mareşal field sports açık hava sporları
fiend /fi:nd/ a. şeytan, iblis, kötü ruh
fierce /fiıs/ s. azılı, acımasız, vahşi, kızgın
fiery /'fayıri/ s. ateşten, ateşli, ateş gibi, kızgın
fiesta /fi'estı/ a. yortu, bayram, fiesta
fifteen /fif'ti:n/ a, s. on beş fifteenth on beşinci
fifth /'fift/ a, s. beşinci
fifty /'fifti/ a, s. elli fiftyfifty yarı yarıya, eşit olarak
fig /fig/ a, bitk. incir; incir ağacı
fight /fayt/ e. fought /fo:t/ savaşmak, çarpışmak; kavga etmek ☆ a. dövüş, kavga; savaş fight off ile mücadele etmek; def etmek fighter kavgacı, savaşçı; ask. avcı uçağı
figment /'figmınt/ a. hayal ürünü ya da uydurma şey
figurative /'figyurıtiv/ s. değişmeceli, mecazi
figure /'figı/ a. biçim, şekil, figür; beden yapısı, boy bos, endam; sayı, rakam figure on planlamak, hesaba katmak figure out çözmek; hesaplamak
filament /'filımınt/ a. filaman, ince tel
file /fayl/ a. eğe, törpü; dosya, klasör ☆ e. eğelemek, törpülemek; dosyalamak; sıralamak
filings /'faylingz/ a. eğe talaşı
fill /fil/ e. doldurmak; dolmak; dolmak, kaplamak; yerine getirmek ☆ a. istiap haddi fill in doldurmak, tamamlamak; bilgi vermek fill up dolmak; doldurmak
fillet /'filit/ a. kemiksiz/kılçıksız et, fileto
fillet /'filit/ e. (eti) fileto kesmek
filling /'filing/ a. doldurma; dolgu, diş dolgusu filling station benzinci, benzin istasyonu
filly /'fili/ a. yavru kısrak, dişi tay
film /film/ a. film; ince tabaka; zar ☆ e. film çekmek, filme almak
filter /'filtı/ a. süzgeç, filtre ☆ e. süzmek, filtreden geçirmek; süzülmek
filth /'filt/ a. pislik filthy pis, kirli; kaba, çirkin
fin /fin/ a, hayb. yüzgeç; palet
final /'faynıl/ s. sonda gelen, sonuncu, son; kesin, kati ☆ a, sp. final, son karşılaşma; dönem sonu sınavı finalist finalist finally sonunda; kesin olarak
finale /fi'na:li/ a, müz. final
finance /'faynens, fi'nens/ a. maliye; iş kurmada gereken para; ç. mali durum ☆ e. paraca desteklemek, finanse etmek financial mali, parasal financier sermayedar
finch /finç/ a, hayb. ispinoz
find /faynd/ e. found /faund/ bulmak; anlamak, fark etmek find out çözmek, keşfetmek, anlamak, öğrenmek finder bulan kimse; vizör finding bulgu; huk. sonuç, karar
fine /fayn/ s. güzel; çok ince; (hava) güzel, açık; sağlıklı, keyfi yerinde; (iş) dikkatli, iyi; (maden) saf, som ☆ be ince ince; çok iyi ☆ a. para cezası ☆ e. para cezasına çarptırmak fine arts güzel sanatlar finely ince ince; çok iyi bir biçimde

finery /'faynıri/ *a.* süslü takılı güzel elbise

finesse /fi'nes/ *a.* (insan ilişkilerinde) yönetme yeteneği, ustalık

finger /'fingı/ *a.* parmak ☆ *e.* parmakla dokunmak **fingernail** tırnak **fingerprint** parmak izi **fingertip** parmak ucu **keep one's fingers crossed** en iyisini dilemek

finicky /'finiki/ *s.* huysuz; güç beğenir

finish /'finiş/ *e.* bitirmek, tamamlamak, sona erdirmek; bitmek ☆ *a.* bitiş, son; cila, perdah, rötuş **finished** bitik, tükenmiş; bitmiş **finish with** ile işini bitirmek, ilişkisini kesmek

finite /'faynayt/ *s.* sonu olan, sonlu, sınırlı

fiord /'fi:o:d/ *a, bkz.* **fjord**

fir /fö:/ *a, bitk.* köknar

fire /'fayı/ *a.* ateş, alev, yanma; yangın; parıltı, parlaklık; ateş etme ☆ *e.* yakmak, tutuşturmak; (silah) ateş etmek, atmak; tahrik etmek, teşvik etmek; *kon.* işten çıkarmak, kovmak, atmak **catch fire** alev almak, tutuşmak **fire alarm** yangın alarmı **fire brigade** itfaiye **fire department** *Aİ.* itfaiye örgütü **fire engine** itfaiye arabası **fire escape** yangın merdiveni **fire station** itfaiye merkezi **on fire** alevler içinde, yanmakta **firearm** ateşli silah **firefly** ateşböceği **fireguard** şömine ızgarası **fireman** itfaiyeci **fireplace** şömine, ocak **fireraising** kundakçılık **fireside** ocak başı **firewood** odun **firework** havai fişek **firing line** ateş hattı

firm /fö:m/ *s.* sert, katı; sağlam; sıkı; kararlı ☆ *a.* firma **firmly** sıkıca, sımsıkı; metanetle

first /fö:st/ *s, a.* birinci, ilk ☆ *be.* önce, ilk önce, başta, ilk kez **at first** başlangıçta, önceleri **first aid** ilkyardım **first class** birinci sınıf, birinci mevki **first floor** *İİ.* birinci kat, *Aİ.* zemin kat **first lady** başbakanın karısı **first of all** en önce, ilkin **first name** isim, ad **first rate** birinci sınıf, en iyi **firsthand** ilk elden, dolaysız **firstly** önce, ilk önce, ilk başta

fiscal /'fiskıl/ *s.* mali

fish /fiş/ *a.* balık; balık eti ☆ *e.* balık tutmak **fisherman** balıkçı **fishing** balıkçılık **fishing line** olta **fishmonger** balık satıcısı, balıkçı **fishy** balık gibi; şüpheli, kuşku uyandıran

fission /'fişın/ *a.* bölünme, yarılma, yarma

fissure /'fişı/ *a.* çatlak, yarık

fist /fist/ *a.* yumruk

fit /fit/ *s.* uygun, elverişli; sağlıklı, zinde ☆ *a.* hastalık nöbeti, sara; galeyan, kriz ☆ *e.* uymak; uydurmak; yakışmak, uymak; tutmak; prova etmek **fitness** zindelik, form; uygunluk

fitting /'fiting/ *a.* terzi provası; bina tesisatı, tertibat

five /fayv/ *a, s.* beş

fix /fiks/ *e.* saptamak, belirlemek, düzenlemek; tutturmak; **(on)** (zihnini) vermek; **(on)** gözlerini dikmek, kararlaştırmak; *kon.* ile ilgilenmek, icabına bakmak

fixation /fik'seyşın/ *a.* yerleştirme, oturtma, takma; saplantı

fixed /fikst/ *s.* sabit, oynamaz; değişmez; belirlenmiş

fixture /'fiksçı/ *a, sp.* fikstür; sabit eşya, demirbaş

fizz /fiz/ *e.* (gazoz gibi) vızlamak, fışırdamak ☆ *a.* fışırtı, vızıltı; *kon.* şampanya

fizzle /'fizıl/ *e.* **(out)** boşa çıkmak

fjord /'fyo:d/ *a, coğ.* fiyort

flabby /'flebi/ *s.* sarkık, pörsük

flag /fleg/ *a.* bayrak, sancak; *den.* bandıra, flama ☆ *e.* canlılığını yitirmek, güçsüzleşmek **flagpole** bayrakdireği

flagon /'flegın/ *a.* bir tür kulplu sürahi

flagrant /'fleygrınt/ *s.* (kötü bir şey) alenen yapan/yapılan

flail /fleyl/ *e.* sağa sola sallamak/sallanmak

flair /fleı/ *a.* özel yetenek, beceri

flake /fleyk/ *a.* ince tabaka, ince parça

flamboyant /flem'boyınt/ *s.* gösterişli, havalı, tantanalı

flame /fleym/ *a.* alev; ateş ☆ *e.* alev alev yanmak

flamingo /flı'mingou/ *a, hayb.* flaman kuşu, flamingo

flammable /'flemıbıl/ s. çabuk yanar, kolay tutuşur

flan /flen/ a. meyveli pasta

flank /flenk/ a. böğür, yan; *ask.* kanat, cenah

flannel /'flenıl/ a. pazen, flanel; fanila

flap /flep/ a. (aşağı sarkan) kapak, flap

flare /fleı/ a. ışık; alev; işaret fişeği ☆ *e.* birden alev almak, parlamak

flared /fleıd/ s. (etek, pantolon) alt kısmı geniş

flash /fleş/ *e.* parlamak, ışıldamak; (telgraf ya da radyo mesajı) yollamak, göndermek; etmek; ☆ *a.* parıltı, ışıltı; flaş **flashback** (film) geriye dönüş **flashbulb** flaş **flasher** (oto) flaşör **flashlight** sinyal, flaş; *Aİ.* cep feneri **flashy** gösterişli

flask /fla:sk/ a. dar boyunlu küçük şişe; termos.

flat /flet/ s. düz, yassı; havasız, patlak; yavan, sıkıcı, tekdüze; mat, donuk; yüzüstü, sırtüstü; *müz.* bemol ☆ *a.* apartman dairesi

flatten /'fletın/ *e.* düzleştirmek, yassılaştırmak; düzleşmek

flatter /'fletı/ *e.* dalkavukluk etmek, yağlamak, yağ çekmek **flattery** dalkavukluk, yağcılık

flavour /'fleyvı/ a. tat, lezzet, çeşni ☆ *e.* tat vermek **flavouring** tatlandırıcı şey, çeşni

flaw /flo:/ a. kusur

flawless /'flo:lis/ s. kusursuz, mükemmel

flaxen /'fleksın/ s. soluk sarı, lepiska

flea /fli:/ a, *hayb.* pire **flea market** bit pazarı

fleck /flek/ a. benek

flee /fli:/ *e.* **fled** /fled/ kaçmak

fleece /fli:s/ a. koyun postu, yapağı ☆ *e.* soymak, yolmak, kazıklamak

fleet /fli:t/ a. filo **merchant fleet** ticaret filosu

flesh /fleş/ a. et; vücut, beden **fleshy** etli; şişmanca, toplu

flex /fleks/ *e.* bükmek, germek ☆ *a.* tel, kordon, esnek kablo **flexibility** bükülgenlik, esneklik **flexible** bükülgen, esnek

flick /flik/ a. fiske, hafif vuruş ☆ *e.* hafifçe vurmak, fiske vurmak

flicker /'flikı/ *e.* titremek, titreşmek, yanıp sönmek ☆ *a.* titreme, titreşme

flight /flayt/ a. uçuş, hava yolculuğu; (kuş, uçak, vb.) sürü; filo; kaçış

flimsy /'flimzi/ s. zayıf, güçsüz; çürük, dayanıksız

flinch /flinç/ *e.* geri çekilmek; kaçınmak; ürkmek

fling /fling/ *e.* **flung** /flang/ fırlatıp atmak, savurmak ☆ *a.* atma, atış; deneme, girişim

flint /flint/ a. çakmaktaşı

flip /flip/ *e.* fiske vurmak ☆ *a.* fiske

flippant /'flipınt/ s. saygısız, küstah

flipper /'flipı/ a. palet

flirt /flö:t/ *e.* flört etmek, kur yapmak

float /flout/ *e.* yüzmek, batmamak; yüzdürmek ☆ *a.* şamandıra, duba

flock /flok/ a. sürü; küme ☆ *e.* toplanmak, üşüşmek

flog /flog/ *e.* dövmek, dayak atmak; kırbaçlamak **flogging** kırbaç cezası, kamçılama

flood /flad/ a. su basması, sel ☆ *e.* su basmak, sel basmak **floodlight** /'fladlayt/ projektör

floor /flo:/ a. zemin, döşeme; kat

flop /flop/ *e.* birdenbire düşmek, çöküvermek; *kon.* (plan, vb.) suya düşmek **floppy** gevşek, sarkık

flora /'flo:rı/ a. bitey, flora

florist /'flo:rist/ a. çiçekçi

flotilla /flı'tilı/ a. küçük filo, filotilla

flounder /'flaundı/ *e.* çırpınmak, çabalamak ☆ *a.* dilbalığı, dere pisisi

flour /flauı/ a. un

flourish /'flariş/ *e.* gelişmek, ilerlemek, savurmak, sallamak ☆ *a.* gelişme; sallama, savurma

flout /flaut/ *e.* zıddına gitmek, burun kıvırmak

flow /flou/ *e.* (sıvı) akmak; sallanmak, sarkmak; çıkmak, doğmak ☆ *a.* akış; akıntı; akın; met, kabarma

flower /'flauı/ a. çiçek ☆ *e.* çiçek açmak **flowerbed** çiçek tarhı **flowered** çiçekli, çiçeklerle süslü **flowerpot** çiçek saksısı **flowery** çiçekli, çiçeklerle süslü

flu /flu:/ *a.* grip
fluctuate /'flakçueyt/ *e.* inip çıkmak, dalgalanmak
flue /flu:/ *a.* boru, baca borusu
fluency /'flu:ınsi/ *a.* (konuşma) akıcılık
fluent akıcı, rahat, pürüzsüz **fluently** akıcı bir biçimde, rahatça
fluid /'flu:id/ *s.* akıcı, akışkan ☆ *a.* sıvı
fluke /flu:k/ *a, kon.* şans, talih
flung /flang/ *bkz.* **fling**
fluorescent /flu'resınt/ *s, fiz.* ışınır, floresan
flurry /'flari/ *a.* coşku, heyecan; ani rüzgâr/kar/yağmur; sağanak ☆ *e.* (birisinin) kafasını karıştırmak
flush /flaş/ *a.* fışkırma, fışkırtma; heyecan; kızarma, coşkunluk ☆ *e.* fışkırmak; fışkırtmak; yüzü kızarmak ☆ *s.* düz, bir hizada; *kon.* varlıklı
fluster /'flastı/ *e.* şaşırtmak, telaşlandırmak ☆ *a.* telaş, şaşkınlık, bocalama
flute /flu:t/ *a, müz.* flüt **flutist** *Aİ.* flütçü
flutter /'flatı/ *e.* (kanat) çırpmak; çırpınmak; telaşlanmak ☆ *a, kon.* telaş, heyecan; *kon.* ufak bahis
flux /flaks/ *a.* akma, akış; değişim, oynaklık
fly /flay/ *e.* **flew** /flu:/, **flown** /floun/ uçmak; uçakla gitmek; çabuk gitmek; uçurmak; uçup gitmek; kaçmak ☆ *a.* sinek **fly in the ointment** küçük ama mide bulandıran bir pürüz
flying /'flaying/ *a.* uçma, uçuş ☆ *s.* uçan **flying saucer** uçandaire
flyover /'flayouvı/ *a.* üstgeçit
foal /foul/ *a.* tay
foam /foum/ *a.* köpük ☆ *e.* köpürmek
focal point /foukıl 'poynt/ *a.* merkez noktası, ilgi merkezi
focus /'foukıs/ *a.* (ç. **focuses, foci** /'fo-uki:/) odak, fokus, merkez; merkez nokta ☆ *e.* bir noktaya toplamak; odak ayarı yapmak
fodder /'fodı/ *a.* kuru ot, saman, yem
foe /fou/ *a, yaz.* düşman
foetus /'fi:tıs/ *a.* cenin, dölüt
fog /fog/ *a.* sis ☆ *e.* sislenmek; (gözlük, vb.) buğulanmak; kafasını karıştırmak **foggy** sisli, dumanlı
foil /foyl/ *a.* yaldız kâğıdı; metal yaprak,

varak; eskrim kılıcı, meç ☆ *e.* işini bozmak, engel olmak
fold /fould/ *e.* katlamak; katlanmak; (eller) kavuşturmak, bağlamak; ☆ *a.* kıvrım **folder** dosya
folio /'fouliou/ *a.* iki ya da dörde katlanmış kâğıt tabakası; bu biçimde katlanmış yapraklardan oluşmuş kitap
folk /fouk/ *a.* halk; insanlar, ahali **folk dance** halk oyunu **folk music** halk müziği **folk singer** halk türküleri sanatçısı **folk song** halk türküsü
folklore /'fouklo:/ *a.* halkbilim, folklor
follow /'folou/ *e.* takip etmek, izlemek; dinlemek, uymak **as follows** aşağıdaki gibi **follower** taraftar, destekçi **follow through** sonunu getirmek, bitirmek **follow up** sonuna kadar götürmek
following /'folouing/ *ilg.* -den sonra, -in ardından ☆ *s.* aşağıdaki; izleyen; ertesi
folly /'foli/ *a.* akılsızlık, aptallık
fond /fond/ *s.* sever, düşkün **be fond of** -e düşkün olmak, -den hoşlanmak **fondly** sevgiyle; safça
fondle /'fondıl/ *e.* okşamak, sevmek
food /fu:d/ *a.* yiyecek, besin, gıda
fool /fu:l/ *a.* aptal, budala, enayi ☆ *e.* kandırmak, aldatmak, aptal yerine koymak **fool about/around** aylak aylak dolaşmak **fool away** çarçur etmek, harcamak **fool with** ile oynamak, kurcalamak **foolery** aptallık **foolhardy** delifişek, çılgın
foolish /'fu:liş/ *s.* aptal, akılsız; saçma, budalaca **foolishly** aptalca **foolishness** aptallık
foot /fut/ *a.* (ç. **feet** /fi:t/) ayak; 30.48 cm.; etek, dip **get/have cold feet** cesaretini yitirmek, korkmak **have one foot in the grave** bir ayağı çukurda olmak **on foot** yayan, yürüyerek **football** futbol; futbol topu **football pools** sportoto **footbridge** yaya köprüsü **foothill** dağ eteğindeki tepe **foothold** ayak basacak sağlam yer, basamak **footing** ayak basacak yer; karşılıklı ilişki **footlights** sahnenin önündeki ışıklar **footnote** dipnot **footpath** keçiyolu,

patika **footprint** ayak izi **footsore** ayakları acımış/şişmiş **footstep** ayak sesi; ayak izi; adım; basamak **footwear** ayakkabı, çizme, vb. ayağa giyilen şeyler

for /fı, fo:/ *ilg.* için; -e olarak; adına, için; uğruna; lehine, lehinde; yüzünden, -den; karşılık; zarfında, -dır; süresince; yerine ☆ *bağ.* çünkü, zira

foray /'forey/ *a.* akın, yağma, baskın

forbad, forbade *bkz.* **forbid**

forbear /fo:'beı/ *e.* **forbore** /fo:'bo:/, **forborne** /fo:'bo:n/ kendini tutmak, çekinmek, sakınmak

forbid /fı'bid/ *e.* **forbad** /fı'bed/ (**forbade** /fı'beyd/), **forbidden** /fı'bidın/ yasaklamak **forbidden** yasak **forbidding** sert; ürkütücü; tehditkâr

force /fo:s/ *a.* güç, kuvvet; zor, baskı, şiddet; etki, nüfuz ☆ *e.* zorlamak; mecbur etmek **by force** zorla **in force** yürürlükteki **forced** zoraki, mecburi **forced landing** mecburi iniş **forceful** güçlü, etkili

forceps /'fo:seps/ *a, hek.* pens, kıskaç

forcible /'fo:sıbıl/ *s.* zorla yapılan

fore /fo:/ *s.* ön

forearm /'fo:ra:m/ *a.* önkol

foreboding /fo:'bouding/ *a.* önsezi

forecast /'fo:ka:st/ *e.* tahmin etmek ☆ *a.* tahmin

forefather /'fo:fa:dı/ *a.* ata, cet

forefinger /'fo:fingı/ *a.* işaretparmağı

forefront /'fo:frant/ *a.* ön taraf, ön sıra

foregoing /'fo:gouing/ *s.* daha önce belirtilen; yukarıdaki

foregone /'fo:gon/ *s.* önceden bilinen, kaçınılmaz, beklenen

foreground /'fo:graund/ *a.* ön plan

forehead /'forid, 'fo:hed/ *a.* alın

foreign /'forin/ *s.* yabancı, dış **foreign affairs** dışişleri **foreign exchange** kambiyo **foreigner** yabancı

foreman /'fo:mın/ *a.* ustabaşı

foremost /'fo:moust/ *s.* en başta gelen, en önemli olan

forename /'fo:neym/ *a.* ad, ilk ad

forensic /fı'rensik/ *s.* mahkemeye ait, adli

forerunner /'fo:ranı/ *a.* haberci, müjdeci

foresee /fo:'si:/ *e.* **foresaw** /fo:'so:/, **foreseen** /fo:'si:n/ önceden görmek, tahmin etmek

foreshadow /fo:'şedou/ *e.* önceden göstermek, belirtisi olmak

foresight /'fo:sayt/ *a.* sağgörü, öngörü, seziş

forest /'forist/ *a.* orman **forester** ormancı **forestry** ormancılık

foretell /fo:'tel/ *e.* **foretold** /fo:'tould/ önceden haber vermek

forever /fı'revı/ *be.* ebediyen, sonsuza kadar, daima

forewarn /fo:'wo:n/ *e.* önceden uyarmak

foreword /'fo:wö:d/ *a.* önsöz

forfeit /'fo:fit/ *e.* kaybetmek, yoksun kalmak ☆ *a.* ceza, kayıp

forge /'fo:c/ *a.* demirhane ☆ *e.* sahtesini yapmak, kalpazanlık yapmak; demir dövmek **forger** sahtekâr; kalpazan **forgery** sahtekârlık; kalpazanlık

forget /fı'get/ *e.* **forgot** /fı'got/, **forgotten** /fı'gotın/ unutmak **forgetful** unutkan

forgivable /fı'gıvıbıl/ *s.* bağışlanabilir, affedilebilir

forgive /fı'giv/ *e.* **forgave** /fı'geyv/, **forgiven** /fı'givın/ affetmek, bağışlamak **forgiveness** af; affetme **forgiving** bağışlayıcı

forgiven /fı'givın/ *bkz.* **forgive**

forgo /'fo:gou/ *e.* bırakmak, vazgeçmek

fork /fo:k/ *a.* çatallı bel, yaba ☆ *e.* çatallaşmak **forked** çatallı **forklift** forklift

forlorn /fı'lo:n/ *s.* üzgün, mahzun

form /fo:m/ *a.* şekil, biçim; görünüş; basılı kâğıt; kondisyon ☆ *e.* biçim vermek; düzenlemek; düzenlenmek

formal /'fo:mıl/ *s.* resmi; biçimsel

formality /fo:'meliti/ *a.* resmiyet; formalite

format /'fo:met/ *a.* kitap boyu, format genel düzen

formation /fo:'meyşın/ *a.* oluşum

former /'fo:mı/ *s.* önceki **formerly** eski den, önceden

formula /'fo:myulı/ *a.* formül; reçete

formulate /'fo:myuleyt/ *e.* açıkça belirt

mek; formülleştirmek
fornicate /'fo:nikeyt/ e. zina yapmak
forsake /fı'seyk/ e. **foresook** /fı'suk/, **forsaken** /fı'seykın/ bırakmak, terk etmek
forswear /fo:'sweı/ e. tövbe etmek, bırakmaya yemin etmek
fort /fo:t/ a. kale
forte /'fo:tey/ a. birinin en iyi yaptığı şey
forth /fo:t/ be. ileri; dışarı **and so forth** vesaire
forthcoming /fo:t'kaming/ s. gelecek, gelecekte olacak
forthwith /fo:t'wid, fo:t'wit/ be. hemen, derhal
fortieth /'fo:ti:t/ a, s. kırkıncı
fortification /fo:tifi'keyşın/ a. güçlendirme, sağlamlaştırma
fortify /'fo:tifay/ e. güçlendirmek, sağlamlaştırmak
fortitude /'fo:tityu:d/ e. dayanıklılık, yüreklilik, metanet
fortnight /'fo:tnayt/ a. iki hafta
fortress /'fo:tris/ a. büyük kale
fortunate /'fo:çınıt/ s. şanslı, talihli; uğurlu, hayırlı **fortunately** Allahtan, şükür ki, şansa
fortune /'fo:çın/ a. şans, talih; kısmet; servet **fortuneteller** falcı
forty /'fo:ti/ a, s. kırk
forum /'fo:rım/ a. forum
forward /'fo:wıd/ s. ön, öndeki; ileri; küstah, şımarık ☆ be, ilg. ileri, ileriye; daha önceye ☆ e. göndermek ☆ a. forvet
fossil /'fosıl/ a. fosil, taşıl
foster /'fo:stı/ e. beslemek, bakmak
foul /faul/s. iğrenç, pis; (hava) bozuk, fırtınalı; çirkin, ayıp; sp. faul
found /faund/ bkz. **find**
found /faund/ e. yapmak, inşa etmek; kurmak; yaptırmak **founder** kurucu
foundation /faun'deyşın/ a. kuruluş, tesis; temel
foundry /'faundri/ a. dökümhane
fountain /'fauntin/ a. çeşme; fıskiye; kaynak, pınar **fountainpen** dolmakalem
four /fo:/ a, s. dört **fourth** dördüncü

fourteen /fo:'ti:n/ a, s. on dört **fourteenth** on dördüncü
fowl /faul/ a. kümes hayvanı
fox /foks/ a. tilki
foyer /'foyey/ a. fuaye, giriş, antre
fraction /'frekşın/ a. küçük parça, bölüm, kesim; mat. kesir
fracture /'frekçı/ a. kırılma; çatlama; kırık, çatlak
fragile /'frecayl/ s. kırılgan; narin
fragment /'fregmınt/ a. parça, kırıntı
fragrance /'freygrıns/ a. güzel koku **fragrant** güzel kokulu
frail /freyl/ s. zayıf, narin; kırılgan, kolay kırılır **frailty** zayıflık, dayanıksızlık, narinlik
frame /freym/ a. iskelet, çatı; beden; çerçeve ☆ e. çerçevelemek **framework** çatı, iskelet, kafes
franc /frenk/ a. frank
franchise /'frençayz/ a. oy hakkı; isim hakkı
frank /frenk/ s. açıksözlü, içten, samimi ☆ e. (mektup) damgalamak
frankfurter /'frenkfö:tı/ a. bir tür sosis
frantic /'frentik/ s. çılgın
fraternity /frı'tö:niti/ a. kardeşlik; birlik, cemiyet, dernek
fraternize /'fretınayz/ e. kardeşçe davranmak, dost olmak
fraud /fro:d/ a. sahtekârlık, dolandırıcılık, hile; dolandırıcı **fraudulent** /'fro:dyulınt/ hileli, hileyle kazanılan
fraught /fro:t/ s. dolu, yüklü
fray /frey/ a, yaz. kavga, arbede, çekişme ☆ e. yıpranmak; yıpratmak
freak /fri:k/ a. hilkat garibesi, ucube; kaçık; kon. koyu hayran, düşkün
freckle /'frekıl/ a. çil
free /fri:/ s. özgür, hür; bağımsız; boş, serbest; parasız, bedava; (davranış) rahat ☆ be. hür olarak; bedava ☆ e. serbest bırakmak, özgürlüğüne kavuşturmak **freedom** özgürlük; bağımsızlık **free and easy** rahat, kaygısız, teklifsiz **freehold** mülk; iyelik hakkı, mülkiyet hakkı **freely** çekinmeden, rahatça; serbestçe; açıkça **freeway** Al. karayolu **free will** irade özgürlüğü
freeze /fri:z/ e. **froze** /frouz/ **frozen** /'f-

rouzın/ donmak; dondurmak; (hava) çok soğuk olmak; donakalmak; (fiyat, ücret, vb.) dondurmak ☆ *a.* donma; don, dondurucu soğuk; (ücret fiyat, vb.) dondurma **freezer** soğutucu, dondurucu **freezing point** donma noktası

freight /freyt/ *a.* taşıma, nakliye; yük

French /frenç/s. Fransız **French fries** *Aİ.* patates kızartması, patates tava **French** Fransızca; **(the)** Fransızlar

frenzy /'frenzi/ *a.* çılgınlık, cinnet, taşkınlık

frequency /'fri:kwınsi/ *a.* sık sık oluş, sıklık; frekans

frequent /'fri:kwınt/ *s.* yaygın, sık sık olan; olağan **frequently** sık sık

fresh /freş/ *s.* taze, körpe; yeni; temiz; taze pişmiş; sağlıklı

freshen /'freşın/ *e.* (rüzgâr) sertleşmek

freshman /'freşmın/ *a, kon.* üniversitede birinci sınıf öğrencisi

friar /'frayı/ *a.* keşiş, papaz

friction /'frikşın/ *a.* sürtme, sürtünme; anlaşmazlık, sürtüşme

Friday /'fraydi/ *a.* cuma

fridge /fric/ *a, kon.* buzdolabı

friend /frend/ *a.* arkadaş, dost **make friends (with)** (ile) arkadaşlık kurmak **friendly** dost, dostça; yardımsever; içten, sıcak **friendship** dostluk, arkadaşlık

frieze /fri:z/ *a.* duvar ya da tavan süsü, friz

frigate /'frigit/ *a, ask.* firkateyn

fright /frayt/ *a.* korku

frighten /'fraytın/ *e.* korkutmak, ürkütmek **frightened** korkmuş, ürkmüş **frightful** korkunç, ürkütücü

frigid /'fricid/ *s.* çok soğuk, buz gibi, dondurucu

frill /fril/ *a.* farbala, fırfır; gereksiz süs **frilly** fırfırlı

fringe /frinc/ *a.* saçak; perçem; kenar

frisk /frisk/ *e.* sıçrayıp oynamak, hoplayıp zıplamak, koşuşmak

frisky /'friski/ *s.* oynak, oyuncu, canlı

frizz /friz/ *e, kon.* (saç) kıvırmak **frizzy** (saç) kıvırcık

fro /frou/ *be:* **to and fro** öteye beriye

frock /frok/ *a.* kadın giysisi

frog /frog/ *a.* kurbağa

from /frım, from/ *ilg.* -den, -dan; -den beri; -den sonra; göz önünde tutulursa, göre

front /frant/ *a.* ön, ön taraf; çehre, yüz; *ask.* cephe ☆ *e.* ile karşı karşıya olmak, -e bakmak **in front of** önünde

frontier /'frantiı/ *a.* sınır, hudut

frost /frost/ *a.* ayaz, don; kırağı ☆ *e.* donmak, buzlanmak **frosty** dondurucu; içten olmayan, soğuk

froth /frot/ *a.* köpük ☆ *e.* köpürmek, köpüklenmek **frothy** köpüklü

frown /fraun/ *e.* kaşlarını çatmak **frown on/upon** uygun görmemek, karşı çıkmak

fruit /fru:t/ *a.* meyve; sonuç, ürün ☆ *e.* meyve vermek **fruitful** sonuç veren, verimli **fruitless** meyvesiz; kısır

fruition /fru:'işın/ *a.* muradına erme, istediğini elde etme, gerçekleşme

frustrate /fra'streyt/ *e.* boşa çıkarmak, engellemek; düş kırıklığına uğratmak **frustration** düş kırıklığı; engelleme, bozma

fry /fray/ *e.* (yağda) kızartmak; kızarmak **frying pan** tava

fuchsia /'fyu:şı/ *a, bitk.* küpeçiçeği

fudge /fac/ *a.* bir çeşit yumuşak şekerleme

fuel /'fyuıl/ *a.* yakıt; yakacak; benzin

fugitive /'fyu:citiv/ *s.* kaçak; akılda tutulması zor; geçici, gidici ☆ *a.* kaçak

fulcrum /'fulkrım/ *a, tek.* (kaldıraç) dayanak noktası, taşıma noktası

fulfil /ful'fil/ *e.* yerine getirmek, yapmak; gerçekleştirmek **fulfilment** yapma, yerine getirme, ifa

full /ful/ *s.* dolu; tam, tüm, bol **to the full** tümüyle **in full** tamamen, tam olarak **full moon** dolunay **full-scale** aslının ölçüsünde; tüm gücünü kullanan **full stop** nokta (.) **full-time** tam gün, tam gün olan/çalışan/yapılan **fully** en az, en azından; tamamen, tam olarak

fumble /'fambıl/ *e.* el yordamıyla aramak, yoklamak; beceriksizce yapmak

fume /fyu:m/ *a.* duman, buhar, gaz ☆ *e.* duman çıkarmak, tütmek; öfkelenmek, köpürmek

fun /fan/ a. oyunculuk, neşe; eğlence, zevk for fun/for the fun of it gırgırına, zevk olsun diye make fun of -e gülmek/güldürmek, alay etmek
function /'fankşın/ a. görev, iş, işlev, fonksiyon; amaç ☆ e. çalışmak, işlemek, iş görmek functional işlevsel, fonksiyonel; iş görür
fund /fand/ a. sermaye, para, fon; stok, birikim ☆ e. para sağlamak, finanse etmek
fundamental /fandı'mentıl/ s. esas, ana, bellibaşlı, temel ☆ a. kural, temel ilke
funeral /'fyu:nırıl/ a. cenaze töreni, gömme; cenaze alayı
funfair /'fanfeı/ a, İİ. eğlence parkı, lunapark
fungus /'fangıs/ a, bitk. mantar
funnel /'fanıl/ a. huni; tek. baca
funny /'fani/ s. gülünç; acayip; garip
fur /fö:/ a. kürk, post
furious /'fyuırıs/ s. öfkeli; azgın
furlong /'fö:long/ a. 201 metre
furnace /'fö:nis/ a. ocak, fırın
furnish /'fö:niş/ e. döşemek, donatmak; tedarik etmek
furniture /fö:niçı/ a. mobilya
furrier /'farıı/ a. kürkçü
furrow /'farou/ a. (toprakta) saban izi
furry /'fö:ri/ s. kürklü; kürk gibi
further /'fö:dı/ be. daha ileri; daha fazla; ayrıca ☆ s. daha çok; başka bir; daha uzaktaki ☆ e. ilerlemesine yardım etmek furthermore bundan başka, ayrıca, üstelik furthermost en uzak, en uzağa
furthest /'fö:dist/ be, s. en uzak
furtive /'fö:tiv/ s. gizli, kaçamak
fury /'fyuıri/ a. korkunç öfke, kızgınlık
fuse /fyu:z/ a, elek. sigorta; ask. tapa ☆ e. (metal) eritmek, eriterek birleştirmek
fuselage /'fyu:zıla:j/ a. uçak gövdesi
fusion /'fyu:jın/ a. birleşme, birleştirme
fuss /fas/ a. gürültü patırtı, yaygara, velvele ☆ e. gereksiz yere telaşlanmak
fussy huysuz, yaygaracı; titiz, mızmız, kılı kırk yaran
futile /'fyu:tayl/ s. boş, boşuna, beyhude
future /'fyu:çı/ a. gelecek in future bundan sonra, artık
fuzzy /'fazi/ s. (saç) kıvırcık, kabarık; (kumaş, vb.) tüylü; bulanık, belirsiz

G

gab /geb/ a, kon. gevezelik
gabardine /'gebıdi:n/ a. gabardin
gabble /'gebıl/ e. çabuk çabuk ve anlaşılmaz biçimde konuşmak
gadget /'gecit/ a, kon. becerikli alet, dalga, zımbırtı
gag /geg/ a. ağız tıkacı; kon. şaka ☆ e. ağzını tıkamak; susturmak
gaggle /'gegıl/ a. kaz sürüsü
gaiety /'geyiti/ a. neşe; şenlik, eğlence
gaily /'geyli/ be. neşeli bir şekilde, neşeyle
gain /geyn/ a. kazanç, kâr; çıkar, yarar; ilerleme, artma ☆ e. kazanmak, elde etmek, edinmek
gait /geyt/ a. yürüyüş, gidiş, yürüyüş biçimi
gala /'ga:lı/ a. gala, şenlik
galaxy /'gelıksi/ a. galaksi the Galaxy Samanyolu
gale /geyl/ a. sert rüzgâr, bora
gall /go:l/ a. safra, öd; kin, nefret; küstahlık; sürtünme sonucu oluşan yara
gallant /'gelınt/ s. yürekli, yiğit, cesur; güzel, görkemli ☆ s. (erkek) kibar, şık gallantry kadınlara karşı incelik, kibarlık; yüreklilik, yiğitlik, cesaret, kahramanlık
galleon /'gelıın/ a. kalyon
gallery /'gelıri/ a. galeri
galley /'geli/ a. kadırga; gemi mutfağı
gallon /'gelın/ a. galon (İİ. 54 lt; Aİ. 78 lt.)
gallop /'gelıp/ a. dörtnal ☆ e. dörtnala gitmek
gallows /'gelouz/ a. darağacı
Gallup poll /'gelıp poul/ a. kamuoyu araştırması
galore /gı'lo:/ be, s. pek çok, bol bol

galvanize /'gelvınayz/ e. galvanize-
mek; canlandırmak
galvanometer /gelvı'nomıtı/ a. galvano-
metre, küçük akımölçer
gambit /'gembit/ a. (satranç) gambit;
hesaplı hareket
gamble /'gembıl/ a. rizikolu iş, kumar
☆ e. kumar oynamak; (**away**) kumarda kaybetmek **gambler** kumarbaz
game /geym/ a. oyun; av; hile; ☆ s. yiğit, gözü pek **game-keeper** av bekçisi
game-licence avlanma ruhsatı
gamma /'gemı/ a. gama **gamma rays**
gama ışınları
gammon /'gemın/ a. tütsülenmiş jambon
gamut /'gemıt/ a, müz. nota dizisi,
gam; bir şeyin tamamı
gander /'gendı/ a. erkek kaz
gang /geng/ a. arkadaş grubu, ekip; çete
gangplank /'gengplenk/ a. iskele tahtası
gangrene /'gengri:n/ a, hek. kangren
gangster /'gengstı/ a. gangster
gangway /'gengwey/ a. dar yol, geçit;
borda iskelesi
gantry /'gentri/ a. (demiryolu) sinyal
köprüsü
gaol /ceyl/ a, İİ. cezaevi, hapishane
gap /gep/ a. boşluk, aralık, yarık; (görüş) ayrılık
gape /geyp/ e. (ağzı açık) alık alık bakmak; açılmak, yarılmak
garage /'gera:j, 'geric/ a. garaj; benzin
istasyonu
garbage /'ga:bic/ a. süprüntü, çöp **garbage can** Aİ. çöp tenekesi
garbled /'ga:bıld/ s. karmaşık, karışık,
yanlış
garden /'ga:dın/ a. bahçe **gardener**
bahçıvan
gargle /'ga:gıl/ e. gargara yapmak ☆
a. gargara
garish /'geıriş/ s. gösterişli, parlak, cafcaflı
garland /'ga:lınd/ a. çelenk
garlic /'ga:lik/ a. sarmısak
garment /'ga:mınt/ a. giyim eşyası, giysi

garnet /'ga:nit/ a. lal taşı
garnish /'ga:niş/ a. süs, garnitür ☆ e.
(yemek) süslemek
garret /'gerit/ a. tavan arası
garrison /'gerisın/ a, ask. garnizon
garter /'ga:tı/ a. jartiyer
gas /ges/ a. (hava) gaz; sıvı gaz; Aİ,
kon. benzin e. gazla zehirlemek; kon.
uzun süre konuşmak **gas mask** gaz
maskesi **gas station** Aİ. benzin istasyonu **step on the gas** gaza basmak
gaseous /'gesiıs/ s. gaz gibi, gazlı
gash /geş/ a. derin yara ☆ e. derin yara açmak
gasket /'geskit/ a. conta
gasoline /'gesıli:n/ a, Aİ, kon. benzin
gasp /ga:sp/ e. güçlükle solumak, soluğu kesilmek; nefes nefeseyken söylemek ☆ a. soluk soluğa konuşma
gassy /'gesi/ s. gazlı, gaz dolu
gastritis /ge'straytis/ a, hek. gastrit, mide yangısı
gastronomy /ge'stronımi/ a. iyi yemek
yeme ve pişirme sanatı, gastronomi
gasworks /'geswö:ks/ a. havagazı fabrikası
gate /geyt/ a. kapı; giriş yeri **gateway** giriş yeri, kapı
gather /'gedı/ e. (**round**) toplanmak;
bir araya gelmek; toplamak, koparmak; (bilgi, vb.) kazanmak; sonuç çıkarmak, anlamak **gathering** toplantı
gauche /gouş/ s. patavatsız, beceriksiz
gaudy /'go:di/ s. gösterişli, çok parlak
gauge /geyc/ a. ölçü, ayar; ölçü aygıtı
☆ e. ölçmek; ölçüp biçmek
gaunt /go:nt/ s. sıska, bir deri bir kemik
gauntlet /'go:ntlit/ a. uzun eldiven
gauze /go:z/ a. tül
gawk /go:k/ e. aval aval bakmak
gay /gey/ s. şen, neşeli; parlak, canlı;
kon. eşcinsel
gaze /geyz/ e. gözünü dikerek bakmak
☆ a. sürekli bakış
gazelle /gı'zel/ a, hayb. ceylan, gazel
gazette /gı'zet/ a. resmi gazete
gear /giı/ a. vites; dişli; tertibat, donatı;
çark **out of gear** boşta **gear lever/-
stick/shift** vites kolu **gearbox** vites ku-

tusu

geisha /'geyşı/ a. geyşa

gel /cel/ e, bkz. jell

gelatine /'celıtin/ a. jelatin

gem /cem/ a. değerli taş, mücevher

Gemini /'cemini, 'ceminay/ a. İkizler burcu

gendarme /'jonda:m/ a. jandarma

gender /'cendı/ a, dilb. cins

genealogy /ci:ni'elıci/ a. soy, soy kütüğü, şecere

general /'cenırıl/ s. genel; yaygın, genel; baş, şef **General Staff** Genelkurmay **general strike** genel grev

general /'cenırıl/ a. general **brigadier general** tuğgeneral **full general** orgeneral **lieutenant general** korgeneral **major general** tümgeneral

generalize /'cenırılayz/ e. genelleştirmek; genelleme yapmak, belirsizleştirmek **generalization** genelleştirme; genelleme **generally** çoğunlukla, genellikle; genelde

generate /'cenıreyt/ e. üretmek

generation /cenı'reyşın/ a. nesil, kuşak; (elektrik, vb.) üretme, üretim

generator /'cenıreytı/ a. üreteç, jeneratör

generic /ci'nerik/ s. cinsle ilgili; genel

generosity /cenı'rosıti/ a. cömertlik

generous /'cenırıs/ s. eli açık, cömert

genesis /'cenisis/ a. başlangıç, başlama noktası

genetic /ci'netik/ s. kalıtsal, kalıtımsal **genetics** genetik, kalıtımbilim

genial /'ci:niıl/ s. hoş, tatlı, cana yakın

genital /'cinitıl/ s. üreme organlarıyla ilgili **genitals** cinsel organlar, üreme organları

genitive /'cenitiv/ a, dilb. -in hali, tamlayan durumu

genius /'ci:niıs/ a. üstün yetenek, deha; dahi

genocide /'cenısayd/ a. soykırım

gentle /'centıl/ s. ince, kibar, nazik; tatlı, yumuşak, hafif, yavaş **gentleman** centilmen; bey, beyefendi **gently** yavaşça; tatlılıkla

gents /cents/ a, İİ, kon. erkekler tuvaleti

genuine /'cenyuin/ s. hakiki, gerçek

geography /ci'ogrıfi/ a. coğrafya **geographer** coğrafyacı **geographical** /ci'ıgrıfikıl/ coğrafi

geology /ci'olıci/ a. yerbilim, jeoloji

geometry /ci'omitri/ a. geometri **geometric** geometrik

geophysics /ci:ou'fiziks/ a. jeofizik, yer fiziği

geopolitics /ci:ou'politiks/ a. jeopolitik

geranium /cı'reyniım/ a, bitk. sardunya

geriatrics /ceri'etriks/ a. yaşlılık hekimliği

germ /cö:m/ a. mikrop; başlangıç

germinate /'cö:mineyt/ e. (tohum) filizlenmek, çimlenmek

gerund /'cerınd/ a, dilb. ulaç, isimfiil

gestation /ce'steyşın/ a. gebelik

gesture /'cesçı/ a. jest, el kol hareketi ☆ e. el kol hareketi yapmak

get /get/ e. **got** /got/ almak, elde etmek; gidip getirmek; gidip almak; olmak, hale gelmek; varmak, ulaşmak; uğraşmak, ilgilenmek ettirmek, yaptırmak; hazırlamak; götürmek; vurmak; anlamak; (hastalık, soğuk) kapmak, tutulmak; kon. kızdırmak, canını sıkmak **get sth done** yaptırmak, ettirmek, başına gelmek **have got** sahip olmak **get about/around** iyileşmek; kon. seyahat etmek, gezmek; (haber, vb.) yayılmak **get across** anlaşılmak, kabul edilmek, benimsenmek **get ahead** ilerlemek, önüne geçmek **get along** gitmek, ayrılmak; geçinmek, iyi ilişkiler içinde olmak; sürdürmek; ilerlemek **get around/round to** vakit bulmak, -e zaman ayırmak **get at** ulaşmak, erişmek; demek istemek **get away** kaçmak **getaway** kon. kaçış, firar **get away with** kötü bir şey yapmak ve cezasından kurtulmak **get back** dönmek, geri gelmek, geri dönmek **get back at sb** kon. -den intikam almak, öc almak **get by** yaşamını sürdürmek; şöyle böyle olmak **get down** yazmak, kaydetmek; güçlükle yutmak; rahatsız etmek, üzmek **get down to** dört elle sarılmak **get in** içeri girmek; varmak; (taşıta) binmek; seçilmek **get into** binmek; öğrenmek, alışmak get (sb) into durumuna koymak; (derde, vb.) sokmak get off (bir araçtan, vb.) inmek; hareket etmek, yola çıkmak; (işten) paydos etmek; cezadan kurtulmak get on anlaşmak, geçinmek; (bir taşıta) binmek; ilerlemek, gitmek get out çıkmak, gitmek; sıvışmak, tüymek, kaçırmak; (sır, vb.) sızmak, yayılma get out of sorumluluktan kaçmak get over (hastalık) iyileşmek, kurtulmak; anlaşılmak; anlaşılmasını sağlamak get round ikna etmek; yararlanmak get through temasa geçmek; bitirmek; tüketmek; anlaşılmasını sağlamak gettogether toplantı, buluşma get together toplanmak, bir araya gelmek get up yataktan kalkmak get up to varmak, yetişmek; (özellikle kötü birşey) yapmak, yapmak üzere olmak

geyser /'gi:zı/ a. gayzer, kaynaç; İİ. şofben

ghastly /'ga:stli/ s. sarı benizli, sapsarı, soluk; korkunç; kon. berbat

gherkin /'gö:kin/ a. turşuluk hıyar

ghetto /'getou/ a. azınlıkların ve yoksulların oturdukları mahalle, geto

ghost /goust/ a. hayalet, hortlak ghostly hayalet gibi

giant /'cayınt/ a. dev

gibbet /'cibit/ a. darağacı

giblets /'ciblits/ a. tavuk, kuş, vb.'nin yürek, ciğer, katı gibi iç organları

giddy /'gidi/ s. başı dönen; hoppa, uçarı

gift /gift/ a. armağan, hediye; Allah vergisi, yetenek gifted yetenekli

gigantic /cay'gentik/ s. devasa, kocaman

giggle /'gigıl/ kıkır kıkır gülmek, kıkırdamak giggle kıkırdama

gild /gild/ yaldızlamak

gill /cil/ a. solungaç

gilt /gilt/ a. yaldız

gin /cin/ a. (içki) cin

ginger /'cıncı/ a, bitk. zencefil ☆ s. kızıl renk, kızıl ginger ale zencefilli gazoz

gipsy /'cipsi/ a. Çingene

giraffe /ci'ra:f/ a, hayb. zürafa

girder /'gö:dı/ a. kiriş, direk

girdle /'gö:dıl/ a. kuşak, kemer, korse

girl /gö:l/ a. kız; kon. kadın; sevgili, kız arkadaş girlfriend sevgili, kız arkadaş girlhood kızlık girlish kız gibi

girth /gö:t/ a. bel ölçüsü, çevre ölçüsü; kolan, çevre

gist /cist/ a. öz, ana fikir, ana noktalar

give /giv/ e. gave /geyv/, given /'givın/ vermek; armağan etmek; ödemek; (hastalık) geçirmek, bulaştırmak; indirmek, atmak giveandtake karşılıklı özveri give away vermek, armağan etmek; ele vermek give back geri vermek give in teslim olmak, boyun eğmek; teslim etmek give off (koku, vb.) çıkarmak, yaymak give out dağıtmak; sona ermek give up vazgeçmek, bırakmak; umudunu kesmek

gizzard /'gizıd/ a. (kuşlarda) katı, taşlık

glacial /'gleyşıl/ s. buz ya da buzulla ilgili

glacier /'glesiı/ a. buzul

glad /gled/ s. mutlu, memnun, hoşnut; memnun edici, sevinçli gladly gönülden, zevkle, istekle, seve seve

gladden /'gledın/ a. sevindirmek, mutlu etmek

glade /gleyd/ e. ormanda ağaçsız alan

gladiator /'gledieytı/ a. gladyatör

glamour /'glemı/ a. çekicilik, alım; büyü, sihir glamorous çekici, göz alıcı

glance /gla:ns/ e. göz atmak, bakmak ☆ a. kısaca bakış; bir bakışta, hemen

gland /glend/ a, anat. bez

glare /gleı/ e. parıldamak; göze batmak; ters ters bakmak ☆ a. parıltı; ters bakış ☆ glaring göz kamaştırıcı

glass /gla:s/ a. cam; cam eşya; bardak glasses gözlük glassware züccaciye, cam eşya glassy cam gibi; (bakış) cansız, donuk

glaze /gleyz/ e. sırlamak; cam takmak; (bakış) anlamsızlaşmak ☆ a. sır, perdah, cila

glazier /'gleyzıı/ a. camcı

gleam /gli:m/ a. ışık, parıltı, pırıltı ☆ e. parıldamak, parlamak

glee /gli:/ a. sevinç, neşe

glib /glib/ s. güzel ve rahat konuşan
glide /glayd/ e. kaymak, akmak, süzülmek; planörle uçmak **glider** planör
glimmer /'glimı/ e. zayıf bir şekilde parlamak ☆ a. donuk ışık; zerre
glimpse /glimps/ e. bir an için görmek, gözüne ilişmek ☆ a. kısa bakış, gözüne ilişme
glint /glint/ e. parıldamak, parlamak ☆ a. parıltı
glisten /'glisın/ e. parıldamak, parlamak
glitter /'glitı/ e. parlamak, parıldamak ☆ a. parıltı **glittering** görkemli, parlak
globe /gloub/ a. top, küre; dünya; gezegen **global** geniş çaplı, ayrıntılı; dünya çapında, evrensel
gloom /glu:m/ a. karanlık; üzüntü, hüzün **gloomy** karanlık; üzüntülü, mahzun, karanlık
glorify /'glo:rifay/ e. övmek; yüceltmek; güzel göstermek
glorious /'glo:rııs/ s. şanlı, şerefli; görkemli, parlak
glory /'glo:ri/ a. şan, ün, şeref; görkem
gloss /glos/ a. parlaklık ☆ a. açıklama, yorum **glossy** parlak ve düz
glossary /'glosıri/ a. ek sözlük
glove /glav/ a. eldiven
glow /glou/ e. parıldamak; içini ateş basmak; kızarmak ☆ a. kızıl ışık, kızıllık; sıcaklık, hararet; çaba, gayret
glower /'glauı/ e. ters ters bakmak
glowworm /'glouwö:m/ a. ateşböceği
glucose /'glu:kous/ a. glikoz
glue /glu:/ a. tutkal, zamk ☆ e. yapıştırmak
glum /glam/ s. asık suratlı, üzgün
glut /glat/ a. bolluk, furya
glutton /'glatın/ a. obur **gluttonous** obur, açgözlü
glycerin(e) /'glisırin/ a. gliserin
gnash /neş/ e. (diş) gıcırdatmak
gnat /net/ a, hayb. sivrisinek, tatarcık
gnaw /no:/ e. kemirmek
go /gou/ e. **went** /went/, **gone** /gan/ gitmek; hareket etmek, kalkmak; ayrılmak; işlemek, çalışmak; sığmak; kırılmak, kopmak; ilerlemek, gelişmek;

götürmek; devam etmek; uymak ☆ a. sınama, deneme; sefer **be going to** -ecek, -acak **go about** (birisiyle) birlikte olmak; dolaşmak **go after** peşinden koşmak, izlemek **go against** -e karşı gelmek **go ahead** ilerlemek, gelişmek; başlamak **go along** aynı fikirde olmak **go by** geçmek, geçip gitmek; -e göre davranmak **go down** inmek; batmak **go for** aramak, çağırmak; saldırmak; hoşlanmak, beğenmek **go in for** katılmak, yer almak; alışkanlık haline getirmek **go into** (yer, iş, vb.'e) girmek; girişmek, ilgilenmek **go off** kesilmek; sönmek; bozulmak, çürümek; (bomba) patlamak **go on** devam etmek; vakit geçirmek **go out** dışarı çıkmak; (ışık, vb.) sönmek; modası geçmek **go over** başarı kazanmak; tutmak, gözden geçirmek, incelemek **go through** gözden geçirmek, incelemek; araştırmak; yoklamak; kabul edilmek; harcamak, tüketmek; katlanmak, çekmek **go over** başarı kazanmak, tutmak; gözden geçirmek, incelemek **go with** uymak, gitmek; birbirini tamamlamak **go without** -sız idare etmek
goad /goud/e. kışkırtmak, dürtmek
goal /goul/ a. amaç, hedef, gaye; sp. kale; gol **goalkeeper** kaleci
goat /gout/ a. keçi, teke
gobble /'gobıl/ e. çabuk çabuk yemek
goblet /'goblit/ a. kadeh
goblin /'goblin/ a. gulyabani, cin
god /god/ a. mabut, put, tapı
God /god/ a. Tanrı, Allah **for God's sake** Allah aşkına; **God forbid/grant that** Allah göstermesin, Allah korusun **God (alone) knows** kon. Allah bilir **God willing** inşallah, Allah isterse **Oh God/My God/Good God** Aman Tanrım **Thank God** Allah'a şükür **godchild** vaftiz çocuğu **goddess** tanrıça **godfather** vaftiz babası
goggle /'gogıl/ e. hayretle bakmak
goggles /'gogılz/ a. koruyucu gözlük
going /'gouing/ a. gidiş, ayrılış, hareket; yol durumu; gidiş hızı ☆ s. şu anki; mevcut, yaşayan; işleyen, çalı-

şan **goingson** olup bitenler, gidişat

gokart /'gouka:t/ a. küçük yarış arabası, gokart

gold /gould/ a. altın; altın rengi; **gold
dust** altın tozu **goldfinch** saka kuşu
goldmine altın madeni **gold smith** kuyumcu

golden /'gouldın/ s. altından, altın; altın rengi **golden handshake** emeklilik
ikramiyesi **golden jubilee** ellinci yıldönümü

golf /golf/ a, sp. golf **golf course/links**
golf sahası **golf club** golf kulübü; golf
sopası

gondola /'gondılı/ a. gondol

gone /gon/ bkz. **go**

gong /gong/ a. gong

good /gud/ s. iyi, güzel; uygun, yerinde; yararlı; yetenekli; sağlıklı, sağlam;
güvenilir, sağlam ☆ a. iyilik **be good
at** -de başarılı olmak **in good time** erken, erkenden **for good** temelli, ebediyen **no good** faydasız, boşuna **good
afternoon** tünaydın **goodbye** allahaısmarladık, hoşça kal **good evening** iyi
akşamlar **goodfornothing** hiçbir işe
yaramaz **goodhumoured** neşeli, şen,
güleryüzlü **goodlooking** yakışıklı **good
morning** günaydın **goodnatured** iyi
huylu **goodness** iyilik **for goodness'
sake** Allah aşkına **My goodness** Tanrım!, Yarabbim! **good night** iyi geceler **goodwill** iyi niyet

goods /gudz/ a. eşya, mal; yük

goofy /'gu:fi/ s. aptal, çatlak, kaçık

goose /gu:s/ a, hayb. kaz

gooseberry /'guzbıri/ a. bektaşiüzümü

gore /go:/ e. boynuzla yaralamak

gorge /go:c/ a, coğ. geçit, boğaz

gorgeous /'go:cıs/ s. harika, çok güzel,
hoş

gorilla /gı'rilı/ a, hayb. goril

gorse /go:s/ a, bitk. karaçalı

gory /'go:ri/ s. kanlı

gosh /goş/ ünl. Allah Allah, vay canına,
hayret

gosling /'gozling/ a, hayb. kaz palazı

goslow /gou'slou/ a, İİ. işi yavaşlatma
eylemi

gospel /'gospıl/ a, kon. hakikat; ilke **the**

Gospel İncil

gossamer /'gosımı/ a. örümcek ağı;
çok ince şey

gossip /'gosip/ a. dedikodu; dedikoducu ☆ e. dedikodu yapmak

got /got/ bkz. **get**

Gothic /'gotik/ s, a. Gotik

gotta /'gotı/ e, kon. -meli, -malı

gotten /'gotın/ bkz. **get**

gouge /gauc/ a. heykeltıraş kalemi;
ucu kıvrık bıçak

goulash /'gu:leş/ a. tas kebabı

gourd /guıd/ a, bitk. sukabağı

gourmet /'guımey/ a. yemek ve içkinin
iyisinden anlayan kimse

gout /gaut/ a, hek. gut, damla sayrılığı

govern /'gavın/ e. yönetmek, idare etmek; etkilemek

governess /'gavınis/ a. mürebbiye

government /'gavımınt/ a. yönetim; hükümet

governor /'gavını/ a. vali; yönetici; şef,
amir; kon. patron, işveren; Aİ. eyalet
başkanı

gown /gaun/ a. uzun kadın giysisi, gece giysisi; cüppe

grab /greb/ e. kapmak ☆ a. kapma

grace /greys/ a. zarafet, güzellik; lütuf;
şükran duası **graceful** zarif, hoş

gracious /'greyşıs/ s. hoş, nazik; (Tanrı) bağışlayıcı, merhametli

gradation /grı'deyşın/ a. derece derece
değişme

grade /greyd/ a. rütbe; derece; cins; Aİ.
eğim, meyil; Aİ. sınıf; not ☆ e. ayırmak, sınıflandırmak

gradient /'greydıınt/ a. eğim, eğiklik,
meyil

gradual /'grecuıl/ s. derece derece
olan, aşamalı **gradually** azar azar

graduate /'grecuit/ a. üniversite mezunu

graduate /'grecueyt/ e. (üniversiteden)
mezun olmak

graduation /grecu'eyşın/ a. mezuniyet;
diploma töreni

graffiti /gre'fi:ti/ a. duvar yazıları

graft /gra:ft/ a, bitk. aşı; hek. (doku) yama ☆ e. (ağaç) aşılamak; hek. doku
yerleştirmek

grain /greyn/ *a.* tahıl, hububat; tane

gram /grem/ *a.* gram

grammar /'gremı/ *a.* dilbilgisi, grammer **grammar school** *ii.* (üniversiteye hazırlayan) orta dereceli okul **grammatical** dilbilgisel

gramme /'grem/ *a, bkz.* **gram**

gramophone /'gremıfoun/ *a.* gramofon

gran /gren/ *a, ii, kon.* büyükanne, nine

granary /'grenıri/ *a.* tahıl ambarı

grand /grend/ *s.* ulu, yüce, görkemli; gösterişli; en önemli, ana; tam; bütün; büyük, yüce **grand piano** kuyruklu piyano

grandad, granddad /grended/ *a, kon.* büyükbaba, dede

grandchild /'grençayld/ *a.* torun

granddaughter /'grendo:tı/ *a.* kız torun

grandeur /'grencı/ *a.* büyüklük, görkem

grandfather /'grenfa:dı/ *a.* büyükbaba, dede

grandiose /'grendious/ *s.* gösterişli, tantanalı, görkemli

grandma /'grenma:/ *a, kon.* büyükanne, nine

grandmother /'grenmadı/ *a.* büyükanne, nine

grandpa /'grenpa:/ *a, kon.* büyükbaba, dede

grandparent /'grenpeırınt/ *a.* büyükbaba ya da büyükanne

grandson /'grensan/ *a.* erkek torun

grandstand /'grendstend/ *a.* tribün

granite /'grenit/ *a.* granit

granny /'greni/ *a, kon.* büyükanne, nine

grant /gra:nt/ *e.* vermek, bahşetmek; onaylamak; varsaymak; kabul etmek; ☆ *a.* bağış; burs; ödenek, tahsisat **take sth/sb for granted** itirazsız kabul etmek

granular /'grenyulı/ *s.* taneli

granulate /'grenyuleyt/ *e.* tanelemek **granulated sugar** tozşeker

granule /'grenyu:l/ *a.* tanecik

grape /greyp/ *a, bitk.* üzüm

grapefruit /'greypfru:t/ *a.* greyfurt, altıntop

grapevine /'greypvayn/ *a, bitk.* asma

graph /gra:f/ *a.* çizge, grafik

graphic /'grefik/ *s.* çizgesel, grafik; (anlatımı, vb.) canlı, açık, tam

grapple /'grepıl/ *e.* (with) boğuşmak

grasp /gra:sp/ *e.* yakalamak, kavramak, tutmak; anlamak, kavramak ☆ *a.* sıkı sıkı tutma, kapma; anlama, kavrama

grass /gra:s/ *a.* ot, çimen; çayır, otlak **grasshopper** çekirge **grassland** otlak **grassy** otlu, çimenli

grate /greyt/ *a.* ocak ızgarası ☆ *e.* rendelemek; gıcırdatmak; gıcırdamak

grateful /'greytfıl/ *s.* minnettar, müteşekkir

grater /'greytı/ *a.* rende

gratify /'gretifay/ *e.* sevindirmek, mutlu etmek

grating /'greyting/ *a.* ızgara, demir parmaklık

gratis /'gretis, 'gra:tis/ *s, be.* bedava, bedavadan, karşılıksız

gratitude /'gretityu:d/ *a.* minnettarlık

gratuitous /grı'tyu:itıs/ *s.* karşılıksız, bedava, karşılık beklemeden; nedensiz

gratuity /grı'tyu:ıti/ *a.* bahşiş

grave /greyv/ *a.* mezar ☆ *s.* ciddi; ağır **gravestone** mezar taşı **graveyard** mezarlık

gravel /'grevıl/ *a.* çakıl

gravitation /grevi'teyşın/ *a.* yerçekimi

gravity /'greviti/ *a.* yerçekimi; ciddiyet, ağırlık, önem

gravy /'greyvi/ *a.* et suyu; salça, sos

gray /grey/ *s, a, Ai, bkz.* **grey**

graze /greyz/ *e.* otlamak; otlatmak; sıyırmak, sıyırıp geçmek ☆ *a.* sıyrık

grease /gri:s/ *a.* (hayvansal) yağ; gres, katıyağ ☆ *e.* yağlamak **greasy** yağlı

great /greyt/ *s.* büyük; kocaman; yüce, ulvi; uzun; sürekli; önemli; yetenekli; *kon.* mükemmel, çok iyi **a great deal** çok **great-grandfather** babasının dedesi **great-grandson** oğlunun/kızının erkek torunu **greatly** çokça, pek **greatness** büyüklük

greed /gri:d/ *a.* açgözlülük **greedy** açgözlü

green /gri:n/ *s.* yeşil; (meyve) ham, olmamış; *kon.* toy; benzi sararmış ☆

a. yeşil renk; yeşil; çayır; ç. yeşil yapraklı sebzeler, yeşillik **green belt** yeşil alan, yeşil kuşak **greenish** yeşilimsi

greengage /'gri:ngeyc/ *a, bitk.* bardakeriği

greengrocer /'gri:ngrousı/ *a.* manav

greenhouse /'gri:nhaus/ *a.* limonluk, ser

greet /gri:t/ *e.* selamlamak, selam vermek; karşılamak **greeting** selam; iyi dilek, tebrik

gregarious /gri'geiriıs/ *s.* sokulgan; sürü halinde yaşayan

grenade /gri'neyd/ *a.* el bombası

grey /grey/ *s.* gri, külrengi; kır saçlı ☆ *a.* külrengi

greyhound /'greyhaund/ *a.* tazı

grid /grid/ *a.* ızgara, parmaklık

grief /gri:f/ *s.* acı, keder, üzüntü

grievance /'gri:vıns/ *a.* yakınma, şikâyet, dert

grieve /gri:v/ *e.* üzülmek, üzmek

grievous /'gri:vıs/ *s.* acı, üzücü

grill /gril/ *a.* ızgara; ızgara et ☆ *e.* ızgarada pişirmek

grim /grim/ *s.* sert, acımasız; *kon.* zevksiz, neşesiz

grimace /gri'meys/ *e.* yüzünü ekşitmek, yüzünü buruşturmak

grime /graym/ *a.* kir tabakası, kir

grin /grin/ *a.* sırıtma, sırıtış ☆ *e.* sırıtmak

grind /graynd/ *e.* **ground** /graund/ öğütmek; gıcırdatmak ☆ *a.* öğütme; sıkıcı zor iş, angarya **grinder** öğütücü **grindstone** bileğitaşı

grip /grip/ *e.* sımsıkı tutmak, kavramak; ilgisini çekmek, etkilemek ☆ *a.* sıkıca tutma, kavrama; sap

gripe /grayp/ *e.* (**at/about**) *kon.* yakınmak, sızlanmak

gripping /'griping/ *s.* dikkat çekici, sürükleyici

grisly /'grizli/ *s.* korkunç, ürkütücü

gristle /'grisıl/ *a, anat.* kıkırdak

grit /grit/ *a.* çakıl; *kon.* azim, kararlılık

groan /groun/ *e.* inlemek ☆ *a.* inilti

grocer /'grousı/ *a.* bakkal **groceries** bakkaliye

groggy /'grogi/ *s, kon.* dizleri tutmayan, halsiz, dermansız, bitkin

groin /groyn/ *a, anat.* kasık

groom /gru:m/ *a.* damat; seyis ☆ *e.* (at) tımar etmek; bir iş için hazırlamak, eğitmek

groove /gru:v/ *a.* yiv, oluk ☆ *a.* yiv açmak

grope /group/ *e.* el yordamıyla aramak, yoklamak

gross /grous/ *s.* şişko, iriyarı; hantal; brüt; kaba ☆ *a.* on iki düzine

grotesque /grou'tesk/ *s.* acayip, garip

grotto /'grotou/ *a.* mağara

grouch /grauç/ *a, kon.* yakınma; dırdır ☆ *e.* yakınmak, şikâyet etmek

ground /graund/ *a.* yer, zemin; toprak; alan, saha; zemin; temel, esas ☆ *e.* (gemi) karaya oturmak; (uçak) kalkışa izin vermemek **groundless** yersiz, nedensiz **groundnut** yerfıstığı

ground /graund/ *bkz.* **grind**

group /gru:p/ *a.* topluluk, grup, küme

grove /grouv/ *a.* koru, ağaçlık

grovel /'grovıl/ *e, hkr.* yerde sürünmek ayaklarına kapanmak

grow /grou/ *e.* **grew** /gru:/, **grown** /groun/ büyümek, gelişmek; olmak; yetiştirmek, üretmek; (sakal) bırakmak uzatmak **grower** yetiştirici

growl /graul/ *a.* hırıltı, hırıldama

grown /graun/ *bkz.* **grow**; **grown-up** yetişkin, olgun

growth /grout/ *a.* büyüme, gelişme; artış

grub /grab/ *e.* toprağı kazmak, eşelemek

grub /grab/ *a.* larva ☆ *e.* kazmak, eşelemek

grubby /'grabi/ *s.* pis, kirli

grudge /grac/ *e.* esirgemek, vermek is tememek, çok görmek; ☆ *a.* kin, ga raz, haset **grudger** kıskanç **grudg ingly** istemeye istemeye

gruelling /gru:iling/ *s.* çok yorucu

gruesome /'gru:sım/ *s.* korkunç, ür künç, tüyler ürpertici

gruff /graf/ *s.* sert, hırçın, kaba

grumble /'grambıl/ *e.* yakınmak, söy lenmek, homurdanmak

grumpy /'grampi/ *s.* huysuz, aksi

grunt /grant/ e. (hayvan) hırıldamak; (insan) homurdanmak ☆ a. hırıltı, homurtu

guarantee /gerın'ti:/ a. güvence, garanti; kefil ☆ e. güvence vermek, garanti etmek, kefil olmak

guarantor /gerın'to:/ a. kefil, garantör

guard /ga:d/ a. koruma; nöbetçi, bekçi ☆ a. nöbet ☆ e. korumak; beklemek; önlemler almak, korunmak on guard nöbette keep guard nöbet beklemek

guarded /'ga:did/ s. (söz) dikkatli

guardian /'ga:dıın/ a. gardiyan, koruyucu; huk. veli, vasi

guerilla, guerrilla /gı'rilı/ a. gerilla

guess /ges/ e. tahmin etmek; sanmak ☆ a. tahmin guesswork tahmin, tahmin işi

guest /gest/ a. misafir; otel müşterisi

guidance /'gaydıns/ a. rehberlik, kılavuzluk; öğüt; yol gösterme

guide /gayd/ a. kılavuz, rehber ☆ e. kılavuzluk etmek, yol göstermek, rehberlik etmek guidebook turist kılavuzu guided missile güdümlü mermi

guild /gild/ a. dernek, lonca

guile /gayl/ a. hile, hilekârlık, kurnazlık

guillotine /'gilıti:n/ a. giyotin; kâğıt kesme makinesi ☆ e. giyotinle başını uçurmak

guilt /gilt/ a. suçluluk guilty suçlu

guinea pig /'gini pig/ a, hayb. kobay; denek

guise /gayz/ a. (aldatıcı) dış görünüş, kılık

guitar /gi'ta:/ a. gitar

gulf /galf/ a. körfez; (görüş) ayrılık

gull /gal/ a, hayb. martı; enayi, saf

gullet /'galit/ a, kon. boğaz, gırtlak

gulp /galp/ e. yutuvermek, aceleyle yutmak; yutkunmak

gum /gam/ a. dişeti; zamk; sakız; çiklet ☆ e. zamkla yapıştırmak

gun /gan/ a. top; tüfek; tabanca gunfire silah sesi; atış gunman silahlı haydut gunner ask. topçu gunpowder barut gun running silah kaçakçılığı

gurgle /'gö:gıl/ a. lıkırtı ☆ e. lıkırdamak

gush /gaş/ e. fışkırmak ☆ a. fışkırma

gust /gast/ a. bora

gusto /'gastou/ a. zevk, haz, heves

gut /gat/ a, anat. bağırsak ☆ e. bağırsaklarını çıkarmak

gutter /'gatı/ a. oluk, suyolu

guy /gay/ a, kon. adam, herif

guzzle /'gazıl/ e. hapur hupur yemek, höpür höpür içmek

gym /cim/ a, kon. spor salonu; jimnastik

gymnasium /cim'neyziım/ a. jimnastik salonu; (Almanya'da) lise

gymnast /'cimnest/ a. jimnastikçi

gymnastics /cim'nestiks/ a. jimnastik

gynaecology /gayni'kolıci/ a, hek. jinekoloji

gypsum /'cipsım/ a. alçıtaşı

gypsy /'cipsi/ a. Çingene

H

haberdasher /'hebıdeşı/ a, İİ. tuhafiye haberdashery /'hebıdeşıri/ a. tuhafiye; tuhafiye dükkânı

habit /'hebit/ a. alışkanlık; alışkı be in the habit of alışkanlığında olmak fall/get into the habit of -e alışmak

habitable /'hebitıbıl/ s. oturmaya elverişli, oturulabilir

habitat /'hebitet/ a. bir hayvan ya da bitkinin yetiştiği doğal ortam

habitation /hebi'teyşın/ a. oturma; konut, oturacak yer

habitual /hı'biçuıl/ s. alışılagelmiş, her zamanki

hack /hek/ e. kesmek, yarmak ☆ a. kira beygiri

hackneyed /'heknid/ s. (söz) bayat, beylik, eskimiş

hacksaw /'hekso:/ a. demir testeresi, vargel testere

had /hıd, hed/ e, bkz. have

haddock /'hedık/ a, hayb. mezgit

haggard /'hegıd/ s. (yüz) yorgun, kırışık, bitkin

haggle /'hegıl/ e. pazarlık etmek, çekişmek, tartışmak

hail /heyl/ *a.* dolu ☆ *e.* dolu yağmak **hailstone** dolu tanesi **hailstorm** dolu fırtınası

hair /heı/ *a.* saç; kıl; tüy **hairbrush** saç fırçası **haircut** saç tıraşı; saç kesimi **hairdo** saç biçimi, saç tuvaleti **hairdresser** kuaför **hairdrier** saç kurutma makinesi **hairgrip** saç tokası **hairnet** saç filesi **hairpiece** takma saç, peruka **hairpin** firkete, saç tokası **hairpin bend** keskin viraj **hairy** kıllı

hale /heyl/ *a.* sağlıklı, dinç, zinde

half /ha:f/ *a.* yarı, buçuk; yarım ☆ *s.* yarı, yarısı; yarım ☆ *be.* yarı yarıya **halfback** hafbek **half-brother** üvey erkek kardeş **half-hearted** isteksiz, gönülsüz, gayretsiz **half-mast** yarı gönder **half-sister** üvey kız kardeş **half time** haftaym, ara **halfway** yarı yolda **half-wit** aptal, geri zekâlı

hall /ho:l/ *a.* salon; (toplantı, vb.'nin yapıldığı) resmi bina; koridor, hol, giriş

hallelujah /heli'lu:yı/ *ünl.* Elhamdülillah! Allah'a şükür!

hallmark /'ho:lma:k/ *a.* altın ya da gümüşte ayar damgası ☆ *e.* ayar damgası vurmak

hallo /hı'lou/ *a, bkz.* **hello**

hallow /'helou/ *e.* kutsamak, kutsallaştırmak

Halloween /helou'i:n/ *a.* Azizler Günü'nün arifesi (31 ekim gecesi)

hallucination /hılu:si'neyşın/ *a.* halüsinasyon, sanrı

hallway /'ho:lwey/ *a, Aİ.* koridor, geçit, hol

halo /'heylou/ *a.* ışık halkası, hale, ağıl

halt /ho:lt/ *e.* durmak; durdurmak ☆ *a.* duruş, durma

halter /'ho:ltı/ *a.* yular, dizgin

halting /'ho:lting/ *s.* ara ara konuşan; duraksayan

halve /ha:v/ *e.* yarıya bölmek; yarıya indirmek

ham /hem/ *a.* jambon

hamburger /'hembö:gı/ *a.* hamburger

hamlet /'hemlit/ *a.* küçük köy

hammer /'hemı/ *a.* çekiç ☆ *e.* çekiçle vurmak, çakmak

hammock /'hemık/ *a.* hamak

hamper /'hempı/ *e.* engellemek, zorluk çıkarmak ☆ *a.* kapaklı sepet

hamster /'hemstı/ *a, hayb.* hamster, cırlak sıçan

hand /hend/ *a.* el; akrep, ibre; yardım, taraf, yan; yardımcı, işçi; işe karışma; kontrol; alkış ☆ *e.* (elden ele) vermek, uzatmak **at hand** yakın; yanında, hazır **by hand** elle; elden **change hands** el değiştirmek **hand in hand** el ele, birlikte **Hands off!** Elleme!, Dokunma! **get/keep one's hand in** (işe) alışmak **give sb a free hand** arzusuna bırakmak **have a hand in** -de katkısı bulunmak **on hand** el altında, hazır **on the one/other hand** bir/diğer yanda **hand down** kuşaktan kuşağa geçmek **hand in** teslim etmek, vermek **hand out** dağıtmak **hand over** teslim etmek, vermek **handbag** el çantası **handball** beyzbol **handbook** el kitabı, rehber **handbrake** el freni **handcuffs** kelepçe **handful** avuç dolusu **handshake** el sıkma, tokalaşma **handwriting** el yazısı

handicap /'hendikep/ *a.* engel; engelli koşu ☆ *e.* engellemek, engel olmak

handicraft /'hendikra:ft/ *a.* el becerisi, el sanatı

handiwork /'hendiwö:k/ *a.* el işi, el becerisi

handkerchief /'henkıçif/ *a.* mendil

handle /'hendıl/ *a.* sap, kulp, kol ☆ *e.* el sürmek, ellemek; ele almak; idare etmek

handsome /'hensım/ *s.* yakışıklı; güzel cömert

handy /'hendi/ *s.* kullanışlı, pratik; *kon.* el altında, hazır **handyman** elinden her iş gelen erkek

hang /heng/ *e.* **hung** /hang/ asmak asılmak, asılı durmak; eğmek; sarkmak; sürtmek ☆ *e.* idam etmek, asmak (bu anlamda düzenli bir fiildir) **hang about/around** *e, kon.* aylak aylak dolaşmak **hang back** çekinmek tereddüt etmek **hang on** sıkıca tutmak, beklemek **hang up** telefonu kapamak **hangman** cellat **hangover** ak

şamdan kalmışlık, humar
hangar /'hengı/ *a.* hangar
hanger /'hengı/ *a.* askı, elbise askısı
hang gliding /'heng glayding/ *a.* uçma sporu
hanging /'henging/ *a.* idam, asma
hanker /'henkı/ *e, kon.* (after/for) özlemini çekmek, can atmak
hanky /'henki/ *a, kon.* mendil
haphazard /hep'hezıd/ *s.* gelişigüzel, plansız, programsız
happen /'hepın/ *e.* olmak, vuku bulmak; başına gelmek, olmak; tesadüfen -mek **happening** olay
happy /'hepi/ *s.* mutlu; memnun, sevinçli **happy-go-lucky** kaygısız, tasasız **happily** mutlulukla, neşeyle; bereket versin ki **happiness** mutluluk
harass /'herıs/ *e.* usandırmak, bezdirmek **harassment** usanç
harbour, harbor /'ha:bı/ *a.* liman; sığınak, barınak ☆ *e.* barındırmak, korumak
hard /ha:d/ *s.* sert, katı; güç, zor; şiddetli; (su) kireçli, acı ☆ *be.* sıkıca, kuvvetlice; hızla; gayretle, harıl harıl, çok **hardback** ciltli kitap **hardboard** kalın mukavva **hard-boiled** (yumurta) çok pişmiş, katı **hard cash** nakit para, madeni para **hard currency** sağlam döviz, sağlam para **hard-core** sabit fikirli, inatçı; müstehçen **hardheaded** mantıklı, açıkgöz **hardhearted** katı yürekli **hard luck** şansızlık, kör talih **hardware** madeni eşya, hırdavat; (bilgisayar) donanım
harden /'ha:dın/ *e.* sertleşmek, katılaşmak; sertleştirmek
hardly /'ha:dli/ *be.* hemen hemen, ancak; güçlükle; hemen hiç; az bir olasılıkla
hardy /'ha:di/ *s.* dayanıklı, güçlü
hare /heı/ *a, hayb.* yabani tavşan
harem /'heırım/ *a.* harem
haricot /'herikou/ *a.* fasulye **haricot bean** kuru fasulye
harm /ha:m/ *a.* zarar, ziyan, hasar; kötülük ☆ *e.* zarar vermek, incitmek **harmful** zararlı **harmless** zararsız
harmonica /ha:'monikı/ *a, müz.* armoni-

ka
harmonize /'ha:mınayz/ *e, müz.* armonisini yapmak; (with) uyum sağlamak
harmony /'ha:mını/ *a, müz.* armoni; uyum, ahenk
harness /'ha:nis/ *a.* koşum takımı ☆ *e.* (atı) koşmak; (doğal güçleri) kullanmak, yararlanmak
harp /ha:p/ *a, müz.* harp **harpist** harpçı **harp on (about)** dönüp dolaşıp aynı şeyi anlatmak
harpoon /ha:'pu:n/ *a.* zıpkın ☆ *e.* zıpkınlamak
harrowing /'herouing/ *s.* üzücü, hırpalayıcı, acı veren
harsh /ha:ş/ *s.* sert; (renk) cırtlak; kaba, zalim, haşin
harvest /'ha:vist/ *a.* hasat, ekin toplama; mahsul, ürün ☆ *e.* biçmek, tarladan kaldırmak
has /hız, hez/ *e, bkz.* **have**
hash /heş/ *a.* kıymalı yemek **make a hash of it** yüzüne gözüne bulaştırmak
hashish /'heşi:ş/ *a.* haşhaş, esrar
haste /heyst/ *a.* acele, telaş
hasten /'heysın/ *e.* acele etmek; acele ettirmek; hemen söylemek
hasty /'heysti/ *s.* acele, aceleyle/telaşla yapılan **hastily** acele ile, hemen
hat /het/ *a.* şapka
hatch /heç/ *e.* (civciv) yumurtadan çıkmak ☆ *a.* ambar ağzı, ambar kapağı; (gemi, uçak) yolcu kapısı
hatchback /'heçbek/ *a.* steyşın araba
hatchet /'heçit/ *a.* küçük balta
hate /heyt/ *a.* nefret ☆ *e.* nefret etmek; *kon.* hoşlanmamak, beğenmemek **hateful** nefret verici, tatsız, iğrenç
hatred /'heytrid/ *a.* nefret, kin
haughty /'ho:ti/ *s.* kibirli, kendini beğenmiş
haul /ho:l/ *e.* çekmek, sürüklemek, taşımak ☆ *a.* çekme, çekiş; bir ağdan çıkan balık miktarı; ganimet, vurgun
haunch /ho:nç/ *a.* kalça, kıç, but
haunt /ho:nt/ *e.* (cin, peri, vb.) uğramak, sık sık görünmek; dadanmak;

hiç aklından çıkmamak ☆ *a.* sık sık gidilen yer, uğrak **haunting** akıldan çıkmayan
have /hıv, hev/ *e.* **had** /hed/ geniş zamanda **(I, you, we, they)** özneleriyle **have; he, she, it** özneleriyle **has** biçiminde çekimlenir.) sahip olmak; yemek, içmek; izin vermek; doğurmak; davet etmek, çağırmak; (rüya) görmek, geçirmek; karşılaşmak **had better** -sa iyi olur **have got** sahip olmak **have (got) to** -meli, -malı, -mek zorunda olmak **have on** giymek; işi olmak; kandırmak, işletmek **have sth done** -tirmek, -tırmak **have done with** bitirmek, son vermek **have/be to do with** -le bir ilgisi olmak
haven /'heyvın/ *a, yaz.* sığınak, liman, barınak
havoc /'hevık/ *a.* hasar, zarar ziyan
hawk /ho:k/ *a, hayb.* doğan, atmaca ☆ *e.* gezgin satıcılık yapmak
hay /hey/ *a.* saman, kuru ot **hay fever** saman nezlesi
hazard /'hezıd/ *a.* tehlike ☆ *e.* riske etmek, tehlikeye atmak
haze /heyz/ *a.* ince sis, duman, pus
hazel /'heyzıl/ *a, bitk.* fındık ağacı ☆ *a, s.* ela **hazel-nut** fındık
hazy /'heyzi/ *s.* bulutlu, sisli, puslu, bulanık
H-bomb /'eyç bom/ *a.* hidrojen bombası
he /hi:/ *adl.* (erkek) o; kendi ☆ *a.* erkek
head /hed/ *a.* baş, kafa; baş taraf; akıl, kafa; lider, başkan; üst kısım; tuğra; (para) tura ☆ *e.* başında olmak, başı çekmek; sorumlu olmak, baş olmak; (topa) kafa vurmak **a/per head** kişi başı, adam başı **come to a head** dönüm noktasına gelmek **go to sb's head** aklını başından almak **have one's head in the clouds** aklı bir karış havada olmak **lose one's head** sapıtmak, pusulayı şaşırmak **off one's head** *kon.* kaçık, üşütük **headache** baş ağrısı **headband** kafa bandı **headdress** başlık **heading** (yazılarda) başlık **headlight** (oto) far **headline**

başlık, manşet; özet haber **headliner** başrol oyuncusu **headmaster** okul müdürü **headphones** kulaklık **headquarters** karargâh; merkez büro
heal /hi:l/ *e.* (yara, vb.) iyileşmek; iyileştirmek; son vermek
health /helt / *a.* sağlık **healthy** sağlıklı
heap /hi:p/ *a.* yığın, küme ☆ *e.* yığmak
hear /hiı/ *e.* işitmek, duymak; haber almak; dinlemek **hear about** duymak, haberini almak **hear from** (mektup, vb.) haber almak **hear of** bahsini işitmek, (adını) duymak
hearing /'hiiring/ *a.* işitme duyusu, işitme; *huk.* duruşma, oturum
hearsay /'hiısey/ *a.* söylenti, şayia
hearse /hö:s/ *a.* cenaze arabası
heart /ha:t/ *a.* kalp, yürek; kalp, gönül, yürek; merkez; kararlılık, yüreklilik; (iskambil) kupa **break sb's heart** kalbini kırmak **by heart** ezbere, ezberden **set one's heart on** -e gönlünü vermek, çok istemek **take (sth) to heart** çok etkilenmek, altüst olmak **heartache** gönül yarası, ıstırap, acı **heart attack** kalp krizi **heartbeat** kalp atışı **heartbreak** ıstırap, acı, derin üzüntü **heartbreaking** kalp kırıcı, çok üzücü **heartbroken** kalbi kırık, kederli **heartburn** *hek.* mide ekşimesi **heart failure** kalp yetmezliği
hearten /'ha:tın/ *e.* yüreklendirmek, cesaret vermek; neşelendirmek
hearth /ha:t / *a.* ocak, şömine
heartily /'ha:tili/ *be.* iştahla, istekle; çok, fazla, fazlasıyla
heartless /'ha:tlıs/ *s.* acımasız, katı yürekli, zalim, kalpsiz
hearty /'ha:ti/ *s.* içten, yürekten, samimi; (yiyecek) doyurucu, bol
heat /hi:t/ *a.* ısı; sıcaklık, sıcak; ısıtma ☆ *e.* ısınmak; ısıtmak **heated** hararetli, ateşli **heater** ısıtıcı **heatwave** sıcak dalgası
heath /hi:t / *a.* fundalık, kır, çalılık; funda, süpürgeotu
heathen /'hi:dın/ *s.* putperest, dinsiz
heather /'hedı/ *a, bitk.* funda, süpürgeotu

eating /'hi:ting/ a. ısıtma sistemi, ısıtma

eave /hi:v/ e. **heaved, hove** /houv/ kaldırmak, yukarı çekmek; kon. fırlatmak; inip kalkmak **heave a sigh** of çekmek

eaven /'hevın/ a. cennet **Heaven** Allah, Yaradan **For Heaven's sake** Allah aşkına **Heaven forbid** Allah göstermesin **Thank Heaven** Tanrıya şükür, bereket versin **heavenly** cennete ilişkin; tanrısal; kon. harika, nefis

eavy /'hevi/ s. ağır; ciddi, ağır; yorucu, güç; (hava) boğucu; (deniz) dalgalı; üzgün **heavy-handed** patavatsız **heavyweight** sp. ağırsıklet

Hebrew /'hi:bru:/ a. İbrani, Yahudi; İbranice ☆ s. İbraniler/İbranice ile ilgili

eckle /'hekıl/ e. sıkıştırmak, sorularla sözünü kesmek

ectare /'hekta:, 'hekteı/ a. hektar

ectic /'hektik/ s. heyecanlı, telaşlı, hareketli

edge /hec/ a. çit, çalı; (against) koruma ☆ e. çitle çevirmek; lafı dolandırmak

edgehog /'hechog/ a, hayb. kirpi

eed /hi:d/ e. dikkat etmek, önemsemek ☆ a. dikkat, önem

eel /hi:l/ a, anat. topuk; ökçe, topuk

efty /'hefti/ s. güçlü kuvvetli, etkili

egemony /hi'gemıni/ a. üstünlük, egemenlik, hegemonya

eight /hayt/ a. yükseklik; coğ. yükselti; doruk, tepe **heighten** yükselmek; yükseltmek, artırmak

eir /eı/ a. varis, mirasçı, kalıtçı **heiress** kadın varis **heirloom** kuşaktan kuşağa geçen değerli şey

elicopter /'helikoptı/ a. helikopter

elium /'hi:lıım/ a, kim. helyum

ell /hel/ a. cehennem ☆ ünl, kon. kahrolasıca! kahretsin! **hellish** kon. berbat

ello /hı'lou/ ünl. merhaba; alo

elm /helm/ a. dümen **helmsman** dümenci

elmet /'helmit/ a. kask, miğfer, tolga

elp /help/ e. yardım etmek; işe yaramak; önlemek; yemek/içecek vermek

☆ a. yardım; yardımcı **Help** İmdat! Yetişin! **helper** yardımcı **helpful** yardımcı, yararlı **helpless** yardıma muhtaç, çaresiz, aciz **helping** yardım; (yemek) porsiyon **can't help** elinde olmamak, -dan, -den edememek

hem /hem/ a. (giysi) kenar, baskı ☆ e. kıvırıp kenarını bastırmak

hemisphere /'hemisfiı/ a. yarıküre

hemlock /'hemlok/ a, bitk. köknara benzer bir çam ağacı; baldıran, ağıotu

hemoglobin /hi:mı'gloubin/ a. hemoglobin

hemorrhage /'hemıric/ a, hek. kanama

hemorrhoid /'hemıroyd/ a, hek. basur, hemoroit

hemp /hemp/ a. kenevir, kendir

hen /hen/ a. tavuk; dişi kuş

hence /hens/ be. bu nedenle, bundan dolayı; şu andan itibaren **henceforth/henceforward** bundan böyle, şimdiden sonra

henchman /'hençmın/ a. dalkavuk

henna /'henı/ a, bitk. kına

hepatitis /hepı'taytis/ a, hek. hepatit, karaciğer yangısı

her /hö:, hı, ı/ adl. (dişil) onu, ona; o ☆ s. onun

herald /'herıld/ a. haberci, müjdeci ☆ e. bir şeyin müjdecisi olmak

heraldry /'herıldri/ a. arma, armacılık

herb /hö:b/ a. (şifalı/yemeklere konan) ot, bitki **herbal** otlarla ilgili **herbalist** şifalı bitkiler yetiştiren/satan kimse

herbivorous /hö:'bivırıs/ s. (hayvan) otobur, otçul

herd /hö:d/ a. hayvan sürüsü **herdsman** çoban, sığırtmaç

here /hıı/ be. burada, buraya **here and there** şurada burada **Here you are** işte, buyurun **hereabouts** buralarda, yakında **hereafter** bundan sonra, gelecekte; ölümden sonraki yaşam, ahret **hereby** şimdi, bu vesileyle, bundan ötürü **harewith** bununla, ilişikte

hereditary /hi'reditıri/ s. kalıtsal

heresy /'herisi/ a. dinsel/toplumsal değerlere aykırı görüş

heritage /'heritic/ a. miras, kalıt

hermetic /hö:'metik/ s. sımsıkı kapalı,

havageçirmez
hermit /'hö:mit/ *a.* münzevi kimse **hermitage** inziva yeri
hernia /'hö:niı/ *a, hek.* fıtık
hero /'hiırou/ *a.* kahraman **heroic** /hı'rouik/ yiğitçe, kahramanca **heroism** /'herouizim/ kahramanlık
heroin /'herouin/ *a.* eroin
heroine /'herouin/ *a.* kadın kahraman
heron /'herın/ *a, hayb.* balıkçıl
herring /'hering/ *a, hayb.* ringa balığı
hers /hö:z/ *adl.* (dişil) onunki, onun
herself /ı'self, hı'self, hö:'self/ *adl.* (dişil) kendisi
hesitant /'hezitınt/ *s.* kararsız, ikircikli
hesitate /'heziteyt/ *e.* tereddüt etmek, duraksamak **hesitation** tereddüt, duraksama
heterogeneous /hetırou'ci:niıs/ *s.* heterojen, çoktürel
hew /hyu:/ *e.* kesmek, yarmak
hexagon /'heksıgın/ *a.* altıgen
hey /hey/ *ünl.* hey
heyday /'heydey/ *a.* en parlak dönem, altın çağ
hi /hay/ *ünl, kon, bkz.* **hello**
hibernate /'haybıneyt/ *e.* kış uykusuna yatmak
hiccup /'hikap/ *a.* hıçkırık ☆ *e.* hıçkırmak, hıçkırık tutmak
hid /hid/ *bkz.* **hide**
hidden /'hidın/ *bkz.* **hide**
hide /hayd/ *e.* **hid** /hid/, **hidden** /'hidın/ saklamak, gizlemek; gizlenmek, saklanmak ☆ *a.* deri, post **hiding** saklama, saklanma; *kon.* dayak, kötek **hiding place** saklanacak yer
hideous /'hidiıs/ *s.* çirkin, berbat, iğrenç, korkunç
hierarchy /'hayıra:ki/ *a.* hiyerarşi, aşama düzeni, sıradüzen
hi-fi /'hayfay, hay'fay/ *a, s.* sesi çok doğal bir biçimde veren (müzik seti, pikap, vb.)
high /hay/ *s.* yüksek; yüce, ulu; (ses) tiz; (zaman) tam **high court** yüksek mahkeme **high fidelity** *bkz.* **hi-fi high jump** yüksek atlama **high school** lise **highbrow** aydın (kimse) **high-class** kaliteli, birinci sınıf **higher education**

yüksek öğrenim **high-handed** despot, zorba **highland** dağlık (bölge) **high-level** çok önemli, zirve **highlight** (resimde) parlak nokta; en önemli/göze çarpan kısım **high-powered** güçlü **high-pressure** yüksek basınçlı; dinamik, enerjik **high-rise** yüksek (yapı) **highway** karayolu **highwayman** eşkıya, soyguncu
highly /'hayli/ *be.* son derece, pek çok
Highness /'haynis/ *a.* (**His/Her/Your**) Ekselansları
hijack /'haycek/ *e.* (uçak, gemi, vb.) kaçırmak **hijacker** uçak, gemi, vb. kaçıran kimse, korsan
hike /hayk/ *a.* (kırda) uzun yürüyüş ☆ *e.* uzun yürüyüşe çıkmak
hilarious /hi'leıriıs/ *s.* çok şamatalı, neşeli **hilarity** neşe, şamata
hill /hil/ *a.* tepe **hillock** küçük tepe, tepecik **hillside** yamaç
hilt /hilt/ *a.* kabza; (**up**) **to the hilt** tamamen
him /im, him/ *adl.* (eril) onu, ona; o
himself /im'self, him'self/ *adl.* (eril) kendisi
hind /haynd/ *s.* arka
hinder /'hindı/ *e.* engellemek
hindrance /'hindrıns/ *a.* engel
Hindu /'hindu:/ *a.* Hinduizm dininden olan kimse, Hindu
hinge /hinc/ *a.* menteşe ☆ *e.* menteşe takmak
hint /hint/ *a.* sezindirme, ima; belirti ☆ *e.* ima etmek, çıtlatmak
hinterland /'hintılend/ *a.* iç bölge
hip /hip/ *a.* kalça
hippie /'hipi/ *a.* hippi
hippo /'hipou/ *a, kon.* suaygırı
hippopotamus /hipı'potımıs/ *a, hayb.* suaygırı
hire /'hayı/ *e.* kiralamak, tutmak ☆ *a.* kira, kiralama **hire out** kiraya vermek **hire purchase, HP** taksit
his /hiz, iz/ *s.* (eril) onun ☆ *adl.* onunki, onun
hiss /his/ *e.* tıslamak, ıslıklamak ☆ *a.* tıslama, ıslık
history /'histıri/ *a.* tarih; tarihsel öykü/olay; geçmiş **historian** tarihçi **historic**

(olay, yer) tarihi **historical** tarihi; tarihle ilgili

hit /hit/ e. vurmak; çarpmak; üzmek; varmak, ulaşmak ☆ a. vurma, vuruş, çarpma; (şarkı, vb.) sevilen/tutulan şey **hit it off (with)** kon. iyi geçinmek

hitch /hiç/ e. bağlamak, takmak; kon. otostop yapmak ☆ a. çekiş; düğüm, bağ; otostop

hitchhike /'hiçhayk/ e. otostop yapmak **hitchhiker** otostopçu

hive /hayv/ a. arı kovanı

hoard /ho:d/ a. istif ☆ e. istif etmek, biriktirmek, stoklamak

hoarfrost /'ho:frost/ a. kırağı

hoarse /ho:s/ s. (ses) kısık, boğuk; kısık sesli

hoary /'ho:ri/ s. (saç) kır, ak

hoax /houks/ a. muziplik, şaka ☆ e. işletmek, gırgır geçmek

hobble /'hobıl/ e. topallamak

hobby /'hobi/ a. hobi, düşkü

hockey /hoki/ a, sp. hokey

hod /hod/ a. tuğla ve harç tenekesi

hoe /hou/ a. çapa, bahçe çapası ☆ e. çapalamak

hoist /hoyst/ e. yükseltmek, kaldırmak; (bayrak) çekmek ☆ a. yükseltme; ağır yük asansörü

hold /hould/ e. **held** /held/ tutmak; tutturmak; düzenlemek; içine almak; elinde tutmak; işgal etmek; inanmak, saymak ☆ a. tutma, tutuş; tutunacak yer; nüfuz, etki **hold back** zapt etmek, tutmak **hold down** (bir işi) yürütmek; aşağıda tutmak **hold off** uzakta tutmak, yaklaştırmamak **hold on** (telefonda) beklemek; devam ettirmek **hold out** dayanmak; uzatmak **hold over** ertelemek **hold to** korumak, bağlı kalmak **hold together** tutturmak, bir arada tutmak **hold up** geciktirmek; yolunu kesip soymak **hold with** uzlaşmak, aynı düşüncede olmak

holding /'houlding/ a. mal, arazi, tahvil **holding company** holding şirketi

holdup /'houldap/ a. (trafik nedeniyle) gecikme; kon. silahlı soygun

hole /houl/ a. delik, çukur; kovuk, in

holiday /'holidey, 'holidi/ a. tatil, dinlen-

ce **on holiday** tatilde

holiness /'houlinis/ a. kutsallık

holler /'holı/ e, Al, kon. bağırmak

hollow /'holou/ s. boş, oyuk; (ses) boğuk ☆ a. çukur

holly /'holi/ a, bitk. çobanpüskülü

holocaust /'holıko:st/ a. büyük tahribat

holy /'houli/ s. kutsal

homage /'homic/ a. saygı, hürmet

home /houm/ a. ev, yuva, aile ocağı; yurt, vatan **at home** evde **be/feel at home** kendini evindeymiş gibi hissetmek **homeland** yurt, ülke **homemade** evde yapılmış, yerli malı **homesick** sıla hasreti çeken **homeward** eve doğru giden **homework** ev ödevi

homely /'houmli/ s. sade, gösterişsiz

homicide /'homisayd/ a. adam öldürme

homogeneous /houmı'ci:nıis/ s. homojen, türdeş, tektürel

homonym /'homınim/ a. okunuş ve yazılışları özdeş, anlamları ayrı sözcük, eşadlı

homosexual /houmı'sekşuıl/ a, s. homoseksüel, eşcinsel

hone /houn/ e. (bıçak, kama, vb.) bilemek

honest /'onist/ s. dürüst, namuslu; içten, açık kalpli **honestly** dürüstçe; gerçekten **honesty** dürüstlük, doğruluk

honey /'hani/ a. bal; Al. tatlım, canım **honeycomb** petek **honeymoon** balayı

honeysuckle /'hanisakıl/ a, bitk. hanımeli

honk /honk/ a. korna sesi ☆ e. ötmek; (korna) öttürmek

honor /'onı/ a, e, Al, bkz. **honour**

honorary /'onırıri/ s. onursal; fahri

honour /'onı/ a. onur, şeref, haysiyet; itibar; iffet ☆ e. onur vermek, şereflendirmek **honourable** namuslu, onurlu; saygıdeğer

hood /hud/ a. kukuleta, başlık; Al. (oto) kaput

hoodwink /'hudwink/ e. kandırmak, aldatmak

hoof /hu:f/ a. toynak

hook /hu:k/ a. çengel, kanca; olta iğnesi; kopça; orak ☆ e. olta ile tutmak;

çengellemek

hooligan /'hu:ligın/ a. serseri, kabadayı

hoop /hu:p/ a. çember

hoot /hu:t/ e. (at/with) ötmek; öttürmek ☆ a. baykuş sesi; yuhalama

hoover /'hu:vı/ a. elektrikli süpürge ☆ e. elektrikli süpürgeyle temizlemek

hop /hop/ e. sekmek; sıçramak; hoplamak ☆ a. sıçrama, sekme; bitk. şerbetçiotu

hope /houp/ e. umut etmek, ummak ☆ a. umut, ümit **hopeful** umut verici; umutlu **hopefully** umarım, inşallah **hopeless** umutsuz; boşuna

hopscotch /'hopskoç/ a. seksek oyunu

horde /ho:d/ a. kalabalık, sürü

horizon /hı'rayzın/ a. ufuk, çevren **horizontal** yatay, düz

hormone /'ho:moun/ a. hormon

horn /ho:n/ a. boynuz; korna, klakson; müz. boru

hornet /'ho:nit/ a, hayb. eşekarısı

horoscope /'horıskoup/ a. yıldız falı, burç

horrible /'horıbıl/ s. korkunç; kon. berbat, iğrenç

horrid /'horid/ s. iğrenç; kon. berbat

horrify /'horifay/ e. korkutmak

horror /'horı/ a. korku, dehşet

hors d'oeuvre /o:'dö:v/ a. ordövr, meze, çerez

horse /ho:s/ a. at, beygir; sp. atlama beygiri **horseback** at sırtı **horse chestnut** atkestanesi **horseman** atlı, binici **horseplay** eşek şakası **horsepower** beygirgücü **horse-racing** at yarışı **horseshoe** at nalı

horticulture /'ho:tikalçı/ a. bahçıvanlık

hose /houz/ a. su hortumu; ç. (külotlu) çorap

hosiery /'hoziıri/ a. çoraplar, iç çamaşırı

hospitable /'hospitıbıl/ s. konuksever

hospital /'hospitıl/ a. hastane

hospitality /hospi'teliti/ a. konukseverlik

hospitalize /'hospitılayz/ e. hastaneye yatırmak, hastaneye kaldırmak

host /houst/ a. ev sahibi, mihmandar; hancı, otelci; sunucu ☆ e. ev sahipliği yapmak, konuk ağırlamak

hostage /'hostic/ a. rehine

hostel /'hostıl/ a. öğrenci yurdu **youth hostel** özellikle genç turistlerin kaldığı otel

hostess /'houstis/ a. ev sahibesi; hostes; konsomatris

hostile /'hostayl/ s. düşmanca, düşman

hostility /ho'stiliti/ a. düşmanlık, kin; ç. savaş

hot /hot/ s. sıcak; biberli, acı; (haber) sıcak, taze **hot-blooded** ihtiraslı, tutkulu **hot dog** sosisli sandviç **hothouse** limonluk, ser, camlık

hotel /hou'tel/ a. otel

hound /haund/ a. av köpeği, tazı

hour /auı/ a. saat **at all hours** gece gündüz, sürekli, her saat **visiting hours** ziyaret saatleri **working hours** çalışma saatleri **hourly** saatte bir, saat başı

house /haus/ a. ev; ev halkı, aile; meclis, kamara ☆ e. barındırmak **houseboat** yüzen ev **housebreaker** ev hırsızı **household** ev halkı **householder** ev sahibi **housekeeper** (otel, ev) idarecisi; kâhya **housekeeping** ev idaresi **housemaid** orta hizmetçisi **housewife** ev kadını **housework** ev işi

housing /'hauzing/ a. iskân; konut sağlama **housing estate** site, toplu konutlar

hovel /'hovıl/ a. mezbele, ahır gibi ev

hover /'hovı/ e. (over/around) havada belli bir noktada durmak; bekleyip durmak

hovercraft /'hovıkra:ft/ a. hoverkraft

how /haw/ be. nasıl; ne kadar; ne kadar, nasıl da ☆ bağ. hangi yolla, nasıl **How come** kon. nasıl olur, neden **How do you do?** Memnun oldum; Nasılsınız? **How long** ne kadar zamandır **How many** kaç tane, kaç **How much** ne kadar; kaç para

however /haw'evı/ be. bununla birlikte, yine de

howl /haul/ e. ulumak, inlemek ☆ a. uluma, inleme, inilti

hub /hab/ a. (oto) tekerlek göbeği

hubbub /'habab/ a. gürültü

huddle /'hadıl/ *e.* bir araya sıkışmak, toplanmak

hue /hyu:/ *a.* renk

huff /haf/ *a.* huysuzluk, dargınlık

hug /hag/ *e.* sevgiyle sarılmak, bağrına basmak ☆ *a.* kucaklama, bağrına basma

huge /hyu:c/ *s.* çok büyük, kocaman

hulk /halk/ *a.* gemi enkazı **hulking** ağır, hantal, iri

hull /hal/ *a.* gemi omurgası, geminin tekne kısmı

hullabaloo /'halıbılu:/ *a.* gürültü, velvele, yaygara

hullo /ha'lou/ *ünl, a, bkz.* **hello**

hum /ham/ *e.* vızıldamak; (şarkı) mırıldanmak

human /'hyu:mın/ *s.* insana ilişkin, insani; insancıl, insanca ☆ *a.* insan **human being** insan, insanoğlu

humane /hyu:'meyn/ *s.* insancıl, sevecen

humanism /'hyu:mınizm/ *a.* hümanizm, insancılık **humanist** hümanist, insancıl

humanitarian /hyu:meni'teırıın/ *a, s.* yardımsever, insancıl

humanities /hyu:'menitiz/ *a.* (yazın, dil, tarih, vb.) konusu insan olan bilimler

humanity /hyu:'meniti/ *a.* insanlık

humble /'hambıl/ *s.* alçakgönüllü, gösterişsiz; fakir

humbug /'hambag/ *a.* saçmalık; *İİ.* nane şekeri

humdrum /'hamdram/ *s.* sıradan, tekdüze, monoton, yavan

humid /'hyu:mid/ *s.* (hava) nemli **humidity** havadaki nem, nem oranı

humiliate /hyu'milieyt/ *e.* küçük düşürmek, utandırmak **humiliation** aşağılama, utandırma

humility /hyu:'militi/ *a.* alçakgönüllülük

humorist /'hu:mırist/ *a.* şakacı kimse; güldürü yazarı

humorous /'hyu:mırıs/ *s.* komik, gülünç, güldürücü

humour /'hyu:mı/ *a.* gülünçlük, komiklik; mizah, güldürü; mizaç, huy ☆ *e.* eğlendirmek; istediğini yerine getir-

mek **sense of humour** mizah/espri anlayışı

hump /hamp/ *a.* kambur; hörgüç; tümsek

humus /hyu:mıs/ *a.* kara toprak, humus

hunch /hanç/ *a.* kambur ☆ *e.* kamburlaştırmak **hunchback** kambur

hundred /'handrıd/ *a, s.* yüz **hundredth** yüzüncü

hunger /'hangı/ *a.* açlık **hunger march** açlık yürüyüşü **hunger strike** açlık grevi

hungry /'hangri/ *s.* aç; acıktırıcı

hunk /hank/ *a.* iri parça

hunt /hant/ *e.* avlamak; araştırmak, aramak ☆ *a.* avlanma, av **hunter** avcı

hurdle /'hö:dıl/ *a.* engel, çit

hurl /hö:l/ *e.* fırlatmak, fırlatıp atmak ☆ *a.* fırlatma, savurma

hurly-burly /'hö:libö:li/ *a.* gürültü, kargaşa, har gür

hurrah /hu'ra:/ *ünl, bkz.* **hurray**

hurray /hu'rey/ *ünl.* yaşa! hurra!

hurricane /'harikın/ *a.* kasırga, bora **hurricane lamp** gemici feneri

hurry /'hari/ *e.* acele etmek; acele ettirmek ☆ *a* acele, telaş **be in a hurry** acelesi olmak **Hurry up!** Çabuk ol

hurt /hö:t/ *e.* acıtmak, incitmek; acımak, incinmek; kalbini kırmak, üzmek; ağrımak

hurtle /'hö:tıl/ *e.* hızla hareket etmek, fırlamak

husband /'hazbınd/ *a.* koca, eş

hush /haş/ *e.* susmak; susturmak ☆ *a.* sessizlik

husk /hask/ *a.* (bitki) dış yapraklar, kabuk **husky** (ses) kısık, boğuk

hustle /'hasıl/ *e.* itip kakmak, acele ettirmek; acele etmek

hut /hat/ *a.* kulübe

hutch /haç/ *a.* küçük hayvan kafesi

hyacinth /'hayısint / *a, bitk.* sümbül

hybrid /'haybrid/ *a.* melez

hydrant /'haydrınt/ *a.* yangın musluğu

hydraulic /hay'drolik/ *s.* hidrolik

hydroelectric /haydroui'lektrik/ *s.* hidroelektrik

hydrogen /'haydrıcın/ *a.* hidrojen

hydrophobia /haydrı'foubiı/ a, hek. kuduz

hyena /hay'i:nı/ a, hayb. sırtlan

hygiene /'hayci:n/ a. sağlık bilgisi; temizlik hygienic sağlıklı, hijyenik, sağlıksal; temiz

hymn /him/ a. ilahi

hyperbole /hay'pö:bıli/ a. abartma, büyütme

hypermarket /'haypıma:kit/ a. hipermarket

hyphen /'hayfın/ a. kısa çizgi, tire

hypnosis /hip'nousis/ a. (ç. -ses /-si:z/) hipnoz hypnotism hipnotizma hypnotize hipnotize etmek

hypocrisy /hi'pokrisi/ a. ikiyüzlülük

hypocrite /'hipıkrit/ s. ikiyüzlü hypocritical ikiyüzlü

hypodermic /haypı'dö:mik/ a. iğne, şırınga ☆ s. deri altı ile ilgili

hypothesis /hay'potisis/ a. hipotez, varsayım hypothetical /haypı'tetikıl/ varsayımlı, varsayıma dayanan

hysteria /hi'stiıriı/ a, hek. isteri hysterical /hi'sterikıl/ s. isterik

I

I, i /ay/ adl. ben

ice /ays/ a. buz; dondurma ice age buzul çağı iceberg buzdağı ice cream dondurma ice skating buz pateni

icy /'aysi/ s. çok soğuk, buz gibi; buzlu

idea /ay'diı/ a. düşünce, fikir; plan; görüş

ideal /ay'diıl/ s. ideal, mükemmel, kusursuz ☆ a. ideal; ülkü idealism idealizm, ülkücülük idealist idealist, ülkücü

idealize /ay'diılayz/ e. mükemmel olarak görmek

identical /ay'dentikıl/ s. (with/to) benzer; aynı

identification /aydentifi'keyşın/ a. tanıma; teşhis; kimlik, hüviyet

identify /ay'dentifay/ e. tanımak, kimliğini saptamak; fark gözetmemek, bir tutmak

identity /ay'dentiti/ a. benzerlik, özdeşlik; kimlik identity (card) kimlik (kartı)

ideology /aydi'olıci/ a. ideoloji

idiocy /'idiısi/ a. aptallık, ahmaklık

idiom /'idiım/ a. deyim idiomatic /-'metik/ deyimsel; deyimlerle dolu

idiot /'idiıt/ a. geri zekâlı kimse; kon. aptal, salak

idle /'aydıl/ s. işsiz, aylak; tembel; yararsız, sonuçsuz, boş

idol /'aydıl/ a. put, tapıncak; çok sevilen kimse/şey

idolatry /ay'dolıtri/ a. puta tapma, putperestlik

idolize /'aydılayz/ e. putlaştırmak, tapmak

if /if/ bağ. eğer, ise if I were you senin yerinde olsam if only keşke as if sanki even if ise bile

igloo /'iglu:/ a. eskimo evi

ignite /ig'nayt/ e. tutuşmak; tutuşturmak

ignition /ig'nişın/ a. tutuşma, tutuşturma; (oto) ateşleme, kontak

ignorance /'ignırıns/ a. bilgisizlik, cahillik, cehalet

ignorant /'ignırınt/ s. bilgisiz, cahil; kon. görgüsüz, kaba, inceliksiz

ignore /ig'no:/ e. aldırmamak, görmemezlikten gelmek

ill /il/ s. hasta; kötü, fena ill-advised düşüncesiz ill-bred görgüsüz ill-fated şansız, talihsiz ill-natured huysuz, ters

illegal /i'li:gıl/ s. yasadışı, yolsuz

illegible /i'lecibıl/ s. okunaksız

illegitimate /ili'citimit/ s. yasalara aykırı; (çocuk) evlilik dışı doğmuş

illicit /i'lisit/ s. yasadışı, yasak

illiterate /i'litırit/ s. okuma yazma bilmeyen

illness /'ilnis/ a. hastalık, sayrılık

illogical /i'locikıl/ s. mantığa aykırı

illuminate /i'lu:mineyt/ e. aydınlatmak illumination ışıklandırma

illusion /i'lu:jın/ a. aldatıcı görünüş; düş, kuruntu, hayal

illustrate /'ilıstreyt/ e. (kitap, sözlük, vb. resimlemek; örneklerle açıklamak

illustration resim; örnek illustrative açıklayıcı, aydınlatıcı
illustrious /i'lastrııs/ s. ünlü
ill will /il'wil/ a. nefret, kin
image /'imic/ a. hayal, görüntü; izlenim, imaj; kopya, eş, aynı
imaginary /i'mecınıri/ s. hayali, düşsel
imagine /i'mecin/ e. hayalinde canlandırmak, hayal etmek; sanmak, düşünmek imagination hayal gücü; kon. düş, düş ürünü imaginative hayal gücü kuvvetli, yaratıcı
imitate /'imiteyt/ e. taklit etmek; örnek almak; benzemek imitation taklit; taklit eser
immaculate /i'mekyulit/ s. tertemiz, lekesiz; kusursuz, tam
immaterial /imı'tiirıil/ s. önemsiz; maddi olmayan, manevi
immature /imı'çuı/ s. olgunlaşmamış
immediate /i'mi:dııt/ s. acele, acil; en yakın immediately hemen, derhal
immense /i'mens/ s. kocaman, muazzam immensely pek çok
immerse /i'mö:s/ e. daldırmak
immigrant /'imigrınt/ a. göçmen
immigrate /'imigreyt/ e. göç etmek immigration göç
imminent /'iminınt/ s. yakın, yakında olacak
immoral /i'morıl/ s. ahlaka aykırı, ahlaksız, terbiyesiz
immortal /i'mo:tıl/ s. ölümsüz; sonsuz, ebedi immortality /-teltti/ ölümsüzlük immortalize ölümsüzleştirmek
immune /i'myu:n/ s. bağışık, muaf immunity bağışıklık; dokunulmazlık
imp /imp/ a. küçük şeytan; yaramaz çocuk, afacan çocuk
impact /'impekt/ a. çarpma, çarpışma
impair /im'peı/ e. zarar vermek, bozmak
impartial /im'pa:şıl/ s. yansız, tarafsız
impassable /im'pa:sıbıl/ s. geçit vermez, geçilmez
impassioned /im'peşınd/ s. ateşli, heyecanlı, coşkun
impatience /im'peyşıns/ a. sabırsızlık impatient sabırsız
impeccable /im'pekıbıl/ s. kusursuz

impede /im'pi:d/ e. engel olmak
impediment /im'pedimınt/ a. engel
impending /im'pending/ s. olması yakın
imperative /im'perıtiv/ s. zorunlu, gerekli ☆ a, dilb. emir, buyruk
imperfect /im'pö:fikt/ s. kusurlu
imperial /im'piırıil/ s. imparatorluk ile ilgili imperialism emperyalizm imperialist emperyalist
impersonal /im'pö:sınıl/ s. kişisel olmayan
impersonate /im'pö:sıneyt/ e. rolüne girmek, canlandırmak, taklidini yapmak
impertinent /im'pö:tinınt/ s. saygısız, kaba, terbiyesiz, küstah
impervious /im'pö:vııs/ s. sugeçirmez
impetuous /im'peçuıs/ s. tez canlı, düşünmeden hareket eden, aceleci
impetus /'impitıs/ a. şiddet, hız, enerji; yüreklendirme
impish /'impiş/ s. şeytani, yaramaz
implant /im'pla:nt/ e. kafasına sokmak, aşılamak
implement /'implimınt/ a. alet
implicate /'implikeyt/ e. (suç, vb.'de) ilişiği olduğunu göstermek
implication /impli'keyşın/ a. (suç) bulaştırma, karıştırma; ima, kinaye
implicit /im'plisit/ s. dolaylı olarak belirten, kapalı, örtük; tam, kesin
implore /im'plo:/ e. yalvarmak, dilemek
imply /im'play/ e. anlamına gelmek; dolayısıyla anlatmak, ima etmek; içermek, kapsamak
impolite /impı'layt/ s. kaba, terbiyesiz
import /im'po:t/ e. ithal etmek, getirtmek ☆ a. ithal, dışalım; ithal malı
importance /im'po:tıns/ a. önem
important /im'po:tınt/ s. önemli
impose /im'pouz/ e. (vergi) koymak; zorla kabul ettirmek imposing görkemli
impossible /im'posıbıl/ s. imkânsız, olanaksız; çekilmez, güç, dayanılmaz
impotent /'impıtınt/ s. yetersiz; iktidarsız
impound /im'paund/ e, huk. haczet-

impractical

360

mek, el koymak
impractical /im'prektikıl/ s. yapılamaz,
uygulanamaz; mantıksız; saçma
impregnable /im'pregnıbıl/ s. alınmaz,
ele geçirilmez, zapt edilemez
impregnate /'impregneyt/ e. hamile bırakmak; emdirmek
impress /im'pres/ e. hayran bırakmak,
etkilemek; kafasına sokmak
impression /im'preşın/ a. etki, izlenim;
baskı impressionism empresyonizm
impressive /im'presiv/ s. etkileyici
imprint /im'print/ e. basmak, damgalamak ☆ a. damga; iz
imprison /im'prizın/ e. hapsetmek imprisonment tutukluluk, hapis
improbable /im'probıbıl/ s. olmayacak, inanılmaz
impromptu /im'promptyu:/ s, be. hazırlıksız, önceden tasarlanmadan
improper /im'propı/ s. uygunsuz, yersiz; yanlış; ahlaksız
improve /im'pru:v/ e. geliştirmek, ilerletmek; gelişmek; iyileşmek improvement ilerleme, gelişme
improvise /'imprıvayz/ e. irticalen söylemek; uyduruvermek, yapıvermek
impudence /'impyudıns/ a. arsızlık,
yüzsüzlük, küstahlık
impudent /'impyudınt/ s. arsız, yüzsüz, saygısız, küstah
impulse /'impals/ a. itme, itiş, itici güç;
içtepi, güdü
impulsive /im'palsiv/ s. itici; atılgan, düşüncesizce hareket eden
impure /im'pyuı/ s. pis, kirli; katışık
in /in/ ilg. içinde; içine; giymiş; sonunda, sonra; göre; bakımından ☆ be.
içeriye, içeride; evde; moda; iktidarda
in all topu topu, hepsi in that mademki; çünkü
inability /inı'biliti/ a. yeteneksizlik; yetersizlik; yapamama
inaccessible /inık'sesıbıl/ s. ulaşılmaz,
erişilmez
inaccurate /in'ekyurit/ s. yanlış, hatalı
inadequate /in'edikwit/ s. yetersiz
inane /i'neyn/ s. anlamsız, saçma, boş
inanimate /in'enimit/ s. cansız, ölü
inapplicable /in'eplikıbıl/ s. uygulana-

maz
inappropriate /inı'proupriıt/ s. uygunsuz
inarticulate /ina:'tikyulit/ s. (konuşma)
anlaşılmaz, belirsiz
inasmuch as /inız'maç ız/ bağ. çünkü,
-dığı için
inaudible /in'o:dıbıl/ s. işitilemez, duyu-
lamaz
inaugurate /i'no:gyureyt/ e. törenle açmak; törenle göreve getirmek
inborn /in'bo:n/ s. doğuştan
incalculable /'in'kelkyulıbıl/ s. hesapla-
namaz
incapable /in'keypıbıl/ s. yeteneksiz,
güçsüz, gücü yetmeyen
incapacitate /inkı'pesiteyt/ e. yetersiz
kılmak, âciz bırakmak
incarnate /in'ka:nit/ s. insan şeklinde
olan incarnation vücut bulma, canlanma; somut örnek
incendiary /in'sendiıri/ s. yangın çıkar-
tan; fesatçı, kışkırtıcı ☆ a. kundakçı
incense /'insens/ a. tütsü, günlük
insense /in'sens/e. kızdırmak
incentive /in'sentiv/ a. dürtü, güdü
incessant /in'sesınt/ s. aralıksız, sürekli
incest /'insest/ a. hısımla cinsel ilişki
inch /inç/ a. inç, pus (2.54 cm.) inch
by inch azar azar, milim milim every
inch tam, komple, sapına kadar
incidence /'insidıns/ a. tekrar oranı
oran
incident /'insidınt/ a. olay incidental tesadüfi; küçük ve önemsiz incidentally tesadüfen, bir ara
incinerate /in'sinıreyt/ e. yakıp kül etmek
incipient /in'sipiınt/ s. yeni başlamış
incision /in'sijın/ a. kesme, yarma; kesik, yarık incisive soruna doğrudan
eğilen, direkt
incisor /in'sayzı/ a. ön diş, kesicidiş
incite /in'sayt/ e. kışkırtmak, körükle
mek
inclination /inkli'neyşın/ a. eğilim; eğik
lik, eğim
incline /in'klayn/ e. eğmek; eğilmek ☆
a. yokuş, bayır, eğim inclined eğimli
yatkın, meyilli

include /in'klu:d/ e. dahil etmek; içine almak, kapsamak, içermek **included** dahil **including** dahil **inclusion** /-jın/ dahil etme; alınma **inclusive** dahil, her şey dahil
incognito /inkog'ni:tou/ s, be. takma adla
incoherent /inkou'hiırınt/ s. tutarsız, anlamsız, abuk sabuk
income /'inkam/ a. gelir, kazanç, akar **income tax** gelir vergisi
incomparable /in'kompırıbıl/ s. eşsiz
incompatible /inkım'petıbıl/ s. birbirine zıt, uyuşmaz, bağdaşmaz
incompetent /in'kompitınt/ s, a. yeteneksiz, yetersiz, beceriksiz (kimse)
incomplete /inkım'pli:t/ s. tamamlanmamış, bitmemiş, eksik
incomprehensible /inkompri'hensıbıl/ s. anlaşılmaz, akıl ermez
inconceivable /inkın'si:vıbıl/ s. tasavvur olunamaz, hayal edilemez, inanılmaz; kon. olanaksız, inanılamaz
inconclusive /inkın'klu:siv/ s. yetersiz, sonuçsuz
incongruous /in'kongruıs/ s. birbirine uymayan, uyuşmaz, bağdaşmaz
inconsiderate /inkın'sidırıt/ s. düşüncesiz, bencil
inconsistent /inkın'sistınt/ s. çelişkili, tutarsız, birbirini tutmayan; değişken, saati saatine uymayan
inconspicuous /inkın'spikyuıs/ s. göze çarpmayan, önemsiz
inconvenience /inkın'vi:niıns/ a. sıkıntı, rahatsızlık ☆ e. zahmet olmak, işini zorlaştırmak
inconvenient /inkın'vi:niınt/ s. rahatsız edici, zahmet verici; elverişsiz
incorporate /in'ko:pıreyt/ e. birleştirmek, dahil etmek; birleşmek **incorporated** anonim **incorporation** birleşme; ortaklık
incorrect /inkı'rekt/ s. yanlış
incorrigible /in'koricıbıl/ s. adam olmaz, düzelmez
increase /in'kri:s/ e. artmak, çoğalmak; artırmak, çoğaltmak ☆ a. artış
increasingly gittikçe
incredible /in'kredıbıl/ s. inanılmaz,

akıl almaz; kon. harika, müthiş
increment /'inkrimınt/ a. artma, artış; zam
incriminate /in'krimineyt/ e. suçlu çıkarmak, suçlu olduğunu göstermek
incubate /'inkyubeyt/ e. kuluçkaya yatmak **incubation** kuluçkaya yatma **incubator** kuluçka makinesi
incur /in'kö:/ e. -e uğramak, girmek, yakalanmak
incurable /in'kyuırıbıl/ s. tedavi edilemez, çaresiz
incursion /in'kö:şın/ a. akın, baskın
indebted /in'detid/ s. borçlu; minnettar
indecent /in'di:sınt/ s. uygunsuz; edepsiz; açık saçık, çirkin
indecision /indi'sijın/ a. kararsızlık
indecisive /indi'saysiv/ s. kararsız
indeed /in'di:d/ be. gerçekten
indefensible /indi'fensıbıl/ s. savunulamaz; bağışlanamaz
indefinite /in'definıt/ s. belirsiz; sınırsız, sonsuz **the indefinite article** dilb. belgisiz tanımlık (a, an)
indelible /in'delibıl/ s. silinmez, çıkmaz
indemnify /in'demnifay/ e. zararını ödemek, tazmin etmek
indemnity /in'demniti/ a. tazminat
indent /in'dent/ e. çentmek, kertmek; (satır) içerden başlamak
independence /indi'pendıns/ a. bağımsızlık
independent /indi'pendınt/ s. bağımsız
indescribable /indis'kraybıbıl/ s. anlatılmaz, tanımlanamaz, tarifsiz
indestructible /indi'straktıbıl/ s. yıkılamaz, yok edilemez
index /'indeks/ a. (ç. -es, indices /'indı-si:z/ dizin, fihrist, indeks; gösterge **index finger** işaretparmağı
Indian /'indiın/ a, s. Hintli; Kızılderili **American Indian** Kızılderili
indicate /'indikeyt/ e. göstermek; belirtmek **indication** belirti; iz, işaret; semptom **indicative** gösterici, belirtici **indicator** oto. sinyal; ibre, gösterge
indices /'indisi:z/ a, ç, bkz. index
indict /in'dayt/ e, huk. suçlamak
indifferent /in'difırınt/ s. aldırışsız, kayıt-

sız **indifference** ilgisizlik, kayıtsızlık

indigestion /indi'cesçın/ *a.* sindirim güçlüğü

indignant /in'dignınt/ *s.* kızgın, dargın

indignity /in'digniti/ *a.* onur kırıcı/küçük düşürücü durum

indirect /indi'rekt/ *s.* dolaylı **indirect speech** *dilb.* dolaylı anlatım

indiscreet /indi'skri:t/ *s.* düşüncesiz, patavatsız, boşboğaz

indiscriminate /indi'skriminit/ *s.* rasgele, gelişigüzel; ayırım yapmayan

indispensable /indi'spensıbıl/ *s.* vazgeçilmez, kaçınılmaz, gerekli

indisposed /indi'spouzd/ *s.* isteksiz; rahatsız, keyifsiz

indisputable /indi'spyu:tıbıl/ *s.* tartışılmaz, kesin, su götürmez

indistinguishable /indi'stingwişıbıl/ *s.* ayırt edilemez, seçilemez

individual /indi'vicuıl/ *s.* bireysel; kişisel, özel; tek ☆ *a.* kişi, birey; *kon.* insan **individually** teker teker

indivisible /indi'vizıbıl/ *s.* bölünmeyen, bölünmez

indoctrinate /in'doktrineyt/ *e.* (fikir) aşılamak, öğretmek, doldurmak

indolence /'indılıns/ *a.* tembellik, uyuşukluk, üşengeçlik

indolent /'indılınt/ *s.* tembel, üşengeç

indoor /'indo:/ *s.* ev içinde olan/yapılan

indoors /'indo:z/ *be.* ev içinde, ev içine

induce /in'dyu:s/ *e.* ikna etmek, kandırmak **inducement** kandırma, ikna, teşvik; neden, güdü

induction /in'dakşın/ *a.* tümevarım **inductive** tümevarımlı

indulge /in'dalc/ *e.* isteklerini yerine getirmek, şımartmak, yüz vermek **indulgence** göz yumma, hoşgörü; şımartma; şımartılma, düşkünlük

industrial /in'dastriıl/ *s.* endüstriyel **industrialist** sanayici, fabrikatör **industrialize** sanayileştirmek; sanayileşmek

industrious /in'dastriıs/ *s.* çalışkan

industry /'indıstri/ *a.* endüstri, sanayi

inebriate /i'ni:brieyt/ *e.* sarhoş etmek

inedible /in'edıbıl/ *s.* yenmez

ineffective /ini'fektiv/ *s.* etkisiz, sonuçsuz

inefficient /ini'fişınt/ *s.* etkisiz, yetersiz, verimsiz

ineligible /in'elicıbıl/ *s.* uygun olmayan, seçilemez

inept /i'nept/ *s.* uygunsuz, yersiz

inequality /ini'kwoliti/ *a.* eşitsizlik; pürüzlülük

inert /i'nö:t/ *s.* hareketsiz, cansız; yavaş, tembel, uyuşuk

inertia /i'nö:şı/ *a.* atalet, süredurum; tembellik, uyuşukluk

inescapable /inis'keypıbıl/ *s.* kaçınılamaz

inevitable /i'nevitıbıl/ *s.* kaçınılmaz

inexcusable /inik'skyu:zıbıl/ *s.* bağışlanamaz, hoş görülemez

inexpensive /inik'spensiv/ *s.* ucuz

inexperience /inik'spiıriıns/ *a.* tecrübesizlik **inexperienced** tecrübesiz, deneyimsiz

inexplicable /inik'splikıbıl/ *s.* açıklanamaz

infallible /in'felibıl/ *s.* yanılmaz, şaşmaz

infamous /'infımıs/ *s.* alçak, rezil; ayıp, iğrenç

infancy /'infınsi/ *a.* bebeklik, çocukluk; başlangıç

infant /'infınt/ *a.* küçük çocuk, bebek

infantile /'infıntayl/ *s.* çocukla ilgili, çocuksu, çocukça

infantry /'infıntri/ *a, ask.* piyade

infect /in'fekt/ *e.* (hastalık) bulaştırmak, geçirmek **infection** mikrop kapma; (hastalık) bulaşma, bulaştırma **infectious** bulaşıcı

infer /in'fö:/ *e.* (from) sonucunu çıkarmak, anlamak

inferior /in'fiıriı/ *s.* (to) aşağı, alt, ikinci derecede, ast

infernal /in'fö:nıl/ *s.* cehennemi, şeytani; *kon.* sinir bozucu

inferno /in'fö:nou/ *a.* cehennem

infertile /in'fö:tayl/ *s.* kısır; çorak

infest /in'fest/ *e.* (with) (fare, vb.) istila etmek, sarmak

infestation /infe'steyşın/ *a.* istila

infidel /'infidıl/ *a.* kâfir, imansız

infidelity /infi'deliti/ a. sadakatsizlik, aldatma

infiltrate /'infiltreyt/ e. süzülmek, girmek

infinite /'infinit/ s. sonsuz, sınırsız

infinitive /in'finitiv/ a, dilb. mastar, eylemlik

infinity /in'finiti/ a. sonsuzluk

infirm /in'fö:m/ s. halsiz, güçsüz

infirmary /in'fö:mıri/ a. revir, hastane

inflame /in'fleym/ e. tutuşturmak, alevlendirmek

inflammable /in'flemıbıl/ s. tutuşur, yanar, yanıcı

inflammation /inflı'meyşın/ a, hek. iltihap, yangı

inflammatory /in'flemıtıri/ s. tahrik eden, alevlendiren, kışkırtıcı

inflate /in'fleyt/ e. şişirmek; şişmek **inflation** enflasyon, para bolluğu; şişkinlik

inflect /in'flekt/ e, dilb. çekmek; kullanıma göre sözcüğün biçimini değiştirmek

inflexible /in'fleksıbıl/ s. eğilmez, bükülmez; değişmez

inflict /in'flikt/ e. (on/upon) uğratmak, çektirmek, vermek

influence /'influıns/ a. etki; nüfuz, sözü geçerlik ☆ e. etkilemek **under the influence of** -in etkisi altında

influential /influ'enşıl/ s. güçlü, etkili

influenza /influ'enzı/ a, hek. grip

influx /'inflaks/ a. istila, akın, üşüşme; içeriye akma

inform /in'fo:m/ e. haberdar etmek, bildirmek, bilgi vermek; ihbar etmek **informant** bilgi veren kimse, bilgi kaynağı **informer** muhbir

informal /in'fo:mıl/ s. resmi olmayan teklifsiz; gündelik

information /infı'meyşın/ a. bilgi, haber; danışma **information desk** danışma

informative /in'fo:mıtiv/ s. bilgi verici, aydınlatıcı

infrared /infrı'red/ s. kızılötesi

infrequency /in'fri:kwınsi/ a. seyreklik

infrequent seyrek, nadir

infringe /in'frinc/ e. çiğnemek, bozmak

infuriate /in'fyuırieyt/ e. çileden çıkarmak

infuse /in'fyu:z/ e. demlemek; aşılamak

ingenious /in'ci:nıs/ s. becerikli, usta, ustaca yapılmış

ingenuity /inci'nyu:iti/ a. zekâ, ustalık, beceri

ingot /'ingıt/ a. külçe

ingrained /in'greynd/ s. kökleşmiş, yerleşmiş

ingratitude /in'gretityu:d/ s. nankörlük

ingredient /in'gri:dıınt/ a. karışımı oluşturan madde

inhabit /in'hebit/ e. -de yaşamak, oturmak **inhabitant** sakin, oturan

inhale /in'heyl/ e. içine çekmek

inherent /in'hiırınt/ s. doğasında olan, doğal

inherit /in'herit/ e. miras olarak almak **inheritance** kalıt, miras

inhibit /in'hibit/ e. tutmak, dizginlemek, engellemek **inhibited** çekingen, utangaç **inhibition** çekingenlik, utangaçlık

inhuman /in'hyu:mın/ s. acımasız, gaddar

initial /i'nişıl/ s. ilk, önceki ☆ a. ilk harf ☆ e. parafe etmek **initially** başlangıçta, ilkin

initiate /i'nişeyt/ e. başlamak, başlatmak; temel bilgileri vermek; göstermek

initiative /i'nişıtiv/ a. ilk adım, başlangıç; inisiyatif **have/take the initiative** ilk adımı atmak, -e ön ayak olmak

inject /in'cekt/ e. iğne yapmak; zerk etmek **injection** iğne, enjeksiyon

injure /'incı/ e. incitmek, yaralamak; zarar vermek, incitmek **injured** yaralı

injury /'incıri/ a. hasar, zarar, ziyan

injustice /in'castis/ a. haksızlık, adaletsizlik **do sb an injustice** haksız davranmak

ink /ink/ a. mürekkep

inkling /'inkling/ a. seziş, kuşku

inland /'inlınd/ s. ülkenin iç kısmında olan, iç

in-laws /'inlo:z/ a. evlilik yoluyla akrabalar

inlet

364

inlet /'inlet, 'inlit/ a. körfezcik, koy; giriş, ağız

inmate /'inmeyt/ a. (hastane, hapishane, vb.) oda arkadaşı

inn /in/ a. han, otel

innate /i'neyt/ s. (nitelik) doğuştan

inner /'inı/ s. iç, içerdeki; merkeze en yakın innermost en içteki

innocent /'inısınt/ s. masum, suçsuz; zararsız; temiz kalpli

innocuous /i'nokyuıs/ s. zararsız, incitmeyen

innovate /'inıveyt/ e. yenilik yapmak innovation yenilik, buluş

innumerable /i'nyu:mırıbıl/ s. sayısız

inoculate /i'nokyuleyt/ e. aşılamak

inoffensive /inı'fensiv/ s. zararsız, incitmeyen

inopportune /in'opıtyu:n/ s. zamansız, sırasız, yersiz, uygunsuz, mevsimsiz

inorganic /ino:'genik/ s. inorganik

inpatient /in'peyşınt/ a. hastanede tedavi gören hasta

input /'input/ a. girdi; giriş

inquest /'inkwest/ a. soruşturma

inquire /in'kwayı/ e. sormak; bilgi almak, sorup öğrenmek, araştırmak inquiring araştırıcı, meraklı

inquiry /in'kwayıri/ a. soruşturma, araştırma

inquisition /inkwi'zişın/ a, hkr. sorgu, sorgulama

inquisitive /in'kwizitiv/ s. başkalarının işleriyle ilgilenen, meraklı

inroads /'inroudz/ a. akın, baskın; gedik

insane /in'seyn/ s. deli, çılgın

insanity /in'senıti/ a. delilik; çılgınlık

inscribe /in'skrayb/ e. yazmak; oymak, hakketmek inscription /in'skripşın/ kitabe, yazıt

insect /'insekt/ a. böcek

insecticide /in'sektisayd/ a. böcek ilacı

insecure /insi'kyuı/ s. güvensiz, endişeli; emniyetsiz, güvenilmez

insensible /in'sensıbıl/ s. bilinçsiz, baygın; bilgisiz, habersiz

insensitive /in'sensitiv/ s. duygusuz, anlayışsız; duyarsız, etkilenmeyen

inseparable /in'sepırıbıl/ s. ayrılmaz, bağlı, yapışık

insert /in'sö:t/ e. sokmak, içine koymak

inshore /in'şo:/ be. kıyıya (doğru)

inside /in'sayd/ a. iç, iç kısım ☆ be. içeriye, içerde inside out tersyüz

insidious /in'sidiıs/ s. sinsi, gizlice zarar veren

insight /'insayt/ a. kavrayış, anlayış

insignificant /insig'nifikınt/ s. değersiz, önemsiz

insincere /insin'siı/ s. içtenliksiz, samimiyetsiz, ikiyüzlü

insinuate /in'sinyueyt/ e. üstü kapalı söylemek, ima etmek, anıştırmak

insipid /in'sipid/ s. tatsız, yavan, lezzetsiz

insist /in'sist/ e. (on/upon) ısrar etmek, dayatmak insistence ısrar; ısrarlılık insistent ısrarlı; sürekli

insolent /'insılınt/ s. arsız, saygısız

insoluble /in'solyubıl/ s. çözünmez, erimez; içinden çıkılmaz, çözülemez

insolvent /in'solvınt/ s, a. borcunu ödeyemeyen

insomnia /in'somniı/ a. uykusuzluk

inspect /in'spekt/ e. denetlemek, incelemek; gözden geçirmek, yoklamak inspection denetim, yoklama inspector müfettiş

inspiration /inspi'reyşın/ a. esin, ilham kon. parlak fikir

inspire /in'spayı/ e. esinlemek, ilham vermek; (with/in) ile doldurmak

instability /instı'biliti/ a. kararsızlık, değişkenlik

install /in'sto:l/ e. (aygıt) döşemek, düzenlemek, kurmak; yerleştirmek installation tesisat, donanım; yerleştirme

instalment /in'sto:lmınt/ a. taksit; kısım, bölüm by instalments taksitle instalment sale taksitle satış

instance /'instıns/ a. örnek for instance mesela, örneğin, sözgelimi in the first instance önce, başlangıç olarak

instant /'instınt/ a. an, dakika ☆ s. hemen olan, acil; (yiyecek) çabuk ve kolay hazırlanabilen instant coffee nes kafe instantly hemen, anında

instead /in'sted/ *be.* (onun) yerine **instead of** -nin yerine

instigate /'instigeyt/ *e.* ön ayak olmak, kışkırtmak **instigation** teşvik, öneri, uyarı **instigator** kışkırtıcı

instil /in'stil/ *e.* (in/into) fikir aşılamak

instinct /'instinkt/ *a.* içgüdü **instinctive** içgüdüsel

institute /'instityu:t/ *a.* enstitü, kurum

institution /insti'tyu:şın/ *a.* kurum, kuruluş, dernek; yerleşmiş gelenek/yasa

instruct /in'strakt/ *e.* öğretmek, okutmak; talimat vermek **instruction** öğretim; talimat, yönerge **instructive** öğretici **instructor** eğitmen, öğretmen

instrument /'instrımınt/ *a.* aygıt, alet; müz. çalgı **instrumental (in)** yardımcı; *müz.* enstrümantal

insufferable /in'safırıbıl/ *s.* (davranış) katlanılmaz, çekilmez

insufficient /insı'fişınt/ *s.* yetersiz, eksik

insular /'insyu:lı/ *s.* dar görüşlü

insulate /'insyuleyt/ *e.* (from/against) izole etmek, yalıtmak; ayırmak **insulation** yalıtım, izolasyon; izolasyon maddesi

insult /in'salt/ *e.* aşağılamak, hakaret etmek ☆ *a.* hakaret

insurance /in'şuırıns/ *a.* sigorta; sigortacılık; sigorta primi

insure /in'şuı/ *e.* sigorta ettirmek; *AI.* garantilemek, sağlama almak

insurgent /in'sö:cınt/ *s, a.* asi, başkaldıran, ayaklanan

insurmountable /insı'mauntıbıl/ *s.* çok büyük, çok güç, yenilemez, başa çıkılmaz

insurrection /insı'rekşın/ *a.* isyan, ayaklanma

intact /in'tekt/ *s.* bozulmamış, tam

intake /'inteyk/ *a.* giriş, ağız

integer /'intıcı/ *a, mat.* tamsayı

integral /'intıgrıl/ *s.* gerekli, önemli; *mat.* integral, tümlev

integrate /'intıgreyt/ *e.* (with/into) bütünleşmek, kaynaşmak; katmak, kaynaştırmak

integrity /in'tegriti/ *a.* güvenilirlik, doğruluk; bütünlük

intellect /'intilekt/ *a.* akıl, zihin **intellectual** /-'lekçuıl/ akli, zihinsel; akıllı, zeki; aydın

intelligence /in'telicıns/ *a.* zekâ; istihbarat, haber alma

intelligent /in'telicınt/ *s.* zeki, akıllı

intelligible /in'telicıbıl/ *s.* anlaşılabilir, açık, net

intend /in'tend/ *e.* tasarlamak, niyet etmek

intense /in'tens/ *s.* şiddetli, güçlü; heyecanlı, ateşli

intensify /in'tensifay/ *e.* yoğunlaşmak; yoğunlaştırmak

intensity /in'tensiti/ *a.* güçlülük, yoğunluk

intensive /in'tensiv/ *s.* yoğun **intensive care** yoğun bakım

intent /in'tent/ *a.* amaç, niyet ☆ *s.* dikkatli; niyetli, azimli, istekli

intention /in'tenşın/ *a.* niyet, maksat; kasıt **intentional** kasıtlı **intentionally** kasten, bile bile

interact /intı'rekt/ *e.* (with) birbirini etkilemek **interaction** etkileşim

intercept /intı'sept/ *e.* yolunu kesmek

interchange /intı'çeync/ *e.* yerlerini değiştirmek; değiş tokuş etmek **interchangeable (with)** birbirinin yerine geçebilir

intercom /'intıkom/ *a.* iç telefon sistemi

intercommunication /intıkomyuni'key-şın/ *a.* dahili haberleşme, iç haberleşme

intercontinental /intıkonti'nentıl/ *s.* kıtalararası

intercourse /'intıko:s/ *a.* (cinsel) birleşme; görüşme, ilişki

interest /'intrist/ *a.* ilgi, merak; ilgi çekme; faiz; yarar; çıkar ☆ *e.* ilgilendirmek; ilgisini çekmek **interested** ilgili, meraklı **interesting** ilginç, entrasan **be interested in** ile ilgilenmek

interfere /intı'fiı/ *e.* burnunu sokmak, karışmak; engel olmak

interior /in'tiırii/ *a, s.* iç

interject /intı'cekt/ *e.* arada söylemek, eklemek **interjection** ünlem

interlock /intı'lok/ *e.* birbirine bağlamak

interlude /'intılu:d/ *a.* ara, teneffüs; (tiyatro, vb.) perde arası; *müz.* ara faslı

intermediary /intı'mi:dıri/ *a.* arabulucu, aracı

intermediate /intı'mi:diıt/ *s.* arada bulunan, ara, orta

intermission /intı'mişın/ *a, Aİ.* perde arası, ara

intermittent /intı'mitınt/ *s.* kesik kesik, aralıklı, süreksiz

intern /in'tö:n/ *e.* enterne etmek, gözaltına almak ☆ *a.* stajyer; stajyer doktor

internal /in'tö:nıl/ *s.* dahili, iç

international /intı'neşınıl/ *s.* uluslararası

interpose /intı'pouz/ *e.* araya girmek, lafa karışmak

interpret /in'tö:prit/ *e.* (konuşarak) tercümanlık yapmak; yorumlamak; anlamını açıklamak **interpretation** yorum, tefsir **interpreter** tercüman

interrogate /in'terıgeyt/ *e.* sorguya çekmek **interrogation** soru; sorgu, sorgulama **interrogative** soru sözcüğü

interrupt /intı'rapt/ *e.* sözünü kesmek; akışını durdurmak **interruption** kesilme, yarıda kesme

intersect /intı'sekt/ *e.* kesişmek, birbiri üzerinden geçmek **intersection** kesişme; kavşak

interval /'intıvıl/ *a.* ara, aralık; perde arası

intervene /intı'vi:n/ *e.* (in) araya girmek, karışmak, müdahale etmek

interview /'intıvyu:/ *a.* mülakat, görüşme; röportaj ☆ *e.* görüşmek; röportaj yapmak

intestine /in'testin/ *a, anat.* bağırsak

intimacy /'intimısi/ *a.* mahremlik, kişisellik; yakın arkadaşlık, dostluk

intimate /'intimit/ *s.* içli dışlı, candan; kişisel, özel

intimidate /in'timideyt/ *e.* korkutmak, gözünü korkutmak, gözdağı vermek

into /'intı, 'intu, 'intu:/ *ilg.* içine, -ye, -ya; haline, biçimine

intolerable /in'tolırıbıl/ *s.* çekilmez, dayanılmaz

intolerant /in'tolırınt/ *s.* hoşgörüsüz

intonation /intı'neyşın/ *a.* ses perdesi, titremleme

intoxicate /in'toksikeyt/ *e.* sarhoş etmek

intractable /in'trektıbıl/ *s.* kontrol edilmesi zor, ele avuca sığmaz

intransitive /in'trensitiv/ *a, s, dilb.* (eylem) geçişsiz

intrepid /in'trepid/ *s.* korkusuz, cesur

intricacy /'intrikısi/ *a.* karışıklık, anlaşılmazlık; karışık şey

intricate /'intrikit/ *s.* karmakarışık

intrigue /in'tri:g/ *e.* ilgisini çekmek; entrika çevirmek ☆ *a.* entrika, dolap

intrinsic /in'trinsik/ *s.* gerçek, aslında olan, esas

introduce /intrı'dyu:s/ *e.* tanıştırmak, tanıtmak; ortaya çıkarmak

introduction /intrı'dakşın/ *a.* tanıtma, tanıtım, takdim; tanıştırma; önsöz; giriş, başlangıç

introductory /intrı'daktıri/ *s.* giriş niteliğinde, tanıtıcı

introvert /'ıntrıvö:t/ *a.* içedönük kimse

intrude /in'tru:d/ *e.* davetsiz olarak girmek **intruder** davetsiz misafir

intuition /intyu'işın/ *a.* sezgi, önsezi

inundate /'inındeyt/ *e.* sel basmak; gark etmek, boğmak

invade /in'veyd/ *e.* istila etmek; akın etmek; baskın yapmak

invalid /'invıli:d, 'invılid/ *s.* hasta, sakat ☆ *s.* hükümsüz, geçersiz

invaluable /in'velyubıl/ *s.* çok değerli, paha biçilmez

invasion /in'veyjın/ *a.* akın, saldırı, istila

invective /in'vektiv/ *a.* hakaret, sövgü

inveigle /in'vi:gıl/ *e.* kandırmak

invent /in'vent/ *e.* icat etmek, bulmak; uydurmak, kıvırmak **invention** icat, buluş **inventive** yaratıcı **inventor** mucit

inventory /'invıntri/ *a.* sayım çizelgesi, envanter

inverse /'invö:s/ *a, s.* ters

invert /in'vö:t/ *e.* tersyüz etmek; sırasını değiştirmek **inverted commas** tırnak işareti

invertebrate /in'vö:tibrit, in'vö:tibreyt/ *s, a, hayb.* omurgasız

jack

invest /in'vest/ *e.* **(in)** para yatırmak, yatırım yapmak
investigate /in'vestigeyt/ *e.* araştırmak, soruşturmak **investigation** araştırma, soruşturma **investigator** müfettiş
invest /in'vest/ *e.* **(para)** yatırmak **investment** yatırım; sağlanan gelir
invidious /in'vidiıs/ *s.* gücendirici, kıskandırıcı, haksız
invigorate /in'vigıreyt/ *s.* güçlendirmek, canlandırmak, dinçleştirmek
invincible /in'vinsıbıl/ *s.* yenilmez
invisible /in'vizıbıl/ *s.* görünmez, görülemez
invitation /invi'teyşın/ *a.* davet, çağrı
invite /in'vayt/ *e.* davet etmek, çağırmak **inviting** davetkâr, çekici, göz alıcı
invoice /'invoys/ *a.* fatura
invoke /in'vouk/ *e.* yakarmak, dua etmek
involuntary /in'volıntıri/ *s.* istenilmeden yapılan, gönülsüzce yapılan
involve /in'volv/ *e.* **(in/with)** karıştırmak, sokmak, bulaştırmak; içermek, kapsamak
inward /'inwıd/ *s.* içeride olan, iç; *Aİ, bkz.* **inwards**
inwards /'inwıdz/ *be.* içeriye doğru
iodine /'ayıdi:n/ *a, kim.* iyot
ion /'ayın/ *a.* iyon
irate /ay'reyt/ *s.* kızgın, öfkeli
iris /'ayıris/ *a, bitk.* süsen çiçeği; *anat.* iris
irksome /'ö:ksım/ *s.* usandırıcı, bıktırıcı, sıkıcı
iron /'ayın/ *a.* demir; ütü ☆ *e.* ütülemek **ironing board** ütü sehpası **ironmonger** hırdavatçı
ironic /ay'ronik/ *s.* alaylı, alaycı, istihzalı
irony /'ayırıni/ *a.* istihza, ince alay
irrational /i'reşınıl/ *s.* akılsız, mantıksız
irregular /i'regyulı/ *s.* **(biçim)** çarpık, eğri; **(zaman)** düzensiz; başıbozuk; *dilb.* düzensiz
irrelevance /i'relivıns/ *a.* konu dışı olma **irrelevant** konu dışı, ilgisiz
irreplaceable /iri'pleysıbıl/ *s.* yeri doldurulamaz

irresistible /iri'zistıbıl/ *s.* karşı konulamaz, dayanılmaz, çok güçlü
irresponsible /iri'sponsıbıl/ *s.* sorumsuz
irrevocable /i'revıkıbıl/ *s.* dönülemez, geri alınamaz, değiştirilemez
irrigate /'irigeyt/ *e.* (toprağı) sulamak
irritable /'iritıbıl/ *s.* çabuk kızan, alıngan
irritant /'iritınt/ *s, a.* tahriş edici (madde)
irritate /'iriteyt/ *e.* kızdırmak, sinirlendirmek; tahriş etmek
is /iz/ *e, bkz.* **be**
Islam /'isla:m/ *a.* İslam, İslamiyet
island /'aylınd/ *a.* ada
isle /ayl/ *a, yaz.* ada
isolate /'aysıleyt/ *e.* ayırmak, izole etmek, yalıtmak **isolated** izole, ayrılmış, tek **isolation** izolasyon, yalıtım, yalnızlık
issue /'işu:, 'isyu:/ *a.* yayımlama; (dergi) sayı; emisyon, piyasaya çıkarma; çıkış ☆ *e.* yayımlamak; donatmak; **(from)** -den gelmek, kaynaklanmak
it /it/ *adl.* o, onu, ona
italics /i'teliks/ *a.* italik yazı
itch /iç/ *e.* kaşınmak; *kon.* can atmak, çok istemek ☆ *a.* kaşıntı; güçlü istek, şiddetli arzu
itchy /'içi/ *s.* kaşıntılı, kaşınan
item /'aytim/ *a.* parça, adet; madde, fıkra **news item** kısa haber, özet haber
itinerary /ay'tinırıri/ *a.* yolculuk planı, yolculuk programı
its /its/ *s.* onun, -ın, -in
itself /it'self/ *adl.* kendisi, kendi
ivory /'ayvıri/ *a.* fildişi
ivy /'ayvi/ *a, bitk.* sarmaşık

J

jab /ceb/ *e.* dürtmek, itmek ☆ *a.* dürtme, itme; *kon.* iğne, şırınga
jabber /'cebı/ *e.* hızlı ve anlaşılmaz bir biçimde konuşmak
jack /cek/ *a.* kriko; (iskambil) vale, ba-

cak

jackal /'ceko:l/ a, hayb. çakal

jacket /'cekit/ a. ceket, mont; patates kabuğu; ciltli kitabın üzerine geçirilen kâğıt kap; Aİ. plak kabı

jackpot /'cekpot/ a. büyük ikramiye

jade /ceyd/ a. yeşimtaşı, yeşim

jagged /'cegid/ s. çentikli, sivri uçlu

jaguar /'cegyuı/ a, hayb. jaguar

jail /ceyl/ a. hapishane, cezaevi

jailer /'ceylı/ a. gardiyan

jam /cem/ a. reçel; sıkışıklık, tıkanıklık ☆ e. sıkıştırmak; tıkamak; bastırmak; sıkışmak

jangle /'cengıl/ e. ahenksiz sesler çıkartmak

janitor /'cenitı/ a. kapıcı, hademe

January /'cenyuıri/ a. ocak (ayı)

jar /ca:/ a. kavanoz; şok, sarsıntı ☆ e. sarsmak; (renk) gitmemek, sırıtmak; (kulak) tırmalamak

jargon /'ca:gın/ a. anlaşılmaz dil, teknik dil

jasmine /'cezmin/ a, bitk. yasemin

jaundice /'co:ndis/ a, hek. sarılık

jaunt /co:nt/ e. (about/around) gezintiye çıkmak ☆ a. kısa gezinti

javelin /'cevılin/ a, sp. cirit; kargı, mızrak

jaw /co:/ a. çene

jay /cey/ a, hayb. alakarga

jazz /cez/ a. caz jazzy göz alıcı, gösterişli

jealous /'celıs/ s. kıskanç jealousy kıskançlık

jeans /ci:nz/ a. blucin, kot pantolon

jeep /ci:p/ a. cip

jeer /ciı/ e. alay etmek, gülmek

jelly /'celi/ a. jöle, pelte; marmelat; jelatin

jellyfish /'celifiş/ a. denizanası

jeopardize /'cepıdayz/ e. tehlikeye atmak jeopardy tehlike

jerk /cö:k/ e. birdenbire çekmek; silkip atmak, silkelemek ☆ a. ani çekiş; itiş, kakış; Aİ, arg. aptal, ayı, kazma

jersey /'cö:zi/ a. kazak

jest /cest/ a. şaka, espri in jest şakadan, gırgırına

jet /cet/ a. jet uçağı; fıskıye; siyah kehribar

jettison /'cetisın/ e. (tehlike anında eşyayı) gemiden atmak

jetty /'ceti/ a. dalgakıran, mendirek

Jew /cu:/ a. Yahudi

jewel /'cu:ıl/ a. değerli taş; mücevher, takı jeweller kuyumcu jewellery mücevherat; kuyumculuk

jiggle /'cigıl/ e, kon. sallamak, çalkalamak

jigsaw /'cigso:/ a. makineli oyma testeresi; bozyap (oyunu) jigsaw puzzle bozyap (oyunu)

jingle /'cingıl/ e. şıngırdamak; şıngırdatmak ☆ a. şıngırtı; basit vezinli şiir

jinx /cinks/ a. uğursuzluk şey/kişi

job /cob/ a. iş, görev, meslek

jockey /'coki/ a. cokey

jog /cog/ e. yavaş yavaş koşmak; itmek, dürtmek jogging yavaş koşu

join /coyn/ e. birleştirmek; birleşmek; katılmak

joiner /'coynı/ a. doğramacı, marangoz joinery doğramacılık, marangozluk

joint /coynt/ a. eklem, ek yeri; et parçası ☆ s. ortak, birleşik

joist /coyst/ a. kiriş

joke /couk/ a. şaka; fıkra play a joke on sb oyun oynamak, işletmek

joker /'coukı/ a. şakacı kimse; (iskambil) joker

jolly /'coli/ s. mutlu, neşeli ☆ be, İİ, kon. çok

jolt /coult/ e. sarsmak ☆ a. şok, sarsıntı

jostle /'cosıl/ e. itip kakmak, dürtüklemek

journal /'cö:nıl/ a. gazete, dergi journalism gazetecilik journalist gazeteci

journey /'cö:ni/ a. seyahat, yolculuk

jowl /caul/ a. gerdan, gıdık

joy /coy/ a. sevinç, mutluluk, neşe joyful neşeli, sevinçli; sevindirici joyous sevinçli joystick (uçak, bilgisayar, vb.'de) manevra kolu

jubilant /'cu:bilınt/ s. neşe dolu, çok sevinçli

jubilee /'cu:bili:, cu:bi'li:/ a. yıldönümü şenliği; jübile diamond jubilee altmışıncı yıldönümü **golden jubilee** ellinci yıldönümü **silver jubilee** yirmi beşinci yıldönümü

Judaism /'cu:deyizım/ *a.* Yahudilik

judge /cac/ *e.* -e yargıçlık etmek; (yarışma, vb.'de) değerlendirmek ☆ *a.* hâkim, yargıç; hakem; bilirkişi

judgment /'cacmınt/ *a.* yargı, hüküm, karar; yargılama; görüş, düşünce **judgment day** kıyamet günü

judicial /cu:'dişıl/ *s.* adli, türel; hukuki, tüzel

judiciary /cu:'dişıri/ *a.* adliye, yargıçlar

judicious /cu:'dişıs/ *s.* sağgörülü, doğru karar veren

judo /'cu:dou/ *a, sp.* judo

jug /cag/ *a.* testi, sürahi

juggernaut /'cagıno:t/ *a, İİ, kon.* büyük kamyon, tır

juggle /'cagıl/ *e.* hokkabazlık yapmak; yolsuzluk yapmak

juice /cu:s/ *a.* meyve/sebze/et suyu; (vücut) salgı **juicy** sulu; *kon.* ilginç, merak uyandırıcı

July /cu'lay/ *a.* temmuz

jumble /'cambıl/ *e.* birbirine karışmak; karmakarışık etmek ☆ *a.* düzensizlik, karmakarışık şey **jumble sale** kullanılmış eşya satışı

jumbo /'cambou/ *s.* kocaman

jump /camp/ *e.* sıçramak, atlamak; üzerinden atlamak; fırlamak ☆ *a.* sıçrama, atlama, zıplama, sıçrayış

jumper /'campı/ *a, İİ.* kazak, süveter

jumpy /'campi/ *s.* sinirli, gergin

junction /'cankşın/ *a.* kavşak

June /cu:n/ *a.* haziran

jungle /'cangıl/ *a.* balta girmemiş orman, cengel

junior /'cu:nii/ *a, s.* yaşça küçük, daha genç; ast

junk /cank/ *a, kon.* ıvır zıvır, döküntü eşya, pılı pırtı

junta /'cantı/ *a.* cunta

Jupiter /'cu:pıtı/ *a.* Jüpiter

jurisdiction /cuiris'dikşın/ *a, huk.* yargılama yetkisi

juror /'cuırı/ *a.* jüri üyesi

jury /'cuıri/ *a, huk.* jüri; yarışma jürisi, jüri

just /cast/ *s.* adil, doğru, dürüst ☆ *be.* tam, tastamam; sadece, yalnız; az önce, demin; güçlükle, darı darına; hemen, şimdi

justice /'castis/ *a.* adalet; adliye, mahkeme; *Aİ.* yargıç **justifiable** savunulabilir, haklı çıkarılabilir

justify /'castifay/ *e.* haklı çıkarmak, doğruluğunu kanıtlamak

jut /cat/ *e.* (out) çıkıntı yapmak

jute /cu:t/ *a, bitk.* hintkeneviri

juvenile /'cu:vınayl/ *s.* genç, gençlere özgü

juxtaposition /cakstıpı'zişın/ *a.* yan yana koyma

K

kaleidoscope /kı'laydıskoup/ *a.* çiçek dürbünü, kaleydoskop

kangaroo /kengı'ru:/ *a, hayb.* kanguru

karate /kı'ra:ti/ *a.* karate

kebab /ki'beb/ *a.* kebap, şiş kebap

keel /ki:l/ *a.* gemi omurgası

keen /ki:n/ *s.* keskin; acı, sert; akıllı **keen on** meraklı, hevesli, hasta

keep /ki:p/ *e.* **kept** /kept/ tutmak; alıkoymak; korumak; saklamak; yerine getirmek; yönetmek; işletmek; geçindirmek. bakmak; engel olmak ☆ *a.* yiyecek, yemek; kale **keep back** söylememek, vermemek **keep down** kontrol altına almak; baskı altında tutmak **keep in** (öğrenciyi) dersten sonra alıkoymak **keep off** -den uzak durmak **keep on** -e devam etmek, sürdürmek; elden çıkarmamak, **keep out** girmemek, uzak durmak; sokmamak, uzak tutmak **keep to** bağlı kalmak, sadık olmak **keep up** ayakta tutmak; bakımını sağlamak; sürdürmek

keeper /'ki:pı/ *a.* bekçi, bakıcı

keg /keg/ *a.* küçük fıçı, varil

kennel /'kenıl/ *a.* köpek kulübesi

kerb /kö:b/ *a.* kaldırımın kenar taşı

kernel /'kö:nıl/ *a.* çekirdek içi; esas, öz

kerosene /'kerısi:n/ *a, Aİ.* gazyağı, gaz

kestrel /'kestrıl/ *a, hayb.* kerkenez

ketchup /'keçıp/ *a.* ketçap, domates sosu

kettle /'ketıl/ *a.* çaydanlık; güğüm; kazan; tencere

key /ki:/ *a.* anahtar; **(to)** çözüm yolu, açıklama; (piyano, daktilo, vb.) tuş; müzik anahtarı ☆ *e.* **(to)** daha uygun hale getirmek, ayarlamak **key ring** anahtarlık

keyboard /'ki:bo:d/ *a.* klavye, tuş

keyhole /'ki:houl/ *a.* anahtar deliği

keynote /'ki:nout/ *a.* temel düşünce, ana ilke, temel, dayanak

khaki /'ka:ki/ *a, s.* haki renk, haki

kick /kik/ *e.* tekmelemek, tekme atmak; (gol) atmak; çifte atmak ☆ *a.* tekme; *kon.* heyecan, coşku

kickoff /'kikof/ *a.* (futbol) başlama vuruşu, ilk vuruş **kick out** kovmak, defetmek

kid /kid/ *a, kon.* oğlak; çocuk ☆ *e, kon.* takılmak, aldatmak, işletmek

kidnap /'kidnep/ *e.* (adam/çocuk) kaçırmak **kidnapper** zorla insan kaçıran kimse

kidney /'kidni/ *a, anat.* böbrek **kidney beans** barbunya; börülce

kill /kil/ *e.* öldürmek; yok etmek **killer** katil **killjoy** neşe kaçıran kimse, oyunbozan

kiln /kiln/ *a.* ocak, fırın

kilo /'ki:lou/ *a, kon.* kilo

kilogram /'kilıgrem/ *a.* kilogram

kilometre /'kilımi:tı, ki'lomıtı/ *a.* kilometre

kilt /kilt/ *a.* İskoç erkeklerinin giydiği eteklik

kimono /ki'mounou/ *a.* kimono

kin /kin/ *a.* akraba, hısım **next of kin** en yakın akraba

kind /kaynd/ *a.* tür, çeşit, cins; tip ☆ *s.* nazik, kibar; iyi kalpli, sevecen; candan, yürekten **a kind of** bir çeşit **It's very kind of you.** Çok naziksiniz. **kind-hearted** iyi kalpli, sevecen **kind of** *kon.* adeta, az çok **kindness** şefkat, sevecenlik; nezaket

kindergarten /'kindıga:tın/ *a.* anaokulu

kindle /'kindıl/ *e.* yakmak, tutuşturmak; yanmak, tutuşmak

kindling /'kindling/ *a.* (gaz, çıra, ot, vb.) tutuşturucu madde

kindly /'kayndli/ *s.* müşfik, sevecen ☆ *be.* nazikçe, kibarca; lütfen

kindred /'kindrid/ *a.* akrabalık, soy

kinetic /ki'netik/ *s, tek.* kinetik, devimsel

king /king/ *a.* kral; (satranç) şah; (iskambil) papaz

kingdom /'kingdım/ *a.* krallık; *bitk, hayb.* âlem

kink /kink/ *a.* halat, tel, ip, saç, vb.'nin dolaşması; acayiplik, tuhaflık

kiosk /'ki:osk/ *a.* küçük kulübe; *İİ.* telefon kulübesi

kiss /kis/ *e.* öpmek ☆ *a.* öpücük, öpüş

kit /kit/ *a.* teçhizat, donatı; avadanlık

kitchen /'kiçın/ *a.* mutfak

kite /kayt/ *a.* uçurtma; *hayb.* çaylak

kitten /'kitın/ *a.* kedi yavrusu, yavru kedi

kiwi /'kiwi:/ *a, hayb.* kivi

kleptomania /kleptı'meynıı/ *a.* çalma hastalığı, kleptomani **kleptomaniac** çalma hastası, kleptoman

knack /nek/ *a, kon.* ustalık, beceri

knead /ni:d/ *e.* yoğurmak; ovmak

knee /ni:/ *a.* diz; (giyside) diz yeri

kneel /ni:l/ *e.* **knelt** /nelt/ **(down/on)** diz çökmek

knickers /'nikız/ *a.* kadın külotu

knife /nayf/ *a.* bıçak; çakı ☆ *e.* bıçaklamak

knight /nayt/ *a.* şövalye **knighthood** şövalyelik

knit /nit/ *e.* örmek; birleşmek, kaynaşmak **knitting** örgü **knitting needle** örgü şişi **knitwear** örgü eşya

knob /nob/ *a.* top, yumru; topuz, tokmak

knock /nok/ *e.* vurmak; çarpmak; *kon.* kusur bulmak, eleştirmek ☆ *a.* vurma, vuruş; *kon.* eleştiri **knock down** vurup yere sermek **knock out** nakavt etmek, yere sermek **knock up** uyandırmak; çok yormak

knock-out /'nokaut/ *a.* nakavt; çekici kimse/şey

knot /not/ *a.* düğüm; budak, boğum

deniz mili **knotty** düğüm düğüm, düğümlü

know /nou/ *e.* **knew** /nyu:/, **known** /noun/ bilmek; tanımak **know-how** ustalık, beceri, teknik

knowledge /'nolic/ *a.* bilgi

known /noun/ *s.* tanınmış, bilinen, tanınan, ünlü

knuckle /'nakıl/ *a.* parmağın oynak yeri

koala /kou'a:lı/ *a, hayb.* koala

Koran /ko:'ra:n, kı'ra:n, 'ko:ren/ *a.* Kuran

kung fu /kang'fu:, kung'fu:/ *a.* kung fu

L

lab /leb/ *a, kon.* laboratuvar

label /'leybıl/ *a.* etiket, yafta ☆ *e.* etiketlemek

laboratory /lı'borıtri/ *a.* laboratuvar

laborious /lı'bo:rııs/ *s.* yorucu, zahmetli, güç

labour /'leybı/ *a.* çalışma, emek, iş; işçi, işçi sınıfı; doğum, doğurma ☆ *e.* çalışmak, uğraşmak; ayrıntılara girmek **labour exchange** iş ve işçi bulma kurumu **labour union** işçi sendikası **labourer** işçi, emekçi

labyrinth /'lebırint / *a.* labirent

lace /leys/ *a.* bağcık, bağ; dantela

lack /lek/ *e.* -sizlik çekmek, -den yoksun olmak ☆ *a.* olmayış, eksiklik

lacquer /'lekı/ *a.* vernik

lad /led/ *a, kon.* delikanlı, genç

ladder /'ledı/ *a.* el merdiveni; çorap kaçığı ☆ *e, ii.* (çorap) kaçmak; kaçırmak

laden /'leydın/ *s.* **(with)** yüklü, dolu

ladle /'leydıl/ *a.* kepçe

lady /'leydi/ *a.* hanımefendi; kadın, bayan **ladybird** uğurböceği **ladykiller** kadın avcısı, çapkın **lady like** hanım hanımcık, kibar

lag /leg/ *e.* yavaş ilerlemek

lager /'la:gı/ *a.* bir tür hafif bira

lagoon /lı'gu:n/ *a, coğ.* denizkulağı, kıyı gölü

laid /leyd/ *bkz.* lay

lain /leyn/ *bkz.* lie

lair /leı/ *a.* vahşi hayvan ini

lake /leyk/ *a.* göl

lamb /lem/ *a.* kuzu; kuzu eti

lame /leym/ *s.* topal, aksak; sakat

lament /lı'ment/ *e.* ağlayıp sızlamak ☆ *a.* ağıt; ağlama, inleme **lamentable** içler acısı, acınacak

lamp /lemp/a. lamba, ışık **lamppost** elektrik direği **lampshade** abajur

lance /la:ns/ *a.* mızrak, kargı

land /lend/ *a.* toprak, kara parçası; ülke; arsa ☆ *e.* karaya çıkmak; iniş yapmak, yere inmek **landlady** ev sahibesi; pansiyoncu kadın **landlocked** kara ile çevrili **landlord** mal sahibi; otelci, pansiyoncu **landmark** sınır taşı; dönüm noktası **landscape** kır manzarası; peyzaj **landslide** heyelan, toprak kayması

lane /leyn/ *a.* dar sokak; yol, şerit

language /'lengwic/ *a.* dil, lisan

lank /lenk/ *s.* (saç) düz ve cansız

lanky /lenki/ *s.* uzun boylu ve zayıf

lantern /'lentın/ *a.* fener

lap /lep/ *a.* kucak; (yarışta) tur ☆ *e.* yalayarak içmek

lapel /lı'pel/ *a.* klapa

lapse /leps/ *a.* küçük kusur, hata, yanlış; ara ☆ *e.* sona ermek; yanılmak

larceny /'la:sıni/ *a, huk.* hırsızlık

larch /la:ç/ *a, bitk.* çam

lard /la:d/ *a.* domuz yağı

larder /'la:dı/ *a.* kiler

large /la:c/ *s.* büyük, iri; geniş; bol **at large** başıboş, serbest; etraflı, ayrıntılı olarak; genelde **large scale** büyük çapta **largely** çoğunlukla **largeness** büyüklük

largesse /la:'ces/ *a.* ihsan, bağış

lark /la:k/ *a, kon.* şaka, gırgır; *hayb.* tarlakuşu

larva /'la:vı/ *a.* larva, tırtıl, kurtçuk

laryngitis /lerin'caytis/ *a, hek.* larenjit, gırtlak yangısı

larynx /'lerinks/ *a, anat.* gırtlak

lascivious /lı'siviıs/ *s.* şehvetli, şehvet düşkünü

laser /'leyzı/ *a.* lazer (aygıtı)

lash /leş/ *e.* kırbaçlamak; (about) aniden hareket etmek; sıkıca bağlamak ☆ *a.* kamçı darbesi; ani ve haşin hareket

lasso /lı'su:, 'lesou/ *a.* kement

last /la:st/ *s.* sonuncu, son; geçen, önceki ☆ *be.* en son ☆ *a.* son ☆ *e.* devam etmek, sürmek; dayanmak **at last** en sonunda **lasting** sürekli, kalıcı

latch /leç/ *a.* kapı mandalı; kapı kilidi

late /leyt/ *s.* geç; sabık, eski; son zamanlardaki, yeni ☆ *be.* geç **lately** son günlerde, son zamanlarda

latent /'leytınt/ *s.* ortada olmayan, gizli

lateral /'letırıl/ *s, tek.* yan, yanal

latest /'leytıst/ *a, kon.* en son haber/moda, vb. **at (the) latest** en geç

lathe /leyd/ *a.* torna tezgâhı

lather /'la:dı/ *a.* sabun köpüğü, köpük ☆ *e.* (sabun) köpürmek; köpürtmek, sabunlamak

Latin /'letin/ *a, s.* Latin, Latince

latitude /'letityu:d/ *a, coğ.* enlem

latrine /lı'tri:n/ *a.* (özellikle kamplarda) hela

latter /'letı/ *s.* sonraki, son **latter day** çağdaş, yeni **latterly** son zamanlarda

lattice /'letis/ *a.* kafes

laugh /la:f/ *e.* (kahkahayla) gülmek ☆ *a.* gülüş, kahkaha **laughable** gülünç, komik **laugh at** -e gülmek; gülüp geçmek **laughter** kahkaha, gülüş

launch /lo:nç/ *e.* (gemi) suya indirmek; (roket) fırlatmak ☆ *a.* (gemiyi) suya indirme

launder /'lo:ndı/ *e.* (giysi) yıkayıp ütülemek

launderette /lo:n'dret/ *a.* çamaşırhane

laundromat /'lo:ndrımet/ *a, Aİ* çamaşırhane

laundry /'lo:ndri/ *a.* çamaşırhane; çamaşır

laurel /'lorıl/ *a, bitk.* defne ağacı

lav /lev/ *a, İİ, kon.* yüznumara

lava /'la:vı/ *a.* lav

lavatory /'levıtıri/ *a.* hela, tuvalet, yüznumara

lavender /'levındı/ *a, bitk.* lavanta

lavish /'leviş/ *s.* savurgan, tutumsuz

law /lo:/ *a.* kanun, yasa; kural; hukuk

law-abiding yasaya saygı gösteren **lawful** yasal **lawless** yasadışı **lawsuit** dava

lawn /lo:n/ *a.* çimen, çimenlik; patiska **lawn mower** çim biçme makinesi

lawyer /'lo:yı/ *a.* avukat

lax /leks/ *s.* umursamaz, kaygısız; savsak

laxative /'leksıtiv/ *a, s.* müshil

lay /ley/ *e.* **laid** /leyd/ yaymak, sermek; koymak; yatırmak; hazırlamak, kurmak; yumurtlamak ☆ *a.* durum, duruş **lay aside** bir kenara koymak **lay-by** *İİ.* (otoyol) park yeri **lay down** belirlemek, saptamak **lay off** işten çıkarmak **lay on** temin etmek; sağlamak **lay up** (hastalık) yatağa düşürmek

layer /'leyı/ *a.* tabaka, kat

layout /'leyaut/ *a.* tertip, düzen; mizanpaj

lazy /'leyzi/ *s.* tembel; ağır, uyuşuk

lead /li:d/ *e.* **led** /led/ götürmek, komuta etmek, yönetmek; sürmek; yaşamak **lead to** -e yol açmak, neden olmak **lead up to** sözü belli bir noktaya getirmek

lead /led/ *a.* kurşun; kalem kurşunu; grafit; anterlin

leader /'li:dı/ *a.* lider, önder **leadership** liderlik

leading /'li:ding/ *s.* başta gelen, en önemli **leading article** başyazı

leaf /li:f/ *a.* (bitki) yaprak; sayfa, yaprak

leaflet /'li:flit/ *a.* broşür

league /li:g/ *a.* dernek; birlik; lig

leak /li:k/ *a.* sızıntı, akıntı; delik, kaçak yeri ☆ *e.* sızdırmak, akıtmak; sızmak **leakage** sızıntı, sızma **leaky** sızıntılı, delik

lean /li:n/ *e.* **leaned** ya da **leant** /lent/ dayanmak, yaslanmak, eğilmek ☆ *s.* çok zayıf, sıska; (et) yağsız; verimsiz, kıt **leaning** eğilim

leanto /'li:ntu:/ *a.* sundurma

leap /li:p/ *e.* **leaped, leapt** /lept/ sıçramak, atlamak ☆ *a.* sıçrayış, atlama **leap year** artıkyıl

learn /lö:n/ *e.* öğrenmek **learned** bilgili **learner** öğrenci **learning** bilgi

373 **liaison**

lease /li:s/ *a.* kira kontratı ☆ *e.* **(out)** kontratla kiralamak
least /li:st/ *be.* en küçük; **en az at least** en azından, hiç olmazsa
leather /'ledı/ *a.* deri
leave /li:v/ *e.* **left** /left/ ayrılmak, bırakmak, terk etmek ☆ *a.* izin **on leave** izinli **by/with your leave** izninizle **leave alone** rahat bırakmak **leave out** atlamak; dahil etmemek
lecture /'lekçı/ *a.* konferans; (üniversitede) ders ☆ *e.* ders vermek; konferans vermek **lecturer** konferansçı; okutman; doçent
led /led/ *bkz.* **lead**
ledger /'lecı/ *a.* defteri kebir
leech /li:ç/ *a, hayb.* sülük; asalak, parazit
leek /li:k/ *a.* pırasa
left /left/ *bkz.* **leave**
left /left/ *s.* sol ☆ *a.* sol taraf ☆ *be.* sola, sol tarafa **left-hand** soldaki, sol **left-handed** solak **leftist** solcu
leftovers /'leftouvız/ *a.* artık yemek
leg /leg/ *a.* bacak; but **pull sb's leg** şaka yapmak, takılmak
legacy /'legısi/ *a.* miras, kalıt
legal /'li:gıl/ *s.* yasal, kanuni **legality** yasallık
legalize /'li:gılayz/ *e.* yasallaştırmak
legation /li'geyşın/ *a.* ortaelçilik
legend /'lecınd/ *a.* söylence, efsane, mit **legendary** efsanevi; ünlü
legible /'lecıbıl/ *s.* okunaklı
legion /'li:cın/ *a.* lejyon
legislate /'lecisleyt/ *e.* **(for/against)** yasa yapmak, yasamak **legislation** yasama
legislative /'lecislıtiv/ *s.* yasamaya ilişkin
legislature /'lecisleyçı/ *a.* yasama meclisi
legitimate /li'citimit/ *s.* yasal; meşru doğmuş; mantıklı, akla yatkın
leisure /'lejı/ *a.* boş vakit **at leisure** boş, serbest; acelesiz **leisurely** acelesiz yapılan, yavaş, sakin
lemon /'lemın/ *a.* limon **lemonade** *İİ.* gazoz; *Aİ.* limonata
lend /lend/ *e.* ödünç vermek, borç ver-

mek
length /lengt/ *a.* uzunluk, boy; süre **at length** en sonunda **lengthen** uzatmak; uzamak **lengthways** /-weyz/, **lengthwise** /-wayz/ uzunluğuna **lengthy** upuzun
lenient /'li:nıınt/ *s.* müşfik, yumuşak
lens /lenz/ *a.* mercek; objektif
lent /lent/ *bkz.* **lend**
lentil /'lentıl/ *a.* mercimek
Leo /'li:ou/ *a.* Aslan burcu
leopard /'lepıd/ *a.* leopar **leopardess** dişi leopar
leper /'lepı/ *a.* cüzzamlı
leprosy /'leprısi/ *a.* cüzzam
lesbian /'lezbiın/ *s.* lezbiyen, sevici
lesion /'li:jın/ *a.* yara, bere
less /les/ *be, s.* daha az
lessen /'lesın/ *e.* azaltmak; azalmak
lesser /'lesı/ *s.* daha az/küçük
lesson /'lesın/ *a.* ders; ibret
lest /lest/ *bağ.* -mesin diye; korkusu ile
let /let/ *e.* izin vermek, bırakmak; kiraya vermek **let alone** rahat bırakmak **let down** yüzüstü bırakmak; düş kırıklığına uğratmak **let go** koyvermek, salıvermek **let in** içeri almak **let off** cezasını affetmek; patlatmak, ateşlemek **let on** söylemek, bildirmek **let out** salıvermek; (sır) ağzından kaçırmak
lethal /'li:tıl/ *s.* öldürücü
lethargy /'letıci/ *a.* uyuşukluk, ilgisizlik
letter /'letı/ *a.* mektup; harf **letterbox** mektup kutusu
lettuce /'letis/ *a.* salata, marul
leukemia /lu:'ki:mıı/ *a, hek.* lösemi, kan kanseri
level /'levıl/ *a.* yüzey, yatay; eşit ☆ *s.* düz; yatay; eşit ☆ *e.* düzlemek; yıkmak **level-headed** makul; dengeli
lever /'li:vı/ *e.* manivela; kaldıraç
levy /'levi/ *a.* zorla toplama
lewd /lu:d/ *s.* şehvet düşkünü; açık saçık
lexicon /'leksikın/ *a.* sözlük
liability /layı'biliti/ *a.* sorumluluk; ödenecek borç; engel
liable /'layıbıl/ *s.* sorumlu; maruz; eğilimli
liaison /li'eyzın/ *a.* bağlantı

liar /'layı/ a. yalancı
lib /lib/ a, kon. özgürlük woman's lib kadın özgürlüğü
libel /'laybıl/ a, huk. onur kırıcı yayın, iftira
liberal /'libırıl/ s. liberal; cömert, eli açık; geniş görüşlü, hoşgörülü liberalism liberalizm
liberate /'libıreyt/ e. serbest bırakmak
liberty /'libıti/ a. özgürlük
Libra /'li:brı/ a. terazi burcu
library /'laybrıri/ a. kütüphane librarian kütüphaneci
licence /'laysıns/ a. ruhsat, izin, ehliyet
license /'laysıns/ e. ruhsat vermek, resmi izin vermek, yetki vermek
lick /lik/ e. yalamak; kon. dayak atmak, pataklamak ☆ a. yalama, yalayış
lid /lid/ a. kapak; gözkapağı
lido /'li:dou/ a. halka açık havuz
lie /lay/ e. lay /ley/, lain /leyn/ yatmak, uzanmak, durmak; (down) yatmak, uzanmak
lie /lay/ e. yalan söylemek ☆ a. yalan
lieutenant /lef'tenınt/ a. teğmen
life /layf/ e. hayat, yaşam; canlılık, hayat change of life menopoz come to life canlanmak, hareketlenmek not on your life dünyada olmaz, kesinlikle hayır, asla lifeboat cankurtaran sandalı lifeguard cankurtaran yüzücü life jacket can yeleği lifeless ölü, cansız; ruhsuz, donuk, ölgün, cansız lifelong ömür boyu lifetime ömür
lift /lift/ e. kaldırmak, yükseltmek ☆ a. kaldırma, yükseltme; İİ. asansör give sb a lift arabasına almak, parasız götürmek lift-off (uçak) kalkış, havalanma
ligament /'ligımınt/ a, anat. kiriş, bağ
light /layt/ a. ışık, aydınlık; lamba; elektrik; (kibrit, çakmak, vb.) ateş ☆ e. lit /lit/ yakmak; yanmak; aydınlatmak; tutuşturmak lighthouse fener kulesi light year ışık yılı
light /layt/ s. hafif; (iş) kolay; önemsiz; aydınlık; (renk) açık light-hearted neşeli, kaygısız lightweight hafifsıklet; hafif, önemsiz
lighten /'laytın/ e. aydınlatmak; aydın-

lanmak; hafifletmek
lighter /'laytı/ a. yakıcı aygıt; çakmak
lightning /'laytning/ a. şimşek; ani/çabuk/kısa süren şey
likable, likeable /'laykıbıl/ s. hoşa giden, cana yakın, sevimli
like /layk/ e. beğenmek, sevmek, hoşlanmak ☆ a, ç. sevilen şeyler likes and dislikes hoşlanılan ve hoşlanılmayan şeyler How do you like Ankara? Ankara'yı nasıl buluyorsunuz? How do you like your coffee? Kahvenizi nasıl istersiniz?
like /layk/ s, ilg. benzer, gibi feel like (canı) istemek like that öyle, o şekilde look like -e benzemek something like gibi bir şey, yaklaşık, civarında What's he like? Nasıl biri? Neye benziyor?
likelihood /'layklihud/ a. olasılık
likely /'laykli/ s. olası, muhtemel; uygun, mantıklı ☆ be. galiba, muhtemelen as likely as not muhtemelen not likely kon. kesinlikle hayır
likeness /'layknis/ a. benzeyiş, benzerlik
likewise /'laykwayz/ be. aynı şekilde; -de, -da, ayrıca, bir de
liking /'layking/ a. (for) sevme, düşkünlük
lilac /'laylık/ a, bitk. leylak; leylak rengi
lily /'lili/ a, bitk. zambak
limb /lim/ a. uzuv, organ; dal
lime /laym/ a. kireç; kalsiyum; bitk. ıhlamur limestone kireçtaşı
limit /'limit/ a. limit, uç, sınır ☆ e. (to) kısıtlamak, sınırlandırmak limitation sınırlama limited sınırlı; (şirket) limitet limitless sınırsız
limousine /'limızi:n/ a. limuzin (araba)
limp /limp/ s. gevşek, yumuşak ☆ e. topallamak ☆ a. topallama
linctus /'linktıs/ a, İİ. öksürük şurubu
linden /'lindın/ a, bitk. ıhlamur ağacı
line /layn/ a. çizgi, hat, yol; dizi, sıra; ip, sicim; telefon hattı; satır, dize; mısra ☆ e. (with) içini kaplamak, astarlamak; dizmek, sıralamak Hold the line, please! (telefonda) Ayrılmayın, lütfen! in line with ile bağıntılı, bağ-

daşık **line up** sıraya girmek; sıraya dizmek

lineage /'liniic/ a. nesil, soy

linear /'liniı/ s. doğrusal, çizgisel

linen /'linin/ a. keten kumaş

liner /'laynı/ a. büyük yolcu gemisi; astar, kaplama maddesi

linesman /'laynzmın/ a, sp. yan hakemi

linger /'lingı/ e. ayrılamamak, oyalanmak; (ağrı, vb.) kolayca geçmemek

lingerie /'lenjıri:/ a. kadın iç çamaşırı

linguist /'lingwist/ a. dilbilimci, dilci; çok dil bilen kişi **linguistic** /-'gwistik/ dilbilimsel, dilsel **linguistics** dilbilim

lining /'layning/ a. astar

link /link/ a. bağlantı, bağ; zincir halkası ☆ e. **(together/up)** bağlamak, birleştirmek

linkage /'linkic/ a. zincir; bağlantı

linseed /'linsi:d/ a, bitk. keten tohumu

lint /lint/ a, hek. sargı bezi, keten tiftiği

lion /'layın/ a. aslan; Aslan burcu **the lion's share** aslan payı

lioness /'layınes/ dişi aslan

lip /lip/ a. dudak **lipstick** dudak boyası, ruj

liquefy /'likwifay/ e. sıvılaşmak; sıvılaştırmak

liqueur /li'kyuı/ a. likör

liquid /'likwid/ a, s. sıvı, likit

liquidate /'likwideyt/ e. kurtulmak, başından savmak; (iş) tasfiye etmek **liquidation** tasfiye

liquor /'likı/ a. alkollü içki; Aİ. (viski, vb.) alkollü sert içki

liquorice /'likıris/ a, bitk. meyankökü

list /list/ a. liste, dizelge ☆ e. listesini yapmak

listen /'lisın/ e. dinlemek ☆ a, kon. dinleme, kulak verme

listener /'lisını/ a. dinleyici

listless /'listlis/ s. yorgun, bitkin, cansız, uyuşuk

lit /lit/ bkz. **light**

literacy /'litırısi/ a. okuryazarlık

literal /'litırıl/ s. tam; kelimesi kelimesine, harfi harfine; yalın, sade

literary /'litırıri/ s. edebi, yazınsal

literate /'litırit/ s. okur yazar

literature /'litırıçı/ a. edebiyat, yazın

lithe /layd / s. esnek, kıvrak

litmus /'litmıs/ a. turnusol

litre /'li:tı/ a. litre

litter /'litı/ a. çöp **litter basket/bin** çöp kutusu

little /'litıl/ s. küçük, ufak; az, kısa; önemsiz, değersiz ☆ be. az miktarda, birazcık ☆ a. az miktar **a little** biraz **little by little** azar azar, yavaş yavaş **make little of** küçümsemek

live /liv/ e. yaşamak; oturmak **live off** -den geçimini sağlamak **live on** ile geçinmek; ile beslenmek

live /layv/ s. diri, canlı; (bomba, vb.) patlamamış; yayın (canlı); (tel) cereyanlı; güncel

livelihood /'layvlihud/ a. geçim, geçinme

lively /'layvli/ s. canlı, hayat dolu, neşeli; gerçeğe uygun

liven /'layvın/ e. **(up)** canlandırmak; canlanmak

liver /'livı/ a, anat. karaciğer

livestock /'layvstok/ a. çiftlik hayvanları, mal

livid /'livid/ s. mor; kon. öfkeden kudurmuş, gözü dönmüş

living /'living/ s. canlı, yaşayan, sağ ☆ a. geçim, yaşayış **living room** oturma odası

lizard /'lizıd/ a, hay. kertenkele

llama /'la:mı/ a, hayb. lama

load /loud/ a. yük; taşınan miktar; elek. şarj ☆ e. yüklemek; doldurmak, şarj etmek

loaf /louf/ a. ekmen somunu

loafer /'loufı/ a. aylaklık eden kimse, aylak

loan /loun/ a. ödünç verilen şey; ödünç verme ☆ e. ödünç vermek

loathe /loud/ e. nefret etmek, iğrenmek, tiksinmek **loathing** tiksinme, iğrenme **loathsome** iğrenç

lobby /'lobi/ a. lobi, hol; kulis faaliyeti

lobe /loub/ a. kulak memesi

lobster /'lobstı/ a, hayb. ıstakoz

local /'loukıl/ s. yerel, yöresel, mahalli; hek. lokal ☆ a. semt birahanesi **local government** yerel yönetim

locality /lou'keliti/ a. yer, yöre
locate /lou'keyt/ e. yerini öğrenmek; yerleştirmek, kurmak **be located** bulunmak **location** yer
loch /lok/ a. göl
lock /lok/ a. kilit; bukle, perçem ☆ e. kilitlemek; kilitlenmek
locker /'lokı/ a. kilitli çekmece ya da dolap
locket /'lokit/ a. madalyon
lockout /'lokaut/ a. lokavt
locomotion /loukı'mouşın/ a. hareket
locomotive /loukı'moutiv/ s. harekete ilişkin ☆ a. lokomotif
locust /'loukıst/ a. çekirge
lodge /loc/ e. (kısa süreli) kirada oturmak; takılıp kalmak ☆ a. kulübe; kapıcı evi; bodrum kat **lodger** pansiyoner, kiracı
lodgings /'locingz/ a. pansiyon
loft /loft/ a. tavan arası
lofty /'lofti/ s. yüce, yüksek
log /log/ a. kütük; (gemi, uçak, vb.) seyir defteri
logarithm /'logıridım/ a. logaritma
logic /'locik/ a. mantık **logical** mantıksal; mantıklı
logistics /lı'cistiks/ a, ask. lojistik
loincloth /'loynklot/ a. peştemal
loins /loynz/ a. bel
loiter /'loytı/ e. (about) duraklayarak, oyalanarak yürümek
loll /lol/ e. (about/around) tembelce oturmak, uzanmak
lollipop /'lolipop/ a. saplı şeker, lolipop
lone /loun/ s. kimsesiz, yalnız, tek
loneliness /'lounlinıs/ a. yalnızlık
lonely /'lounli/ s. yalnız ve mutsuz, kimsesiz; ıssız
lonesome /'lounsım/ s, Aİ. yalnız; ıssız
long /long/ s. uzun ☆ be. uzun zamandır; süresince, boyunca **as/so long as** eğer, şartıyla **long ago** uzun süre önce **not long ago** yakın zamanlarda **so long** kon. hoşça kal **long-distance** uzun mesafe; (telefon) şehirlerarası **long-range** uzun menzilli **longsighted** hipermetrop **longstanding** uzun süredir var olan, çok eski **long-term** uzun vadeli **longways** uzunlamasına

long /long/ e. **(for/to)** çok istemek, can atmak **long for** -e can atmak, -i özlemek **longing** özlem
longitude /'loncityu:d/ a, coğ. boylam
longwinded /long'windid/ s. uzun ve sıkıcı, sözü bitmez
look /luk/ e. bakmak; görünmek; **(like)** benzemek ☆ a. bakış; yüz ifadesi ç. görüntü, görünüş **look after** bakmak, gözetmek **look down on** hor görmek, küçümsemek **look for** aramak **look forward to** dört gözle beklemek, iple çekmek **look into** araştırmak, incelemek **look out** dikkat etmek **look over** göz gezdirmek, kısaca incelemek **look through** gözden geçirmek, incelemek **look up** iyiye gitmek; (kitaptan) bulmak, aramak; ziyaret etmek **look up to** -e saygı göstermek
loom /lu:m/ a. dokuma tezgâhı ☆ e. **(up)** daha büyük ve korkunç gözükmek
loop /lu:p/ a. ilmik, ilik ☆ e. ilmik yapmak; bağlamak
loose /lu:s/ s. bağsız, serbest, başıboş; gevşek, sıkı olmayan; dağınık; (giysi) bol; şüpheli; hafifmeşrep **let loose** serbest bırakmak **loosen** gevşetmek; çözmek
loot /lu:t/ a. ganimet, yağma ☆ e. yağma etmek **looter** çapulcu, yağmacı
lop /lop/ e. kesmek; (ağaç) budamak
lord /lo:d/ a. efendi, sahip; lord **The Lord** Allah, Tanrı **The House of Lords** Lordlar Kamarası **lordship** lortluk; lort
lorry /'lori/ a. kamyon
lose /lu:z/ e. lost /lost/ kaybetmek, yitirmek; yenilmek, kazanamamak; (elden) kaçırmak **lose oneself** kendini kaybetmek **lose one's head** kontrolünü kaybetmek **lose one's temper** tepesi atmak **loser** mağlup, yenilen
loss /los/ a. kaybetme; kayıp; zarar, ziyan **at a loss** şaşkın, afallamış; zararına
lost /lost/ bkz. lose; s. kayıp; yitirilmiş; boşa gitmiş **get lost** kaybolmak
lot /lot/ a, kon. çok miktar; hepsi, tümü; grup; kur'a; adçekme; talih, kısmet, yazgı **a lot of, lots of** birçok, bir sürü a

lot pek çok, epey **draw lots** kura çekmek, adçekmek
lotion /'louşın/ *a.* losyon
lottery /'lotıri/ *a.* piyango
lotus /'loutıs/ *a, bitk.* nilüfer
loud /laud/ *s.* yüksek sesli, gürültülü; cırtlak, çiğ, cafcaflı ☆ *be.* yüksek sesle **loudspeaker** hoparlör
lounge /launc/ *a.* salon; hol; fuaye ☆ *e.* (about/around) tembelce uzanmak, yayılıp oturmak **lounge suit** (erkek) günlük kıyafet
louse /laus/ *a.* (ç. **lice** /lays/) bit
lousy /'lauzi/ *s, kon.* berbat, rezil; bitli
lout /laut/ *a.* hödük, ayı
love /lav/ *a.* aşk, sevgi, sevi; sevgili; *il.* canım; (tenis) sıfır ☆ *e.* sevmek; ile sevişmek **be in love with** -e âşık olmak, -yı sevmek **fall in love with** -e âşık olmak **make love** sevişmek **love affair** aşk macerası **lover** âşık, sevgili **lovemaking** sevişme **loving** seven
lovely /'lavli/ *s.* güzel, hoş; *kon.* nefis, harika
low /lou/ *s.* alçak; düşük; zayıf; (ses) az; rezil, aşağılık; adi **lownecked** alçak yakalı, dekolte **low-pitched** (ses) pes
low /lou/ *e.* (inek) böğürmek ☆ *a.* böğürtü
lower /louı/ *s.* alt ☆ *e.* azaltmak, kısmak; azalmak; indirmek; (kendini) küçük düşürmek **lower class** aşağı tabaka
lowland /'loulınd/ *a.* ova
loyal /'loyıl/ *s.* vefalı, sadık **loyalty** bağlılık, sadakat
lozenge /'lozinc/ *a.* pastil
lubricant /'lu:brikınt/ *a.* yağlayıcı madde
lubricate /'lu:brikeyt/ *e.* yağlamak
lucid /'lu:sid/ *s.* kolay anlaşılır, açık
luck /lak/ *a.* şans, talih; uğur **bad luck** aksilik, şanssızlık **Good luck!** Bol şanslar! **luckily** çok şükür, bereket versin ki **lucky** şanslı, talihli; uğurlu
lucrative /'lu:krıtiv/ *s.* kârlı, kazançlı
ludicrous /'lu:dikrıs/ *s.* gülünç
lug /lag/ *e, kon.* zorlukla çekmek
luggage /'lagic/ *a.* bagaj

lukewarm /lu:k'wo:m/ *s.* (sıvı) ılık
lull /lal/ *e.* yatıştırmak; yatışmak
lullaby /'lalıbay/ *a.* ninni
lumbago /lam'beygou/ *a, hek.* bel ağrısı
lumber /'lambı/ *e.* hantal hantal yürümek **lumberjack** oduncu
luminous /'lu:minıs/ *s.* parlak, aydınlık
lump /lamp/ *a.* toprak; yumru, şiş; (şeker) küp **lumpy** yumru yumru, pütürlü
lunar /'lu:nı/ *s.* ayla ilgili, aya ait **lunar month** kameri ay, 28 günlük ay
lunatic /'lu:nıtik/ *a, s.* deli, kaçık **lunatic asylum** tımarhane
lunch /lanç/ *a.* öğle yemeği
luncheon /'lançın/ *a.* öğle yemeği
lung /lang/ *a.* akciğer
lunge /lanc/ *a.* hamle, saldırış
lurch /lö:ç/ *a.* yalpa ☆ *e.* yalpalamak
lure /luı/ *e.* ayartmak, çekmek
lurid /'luırid/ *s.* parlak; korkunç
lurk /lö:k/ *e.* gizlenmek, pusuya yatmak
luscious /'laşıs/ *s.* tatlı, nefis
lush /laş/ *s.* (bitki) verimli, bol, gür
lust /last/ *a.* şehvet **lustful** şehvetli
lustre /'lastı/ *a.* parlaklık, parıltı
lute /lu:t/ *a, müz.* ut, kopuz
luxuriant /lag'zyuıriınt/ *s.* bereketli, bol
luxurious /lag'zyuıriıs/ *s.* konforlu, lüks
luxury /'lakşıri/ *a.* konfor, lüks
lynch /linç/ *e.* linç etmek
lynx /links/ *a, hayb.* vaşak
lyre /layı/ *a.* lir
lyric /'lirik/ *a.* lirik şiir ☆ *s.* lirik **lyrical** lirik, heyecanlı, coşkun **lyricist** şarkı sözü yazarı **lyrics** güfte, şarkı sözleri

M

ma /ma:/ *a, kon.* anne, ana
ma'am /mem, ma:m/ *a.* madam, bayan
macabre /mı'ka:brı/ *s.* korkunç
macadam /mı'kedım/ *a.* şose
macaroni /mekı'rouni/ *a.* makarna

mace /meys/ a. gürz, topuz; tören asası

Mach /mek/ a. mak, uçağın ses hızına oranla hızı

machine /mı'şi:n/ a. makine machinegun makineli tüfek machinist makinist

machinery /mı'şi:nıri/ a. makineler; mekanizma

mackerel /'mekırıl/ a, hayb. uskumru

mackintosh /'mekintoş/ a. yağmurluk

mad /med/ s. deli, çılgın; kon. kızgın, kudurmuş drive sb mad kızdırmak, deli etmek go mad delirmek like mad kon. deli gibi madman deli madly deli gibi, çılgınca; kon. çok madness delilik, çılgınlık

madam /'medım/ a. bayan, hanımefendi

madden /'medın/ e. çıldırtmak, deli etmek, kudurtmak

made /meyd/ bkz. make; s. -den yapılmış, -den

Madonna /mı'donı/ a. Meryem Ana

madrigal /'medrigıl/ a. çalgısız söylenen çok sesli şarkı, madrigal

maestro /'maystrou/ a. orkestra şefi, maestro

magazine /megı'zi:n/ a. dergi, magazin; depo, cephane; şarjör

maggot /'megıt/ a. kurtçuk, kurt

magic /'mecik/ a. büyü; büyücülük ☆ s. büyülü magical büyülü magician /mı'cişın/ büyücü, sihirbaz

magistrate /'mecistreyt/ a. sulh yargıcı

magnanimous /meg'nenimıs/ s. yüce gönüllü, bağışlayıcı

magnate /'megneyt/ a. patron, kodaman

magnet /'megnit/ a. mıknatıs magnetic /meg'netik/ mıknatıslı magnetism manyetizma magnetize mıknatıslamak; çekmek, büyülemek

magnificent /meg'nifisınt/ s. görkemli, olağanüstü, muhteşem

magnify /'megnifay/ e. büyütmek magnifying glass büyüteç

magnitude /'megnityu:d/ a. büyüklük; önem

magnolia /meg'nouliı/ a, bitk. manolya

magpie /'megpay/ a, hayb. saksağan

maharaja /ma:hı'ra:cı/ a. mihrace

mahogany /mı'hogıni/ a. mahun, maun

maid /meyd/ a. bayan hizmetçi

maiden /'meydın/ a, yaz. evlenmemiş kız maiden name kızlık soyadı

mail /meyl/ a. posta; zırh ☆ e. postayla göndermek mailbox Aİ. posta kutusu mailman Aİ. postacı

maim /maym/ e. sakatlamak

main /meyn/ s. asıl, ana, temel mainland ana toprak, kara mainly başlıca; çoğunlukla

maintain /meyn'teyn/ e. sürdürmek; geçindirmek; bakmak; korumak, bakmak; savunmak

maintenance /'meyntınıns/ a. bakım; geçim; savunma

maize /meyz/ a, İİ. mısır

majestic /mı'cestik/ s. görkemli, muhteşem, şahane

majesty /'mecisti/ a. görkem, haşmet, heybet His Majesty Kral Hazretleri

major /'meycı/ s. daha büyük, daha önemli ☆ a. ask. binbaşı; huk. büyük, reşit, ergin; (üniversitede) ana dal; müz. majör

majority /mı'coriti/ a. çoğunluk; sayı farkı, fark; huk. rüşt

make /meyk/ e. made /meyd/ yapmak; hazırlamak, düzeltmek; (para, başarı, vb.) kazanmak; yaratmak; elde etmek, sağlamak; -dırmak, -tirmek ☆ a. yapı, biçim; marka, çeşit make for -e doğru yol almak; -e neden olmak make off kaçmak, tüymek make off with çalmak make out (güçlükle) anlamak, çözmek; yazmak make over devretmek, bırakmak; dönüştürmek, çevirmek make up uydurmak; hazırlamak; tamamlamak, makyaj yapmak make up for affettirmek, telafi etmek make up to gözüne girmeye çalışmak make-believe yapmacık, sahtelik maker yapımcı make-up makyaj; bileşim; mizaç, huy

maladjusted /melı'castid/ s. (çevreye) uyamayan, uyumsuz

malady /'melıdi/ a. hastalık, illet

malaria /mı'leırıı/ a, hek. sıtma

male /meyl/ a, s. erkek

malice /'melis/ a. kötülük, kin; düşmanlık malicious /'mı'lişıs/ kötücül, kinci

malignant /mı'lignınt/ s. kötü niyetli

mallard /'melıd/ a, hayb. yabanördeği

malleable /'meliıbıl/ s. (maden) dövülgen; (insan) yumuşak, uysal

mallet /'melit/ a. tokmak

malnutrition /melnyu'trişin/ a. kötü beslenme

malt /mo:lt/ a. biralık arpa, malt

maltreat /mel'tri:t/ e. kötü davranmak, zulmetmek

mammal /'memıl/ a, hayb. memeli

mammoth /'memıt/ a, hayb. mamut

nan /men/ a. (ç. men /men/) adam, erkek; insan, kişi; insanlık manhood erkeklik the man in the street sokaktaki adam man-eater yamyam man of the world görmüş geçirmiş kimse man-made insan yapımı; sentetik man-of-war savaş gemisi

nanacle /'menıkıl/ a. kelepçe

nanage /'menic/ e. yönetmek, idare etmek; başarmak, becermek; menajerliğini yapmak manageable yönetilebilir; kullanışlı

nanagement /'menicmınt/ a. yönetim, idare; yönetim kurulu

nanager /'menicı/ a. müdür; yönetici manageress müdire, kadın yönetici managerial idari, yönetimle ilgili

nandate /'mendeyt/ a. buyruk, emir; vekillik

nandatory /'mendıtıri/ s. zorunlu

nandolin /mendı'lin/ a, müz. mandolin

nane /meyn/ a. yele

nanganese /'mengıni:z/ a, kim. manganez

nange /meync/ a. uyuz hastalığı

nanger /'meyncı/ a. yemlik

nangle /'mengıl/ e. parçalamak, ezmek, yırtmak

nango /'mengou/ a, bitk. mango, hintkirazı

nania /'meynıı/ a. manyaklık, delilik; düşkünlük maniac manyak, deli

nanicure /'menikyuı/ a. manikür

nanifest /'menifest/ s. açık, belli ☆ e.

göstermek, ortaya koymak

manifesto /meni'festou/ a. bildirge, bildiri

manifold /'menifould/ s. türlü türlü, çok

manipulate /mı'nipyuleyt/ e. beceriyle kullanmak, ustalıkla yönetmek

mankind /men'kaynd/ a. insanlık, insanoğlu

manly /'menli/ s. mert, yiğit, erkek

manner /'menı/ a. tarz, biçim, yol; davranış manners görgü all manner of her tür

mannerism /'menırizım/ a. kişisel özellik

manoeuvre /mı'nu:vı/ a. manevra; hile, dolap

manor /'menı/ a. malikâne

manpower /'menpauı/ a. el emeği, insan gücü

mansion /'menşın/ a. konak

manslaughter /'menslo:tı/ a, huk. kasıtsız adam öldürme

mantelpiece /'mentlpi:s/ a. şömine rafı

mantle /'mentıl/ a. kolsuz manto, harmani; örtü

manual /'menyuıl/ s. elle yapılan, ele ait, el ☆ a. el kitabı, kılavuz

manufacture /menyu'fekçı/ a. imal, yapım; ürün ☆ e. imal etmek, yapmak manufacturer imalatçı, yapımcı

manure /mı'nyuı/ a. gübre

manuscript /'menyuskript/ a. yazma, el yazması

many /meni/ s, adl, a. çok, birçok how many kaç tane? many's the time birçok kereler too many çok fazla

map /mep/ a. harita

maple /'meypıl/ a, bitk. akçaağaç

mar /ma:/ e. bozmak, lekelemek

marathon /'merıtın/ a. maraton

marauding /mı'ro:ding/ s. yağmacı, çapulcu

marble /'ma:bıl/ a. mermer; bilye, misket

March /ma:ç/ a. mart

march /ma:ç/ a. askeri yürüyüş; yürünen mesafe; ilerleme; müz. marş ☆ e. düzenli adımlarla yürümek; ilerlemek

marchioness /ma:şı'nes/ a. markiz
mare /meı/ a, hayb. kısrak
margarine /ma:cı'ri:n/ a. margarin
margin /'ma:cin/ a. sınır, kenar; sayfa kenarındaki boşluk marginal kenarda olan
marigold /'merigould/ a. kadife çiçeği
marina /mı'ri:nı/ a. marina, küçük liman
marine /mı'ri:n/ s. deniz/denizcilik ile ilgili ☆ a. bahriye, denizcilik; bahriyeli
marionette /meriınet/ a. kukla
marital /'meritıl/ s. evlilikle ilgili marital status medeni hal
maritime /'meritaym/ s. denizle ilgili; denizcilikle ilgili, denizcilik ... maritime power donanması olan devlet
mark /ma:k/ a. işaret, nişan, çizgi; (okul) not, numara; damga; marka ☆ e. işaretlemek; damgalamak; not vermek marked göze çarpan marker işaretleyen şey
mark /ma:k/ a. Alman parası, mark
market /'ma:kit/ a. çarşı, pazar; piyasa; borsa be on the market satışa çıkarılmak black market karaborsa market analysis piyasa araştırması marketplace pazaryeri market price piyasa fiyatı market research piyasa araştırması marketing pazarlama
marksman /'ma:ksmın/ a. nişancı
marl /'ma:l/ a. marn, kireçli toprak
marmalade /'ma:mıleyd/ a. marmelat
maroon /mı'ru:n/ a, s. kestane rengi
marquee /ma:'ki/ a. büyük çadır, otağ
marquis /'ma:kwis/ a. marki
marriage /'meric/ a. evlenme; evlilik
married /'merid/ s. evli get married (to) ile evlenmek
marrow /'merou/ a, bitk. sakızkabağı; ilik, öz
marry /'meri/ e. evlendirmek; evlenmek
Mars /ma:z/ a. Mars
marsh /ma:ş/ a. bataklık marshy bataklık
marshal /'ma:şıl/ a, ask. mareşal; teşrifatçı; Aİ. (polis, itfaiye, vb.) şef ☆ e. dizmek, sıralamak; yol göstermek
martial /'ma:şıl/ s. savaşla ilgili; savaş-

çı martial law sıkıyönetim
martin /'ma:tin/ a, hayb. kırlangıç
martyr /'ma:tı/ a. şehit ☆ e. şehit etmek martyrdom şehitlik
marvel /'ma:vıl/ a. şaşılacak şey, mucize marvellous harika, müthiş, fevkalade
Marxist /'ma:ksist/ a, s. Marksist Marksçı Marxism Marksizm
mascara /ma'ska:rı/ a. rimel, maskara
mascot /'meskıt/ a. uğur, maskot
masculine /'meskyulin/ s. erkeksi; dilb eril
mash /meş/ a. lapa, ezme; kon. pata tes püresi ☆ e. ezmek
mask /ma:sk/ a. maske; örtü; yüz kalıb ☆ e. maske takmak; gizlemek
masochist /'mesıkist/ a. mazoşist, öze zer masochism mazoşizm, özezerlik
mason /'meysın/ a. duvarcı; taşçı; ma son masonry duvarcılık; masonluk taş
masquerade /meskı'reyd/ a. maske balo; gerçeği gizleme
mass /mes/ a. yığın, küme; çokluk; küt le mass media kitle iletişim mass pro duction seri üretim the masses çal şan sınıf, emekçiler
massacre /'mesıkı/ a. katliam, kırım ☆ e. katliam yapmak
massage /'mesa:j/ a. masaj ☆ a. ma saj yapmak
masseur /me'sö:/ a. masör
massive /'mesiv/ s. iri, kocaman; güç lü; som, yekpare
mast /ma:st/ a. gemi direği; gönder
master /'ma:stı/ a. sahip; patron; mü dür; (erkek) öğretmen; usta ☆ e. hâ kim olmak, iyi bilmek masterful ded ğini yaptıran, egemen master ke maymuncuk masterly ustaca, mü kemmel mastermind çok zeki kims masterpiece şaheser, başyapıt
masturbate /'mestıbeyt/ e. mastürbas yon yapmak masturbation mastü basyon
mat /met/ a. hasır; paspas; altlık ☆ s donuk, mat
matador /'metıdo:/ a. boğa güreşçis matador

match /meç/ a. kibrit; fitil; eş, denk; benzer; maç, karşılaşma ☆ e. birbirine uymak matchbox kibrit kutusu matching uyumlu matchless eşsiz, benzersiz matchmaker çöpçatan
mate /meyt/ a. arkadaş, dost; *il, kon.* ahbap, arkadaş; (hayvan) eş; satranç (mat) ☆ e. çiftleşmek; çiftleştirmek
material /mı'tiırııl/ a. madde; malzeme, gereç; kumaş ☆ s. maddi materialism materyalizm, özdekçilik materialist materyalist
maternal /mı'tö:nıl/ s. anaya özgü, ana ...; (akrabalık) ana tarafından
maternity /mı'tö:niti/ a. analık; gebelik maternity hospital doğumevi
mathematics /meti'metiks/ a. matematik mathematical matematiksel; *mec.* tam, kesin mathematician matematikçi
maths /mets/ a, *İİ, kon.* matematik
matiné /'metiney/ a. matine
matrimony /'metrimıni/ a. evlilik
matt /met/ s. donuk, mat
matter /'metı/ a. madde, cisim; iş, sorun, konu, mesele; konu, içerik; aksilik, dert; cerahat, irin; mesele, sorun ☆ e. önemi olmak a matter of ... meselesi a matter of course olağan bir şey, sıradan olay a matter of death ölüm kalım meselesi as a matter of fact aslında, işin doğrusu; nitekim What's the matter? Ne var? Ne oluyor? It doesn't matter. Önemi yok. printed matter basılı yazı, matbua
matting /'meting/ a. hasır
mattock /'metık/ a. kazma
mattress /'metris/ a. döşek, şilte
mature /mı'çuı/ s. olgun ☆ e. olgunlaşmak maturity olgunluk
maul /mo:l/ e. hırpalamak; yaralamak
mausoleum /mo:sı'liım/ a. anıtkabir
mauve /mouv/ a, s. leylak rengi
maxim /'meksim/ a. özdeyiş
maximum /'meksimım/ a. en yüksek derece ☆ s. en yüksek, maksimum
may /mey/ e. (olasılık, izin ve dilek belirtir) -ebilmek, -abilmek
May /mey/ a. mayıs
maybe /'meybi/ *be.* belki

mayonnaise /meyı'neyz/ a. mayonez
mayor /meı/ a. belediye başkanı
maze /meyz/ a. labirent
me /mi, mi:/ *adl.* beni; bana; ben
meal /mi:l/ a. yemek, öğün
mean /mi:n/ e. anlamına gelmek, demek olmak; demek istemek, kastetmek; niyet etmek ☆ s. pinti, cimri; adi; alçak; ortalama ☆ a. orta; ortalama; ç. servet, para; ç. vasıta; araç by any means her ne şekilde olursa olsun by no means kesinlikle, hiç by means of vasıtasıyla, yardımıyla
meander /mi'endı/ a. dolambaç
meaning /'mi:ning/ a. anlam meaningful anlamlı meaningless anlamsız
meant /ment/ *bkz.* mean
meantime /'mi:ntaym/ *be.* bu arada in the meantime bu arada
meanwhile /'mi:nwayl/ *be.* bu arada
measles /'mi:zılz/ a, *hek.* kızamık
measure /'mejı/ a. ölçü; tedbir, önlem ☆ e. ölçmek measurement ölçüm; ölçü
meat /mi:t/ a. et meatball köfte
mechanic /mi'kenik/ a. makinist; tamirci mechanical makineyle ilgili, mekanik mechanics mekanik
mechanism /'mekınizım/ a. mekanizma
mechanize /'mekınayz/ e. makineleştirmek
medal /medıl/ a. madalya
medallion /mi'deliın/ a. madalyon
meddle /'medıl/ e. karışmak, burnunu sokmak
media /'mi:diı/ a. kitle iletişim araçları
mediate /'mi:dieyt/ e. arabuluculuk etmek mediator arabulucu
medical /'medikıl/ s. tıbbi
medicate /'medikeyt/ e. içine ilaç katmak
medicinal /mi'disınıl/ s. iyileştirici
medicine /'medsın/ a. ilaç; tıp, hekimlik
medieval /medi'i:vıl/ s. ortaçağ ..., ortaçağa ait
mediocre /mi:di'oukı/ s. orta, şöyle böyle
meditate /'mediteyt/ e. enine boyuna

düşünmek; tasarlamak

medium /'mi:dıım/ *a.* (ç. **media** /'mi:-
dıı/) çevre, ortam; vasıta, araç; orta
durum, orta derece **medium sized** orta boylu

medley /'medli/ *a.* karışım; *müz.* potpuri, medley

meek /mi:k/ *s.* uysal, alçakgönüllü

meet /mi:t/ *e.* **met** /met/ rastlamak,
karşılaşmak; karşılamak; tanışmak;
buluşmak; toplanmak

meeting /'mi:ting/ *a.* buluşma; toplantı

megaphone /'megıfoun/ *a.* megafon

melancholy /melınkıli/ *a.* melankoli, hüzün ☆ *s.* hüzünlü

mellow /'melou/ *s.* olgun, tatlı, sulu; yumuşak, tatlı

melodious /mi'loudiıs/ *s.* kulağa hoş
gelen, uyumlu, melodik

melodrama /'melıdra:mı/ *a.* melodram

melon /'melın/ *a, bitk.* kavun

melt /melt/ *e.* erimek; eritmek; kaybolmak **melt away** eriyip kaybolmak

member /'membı/ *a.* üye; organ; uzuv
membership üyelik; üyeler

membrane /'membreyn/ *a.* ince zar

memo /'memou/ *a.* kısa not

memoirs /'memwa:z/ *a.* yaşam öyküsü

memorable /'memırıbıl/ *s.* anılmaya değer

memorandum /memı'rendım/ *a.* not;
nota, muhtıra; tezkere, memorandum

memorial /mı'mo:rııl/ *a.* anıt

memorize /'memırayz/ *e.* ezberlemek

memory /'memıri/ *a.* hafıza; anı, hatıra
in memory of -ın anısına

menace /'menis/ *a.* tehdit, tehlike ☆
e. tehdit etmek

mend /mend/ *e.* onarmak, tamir etmek; yamamak; düzeltmek **on the
mend** iyileşen, düzelen

menstruation /menstru'eyşın/ *a.* âdet,
aybaşı

mental /'mentıl/ *s.* zihinsel, akli **mental
hospital** akıl hastanesi **mental illness**
akıl hastalığı

mentality /men'teliti/ *a.* düşünüş, zihniyet; akıl, zekâ, zihin

menthol /'mentol/ *a.* mentol

mention /'menşın/ *e.* -den söz etmek,

bahsetmek, anmak **Don't mention it!**
Bir şey değil! Estağfurullah!

menu /'menyu:/ *a.* yemek listesi, mönü

mercenary /'mö:sınıri/ *a.* paralı asker

merchandise /'mö:çındayz/ *a.* ticaret
eşyası, mal

merchant /'mö:çınt/ *a.* tüccar, tacir

merciful /'mö:sifıl/ *s.* sevecen, bağışlayıcı, merhametli

merciless /'mö:silis/ *s.* merhametsiz,
acımasız, amansız

mercury /'mö:kyuri/ *a.* cıva

Mercury /'mö:kyuri/ *a.* Merkür

mercy /'mö:si/ *a.* merhamet, acıma

mere /miı/ *s.* sırf, sadece, yalnız **the
merest** en ufak, en önemsiz **merely**
sadece, yalnızca

merge /mö:c/ *e.* birleştirmek; birleşmek **merger** birleşme

meridian /mı'ridiın/ *a.* meridyen

merit /'merit/ *a.* değer, liyakat; erdem

mermaid /'mö:meyd/ *a.* denizkızı

merriment /'merimınt/ *a.* şenlik, neşe,
keyif

merry /'meri/ *s.* neşeli, şen, güleç
merry-go-round atlıkarınca

mesh /meş/ *a.* ağ gözü; tuzak ☆ *e.*
(çark dişleri) birbirine geçmek

mess /mes/ *a.* karışıklık, dağınıklık; kirlilik, pislik; *ask.* yemekhane; *ask.* karavana **make a mess of** yüzüne gözüne
bulaştırmak, berbat etmek

message /'mesic/ *a.* haber, mesaj

messenger /'mesıncı/ *a.* haberci, ulak

messiah /mi'sayı/ *a.* kurtarıcı; İsa Peygamber

met /met/ *bkz.* **meet**

metabolism /mi'tebılizım/ *a.* metabolizma

metal /'metıl/ *a.* metal, maden **metallic**
/mi'telik/ madeni

metallurgy /'metılö:ci, mi'telıci/ *a.* me-
talürji, metalbilim

metaphor /'metıfı/ *a.* eğretileme, isti-
are

meteor /'mi:tiı/ *a.* göktaşı, meteor **me-
teorite** /-rayt/ göktaşı

meteorology /mi:tiı'rolıci/ *a.* meteoroloji, havabilgisi

meter /'mi:tı/ *a.* ölçme aygıtı, sayaç, saat; *Al.* metre
method /'metıd/ *a.* yöntem **methodical** /mi'todıkıl/ sistemli, yöntemli
meticulous /mi'tikyulıs/ *s.* titiz
metre /'mi:tı/ *a.* metre; ölçü, vezin **metric** /'metrik/ metrik
metropolis /mi'tropılis/ *a.* büyük şehir, anakent, metropol; başkent. **metropolitan** başkentle/büyük şehirle ilgili
mettle /'metıl/ *a.* yiğitlik, cesaret
mew /nyu:/ *e.* miyavlamak ☆ *a.* miyavlama
miaow /mi'au/ *a.* miyav, miyavlama ☆ *e.* miyavlamak
mica /'maykı/ *a.* mika
microbe /'maykroub/ *a.* mikrop
microchip /'maykrıçip/ *a.* miniyonga, mikroçip
microfilm /'maykrıfilm/ *a.* mikrofilm
microorganism /maykrou'o:gınizım/ *a.* mikroorganizma
microphone /'maykrıfoun/ *a.* mikrofon
microprocessor /maykrou'prousesı/ *a.* (bilgisayar) mikroişlem birimi, mikroişlemci
microscope /'maykrıskoup/ *a.* mikroskop
microwave /'maykrıweyv/ *a.* mikrodalga
mid /mid/ *s.* ortasında
midday /mid'dey/ *a.* öğle vakti ☆ *s.* öğle
middle /'midıl/ *a.* orta; vasat; merkezi **Middle Ages** ortaçağ **middle class** orta sınıf **Middle East** Ortadoğu **in the middle of sth/doing sth** ile meşgul, -mekte, -makta **middleman** komisyoncu, aracı **middleweight** (boks) ortasıklet
midge /mic/ *a, hayb.* tatarcık
midget /'micit/ *s.* cüce; çok küçük
midland /'midlınd/ *a.* bir ülkenin iç kısmı **the Midlands** orta İngiltere
midnight /'midnayt/ *a.* gece yarısı
midriff /'midrif/ *a, anat.* diyafram
midway /mid'wey/ *s, be.* yarı yolda, ortasında
midwife /'midwayf/ *a.* ebe
might /mayt/ *bkz.* **may**; *a.* kudret, güç

mighty güçlü, kudretli
migraine /'mi:greyn, 'maygreyn/ *a, hek.* migren
migrant /'maygrınt/ *a.* göçmen
migrate /may'greyt/ *e.* göç etmek, göçmek **migration** göç
mike /mayk/ *a, kon.* mikrofon
mild /mayld/ *s.* yumuşak başlı, uysal; ılımlı
mildew /'mildyu:/ *a.* küf
mile /mayl/ *a.* mil (1609 m.) **milestone** kilometre taşı; dönüm noktası
mileage /'maylic/ *a.* mil hesabıyla uzaklık
militant /'militınt/ *s.* saldırgan, savaşçı ☆ *a.* militan
military /'militıri/ *s.* askeri
militia /mi'lişı/ *a.* milis
milk /milk/ *a.* süt ☆ *e.* sağmak **milkman** sütçü **milky** sütlü **the Milky Way** Samanyolu
mill /mil/ *a.* değirmen; imalathane ☆ *e.* öğütmek; çekmek
millennium /mi'leniım/ *a.* bin yıl
miller /'milı/ *a.* değirmenci
millet /'milit/ *a.* darı
milliner /'milinı/ *a.* kadın şapkacısı
million /'milyın/ *a.* milyon
millionaire /milyı'neı/ *a.* milyoner
mime /maym/ *a.* pandomim; pandomim oyuncusu ☆ *e.* pandomim yapmak
mimic /'mimik/ *a.* taklitçi ☆ *e.* taklidini yapmak
minaret /minı'ret/ *a.* minare
mince /mins/ *e.* kıymak, doğramak ☆ *a.* kıyma
mind /maynd/ *a.* akıl; düşünce; kanı; hatır, bellek; dikkat **change one's mind** fikrini değiştirmek **in one's right mind** aklı başında **make up one's mind** kararını vermek **out of one's mind** deli
mind /maynd/ *e.* bakmak, ilgilenmek; aldırış etmek, önemsemek; sakıncalı bulmak **do/would you mind** sizce bir sakıncası var mı **mind you** şunu da göz önünde bulundurun ki **Mind your own business** Sen kendi işine bak. **Never mind** Boş ver; Önemi yok; Al-

mine   384

dırma; Sağlık olsun **mindful** -e dikkat
eden, önem veren **mindless** akılsız,
aptal; aldırış etmeyen
mine /mayn/ *adl.* benimki ☆ *a.* maden ocağı; *ask.* mayın ☆ *e.* (maden,
vb.) çıkarmak; mayın döşemek **mine-
field** mayın tarlası **miner** madenci
mineral /'minırıl/ *a, s.* mineral **mineral
water** madensuyu
mingle /'mingıl/ *e.* karıştırmak; karışmak
mini /'mini/ *s.* küçük, mini
miniature /'miniıçı/ *a.* minyatür
minibus /'minibas/ *a.* minibüs
minimal /'minimıl/ *s.* en az, en küçük
minimize /'minimayz/ *e.* en aza indirgemek, azaltmak
minimum /'minimım/ *s.* en küçük, en
az ☆ *a.* en küçük miktar **minimum
wage** asgari ücret
mining /'mayning/ *a.* madencilik
minister /'ministı/ *a.* bakan; orta elçi;
papaz
ministry /'ministri/ *a.* bakanlık; papazlık
mink /mink/ *a, hayb.* vizon; vizon kürk
minor /'maynı/ *s.* daha az; önemsiz, küçük; *müz.* minör ☆ *a, huk.* ergin olmayan çocuk
minority /may'noriti/ *a.* azınlık
minster /'minstı/ *a.* büyük kilise
minstrel /'minstrıl/ *a.* ortaçağ halk ozanı
mint /mint/ *a, bitk.* nane; darphane
minus /'maynıs/ *a, s, ilg.* eksi
minute /'minit/ *a.* dakika; kısa süre, an
minutes /'minits/ *a.* tutanak
miracle /'mirıkıl/ *a.* mucize **miraculous**
/mi'rekyulıs/ mucizevi, şaşılacak
mirage /'mira:j/ *a.* serap, ılgın
mirror /'mirı/ *a.* ayna
misadventure /misıd'vençı/ *a.* kaza, talihsizlik
misapprehend /misepri'hend/ *e.* yanlış
anlamak
misbehave /misbi'heyv/ *e.* terbiyesizlik
etmek, kötü davranmak
miscalculate /mis'kelkyuleyt/ *e.* yanlış
hesaplamak
miscarriage /mis'keric/ *a.* çocuk düşür-

me, düşük; başarısızlık
miscarry /mis'keri/ *e.* (çocuk) düşürmek; başarısız olmak, boşa gitmek
miscellaneous /misı'lenyiıs/ *s.* çeşitli
mischance /mis'ça:ns/ *a.* şanssızlık, talihsizlik
mischief /'misçif/ *a.* kötülük; yaramazlık **mischievous** zararlı; yaramaz
misconduct /mis'kondakt/ *a.* kötü davranış; kötü yönetim; zina
misdemeanour /misdi'mi:nı/ *a.* hafif
suç
miser /'mayzı/ *a.* cimri, para canlısı
miserable /'mizırıbıl/ *s.* sefil, perişan;
mutsuz; kötü, berbat
misery /'mizıri/ *a.* sefalet, perişanlık,
dert; yoksulluk
misfire /mis'fayı/ *e.* (silah) tutukluk yapmak; bekleneni vermemek
misfortune /mis'fo:çın/ *a.* şanssızlık, talihsizlik; felaket, kaza
misgiving /mis'giving/ *a.* kuşku, kaygı
mishap /'mishep/ *a.* talihsizlik, kaza
misinterpret /misin'tö:prit/ *e.* yanlış anlamak, yanlış yorumlamak
mislay /mis'ley/ *e.* **misled** /misled/ *e.*
nereye koyduğunu unutmak
mislead /mis'li:d/ *e.* **misled** /misled/ *e.*
yanıltmak; baştan çıkarmak
mismanage /mis'menic/ *e.* kötü yönetmek
misogynist /mi'socinist/ *a.* kadın düşmanı
misplace /mis'pleys/ *e.* yanlış yere koymak
misprint /mis'print/ *a.* baskı hatası
mispronounce /misprı'nauns/ *e.* yanlış
telaffuz etmek
miss /mis/ *e.* vuramamak, ıskalamak;
kaçırmak; özlemek ☆ *a.* vuramama,
ıskalama **miss out** atlamak, kaçırmak
missing namevcut, eksik
miss /mis/ *a.* hanımefendi, bayan
missile /'misayl/ *a.* füze; mermi
mission /'mişın/ *a.* özel görev; kurul
missionary misyoner
misspell /mis'spel/ *e.* **misspelt** /mis's-
pelt/ harflerini yanlış söylemek
mist /mist/ *a.* sis, duman; buğu **misty**
sisli, dumanlı

mistake /mis'teyk/ *e.* **mistook** /mi'-stuk/, **mistaken** /mi'steykın/ yanlış anlamak; başkasına benzetmek ☆ *a.* hata, yanlış, yanlışlık; kusur **make a mistake** hata yapmak **mistaken** yanlış, hatalı, yersiz

Mister /'mistı/ *a.* Bay

mistletoe /'misıltou/ *a, bitk.* ökseotu

mistook /mi'stuk/ *bkz.* **mistake**

mistress /'mistris/ *a.* evin hanımı; kadın öğretmen; metres

mistrust /mis'trast/ *e.* güvenmemek ☆ *a.* güvensizlik

misunderstand /misandı'stend/ *e.* **misunderstood** /misandı'stud/ yanlış anlamak **misunderstanding** yanlış anlaşılma

misuse /mis'yu:z/ *e.* yanlış yerde kullanmak; kötü kullanmak ☆ *a.* yanlış kullanma; kötüye kullanma

mitigate /'mitigeyt/ *e.* hafifletmek, azaltmak

mitten /'mitın/ *a.* parmaksız eldiven

mix /miks/ *e.* karıştırmak; karışmak; kaynaşmak, uyum sağlamak **mixed** karışık, karma **mixer** karıştırıcı, mikser

mixture /'miksçı/ *a.* karışım; karışma, karıştırma

moan /moun/ *a.* inilti ☆ *e.* inlemek

mob /mob/ *a.* ayaktakımı; kalabalık

mobile /'moubayl/ *s.* hareket eden, oynak; seyyar, gezici

mobilize /'moubilayz/ *e.* silah altına almak, seferber etmek **mobilization** seferberlik

moccasin /'mokısin/ *a.* makosen

mock /mok/ *e.* alay etmek ☆ *s.* yapmacık, sahte **mockery** alay; gülünç taklit

modal /'moudıl/ *s, dilb.* kiplerle ilgili, kip; *müz.* makamla ilgili

mode /moud/ *a.* tarz, yol, biçim

model /'modıl/ *a.* örnek, model; model, manken; kalıp ☆ *e.* modelini yapmak, örneğini çıkarmak; mankenlik yapmak **model on/upon** -e örnek almak

moderate /'modırit/ *s.* orta; görüşleri aşırıya kaçmayan, ılımlı

moderate /'modıreyt/ *e.* hafifletmek,

azaltmak; hafiflemek, azalmak

moderation /modı'reyşın/ *a.* ılımlılık

modern /'modın/ *s.* çağdaş, modern **modernize** yenileştirmek, modernize etmek

modest /'modist/ *s.* alçakgönüllü; sade, gösterişsiz **modesty** alçakgönüllülük

modify /'modifay/ *e.* değişiklik yapmak, değiştirmek **modification** /-fi'-keyşın/ değiştirme; değişiklik

module /'modyu:l/ *a.* ölçü birimi; modül

mohair /'mouheı/ *a.* tiftik

Mohammedan /mou'hemidın/ *a, s.* Müslüman

moist /moyst/ *s.* rutubetli, nemli

moisten /'moysçın/ *e.* ıslatmak; ıslanmak, yaşarmak

moisture /'moysçı/ *a.* rutubet, nem

molar /'moulı/ *a.* azıdişi

mole /moul/ *a.* ben; dalgakıran; *hayb.* köstebek

molecule /'molikyu:l/ *a.* molekül, özdecik

molest /mı'lest/ *e.* rahatsız etmek; sarkıntılık etmek

mollusc /'molısk/ *a, hayb.* yumuşakça

molten /'moultın/ *s.* erimiş, dökme

mom /mom/ *a, AI, kon.* anne

moment /'moumınt/ *a.* kısa süre, an; önem **at the moment** şu anda, şimdi **at that moment** o anda **momentary** bir anlık, geçici

momentous /mou'mentıs/ *s.* önemli

momentum /mou'mentım/ *a.* fiz. moment, devinirlik; hız

monarch /'monık/ *a.* tekerk, mutlak hükümdar **monarchic** /'mına:kik/ monarşik **monarchy** tekerki, monarşi

monastery /'monıstri/ *a.* manastır

Monday /'mandi, 'mandey/ *a.* pazartesi

monetary /'manitıri/ *s.* parasal

money /'mani/ *a.* para **money box** kumbara **money order** posta havalesi, banka havalesi

mongrel /'mangrıl/ *a.* melez, kırma

monitor /'monitı/ *a.* sınıf başkanı; monitör, denetlik

monk /mank/ *a.* keşiş, rahip

monkey /'manki/ *a.* maymun **monkey business** *kon.* dolap, hile, üçkâğıt

monochrome /'monıkroum/ *s.* tek renkli; (TV) siyah-beyaz

monogamy /mı'nogımi/ *a.* tekeşlilik, monogami

monologue /'monılog/ *a.* monolog

monopolize /mı'nopılayz/ *e.* tekeline almak

monopoly /mı'nopıli/ *a.* tekel

monotonous /mı'notınıs/ *s.* tekdüze, monoton **monotony** tekdüzelik, monotonluk

monster /'monstı/ *a.* canavar; dev

monstrous /'monstrıs/ *s.* kocaman; korkunç, iğrenç

montage /'monta:j/ *a.* kurgu, montaj

month /mant / *a.* ay **monthly** ayda bir, aylık

monument /'monyumınt/ *a.* anıt **monumental** /-'mentıl/ anıtsal

moo /mu:/ *a.* böğürme ☆ *e.* böğürmek

mood /mu:d/ *a.* ruh hali; aksilik, huysuzluk; *dilb.* kip **moody** değişken; huysuz

moon /mu:n/ *a.* ay **full moon** dolunay **new moon** hilal **once in a blue moon** kırk yılda bir **moonlight** ay ışığı

moor /muı/ *a.* çalılık arazi, kır ☆ *e,* *den.* palamarla bağlamak **moorings** gemi bağlama yeri

moose /mu:s/ *a, hayb.* Amerika geyiği, mus

mop /mop/ *a.* saplı tahta bezi; *kon.* dağınık saç ☆ *e.* saplı bezle silmek

mope /moup/ *e.* neşesiz olmak, kederli olmak

moped /'mouped/ *a.* motorlu bisiklet

moral /'morıl/ *a.* ahlaki, törel; dürüst; manevi ☆ *a.* ahlak dersi **morals** ahlak

morale /mı'ra:l/ *a.* moral

morality /mı'reliti/ *a.* ahlaklılık, erdem

morass /mı'res/ *a.* bataklık

more /mo:/ *s.* daha çok ☆ *be.* daha (çok) **and what's more** üstelik **any more** artık **more and more** gittikçe, gitgide **more or less** aşağı yukarı, yaklaşık **no more** bir daha hiç, artık hiç **the more ... the more ...** ne kadar ... o kadar ...

morello /mı'relou/ *a, bitk.* vişne

moreover /mo'rouvı/ *be.* bundan başka, üstelik, zaten

morgue /mo:g/ *a.* morg

morning /'mo:ning/ *a.* sabah **Good morning!** Günaydın!

moron /'mo:ron/ *a.* geri zekâlı; *hek.* moron

morose /mı'rous/ *s.* somurtkan, suratsız

morpheme /'mo:fi:m/ *a, dilb.* morfem, biçimbirim

morphine /'mo:fi:n/ *a.* morfin

Morse code /mo:s'koud/ *a.* Mors alfabesi

morsel /'mo:sıl/ *a.* lokma, parça

mortal /'mo:tıl/ *s.* fani, ölümlü; ölümcül; *kon.* çok büyük, aşırı ☆ *a.* fani, ölümlü, insan **mortality** /-'teliti/ ölümlülük; ölüm oranı

mortar /'mo:tı/ *a.* harç; *ask.* havan topu ☆ *e.* harç ile sıvamak

mortgage /'mo:gic/ *a.* rehin, ipotek ☆ *e.* rehine koymak, ipotek etmek

mortify /'mo:tifay/ *e.* küçük düşürmek, utandırmak

mortuary /'mo:çuıri/ *a.* morg

mosaic /mou'zeyik/ *a.* mozaik

Moslem /'mozlim/ *a, s.* Müslüman

mosque /mosk/ *a.* cami

mosquito /mı'ski:tou/ *a.* sivrisinek

moss /mos/ *a.* yosun **mossy** yosunlu

most /moust/ *s.* en çok; hemen hepsi, çoğu ☆ *be.* en çok, en, son derece, pek ☆ *a.* en çok miktar, çoğunluk **at (the) most** en çok, olsa olsa **mostly** çoğunlukla, çoğu kez

motel /mou'tel/ *a.* motel

moth /mot / *a.* güve; pervane

mother /'madı/ *a.* ana, anne **motherhood** annelik **mother-in-law** kaynana **motherland** anayurt, anavatan **mother tongue** ana dili **motherly** ana gibi, anaya özgü

motif /mou'ti:f/ *a.* motif, örge

motion /'mouşın/ *a.* hareket, devinim; işaret; önerge; *tek.* işleme, çalışma

387   **multitude**

motion picture sinema filmi slow motion ağır çekim motionless hareketsiz
motivate /'moutiveyt/ e. harekete geçirmek motivation güdüleme, güdü, motivasyon
motive /'moutiv/ a. neden, güdü, dürtü ☆ s. hareket ettirici
motocross /'moutoukros/ a. motosiklet yarışı, motokros
· motor /'moutı/ a. motor; motorlu araç ☆ s. hareket ettirici motorbike motosiklet motorboat deniz motoru motorcar otomobil, araba motorcycle motosiklet motoring araba kullanma, sürücülük; otomobil sporu motorist otomobil sürücüsü motorize /-rayz/ motor takmak, motorize etmek motorway karayolu, otoyol
motto /'motou/ a. parola, slogan
mould /mould/ a. kalıp; küf ☆ e. kalıba dökmek; küflenmek
moulder /'mouldı/ e. çürümek, dökülmek
moult /moult/ e. tüylerini dökmek
mount /maunt/ a. dağ, tepe; binek hayvanı ☆ e. binmek; çıkmak; artmak
mountain /'mauntin/ a. dağ mountaineer /-'niı/ dağcı mountaineering dağcılık mountainous dağlık
mourn /mo:n/ e. (for/over) yasını tutmak mourner yaslı kimse mournful yaslı
mourning /'mo:ning/ a. yas; yas giysisi
mouse /maus/ a. (ç. mice /mays/) fare mousetrap fare kapanı
moustache /mı'sta:ş/ a. bıyık
mouth /maut / a. ağız mouthful ağız dolusu lokma mouthorgan ağız mızıkası, armonika mouthpiece ağızlık mouth-watering ağız sulandırıcı
movable /'mu:vıbıl/ s. menkul, taşınır
move /mu:v/ e. hareket ettirmek, kımıldatmak, oynatmak; taşımak; işletmek; duygulandırmak, etkilemek ☆ a. hareket, kımıldama; göç, taşınma; (satranç) oynama sırası, hamle, el; hareket; önlem move in eve taşınmak move off uzaklaşmak, gitmek move out evden taşınmak
movement /'mu:vmınt/ a. hareket; kı-

mıldanma; *müz.* tempo, ritm; mekanizma
movie /'mu:vi/ a, Aİ, kon. film; sinema go to the movies sinemaya gitmek
mow /mou/ e. biçmek
mower /'mouı/ a. çim biçme makinesi
Mr /'mistı/ a. Bay, By
Mrs /'misiz/ a. (evli) Bayan, Bn
Ms /miz, mız/ a. (evli ya da bekâr) Bayan, Bn
much /maç/ s, be. çok ☆ a. çok şey as much as ... kadar how much ne kadar; kaç para? much the same hemen hemen aynı so much o kadar çok make much of çok önem vermek; anlamak
muck /mak/ a. pislik; kir; gübre muck up kirletmek, pisletmek
mucus /'myu:kıs/ a. sümük
mud /mad/ a. çamur mudguard çamurluk muddy çamurlu
muddle /madıl/ a. dağınıklık; şaşkınlık ☆ e. karıştırmak, bozmak; hayrete düşürmek muddlehead sersem; kalın kafalı
muffle /'mafıl/ e. (sesi) boğmak, hafifletmek muffler atkı, fular; Aİ. susturucu
mug /mag/ a. kulplu bardak, maşrapa; *arg.* yüz, surat; İİ, kon. enayi, avanak ☆ e. saldırıp soymak
muggy /'magi/ s. (hava) kapalı, boğucu, bunaltıcı
Muhammadan /mu'hemıdın/ a, s. Müslüman
mulberry /'malbıri/ a, bitk. dut
mule /myu:l/ a, hayb. katır
mullah /'malı/ a. molla
mullet /'malit/ a, hayb. tekir balığı
multilateral /malti'letırıl/ s. çok yanlı
multiple /'maltipıl/ s. çok, birçok, çeşitli ☆ a, mat. kat
multiplication /maltipli'keyşın/ a, mat. çarpım; artış, çoğalma multiplication table çarpım tablosu
multiply /'maltiplay/ e, mat. (by) çarpmak; çoğalmak; çoğaltmak; üremek
multistorey /malti'sto:ri/ s. (bina) çok katlı
multitude /'maltityu:d/ a. çok sayı, çok-

luk, kalabalık
mum /mam/ *a, İİ, kon.* anne
mumble /'mambıl/ *e.* mırıldanmak, ağzında gevelemek
mummify /'mamifay/ *e.* mumyalamak
mummy /'mami/ *a.* mumya
mummy /'mami/ *a, İİ, kon.* anne
mumps /mamps/ *a, hek.* kabakulak
munch /manç/ *e.* hatır hutur yemek
mundane /man'deyn/ *s.* günlük, olağan
municipal /myu:'nisipıl/ *s.* belediye/-kent ile ilgili municipality /myu:nisi'peliti/ belediye
munitions /myu:'nişınz/ *a, ask.* mühimmat, cephane
mural /'myuırıl/ *a.* duvara yapılmış resim, duvar resmi, fresk
murder /'mö:dı/ *a.* adam öldürme, cinayet ☆ *e.* katletmek, öldürmek; *kon.* berbat etmek, içine etmek murderer katil murderous öldürücü
murky /'mö:ki/ *s.* karanlık
murmur /'mö:mı/ *a.* mırıldanma, mırıltı; söylenme ☆ *e.* mırıldanmak; homurdanmak, söylenmek
muscle /'masıl/ *a.* kas, adale
muscular /'maskyulı/ *s.* kaslarla ilgili; kaslı, adaleli, güçlü
muse /myu:z/ *e.* (over/up/upon) derin derin düşünmek, derin düşüncelere dalmak
museum /myu:'zıım/ *a.* müze
mushroom /'maşru:m/ *a, bitk.* mantar
music /'myu:zik/ *a.* müzik; nota, makam music centre/set müzik seti music hall müzikhol musical müzikal; müzikli; müziksever; hoş, uyumlu
musician /myu:'zişın/ *a.* müzisyen
musk /mask/ *a, bitk.* misk
Muslim /'mazlim/ *a, s.* Müslüman
muslin /'mazlin/ *a.* muslin
mussel /'masıl/ *a.* midye
must /mıst, mast/ *e.* (zorunluluk, gereklilik belirtir) -meli, -malı; (tahmin belirtir) -meli, -malı ☆ *a.* gerekli şey, yapılması gereken şey
mustard /'mastıd/ *a.* hardal
muster /'mastı/ *e.* toplanmak; toplamak

musty /'masti/ *s.* küf kokulu, küflü
mutation /myu:'teyşın/ *a.* değişme, dönüşme; *biy.* değişinim
mute /myu:t/ *s.* sessiz; *dilb.* (harf) okunmayan ☆ *a.* dilsiz
mutilate /'myu:tileyt/ *e.* kötürüm etmek, sakatlamak; bozmak
mutiny /'myu:tini/ *a.* (denizci, asker) isyan, ayaklanma mutineer isyancı, asi
mutter /'matı/ *e.* mırıldanmak; söylenmek, homurdanmak ☆ *a.* mırıltı
mutton /matın/ *a.* koyun eti
mutual /'myu:çuıl/ *s.* ortak; karşılıklı
muzzle /'mazıl/ *a.* hayvan burnu; top/-tüfek ağzı
my /may/ *s.* benim
myopia /may'opıı/ *a.* miyopluk myopic /may'opik/ miyop
myriad /'mirııd/ *s.* çok, sayısız
myrtle /'mö:tıl/ *a, bitk.* mersin ağacı
myself /may'self/ *adl.* ben, kendim, kendimi, kendime by myself yalnız başıma, kendi kendime
mysterious /mi'stiirııs/ *s.* esrarengiz, gizemli
mystery /'mistıri/ *a.* sır, giz; anlaşılmaz şey, gizem, esrar
mystic /'mistik/ *s.* gizemli, mistik; gizemcilikle ilgili ☆ `a.* gizemci mysticism /-sizım/ tasavvuf, gizemcilik
mystify /'mistifay/ *e.* şaşırtmak
myth /mit/ *a.* efsane, söylence mythical efsanevi, söylencesel
mythology /mi'tolıci/ *a.* mitoloji, söylenbilim mythological mitolojik

N

nab /neb/ *e, kon.* yakalamak, kapmak
nag /neg/ *a.* ufak at, midilli ☆ *e.* söylenip durmak, dırdır etmek
nail /neyl/ *a.* tırnak; çivi ☆ *e.* çivilemek hit the nail on the head taşı gediğine koymak, tam üstüne basmak
naive /nay'i:v/ *s.* saf, bön, toy
naked /'neykid/ *s.* çıplak
name /neym/ *a.* ad, isim; ün, şöhret;

ünlü kişi ☆ *e.* ad koymak; seçmek, atamak **family name** soyadı **by name** ismen, adıyla **in the name of** adına, namına **call sb names** -e sövüp saymak **know sb by name** -i ismen tanımak **make a name for oneself** ün kazanmak **nameless** adsız, isimsiz; tarifi olanaksız, anlatılamaz **namely** yani, şöyle ki **nameplate** tabela **namesake** adaş

nanny /'neni/ *a.* dadı

nap /nep/ *e.* kestirmek, şekerleme yapmak ☆ *a.* kısa uyku, kestirme

nape /neyp/ *a.* ense

napkin /'nepkin/ *a.* peçete

nappy /'nepi/ *a.* bebek bezi

narcissism /'na:sisizm/ *a.* narsisizm, özseverlik

narcissus /na:'sisis/ *a, bitk.* nergis

narcotic /na:'kotik/ *a, s.* uyuşturucu

narrate /nı'reyt/ *e.* anlatmak, aktarmak **narration** anlatım; öyküleme; öykü, hikâye **narrative** öykü, anlatı **narrator** anlatıcı

narrow /'nerou/ *s.* dar; ensiz; sınırlı; kıt kanaat ☆ *e.* daralmak; daraltmak **narrow-minded** dar görüşlü, bağnaz

nasal /'neyzıl/ *s.* burunla ilgili; *dilb.* genzel, genizsel

nasty /'na:sti/ *s.* kötü, tatsız; açık saçık, ayıp; pis, iğrenç

natal /neytıl/ *s.* doğumla ilgili

nation /'neyşın/ *a.* millet, ulus

national /'neşınıl/ *s.* ulusal **national anthem** milli marş **national park** milli park **nationalism** milliyetçilik, ulusçuluk **nationalist** milliyetçi, ulusçu **nationality** milliyet, ulusallık; uyrukluk, tabiiyet; ulus

nationalize /'neşınılayz/ *e.* devletleştirmek, kamulaştırmak

nationwide /neyşın'wayd/ *s.* yurt çapında, tüm yurtta gerçekleşen

native /'neytiv/ *s.* yerli, doğuştan ☆ *a.* yerli

natural /'neçırıl/ *s.* doğal; olağan; doğuştan **natural history** tabiat bilgisi, doğa bilgisi **natural resources** doğal kaynaklar **natural sciences** doğal bilimler **naturally** doğal olarak

naturalist /'neçırılist/ *a.* doğa bilimleri uzmanı, natüralist, doğalcı

naturalize /neçırılayz/ *e.* yurttaşlığa kabul etmek

nature /'neyçı/ *a.* tabiat, doğa; yaradılış, mizaç; tür, çeşit

naught /no:t/ *a.* hiç, hiçbir şey, sıfır

naughty /'no:ti/ *s.* yaramaz, haylaz

nausea /'no:ziı/ *a.* mide bulantısı

nautical /'no:tikıl/ *s.* gemicilik/deniz/-denizcilikle ilgili **nautical mile** deniz mili

naval /'neyvıl/ *s.* bahriyeye/donanmaya ait

navel /'neyvıl/ *a.* göbek

navigable /'nevigıbıl/ *s.* gemilerin yüzebileceği kadar derin

navigate /'nevigeyt/ *e.* (gemi, uçak, vb.) kullanmak; gemiyle gezmek; kaptanlık etmek **navigation** denizcilik, gemicilik, dümencilik **navigator** (gemi, uçak, vb.) rotacı, dümenci

navy /'neyvi/ *a.* deniz kuvvetleri; deniz filosu, donanma **navy blue** lacivert

near /niı/ *s.* yakın ☆ *be, ilg.* yakın, yakında, yanında, yakınında ☆ *e.* yaklaşmak **nearby** yakın, yakında **nearly** hemen hemen, neredeyse **nearness** yakınlık **nearsighted** miyop

neat /ni:t/ *s.* temiz, derli toplu; tertipli, düzensever; (içki) sek; *Aİ, kon.* çok iyi

nebula /'nebyulı/ *a.* bulutsu, nebula

necessary /'nesisıri/ *s.* gerekli, zorunlu; kaçınılmaz **necessarily** mutlaka

necessitate /ni'sesiteyt/ *e.* gerektirmek, zorunlu kılmak

necessity /ni'sesiti/ *a.* zorunluluk; ihtiyaç, gereksinim; yoksulluk

neck /nek/ *a.* boyun; elbise yakası; *coğ.* dil, kıstak ☆ *e, kon.* (cinsel birleşme yapmadan) sevişmek **up to one's neck** *kon.* boğazına kadar **necktie** *Aİ.* kravat

neckerchief /'nekıçif/ *a.* boyun atkısı

necklace /'neklis/ *a.* kolye, gerdanlık

nectar /'nektı/ *a.* nektar

née /ney/ *be.* kızlık soyadıyla

need /ni:d/ *a.* lüzum, gerek; ihtiyaç, gereksinim ☆ *e.* -e ihtiyacı olmak, gereksinim duymak; gerektirmek; gerekmek **needful** gerekli **needless** gereksiz

needle /'ni:dıl/ *a.* iğne; şiş, tığ; ibre; şırınga, enjektör **needlework** iğne işi, işleme

negative /'negıtiv/ *s.* negatif, olumsuz; *mat.* eksi ☆ *a.* olumsuz yanıt; (film) negatif

neglect /ni'glekt/ *e.* ihmal etmek, savsaklamak, sermek; yapmamak, yapmayı unutmak ☆ *a.* savsaklama, ihmal **neglectful** ihmalci **negligence** /'neglicıns/ ihmal, dikkatsizlik, kayıtsızlık **negligent** /'neglicınt/ ihmalci, dikkatsiz **negligible** /'neglicıbıl/ önemsiz, kayda değmez

negotiable /ni'gouşıibıl/ *s.* ciro edilebilir, devredilebilir, satılabilir; *kon.* (yol, vb.) geçilebilir

negotiate /ni'gouşieyt/ *e.* görüşmek; başarmak; akdetmek; ciro etmek, satmak **negotiation** görüşme; ciro etme, devretme **negotiator** delege, görüşmeci

Negro /'ni:grou/ *a.* zenci

neigh /ney/ *e.* kişnemek ☆ *a.* kişneme

neighbour /'neybı/ *a.* komşu

neighbourhood /'neybıhud/ *a.* komşular, konu komşu; çevre, yöre, semt

neither /'naydı/ *s.* (ikisinden) hiçbiri, hiçbir ☆ *adl.* hiçbiri **neither ... nor** ne ... ne de

neon /'ni:on/ *a.* neon **neon sign** ışıklı reklam

nephew /'nevyu:, 'nefyu:/ *a.* erkek yeğen

nepotism /'nepıtizım/ *a.* yakınlarını kayırma, dayıcılık

nerve /nö:v/ *a.* sinir; *kon.* arsızlık, yüzsüzlük **get on sb's nerves** -in sinirine dokunmak

nervous /'nö:vıs/ *s.* sinirleri gergin, heyecanlı, ürkek; sinirsel **nervous breakdown** sinir krizi **nervous system** sinir sistemi

nest /nest/ *a.* yuva

nestle /'nesıl/ *a.* rahatça yerleşmek, kurulmak; barındırmak, sığındırmak

net /net/ *a.* ağ; file; tuzak ☆ *s.* net, katıksız, kesintisiz ☆ *e.* (ağ ile) yakalamak **network** şebeke

nettle /'netıl/ *a, bitk.* ısırgan

neurology /nyu'rolıci/ *a.* sinirbilim, nevroloji

neurosis /nyu'rousis/ *a.* nevroz, sinirce

neurotic /nyu'rotik/ *a.* nevrozlu, sinirceli

neuter /'nyu:tı/ *s, dilb.* eril/dişil olmayan; yansız; nötr, cinsiyetsiz

neutral /'nyu:trıl/ *s.* yansız, tarafsız; *kim.* yansız, nötr; cinssiz; (vites) boşta **neutralize** etkisiz bırakmak; yansızlaştırmak

neutron /'nyu:trın/ *a.* nötron

never /'nevı/ *be.* asla, hiçbir zaman; hiç **Never mind!** Zararı yok! Boş ver! Aldırma!

nevertheless /nevıdı'les/ *be.* bununla birlikte, yine de

new /nyu:/ *s.* yeni; taze; acemi **newborn** yeni doğmuş **newcomer** yeni gelen **newly** geçenlerde, yeni; yeni bir biçimde **newlywed** yeni evli

news /nyu:z/ *a.* haber **news agency** haber ajansı **news conference** basın toplantısı **newsagent** gazete/dergi, vb. satıcısı **newscast** haber yayını **newspaper** gazete **newsprint** gazete kâğıdı **newsreel** aktüalite/haber filmi **newsstand** gazete bayii **newsvendor** gazete satıcısı

newt /nyu:t/ *a, hayb.* semender

next /nekst/ *s.* en yakın; bir sonraki, gelecek, önümüzdeki **next-door** bitişik ev(deki), yandaki **next to** -e bitişik, -in yanında

nib /nib/ *a.* uç, kalem ucu

nibble /'nibıl/ *e.* dişlemek, ısırmak

nice /nays/ *s.* hoş, sevimli, güzel; nefis, iyi; nazik, ince **nice looking** çekici, güzel **nicely** hoş bir biçimde

niche /niç, ni:ş/ *a.* duvarda oyuk; uygun yer/iş/mevki

nick /nik/ *a.* çentik, sıyrık ☆ *e.* çentmek, sıyırmak; *İİ, kon.* aşırmak, yürütmek

nickel /'nikıl/ *a, kim.* nikel; beş sent

nickname /'nikneym/ *a.* takma ad

nicotine /'nikıti:n/ *a.* nikotin

niece /'ni:s/ *a.* kız yeğen
night /nayt/ *a.* gece; akşam **all night (long)** bütün gece boyunca **Good night!** İyi geceler! **night after night** her gece **night school** akşam okulu **night shift** gece vardiyası **night watchman** gece bekçisi **nightclub** gece kulübü **nightdress** gecelik **nightgown** gecelik **nightie** *kon.* gecelik **nightly** her gece, her gece olan
nightingale /'naytingeyl/ *a.* bülbül
nightmare /'naytmeı/ *a.* kâbus
nil /nil/ *a.* hiç, sıfır
nimble /'nimbıl/ *s.* çevik, atik
nine /nayn/ *a, s.* dokuz **ninth** dokuzuncu
nineteen /nayn'ti:n/ *a, s.* on dokuz **nineteenth** on dokuzuncu
ninety /'naynti/ *a, s.* doksan **ninetieth** doksanıncı
nip /nip/ *a.* çimdik; soğuk, ayaz ☆ *e.* çimdiklemek; ısırmak; kesmek, budamak **nip in the bud** engellemek, baltalamak
nipple /'nipıl/ *a.* meme ucu; biberon emziği
nippy /'nipi/ *s.* soğuk; atik, acele, hızlı
nit /nit/ *a.* bit, vb. yumurtası, sirke
nitrate /'naytreyt/ *a, kim.* nitrat
nitrogen /'naytrıcın/ *a, kim.* nitrojen
no /nou/ *be.* hayır, olmaz, yok ☆ *s.* hiç ☆ *a.* yok yanıtı
nobility /nou'biliti/ *a.* soyluluk
noble /'noubıl/ *s.* soylu, aristokrat; yüce, asil **nobleman** soylu, asilzade
nobody /'noubıdi/ *adl.* hiç kimse
nod /nod/ *e.* (onay, selam için) başını sallamak; *kon.* uyuklamak ☆ *a.* baş sallama
noise /noyz/ *a.* gürültü, patırtı, ses, seda **noisy** gürültülü, patırtılı, gürültücü
nomad /'noumed/ *a.* göçebe **nomadic** göçebe
nominal /'nominıl/ *s.* (fiyat) itibari; *dilb.* adlarla ilgili; önemsiz, düşük
nominate /'nomineyt/ *e.* aday olarak göstermek; atamak, tayin etmek
nominative /'nominıtiv/ *a, dilb.* yalın hal
nonaligned /nonı'laynd/ *s.* (ülke) bağlantısız
noncommissioned officer /nonkımişınd 'ofisı/ *a.* astsubay, gedikli erbaş
none /nan/ *adl.* hiçbiri; hiç ☆ *be.* hiç **none but** sadece, yalnız
nonentity /no'nentiti/ *a.* önemsiz/değersiz kişi
nonflammable /non'flemıbıl/ *s.* yanmaz
nonplus /non'plas/ *e.* şaşırtmak
nonsense /'nonsıns/ *a.* anlamsız söz, saçmalık; aptalca davranış **nonsensical** abuk subuk, aptalca
nonsmoker /non'smoukı/ *a.* sigara içmeyen kimse; *İİ.* sigara içilmeyen kompartıman
nonstick /non'stik/ *s.* (tava) yapışmaz
nonstop /non'stop/ *s, be.* (yolculuk) direkt, aktarmasız; aralıksız
noodle /'nu:dıl/ *a.* şehriye
nook /nuk/ *a.* köşe, kuytu yer
noon /nu:n/ *a.* öğle vakti, öğle
no one /'nou wan/ *adl.* hiç kimse
noose /nu:s/ *a.* (darağacı, vb.) ilmik
nor /no:/ *bağ.* ne de
norm /no:m/ *a.* örnek, norm; ölçü
normal /'no:mıl/ *s.* normal, olağan; ortalama **normally** normal olarak, genelde
north /no:t/ *a, s.* kuzey ☆ *be.* kuzeye doğru **northeast** kuzeydoğu **northeaster** kuzeydoğu rüzgârı, poyraz **northerly** /'no:dıli/ kuzeyden gelen/esen **northern** /'no:dın/ kuzey ... **North Pole** Kuzey Kutbu **northwards** /'no:twıdz/ kuzeye doğru **northwest** /no:t'west/ kuzeybatı
nose /nouz/ *a.* burun **follow one's nose** dosdoğru gitmek; doğru görüneni yapmak **have a nose for** sezgisi güçlü olmak **turn up one's nose at** burun kıvırmak, beğenmemek **under sb's (very) nose** burnunun dibinde
nostalgia /no'stelcı/ *a.* nostalji, geçmişe özlem
nostril /'nostril/ *a.* burun deliği
not /not/ *be.* değil, yok **Not at all** bir şey değil, rica ederim
notable /'noutıbıl/ *s.* dikkate değer; tanınmış ☆ *a.* ileri gelen/saygın/tanın-

mış kişi **notably** özellikle; epeyce
notary /'noutıri/ *a.* noter
notation /nou'teyşın/ *a.* rakamlar ve
işaretler sistemi
notch /noç/ *a.* çentik, kertik ☆ *e.* çentmek, kertik açmak
note /nout/ *a.* not; nota, muhtıra; *müz.*
nota; senet; banknot; önem ☆ *e.* not
etmek, kaydetmek; dikkat etmek,
önem vermek; farkına varmak **of note**
tanınmış, ünlü **compare notes** fikir
alışverişinde bulunmak **notebook** defter **noted** ünlü, tanınmış **noteworthy**
dikkate değer, önemli
nothing /'nating/ *a.* hiçbir şey; önemsiz kimse/şey; sıfır **for nothing** bedava, parasız; boşuna, boşa **nothing
but** sadece **nothing for it** başka çare
yok **nothing to do with** ile ilgisi yok
notice /'noutis/ *a.* duyuru; bildiri; uyarı;
dikkat ☆ *e.* -e dikkat etmek; farkına
varmak, gözüne ilişmek **give notice**
önceden haber vermek **take notice of**
dikkate almak **noticeable** göze çarpan, önemli **notice board** ilan tahtası
notification /noutifi'keyşın/ *a.* tebliğ, bildiri, bildirge
notify /'noutifay/ *e.* bildirmek, haberdar
etmek, haber vermek
notion /'nouşın/ *a.* fikir, görüş, kanı
notorious /nou'to:rııs/ *s.* kötü tanınmış,
adı çıkmış, kötü şöhretli
notwithstanding /notwit'stending/ *ilg.*
-e rağmen, -e karşın ☆ *be.* buna rağmen, yine de
nougat /'nu:ga:/ *a.* koz helva, nuga
nought /no:t/ *a, İİ.* sıfır; hiç
noun /naun/ *a, dilb.* isim, ad
nourish /'nariş/ *e.* beslemek; desteklemek **nourishment** besin, gıda, yiyecek
novel /'novıl/ *a.* roman **novelist** romancı
novelty /'novılti/ *a.* yenilik
November /nou'vembı/ *a.* kasım
novice /'novis/ *a.* acemi, çırak, toy
now /nau/ *be.* şimdi ☆ *bağ.* mademki, -dığı için **by now** şimdiye dek **from
now on** bundan böyle, bundan sonra
just now az önce, demin **now and**

then/again ara sıra, bazen, arada bir
nowadays /'nauıdeyz/ *be.* bu günlerde,
şimdilerde, bu aralar
nowhere /'nouweı/ *be.* hiçbir yerde/yere
noxious /'nokşıs/ *s.* zararlı, tehlikeli
nozzle /'nozıl/ *a.* ağızlık, meme
nuclear /'nyu:klıı/ *s.* nükleer, çekirdeksel **nuclear disarmament** nükleer silahsızlanma **nuclear energy** nükleer
enerji
nucleus /'nyu:klııs/ *a.* çekirdek; öz
nude /nyu:d/ *s.* çıplak
nudge /nac/ *e.* dirsekle dürtmek
nudity /'nyu:diti/ *a.* çıplaklık
nugget /'nagit/ *a.* (altın, vb.) külçe
nuisance /'nyu:sıns/ *a.* sıkıntı veren
şey/kimse, baş belası
null /nal/ *s.* geçersiz; boş, sıfır **null
and void** geçersiz, hükümsüz
numb /nam/ *s.* uyuşmuş, uyuşuk
number /'nambı/ *a.* sayı; rakam; numara; miktar ☆ *e.* saymak; numaralamak **a number of** birkaç, birtakım
numberplate (oto) plaka
numeral /'nyu:mırıl/ *s.* sayısal ☆ *a.* sayı
numerical /nyu:'merikıl/ *s.* sayısal
numerous /'nyu:mırıs/ *s.* birçok, sayısız
nun /nan/ *a.* rahibe **nunnery** rahibe
manastırı
nuptial /'napşıl/ *s.* evlenme/düğün ile
ilgili
nurse /nö:s/ *a.* hemşire, hastabakıcı ☆
e. (çocuğa, hastaya) bakmak; ilgilenmek; emzirmek
nursery /'nö:sırı/ *a.* çocuk odası; çocuk
yuvası, kreş; fidanlık **nursery school**
anaokulu
nursing /'nö:sing/ *a.* hemşirelik **nursing home** özel sağlık yurdu
nurture /'nö:çı/ *a.* (çocuk) büyütme,
bakım, eğitim ☆ *e.* büyütmek, yetiştirmek
nut /nat/ *a.* fındık; ceviz; vida somunu
nutshell fındık kabuğu; *kon.* özet, kısa açıklama
nutmeg /'natmeg/ *a.* küçük hindistancevizi

nutrient /'nyu:triınt/ s, a. besleyici (gıda)
nutrition /nyu:'trişın/a. beslenme; yiyecek, gıda **nutritious** besleyici
nuts /nats/ s, kon. deli, çılgın
nylon /'naylon/a. naylon
nymph /nimf/ a. peri

O

oak /ouk/ a. meşe ağacı
oar /o:/ a. kürek, sandal küreği
oat /out/ a. yulaf tanesi; ç. yulaf **oatmeal** yulaf unu
oath /out / a. ant, yemin; küfür
obdurate /'obcurit/ s. inatçı
obedient /ı'bi:dıınt/ s. söz dinler, uysal **obedience** itaat, söz dinleme
obelisk /'obılisk/ a. dikilitaş
obese /ou'bi:s/ s. çok şişman
obey /ou'bey/ e. denileni yapmak, söz dinlemek; riayet etmek, uymak
obituary /ı'biçuıri/ a. ölüm ilanı
object /'obcikt/ a. nesne, şey, madde; amaç; mevzu, konu; dilb. nesne
object /'ıbcekt/ e. (to) karşı çıkmak, itiraz etmek **objection** itiraz; sakınca, engel
objective /ıb'cektiv/ s. tarafsız, yansız; nesnel ☆ a. amaç, hedef; mercek, objektif **objectively** nesnel olarak
obligation /obli'geyşın/ a. zorunluluk, mecburiyet; yükümlülük; ödev; senet
obligatory /ı'bligıtıri/ s. zorunlu
oblige /ı'blayc/ e. zorunda bırakmak; lütufta bulunmak; minnettar bırakmak **I'm much obliged to you.** Size minnettarım. **obliging** yardıma hazır
oblique /ı'bli:k/ s. eğri, eğik
oblivion /ı'bliviın/ a. unutulma
oblong /'oblong/ s, a. dikdörtgen
obnoxious /ıb'nokşıs/ s. pis, iğrenç
oboe /'oubou/ a, müz. obua
obscene /ıb'si:n/ s. açık saçık, müstehcen **obscenity** /ıb'seniti/ müstehcenlik; müstehcen şey
obscure /ıb'skyuı/ s. anlaşılması güç;

karanlık; pek tanınmamış **obscurity** karanlık; anlaşılmazlık; tanınmamışlık
observance /ıb'zö:vıns/ a. yerine getirme, yapma; görenek
observant /ıb'zö:vınt/ s. dikkatli
observation /obzı'veyşın/ a. inceleme; gözlem; gözetleme
observatory /ıb'zö:vıtıri/ a. rasathane, gözlemevi
observe /ıb'zö:v/ e. dikkat etmek, gözlemek; incelemek, gözlemlemek; gözetlemek **observer** gözlemci
obsess /ıb'ses/ e. hiç aklından çıkmamak, kafasına takılmak **obsession** saplantı, sabit fikir, tutku
obsolete /'obsıli:t/ s. eskimiş, eski, modası geçmiş
obstacle /'obstıkıl/ a. engel
obstetrician /obsti'trişın/ a. doğum uzmanı
obstinate /'obstinit/ s. inatçı
obstruct /ıb'strakt/ e. tıkamak; engellemek **obstruction** engelleme
obtain /ıb'teyn/ e. elde etmek, edinmek, sağlamak; almak
obtrusive /ıb'tru:siv/ s. sıkıntı veren, sırnaşık, yılışık; göze batan
obtuse /ıb'tyu:s/ s. aptal, kalın kafalı; (açı) geniş
obvious /'obviıs/ s. apaçık, belli
occasion /ı'keyjın/a. fırsat; münasebet, vesile; neden; hal, durum; önemli gün, olay **on the occasion of** münasebetiyle, dolayısıyla
occasional /ı'keyjınıl/ s. arada sırada olan **occasionally** ara sıra, bazen
occult /'okalt/ s. gizli; gizemli
occupant /'okyupınt/ a. bir yerde oturan kimse, sakin
occupation /okyu'peyşın/ a. meslek, iş; işgal **occupational** meslekle ilgili
occupy /'okyupay/ e. işgal etmek, zapt etmek; -de oturmak; meşgul etmek
occur /ı'kö: / e. vuku bulmak, olmak; bulunmak, yer almak **occurrence** /ı'karıns/ olay
ocean /'ouşın/ a. okyanus
oceanography /ouşın'ogrıfi/ a. oşinografi, okyanusbilim
o'clock /ı'klok/ be. (tam saatlerde kulla-

nılır) saat . . .

octagon /'oktıgın/ *a, mat.* sekizgen

octave /'oktiv, 'okteyv/ *a, müz.* oktav

october /ok'toubı/ *a.* ekim (ayı)

octopus /'oktıpıs/ *a, hayb.* ahtapot

odd /od/ *s.* acayip, tuhaf, garip; (sayı) tek; küsur; (ayakkabı, eldiven, vb.) tek **oddity** tuhaflık, acayiplik; garip kişi/şey, antika **oddly** garip biçimde **oddly enough** ne gariptir ki

odds /'odz/ *a.* olasılık, şans, ihtimaller; (bahiste) ikramiye oranı **at odds (with)** ile anlaşmazlık içinde **odds and ends** ufak tefek şeyler, ıvır zıvır

odious /'oudiıs/ *s.* iğrenç, nefret uyandırıcı, tiksindirici

odour /'oudı/ *a.* (ter, vb.) koku

odyssey /'odisi/ *a.* uzun ve serüvenli yolculuk

oesophagus /i'sofıgıs/ *a, anat.* yemek borusu

of /ov, ıv/ *ilg.* -in, -ın, -nin, -nın

off /of/ *ilg.* -den; ayrılan, sapan; -den uzak, uzağa; açıkta, açıklarında; isteksiz, soğumuş ☆ *be.* uzak. uzakta, uzağa; tümüyle ☆ *s.* kesilmiş, kesik; çalışmayan, izinli; sağdaki; kokmuş, bozuk; cansız, ölü **off and on** ara sıra **off chance** zayıf bir olasılık **off season** ölü sezon

offence /ı'fens/ *a.* suç; hakaret, gücendirme; saldırı

offend /ı'fend/ *e.* suç işlemek; gücendirmek, kırmak; rahatsız etmek

offensive /ı'fensiv/ *s.* pis, kötü, çirkin; saldırıyla ilgili

offer /'ofı/ *e.* teklif etmek; arz etmek, sunmak ☆ *a.* teklif; sunma, takdim, arz **offering** bağış, adak, kurban; teklif

offhand /of'hend/ *s.* düşünmeden yapılmış, hazırlıksız ☆ *be.* hazırlıksız, düşünmeden

office /'ofis/ *a.* yazıhane, büro, ofis; devlet dairesi; bakanlık **office block** iş hanı

officer /'ofisı/ *a.* görevli, memur; polis memuru; subay

official /ı'fişıl/ *s.* resmi ☆ *a.* memur **officially** resmi olarak

off-license /'oflaysıns/ *a, İİ.* içki satılan dükkân

offset /'ofset/ *a.* ofset, ofset baskı ☆ *e.* dengelemek, denkleştirmek

offshoot /'ofşu:t/ *a, bitk.* sürgün, dal

offshore /of'şo:/ *be, s.* kıyıdan uzak

offside /of'sayd/ *a, sp.* ofsayt

offspring /'ofspring/ *a.* çoluk çocuk, döl

often /'ofın, 'oftın/ *be.* sık sık, çoğu kez

ogre /'ougı/ *a.* dev; korkunç kimse

oil /oyl/ *a.* yağ, sıvı yağ; yağlıboya; petrol; zeytinyağı ☆ *e.* yağ sürmek, yağlamak **oil painting** yağlıboya resim (sanatı) **oil well** petrol kuyusu **oilcloth** muşamba **oily** yağlı

ointment /'oyntmınt/ *a.* merhem

OK, okay /ou'key/ *be, kon.* peki, tamam, oldu ☆ *e, kon.* onaylamak ☆ *s.* iyi, uygun, idare eder ☆ *a.* onay, olur

old /ould/ *s.* yaşlı; . . . yaşında; eski; deneyimli, pişkin **How old are you?** Kaç yaşındasınız? **grow old** yaşlanmak **old age pension** yaşlılık maaşı **old-fashioned** modası geçmiş, demode **old hand** deneyimli kimse, eski kurt

olive /'oliv/ *a, bitk.* zeytin; zeytin ağacı

Olympic /ı'limpik/ *s.* olimpik **Olympic Games** Olimpiyat oyunları, Olimpiyatlar

omelette /'omlit/ *a.* omlet

omen /'oumın/ *a.* kehanet; alamet

omission /ou'mişın/ *a.* dahil etmeme, atlama

omit /ou'mit/ *e.* ihmal etmek, atlamak; geçmek

on /on/ *ilg.* üstünde, üstüne; -de, -da; hakkında, üzerine; yönünde, doğru; uyarınca, göre ☆ *be.* ileriye; aralıksız, durmadan **on and on** durmadan, boyuna

once /wans/ *be.* bir kez, bir kere; bir zamanlar, eskiden **all at once** aniden, birdenbire; derhal, hemen **at once** derhal, hemen **once again** bir kere daha **once and for all** ilk ve son defa **once in a while** arada bir, bazen **once more** bir kez daha, yine **once or twice** bir iki kez **once upon a time** bir zamanlar; bir varmış bir yokmuş oncoming /'onkaming/ s. ilerleyen, yaklaşan

one /wan/ a, s. bir; tek ☆ a. bir sayısı; bir tane ☆ adl. biri, birisi; insan one by one birer birer one another birbirini

oneself /wan'self/ adl. kendisi, kendi kendine by oneself yalnız başına

one-way /wan'wey/ s. tek yönlü; (bilet) gidiş

onion /'anyın/ a, bitk. soğan

only /'ounli/ s. biricik, tek ☆ be. ancak, yalnız ☆ bağ. ama, ne var ki, ancak if only ah bir, ah keşke only too çok, tamamen

onset /'onset/ a. saldırı; başlangıç

onshore /on'şo:/ s, be. denizden karaya

onslaught /'onslo:t/ a. şiddetli saldırı

onto /'ontu/ ilg. üstüne, üzerine

onus /'ounıs/ a. yük, sorumluluk

onward /'onwıd/ s. ilerleyen ☆ be. ileri

onyx /'oniks/ a. damarlı akik, oniks

ooze /u:z/ a. sızıntı ☆ e. sızmak; sızdırmak

opaque /ou'peyk/ s. ışık geçirmez

open /oupın/ s. açık; çözümlenmemiş, askıda; ödenmemiş ☆ e. açmak; açılmak open-air açık hava open-air theatre açık hava tiyatrosu open out açmak, sermek; gelişmek opener açacak open-handed eli açık, cömert openhearted açık kalpli, içten open-minded açık fikirli

opening /'oupıning/ a. açılış; ağız, kapı; açık alan

opera /'opırı/ a. opera

operate /'opıreyt/ e. işletmek, çalıştırmak; işlemek, çalışmak; ameliyat etmek operating theatre ameliyat odası

operation /opı'reyşın/ a. işletme; işleme, çalışma; ameliyat; ask. harekât operational kullanıma hazır

operative /'opırıtiv/ s. işleyen, çalışan; etkin, etkili; geçerli

operator /'opıreytı/ a. operatör, işletmen

operetta /opı'retı/ a. operet

opinion /ı'pinyın/ a. fikir, düşünce, kanı in my opinion bence, kanımca public opinion kamuoyu

opium /'oupiım/ a. afyon

opponent /ı'pounınt/ a. aleyhtar, muhalif, rakip

opportune /'opıçu:n/ s. elverişli, uygun

opportunity /opı'tyu:niti/ a. fırsat, elverişli zaman

oppose /ı'pouz/ e. karşı koymak, karşı çıkmak as opposed to -in aksine

opposite /'opızit/ a. karşıt, zıt, karşı ☆ s. karşıt, zıt, ters, aksi; karşısında opposite sex karşı cins

opposition /opı'zişın/ a. muhalefet; karşı koyma, direnme; rekabet; zıtlık, karşıtlık

oppress /ı'pres/ e. bunaltmak, sıkıntı vermek; baskı uygulamak, eziyet etmek oppression baskı, zulüm; sıkıntı oppressive ezici, ağır; bunaltıcı oppressor zalim, zorba

optic /'optik/ s. gözle ilgili optics /'optiks/ ışıkbilgisi, optik optical /'optikıl/ görme duyusuyla ilgili optician /op'tişın/ gözlükçü

optimism /'optimizım/ a. iyimserlik optimist iyimser kimse optimistic iyimser

optimum /'optimım/ s. en iyi/yüksek/uygun

option /'opşın/ a. seçme hakkı, tercih hakkı; seçenek optional isteğe bağlı, seçmeli

or /o:/ bağ. veya, ya da, veyahut, yoksa or else yoksa or so . . . civarında

oral /'o:rıl/ s. sözel, sözlü, ağızdan; ağızdan, oral

orange /'orinc/ a, bitk. portakal ☆ a, s. portakalrengi, turuncu

orangutang /o:rengu'teng/ a, hayb. orangutan

oration /ı'reyşın/ a. söylev, nutuk

orator /'orıtı/ a. hatip, konuşmacı oratory hitabet, güzel konuşma sanatı

oratorio /orı'to:riou/ a, müz. oratoryo

orbit /'o:bit/ a. yörünge ☆ e. yörüngede dönmek

orchard /o:çıd/ a. meyve bahçesi

orchestra /'o:kistrı/ a. orkestra

orchid

orchid /'o:kid/ a, bitk. orkide
ordeal /o:'di:l/ a. çetin sınav, ateşten
gömlek
order /'o:dı/ a. düzen, tertip; sıra, dizi;
usul, yol, kural; sipariş, ısmarlama; havale; emir, buyruk ☆ e. buyurmak,
emretmek; ısmarlamak; sipariş vermek; düzenlemek, tertiplemek in order that -mesi için in order to -mek
için out of order bozuk; çalışmaz; düzensiz make to order sipariş üzerine
yapmak put in order düzene koymak
order sb around -e gereksiz emirler
yağdırmak
orderly /'o:dılı/ s. düzenli, derli toplu,
tertipli; sistemli; uslu, uysal ☆ a.
emir eri; hastane hademesi
ordinal /'o:dinıl/ a, mat. sıra sayısı
ordinance /'o:dinıns/ a. buyruk, emir;
yasa, yönetmelik
ordinary /'o:dınri/ s. alışılmış, olağan
ore /o:/ a. maden cevheri
organ /'o:gın/ a. uzuv, organ; alet,
araç; yayın organı; müz. org
organic /o:'genik/ s. organik; organlar-
la ilgili
organism /'o:gınizim/ a. organizma
organization /o:gınay'zeyşın/ a. örgüt;
örgütlenme; organizasyon
organize /'o:gınayz/ e. kurmak, örgütlemek; düzenlemek
orgasm /'o:gezım/ a. orgazm, doyu-
num, cinsel doyum
orgy /'o:ci/ a. seks partisi; âlem, cümbüş
orient /'o:riınt/ a. doğu; doğu ülkeleri,
Asya; Uzakdoğu oriental doğuya özgü, doğu . . .
orientate /'o:riınteyt/ e. yönlendirmek
orientation yönlendirme
orifice /'orifis/ a. ağız, delik
origin /'oricin/ a. başlangıç, kaynak;
kök, köken
original /ı'ricinıl/ s. orijinal, özgün; yaratıcı ☆ a. asıl, orijinal originality orijinallik, özgünlük; yaratıcılık originally
aslında; özgün bir biçimde
originate /ı'ricineyt/ e. kaynaklanmak,
çıkmak, başlamak; başlatmak
ornament /'o:nımınt/ a. süs, süs eşyası

☆ e. süslemek
ornate /o:'neyt/ s. çok süslü
ornithology /o:ni'tolıci/ a. kuş bilimi
orphan /'o:fın/ a. öksüz, yetim, kimsesiz orphanage yetimlik, öksüzlük; ye-
timler yurdu
orthodox /'o:tıdoks/ s. herkesin inandı-
ğına inanan, ortodoks
orthography /o:'togrıfi/ a. imla, yazım
orthopaedic /o:tı'pi:dik/ s. ortopedik
orthopaedics ortopedi
oscillate /'osileyt/ e. sallanmak, salınmak oscillation salınım
ostentation /ostın'teyşın/ a. gösteriş,
çalım
ostrich /'ostriç/ a, hayb. devekuşu
other /'adı/ s. diğer, öteki; başka ☆
adl. diğeri, öbürü; başkası ☆ be. başka türlü every other day gün aşırı the
other day geçen gün each other birbirini, birbirine other than hariç, dışında
otherwise /'adıwayz/ be. başka türlü;
yoksa; başka bakımlardan
otter /'otı/ a, hayb. susamuru; samur
kürk
ought /o:t/ e. (ödev/tavsiye belirtir)
-meli, -malı, gerek, iyi olur
ounce /auns/ a. ons (28.35 gr.)
our /a:, auı/ s. bizim
ours /'auız/ adl. bizimki
ourselves /auı'selvz/ adl. biz, kendimiz
by ourselves tek başımıza, yalnız
oust /aust/ a. dışarı atmak
out /aut/ be. dışarı, dışarıya; dışarıda;
yüksek sesle ☆ s. dışarıdaki, dış,
uzakta bulunan; iktidarda olmayan;
olanaksız out of -den dışarı; -in dışında; -den dolayı; -den yapılmış
out-of-date modası geçmiş, eski
out-of-doors dışarıda out-of-the way
ücra, uzak, sapa
outboard motor /autbo:d 'moutı/ a. dıştan takılan motor
outbreak /'autbreyk/ a. patlak verme
çıkma; salgın
outbuilding /'autbilding/ a. ek bina
outburst /'autbö:st/ a. patlama, patlak
verme
outcast /'autka:st/ a, s. toplumdan atıl

mış, serseri

outcome /'autkam/ a. sonuç

outcry /'autkray/ a. halk protestosu; haykırma

outdated /aut'deytid/ s. modası geçmiş

outdo /aut'du:/ e. **outdid** /autdid/, **outdone** /autdan/ -den üstün olmak, yenmek, geçmek

outdoor /aut'do:/ s. açık havada, açık hava ... **outdoors** açık havada, dışarıda

outer /'autı/ s. harici, dış, dıştaki **outer space** uzay

outermost /'autımoust/ s. en dıştaki, en uzaktaki

outfit /'autfit/ a. teçhizat, takım, donatı; kon. grup, ekip

outgoing /aut'gouing/ s. giden, ayrılan; cana yakın

outgrow /aut'grou/ e. **outgrew** /aut'g-ru:/, **outgrown** /aut'groun/ -den daha çabuk büyümek; (büyüdüğü için giysilerine) sığmamak

outing /'auting/ a. gezinti, gezi

outlandish /aut'lendiş/ s. garip, acayip

outlaw /'autlo:/ a. kanun kaçağı, haydut

outlet /'autlet/ a. çıkış yeri, delik, ağız

outline /'autlayn/ a. ana hatlar; özet ☆ e. şeklini/taslağını çıkarmak

outlook /'autluk/ a. görünüm; bakış açısı

outlying /'autlaying/ s. uzak

outnumber /aut'nambı/ e. sayıca üstün olmak

outpatient /'autpeyşınt/ a. ayakta tedavi edilen hasta

outpost /'autpoust/ a. ileri karakol

output /'autput/ a. verim; ürün; bilgisayardan alınan bilgi, çıktı

outrage /'autreyc/ e. hakaret; rezalet; tecavüz **outrageous** terbiyesiz, çirkin

outright /aut'rayt/ be. tam, bütün; açık belli

outset /'autset/ a. başlangıç

outside /aut'sayd/ ilg. dışında; dışına ☆ be. dışarıda; dışarıya ☆ s. dış ☆ a. dış (taraf); dış görünüş

outsider /aut'saydı/ a. bir grubun dışın-

da olan kimse, yabancı; kazanma olasılığı az olan yarışmacı/hayvan

outsize /'autsayz/ s. (giysi) büyük boy

outskirts /'autskö:ts/ a. kentin dışı, dış mahalle, varoş

outsmart /aut'sma:t/ e, kon. kurnazlıkla üstesinden gelmek, hakkından gelmek, yenmek, alt etmek

outspoken /aut'spoukın/ s. dobra dobra konuşan, açıksözlü

outstanding /aut'stending/ s. göze çarpan, önemli; ödenmemiş

outstrip /aut'strip/ e. -den daha iyi yapmak, geçmek, geride bırakmak

outward /'autwıd/ s. dış ☆ be. (aynı zamanda **outwards**) dışarıya **outwardly** görünüşte

outweigh /aut'wey/ e. -den daha ağır basmak, -den daha önemli olmak

outwit /aut'wit/ e. kurnazlıkla alt etmek, yenmek

oval /'ouvıl/ s. yumurta biçiminde, oval

ovary /'ouvıri/ a. yumurtalık; bitk. tohumluk

ovation /ou'veyşın/ a. coşkunca alkış

oven /'avın/ a. fırın

over /'ouvı/ ilg. üzerinde, üstünde; üzerine, üstüne; öbür tarafına, öbür tarafında; -den çok; baştan başa, her yerine; sonuna dek, süresince; hakkında, konusunda ☆ be. yukarıya; yukarıda; bitmiş; adamakıllı, iyice; karşı tarafa, öbür tarafa **all over** her tarafında; her tarafına **all over again** yeni baştan **over and above** -den başka **over and over** defalarca

over- /ouvı/ önek gereğinden çok, aşırı derecede; aşağıya, yere

overall /ouvır'o:l/ be, s. tüm, toplam; ayrıntılı, kapsamlı

overalls /'ouvıro:lz/ a. işçi tulumu, tulum

overbearing /ouvı'beıring/ s. mütehakkim, buyurucu

overboard /'ouvıbo:d/ be, den. gemiden denize

overcast /ouvı'ka:st/ s. bulutlu, kapalı

overcharge /ouvı'ça:c/ e. fazla fiyat istemek, kazıklamak

overcoat /'ouvıkout/ a. palto

overcome /ouvı'kam/ e. overcame /o-uvıkeym/, overcome üstesinden gelmek, alt etmek; galip gelmek

overdo /ouvı'du:/ e. overdid /ouvıdid/, overdone /ouvıdan/ abartmak, şişirmek; fazla pişirmek

overdose /'ouvıdous/ a. aşırı doz

overdraft /'ouvıdra:ft/ a. hesabından fazla para çekme izni, açık kredi

overdraw /ouvı'dro:/ e. overdrew /ouvıdru:/, overdrawn /auvıdro:n/ (bankadaki hesabından) fazla para çekmek

overdue /ouvı'dyu:/ s. vadesi geçmiş; rötarlı, geçikmiş

overflow /ouvı'flou/ e. taşmak ☆ a. taşma; taşkın; oluk

overgrown /ouvı'groun/ s. yabanıl bitkilerle kaplı; fazla/hızlı büyümüş

overhang /ouvı'heng/ e. overhung /o-uvıhang/ sarkmak

overhaul /ouvı'ho:l/ e. elden geçirmek, onarmak; yetişip geçmek

overhead /ouvı'hed/ s, be. yukarıda, tepede

overheads /'ouvıhedz/ a. işletme giderleri

overhear /ouvı'hiı/ e. overheard /-'hö:d/ kulak misafiri olmak, gizlice dinlemek

overjoyed /ouvı'coyd/ s. çok sevinçli

overland /ouvı'lend/ s. karayolu ile yapılan ☆ be. karadan

overlap /ouvı'lep/ e. üst üste binmek; kısmen kaplamak

overload /ouvı'loud/ e. aşırı yüklemek; fazla elektrik kullanmak

overlook /ouvı'luk/ e. -e nazır olmak, bakmak; gözden kaçırmak, görememek; göz yummak

overnight /ouvı'nayt/ be. geceleyin

overpower /ouvı'pauı/ e. yenmek

overrate /ouvı'reyt/ e. fazla değer vermek

overseas /ouvı'si:z/ be, s. denizaşırı

overshadow /ouvı'şedou/ e. gölge düşürmek, gölgelemek

oversight /'ouvısayt/ a. dikkatsizlik, gözden kaçırma, dalgınlık

oversleep /ouvı'sli:p/ e. uyuya kalmak

overt /'ouvö:t/ s. açıkça yapılan

overtake /ouvı'teyk/ e. overtook /ouvı'tuk/, overtaken /ouvı'teykın/ yetişip geçmek, sollamak; ansızın yakalamak, bastırmak

overthrow /ouvı'trou/ e. overthrew /o-uvı'tru:/, overthrown /ouvı'troun/ (hükümet, vb.) devirmek, yıkmak

overtime /'ouvıtaym/ a, be. fazla mesai

overture /'ouvıçuı/ a, müz. uvertür; ç. görüşme önerisi, öneri

overturn /'ouvıtö:n/ e. devirmek

overweight /ouvı'weyt/ s. (belli bir kilodan) ağır

overwhelm /ouvı'welm/ e. yenmek, ezmek, bastırmak; gark etmek, boğmak overwhelming çok büyük, ezici

overwork /ouvı'wö:k/ e. fazla çalışmak; fazla çalıştırmak ☆ a. fazla çalışma

ovum /'ouvım/ a, /ç, ova /'ouvı/ biy. yumurta

owe /ou/ e. borcu olmak, borçlu olmak

owing /'ouing/ s. ödenmemiş owing to -den dolayı, yüzünden

owl /aul/ a, hayb. baykuş, puhu

owlet /'aulit/ a, hayb. baykuş yavrusu

own /oun/ s, adl. kendi, kendisinin ☆ e. sahip olmak have/get one's own back öcünü almak on one's own tek başına, yalnız

owner /'ounı/ a. mal sahibi owner-driver kendi aracını kullanan sürücü ownerless sahipsiz owner-occupied sahibinin oturduğu ownership mülkiyet, sahiplik

ox /oks/ a. /ç. owen /'oksın/ hayb. öküz

oxcart /'okska:t/ a. öküz arabası, kağnı

oxidation /oksi'deyşın/ a. oksidasyon

oxide /'oksayd/ a, kim. oksit

oxygen /'oksicın/ a, kim. oksijen oxygen mask oksijen maskesi oxygen tent oksijen çadırı

oyez /ou'yes/ ünl, huk. dikkat!, dinleyin!

oyster /'oystı/ a, hayb. istiridye oyster bank istiridye yatağı oyster catcher istiridye avcısı, denizsaksağanı

ozone /'ouzoun/ a, kim. ozon ozone layer ozon tabakası

P

pace /peys/ a. adım; yürüyüş ☆ e. adımlamak keep pace with kon. ayak uydurmak
pacific /pı'sifik/ s. barışsever, barışçı
pacifism /'pesifizım/ a. barışseverlik pacifist barışsever
pacify /'pesifay/ e. yatıştırmak
pack /pek/ a. bohça, çıkın; paket; sürü; (iskambil) deste ☆ e. paketlemek; sarmak; tıka basa doldurmak
package /'pekic/ a. paket, bohça, ambalaj package tour (acentanın ayarladığı) grup turu
packet /'pekit/ a. paket
packing /'peking/ a. paketleme, ambalaj
pact /pekt/ a. antlaşma, pakt
pad /ped/ a. yastık; kâğıt destesi, bloknot; ıstampa ☆ e. içini doldurmak padding vatka; kıtık
paddle /'pedıl/ a. kısa kürek, (masa tenisi) raket paddle steamer yandan çarklı gemi
paddock /'pedık/ a. küçük çayır alan
paddy /'pedi/ a. çeltik tarlası
padlock /'pedlok/ a. asma kilit
pagan /'peygın/ a, s. putperest
page /peyc/ a. sayfa
pageant /'pecınt/ a. kutlama töreni; gösteri pageantry parlak gösteri
paid /peyd/ bkz. pay
pain /peyn/ a. ağrı, sızı; acı, ıstırap; zahmet, külfet pain in the neck/ass kon. baş belası, dert painful acı veren, ağrılı painkiller ağrı kesici painless acısız, ağrısız painstaking dikkatli, özenli
paint /peynt/ e. boyamak; resmini yapmak; badana yapmak; makyaj yapmak ☆ a. boya paintbrush boya fırçası painter ressam; badanacı, boyacı painting ressamlık; yağlıboya resim, tablo

pair /peı/ a. çift; karı koca in pairs ikişer ikişer
pajamas /pı'ca:mız/ a, Aİ. pijama
pal /pël/ a, kon. arkadaş, ahbap
palace /'pelis/ a. saray
palate /'pelit/ a. damak; ağız tadı
palatial /pı'leyşıl/ s. saray gibi, görkemli
pale /peyl/ a. soluk; solgun, cansız
palette /'pelit/ a. ressam paleti
pall /po:l/ a. tabut örtüsü ☆ e. usandırmak, bıktırmak, sıkmak
pallid /'pelid/ s. solgun, benzi atmış
palm /pa:m/ a, bitk. palmiye; hurma ağacı; avuç içi, aya
palmist /'pa:mist/ a. el falcısı palmistry el falı
palpitate /'pelpiteyt/ e. (yürek) hızlı ve düzensizce atmak
palsy /'po:lzi/ a. 'inme, felç
pamper /'pempı/ e. üzerine çok düşmek, şımartmak
pamphlet /'pemflit/ a. kitapçık, broşür
pan /pen/ a. tava; lavabo taşı ☆ e. elemek, süzmek; (kamerayı) sağa sola çevirmek
pancake /'penkeyk/ a. tava keki, gözleme
pancreas /'penkriıs/ a, anat. pankreas
panda /'pendı/ a, hayb. panda
pandemonium /pendi'mouniım/ a. şamata, curcuna, tantana
pane /peyn/ a. pencere camı
panel /'penıl/ a. kapı aynası; pano; jüri heyeti panel discussion açıkoturum
pang /peng/ a. ani ağrı, sancı, acı
panic /'penik/ a. panik, ürkü ☆ e. paniğe uğratmak; paniğe kapılmak
pannier /'peniı/ a. küfe, sepet
panorama /penı'ra:mı/ a. panorama; toplu görünüm
pansy /'penzi/ a, bitk. hercaimenekşe
pant /pent/ e. sık sık nefes almak, nefes nefese kalmak; nefes nefese söylemek
panther /'pentı/ a, hayb. panter; Aİ. puma
panties /'pentiz/ a, kon. kadın külotu
pantomime /'pentımaym/ a. pandomim

pantry /'pentri/ a. kiler
pants /pents/ a, İİ. kadın külotu; Aİ.
pantalon
paper /'peypı/ a. kâğıt; kon. gazete; yazı, bildiri; ç. evrak; sınav soruları ☆
e. duvar kâğıdıyla kaplamak on paper kâğıt üzerinde paper clip ataş
paperback kâğıt kapaklı kitap paperbag kesekağıdı paperwork kırtasiyecilik
paprika /'peprikı/ a. kırmızıbiber
papyrus /pı'payırıs/ a. papirüs
par /pa:/ a. nominal değer, itibari kıymet, eşit düzey
parable /'perıbıl/ a. mesel, ibret alınacak öykü
parachute /'perişu:t/ a. paraşüt ☆ e.
paraşütle atlamak parachutist paraşütçü
parade /pı'reyd/ a. geçit töreni; gösteriş ☆ e, ask. sıraya dizilmek; gösteriş yapmak
paradise /'perıdays/ a. cennet
paradox /'perıdoks/ a. paradoks, yanıltmaç
paraffin /'perıfin/ a. parafin
paragraph /'perıgra:f/ a. paragraf
parallel /'perılel/ s. paralel, koşut ☆ a.
paralel çizgi; benzerlik; coğ. enlem
parallel /'perılel/ e. benzemek, eşit olmak
paralyse /'perılayz/ e. felç etmek, felce uğratmak
paralysis /pı'relisis/ a. inme, felç
paralytic /perı'litik/ a. felçli kimse
paramount /'perımaunt/ s. üstün, yüce, en büyük, en önemli
paranoia /perı'noyı/ a, ruhb. paranoya
paranoid /'perınoyd/ paranoyak
parapet /'perıpit/ a. korkuluk, siper
paraphernalia /perıfı'neyliı/ a. takım
taklavat, donatı
paraphrase /'perıfreyz/ e. başka sözcüklerle açıklamak, açımlamak ☆ a.
açımlama
parasite /'perısayt/ a. asalak
parasol /'perısol/ a. güneş şemsiyesi
paratroops /'perıtru:ps/ a, ask. paraşütçü kıtası paratrooper /'perıtru:pı/ paraşütçü

parcel /'pa:sıl/ a. paket, koli parcel out
taksim etmek, bölümlere/hisselere
ayırmak parcel post paket postası
parch /pa:ç/ e. (güneş) kavurmak; (susuzluktan) kavrulmak
parchment /'pa:çmınt/ a. tirşe, parşömen
pardon /'pa:dın/ a. af, bağışlama ☆
e. bağışlamak, affetmek I beg your
pardon Affedersiniz, Efendim?
pare /peı/ e. kabuğunu soymak
parent /'peırınt/ a. ana ya da baba, veli; ç. ana baba, ebeveyn parenthood
analık ya da babalık
parenthesis /pı'rentisis/ a. ayraç, parantez; ara söz
parity /'periti/ a. eşitlik, denklik
park /pa:k/ a. park, yeşil alan ☆ e.
park etmek; kon. koymak, bırakmak
parking /pa:king/ a. park yapma No
Parking Park yapılmaz parking lot Aİ.
otopark parking meter parkmetre,
otopark sayacı parking space park yeri
parley /'pa:li/ a. zirve toplantısı, barış
görüşmesi
parliament /'pa:lımınt/ a. parlamento,
meclis parliamentarian /-mın'teırıın/
parlamenter parliamentary /-mentırı/
parlamentoya ait
parlour /'pa:lı/ a. salon beauty parlor
Aİ. güzellik salonu
parody /'perıdi/ a. parodi, gülünçleme;
adi kopya
parole /pı'roul/ a. şartlı tahliye
parquet /'pa:key/ a. parke
parrot /'perıt/ a, hayb. papağan
parry /'peri/ e. savuşturmak; geçiştirmek
parsley /'pa:sli/ a. maydanoz
parsnip /'pa:snip/ a. yabani havuç
parson /'pa:sın/ a. papaz
part /pa:t/ a. bölüm, kısım, parça; pay;
yan, taraf; görev; rol; müz. fasıl for my
part kendi hesabıma, bence for the
most part çoğunlukla in part kısmen
part of speech sözcük türü play a
part rol oynamak part with -den ayrılmak
partial /'pa:şıl/ s. bölümsel, kısmi; taraf-

gir, yan tutan; düşkün **partiality** /-'eli-ti/ *a.* yan tutma, tarafgirlik; düşkünlük **partially** kısmen; yan tutarak

participate /pa:'tisipeyt/ *e.* katılmak, iştirak etmek **participant** /-pınt/ katılımcı, iştirakçi **participation** katılma, katılım

participle /'pa:tisipıl/ *a, dilb.* ortaç

particle /'pa:tikıl/ *a.* parça, zerre, tane; *dilb.* işlevsel sözcük, ilgeç, tanımlık, bağlaç

particular /pı'tıkyulı/ *s.* belirli; özel; mahsus, özgü; titiz; tam, ayrıntılı **in particular** özellikle **particularly** özellikle **particulars** ayrıntılar, detaylar

partisan /pa:ti'zen/ *a.* yandaş, taraftar, partizan; *ask.* çeteci

partition /pa:'tişın/ *a.* bölünme, ayrılma; bölme, ince duvar

partly /'pa:tli/ *be.* kısmen

partner /'pa:tnı/ *a.* ortak; eş; kavalye, dam **partnership** ortaklık

partridge /'pa:tric/ *a, hayb.* keklik

party /'pa:ti/ *a.* eğlenti, parti; (siyasi) parti; taraf, yan

pasha /'peşı/ *a.* paşa

pass /pa:s/ *a.* geçit, boğaz; paso, şebeke; giriş-çıkış izni; pas; geçiş; sınavda geçme ☆ *e.* geçmek, ilerlemek; (sınav) başarmak, geçmek; hüküm vermek, karar vermek; (futbol) pas vermek; sayılmak, sanılmak **pass away/on** geçmek; ölmek **pass by** yanından/önünden geçmek; önememememek, boş vermek **pass for** olarak sayılmak, . . . sanılmak **pass off** geçmek, dinmek, bitmek; meydana gelmek, olmak **pass on** -e vermek; ölmek **pass out** kendinden geçmek, bayılmak

passable /'pa:sıbıl/ *s.* iyi, geçer; (yol, ırmak, vb.) geçit verir, geçilebilir

passage /'pesic/ *a.* geçiş; pasaj, koridor; paragraf, parça; deniz yolculuğu

passenger /'pesincı/ *a.* yolcu

passion /'peşın/ *a.* ihtiras, tutku, hırs **passionate** ihtiraslı, tutkulu; ateşli, şiddetli

passive /'pesiv/ *s.* pasif; *dilb.* edilgen **passive voice** *dilb.* edilgen çatı

passport /'pa:spo:t/ *a.* pasaport

password /'pa:swö:d/ *a.* parola

past /pa:st/ *s.* geçmiş; geçen ☆ *ilg.* -den sonra, -ın ötesinde ☆ *a.* geçmiş zaman, geçmiş; bir kimsenin geçmişi; *dilb.* geçmiş zaman

paste /peyst/ *a.* hamur; macun; kola; çiriş **pasteboard** mukavva

pastel /'pestıl/ *a.* pastel boya kalemi; soluk renk, pastel renk

pasteurize /'pesçırayz/ *e.* pastörize etmek

pastille /pe'sti:l/ *a, hek.* pastil

pastime /'pa:staym/ *a.* eğlence, oyun

pastor /'pa:stı/ *a.* papaz

pastrami /pestra:mi/ *a.* pastırma

pastry /'peystri/ *a.* hamur işi; pasta

pasture /'pa:sçı/ *a.* ot; otlak, çayır

pasty /'pesti/ *a.* etli börek ☆ *s.* (yüz) solgun

pat /pet/ *a.* hafifçe vurma, okşama ☆ *e.* elle hafifçe vurmak, hafifçe okşamak

patch /peç/ *a.* yama; *hek.* yakı; benek, ben ☆ *e.* yamamak **patchwork** yama işi **patchy** yarım yamalak, şöyle böyle

patent /'peytnt/ *a.* patent

paternal /pı'tö:nıl/ *s.* babayla ilgili; (akrabalık) baba tarafından

paternity /pı'tö:niti/ *a.* babalık

path /pa:t/ *a.* keçiyolu, patika; yol

pathetic /pı'tetik/ *s.* acıklı, dokunaklı **pathological** patolojik

pathway /'pa:twey/ *a.* patika

patience /'peyşıns/ *a.* sabır

patient /'peyşınt/ *s.* sabırlı ☆ *a.* hasta

patriarch /'peytria:k/ *a.* patrik, piskopos; aile reisi, kabile reisi

patriarchy /'peytria:ki/ *a.* ataerkil toplum düzeni **patriarchal** ataerkil

patriot /'petriıt/ *a.* yurtsever **patriotic** /-'otik/ yurtsever **patriotism** yurtseverlik

patrol /pı'troul/ *a, ask.* devriye **patrolman** *Aİ.* devriye polisi

patron /'peytrın/ *a.* hami, koruyucu; sürekli müşteri **patronage** /'petrınic/ himaye, koruma; sürekli müşteriler

patter /'petı/ *a.* pıtırtı, ses

pattern /'petın/ *a.* numune, örnek; elbise patronu; şablon; kalıp

paunch /po:nç/ *a.* şiş göbek

pauper /'po:pı/ *a.* yoksul, fakir

pause /po:z/ *a.* mola, ara; durak, durgu ☆ *e.* duraklamak, ara vermek

pave /peyv/ *e.* kaldırım döşemek

pavement /'peyvmınt/ *a, İİ.* kaldırım

pavilion /'pı'vilyın/ *a.* büyük çadır; pavyon; köşk

paw /po:/ *a.* pençe ☆ *e.* pençelemek

pawn /po:n/ *a.* (satranç) piyon, piyade; kukla, piyon, alet; rehin ☆ *e.* rehine vermek, rehine koymak **pawnbroker** rehinci, tefeci **pawnshop** rehinci dükkânı

pay /pey/ *e.* **paid** /peyd/ ödemek; yarar sağlamak; karşılığını vermek ☆ *a.* ödeme; ücret, maaş **pay attention (to)** dikkat etmek **pay a visit** ziyaret etmek **pay back** geri vermek, ödemek **pay sb back** -den bşin acısını çıkartmak **pay off** (borç) tümüyle kapatmak; ücretini verip kovmak **pay up** borcunu kapatmak **payable** ödenecek, ödenmesi gerek; ödenebilir **payday** maaş günü **payee** alacaklı **payment** ödeme; ücret, maaş **payroll** ücret bordrosu

pea /pi:/ *a, bitk.* bezelye

peace /pi:s/ *a.* barış; rahat, huzur; asayiş, güvenlik **at peace** barış halinde **break the peace** asayişi bozmak **hold one's peace** sesini çıkarmamak, susmak **keep the peace** asayişi korumak **peaceable** barışçıl **peaceful** barışsever; sakin, huzurlu

peach /pi:ç/ *a.* şeftali

peacock /'pi:kok/ *a.* tavuskuşu

peahen /'pi:hen/ *a.* dişi tavuskuşu

peak /pi:k/ *a.* uç, doruk, zirve

peal /pi:l/ *a.* çan sesi; gürültü

peanut /'pi:nat/ *a.* amerikanfıstığı, yerfıstığı **peanut butter** krem fıstık

pear /peı/ *a, bitk.* armut

pearl /pö:l/ *a.* inci **mother-of-pearl** sedef

peasant /'pezınt/ *a.* köylü **peasantry** köylü sınıfı

pebble /'pebıl/ *a.* çakıl taşı

peck /'pek/ *e.* gagalamak ☆ *a.* gagalama

peculate /'pekyuleyt/ *e.* zimmetine para geçirmek

peculiar /pi'kyu:lıı/ *s.* acayip, tuhaf; **(to)** özgü, mahsus **peculiarity** /-li'eriti/ özellik; acaiplik

pedagogy /'pedıgoci/ *a.* pedagoji, eğitbilim **pedagogue** eğitimci

pedal /pedıl/ *a.* ayaklık, pedal

pedant /'pednt/ *a.* kılı kırk yaran

peddle /'pedıl/ *e.* seyyar satıcılık yapmak **peddler** seyyar satıcı

pedestal /'pedistıl/ *a.* (heykel, sütun, vb.) taban, kaide

pedestrian /pi'destrıın/ *a.* yaya **pedestrian crossing** yaya geçidi

pediatrician /pi:dıı'trişın/ *a, hek.* çocuk doktoru

pedicure /'pedikyuı/ *a.* ayak bakımı, pedikür

pedigree /'pedigri:/ *a.* soyağacı; soy

peel /pi:l/ *e.* kabuğunu soymak; (kabuğu) soyulmak ☆ *a.* (meyve, sebze,) kabuk

peep /pi:p/ *e, kon.* gizlice bakmak, dikizlemek ☆ *a.* gizlice bakış, dikiz

peer /pıı/ *a.* eş, emsal; asilzade ☆ *e.* dikkatle bakmak

peg /peg/ *a.* ağaç çivi; mandal; kanca, askı

pejorative /pi'corıtiv/ *s.* küçük düşürücü, kötüleyici, yermeli

pelican /'pelikın/ *a, hayb.* pelikan

pelt /pelt/ *a.* post, deri, kürk

pelvis /'pelvis/ *a, anat.* pelvis, leğen

pen /pen/ *a.* tükenmezkalem; dolmakalem; ağıl; kümes **pen-friend** mektup arkadaşı **penknife** çakı **pen name** takma ad

penal /'pi:nıl/ *s.* cezai

penalty /'penılti/ *a.* ceza; *sp.* penaltı **pay the penalty** cezasını çekmek

penance /'penıns/ *a.* ceza; kefaret

pence /pens/ *İİ, bkz.* **penny**

pencil /'pensıl/ *a.* kurşunkalem

pendant /'pendınt/ *a.* pandantif

pending /'pending/ *s.* kararlaştırılmamış, askıda

pendulum /'pendyulım/ *a.* sarkaç

penetrate /'penitreyt/ *e.* içine girmek, işlemek; sızmak **penetrating** içe işleyen, keskin; kavrayışlı, akıllı

penguin /'pengwin/ *a.* penguen

penicilin /peni'silin/ *a.* penisilin

peninsula /pi'ninsyulı/ *a, coğ.* yarımada

penis /'pi:nis/ *a.* penis, kamış

penitence /'penitıns/ *a.* pişmanlık, tövbe **penitent** pişman, tövbeli

pennant /'penınt/ *a.* flama, flandra

penniless /'penilıs/ *s.* züğürt, meteliksiz

penny /'peni/ *a.* (ç. **pennies** /'peniz/) Pound'un yüzde biri, peni; *Al.* sent

pension /'penşın/ *a.* emekli maaşı **pensioner** emekli (aylığı alan kimse)

pensive /'pensiv/ *s.* düşünceli, dalgın

pentagon /'pentıgın/ *a.* beşgen

pentathlon /pen'tetlın/ *a, sp.* pentatlon

penthouse /'penthaus/ *a.* çatı katı

people /'pi:pıl/ *a.* insanlar, kalabalık; halk; kişi, kimse; millet, ulus

pepper /'pepı/ *a.* biber **black pepper** kara biber **hot pepper** çok acı biber **red pepper** kırmızı biber **peppercorn** tane biber **peppermint** nane; nane şekeri **peppery** biberli; çabuk kızan

per /pı, pö:/ *ilg.* her biri için, başına; vasıtasıyla, eliyle **per annum** yılda **per capita** kişi başına (düşen) **per cent** yüzde

perambulator /pı'rembyuleytı/ *a.* çocuk arabası

perceive /pı'si:v/ *e.* algılamak, kavramak, anlamak, görmek

percentage /pı'sentic/ *a.* yüzdelik, yüzde oranı; komisyon, yüzdelik

perceptible /pı'septıbıl/ *s.* algılanabilir, duyulabilir, görülebilir

perception /pı'sepşın/ *a.* algı, kavrayış, seziş

perceptive /pı'septiv/ *s.* kavrayışlı, zeki

perch /pö:ç/ *a.* tünek; yüksek yer; *hayb.* tatlı su levreği ☆ *e.* konmak, tünemek

percolate /'pö:kıleyt/ *e.* **(through)** süzülmek, sızmak; süzmek **percolator** süzgeçli kahve ibriği

percussion /pı'kaşın/ *a.* vurma, çarpma

perennial /pı'reniıl/ *s.* bir yıl süren; (bitki) uzun ömürlü

perfect /'pö:fikt/ *s.* mükemmel, kusursuz, eksiksiz; tam ☆ *e.* /pı'fekt/ mükemmelleştirmek **perfection** mükemmellik; tamamlama; eşsiz örnek **perfectly** mükemmel bir şekilde; tamamen

perfidious /pı'fidiıs/ *s.* hain, kalleş, vefasız

perfidy /'pö:fidi/ *a.* vefasızlık, hainlik, kalleşlik

perforate /'pö:fıreyt/ *e.* delmek

perform /pı'fo:m/ *e.* yapmak, yerine getirmek; oynamak, temsil etmek; rol almak; *müz.* çalmak **performance** ifa, icra, yerine getirme; gösteri, oyun; performans **performer** sanatçı, oyuncu, müzisyen

perfume /'pö:fyu:m/ *a.* koku; parfüm

perhaps /pı'heps/ *be.* belki

peril /'peril/ *a.* tehlike

perimeter /pı'rimitı/ *a, mat.* çevre

period /'piiriıd/ *a.* dönem, devre; devir, çağ; süre; âdet, aybaşı; ders; *Al.* nokta **periodic** /piiri'odik/ periyodik **periodical** /piiri'odikıl/ sürekli yayın

periphery /pı'rifıri/ *a.* muhit, çevre

periscope /'periskoup/ *a.* periskop

perish /'periş/ *e.* ölmek, yok olmak; *il.* bozulmak **perishable** (yiyecek) çabuk bozulan

perjure /'pö:cı/ *e.* **perjure oneself** yalan yere yemin etmek

perk /pö:k/ *a, kon.* avanta

perm /pö:m/ *a, kon.* perma ☆ *e, kon.* perma yapmak

permanence /'pö:mınıns/ *a.* süreklilik

permanent /'pö:mınınt/ *s.* sürekli **permanent wave** perma(nant)

permissible /pı'misıbıl/ *s.* izin verilebilir

permission /pı'mişın/ *a.* müsaade, izin

permit /pı'mit/ *e.* izin vermek

permutation /pö:myu'teyşın/ *a, mat.* permutasyon

perpendicular /pö:pın'dikyulı/ *s.* dik, dikey ☆ *a.* dikey çizgi, dikey, dikme

perpetual /pı'peçuıl/ *s.* kalıcı; sürekli

perpetuate /pı'peçueyt/ *e.* sürdürmek; ölümsüzleştirmek, korumak

perplex

perplex /pı'pleks/ e. şaşırtmak

perplexity /pı'pleksiti/ a. şaşkınlık

persecute /'pö:sikyu:t/ e. zulmetmek; rahat vermemek persecution zulüm, eziyet

persevere /pö:si'vıı/ e. sebat etmek, azimle devam etmek perseverance sebat, azim

persist /pı'sist/ e. ısrar etmek, üstelemek; devam etmek, kalmak persistence ısrar, inat; sebat persistent inatçı, ısrarlı; sürekli

person /'pö:sın/ a. kişi, şahıs; insan, kimse; kon. şahıs personable yakışıklı, güzel

personal /'pö:sınıl/ s. kişisel; özel; bedensel personal pronoun dilb. şahıs zamiri personality kişilik, şahsiyet; önemli kişi

personify /pı'sonifay/ e. kişilik vermek; -in simgesi olmak personification kişileştirme; canlı örnek, simge

personnel /pö:sı'nel/ a. personel, görevliler

perspective /pı'spektiv/ a. perspektif

perspiration /pö:spi'reyşın/ a. ter

perspire /pı'spayı/ e. terlemek

persuade /pı'sweyd/ e. ikna etmek; inandırmak

persuasion /pı'sweyjın/ a. ikna; inanç

persuasive /pı'sweysiv/ s. ikna edici, inandırıcı

pert /pö:t/ s. sulu, cıvık, şımarık

pertain /pı'teyn/ e. (to) -e ait olmak

pervade /pı'veyd/ e. yayılmak, kaplamak

perverse /pı'vö:s/ s. huysuz, ters; sapık perversion sapıklık

pervert /pı'vö:t/ e. baştan çıkarmak, ayartmak

pessimism /'pesimizım/ a. kötümserlik pessimist kötümser

pest /pest/ a, kon. baş belası, musibet

pester /'pestı/ e. rahatsız etmek, sıkmak

pesticide /'pestisayd/ a. böcek zehiri

pet /pet/ a. evde beslenen hayvan; sevgili, gözde ☆ e. okşamak, sevmek; kon. sevişmek, oynaşmak

petal /'petıl/ a, bitk. taçyaprağı

petition /pi'tişın/ a. dilekçe; toplu dilekçe; talep ☆ e. dilekçe vermek

petrify /'petrifay/ e. taşlaşmak; taşlaştırmak; kon. şok etmek

petrol /'petrıl/ a. benzin petrol station benzin istasyonu, benzinci

petroleum /pi'troulıım/ a. petrol

petticoat /'petikout/ a. içeteklik

petty /'peti/ s. önemsiz, küçük; aşağılık, miskin petty officer deniz astsubayı

petulant /'peçulınt/ s. huysuz, hırçın

pew /pyu:/ a. uzun bank/sıra

phantom /'fentım/ a. hayalet

pharaoh /'feırou/ a. firavun

pharmacy /'fa:mısi/ a. eczacılık; eczane pharmacist /'fa:mısist/ eczacı

phase /feyz/ a. evre, safha

pheasant /'fezınt/ a, hayb. sülün

phenomenal /fi'nominıl/ s. olağanüstü, şaşılacak, süper

phenomenon /fi'nominın/ a. fenomen, görüngü; harika şey/kimse

philanthropic /filın'tropik/ s. insansever, hayırsever

philately /fi'letıli/ a. pulculuk, pul toplama

philology /fi'lolıci/ a. filoloji

philosophy /fi'losıfi/ a. felsefe

philosopher /fi'losıfı/ a. filozof

philosophical /filı'sofikıl/ s. felsefi; (kişi) mantıklı

phlegm /flem/ a. balgam, sümük

phlegmatic /fleg'metik/ s. sakin, soğukkanlı, heyecanlanmaz

phobia /'foubiı/ a. fobi, ürkü

phoenix /'fi:niks/ a. Anka kuşu

phone /foun/ a. kon. telefon ☆ e, kon. telefon etmek

phoneme /'founi:m/ a, dilb. sesbirim

phonetic /fı'netik/ s. sesçil, fonetik phonetics sesbilim, sesbilgisi

phonology /fı'nolıci/ a. sesbilim

phosphate /'fosfeyt/ a, kim. fosfat

phosphorus /'fosfırıs/ a, kim. fosfor

photo /'foutou/ a, kon. fotoğraf

photocopy /'foutoukopi/ a. fotokopi ☆ e. fotokopi çekmek photocopier fotokopi makinesi

photogenic /foutou'cenik/ s. fotojenik

405 **pine**

photograph /'foutıgra:f/ a. fotoğraf ☆
e. fotoğrafını çekmek **photographer**
fotoğrafçı **photography** fotoğrafçılık
phrase /freyz/ a, dilb. birkaç sözcükten
oluşan anlamlı birim, sözcük öbeği,
dizilim **phrasebook** seyahat rehberi;
konuşma kılavuzu
physical /'fizikıl/ s. fiziksel; bedensel
physical education beden eğitimi
physician /fi'zişın/ a. doktor, hekim
physicist /'fizisist/ a. fizikçi
physics /'fiziks/ a. fizik
physiology /fizi'olıci/ a. fizyoloji
physiological /fiziı'locikıl/ s. fizyolojik
physiotherapy /fiziou'terıpi/ a. fizyoterapi
physique /fi'zi:k/ a. vücut yapısı, fizik
piano /pi'enou/ a. piyano **pianist** /'piı-
nist, 'pya:nist/ piyanist
pick /pik/ e. seçmek, seçip ayırmak;
toplamak, koparmak; ayıklamak; kazmak, delmek; karıştırmak ☆ a. kazma; kürdan; seçme **Take your pick.**
Seçimini yap. **pick sb's pocket** birinin
cebinden bir şey yürütmek
pickaxe /'pikeks/ a. kazma
picket /'pikit/ a. grev gözcüsü; kazık;
ask. ileri karakol ☆ e. gözcülük etmek
pickle /'pikıl/ a. turşu ☆ e. turşusunu
kurmak **in a pickle** kon. zor durumda
pickpocket /'pikpokit/ a. yankesici
pick-up /'pikap/ a. kamyonet; pikap kolu
picnic /'piknik/ a. piknik ☆ e. piknik
yapmak
pictorial /pik'to:riıl/ s. resimli, resmedil-
miş
picture /'pikçı/ a. resim, tablo; film; görüntü; **pictures** sinema ☆ e. resmini
yapmak, çizmek; düşlemek, hayal etmek
picturesque /pikçı'resk/ s. pitoresk;
(dil) net, açık, canlı
piddling /'pidling/ s. küçük, önemsiz
pidgin /'picin/ a. karma dil, tarzanca
pie /pay/ a. börek, çörek, tart, turta
piebald /'paybo:ld/ a, s. (at) alaca, benekli
piece /pi:s/ a. parça; oyun; (satranç, da-

ma) taş; numune, örnek; madeni para **a piece of cake** kon. çocuk oyuncağı **fall to pieces** parçalanmak, dağılmak **go (all) to pieces** eli ayağına dolaşmak **in one piece** kon. hasar görmemiş, sağlam **pull to pieces** anlam-
sızlığını belirtmek
piecemeal /'pi:smi:l/ s, be. parça parça, azar azar, bölüm bölüm
pier /piı/ a. iskele; destek, payanda
pierce /'piıs/ e. delmek, delip geçmek
piercing (ses) keskin, tiz; (soğuk) içe
işleyen
piety /'payıti/ a. dindarlık
pig /pig/ a, hayb. domuz; pisboğaz
pig-headed inatçı **pigtail** saç örgüsü
piggy ufak domuz
pigeon /'picin/ a, hayb. güvercin
pigment /'pigmınt/ a. boya maddesi,
pigment
pigmy /'pigmi/ a. cüce, bodur
pike /payk/ a. mızrak, kargı; turnabalığı
pile /payl/ a. yığın, küme; kazık, direk;
tüy, hav; pil ☆ e. yığmak
pilgrim /'pilgrim/ a. hacı **pilgrimage**
/-mic/ a. hac, hacılık **go on/make a
pilgrimage** hacca gitmek
pill /pil/ a. hap; doğum kontrol hapı
pillar /'pilı/ a. sütun; direk **pillar-box**
posta kutusu
pillow /'pilou/ a. yastık **pillow case/slip**
yastık kılıfı
pilot /'paylıt/ a. pilot; den. kılavuz ☆
e. pilotluk yapmak; kılavuzluk yapmak
pimp /pimp/ a. pezevenk
pimple /'pimpıl/ a. sivilce
pin /pin/ a. topluiğne; broş, iğne; firkete ☆ e. iğnelemek, iliştirmek; kıpırda-
yamaz hale sokmak, sıkıştırmak **pins
and needles** kon. karıncalanma
pinafore /'pinıfo:/ a. göğüslük, önlük
pincers /'pinsız/ a. kerpeten; kıskaç
pinch /pinç/ e. kıstırmak, sıkıştırmak;
çimdiklemek; kon. araklamak yürütmek ☆ a. çimdik; tutam **at/in a
pinch** gerekirse **feel the pinch** darda
olmak
pine /payn/ a, bitk. çam ☆ e. (away)
güçten kuvvetten düşmek

pineapple /'paynepıl/ *a, bitk.* ananas

ping-pong /'pingpon/ *a, kon.* ping-pong, masatenisi

pink /pink/ *s.* pembe pinkish pembemsi

pinnacle /'pınıkıl/ *a.* doruk, zirve; sivri tepeli kule

pint /paynt/ *a.* galonun sekizde biri (*İİ.* 0, 568 lt; *Aİ.* 0, 473 lt)

pioneer /payı'niı/ *a.* öncü ☆ *e.* öncülük etmek

pious /'payıs/ *s.* dindar

pip /pip/ *a.* meyve çekirdeği

pipe /payp/ *a.* boru; pipo; kaval ☆ *e.* borularla taşımak; kaval/gayda çalmak pipeline boru hattı

piper /'paypı/ *a.* kavalcı; gaydacı

piquant /'pi:kınt/ *s.* acı/keskin

piracy /'payırısi/ *a.* korsanlık

piranha /pi'ra:nyı, pi'ra:nı/ *a, hayb.* piranha

pirate /'payırıt/ *a.* korsan ☆ *e.* korsan satış yapmak

pirouette /piru'et/ *a.* (balede) tek ayak üzerinde dönüş, piruet

Pisces /'paysi:z/ *a.* Balık burcu

piss /pis/ *e.* işemek ☆ *a.* çiş, sidik; işeme

pistachio /pi'sta:şiou/ *a.* fıstık

pistol /'pistıl/ *a.* tabanca

piston /'pistın/ *a.* piston

pit /pit/ *a.* çukur; maden ocağı; (tiyatro) parter

pitch /piç/ *a, sp.* saha, alan; fırlatma, atış; *müz.* perde; derece; zift ☆ *e.* konmak, konaklamak; (çadır) kurmak; (top, vb.) atmak; *müz.* sesin perdesini ayarlamak pitch-black zifiri karanlık

pitcher /'piçı/ *a.* testi, sürahi, ibrik

pith /pit / *a, bitk.* öz; öz pithy özlü; anlamlı

pitiable /'pitiıbıl/ *s.* acınacak

pitiful /'pitifıl/ *s.* acıklı, acınacak; merhametli

pittance /'pitıns/ *a.* çok düşük ücret

pity /'piti/ *a.* merhamet, acıma ☆ *e.* merhamet etmek, acımak for pity's sake Allah aşkına, ne olur have/take pity on (sb) -e acımak What a pity!

Ne yazık!

pivot /'pivıt/ *a.* eksen, mil ☆ *e.* bir eksen çevresinde dönmek

pixy /'piksi/ *a, bkz.* pixie

pizza /'pi:tsı/ *a.* pizza

placard /'pleka:d/ *a.* duvar ilanı, afiş, pankart, poster

place /pleys/ *a.* yer; oturacak yer, koltuk; memuriyet, görev; *mat.* hane, basamak ☆ *e.* koymak, yerleştirmek; (para) yatırmak; kim olduğunu çıkarmak, anımsamak in place yerinde in the first place her şeyden önce out of place yersiz, münasebetsiz place of birth doğum yeri take place meydana gelmek, olmak

placid /'plesid/ *s.* sakin, durgun

plague /pleyg/ *a.* veba; baş belası, dert

plaice /pleys/ *a, hayb.* pisibalığı

plain /pleyn/ *a.* ova ☆ *s.* düz; yalın, sade, süssüz; açık, kolay anlaşılır; alımsız, çirkin in plain words açıkçası plainspoken açıksözlü plainly açıkça; süssüz biçimde

plaint /pleynt/ *a.* huk. dava plaintiff davacı

plait /pleyt/ *a.* örgü, saç örgüsü ☆ *e.* (saç, vb.) örmek

plan /plen/ *a.* plan, kroki, taslak; proje, tasarı; niyet ☆ *e.* planlamak, tasarlamak; planını çizmek; düzenlemek

plane /pleyn/ *a, kon.* uçak; planya, rende; *mat.* düzlem; seviye, düzey; *bitk.* çınar ☆ *e.* rendelemek ☆ *s.* düz; dümdüz plane geometry düzlem geometri

planet /'plenit/ *a.* gezegen

plank /plenk/ *a.* uzun tahta, kalas

plant /pla:nt/ *a.* bitki; fabrika; atelye; tesis ☆ *e.* dikmek, ekmek; tesis etmek, kurmak

plantation /plen'teyşın/ *a.* fidanlık; büyük çiftlik

plaque /plek/ *a.* plaket, levha

plashy /'pleşi/ *s.* çamurlu, ıslak

plasma /'plezmı/ *a, biy.* plazma, kansu

plaster /'pla:stı/ *a.* sıva; plaster; *hek.* yakı ☆ *e.* sıvamak; yapıştırmak plaster cast alçı plaster of Paris alçı plasterer sıvacı

plastic /'plestik/ *a, s.* plastik **plastic surgery** estetik ameliyat/cerrahlık **the plastic arts** plastik sanatlar

plate /pleyt/ *a.* tabak; levha, klişe; *sp.* kupa; fotoğraf klişesi ☆ *e.* (metal) kaplamak

plateau /'pletou/ *a, coğ.* yayla

platform /'pletfo:m/ *a.* peron; kürsü; (seçimden önce) parti programı

plating /'pleyting/ *a.* kaplama

platinum /'pletinım/ *a.* platin

platonic /plı'tonik/ *s.* (iki kişi arasındaki sevgi/arkadaşlık) fiziksel olmayan, duygusal

platoon /plı'tu:n/ *a, ask.* müfreze, takım

plausible /'plo:zibıl/ *s.* makul, akla yatkın; inandırıcı

play /pley/ *a.* oyun, eğlence; piyes; şaka, oyun; kumar ☆ *e.* oynamak; eğlenmek; (müzik aleti) çalmak; sahnelemek, temsil etmek **play dead** ölü numarası yapmak **play for time** kasten zaman geçirmek **play it by ear** oluruna bırakmak **play it cool** soğukkanlılığını yitirmemek **play (it) safe** işi sağlama almak **play on words** cinas, sözcük oyunu **play the fool** aptalca davranmak **play the game** adil ve dürüst olmak **play with fire** ateşle oynamak **play back** (şarkı, vb.) yeniden çalmak, tekrarlamak **playboy** eğlence peşinde koşan zengin delikanlı **playday** tatil günü **player** oyuncu **playful** şen, şakacı **playground** çocukların oyun alanı **playhouse** tiyatro **playing card** iskambil kâğıdı **playmate** oyun arkadaşı **play-off** beraberliği bozmak için oynanan oyun **plaything** oyuncak **playwright** oyun yazarı

plea /pli:/ *a.* yalvarma, rica; özür; savunma, itiraz

plead /pli:d/ *e.* yalvarmak; özür dilemek; dava açmak; savunmak; suçlamak **plead guilty/not guilty** suçlu olduğunu kabul etmek (etmemek)

pleasant /'plezınt/ *s.* hoş, tatlı; sevimli, cana yakın

pleasantry /'plezıntri/ *a.* şaka, espri

please /pli:z/ *e.* memnun etmek, sevindirmek; hoşuna gitmek, istemek ☆ *be.* lütfen **if you please** isterseniz; lütfen, rica ederim **pleased** memnun, hoşnut **pleasing** hoş, tatlı

pleasure /'plejı/ *a.* zevk, haz; keyif, eğlence **pleasurable** zevk veren, hoş

pleat /pli:t/ *a.* kıvrım, pli, plise

plebiscite /'plebisit/ *a.* halkoylaması

plectrum /'plektrım/ *a, müz.* mızrap, pena

pledge /plec/ *a.* rehin; söz, güvence; kanıt, işaret ☆ *e.* rehine koymak; söz vermek; güvence vermek, taahhüt etmek

plentiful /'plentifıl/ *s.* bereketli, bol

plenty /'plenti/ *a.* bolluk, çokluk; bol miktar **plenty of** pek çok

pliable /'playıbıl/ *s.* bükülgen, yumuşak; itaatkâr, uysal

pliers /'playız/ *a.* kerpeten, pens

plight /playt/ *a.* kötü durum, çıkmaz

plod /plod/ *e.* ağır ağır yürümek

plot /plot/ *a.* arsa, parsel; entrika, suikast; (roman, vb.'de) olay örgüsü ☆ *e.* komplo kurmak; haritada göstermek; işaretlemek

plough /plau/ *a.* saban, pulluk ☆ *e.* sabanla sürmek, çift sürmek; yol açmak **the Plough** Büyükayı

pluck /plak/ *e.* koparmak; yolmak; (telli çalgı) çalmak ☆ *a.* cesaret, yiğitlik

plug /plag/ *a.* tapa, tıkaç; (elektrik) fiş; buji ☆ *e.* tıkamak

plum /plam/ *a, bitk.* erik

plumb /plam/ *a.* çekül, şakul

plumber /'plamı/ *a.* su tesisatçısı, muslukçu

plumbing /'plaming/ *a.* su tesisatı; boru tesisatçılığı, muslukçuluk

plume /plu:m/ *a.* kuştüyü

plunder /'plandı/ *e.* yağma etmek, yağmalamak ☆ *a.* yağma, yağmacılık

plunge /planc/ *a.* dalma, dalış ☆ *e.* daldırmak, batırmak, sokmak

plural /'pluırıl/ *a, s, dilb.* çoğul

plus /plas/ *a.* artı işareti ☆ *s.* artı; artı, pozitif; -in üstünde

plush /plaş/ *a.* pelüş

Pluto /'plu:tou/ *a.* Plüton

ply /play/ *e.* düzenli sefer yapmak; çalışmak, iş yapmak ☆ *a.* kat, katmer

plywood /'playwud/ *a.* kontrplak

pneumatic /nyu:'metic/ *s.* pnömatik, havalı

pneumonia /nyu:'moniı/ *a, hek.* zatürree, akciğer yangısı

pocket /'pokit/ *a.* cep; torba, kese ☆ *e.* cebe koymak **pocket money** cep harçlığı **pocketbook** cep defteri; cep kitabı

pockmark /'pokma:k/ *a.* çopur, iz

pod /pod/ *a.* bezelye, fasulye, vb. kabuğu ☆ *e.* kabuğunu soymak

podgy /'poci/ *s.* bodur, tıknaz

poem /'pouim/ *a.* şiir

poet /'pouit/ *a.* şair **poetic** şiirsel

poetry /'pouitri/ *a.* şiir; şiir sanatı; şiirler

poignant /'poynyınt/ *s.* üzücü, dokunaklı, acı; acı, keskin

point /poynt/ *a.* nokta; uç; durum; sayı, puan; *mat.* virgül; derece; husus; anlam; konu; özellik; namlu; *coğ.* burun ☆ *e.* işaret etmek; doğrultmak; ucunu göstermek; noktalamak; yöneltmek; virgülle hanelere ayırmak **point of view** görüş, bakım **to the point** konu ile ilgili **be on the point of** -mek üzere olmak **come to the point** asıl konuya gelmek **make a point of** üzerinde durmak, önem vermek **point out** göstermek, belirtmek **pointed** sivri uçlu; anlamlı **pointer** işaret değneği; gösterge; öğüt **pointless** anlamsız; yararsız

poise /poyz/ *a.* özgüven; denge ☆ *e.* dengesiz biçimde yerleştirmek

poison /'poyzın/ *a.* zehir ☆ *e.* zehirlemek **poisonous** zehirli

poke /pouk/ *e.* sokmak; dürtmek **poke one's nose into sth** burnunu sokmak

poker /'poukı/ *a.* ocak demiri; poker

polar /'poulı/ *s.* kutupsal, kutuplarla ilgili **polar bear** kutup ayısı

polarize /'poulırayz/ *e.* (iki ayrı noktada) toplamak; *fiz.* polarmak

pole /poul/ *a.* direk, sırık; kutup; *fiz.* kutup **pole star** Kutupyıldızı **pole vault** *sp.* sırıkla atlama

police /pı'li:s/ *a.* polis (örgütü), emniyet **police station** karakol **policeman**

polis memuru **policewoman** kadın polis

policy /'polisi/ *a.* siyaset, politika; poliçe

polio /'pouliou/ *a, hek.* çocuk felci

polish /'poliş/ *e.* parlatmak, cilalamak ☆ *a.* cila, perdah; ayakkabı boyası; kibarlık, incelik

polite /pı'layt/ *s.* nazik, kibar **politely** nazikçe **politeness** nezaket, kibarlık

politic /'politik/ *s.* akıllı, kurnaz; ihtiyatlı, tedbirli

political /pı'litikıl/ *s.* siyasal, politik; politikayla ilgilenen

politician /poli'tişın/ *s.* politikacı

politics /'politiks/ *a.* siyaset, politika; politik görüşler

polka /'polkı/ *a, müz.* polka

poll /poul/ *a.* seçim; oylama, oy verme; oy sayısı; kamuoyu yoklaması ☆ *e.* oy almak; oy vermek

pollen /'polın/ *a, bitk.* polen, çiçektozu

pollute /pı'lu:t/ *e.* kirletmek **pollution** kirlenme, kirlilik

polo /'poulou/ *a, sp.* polo **polo neck** boğazlı yaka

polyandry /poli'endri/ *a.* çokkocalılık, poliandri

polyester /'poliestı/ *a.* polyester

polygamy /pı'ligımi/ *a.* çokkarılılık, poligami

polygon /'poligon/ *a.* poligon, çokgen

polytechnic /poli'teknik/ *a.* sanat/fen kolu

pomade /pı'ma:d, pı'meyd/ *a.* pomat, saç merhemi, briyantin

pomegranate /'pomigrenit/ *a, bitk.* nar

pomp /pomp/ *a.* gösteri; görkem

pompous /'pompıs/ *s.* kendini beğenmiş; ağdalı, cafcaflı

pond /pond/ *a.* gölcük; havuz

ponder /'pondı/ *e.* düşünüp taşınmak

ponderous /'pondırıs/ *s.* ağır

pony /'pouni/ *a, hayb.* midilli **ponytail** (saç) at kuyruğu

poodle /'pu:dıl/ *a.* fino köpeği

pool /pu:l/ *a.* havuz; gölcük; su birikintisi; Amerikan bilardosu **the (football) pools** spor toto

poor /puı/ *s.* yoksul, fakir; zavallı; yeter-

siz; kıt **poorly** hasta, rahatsız
pop /pop/ *e.* pat diye ses çıkarmak,
patlamak ☆ *a.* patlama sesi, pat;
kon. gazoz; *müz.* pop **popcorn** patla-
mış mısır **pop-eyed** patlak gözlü **pop
in** ansızın girmek, uğramak **pop out**
ansızın çıkmak
pope /poup/ *a.* papa
poplar /'poplı/ *a, bitk.* kavak
poppy /'popi/ *a, bitk.* gelincik; afyon,
haşhaş
populace /'popyulıs/ *a.* halk, ayaktakımı, avam
popular /'popyulı/ *s.* sevilen, tutulan,
popüler; halka özgü; genel, yaygın
popularity /popyu'leriti/ *a.* sevilme, tutulma, popülerlik
populate /'popyuleyt/ *e.* bir yerde yerleşmek; insan yerleştirmek
population /popyu'leyşın/ *a.* nüfus;
ahali, halk
populism /'popyulizım/ *a.* halkçılık
porcelain /'po:slin/ *a.* porselen, çini
porch /po:ç/ *a.* kapı önü sundurması
porcupine /'po:kyupayn/ *a, hayb.* kirpi
pore /po:/ *a.* gözenek
pork /po:k/ *a.* domuz eti
porn /po:n/ *a, kon.* pornografi
pornography /po:'nogrıfi/ *a.* pornografi
porous /'po:rıs/ *s.* gözenekli, geçirgen
porridge /'poric/ *a.* yulaf lapası
port /po:t/ *a.* liman; liman kenti; *den.*
lombar; porto şarabı **port of call** uğra-
nılacak liman **port of departure** çıkış
limanı **port of destination** gidilecek liman
portable /'po:tıbıl/ *s.* taşınabilir, portatif
porter /'po:tı/ *a.* hamal; kapıcı
portfolio /po:t'fouliou/ *a.* evrak çantası;
bakanlık
portion /'po:şın/ *a.* parça, bölüm; porsiyon; pay, hisse
portrait /'po:trit/ *a.* insan resmi, portre
portray /'po:trey/ *e.* resmini yapmak;
tasvir etmek; (rol) oynamak
pose /pouz/ *e.* poz vermek ☆ *a.* duruş, poz; yapmacık tavır
position /pı'zişın/ *a.* durum; mevki, yer;
iş, görev ☆ *e.* yerleştirmek; yerini belirlemek **be in a position to** -cek du-

rumda olmak
positive /'pozitiv/ *s.* olumlu; mutlak, kesin; tam, gerçek; *mat.* artı, pozitif; (fotoğraf) pozitif
possess /pı'zes/ *e.* sahip olmak, -si olmak **possessor** mal sahibi
possession /pı'zeşın/ *a.* iyelik, sahiplik;
ç. mal mülk, servet
possessive /pı'zesiv/ *s.* sahip olmak isteyen; iyelik gösteren; *dilb.* iyelik durumu
possibility /posi'biliti/ *a.* ihtimal; olasılık; olabilirlik
possible /'posibıl/ *s.* mümkün, olanaklı; muhtemel, olabilir, olası **possibly**
belki; imkân dahilinde
post /poust/ *a.* posta, postane ☆ *e.*
postaya atmak, postalamak **by post**
posta ile **post-box** posta kutusu **postcard** kartpostal **postcode** posta kodu
postman postacı **postmaster** postane müdürü **post-office** postane
post /poust/ *a.* direk, kazık; iş, görev;
nöbet; *ask.* garnizon, kışla; karakol ☆
e. ilan etmek, yerleştirmek, dikmek;
tayin etmek
postage /'poustic/ *a.* posta ücreti
postal /'poustıl/ *s.* posta ile ilgili **post-
al/money order** posta havalesi
poster /'poustı/ *a.* poster, afiş
posterior /po'stiirıı/ *s.* gerideki; sonraki
posterity /po'steriti/ *a.* gelecek kuşak-
lar; nesil, döl
postgraduate /poust'grecuit/ *a, s.* lisansüstü (yapan öğrenci)
postmortem /poust'mo:tım/ *a.* otopsi
postnatal /poust'neytıl/ *s.* doğumdan
sonrasıyla ilgili
postpone /pıs'poun/ *e.* ertelemek
postscript /'poustskript/ *a.* (mektupta)
not, dipnot
posture /'posçı/ *a.* duruş
posy /'pouzi/ *a.* çiçek demeti
pot /pot/ *a.* çömlek, kap; saksı; *kon.*
(para) bol miktar; *kon.* ıska; *kon.* kupa ☆ *e.* saksıya koymak; vurup öldürmek, avlamak
potato /pı'teytou/ *a.* patates **potato
chips** *Aİ.* cips
potency /'poutınsi/ *a.* güç, iktidar

potent /'poutınt/ s. güçlü, kuvvetli
potential /pı'tenşıl/ s. potansiyel, gizil ☆ a. güç, potansiyel; fiz. gizligüç, potansiyel; elek. gerilim
potter /'potı/ a. çömlekçi pottery çanak çömlek; çömlekçilik
pouch /pauç/ a. kese, torba
poultice /'poultis/ a. yara lapası
poultry /'poultri/ a. kümes hayvanları
pounce /pauns/ e. (at/on/upon) aniden saldırmak, atılmak
pound /paund/ a. İngiliz lirası, Sterlin, Paund; libre (453,6 gr.) ☆ e. dövmek, ezmek; çarpmak; (kalp) küt küt atmak
pour /po:/ e. dökmek, akıtmak; dökülmek, akmak; (çay, vb.) koymak; bardaktan boşanırcasına yağmak
pout /paut/ e. somurtmak, surat asmak ☆ a. somurtma
poverty /'povıti/ a. yoksulluk, fakirlik; yetersizlik poverty-stricken çok yoksul, gariban
powder /'paudı/ a. toz; pudra; barut powder room (sinema, otel) bayanlar tuvaleti
power /'pauı/ a. kuvvet, güç; etki, nüfuz; yetenek; devlet; sözü geçerlik; mat. kuvvet, üst power plant Aİ. elektrik santralı power station İİ. elektrik santralı powerful güçlü; etkili powerless güçsüz, kuvvetsiz
practicable /'prektikıbıl/ s. uygulanabilir, yapılabilir
practical /'prektikıl/ s. pratik, uygulamalı; kullanışlı; becerikli practical joke muziplik, eşek şakası practically hemen hemen; uygun olarak, pratik olarak
practice /'prektis/ a. alıştırma; uygulama; antrenman; alışkanlık out of practice körelmiş, pratiğini yitirmiş
practise /'prektis/ e. pratik yapmak, antrenman yapmak; uygulamak, yapmak, denemek; çalışmak
practitioner /prek'tişını/ a. doktor; avukat
pragmatic /preg'metik/ s. pragmatik, pratik pragmatism yararcılık, pragmatizm

prairie /'preıri/ a. bozkır
praise /preyz/ a. övme, övgü; şükran ☆ e. övmek; şükretmek praiseworthy övülmeye değer
pram /prem/ a, İİ. çocuk arabası
prance /pra:ns/ e. kasıla kasıla yürümek
prank /prenk/ a. muziplik, şaka, oyun
prattle /'pretıl/ e. çocukça/saçma sapan konuşmak
prawn /pro:n/ a. büyük karides
pray /prey/ e. dua etmek, yakarmak
prayer /'preı/ a. dua, yakarı, yakarış
preach /pri:ç/ e. vaaz etmek, vaaz vermek; öğütlemek, öğüt vermek
preacher vaiz
preamble /'pri:embıl/ a. giriş, önsöz
precaution /pri'ko:şın/ a. tedbir, önlem
precede /pri'si:d/ e. -den önce gelmek; -den üstün olmak preceding önceki
precedent /'presidınt/ a. teamül, geçmiş örnek, emsal
precious /'preşıs/ s. kıymetli, değerli
precipice /'presipis/ a. uçurum, yar
precipitate /pri'sipiteyt/ e. hızlandırmak; kim. çökelmek; kim. çökeltmek ☆ a, kim. çökelti ☆ s. acele, apar topar, telaşlı precipitation telaş, acele; yağış; kim. çökelme
précis /'preysi:/ a. özet
precise /pri'says/ s. tam, doğru, kesin; titiz, kusursuz precisely tam olarak, tam; evet, öyle, aynen öyle
precision /pri'sijın/ a. kesinlik, doğruluk
precocious /pri'kouşıs/ s. erken gelişmiş, erken büyümüş
predator /'predıtı/ a, hayb. yırtıcı hayvan
predecessor /'pri:disesı/ a. öncel, selef; ata
predetermine /pri:di'tö:min/ e. önceden belirlemek
predicament /pri'dikımınt/ a. zor durum, çıkmaz
predicate /'predikit/ a, dilb. yüklem
predicative /pri'dikıtiv/ s, dilb. yüklemin parçası olarak kullanılan, yüklemcil
predict /pri'dikt/ e. önceden bildirmek predictable tahmin edilebilir predic-

tion kehanet
predispose /pri:dis'pouz/ e. etkilemek
predominant /pri'domınınt/ s. üstün, baskın, hâkim, ağır basan
preeminent /pri:'eminınt/ s. üstün
prefabricate /pri:'febrikeyt/ e. parçalarını önceden hazırlamak **prefabricated** (ev, gemi, vb.) prefabrik
preface /'prefis/ a. önsöz
prefer /pri'fö: / e. tercih etmek, yeğlemek
preferable /'prefırıbıl/ s. tercih edilir, daha uygun **preferably** tercihan
preference /'prefırıns/ a. tercih, yeğleme; öncelik hakkı, üstünlük
preferential /prefı'renşıl/ s. tercihli, ayrıcalıklı
prefix /'pri:fiks/ a, dilb. önek
pregnant /'pregnınt/ s. gebe, hamile; anlamlı **pregnancy** gebelik, hamilelik
prehistory /pri:'histıri/ a. tarihöncesi bilimi, prehistorya
prejudice /'precıdis/ a. önyargı, peşin hüküm **prejudiced** önyargılı
preliminary /pri'liminıri/ s. başlangıç niteliğinde, ilk, ön
prelude /'prelyu:d/ a, müz. prelüd, peşrev; başlangıç
premature /'premıçı/ s. erken, vakitsiz, mevsimsiz; erken doğmuş
premeditate /pri:'mediteyt/ e. önceden tasarlamak
premier /'premiı/ s. ilk, birinci, baştaki, baş ☆ a. başbakan
premiere /'premieı/ a. gala
premise /'premis/ a. dayanak noktası **premises** bina ve müştemilatı
premium /'pri:mıım/ a. sigorta primi; ödül, prim **at a premium** nadir, zor bulunur
prenatal /pri:'neytıl/ s. doğum öncesine ait
prep /prep/ a, İİ, kon. ev ödevi; ders çalışma, derse hazırlanma **prep class** kon. hazırlık (sınıfı)
preparation /prepı'reyşın/ a. hazırlama, hazırlanma, hazırlık
preparatory /pri'perıtıri/ a. hazırlayıcı **preparatory school** hazırlık okulu
prepare /pri'peı/ e. hazırlamak; hazır-
lanmak
preposition /prepı'zişın/ a, dilb. edat, ilgeç
preposterous /pri'postırıs/ s. mantıksız, saçma, akla sığmaz
prerogative /pri'rogıtiv/ a. imtiyaz, ayrıcalık
prescribe /pri'skrayb/ a. buyurmak, emretmek; (doktor) reçete yazmak
prescription /pri'skripşın/ a, hek. reçete; buyruk, emir
presence /'prezıns/ a. hazır bulunma; huzur, varlık; görünüş
present /'prezınt/ a. armağan, hediye ☆ s. mevcut, bulunan; şimdiki, şu anki **at present** şu anda, şimdi **for the present** şu anda, şimdilik
present /pri'zent/ e. sunmak, takdim etmek; tanıtmak, takdim etmek
presentable /pri'zentıbıl/ s. uygun, düzgün, yerinde
presentation /prezın'teyşın/ a. sunma, takdim; tanıtma; gösterme
presently /'prezıntli/ be. birazdan
preservation /prezı'veyşın/ a. koruma, korunma
preservative /pri'zö:vıtiv/ s. koruyucu
preserve /pri'zö:v/ e. korumak; saklamak; konservesini yapmak
preside /pri'zayd/ e. başkanlık etmek
presidency /'prezidınsi/ a. başkanlık
president /'prezidınt/ a. başkan; rektör; cumhurbaşkanı
press /pres/ a. sıkıştırma, baskı; basın, gazeteciler; basımevi; tazyik; (el) sıkma; sıkma makinesi, pres; iş çokluğu; (giyside) ütü ☆ e. bastırmak, basmak; sıkıştırmak; sıkıp suyunu çıkarmak; ütülemek; ısrar etmek, üstelemek **press agent** basın sözcüsü **press conference** basın toplantısı
pressure /'preşı/ a. basınç, tazyik; baskı, zorlama **pressure cooker** düdüklü tencere
prestige /pre'sti:j/ a. saygınlık
presumably /pri'zyu:mıbli/ be. herhalde, galiba, tahminen, belki de
presume /pri'zyu:m/ e. saymak, varsaymak, farz etmek; cüret etmek
presumption /pri'zampşın/ a. varsa-

yım, tahmin; cüret, küstahlık

presuppose /pri:sı'pouz/ *e.* önceden varsaymak; koşul olarak gerektirmek

pretend /pri'tend/ *e.* -miş gibi yapmak; numara yapmak, rol yapmak; kendine . . . süsü vermek

pretension /pri'tenşın/ *a.* hak iddia etme, iddia; gösteriş

pretentious /pri'tenşıs/ *s.* kendini beğenmiş, gösterişli

pretext /'pri:tekst/ *a.* bahane, kulp

pretty /'priti/ *s.* hoş, güzel, sevimli ☆ *be.* oldukça, epey **pretty much/well** hemen hemen

pretzel /'pretsıl/ *a.* çubuk kraker

prevail /pri'veyl/ *e.* yenmek, üstün gelmek; egemen olmak

prevalent /'prevılınt/ *s.* yaygın, genel

prevent /pri'vent/ *e.* **(from)** önlemek, engellemek **preventive** önleyici, koruyucu

preview /'pri:vyu:/ *a.* (film, vb.'nin) halka gösterilmeden önce özel olarak gösterilmesi, özel gösterim

previous /'pri:viıs/ *s.* önceki, evvelki **previously** önceden

prey /prey/ *a.* av

price /prays/ *a.* fiyat, eder; değer, kıymet; ödül ☆ *e.* fiyat koymak **price tag** fiyat etiketi **priceless** paha biçilmez

prick /prik/ *a.* delik; delme, batırma; iğne, diken batması ☆ *e.* batmak, delmek; sokmak, iğnelemek

prickle /'prikıl/ *a.* diken, sivri uç ☆ *e.* iğnelenmek, karıncalanmak **prickly** dikenli; huysuz

pride /prayd/ *a.* gurur; onur; övünme; övünç **pride oneself on** ile öğünmek

priest /pri:st/ *a.* papaz, rahip **priesthood** papazlık

prim /prim/ *a.* kurallara fazla bağlı, formaliteci

primarily /'praymırıli/ *be.* her şeyden önce, aslında

primary /'praymıri/ *s.* baş, başlıca, ana, temel; birinci **primary school** ilkokul

primate /'praymit/ *a.* başpiskopos

primate /'praymeyt/ *a, hayb.* primat

prime /praym/ *s.* birinci, ilk, baş; en ka-

lite, en iyi ☆ *e.* hazırlamak; (boya) astar vurmak **Prime Minister** Başbakan **prime number** *mat.* asal sayı

primer /'praymı/ *a.* ilk okuma kitabı; *ask.* kapsül; astar boya

primitive /'primitiv/ *s.* ilkel

primrose /'primrouz/ *a, bitk.* çuhaçiçeği

prince /prins/ *a.* prens

princess /prin'ses/ *a.* prenses

principal /'prinsipıl/ *s.* başlıca, esas, temel ☆ *a.* okul müdürü; yönetici, başkan, şef; anapara

principality /prinsi'peliti/ *a.* prenslik

principle /'prinsipıl/ *a.* ilke, prensip; köken; *ç.* ahlak, dürüstlük

print /print/ *e.* basmak; yayımlamak ☆ *a.* iz; tabı, bası; damga, kalıp; basılmış yazı, matbua; emprime, basma kumaş **in print** basılı **out of print** baskısı tükenmiş **printer** matbaacı; printer **printing** baskı; matbaacılık **printing press** basım makinesi

prior /'prayı/ *s.* önce, önceki

priority /pray'oriti/ *a.* öncelik, üstünlük

prism /'prizm/ *a.* prizma, biçme **prismatic** /-'metik/ prizmatik

prison /'prizın/ *a.* cezaevi, hapishane **prisoner** tutuklu, mahpus; tutsak, esir **prisoner of war** savaş esiri

privacy /'privısi, 'prayvısi/ *a.* mahremiyet, gizlilik

private /'prayvit/ *s.* özel; kişisel; gizli ☆ *a.* er, asker **in private** gizlilikle **private detective/investigator** özel dedektif **private enterprise** özel teşebbüs **private school** özel okul **privately** gizli olarak

privatize /'prayvıtayz/ *e.* özelleştirmek

privilege /'privilic/ *a.* ayrıcalık, imtiyaz **privileged** ayrıcalıklı

prize /prayz/ *a.* ödül; ikramiye ☆ *e.* çok değer vermek

pro /prou/ *a, kon.* profesyonel

probability /probı'biliti/ *a.* ihtimal, olasılık

probable /'probıbıl/ *s.* muhtemel, olası **probably** büyük olasılıkla, muhtemelen

probation /prı'beyşın/ *a.* deneme; *huk.*

gözaltında tutma koşuluyla salıverme
probe /proub/ *a, hek.* sonda; araştırma; insansız uzay roketi
problem /'problım/ *a.* problem, sorun; *mat.* problem
procedure /prı'si:cı/ *a.* prosedür, yordam
proceed /prı'si:d/ *e.* ilerlemek; (with) devam etmek, sürdürmek
proceeding /prı'si:ding/ *a.* ilerleme; hareket tarzı; işlem, yöntem
process /'prouses/ *a.* oluşum, süreç; yöntem, işlem, yol; gidiş, seyir; *huk.* dava ☆ *e.* belli bir işleme tabi tutmak; bilgisayarda denetlemek
procession /prı'seşın/ *a.* geçit töreni; tören alayı
proclaim /prı'kleym/ *e.* duyurmak, ilan etmek proclamation /proklı'meyşın/ beyanname, bildirge; ilan, duyuru
procure /prı'kyuı/ *e.* sağlamak, elde etmek, edinmek
prod /prod/ *e.* dürtmek; kışkırtmak, özendirmek, gaz vermek
prodigal /'prodigıl/ *s.* savurgan
prodigious /prı'dicıs/ *s.* şaşılacak, olağanüstü, harika
prodigy /'prodici/ *a.* olağanüstü şey
produce /prı'dyu:s/ *e.* üretmek, yapmak; yetiştirmek; neden olmak; (film) sahneye koymak producer üretici; yapımcı
product /'prodakt/ *a.* ürün; sonuç; *mat.* çarpım
production /prı'dakşın/ *a.* üretim, yapım; ürün; eser
productive /prı'daktiv/ *s.* verimli; yaratıcı
productivity /prodak'tiviti/ *a.* verimlilik
profane /prı'feyn/ *s.* kutsal şeylere karşı saygısız profanity /prı'feniti/ kutsal şeylere karşı saygısızlık
profess /prı'fes/ *e.* açıkça söylemek, açıklamak, itiraf etmek
profession /prı'feşın/ *a.* iş, meslek, uğraş; itiraf, beyan
professional /prı'feşınıl/ *s.* profesyonel; mesleki ☆ *a.* profesyonel
professor /prı'fesı/ *a.* profesör; *Aİ.* (üniversitede) öğretmen

proficiency /prı'fişınsi/ *a.* ustalık, yeterlik proficient (at/in) usta, becerikli
profile /'proufayl/ *a.* yandan görünüş, profil; kısa özgeçmiş; kesit keep a low profile dikkat çekmekten sakınmak
profit /'profit/ *a.* kazanç, kâr; yarar, fayda profit and loss account kâr zarar hesabı profit sharing kâr bölüşümü profitable kazançlı, kârlı, yararlı
profound /prı'faund/ *s.* derin; bilgili, etkileyici profoundly derinden; çok, son derece
profuse /prı'fyu:s/ *s.* çok, bol profusion bolluk
programme /'prougrem/ *a.* program, izlence programmer bilgisayar programcısı
progress /'prougres/ *a.* ilerleme; gelişme in progress yapılmakta; sürmekte progress /prı'gres/ *e.* ilerlemek; gelişmek, kalkınmak
progression /prı'greşın/ *a.* ilerleme
progressive /prı'gresiv/ *s.* ilerleyen; kalkınan, gelişen; ilerici
prohibit /prı'hibit/ *e.* yasaklamak
prohibition /prouhi'bişın/ *a.* yasak
prohibitive /prı'hibitiv/ *s.* yasaklayıcı
project /'procekt/ *a.* proje; tasarı
project /prı'cekt/ *e.* atmak, fırlatmak; yansıtmak; *mat.* izdüşürmek
projectile /prı'cektayl/ *a.* mermi, roket
projection /prı'cekşın/ *a.* atma, fırlatma; *mat.* izdüşüm; çıkıntı
projector /prı'cektı/ *a.* projektör, gösterici; projektör, ışıldak
proletariat /prouli'teırııt/ *a.* işçi sınıfı, emekçi sınıfı proletarian emekçi, işçi
prolific /prı'lifik/ *s.* verimli; doğurgan
prologue /'proulog/ *a.* öndeyiş, giriş
prolong /'proulong/ *e.* uzatmak
prominent /'prominınt/ *s.* göze çarpan, belirgin; ünlü, seçkin; önemli; çıkıntı; fırlak prominence ün; önem; çıkıntı
promise /'promis/ *e.* söz vermek, vaat etmek ☆ *a.* söz, vaat; taahhüt; umut, beklenti break a promise sözünü tutmamak give/make a promise söz vermek keep a promise sözünü

tutmak **promising** umut verici, geleceği parlak

promontory /'promıntıri/ *a, coğ.* burun

promote /prı'mout/ *e.* yükseltmek, terfi ettirmek; ilerletmek; reklamını yapmak **promoter** teşvikçi, destekleyici; teşebbüs sahibi, kurucu

promotion /prı'mouşın/ *a.* yükselme, terfi; destek, teşvik

prompt /prompt/ *e.* -e sevk etmek, teşvik etmek; suflörlük yapmak ☆ *s.* seri, çabuk, tez, dakik

prone /proun/ *s.* yüzükoyun

prong /prong/ *a.* çatal dişi

pronoun /'prounaun/ *a, dilb.* zamir, adıl

pronounce /prı'nauns/ *e.* telaffuz etmek, söylemek; resmen bildirmek **pronounced** göze çarpan, belirgin **pronouncement** bildiri, beyan, ilan

pronunciation /prınansi'eyşın/ *a.* telaffuz, sesletim

proof /pru:f/ *a.* kanıt, delil; deneme, sınama; içkinin alkol derecesinin ölçüsü; prova ☆ *s.* -e dayanıklı, geçirmez, işlemez

prop /prop/ *a.* destek

propaganda /propı'gendı/ *a.* yaymaca, propaganda

propagate /'propıgeyt/ *e.* üremek, çoğalmak; çoğaltmak, üretmek

propel /prı'pel/ *e.* ileriye doğru sürmek **propeller** pervane

proper /'propı/ *s.* doğru dürüst, uygun, nazik, terbiyeli **proper noun** *dilb.* özel ad

property /'propıti/ *a.* mal; mülk, arazi, emlak; özellik **lost property** kayıp eşya **property tax** emlak vergisi

prophecy /'profisi/ *a.* kehanet

prophesy /'profisay/ *e.* kehanette bulunmak

prophet /'profit/ *a.* peygamber; kâhin

proportion /prı'po:şın/ *a.* oran; orantı; pay; ç. boyutlar **in proportion to** -e oranla **proportional** orantılı

proposal /prı'pouzıl/ *a.* öneri, teklif; evlenme teklifi

propose /prı'pouz/ *e.* önermek; evlenme teklif etmek

proposition /propı'zişın/ *a.* öneri; mesele; sorun; *mat.* önerme

proprietary /prı'prayıtıri/ *s.* tescilli, patentli

proprietor /prı'prayıtı/ *a.* mal sahibi

propriety /prı'prayiti/ *a.* uygunluk, doğruluk

propulsion /prı'palşın/ *a.* itici güç

prose /prouz/ *a.* düzyazı, nesir

prosecute /'prosikyu:t/ *e, huk.* hakkında kovuşturma açmak, kovuşturmak **prosecution** kovuşturma; dava; davacı **prosecutor** davacı **public prosecutor** cumhuriyet savcısı

prospect /'prospekt/ *a.* beklenti, umut; görünüş

prospect /prı'spekt/ *e.* (altın, vb.) aramak

prospective /prı'spektiv/ *s.* umulan, beklenen

prospectus /prı'spektıs/ *a.* prospektüs

prosper /'prospı/ *e.* başarılı olmak **prosperity** /pro'speriti/ refah, gönenç **prosperous** başarılı, müreffeh, gönençli

prostitute /'prostityu:t/ *a.* fahişe

prostrate /'prostreyt/ *s.* yüzükoyun yatmış; bitkin, tükenmiş

protect /prı'tekt/ *e.* korumak, saklamak **protection** koruma; koruyucu **protective** koruyucu **protector** koruyucu

protein /'prouti:n/ *a.* protein

protest /'proutest/ *a.* itiraz, karşı çıkma; *tic.* protesto

protest /prı'test/ *e.* karşı çıkmak, itiraz etmek; iddia etmek

Protestant /'protistınt/ *a.* Protestan

protocol /'proutıkol/ *a.* protokol; tutanak

proton /'prouton/ *a, fiz.* proton

prototype /'proutıtayp/ *a.* ilk örnek, prototip

protract /prı'trekt/ *e.* (süresini) uzatmak **protractor** *mat.* iletki

protrude /prı'tru:d/ *e.* çıkıntı yapmak; dışarı çıkarmak

proud /praud/ *s.* **(of)** gururlu, kıvanç duyan; gururlu, mağrur; kendini beğenmiş; görkemli **proud flesh** yara etrafındaki şiş

415 **pungent**

prove /pru:v/ *e.* kanıtlamak; çıkmak, bulunmak; *mat.* sağlamasını yapmak
proverb /'provö:b/ *a.* atasözü
provide /prı'vayd/ *e.* sağlamak; hazırlıklı bulunmak, önlem almak **provided,** **providing that** yeter ki, -mek koşuluyla **provide for** geçimini sağlamak
province /'provins/ *a.* il; ç. taşra; ilgi alanı, uzmanlık
provincial /prı'vinşıl/ *s.* taşralı; kaba, görgüsüz
provision /prı'vijın/ *a.* tedarik, hazırlık; ç. erzak; hüküm, madde **provisional** geçici
provocation /provı'keyşın/ *a.* kışkırtma
provoke /prı'vouk/ *e.* kışkırtmak; -e neden olmak **provoking** sinir bozucu, can sıkıcı
prow /prau/ *a, den.* pruva
prowl /praul/ *e.* sinsi sinsi dolaşmak
proximity /prok'simiti/ *a.* yakınlık
proxy /'proksi/ *a.* vekil; vekâlet
prudent /'pru:dınt/ *s.* ihtiyatlı, öngörülü
prune /pru:n/ *a.* kuru erik ☆ *e.* budamak
psalm /sa:m/ *a.* ilahi
pseudonym /'syu:dınim/ *a.* takma ad
psychiatry /say'kayıtri/ *a.* psikiyatri, ruh hekimliği **psychiatrist** psikiyatrist, ruh hekimi **psychic(al)** /'saykik(l)/ *s.* ruhsal
psychoanalysis /saykouı'nelisis/ *a.* psikanaliz, ruhçözümleme **psychoanalyst** /-nılist/ psikanalist
psychology /say'kolıci/ *a.* psikoloji, ruhbilim **psychological** /saykı'locikıl/ psikolojik, ruhbilimsel **psychologist** /say'kolıcist/ ruhbilimci
psychotic /say'kotik/ *a, s.* psikozlu
pub /pab/ *a.* birahane, pub
puberty /'pyu:bıti/ *a.* ergenlik, erinlik
public /'pablik/ *s.* halka ait; genel; devlete ait, ulusal ☆ *a.* kamu, halk **in public** alenen, herkesin önünde **public opinion** kamuoyu **public relations** halkla ilişkiler **public school** *İİ.* özel okul; *Aİ.* parasız okul **publicly** açıkça
publication /pabli'keyşın/ *a.* yayım, yayımlama; yayın

publicity /pa'blisiti/ *a.* tanıtma, reklam; halkın dikkati
publicize /'pablisayz/ *e.* reklamını yapmak; halka tanıtmak
publish /'pabliş/ *e.* yayımlamak, basmak; açığa vurmak **publisher** yayımcı, yayınevi
pucker /'pakı/ *e.* büzmek, buruşturmak
pudding /'puding/ *a.* puding, muhallebi
puddle /'padıl/ *a.* su birikintisi, gölcük
puff /paf/ *a.* (sigara) fırt; üfürük; esinti; soluk ☆ *e.* üflemek, püflemek; (sigara) içmek; (buhar, duman, vb.) çıkarmak
pull /pul/ *e.* çekmek; koparmak ☆ *a.* çekme, çekiş; yudum; fırt; *kon.* iltimas, torpil **pull down** yıkmak, indirmek **pull in** (tren) istasyona girmek; (taşıt) kenara çekmek **pull off** çıkarmak, soymak; başarmak **pull up** sökmek, yolmak; durmak
pulley /'puli/ *a.* makara, kasnak
pullover /'pulouvı/ *a.* kazak
pulp /palp/ *a.* meyve eti
pulpit /'pulpit/ *a.* kürsü, mimber
pulsate /'palseyt/ *e.* (yürek, nabız, vb.) atmak, çarpmak
pulse /pals/ *a.* nabız, nabız atışı; bakliyat
pulverize /'palvırayz/ *e.* ezmek, toz haline getirmek
puma /'pyu:mı/ *a, hayb.* puma
pump /pamp/ *a.* pompa; tulumba ☆ *e.* pompalamak
pumpkin /'pampkin/ *a, bitk.* balkabağı
pun /pan/ *a.* cinas, sözcük oyunu
punch /panç/ *e.* yumruklamak; zımbalamak ☆ *a.* yumruk; zımba; matkap, delgi; punç; güç, etki **puncher** zımba; kovboy
punctual /'pankçuıl/ *s.* dakik
punctuate /'pankçueyt/ *e, dilb.* noktalama işaretlerini koymak; (sözü, vb.) ikide bir kesmek **punctuation** noktalama **punctuation mark** *dilb.* noktalama işareti
puncture /'pankçı/ *a.* küçük delik; (lastikte, vb.) patlak
pungent /'pancınt/ *s.* sert, acı, keskin

punish /'paniş/ *e.* cezalandırmak, ceza vermek **punishment** ceza
pup /pap/ *a.* yavru fok; yavru köpek
pupil /'pyu:pıl/ *a.* öğrenci; *anat.* gözbebeği
puppet /'papit/ *a.* kukla
puppy /'papi/ *a.* köpek yavrusu
purchase /'pö:çis/ *e.* satın almak ☆ *a.* satın alma, alım; satın alınan şey **purchaser** müşteri, alıcı
pure /pyuı/ *s.* katıksız, arı, saf; temiz; safkan; masum, namuslu; kuramsal **purely** tamamen, sırf, yalnız
puree /'pyuırey/ *e.* püre, ezme
purgatory /'pö:gıtıri/ *a.* Araf
purge /pö:c/ *a.* temizleme, tasfiye; *hek.* müshil ilacı ☆ *e.* temizlemek, arıtmak
purify /'pyuırifay/ *e.* temizlemek, arındırmak, arıtmak
puritan /'pyuıritın/ *a, s.* yobaz, bağnaz, sofu
purity /'pyuıriti/ *a.* saflık, temizlik, arılık
purl /pö:l/ *a.* ters ilmik
purple /'pö:pıl/ *a, s.* mor
purpose /'pö:pıs/ *a.* amaç, gaye, maksat; niyet, kasıt **on purpose** kasten, bile bile
purr /pö:/ *e.* (kedi) mırlamak ☆ *a.* kedi mırlaması, mırıltı
purse /pö:s/ *a.* küçük para çantası, para kesesi; *Aİ.* kadın el çantası
pursue /pı'syu:/ *e.* kovalamak, peşine düşmek, izlemek; devam etmek, sürdürmek
pursuit /pı'syu:t/ *a.* kovalama, takip, peşine düşme; meşgale, uğraş, iş
pus /pas/ *a.* cerahat, irin
push /puş/ *e.* itmek; basmak, bastırmak; sıkıştırmak, zorlamak ☆ *a.* itme, itiş, kakma, dürtme; çaba, gayret; girginlik **pushchair** çocuk arabası **pusher** fırsatçı; uyuşturucu satıcısı
pussy /'pusi/ *a, kon.* kedi, pisi pisi
put /put/ *e.* put /put/ koymak, yerleştirmek; sokmak; sormak; açıklamak, belirtmek **put aside** biriktirmek **put away** yerine koymak, kaldırmak **put back** geciktirmek; ertelemek **put down** yere koymak, indirmek; sustur-

mak; yazmak; azaltmak **put forward** ileri sürmek **put in for** adaylığını koymak, başvurmak **put off** ertelemek; şaşırtmak; atlatmak, oyalamak **put on** giymek, takmak; tavır takınmak; eklemek; sahneye koymak **put out** söndürmek; üzmek; çıkarmak; şaşırtmak **put through** başarmak, gerçekleştirmek; (telefon) bağlamak **put up** inşa etmek, kurmak; misafir etmek; ağırlamak; (fiyat, vb.) arttırmak; (ilan. vb.) asmak **put up with** tahammül etmek, katlanmak
putrid /'pyu:trid/ *s.* çürük, bozuk
puzzle /'pazıl/ *e.* şaşırtmak; şaşırmak ☆ *a.* bilmece, bulmaca; muamma
pygmy /'pigmi/ *a.* pigme; cüce
pyjamas /pı'ca:mız/ *a.* pijama
pylon /'paylın/ *a.* çelik elektrik direği
pyramid /'pirımid/ *a, mat.* piramit; ehram, piramit
pyrex /'payreks/ *a.* ateşe dayanıklı cam eşya
pyrotechnics /payırou'tekniks/ *a.* fişekçilik; havai fişek gösterisi
python /'paytın/ *a, hayb.* piton yılanı

Q

quack /kwek/ *a.* ördek sesi, vak; yalancı doktor, şarlatan
quadrangle /'kwodrengıl/ *a.* bahçe; *mat.* dörtgen
quadraphonic /kwodrı'fonik/ *s.* (ses) dört kanallı, kuadrofonik
quadrilateral /kwodri'letırıl/ *s, a.* dörtgen
quadrillion /kwo'drilıın/ *a.* katrilyon
quadruped /'kwodruped/ *a, hayb.* dört ayaklı hayvan
quadruple /'kwodrupıl/ *e.* dörtle çarpmak; dört katı olmak
quagmire /'kwegmayı/ *a.* bataklık
quail /kweyl/ *a, hayb.* bıldırcın
quake /kweyk/ *e.* titremek
qualification /kwolifi'keyşın/ *a.* nitelik, yeterlik; niteleme

qualify /'kwolifay/ e. hak kazandırmak, yetki vermek; nitelemek, karakterize etmek; sınırlandırmak, değiştirmek, hafifletmek qualified nitelikli, kalifiye qualitative /'kwolitıtiv/ s. nitel

quality /'kwoliti/ a. nitelik, kalite, vasıf; özellik

qualm /kwa:m/ a. mide bulantısı; kuşku, huzursuzluk, endişe, kuruntu

quantitative /'kwontitıtiv/ s. nicel

quantity /'kwontiti/ a. nicelik; miktar

quarantine /'kworınti:n/ a. karantina

quarrel /'kworıl/ a. kavga, çekişme, bozuşma ☆ e. kavga etmek, kapışmak, atışmak, bozuşmak quarrelsome kavgacı

quarry /'kwori/ a. av; taş ocağı

quart /kwo:t/ a. galon'un dörtte biri, kuart (1, 137 lt.)

quarter /'kwo:tı/ a. çeyrek; çeyrek saat; üç aylık süre; Al. 25 sent; mahalle, bölge; ask. kışla, konak quarter-master ask. levazım subayı; den. serdümen quarterfinal çeyrek final quarterly üç ayda bir olan, üç aylık

quartet /kwo:'tet/ a, müz. dörtlü, kuartet

quartz /kwo:ts/ a. kuvars

quash /kwoş/ e. bozmak, kaldırmak

quaver /'kweyvı/ a, müz. (ses) titremek

quay /ki:/ a. rıhtım, iskele

queasy /'kwi:zi/ s. midesi bulanmış, kusacak halde

queen /'kwi:n/ a. kraliçe; (iskambil) kız, dam; (satranç) vezir

queer /kwiı/ s. acayip, tuhaf, garip; kon. kaçık, üşütük

quell /kwel/ e. bastırmak, ezmek, önünü almak

quench /kwenç/ e. (susuzluk, vb.) gidermek; (ateş) söndürmek

query /'kwiiri/ a. soru; kuşku ☆ e. sormak; -den kuşkulanmak

question /'kwesçın/ a. soru; sorgu; konu, sorun ☆ e. sorguya çekmek; kuşkulanmak come into question gündeme gelmek in question söz konusu olan out of the question söz konusu olamaz question mark soru işareti questionable kuşku uyandıran

questionnaire /kwesçı'neı/ a. anket

queue /kyu:/ a, ii. kuyruk, sıra ☆ e, ii. kuyruk olmak join the queue kuyruğa girmek jump the queue kuyruktakilerin önüne geçmek

quibble /'kwibıl/ e. önemsiz konular üzerinde tartışmak

quick /kwik/ s. çabuk, hızlı; tez, çabuk; anlayışlı, zeki quickly çabucak, süratle

quicken /'kwikın/ e. çabuklaşmak, hızlanmak; çabuklaştırmak

quicksand /'kwiksend/ a. bataklık

quicksilver /'kwiksilvı/ a, kim. cıva

quiet /'kwayıt/ s. sessiz, sakin; sessiz; durgun

quill /kwil/ a. iri kuş tüyü

quilt /kwilt/ a. yorgan

quince /kwins/ a. ayva

quinine /'kwini:n/ a, hek. kinin

quip /kwip/ a. alaylı şaka, iğneli söz

quit /kwit/ e. quit, quitted -den ayrılmak, terk etmek; bırakmak

quite /kwait/ be. tümüyle, büsbütün; az çok, oldukça

quiver /'kwivı/ a. ok kılıfı, sadak, okluk ☆ e. titremek

quiz /kwiz/ a. kısa sınav, yoklama; bilgi yarışması ☆ e. sorular sormak, sorguya çekmek

quizzical /'kwizikıl/ s. şakacı, alaycı

quota /'kwoutı/ a. pay; kota, kontenjan

quotation /kwou'teyşın/ a, yaz. alıntı, iktibas; piyasa rayici, fiyat quotation mark dilb. tırnak işareti

quote /kwout/ e. alıntı yapmak, iktibas etmek; zikretmek; tic. fiyat vermek ☆ a, kon. iktibas, alıntı; sunulan fiyat

quotient /'kwouşınt/ a, mat. bölüm

R

rabbi /'rebay/ a. haham

rabbit /'rebit/ a. tavşan

rabble /'rebıl/ a. düzensiz kalabalık

rabies /'reybi:z/ a. kuduz hastalığı

race /reys/ a. yarış; su akıntısı; ırk, soy;

racial 418

ç. at yarışı ☆ e. yarışmak **the human race** insan nesli **racecourse** (hipodromda) koşu alanı **racetrack** yarış pisti, koşuyolu
racial /'reyşıl/ s. ırkla ilgili, ırksal **racialism** ırkçılık **racialist** ırkçı **racism** /'reysizım/ ırkçılık **racist** ırkçı
rack /rek/ a. parmaklıklı raf, askı
racket /'rekit/ a, kon. gürültü, patırtı
racket, racquet /'rekit/ a. raket
radar /'reyda:/ a. radar
radial /'reydiıl/ s. ışınsal; yarıçapla ilgili
radiance /'reydiıns/ a. parlaklık, aydınlık; neşe, sevinç
radiant /'reydiınt/ s. ışık saçan parlak; ısı yayan; neşe saçan, sevinçli
radiate /'reydieyt/ e. ışık saçmak; ısı yaymak; (neşe, vb.) saçmak
radiation /reydi'eyşın/ a. ısı/ışın saçma; radyasyon, ışınım
radiator /'reydieytı/ a. radyatör
radical /'redikıl/ s. köklü; radikal, köktenci; mat. kökle ilgili
radio /'reydiou/ a. radyo
radioactive /reydiou'ektiv/ s. ışınetkin, radyoaktif **radioactivity** ışınetkinlik, radyoaktivite
radiograph /'reydiougra:f/ a. röntgen filmi, radyograf
radiography /reydi'ogrıfi/ a. ışınçekim, radyografi
radiology /reydi'olıci/ a. röntgenbilim, radyoloji
radish /'rediş/ a, bitk. turp
radium /'reydiım/ a, kim. radyum
radius /'reydiıs/ a, mat. yarıçap; anat. önkol kemiği
raffle /'refıl/ a. piyango, çekiliş
raft /ra:ft/ a. sal
rag /reg/ a. bez parçası, paçavra; eşek şakası ☆ e. eşek şakası yapmak; dalga geçmek
rage /reyc/ a. öfke, hiddet; düşkünlük, tutku
ragged /'regid/ s. yırtık pırtık, eski püskü
raid /reyd/ a. akın, baskın **raider** akıncı
rail /reyl/ a. parmaklık; ray; demiryolu **railing** parmaklık **railroad** demiryolu **railway** İİ. demiryolu

rain /reyn/ a. yağmur ☆ e. (yağmur) yağmak **rainbow** gökkuşağı, alkım, ebekuşağı **raincoat** yağmurluk **raindrop** yağmur damlası **rainfall** yağış miktarı, yağış **rainproof** yağmur geçirmez **rain forest** tropikal orman **rains** muson yağmurları; muson **rainy** yağmurlu
raise /reyz/ e. kaldırmak, yükseltmek; bina etmek, dikmek; büyütmek, yetiştirmek, toplamak; neden olmak, uyandırmak ☆ a, Aİ. ücret artışı, zam
raisin /'reyzın/ a. kuru üzüm
rake /reyk/ a. tırmık ☆ e. tırmıklamak, taramak **rake in money** çok para kazanmak
rally /'reli/ e. bir araya toplanmak; iyileşmek, düzelmek, toparlanmak ☆ a. toplantı; otomobil yarışı, ralli; (tenis) uzun sayı mücadelesi
ram /rem/ a, hayb. koç; Koç burcu
Ramadan /'remıden, 'remıda:n/ a. ramazan
ramification /remifi'keyşın/ a. dallanıp budaklanma
ramp /remp/ a. yokuş, rampa
rampage /rem'peyc, 'rempeyc/ e. sağa sola saldırmak, kudurmak
rampart /'rempa:t/ a. siper, sur
ramshackle /'remşekıl/ s. köhne, harap, viran
ran /ren/ bkz. run
ranch /ra:nç/ a. büyük çiftlik
rancour /'renkı/ a. kin, hınç
random /'rendım/ s. rasgele, gelişigüzel **at random** öylesine, amaçsızca
range /reync/ a. sıra, dizi; menzil; atış alanı ☆ e. dizmek; dizilmek; uzanmak **ranger** orman bekçisi
rank /renk/ a. sıra, dizi; rütbe; sınıf, tabaka ☆ e. sıralamak, dizmek; yer almak, sayılmak
rankle /'renkıl/ e. (acısı) içinden çıkmamak, sürmek, yüreğine dert olmak
ransack /'rensek/ e. altını üstüne getirmek; yağmalamak
ransom /'rensım/ a. fidye **a king's ransom** büyük para
rap /rep/ a. hafifçe vuruş; kon. suç, ceza

rape /reyp/ *a.* ırza geçme, ırza tecavüz; bozma, mahvetme ☆ *e.* ırzına geçmek

rapid /'repid/ *s.* hızlı; (yokuş) dik

rapidly /'repidli/ *be.* hızla, süratle

rapt /rept/ *s.* kendini vermiş şekilde, can kulağıyla

rapture /'repçı/ *a.* büyük sevinç, esrime **go to raptures** (sevincinden) havalara uçmak

rare /reı/ *s.* nadir, seyrek; (et) az pişmiş **rarely** nadiren, seyrek olarak

rarity /'reıriti/ *a.* nadirlik, seyreklik; ender bulunur şey

rascal /'ra:skıl/ *a.* namussuz, alçak; yaramaz, kerata

rash /reş/ *s.* düşüncesiz, aceleci

rasp /ra:sp/ *a.* raspa, kaba törpü

raspberry /'ra:zbıri/ *a.* ahududu, ağaççileği

rat /ret/ *a.* iri fare, sıçan; hain, dönek

rate /reyt/ *a.* oran, nispet; çeşit ☆ *e.* kıymet biçmek; vergi koymak **at any rate** her nasılsa **rate of exchange** döviz kuru **rate of interest** faiz oranı

rather /'ra:dı/ *be.* oldukça, epeyce; tercihan, daha çok; daha doğrusu; aksine, tersine

ratify /'retifay/ *e.* onaylamak

rating /'reyting/ *a.* beğenilme, tutulma, reyting; *ii.* deniz eri, tayfa

ratio /'reyşiou/ *a.* oran, nispet

ration /'reşın/ *a.* istihkak, pay

rational /'reşınıl/ *s.* aklı başında, mantıklı; *mat.* rasyonel, oranlı

rationalism /'reşınılizim/ *a, fel.* usçuluk, rasyonalism **rationalist** akılcı

rationalize /'reşınılayz/ *e.* kılıf uydurmak; *ii.* (yöntem) geliştirmek, verimlileştirmek

rattle /'retıl/ *a.* bebek çıngırağı, kaynanazırıltısı, cırcır ☆ *e.* şıngırdamak, tıngırdamak **rattlesnake** çıngıraklıyılan

raucous /'ro:kıs/ *s.* (ses) kısık, boğuk

ravage /'revic/ *e.* mahvetmek, kırıp geçirmek; yağmalamak, soymak

rave /reyv/ *e.* deli gibi abuk sabuk konuşmak, saçmalamak, sayıklamak

raven /'reyvın/ *a, hayb.* kuzgun

ravenous /'revinıs/ *s.* kurt gibi aç

ravine /rı'vi:n/ *a, coğ.* dar ve derin koyak

ravioli /revi'ouli/ *a.* bir tür mantı

ravish /'reviş/ *e, yaz.* ırzına geçmek; zevk vermek, esritmek

raw /ro:/ *s.* çiğ; işlenmemiş, ham; deneyimsiz, acemi; (hava) soğuk ve yağışlı

ray /rey/ *a.* ışın

rayon /'reyon/ *a.* yapay ipek, rayon

raze /reyz/ *e.* yıkıp yerle bir etmek

razor /'reyzı/ *a.* ustura; tıraş makinesi

re /ri:/ *ilg.* (iş mektuplarında) -e dair, hakkında, ile ilgili olarak

re /rey/ *a, müz.* re notası

reach /ri:ç/ *e.* ulaşmak, erişmek; yetişmek, değmek ☆ *a.* uzanma; menzil; anlayış, kavrayış **out of reach** erişilmez, yetişilmez

react /ri'ekt/ *e.* tepki göstermek; *kim.* tepkimek; karşılık vermek

reaction /ri'ekşın/ *a.* tepki, reaksiyon; *kim.* tepkime; gericilik

read /ri:d/ *e.* **red** /red/ okumak; anlamak; öğrenim görmek; (termometre, vb.) göstermek **read between the lines** kapalı anlamını bulmak **readable** okumaya değer; (yazı) okunaklı

reader /'ri:dı/ *a.* okuyucu, okur; *ii.* doçent; düzeltmen; okuma kitabı

readily /'redili/ *be.* isteyerek, seve seve, gönülden **readiness** isteklilik; hazır olma

reading /'ri:ding/ *a.* okuma; yorum; okuma parçası

ready /'redi/ *s.* hazır; istekli; kolay, çabuk, seri; eli çabuk **ready-made** (giysi) hazır

real /rıl/ *s.* gerçek, hakiki **real estate** taşınmaz mal, gayrimenkul

realism /'rılizim/ *a.* gerçekçilik

realist /'rılist/ *a.* gerçekçi **realistic** realist, gerçekçi

reality /ri'eliti/ *a.* gerçek, hakikat; gerçekçilik **in reality** gerçekte, aslında

realize /'rılayz/ *e.* farkına varmak, anlamak, kavramak, gerçekleştirmek **realization** farkına varma; gerçekleştirme

realtor /'rılltı/ *a, Aİ.* emlakçı

really /'riıli/ *be.* gerçekten, sahiden
realm /relm/ *a.* krallık; alan, ülke
reap /ri:p/ *e.* (ekin) biçmek
rear /riı/ *a.* geri, arka, art ☆ *e.* yetiştirmek, büyütmek; kaldırmak
reason /'ri:zın/ *e.* neden, sebep; akıl, sağduyu; gerekçe ☆ *e.* muhakeme etmek; -den sonuç çıkarmak; tartışmak, görüşmek **beyond/past all reason** mantıksız, aşırı **bring sb to reason** yola getirmek, aklını başına getirmek **by reason of** yüzünden, dolayı **listen to/hear reason** laf dinlemek **lose one's reason** aklını bozmak **with reason** haklı olarak **within reason** makul ölçüler içinde
reasonable /'ri:zınıbıl/ *s.* akla uygun, makul; akıllı
reasoning /'ri:zıning/ *a.* mantıklı düşünme; muhakeme
reassurance /riı'şuırıns/ *a.* rahatlatma, güven verme
reassure /ri:ı'şuı/ *e.* güven vermek; korku, kaygı, vb.'den kurtarmak
rebel /'rebıl/ *e.* baş kaldırmak, isyan etmek, ayaklanmak **rebellion** ayaklanma, isyan **rebellious** asi, isyancı
rebirth /ri:'bö:t/ *e.* yeniden doğma
rebound /ri'baund/ *e.* geri sıçramak, çarpıp geri gelmek, sekmek ☆ *a.* (basketbol) ribaund
rebuff /ri'baf/ *a.* tersleme, ret
rebuild /ri:'bild/ *e.* yeniden inşa etmek
rebuke /ri'byu:k/ *e.* azarlamak
recall /ri'ko:l/ *e.* geri çağırmak; anımsamak ☆ *a.* geri çağırma; anımsama
recapitulate /ri:kı'piçuleyt/ *e.* özetlemek
recede /ri'si:d/ *e.* geri çekilmek
receipt /ri'si:t/ *a.* makbuz, fiş, fatura; alma; ç. gelir, hasılat
receive /ri'si:v/ *e.* almak; -e uğramak; yemek; evine almak; konuk etmek; karşılamak **receiver** alıcı; ahize, almaç; tahsildar
recent /'ri:sınt/ *s.* yeni, yakında olan, son günlerdeki, son **recently** son günlerde, son zamanlarda
receptacle /ri'septıkıl/ *a.* kap
reception /ri'sepşın/ *a.* alma; karşılama, kabul; kabul töreni; resepsiyon
receptionist resepsiyon görevlisi
receptive /ri'septiv/ *s.* çabuk kavrayan, anlayışlı
recess /ri'ses/ *a.* paydos, tatil, ara; iç taraf
recession /ri'seşın/ *a.* geri çekilme, gerileme
recipe /'resipi/ *a.* yemek tarifi; reçete
recipient /ri'sipiınt/ *a.* alıcı
reciprocal /ri'siprıkıl/ *s.* karşılıklı, iki taraflı
recital /ri'saytıl/ *a.* anlatma; *müz.* resital
recite /ri'sayt/ *e.* ezberden okumak; anlatmak
reckless /'reklıs/ *s.* korkusuz, pervasız, kayıtsız, umursamaz
reckon /'rekın/ *e.* hesaplamak, saymak; sanmak, tahmin etmek **reckoning** hesap; *den.* mevki tahmini **day of reckoning** hesap günü, kıyamet günü
reclaim /ri'kleym/ *e.* düzeltmek, iyileştirmek; geri istemek
recline /ri'klayn/ *e.* yaslanmak; uzanmak
recognize /'rekıgnayz/ *e.* tanımak
recognizable tanınabilir **recognition** /-'nişın/ tanıma, tanınma, kabul
recoil /'rikoyl/ *e.* geri çekilmek; (silah) geri tepmek
recollect /rekı'lekt/ *e.* anımsamak, hatırlamak **recollection** anımsama, hatırlama; hatırlanan şey, anı
recommend /rekı'mend/ *e.* önermek, tavsiye etmek; öğütlemek **recommendation** tavsiye; öğüt
recompense /'rekımpens/ *e.* karşılığını vermek, ödemek, telafi etmek ☆ *a.* karşılık, tazminat
reconcile /'rekınsayl/ *e.* barıştırmak, uzlaştırmak; (düşünce, görüş, vb.) bağdaştırmak; **(to)** kabul ettirmek, razı etmek
reconnaissance /ri'konisıns/ *a, ask.* keşif
reconnoitre /rekı'noytı/ *a, ask.* keşfe çıkmak
reconstitute /ri:'konstityu:t/ *e.* tekrar kurmak, yenilemek
reconstruct /ri:kın'strakt/ *e.* yeniden

kurmak, yeniden inşa etmek
record /ri'ko:d/ e. yazmak, kaydetmek, deftere kaydetmek; (aygıt) kaydetmek; (görüntü, ses) almak, kayıt yapmak
record /'reko:d/ a. kayıt; tutanak; sicil; rekor; plak
recorder /ri'ko:dı/ a. kayıt aygıtı, teyp; kayıt memuru
recording /ri'ko:ding/ a. kayıt
recover /ri'kavı/ e. iyileşmek, toparlanmak; yeniden elde etmek ☆ a. geri alma; iyileşme, düzelme
recreation /rekri'eyşın/ a. eğlence, dinlenme
recruit /ri'kru:t/ a. acemi er; yeni üye ☆ e. işe almak, çalıştırmak; askere almak; üye yapmak
rectangle /'rektengıl/ a. dikdörtgen **rectangular** /rek'tengyulı/ dikdörtgen biçiminde
rectify /'rektifay/ e. düzeltmek; kim. arıtmak, damıtmak **rectifier** doğrultucu, düzeltici; redresör
rector /'rektı/ a. rektör; papaz
rectum /'rektım/ a, anat. düzbağırsak, göden, rektum
recuperate /ri'kyu:pıreyt/ e. iyileşmek, sağlığına kavuşmak
recur /ri'kö:/ e. tekrar meydana gelmek, yinelenmek **recurrence** /ri'karıns/ yineleme, tekrar olma
red /red/ s. kırmızı; (saç) kızıl; (cilt) pembe **Red Crescent** Kızılay **Red Cross** Kızılhaç **Red Indian** Kızılderili **red tape** bürokrasi, kırtasiyecilik see **red** tepesi atmak, gözü dönmek **red-blooded** yürekli, gözü pek
redcurrant /red'karınt/ a, bitk. frenküzümü
redden /'redın/ e. kızarmak; kızartmak, kırmızılaştırmak
reddish /'rediş/ s. kırmızımsı, kırmızımtırak
redhead /'redhed/ a, kon. kızıl saçlı kadın, kızıl
redress /ri'dres/ e. düzeltmek
reduce /ri'dyu:s/ e. azaltmak, indirmek; kon. kilo vermek **reduction** /ri'dakşın/ azaltma, indirme; indirim, tenzi-

lat
redundant /ri'dandınt/ s. gereksiz, lüzumsuz, fazla, aşırı, bol; işten çıkarılan
reed /ri:d/ a, bitk. kamış, saz
reef /ri:f/ a, den. camadan; coğ. resif
reek /ri:k/ a. kötü koku ☆ e. kötü kokmak
reel /ri:l/ a. makara, bobin; çıkrık; (teyp) makara ☆ e. sallanmak, sendelemek
refectory /ri'fektıri/ a. yemekhane
refer /ri'fö:/ e. (to) -den söz etmek; ilgili olmak; kapsamak; göndermek
referee /refı'ri:/ a, sp. hakem; huk. bilirkişi
reference /'refırıns/ a. bahsetme, söz etme; başvurma; referans, bonservis **in/with reference to** -e dair, -e ilişkin **reference book** başvuru kitabı
referendum /refı'rendım/ a. halk oylaması, referandum
refill /ri:'fil/ e. yeniden doldurmak ☆ a. yedek (kâğıt, pil, kalem içi, kurşun, vb.)
refine /ri'fayn/ e. arıtmak, tasfiye etmek, rafine etmek **refined** arıtılmış, rafine; kibar, zarif **refinery** arıtımevi, rafineri
reflect /ri'flekt/ e. yansıtmak **reflection** yansıma; yankı **reflective** düşünceli **reflector** yansıtaç, reflektör
reflex /'ri:fleks/ a. refleks, tepki
reflexive /ri'fleksiv/ s, dilb. dönüşlü
reform /ri'fo:m/ e. düzeltmek; düzelmek; -de reform yapmak ☆ a. reform, düzeltme **reformer** ıslahatçı, reformcu
refract /ri'frekt/ e. (ışık) kırmak, kırıp yansıtmak **refraction** kırılma
refrain /ri'freyn/ e. kendini tutmak ☆ a. nakarat
refresh /ri'freş/ e. canlandırmak; serinletmek; yenilemek, tazelemek; yenilenmek, canlanmak **refreshing** canlandırıcı, dinçleştirici; serinletici **refreshment** canlanma, güçlenme; ç. yiyecek ve içecek
refrigerate /ri'fricıreyt/ e. soğutmak; serinletmek **refrigerator** buzdolabı

refuge /'refyu:c/ a. sığınak, barınak; re-
füj **take refuge (in)** sığınmak
refugee /refyu'ci:/ a. mülteci
refund /ri'fand/ e. (parayı) geri vermek
☆ a. geri verilen para, geri ödeme
refusal /ri'fyu:zıl/ a. ret, geri çevirme
refuse /ri'fyu:z/ e. reddetmek, kabul etmemek, geri çevirmek
regain /ri'geyn/ e. yeniden elde etmek
regal /'ri:gıl/ s. kral ya da kraliçe gibi;
krallara layık, şahane
regard /ri'ga:d/ e. bakmak; gibi görmek, olarak ele almak; göz önünde
tutmak ☆ a. saygı, itibar; önemse-
me, aldırış; saygı, dikkat; bakış; ç. selam, iyi dilekler **in/with regard to** hakkında, -e gelince **regarding** hakkında,
ilişkin **regardless** ne olursa olsun,
mutlaka **regardless of** -e bakmaksı-
zın, -e aldırmadan
regent /'ri:cınt/ a. kral naibi
regime /rey'ci:m/ a. yönetim; rejim, perhiz
regiment /'recimınt/ a, ask. alay
region /'ri:cın/ a. bölge, yöre **in the region of** yaklaşık, civarında **regional**
bölgesel, yöresel
register /'recistı/ a. sicil, kütük; kayıt
defteri; dosya; liste ☆ e. kaydetmek;
(aygıt) göstermek **cash register** yazar
kasa **registered** (mektup) taahhütlü;
tescilli
registrar /reci'stra:/ a. sicil memuru, nüfus memuru
registration /reci'streyşın/ a. kayıt, tescil **registration number** plaka numarası
registry /'recistri/ a. sicil dairesi **registry
office** evlendirme dairesi
regret /ri'gret/ e. pişman olmak; üzülmek ☆ a. üzüntü; pişmanlık **regretful** üzüntülü **regrettable** üzücü, acınacak
regular /'regyulı/ s. düzgün, muntazam; nizami; muvazzaf **regularity** dü-
zenlilik, intizam **regularly** düzenli olarak
regulate /'regyuleyt/ e. düzenlemek;
ayarlamak **regulation** düzenleme;
ayarlama; ç. yönetmelik, tüzük **regula-**

tor ayarlayıcı, regülatör
rehabilitate /ri:hı'biliteyt/ e. yenileştirmek; onarmak; sağlığına kavuştur-
mak **rehabilitation** yenileme; onarım;
rehabilitasyon
rehearse /ri'hö:s/ e. (tiyatro) prova etmek **rehearsal** prova; anlatma, sayıp
dökme
reign /reyn/ a. hükümdarlık, saltanat ☆
e. saltanat sürmek; oluşmak, olmak
reimburse /ri:im'bö:s/ e. (parasını) geri
vermek, ödemek
rein /reyn/ a. dizgin
reincarnate /ri:in'ka:neyt/ e. öldükten
sonra yeni bir bedende diriltmek; (ru-
ha) yeni bir beden vermek **reincarna-
tion** başka bir bedende dirilme
reindeer /'reyndı/ a, hayb. ren geyiği
reinforce /ri:in'fo:s/ e. güçlendirmek,
takviye etmek **reinforcement** güçlendirme, takviye, destek ç, ask. takviye
birliği
reiterate /ri:'itıreyt/ e. (birkaç kez) yinelemek, tekrarlamak
reject /ri'cekt/ e. reddetmek, geri çevirmek **rejection** ret, geri çevirme
rejoice /ri'coys/ e. çok sevinçli olmak
rejoicing büyük sevinç, şenlik
rejuvenate /ri'cu:vıneyt/ e. gençleştirmek
relapse /ri'leps/ e. kötüye gitmek, kötüleşmek ☆ a. kötüleşme; (kötü yola)
sapma
relate /ri'leyt/ e. anlatmak, nakletmek;
(to) ile bağdaştırmak, ilişki kurmak
relation /ri'leyşın/ a. akraba; ilgi, ilişki,
bağlantı **in relation to** hakkında, -e
ilişkin **relationship** akrabalık; ilgi, ilişki, bağlantı
relative /'relıtiv/ a. akraba ☆ s. nispi,
göreli; ilişkin **relative clause** sıfat yantümcesi **relative pronoun** dilb. ilgi adılı **relatively** oranla, nispeten; oldukça
relativity /relı'tiviti/ a. izafiyet, görelik
relax /ri'leks/ e. gevşemek, rahatlamak;
gevşetmek, dinlendirmek **relaxation**
gevşeme, yumuşama; gevşetme; gevşeklik
relay /'ri:ley/ a. nöbetleşe çalışan ekip,
vardiya, posta; yedek malzeme ☆ e.

naklen yayınlamak
release /ri'li:s/ e. serbest bırakmak ☆
a. serbest bırakma, salma, tahliye **on
general release** (film) gösterimde
relegate /'religeyt/ e. aşağı bir durum,
mevkiye indirmek
relent /ri'lent/ e. yumuşamak, acıyıp
merhamete gelmek, yumuşamak
relevant /'relivınt/ s. konu ile ilgili; amaca uygun **relevance** ilgi, uygunluk
reliable /ri'layıbıl/ s. güvenilir; güvenli
reliability güvenilirlik
relic /'relik/ a. kalıntı; hatıra, andaç
relief /ri'li:f/ a. ferahlama, rahatlama;
kurtarma; teselli; iç ferahlığı; yardım;
çare, derman; ask. nöbet değiştirme;
kabartma, rölyef
relieve /ri'li:v/ e. ferahlatmak, hafifletmek, yatıştırmak; ask. nöbet değiştirmek
religion /ri'licın/ a. din; mezhep; inanç,
iman
religious /ri'licıs/ s. dinsel, dini; dindar
relinquish /ri'linkwiş/ e. vazgeçmek, bırakmak, feragat etmek
relish /'reliş/ a. istek, zevk, iştah; çeşni,
lezzet ☆ e. hoşlanmak, zevk almak,
hoşnut olmak
reluctant /ri'laktınt/ s. isteksiz, gönülsüz **reluctance** isteksizlik, gönülsüz-
lük
rely /ri'lay/ e. **(on)** güvenmek
remain /ri'meyn/ e. kalmak **remainder**
artan; kalan **remains** kalıntılar; ceset
remark /ri'ma:k/ e. söylemek, belirtmek ☆ a. söz, düşünce, görüş re-
markable dikkate değer, göze çarpan, olağanüstü
remedial /ri'mi:dııl/ s. iyileştiren
remedy /'remidi/ a. çare; ilaç, deva
remember /ri'membı/ e. hatırlamak; aklında tutmak; **(to)** -den selam götürmek **remembrance** anma, hatırlama,
yâd etme; anı, hatıra; andaç, yadigâr
remind /ri'maynd/ e. hatırlatmak, aklına getirmek
reminisce /remi'nis/ e. eski günlerden
konuşmak **reminiscence** geçmişi hatırlama
reminiscent /remi'nisınt/ s. -i hatırla-

tan, benzeri
remission /ri'mişın/ a. bağışlama, af
remit /ri'mit/ e. (borç, ceza, vb.'den)
kurtarmak; postayla (para, çek, vb.)
göndermek **remittance** para havalesi, gönderilen para
remnant /'remnınt/ a. artık, kalıntı
remonstrate /'remınstreyt/ e. şikâyet etmek, itiraz etmek
remorse /ri'mo:s/ a. vicdan azabı, kahır
without remorse acımasızca **remorse-
ful** pişman **remorseless** acımasız
remote /ri'mout/ s. uzak **remote control** uzaktan kumanda
remove /ri'mu:v/ e. çıkarmak; kaldırmak, alıp götürmek; temizlemek, silmek; taşınmak, gitmek **removable** taşınabilir **removal** kaldırma; çıkarma;
taşınma
remunerate /ri'myu:nıreyt/ e. emeğinin
karşılığını ödemek **remuneration** ücret, karşılık **remunerative** kazançlı
Renaissance /ri'neysıns/ a. Rönesans
render /'rendı/ e. (yardım, vb.) vermek,
sunmak; hale getirmek; **(into)** -e tercüme etmek
rendezvous /'rondivu:, 'rondeyvu:/ a.
buluşma, randevu; buluşma yeri
rendition /ren'dişın/ a. icra, sunma,
temsil
renegade /'renigeyd/ a. hain, dönek
renew /ri'nyu:/ e. yenilemek **renewable**
yenilenebilir **renewal** yenileme
renounce /ri'nauns/ e. vazgeçmek, terk
etmek; bırakmak, feragat etmek
renovate /'renıveyt/ e. yenilemek, onarmak
renown /ri'naun/ a. ün, ad, şan, şöhret
rent /rent/ a. kira ☆ e. kiralamak
rental /'rentıl/ a. kira bedeli, kira
renunciation /rinansi'eyşın/ a. vazgeç-
me, feragat
reorganize /ri:'o:gınayz/ e. yeniden düzenlemek
repair /ri'peı/ e. onarmak, tamir etmek
☆ a. onarım, tamirat **under repair**
onarımda
reparation /repı'reyşın/ a. tazminat
repatriate /ri:'petrieyt/ e. yurduna geri
göndermek

repay   424

repay /ri'pey/ e. (para) geri vermek; altında kalmamak
repayable geri ödenebilir repayment geri ödeme
repeal /ri'pi:l/ e. yürürlükten kaldırmak, feshetmek ☆ a. fesih, iptal
repeat /ri'pi:t/ e. tekrarlamak, yinelemek repeat a course/year bir yıl daha aynı sınıfta okumak repeatedly defalarca, tekrar tekrar
repel /ri'pel/ e. geri püskürtmek; iğrendirmek repellent sinek, vb. kovucu madde
repent /ri'pent/ e. pişman olmak repentance pişmanlık
repercussion /ri:pı'kaşın/ a. geri tepme
repertoire /'repıtwa:/ a. repertuvar; dağarcık
repetition /repi'tişın/ a. tekrar, yineleme
replace /ri'pleys/ e. eski yerine koymak; (with/by) değiştirmek; -in yerini almak replacement yerine koyma; vekil, yedek
replay /ri:'pley/ e. (maç) tekrarlamak; (müzik) tekrar çalmak ☆ a. tekrar oynanan maç; (görüntü, ses, kayıt, vb.) tekrar
replica /'replikı/ a. kopya
reply /ri'play/ e. karşılık vermek, yanıtlamak ☆ a. yanıt; karşılık in reply yanıt olarak
report /ri'po:t/ a. rapor; gazete haberi, haber; bildiri; söylenti; not karnesi; diploma ☆ e. rapor vermek/yazmak; bildirmek; anlatmak, söylemek reported speech dilb. dolaylı anlatım reporter gazete muhabiri; raportör
represent /repri'zent/ e. temsil etmek, göstermek; simgelemek; huk. -in vekili olmak; rolünü oynamak representation tasvir; oyun, temsil; mümessillik; simge; gösterme
representative /repri'zentıtiv/ s. temsil eden; temsili; örnek, tipik, karakteristik ☆ a. temsilci, vekil, milletvekili House of Representatives Temsilciler Meclisi
repress /ri'pres/ e. bastırmak, önlemek repression bastırma, tutma

reprimand /'reprima:nd/ a. (resmi) tekdir, kınama ☆ e. (resmi olarak) kınamak
reprint /ri:'print/ e. (kitap) yeniden basmak ☆ a. yeni baskı
reproach /ri'prouç/ a. azar, kınama ☆ e. azarlamak, kınamak
reproduce /ri:prı'dyu:s/ e. üremek, çoğalmak; kopye etmek; (oyun) yeniden oynamak reproduction üreme; çoğaltma; röprodüksiyon; özdeşbaskı
reptile /'reptayl/ a, hayb. sürüngen
republic /ri'pablik/ a. cumhuriyet republican cumhuriyete ait; cumhuriyetçi
repugnant /ri'pagnınt/ s. çirkin, iğrenç
repulse /ri'pals/ e. püskürtmek, kovmak; iğrendirmek repulsion iğrenme, tiksinti repulsive iğrenç
reputable /'repyutıbıl/ s. ünlü, tanınmış
reputation /repyu'teyşın/ a. ün, şöhret
request /ri'kwest/ a. rica, dilek, istek ☆ e. rica etmek, dilemek
require /ri'kwayı/ e. gerektirmek; istemek; emretmek; buyurmak requirement ihtiyaç, gereksinim; icap, gerek
requisite /'rekwizit/ s. gerekli, zorunlu
rescue /'reskyu:/ e. kurtarmak ☆ a. kurtarma, kurtuluş
research /ri'sö:ç/ a. araştırma ☆ e. araştırma yapmak researcher araştırmacı
resemblance /ri'zemblıns/ a. benzerlik
resemble /ri'zembıl/ e. benzemek
resent /ri'zent/ e. kızmak, içerlemek
reservation /rezı'veyşın/ a. yer ayırtma, rezervasyon; şart, koşul; kuşku
reserve /ri'zö:v/ e. ayırmak, saklamak; ayırtmak ☆ a. yedek, rezerv; çekingenlik; fon, karşılık reserved çekingen; sessiz; tutulmuş, ayırtılmış
reservoir /'rezıvwa:/ a. su deposu
reside /ri'zayd/ e. -de ikamet etmek, oturmak
residence /'rezidıns/ a. konut; oturma, ikamet residence permit oturma izni
resident /'rezidınt/ s, a. sakin, oturan residential /-'denşıl/ oturmaya elverişli

retaliate

residual /ri'zicuıl/ s. artan, kalan
residue /'rezidyu:/ a. kalan, artık; kim. tortu
resign /ri'zayn/ e. istifa etmek, çekilmek **resign oneself to** -e razı olmak, katlanmak **resigned** boyun eğmiş, uysal
resignation /rezig'neyşın/ a. istifa, çekilme; boyun eğme, kabullenme
resilience /ri'zilıns/ a. esneklik **resilient** esnek
resin /'rezin/ a. çam sakızı, reçine
resist /ri'zist/ e. karşı koymak, direnmek; dayanmak **resistance** direnme; dayanma; *fiz.* direnç **resistant** direnen, dayanıklı **resistor** rezistans, direnç
resolute /'rezılu:t/ s. azimli
resolution /rezı'lu:şın/ a. kararlılık, azim; önerge; çözüm
resolve /ri'zolv/ e. karar vermek; çözmek; ortadan kaldırmak
resonant /'rezınınt/ s. çınlayan, yankılanan **resonance** tınlama; *fiz.* seselim, rezonans
resort /ri'zo:t/ a. dinlence yeri, mesire ☆ e. sık sık uğramak, gitmek
resound /ri'zaund/ e. çınlamak, yankılanmak **resounding** çınlayan, yankılanan; çok büyük
resource /ri'zo:s, ri'so:s/ a. kaynak, zenginlik; çare; beceriklilik **resourceful** becerikli, açıkgöz
respect /ri'spekt/ a. saygı; münasebet; bakım; ç. selamlar, saygılar ☆ e. saygı göstermek **in respect of** -e gelince **with respect to** ile ilgili olarak; göre; -e gelince
respectable /ri'spektıbıl/ s. saygıdeğer; epey, oldukça
respectful /ri'spektfıl/ s. saygılı
respective /ri'spektiv/ s. her biri, kendi **respectively** anılan sıraya göre, biri . . . öteki . . .
respiration /respi'reyşın/ a. solunum
respite /'respit, 'respayt/ a. mola, soluklanma
resplendent /ri'splendınt/ s. parlak, pırıl pırıl, görkemli, göz kamaştırıcı
respond /ri'spond/ e. yanıt vermek, ya-

nıtlamak; **(by/with)** karşılık vermek **respond to** sonucu olarak iyiye gitmek
response /ri'spons/ a. yanıt; karşılık
responsibility /risponsı'biliti/ a. sorumluluk
responsible /ri'sponsıbıl/ s. **(for/to)** -den sorumlu; sorumluluk gerektiren; güvenilir
responsive /ri'sponsiv/ s. karşılık veren
rest /rest/ a. dinlenme; rahat, huzur; *müz.* durak ☆ e. dinlenmek; dayanmak, yaslanmak; dayamak, yaslamak **restful** dinlendirici **restless** yerinde duramayan, kıpır kıpır
rest /rest/ a. arta kalan, artık; diğerleri, ötekiler
restaurant /'restront/ a. lokanta
restitution /resti'tyu:şın/ a. iade, sahibine geri verme
restive /'restiv/ s. dik kafalı, inatçı
restoration /restı'reyşın/ a. onarım, yenileme, restorasyon
restorative /ri'sto:rıtiv/ s. güçlendiren, sağlık veren
restore /ri'sto:/ e. geri vermek; onarmak, yenilemek; yeniden canlandırmak
restrain /ri'streyn/ e. tutmak, alıkoymak, engellemek; sınırlamak, bastırmak **restrained** kontrollü **restraint** kendini tutma
restrict /ri'strikt/ e. sınırlamak, kısıtlamak **restriction** sınırlama **restrictive** sınırlayıcı
result /ri'zalt/ a. sonuç ☆ e. **(from)** meydana gelmek, çıkmak, doğmak; **(in)** ile sonuçlanmak **as a result (of)** yüzünden, nedeniyle **resultant** sonucu olan
résumé /'rezyumey, 'reyzyumey/ a. özet; özgeçmiş
resurrection /rezı'rekşın/ a. yenileme, canlanma
retail /'ri:teyl/ e. perakende satmak; **(at)** perakende olarak ☆ a. perakende satış **retailer** perakendeci
retain /ri'teyn/ e. alıkoymak, tutmak
retaliate /ri'telieyt/ e. misillemede bulunmak

retard /ri'ta:d/ e. geciktirmek, yavaşlatmak

retarded /ri'ta:did/ s. (çocuk) yavaş gelişen, geri zekâlı

retention /ri'tenşın/ a. (akılda, vb.) tutma

reticent /'retisınt/ s. suskun, ağzı sıkı

retina /'retinı/ a. retina, ağkatman

retinue /'retinyu:/ a. maiyet, heyet

retire /ri'tayı/ e. (geri) çekilmek; emekliye ayrılmak, emekli olmak; emekliye
ayırmak **retired** emekli **retirement**
emeklilik **retiring** çekingen, içine kapanık

retort /ri'to:t/ e. sert yanıt vermek ☆ a.
sert yanıt, karşılık; *kim.* imbik

retouch /ri:'taç/ e. rötuş yapmak

retrace /ri'treys, ri:'treys/ e. tekrarlamak, geriye/kaynağına gitmek

retreat /ri'tri:t/ a. geri çekilme; *ask.* ricat ☆ e. geri çekilmek

retribution /retri'byu:şın/ a. ceza

retrograde /'retrıgreyd/ s. gerileyen

retrospect /'retrıspekt/ a. geçmişe bakış **in retrospect** geçmişe bakıldığın-
da **retrospective** geçmişle ilgili; *huk.*
önceki olayları kapsayan

return /ri'tö:n/ e. dönmek, geri gelmek;
geri vermek, iade etmek; geri çevirmek; karşılık vermek ☆ a. dönüş; geri gönderme; seçim; karşılık **by return** ilk postayla **in return (for)** -e karşılık, karşılığında **return ticket** gidiş--
dönüş bileti

reunion /ri:'yu:niın/ a. yeniden bir araya gelme

revalue /ri:'velyu:/ e. (bir ülke parası-
nın) değerini yükseltmek

revel /'revıl/ e. eğlenmek, âlem yapmak; **(in)** -den haz duymak ☆ a. eğlence, cümbüş

revelation /revı'leyşın/ a. açığa vurma,
ifşa

revenge /ri'venc/ a. öç, intikam ☆ e.
-in öcünü almak

revenue /'revinyu:/ a. gelir, hükümetin
vergi geliri

reverberate /ri'vö:bıreyt/ e. yankılanmak

revere /ri'viı/ e. derin saygı göstermek

reverence /'revırıns/ a. derin saygı

reverend /'revırınd/ s. (papaz) saygıdeğer, muhterem, sayın, aziz

reverent /'revırınt/ s. saygılı

reversal /ri'vö:sıl/ a. ters dönme

reverse /ri'vö:s/ s. ters, arka, aksi; karşıt, zıt ☆ e. ters çevirmek; baş aşağı
çevirmek; geri gitmek; geri hareket ettirmek ☆ a. ters taraf, ters yüz; zıt,
zıttı, tersi; terslik; başarısızlık; geri vites

revert /ri'vö:t/ e. **(to)** yeniden dönmek

review /ri'vyu/ a. gözden geçirme, inceleme; eleştiri, dergi ☆ e. gözden
geçirmek, yeniden incelemek; eleştirmek; *ask.* teftiş etmek

revise /ri'vayz/ e. gözden geçirip düzeltmek; (görüş, vb.) değiştirmek; *İİ.*
(ders) tekrarlamak, bir daha gözden
geçirmek **revision** gözden geçirip düzeltme; tekrar

revive /ri'vayv/ e. canlandırmak; canlanmak **revival** yeniden canlanma

revoke /ri'vouk/ e. geri almak, geçersiz
kılmak

revolt /ri'voult/ e. **(against)** başkaldırmak, isyan etmek ☆ a. başkaldırma,
ayaklanma, isyan

revolution /revı'lu:şın/ a. ihtilal, devrim
revolutionary devrimci **revolutionize**
-de devrim yaratmak

revolve /ri'volv/ e. dönmek; döndürmek

revolver /ri'volvı/ a. tabanca

revue /ri'vyu:/ a. revü

revulsion /ri'valşın/ a. (düşüncelerde)
ani değişiklik, sapma

reward /ri'wo:d/ e. ödül vermek ☆ a.
ödül

rewrite /ri:'rayt/ e. yeniden yazmak

rhapsody /'repsıdi/ a, *müz.* rapsodi

rheumatism /'ru:mıtizım/ a, *hek.* romatizma

rhinoceros /ray'nosırıs/ a, *hayb.* gergedan

rhyme /raym/ a. uyak, kafiye ☆ e. ile
uyak oluşturmak

rhythm /'ridım/ a. ritim; vezin **rhythmic**
ritmik

rib /rib/ a, *anat.* kaburga kemiği

ribbon /'ribın/ a. kurdele; şerit

rice /rays/ *a, bitk.* pirinç; pilav
rich /riç/ *s.* zengin; bitek, verimli, bereketli; (yemek) yağlı, ağır; *kon.* gülünç, komik **the rich** zenginler **riches** varlık, zenginlik, servet **richness** zenginlik
rickets /'rikits/ *a.* kemik hastalığı, raşitizm
rickety /'rikiti/ *s.* zayıfça tutturulmuş, çürük
rid /rid/ *e.* **rid** /rid/ **(of)** -den kurtarmak, temizlemek **get rid of** -den kurtulmak, -den yakasını sıyırmak, başından atmak
riddle /'ridıl/ *a.* bilmece; kalbur ☆ *e.* kalburdan geçirmek, elemek; **(with)** delik deşik etmek
ride /rayd/ *e.* **rode** /roud/, **ridden** /'ridın/ (at, bisiklet, motosiklet, vb.) sürmek, binmek; ata binmek; **(in)** yolculuk etmek ☆ *a.* gezinti, tur **rider** binici, atlı, sürücü
ridge /ric/ *a.* sırt, bayır; dağ sırası
ridicule /'ridikyu:l/ *a.* eğlenme, alay ☆ *e.* ile alay etmek, gülmek
ridiculous /ri'dikyulıs/ *s.* gülünç, saçma
rifle /'rayfıl/ *e.* soymak, yağma etmek ☆ *a.* tüfek
rift /rift/ *a.* yarık, çatlak
rig /rig/ *e.* (gemi) donatmak; -e hile karıştırmak ☆ *a.* (gemi) arma, donanım; *kon.* kılık kıyafet; alet
right /rayt/ *s.* doğru; haklı; gereken, aranan; dik; sağ ☆ *be.* doğru (olarak); doğruca, tümüyle ☆ *a.* hak; yetki; doğru, gerçek; sağ ☆ *e.* doğrultmak, düzeltmek **all right** tamam, olur, hay hay; uygun **right away** hemen, birazdan **right here** tam burada/buraya **by rights** hakka bakılırsa **right-hand** sağdaki **right-handed** sağ elle kullanılan **right-minded** doğru düşünceli **rightist** sağcı **rightly** doğru olarak; haklı olarak
righteous /'rayçıs/ *s.* dürüst, doğru
rightful /'raytfıl/ *s.* yasal, meşru
rightly /'raytli/ *be.* doğru olarak; gereği gibi, hakkıyla; *kon.* kesinlikle
rigid /'ricid/ *s.* sert, katı
rigorous /'rigırıs/ *s.* sert, şiddetli

rigour /'rigı/ *a.* sertlik, katılık
rim /rim/ *a.* kenar; çerçeve
rind /raynd/ *a.* kabuk
ring /ring/ *e.* **rang** /reng/, **rung** /rang/ (zil, vb.) çalmak, çınlatmak; çınlamak; çember içine almak ☆ *a.* halka; yüzük; çember; zil sesi; hale **give sb a ring** -e telefon etmek **ring off** telefonu kapatmak **ring sb up** -e telefon etmek
ringleader /'ringli:dı/ *a.* çete başı, elebaşı
ringlet /'ringlit/ *a.* saç lülesi
rink /rink/ *a.* paten alanı, buz alanı
rinse /rins/ *e.* çalkalamak; durulamak
riot /'rayıt/ *a.* ayaklanma, isyan; kargaşa ☆ *e.* ayaklanmak, isyan etmek; kargaşa yaratmak **riotous** isyan çıkaran, huzuru bozan; gürültülü
rip /rip/ *e.* yırtmak; yırtılmak; yarmak ☆ *a.* yarık, yırtık, sökük ☆ *a.* anafor, girdap
ripe /rayp/ *s.* olmuş, olgun
ripen /'raypın/ *e.* olgunlaşmak
ripple /'ripıl/ *a.* küçük dalga; şapırtı, şarıltı
rise /rayz/ *e.* **rose** /rouz/, **risen** /'rizın/ doğmak; yükselmek, çıkmak; artmak ☆ *a.* doğuş, yükseliş; artış, çoğalma; çıkış **give rise to** -e neden olmak **rise against** -e başkaldırmak
risen /'rizın/ *bkz.* rise
risk /risk/ *a.* tehlike, risk; riziko ☆ *e.* tehlikeye atmak; göze almak **at one's own risk** tehlikeyi göze almış **risky** riskli, rizikolu
rite /rayt/ *a.* (dini) töre, âdet **ritual** dini törenle ilgili
rival /'rayvıl/ *a, s.* rakip ☆ *e.* -e rakip olmak, ile rekabet etmek **rivalry** rekabet, rakiplik
river /'rivı/ *a.* nehir, ırmak
rivet /'rivit/ *a.* perçin çivisi
road /roud/ *a.* yol, cadde
roam /roum/ *e.* gezinmek, dolanmak
roar /ro:/ *e.* gürlemek; kükremek ☆ *a.* kükreme; gürleme
roast /roust/ *e.* kızartmak; kavurmak ☆ *a.* kızartma; kızartma et
rob /rob/ *e.* soymak; çalmak **robber**

soyguncu **robbery** soygun
robe /roub/ *a.* cüppe; kaftan; bornoz
robin /'robin/ *a, hayb.* kızılgerdan
robot /'roubot/ *a.* robot
rock /rok/ *e.* sallamak; sallanmak; şaşırtmak, sarsmak ☆ *a.* kaya; kayalık **rocking chair** sallanan sandalye
rocket /'rokit/ *a.* roket, füze
rod /rod/ *a.* değnek, çubuk; rod
rode /roud/ *bkz.* ride
roe /rou/ *a.* karaca; balık yumurtası
rogue /roug/ *a.* namussuz, hilekâr
role /roul/ *a.* rol
roll /roul/ *a.* tomar, top, rulo; sandviç ekmeği; silindir, merdane; liste, defter, sicil, kayıt; gürültü; yuvarlama ☆ *e.* yuvarlamak; yuvarlanmak; sarmak, dürmek; silindirle düzlemek **roll call** yoklama **roll in** yığınla gelmek, yağmak **roll up** gelmek, varmak
roller /'roulı/ *a.* silindir, merdane
rolling /'rouling/ *s.* (arazi) inişli çıkışlı **rolling pin** oklava
Roman /'roumın/ *s.* eski Roma'ya ilişkin **Roman numerals** Romen rakamları
romance /rou'mens, rı'mens/ *a.* aşk macerası
romantic /rou'mentik, rı'mentik/ *s.* romantik **romanticism** romantizm
romp /romp/ *a.* sıçrayıp oynama, hoplayıp zıplama
roof /ru:f/ *a.* çatı, dam
rook /ruk/ *a.* (satranç) kale; *hayb.* ekinkargası; hileci, üçkâğıtçı
room /ru:m, rum/ *a.* oda; yer, boş yer; ç. daire, apartman **roommate** oda arkadaşı **roomy** geniş, ferah
roost /ru:st/ *a.* tünek
rooster /'ru:stı/ *a, Aİ.* horoz
root /ru:t/ *a.* kök; köken ☆ *e.* kök salmak, kökleşmek
rope /roup/ *a.* ip, halat ☆ *e.* iple/halatla bağlamak
rosary /'rouzıri/ *a.* tespih
rose /rouz/ *bkz.* rise; *a.* gül
rosé /'rouzey/ *a.* pembe şarap, roze şarabı
rosette /rou'zet/ *a.* rozet
rosemary /'rouzmıri/ *a, bitk.* biberiye

rose-water /'rouzwo:tı/ *a.* gülsuyu
rosy /'rouzi/ *s.* gül renkli, pembe, pembemsi; umut verici, parlak
rot /rot/ *e.* çürümek ☆ *a.* çürük
rotate /rou'teyt/ *e.* (bir eksen üzerinde) dönmek; döndürmek **rotation** dönme
rotor /'routı/ *a.* döneç, rotor
rotten /'rotın/ *s.* çürük, bozuk
rouge /ru:j/ *a.* allık
rough /raf/ *s.* pürüzlü, pürtüklü; engebeli; taşlık; kaba dokunmuş ☆ *be.* kabaca ☆ *e.* taslağını yapmak **roughly** kaba bir biçimde; aşağı yukarı
roulette /ru:'let/ *a.* rulet
round /raund/ *s.* yuvarlak ☆ *be.* etrafa, etrafta ☆ *ilg.* çevresinde, çevresine; her tarafına ☆ *a.* yuvarlak şey, daire; *ask.* devriye; (boks) raund; *hek.* vizite ☆ *e.* yuvarlaklaştırmak; dönmek **a round dozen** tam bir düzine **go/make the rounds** sırasıyla ziyaret etmek **round off** bitirmek, tamamlamak **round up** bir araya toplamak
roundabout /'raundıbaut/ *a, İİ.* atlıkarınca ☆ *s.* dolambaçlı, dolaylı
round-trip /raund'trip/ *s, Aİ.* (bilet) gidiş-dönüş
rouse /rauz/ *e.* uyandırmak
rout /raut/ *a.* bozgun
route /ru:t/ *a.* rota, yol
routine /ru:'ti:n/ *a.* alışkanlık haline gelmiş şey, âdet; usül
row /rou/ *a.* sıra, dizi; kavga, patırtı, hır; kürek çekme; sandal gezintisi ☆ *e.* kürek çekerek götürmek; kavga etmek, atışmak **rowing** kürek çekme
rowdy /'raudi/ *s.* zorba, kaba
royal /'royıl/ *s.* krala/krallığa ait
royalist kralcı
royalty /'royılti/ *a.* krallık; telif hakkı ücreti
rub /rab/ *e.* ovmak, ovalamak; sürtmek, sürtünmek ☆ *a.* ovma, sürtme **rub along** iyi geçinmek **rub down** aşındırmak; kurulamak **rub in** ovarak yedirmek **rub out** silmek
rubber /'rabı/ *a.* lastik, kauçuk; silgi
rubbish /'rabiş/ *a.* süprüntü, çöp; *kon.* saçmalık, saçma, zırva
rubble /'rabıl/ *a.* moloz

ruby /'ru:bi/ *a.* yakut
rucksack /'raksek/ *a.* sırt çantası
rudder /'radı/ *a.* dümen; kılavuz, rehber
ruddy /'radi/ *s.* (yüz) sağlıklı, pembe
rude /ru:d/ *s.* terbiyesiz, kaba
ruff /raf/ *a.* kırmalı yaka
ruffian /'rafiın/ *a.* kötü/kaba adam
ruffle /'rafıl/ *e.* buruşturmak, kırıştırmak; bozmak; sinirlendirmek
rug /rag/ *a.* küçük halı, kilim; battaniye, örtü
rugged /'ragid/ *s.* engebeli; pürüzlü
ruin /'ru:in/ *a.* yıkılma, yıkım, yıkıntı ç. kalıntılar, ören ☆ *e.* mahvetmek, harap etmek
rule /ru:l/ *a.* kural, ilke; usul, yol, yöntem, âdet; yönetim ☆ *e.* yönetmek; hüküm sürmek; cetvelle çizmek **as a rule** genelde, çoğunlukla **rule out** çıkarmak, silmek **ruler** hükümdar; cetvel **ruling** yargı, hüküm
rum /ram/ *a, İİ.* rom; *Aİ.* alkollü içki
rumble /'rambıl/ *a.* gürleme ☆ *e.* gürlemek
ruminate /'ru:mineyt/ *e, hayb.* geviş getirmek
rummage /'ramic/ *e.* altüst edip aramak
rumour /'ru:mı/ *a.* söylenti
rump /ramp/ *a.* sağrı; but, sığır butu
rumple /'rampıl/ *e.* buruşturmak, kırıştırmak; karmakarışık etmek
run /ran/ *e.* ran /ren/, run /ran/ koşmak; işlemek, çalışmak; çalıştırmak, işletmek; yarışmak; kaçmak ☆ *a.* koşma; koşu; oynama/gösterim süresi; çorap kaçığı; çeşit **run across** -e rastlamak **run after** peşinden koşmak **runaway** kaçak **run away with** alıp götürmek, çalmak, aşırmak; birlikte kaçmak **run into** -e rastlamak; çarpmak çarpışmak; girmek, düşmek **run low** azalmak **runner-up** (koşu, yarış, vb.) ikinci gelen kimse/takım **run off** kaçmak; akıtmak; yayınlamak, basmak **run on** devam etmek, sürmek; (zaman) geçmek **run out of** -i tüketmek, bitirmek; bitmek, tükenmek, -siz kalmak **run over** çiğnemek, ezmek; göz

gezdirmek
rung /rang/ *bkz.* ring
runner /'ranı/ *a.* koşucu; haberci; ulak; kaçakçı
runway /'ranwey/ *a.* uçak pisti
rupture /'rapçı/ *a.* kırılma, kopma, yırtılma; *hek.* fıtık
rural /'ruırıl/ *s.* kırsal
rush /raş/ *e.* acele etmek; koşmak, seğirtmek; acele ettirmek; aceleye getirmek ☆ *a.* acele; hamle, hücum, saldırış; rağbet, istek; saz, hasırotu **the rush hours** trafiğin yoğun olduğu saatler
rusk /rask/ *a.* peksimet
rust /rast/ *a.* pas; pas rengi ☆ *e.* paslanmak; paslandırmak **rusty** paslı
rustic /'rastik/ *s.* kırlara, köylere ilişkin
rustle /'rasıl/ *a.* hışırtı ☆ *e.* hışırdamak
rut /rat/ *a.* tekerlek izi
ruthless /'ru:tlis/ *s.* acımasız
rye /ray/ *a, bitk.* çavdar **rye bread** çavdar ekmeği

S

sable /'seybıl/ *a, hayb.* samur
sabotage /'sebıta:j/ *a.* baltalama, sabotaj **saboteur** sabotajcı
sabre /'seybı/ *a, İİ.* süvari kılıcı
sack /sek/ *a.* çuval, torba; *kon.* işten kovulma; yağma, çapul ☆ *e, kon.* işten kovmak, sepetlemek
sacrament /'sekrımınt/ *a.* (Hıristiyanlıkta) dinsel tören
sacred /'seykrid/ *s.* dinsel; kutsal
sacrifice /'sekrifays/ *a.* kurban; özveri, fedakârlık ☆ *e.* kurban etmek; feda etmek, gözden çıkarmak
sacrilege /'sekrilic/ *a.* kutsal kişi ya da şeylere saygısızlık, küfür
sad /sed/ *s.* üzgün, üzüntülü, kederli; acıklı **sadly** üzüntüyle; ne yazık ki
sadden /'sedın/ *e.* üzmek; üzülmek
saddle /'sedıl/ *a.* eyer, semer; (bisiklet, vb.) sele; sırt ☆ *e.* eyerlemek **saddlebag** heybe

sadism /'seydizım/ a. sadizm **sadist** sadist

safari /sı'fa:ri/ a. safari

safe /seyf/ s. emin; emniyetli, güvenilir; tehlikesiz; sağlam ☆ a. (demir) kasa **safeguard** koruyucu şey **safety** güvenlik, emniyet **safety belt** emniyet kemeri **safety glass** dağılmaz cam **safety pin** çengelliiğne

sag /seg/ e. bel vermek, eğilmek, bükülmek, çökmek, sarkmak

saga /'sa:gı/ a. destan

sagacious /sı'geyşıs/ s. akıllı, sağ görülü

sage /seyc/ a, bitk. adaçayı; bilge

Sagittarius /seci'teıriıs/ a. Yay (burcu)

said /sed/ bkz. say; s. adı geçen, sözü edilen

sail /seyl/ a. yelken; deniz yolculuğu; yelkenli ☆ e. yelkenli, gemi, vb. ile gitmek; su üzerinde seyretmek **sailboard** rüzgâr sörfü **sailing** gemicilik; yelkencilik; deniz yolculuğu **sailor** denizci, gemici

saint /seynt/ a. aziz, ermiş

sake /seyk/ a. hatır **for God's sake** kon. Allah aşkına **for the sake of** -in hatırı için, -in uğruna; amacıyla

salad /'selıd/ a. salata

salami /sı'la:mi/ a. salam

salary /'selıri/ a. aylık, maaş

sale /seyl/ a. satış; indirimli satış; ucuzluk; talep, sürüm; mezat **for sale** satılık **on sale** satılık **sales talk** esnaf ağzı **salesclerk** Aİ. tezgâhtar **salesman** satıcı, satış memuru **saleswoman** satıcı, satış memuresi

saline /'seylayn/ s. tuzlu, tuzla ilgili

saliva /sı'layvı/ a. tükürük, salya **salivary glands** tükürük bezleri

salivate /'seliveyt/ e. tükürük salgılamak, ağzı salyalanmak

sallow /'selou/ s. (ten) soluk, sağlıksız

salmon /'semın/ a, hayb. som balığı

saloon /sı'lu:n/ a, Aİ. büyük araba; Aİ. bar, meyhane; İİ. salon bar

salt /so:lt/ a. tuz ☆ e. tuz katmak, tuzlamak **saltcellar** tuzluk **saltshaker** Aİ. tuzluk **saltwater** tuzlu suya ait, deniz suyuna ait **salty** tuzlu, tuzlanmış **salt**

lake tuz gölü

salutation /selyu'teyşın/ a. selamlama, selam

salute /sı'lu:t/ e. selamlamak, selam vermek ☆ a. selam; karşılama

salvage /'selvic/ a. kurtarma; kurtarılan mal ☆ e. (yangından, kazadan) kurtarmak

salvation /sel'veyşın/ a. kurtarma, kurtarılma; kurtuluş, selamet

salve /sa:v, selv/ a. merhem

salver /'selvı/ a. gümüş tepsi

same /seym/ s. aynı; benzer; tıpkısı **all the same, just the same** yine de **at the same time** aynı zamanda; bununla birlikte **It's all the same to me.** Benim için fark etmez. **same to you** kon. sana da, size de, aynen

samovar /'semıva:/ a. semaver

sample /'sa:mpıl/ a. örnek, model

samurai /'semuray/ a. Japon savaşçısı, samuray

sanatorium /senı'to:riım/ a. sanatoryum, sağlıkevi

sanctimonious /senkti'mouniıs/ s. yalancı sofu, dindarlık taslayan

sanction /'senkşın/ a. onay, onaylama, tasdik; yaptırım, ceza

sanctity /'senktiti/ a. kutsallık

sanctuary /'senkçuıri/ a. kutsal yer, tapınak; sığınak

sand /send/ a. kum; ç. kumsal, plaj **sandy** kumlu; (saç) kum rengi **sandbag** kum torbası **sandpaper** zımpara kâğıdı **sandstorm** kum fırtınası

sandal /'sendıl/ a. sandal, sandalet, burnu açık terlik

sandwich /'senwiç/ a. sandviç **sandwich board** sırta ve göğüse asılan reklam yaftası

sane /seyn/ s. aklı başında, akıllı

sanitary /'senitıri/ s. sağlıklı, sıhhi **sanitary napkin/towel** âdet bezi

sanitation /seni'teyşın/ a. sağlık koruma

sanity /'seniti/ a. akıl sağlığı

sap /sep/ a, bitk. besisuyu, özsu

sapphire /'sefayı/ a. gökyakut, safir

sarcasm /'sa:kezım/ a. acı alay **sarcastic** iğneleyici, alaylı

sardine /sa:'di:n/ *a, hayb.* sardalye
sash /seş/ *a.* kuşak; pencere çerçevesi
satan /'seytın/ *a.* şeytan
satchel /'seçıl/ *a.* sırtta taşınan okul çantası
satellite /'setilayt/ *a.* uydu
satiate /'seyşieyt/ *e.* doyurmak
satin /'setin/ *a.* saten, atlas
satire /'setayı/ *a, yaz.* taşlama, yergi, yerme, hiciv **satirical** yergili, hicivli
satisfaction /setis'fekşın/ *a.* memnuniyet, hoşnutluk; tatmin, doyum; tazmin, ödeme
satisfactory /setis'fektırı/ *s.* doyurucu, tatmin edici, yeterli, tatminkâr
satisfy /'setisfay/ *e.* tatmin etmek, doyurmak; memnun etmek, sevindirmek; yetmek; karşılamak
saturate /'seçıreyt/ *e, kim.* doyurmak
Saturday /'setıdi, 'setıdey/ *a.* cumartesi
Saturn /'setın/ *a.* Satürn
sauce /so:s/ *a.* salça, sos; *kon.* yüzsüzlük, arsızlık
saucepan /'so:spın/ *a.* kulplu tencere
saucer /'so:sı/ *a.* çay tabağı, fincan tabağı
sauna /'so:nı/ *a.* sauna
sausage /'sosic/ *a.* sucuk, sosis
savage /'sevic/ *s.* yabani, vahşi, yırtıcı **savagery** vahşilik, yabanıllık, yırtıcılık
savanna /sı'venı/ *a.* bozkır, savan
save /seyv/ *e.* kurtarmak; (para) biriktirmek; kaybını önlemek, kazandırmak
saving /'seyving/ *s.* tutumlu; koruyan ☆ *a.* kurtarma; ç. biriktirilen para, tasarruf ☆ *ilg.* -den başka **savings account** tasarruf hesabı
saviour /'seyviı/ *a.* kurtarıcı
savour /'seyvı/ *a.* tat, lezzet, çeşni; koku **savoury** lezzetli; hoş
saw /so:/ *bkz.* see
saw /so:/ *a.* testere, bıçkı ☆ *e.* testere ile kesmek, biçmek **sawdust** talaş **sawmill** bıçkı fabrikası **sawyern** bıçkıcı
saxophone /'seksıfoun/ *a.* saksofon
say /sey/ *e.* **said** /sed/ demek, söylemek **that is to say** yani, bu demek oluyor ki **they say** diyorlar ki **you don't say (so)** *kon.* Yok ya!, Hadi ya!

have one's say fikrini bildirmek
saying /'seying/ *a.* söz, özdeyiş, atasözü
scab /skeb/ *a.* yara kabuğu
scabbard /'skebıd/ *a.* (kılıç, vb.) kın
scabies /'skeybiz/ *a, hek.* uyuz
scaffold /'skefıld, 'skefould/ *a.* yapı iskelesi; darağacı
scald /sko:ld/ *e.* kaynar suyla haşlamak ☆ *a.* haşlanma sonucu oluşan yanık
scale /skeyl/ *a.* ölçek; ölçü, çap; derece; cetvel; *müz.* ıskala, gam; balık, vb. pulu; terazi gözü, kefe ☆ *e.* tırmanmak, çıkmak **scale up (down)** belli bir oranda büyütmek (küçültmek)
scales /skeylz/ *a.* terazi
scallop /'skolıp/ *a, hayb.* tarak
scalpel /'skelpıl/ *a, hek.* küçük bıçak, skalpel, bistüri
scamp /skemp/ *e.* hızla koşmak, kaçmak, seğirtmek
scan /sken/ *e.* incelemek; gözden geçirmek; *yaz.* dizeleri duraklara ayırmak
scandal /'skendıl/ *a.* skandal, rezalet; kara çalma, iftira, dedikodu **scandalous** rezil, utanılacak
scant /skent/ *s.* az, kıt **scanty** az, kıt
scapegoat /'skeypgout/ *a.* başkasının suçunu yüklenen kimse, şamar oğlanı, abalı
scar /ska:/ *a.* yara izi ☆ *e.* yara izi bırakmak
scarce /skeıs/ *s.* seyrek, az bulunur, kıt **scarcely** hemen hiç, pek az, güçlükle **scarcity** azlık, kıtlık
scare /skeı/ *a.* ani korku ☆ *e.* korkutmak; **(off/away)** korkutup kaçırmak **scarecrow** bostan korkuluğu
scarf /ska:f/ *a.* eşarp, atkı, kaşkol
scarlet /'ska:lit/ *a, s.* al, kırmızı **scarlet fever** *hek.* kızıl
scary /'skeıri/ *s, kon.* korkutucu, ürkütücü, korkunç
scathing /'skeyding/ *s.* sert, kırıcı
scatter /'sketı/ *e.* saçmak, serpmek, dağıtmak
scavenger /'skevincı/ *a.* leş yiyen hayvan; çöp karıştıran kimse
scenario /si'na:riou/ *a.* senaryo
scene /si:n/ *a.* sahne; olay yeri; sahne,

tablo; dekor; manzara **behind the scenes** perde arkasından, gizlice **make a scene** olay/rezalet çıkarmak **scenery** görünüm, manzara; sahne dekoru

scent /sent/ *a.* güzel koku; *İİ.* parfüm ☆ *e.* kokusunu almak; sezmek

sceptic /'skeptik/ *a.* kuşkucu **sceptical** şüpheci, kuşkulu

sceptre /'septı/ *a.* hükümdar asası

schedule /'şedyu:l/ *a.* program; liste; cetvel; *Aİ.* (tren, otobüs, vb.) tarife **on schedule** planlanan saatte, beklenen saatte **scheduled flight** tarifeli uçuş

schema /'ski:mı/ *a.* şema **schematic** şematik, sistemli

scheme /ski:m/ *a.* entrika, dolap, dalavere; plan, proje, tasarı

schizophrenia /skitsou'fri:nıı, skitsı'fri:nıı/ *a, ruhb.* şizofreni **schizophrenic** şizofren

scholar /'skolı/ *a.* bilgin; burslu öğrenci; *kon.* tahsilli kimse **scholarship** bilginlik; burs

school /sku:l/ *a.* okul; ekol; fakülte, yüksekokul; *Aİ.* üniversite **schoolboy** erkek öğrenci **schoolchildren** okul çocukları **schoolgirl** kız öğrenci **schooling** eğitim, öğretim **schoolmaster** *İİ.* erkek öğretmen **schoolmate** okul arkadaşı **schoolmistress** *İİ.* bayan öğretmen **schoolwork** dersler, okul çalışmaları **school report** karne

science /'sayıns/ *a.* bilim, ilim; fen, teknik **science fiction** bilimkurgu **scientific** bilimsel **scientist** bilgin, bilim adamı

scissors /'sizız/ *a.* makas

scoff /skof/ *e.* alay etmek, gülmek; *kon.* hapur hupur yemek

scold /skould/ *e.* azarlamak, paylamak **scolding** azar, paylama

scone /skon, skoun/ *a.* bir tür yağlı çörek

scoop /sku:p/ *a.* kepçe; kürek; (gazetecilikte) haber atlatma ☆ *e.* kepçeyle çıkarmak; (gazetecilikte) haber atlatmak

scooter /'sku:tı/ *a.* küçük motosiklet, skuter; trotinet

scope /skoup/ *a.* anlama yeteneği; hareket serbestliği; fırsat; faaliyet alanı

scorch /sko:ç/ *e.* (güneş, vb.) yakmak, kavurmak; alazlamak

score /sko:/ *a.* çizgi, kertik, çentik; sıyrık; sayı, puan, skor; sebep; *müz.* partisyon ☆ *e.* (sayı, puan) kazanmak, almak; (gol) atmak; çentmek **scoreboard** puan tahtası, skorbord **scorer** *sp.* golcü, skorer; puanları kaydeden kimse

scorn /sko:n/ *a.* küçümseme ☆ *e.* hor görmek, tepeden bakmak **scornful** hor gören, küçümseyen

Scorpio /'sko:piou/ *a.* Akrep burcu

scorpion /'sko:pıın/ *a, hayb.* akrep

scoundrel /'skaundrıl/ *a.* alçak, kötü adam, hergele

scour /skauı/ *e.* (**down/out/off**) ovarak temizlemek; süratle köşe bucak aramak

scourge /skö:c/ *a.* kırbaç, kamçı; bela, musibet, felaket

scout /skaut/ *a.* izci; keşif eri, öncü; gözcü

scowl /skaul/ *e.* kaşlarını çatmak ☆ *a.* kaş çatma

scrabble /'skrebıl/ *e, kon.* (**about**) eşeleyip aramak; kargacık burgacık yazmak

scramble /'skrembıl/ *e.* tırmanmak; çekişmek, kapışmak; (yumurta) çırpıp yağ ve sütle pişirmek ☆ *a.* tırmanma; kapışma, dalaşma

scrap /skrep/ *a.* kırıntı; döküntü; ıskarta ☆ *e.* ıskartaya çıkarmak, atmak; *kon.* kapışmak, dalaşmak **scrapbook** koleksiyon defteri, albüm

scrape /skreyp/ *e.* kazımak; sıyırmak; sürtünmek ☆ *a.* kazıma; sürtme; sıyrık, çizik; *kon.* müşkül durum **scraper** raspa; greyder

scratch /skreç/ *e.* tırmalamak; çizmek; kaşımak; (listeden) çıkarmak ☆ *a.* tırmık, çizik, sıyrık; cızırtı; kaşıma; karalama **from scratch** *kon.* sıfırdan başlayarak **up to scratch** *kon.* kaliteli, iyi **scratchy** (plak, kayıt, vb.) cızırtılı

scrawl /skro:l/ *e.* karalamak, çızıktırmak ☆ *e.* kargacık burgacık yazı

433   **secrecy**

scream /skri:m/ e. çığlık atmak, feryat
etmek ☆ a. feryat, çığlık
screech /skri:ç/ a. çığlık ☆ e. bağırmak
screen /skri:n/ a. perde; ekran; paravana; bölme; pano; ocak siperi; kalbur,
elek ☆ e. gizlemek, korumak; elemek, seçmek **screenplay** senaryo
screw /skru:/ a. vida; pervane, uskur ☆
e. vidalamak; çevirmek, çevirerek sıkıştırmak **screwdriver** tornavida
scribble /'skribıl/ e. karalamak, çiziktirmek ☆ a. karalama, çiziktirme
scribe /skrayb/ a. yazıcı
script /skript/ a. el yazısı; alfabe, abece; senaryo **script writer** (radyo, TV)
oyun yazarı
scripture /'skripçı/ a. Kutsal Kitap
scroll /skroul/ a. (kâğıt) tomar
scrub /skrab/ a, bitk. bodur çalılık, fundalık ☆ e. ovarak yıkamak, fırçalaya-
rak temizlemek
scruple /'skru:pıl/ a. vicdan; bilinç ☆
e. vicdanı el vermemek; kaçınmak
scrupulous /'skru:pyulıs/ s. vicdanlı,
adil; dikkatli, titiz
scrutinize /'skru:tinayz/ e. iyice incelemek, irdelemek
scrutiny /'skru:tini/ a. dikkatli inceleme,
araştırma
scuba /'skyu:bı/ a. oksijen tüplü dalma
aygıtı
scuff /skaf/ e. sürtmek, çizmek
scuffle /'skafıl/ e. itişip kakışmak
sculptor /'skalptı/ a. yontucu, heykeltıraş
sculpture /'skalpçı/ a. yontuculuk, heykeltıraşlık, heykel sanatı; yontu, heykel ☆ e. yontusunu yapmak, oymak
scum /skam/ a. kir tabakası
scurry /'skari/ e. acele etmek, seğirtmek
scurvy /'skö:vi/ a, hek. iskorbüt
scythe /sayd/ a. tırpan
sea /si:/ a. deniz at sea denizde, gemide by sea deniz yoluyla sea lion deniz aslanı sea urchin denizkestanesi
seabed deniz dibi seacoast sahil sea-
food yenilebilen deniz ürünü seagull
martı seahorse denizatı seaman de-

nizci; gemici seaport liman seashell
deniz hayvanı kabuğu seashore de-
niz kıyısı seasick deniz tutmuş sea-
side deniz kıyısı seaurchin deniz kes-
tanesi seaward denize doğru seaweed yosun, deniz sazı
seal /si:l/ a. mühür, damga; conta;
hayb. fok, ayıbalığı ☆ e. mühürlemek; damgalamak; onaylamak
seam /si:m/ a. dikiş yeri; ek yeri
sear /sıı/ e. yakmak, kavurmak, dağlamak
search /sö:ç/ e. araştırmak; -nın üstünü
aramak; sondalamak ☆ a. arama,
araştırma in search of -in arayışı içinde searching inceden inceye araştı-
ran, sıkı searchlight ışıldak
season /'si:zın/ a. mevsim; sezon; dönem; zaman ☆ e. (with) yemeğe baharat koymak; (odunu) kurutmak in
season (meyve, sebze) tam mevsimi,
olgun out of season (meyve, sebze)
mevsimsiz, zamansız season ticket
abonman bileti seasonal mevsimlik
seasoning (tuz, biber gibi) yemeğe
tat veren şey
seat /si:t/ a. oturacak yer, iskemle, koltuk; köşk, konak, yalı; (tiyatro) koltuk;
makat ☆ e. oturtmak; yerleştirmek
seat belt emniyet kemeri
secateurs /'sekıtö:z/ a, İİ. bahçıvan makası
secede /si'si:d/ e. üyelikten çekilmek,
ayrılmak secession /si'seşın/ üyelikten çekilme, ayrılma
seclude /si'klu:d/ e. inzivaya çekmek,
başkalarından uzak tutmak secluded
münzevi; gözden uzak seclusion /-'-
jın/ inziva
second /'sekınd/ s. ikinci; diğer, öteki
☆ a. saniye; yardımcı, muavin; tapon mal on second thought iyice dü-
şündükten sonra second-best ikinci
kalite second-class ikinci sınıf; ikinci
mevki second-hand elden düşme,
kullanılmış second-rate ikinci derecede secondly ikinci olarak
secondary /'sekındıri/ s. ikinci derecede, ikincil secondary school ortaokul •
secrecy /'si:krisi/ a. sır saklama; gizlilik

secret /'si:krit/ s. gizli; saklı ☆ a. gizli şey, giz, sır in secret gizlice keep a secret sır saklamak secret agent gizli ajan

secretary /'sekrıtıri/ a. sekreter, yazıcı, yazman; bakan secretarial /sekrı'teırııl/ sekreterlikle ilgili secretariat /sekrı'teırııt/ sekreterlik, sekreterya

secrete /si'kri:t/ e, biy. salgılamak, salmak; gizlemek

secretition /'si:krişın/ a. salgılama; salgı; gizleme

sect /sekt/ a. tarikat, mezhep

section /'sekşın/ a. parça, bölüm; bölge; kesim; mat. kesit sectional bölgesel

sector /'sektı/ a. sektör; kesim; daire dilimi, kesme; ask. bölge

secular /'sekyulı/ s. laik; dünyevi

secure /si'kyuı/ s. emin, güvenli, sağlam, kopmaz

security /si'kyuıriti/ a. emniyet, güvenlik; teminat, güvence securities menkul kıymetler, senetler

sedate /si'deyt/ s. sakin, ağırbaşlı

sedative /'sedıtiv/ s, hek. sakinleştirici

sedentary /'sedıntıri/ s. oturularak yapılan; bir yere yerleşmiş, yerleşik

sediment /'sedimınt/ a. tortu, çöküntü

seduce /si'dyu:s/ e. baştan çıkarmak, ayartmak; iğfal etmek seduction baştan çıkarma; iğfal seductive baştan çıkarıcı

see /si:/ e. saw /so:/, seen /si:n/ görmek; anlamak, kavramak; ziyaret etmek; görüşmek I see anlıyorum let me see bir düşüneyim, bir bakayım see about ile ilgilenmek, uğraşmak see off yolcu etmek, uğurlamak, geçirmek see out bitirmek, sonunu getirmek see over gözden geçirmek see to ilgilenmek, bakmak seeing that -dığı için, -e göre

seed /si:d/ a, bitk. tohum ☆ e. tohum ekmek seedbed fidelik seedling fide

seek /si:k/ e. sought /so:t/ aramak, araştırmak; sormak; istemek

seem /si:m/ e. görünmek, gözükmek; gibi gelmek it seems that gibi görünüyor seeming görünüşte, sözde

seemly /'si:mli/ s. uygun, yakışır, münasip

seep /si:p/ e. (sıvı) sızmak

seesaw /'si:so:/ a. tahterevalli

segment /'segmınt/ a. parça, dilim

segregate /'segrigeyt/ e. ayırmak segregation ayrım; toplumsal kopma

seismic /'sayzmik/ s. depreme ilişkin

seismograph /'sayzmıgra:f/ a. depremyazar, sismograf

seize /si:z/ e. tutmak, kapmak; el koymak; gasp etmek; tutuklamak

seizure /'si:jı/ a. el koyma; yakalama; zapt; hek. ani nöbet, kriz

seldom /'seldım/ be. nadiren, seyrek

select /si'lekt/ e. seçmek, seçip ayırmak ☆ a. seçme, seçkin selection seçme; seçme parçalar selective ayıran, seçici selector seçici

self- /self/ önek kendi, öz self-abuse kendini aşağılama; mastürbasyon self-confident kendinden emin, kendine güvenen self-contained ağzı sıkı; (daire) müstakil, bağımsız; kendine hâkim olan self-control kendine hâkim olma, özdenetim self-defence kendini savunma, meşru müdafaa self-determination bir ulusun kendi yönetim biçimine kendisinin karar vermesi self-employed serbest meslek sahibi self-evident apaçık, ortada self-important kendini beğenmiş self-interest kişisel çıkar, bencillik self-possessed temkinli, serinkanlı self-reliance özgüven self-respect izzetinefis, özsaygı self-righteous kendini beğenmiş self-service selfservis self-supporting kendi kendini geçindiren self-willed inatçı, dik kafalı

selfish /'selfiş/ s. bencil selfishness bencillik

sell /sel/ e. sold /sould/ satmak; satılmak sell off elden çıkarmak, satıp savmak sell out (bilet, vb.) hepsini satmak seller satıcı, bayi best-seller en çok satan kitap, vb.

sellotape /'selıteyp/ a. seloteyp

semantic /si'mentik/ s. anlamsal, anlambilimsel semantics anlambilim

semen /'si:mın/ a. meni, bel

semester /si'mestı/ *a.* dönem, devre, sömestr, yarıyıl

semi /'semi/ *önek* yarı, yarım **semicircle** yarım daire **semicolon** noktalı virgül **semiconductor** yarı iletken **semidetached** bir duvarı yandaki eve bitişik **semifinal** yarıfinal

seminar /'semina:/ *a.* seminer

Semitic /si'mitik/ *s.* Samilerle ilgili, Sami

senate /'senit/ *a.* senato **senator** senatör

send /send/ *e.* sent /sent/ göndermek, yollamak **send away** (başka bir yere) göndermek **send for** çağırmak, getirtmek **send off** uğurlamak; yolcu etmek **send out** dağıtmak, göndermek **sender** gönderen

senile /'si:nayl/ *s.* bunak

senior /'si:niı/ *s.* yaşça daha büyük; kıdemli ☆ *a.* daha yaşlı olan kişi; son sınıf öğrencisi

sensation /sen'seyşın/ *a.* his, duyu; heyecan yaratan olay, sansasyon **sensational** heyecanlı; *kon.* harika, müthiş

sense /sens/ *a.* duyu, duyum; duygu; anlam; akıl, zekâ ☆ *e.* hissetmek, sezmek **make sense** bir anlamı olmak, anlaşılır olmak **senseless** baygın; anlamsız

sensibility /sensı'biliti/ *a.* duyarlık

sensible /'sensıbıl/ *s.* makul; akıllı, aklı başında; fark edilir .

sensitive /'sensitiv/ *s.* duyarlı **sensitivity** duyarlık

sensual /'senşuıl/ *s.* nefsi; bedensel; şehvetli **sensuality** şehvet

sensuous /'senşuıs/ *s.* duyumsal

sent /sent/ *bkz.* **send**

sentence /'sentıns/ *a, dilb.* tümce, cümle; *huk.* yargı, karar, hüküm ☆ *e.* **(to)** *huk.* mahkûm etmek

sentiment /'sentimınt/ *a.* duygu, his; fikir, düşünce, kanı

sentimental /senti'mentıl/ *s.* duygusal

sentinel /'sentinıl/ *a.* nöbetçi, gözcü

sentry /'sentri/ *a.* nöbetçi er

separate /'sepırıt/ *s.* ayrı ☆ *e.* /'sepıreyt/ ayırmak; ayrılmak **separately** /'sepırıtli/ *be.* ayrı ayrı **separation** /se-

pır'eyşın/ *a.* ayrılış; ayrılık

September /sep'tembı/ *a.* eylül

septic /'septik/ *s.* mikroplu

sepulchre /'sepılkı/ *a.* mezar, gömüt

sequel /'si:kwıl/ *a.* bir şeyin devamı, arkası; sonuç, son

sequence /'si:kwıns/ *a.* sıra, art arda gelme; dizi, sıra; seri, silsile, zincir, dizi **sequence of tenses** zamanların uyumu

serenade /seri'neyd/ *a.* serenat

serene /si'ri:n/ *s.* durgun, sessiz, sakin

sergeant /'sa:cınt/ *a, ask.* çavuş; komiser muavini **sergeant major** *ask.* başçavuş

serial /'siırıl/ *s.* seri, tefrika, (radyo, TV) dizi

series /'siıriz/ *a.* sıra, dizi, seri

serious /'siıriıs/ *s.* ciddi, ağırbaşlı; ağır, tehlikeli; şaka yapmayan **seriously** ciddi olarak

sermon /'sö:mın/ *a.* dinsel konuşma, vaaz

serpent /'sö:pınt/ *a, yaz.* yılan

serum /'siırım/ *a.* serum

servant /'sö:vınt/ *a.* hizmetçi, uşak; kul **civil servant** devlet memuru

serve /sö:v/ *e.* hizmet etmek; servis yapmak, bakmak; vazifesini görmek, yerine geçmek; amaca uymak

service /'sö:vis/ *a.* hizmet; servis; görev; hizmetçilik; ayin, tören **at your service** emrinize amade, emrinizde **of service** yardımcı, yararlı **serviceable** işe yarar, elverişli; dayanıklı

serviette /sö:vi'et/ *a, İİ.* peçete, sofra peçetesi

servile /'sö:vayl/ *s.* köle gibi

servitude /'sö:vityu:d/ *a.* kölelik

session /'seşın/ *a.* oturum, celse; toplantı; *Aİ.* (üniversitede) dönem

set /set/ *e.* koymak; yerleştirmek; oturtmak; saptamak; belirlemek; ayarlamak; dikmek; sertleştirmek; düzeltmek; (güneş) batmak; pıhtılaşmak; koyulaşmak ☆ *a.* takım; sıra, dizi; alıcı, aygıt; (sinema) set; (güneş) batma ☆ *s.* sabit, değişmez **set about** başlamak **set aside** ayırmak, saklamak **set back** ilerlemesini engellemek **set**

down yazmak, kaydetmek; *il.* durup **yolcu** indirmek **set fire to** ateşe vermek **set free** serbest bırakmak **set in** başlamak **set off** yola çıkmak; (bomba, vb.) patlatmak; atmak **set up** (iş, vb.) kurmak; dikmek **setback** engel **set-up** organizasyon, yapı

settee /se'ti:/ *a.* kanepe

setting /'seting/ *a.* çevre; sahne, dekor; ayar; çerçeve, yuva

settle /'setıl/ *e.* yerleşmek; konmak; yerleştirmek; yatıştırmak; halletmek; karara bağlamak; (hesap) ödemek **settle down** yerleşmek; uslanmak **settle for** razı olmak **settle in** (yeni bir ortama) alışmak **settle up** (borcunu) ödemek, (hesabını) kapatmak; (iş) çözmek, halletmek **settled** sabit, değişmez, belirli **settlement** yerleşme, yerleşim; ödeme; çözümleme; yeni koloni; anlaşma **settler** yeni yerleşen kimse, göçmen

seven /'sevın/ *a, s.* yedi **seventh** yedinci

seventeen /sevın'ti:n/ *a, s.* on yedi **seventeenth** on yedinci

seventy /'sevınti/ *a, s.* yetmiş **seventieth** yetmişinci

sever /'sevı/ *e.* kesmek; koparmak; ayırmak

several /'sevırıl/ *s.* birkaç; birçok; ayrı ayrı, farklı

severe /si'vıı/ *s.* sert; ciddi, ağır **severity** /sı'verıti/ sertlik; ciddiyet, tehlike

sew /sou/ *e.* **sewed, sewn** /soun/ dikiş dikmek; dikmek

sewage /'syu:ic, 'su:ic/ *a.* lağım pisliği

sewer /'syu:ı, 'su:ı/ *a.* lağım

sex /seks/ *a.* cinsiyet; cinsellik; cinsel ilişki, seks **sex appeal** cinsel çekicilik, seksapel **sexy** seksi

sextant /'sekstınt/ *a.* sekstant

sexton /'sekstın/ *a.* kilise hademesi, zangoç

sexual /'sekşuıl, 'seksyuıl/ *s.* cinsel; *bitk.* eşeyli **sexual intercourse** cinsel birleşme **sexuality** cinsel özellikler

shabby /'şebi/ *s.* eski püskü, pejmürde; kılıksız; aşağılık, adi

shack /şek/ *a.* kulübe

shackle /'şekıl/ *a.* köstek; pranga, zincir; engel

shade /şeyd/ *a.* gölge; gölgelik yer; abajur, karpuz; nüans, ayırtı ☆ *e.* gölge vermek; korumak **shadow cabinet** gölge kabine

shadow /'şedou/ *a.* gölge; karanlık; iz, eser ☆ *e.* gölgelendirmek; karartmak; gözetlemek **shadowy** gölgeli; belli belirsiz

shady /'şeydi/ *s.* gölgeli, karanlık; *kon.* namussuz, üçkâğıtçı, güvenilmez

shaft /şa:ft/ *a.* mil, şaft; ok; sütun gövdesi; ışın; hava bacası

shaggy /'şegi/ *s.* (saç) kabarık, taranmamış

shake /şeyk/ *e.* sallamak; silkelemek; çalkalamak; sarsmak; sallanmak ☆ *a.* sarsıntı, sallama **shake hands** el sıkışmak **shake off** -den kurtulmak, yakasını kurtarmak **shake out** silkelemek **shake up** çalkalamak; sarsmak; gözünü açmak, uyandırmak; sertliğini gidermek **shake-up** köklü değişiklik **shaker** *Aİ.* tuzluk/biberlik **shaky** titrek, sarsak; şüpheli; sallantıda

shaken /'şeykın/ *bkz.* shake

shall /şıl, şel/ *e.* (olumsuz biçimi **shan't** /şa:nt/ (yardımcı fiil olarak) -ecek, -acak; (kural/yasa/emir/söz belirtir) -ecek, -acak; (**I** ve **we** ile öneri belirtir) -eyim mi, -elim mi

shallow /'şelou/ *s.* sığ; yüzeysel; dar

sham /şem/ *a.* taklit, yapmacık, yalan ☆ *e.* numara yapmak, rol yapmak

shame /şeym/ *a.* utanç; utanma; sıkılma; ayıp; yazık; şanssızlık **put sb/sth to shame** -den utandıracak derecede üstün olmak **Shame on you!** Ayıp! Utan! **for shame!** ayıp, yazıklar olsun! **What a shame!** Ne yazık! **shamefaced** utanmış **shameless** utanmaz, yüzsüz

shampoo /şem'pu:/ *a.* şampuan ☆ *e.* şampuanlamak

shamrock /'şemrok/ *a, bitk.* yonca

shank /şenk/ *a.* bacak; incik; sap

shanty /'şenti/ *a.* kulübe; gemici şarkısı

shape /şeyp/ *a.* biçim, şekil; kalıp; *kon.* form, kondisyon; maske, kisve ☆ *e.*

biçimlendirmek; oluşturmak; uydurmak **take shape** biçimlenmek, gerçekleşmek **shapeless** biçimsiz; çirkin **shapely** biçimli, yakışıklı
share /şeı/ a. pay, hisse; hisse senedi ☆ *e.* paylaşmak; paylaştırmak, bölüştürmek **shareholder** hissedar
shark /şa:k/ a. köpekbalığı; dolandırıcı
sharp /şa:p/ s. keskin; sivri; dokunaklı; sert; zeki, uyanık; buruk, ekşi; tiz, keskin ☆ *be.* tam; *müz.* diyez nota; diyez işareti **sharpen** bilemek, sivriltmek, keskinleştirmek **sharpener** bileyici; kalemtıraş
shatter /şetı/ e. kırmak; kırılmak
shave /şeyv/ e. tıraş olmak; tıraş etmek; rendelemek, kesmek; soymak, yüzmek ☆ *a.* tıraş **a close/narrow shave** kıl payı kaçış, kurtuluş **shaver** tıraş makinesi **shaving** tıraş; ç. talaş, yonga
shawl /şo:l/ a. şal, atkı
she /şi, şi:/ adl. o
shear /şıı/ e. **sheared, shorn** /şo:n/ kırkmak, kesmek
shears /'şıız/ a. yün kırkma makası, büyük makas
sheath /şi:t / a. kın, kılıf; prezervatif
shed /şed/ e. dökmek, saçmak, akıtmak; yaymak ☆ *a.* baraka, kulübe; hangar **shed crocodile tears** sahte gözyaşı dökmek
sheen /şi:n/ a. parlaklık
sheep /şi:p/ a. (ç. sheep) koyun **sheepish** utangaç, çekingen **sheepskin** koyun postu, pösteki
sheer /şıı/ s. katıksız, sırf, halis; dimdik; incecik
sheet /şi:t/ a. çarşaf, yatak çarşafı; tabaka; yaprak
sheikh /şeyk/ a. şeyh
shelf /şelf/ a. raf; *coğ.* şelf, sığlık
shell /şel/ a. deniz kabuğu; kabuk; topçu mermisi **shellfish** kabuklu deniz hayvanı
shelter /'şeltı/ a. sığınak, barınak ☆ *e.* barındırmak; sığınmak
shelve /şelv/ e. rafa koymak; ertelemek
shepherd /'şepıd/ a. çoban
sheriff /'şerif/ a. (Amerika'da) şerif, polis şefi
sherry /'şeri/ a. beyaz İspanyol şarabı, şeri
shield /şi:ld/ a. kalkan; siper
shift /şift/ a. değişme, değiştirme; vardiya, nöbet ☆ *e.* değiştirmek; (suç, vb.) yüklemek
shilling /şiling/ a. şilin
shimmer /'şimı/ a. titrek ışık, parıltı ☆ *e.* parıldamak, titrek ışıkla parıldamak
shin /şin/ a, *anat.* incik
shine /şayn/ e. **shone** /şon/ parlamak; parlatmak ☆ *a.* parlaklık; cila **shiny** parlak, gıcır gıcır
ship /şip/ a. gemi, vapur ☆ *e.* gemiyle taşımak/göndermek; gemiye yüklemek **shipment** (mal) gönderme; gönderilen mal **shipper** nakliyeci **shipping** gemiler; gemicilik; nakliye **shipwreck** karaya oturma; deniz kazası **shipyard** tersane
shirk /şö:k/ e. kaçmak, kaytarmak
shirt /şö:t/ a. gömlek
shiver /'şivı/ a. titreme, ürperti ☆ *e.* titremek, ürpermek
shoal /şoul/ a. sığlık; balık sürüsü
shock /şok/ a. darbe, vuruş; sarsıntı; şok ☆ *e.* çok şaşırtmak, sarsmak; şok etmek **shocking** şaşırtıcı; korkunç; iğrenç, berbat
shoddy /'şodi/ s. adi, kalitesiz
shoe /şu:/ a. ayakkabı; at nalı **shoehorn** ayakkabı çekeceği **shoelace** ayakkabı bağı **shoemaker** ayakkabıcı **shoestring** *Al.* ayakkabı bağı
shone /şon/ *bkz.* shine
shoo /şu:/ ünl. hoşt, pist, kış ☆ *e.* kovmak, kışkışlamak
shoot /şu:t/ e. **shot** /şot/ ateş etmek; (silahla) vurmak; filme almak, çekmek; *sp.* şut çekmek; filizlenmek, sürmek ☆ *a, bitk.* filiz, sürgün; atış; av alanı **shooting star** göktaşı
shop /şop/ a. dükkân, mağaza; atölye ☆ *e.* alışverişe çıkmak, alışveriş yapmak **shopkeeper** dükkâncı **shoplift** dükkânlardan eşya çalmak **shop assistant** satıcı, tezgâhtar **shopping** alışveriş **go shopping** alışverişe çıkmak **shopping-centre** alışveriş merkezi

shore 438

shore /şo:/ a. kıyı, sahil; kara
short /şo:t/ s. kısa; kısa boylu; bodur;
az, eksik, yetersiz; (çörek, vb.) gevrek
☆ be. birdenbire in short kısacası
short of -in dışında, hariç fall/run
short of yetmemek, tükenmek short
wave (radyo) kısa dalga short-range
kısa dönemli short-term kısa dönemli
shortage yokluk, kıtlık shortbread şekerli galeta shortcoming kusur, eksiklik shortcut kestirme, kısa yol short-
en kısaltmak shorthand steno shortly
kısaca; yakında shortsighted miyop;
ileriyi göremeyen
shorts /şo:ts/ a. kısa pantalon, şort
shot /'şot/ a. atış, atım; gülle, top; menzil, erim; girişim, fotoğraf resim, film;
sp. şut big shot önemli kimse shotgun av tüfeği, çifte
should /şıd, şud/ e. (öneri ya da gereklilik belirtir) -meli, -malı; (beklenti ya
da olasılık belirtir) -meli, -mesi gerek;
(dolaylı anlatımda shall'in yerine kul-
lanılır) -ecek, -acak; -mesi, -ması; (koşul cümlelerinde) -ecek (olursa)
shoulder /'şouldı/ a. omuz ☆ e. omuzlamak shoulder blade anat. kürekkemiği
shout /şaut/ e. bağırmak; seslenmek
☆ a. bağırma, bağırış
shove /şav/ e. ittirmek
shovel /'şavıl/ a. kürek
show /şou/ e. showed, shown /şoun/
göstermek; (film) oynamak; sergilemek; kanıtlamak ☆ a. gösteri, oyun;
gösteriş; görünüş; sergi show business eğlence sanayii show off gösteriş yapmak, hava atmak show up ortaya koymak; ortaya çıkarmak, çıkagelmek; görünmek showcase vitrin showroom sergi salonu showman tiyatro,
sirk, vb. müdürü; şovmen showy gö-
zalıcı, gösterişli
shower /'şauı/ a. sağanak; duş
shown /şoun/ bkz. show
showing /'şouing/ a. gösterme, gösterim, sergileme
showing-off /'şouingof/ a. gösteriş, caka, fiyaka, hava
showy /'şoui/ s. (fazla) dikkat çeken,

cart, cırtlak, cafcaflı, havalı
shrank /şrenk/ bkz. shrink
shrapnel /'şrepnıl/ a. şarapnel
shred /şred/ a. parça, dilim
shrewd /şru:d/ s. zeki, kurnaz
shriek /şri:k/ e. çığlık atmak ☆ a. çığlık
shrill /şril/ s. tiz sesli, keskin
shrimp /şrimp/ a, hayb. karides, teke
shrine /şrayn/ a. türbe
shrink /şrink/ e. shrank /şrenk/,
shrunk /şrank/ büzülmek; büzmek;
daraltmak shrink from -den çekinmek shrinkage çekme, daralma
shrivel /'şrivıl/ e. kuruyup büzülmek,
buruşmak, kıvrılmak, pörsümek
shroud /şraud/ a. kefen; örtü
shrub /şrab/ a. funda, çalı shrubbery
çalılık
shrug /şrag/ e. omuz silkmek
shudder /'şadı/ e. ürpermek, titremek
shuffle /'şafıl/ e. (oyun kâğıdı) karıştırmak, karmak
shun /şan/ e. çekinmek, kaçmak, uzak
durmak, sakınmak
shut /şat/ e. shut /şat/ kapamak, kapatmak; kapanmak shut down (fabri-
kayı, işi, vb.) kapatmak shut up susmak, kapamak
shutter /'şatı/ a. kepenk, panjur
shuttle /'şatıl/ a. mekik; uzay mekiği ☆
e. gidip gelmek, mekik dokumak
shy /şay/ s. utangaç, çekingen; ürkek
sick /sik/ s. hasta; midesi bulanmış;
(of) bıkmış, bezmiş; mide bulandırıcı
make sb sick kon. gıcık etmek, kıl etmek sick pay hastalık parası sickness
hastalık; bulantı, kusma
sicken /'sikın/ e. midesini bulandırmak;
hastalanmak sickening iğrenç
sickle /'sikıl/ a. orak
sickly /'sikli/ s. hastalıklı; iğrenç
side /sayd/ a. yan; kenar; yüz, taraf; bölüm, kısım; yön; sp. taraf, takım;
(dağ, vb.) yamaç, etek; böğür ☆ s.
yan side by side yan yana side effect
yan etki side street yan sokak sideboard büfe sideboards, Aİ. sideburns
(saç) favoriler sidelong yanlamasına,
yan sidewalk Aİ. yaya kaldırımı side-

439 **sister**

wards yana doğru, yanlamasına, yan yan
siege /si:c/ a. kuşatma
sieve /siv/ a. kalbur, kevgir, elek
sift /sift/ e. elemek, kalburdan geçirmek
sigh /say/ a. iç çekme ☆ e. iç çekmek
sight /sayt/ a. görme, görüş; manzara, görünüş; nişangâh; ç. görülmeye değer yerler at first sight ilk görüşte catch sight of gözüne ilişmek in sight görünürde out of sight gözden uzak lose sight of gözden kaybetmek sightseeing görülmeye değer yerleri gezip dolaşma
sign /sayn/ a. işaret, gösterge; belirti, iz; levha; tabela ☆ e. imzalamak; işaret etmek signpost yol gösteren levha, işaret direği
signal /'signıl/ a. işaret, sinyal ☆ e. işaret etmek, işaretle bildirmek
signatory /'signıtıri/ a. imza sahibi
signature /'signıcı/ a. imza
signet /'signit/ a. mühür
significance /sig'nifikıns/ a. önem; anlam significant önemli; anlamlı
signify /'signifay/ e. bildirmek, belirtmek; anlamına gelmek
silence /'saylıns/ a. sessizlik; durgunluk silencer susturucu
silent /'saylınt/ s. sessiz; gürültüsüz; suskun
silhouette /silu:'et/ a. gölge, karaltı, siluet
silk /silk/ a. ipek silken ipekli silkworm ipekböceği silky ipekli, ipek gibi, ipeksi
sill /sil/ a. eşik
silly /'sili/ s. aptal, ahmak, akılsız, budala; ahmakça
silo /'saylou/ a. silo
silt /silt/ a. alüvyon, balçık
silver /'silvı/ a, s. gümüş ☆ e. gümüş kaplamak silver paper yaldızlı kâğıt silversmith gümüşçü silvery gümüş gibi; (ses) tatlı ve berrak silverware gümüş eşya
similar /'similı/ s. benzer
similarity /simi'leriti/ a. benzerlik
simile /'simili/ a, yaz. teşbih, benzetme

simmer /'simı/ e. yavaş yavaş kaynamak
simple /'simpıl/ s. basit; kolay; yalın, süssüz simply sade bir şekilde; tümüyle; yalnız
simplicity /sim'plisiti/ a. basitlik, yalınlık; kolaylık; saflık, bönlük
simplify /'simplifay/ e. kolaylaştırmak, basitleştirmek; mat. sadeleştirmek
simulate /'simyuleyt/ e. taklit etmek, numara yapmak, gibi görünmek
simultaneous /simıl'teyniıs/ s. aynı zamanda yapılan, eşzamanlı
sin /sin/ a. günah; suç commit a sin günah işlemek sinful günahkâr
since /sins/ bağ. -den beri, mademki; -dığı için ☆ be. o zamandan beri, önce ☆ ilg. -den beri ever since o zamandan beri
sincere /sin'siı/ s. samimi, içten, candan sincerely içtenlikle Yours sincerely (mektup sonunda) Saygılarımla sincerity içtenlik, candanlık, samimiyet
sinew /'sinyu:/ a, anat. kiriş, sinir
sing /sing/ e. sang /seng/, sung /sang/ (şarkı) söylemek; ötmek, şakımak; uğuldamak singer şarkıcı
single /'singıl/ s. tek, bir; tek kişilik; bekâr ☆ a, İİ. gidiş bileti; 45'lik plak; kon. tek kişilik oda single ticket gidiş bileti single handed tek başına, yalnız single minded azimli singles (tenis, vb.) tekler maçı singly teker teker, tek başına
singular /'singyulı/ s, a. tekil singular noun tekil isim
sinister /'sinistı/ s. uğursuz
sink /sink/ e. sank /senk/, sunk /sank/ batmak; batırmak; çekmek; alçalmak ☆ a. lavabo, musluk taşı; lağım
sinus /'saynıs/ a, anat. boşluk
sip /sip/ e. yudumlamak ☆ a. yudum
siphon /'sayfın/ a. sifon
sir /sö: / a. efendim, efendi
siren /'sayırın/ a. canavar düdüğü, siren
sirloin /'sö:loyn/ a. sığır filetosu
sister /'sistı/ a. kız kardeş; hemşire, hastabakıcı; rahibe sisterhood kız kar-

deşlik **sister-in-law** görümce, baldız, yenge, elti

sit /sit/ *e.* **sat** /set/ oturmak; toplanmak; **(for)** (sınava) girmek, sınav olmak **sit about/around** *kon.* hiçbir şey yapmamak **sit back** boş boş oturmak **sit in** vekâlet etmek **sit out** sonuna kadar kalmak; yer almamak **sit up** geç saatlere kadar oturmak; dik oturmak

site /sayt/ *a.* yer, mevki; arsa

sitting /'siting/ *a.* oturuş; poz verme; oturum, celse **sitting room** oturma odası

situated /'siçueytid/ *s.* bulunan, yerleşmiş

situation /siçu'eyşın/ *a.* yer, konum; durum, hal; iş, memuriyet

six /siks/ *a, s.* altı **sixth** altıncı **sixth sense** altıncı his

sixteen /sik'sti:n/ *a, s.* on altı **sixteenth** on altıncı

sixty /'siksti/ *a, s.* altmış **sixtieth** altmışıncı

size /sayz/ *a.* büyüklük; (elbise) beden, boy; ölçü, ebat; (ayakkabı) numara **sizeable** oldukça büyük

sizzle /'sizıl/ *e.* cızırdamak ☆ *a.* cızırtı

skate /skeyt/ *a.* paten ☆ *e.* patenle kaymak **skateboard** kaykay

skeleton /'skelitın/ *a.* iskelet; çatı

sketch /skeç/ *a.* taslak; kroki; skeç

skewer /'skyu:ı/ *a.* kebap şişi

ski /ski:/ *a.* kayak ☆ *e.* kayak yapmak

skid /skid/ *a.* kayma, yana kayma; kızak; takoz ☆ *e.* (otomobil, vb.) yana doğru savrulmak

skill /skil/ *s.* beceri, ustalık **skilled** kalifiye, usta

skim /skim/ *e.* köpüğünü/kaymağını almak; üzerinden kaymak, sıyırıp geçmek **skim milk** kaymağı alınmış süt

skin /skin/ *a.* deri, cilt; post, pösteki; kabuk ☆ *e.* derisini yüzmek; kabuğunu soymak **skinhead** dazlak **skinny** bir deri bir kemik, sıska

skip /skip/ *e.* hoplamak, sıçramak, zıplamak, sekmek ☆ *a.* hoplayıp sıçrama, sekme

skipper /'skipı/ *a, kon.* kaptan

skirmish /'skö:miş/ *a.* çatışma, çarpışma; çekişme

skirt /skö:t/ *a.* etek, eteklik; kenar

skulk /skalk/ *e.* sinsi sinsi dolaşmak

skull /skal/ *a.* kafatası

skunk /skank/ *a, hayb.* kokarca

sky /skay/ *a.* gökyüzü **skyjack** uçak kaçırmak **skylark** *hayb.* tarlakuşu **skyline** ufuk çizgisi **skyscraper** gökdelen

slab /sleb/ *a.* kalın dilim, kat

slack /slek/ *s.* gevşek, sarkık; ağır; dikkatsiz; (iş) durgun, kesat

slag /sleg/ *a.* cüruf, dışık

slake /sleyk/ *e.* (susuzluk) gidermek

slalom /'sla:lım/ *a, sp.* slalom

slam /slem/ *a.* kapıyı çarparak kapama; (briçte) şlem ☆ *e.* çarparak kapamak; hızla vurmak; *kon.* şiddetle eleştirmek

slander /'slendı/ *a.* karalama, iftira ☆ *e.* karalamak, iftira etmek

slang /sleng/ *a.* argo

slant /sla:nt/ *e.* eğilmek; eğmek; eğimli olmak ☆ *a.* eğim; görüş; yan bakış

slap /slep/ *e.* tokatlamak; yere çarpmak, yere çalmak ☆ *a.* tokat

slash /sleş/ *e.* kesmek, yarmak; *kon.* iyice indirmek ☆ *a.* uzun kesik, yarık; yırtmaç

slaughter /'slo:tı/ *a.* hayvan kesme, kesim; katliam, kırım ☆ *e.* (hayvan) kesmek; kan dökmek, katliam yapmak **slaughterhouse** mezbaha, kesimevi

slave /sleyv/ *a.* köle **slavery** kölelik

slay /sley/ *e.* vahşice öldürmek, katletmek

sledge /slec/ *a.* kızak

sledgehammer /'slechemı/ *a.* balyoz

sleek /sli:k/ *s.* düz, parlak, bakımlı

sleep /sli:p/ *e.* **slept** /slept/ uyumak ☆ *a.* uyku **go to sleep** uyumak **put to sleep** uyutmak, yatırmak **sleeping car** yataklı vagon **sleepless** uykusuz **sleepy** uykulu **sleeping pill** uyku hapı **sleepwalker** uyurgezer

sleet /sli:t/ *a.* sulusepken ☆ *e.* sulusepken yağmak

sleeve /sli:v/ *a.* giysi kolu, yen; manşon, kol

sleigh /sley/ *a.* atlı kızak
sleight /sleyt/ *a.* el çabukluğu, marifet
sleight of hand el çabukluğu
slender /'slendı/ *s.* incecik, narin, ince;
az, yetersiz
slept /slept/ *bkz.* **sleep**
slice /slays/ *a.* dilim; hisse, pay ☆ *e.*
dilimlemek, dilmek
slick /slik/ *s.* düz; kaygan; yüze gülücü;
üçkâğıtçı ☆ *a.* ince petrol tabakası
slid /slid/ *bkz.* **slide**
slide /slayd/ *e.* **slid** /slid/ kaymak; kaydırmak ☆ *a.* kayma; kaydırak; sür-
gü; heyelan; diyapozitif, slayt; saç tokası **slide ruler** sürgülü hesap cetveli
slight /slayt/ *s.* ince, narin, zayıf; ufak,
önemsiz ☆ *e.* önemsememek, hor
görmek, küçümsemek **slightly** biraz,
azıcık
slim /slim/ *s.* narin, ince; zayıf, az
slime /slaym/ *a.* balçık; çamur
sling /sling/ *e.* **slung** /slang/ atmak ☆
a. sapan; *den.* izbiro; kol askısı
slink /slink/ *e.* **slung** /slank/ sıvışmak
slip /slip/ *a.* kayma; yanlışlık, hata;
kombinezon; yastık yüzü ☆ *e.* kaymak; (gizlice) sıvışmak, kaçmak **slip
of the tongue** dil sürçmesi **slip on**
(giysi) giyivermek, geçirivermek **slip
one's notice** gözünden kaçmak **slip
up** yanılmak, sürçmek
slipper /'slipı/ *a.* terlik
slippery /'slipıri/ *s.* kaygan; kaypak
slit /slit/ *e.* yarmak, uzunluğuna kesmek ☆ *a.* kesik, yarık; dar aralık
slither /'slidı/ *e.* kaymak
sliver /'slivı/ *a.* kıymık; ince dilim
slogan /'slougın/ *a.* slogan
slop /slop/ *a.* lapa, sulu yemek ☆ *e.*
dökmek; dökülmek
slope /sloup/ *e.* eğimli olmak ☆ *a.* yokuş, bayır; eğim, meyil
sloppy /'slopi/ *s.* çamurlu; baştan savma, uyduruk; aptalca, saçma
slosh /sloş/ *e.* sudan/çamurdan geçmek; (sıvı) taşmak
slot /slot/ *a.* yarık, delik; *kon.* (radyo,
vb.) program **slot machine** (içine para atılarak içki, sigara, vb. alınan) otomatik makine; kollu kumar makinesi

sloth /slout/ / *a.* tembellik, miskinlik
slough /slau/ *a.* bataklık; kötü durum
☆ *e.* **(off)** (yılan, vb.) deri değiştirmek
sloven /'slavın/ *a.* pasaklı, kılıksız
slow /slou/ *s.* yavaş, ağır; (saat) geri;
güç anlayan ☆ *be.* yavaş yavaş **slow
down/up** yavaşlamak; yavaşlatmak
slow motion ağır çekim **slowly** yavaş
yavaş
sludge /slac/ *a.* sulu çamur
slug /slag/ *a.* kabuksuz sümüklüböcek
sluggish /'slagiş/ *s.* uyuşuk, tembel
slum /slam/ *a, kon.* gecekondu mahal-
lesi, kenar mahalle
slump /slamp/ *e.* birdenbire düşmek
☆ *a.* (ticaret, fiyat, vb.'de) durgunluk, kriz
slung /slang/ *bkz.* **sling**
slunk /slangk/ *bkz.* **slink**
slur /slö:/ / *a.* tahkir, leke
slush /slaş/ *a.* sulu çamur; yarı erimiş
kar
slut /slat/ *a.* pasaklı kadın
sly /slay/ *s.* sinsi, kurnaz; muzip
smack /smek/ *e.* şaplak atmak, tokatlamak; **(of)** kokmak, tadı vermek; şapır-
tıyla öpmek ☆ *a.* şamar, tokat, şaplak; hafif çeşni, tat; şapırtılı öpücük
small /smo:l/ *s.* küçük, ufak; önemsiz
small change bozuk para **small intestine** incebağırsak **small talk** sohbet,
laklak, muhabbet
smart /sma:t/ *s.* zarif, şık; yakışıklı; gösterişli; kurnaz, usta; çevik, canlı ☆ *e.*
ağrımak, sızlamak, acıtmak
smarten /sma:tın/ *e.* **(up)** güzelleştirmek
smash /smeş/ *e.* paramparça etmek;
parçalanmak, paramparça olmak; (rekor) kırmak ☆ *a.* kırılma, parçalan-
ma; şangırtı; çarpışma, kaza
smattering /'smetıring/ *a.* çat pat bilgi,
yüzeysel bilgi
smear /smiı/ *a.* leke; karalama, iftira ☆
e. sürmek, bulaştırmak; lekelemek
smell /smel/ *e.* **smelt** /smelt/ koklamak; kokmak ☆ *a.* koku; koklama
smelt /smelt/ *bkz.* **smell**
smile /smayl/ *e.* gülümsemek ☆ *a.* gü-

lümseme
smirk /smö:k/ e. sırıtmak ☆ a. sırıtış
smith /smit / a. demirci
smock /smok/ a. iş gömleği, önlük
smog /smog/ a. dumanlı sis, sanayi sisi
smoke /smouk/ a. duman; (sigara) içme ☆ e. (sigara, pipo, vb.) içmek;
tütmek; (balık, et, vb.) tütsülemek
smoker sigara içen; sigara içenlere
ayrılmış bölüm smoky dumanlı; duman rengi
smooth /smu:d / s. düz, düzgün; sarsıntısız; (tat) hoş; akıcı ☆ e. düzlemek smoothly pürüzsüzce
smother /'smadı/ e. boğulmak; boğmak
smoulder /'smouldı/ e. için için yanmak; için için köpürmek
smudge /smac/ e. kirlenmek; kirletmek
☆ a. is lekesi
smug /smag/ s. kendini beğenmiş
smuggle /'smagıl/ e. kaçakçılık yapmak, kaçırmak smuggler kaçakçı
smuggling kaçakçılık
smut /smat/ â. is, kurum; küf
snack /snek/ a. hafif yemek snack bar
hafif yemek yeren yer
snag /sneg/ a. beklenmedik engel ya
da güçlük
snail /sneyl/ a. salyangoz
snake /sneyk/ a. yılan
snap /snep/ e. çatırtıyla kopmak, kırılmak; gürültüyle kapamak; birdenbire
ısırmak, dişlemek; kon. fotoğrafını
çekmek ☆ a. kopma; kırılma; çatırtı;
ısırma; kopça, çıtçıt; enstantane, şipşak resim snapshot atılgan, canlı, çevik snapshot enstantane fotoğraf, şipşak
snare /sneı/ a. tuzak, kapan
snarl /sna:l/ e. hırlamak ☆ a. hırlama
snatch /sneç/ e. kapmak, kavramak ☆
a. kapış, kapma; gayret; kısa süre, an
sneak /sni:k/ e. sinsice/gizlice ilerlemek; süzülmek; kon. (öğretmene,
vb.) gammazlamak ☆ a. muhbir,
gammaz sneaky sinsi
sneakers /'sni:kız/ a, Aİ. bez spor ayakkabı, kes
sneer /sniı/ e. dudak bükmek, küçüm-

semek ☆ a. dudak bükme, küçümseme, alay
sneeze /sni:z/ e. aksırmak ☆ a. aksırık
sniff /snif/ e. burnunu çekmek; koklamak ☆ a. burnunu çekme; havayı
koklama
snigger /'snigı/ e. kıs kıs gülmek ☆ a.
kıs kıs gülüş
snip /snip/ a. kırpma, kırkma ☆ e. ma-
kasla kesmek, kırpmak
snipe /snayp/ e. siperden ateş etmek
snob /snob/ a. züppe snobbery züppelik
snooker /'snu:kı/ a. bir tür bilardo oyunu
snoop /snu:p/ e. burnunu sokmak
snooze /snu:z/ a, kon. kısa uyku, şekerleme ☆ e, kon. kestirmek, şekerleme yapmak
snore /sno:/ a. horlama, horultu ☆ e.
horlamak
snorkel /'sno:kıl/ a. şnorkel
snort /sno:t/ e. burnundan solumak, horuldamak
snout /snaut/ a, hayb. (domuz, vb.) burun
snow /snou/ a. kar ☆ e. kar yağmak
snowball kartopu snowdrop bitk. kar-
delen snowfall kar yağışı snow-flake
kar tanesi snowman kardan adam
snowplough kar temizleme makine-
si/aracı snowstorm kar fırtınası snowy
karlı; bembeyaz
snub /snab/ e. küçümsemek, aşağılamak ☆ a. aşağılama, küçümseme
snuff /snaf/ a. enfiye
snug /snag/ s. rahat ve sıcaklık; (giysi)
tam oturan
snuggle /'snagıl/ e. sokulmak
so /sou/ be. böyle, öyle; bu kadar, bu
derece; bu nedenle, onun için; de,
da; demek (ki); pek, çok ☆ bağ.
-mesi için; -sin diye so as to -mek
için, -cek biçimde, -mek amacıyla So
long kon. Güle güle, Hoşça kal. So
what kon. Bana ne; Ne yani; Ne olmuş so-and-so falan kişi/şey, filanca
so-called sözde, sözümona so-so şöyle böyle Just/Quite so İİ. Evet, Aynen

443   **song**

öyle
soak /souk/ *e.* sırılsıklam etmek; ıslatmak; ıslanmak ☆ *a.* ıslatma, ıslanma
soap /soup/ *a.* sabun
soar /so:/ *e.* süzülmek, süzülerek yükselmek
sob /sob/ *a.* hıçkıra hıçkıra ağlamak ☆ *a.* hıçkırık
sober /'soubı/ *s.* ayık; ölçülü; ciddi, ağırbaşlı; yalın **sober up** ayılmak; ayıltmak
soccer /'sokı/ *a, ii.* futbol
sociable /'souşıbıl/ *s.* sokulgan, girgin, arkadaş canlısı; hoşsohbet
social /'souşıl/ *s.* toplumsal, sosyal; toplu halde yaşayan **social democracy** sosyal demokrasi **social science** sosyal bilimler **social security** sosyal güvenlik; sosyal sigorta **social services** sosyal hizmetler **social worker** sosyal hizmet görevlisi
socialism /'souşılizım/ *a.* toplumculuk, sosyalizm **socialist** toplumcu, sosyalist
society /sı'sayiti/ *a.* toplum; topluluk; dernek; kurum; şirket; arkadaşlık; sosyete
sociology /sousi'olıci/ *a.* toplumbilim, sosyoloji **sociologist** toplumbilimci, sosyolog
sock /sok/ *a.* kısa çorap
socket /'sokit/ *a.* priz, duy; oyuk, yuva
sod /sod/ *a.* çim
soda /'soudı/ *a.* soda **soda water** gazoz, maden sodası
sodden /'sodın/ *s.* sırılsıklam
sodium /'soudiım/ *a, kim.* sodyum
sofa /'soufı/ *a.* kanepe, sedir
soft /soft/ *s.* yumuşak; ılık, tatlı; müşfik, sevecen; yumuşak başlı, uysal; *kon.* aptal; yavaş **soft-boiled** (yumurta) rafadan **soft drink** alkolsüz içki **soft/-easy touch** yolunacak kaz **soften** yumuşatmak; yumuşamak **soft-hearted** yufka yürekli
software /'softweı/ *a.* (bilgisayar) yazılım
soggy /'sogi/ *s.* çok ıslak, sırılsıklam
soil /soyl/ *a.* toprak

solace /'solis/ *a.* avuntu, teselli
solar /'soulı/ *s.* güneşle ilgili **solar system** güneş sistemi **solar year** güneş yılı
solarium /sou'leırıım/ *a.* solaryum, güneşlik
solder /'soldı/ *a.* lehim ☆ *e.* lehimlemek
soldier /'soulcı/ *a.* er, asker
sole /soul/ *a.* taban, pençe ☆ *s.* yalnız, tek ☆ *a.* dilbalığı
solemn /'solım/ *s.* törenle yapılan; resmi; kutsal; ağırbaşlı, ciddi
solemnity /sı'lemniti/ *a.* ciddiyet, resmiyet; tantanalı tören
solicit /sı'lisit/ *e.* rica etmek, istemek
solicitor /sı'lisitı/ *a.* avukat; istekli, talip
solid /'solid/ *s.* katı; sağlam; yekpare; som; devamlı, aralıksız ☆ *a.* katı madde
solidarity /soli'deriti/ *a.* dayanışma
solidify /sı'lidifay/ *e.* katılaştırmak; katılaşmak; sağlamlaştırmak
solitary /'solitıri/ *s.* yalnız; ıssız
solitude /'solityu:d/ *a.* yalnızlık
solo /'soulou/ *a, müz.* solo **soloist** solist
solstice /'solstis/ *a.* gündönümü
soluble /'solyubıl/ *s.* çözünür
solution /sı'lu:şın/ *a.* çözüm; *kim.* çözünme; *kim.* çözelti, eriyik
solve /solv/ *e.* çözmek, halletmek
solvent /'solvınt/ *s.* borcunu ödeyebilen, muteber ☆ *a, kim.* çözücü, eriten
some /sım, sam/ *s.* biraz; birkaç; bazı, kimi; (herhangi) bir ☆ *adl.* bazısı, bazıları, kimi; bir miktar, biraz **somebody** biri, birisi **someday** bir gün, ilerde, gelecekte **somehow** her nasılsa, bir yolla; nasıl oluyorsa; her nedense, nedense **something** bir şey **something like** gibi; *ii, kon.* yaklaşık, civarında **sometime** bir ara **sometimes** bazen, ara sıra **somewhat** biraz, oldukça **somewhere** bir yere; bir yerde
somersault /'samıso:lt/ *a.* takla ☆ *e.* takla atmak
son /san/ *a.* oğul **son-in-law** damat
sonata /sı'na:tı/ *a, müz.* sonat
song /song/ *a.* şarkı, türkü

sonic /'sonik/ s. sesle ilgili
sonnet /'sonit/ a, yaz. sone
soon /su:n/ be. yakında, birazdan; neredeyse; erken as soon as (yap)-ar (yap)-maz soon after -den hemen sonra sooner or later er geç sooner than -mektense
soot /sut/ a. is, kurum sooty isli
soothe /su:d / e. yatıştırmak, dindirmek
sophisticated /sı'fistikeytid/ s. görmüş geçirmiş; pişkin; karmaşık, gelişmiş
sophomore /'sofımo:/ a. lise ya da üniversitede ikinci sınıf öğrencisi
soppy /'sopi/ s, İİ, kon. içli, aşırı duyarlı
soprano /sı'pra:nou/ a, müz. soprano
sorbet /'so:bit/ a. şerbet
sorcerer /'so:sırı/ a. büyücü, sihirbaz sorcery büyü; büyücülük
sordid /'so:did/ s. kirli, pis; alçak, aşağılık; çıkarcı, paragöz
sore /so:/ s. acıyan, ağrıyan; kırgın, küskün ☆ a. yara sorely şiddetle, çok
sorrow /'sorou/ a. üzüntü, keder, acı
sorry /'sori/ s. üzgün; pişman ☆ ünl. üzgünüm; maalesef; affedersiniz; İİ. efendim? be sorry (for) üzgün olmak, üzülmek feel sorry (for) (-e) acımak, için üzülmek
sort /so:t/ a. tür, çeşit ☆ e. sınıflandırmak sort of kon. bir yerde, bir bakıma sort out İİ. düzeltmek, çözmek, halletmek; seçmek; ayıklamak
soufflé /'su:fley/ a. sufle
sought /so:t/ bkz. seek
soul /soul/ a. ruh, can; öz, esas; kimse soulful içli, duygulu soulless ruhsuz, duygusuz
sound /saund/ a. ses; gürültü; etki, izlenim ☆ e. (gibi) gelmek/görünmek; çalmak, öttürmek; ses çıkarmak ☆ s. sağlam; emin; güvenilir; (uyku) derin ☆ be. (uyku) derin, deliksiz, mışıl mışıl soundproof sesgeçirmez soundtrack film müziği
soup /su:p/ a. çorba
sour /sauı/ s. ekşi; (süt) ekşimiş, kesilmiş; ters, hırçın, huysuz
source /so:s/ a. kaynak; memba
south /saut / a. güney southbound gü-

neye giden southeast güneydoğu southern güneye ait, güney southward güneye giden southwest güneybatı
souvenir /su:vı'niı/ a. andaç, hatıra
sovereign /'sovrin/ a. hükümdar ☆ s. yüce, en yüksek; egemen, hâkim
sovereignty /'sovrınti/ a. egemenlik, hâkimiyet, bağımsızlık
sow /sou/ e. sowed, sown /soun/ (tohum) ekmek
soya bean /'soyı bi:n/ a. soya fasulyesi
spa /spa:/ a. kaplıca
space /speys/ a. uzay; alan, meydan; yer; aralık; açıklık; süre space shuttle uzay mekiği spacecraft uzay aracı spaceship uzaygemisi
spacious /'speyşıs/ s. geniş, ferah, havadar
spade /speyd/ a. bahçıvan beli; (iskambil) maça
spaghetti /spı'geti/ a. çubuk makarna, spagetti
span /spen/ a. karış; aralık; an
spangle /'spengıl/ a. pul, payet
spank /spenk/ e. kıçına şaplak atmak
spanner /'spenı/ a. somun anahtarı
spar /spa:/ a, den. seren, direk
spare /speı/ s. yedek, fazla; az, kıt, yetersiz, serbest, boş ☆ e. esirgemek; -siz olabilmek, -siz yapabilmek, -den kurtarmak spare part yedek parça spare time boş zaman
spark /spa:k/ a. kıvılcım; zerre; işaret, iz ☆ e. kıvılcım saçmak sparking plug buji
sparkle /'spa:kıl/ a. parlayış, parıltı ☆ e. pırıldamak sparkling parlak
sparrow /'sperou/ a. serçe
sparse /spa:s/ s. seyrek
spasm /'spezım/ a, hek. spazm, kasılma
spat /spet/ bkz. spit
spate /speyt/ a. sel, sağanak
spatter /'spetı/ a. (çamur, vb.) sıçratmak ☆ a. serpinti, sağanak
spatula /'spetyulı/ a. spatül, mala
spawn /spo:n/ a. balık yumurtası ☆ e. (balık, kurbağa, vb.) yumurtlamak
speak /spi:k/ e. spoke /spouk/, spo-

ken /spoukın/ konuşmak; konuşma yapmak **speak for** -ın adına konuşmak **speak of** -den söz etmek **speak out** sesini yükselterek konuşmak **speak up** daha yüksek sesle konuşmak; fikrini belirtmek **speaker** konuşmacı; sözcü; hoparlör, kolon

spear /spiı/ a. kargı, mızrak; zıpkın

spearmint /'spiımint/ a, bitk. nane

special /'speşıl/ s. özel **specially** özellikle

specialist /'speşılist/ a. uzman

speciality /speşi'eliti/ a. özellik

specialize /'speşılayz/ e. uzmanlaşmak

species /'spi:şi:z/ a, bitk, hayb. tür, cins

specific /spi'sifik/ s. özgül; özel, belirli; bir türe özgü

specification /spesifi'keyşın/ a. belirtme; ç. ayrıntılar

specify /spesifay/ e. kesinlikle belirtmek

speck /spek/ a. nokta, benek; zerre

speckle /'spekıl/ a. ufak benek, leke, nokta, çil **speckled** çilli

spectacle /'spektıkıl/ a. gösteri, oyun; manzara, görünüm **spectacles** gözlük

spectacular /spek'tekyulı/ s. olağanüstü, mükemmel

spectator /spek'teytı/ a. izleyici, seyirci

spectrum /'spektrım/ a, fiz. tayf

speculate /'spekyuleyt/ e. tahmin etmek; tic. spekülasyon yapmak **speculation** kuram; tahmin; spekülasyon, vurgun **speculative** kuramsal **speculator** spekülatör, vurguncu

sped /sped/ bkz. **speed**

speech /spi:ç/ a. konuşma; söz, söylev **speechless** dili tutulmuş

speed /spi:d/ a. hız; vites ☆ e. **sped** /sped/ hızla gitmek **speed up** hızlanmak; hızlandırmak **speedboat** sürat motoru **speedometer** hızölçer, hız göstergesi **speedway** motosiklet ya da otomobil yarışı pisti; Aİ. sürat yolu, ekspres yol **speedy** hızlı, çabuk, seri

spell /spel/ e. **spelt** /spelt/ harf harf söylemek ☆ a. sihir, büyü; nöbet; süre, dönem **spellbound** büyülenmiş **spelling** imla, yazım

spend /spend/ e. **spent** /spent/ (para) harcamak; (vakit) geçirmek

spendthrift /'spendtrift/ a. müsrif, savurgan

spent /spent/ bkz. **spend**; s. kullanılmış

sperm /spö:m/ a. atmık, sperm, meni

sphere /sfiı/ a. yuvar, küre; alan **spherical** küresel

sphinx /sfinks/ a. sfenks

spice /spays/ a. bahar, baharat **spicy** baharatlı; açık saçık, muzır

spider /'spaydı/ a. örümcek

spike /spayk/ a. sivri (demir, vb.) uç; sivri uçlu şey; başak

spill /spil/ e. **spilt** /spilt/ dökmek; dökülmek; üstünden atmak ☆ a. dökme; (at vb.'den) düşürme

spin /spin/ e. **spun** /span/ (iplik) eğirmek; bükmek; döndürmek, çevirmek ☆ a. fırıl fırıl dönme; kon. gezinti

spinach /'spinic, 'spiniç/ a. ıspanak

spinal /'spaynıl/ s, anat. belkemiğiyle ilgili **spinal cord** anat. omurilik

spindle /'spindıl/ a. iğ; mil, dingil

spine /spayn/ a, anat. omurga, belkemiği; hayb, bitk. diken **spineless** omurgasız; korkak, yüreksiz

spiral /'spayırıl/ a. helezon, helis; hek. spiral ☆ s. sarmal, helezoni

spirit /'spirit/ a. ruh, can; peri, cin; huy, karakter; ispirto; şevk, canlılık; **spirits** sert içki, alkol **spirited** ateşli, canlı; huylu **in low/poor spirits** neşesiz, keyifsiz

spiritual /'spiriçuıl/ s. ruhsal, manevi; dini, kutsal; ruhani

spit /spit/e. **spat** /spet/ tükürmek, çiselemek ☆ a. şiş, kebap şişi; coğ. dil; tükürük, salya

spite /spayt/ a. kin, garez **in spite of** -e rağmen, -i umursamadan **spiteful** kinci

spittle /'spitıl/ a. tükürük, salya

splash /'spleş/ e. (su, çamur, vb.) sıçramak; sıçratmak ☆ a. sıçrayan çamur; leke; şapırtı

spleen /spli:n/ a. dalak

splendid /'splendid/ s. görkemli, gösterişli; muhteşem kon. mükemmel, çok iyi splendour /'splendı/ a. görkem, ihtişam

splice /'splays/ e. (örerek, yapıştırarak) tutturmak

splinter /'splintı/ a. kıymık

split /split/ e. split /split/ yarmak; yarılmak; bölmek; bölünmek ☆ a. yarık, çatlak; bölünme, ihtilaf split hairs kılı kırk yarmak

spoil /spoyl/ e. spoilt /spoylt/ berbat etmek, mahvetmek; yüz vermek, şımartmak

spoilt /spoylt/ bkz. spoil

spoke /spouk/ bkz. speak

spoken /spoukın/ bkz. speak

spokesman /'spouksmın/ a. sözcü

sponge /spanc/ a. sünger; kon. otlakçı, beleşçi ☆ e. sırtından geçinmek

sponsor /'sponsı/ a. spor kulübü, radyo, TV programları vb.'nin masraflarını karşılayıp reklamını yapan firma ☆ e. kefil olmak; himaye etmek

spontaneous /spon'teyniıs/ s. kendiliğinden olan; doğal, içten gelen spontaneously kendiliğinden

spook /spu:k/ a, kon. hayalet, hortlak

spool /spu:l/ a. makara, bobin

spoon /spu:n/ a. kaşık ☆ e. kaşıklamak spoonful kaşık dolusu

sporadic /spı'redik/ s. tek tük, seyrek

sport /spo:t/ a. spor; eğlence, oyun sports spor karşılaşması sports car spor araba sportsman sporcu; sportmen sportsmanship sportmenlik sports wear spor giysi

spot /spot/ a. nokta, benek, leke, yer ☆ e. beneklemek, lekelemek; ayırt etmek, tanımak; bulmak spotless lekesiz, tertemiz spotted benekli spotty benekli

spouse /spaus, spauz/ a, huk. eş, karı ya da koca

spout /spaut/ e. fışkırtmak; fışkırmak; kon. heyecanla okumak/konuşmak ☆ a. bir kabın ağzı; ağız, fışkıran su

sprain /spreyn/ e. burkmak ☆ a. burkulma

sprang /spreng/ bkz. spring

sprawl /spro:l/ e. yayılarak oturmak

spray /sprey/ a. serpinti; püskürtme ara-

cı, sprey ☆ e. (toz halinde) serpmek, püskürtmek

spread /spred/ e. spread /spred/ yaymak; sermek; sürmek ☆ a. yayılma; dağılma; örtü; genişlik

spree /spri:/ a. cümbüş, âlem

sprig /sprig/ a. sürgün, fışkın

sprightly /'spraytli/ s. neşeli, şen

spring /spring/ e. sprang /spreng/, sprung /sprang/ sıçramak, fırlamak; ortaya çıkıvermek; yaylanmak; çıkmak, doğmak ☆ a. sıçrayış; fırlama; yay, zemberek; ilkbahar; pınar, kaynak; köken spring up baş göstermek, çıkıvermek, türemek springboard sıçrama tahtası, tramplen springtime ilkbahar

sprinkle /'sprinkıl/ e. serpmek; saçmak; çiselemek sprinkler pülverizatör; püskürteç

sprint /sprint/ e. tabana kuvvet koşmak ☆ a. sürat koşusu

sprite /sprayt/ a. peri, cin

sprout /spraut/ e. filizlenmek; çıkarmak ☆ a, bitk. filiz, tomurcuk, sürgün; brüksellahanası

spruce /spru:s/ a, bitk. ladin ağacı

sprung /sprang/ bkz. spring

spry /spray/ s. dinç, canlı, çevik

spun /span/ bkz. spin

spume /spyu:m/ a. köpük

spur /spö: / a. mahmuz; dürtü, güdü ☆ e. mahmuzlamak; kışkırtmak

spurn /spö:n/ e. tekme ile kovmak; reddetmek, burun kıvırmak

spurt /spö:t/ e. fışkırmak; fışkırtmak ☆ a. fışkırma; ani hamle

spy /spay/ a. casus ☆ e. casusluk etmek, gözetlemek

squabble /'skwobıl/ a. ağız kavgası, atışma ☆ e. dalaşmak; çekişmek

squad /skwod/ a. ekip, takım; ask. manga

squadron /'skwodrın/ a, ask. filo; süvari bölüğü

squalid /'skwolid/ s. pis, bakımsız

squall /skwo:l/ e. yaygara koparmak, feryat etmek ☆ a. yaygara, feryat

square /skweı/ a. kare; alan, meydan; gönye; mat. kare; kon. örümcek kafalı

☆ s. kare biçiminde; dik açılı; dürüst, doğru ☆ e. dört köşe yapmak; *mat.* karesini almak **square root** kare kök **square up** *kon.* hesabı ödemek **squarely** dürüstçe; tam karşıda
squash /skwoş/ e. ezmek, sıkmak; son vermek, bastırmak ☆ a. ezme; meyve suyu; kalabalık; balkabağı; *sp.* bir tür kapalı tenis oyunu
squat /skwot/ e. çömelmek; bir yere izinsiz yerleşmek ☆ s. bodur, bücür
squaw /skwo:/ a. Kızılderili kadın
squawk /skwo:k/ e. cırlamak; gıcırdamak ☆ a. cırlama; gıcırtı
squeal /skwi:l/ e. ciyaklamak; haykırmak; *arg.* ihbar etmek, ele vermek ☆ a. ciyaklama; haykırış
squeamish /'skwi:miş/ s. midesi bulanan; güç beğenir
squeeze /skwi:z/ e. sıkmak, sıkıştırmak; tıkışmak ☆ a. sıkma, sıkıştırma
squelch /skwelç/ e. susturmak, bastırmak
squib /skwib/ a. fişek, maytap; yergi, hiciv
squid /skwid/ *a, hayb.* mürekkepbalığı
squint /skwint/ e. gözlerini kısmak; şaşı bakmak
squire /skwayı/ a. köy ağası, bey
squirm /skwö:m/ e. kıvranmak
squirrel /'skwirıl/ *a, hayb.* sincap
squirt /skwö:t/ e. fışkırmak; fışkırtmak
stab /steb/ a. bıçaklama; bıçak yarası ☆ e. bıçaklamak; (bıçak, ağrı, vb.) saplamak
stability /stı'biliti/ a. sağlamlık; denge; değişmezlik
stabilize /'steybilayz/ e. dengede tutmak; sağlamlaştırmak
stable /'steybıl/ s. değişmez, sabit; sağlam ☆ a. ahır
stack /stek/ a. yığın, istif; baca
stadium /'steydiım/ a. stadyum
staff /sta:f/ a. personel, çalışanlar, kadro; kurmay; değnek, sopa
stag /steg/ a. erkek geyik
stage /steyc/ a. sahne; tiyatro; aşama, evre ☆ e. sahneye koymak
stagger /'stegı/ e. sendelemek; şaşırtmak, afallatmak ☆ a. sendeleme,

sallanma
stagnant /'stegnınt/ s. durgun
stagnate /steg'neyt/ e. durgunlaşmak
staid /steyd/ s. ciddi, sıkıcı
stain /steyn/ e. lekelemek; lekelenmek; boyamak ☆ a. leke; benek; boya, vernik **stainless** lekesiz, temiz; paslanmaz **stainless steel** paslanmaz çelik
stair /steı/ a. merdiven basamağı **stairs** merdiven **staircase, stairway** merdiven
stake /steyk/ a. kazık; direk; kumarda ortaya konulan para, miza ☆ e. kazığa bağlamak; kumarda para koymak
stalactite /stelıktayt/ a. sarkıt
stalagmite /'stelıgmayt/ a. dikit
stale /steyl/ s. bayat; adi; yıpranmış
stalemate /'steylmeyt/ a. (satranç) pat
stalk /sto:k/ a. gizlice yaklaşmak; azametle yürümek ☆ a, bitk. sap
stall /sto:l/ a. ahır (bölmesi); satış yeri, sergi; (tiyatro) koltuk ☆ e. durmak, stop etmek; stop ettirmek; ahıra kapatmak; *kon.* oyalanmak, geciktirmek
stallion /'steliın/ a. aygır, damızlık at
stamina /'steminı/ a. dayanıklılık
stammer /'stemı/ e. kekelemek ☆ . kekeleme; kekemelik
stamp /stemp/ e. damgalamak; pul yapıştırmak; (para) basmak; tepinmek ☆ a. pul, posta pulu; damga; ıstampa; iz, işaret
stampede /'stempi:d/ a. bozgun, panik
stand /stend/ e. **stood** /stud/ ayakta durmak, dikelmek; durmak, bulunmak; dayanmak; katlanmak ☆ a. duruş; sehpa, askı, ayaklık, tezgâh, satış sergisi; durak; tribün; (mahkemede) tanık yeri **stand by** yanında durmak; hazır beklemek **stand for** anlamına gelmek; desteklemek **stand on one's own (two) feet** kendi yağı ile kavrulmak **stand out** göze çarpmak; kendini göstermek **stand up** ayağa kalkmak **stand up for** -ı desteklemek **stand up to** cesaretle karşılamak, göğüs germek **standby** hazır bekleyen şey/kimse **stand-in** dublör **standstill** sekte vurma
standard /'stendıd/ a. standart; bay-

rak, sancak ☆ *s.* standart, tekbiçim
standard of living yaşam standartı
standardize standardize etmek
standing /'stending/ *s.* ayakta duran;
durgun; daimi ☆ *a.* süreklilik, devam; geçerlilik; saygınlık
stanza /'stenzı/ *a, yaz.* şiir kıtası, kesim
staple /'steypıl/ *a.* zımba teli; başlıca
ürün; hammadde **stapler** tel zımba
star /sta:/ *a.* yıldız ☆ *e.* başrolü oynamak **starboard** *den.* sancak **starfish**
denizyıldızı **stars and stripes** ABD
bayrağı **starlight** yıldız ışığı **starring**
başrolde
starch /sta:ç/ *a.* nişasta; kola **starchy** nişastalı; kolalı; sert, katı
stare /steı/ *e.* dik dik bakmak ☆ *a.* sabit bakış
stark /sta:k/ *s.* sert, katı; sade, yalın; ıssız **stark naked** *kon.* anadan doğma
starling /'sta:ling/ *a, hayb.* sığırcık
start /sta:t/ *e.* başlamak; başlatmak; yola çıkmak; ürkmek, irkilmek ☆ *a.*
başlangıç, başlama; kalkış, hareket;
sp. çıkış, start; sıçrama, irkilme;
avans; ürkme **to start with** önce; başlangıçta **start off** hareket etmek, yola
koyulmak **start out** *kon.* -mek niyetinde olmak **starter** (oto) marş; yarışa
katılan kişi/at; *sp.* starter, çıkışçı; meze türünden ilk yemek
startle /'sta:tıl/ *e.* korkutmak, ürkütmek, ürkmek
starve /sta:v/ *e.* açlıktan ölmek; açlıktan öldürmek; *kon.* kurt gibi acıkmak
starvation açlıktan ölme
state /steyt/ *a.* durum, hal; devlet, hükümet; eyalet ☆ *e.* belirtmek, bildirmek **statement** söz, ifade; demeç; hesap
statesman /'steytsmın/ *a.* devlet adamı
static /'stetik/ *s.* durağan, statik **statics**
dinginlikbilim, statik
station /'steyşın/ *a.* istasyon; durak;
yer; karakol, merkez
stationary /'steyşınıri/ *s.* yerinde duran,
durağan, sabit
stationer /'steyşını/ *a.* kırtasiyeci **stationery** kırtasiye
statistics /stı'tistiks/ *a.* istatistik

statistician /stetis'tişın/ *a.* istatistikçi
statue /'steçu:/ *a.* yontu, heykel
statuette /steçu'et/ *a.* heykelcik, küçük
yontu
status /'steytıs/ *a.* durum, hal; toplumsal ya da mesleki durum, konum,
mevki
statute /'steçu:t/ *a.* yasa, kural
stave /steyv/ *a.* fıçı tahtası; değnek; şiir
kıtası **stave in** kurmak, delmek **stave
off** uzaklaştırmak, savmak
stay /stey/ *e.* kalmak; durmak; durdurmak, ertelemek; dayanmak; bastırmak, geçiştirmek ☆ *a.* kalış, kalma;
huk. erteleme **stay in** dışarı çıkmamak, evde kalmak **stay on** kalmaya
devam etmek **stay out** (evden) dışarda kalmak; grevi sürdürmek **stay put**
yerinden kımıldamamak
steadfast /'stedfa:st/ *s.* sadık, dönmez
steady /'stedi/ *s.* sallanmaz, sağlam,
sabit; şaşmaz; düzgün, muntazam
steadily durmadan, gittikçe; muntazaman
steak /steyk/ *a.* biftek
steal /sti:l/ *e.* **stole** /stoul/, **stolen** /'stoulın/ çalmak, aşırmak; hırsızlık yapmak; gizlice hareket etmek
stealth /'stelt / *a.* gizli iş
steam /sti:m/ *a.* buhar; buğu; güç, enerji; öfke ☆ *e.* buhar salıvermek; buğuda/buharda pişirmek **steam engine**
buhar makinesi **steamer** buharlı vapur **steamy** buharlı; buğulu
steel /sti:l/ *a.* çelik **steelworks** çelik fabrikası
steep /sti:p/ *s.* dik, yalçın; *kon.* aşırı,
yüksek ☆ *e.* suya batırmak; ıslatmak
steeple /'sti:pıl/ *a.* çan kulesi
steeplechase /'sti:pılçeys/ *a.* engelli koşu/at yarışı
steer /stiı/ *e.* dümen kullanmak; yönetmek ☆ *a.* boğa, öküz **steering
wheel** direksiyon
stem /stem/ *a.* ağaç gövdesi; sap; *dilb.*
gövde; *den.* pruva ☆ *e.* (akışını) durdurmak
stench /stenç/ *a.* pis koku
stencil /'stensıl/ *a.* şablon; kalıp; marka; mumlu kâğıt

stenographer /stı'nogrıfı/ *a.* stenograf
stenography /stı'nogrıfi/ *a.* steno
step /step/ *a.* adım; basamak; ayak sesi; ayak izi ☆ *e.* adım atmak, girmek; basmak **step by step** adım adım, yavaş yavaş **step in** müdahale etmek **step up** artırmak **step/tread on someone's toes/corns** birinin damarına basmak **stepbrother** üvey erkek kardeş **stepchild** üvey çocuk **stepladder** seyyar merdiven, portatif merdiven **stepparent** üvey anne ya da baba **stepping stone** atlama tahtası/taşı **stepsister** üvey kız kardeş
steppe /step/ *a.* bozkır, step
stereo /'steriou, 'stiıriou/ *a.* stereo pikap/teyp/cihaz, müzik seti
stereoscope /'steriıskoup/ *a.* stereoskop
stereotype /'steriıtayp/ *a.* klişeleşmiş örnek, beylik olay
sterile /'sterayl/ *s.* kısır, dölsüz; verimsiz; mikropsuz, steril
sterilize /'sterilayz/ *e.* kısırlaştırmak; sterilize etmek
sterling /'stö:ling/ *a.* sterlin
stern /stö:n/ *s.* sert, haşin; acımasız ☆ *a, den.* kıç
stethoscope /'stetıskoup/ *a, hek.* stetoskop
stew /styu:/ *a.* türlü, güveç, yahni ☆ *e.* hafif ateşte kaynatmak
steward /'styu:ıd/ *a.* kâhya; erkek hostes; kamarot
stewardess /styu:ı'des/ *a.* hostes; kadın kamarot
stick /stik/ *e.* **stuck** /stak/ saplamak; saplanmak; koymak; sokmak; takmak; yapışmak; yapıştırmak; çıkmaza sokmak ☆ *e. a.* sopa, değnek; baston **stick around** *kon.* beklemek, kalmak **stick at** *-den* çekinmek **stick out** dışarı çıkarmak, uzatmak **stick to** bağlı kalmak, tutmak **stick together** *kon.* birbirine sadık kalmak **stick up** dik durmak **sticker** yapışkan adam; çıkartma **sticking plaster** plaster, yapışkan yakı **sticky** yapışkan; *kon.* güç, zor
stiff /stif/ *s.* eğilmez, bükülmez; pekişmiş; sıkı; koyu; güç, zor; şiddetli

stiffen /'stifın/ *e.* sertleştirmek; kasmak; kasılmak
stifle /'stayfıl/ *e.* boğmak, boğulmak; bastırmak, tutmak
stigma /'stigmı/ *a.* damga; ayıp; *bitk.* tepecik
stile /stayl/ *a.* turnike
still /stil/ *s.* hareketsiz; sessiz, durgun; (şarap, vb.) köpüksüz ☆ *be.* hâlâ; yine de, buna rağmen; (daha) da
still /stil/ *a.* imbik
stimulant /'stimyulınt/ *a.* uyarıcı
stimulate /'stimyuleyt/ *e.* uyarmak, kışkırtmak, harekete geçirmek; teşvik etmek, özendirmek **stimulation** dürtme, teşvik; uyarma
stimulus /'stimyulıs/ *a.* uyarıcı
sting /sting/ *e.* **stung** /stang/ (arı, vb.) sokmak; acıtmak, sızlatmak ☆ *a.* sokma, ısırma; (arı, akrep, vb.) iğne; ısırgan tüyü
stingy /'stinci/ *s, kon.* cimri, pinti
stink /stink/ *e.* **stank (stunk)** /stenk (stank)/ pis kokmak ☆ *a.* pis koku
stint /stint/ *e.* esirgemek; cimrilik etmek
stipulate /'stipyuleyt/ *e.* şart koşmak, öngörmek **stipulation** şart koşma, şart
stir /stö:/ *e.* karıştırmak; kıpırdamak, kımıldamak; kıpırdatmak, kımıldatmak; harekete geçirmek ☆ *a.* karıştırma; hareket, canlılık, telaş **stirring** heyecanlandırıcı
stirrup /'stirıp/ *a.* üzengi
stitch /stiç/ *a.* dikiş; ilmik ☆ *e.* dikmek; dikiş dikmek
stoat /stout/ *a, hayb.* kakım, as
stock /stok/ *a.* stok, mevcut mal; hisse senedi; ağaç gövdesi; çiftlik hayvanları; sap, kabza; *bitk.* şebboy çiçeği ☆ *s.* beylik, basmakalıp **in stock** elde mevcut **out of stock** mevcudu kalmamış **stockbroker** borsa tellalı **stock exchange** borsa
stocking /'stoking/ *a.* uzun çorap
stocky /'stoki/ *s.* bodur, tıknaz
stoke /stouk/ *e.* ateşe kömür, vb. atmak, canlandırmak
stole /stoul/ *a.* etol, şal

stole, stolen /stoul, stoulın/ *bkz.* **steal**

stomach /'stamık/ *a.* mide; karın; iştah **stomachache** karın ağrısı

stomp /stomp/ *e, kon.* paldır küldür yürümek/dans etmek

stone /stoun/ *a.* taş; mücevher; meyve çekirdeği; 6350 gr.'lık ağırlık ölçüsü ☆ *e.* taşlamak, taşa tutmak; çekirdeğini çıkarmak **Stone Age** taş devri **stone-deaf** duvar gibi sağır

stony /'stouni/ *s.* taşlık, taşlı; taş gibi, acımasız

stool /stu:l/ *a.* tabure; dışkı

stoop /stu:p/ *e.* öne doğru eğilmek; kambur durmak; alçalmak, tenezzül etmek ☆ *a.* eğilme; alçalma

stop /stop/ *e.* durmak; durdurmak; önlemek, engellemek, durdurmak, mani olmak; kesilmek; tıkamak ☆ *a.* durma; durdurma, durak; nokta; engel **stop by** uğramak, ziyaret etmek **stop light** stop lambası; (trafik ışığı) kırmızı ışık **stopcock** vana **stopover** (yolculukta) mola **stoppage** durdurma, durma; tıkama **stopwatch** kronometre

storage /'sto:ric/ *a.* depolama, depo etme; ambar, depo; ardiye ücreti

store /sto:/ *a.* stok; *Aİ.* dükkân, mağaza; ambar, depo; ç. erzak ☆ *e.* depolamak, ambara koymak; saklamak **storehouse** ambar, depo **storeroom** ambar, depo, kiler

storey /'sto:ri/ *a.* (binada) kat

stork /sto:k/ *a.* leylek

storm /sto:m/ *a.* fırtına; öfke; ani duygusal taşkınlık; yüksek ses ☆ *e.* fırtına patlamak; kıyameti koparmak; *ask.* hücum etmek **stormy** fırtınalı

story /'sto:ri/ *a.* öykü, hikâye

stout /staut/ *s.* iri yarı; kalın; sağlam ☆ *a.* sert bira

stove /stouv/ *a.* soba; fırın, ocak

stow /stou/ *e.* istif etmek, yerleştirmek **stowaway** kaçak yolcu

straddle /'stredıl/ *e.* bacaklarını iyice açıp oturmak/dikilmek

straight /streyt/ *s.* düz, doğru; dik, dimdik; düzenli; dürüst; saf, sek ☆ *be.* düz, doğru; direkt; hemen ☆ *a.* (yarış, vb.'de) düzlük

straighten /'streytın/ *e.* düzeltmek, doğrultmak; düzelmek

straightforward /streyt'fo:wıd/ *s.* doğru sözlü, açık sözlü

strain /streyn/ *a.* gerginlik; burkulma, burkulup incinme; soy, ırk, nesil; soydan gelen özellik, iz; biçim, tarz; melodi, ezgi ☆ *e.* (at) germek, asılmak; zorlanmak; zorlamak; zarar vermek; (against) vücuduyla bastırmak

strainer /'streynı/ *a.* süzgeç

strait /streyt/ *a, coğ.* boğaz; ç. sıkıntı, darlık, güç durum

straitlaced /streyt'leyst/ *s, hkr.* bağnaz

strand /strend/ *a.* kıyı, sahil, yalı; tel, iplik ☆ *e.* karaya oturmak; karaya oturtmak

strange /streync/ *s.* tuhaf, garip, acayip; yabancı **stranger** yabancı, el; bir işin yabancısı kişi **strangeness** acayiplik

strangle /'strengıl/ *e.* boğazlamak

strap /strep/ *a.* kayış; şerit, bant ☆ *e.* kayışla bağlamak

strapping /'streping/ *s.* iri yarı

strategic /strı'ti:cik/ *s.* stratejik

strategy /'stretici/ *a.* strateji

stratosphere /'stretısfiı/ *a.* katyuvarı, stratosfer

stratum /'streytım/ *a.* katman, tabaka; kat; toplumsal sınıf, tabaka

straw /stro:/ *a.* saman; kamış, çubuk; önemsiz şey **the last straw** bardağı taşıran son damla

strawberry /stro:bırı/ *a, bitk.* çilek

stray /strey/ *e.* yolunu yitirmek; doğru yoldan ayrılmak ☆ *a.* gruptan ayrılmış, kaybolmuş

streak /stri:k/ *a.* yol, çizgi, çubuk ☆ *e.* çizgilemek, yol yol yapmak; hızla geçmek

stream /stri:m/ *a.* akarsu, çay, dere; akıntı; akım; sel; gidiş ☆ *e.* akmak; dalgalanmak **streamer** flama, fors

streamline /'stri:mlayn/ *e.* (işyeri, vb.) verimlilik düzeyini artırmak; aerodinamik şekil vermek

street /stri:t/ *a.* sokak, cadde

strength /strengt/ *a.* güç, kuvvet; dayanıklılık; sertlik; şiddet **strengthen** güç-

lendirmek, sağlamlaştırmak
strenuous /'strenyuıs/ s. güç, yorucu; faal, etkili
stress /stres/ a. gerilim, gerginlik, sıkıntı, stres; baskı, etki; önem; *dilb.* vurgu ☆ e. vurgulamak
stretch /streç/ e. germek, uzatmak; gerilmek, uzamak; yayılmak; gerinmek ☆ a. germe; gerilme; alan; süre
stretcher /'streçı/ a. sedye
stricken /'strikın/ s. (dert, hastalık, vb.'den) çeken, yakalanmış
strict /strikt/ s. sıkı; dikkatli; tam; katı, değişmez; titiz
stridden /'stridın/ *bkz.* stride
stride /strayd/ e. **strode** /stroud/, **stridden** /'stridın/ uzun adımlarla yürümek ☆ a. uzun adım
strife /strayf/ a. sorun, kavga, çekişme
strike /strayk/ e. **struck** /strak/ vurmak; aklına gelivermek; bulmak; (para, vb.) basmak; (kibrit) çakmak; (saat) çalmak; grev yapmak ☆ a. grev; (petrol, vb.) bulmak; *ask.* hava saldırısı **be on strike** grevde olmak **go on strike** grev yapmak **strike off** listeden çıkartmak, silmek **strike on/upon** buluvermek, bulmak **strike up** çalmaya başlamak; (dostluk) kurmak **striker** grevci; vurucu **striking** çarpıcı, göz alıcı
string /'string/ a. sicim, ip; tel; bağ, şerit; dizi ☆ e. **strung** /strang/ ipliğe dizmek, geçirmek **stringed** telli; ipe dizilmiş **stringed instrument** *müz.* telli çalgı
stringent /'strincınt/ s. (kural) uyulması zorunlu, katı; para sıkıntısı çeken, darda
strip /strip/ e. (giysi, kabuk, vb.) soymak; yolmak; soyunmak ☆ a. şerit; *sp.* forma **stripper** striptizci **striptease** striptiz
stripe /strayp/ a. kumaş yolu, çizgi, çubuk; biçim, tip **striped** çizgili, yollu
strive /strayv/ e. **strove** /strouv/, **striven** /strivın/ çabalamak, uğraşmak
striven /'strivın/ *bkz.* strive
strode /stroud/ *bkz.* stride
stroke /strouk/ a. vuruş, çarpma; inme;

felç; yüzme tarzı, kulaç; okşama ☆ e. okşamak; (topa) vurmak
stroll /stroul/ e. gezinmek, dolaşmak ☆ a. gezinti
strong /strong/ s. güçlü, kuvvetli; metin; sağlam; (tadı, kokusu) sert, koyu **stronghold** kale
strove /strouv/ *bkz.* strive
struck /strak/ *bkz.* strike
structural /'strakçırıl/ s. yapısal
structure /'strakçı/ a. yapı, kuruluş; bina, yapı; bünye
struggle /'stragıl/ a. çaba, uğraş, gayret, mücadele ☆ e. çabalamak, uğraşmak
strum /stram/ e, kon. acemice çalmak, zımbırdatmak, tıngırdatmak
strung /strang/ *bkz.* string
strut /strat/ e. kasıla kasıla yürümek
stub /stab/ a. sigara izmariti; dip koçanı; kütük **stub out** (sigara) söndürmek
stubble /'stabıl/ a. ekin anızı
stubborn /'stabın/ s. inatçı, direngen
stubby /'stabi/ s. kısa ve kalın; güdük
stuck /stak/ *bkz.* stick; s. şaşırıp kalmış; saplanmış; takılmış
stud /stad/ a. damızlık at, aygır; hara; iri başlı çivi; yaka düğmesi ☆ e. çivilemek
student /'styu:dınt/ a. öğrenci
studio /'styu:diou/ a. stüdyo
studious /'styu:diıs/ s. çalışkan; dikkatli
study /'stadi/ a. çalışma, okuma; inceleme; taslak; çalışma odası ☆ e. okumak, çalışmak; öğrenimi görmek; incelemek
stuff /staf/ a. madde; kumaş; şey ☆ e. doldurmak, tıkmak; tıkamak; *kon.* tıka basa yemek; (tavuk, vb. yiyecek) içini doldurmak **stuffy** havasız
stumble /'stambıl/ a. tökezlemek; *kon.* dili sürçmek, kekelemek
stump /stamp/ a. kütük ☆ e, kon. şaşkına çevirmek, sersemletmek
stun /stan/ e. afallatmak; bayıltmak **stunning** çok çekici, hoş
stung /stang/ *bkz.* sting
stunk /stangk/ *bkz.* stink

stunt /stant/ *e.* engellemek, gelişmesini engellemek, bodur bırakmak ☆ *a.* numara, hüner, gösteri **stunt man** (tehlikeli sahnelerde oynayan) dublör

stupefy /'styu:pifay/ *e.* sersemletmek, bunaltmak; şaşırtmak

stupendous /styu:'pendıs/ *s.* muazzam, harikulade, müthiş, büyük

stupid /'styu:pid/ *s.* aptal, salak, ahmak; saçma, aptalca

stupor /'styu:pı/ *a.* uyuşukluk, sersemlik

sturdy /'stö:di/ *s.* gürbüz; azimli

stutter /'statı/ *e.* kekelemek

sty /stay/ *a.* domuz ahırı; (göz) arpacık

style /stayl/ *a.* tarz, üslup, stil, biçem; moda; tip; tavır ☆ *e.* biçimlendirmek **stylish** şık, zarif, modaya uygun **stylist** modacı, desinatör

suave /swa:v/ *s.* nazik, tatlı

sub /sab/ *a, kon.* üye aidatı; denizaltı

subconscious /sab'konşıs/ *a, s.* bilinçaltı

subdivide /sabdi'vayd/ *e.* tekrar bölmek **subdivision** /-di'vijın/ altbölüm

subdue /sıb'dyu/ *e.* boyunduruk altına almak; yumuşatmak, azaltmak

subject /'sabcikt/ *a.* kul, bende; konu, mevzu; ders; denek; *dilb.* özne ☆ *s.* tabi; bağlı ☆ *e.* **(to)** tabi tutmak

subjective /sıb'cektiv/ *s.* öznel

subjunctive /sıb'canktiv/ *a, dilb.* dilek kipi ☆ *s.* dilek kipiyle ilgili

sublime /sı'blaym/ *s.* yüce, ulu

submarine /sabmı'ri:n/ *a.* denizaltı

submerge /sıb'mö:c/ *e.* batırmak, daldırmak; batmak, dalmak

submission /sıb'mişın/ *a.* boyun eğme, uyma, itaat; teklif, sunuş

submissive /sıb'misiv/ *s.* uysal, boyun eğen, itaatkâr

submit /sıb'mit/ *e.* boyun eğmek, itaat etmek; ileri sürmek, önermek, sunmak

subordinate /sı'bo:dinit/ *s.* bağlı, tabi; ikinci derecede ☆ *a.* ast

subscribe /sıb'skrayb/ *e.* **(to)** abone olmak; bağışta bulunmak; onaylamak **subscriber** abone **subscription** /sıb'skripşın/ abone ücreti; üye aidatı

subsequent /'sabsikwınt/ *s.* sonra gelen, sonraki **subsequently** sonradan

subside /sıb'sayd/ *e.* alçalmak, inmek; yatışmak, azalmak

subsidiary /sıb'sidiıri/ *a.* bayi, şube ☆ *s.* tali, yardımcı

subsidize /'sabsidayz/ *e.* (hükümet, vb.) para vermek, desteklemek

subsistence /sıb'sistıns/ *a.* geçim; varlık

substance /'sabstıns/ *a.* madde, materyal, cisim, özdek; **(the)** önemli bölüm, öz

substandard /sab'stendıd/ *s.* belli düzeyin altında, standartın altında

substantial /sıb'stenşıl/ *s.* dayanıklı, sağlam; özlü; gerçek; büyük, önemli

substantiate /sıb'stenşieyt/ *e.* kanıtlamak, doğrulamak

substitute /'sabstityu:t/ *a.* vekil, temsilci ☆ *e.* vekâlet etmek; yerine koymak/kullanmak **substitution** yerine koyma, ornatma

subterfuge /'sabtıfyu:c/ *a.* kaçamak, bahane; hile, dalavere

subterranean /sabtı'reyniın/ *s.* yeraltı

subtitles /'sabtaytlz/ *a.* (film) altyazı

subtle /'satıl/ *s.* güç algılanan, güç fark edilen, ince; kurnaz, zeki

subtract /sıb'trekt/ *e.* **(from)** çıkarmak **subtraction** *mat.* çıkarma; eksiltme

suburb /'sabö:b/ *a.* varoş, banliyö, yörekent **suburban** /sı'bö:bın/ banliyöde oturan; banliyö

subvert /sıb'vö:t/ *e.* (iktidardakileri) devirmeye çalışmak **subversive** /-vö:-siv/ yıkıcı

subway /'sabwey/ *a.* yeraltı geçidi; *Aİ.* metro, altulaşım

succeed /sık'si:d/ *e.* **(in)** başarmak, başarıya ulaşmak; -den sonra gelmek, izlemek; varis olmak

success /sık'ses/ *a.* başarı; başarılı kimse/şey **successful** başarılı

succession /sık'seşın/ *a.* birbirini izleme; yerine geçme **in succession** ardı ardına, sıra ile **successive** ardı ardına, sıra ile **successor** halef, ardıl

succinct /sık'sinkt/ *s.* az ve öz

succulent /'sakyulınt/ *s.* (meyve, vb.)

sulu

succumb /sɪ'kam/ *e.* **(to)** yenilmek, dayanamamak, boyun eğmek

such /saç/ *s.* öyle, böyle, bu gibi; öylesine; o kadar; bu gibi, bu tür **such as** gibi **such that** öyle ... **such-and such** falan filan **suchlike** benzeri şeyler, böylesi

suck /sak/ *e.* emmek ☆ *a.* emme

sucker /'sakɪ/ *a.* emen, emici; *bitk.* sürgün; *Aİ.* enayi, budala

suckle /'sakɪl/ *e.* emzirmek

suction /'sakşın/ *a.* emme; *fiz.* emiş gücü **suction pump** emme basma tulumba

sudden /'sadın/ *s.* ani, beklenmedik **all of a sudden** ansızın, birdenbire **suddenly** aniden, birdenbire

suds /sadz/ *a.* sabun köpüğü

sue /su:, syu:/ *e, huk.* dava etmek, dava açmak

suede /sweyd/ *a.* süet

suffer /'safı/ *e.* acı çekmek; zarara uğramak; -e uğramak **sufferer** acı çeken kimse, hasta **suffering** acı, güçlük

suffice /sɪ'fays/ *e.* yetmek, yeterli olmak

sufficiency /sɪ'fişınsi/ *a.* yeterlilik

sufficient /sɪ'fişınt/ *s.* yeterli

suffix /'safiks/ *a, dilb.* sonek

suffocate /'safıkeyt/ *e.* (havasızlıktan) boğulmak; boğmak

sugar /'şugı/ *a.* şeker; *kon.* şekerim, tatlım **sugar beet** şekerpancarı **sugar cube/lump** kesmeşeker **sugarcane** şekerkamışı

suggest /sɪ'cest/ *e.* önermek; fikrini vermek, akla getirmek **suggestion** öneri; eser, iz

suicide /'su:isayd, 'syu:isayd/ *a.* intihar

suit /su:t, syu:t/ *a.* takım elbise, takım; *huk.* dava ☆ *e.* uymak, uygun olmak; yakışmak, açmak; uygun düşürmek, uydurmak **suitable** uygun, elverişli **suitcase** bavul, valiz

suite /swi:t/ *a.* (otel, vb.) daire; *müz.* süit

sulk /salk/ *e.* somurtmak, surat asmak **sulky** somurtkan, küskün

sullen /'salın/ *s.* (yüz) asık; somurtkan

sulphur /'salfı/ *a, kim.* kükürt

sultan /'saltın/ *a.* sultan

sultana /sul'ta:nı/ *a.* sultan karısı/kızı; çekirdeksiz kuru üzüm

sultry /'saltri/ *s.* (hava) bunaltıcı

sum /sam/ *a.* toplam, tutar; *mat.* problem **sum up** toplamak; özetlemek

summary /'samıri/ *e.* özet **summarize** /-'rayz/ özetlemek

summer /'samı/ *a.* yaz **summerhouse** çardak **summertime** yaz mevsimi

summit /'samit/ *a.* zirve, doruk

summon /'samın/ *e.* **(to)** getirtmek, celp etmek **summons** celp, çağrı

sun /san/ *a.* güneş ☆ *e.* güneşlenmek **sunbathe** güneş banyosu yapmak **sunburn** güneş yanığı **sundown** gün batımı **sunflower** ayçiçeği **sunglasses** güneş gözlüğü **sunlight** güneş ışığı **sunny** güneşli **sunrise** gündoğumu **sunset** günbatımı **sunshade** güneş şemsiyesi, güneşlik **sunshine** güneş ışığı **sunstroke** güneş çarpması **suntan** güneş yanığı, bronzlaşma

sundae /'sandey/ *a.* meyveli dondurma

Sunday /'sandi, 'sandey/ *a.* pazar (günü)

sundry /'sandri/ *s.* çeşitli, türlü türlü

sung /sang/ *bkz.* sing

sunk /sangk/ *bkz.* sink

sunken /'sankın/ *s.* batmış, batık; çukur

super /'su:pı, 'syu:pı/ *s, kon.* süper, müthiş

superb /su:'pö:b/ *s.* mükemmel, harika, süper

superficial /su:pı'fişıl/ *s.* yüzeysel

superfluous /su:'pö:fluıs/ *s.* lüzumsuz, fazla, gereksiz

superhuman /su:pı'hyu:mın/ *s.* insanüstü

superimpose /su:pır'impouz/ *e.* **(on)** üstüne koymak, eklemek

superintend /su:pırin'tend/ *e.* yönetmek; denetlemek **superintendent** yönetici; müfettiş; *İİ.* polis memuru

superior /su:'piırı/ *s.* (sınıf, mevki, vb.) üst, yüksek; üstün nitelikli; üstünlük taslayan ☆ *a.* amir, üst **superiority**

/-'oriti/ üstünlük

superlative /syu:'pö:lıtiv/ *s, a.* en üstün; en yüksek **superlative degree** *dilb.* en üstünlük derecesi

supermarket /'su:pıma:kit/ *a.* süpermarket

supernatural /su:pıneçırıl/ *s.* doğaüstü

supersede /su:pı'si:d/ *e.* yerine geçmek

supersonic /su:pı'sonik/ *s.* sesten hızlı

superstition /su:pı'stişın/ *a.* batıl inanç **superstitious** batıl inançlı

supervise /'su:pıvayz/ *e.* nezaret etmek, denetlemek

supervision /su:pı'vijın/ *a.* nezaret, denetim

supervisor /'su:pıvayzı/ *a.* müfettiş; (üniversitede) danışman

supper /'sapı/ *a.* akşam yemeği

supplant /sı'pla:nt/ *e.* yerine geçmek, ayağını kaydırıp yerini kapmak

supple /'sapıl/ *s.* bükülgen, esnek

supplement /'saplimınt/ *a.* ilave, ek ☆ *e.* **(by/with)** -e eklemeler yapmak **supplementary** ilave olan, ek

supply /sı'play/ *e.* vermek, tedarik etmek, sağlamak ☆ *a.* tedarik, temin; mevcut, stok **supply and demand** arz ve talep **supplier** tedarik eden kimse/firma **supplies** levazım, erzak, gereçler

support /sı'po:t/ *e.* (ağırlığını) çekmek; desteklemek; geçindirmek, bakmak ☆ *a.* destek **supporter** taraftar

suppose /sı'pouz/ *e.* zannetmek, sanmak **be supposed to** -meli, -malı, -mesi gerek **supposedly** söylendiğine göre **supposing** eğer

supposition /sapı'ziişın/ *a.* varsayım; farz, sanı

suppress /sı'pres/ *e.* bastırmak, önlemek

supreme /su:'pri:m/ *s.* en yüksek **Supreme Court** Yüce Divan, Anayasa Mahkemesi **supremacy** üstünlük

sure /şuı/ *s.* emin, şüphesiz, kesin; muhakkak, kuşkusuz **for sure** kesinlikle öyle, mutlaka **make sure** emin olmak **surely** elbette, kuşkusuz

surety /'şuıriti/ *a.* kefalet, teminat, güvence, garanti; kefil

surf /sö:f/ *a.* çatlayan dalgalar **surfing** sörf

surface /'sö:fis/ *a.* yüzey; dış görünüş **on the surface** görünüşte, dıştan

surfeit /'sö:fit/ *a.* aşırı miktar

surge /sö:c/ *a.* dalgalanma ☆ *e.* dalgalanmak; yükselmek

surgeon /'sö:cın/ *a, hek.* cerrah

surgery /'sö:cıri/ *a, hek.* cerrahlık, ameliyat; *İİ.* muayenehane

surgical /'sö:cikıl/ *s, hek.* cerrahi

surly /'sö:li/ *s.* ters, sert, huysuz

surmount /sı'maunt/ *e.* üstesinden gelmek, alt etmek, yenmek

surname /'sö:neym/ *a.* soyad

surpass /sı'pa:s/ *e.* geçmek, aşmak

surplus /'sö:plıs/ *a, s.* artık

surprise /sı'prayz/ *a.* sürpriz; şaşkınlık; *ask.* baskın ☆ *e.* şaşırtmak; *ask.* baskın yapmak **surprising** şaşırtıcı

surrender /sı'rendı/ *e.* teslim olmak; teslim etmek

surround /sı'raund/ *e.* kuşatmak, etrafını sarmak, çevirmek **surrounding** kenar, çevredeki, civardaki **surroundings** çevre

surveillance /sö:'veylıns/ *a.* gözetim, gözaltı **under surveillance** gözaltında

survey /sı'vey/ *e.* bakmak, incelemek, dikkatle göz gezdirmek ☆ *a.* /'sö:vey/ inceleme; gözden geçirme; yüzölçümü, ölçüm

survival /sı'vayvıl/ *a.* hayatta kalma, yaşamı sürdürme

survive /sı'vayv/ *e.* hayatta kalmak; sağ salim çıkmak, -den sağ kurtulmak **survivor** ölümden dönen kimse, hayatta kalan

susceptible /sı'septıbıl/ *s.* **(to)** kolay etkilenen, etki altında kalan

suspect /sı'spekt/ *e.* şüphelenmek, kuşkulanmak, zannetmek

suspect /'saspekt/ *a.* sanık ☆ *s.* şüpheli, su götürür

suspend /sı'spend/ *e.* asmak; ertelemek, askıya almak; (okul, vb.'den) uzaklaştırmak

suspenders /sı'spendız/ *a, İİ.* çorap askısı *Aİ.* pantolon askısı

suspense /sı'spens/ a. askıda kalma, kararsızlık; şüpheli beklenti
suspension /sı'spenşın/ a. asma; erteleme; kim. süspansiyon; askı donanımı, süspansiyon **suspension bridge** asma köprü
suspicion /sı'spişın/ a. şüphe, kuşku **suspicious** şüpheli, kuşkulu
sustain /sı'steyn/ e. güçlü tutmak, güç vermek; uzun süre korumak; (acı, vb.) çekmek
sustenance /'sastınıns/ a. besleme, güç verme; gıda, besin
swab /swob/ a. temizleme bezi
swagger /'swegı/ e. kasıla kasıla yürümek
swallow /'swolou/ e. yutmak ☆ a. yutma, yudum; kırlangıç
swamp /swomp/ a. bataklık, batak
swan /swon/ a. kuğu
swank /swenk/ e, kon. caka satmak, gösteriş yapmak
swap /swop/ e, kon. değiş tokuş etmek, değiştirmek ☆ a. değiş tokuş, takas
swarm /swo:m/ a. (arı, vb.) küme, oğul; sürü, kalabalık
swarthy /'swo:di/ s. esmer, yağız
swat /swot/ e. (böcek, sinek, vb.) ezmek
sway /swey/ e. sallamak; sallanmak; etkilemek
swear /sweı/ e. **swore** /swo:/, **sworn** /swo:n/ yemin etmek, ant içmek; küfretmek **swearword** küfür, sövgü
sweat /swet/ a. ter; zor iş, angarya ☆ e. terlemek; alın teri dökmek, çok çalışmak **sweaty** terli; terletici
sweater /'swetı/ a. kazak
sweatshirt /'swetşö:t/ a. uzun kollu pamuklu kazak
swede /swi:d/ a, bitk. şalgam
sweep /swi:p/ e. **swept** /swept/ süpürmek, süpürerek temizlemek; sürüklemek; sürtmek, sürtünmek ☆ a. süpürme; saha, alan; baca temizleyicisi **sweeper** süpürücü **sweeping** geniş içerikli; genel
sweet /swi:t/ s. tatlı; taze ☆ a, ii. tatlı; şekerleme **sweet corn** ii. mısır **sweet-**

heart sevgilim **sweeten** tatlandırmak **sweetness** tatlılık
swell /swel/ e. **swelled** /sweld/ **swollen** /swolın/ şişmek, kabarmak; şişirmek, kabartmak ☆ a. şişkinlik; denizin dalgalanması; sesin yükselmesi **swelling** kabarık, şiş, şişlik
swerve /swö:v/ e. aniden yana sapmak; (amaçtan) sapmak; saptırmak, döndürmek
swift /swift/ s. çabuk, atik, tez, hızlı
swill /swil/ e. (out/down) bol suyla çalkalamak/yıkamak
swim /swim/ e. **swam** /swem/, **swum** /swam/ yüzmek ☆ a. yüzme **swimming** yüzme, yüzme sporu, yüzücülük **swimming bath** ii. (halka açık) yüzme havuzu **swimming costume** kadın mayosu **swimming trunks** erkek mayosu, mayo **swimsuit** kadın mayosu
swindle /'swindıl/ e. (out of) dolandırmak ☆ a. dolandırıcılık
swing /swing/ e. **swung** /swang/ sallanmak; sallamak; dönmek ☆ a. sallanış, sallanma; salıncak
swipe /swayp/ a. kuvvetli darbe ☆ e. çalmak, aşırmak
swirl /swö:l/ e. girdap yaparak dönmek ☆ a. girdap
swish /swiş/ e. ıslık sesi çıkarmak; hışırdamak ☆ a. hışırtı
switch /swiç/ a. şalter, devre anahtarı, elektrik düğmesi; (beklenmedik) değişiklik; Aİ. demiryolu makası ☆ e. düğmeye basıp açmak/kapamak; değiştirmek **switch over** (TV, radyo) kanal değiştirmek **switchboard** telefon santralı
swivel /'swayvıl/ e. (round) kendi etrafında dönmek; döndürmek
swollen /'swoulın/ bkz. swell; s. şişmiş, şiş, kabarık
swoop /swu:p/ e. üstüne çullanmak ☆ a. üstüne çullanma
sword /so:d/ a. kılıç **swordfish** kılıçbalığı
swore, sworn /swo:, swo:n/ bkz. swear
swum /swam/ bkz. swim
swung /swang/ bkz. swing

sycamore /'sikımo:/ a, bitk. firavununinciri; Aİ. çınar
syllable /'silıbıl/ a, dilb. hece, seslem
syllabus /'silıbıs/ a. müfredat programı
symbol /'simbıl/ a. sembol, simge symbolic /sim'bolik/ sembolik symbolize /'simbılayz/ sembolize etmek
symmetry /'simitri/ a. simetri, bakışım symmetrical /si'metrikıl/ simetrik
sympathetic /simpı'tetik/ s. karşısındakinin duygularına katılan, duygudaş
sympathize /'simpıtayz/ e. (with) duygularını paylaşmak
sympathy /'simpıti/ a. acıma, şefkat, halden anlama; başkalarının duygularını paylaşma/anlama
symphony /'simfıni/ a, müz. semfoni symphonic /sim'fonik/ senfonik
symptom /'simptım/ a. araz, bulgu
synagogue /'sinıgog/ a. sinagog, havra
synchronize /'sinkrınayz/ e. (saat) aynı zamana ayarlamak; eş zamanlı/eş hızlı olmak
syndicate /'sindikit/ a. sendika, kartel
syndrome /'sindroum/ a, hek. hastalık belirtileri, tüm semptomlar, sendrom
synonym /'sınınim/ a. eşanlamlı sözcük, eşanlamlı synonymous /si'nonimıs/ eşanlamlı
synopsis /si'nopsis/ a. özet
syntax /'sinteks/ a, dilb. sentaks, sözdizim
synthesis /'sintisis/ a. (ç. -theses /-si:z/) sentez, bireşim
synthetic /sin'tetik/ a. sentetik, yapay
syphilis /'sifilis/ a, hek. frengi
syringe /si'rinc/ a. şırınga
syrup /'sirıp/ a. şurup
system /'sistım/ a. sistem systematic /sistı'metik/ s. sistemli, sistematik systems analyst sistem analisti

T

tab /teb/ a. etiket; giysinin asma yeri
table /'teybıl/ a. masa; yemek, sofra; tablo, çizelge table tennis sp. masatenisi tablecloth sofra örtüsü table d'hote tabldot tablespoon servis kaşığı tableware sofra takımı
tablet /'teblit/ a, hek. tablet; kitabe, yazıt
taboo /tı'bu:, te'bu:/ a. tabu, yasak
tabulate /'tebyuleyt/ e. cetvel haline koymak, çizelgelemek
tacit /'tesit/ s. söylenmeden anlaşılan
tack /tek/ a. ufak çivi, raptiye ☆ e. teyellemek; den. orsa etmek
tackle /'tekıl/ a. halat takımı; takım, donatı; sp. markaj ☆ e. uğraşmak, üstesinden gelmek; sp. topu kapmak
tact /tekt/ a. davranış inceliği, sezinç tactful nazik, sezinçli tactless patavatsız, düşüncesiz, densiz
tactic /'tektik/ a. taktik, yönlem tactical taktik tactics taktik
tadpole /'tedpoul/ a, hayb. iribaş
tag /teg/ a. etiket, fiş ☆ e. etiketlemek
tail /teyl/ a. kuyruk; bozuk paranın resimsiz tarafı ☆ e, kon. peşine düşmek, gizlice işlemek heads or tails yazı mı, tura mı
tailor /'teylı/ a. terzi tailor-made ısmarlama dikilmiş; uygun
taint /teynt/ e. leke, nokta, iz
take /teyk/ e. took /tuk/, taken /teykın/ almak; götürmek; tutmak; kazanmak; almak; (sınav) girmek; (fotoğraf) çekmek; kabullenmek; (içine) almak, taşımak; tahammül etmek; binmek, ile gitmek take after -e benzemek take apart sökmek takeaway hazır yemek satan dükkân take back geri almak take down sökmek, parçalarına ayırmak; yazmak take in içeriye almak; içine almak; (giysi) daraltmak; anlamak; kandırmak takeoff havalanma, kalkış take off çıkarmak; (uçak) havalanmak take on işe almak, işe başlatmak; ile dövüşmek; üstlenmek take out içinden çıkarmak; bir yere götürmek; edinmek takeover devralma, ele geçirme take over devralmak take to kanı kaynayıvermek; -e başlamak take up girişmek, başlamak; (yer, zaman, vb.) kaplamak; sürdürmek

457   **tear**

taking /'teyking/ s, kon. çekici
takings /'teykingz/ a. kazanç, hasılat
talcum powder /'telkım paudı/ a. talk
pudrası
tale /teyl/ a. hikâye, masal; dedikodu
talent /'telınt/ a. doğal yetenek, istidat
talented yetenekli
talk /to:k/ e. konuşmak, söylemek; görüşmek ☆ a.
konuşma, görüşme;
sohbet; konuşma biçimi talkative konuşkan, çenesi düşük talk down to biriyle küçümseyici bir biçimde konuşmak talk into -meye ikna etmek talk out of -den vazgeçirmek talk over görüşmek, tartışmak
tall /to:l/ s. uzun boylu; ... boyunda;
yüksek tall order olmayacak iş tall
story inanılması güç hikâye
tallow /'telou/ a. donyağı
talon /'telın/ a, hayb. pençe
tambourine /tembı'ri:n/ a, müz. tef
tame /teym/ s. evcil; yumuşak başlı, uysal ☆ e. evcilleştirmek tamer vahşi
hayvan eğiticisi
tamper /'tempı/ e. (with) karıştırmak,
kurcalamak, oynamak
tan /ten/ e. (hayvan derisi) tabaklamak; güneşte yanmak, bronzlaşmak
☆ a. güneş yanığı; sarımsı kahverengi
tang /teng/ a. keskin koku/tat
tangent /'tencınt/ a, mat. tanjant, teğet
tangerine /tencı'ri:n/ a, bitk. mandalina
tangible /'tencıbıl/ s. dokunulabilir, elle
tutulur, somut; gerçek
tangle /'tengıl/ e. karmakarışık etmek,
arapsaçına çevirmek ☆ a. karmakarışık şey, düğüm
tango /'tengou/ a, müz. tango
tank /tenk/ a, ask. tank; (gaz, sıvı, vb.)
depo, tank, sarnıç
tankard /'tenkıd/ a. maşrapa
tanker /'tenkı/ a. tanker
tantalize /'tentılayz/ e. boşuna ümit
vermek
tantrum /'tentrım/ a. öfke nöbeti
tap /tep/ a. musluk; tapa, tıkaç; hafif vuruş ☆ e. hafifçe vurmak; tapa ya da
musluğu açmak
tape /teyp/ a. şerit; bant tape recorder

teyp
taper /'teypı/ e. sivrilmek; inceltmek ☆
a. ince ve uzun mum
tapestry /'tepistri/ a. duvar halısı
tar /ta:/ a. asfalt; katran
tardy /'ta:di/ s. geç, gecikmiş
target /'ta:git/ a. hedef; amaç, erek
tariff /'terif/ a. tarife
tarmac /'ta:mek/ a. asfalt pist/alan
tarnish /'ta:niş/ e. karartmak, donuklaştırmak; donuklaşmak
tart /ta:t/ a. turta ☆ s. keskin, acı
tartar /'ta:tı/ a. şirret, bela tartar sauce
sos tartar, balık sosu
task /ta:sk/ a. vazife, görev, iş
taste /teyst/ e. tatmak, tadına bakmak;
tat almak ☆ a. tat; tadımlık; beğeni,
zevk tasteless tatsız; zevksiz tasty lezzetli, tatlı
tatters /'tetız/ a. paçavra, parça
tattoo /te'tu:, tı'tu:/ e. dövme yapmak
☆ a. dövme
taught /to:t/ bkz. teach
taunt /to:nt/ e. alay etmek, sataşmak
☆ a. alay, sataşma, iğneleme
Taurus /'to:rıs/ a. Boğa burcu
taut /to:t/ s. sıkı, gergin
tavern /'tevın/ a. taverna
tawny /'to:ni/ s. esmer, sarımsı kahverengi
tax /teks/ e. vergi koymak; külfet olmak, yük olmak ☆ a. vergi; külfet,
yük taxable vergiye tabi taxation vergilendirme tax-free vergiden muaf
taxi /'teksi/ a. taksi taxi rank, taxi
stand taksi durağı taximeter taksimetre
tea /ti:/ a. çay teabag poşet çay teacup çay fincanı tea leaf çay yaprağı
teapot çaydanlık tea spoon çay kaşığı
teach /ti:ç/ e. taught /to:t/ öğretmek;
ders vermek teacher öğretmen, hoca
teaching öğretim; ders, öğreti; öğretmenlik
team /ti:m/ a. takım; grup, ekip team
up with birlikte çalışmak teamwork
ekip çalışması
tear /tiı/ a. gözyaşı
tear /teı/ e. tore /to:/, torn /to:n/ yırt-

mak; koparmak; yırtılmak, kopmak; yolmak; *kon.* çılgın gibi koşmak ☆ *a.* yırtık **tear up** parça parça etmek
tease /'ti:z/ *e.* sataşmak, takılmak ☆ *a.* muzip, şakacı kimse **teaser** muzip; şakacı kimse; *kon.* zor bir soru/sorun
teat /ti:t/ *a.* biberon emziği
technical /'teknikıl/ *s.* teknik
technician /tek'nişın/ *a.* teknisyen
technique /tek'ni:k/ *a.* teknik, yordam
technology /tek'nolıci/ *a.* teknoloji **technological** teknolojik
teddy bear /'tedi beı/ *a.* oyuncak ayı
tedious /'ti:dııs/ *s.* can sıkıcı, usandırıcı
teem /ti:m/ *e.* **(with)** dolu olmak, kaynaşmak ☆ *e, kon.* bardaktan boşanırcasına yağmak
teenage /'ti:neyc/ *s.* 13-19 yaş arası gençlerle ilgili **teenager** 13-19 yaş arası genç
teens /'ti:nz/ *a.* 13-19 arasındaki yaş
tee shirt /'ti:şö:t/ *a.* tişört
teeth /ti:t / *a.* dişler **teethe** /ti:d / (bebek) diş çıkarmak
teetotal /ti:'toutıl/ *s.* yeşilaycı, içki içmeyen
telecast /'telika:st/ *a.* televizyon yayını
telecommunications /telikımyu:ni'keyşınz/ *a.* telekomünikasyon, iletişim
telegram /'teligrem/ *a.* telgraf, telyazı
telegraph /'teligra:f/ *a.* telgraf
telepathy /ti'lepıti/ *a.* telepati
telephone /'telifoun/ *a.* telefon ☆ *e.* telefon etmek **telephone booth** telefon kulübesi **telephone directory** telefon rehberi **telephone exchange** telefon santrali
telephonist /tı'lefınist/ *a.* santral memuru
telescope /'teliskoup/ *a.* teleskop
televise /'telivayz/ *e.* televizyonda göstermek, yayınlamak
television /'telivijın/ *a.* televizyon
telex /'teleks/ *a.* teleks; teleks haberi
tell /tel/ *e.* **told** /tould/ söylemek; anlatmak; bildirmek; ayırt etmek, tanımak; etki etmek, etkili olmak **tell off** azarlamak, paylamak **teller** veznedar; (oy) sayıcı **telling** etkili
telltale /'telteyl/ *a, kon.* muhbir, ispiyon-

cu ☆ *s.* belli eden, açığa vuran
telly /'teli/ *a, İİ, kon.* televizyon
temper /'tempı/ *a.* hal, keyif; huy, mizaç; kızgınlık ☆ *e.* (metal) sertleştirmek, tavlamak; hafifletmek, yumuşatmak **fly/get into a temper** aniden tepesi atmak **keep one's temper** sakinliğini korumak **lose one's temper** tepesi atmak, kızmak
temperament /'tempırımınt/ *a.* mizaç, yaradılış **temperamental** /-'mentıl/ saati saatine uymayan
temperate /'tempırit/ *s.* ılımlı, ölçülü; ılıman, ılık, mutedil
temperature /'tempırıçı/ *a.* sıcaklık (derecesi); *hek.* vücut ısısı, ateş **have/run a temperature** ateşlenmek, ateşi olmak **take sb's temperature** ateşini ölçmek
tempest /'tempist/ *a.* fırtına
temple /'tempıl/ *a.* tapınak; *anat.* şakak
tempo /'tempou/ *a.* tempo
temporal /'tempırıl/ *s.* zamanla ilgili; maddi; geçici
tawny /'to:ni/ *s.* esmer, sarımsı kahverengi
tax /teks/ *e.* vergi koymak; külfet olmak, yük olmak ☆ *a.* vergi; külfet, yük **taxable** vergiye tabi **taxation** vergilendirme **tax-free** vergiden muaf
taxi /'teksi/ *a.* taksi **taxi rank, taxi stand** taksi durağı **taximeter** taksimetre
tea /ti:/ *a.* çay **teabag** poşet çay **teacup** çay fincanı **tea leaf** çay yaprağı **teapot** çaydanlık **tea spoon** çay kaşığı
teach /ti:ç/ *e.* **taught** /to:t/ öğretmek; ders vermek **teacher** öğretmen, hoca **teaching** öğretim; ders, öğreti; öğretmenlik
team /ti:m/ *a.* takım; grup, ekip **team up with** birlikte çalışmak **teamwork** ekip çalışması
tear /tiı/ *a.* gözyaşı
tear /teı/ *e.* **tore** /to:/, **torn** /to:n/ yırtmak; koparmak; yırtılmak, kopmak; yolmak; *kon.* çılgın gibi koşmak ☆ *a.* yırtık **tear up** parça parça etmek
tease /ti:z/ *e.* sataşmak, takılmak ☆ *a.*

muzip, şakacı kimse **teaser** muzip; şakacı kimse; *kon.* zor bir soru/sorun
teat /ti:t/ *a.* biberon emziği
technical /'teknikıl/ *s.* teknik
technician /tek'nişın/ *a.* teknisyen
technique /tek'ni:k/ *a.* teknik, yordam
technology /tek'nolıci/ *a.* teknoloji **technological** teknolojik
teddy bear /'tedi beı/ *a.* oyuncak ayı
tedious /'ti:dıis/ *s.* can sıkıcı, usandırıcı
teem /ti:m/ *e.* (**with**) dolu olmak, kaynaşmak ☆ *e, kon.* bardaktan boşanırcasına yağmak
teenage /'ti:neyc/ *s.* 13-19 yaş arası gençlerle ilgili **teenager** 13-19 yaş arası genç
teens /'ti:nz/ *a.* 13-19 arasındaki yaş
tee shirt /'ti:şö:t/ *a.* tişört
teeth /ti:t / *a.* dişler **teethe** /ti:d / (bebek) diş çıkarmak
teetotal /ti:'toutıl/ *s.* yeşilaycı, içki içmeyen
telecast /'telika:st/ *a.* televizyon yayını
telecommunications /telikımyu:ni'keyşınz/ *a.* telekomünikasyon, iletişim
telegram /'teligrem/ *a.* telgraf, telyazı
telegraph /'teligra:f/ *a.* telgraf
telepathy /ti'lepıti/ *a.* telepati
telephone /'telifoun/ *a.* telefon ☆ *e.* telefon etmek **telephone booth** telefon kulübesi **telephone directory** telefon rehberi **telephone exchange** telefon santrali
telephonist /tı'lefınist/ *a.* santral memuru
telescope /'teliskoup/ *a.* teleskop
televise /'telivayz/ *e.* televizyonda göstermek, yayınlamak
television /'telivijın/ *a.* televizyon
telex /'teleks/ *a.* teleks; teleks haberi
tell /tel/ *e.* **told** /tould/ söylemek; anlatmak; bildirmek; ayırt etmek; tanımak; etki etmek, etkili olmak **tell off** azarlamak, paylamak **teller** veznedar; (oy) sayıcı **telling** etkili
telltale /'telteyl/ *a, kon.* muhbir, ispiyoncu ☆ *s.* belli eden, açığa vuran
telly /'teli/ *a, İİ, kon.* televizyon
temper /'tempı/ *a.* hal, keyif; huy, mizaç; kızgınlık ☆ *e.* (metal) sertleştir-

mek, tavlamak; hafifletmek, yumuşatmak **fly/get into a temper** aniden tepesi atmak **keep one's temper** sakinliğini korumak **lose one's temper** tepesi atmak, kızmak
temperament /'tempırımınt/ *a.* mizaç, yaradılış **temperamental** /-'mentıl/ saati saatine uymayan
temperate /'tempırit/ *s.* ılımlı, ölçülü; ılıman, ılık, mutedil
temperature /'tempırıçı/ *a.* sıcaklık (derecesi); *hek.* vücut ısısı, ateş **have/run a temperature** ateşlenmek, ateşi olmak **take sb's temperature** ateşini ölçmek
tempest /'tempist/ *a.* fırtına
temple /'tempıl/ *a.* tapınak; *anat.* şakak
tempo /'tempou/ *a.* tempo
temporal /'tempırıl/ *s.* zamanla ilgili; maddi; geçici
temporary /'tempırıri/ *s.* geçici **temporarily** geçici olarak
tempt /tempt/ *e.* ayartmak, baştan çıkarmak, teşvik etmek; cezbetmek **tempting** çekici
temptation /temp'teyşın/ *a.* baştan çıkarma, ayartma; çekici şey
ten /ten/ *a, s.* on **tenth** onuncu
tenacious /ti'neyşıs/ *s.* inatçı, direngen; (hafıza) güçlü
tenancy /'tenınsi/ *a.* kira süresi; kiracılık
tenant /'tenınt/ *a.* kiracı
tend /tend/ *e.* (**to**) meyletmek, eğilimi olmak; yönelmek; bakmak, ilgilenmek
tendency /'tendınsi/ *a.* eğilim
tender /'tendı/ *s.* yumuşak, gevrek, körpe; duyarlı, hassas; sevecen, müşfik, şefkatli; dokununca acıyan ☆ *a.* teklif ☆ *e.* teklif etmek, sunmak
tendon /'tendın/ *a, anat.* kiriş
tenement /'tenimınt/ *a.* çok kiracılı ucuz apartman
tennis /'tenis/ *a, sp.* tenis **tennis court** tenis sahası
tenor /'tenı/ *a, müz.* tenor
tense /tens/ *s.* gergin ☆ *a, dilb.* zaman
tension /'tenşın/ *a.* gerginlik; gerilim

tent /tent/ a. çadır

tentacle /'tentikıl/ a, hayb. dokunaç

tentative /'tentıtiv/ s. deneme niteliğinde, öneri niteliğinde, geçici

tenuous /'tenyuıs/ s. çok zayıf, az, hafif

tenure /'tenyı, 'tenyuı/ a. tasarruf hakkı; kullanım süresi

tepid /'tepid/ s. ılık

tequila /ti'ki:lı/ a. tekila

term /tö:m/ a. (okul) dönem; süre; terim; ç. şartlar, koşullar; ç. ilişkiler, ara be on good (bad) terms with ile arası iyi (kötü) olmak come to terms with ile anlaşmak in terms of -e göre; bir dille

terminal /'tö:minıl/ s. uçta bulunan, uç, son; ölümcül ☆ a. terminal; son durak; elek. kutup

terminate /'tö:mineyt/ e. bitirmek, son vermek; bitmek termination son, bitme

terminology /tö:mi'nolıci/ a. terminoloji

terminus /'tö:minıs/ a. son durak

termite /'tö:mayt/ a, hayb. beyaz karınca, termit

terrace /'teris/ a. sıra evler; teras, taraça; set; sp. tribün basamağı

terrain /te'reyn, ti'reyn/ a. arazi

terrestrial /ti'restriıl/ s. karaya ait, karasal; dünyevi, dünya ile ilgili

terrible /'terıbıl/ s. korkunç; kon. rezil, berbat terribly çok

terrier /'teriı/ a. teriyer, av köpeği

terrific /tı'rifik/ s, kon. çok iyi, mükemmel, harika, süper; korkunç, müthiş, süper

terrify /'terifay/ e. çok korkutmak

territorial /teri'to:riıl/ s. karaya ait, karasal territorial waters karasuları

terror /'terı/ a. tedhiş, terör; dehşet, korku; kon. baş belası terrorism terörizm, tedhişçilik terrorist terörist, tedhişçi terrorize korkutmak, yıldırmak

terse /tö:s/ s. (söz) kısa ve özlü

test /test/ a. sınav, test; deneme, sınama; ölçü, ayar; muayene; deney; kim. çözümleme ☆ e. muayene etmek; denemek, sınamak; araştırmak test tube deney tüpü test-tube baby tüp bebek

testament /'testımınt/ a. vasiyetname New Testament Yeni Ahit Old Testament Eski Ahit

testicle /'testikıl/ a. testis, erbezi, taşak

testify /'testifay/ e. tanıklık etmek; kanıtlamak, doğrulamak

testimonial /testi'mouniıl/ a. bonservis; takdirname, başarı belgesi

testimony /'testimıni/ a, huk. tanıklık; ifade

tetanus /'tetınıs/ a, hek. tetanos, kazıklıhumma

tether /'tedı/ a. hayvan zinciri/ipi at the end of one's tether dayanacak sabrı/gücü kalmamış

text /tekst/ a. metin, parça; konu textbook ders kitabı

textile /'tekstayl/ a. tekstil, dokuma; dokuma kumaş ☆ s. tekstille ilgili

texture /'teksçı/ a. dokuma, örgü; bünye, yapı, doku

than /dın, den/ bağ. -den, -dan

thank /tenk/ e. teşekkür etmek ☆ a. teşekkür, şükran thank God/goodness/heaven Allah'a şükür, çok şükür thank you teşekkür ederim, sağ olun thanks to -in sayesinde thankful müteşekkir, minnettar thankless nankör, iyilikbilmez thanks teşekkürler thanksgiving şükür, şükran, minnet thanksgiving day Şükran Yortusu

that /det/ s, adl. şu, o ☆ be, kon. o kadar, öylesine that's that (işte) o kadar

that /dıt, det/ bağ. ki, -dığı(nı), -diği(ni) ☆ adl. ki o, -en, -an; ki onu, ki ona, -dığı, -diği

thaw /to:/ e. erimek; eritmek; yakınlaşmak, samimileşmek, açılmak

the /dı, di, di:/ belgili tanımlık (tekil ya da çoğul adlardan önce gelerek onlara belirlilik kavramı verir)

theatre /'tiıtı/ a, İİ. tiyatro theatrical tiyatroya ait; yapmacık, abartmalı

theft /teft/ a. hırsızlık

their /dı, deı/ s. onların

theirs /deız/ adl. onların, onlarınki

them /dım, dem/ adl. onları, onlara, onlar

theme /ti:m/ a. konu, anakonu, tema; *müz.* tema **theme song/tune** film müziği

themselves /dım'selvz/ *adl.* kendileri, kendilerini, kendilerine **by themselves** kendi kendilerine

then /den/ *be.* o zaman, o zamanlar, o süre içinde; sonra, ondan sonra, daha sonra; bu durumda, öyleyse, madem öyle **now and then** ara sıra

thenceforth /dens'fo:t/ *be.* o zamandan beri

theology /ti'olıci/ a. ilahiyat, teoloji **theologian** ilahiyatçı **theological** teolojik

theorem /'tiırım/ a. teorem, sav

theoretical /tiı'retikıl/ *s.* teorik, kuramsal

theory /'tiıri/ a. teori, kuram **in theory** teoride, teorik olarak

therapeutic /terı'pyu:tik/ *s.* tedaviye ait; iyileştirici, sağaltıcı

theraphy /'terıpi/ a. tedavi, sağaltım **therapist** terapist, sağaltman

there /deı/ *be.* orada, oraya, orayı ☆ *ünl.* işte **there is/are** var **There you are** demedim mi, buyur bakalım, gördün mü; buyur, al, işte **thereabouts** oralarda; o sıralarda; ona yakın **thereafter** ondan sonra **thereby** o suretle, suretiyle **therefore** bu yüzden, bu nedenle, onun için **therein** bu bakımdan **thereof** onun üzerine **thereto** ona **thereupon** bunun üzerine, o an

thermal /'tö:mıl/ *s.* termik, ısıl

thermometer /tı'momıtı/ a. termometre, sıcakölçer

thermos /'tö:mıs/ a. termos

thermostat /'tö:mıstet/ a. termostat, ısıdenetir

thesaurus /ti'so:rıs, 'tesırıs/ a. kavramlar dizini (kitabı)

thesis /'ti:sis/ a. (ç. -ses /-si:z/ iddia, sav; inceleme

they /dey/ *adl.* onlar

thick /tik/ *s.* kalın; (sıvı) koyu, katı; sık; yoğun; (ses) boğuk **thickheaded** kalın kafalı **thickness** kalınlık; koyuluk; sıklık; yoğunluk

thicken /'tikın/ *e.* kalınlaştırmak; kalın-

laşmak; koyulaştırmak; koyulaşmak

thief /ti:f/ a. hırsız

thigh /tay/ a, *anat.* uyluk, but

thimble /'timbıl/ a. yüksük

thin /tin/ *s.* ince; zayıf, cılız; sulu, cıvık; (bahane) sudan **thinskinned** duyarlı, alıngan

thing /ting/ a. şey, nesne; olay; yaratık, canlı; ç. eşya, giyecekler

think /tink/ *e.* **thought** /to:t/ düşünmek; sanmak **think about** düşünmek **think of** düşünmek, tasarlamak; hatırlamak **think out/through** düşünüp taşınmak **think over** üzerinde düşünüp taşınmak **thinker** düşünür **thinking** düşünceli; düşünce

third /tö:d/ a, *s.* üçüncü ☆ a. üçte bir **thirdly** üçüncü olarak **third rate** kalitesiz, adi

thirst /tö:st/ a. susuzluk **thirsty** susamış; susatıcı

thirteen /tö:'ti:n/ a, *s.* on üç **thirteenth** on üçüncü

thirty /tö:ti/ *s, a.* otuz **thirtieth** otuzuncu

this /dis/ *s, adl.* (ç. **these** /di:z/) bu **like this** böyle, bu şekilde, bunun gibi

thistle /'tisıl/ a, *bitk.* devedikeni

thong /tong/ a. sırım; kayış

thorax /'to:reks/ a, *hayb.* göğüs

thorn /to:n/ a. diken; dikenli bitki **thorny** dikenli

thorough /'tarı/ *s.* tam, eksiksiz, baştan aşağıya; titiz **thoroughbred** safkan, soylu **thoroughfare** işlek cadde **thoroughly** tümüyle, adamakıllı

those /douz/ *adl.* şunlar, onlar ☆ *s.* şu, o

though /dou/ *bağ.* -e rağmen, -e karşın, -se bile ☆ *be.* yine de, her şeye rağmen **as though** -mış gibi

thought /to:t/ a. düşünce; görüş, kanı; endişe **on second thoughts** sonradan düşününce **thoughtful** düşünceli, dalgın **thoughtless** düşüncesiz

thousand /'tauzınd/ *a, s.* bin **thousandth** bininci

thrash /treş/ *e.* (sopa/kırbaç ile) dövmek; yenmek **thrash out** tartışarak çözümlemek **thrashing** dayak atma, dayak

thread /tred/ a. iplik; lif, tel; yiv ☆ e. (iğneye) iplik geçirmek **threadbare** eski püskü, yıpranmış

threat /tret/ a. tehdit; tehlike

threaten /'tretın/e. tehdit etmek; belirtisi olmak **threatening** tehdit edici

three /tri:/ a, s. üç **three-dimensional** üç boyutlu

thresh /treş/ e. harman dövmek

threshold /'treşhould, 'treşould/ a. eşik; başlangıç **on the threshold of** -in eşiğinde

threw /tru:/ bkz. throw

thrift /trift/a. tutum, idare **thrifty** tutumlu, idareli

thrill /tril/ a. heyecan; korku ☆ e. heyecanlanmak **thriller** heyecanlı kitap/oyun/film

thrive /trayv/e. iyiye gitmek; başarılı olmak; büyümek

throat /trout/ a. boğaz; gırtlak

throb /trob/ e. küt küt atmak, zonklamak

throes /trouz/ a. şiddetli ağrı, sancılar

throne /troun/ a. taht

throng /trong/ a. kalabalık

throttle /'trotıl/ e. boğazlamak, boğmak, gırtlaklamak ☆ a. kısma valfı, kelebek

through /tru:/ ilg. -den geçerek, içinden, arasından; yoluyla, sayesinde; vasıtasıyla, eliyle; -den; yüzünden, nedeniyle; her yanında, her yanına; başından sonuna dek; süresince ☆ be. başından sonuna kadar; baştan başa; tümüyle ☆ s. direkt, aktarmasız; engelsiz **through and through** tamamen, tümüyle **be through** bitirmek

throughout /tru:'aut/ be. baştanbaşa; başından sonuna kadar, hep

throw /trou/ e. **threw** /tru:/, **thrown** /troun/ atmak, fırlatmak ☆ a. atma, atış, fırlatma **throw about** saçmak, dağıtmak **throw away** boşa harcamak, çarçur etmek **throw off** üstünden atmak, çıkarmak; -den kurtulmak **throw on** üzerine giyivermek **throw out** ileri sürmek, söylemek; reddetmek; kov-

mak **throw over** ile ilişkisini kesmek **throw together** acele yapıvermek **throw up** kusmak; bırakmak, vazgeçmek

thrown /troun/ bkz. throw

thru /tru:/ bkz. through

thrush /traş/ a, hayb. ardıçkuşu; hek. pamukçuk

thrust /trast/ e. thrust /trast/ sokmak, saplamak; itmek, dürtmek

thud /tad/ a. gümbürtü, pat, küt ☆ e. pat diye vurmak

thug /tag/a. cani, katil, haydut

thumb /tam/ a. başparmak **thumbtack** raptiye

thump /tamp/ e. yumruklamak, güm güm vurmak; (kalp) küt küt atmak

thunder /'tandı/ a. gök gürültüsü ☆ e. (gök) gürlemek; bağırmak, gürlemek **thunderbolt** yıldırım **thunderstorm** yıldırımlı fırtına **thunderstruck** yıldırım çarpmışa dönmüş, şaşkın

Thursday /'tö:zdi, 'tö:zdey/ a. perşembe

thus /das/ be. böylece; bu sonuçla **thus far** şu ana kadar

thyme /taym/ a, bitk. kekik

thyroid /'tayroyd/ a. tiroit, kalkanbezi

tick /tik/ a. tıkırtı, tiktak; "doğru" işareti; ii, kon. an, saniye; hayb. kene ☆ tıkırdamak, tıklamak; doğru işareti koymak **tick off** işaret koymak; kon. paylamak, azarlamak

ticket /'tikit/ a. bilet; etiket; (trafik) para cezası **ticket collector** biletçi **ticket office** bilet gişesi

tickle /'tikıl/ e. gıdıklamak; eğlendirmek **ticklish** hemen gıdıklanır; zor, özel dikkat isteyen, nazik

tide /tayd/ a. gelgit; akış, eğilim

tidy /'taydi/ s. derli toplu, temiz; kon. oldukça büyük ☆ e. (up) derleyip toplamak, çekidüzen vermek

tie /tay/ a. kravat; bağ; beraberlik, sonuç eşitliği; düğüm ☆ e. bağlamak; bağlanmak; sp. berabere kalmak

tier /'tayı/ a. kat, sıra, dizi

tiff /tif/ a. atışma, tartışma

tiger /'taygı/ a. kaplan

tight /tayt/ s. sıkı, sımsıkı; gergin; zor,

güç; geçirmez, sızdırmaz; *kon.* cimri, eli sıkı; *kon.* sarhoş ☆ *be.* sımsıkı sit **tight** olduğu yerde kalmak **tighten** sıkmak, germek; sıkıştırmak, gerginleştirmek

tights /tayts/ *a.* külotlu çorap

tile /tayl/ *a.* kiremit; çini

till /til/ *ilg, bağ.* -e kadar, -e dek ☆ *a.* para çekmecesi, kasa

tilt /tilt/ *e.* eğmek; eğilmek ☆ *a.* eğiklik

timber /'timbı/ *a.* kereste

time /taym/ *a.* zaman, vakit; müddet, süre; *müz.* tempo; devir, çağ; defa, kere; *mat.* kere, çarpı ☆ *e.* saat tutmak, süresini ölçmek; zamanlamak, ayarlamak **all the time** durmadan, sürekli, boyuna **at the same time** aynı zamanda; yine de, mamafih **at times** bazen **behind the times** eski kafalı **by the time** -dığı zaman **for a time** kısa bir süre **for the time being** şimdilik **from time to time** ara sıra, bazen **in time** vaktinde, erkence; zamanla **keep up with the times** zamana ayak uydurmak **many a time** sık sık **on time** vaktinde, tam vaktinde **once upon a time** bir zamanlar; bir varmış bir yokmuş **pass the time of day** laklak etmek **play for time** zaman geçirmek, oyalanmak **take one's time** acele etmemek **time after time** sık sık, tekrar tekrar **time and (time) again** sık sık, tekrar tekrar **time bomb** saatli bomba **time card** fabrika çalışma kartı **time exposure** poz **timekeeper** saat hakemi **timeless** değişmeyen, ebedi, sonsuz **timely** tam vaktinde, yerinde, uygun **timer** saat hakemi; kronometre **timetable** tren vb. tarifesi; ders programı **timing** zamanlama **What's the time? What time is it?** Saat kaç?

timid /'timid/ *s.* çekingen, sıkılgan

tin /tin/ *a.* kalay; teneke; teneke kutu; konserve kutusu; *arg.* para, mangiz ☆ *e.* (yiyecek, vb.) konservelemek, kutulamak **tin opener** *İİ.* konserve açacağı

tincture /'tinkçı/ *a.* boya; tentür

tinge /tinc/ *a.* az miktar, nebze

tingle /'tingıl/ *e.* ürpermek, diken diken olmak

tinker /'tinkı/ *a.* tenekeci

tinkle /'tinkıl/ *a.* çıngırtı ☆ *e.* çınlamak

tint /tint/ *a.* hafif renk; renk tonu

tiny /'tayni/ *s.* küçücük, minicik

tip /tip/ *a.* (burun, parmak, vb.) uç; çöplük; bahşiş; tavsiye ☆ *e.* eğmek, yana yatırmak; eğilmek; devirmek; devrilmek **on the tip of one's tongue** dilinin ucunda olmak

tipple /'tipıl/ *a, kon.* içki

tipsy /'tipsi/ *a.* çakırkeyf

tiptoe /'tiptou/ *a:* **on tiptoe** ayaklarının ucuna basarak ☆ *e.* ayaklarının ucuna basarak yürümek

tire /tayı/ *e.* yormak; yorulmak **be tired of** -den bıkmak **get tired** yorulmak

tired yorgun **tireless** yorulmak bilmez, bitmez tükenmez **tiresome** yorucu **tiring** yorucu

tissue /'tişu:, 'tisyu:/ *a, anat.* doku; ince kumaş; kâğıt mendil

tit /tit/ *a, hayb.* baştankara

titivate /'titiveyt/ *e, kon.* çeki düzen vermek, toparlamak

title /'taytıl/ *a.* başlık, ad; unvan; *huk.* hak, istihkak; *sp.* şampiyonluk

titter /'titı/ *e.* kıkır kıkır gülmek

to /tı, tu, tu:/ *ilg.* -e doğru, -e; -e kadar, -e; -e karşı, -e; (saat) kala, var; her birinde; -mek, -mak

toad /toud/ *a, hayb.* karakurbağası

toast /toust/ *a.* kızarmış ekmek; sağlığına içme, kutlama ☆ *a.* kızartmak; sağlığına içmek **toaster** ekmek kızartma makinesi

tobacco /tı'bekou/ *a.* tütün **tobacconist** tütüncü

toboggan /tı'bogın/ *a.* kar kızağı

today /tı'dey/ *a, be.* bugün

toddle /'todıl/ *e.* tıpış tıpış yürümek

toe /tou/ *a.* ayak parmağı **on one's toes** harekete hazır, tetikte **toenail** ayak tırnağı

toffee /'tofi/ *a.* bonbon, şekerleme

together /tı'gedı/ *be.* bir araya, bir arada; birlikte, beraber; aynı anda, birden **togetherness** birliktelik, beraberlik

toil /toyl/ e. çok çalışmak, yorulmak ☆ a. zor iş

toilet /'toylit/ a. hela, tuvalet

toiletries /'toylitriz/ a. tuvalet takımı, tuvalet eşyaları

token /'toukın/ a. belirti, iz, gösterge; jeton; kart, marka, fiş

told /tould/ bkz. tell

tolerable /'tolırıbıl/ s. dayanılabilir, çekilir; şöyle böyle, orta

tolerance /'tolırıns/ a. tahammül, dayanıklılık; müsamaha, hoşgörü tolerant hoşgörülü; tahammüllü

tolerate /'tolıreyt/ e. müsamaha etmek, hoş görmek; tahammül etmek, katlanmak toleration müsamaha, hoşgörü

toll /toul/ a. (yol, köprü, vb.) geçiş ücreti; bedel; çan sesi ☆ e. (çan) çalmak tollgate geçiş ücreti ödenen yer

tomato /tı'ma:tou/ a, bitk. domates

tomb /tu:m/ a. mezar, kabir; türbe tombstone mezar taşı

tomorrow /tı'morou/ a, be. yarın

ton /tan/ a. ton (İİ. 1016.047 kg.; Aİ. 907.2 kg); ton (1000 kg.); den. tonilato; kon. yığın, sürü, büyük miktar, ton

tone /toun/ a. ses; ses tonu, ton; müz. perde, ton; renk tonu, ton; tarz, tavır tone down tonunu hafifletmek, yumuşatmak tone in with ile uyum sağlamak, uymak

tongs /tongz/ a. maşa

tongue /tang/ a. dil; lisan hold one's tongue çenesini tutmak, dilini tumak tongue twister tekerleme tongue-tied dili tutulmuş; ağzı var dili yok

tonic /'tonik/ a. tonik; kuvvet ilacı

tonight /tı'nayt/ a, be. bu gece

tonnage /'tanic/ a. tonaj, tonilato

tonsil /tonsil/ a, hek. bademcik

too /tu:/ be. (gereğinden) çok, fazla, aşırı; de, da, dahi

tool /tu:l/ a. alet

tooth /tu:t / a. (ç. teeth /ti:t /) diş toothache diş ağrısı toothpaste diş macunu toothpick kürdan

top /top/ a. tepe, doruk, üst; baş; örtü, kapak; topaç ☆ s. en yüksek, en üst ☆ e. üstünü örtmek, kapamak; -den üstün gelmek, geçmek from top to bottom baştan aşağı, tümüyle on top of üstüne, üstünde, ayrıca, üstelik top secret çok gizli topcoat palto topless (kadın) göğüsleri açık, üstsüz topmost en üstteki, en yüksek

topaz /'toupez/ a. sarı yakut, topaz

topic /'topik/ a. konu

topography /tı'pogrıfi/ a. topografya, yerbetim

topple /'topıl/ e. sendelemek, düşmek; devirmek, düşürmek

topsy-turvy /topsi'tö:vi/ s, be. karman çorman

torch /to:ç/ a. el feneri; meşale

torment /'to:ment/ a. büyük acı, sancı, eziyet ☆ e. acı çektirmek, eziyet etmek

torn /to:n/ bkz. tear; s. ayrı, bölünmüş

tornado /to:'neydou/ a. kasırga

torpedo /to:'pi:dou/ a, ask. torpil

torrent /'torınt/ a. sel

torrid /'torid/ s. çok sıcak, yakıcı

torsion /'to:şın/ a. bükme, bükülme

tortoise /'to:tıs/ a. kaplumbağa

tortuous /'to:çuıs/ s. dolambaçlı, dönen; kaçamaklı, dolaylı

torture /'to:çı/ a. işkence ☆ e. işkence etmek

toss /tos/ e. atmak; yazı-tura atmak; sallamak; sallanmak ☆ a. sallama, sallanma; atma, fırlatma; yazı-tura

tot /tot/ e. (up) toplamak, ilave etmek ☆ a. ufak çocuk; bir yudum içki

total /'toutıl/ s. toplam, bütün ☆ a. toplam; tutar ☆ e. toplamını bulmak; toplamak; tutmak, etmek totally bütün bütün, tümüyle

totalitarian /touteli'teıriın/ a. totaliter, erktekelci

totem /'toutım/ a. totem, ongun

totter /'totı/ e. sendelemek, yalpalamak

touch /taç/ e. değmek; dokunmak, ellemek; etkilemek, duygulandırmak ☆ a. dokunma; temas, değme; az miktar; sp. taç; duygululuk, hassasiyet, incelik touch wood nazar değmesin diye tahtaya vurmak in touch with -den haberdar get in touch with ile temasa geçmek keep in touch with

465
transatlantic

ile teması sürdürmek, ile ilişkiyi kesmemek **touch down** (uçak) yere inmek **touch on/upon** (konuya) değinmek **touch up** rötuş yapmak

touching /taçing/ s. dokunaklı, acıklı, duygulandırıcı

touchy /taçi/ s. alıngan

tough /taf/ s. sert, kart; dayanıklı, dirençli güçlü; çetin, zor, güç ☆ a, kon. kabadayı, bıçkın **toughen** sertleşmek; sertleştirmek

toupee /'tu:pey/ a. küçük peruka

tour /tuı/ a. tur, gezi; turne ☆ e. gezmek, dolaşmak

tourism /'tuırizım/ a. turizm **tourist** turist

tournament /'tuınımınt, 'to:nımınt/ a. turnuva, yarışma

tourniquet /'tuınikey, 'to:nikey/ a. kanamayı durdurucu sargı, sargı bezi

tousle /'tauzıl/ e. (saç, vb.) karıştırmak

tow /tou/ e. (taşıt) yedekte çekmek ☆ a yedekte çekme **in tow** kon. yakın takipte

toward(s) /tı'wo:d(z)/ ilg. -e doğru, yönünde; -e karşı; -e doğru, sularında

towel /'tauıl/ a. havlu

tower /'tauı/ a. kule; burç **tower block** apartman, yüksek bina

town /taun/ a. şehir, kent; kasaba **town council** belediye meclisi **town planning** şehir planlaması

toxic /'toksik/ s. zehirli

toxin /'toksin/ a. toksin

toy /toy/ a. oyuncak **toyshop** oyuncakçı dükkânı

trace /treys/ e. izini sürmek, izlemek; ortaya çıkarmak; kopyasını çıkarmak ☆ a. iz; kalıntı; az miktar, zerre **tracing** kopya

track /trek/ a. iz; patika; ray; pist, yarış pisti; parça, şarkı; palet, tırtıl ☆ e. izini takip etmek, izini sürmek **keep track (of)** -den haberdar olmak **on the right track** doğru yolda **tracking events** atletizm karşılaşmaları **tracksuit** eşofman

tract /trekt/ a. arazi, alan, toprak; anat. sistem, aygıt

traction /'trekşın/ a. çekme, çekilme

tractor /'trektı/ a. traktör

trade /treyd/ a. ticaret, alışveriş; meslek, sanat, iş ☆ e. (in/with) ticaret yapmak, iş yapmak **trade name** ad, marka **trade union** sendika **trade wind** alize rüzgârı **trademark** alameti farika, marka **trader** tüccar, tacir; borsa simsarı **tradesman** esnaf

tradition /trı'dişın/ a. gelenek, anane **traditional** geleneksel

traffic /'trefik/ a. trafik; ticaret **traffic jam** trafik sıkışıklığı **traffic lights** trafik ışıkları **traffic signs** trafik işaretleri

tragedy /'trecidi/ a. trajedi, ağlatı; facia, felaket

tragic /'trecik/ s. trajik; üzücü; kon. müthiş, korkunç

trail /treyl/ a. iz, koku; patika, keçiyolu ☆ e. izini sürmek; peşinden sürüklemek; sürüklenmek

trailer /'treylı/ a. römork, treyler; fragman, tanıtma filmi; Aİ. karavan

train /treyn/ a. tren; kafile, kervan ☆ e. yetiştirmek, eğitmek; sp. antrenman yapmak; (on/upon) -e nişan almak **trainee** stajyer; öğrenci **trainer** antrenör, çalıştırıcı **training** terbiye, eğitim; sp. antrenman, çalışma

trait /treyt/ a. özellik, karakter

traitor /'treytı/ a. hain

trajectory /trı'cektıri/ a. yörünge

tram /trem/ a. tramvay

tramp /tremp/ a. serseri; uzun yürüyüş ☆ e. ağır adımlarla yürümek; yürüyüp geçmek, çiğnemek

trample /'trempıl/ e. basmak, ezmek, çiğnemek

trampoline /'trempıli:n/ a. tramplen

trance /tra:ns/ a. kendinden geçme, esrime, trans

tranquil /'trenkwil/ s. sakin, sessiz; durgun

tranquillizer /'trenkwilayzı/ a. sakinleştirici, yatıştırıcı ilaç

transact /tren'zekt/ e. (iş) görmek, bitirmek, yapmak

transaction /tren'zekşın/ a. iş görme, yapma; iş, muamele, işlem

transatlantic /trenzıt'lentik/ s. transatlantik, Atlantik Okyanusu'na ait, Atlantikaşırı

transcend /tren'send/ *e.* geçmek, aşmak **transcendent** üstün, ulu, yüce

transcribe /tren'skrayb/ *e.* kopya etmek, suretini çıkarmak; *müz.* uyarlamak **transcript** kopya, suret

transfer /trens'fö: / *e.* nakletmek, taşımak; taşınmak; *sp.* transfer etmek, transfer olmak; aktarma yapmak; *huk.* devretmek ☆ *a, sp.* transfer; *huk.* devir; aktarma bileti; nakil

transform /trens'fo:m/ *e.* biçimini değiştirmek, dönüştürmek **transformation** dönüşüm **transformer** transformatör, trafo

transfuse /trens'fyu:z/ *e.* (kan) nakletmek

transgress /trenz'gres/ *e.* (sınırı) aşmak; bozmak, çiğnemek

transient /'trenziınt/ *s.* geçici, süreksiz

transistor /tren'zistı/ *a.* transistor

transit /'trensit, 'trenzit/ *a.* taşıma, aktarma; geçiş

transition /tren'zişın/ *a.* geçiş

transitive /'trensitiv/ *s, a, dilb.* geçişli (eylem)

translate /trenz'leyt, trens'leyt/ *e.* tercüme etmek, çevirmek **translation** tercüme, çeviri **translator** tercüman, çevirmen

translucent /trenz'lu:sınt/ *s.* yarısaydam

transmission /trenz'mişın/ *a.* gönderme, iletme; geçirme, taşıma; (radyo, TV) yayın; transmisyon, vites

transmit /trenz'mit/ *e.* göndermek; yayınlamak; geçirmek, iletmek; (hastalık, vb.) geçirmek, bulaştırmak **transmitter** verici, iletici

transparent /tren'sperınt/ *s.* saydam; açık, net **transparency** saydamlık; slayt

transpire /tren'spayı/ *e.* ortaya çıkmak, bilinmek; *kon.* olmak, vuku bulmak

transplant /'trenspla:nt/ *e.* (bitki) başka bir yere dikmek/aktarmak; (organ, saç, vb.) nakletmek **transplantation** nakil, aktarma

transport /'trenspo:t/ *a.* nakil, taşıma; taşımacılık; araç ☆ *e.* taşımak, götür-

mek, nakletmek; sürgüne göndermek **transportation** taşıma, taşımacılık; araç, taşıt; sürgün

transpose /tren'spouz/ *e.* yerlerini/sırasını değiştirmek; *müz.* perdesini değiştirmek

trap /trep/ *a.* tuzak; kapan; *kon.* ağız ☆ *e.* tuzağa düşürmek

trapeze /trı'pi:z/ *a.* trapez

trash /treş/ *a.* değersiz şey, adi şey; *Aİ.* süprüntü; *Aİ.* ayaktakımı **trashy** değersiz

trauma /'tro:mı, 'traumı/ *a, hek.* travma

travel /'trevıl/ *e.* seyahat etmek, yolculuk yapmak; yol almak, gitmek; *kon.* kaçmak, tüymek ☆ *a.* seyahat, yolculuk **travel agency/bureau** seyahat acentası **traveller** seyyah, yolcu; pazarlamacı **traveller's cheque** seyahat çeki

traverse /'trevö:s/ *e.* içinden/üzerinden geçmek

travesty /'trevisti/ *a.* kötü/gülünç taklit

trawl /tro:l/ *a.* tarak ağı, trol ☆ *e.* tarak ağıyla balık tutmak **trawler** tarak ağlı balıkçı gemisi

tray /trey/ *a.* tepsi; tabla

treacherous /'treçırıs/ *s.* hain, dönek; tehlikeli **treachery** hainlik, ihanet

treacle /'tfi:kıl/ *a.* şeker pekmezi

tread /tred/ *e.* **trod** /trod/, **trodden** /trodın/ üzerinde yürümek; basmak, çiğnemek, ezmek ☆ *a.* ayak basışı/sesi; lastik tırtılı; merdiven basamağı

treadle /'tredıl/ *a.* pedal, ayaklık

treason /'tri:zın/ *a.* vatan hainliği

treasure /'trejı/ *a.* hazine, define ☆ *e.* çok değer vermek

treasurer /'trejırı/ *a.* haznedar, veznedar

treasury /'trejıri/ *a.* hazine; maliye dairesi

treat /tri:t/ *e.* muamele etmek, davranmak; ele almak; düşünmek, saymak, görmek; **(to)** ikram etmek, ısmarlamak; kimyasal işleme tabi tutmak; tedavi etmek ☆ *a.* zevk, hoş şey, hoş sürpriz

treatise /'tri:tis, 'tri:tiz/ *a.* bilimsel inceleme, tez

treatment /'tri:tmınt/ *a.* muamele, davranış; tedavi

treaty /'tri:ti/ *a.* antlaşma

treble /'trebıl/ *a, müz.* soprano; tiz ☆ *s, be.* üç misli, üç kat

tree /tri:/ *a.* ağaç

tremble /'trembıl/ *e.* titremek; ürpermek ☆ *a.* titreme; ürperme, ürperti

tremendous /tri'mendıs/ *s.* çok büyük, kocaman; harika, olağanüstü **tremendously** son derece, çok

tremor /'tremı/ *a.* titreme

trench /trenç/ *a.* hendek, çukur; *ask.* siper

trend /trend/ *a.* eğilim; akım

trepidation /trepi'deyşın/ *a.* telaş, kaygı

trespass /'trespıs, 'trespes/ *e.* (başkasının arazisine) izinsiz girmek

trestle /'tresıl/ *a.* masa ayaklığı, sehpa

trial /'trayıl/ *a, huk.* duruşma, yargılama; deneme, sınama; baş belası, dert **on trial** yargılanmakta; deneme için **trial and error** deneme-yanılma yöntemi

triangle /'trayengıl/ *a.* üçgen **triangular** üçgen, üç köşeli

tribe /trayb/ *a.* kabile, boy, oymak, aşiret **tribesman** oymak üyesi

tribunal /tray'byu:nıl/ *a, huk.* mahkeme

tributary /'tribyutıri/ *a, coğ.* kol, akarsu, geleğen

tribute /'tribyu:t/ *a.* takdir, övgü; baç, haraç, vergi

trick /trik/ *a.* hüner, numara, el çabukluğu; marifet, ustalık, beceri, incelik; muziplik, şeytanlık; (iskambil) el; hile, düzen, dolap, oyun, dalavere; **do the trick** *kon.* işini görmek, amacını karşılamak ☆ *e.* **(into)** aldatmak, kandırmak **tricky** kurnaz; hileli, aldatıcı; ustalık isteyen, zor

rifle /'trayfıl/ *a.* değersiz şey; meyveli tatlı, bir tür jöle **trifle with** hafife almak **trifling** önemsiz, değersiz

rigger /'trigı/ *a.* tetik

rigonometry /trigı'nomitri/ *a.* trigonometri

rill /tril/ *a.* ses titremesi

trillion /'trilyın/ *a.* trilyon; *Aİ.* bilyon

trim /trim/ *e.* **(off)** kesip düzeltmek, budamak; **(with)** süslemek; kısmak; yenmek ☆ *s.* düzenli, derli toplu ☆ *a.* kesme, kırkma; intizam, düzen; form, kondisyon **trimming** süs; garnitür; kesilmiş parça

trinket /'trinkit/ *a.* incik boncuk, değersiz ziynet

trio /'tri:ou/ *a.* üçlü

trip /trip/ *e.* düşürmek; tökezlemek, sendelemek; hata yapmak; **(up)** yanıltmak ☆ *a.* gezi, gezinti, kısa yolculuk; takılma, tökezleme; düşme; hata, yanılma

tripe /trayp/ *a.* işkembe; *kon.* zırva

triple /'tripıl/ *s.* üç misli, üç kat; üçlü

triplet /'triplit/ *a.* üçüz

tripod /'traypod/ *a.* üç ayaklı sehpa

trite /trayt/ *s.* basmakalıp, beylik

triumph /'trayımf/ *a.* zafer, yengi

trivial /'triviıl/ *s.* önemsiz, değersiz

trod, trodden /trod/ *bkz.* tread

trolleybus /'trolibas/ *a.* troleybüs

trombone /trom'boun/ *a, müz.* trombon

troop /tru:p/ *a.* küme, takım, sürü, grup; *ç.* askerler; *ask.* bölük, tabur, alay **trooper** süvari eri; *Aİ.* eyalet polisi

trophy /'troufi/ *a.* ödül; ganimet, av

tropic /'tropik/ *a.* dönence; *ç.* tropikal bölge **tropical** tropikal; çok sıcak

trot /trot/ *a.* tırıs ☆ *a.* tırıs gitmek; tırısa kaldırmak; *kon.* gitmek, kaçmak

trouble /'trabıl/ *e.* üzmek, başını ağrıtmak, telaşlandırmak, sıkmak; rahatsız etmek, zahmet vermek; zahmet etmek **fish in troubled waters** bulanık suda balık avlamak ☆ *a.* ıstırap, üzüntü, sıkıntı; dert, bela; müşkül durum, rahatsızlık, hastalık, zahmet **ask/look for trouble** bela aramak **be in trouble** başı dertte olmak **get oneself into trouble** başını derde sokmak **troublemaker** baş belası, fitneci, sorun çıkaran kimse **troublesome** zahmetli, güç; sıkıcı, sıkıntılı

trough /trof/ *a.* yalak, tekne

troupe /tru:p/ *a.* şarkıcı/dansçı/oyuncu

grubu
trousers /'trauzız/ *a.* pantolon
trout /traut/ *a.* alabalık
trowel /'trouıl/ *a.* mala
truant /'truınt/ *a.* okul kaçağı **play truant** okuldan kaçmak, dersleri kırmak
truce /tru:s/ *a.* ateşkes
truck /track/ *a, Aİ.* kamyon; *İİ.* yük vagonu
trudge /trac/ *e.* yorgun argın yürümek
true /tru:/ *s.* doğru, gerçek; halis, hakiki, katışıksız; içten, samimi; sadık, vefalı **come true** gerçekleşmek **true to -e** uygun, ile bağdaşan
truly /'tru:li/ *be.* gerçekten, hakikaten; içtenlikle **yours truly** (mektup sonlarında) saygılarımla
trump /tramp/ *a.* (iskambil) koz ☆ *e.* (iskambil) koz çakmak, kozla almak
trumpet /'trampit/ *a, müz.* trompet, boru
truncheon /'trançın/ *a.* cop
trunk /trank/ *a.* ağaç gövdesi; beden; gövde; fil hortumu; *Aİ.* araba bagajı; *ç.* erkek mayosu **trunk road** anayol
truss /tras/ *e.* (**up**) sımsıkı bağlamak ☆ *a.* kiriş, makas, destek; *hek.* kasık bağı
trust /trast/ *a.* güven; sorumluluk; *huk.* mutemetlik ☆ *e.* güvenmek, inanmak; ümit etmek, ummak **trustee** mütevelli; emanetçi **trustworthy** güvenilir
truth /tru:t/ *a.* gerçek, hakikat; doğruluk, gerçeklik; içtenlik; dürüstlük **truthful** doğru; doğru sözlü, dürüst
try /tray/ *e.* denemek; sınamak; uğraşmak, çalışmak; *huk.* yargılamak ☆ *a.* deneme, kalkışma, girişim **try on** (giysi) prova etmek, giyip denemek **try out** denemek **trying** yorucu, bıktırıcı
tsar /za:, tsa:/ *a.* çar
t-shirt /'ti: şö:t/ *a.* tişört
tub /tab/ *a.* tekne, leğen; *kon.* küvet
tuba /'tyu:bı/ *a, müz.* tuba
tube /tyu:b/ *a.* tüp; boru; *İİ.* metro, yeraltı treni
tuber /'tyu:bı/ *a, bitk.* yumrukök

tuberculosis /tyu:bö:kyu'lousis/ *a, hek.* tüberküloz, verem
tubular /'tyu:byulı/ *s.* tüp/boru şeklinde, borulu
tuck /tak/ *e.* (içine) sokmak; tıkmak; katlamak ☆ *a.* pli, kırma
Tuesday /'tyu:zdi:/ *a.* salı
tuft /taft/ *a.* küme, öbek, top; püskül
tug /tag/ *e.* şiddetle çekmek, asılmak; sürüklemek ☆ *a.* kuvvetli çekiş; römorkör **tugboat** römorkör
tuition /tyu:'işın/ *a.* öğretim; okul harcı/taksiti
tulip /'tyu:lip/ *a.* lale
tumble /'tambıl/ *e.* düşmek, yuvarlanmak; *kon.* jetonu düşmek ☆ *a.* düşme; karışıklık, kargaşa
tummy /'tami/ *a, kon.* karın, mide
tumor /'tyu:mı/ *a, Ai, bkz.* **tumour**
tumour /'tyu:mı/ *a, hek.* tümör, ur
tumult /'tyu:malt/ *a.* kargaşa, gürültü, patırtı, heyecan
tuna /'tyu:nı/ *a.* tonbalığı, orkinos
tune /tyu:n/ *a.* nağme, hava, ezgi; akort; uyum ☆ *e.* akort etmek; (makineyi) ayarlamak, düzen vermek **in tune** akortlu; uyumlu **out of tune** akortsuz **tuneful** ahenkli **tuner** tuner, alıcı cihaz, radyo; akortçu
tunic /'tyu:nik/ *a.* tunik; asker/polis ceketi
tunnel /'tanıl/ *a.* tünel
turban /'tö:bın/ *a.* sarık; türban
turbot /'tö:bot/ *a, hayb.* kalkan
turbulence /'tö:byulıns/ *a.* hava akımı; sertlik
tureen /tyu'ri:n/ *a.* büyük çorba kâsesi
turf /tö:f/ *a.* çimenlik, çimen, çim
Turk /tö:k/ *a.* Türk
turkey /'tö:ki/ *a.* hindi
Turkish /'tö:kiş/ *s.* Türk; Türkçe **Turkish bath** hamam **Turkish delight** lokum
turmoil /'tö:moyl/ *a.* kargaşa, karışıklık, telaş
turn /tö:n/ *e.* çevirmek, döndürmek; çevrilmek, dönmek; sapmak; saptırmak; yöneltmek; üstüne tutmak; kıvırmak, katlamak; dönüştürmek; ekşitmek; varmak, ulaşmak ☆ *a.* devir

dönüş; dönemeç; değişim, değişiklik; sıra; nöbet; yetenek; *kon.* korkutma, sarsma **at every turn** her defasında **in turn** sıra ile **out of turn** sıra dışında, sırasız **take turns** sıra ile (nöbetleşe) yapmak **turn against** karşı çıkmak **turn away** geri çevirmek **turn back** geri dönmek; (sayfa, vb.) kıvırmak **turn down** sesini kısmak; gücünü azaltmak; geri çevirmek **turn in** teslim etmek, vermek; *kon.* yatmak **turn off** söndürmek, kapamak, kesmek; *kon.* keyfini kaçırmak, sıkmak **turn on** açmak; saldırmak; *kon.* (cinsel açıdan) etkilemek, ilgisini uyandırmak **turn out** söndürmek, kapatmak; üretmek; boşaltmak; olmak, çıkmak; giydirmek; çıkıp gelmek, toplanmak **turn over** çevirmek; devretmek, bırakmak; (motor) sessiz çalışmak; üzerinde düşünmek **turn to** -e başvurmak **turn up** gelmek; ortaya çıkmak; biraz daha açmak **turnout** toplantı mevcudu, katılanlar; kılık kıyafet **turnover** sermaye devri, ciro; meyveli turta

turnstile /'tö:nstayl/ *a.* turnike
turner /'tö:nı/ *a.* tornacı
turning /'tö:ning/ *a.* dönüş; dönemeç **turning point** dönüm noktası
turnip /'tö:nip/ *a.* şalgam
turquoise /'tö:kwoyz/ *s, a.* turkuaz
turret /'tarit/ *a.* küçük kule; *ask.* taret
turtle /'tö:tıl/ *a.* su kaplumbağası
tussle /'tasıl/ *e.* (with) *kon.* kapışmak, döğüşmek ☆ *a, kon.* kapışma, döğüşme, kavga
tutor /'tyu:tı/ *a.* özel öğretmen; *İİ.* (üniversitede) öğretmen
tuxedo /tak'si:dou/ *a, Aİ.* smokin
twang /tweng/ *a.* genizden konuşma; tıngırtı
tweak /twi:k/ *e.* (kulak, burun, vb.) burkuvermek, bükmek
tweed /twi:d/ *a.* tüvit, iskoç kumaşı
tweezers /'twi:zız/ *a.* cımbız
twelve /twelv/ *a, s.* on iki **twelfth** on ikinci
twenty /'twenti/ *a, s.* yirmi **twentieth** yirminci
twice /tways/ *be.* iki kere; iki katı

twiddle /'twidıl/ *e.* döndürmek
twig /twig/ *a.* ince dal
twilight /'twaylayt/ *a.* alacakaranlık
twin /twin/ *a.* ikiz; ikili, çifte
twine /twayn/ *a.* kınnap, kalın sicim
twinge /twinc/ *a.* sancı
twinkle /'twinkıl/ *e.* parıldamak ☆ *a.* parıltı
twirl /twö:l/ *e.* hızla dönmek; hızla döndürmek ☆ *a.* hızla dönüş
twist /twist/ *e.* bükmek; burkmak; döndürmek; bükülmek ☆ *a.* bükme, bükülme; burkma, burkulma; dönemeç; sicim, ibrişim
twitch /twiç/ *e.* aniden çekmek; seğirtmek ☆ *a.* seğirme, kıpırtı; ani çekiş
twitter /'twitı/ *e.* cıvıldamak ☆ *a.* cıvıltı
two /tu:/ *a, s.* iki **in two** iki parça, iki parçaya **one or two** bir iki, birkaç **put two and two together** bağdaştırarak sonuç çıkarmak **twofaced** ikiyüzlü **two-fold** iki misli, iki kat **two-piece** iki parçalı **two-way** çift yönlü, gidiş-geliş
tycoon /tay'ku:n/ *a.* kodaman, büyük işadamı
type /tayp/ *a.* tip, çeşit, tür; matbaa harfi; örnek ☆ *e.* daktilo ile yazmak; daktilo kullanmak **typewriter** daktilo, yazı makinesi **typist** daktilograf
typhoid /'tayfoyd/ *a, hek.* tifo
typhoon /tay'fu:n/ *a.* tayfun
typhus /'tayfıs/ *a, hek.* tifüs
typical /'tipikıl/ *s.* tipik
typify /'tipifay/ *e.* -in tipik bir örneği olmak
tyranny /'tirıni/ *a.* zorbalık, zulüm; zorba hükümet
tyrant /'tayırınt/ *a.* zorba; zorba hükümdar, tiran
tyre /tayı/ *a.* (oto) dış lastik
tzar /za:, tsa:/ *a.* çar

U

udder /'adı/ *a.* hayvan memesi
ugly /'agli/ *s.* çirkin; iğrenç; ters, aksi
ulcer /'alsı/ *a, hek.* ülser

ultimate /'altimit/ *s.* son, en son; *kon.* mükemmel, en büyük **ultimately** en sonunda

ultimatum /alti'meytım/ *a.* ültimatom

ultraviolet /altrı'vayılit/ *s.* ultraviyole, morötesi

umbrella /am'brelı/ *a.* şemsiye

umpire /'ampayı/ *a.* (tenis) hakem

unable /an'eybıl/ *s.* yapamaz, gücü yetmez

unabridged /anı'bricd/ *s.* (yazı) kısaltılmamış

unaccountable /anı'kauntıbıl/ *s.* şaşırtıcı, açıklanamaz, anlaşılmaz

unaccustomed /anı'kastımd/ *s.* garip; **(to)** alışmamış, yadırgayan

unanimous /yu:'nenimıs/ *s.* hemfikir, aynı fikirde, ortak

unarmed /an'a:md/ *s.* silahsız

unassuming /anı'syu:ming/ *s.* alçakgönüllü, gösterişsiz, sessiz

unattended /anı'tendid/ *s.* yalnız, kimsesiz, başıboş

unaware /anı'weı/ *s.* habersiz, farkında olmayan **unawares** ansızın

unbalanced /an'belınst/ *s.* dengesiz

unbearable /an'beırıbıl/ *s.* dayanılmaz, çekilmez

unbelievable /anbi'li:vıbıl/ *s.* inanılmaz, şaşırtıcı

unborn /an'bo:n/ *s.* henüz doğmamış

unbutton /an'batın/ *e.* düğmelerini çözmek

uncertain /an'sö:tın/ *s.* kuşkulu, şüpheli; kararsız; kesin olmayan

uncharitable /an'çeritıbıl/ *s.* hoşgörüsüz, acımasız, sert

unchecked /an'çekt/ *s.* serbest bırakılmış, kontrolünden çıkmış, başıboş

uncle /'ankıl/ *a.* amca; enişte; dayı

uncomfortable /an'kamftıbıl/ *s.* rahatsız, konforsuz

uncommon /an'komın/ *s.* nadir, seyrek; acayip, olağandışı

uncompromising /an'komprımayzing/ *s.* uzlaşmaz, kararından dönmez

unconcerned /ankın'sö:nd/ *s.* ilgisiz; kaygısız

unconditional /ankın'dişınıl/ *s.* kayıtsız şartsız, mutlak

unconscious /an'konşıs/ *s.* baygın, kendinde değil; bilmeden, kasıtsız ☆ *a.* bilinçaltı

uncork /an'ko:k/ *e.* (şişenin) tıpasını açmak

uncountable /'ankauntıbıl/ *s.* sayılamayan

uncover /an'kavı/ *e.* (örtüsünü, kapağını) açmak; ortaya çıkarmak

uncut /an'kat/ *s.* kesilmemiş; (film, kitap, vb) kısaltılmamış, makaslanmamış

undaunted /an'do:ntid/ *s.* yiğit, gözü pek, korkusuz, yılmaz

undecided /andi'saydid/ *s.* kararlaştırılmamış; askıda, kararsız

undeniable /andi'nayıbıl/ *s.* inkâr edilemez, yadsınamaz, kesin

under /'andı/ *be.* altında, altına ☆ *ilg.* altında, altına, altından; -den az, -den aşağı, -in altında; -in yönetiminde **under age** reşit olmamış **under cover (of)** -e sığınmış/gizlenmiş

undercarriage /'andıkeric/ *a.* (uçak) iniş takımı, tekerlekler

undercharge /andı'ça:c/ *e.* değerinden az para istemek

underclothes /'andıkloudz/ *a.* iç çamaşırı

undercoat /'andıkout/ *a.* astar boya

undercut /andı'kat/ *e.* başkalarından daha ucuza satmak

underdeveloped /andıdı'velıpt/ *s.* az gelişmiş **underdeveloped country/nation** az gelişmiş ülke

underdog /'andıdog/ *a.* ezilen kişi, mazlum

underdone /andı'dan/ *s.* az pişmiş

underestimate /andır'estimeyt/ *e.* az/düşük olarak tahmin etmek

underfoot /andı'fut/ *be.* ayak altında

undergo /andı'gou/ *e.* **underwent** /andı'went/, **undergone** /andı'gon/ -e uğramak, çekmek, geçirmek

underwent /andı'went/ *bkz.* **undergo**

undergraduate /andı'grecyuit/ *a.* üniversite öğrencisi

underground /'andıgraund/ *s.* yeraltı; gizli ☆ *a, il.* yeraltı treni, metro

undergrowth /'andıgrout/ *a, bitk.* ormanaltı bitkileri

underline /andı'layn/ e. altını çizmek; vurgulamak, belirtmek

undermanned /andı'mend/ s. personeli yetersiz, az çalışanı olan

undermine /andı'mayn/ e. baltalamak, yıkmak, temelini çürütmek

underneath /andı'ni:t / ilg, be. altına, altından, altında ☆ a. bir şeyin alt bölümü, alt

undernourish /andı'nariş/ e. kötü beslemek, yeterli beslememek

underpants /'andıpents/ a. külot, don

underpass /'andıpa:s/ a. yeraltı geçidi

underprivileged /andı'privilicd/ s. temel sosyal haklardan yoksun

underrate /andı'reyt/ e. hafife almak, küçümsemek, gereğinden az değer vermek

undershirt /andı'şö:t/ a, Aİ. atlet, fanila

underside /'andısayd/ a. alt kısım, alt bölüm, alt, taban

undersigned /'andısaynd/ s. aşağıda imzası bulunan

understand /andı'stend/ e. **understood** /andı'stud/ anlamak **understandable** anlaşılır, kavranır **understanding** anlayış; anlama; anlayışlı

understatement /andı'steytmınt/ a. (anlatmaya) yetersiz kalan ifade

understood /andı'stud/ bkz. **understand**

undertake /andı'teyk/ e. **undertook** /andı'tuk/, **undertaken** /andı'teykın/ üzerine almak, üstlenmek, sorumluluğunu almak; (işe) girişmek, başlamak

undertaker /'andıteykı/ a. cenaze kaldırıcısı

underwater /andı'wo:tı/ s, be. sualtı; sualtında

underwear /'andıweı/ a. iç çamaşırı

underweight /andı'weyt/ s. normalden hafif

underworld /'andıwö:ld/ a. ölüler diyarı; yeraltı dünyası, suçlular dünyası

undesirable /andi'zayırıbıl/ s. istenmeyen, hoşa gitmeyen, nahoş

undeveloped /andi'velıpt/ s. (yer) gelişmemiş

undistinguished /andi'stingwişt/ s. sıradan, vasat; üstün özellikleri olmayan

undivided /andi'vaydid/ s. tam, bölünmemiş

undo /an'du:/ e. **undid** /andid/, **undone** /andan/ çözmek, açmak; mahvetmek, yok etmek **undoing** felaket nedeni, mahvolma sebebi

undone /an'dan/ bkz. **undo**; s. yapılmamış, tamamlanmamış; çözülmüş, açılmış, bağlanmamış

undoubted /an'dautid/ s. kesin, su götürmez, kuşku götürmez, şüphesiz

undress /an'dres/ e. soyunmak; soymak, giysilerini çıkarmak

undue /an'dyu:/ s. aşırı, çok fazla; yersiz

unearth /an'ö:t / e. kazıp çıkarmak

unearthly /an'ö:tli/ s. doğaüstü, esrarengiz, korkunç; kon. yersiz, vakitsiz, uygunsuz

uneasy /an'i:zi/ s. sıkıntılı, tedirgin, rahatsız, endişeli

uneducated /an'ecukeytid/ s. tahsilsiz, eğitimsiz

unemployed /anim'ployd/ s. işsiz **the unemployed** işsizler **unemployment** işsizlik

unenviable /an'enviıbıl/ s. hoşa gitmeyen, nahoş

unequal /an'i:kwıl/ s. eşit olmayan; yetersiz, yeterli seviyede olmayan

uneven /an'i:vın/ s. düz olmayan, yamuk, eğri; değişken, kararsız

unfaithful /an'feytfıl/ s. vefasız; eşine sadık olmayan, eşini aldatan

unfavourable /an'feyvırıbıl/ s. uygun olmayan, elverişsiz, aksi, ters, kötü

unfold /an'fould/ e. (katlanmış bir şeyi) açmak; göz önüne sermek; göz önüne serilmek, çözülmek, ortaya çıkmak

unforgettable /anfı'getıbıl/ s. unutulmaz

unfortunate /an'fo:çunit/ s. talihsiz, bahtsız, şanssız; yersiz, uygunsuz **unfortunately** maalesef, ne yazık ki

unfounded /an'faundid/ s. asılsız, temelsiz

unfurl /an'fö:l/ *e.* (yelken, bayrak, vb.) açmak, fora etmek

ungrateful /an'greytfıl/ *s.* nankör

unguarded /an'ga:did/ *s.* sakınmasız, ihtiyatsız

unhappy /an'hepi/ *s.* mutsuz; uygunsuz, yersiz

unhealthy /an'helti/ *s.* sağlıksız; sağlığa zararlı; *kon.* tehlikeli

unheard /an'hö:d/ *s.* duyulmamış, dinlenmemiş

unidentified /anay'dentifayd/ *s.* kimliği belirlenememiş, kimliği saptanmamış

uniform /'yu:nifo:m/ *a.* üniforma ☆ *s.* tek biçimli, aynı

unify /'yu:nifay/ *e.* bir örnek yapmak; bütünleştirmek

uninterested /an'intristid/ *s.* (in) ilgisiz

uninterrupted /anıntı'raptid/ *s.* devamlı, kesintisiz

union /'yu:niın/ *a.* birleşme, birleştirme; birlik; sendika; dernek; federasyon **the Union Jack** İngiliz bayrağı

unique /yu:'nik/ *s.* tek, biricik; *kon.* nadir, az bulunur, eşsiz

unison /'yu:nisın/ *a.* uyum, ahenk, birlik

unit /'yu:nit/ *a.* birim; ünite; *ask.* birlik

unite /yu:'nayt/ *e.* birleşmek; birleştirmek; birlikte olmak

united /yu:'naytid/ *s.* birleşmiş, birleşik; ortak amaçlı **United Nations** Birleşmiş Milletler

unity /'yu:niti/ *a.* birlik; birleşme

universal /yu:ni'vö:sıl/ *s.* evrensel, genel

universe /'yu:nivö:s/ *a.* evren

university /yu:ni'vö:siti/ *a.* üniversite

unkind /an'kaynd/ *s.* düşüncesiz, kaba, kırıcı; zalim, sert

unknown /an'noun/ *a, s.* bilinmeyen, meçhul, tanınmayan

unlawful /an'lo:fıl/ *s.* yasadışı, yolsuz

unless /an'les, ın'les/ *bağ.* -medikçe, -madıkça, -mezse

unlike /an'layk/ *ilg.* -den farklı; -e benzemeyen

unlikely /an'laykli/ *s.* muhtemel olmayan, olasısız

unload /an'loud/ *e.* (yük, silah, film, vb.) boşaltmak

unlock /an'lok/ *e.* kilidini açmak

unloose /an'lu:s/ *e, yaz.* gevşetmek; çözmek

unlucky /an'laki/ *s.* şanssız, talihsiz

unmarried /an'merid/ *s.* evlenmemiş, bekâr

unnatural /an'neçırıl/ *s.* doğal olmayan; anormal; sapık, anormal

unnecessary /an'nesısiri/ *s.* gereksiz

unpack /an'pek/ *e.* (bavul, paket, vb.) açmak, boşaltmak; eşyalarını çıkarmak

unpleasant /an'plezınt/ *s.* nahoş, tatsız, çirkin; kaba

unprecedented /an'presidentid/ *s.* eşi görülmemiş, emsalsiz

unprofessional /anprı'feşınıl/ *s.* (davranış) meslek kurallarına aykırı

unprovoked /anprı'voukt/ *s.* kışkırtılmadan yapılmış

unqualified /an'kwolifayd/ *s.* vasıfsız, ehliyetsiz, yetersiz

unquestionable /an'kwesçınıbıl/ *s.* su götürmez, kesin, tartışmasız

unravel /an'revıl/ *e.* (iplik, giysi, vb.) çözmek, sökmek; çözülmek, sökülmek

unreal /an'riıl/ *s.* gerçek olmayan, düşsel

unreasonable /an'ri:zınıbıl/ *s.* mantıksız, saçma; (fiyat, vb.) aşırı

unreliable /anri'layıbıl/ *s.* güvenilmez

unrest /an'rest/ *a.* huzursuzluk, kargaşa

unroll /an'roul/ *e.* (örtü, vb.) açmak, yaymak

unsaid /an'sed/ *s.* söylenmemiş, dile getirilmemiş

unsavoury /an'seyvıri/ *s.* rezil, aşağılık, çirkin, ahlaksız

unscathed /an'skeydd/ *s.* hasar görmemiş

unscrupulous /an'skru:pyulıs/ *s.* ahlaksız, vicdansız

unseat /an'si:t/ *e.* görevden almak; (at) binicisini düşürmek

unseemly /an'si:mli/ *s.* uygunsuz, yakışık almaz

473

urge

unsettle /an'setıl/ *e.* huzurunu kaçırmak
unshakeable /an'şeykıbıl/ *s.* (inanç)
sarsılmaz, sağlam
unsightly /an'saytli/ *s.* göz zevkini bozan, çirkin
unskilled /an'skild/ *s.* vasıfsız, beceriksiz
unsophisticated /ansı'fistikeytid/ *s.* deneyimsiz, toy; mütevazı, basit, sıradan
unsound /an'saund/ *s.* (düşünce) sağlam temele oturmayan; çürük
unspeakable /an'spi:kıbıl/ *s.* korkunç,
müthiş, sözle anlatılmaz
unstuck /an'stak/ *s.* bağlı/yapışık olmayan, kopuk
untidy /an'taydi/ *s.* düzensiz, dağınık
untie /an'tay/ *e.* çözmek
until /an'til, ın'til/ *bağ, ilg.* -e kadar, -e
dek, -inceye kadar
untimely /an'taymli/ *s.* vakitsiz, zama-
nından önce, mevsimsiz; uygunsuz,
yersiz
untold /an'tould/ *s.* muazzam, sayısız,
büyük; anlatılmamış
untruth /an'tru:t/ *a.* yalan **untruthful**
yalancı; yalan, uydurma
unused /an'yu:zd/ *s.* kullanılmamış ☆
s. /an'yu:st/ **(to)** alışmamış, alışık olmayan
unusual /an'yu:juıl, an'yu:jıl/ *s.* olağan
olmayan, alışılmamış, ender, görül-
medik **unusually** ender olarak; çok,
aşırı derecede
unveil /an'veyl/ *e.* örtüsünü açmak; ortaya çıkarmak
unwell /an'wel/ *s.* hasta, rahatsız, kötü
unwieldy /an'wi:ldi/ *s.* hantal, ağır
unwind /an'waynd/ *e.* (yumak) çözmek, açmak; çözülmek, açılmak; *kon.*
gevşemek, rahatlamak
unzip /an'zip/ *e.* fermuarını açmak
up /ap/ *be.* yukarıya; yukarıda, yüksek-
te ☆ *ilg.* yukarısında, yukarısına ☆
s. yukarı giden **up against** yüz yüze
up and about ayakta, yataktan çıkmış **up to** ilg. -e kadar; -e uygun, yeterli; -e bağlı, -e kalmış **up to date**
çağdaş, modern **What's up** *kon.* Ne

oluyor? Ne var? Ne oldu? Sorun ne?
upbringing /'apbringing/ *a.* çocuk bakım ve eğitimi, yetişme, yetişim
update /ap'deyt/ *e.* modernleştirmek,
çağdaşlaştırmak
uphill /ap'hil/ *s, be.* yokuş yukarı
uphold /ap'hould/ *e.* **upheld** /apheld/
onaylamak; desteklemek
upholster /ap'houlstı/ *e.* (koltuk) döşemek, kaplamak **upholstery** döşemeci-
lik; döşemelik eşya
upkeep /'apki:p/ *a.* bakım
upland /'aplınd/ *a.* yayla, yüksek arazi
upon /ı'pon/ *ilg.* üzerinde, üzerine
upper /'apı/ *s.* üst, üstteki
uppermost /'apımoust/ *be, s.* en başta
gelen, başlıca
upright /'aprayt/ *s.* e, dik, dimdik; dikey; doğru, dürüst, namuslu
uprising /'aprayzing/ *a.* başkaldırı,
ayaklanma, isyan
uproar /'apro:/ *a.* gürültü, şamata
uproot /ap'ru:t/ *e.* kökünden sökmek
upset /ap'set/ *e.* **upset** /apset/ devirmek, altüst etmek, bozmak; keyfini
kaçırmak, üzmek ☆ *s.* üzgün, üzüntülü; rahatsız, hasta; (mide) bulanmış, ☆ *a.* devirme, devrilme; altüst
olma; (mide) bozukluk, rahatsızlık
upshot /'apşot/ *a.* netice, sonuç
upside down /apsayd 'daun/ *be.* alt
üst, karmakarışık; tepetaklak, baş aşağı, ters
upstairs /ap'steız/ *be, s.* yukarıya, üst
kata, yukarıda, üst katta ☆ *a.* üst kat
upstream /ap'stri:m/ *be, s.* akıntıya karşı
uptight /'aptayt/ *s, kon.* eli ayağına do-
laşmış, telaşlı, heyecanlı
upward /'apwıd/ *s.* artan, yükselen
upwards /'apwıdz/ *be.* yukarıya doğru
uranium /yu'reyniım/ *a, kim.* uranyum
Uranus /yu'reynıs/ *a.* Uranüs
urban /'ö:bın/ *s.* kent ile ilgili, şehirsel,
kentsel
urbane /ö:'beyn/ *s.* nazik, yumuşak
urchin /'ö:çin/ *a.* afacan, yumurcak
urge /ö:c/ *e.* **(on)** teşvik etmek; **(on)** ileri sürmek; ısrar etmek ☆ *a.* dürtü,
şiddetli istek, gereksinim

urgent /'ö:cınt/ *s.* acil, ivedi **urgently** acele ile

urinate /'yuırineyt/ *e.* işemek

urine /'yuırin/ *a.* idrar, sidik

urn /ö:n/ *a.* semaver

us /ıs, as/ *adl.* bizi, bize, biz

usage /'yu:zic, 'yu:sic/ *a.* kullanım, kullanış

use /yu:s/ *a.* kullanma, kullanım; fayda; âdet, alışıklık **in use** kullanılan **out of use** kullanılmayan **come into use** kullanılmaya başlanmak **useful** yararlı **useless** yararsız

use /yu:z/ *e.* kullanmak **used** kullanılmış **user** kullanan kimse/şey

used /yu:st/ **be used to** -e alışık olmak **get used to** -e alışmak **used to** (eskiden) -erdi, -ardı

usher /'aşı/ *a.* teşrifatçı; (sinema, tiyatro, vb.) yer gösterici ☆ *e.* (in/out) eşlik etmek, götürmek; içeri getirmek

usual /'yu:juıl, 'yu:jıl/ *s.* her zamanki, alışılmış, olağan **as usual** her zaman olduğu gibi **usually** çoğunlukla, genellikle

usurp /yu:'zö:p/ *e.* gasp etmek, zorla almak

utensil /yu:'tensıl/ *a.* alet; kap

uterus /'yu:tırıs/ *a, anat.* dölyatağı

utility /yu:'tiliti/ *a.* yarar, fayda, **public utilities** kamu kuruluşları

utilize /'yu:tilayz/ *e.* kullanmak, yararlanmak, değerlendirmek

utmost /'atmoust/ *a, s, yaz.* elden gelen en büyük (gayret)

utter /'atı/ *s.* halis, tam, su katılmadık ☆ *e.* söylemek, demek; (çığlık, vb.) atmak **utterance** ifade, sözce

U-turn /'yu:tö:n/ *a.* U dönüşü

V

vacancy /'veykınsi/ *a.* boş (oda, yer); açık kadro

vacant /'veykınt/ *s.* boş; açık, münhal

vacate /vı'keyt/ *e.* boşaltmak, tahliye etmek

vacation /vı'keyşın/ *a.* tatil

vaccinate /'veksineyt/ *e.* aşı yapmak **vaccine** aşı **vaccination** aşılama, aşı

vacillate /'vesileyt/ *e.* bocalamak, tereddüt etmek

vacuum /'vekyuım/ *a.* boşluk; vakum ☆ *e, kon.* elektrik süpürgesiyle temizlemek **vacuum cleaner** elektrik süpürgesi

vagabond /'vegıbond/ *a.* serseri

vagina /vı'caynı/ *a, anat.* dölyolu, vajina

vagrant /'veygrınt/ *a, s.* serseri

vague /veyg/ *s.* belirsiz, anlaşılmaz

vain /veyn/ *s.* boş, yararsız; kibirli, kendini beğenmiş **in vain** boşuna, boş yere

Valentine's Day /'velıntaynz dey/ *a.* 14 şubat sevgililer günü

valet /'velit/ *a.* uşak; (otel) oda hizmetçisi

valid /'velid/ *s.* geçerli; yasal, meşru

validate /'velideyt/ *e.* geçerli kılmak, onaylamak

validity /vı'lidıti/ *a.* geçerlik

valley /'veli/ *a, coğ.* vadi, koyak

valuable /'velyubıl/ *s.* değerli, kıymetli **valuables** değerli şeyler, mücevherat, vb.

valuation /velyu'eyşın/ *a.* (of) değer biçme, kıymet takdiri; biçilen değer

value /'velyu:/ *a.* değer; önem, itibar; anlam ☆ *e.* değer biçmek; önem vermek **Value Added Tax, VAT** katma değer vergisi

valve /velv/ *a.* valf, supap; radyo lambası

vampire /'vempayı/ *a.* vampir

van /ven/ *a.* kamyonet; *ii.* eşya ya da yük vagonu

vandal /'vendıl/ *a.* yararlı ya da güzel şeyleri tahrip eden kimse, vandal **vandalism** vandalizm, yıkıcılık **vandalize** kırıp dökmek

vane /veyn/ *a.* rüzgâr gülü

vanguard /'venga:d/ *a, ask.* öncü kolu; elebaşı

vanilla /vı'nilı/ *a.* vanilya

vanish /'veniş/ *e.* gözden kaybolmak; yok olmak

vanity /'veniti/ a. kendini beğenmişlik, kibir; boşunalık, beyhudelik

vaporize /'veypırayz/ e. buharlaştırmak; buharlaşmak

vapour /'veypı/ a. buğu; buhar

variable /'veıriıbıl/ s. değişken

variant /'veıriınt/ s. değişik ☆ a. deği-şik biçim, varyant

variation /veıri'eyşın/ a. değişme miktarı, değişme derecesi; değişim, değişme, varyasyon

varied /'veırid/ s. değişik; çeşitli

variety /vı'rayıti/ a. değişiklik, çeşitlilik; (of) tür, nevi; varyete, şov

various /'veırııs/ s. çeşitli, değişik, türlü türlü; çok sayıda, birçok

varnish /'va:niş/ a. vernik; cila; parlaklık ☆ e. cila sürmek; verniklemek

vary /'veıri/ e. değiştirmek, değişmek

vase /va:z/ a. vazo

vast /va:st/ s. çok geniş, engin; çok vastly çok

vat /vet/ a. fıçı, tekne

vault /vo:lt/ a. yeraltı mezarı; kubbe ☆ e. üzerinden atlamak

veal /vi:l/ a. dana eti

veer /vıı/ e. yön değiştirmek, dönmek

vegetable /'vectıbıl/ a. sebze

vegetarian /veci'teıriın/ a. vejetaryen, etyemez

vegetate /'veciteyt/ e. ot gibi yaşamak

vegetation /veci'teyşın/ a. bitki örtüsü, bitey

vehement /'viımınt/ s. öfkeli, şiddetli, sert

vehicle /'vi:ikıl/ a. taşıt, vasıta; araç

veil /veyl/ a. peçe, yaşmak; perde; duvak; paravana

vein /veyn/ a, anat. damar

velocity /vi'lositi/ a. sürat, hız

velvet /'velvit/ a. kadife

vendetta /ven'detı/ a. kan davası

veneer /vi'nıı/ a. kaplama maddesi; yapma tavır, sahte görünüş

venerable /'venırıbıl/ s. saygıdeğer

venerate /'venıreyt/ e. saygı göstermek

venereal /vı'nıırııl/ s. cinsel ilişkiyle ilgili; zührevi venereal disease zührevi hastalık

vengeance /'vencıns/ a. öç, intikam

take vengeance intikam almak with a vengeance şiddetle, alabildiğine

venison /'venisın/ a. geyik/karaca eti

venom /'venım/ a. (yılan, vb.) zehiri

vent /vent/ a. delik, ağız

ventilate /'ventileyt/ e. havalandırmak ventilation havalandırma ventilator vantilatör, havalandırma sistemi

venture /'vençı/ e. tehlikeye atmak; cüret etmek, göze almak ☆ a. tehlikeli girişim, macera

Venus /'vi:nıs/ a. Venüs gezegeni, Zühre

veranda /vı'rendı/ a. balkon, veranda

verb /vö:b/ a, dilb. fiil, eylem

verbal /'vö:bıl/ s. sözlü, sözel

verdict /'vö:dikt/ a, huk. jüri kararı

verge /vö:c/ a. kenar, sınır, hudut verge on/upon -in eşiğinde olmak

verify /'verifay/ e. doğruluğunu kanıtlamak

veritable /'veritıbıl/ s. gerçek, tam

vermilion /vı'miliın/ a, s. alev kırmızısı

vermin /'vö:min/ a. zararlı böcek ya da hayvanlar

vermouth /'vö:mıt / a. vermut

vernacular /vı'nekyulı/ a. anadil; lehçe

verruca /vı'ru:kı/ a. nasır

versatile /'vö:sıtayl/ s. çok yönlü; çok işe yarayan, çok kullanımlı

verse /vö:s/ a. şiir, koşuk; mısra; ayet

version /'vö:şın/ a. yorum; çeviri; uyarlama

versus /'vö:sıs/ ilg. -e karşı

vertebra /'vö:tibrı/ a. (ç. -brae /-bri:/) omurga vertebrate /'vö:tibrit/ omurgalı

vertical /'vö:tikıl/ s. dikey, düşey

vertigo /'vö:tigou/ a. baş dönmesi

very /'veri/ be. çok, pek; gerçekten; tümüyle ☆ s. aynı, tıpkısı; tam; hatta, bile

vessel /'vesıl/ a. kap, tas; gemi, tekne blood vessel damar

vest /vest/ a, İİ. atlet, fanila; Aİ. yelek

vestibule /'vestibyu:l/ a. antre, hol

vestige /'vestic/ a. iz, eser

vet /vet/ a, kon. veteriner, baytar

veteran /'vetırın/ a, s. (of) kıdemli, eski; emektar; gazi

veterinary 476

veterinary /'vetırinıri/ s. hayvan hastalıklarıyla ilgili **veterinary surgeon** İİ. veteriner

veto /'vi:tou/ a. veto ☆ e. veto etmek

vex /veks/ e. kızdırmak, canını sıkmak

via /'vayı/ ilg. yolu ile, -den geçerek; kon. aracılığıyla

viable /'vayıbıl/ s. uygulanabilir; varlığını sürdürebilir

viaduct /'vayıdakt/ a. viyadük, köprü

vibrate /vay'breyt/ e. titremek; titretmek **vibration** titreşim; titreme

vicar /'vikı/ a. papaz

vice /vays/ a. ahlaksızlık; kötülük; kon. kötü alışkanlık; mengene

vice versa /vaysı 'vö:sı/ be. tersine; karşılıklı olarak

vicinity /vi'siniti/ a. semt, çevre, yöre

vicious /'vişıs/ s. kötü amaçlı **vicious circle** kısır döngü

victim /'viktim/ a. kurban

victor /'viktı/ a. kazanan, galip; fatih

Victorian /vik'to:riın/ s, a. Kraliçe Viktorya dönemine ait

victorious /vik'to:riıs/ s. muzaffer, galip

victory /'viktıri/ a. zafer, utku, galibiyet

video /'vidiou/ a, s. video **videotape** videoteyp, video bandı

view /vyu:/ a. görüş, görünüş; manzara; bakış; düşünce; kanı ☆ e. incelemek; bakmak; muayene etmek **in view of** -i göz önünde bulundurarak **on view** sergilenmekte **point of view** görüş **with a view to** amacıyla, -mek için **viewer** televizyon izleyen kimse, seyirci

viewy /'vyu:i/ s gösterişli

vigil /'vicil/ a. (nöbet, vb. için) geceleyin uyumama, nöbet tutma

vigilant /'vicilınt/ s. uyanık, tetikte

vigour /'vigı/ a. güç, kuvvet, dinçlik; gayret **vigorous** güçlü, dinç, enerjik

vile /vayl/ s. aşağılık, adi; iğrenç

villa /'vilı/ a. villa

village /'vilic/ a. köy **villager** köylü

villain /'vilın/ a. kötü adam

vindicate /'vindikeyt/ e. haklı çıkarmak, doğruluğunu kanıtlamak

vindictive /vin'diktiv/ s. kinci

vine /vayn/ a, bitk. asma, bağ kütüğü; sarmaşık **vineyard** üzüm bağı

vinegar /'vinigı/ a. sirke

vintage /'vintic/ a. bağbozumu

viola /vi'oulı/ a, müz. viyola

violate /'vayıleyt/ e. bozmak, çiğnemek; tecavüz etmek **violation** ihlal, bozma; tecavüz

violent /'vayılınt/ s. sert, şiddetli; zorlu

violet /'vayılıt/ a. menekşe

violin /vayı'lin/ a, müz. keman, viyolon

viper /'vaypı/ a, hayb. engerek

virgin /'vö:cin/ a. bakire, kız ☆ s. bakire; el değmemiş, saf; doğal; bakir **virginity** bekâret, erdenlik

Virgin Mary /vö:cin 'meıri/ a. Meryem Ana

Virgo /'vö:gou/ a. Başak burcu

virile /'virayl/ s. güçlü; erkekçe; (cinsel yönden) iktidarlı

virtual /'vö:çuıl/ s. ismen olmasa da fiilen var olan, gerçek, asıl **virtually** hemen hemen, neredeyse

virtue /'vö:çu:/ a. fazilet, erdem; üstünlük **by virtue of** -den dolayı, -in sayesinde **virtuous** /-çuıs/ erdemli; dürüst

virus /'vayırıs/ a. virüs

visa /'vi:zı/ a. vize

vis-à-vis /vi:z a:'vi:, vi:zı'vi:/ ilg. -e bakınca; yüz yüze

viscous /'viskıs/ s. (sıvı) yapışkan

visible /'vizıbıl/ s. görülebilir, görünür

vision /'vijın/ a. görme; görüş; ileriyi görme; hayal, düş

visionary /'vijınıri/ s. ileriyi gören; düşsel, hayali ☆ a. hayalperest

visit /'vizit/ e. ziyaret etmek, görmeye gitmek ☆ a. ziyaret; teftiş; muayene, vizite

visitor /'vizitı/ a. ziyaretçi

visor /'vayzı/ a. (kasket) siperlik, siper

visual /'vijuıl/ s. görsel **visual aid** görsel eğitim aracı

vital /'vaytıl/ s. (yaşam için) gerekli; çok önemli; yaşam dolu, canlı

vitality /vay'teliti/ a. hayatiyet, canlılık, dirilik

vitally /'vaytıli/ be. en yüksek derecede

vitamin /'vitımin, 'vaytımin/ a. vitamin

vivacious /vi'veyşıs/ s. şen şakrak

vivid /'vivid/ s. parlak, canlı; güçlü; can-

lı, akılda kalıcı
vixen /'viksın/ *a, hayb.* dişi tilki; cadaloz kadın
vocabulary /vı'kebyulıri, vou'kebyulıri/ *a.* kelime hazinesi; kısa sözlük
vocal /'voukıl/ *s.* sesle ilgili **vocal cords** ses telleri **vocalist** şarkıcı
vocation /vou'keyşın/ *a.* meslek, iş **vocational** mesleki
vodka /'vodkı/ *a.* votka
vogue /voug/ *a.* moda
voice /voys/ *a.* ses **give voice to** ifade etmek, dile getirmek **with one voice** hep bir ağızdan
void /voyd/ *s.* boş; geçersiz ☆ *a.* boşluk ☆ *e.* geçersiz kılmak; boşaltmak
volatile /'volıtayl/ *s.* değişken, dönek; (sıvı) uçucu
volcano /vol'keynou/ *a.* volkan, yanardağ
volley /'voli/ *a.* yaylım ateş; *sp.* topa yere düşmeden vurma, vole **volleyball** voleybol
volt /voult/ *a.* volt **voltage** voltaj
voluble /'volyubıl/ *s.* konuşkan, dilli
volume /'volyu:m/ *a.* hacim; cilt; miktar; (ses) güç, şiddet
voluntary /'volıntıri/ *s.* gönüllü; iradi, istençli, kasıtlı
volunteer /volın'tiı/ *a.* gönüllü ☆ *e.* bir hizmete gönüllü olarak girmek
voluptuous /vı'lapçuıs/ *s.* şehvetli; seksi
vomit /'vomit/ *e.* kusmak ☆ *a.* kusmuk
voodoo /'vu:du:/ *a.* büyü, büyü dini
vortex /'vo:teks/ *a.* girdap
vote /vout/ *a.* oy; **(the)** oy hakkı ☆ *e.* oy vermek; seçmek; önermek; *kon.* bildirmek, ilan etmek **voter** seçmen
vouch /vauç/ *e.* **(for)** kefil olmak; doğrulamak, tasdik etmek **voucher** senet, makbuz, belge
vow /vau/ *a.* yemin, ant ☆ *e.* yemin etmek, ant içmek
vowel /'vauıl/ *a.* ünlü, sesli harf
voyage /'voyic/ *a.* seyahat, yolculuk, gezi
vulgar /'valgı/ *s.* kaba, terbiyesiz, bayağı; zevksiz, adi

vulnerable /'valnırıbıl/ *s.* hassas; korunmasız, savunmasız, zayıf
vulture /'valçı/ *a, hayb.* akbaba

W

wad /wod/ *a.* tapa, tıkaç
waddle /'wodıl/ *e.* badi badi yürümek
wade /weyd/ *e.* (su, çamur, vb. içinde) güçlükle ilerlemek
wafer /'weyfı/ *a.* ince bisküvi
waffle /'wofıl/ *a.* bir tür gözleme; *İİ, kon.* zırvalama
wag /weg/ *a.* sallama ☆ *e.* sallamak
wage /weyc/ *a.* ücret
wager /'weycı/ *a.* bahis ☆ *e.* bahse girmek
waggon /'wegın/ *a.* yük arabası; kağnı; *İİ.* yük vagonu
wail /weyl/ *e.* ağlamak, feryat etmek ☆ *a.* ağlama, feryat
waist /weyst/ *a.* bel **waistband** kemer, kuşak **waistcoat** yelek
wait /weyt/ *e.* **(for)** beklemek ☆ *a.* bekleme **keep sb waiting** -i bekletmek **lie in wait** pusuya yatmak **wait on** hizmet etmek, bakmak **waiting room** bekleme salonu
waiter /'weytı/ *a.* garson **waitress** bayan garson
wake /weyk/ *e.* **woke** /wouk/, **woken** /'woukın/ **(up)** uyanmak; uyandırmak ☆ *a.* dümen suyu **wakeful** uyanık, uyuyamayan; uykusuz
waken /'weykın/ *e.* uyandırmak; uyanmak
walk /wo:k/ *e.* yürümek; gezinmek, dolaşmak; yürüyüşe çıkarmak, gezdirmek; yürüyerek eşlik etmek ☆ *a.* yürüyüş, gezinti; yürüme; kaldırım, yol **walk of life** sosyal durum, meslek **go for a walk** yürüyüşe çıkmak **walk/off with** *kon.* (ödül, vb.) kolayca kazanmak; *kon.* çalmak, yürütmek **walkout** grev; (toplantı, vb.'ni) terk etme **walk out on** *kon.* yüzüstü bırakmak, terk etmek **walking** yürüme, yürüyüş **walk-**

ing stick baston
walkie-talkie /wo:ki'to:ki/ *a*. portatif alı-
cı-verici aygıt
wall /wo:l/ *a*. duvar; sur **wallchart** öğretim aracı olarak kullanılan duvar res-
mi **wallpaper** duvar kâğıdı
wallet /'wolit/ *a*. cüzdan
walnut /'wo:lnat/ *a*. ceviz; ceviz ağacı
walrus /'wo:lrıs/ *a, hayb*. mors
waltz /wo:ls/ *a, müz*. vals
wander /'wondı/ *e*. dolaşmak, gezmek;
ayrılmak, sapmak; **(off)** konudan ayrılmak **wanderer** amaçsızca dolaşan
kimse, avare
wane /weyn/ *e*. azalmak, eksilmek; sönmek; (ay) gittikçe küçülmek
want /wont/ *e*. istemek; -e gereksinimi
olmak; gerektirmek ☆ *a*. istek; gereksinim, ihtiyaç, lüzum; yokluk **want
for** -e ihtiyaç duymak, aramak **be
wanting** eksik olmak **wanted** aranan
wanting eksik, noksan
wanton /'wontın/ *s*. değişken, kaprisli;
kontrolsüz; mantıksız, nedensiz
war /wo:/ *a*. savaş **warfare** savaş; mücadele **warhead** patlayıcı savaş başlığı
warlike savaşçı; savaşla ilgili **warship**
savaş gemisi **wartime** savaş zamanı
warble /'wo:bıl/ *e*. ötmek, şakımak
warbler çalıbülbülü, ötleğen
ward /wo:d/ *a*. koğuş; semt, bölge; vesayet; vesayet altındaki kimse
warden /'wo:dın/ *a*. bekçi; muhafız
warder /'wo:dı/ *a*. gardiyan, bekçi
wardrobe /'wo:droub/ *a*. gardırop
warehouse /'weıhaus/ *a*. depo, ambar
wares /weız/ *a*. mal, eşya
warm /wo:m/ *s*. sıcak; sıcak tutan; içten, candan; hoş; neşeli, dostça ☆
e. ısıtmak; ısınmak **warm to/towards**
kon. sevmeye başlamak, hoşlanmak,
ısınmak; ilgilenmek, ilgilenmeye başlamak **warm up** ısınmak; ısıtmak
warm-blooded sıcakkanlı; enerjik, tutkulu **warm-hearted** iyi kalpli, cana yakın
warmth /wo:mt / *a*. sıcaklık; içtenlik
warn /wo:n/ *e*. uyarmak, ikaz etmek
warning uyarı, ikaz, tembih
warp /wo:p/ *a*. eğrilik, çarpıklık; çözgü;

den. palamar ☆ *e*. eğrilmek, yamulmak; eğriltmek
warrant /'worınt/ *a*. yetki; ruhsat; teminat, garanti ☆ *e*. mazur göstermek;
garanti etmek **search warrant** arama
emri **warranty** garanti belgesi
warrior /'woriı/ *a*. savaşçı; asker
wart /wo:t/ *a*. siğil
wary /'weıri/ *s*. ihtiyatlı; uyanık
was /wız/ **woz**/ *e*. (be eyleminin **I, he,
she, it** özneleriyle kullanılan geçmiş
zaman biçimi) -dı, -di
wash /woş/ *e*. yıkamak; yıkanmak ☆
a. yıkama; yıkanma; çamaşır; dal-
ga/su sesi **washable** yıkanır, yıkanabi-
lir **washbasin** lavabo **washbowl** *Aİ*. lavabo **washer** yıkayıcı; çamaşır makinesi **washing** yıkama, yıkanma; çamaşır **washing machine** çamaşır makinesi **washing-up** İİ, *kon*. bulaşık yıkama,
bulaşıklar **wash out** (kir, vb.) yıkaya-
rak çıkarmak, temizlemek **wash up** *İİ*.
bulaşık yıkamak; *Aİ*. elini yüzünü yıkamak
wasp /'wosp/ *a*. eşekarısı
wastage /weyst/ *a*. israf, sarfiyat
waste /weyst/ *a*. israf, savurganlık; artık
madde; boş arazi, çöl ☆ *s*. artık;
boş, çorak ☆ *e*. israf etmek, çarçur
etmek **go/run to waste** israf olmak, ziyan olmak **lay waste** harap etmek, yıkıp yakmak **wastebasket** çöp sepeti
wasteful savurgan, müsrif **wastepaper basket** kâğıt sepeti **waste pipe**
künk
watch /woç/ *e*. seyretmek, izlemek;
göz kulak olmak; beklemek; dikkat etmek; gözetlemek ☆ *a*. kol saati; cep
saati; gözetleme; nöbet; nöbetçi, bekçi; nöbetçilik **watchband** saat kayışı
watchdog bekçi köpeği **watch for** beklemek, kollamak **watchful** tetikte, uyanık, dikkatli **watchmaker** saatçi **watchman** bekçi gözcü **watch out** *kon*. dikkat etmek **watchword** parola; slogan
water /'wo:tı/ *a*. su ☆ *e*. sulamak; sulandırmak; sulanmak **by water** deniz
yoluyla **fresh water** tatlı su **hard water** acı su **spring water** memba suyu
water down sulandırmak **watercolour**

weld

suluboya **watercourse** su yolu, dere
waterfall çağlayan, şelale **waterfront**
rıhtım **waterline** (gemilerde) su düze-
yi **watermelon** karpuz **watermill** su
değirmeni **waterproof** sugeçirmez, su
sızdırmaz **water-ski** su kayağı **waterway** su yolu/kanal/geçit **waterwheel**
su çarkı **waterworks** su dağıtım tesisatı **watery** sulu, cıvık, çok sulu; (renk)
soluk
watt /wot/ a. vat
wave /weyv/ e. sallamak; sallanmak; el
sallamak ☆ a. dalga; (el) sallama
wavelength dalga boyu **wavy** (saç)
dalgalı
wax /weks/ a. balmumu; kulak kiri
way /wey/ a. yol; yön, taraf; mesafe; şekil; yöntem, yol; imkân, olasılık **by
the way** sırası gelmişken, bu arada
by way of yolu ile; amacıyla, niyetiyle
get under way başlamak **give way** boyun eğmek **in a way** bir bakıma **in
some ways** bazı bakımlardan **make
way for** -e yol açmak **no way** hayatta
olmaz **out of the way** olağandışı,
anormal **put sb out of the way** ortadan kaldırmak; başından atmak **right
of way** (trafikte) geçiş hakkı **way in** giriş **way out** çıkış
waylay /'weyley/ e. yolunu kesmek, durdurmak
wayside /'weysayd/ a. yol kenarı
wayward /'weywıd/ s. kararsız, değişken
we /wi, wi:/ adl. biz
weak /wi:k/ s. güçsüz, zayıf; yetersiz;
(çorba, çay) sulu, açık **weakness** zayıflık, güçsüzlük; zaaf; kusur, hata
weaken /'wi:kın/ e. zayıflamak; zayıflat-
mak
wealth /welt/ a. varlık, servet, para;
bolluk, çokluk **wealthy** zengin, varlıklı
wean /wi:n/ e. sütten kesmek
weapon /'wepın/ a. silah
wear /weı/ e. **wore** /wo:/, **worn** /wo:n/
giymek; takmak; takınmak; aşınmak,
yıpranmak; aşındırmak ☆ a. giyme,
giyinme; giysi, giyim; aşınma, eskime
wear away zamanla aşınmak; aşındırmak **wear down** aşınmak; aşındır-

mak, yıpratmak; yenmek **wear off**
azalmak, hafiflemek, geçmek **wear
on** uzamak, bitmek bilmemek **wear
out** giyip eskitmek; iyice eskitmek;
çok yormak
weary /'wiıri/ s. yorgun; yorucu
weather /'wedı/ a. hava ☆ e. (fırtına,
güçlük, vb.'yi) atlatmak, savuşturmak; soldurmak, aşındırmak; solmak,
aşınmak
weave /wi:v/ e. **wove** /wouv/, **woven**
/'wouvın/ dokumak; örmek ☆ a. do-
kuma; örme **weaver** dokumacı **weaving** dokuma
web /web/ a. ağ; dokuma
wed /wed/ e, yaz. evlenmek
wedding /'weding/ a. nikâh, düğün
wedge /wec/ a. kama, kıskı, takoz
wedlock /'wedlok/ a. evlilik
Wednesday /'wenzdi/ a. çarşamba
weed /wi:d/ a. yabani ot, zararlı ot; kon.
zayıf kimse
week /wi:k/ a. hafta **weekday** hafta içi,
iş günü **weekend** hafta sonu **weekly**
haftalık, haftada bir
weep /wi:p/ e. **wept** /wept/ ağlamak
weft /weft/ a. atkı, argaç
weigh /wey/ e. (ağırlığını) tartmak; ağır-
lığında olmak **weigh anchor** demir almak **weigh down** ağırlığıyla aşağıya
itmek, basmak **weigh on** üzmek, düşündürmek **weighing machine** kantar, baskül
weight /weyt/ a. ağırlık; tartı; sp. halter;
önem, değer; sıkıntı, yük **lose weight**
kilo vermek **over weight** fazla kilolu
put on weight kilo almak, şişmanlamak **under weight** zayıf, normal kilo-
nun altında **weighty** önemli, ciddi
weir /wiı/ a. su bendi
weird /wiıd/ s. garip, tuhaf
welcome /'welkım/ ünl. Hoş geldiniz. ☆
e. içtenlikle karşılamak; kabul etmek
☆ a. hoş karşılama ☆ s. hoşa giden, istenilen, sevindirici; serbest
make (sb) welcome (bir misafiri) ağırlamak **You're welcome** Rica ederim,
Bir şey değil
weld /weld/ e. kaynak yaparak birleştirmek ☆ a. kaynak **welder** kaynakçı

welfare /'welfeı/ a. refah, gönenç; Aİ.
yoksullara yapılan hükümet yardımları

well /wel/ be. iyi; güzel; adamakıllı, iyice; hakkıyla; pek, çok; hayli, oldukça
☆ s. sağlığı yerinde, iyi; uygun, yerinde; elverişli ☆ ünl. şey!; ha!; pekâlâ! ☆ a. kuyu; memba, pınar as well
dahi, de, da as well as hem . . . hem
de, olduğu kadar, ile birlikte well off
zengin, varlıklı do well başarılı olmak

well /wel/ önek iyi, doğru, dürüst, adamakıllı well-advised akıllı, sağgörülü
well-behaved terbiyeli well-being
mutluluk, gönenç, iyilik well-bred kibar, terbiyeli well-done iyi pişmiş
well-informed bilgili, kültürlü; kulağı
delik, her şeyi bilen well-intentioned
iyi niyetli well-known tanınmış, ünlü
well-read çok okumuş, kültürlü, bilgili
well-spoken konuşması düzgün
well-timed vaktinde, uygun
well-to-do kon. zengin well-wisher iyilik/mutluluk dileyen kimse

wellington /'welingtın/ a. çizme

went /went/ bkz. go

wept /wept/ bkz. weep

were /wı, wö: / e. (be eyleminin we,
you, they özneleriyle kullanılan geçmiş zaman biçimi) -idik, idin(iz), -idiler

west /west/ a. batı ☆ be. batıya doğru
westbound batıya giden westerly batıdaki; batıdan gelen

western /'westın/ s. batı ☆ a. kovboy
filmi/romanı

wet /wet/ s. ıslak, yaş; (boya) kurumamış; yağmurlu ☆ a. yağmur, yağmurlu hava; ıslaklık ☆ e. ıslatmak; ıslatmak

whack /wek/ a. küt diye vurma; vuruş
sesi, küt, pat; kon. pay, hisse

whale /weyl/ a. hayb. balina whaler balina avcısı; balina avlama gemisi

wharf /wo:f/ a. iskele, rıhtım

what /wot/ s, adl. ne; hangi What for
Ne için What if ya ... ise What ...
like? Nasıl? Nasıl bir şey? What next
Başka? Daha neler? What's more Üstelik, Dahası What of it/So what?

kon. ne olmuş yani, ne çıkar

whatever /wo'tevı/ adl. her ne, her hangi ☆ s. ne, hangi; hiçbir, hiç

whatsoever /wotsou'evı/ s, adl, bkz.
whatever

wheat /wi:t/ a. buğday

wheedle /'wi:dıl/ e. tatlı dille ikna etmek

wheel /wi:l/ a. tekerlek; direksiyon
wheelbarrow el arabası wheelchair tekerlekli sandalye

wheeze /wi:z/ e. hırıltıyla solumak ☆
a. hırıltı

when /wen/ be. ne zaman ☆ bağ. -dığı zaman; -ınca, -ince; -dığı halde;
takdirde, eğer

whenever /we'nevı/ be, bağ. her ne zaman

where /weı/ be. nereye; nerede; nereden ☆ bağ. ki o yere; ki o yerde; -dığı; -diği whereabouts nereye, nerelerde ☆ a. (bulunduğu) yer

whereas /weı'rez/ bağ. oysa; mademki

wherever /weı'revı/ be, bağ. her nereye, her nerede, nereye, nerede

wherewithal /'weıwido:l/ a. gerekli para, vb.

whet /wet/ e. bilemek; (iştah) açmak
whet sb's appetite iştahını iyice kabartmak

whether /'wedı/ bağ. -meyip, -mediğini

which /wiç/ s. hangi ☆ adl. hangisi(ni); ki o, -en, -an; ki onu/ona, -dığı, -diği

whichever /wi'çevı/ s, adl. herhangi,
hangi; herhangi bir(i)

whiff /wif/ a. esinti; koku

while /wayl/ bağ. -ken; -e rağmen, karşın ☆ a. süre, zaman after a while biraz sonra for a while bir süre worth
(one's) while (harcanacak zamana)
değer

whilst /waylst/ bağ, İİ, bkz. while

whim /wim/ a. kapris whimsical /'wimzikıl/ kaprisli

whimper /'wimpı/ e. sızlamak, sızlanmak ☆ a. ağlama, sızlama

whine /wayn/ e. sızlanmak, zırıldamak;
zırlamak

481 winch

whinny /'wini/ e. kişnemek ☆ a. kişneme
whip /wip/ a. kırbaç, kamçı; parlamentoda parti denetçisi ☆ e. kırbaçlamak; (yumurta, krema, vb.) çırpmak; kon. yenmek whip up tahrik/teşvik etmek; yapıvermek
whirl /wö:l/ e. fırıl fırıl döndürmek; fırıl fırıl dönmek ☆ a. hızla dönme whirlpool girdap whirlwind hortum, kasırga
whirr /wö: / a. kanat, pervane, vb. sesi, pır pır ☆ e. pır pır etmek
whisk /wisk/ a. toz fırçası; (yumurta, vb.) çırpma aleti ☆ e. silkmek, sallamak; apar topar götürmek; çırpmak
whisker /'wiskı/ a. kedi, fare, vb. bıyığı; ç. favori
whisky /'wiski/ a. viski
whisper /'wispı/ a. fısıltı ☆ e. fısıldaşmak; fısıldamak
whistle /'wisıl/ a. ıslık; düdük ☆ e. ıslık çalmak; düdük çalmak
white /wayt/ s. beyaz; soluk benizli; (kahve) sütlü ☆ a. beyaz renk; yumurta akı the White House Beyaz Saray white-collar büroda çalışan whiten beyazlaşmak; beyazlaştırmak
whitewash /'waytwoş/ a. badana ☆ e. badanalamak
whither /'widı/ be. nereye; ki oraya, -diği
whittle /'witıl/ e. yontmak whittle down azaltmak
whiz /wiz/ a. vızıltı ☆ e, kon. vın diye gitmek; vızıldamak
who /hu:/ adl. kim; kime; kimi; ki o, -en, -an; ki onu/ona, -dığı, -diği
whoever /hu:'evı/ adl. her kim; her kim ise, kim olursa olsun
whole /houl/ s. bütün; tüm; mat. tam, kesirsiz ☆ a. bütün on the whole neticede, genelde whole-hearted candan, içten wholly tümüyle, bütün bütün
wholesale /'houlseyl/ a. toptan satış ☆ s, be. toptan; toplu wholesaler toptancı
wholesome /'houlsım/ s. sağlığa yararlı
whom /hu:m/ adl. kim, kimi, kime; ki o/onu/ona, -dığı, -diği
whoop /hu:p, wu:p/ a. (neşeyle) bağırma, bağırış ☆ e. bağırmak, bağrışmak
whore /ho:/ a. fahişe, orospu
whose /hu:z/ adl. kimin; ki onun, -en, -an; (nesneler için) ki onun, -en, -an
why /way/ be. niçin, neden, niye the reason why -in nedeni Why not (öneri belirtir) neden olmasın
wick /wik/ a. fitil
wicked /'wikid/ s. kötü; kon. yaramaz, muzip
wicket /'wikit/ a. (kriket) kale
wide /wayd/ s. geniş; engin, açık ☆ be. iyice; tamamen; (hedeften) uzağa widely geniş çapta, adamakıllı, iyice widen genişlemek; genişletmek widespread yaygın
widow /'widou/ a. dul kadın widower dul erkek
width /widt / a. genişlik; en
wield /wi:ld/ e. kullanmak
wife /wayf/ a. karı, hanım, eş
wig /wig/ a. peruka
wiggle /'wigıl/ e. kıpır kıpır oynatmak, kıpırdatmak
wigwam /'wigwem/ a. Kızılderili çadırı
wild /wayld/ s. vahşi, yabani; hiddetli, kızgın; şiddetli, sert; fırtınalı; çılgın; deli wildcat yaban kedisi wilderness ekilmemiş boş arazi wildlife vahşi doğa wildly çılgınca
will /wil/ e. would /wud/ -ecek, -acak Will you ...? -er misiniz? -ar mısınız?
will /wil/ a. irade, istem, istenç; vasiyetname ☆ e. niyet etmek, istemek; vasiyetle bırakmak at will istediği zaman
willing /'wiling/ s. gönüllü; razı, istekli willingly seve seve
willow /'wilou/ a, bitk. söğüt
wilt /wilt/ e. (çiçek, vb.) solmak; soldurmak
wily /'wayli/ s. kurnaz, cingöz
win /win/ e. won /wan/ kazanmak ☆ a. galibiyet, yengi winner kazanan winnings kazanılan para, kazanç
wince /wins/ e. irkilmek
winch /winç/ a. vinç

wind

wind /wind/ *a.* rüzgâr, yel; nefes, soluk; (midede) gaz; boş laf; *müz.* üflemeli çalgılar ☆ *e.* soluğunu kesmek **windfall** rüzgârla düşen meyve; beklenmedik para/şans **windmill** yel değirmeni **windscreen** (oto) ön cam **windy** rüzgârlı; geveze

wind /waynd/ *e.* **wound** /waund/ sarmak, dolamak; sarılmak, dolanmak **wind up** saat kurmak

window /'windou/ *a.* pencere, cam; vitrin **window dressing** vitrin dekorasyonu **window-shopping** vitrin gezmesi **windowpane** pencere camı **windowsill** pencere eşiği

wine /wayn/ *a.* şarap

wing /wing/ *a.* kanat; kol; *sp.* kanat oyuncusu ☆*e.* uçurmak; hafifçe yaralamak

wink /wink/ *e.* göz kırpmak; parıldamak ☆ *a.* göz kırpma

winsome /'winsım/ *s.* güzel, çekici

winter /'wintı/ *a.* kış

wipe /wayp/ *e.* silmek ☆ *a.* silme, temizleme **wipe off** silip çıkarmak; -den kurtarmak **wipe out** ortadan kaldırmak, öldürmek, temizlemek **wipe up** bulaşıkları kurulamak

wiper /'waypı/ *a.* (oto) silecek

wire /'wayı/ *a.* tel; *kon.* telgraf ☆ *e.* elektrik teli, vb. bağlamak; telgraf göndermek

wireless /'wayılis/ *a, İİ, esk.* radyo ☆ *s.* telsiz, kablosuz

wiring /'wayıring/ *a.* elektrik tertibatı

wisdom /'wizdım/ *a.* akıl; bilgelik **wisdom tooth** akıldişi

wise /wayz/ *s.* akıllı; bilgili; deneyimli; kurnaz

wish /wiş/ *e.* (şu anda olanaksız bir şey) istemek, dilemek ☆ *a.* dilek, istek **wishful** arzulu, istekli; hasret dolu **wishful thinking** hüsnükuruntu **wishbone** lades kemiği

wisp /wisp/ *a.* tutam; demet

wit /wit/ *a.* akıl, zekâ; nükte; nükteci **witty** nükteli, nükteci

witch /'wiç/ *a.* büyücü kadın; büyüleyici güzellikte kadın **witchcraft** büyücülük

with /wid, wit / *ilg.* ile, -le, -la; -li, -lı; -e rağmen; -in lehinde, -den yana; nedeniyle, sayesinde

withdraw /wid'dro:, wit'dro:/ *e.* **withdrew** /-'dru:/, **withdrawn** /-dro:n/ geri çekmek; geri almak; çekilmek; (para) çekmek **withdrawal** geri çekme/alma; geri çekilme

withdrawn /wid'dro:n, wit'dro:n/ *bkz.* **withdraw**; *s.* içine kapanık

withdrew /wid'dru:/ *bkz.* **withdraw**

wither /'widı/ *e.* solmak, kurumak; soldurmak, kurutmak; sönmek, yok olmak

withheld /wid'held/ *bkz.* **withhold**

withhold /wid'hould, wit'hould/ *e.* **withheld** /'wid'held/ saklamak, vermemek

within /wi'din/ *ilg.* içinde

without /wi'daut/ *ilg.* -sız, -siz; -meden, -meksizin

withstand /wid'stend, wit'stend/ *e.* **withstood** /-'stud/ karşı koymak, direnmek

witness /'witnis/ *a.* tanık, şahit; tanıklık; kanıt, delil ☆ *e.* tanık olmak; tanıklık etmek; göstermek, kanıtlamak

wizard /'wizıd/ *a.* sihirbaz, büyücü

wizened /'wiznd/ *s.* buruşuk, buruşmuş

wobble /'wobıl/ *e.* sallanmak; sallamak

woe /wou/ *a.* üzüntü, dert, keder

woke(n) /wouk(ın)/ *bkz.* **wake**

wolf /wulf/ *a, hayb.* kurt

woman /'wumın/ *a.* (ç. **women** /'wimin/) kadın **womanhood** kadınlık

womb /wu:m/ *a, anat.* rahim, dölyatağı

wonder /'wandı/ *a.* şaşkınlık, merak, hayret; harika ☆ *s.* harika ☆ *e.* hayret etmek, şaşmak **wonderful** harika, olağanüstü

wood /wud/ *a.* odun, tahta, kereste; orman, koru **woodcock** çulluk **woodcutter** oduncu **wooded** ağaçlık, ormanlık **wooden** tahta, ahşap; odun gibi **woodland** ormanlık ülke/bölge/arazi **woodpecker** ağaçkakan **woodwind** (tahtadan yapılmış) üflemeli çalgılar **woodwork** doğramacılık, dülgerlik; ahşap kısımlar, doğrama işleri **wood-**

worm ağaçkurdu, tahtakurdu **woody** ağaçlık, ormanlık

wool /wul/ *a.* yün; yapağı **woollen** yünlü **woollens** yünlü giysiler, yünlüler **woolly** yünlü; yün gibi

word /wö:d/ *a.* kelime, sözcük; söz; mesaj, haber, bilgi **break one's words** sözünü tutmamak **eat one's words** tükürdüğünü yalamak **have a word with** ile görüşmek **in a word** kısacası **in other words** başka bir deyişle **keep one's word** sözünü tutmak, sözünde durmak **say the word** *kon.* izin vermek, onaylamak **take sb's word for it** söylediğine inanmak/kabul etmek **word for word** kelimesi kelimesine **word processor** kelime işlem aygıtı **wording** anlatım biçimi **wordy** sözü fazla uzatan

wore /wo:/ *bkz.* **wear**

work /wö:k/ *a.* iş, çalışma; eser, yapıt; ç. fabrika; ç. mekanizma ☆ *e.* çalışmak; çalıştırmak; işe yaramak; işlemek; işletmek; başarılı olmak, yürümek **at work** işte, iş başında **all in the day's work** normal, beklendiği gibi **out of work** işsiz, boşta **set to work** başlamak, koyulmak **work force** toplam işçi sayısı **work out** hesaplamak; istenildiği gibi olmak; sonuçlanmak; idman yapmak **work up** geliştirmek, ilerletmek; gelişmek; heyecanlandırmak, kamçılamak **workbook** alıştırma kitabı **workday** işgünü **workout** idman, antrenman **workshop** atölye

workable /'wö:kıbıl/ *s.* çalışır; işe yarar, uygulanabilir

worker /'wö:kı/ *a.* işçi

working /'wö:king/ *a.* çalışma; ç. çalışma/işleme sistemi, işleyiş ☆ *s.* çalışan, işleyen **working capital** işletme sermayesi **working conditions** çalışma şartları **working hours** çalışma saatleri

workman /'wö:kmın/ *a.* işçi **workmanship** işçilik, ustalık

world /wö:ld/ *a.* dünya; evren **worldly** dünyevi, maddi **worldwide** dünya çapında

worm /wö:m/ *a.* kurt, solucan

worn /wo:n/ *bkz.* **wear**

worried /'warid/ *s.* endişeli, kaygılı, üzgün ☆ *e.* kaygılanmak, merak etmek; kaygılandırmak, rahatsız etmek ☆ *a.* kaygı, üzüntü, sıkıntı

worse /wö:s/ *s, be.* daha kötü, beter; daha hasta

worsen /'wö:sın/ *e.* daha da kötüleşmek; daha da kötüleştirmek

worship /'wö:şip/ *e.* tapmak; ibadet etmek ☆ *a.* ibadet, tapınma; hayranlık

worst /wö:st/ *s, be.* en kötü ☆ *a.* en kötü şey

worth /wö:t / *s.* değerinde, eder ☆ *a.* değer **worthless** değersiz; adi, karaktersiz **worthwhile** harcanan emeğe değer, yapmaya değer

worthy /'wö:di/ *s.* layık, değer

would /wud/ *e.* (**will**'in geçmiş biçimi olarak) -cekti, -caktı; -erdi, -ardı

wound /wu:nd/ *a.* yara ☆ *e.* yaralamak

wound /wu:nd/ *bkz.* **wind**

wove /wouv/ *bkz.* **weave**

woven /'wouvın/ *bkz.* **weave**

wow /wau/ *ünl, kon.* vay, vay canına

wrangle /'rengıl/ *a.* gürültülü tartışma, ağız dalaşı ☆ *e.* atışmak, ağız dalaşı yapmak

wrap /rep/ *e.* sarmak; sarmalamak; katlamak, koymak, yaymak ☆ *a.* örtü, atkı **wrapped up in** kendini -e vermiş **wrapper** sargı; sabahlık **wrapping** ambalaj, sargı

wreak /ri:k/ *e.* (öfke, hırs, vb.) salmak

wreath /ri:t / *a.* çelenk; taç

wreathe /ri:d / *e.* sarmak, kaplamak; (duman, vb.) süzülmek

wreck /rek/ *a.* gemi enkazı; enkaz, mahvolmuş şey/kimse ☆ *e.* enkaz haline getirmek; mahvetmek **wreckage** /'rekic/ enkaz, yıkıntı

wren /ren/ *a.* çalıkuşu

wrench /renç/ *e.* burkmak ☆ *a.* burkma, burkulma; İngiliz anahtarı

wrestle /'resıl/ *e.* güreşmek ☆ *a.* güreş **wrestler** güreşçi **wrestling** güreş

wretch /reç/ *a.* zavallı kimse

wretched /'reçid/ *s.* perişan, zavallı; berbat

wring 484

wring /ring/ e. wrung /rang/ burmak;
sıkmak ☆ a. burma, sıkma
wrinkle /'rinkıl/ a. kırışıklık; kon. ipucu
☆ e. kırıştırmak; kırışmak
wrist /rist/ a. bilek wristwatch kol saati
writ /rit/ a. ferman, ilam, buyruk
write /rayt/ e. wrote /rout/, written /'ri-
tın/ yazmak write down kaydetmek,
yazmak write in mektupla başvurmak
writer /'raytı/ a. yazar
writhe /rayd / e. kıvranmak
writing /'rayting/ a. yazı
written /ri'tın/ bkz. write
wrong /rong/ s. yanlış; ters; haksız; bozuk What's wrong with ... -in nesi var
go wrong kötü sonuçlanmak, ters gitmek wrongdoer haksızlık eden kimse; günahkâr wrongful haksız; yasadışı, yolsuz
wrote /rout/ bkz. write
wrung /rang/ bkz. wring
wry /ray/s. eğri, çarpık

X

xenophobia /zenı'foubıı/ a, ruhb. yabancı düşmanlığı
Xmas /'krismıs, 'eksmıs/ a, kon. Noel
X-ray /'eksrey/ e. röntgenini çekmek ☆
a. röntgen ışını; röntgen filmi; röntgen muayenesi
xylophone /'zaylıfoun/ a, müz. ksilofon

Y

yacht /yot/ a. yat yacht-club yat kulübü
yachting yatçılık yachtsman yatçı
yak /yek/ a, hayb. tibet sığırı ☆ e, kon.
laklak etmek
yank /yenk/ e, kon. birden hızla çekmek
Yankee /'yenki:/ a, kon. (Kuzey) Amerikalı

yap /yep/ e. havlamak; zırvalamak ☆
a. havlama; gevezelik
yard /ya:d/ a. yarda (0.914 m.); den. seren; avlu yard stick bir yardalık ölçü
çubuğu
yarn /ya:n/ a. iplik; kon. hikâye, masal,
maval
yawl /yo:l/ a. filika
yawn /yo:n/ e. esnemek ☆ a. esneme
yeah /yeı/ be, kon. evet
year /yiı, yö: / a. yıl, sene all the year
round bütün yıl boyunca yearly yılda
bir kez olan; yıllık
yearn /yö:n/ e. özlemek, göresimek,
can atmak yearning arzu, özlem; arzulu, özlemli
yeast /yi:st/ a. maya
yell /yel/ e. (at/out) bağırmak, haykırmak ☆ a. bağırış, feryat, çığlık
yellow /'yelou/ a. sarı; kon. ödlek, korkak yellow fever hek. sarı humma yellow pages sarı sayfalar, işyerlerinin telefon numaralarını içeren rehber
yellowish sarımsı, sarımtırak
yen /yen/ a. yen, Japon parası
yes /yes/ be. evet
yesterday /'yestıdi, 'yestıdey/ be. dün
yet /yet/ be. henüz, daha; şu ana kadar, hâlâ ☆ bağ. ama, yine de; aynı
zamanda as yet şu/o ana kadar
yield /yi:ld/ e. teslim olmak; (kâr) getirmek; çökmek, bel vermek, eğilmek;
ürün vermek ☆ a. ürün; kazanç, gelir
yoga /'yougı/ a. yoga
yoghurt /'yogıt/ a. yoğurt
yoke /youk/ a. boyunduruk; bağ
yolk /youk/ a. yumurta sarısı
yore /yo:/ a. eski zaman, geçmiş
you /yı, yu, yu:/ adl. sen, siz; seni, sizi;
sana, size
young /yang/ s. genç; yeni, taze, körpe
☆ a. (the) gençler, gençlik; (hayvan) yavru youngster çocuk, delikanlı
your /yı; yo:/ s. senin, sizin
yours /yo:z/ adl. senin, sizin, sizinki
yourself /yı'self, yo:'self/ adl. (ç. -selves
/-'selvz/) kendin, kendiniz, kendine,
kendini by yourself tek başına

zoom

youth /yu:t / *a.* gençlik; gençler **youthful** genç; dinç

Z

zeal /zi:l/ *a.* gayret, azim, istek **zealous** /'zelıs/ gayretli, istekli, şevkli
zebra /'zi:brı/ *a.* zebra **zebra crossing** yaya geçidi
zenith /'zenit / *a.* başucu; doruk, zirve
zeppelin /'zepılin/ *a.* zeplin
zero /'ziırou/ *a.* sıfır
zest /zest/ *a.* tat, lezzet, çeşni; zevk, hoşlanma
zigzag /'zigzeg/ *a.* zikzak ☆ *e.* zikzak yapmak
zinc /zink/ *a, kim.* çinko

zip /zip/ *a.* fermuar; vızıltı; gayret ☆ *e.* fermuarla açmak/kapatmak; vınlamak **zip code** *Aİ.* posta bölge kodu **zip-fastener, zipper** fermuar
zippy /'zipi/ *s.* hareketli, enerjik
zither /'zidı/ *a, müz.* kanun
zodiac /'zoudiek/ *a.* burçlar kuşağı, zodyak
zone /zoun/ *a.* kuşak; bölge
zoo /zu:/ *a.* hayvanat bahçesi
zoology /zou'olıci, zu'olıci/ *a.* hayvanbilim, zooloji **zoological** /zouı'locikıl/ zoolojik **zoological garden** hayvanat bahçesi **zoologist** /zou'olıcist/ hayvanbilimci, zoolog
zoom /zu:m/ *e.* vınlamak; (uçak) dikine yükselmek; *kon.* (araba) rüzgâr gibi gitmek; zum yapmak ☆ *a.* (uçak) dikine yükselme **zoom past** önünden ok gibi geçmek